Colonial Wars of North America, 1512–1763

MILITARY HISTORY OF THE UNITED STATES (VOL. 5)
GARLAND REFERENCE LIBRARY OF THE HUMANITIES (VOL. 1245)

Colonial Wars of North America, 1512–1763
An Encyclopedia

Editor
Alan Gallay

GARLAND PUBLISHING, INC.
New York & London
1996

Library of Congress Cataloging-in-Publication Data

Colonial wars of North America, 1512–1763 : an encyclopedia / editor,
   Alan Gallay
       p.   cm. — (Garland reference library of the humanities ; vol.
1245. Military history of the United States ; v. 5)
   Includes bibliographical references and index.
   ISBN 0-8240-7208-1 (alk. paper)
   1. North America—History, Military—Encyclopedias. 2. West Indies—
History, Military—Encyclopedias.   I. Gallay, Alan. II. Series: Garland
reference library of the humanities ; vol. 1245. III. Series: Garland reference
library of the humanities. Military history of the United States ; vol. 5.
E46.5.C65 1996
970—dc20
                            95-43577
                            CIP

Cover design by Lawrence Wolfson Design, New York.
Cover photograph courtesy of Bettman Archive.

Printed on acid-free, 250-year-life paper
Manufactured in the United States of America

For my parents, Harold and Leona Gallay

Contents

Illustrations

Preface

Colonial Wars of North America, 1512–1763: An Encyclopedia fills an important gap in available reference volumes for early American history. Much of the subject matter included in the encyclopedia has not appeared in other reference works and has received little or no attention in the secondary sources. Designed to provide ready reference on a variety of historical issues, peoples, and events, the encyclopedia not only provides useful essays on traditional topics of interest to scholars and students but also rescues the obscure and points the way to new areas of inquiry.

Geographic coverage is extensive, encompassing the present United States (including areas often overlooked in general histories, such as the Spanish Southwest and Russian Alaska), as well as relevant essays on Canada, the West Indies, and elsewhere. Beginning with the Spanish conquistadors and extending through Pontiac's War in 1763, this encyclopedia broadly defines warfare to include the military and diplomatic histories of a great variety of early American peoples. Native Americans, Europeans, and Africans all actively participated in the wars of colonial America, and it has been the intention of the editor of this work to purposely eschew an Anglocentric focus. The essays provide a wealth of information in the form of group and colony histories, biographies, and essays on forts, locales, conflicts, treaties, and intercultural relationships. Additionally, there are numerous essays on topics related to warfare, such as weaponry, technology, supply, and medical services.

With almost 700 essays written by more than 135 contributors from several different countries, it was inevitable that problems of nomenclature would arise. These problems are compounded by the multiplicity of terms and alternative spellings in both historical and contemporary works for wars, battles, treaties, forts, and peoples. Although spelling has been altered to a single standard in many instances, I have left intact the variety of terms used to describe a single item. For example, reference in the encyclopedia is made to the "Lenni Lenape," but readers looking for the main entry will find the notation: "*See* Delaware." Extensive cross-referencing and the index will assist readers through the maze of multiple terms for single items.

The selection of titles for essays was at times a daunting task, and I appreciate the assistance provided by the authors. Some titles have been altered from common usage to provide clarity to the item described. "Pontiac's Rebellion," for instance, has been transposed into "Pontiac's War," for rebellion refers to a conflict between a subject people and their rulers (or conquerors), which in this case does not describe the historical situation.

For the nomenclature that describes the wars for empire between England and France from 1689 to 1763, I generally have selected the term most often used to describe the American theater of conflict in United States histories. Thus, the "War of the League of Augsburg" is referred to as "King William's War"; the "War of the Spanish Succession" is termed "Queen Anne's War"; the "War of the Austrian Succession" becomes "King George's War." On the other hand, the "French and Indian War"—an American term—has been replaced by the "Seven Years' War" to reflect current historiographical usage and denote this war's more global nature than the earlier conflicts.

There are many people to thank who worked on this encyclopedia. It has been a *group* effort. As editor, I have fully appreciated the enthusiasm and professional competence that the authors brought to their essays. It was a pleasure to work with so many fine scholars from different walks of life, countries, and historical perspectives.

Additionally, I would like to note my grateful appreciation to Steven C. Eames, who contributed more than 20 essays. Andrew P. Ivy selflessly donated much time and effort assisting in the selection and preparation of the illustrative material—another collaborative effort that adds to the richness of the work. Jane Landers, in addition to contributing several essays, helped locate scholars to contribute entries on New Spain. The Bureau of Faculty Research at Western Washington University provided a summer research grant and money for photocopying. Again, I am most grateful for all the help.

My parents, Harold and Leona Gallay, to whom this encyclopedia is dedicated, first introduced and nurtured my love for colonial American history. When I was four years old, they took me to Fort Ticonderoga in New York (before it burned down) and I was hooked—embedded with a lasting memory. Through the childhood years they took me to numerous other historical sites from Maine to Mississippi—thus producing one of the few college freshmen who had a firm idea of his career path.

My wife, Carolina Coleman, and my daughter, Cyrana, deserve my thanks for the constant stream of love that keeps my priorities in proper perspective.

Alan Gallay
Bellingham, Washington

Introduction

Warfare played a crucial and ubiquitous role in the European colonization of North America. From the first conquistadors on American shores to the last of the imperial wars before the colonies sought their independence, Europeans used arms to establish colonies and to secure, protect, and dominate trade, as well as subjugate and enslave peoples. Not all of the various interests and nations involved in overseas expansion thought of themselves as on a militant quest to conquer—though conquest was indeed in the minds of many—but military force was seen as the most expeditious and logical way to attain goals overseas. This introduction will provide an overview of the sources of conflict and the early American peoples and regions involved.

The sixteenth- and seventeenth-century European imperialists carried the sword for the greater glory of God, monarch, family, and themselves. They never questioned their right to colonize, though they did debate how native peoples should be treated. For the European powers, overseas expansion was an extension of the endemic military conflicts in Europe. They developed mercantile empires that, by their very nature, further promoted armed conflict in both the New and Old Worlds. Spain, France, and England—the three most important imperial powers in what became the United States—each hoped to build a closed empire that would keep their colonial riches to themselves. The colonies would provide raw materials for the mother country, which, in turn, would provide manufactured goods and protection for the colonies. Perceiving that the world's wealth was finite, each imperial power jealously guarded its own empire while hoping to weaken their competitors. They perceived that any advantage accrued to one nation was a disadvantage to another, and they should use force, stealth, or any other means to limit, check, or reduce a foe's holdings and obtain a subsequent gain for themselves.

Every move by one power had to be countered by another. When the Dutch built Fort Good Hope on the Connecticut River in the 1630s, the English countered by erecting Fort Saybrook a few miles away; when the French entered the mouth of the Mississippi at the end of the seventeenth century, the Spanish quickly responded by settling Pensacola; when the French extended their colonial holdings into western Louisiana and the Missouri country, the Spanish built forts in east Texas and sent troops to the Midwest; and when the French spread their influence among aboriginal peoples of the Mississippi Valley by sending traders and priests, the English followed suit by sending their traders there as well. The European powers wasted little time taking advantage of a perceived or real weakness in a competing colonial power. As Spanish power receded north of the St. Johns River in Florida, the English steadily encroached, first with forts, and then by establishing the new colony of Georgia in Spain's claimed domain. When the French could not sufficiently supply their Choctaw allies, English South Carolina stepped in with trade goods hoping to wean the Choctaw from the French—thereby helping promote a civil war among the Choctaw.

The building of empires tied the New World to the Old. Spain used the gold and silver of Mexico, Peru, and elsewhere in South America to fund its wars in Europe; the imperial wars between England and France were paralleled by colonial wars—English gains in North America and the West Indies were often exchanged for French gains in Europe. Aboriginal peoples were caught in the European competition but, through superior diplomacy and their own military power, often made the best of a dangerous situation. Some learned to play the Europeans against one another; others contracted alliances with a particular European state and thereby bettered their position against other colonizers and indigenous neighbors; on the other hand, they more often bore the brunt of European hostilities and faced defeat and annihilation by a combination of European and Amerindian forces.

Not all of the warfare in early America resulted from the imperial contests spawned in Europe. Although often drawn into the imperial wars, the European colonists also instigated armed conflicts in the New World. Whether pressuring Native Americans for land, conducting slave raids on aboriginal peoples, or abusing them in trade, colonists often attacked or otherwise provoked their indigenous neighbors to war. Sometimes governments, both colonial and imperial, tried to restrict their colonists' militant behavior—for government officers learned that war was expensive and peaceful trade relations with Amerindians could reap more benefits than conquest. However, governments rarely used force in defense of aborigines and against European colonists. Before the Yamasee War (1715–1717), for instance, the South Carolina government had long recognized that colonial traders were at fault in taking advantage of the Yamasee in trade and illegally enslaving them. The government set up an investigative commission that collected reams of evidence regarding the baleful treatment of the Yamasee, who defended Carolina's southern frontier against the Spanish and hostile Amerindians. The government, however, was never willing to do more than slap the wrists of guilty parties, and by 1715, found itself engulfed in a war with the Yamasee and numerous other tribes wronged by traders and other colonists.

The imperial nations found it difficult to rule their colonies effectively with an ocean between the Old World and New. Slow communication often masked problems such as corrupt, self-interested practices of colonial administrators. Even when aware of activities that worked against imperial interests, home governments lacked the will, power, and skill to forcefully control their appointees and colonists. Government officials, soldiers, and colonists smuggled goods with European enemies—even during times of war. In times of peace, the home governments had difficulty restraining their colonists from attacking European foes. To escape censure, colonial officials and traders employed indigenous peoples to carry out forays against enemy Europeans and their Amerindian allies. In addition to the effectiveness of indigenous arms, aborigines could also be blamed for making these peacetime attacks.

The colonists, for the most part not comprised of professional soldiery, accepted the expediency of armed conflict to attain their ends. They did not perceive the use of military power against their neighbors as a moral question. Force was somewhat limited by government, but depended more on capability and resources. These last two factors forced the peoples of early America to interact in myriad types of relationships, many of them peaceful, all of them varying from moment to moment and place to place. The inability of any single group among the various colonists and indigenous peoples to assert hegemonic power resulted in great fluidity in intercultural relations. Europeans and Amerindians learned to use diplomacy, trade, and tact to achieve their ends, though force or its perceived use played an important role as each group considered what they could and could not accomplish.

The history of colonial America is not simply the story of European powers facing off against one another, while brutally exploiting the indigenous peoples within their reach. As is evident in this encyclopedia, military conflict, which included the armed subjection of native peoples, forms a large part of the story, but hardly the whole. The European colonists struggled to survive, and once survival seemed assured, they turned to domestic development; but demographic pressures— the arrival of thousands of immigrants and internal population growth—led to continual expansion and new conflicts. The early American peoples, particularly those east of the Mississippi and outside the relatively secure (after the seventeenth century) Atlantic coastal area from Virginia through southern New England, experienced warfare or the threat of warfare as a near-constant factor in their lives. The haunting specter of military conflict affected settlement patterns, domestic life, politics, and virtually every other area of human experience among European settlers and Amerindians alike. At any time, a war party of Iroquois from the Finger Lakes region of New York could ambush a Chickasaw hunting party near the Mississippi River; a group of New Hampshire rangers might pursue scalps from a band of Western Abenaki fleeing along Lake Champlain; yet another Anglo-French war could engulf everyone. The Europeans surely did not introduce warfare to America, but they did enlarge its scope and increase the level of firepower. They provoked numerous conflicts through greed for land and trade. Their desire to expand their colonies at the expense of their European and indigenous neighbors guaranteed that conflict would remain endemic—and it did.

The Spanish conquistadors were the first Europeans to attempt the building of an empire in the present United States. They began their quest heavily armed and armored, and met with repeated difficulties. They invaded at Tampa Bay, moved inland and northward, then encountered nearly impassable terrain and often hostile receptions from the natives, who took advantage of the conquistadors' incompetence. Contemporary Spanish critics of these failures noted that the conquistadors operated in an almost mindless fashion, blindly pursuing El Dorado, abusing the indigenous population through enslavement and forced prostitution, and making no concerted effort to establish a permanent Spanish presence. However, even those expeditions that attempted to establish stable and permanent colonies on the Gulf and Atlantic coasts met with failure. Only after a half-century of unsuccessful attempts did the Spanish marshal their resources to secure a colony in Florida under Pedro Menéndez de Avilés in 1565. In the next century, Spanish outposts spread up the Atlantic coast to Carolina, with some priests making it as far north as Virginia, following the crown's insistence that the cross accompany the sword. A string of missions across north-central Florida and on the Georgia Sea Islands built to protect themselves and their Amerindian clients were the most potent statement of Spanish power in the Southeast. The Spanish at first withheld arms from the indigenous inhabitants, but the arrival of an aggressive English colony at Carolina in 1670 put the Spanish on the defensive and forged a closer military connection with their Amerindian allies.

The Spanish crown found Florida a burden. Its riches remained an illusion, but its value as protection for the Florida Strait, through which New World gold shipments passed on their way to Spain, and the peninsula's significance as a line of defense against the English, led the Spanish to maintain their colony. The English, in whose hands Florida could become a launching pad for assaults against Cuba and Mexico, with allied natives attacked and destroyed the mission system between 1670 and 1705. Expeditions organized in Carolina and often led or sponsored by men in the highest levels of government were undertaken to capture Florida Amerindians and reduce them to slavery. Spain found itself unable to protect its mission allies as the English and allied Amerindian slavers ravaged Florida all the way to the Keys. Spain's Florida colony was all but destroyed, yet it managed to hold on despite English attempts at complete eradication.

The Spanish position in the American Southwest was not gravely threatened by other European powers, although France checked Spanish expansion eastward from Texas and the English briefly harassed them in California. In the West, the Native American population posed the greatest problem to Spain, particularly in New Mexico. But without having to contend with England and France in the region, they expanded into California and north to the Pacific Northwest.

The English challenged Spain's New World empire. After aborted attempts to colonize at Roanoke in the 1580s, they permanently established a colony at Jamestown in 1607. These first colonies were designed in part as military bases to attack New Spain. With the discovery of a marketable commodity, tobacco, the Virginia colony expanded by attracting new settlers, and English colonization extended into other areas, such as Maryland and Massachusetts. England's ability to build a strong demographic base distinguished its colonies from those of the other European powers. Thousands of Englishmen flocked to North America to begin a new way of life. Moreover, England, unlike Spain, allowed dissidents to settle in its colonies believing troublemakers, the unemployed, and unwanted, though a problem at home, could well serve the empire abroad. Furthermore, England allowed oppressed Protestants from other European nations to settle in its colonies and become full citizens. The settlers came to the New World for a variety of reasons and from a variety of social groups. Many, if not most, believed in their right to take land from the aboriginal inhabitants for their own use.

Between England's Chesapeake and New England colonies, the Dutch and Swedes established their own North American settlements. In the 1620s and 1630s, the Dutch colonized in the Hudson River valley, western Connecticut, and southward to the Delaware River valley, where the Swedes also settled in 1637. New Netherland and New Sweden, when not in conflict with each other, also had to contend with powerful Amerindian peoples. The Dutch pushed the Swedes out of North America, but were faced with English expansion from New England and Maryland. Three Dutch wars with England in the 1660s and 1670s, mostly fought as trade wars on the high seas, effectively ended Dutch colonization in North America.

The French originally attempted colonization in Florida, but were soundly defeated by the Spanish in 1565. They then turned their attention to Canada—distant from the threat of Spanish power. From Quebec, and later Montreal, they established a fur-trading empire that expanded to the Great Lakes, west as far as the Dakotas, northwest to Hudson Bay, and east to the maritime provinces. They returned to the Southeast at the end of the seventeenth century, and from bases at Mobile and New Orleans, built their Louisiana colony. Between Canada and the Gulf coast, the French tied their far-flung colonies together with settlements and trading posts in Arkansas, Illinois, and the Missouri River valley. Though able to tap into important aboriginal trading networks in the interior continent, numerous difficulties beset them. The Iroquois initially posed the greatest problems in the seventeenth century, as aborigines and Europeans competed for control of the fur trade. Toward the end of the seventeenth century, the great wars of empire with England, to be discussed below, drained French resources. French inability to attract colonists from Europe, coupled with its preoccupation with European affairs, kept its colonies in a weakened condition relative to the English colonies. In the Southeast, Spain was only occasionally a hindrance, and at times a great help, as Louisiana often received needed supplies from Pensacola or from Mexico. But the colony's disastrous wars with the Natchez and then the Chickasaw kept Louisiana weak from 1729 until French removal from North America at the end of the Seven Years' War.

For Native American peoples, disease often wreaked more havoc than warfare. Combined, they were potent enemies. Demographically weakened bands were forced to unite and confederate with other indigenous groups. Some moved their settlements close to the Europeans and became known by the English as settlement Indians, and by the French as *petite nations*. Some Amerindians found their greatest threats came from indigenous neighbors who competed for control of marketable commodities, or who attacked them to replenish their own declining ranks or for sale to the Europeans as slaves, or for any number of reasons that had little or no connection to the Europeans. Native Americans had their ancient enmities just as the Europeans did. The Choctaw and the Chickasaw, the Creek and the Cherokee, for instance, had long-standing disputes that continued through much of the colonial era and resisted occasional European attempts at mollification.

On the northern frontier, Amerindians were involved in two major wars with the Puritan New England colonies in the seventeenth century, the Pequot War (1636–1637) and King Philip's War (1675–1676). These wars devastated Amerindians and Europeans as well. The native population of southern New England was severely reduced by the wars and disease, and many of the survivors were enslaved, placed on reservations, or became refugees and left the region.

Native American power remained potent outside of southern New England, Virginia, and the Atlantic coast. The Abenaki, Cherokee, Chickasaw, Choctaw, Creek, and Iroquois were among the militarily strong native peoples feared by their European neighbors. All of these peoples recognized that survival necessitated continual ties to the flow of European trade goods, and though they might hope to stay out of the European wars, to varying extents these conflicts affected them all.

During the period of the great wars of empire—King William's War (1689–1697), Queen Anne's War (1702–1713), King George's War (1744–1748), and the Seven Years' War (1756–1763, which actually began in America in 1754, the later starting date referring to the European phase of the conflict)—France and England jockeyed for position to improve their New World holdings. Raids and counter-raids, particularly along the Canadian–New England and New York frontier, were supplemented by invasion and counter-invasion by large land and naval forces. Armed conflict also accompanied the periods between the declared wars. The British and French built hundreds of forts and garrisons to protect communities, trade, and lines of communication. Rangers and scouts patrolled frontiers, bounties were offered and awarded for enemy scalps, and civilians were captured from their homes for ransom. New techniques of fighting, arming, dress, and maneuvering were adapted by the Euramericans (and often from the Amerindian example). The last of these wars, the Seven Years' War, became the watershed event for many of the peoples who inhabited the vast stretch of territory from the Atlantic to the Mississippi Valley, and from Canada to the Gulf of Mexico. The defeat and removal of France from North America secured the English colonies, which no longer needed the mother country for protection, permitting some of the colonies to make the break that occurred a little more than a decade later. Another result: the Spanish temporarily lost Florida to the English and moved into Louisiana, from which they focused attention on securing their empire in the Southwest and California. Amerindian peoples did not lose their power with the French defeat and many indigenous nations remained strong for decades to come. But the English, and then the new American nation, learned to use trade as a weapon for expansion in the West. It is important to iterate that the power of many indigenous groups did not disappear at the end of the Seven Years' War, but their position was undermined by not having the French to provide supplies. The English colonies were too weak to conquer the powerful nations of the interior continent, but they were more secure against attack from without. After the American Revolution, the English presence in Canada, and the Spanish return to Florida and continued occupation of Louisiana, forged some help for indigenous groups resisting the westward movement of the United States. But the French defeat in the Seven Years' War and the disappearance of the check the French presence placed on the English colonists set in motion the expansion of the United States across the Appalachians. Armed settlement signaled the ultimate defeat and removal of most of the indigenous peoples who lived east of the Mississippi River.

Another major group of peoples who participated in colonial American warfare and whose participation is often overlooked were African Americans—for whom there is not the same plenitude of sources as exist for Euramericans and Amerindians. Africans accompanied the very first conquistadors, served as soldiers and auxiliaries in several conflicts (see, for instance, the Yamasee War and the Chickasaw War), provided a free black militia for Spanish St. Augustine, allied with Native Americans (as in the Natchez War with France, 1729–1733), and initiated conflicts to escape slavery (as in the Stono Rebellion). African Americans posed a grave military threat to all of the southern colonies—a potential fifth column that could unite with the enemies of their masters. The story of African American participation in the military history of colonial America is just beginning to be told. The significance of many colonial conflicts will become much clearer as the role of free and enslaved blacks is studied. At the very least, we can note that Europeans recognized their military value and included them among their forces. Moreover, warfare provided African Americans an opportunity to better their social position and, at times, a chance for freedom.

The history of the colonial wars and of the many peoples involved in them is largely retold in this encyclopedia. It is a story of individuals and peoples struggling to survive under the most abject circumstances. In earlier times, some of these episodes were romanticized and glamorized by novelists and historians. This celebration of the martial past, however, has led more recent generations to turn away from the serious study of warfare, believing that its study brought about the glorification and romanticization they despised. We would do well, however, to refocus our attention to the history of armed conflict that pervaded our nation's childhood. There is much to learn about who we are and where we have come from. With the recognition that participants on all sides were our own ancestors, we can see their story is our own and should not be ignored or forgotten. Warfare, for many, was the most important factor in their lives. We owe it to them, as well as to ourselves, to recount their experiences, and learn from them.

Chronology

1512	Juan Ponce de Leon "discovers" Florida for Spain
1519	Initial Spanish entry into Texas
1526	Lucas Vázquez de Ayllón expedition to Florida
1528	Panfílo de Narváez expedition to Florida
1539–1541	Hernando de Soto leads expedition through the Southeast
1540	Francisco Vázquez de Coronado leads Spanish expedition from California to Kansas
1556	Juan Pardo leads Spanish expedition to the Carolinas
1557	Juan Pardo leads second Spanish expedition to the Carolinas
1559	Tristan de Luna attempts settlement at Pensacola, Florida
1562	French under Jean Ribault establish settlements in Florida and Port Royal, South Carolina
1564	René de Laudonnièrre establishes French colony at Fort Caroline, Florida, and reinforces South Carolina settlement
1565	Pedro Menéndez de Avilés destroys French colony in Florida and establishes oldest permanent European settlement in present United States at St. Augustine, Florida
1585	English temporarily settle Roanoke Island in present-day North Carolina
1586	Sir Francis Drake leads British attack on St. Augustine
1597	Guale revolt against Spanish at Tolomato Presidio (Georgia)
1598	Juan de Oñate leads Spanish expedition to California from Mexico
1601	Juan de Oñate leads Spanish expedition to Quivera, Kansas

1607	Founding of Jamestown, Virginia, first permanent English settlement in present United States
1608	Samuel de Champlain establishes first permanent French trading post in Canada, at Quebec
1609	Champlain assists Algonquin-Huron attack on Mohawks
1609	Henry Hudson explores Hudson River
1620 December 16	Pilgrims land at Plymouth Bay
1622–1632	Virginia-Indian War
1623 April 4–7	Plymouth raid on Massachusetts Indian village of Wessagusset
1623	Dutch establish first permanent settlement in New Jersey
1624	Dutch build Fort Orange at Albany (New York)
1624–1628	Mohawk-Mahican War
1626	New Amsterdam established on Manhattan Island
1630	Fort Swanendael built by Dutch is first European settlement in present-day Delaware
1630	Puritans settle at Massachusetts Bay
1633	Founding of Maryland
1636–1637	Pequot War in New England
1636	Endicott expedition against Pequot
1637	Ancient and Honorable Artillery Company of Massachusetts formed
1637 December 31	New Sweden established on Delaware Bay
1639–1645	Kieft's War between Dutch and Delaware
1641–1701	Iroquois Wars between the Five Nations and New France and its allies
1643	Dutch-Mohawk Treaty
1643 September 7	New England Confederation formed of Connecticut, New Haven, Plymouth, and Massachusetts Bay Colony
1644	Roger Williams secures parliamentary patent for Rhode Island
1644–1646	Virginia-Indian War
1645	Treaty of Trois Rivières provides temporary truce between Mohawks and French

1647	Apalachee Revolt against Spanish in Florida
1650	Hartford Treaty settles border between New Netherland and New England
1651 November 5	Swedes capture Fort Casimir (Delaware) from Dutch
1652–1654	First Anglo-Dutch War
1654–1656	Oliver Cromwell's "Western Design" implemented to seize Spanish possessions in West Indies
1655–1657	Peach War between Delaware and Dutch
1655 September 26	Dutch retake Fort Casimir (Delaware) from Swedes
1656	Timucuans revolt against Spanish in Florida
1659–1660, 1663–1664	Esopus War between Esopus and Dutch
1664 September 8	English capture New Netherland
1665–1667	Second Anglo-Dutch War
1670	English settle Carolina and Pennsylvania
1672–1674	Third Anglo-Dutch War
1673–1674	Jacques "Pére" Marquette and Louis Jolliet explore Mississippi Valley
1674	Dutch recapture New York
1674 March 6	Treaty of Westminster restores New York to English
1674–1675	Chacato "Troubles" in Florida
1675	Virginia and Maryland attack Susquehannocks
1675–1676	King Philip's War in New England
1675	Indians burn Springfield (Massachusetts)
1675 September 18	Bloody Brook Massacre near Deerfield (Massachusetts)
1675 December 19	Defeat and brutal murder of hundreds of Narragansetts at Great Swamp (Rhode Island)
1676	Bacon's Rebellion (Virginia)
1676 May 19	English victory over Philip at Falls Fight
1677/1680	Virginia-Indian Treaty
1677	Signing of "Covenant Chain" treaty between Iroquois and English

1680	New Hampshire established as a royal colony
1680	South Carolina war with Westo
1680	Pueblo Indian Revolt against Spanish
1680	René-Robert Cavalier de La Salle builds first European fort in Illinois country, Fort Crevecoeur (Illinois)
1681	Renewal of war between South Carolina and Westo
1686–1689	Dominion of New England established
1687	Jacques-René de Brísay de Denonville leads French attack on five Seneca villages
1688–1689	English "Glorious" Revolution
1689–1691	Leisler's Rebellion (New York)
1689–1697	King William's War
1689	Abenaki attack Pemaquid (Maine)
1689 June	Abenaki attack Dover (New Hampshire)
1689 August 4	1,500 Iroquois attack French village of Lachine, Canada
1689 September 21	Battle of Brackett's Woods (Maine)
1690 February	Franco-Indian raiding party decimates Schenectady (New York)
1690 March	Franco-Indian raiding party totally surprises garrison at Salmon Falls (New Hampshire)
1690 August 13	John Schuyler leads attack on La Prairie, Canada
1690	English defeat French at Port Royal, Canada
1690	New England expedition against Canada fails
1691 June	200 warriors from Norridgewock attack Wells (Maine)
1691 August 1	Peter Schuyler leads raid on La Prairie, Canada
1692 February 6	Indian attack on York (Maine)
1692 June	Franco-Abenaki attack on Wells (Maine)
1694 July 18	300 French-led Penobscots decimate Oyster River (Durham, New Hampshire)
1696 August	Destruction of Fort William Henry (Maine) by French
1696	Pueblo Indian Revolt

1697 March 15	Haverhill (Massachusetts) attacked by Indians—Hannah Duston taken captive
1697 March 30	Hannah Duston and two others kill and scalp Indian captors and become heroes in New England
1697	Treaty of Ryswick
1699	Pierre Le Moyne d'Iberville occupies Gulf coast for France
1699 September 6	French turn back English frigate at "English Bend," successfully asserting claim over England to Mississippi River
1700, 1701	Iroquois treaties with England and France end 70 years of warfare between the Five Nations and Great Lakes Indians allied to France
1702–1713	Queen Anne's War
c. 1702–1776	Creek-Choctaw Wars
1704 February	Franco-Indian attack on Deerfield (Massachusetts)
1704	James Moore leads Carolina and Creek forces against Apalachee
1705 February 8	Haverhill (Massachusetts) faces second major Indian attack
1706 September	Franco-Spanish assault on Charles Town (South Carolina) fails
1707	British attack Pensacola (Florida)
1707	Failed British attack on French at Port Royal, Canada
1708 August 29	Haverhill (Massachusetts) attacked for third and final time
1709	British expedition against Canada aborted
1710	British conquest of Port Royal, Canada
1711	Hovenden Walker ends disastrous British attempt against Quebec
1711–1713	Tuscarora War
1713 July 28	Treaty of Portsmouth: Penobscot, Kennebec, and Maliseet recognize their allegiance to Great Britain
1713	Treaty of Utrecht: France surrenders Acadia, Hudson Bay, Newfoundland, and its half of St. Kitts to Great Britain
1715–1717	Yamasee War
1716	Spain establishes its first permanent settlement in Texas
1716	Clash between Natchez and French

1717	Fort Toulouse (Alabama) built by French among the Upper Creek helps both withstand growing English power in the Southeast
1718	New Orleans founded
1718	San Antonio occupied by Spain
1718 December	French take Pensacola (Florida) from Spanish
1718–1721	Anglo-Spanish War
1719 August	Spanish retake Pensacola (Florida)
1719 August 18–19	Failed Spanish attack on French at Mobile Bay (Alabama)
1719 September	French retake Pensacola (Florida)
1720–1722	Aguayo expedition secures east Texas for Spain from France
1722 November 25	France relinquishes Pensacola to Spain
1723	Clash between French and Natchez
1722–1727	Dummer's War between Abenaki and English
1724 August 24	Jesuit priest Sebastien Rale killed in English attack on Norridgewock (Maine)
1725 May 8	Lovewell's Fight (Maine)
1726–1727	Dummer's Treaty between Massachusetts and the Indians of Maine and the Maritime Provinces
1728 March	British-Indian forces under John Palmer attack Yamasee villages outside St. Augustine (Florida)
1729–1730	Fox Indians decimated by French and Indian allies
1729–1733	Natchez War with France
1733	English settle Georgia
1736	Ojibwa-Dakota conflict
1736	Chickasaw War with French
1736	Chickasaw defeat French at Battle of Ackia (Tennessee)
1737	Walking Purchase (Pennsylvania)
1739–1744	Anglo-Spanish War
1739	British and colonial troops attack Porto Bello on the Isthmus of Panama
1739–1740	Chickasaw War with French renewed

1739	Stono Rebellion (South Carolina)
1740 May–July	James Oglethorpe leads failed invasion of Spanish Florida
1740–1754	Creek-Cherokee Wars
1741	British expedition against Cartagena fails
1742 July	Oglethorpe turns back Spanish at Battle of Bloody Marsh (Georgia)
1743 August	Oglethorpe unsuccessfully attacks St. Augustine (Florida)
1744	Treaty of Lancaster (Pennsylvania) between Iroquois and Virginia and Maryland
1744–1748	King George's War
1744 May	Battle of Canso, Nova Scotia
1744 August	Fort Massachusetts (Massachusetts) burned to the ground by Franco-Indian force
1745 May–June	British successfully siege Louisbourg
1745 November	Battle of Saratoga (New York), Franco-Indian force carries off more than 100 prisoners
1746–1747	British expedition against Canada aborted
1746–1750	Choctaw civil war
1747 February 11	Battle of Grand Pré, 300 Canadians plus Indian allies force England out of northern Nova Scotia
1747 April 4	Fort at Number Four, Charlestown (New Hampshire) withstands Franco-Indian attack
1747	Indian uprising against French in the Great Lakes region
1748	Treaty of Aix-la-Chapelle returns Louisbourg to France
1748	Ohio Company created
1752	Choctaw-Chickasaw War
1752	Treaty of Logstown (Pennsylvania), reaffirms Treaty of Lancaster (1744) and permits British settlement east and south of the Ohio River
1752 June 1	Fox attack Cahokia-Michigamea
1752 June 21	Ottawas and 200 *coureurs de bois* drive English out of Pickawillany (Ohio)
1754 Spring	French construct Fort Duquesne (Pennsylvania) at the juncture of Allegheny and Monongahela Rivers

1754 Spring–Summer	George Washington leads Virginia troops into Ohio country where they defeat French party and then, in turn, are defeated at Fort Necessity (Pennsylvania)
1754 June 19–July 11	Albany Conference
1754–1763	Seven Years' War
1754 September	Shawnee attack Buffalo Creek (South Carolina)
1755 June 16	Fort Beauséjour, Nova Scotia, falls to British
1755 July 9	Edward Braddock defeated by French at the Monongahela
1755 September	Baron Jean-Armand Dieskau leads failed French attack against British on Lake George (New York)
1756 March 27	Fort Bull (New York) falls to French forces
1756 August 3	Fort Granville (Pennsylvania) falls to French forces
1756 August	Battle of Oswego (New York), Louis-Joseph de Montcalm takes 1,700 prisoners
1756 September	Battle of Kittanning (Pennsylvania)
1756 December	William Pitt takes over British war effort
1757 August 3	French siege of Fort William Henry (New York) ends successfully
1757 November	Battle of German Flats (New York), yields French 150 captives
1758 March 13	Battle on Snowshoes (New York), Rogers' Rangers overwhelmed
1758 June–July	British successfully siege Louisbourg
1758 July 8	Battle of Ticonderoga (New York), Montcalm defeats larger British army under James Abercromby
1758 August 27	Surrender of Fort Frontenac, Canada, to John Bradstreet
1759 June–September	Battle of Quebec, death of Montcalm and British General James Wolfe
1759 July 6–25	British successfully siege Fort Niagara (New York)
1759 July 24	Battle of La Belle Famille (New York), French relief force defeated on way to Niagara
1759 October	Rogers' Rangers attack Abenaki mission at St. Francis, Canada
1759–1761	Cherokee War
1760 February	Cherokee attack Fort Prince George (South Carolina) to free hostages, who are then massacred

1760 February 27	Cherokee fail to take Fort Dobbs (North Carolina)
1760 March–August 7	Cherokee successfully siege Fort Loudoun (Tennessee), kill all but one captive
1760 May	French fail to recapture Quebec
1760 June 16	Battle of Sainte-Thérèse, Rogers' Rangers raid into Canada
1760 August 25	British capture Fort Lévis (New York)
1760 September 8	British take Montreal
1761	Spain agrees to enter Seven Years' War in May 1762 on side of French
1761 August	Havana surrenders to British forces
1762 June	British garrison at St. John's, Newfoundland, surrenders to French forces
1762 September 18	British retake St. John's, capture 689 prisoners
1762 November 13	Treaty of Fontainbleau: France cedes New Orleans and all territorial claims west of the Mississippi River to Spain
1763–1764	Pontiac's War
1763 February 10	Treaty of Paris ends Seven Years' War
1763 May 16	Defeat of British at Fort Sandusky (Ohio) by Wyandot, Ottawa, and allied Indians
1763 June	Fort Michilimackinac (Michigan) falls to Indians
1763 July 28–August 1	Fort Pitt (Pennsylvania) attacked by Ottawa, Wyandot, and Delaware
1763 August 5–6	Henry Bouquet leads British troops to victory over allied Indians in only field engagement of Pontiac's War, Battle of Bushy Run (Pennsylvania)
1763 October 7	Proclamation Act limits western movement of English colonists
1763	Augusta Congress (Georgia)
1763 December	Paxton Boys murder 20 Indians in Lancaster County (Pennsylvania)

Contributors

William L. Anderson
Department of History, Western Carolina University

Richard Aquila
Department of History, Ball State University

Juan I. Arnaud-Rabinal
Dpto. de Historia de America, Universidad de Sevilla, Spain

José Ignacio Avellaneda
Department of History, University of Florida

John F. Battick
Department of History, University of Maine

Alberto Bernardez-Alvarez
Dpto. de Historia de America, Universidad de Sevilla, Spain

Lance A. Betros
Fayetteville, Georgia

Debra R. Boender
Ellicott City, Maryland

Larry G. Bowman
Department of History, University of North Texas

Kathryn E. Holland Braund
Auburn, Alabama

Colin G. Calloway
Department of History, University of Wyoming

Edward J. Cashin
Department of History and Anthropology, Augusta College

Alfred A. Cave
Department of History, University of Toledo

Joyce E. Chaplin
Department of History, Vanderbilt University

Boyd Childress
Ralph Brown Draughon Library, Auburn University

Donald E. Chipman
Department of History, University of North Texas

Charles E. Clark
Department of History, University of New Hampshire

Thomas Costa
Department of History, Clinch Valley College

Samuel Willard Crompton
Northampton, Massachusetts

Evelyn C. Darrow
Wilson Library, Western Washington University

John Morgan Dederer
Stratford, Connecticut

Joseph A. Devine, Jr.
Department of History, Stephen F. Austin State University

Louis De Vorsey, Jr.
Department of Geography, University of
Georgia

Gregory E. Dowd
Department of History, University of Notre
Dame

Ronald P. Dufour
Department of History, Rhode Island College

Richard Dukes
Columbia, South Carolina

Brian Leigh Dunnigan
Executive Director, Old Fort Niagara
Association

Steven C. Eames
Department of History, St. Anselm College

Leroy V. Eid
Department of History, University of Dayton

Carl J. Ekberg
Department of History, Illinois State
University

John S. Erwin
School of Social Science, Olney Central
College

David R. Farrell
Department of History, University of Guelph,
Canada

John E. Ferling
Department of History, West Georgia College

Mark F. Fernandez
Department of History, Loyola University

Doris B. Fisher
School of Arts and Sciences, Clayton State
College

Michael James Foret
Department of History, University of
Wisconsin–Stevens Point

Chris Friday
Department of History, Western Washington
University

Alan Gallay
Department of History, Western Washington
University

Patricia Galloway
Mississippi State Department of Archives and
History

George Geib
Department of History, Butler University

Charles T. Gehring
New Netherland Project, New York State
Library

William G. Godfrey
Department of History, Mount Allison
University, Canada

Richard C. Goode
Department of History, David Lipscomb
University

Elizabeth Gossman
Issaquah, Washington

Gretchen L. Green
Department of History, University of
Missouri-Kansas City

Julian Gwyn
Department of History, University of Ottawa,
Canada

Leslie Hall
Wilson Library, Western Washington
University

John D. Hamilton
Curator, Museum of Our National Heritage

Kimberly S. Hanger
Department of History, University of Tulsa

John H. Hann
San Luis Archaelogical and Historic Site,
Tallahassee, Florida

Alan Harfield
Barton-on-Sea, Hampshire, England

Raymond E. Hauser
Department of History, Waubonsee
Community College

Jeanne T. Heidler
Department of History, USAF Academy

James Hill
Columbia, South Carolina

Eric Hinderaker
Department of History, University of Utah

James H. Hitchman
Department of History, Western Washington
University

Donald J. Horton
Department of History, University of
Waterloo, Canada

Ronald W. Howard
Department of History, Mississippi College

Anthony P. Inguanzo
Bronx, New York

Larry E. Ivers
Eagle Grove, Iowa

Harvey H. Jackson
Department of History, Jacksonville State
University

Cornelius J. Jaenen
Department of History, University of Ottawa,
Canada

Richard R. Johnson
Department of History, University of
Washington

Sherry Johnson
Department of History, Florida International
University

John M. Keefe
Lansing, Kansas

Mary Kimbrough
Department of Foreign Languages and
Literature, Texas Southern University

Paul E. Kopperman
Department of History, Oregon State
University

Mark V. Kwasny
Department of History, Ohio State
University–Newark

Jane Landers
Department of History, Vanderbilt University

James S. Leamon
Department of History, Bates College

Adam Norman Lynde
Philadelphia, Pennsylvania

John P. McCarthy
Principal Archaeologist, John Milner
Associates, West Chester, Pennsylvania

Martha W. McCartney
Williamsburg, Virginia

D. Peter MacLeod
Department of History, University of Ottawa,
Canada

Malcolm MacLeod
Department of History, Memorial University
of Newfoundland, Canada

John R. McNeil
Department of History, Georgetown
University

Russell M. Magnaghi
Department of History, Northern Michigan
University

Peter C. Mancall
Department of History, University of Kansas

Jack D. Marietta
Department of History, University of Arizona

Alfred J. Marini
Nova High School, Davie, Florida

Roy Marokus
Amarillo, Texas

Ronald Martin
Department of History, Rancho Santiago
College

Pedro M. Martin-Escudero
Dpto. de Historia de America, Universidad de
Sevilla, Spain

Gregory D. Massey
Department of History and Political Science, Freed-Hardeman University

Richard I. Melvoin
Assistant Dean of Admissions and Financial Aid, Harvard University

Donna Merwick
Department of History, University of Melbourne, Australia

Richard Middleton
Department of Modern History, The Queen's University of Belfast, Northern Ireland

Leslie Miller
Athens, Georgia

Dale B. Miquelon
Department of History, University of Saskatchewan, Canada

Michael J. Mullin
Department of History, Augustana College

John F. Murphy, Jr.
Longport, New Jersey

Bert M. Mutersbaugh
Department of History, Eastern Kentucky University

Michael W. Nagle
Bellingham, Washington

June Namias
Department of History and Geography, University of Alaska Anchorage

Martin L. Nicolai
Department of History, Queen's University, Canada

Gregory H. Nobles
School of History, Technology, and Society, Georgia Institute of Technology

James H. O'Donnell, III
Department of History, Marietta College

Sean O'Neill
History Department, Grand Valley State University

Paul Otto
Department of History, Calvin College

Susan R. Parker
Historic St. Augustine Preservation Board, St. Augustine, Florida

T.C. Parramore
Department of History, Meredith College

William Pencak
Department of History, Pennsylvania State University

Joseph L. Peyser
Department of Foreign Languages, Indiana University at South Bend

Felipe del Pozo-Redondo
Dpto. de Historia de America, Universidad de Sevilla, Spain

Thomas L. Purvis
Associate Editor, *American National Biography*

John G. Reid
Department of History, St. Mary's University, Canada

Daniel K. Richter
Department of History, Dickinson College

Alan Rogers
Department of History, Boston College

Helen C. Rountree
Department of Sociology, Old Dominion University

Lawrence S. Rowland
Department of History, University of South Carolina at Beaufort

John A. Schutz
Department of History, University of Southern California

John F. Schwaller
Department of History, Florida Atlantic University

Robert A. Selig
Department of History, Grand Valley State University

William L. Shea
Department of Social and Behavioral
Sciences, University of Arkansas at
Monticello

Sheila L. Skemp
Department of History, University of
Mississippi

Nicholas N. Smith
Ogdensburg, New York

J. Russell Snapp
Department of History, Davidson College

Jeffrey B. Snyder
Archaeologist, John Milner Associates, West
Chester, Pennsylvania

Ian K. Steele
Department of History, University of Western
Ontario, Canada

Peter Stern
Alexander Library, Rutgers University

Jim Sumner
Curator, North Carolina Museum of History

Carl E. Swanson
Department of History, East Carolina
University

Jesús F. de la Teja
Department of History, Southwest Texas
State University

Linda M. Thorstad
Baton Rouge, Louisiana

Kathryn L. Utter
Sedro Woolley, Washington

David William Voorhees
Papers of Jacob Leisler, Department of
History, New York University

Louis M. Waddell
Papers of Henry Bouquet, Pennsylvania
Historical and Museum Commission

Harry M. Ward
Department of History, University of
Richmond

Gregory A. Waselkov
Department of Sociology and Anthropology,
University of South Alabama

Robert M. Weir
Department of History, University of South
Carolina

David L. Whitesell
Tacoma, Washington

Joe Bassette Wilkins
Division of History and Social Sciences,
Livingston University

Richard P.W. Williams
Washington, D.C.

Paul Woehrmann
Milwaukee Public Library, Milwaukee,
Wisconsin

David T. Zabecki
Freiburg, Germany

Abatis

An obstacle around a defensive position. It consists of felled trees sharpened on one end. The sharpened end as well as the branches point toward the enemy, while the other end is dug into the ground for support. Its purpose is to make an enemy attack, especially by cavalry, more difficult, and to slow down an infantry attack by forcing the attacker to cut a path through the abatis.

Robert A. Selig

Abenaki

The Abenaki Indians of northern New England occupied a crucial and precarious position during the era of the colonial wars. Located in what became the borderland between New England and New France, they played an important role in the French and Indian Wars and were vitally affected by the outcome of the conflicts.

The Abenakis—the "people of the dawn-land"—were loosely-related Algonquian-speaking tribes who inhabited the area of present-day Maine, New Hampshire, Vermont, and southern Quebec. In Maine, the Penobscots, Kennebecs, Wawenocks, and Androscoggins constituted a formidable power on New England's eastern frontier. The Pigwackets, Ossipees, and Winnipesaukes occupied an intermediate position in the White Mountain region of western Maine and New Hampshire, while Pennacook villages nestled in the Merrimack Valley. The Sokokis and Cowasucks occupied the upper Connecticut Valley, and the Missisquois and other groups of Vermont Abenakis inhabited the Champlain Valley. During the era of the colonial wars, new Abenaki communities grew up on the banks of the St. Lawrence around the

French mission villages at St. Francis and Bécancour. In time, the Passamaquoddies of eastern Maine and the Micmac and Maliseet of the Maritime Provinces became associated with the Abenakis as members of the Wabanaki Confederacy, and the English often referred to all the tribes of Maine as simply "the Eastern Indians." Although the tribes were distinct and autonomous, they tended to be fluid and seasonal concentrations of population. The family band was the basic unit of Abenaki society, subsistence, and politics.

The Abenakis were among the first Native Americans to encounter Europeans, and they displayed evidence of previous contact by the time Giovanni da Verrazano met them in 1524. The French explorer Samuel de Champlain initiated peaceful relations with them in 1604–1605; about the same time the English alienated them by kidnapping five Abenakis and taking them to England. Smallpox and other diseases introduced by Europeans hit the Abenakis hard in 1617 and throughout the era of the colonial wars.

The pattern of amicable relations with the French and increasingly hostile relations with the English continued in subsequent years. While the English had the edge in the trade goods upon which the Abenakis became heavily dependent, the French secured the allegiance of the tribes because they did not covet Abenaki lands and because Jesuit missionaries like Sebastien Rale came to wield significant spiritual and political influence in Abenaki villages.

The growing English threat to Abenaki land and culture pushed the Abenakis further into the arms of the French. Abenakis fought the English in the northern phases of King Philip's War (1675–1676) and some Abenakis sought refuge from the conflict by migrating to French mission villages in Canada.

As Anglo-French imperial rivalry spilled over into open warfare in North America, the Abenakis allied with the French in common cause against English expansion. For the most part, the Abenakis waged guerrilla warfare against the English, harrying the frontier settlements in small-scale raids, and often carrying off captives whom they adopted into the tribe or sold to the French.

Abenaki warriors fought on their own and with French officers in King William's War (1689–1697) and in Queen Anne's War (1702–1713). After each war, the English made treaties with the Abenakis which they described as "acts of submission," and blamed the Abenakis for the hostilities.

From 1722 to 1727, a time of formal peace between England and France, the Abenakis fought against Massachusetts and New Hampshire in Dummer's War. The English destroyed Abenaki villages at Penobscot and Norridgewock in Maine, but the Vermont Abenakis led by Grey Lock harried the Massachusetts frontier with impunity. The war petered out in a series of conferences in which the eastern Abenakis agreed to the terms of Dummer's Treaty.

The outbreak of King George's War (1744–1748) once again saw the Abenakis and the French launch a joint war effort. French officers "sang the war song" in Abenaki villages, and a stream of Abenaki war parties from the French missions pinned back the New England frontier.

During the Seven Years' War (1754–1763), Abenakis served with the French forces in almost every major campaign, as well as conducting their own raids against the English, and Penobscot warriors were blamed for perpetrating the massacre of English soldiers after the surrender of Fort William Henry. As the tide of the war swung in favor of the redcoats, the Abenakis saw the conflict carried deeper into their territory. In 1759, Robert Rogers burned the Abenaki village at St. Francis, which had been the scourge of New England for half a century, although his victory was by no means as complete as he claimed, and his command suffered heavy casualties on the return journey.

With the defeat of France, the Abenakis were left without allies to face the flood of settlement that English victory unleashed. It was common Abenaki strategy for villages to disperse into family bands in time of warfare and many of the tribes had become scattered. Some bands had taken up residence in Canada during the course

of the wars, adding their numbers to the composite Abenaki communities at St. Francis and Bécancour. Others pulled back into the farthest reaches of their territory to avoid contact and conflict with the invaders. Those bands who remained in their homelands experienced hard times adjusting to the reality of English conquest and the presence of English settlers.

Wedged between the competing English and French colonies, the Abenakis' involvement in the Anglo-French wars was inevitable. Their effectiveness as allies of the French in launching raids on the New England frontier earned them notoriety and condemnation in New England. Contemporary chroniclers, and later historians like Francis Parkman, portrayed the Abenakis as bloodthirsty savages who carried out the orders of their unscrupulous French masters. In reality, the Abenakis fought for their own survival, regarded the English as aggressive and treacherous, and made it clear time and again that they were the independent allies, not the subjects, of the king of France.

Colin G. Calloway

References

Colin G. Calloway, *The Western Abenakis of Vermont, 1600–1800: War, Migration, and the Survival of an Indian People* (1990); Gordon M. Day, *The Identity of the St. Francis Indians* (1981); William A. Haviland and Marjory W. Power, *The Original Vermonters: Native Inhabitants Past and Present* (1981); Kenneth M. Morrison, *The Embattled Northeast: The Elusive Ideal of Alliance in Abenaki-Euramerican Relations* (1984); André Sévigny, *Les Abenaquis: Habitats et Migrations* (1976).

See also DUMMER'S TREATY; DUMMER'S WAR; NORRIDGEWOCK, BATTLE OF; RALE, SEBASTIEN; ST. FRANCIS, BATTLE OF; SOKOKI

Abercromby, James (1706–1781)

James Abercromby was born in Banffshire, Scotland. Commissioned ensign, 25th Foot Regiment, in 1717, he entered the army at perhaps the worst moment for a gentleman seriously interested in a military career. Though the Jacobite rebellion necessitated its expansion in 1715, the army had declined in real numbers since the end of the War of the Spanish Succession in 1713. Britain now entered the period of Walpole's peace, and though promoted lieutenant, 30th Foot, in 1724, Abercromby did not obtain his captaincy, albeit in the 1st Foot, until 1736. His entry to Parliament as M.P. for Banffshire, in the interest of his brother-in-law, William Duff, Lord Braco, reflected Abercromby's recognition of his meagre prospects for promotion at the time. For his loyal support of government measures, Abercromby was made king's printer in Scotland, and appointed lieutenant governor of Stirling Castle in 1739.

The outbreak of the War of the Austrian Succession (1740–1748) gave Abercromby the opportunity to advance his military career. Promoted major in 1742 and lieutenant colonel in 1744, Abercromby became colonel of the 1st Foot in 1746, when he served as deputy quartermaster general on the L'Orient expedition. Wounded at Hulst in the Netherlands the following year, Abercromby retired from active duty until the eve of the Seven Years' War (1754–1763). Abercromby took command of the 50th Foot in 1755, and in 1756 was appointed deputy to Lord Loudoun, a close friend and commander in chief in North America. Appointed colonel of the 44th, whose previous commander, Sir Peter Halkett, had died on the Monongahela, Abercromby found his new regiment "in want of many things, and soon [to] be naked." The general proved to be an able subordinate in the often rough and tumble North American command. Wrote Loudoun: "M.G. Abercromby is a good officer, and a very good second man any where, whatever he is employed in." Alexander Colden also found Abercromby "the most easy and free of any general I ever had the honour to be acquainted with and did not take any of that state and grandeur upon him that [William] Shirley does, everyone that came to wait on him had free access to him."

After two years of war in North America, considerable preparation was still required to mount an expedition against Canada. Loudoun's activities in 1757 were therefore limited to uninspiring but necessary logistic paperwork. For this he was rewarded with recall to England on 30 December 1757, when Secretary of State William Pitt wrote Loudoun, Abercromby, and the colonial governors of the appointment of Abercromby as commander in chief, North America, and colonel of the 60th Foot. The difficulties of communication in the age of sail are best exemplified by the fact that Abercromby did not receive notice of his appointment until 7 March 1758.

Loudoun's comment that Abercromby was "a very good second man" was to prove prophetic. In fact, Abercromby was not the independent commander in chief that Braddock or Loudoun had been. The show was run from London by William Pitt, and for not the last time, England would suffer the consequences of a "war minister" with too much inspiration but little enough understanding of local circumstances. In orders dated 30 December 1757, Pitt directed Abercromby to personally conduct the invasion of Canada via Lake Champlain. Louisbourg, however, was the jewel of the 1758 campaign, and that operation was under the command of Abercromby's subordinate, Jeffrey Amherst. Amherst's force was to number 14,000 regulars, drawn largely from forces already in America. Abercromby's numbers for the invasion were further reduced with the creation of an expeditionary force against Fort Duquesne on the Ohio, under Colonel John Forbes. Thus, when Abercromby's army gathered on Lake George in late June, it numbered barely 6,000 regulars. His weaknesses were supposed to be corrected by provincials, but since the previous spring he had had difficulty in obtaining full quotas from the more distant provinces, while the refusal of those on hand to perform certain duties, such as garrison smallpox-torn Albany, had necessitated the further reduction of his regulars through extraneous duties.

Abercromby's force was an impressive sight on 6 July as 800 batteaux, carrying 22 men each, and 90 whaleboats with ten men each, landed three miles south of Fort Carillon (Ticonderoga). Tragically, Viscount Howe, Abercromby's second-in-command, was killed when his force of light infantry collided with a party of French regulars and Indians. The ensuing confusion in gathering gloom put a halt to the English advance. The next day, 7 July, was spent collecting stragglers and driving in French advanced posts. Early in the morning of the 8th, Abercromby's engineers advised him that the French works could be taken if they were attacked before completed. Much to the regret of nearly 1,500 regulars who would subsequently be killed and wounded, Abercromby agreed. The repeated attacks lasted for four hours, with no impression being made on the French works, when Abercromby finally decided that, "for the preservation of the remainder of so many brave men," he would withdraw.

Though Abercromby was active in protecting the frontiers from the invasion to which his defeat had opened them, his self-confidence as commander, as well as the army's confidence in him, collapsed. With little regret from either, he was recalled by London on 18 September 1758. James Abercromby was promoted lieutenant general in 1759, and general in 1772. He did not see service in the Revolutionary War, but died in Glassaugh, in 1781, still colonel of the 44th and lieutenant governor of Stirling Castle.

Adam Norman Lynde

References

British Public Record Office, W01/1 Commander in Chief, North America; Richard Harrison Papers, New York Historical Society; G.S. Kimball, ed., *Correspondence of William Pitt* (1906); Douglas Edward Leach, *Arms for Empire. A Military History of the British Colonies in North America, 1607–1763* (1973); Stanley Pargellis, *Military Affairs in North America, 1748–1765* (1969).

See also TICONDEROGA, BATTLE OF

Acadia

Although it was not accurately mapped to the French, Acadia comprised all of what is now Nova Scotia, New Brunswick, Prince Edward Island, and parts of Quebec and Maine. Acadia, or parts of it, was included in the 1603 French grant to Pierre du Gua de Monts. Part of De Monts' grant was also included in the 1620 grant to the Council of New England. Perhaps as a way of showing his authority over the disputed territory, Chief Unongoit in 1625 deeded a large tract of Acadia, including Pemaquid, to English settler John Brown. The English strengthened their claim to the area when Plymouth Pilgrims established a trading post on the Kennebec in 1629 and other English settlers traded with the Indians further down the coast. In 1631, the New England Council granted Pemaquid to Aldworth and Elbridge, wealthy merchants of Bristol. Englishmen from these eastern Maine settlements had easy access to the fine fishing grounds claimed by the Acadian French. The area between the Bay of Fundy and Machias remained a no-man's-land, except for the Indians, separating the French and English settlements. Although the French claimed that the boundary between Acadia and New England was the Kennebec River, no attempt was made to enforce their claim until 1687 when Louis-Alexandre des Friches de Meneval was appointed governor of Acadia.

In 1687 new governors were appointed to both Massachusetts and Acadia. Both were strong militarists determined to protect the interests of their colonies. Governor Edmund Andros of Massachusetts decided to assert his authority over his claimed territory by attacking St. Castin's trading post on the Penobscot. Meneval retaliated with raids on English settlements. During King William's War, in 1689, the French king defiantly granted Antoine de Lamothe Cadillac a tract of land at Frenchman's Bay that included Mt. Desert Island.

The role of Acadia during King William's War was principally to send Indians to raid northern New England frontier settlements. Queen Anne's War followed, in which English forces attacked Acadian towns of Fort Beauséjour, Salmon Falls, Grand Pré, and Port Royal. Peace was signed with the Treaty of Utrecht giving England all of Acadia except Nova Scotia.

French priests played a major role in convincing Acadian Indians to attack English frontier settlements. It was no secret that Abbe Le Loutre, missionary to the Micmac, stirred up Maliseet and Micmac Indians to conduct raids in northern New England. The French population of Acadia was so small that they had to rely on Indian warriors. Acadians felt that English expansion threatened them, resulting in Indian raids on New England frontier settlements, particularly in the period 1721–1726, and again from 1745–1763.

Although Acadia and New England were enemies, the Acadians depended on trade goods from Massachusetts. Archaeological digs at many Acadian and Quebec sites have turned up pottery made at Newburyport, Massachusetts, and other New England goods. This trade was threatened by Micmac and Maliseet Indians who sometimes captured coastal vessels. After the British captured Fort Beauséjour in 1755, about 6,000 Acadians who refused to take an oath of allegiance to the English king were removed to southern American colonies. The Acadian bastion of Louisbourg was the next objective. A large expedition under William Pepperrell, Jr. successfully captured it on 26 July 1758, despite stout French resistance. After the removal of France from Canada, Nova Scotia looked to Boston as a cultural and trade center. These ties remained very strong until the American Revolution.

Nicholas N. Smith

References

John B. Brebner, *New England's Outpost: Acadia Before the Conquest of Canada* (1927); Gerald E. Morris, ed., *The Maine Bicentennial Atlas, an Historical Survey* (1976); Beamish Murdoch, *A History of Nova Scotia or Acadia*, 3 vols. (1867); L.F.S. Upton, *Micmacs and Colonists: Indian-White Relations in the Maritimes, 1713–1867* (1979); John Clarence Webster, *Acadia at the End of the Seventeenth Century* (1934).

See also ACADIA, BRITISH CONQUEST OF (1710); ACADIA, NEW ENGLAND ATTACK ON (1690); ACADIA, NEW ENGLAND ATTACK ON (1707); FORT BEAUSÉJOUR; GRAND PRÉ, BATTLE OF; LE LOUTRE, ABBE JEAN LOUIS; LOUISBOURG; PORT ROYAL (CANADA); UTRECHT, TREATY OF

Acadia, British Conquest of (1710)

The British conquest of Acadia, accomplished militarily in 1710 and confirmed by the Treaty of Utrecht (1713), was a turning point in French-British military affairs in North America. It was a crucial part of the process—culminating in the fall of Canada in 1757–1760—by which British arms prevailed. The planning of the 1710 expedition had its origins in events of earlier years. A seaborne attack on Port Royal, Canada, by New England militia in 1707 had been a disaster, and had prompted Governor Joseph Dudley of Massachusetts to conclude that British regular troops should be employed in any future assault. At the same time, Samuel Vetch, a Scottish military officer with merchant connections in Boston and New York, was in London to attempt to persuade the British government of the merits of a thoroughgoing effort to expel the French from North America. In 1708, the Board of Trade endorsed Vetch's proposals, and 1709 was selected as the year for an elaborate, two-faceted attack on the French by British and colonial troops. While one contingent would leave Boston by sea to fall upon Port Royal and then Quebec, another force would march overland to attack Montreal. By the spring of 1709, Vetch was in Boston with a colonel's commission and a promise of the governorship of the conquered Canada. Unfortunately for him, and for the colonies which raised troops for the expedition and paid them through the summer, British priorities shifted and only in October did word arrive in Boston that "divers weighty considerations" had

prevented dispatch of the British force. Hasty attempts to organize a late autumn attack on Port Royal, to make some productive use of the preparations made, failed to mature.

Out of the climate of disillusionment created by the fiasco of 1709 came steady pressure from Boston for British support of an assault on Port Royal, if not on Canada, the next year. For New England, as opposed to New York, Acadia was as great a concern as Canada. Privateering attacks from Port Royal on New England shipping had been increasingly successful, and New Englanders also held Acadian colonial authorities responsible for Abenaki raids on their frontiers. In early 1710, with the consent of the General Court, Dudley instructed the Massachusetts agent in London to press for an expedition against this "perfect Dunkirk, and Nest of Robbers." This time the response was more active. In mid-July, a force of some 400 British marines disembarked in Boston, commanded by Colonel Francis Nicholson. A former lieutenant governor of Virginia, Nicholson had been among the prospective commanders of the 1709 expedition and was now named commander in chief. Vetch was designated governor of the conquered Acadia, or Nova Scotia as it would then be known.

The departure of the fleet for Port Royal was delayed for several weeks by organizational problems in raising and equipping the 1,500 colonial troops—the majority from Massachusetts, but with contingents from Connecticut, Rhode Island, and New Hampshire—who combined with the marines and a group of trained colonial grenadiers. After leaving Boston on 18 September, however, the expedition went according to plan. The fleet reached Port Royal on the 24th, and the marines and grenadiers led the disembarkation the following day. The attackers were aware that the fort was in a state of disrepair and was inadequately garrisoned. Acadia and its governor, Daniel d'Auger de Subercase, were feeling the effects of the increasing exhaustion of France after an extended period of European and North American warfare. Supplies and reinforcements had not arrived from France in significant quantity for the two previous years, and Subercase had to face the 1710 attack with an ill-assorted and poorly equipped garrison of fewer than 300. "I will do all that is expected of me," was the governor's plea to the French minister of marine, "but ultimately, Monseigneur, I beg you to realize that I cannot do the impossible." Among the impossibilities was the launching of a serious attack on the disembarking troops. Unlike in 1707, when Subercase had personally led a series of effective forays which contributed importantly to the discomfiture and eventual withdrawal of the invaders of that year, the governor now had to remain within the walls of the fort and employ what little artillery he had. It had little effect, and the British unhurriedly went about the business of deploying their own guns and mortars. When they had done so, they began a bombardment that brought about desertions from the garrison, pressure for surrender from the Acadian colonists, and eventually a unanimous verdict among Subercase's senior officers that capitulation was inevitable. Terms were agreed upon on 2 October.

The French surrender of Port Royal was carried out with as much bravado as circumstances permitted. As agreed, the regular troops of the garrison marched out with colors flying, and Subercase was said to have informed Nicholson that he hoped to return to visit him in the following spring. In reality, as the ragged soldiers embarked for France, where Subercase would have his conduct examined by a court-martial that acquitted him of negligence, the prospect of a full-scale French counterattack was remote. Both Canada and French Newfoundland were hard pressed to ensure their own defense, and notions of an expedition from France itself remained vague. Nevertheless, there were real questions as to how effective the British conquest would be. The new union flag flew over the fort and settlement now renamed Annapolis Royal, in honor of Queen Anne, in the similarly restyled colony of Nova Scotia. Nicholson and his council of war lost no time in proclaiming that this was a territory to which the British crown had "an undoubted right of inheritance as well as conquest." The native Micmac inhabitants, however, were unimpressed by any such assertion. Although they had held aloof from the battle that had led to the French surrender, Micmac forces—with reinforcement from some 40 Abenaki who had inflicted defeat on a substantial British detachment in the spring of 1711—effectively harassed the British garrison thereafter. With the Acadian inhabitants, the British relationship was uneasy. Some Acadians at Annapolis Royal cooperated, while others resisted passively or actively. His garrison depleted by disease and desertion, and supplies running low, Samuel Vetch reported to London in the summer of 1712 that he was "allmost . . . in dispair." Soon, he warned, Nova Scotia might have to be abandoned.

Vetch's gloom proved to be excessive, except with respect to his own office: he was dismissed in the following year and replaced by Francis Nicholson. The Treaty of Utrecht facilitated the continuation of the British presence in Nova Scotia by turning over to Britain the French claim to Acadia, except for French retention of Cape Breton Island and the island of Saint John (later known as Prince Edward Island). The Micmac still had no reason to recognize the legitimacy of British pretensions, but as between the two European powers the treaty had confirmed the military conquest of 1710. The conquest was a fragile victory for Great Britain, but it was also a serious setback for France. It represented an important phase in the loosening of the French grip on the northernmost parts of North America.

John G. Reid

References

René Baudry, "Daniel d'Auger de Subercase," *Dictionary of Canadian Biography,* ed. by George W. Brown, et al., 12 vols. (1966–1990), 2:35–39; Naomi Griffiths, *The Acadians: Creation of a People* (1973); Dale Miquelon, *New France, 1701–1744: "A Supplement to Europe"* (1987); George A. Rawlyk, *Nova Scotia's Massachusetts: A Study of Massachusetts–Nova Scotia Relations, 1630 to 1784* (1973); G.M. Waller, *Samuel Vetch: Colonial Enterpriser* (1960).

See also QUEEN ANNE'S WAR; VETCH, SAMUEL

Acadia, New England Attack on (1690)

The decision to launch a seaborne attack on French Acadia by New England forces in the spring of 1690 had its origins in events of the previous three years. The English revolution of 1688–1689 had led to war between England and France in May 1689. The fragile coexistence between English and French in eastern North America which had prevailed since the Treaty of Whitehall, 1686, now broke down. At the same time, English-Abenaki hostilities in the Abenaki territory continued as they had done since 1688. In August 1689, Abenaki forces reduced the English fort at Pemaquid, between the Penobscot and Kennebec Rivers. Observed by French missionaries, this impressive display of military strength led to the conclusion of a formal alliance between French and Abenaki, as opposed to the loose network of religious and kinship ties that had previously existed. Already there were influential New Englanders who believed that the French and Abenaki were acting in collaboration, and resentment had also grown in Massachusetts fishing centers over the efforts of a new governor of Acadia—Louis-Alexandre des Friches de Meneval—who since 1687 had been endeavoring to refortify Port Royal and exclude New England fishing vessels from Acadian waters. By December 1689, the Massachusetts General Court was receiving complaints of the "great depredations" of the French at Port Royal, and was discussing the possibility of a raid on Acadia.

Factional quarrels in Boston delayed the laying of firm plans. Port Royal was, in any case, much less formidable militarily than the New Englanders suspected, with Meneval reduced to virtual despair by the shortage of supplies from France and discontent among his officers and troops. The proposed attack might never have taken place had it not been for raids launched by French and native forces from Canada early in 1690 on Schenectady, New York, Salmon Falls, New Hampshire, and eventually on Casco, Maine. Each of these assaults was devastatingly successful and caused much loss of life among the colonists. News of the Salmon Falls raid, reaching Boston in late March—even though it had had no connection with Port Royal—finally prompted the naming of a commander for the attack on Acadia, in the person of Sir William Phips. Originally from a small English community on the Kennebec River, Phips had assiduously promoted his career in London and Boston. His religious conversion in early 1690 solidified his credentials with the Massachusetts political elite. As a commander, Phips was untried, though his instructions were thoroughgoing: he was enjoined to bring about the surrender of Port Royal and other French centers in Acadia, or in the event of their refusal to surrender he was to "assault, fight, take, kill, destroy, utterly extirpate, and root out the said common Enemy."

The raid itself was less dramatic than the instructions might have suggested, though it was successful in its own way. Phips left Boston in late April with a regiment of militia 446 strong, and a fleet of seven vessels. Following inconclusive skirmishes at Penobscot, Machias, and Passamaquoddy Bay, the expedition reached Port Royal on 9 May. Within two days, the despondent Meneval was persuaded to capitulate on terms that guaranteed the safety of the Acadian colonists, their possessions, and of the Port Royal church. The terms were quickly breached by the victors, who set about plundering the settlement. "We . . . rifled the Church, Pull'd down the High-Altar, breaking their Images," wrote Phips of the beginning of this two-day riot of looting. By 14 May, Phips was ready to turn to more solemn business. Asserting the English claim to ownership of what New Englanders customarily referred to as Nova Scotia, he summoned the Acadian inhabitants to take an oath of allegiance to the English crown. According to Phips, many did so, and with "great Acclamations and Rejoicings." Phips then set up a small council of Acadian residents, headed by a sergeant in the defeated garrison, Charles La Tourasse, to govern in the English interest. After vessels had been sent to attack other Acadian coastal communities, the New Englanders gathered up the plunder and some prisoners—including the unfortunate Meneval, who would endure almost a year of captivity—and regained Boston harbor by month's end.

The 1690 raid on Acadia brought enrichment to many of the New England participants who returned with booty, and it greatly advanced the career of Phips. Despite the failure of a larger expedition under his command, later in 1690, to take the French stronghold of Quebec, he became governor of Massachusetts in 1692. The results for the Acadians were necessarily less salutary. The governing council appointed in Port Royal was not a serious assertion of English rule. La Tourasse quickly reported what had taken place to a new French commandant in Acadia—Joseph Robinau de Villebon—who was in the process of establishing his headquarters in the St. John River Valley. Villebon authorized La Tourasse to continue the sham, later reporting to France that he had "carried out all my orders with the greatest exactitude." But there was also a more destructive aftermath for the Acadians. In June, Port Royal was attacked by warships from New York. The attack not only brought more pillage, but also the killing of livestock and—according to Villebon—the hanging of two Acadians and the deaths of the entire family of one of them in their burning house.

It was this harsh epilogue to the initial raid of May 1690 that most clearly indicated the significance of the events of that spring. The Phips descent on Port Royal had its elements of *opéra-bouffe*. Yet it was part of the inauguration of a new phase of French-English hostility in eastern North America. Previous informal efforts at coexistence were breaking down in the face of imperial conflicts and bitterness engendered by the destructive raiding warfare by land and sea in 1689–1690 and thereafter. The ensuing years would be bloody and destructive, and the New England assault on Acadia of May 1690—while itself remarkable for plunder rather than extensive bloodshed—pointed the way to that difficult future.

John G. Reid

References

John Bartlet Brebner, *New England's Outpost: Acadia Before the Conquest of Canada* (1927); George A. Rawlyk, *Nova Scotia's Massachusetts: A Study of Massachusetts–Nova Scotia Relations, 1630 to 1784* (1973); John G. Reid, *Acadia, Maine, and New Scotland: Marginal Colonies in the Seventeenth Century* (1981); C.P. Stacey, "Sir William Phips," *Dictionary of Canadian Biography,* ed. by George W. Brown, et al., 12 vols. (1966–1990), 1:544–546.

See also KING WILLIAM'S WAR; PHIPS, WILLIAM

Acadia, New England Attack on (1707)

With the recurrence of war between England and France in 1702, exchanges between New Englanders and the forces of the French and their native allies became increasingly bitter. Land raids into New England led the Massachusetts General Court by early 1704 to call for the raising of a force "to insult the Eastern Coast of Nova Scotia and Port Royal." The resulting expedition commanded by Benjamin Church did serious damage to a number of Acadian settlements, but did not assault Port Royal. By 1706, matters had become more complex. Six Boston merchants were found by the General Court to have traded illegally with Acadians and Micmac. The scandal even reached close to Governor Joseph Dudley, and Dudley's subsequent endorsement of a raid in force on Acadia represented an effort both to appease public opinion and to rescue his own reputation. The force that left Boston in May 1707, commanded by John March, included some 1,300 soldiers and sailors on a 24-vessel fleet. Most of the troops were from Massachusetts: intensive efforts to recruit from the other New England colonies had yielded only small contingents from New Hampshire and Rhode Island, and none at all from Connecticut.

When the New Englanders disembarked before Port Royal on 26 May 1707 and began to move toward the fort, their number was more than double that of the garrison. Repeated harassment by small groups of French troops, however, coordinated by Governor Daniel d'Auger de Subercase, kept the attackers from pressing home their numerical advantage. At a chaotic series of councils of war in early June, March was persuaded that Port Royal could not be taken and the fleet retreated to Casco Bay. The commander then pleaded in a letter to Dudley that the governor should not "misconstrue our Actions." Misconstruction or not, popular outrage in Boston forced the governor's hand. The fleet was ordered back to Port Royal in July, and March was replaced as commander by a committee of three other officers. The renewed attack was another disaster, and the scheme finally collapsed in a welter of recrimination. Failure as it was, the attack of 1707 was not unimportant. Governor Dudley, disgusted at "the disorderly Temper" of the New England forces, drew the conclusion that any future expedition would need to be strengthened by British regular troops. Three years later he got his wish. Thus, the failure of 1707 exerted a significant influence on the planning of the more successful expedition of 1710.

John G. Reid

References

John Bartlet Brebner, *New England's Outpost: Acadia Before the Conquest of Canada* (1927); Philip S. Haffenden, *New England in the English Nation, 1689–1713* (1974); George A. Rawlyk, *Nova Scotia's Massachusetts: A Study of Massachusetts–Nova Scotia Relations, 1630 to 1784* (1973).

See also HILTON, WINTHROP; MARCH, JOHN; QUEEN ANNE'S WAR

Ackia, Battle of (1736)

French and Indian forces under command of Jean-Baptiste Le Moyne de Bienville fought Chickasaws at their village of Ackia on 26 May 1736 after Pierre d'Artaguette's defeat at the Battle of Ogoula Tchetoka two months earlier.

Unaware of Artaguette's defeat and Chickasaw knowledge of his plans, Bienville's army of approximately 500 soldiers, voyageurs, settlers, Indians, and armed Negroes commanded by free black officers arrived at the rendezvous point with no word or sign of Artaguette. Because of Chickasaw preparation and a lack of coordination between Bienville and his Choctaw allies, Bienville was defeated almost as decisively as Artaguette; a total defeat was prevented only by the actions of Alabama Mingo's Choctaw warriors, who carried off wounded Frenchmen, and lost 22 of their own men in the effort. This second defeat fueled French determination to destroy the Chickasaws and was a prime motivation for the Chickasaw campaign of 1739–1740.

Michael James Foret

References

James R. Atkinson, "The Ackia and Ogoula Tchetoka Chickasaw Village Locations in 1736 during the French-Chickasaw War," *Mississippi Archaeology,* 20 (1985):53–72; Michael James Foret, "On the Marchlands of Empire: Trade, Diplomacy, and War on the Southeastern Frontier, 1733–1763," Ph.D. Dissertation, College of William and Mary (1990):131–169.

Joseph Peyser, "1740 French Map Pinpoints Battle Site in Mississippi," *Mapline,* 39 (1985):1–4; ———, "The Chickasaw Wars of 1736 and 1740: French Military Drawings and Plans Document the Struggle for the Lower Mississippi," *Journal of Mississippi History,* 44 (1982):1–25.

See also AFRICAN AMERICANS; CHICKASAW WARS; LE MOYNE DE BIENVILLE, JEAN-BAPTISTE; OGOULA TCHETOKA, BATTLE OF

Adair, James (c. 1709–c. 1783)

James Adair was one of several unusually gifted Celts who came to make his fortune among the Indians of the Southeast; he was better known than most because he wrote *The History of the American Indians* (1775), which is still used today as a valuable source of ethnographic facts about the Indians of the Southeast in the eighteenth century. In spite of Adair's thoroughly-argued conviction that the Indians descended from the Lost Tribes of Israel, Adair was well qualified to write it, since he spent some 30 years as an Indian trader among the Chickasaws,

Creek, and Choctaws. But Adair was not only a trader; he pursued his own interests and sometimes consented to serve as a tool of official Indian policy. He complained loudly of the incompetence of others when his goals were thwarted.

Apparently a younger son of the Scotch-Irish Adair family, James Adair came to South Carolina in 1735, engaging in the Indian trade with the Cherokees and Catawbas; through those contacts establishing trade first with the Chickasaws of South Carolina, then with the major part of that nation on the upper reaches of the Tombigbee River by 1744. At about that time he was enlisted by Governor James Glen of South Carolina in a plan to win over the Choctaws as part of Carolina's actions against the French in King George's War. He claimed that his negotiations with the Choctaw war chief Red Shoe in 1745 were probably influential in exacerbating Choctaw-French relations and instigating the murder of several Frenchmen by Red Shoe's faction.

Adair did not receive the promised monopoly of the Choctaw trade, so he was bitterly amused to see Glen's "Sphynx Company" fail miserably at exploiting it, as Red Shoe's death led to the outbreak of civil war among the Choctaws. Probably responsible for several pamphlets and memorials published against Glen in Charles Town, Adair was unsuccessful in his applications for reward for his actions, and he returned to the Cherokee trade to mend his fortunes in 1750. He must have maintained his ties with his friends, the eastern Chickasaws, however, because he led them in 1760 to support Archibald Montgomery at Fort Prince George after the Cherokee revolt of that year. In 1761, he returned to the western Chickasaw trade, making some success as the British took over eastern Louisiana in 1763, and trade could be based in Mobile.

Adair certainly hoped to be made official agent to the southeastern tribes, but doubtless his frequently impolitic behavior caused him to be passed over in favor first of Edmond Atkin in 1759, then of John Stuart in 1763, neither of whom he considered qualified. He left the Chickasaws in 1768 to promote his book and request a missionary for the Chickasaws in New York. In 1775, he was in London supervising the printing of his book. Returning to Carolina, he may have settled and married among the Overhill Cherokees, as place-names and Cherokee genealogies suggest.

Patricia Galloway

References

James Adair, *History of the American Indians* (1775); Samuel Cole Williams, "Introduction," in Williams, ed., *Adair's History of the American Indians*, rpt. 1966.

Admiralty Law

The imperial government in London developed admiralty law to regulate the capturing of enemy vessels and cargoes (which were referred to as prizes) by the Royal Navy and privateers. Admiralty law included royal instructions and parliamentary statutes adjudicated by the High Court of Admiralty in England and by vice-admiralty courts in the American colonies.

Royal instructions governed the conduct of British warships when taking prizes. They established criteria for issuing letters of marque, which were essentially licenses to seize enemy vessels, and thus distinguished privateering from the illegal activity of piracy. The instructions required that all prizes be tried in admiralty courts, and also addressed the number of witnesses, treatment of prisoners, and safeguarding of cargoes.

In addition to royal instructions, Parliament enacted legislation to govern privateering. During seventeenth-century imperial conflicts, no comprehensive statutes existed to control prize adjudication. This allowed England's monarch great latitude to influence prize cases and created an atmosphere of uncertainty for privateer owners. Beginning in Queen Anne's War (1702–1713), Parliament passed a series of acts to regulate prize adjudication. These laws established a uniform legal process for condemning prizes captured by British warships.

Admiralty courts adjudicated maritime disputes. Like their British counterparts, colonial vice-admiralty courts decided prize cases (and other maritime causes) following the international admiralty tradition of the civil law, which did not include juries. The prize courts were popular tribunals with the owners and crews of British warships because they rendered verdicts in favor of privateers and naval vessels in the great majority of cases. Condemnation rates over 90 percent were common.

Carl E. Swanson

References

Michael Craton, "The Role of the Caribbean Vice-Admiralty Courts in British Imperialism," *Caribbean Studies*, XI (1971):5–20; Helen J. Crump, *Colonial Admiralty Jurisdiction in the Seventeenth Century* (1931); Richard Pares, *Colonial Blockade and Neutral Rights, 1739–1763* (1938); Carl E. Swanson, *Predators and Prizes: American Privateering and Imperial Warfare, 1739–1748* (1991); Carl Ubbelohde, *The Vice-Admiralty Courts and the American Revolution* (1960).

African Americans

African Americans were active participants in the colonial wars of America, particularly in the Southeast. The English, French, and Spanish all employed blacks in their military campaigns, and in several instances blacks allied with Native Americans in warfare. Moreover, the potential alliance of blacks and Indians shaped the course of the South's development and the diplomacy of its people.

European armies in the Southeast, as early as the first conquistador armies, ordinarily employed black slaves as teamsters for the movement of supplies on campaigns. Black slaves also accompanied armies as the servants of officers and other soldiers. By the early eighteenth century, the English had taken the next step of arming slaves for the defense of their colonies, as in the Yamasee War when white Carolinians became desperate to hold off hostile Native Americans who had ravaged their frontier. The Yamasee already had liberated hundreds of slaves from Carolina plantations and the Carolinians probably surmised that it would be better to arm slaves against the Yamasee than lose them in raids. Many of the slaves liberated by the Yamasee were formed into a free militia by the Spanish at Fort Mose outside of St. Augustine. They and later runaways helped protect the Spanish colony. On subsequent incursions by the British into Florida, particularly during the Anglo-Spanish War of 1740, the British recaptured runaways in Florida and returned them to slavery. However, the free black militia survived and the Spanish removed these black soldiers from the Southeast on the cession of Florida in 1763, with many then serving as militia in the Spanish Caribbean.

The British had no trouble recognizing the military value of their slaves even before the Yamasee War, for blacks' knowledge of the military arts and their desire for freedom earlier had combined against British interests. By 1711, during the Tuscarora War, South Carolinian John Barnwell led English troops into North

Carolina and discovered to his dismay that a runaway black from Virginia named Henry had helped the Tuscarora design a "well constructed fortification." At the making of the peace, Barnwell insisted that the Tuscarora hand over 25 runaways under their protection. More than 20 years after the war, South Carolina officials still complained about Tuscarora liberating slaves from their plantations and contemplated a war of extirpation against them.

Runaways not only provided military expertise and a willingness to fight in alliance with indigenous peoples, but also a host of skills that could influence the military decisions of aboriginal peoples. They served as translators, diplomats, and advisors. At one point during the Yamasee War the governor of South Carolina expected the Cherokee to join them against the Creek, but he learned that "2 Rogues of Negroes run away from ye English and came and told [the Cherokee] a parcel of lies which hindered their coming." Another nation that joined South Carolina's enemies in the Yamasee War was the Waccamaw, who numbered fewer than 100 men in 1720. The single surviving source recording the Waccamaw conflict with the colony noted that blacks had instigated the Indians against the whites.

The influence of runaway slaves in Native American communities was readily apparent to the French and Spanish, who both employed blacks in frontier diplomacy. The French, for instance, used a black "messenger" to convince a party of 70 Creek warriors not to attack the Yamasee in Florida. The Spanish also used black translators to parley with the Creek.

England and France both worked diligently to keep their slaves and their aboriginal neighbors apart and mutually hostile to prevent military alliances. South Carolina officials repeatedly passed laws barring African Americans from employment in the Indian trade, where they could learn Indian languages and gain a familiarity that could undermine the colony's security. Nevertheless, the traders continued to employ blacks despite the laws and the stiff penalties those laws provided. Runaways never ceased to search for refuge among indigenous peoples and to counter colonial officials' arguments with their own. In 1751, Carolina trader Richard Smith, for instance, reported that three runaway blacks told the Keowees "that the white People was coming up to destroy them all, and that they had got some Creek Indians to assist them." Smith believed that the run-

aways spoke the truth, "and the more [so] for that the old Warrior of Keowee said some Negroes had applied to him, and told him that there was in all Plantations many Negroes more than white People, and that for the sake of Liberty they would join them."

Nowhere did a black-Indian military alliance pose a greater threat to the survival of a European colony than in the Natchez War. More than 100 black slaves helped the Natchez in their attack on the French in 1729. When a French-led party of Choctaw counterattacked, the liberated slaves stuck by their Natchez allies, leading Louisiana Governor Etienne Périer to ruefully report to his superiors that the defeat of the Natchez "would have been complete if it had not been for the negroes who prevented the Choctaws from carrying off the powder and who by their resistance had given the Natchez time to enter the[ir] two forts."

The French so feared black-Indian cooperation during the war that the governor recruited a party of blacks to murder a small group of Indians whom the governor knew were innocent of any conspiracy against the colony. Périer justified his actions in a letter to his superior in France. "Even the Chaouchas who were a nation of 30 men below New Orleans made our colonists tremble . . . which made me decide to have them destroyed by our own negroes which they executed with as much promptness as secrecy. This example carried out by our negroes has kept the other little nations up the river in a respectful attitude."

During the French wars with the Chickasaw that followed, free blacks were given the chance to prove their military prowess to the French. At the Battle of Ackia, one of several French defeats by the Chickasaw, the French marched behind mantelets carried by blacks. When in the midst of the fighting the blacks dropped the mantelets and fled, a free black named Simon, in a display of heroism and martial valor "distinguished himself by a singularly bold feat performed before the whole army." Simon ran up the hill to the Chickasaw fort, and with musket balls "raining around him, he held on, and reaching a troop of horses at pasture, picked out a fine mare, sprung on her back, and rode to camp unscathed." French observers noted that Simon's performance was done solely to show the French that blacks could make brave warriors. Perhaps Simon's bravery is what led the French in the future to avoid using black troops in Louisiana—a slave population that was confident in its martial powers posed a grave threat to the colony.

The presence of African Americans in the Southeast had great impact upon the region's military history. Without black soldiers and black labor the European forces would have been much the weaker, especially at critical moments when resources were strained. Black labor played a significant role in the construction of fortifications and other defensive networks, and the threat of black-Indian alliances loomed throughout the entire colonial period. British dependence on slavery shaped relations with its indigenous and European neighbors. Vigilant efforts had to be made to prevent black-Indian alliances. The French, too, feared the specter of their slaves cooperating with indigenous enemies. The Natchez War shook the colony to its foundation, and an alleged slave conspiracy in New Orleans during the war was blamed on the Chickasaw.

The participation of African Americans in military enterprises was limited by the fact that they had no homeland of their own in the Southeast. Except for raiding Maroon communities, blacks had little or no hope of forging their own free communities. In Florida, free blacks did succeed in establishing a community, but its existence depended on the tenuous Spanish settlement. The potential for establishing larger free black communities existed; Governor James Glen of South Carolina was but one of several British officials who noted that if neighboring aboriginal communities were extirpated or forced from their lands, then black Maroon communities would replace them. Thus, settlement Indians were induced by large rewards to return runaways, which helped limit the potential military power of African Americans. Still, black runaways found refuge among the larger indigenous nations of the interior continent, despite the rewards and pressures placed by the European powers upon native communities. Although many southeastern Indians came to own African American slaves, others, and sometimes the Indian slaveholders themselves, provided refuge and formed military alliances with blacks well into the nineteenth century.

Alan Gallay

References

J.H. Easterby, R. Nicholas Oldsberg, and Terry Lipscomb, eds., *The Colonial Records of South Carolina: The Journal of the Commons House of Assembly,* 14 vols. (1951–); Jane Landers, "Gracia Real de Santa Teresa de Mose: A Free Black Town in Spanish Colonial Florida," *American Historical Review,* 95 (1990):9–30.

W.L. McDowell, Jr., ed., *The Colonial Records of South Carolina,* Series 2, *Documents Relating to Indian Affairs, May 21, 1750–August 7, 1754* (1958); Chapman Milling, *Red Carolinians* (1940); Dunbar Rowland and A.B. Sanders, eds., *Mississippi Provincial Archives, French Dominion, 1729–1740* (1927); Reuben G. Thwaites, ed., *The Jesuit Relations and Allied Documents,* Vol. 68 (1896–1901).

See also BLACK AND INDIAN MILITIAS; MENÉNDEZ, FRANCISCO; NATCHEZ WAR; STONO REBELLION

Aguayo Expedition (1720–1722)

The Aguayo expedition was organized by Joseph de Azlor y Virto de Vera, second marqués de San Miguel de Aguayo, to secure east Texas after a brief French incursion in 1719. The expedition resulted in a stronger Spanish presence in Texas and the establishment of two new presidios and numerous missions.

In response to a small French force from Natchitoches, Louisiana, overrunning Mission San Miguel de los Adaes, the easternmost Spanish establishment in Texas, the Spanish abandoned the region. Aguayo offered to raise a military force strong enough to drive the French out and secure the province. Receiving a vice-regal commission as governor of Coahuila and Texas to raise 500 men, he sent an advance unit to reinforce San Antonio in 1720, and in 1721 crossed into Texas with a mounted infantry battalion. While a detachment under Domingo Ramón took possession of the Gulf coast near the former site of René-Robert Cavelier, sieur de La Salle's colony. Aguayo proceeded to east Texas where he reoccupied the missions and Presidio de los Tejas and established a new garrison close to Mission San Miguel.

By the time the Aguayo expedition arrived in Texas, the French had long since retreated. When the force arrived at the border with Louisiana, it found the French unwilling to do more than verbally protest Aguayo's decision to establish a Spanish presence so close to Natchitoches. Aguayo did not believe the French threat entirely gone and left much of his force behind as a garrison. When the expedition entered Texas, the province's active Spanish establishments consisted of the presidio and two missions at San Antonio; when it left, the province contained four presidios and ten missions and more than 260 soldier/settlers, many with families. The expedition has been credited with finally settling the Texas ownership question in favor of the Spanish.

Jesús F. de la Teja

References
    Richard G. Santos, ed. and trans., *Aguayo Expedition into Texas, 1721: An Annotated Translation of the Five Versions of the Diary Kept by Br. Juan Antonio de la Peña* (1981).

See also FRANCE-SPAIN RELATIONS; TEXAS

Aix-la-Chapelle, Treaty of (1748)
The treaty of Aix-la-Chapelle signaled an intermission rather than a conclusion in the power struggles of the eighteenth century. Although the War of the Austrian Succession (1739–1748) affected all the European countries and their colonies, Britain and France more than any other powers had the ability to decide when to end the war, and by 1747 both were exhausted and ready for peace. Britain was no longer able to contend with the French armies, led by Maréchal Saxe, one of the ablest of eighteenth-century generals, who had triumphed at Fontenoy (11 May 1745), Raucoux (11 October 1746), and Lawfeldt (2 July 1747). France had captured Brussels (1746) and Bergen-op-Zoom (1747) and was about to overrun the Dutch Republic. Saxe seemed likely to achieve what had eluded Louis XIV: domination of the Low Countries across from England. In contrast to France's successes in Europe, the war in the New World and on the oceans had been a series of disasters: the loss of Louisbourg in 1745 endangered Canada; storms had shattered the duc d'Anville's fleet sent to America in 1746; and two fleets had been defeated in 1747. France was as eager as Britain for peace.

    After months of negotiations, Britain, France, and the Netherlands signed the final treaty on 18 October 1748, and the other major signatories, Austria, Spain, and Sardinia, acceded within the next few weeks. Britain returned Louisbourg to France, and the French surrendered their conquests in the Austrian Netherlands, the United Provinces, and Ma-

dras. Knowledgeable people had expected Britain to give up something, either Gibraltar or Cape Breton, and Parliament's appropriation of £236,000 in 1747 to reimburse Americans for taking Louisbourg was a forewarning of what would be done with that fortress, but the cession of Louisbourg, however inevitable, was disappointing to Americans. Britain kept the infamous *asiento* four more years, and France ceased supporting the Stuart pretenders. Austria emerged from the war as the major loser: the treaty guaranteed Prussia's ownership of Silesia, which Frederick the Great had seized in 1740. Austria was disgusted with Britain's inability to help it; this contributed to the "Diplomatic Revolution" which allied Austria with France in the next war. Britain and France settled nothing about boundaries between their American possessions. They did appoint commissioners to discuss the matter, but a real decision was left to the next war.

Joseph A. Devine, Jr.

References
    Richard Lodge, *Studies in Eighteenth-Century Diplomacy, 1740–1748* (1930); Richard Pares, "American vs. Continental Warfare, 1739–1763," *English Historical Review,* Vol. LI (1936):429–465; Herbert Richmond, *Statesmen and Sea Power* (1946); Jack M. Sosin, "Louisbourg and the Peace of Aix-la-Chapelle, 1748," *William and Mary Quarterly,* 3d Ser., XIV (1957):516–535.

See also KING GEORGE'S WAR

Alaska
See RUSSIAN AMERICA

Albany Conference (19 June–11 July 1754)
The Albany Conference, one in a series of intercolonial congresses called for the purpose of coordinating defense efforts and Indian affairs, had special importance in that it additionally was the first gathering of delegates from the colonies to consider the establishment of a general rather than a regional intercolonial confederacy.

    A circular letter from the Board of Trade of 18 September 1753 requested Sir Danvers Osborn, governor of New York, to hold an Indian conference to be attended by commissioners from New York, Massachusetts, New Hampshire, New Jersey, Pennsylvania, and Maryland; shortly afterwards the call went out to all the colonies, except Delaware, which had the same governor as Pennsylvania and Georgia, then a fledging frontier province.

Twenty-four commissioners from seven colonies met at the city hall in Albany on 19 June. New Jersey, Virginia, North Carolina, and South Carolina did not send delegates, though, at the request of Governor Robert Dinwiddie, Virginia was unofficially represented by the acting governor of New York, James DeLancey. The delegates to the conference consisted of 14 colony legislators, four New York councilors, and six governors. Only the Massachusetts commissioners had power to conclude a union. One hundred fifty Iroquois also were present. Much of the work of the conference pertained to Indian relations, particularly recognizing Indian land rights and providing for a British-American military buildup on the frontier.

Several commissioners, most notably Benjamin Franklin, Thomas Hutchinson, and Richard Peters, submitted plans of union for consideration. A plan by a non-commissioner, Thomas Pownall, "Considerations toward a General Plan of Measures for the Colonies," also figured in the discussions. Franklin's "Short Hints," originally prepared in 1751, however, formed the basis for the plan of union that emerged from the conference. The "Albany Plan of Union" was reported out of a special committee (consisting of Thomas Hutchinson, Theodore Atkinson, William Pitkin, Samuel Hopkins, Benjamin Franklin, William Smith, and Benjamin Taxker, each representing their respective colonies) on 8 July, and the following day it was "pretty unanimously" adopted.

The Albany Plan of Union called for a president general, appointed by the crown, with powers of enforcement of laws passed by the Grand Council, a veto which could not be over-ridden, and nomination and commissioning of all military officers (subject to approval by the Grand Council). The Grand Council, with legislative authority, consisted of 48 members who would serve three-year terms and be eligible for reelection. During the first three years the number of delegates per colony was to be in proportion to a colony's size and population; afterward the delegations were to be set at seven for Massachusetts and Virginia each, six for Pennsylvania, five for Connecticut, four each for New York, Maryland, North Carolina, and South Carolina, three for New Jersey, and two

each for New Hampshire and Rhode Island. The Grand Council could elect its speaker, and commissioners would receive per diem and travel expense allowances. The Grand Council could name civil officers of the confederacy, such as tax collectors and the treasurer, subject to approval by the president general.

The president general and the Grand Council shared certain joint powers, which included direction of Indian affairs, declaration of peace or war with the Indians, purchase of Indian lands outside colonial boundaries, establishment of new settlements on such lands, enactment of laws affecting new settlements until the king could establish separate colonies, and to raise taxes for defraying Indian and military expenses, erecting forts, raising troops, and building and equipping naval vessels. Most revenue would come from excise taxes on luxury goods. For the plan to go into effect, approval was required from the colonial assemblies and by Parliament.

The Albany Plan of Union was little discussed by the British ministry, which saw fit not to send it to Parliament. The weak leadership did not want to support a plan that was deemed controversial. Moreover, Parliament was not scheduled to convene until November 1754, and it was considered a more pressing matter to attend to the development of military strength in the colonies in the war against France. Among criticisms of the Albany Plan of Union by the British ministry were the lack of power of the president general to prorogue the Grand Council or select its speaker, and that the Grand Council represented a strengthening of legislative authority in the colonies. What the colonists did not know was that the ministry had already thoroughly explored the feasibility of colonial union, and was apprehensive that any federal union might kindle an independence movement.

The Pennsylvania legislature rejected the plan of union on 7 August 1754, and the other colonies either followed suit or took no action at all. Various objections raised in the colonies against union included: fear of losing control by the colonial assemblies; opposition to increased taxation; concern that special interests, such as those of the land companies, would be affected; possible infringement upon charter rights, including stipulations in several charters that boundaries be from sea-to-sea; lack of currency in the colonies for taxation; colonial interest more in defense, Indian alliance, and regulation of the fur trade rather than in union itself; that smaller colonies, such as Rhode Island, were underrepresented; objection to the president general's veto; and fear that the territory embraced by the 11 colonies was too large and its population too great for single administration.

Despite the failure to establish an intercolonial union, the Albany Conference set the precedent for the holding of congresses representing the majority of the colonies. It also established an agenda for the need of cooperation in Indian and military affairs, brought forward the issue of what should be the nature of the colonial contribution to the war effort in America, and planted in the minds of Americans the idea of federal union. Benjamin Franklin was one who labored to make Americans aware of the interdependence among the colonies. His "Join or Die" cartoon in the 9 May 1754 issue of the *Pennsylvania Gazette* depicted a jointed snake in eight pieces, labeled with the initials of New England, New York, New Jersey, Pennsylvania, Maryland, Virginia, North Carolina, and South Carolina. Most colonial newspapers reprinted this emblem, 1754–1755.

Harry M. Ward

References

Lawrence H. Gipson, *The British Empire Before the American Revolution,* Vols. 4 and 5 (1936–1970); Leonard W. Larabee, ed., *The Papers of Benjamin Franklin,* Vols. 4 and 5 (1961 and 1962); Robert C. Newbold, *The Albany Congress and Plan of Union of 1754* (1955); Alison G. Olson, "The British Government and Colonial Union, 1754," *William and Mary Quarterly,* 3d Ser., 27 (1960):22–34; Harry M. Ward, *"Unite or Die": Intercolony Relations, 1690–1763* (1971).

See also FRANKLIN, BENJAMIN; INTERCOLONIAL RELATIONS

Fort Algernon (Virginia)

One of the earliest English forts built in Virginia, Fort Algernon was constructed in 1609 on Old Point Comfort at the lower end of the peninsula between the James River and the York River. Erected by order of George Percy, president of the Virginia Council, to provide a watch on coastal shipping, the fort consisted of an earthwork and wooden stockade. Spaniard Diego de Molina, imprisoned there in 1612, described it as "a weak structure of boards ten hands high." The fort included storehouse, magazine, and barracks for a garrison of 25 to 40 men and was armed with four to 11 cannon of varying sizes.

After accidentally burning in 1612, the fort was rebuilt, but by 1617 it had fallen into disrepair and debates over its refurbishment occupied the Virginia assembly during the 1620s. Another fort was constructed at the site in 1632, but it was abandoned by the 1660s.

Thomas Costa

References

Richard P. Weinhart and Colonel Robert Arthur, *Defender of the Chesapeake: The Story of Fort Monroe,* 3rd ed. (1989).

Fort Allen (Pennsylvania)

On 26 November 1755, in response to a series of Indian attacks along the northern frontier of Pennsylvania, the colony allocated £60,000 for the erection of a string of posts running along the Blue Mountains. Fort Allen was one of the resulting outposts. Located on the Lehigh River ten miles above the Lehigh Gap, it stood on the site of Gnadenhütten, the Moravian mission which was attacked and destroyed on 24 November by a band of 12 Munsee warriors from Assinnissink. A month later a detachment of 40 militiamen, sent to Gnadenhütten to protect the remaining property and stored grain, was routed by Delawares, and the site was abandoned once again. Benjamin Franklin, one of the commissioners appointed to oversee the fort-building projects, returned with another company to complete the fort's construction. Franklin sketched a design of the fort for its builders to follow, and before the end of January he reported that "our fort (if such a magnificent name may be given to so miserable a stockade) was finished in a week, tho' it rained so hard every other day that the men could not work."

Fort Allen had an unusual rectangular shape. It was a palisaded structure about 125 feet long by 50 feet wide, which enclosed three log buildings to house the garrison and its stores. It was garrisoned from the time of its completion in 1756 until 1761 by the Pennsylvania Regiment, a colonial militia force comprised of three battalions and about 1,300 men that ranged among the outlying forts, settlements, and farms throughout the duration of the war. Although the site appeared strategically important when it was first occupied, it saw no military activity after its construction. It did, however, offer accommodations to parties of Indians traveling to and from Easton for conferences in 1756 and 1757. In 1758, the governor of the colony rejected a petition to abandon the fort and move its garrison to a more strategic location. Aside from a brief occupation by a detachment of soldiers in 1763, the fort was abandoned after 1761. In 1787 a visitor to the site could find no trace of the fort.

Eric Hinderaker

References
    Benjamin Franklin, *The Autobiography of Benjamin Franklin*, rpt. 1958; Thomas L. Montgomery, ed., *Report of the Commission to Locate the Site of the Frontier Forts of Pennsylvania*, 2nd ed., 2 vols. (1916); C. Hale Sipe, *The Indian Wars of Pennsylvania* (1929); Charles Morse Stotz, *Outposts of the War for Empire: The French and English in Western Pennsylvania; Their Armies, Their Forts, Their People, 1749–1764* (1985).

See also FORT DUPUI (PENNSYLVANIA); FORT HENRY (PENNSYLVANIA); FORT LEBANON (PENNSYLVANIA); FORT NORRIS (PENNSYLVANIA)

Altamaha River

The Oconee and Ocmulgee Rivers meet in southeastern Georgia to form the Altamaha River. The Altamaha then flows southeasterly through the Georgia pine barrens and coastal lowlands for more than 85 miles to the Atlantic Ocean. The Altamaha River takes its name after a Yamasee Indian town that was located near the lower reaches of the river during the sixteenth century. During the early eighteenth century the British built and garrisoned Fort King George (1721–1727) on the north bank near its mouth. After the founding of the British colony of Georgia, a settlement of Scottish Highlanders built and occupied the town of Darien, near abandoned Fort King George. About 1737, an Indian trading post, called Mount Venture, was established on the south bank of the river about 55 miles above Darien. Mount Venture and its garrison of Georgia rangers was destroyed by Yamasee Indians during a November 1742 raid. In 1746, a new trading post was constructed on the north side of the forks of the Altamaha, probably near its source. During the French and Indian War

(1754–1763), Georgia built Fort Barrington (c. 1756–1760) on the east bank about 30 miles above Darien, and garrisoned it with rangers.

Larry E. Ivers

References
    Verner W. Crane, *The Southern Frontier, 1670–1732* (1929); Larry E. Ivers, *British Drums on the Southern Frontier: The Military Colonization of Georgia, 1733–1749* (1974).

Amherst, Jeffrey, First Baron Amherst (1717–1797)

Jeffery Amherst was the son of Jeffery Amherst, a prosperous barrister, and Elizabeth Kerrill. At the age of 12 he became a page in the house of the first duke of Dorset. His early military career remains obscure, but we do know that he spent his formative years in Ireland as a lieutenant in a cavalry regiment under the tutelage of Sir John Ligonier. Amherst saw his first active service in Germany as aide-de-camp under Ligonier during the War of the Austrian Succession. In December 1745, he was appointed a captain in the 1st Foot Guard's Regiment, a position which carried with it the rank of lieutenant colonel in the army at large. In 1747, he was made aide-de-camp of the duke of Cumberland, who had been recently appointed commander in chief of the allied forces in Europe. After the signing of the Treaty of Aix-la-Chapelle, Amherst returned to England.

His career soon continued its solid, steady rise. In 1756, he was appointed commissary in charge of the administration of the 8,000 Hessian troops taken into British pay at the start of the Seven Years' War. He spent just a few months in Germany performing the required duties of this position—largely financial in nature—and returned to England in May with some of the Hessians, in preparation for a feared French invasion. He was subsequently appointed a colonel in the 15th Foot Regiment, a non-command position, and returned to Germany with the Hessians in March 1757. In October of that year, Ligonier succeeded the duke of Cumberland as commander in chief of the British army, and he quickly appointed his former protégé as commander of the Louisbourg expedition. Amherst's appointment was remarkable, since he was very junior in the army and all of his operational experience had been on staff. Apparently Ligonier, Pitt, and Newcastle all used their considerable influence to win Amherst the position. Amherst finally sailed on 16 March 1758, and in late May joined the fleet commanded by Admiral Edward Boscawen, just outside Halifax harbor. The Louisbourg siege was part of a larger British plan to secure a decisive final victory over the French forces in North America. Through a combination of luck, patience, thorough preparation, and careful deployment of forces, Amherst carried the day in a decisive if somewhat drawn-out victory. The stubborn French defense, however, meant that final victory would have to wait still another year. But in the meantime, Amherst became something of a hero to the New Englanders, and towns in Massachusetts and New Hampshire were named after him. Louisbourg, of course, had always been regarded to be of the greatest strategic importance to both the British and the colonists; at its capture, for instance, Pitt sent a letter with the news by mounted messenger to his wife so she would be among the first to hear.

While still at Louisbourg, Amherst received news of the reverses suffered by General James Abercromby at Fort Carillon. He promptly moved to the latter's assistance with five battalions, leaving a garrison at Louisbourg and sailing to Boston, marching from there to Albany, and thence to Abercromby's aid at Lake George. He also sent detachments under James Wolfe to destroy French settlements in the Gulf of St. Lawrence, and others under Lord Rollo to capture the Ile Saint-Jean. He ordered Robert Monckton, finally, to take control of the communities in the St. John River Valley in New Brunswick. When Amherst arrived at Lake George, however, he quickly saw that he could be of no real help there, so he made his way back to Halifax. It was there, on 9 November, that he heard of Abercromby's defeat, a loss that led to the latter's recall. With Abercromby in disgrace, Amherst was now appointed commander in chief of the forces in America, and he wintered in New York, making plans and logistical arrangements for the 1759 campaign. Here, too, he was welcomed as a hero, and he received official congratulations for his accomplishments from the commander in chief of the British army.

As the fateful new year dawned, Amherst realized that a two-pronged attack on Canada held the greatest potential for final success, a conclusion supported by both Pitt and Ligonier. Detailed orders and campaign plans from Pitt

finally reached Amherst in March 1759. Wolfe was appointed to command the principal expedition up the St. Lawrence River against Quebec, while Amherst would invade from the south with both regular and provincial troops on the route followed earlier and unsuccessfully by Loudoun and Abercromby. Pitt also ordered Amherst to cooperate with Vice Admiral Sir Charles Saunders in a joint attack by land and water against the French settlements on the Mississippi and the Mobile, once the northern campaigns were suspended in the autumn. For these ambitious plans Amherst mobilized a total force of some 16,000 troops. He allotted 5,000 to General John Prideaux for a move against Oswego and Fort Niagara; if successful, this effort would sever the communications lifeline of the French garrisons south of Lake Erie. He kept the remainder of the force for the move up Lake Champlain. Amherst also received assurance from Sir William Johnson of the necessary Indian support; he did not, however, share the details of his plans with Johnson, to insure secrecy from the Indians, lest they leak information to the French. At this point he was completely confident, expecting that even if the French moved all their troops to defend Quebec, Montreal would be left exposed and vulnerable. As always, he was also careful and thorough, stockpiling supplies, laying out encampments, and constructing boats. He also showed concern for the health of his men; instead of liquor, for instance, he encouraged them to drink what he called a "wholesome beverage" of "melasses and the tops of spruce fir, boiled together in a proper quantity of water"—what was known as spruce beer. It was designed as an antiscorbutic and an antidote against the distemper caused by excessive drinking. On 21 June, a month behind schedule, he finally assembled his army of 6,236 regular and provincial troops at Lake St. Sacrament. He then spent another month constructing a fort on the site of the old Fort William Henry. Weather slowed him further and he was plagued by desertions. Finally, on 21 July, he embarked on the principal course of his march, with a total of approximately 11,000 men. He moved to Fort Carillon (Ticonderoga), where the French resisted for several days, hoping at least to slow the British advance. After taking Carillon and rebuilding it, Amherst decided to construct an elaborate fortress at Crown Point beside the French-dismantled walls of Fort Saint Frédéric, which had been blown up and abandoned on

A

31 July. He also regularly sent out scouting parties of Indians and rangers to ensure that he would not be taken by surprise. In the middle of September, for instance, a force of 200 rangers, regulars, and Indians left Crown Point for a diversionary raid against the French Indian village of St. Francis, about 100 miles above Quebec. On 6 October, the British force slaughtered a large number of the village's inhabitants, seriously weakening the French protective shield. Amherst's slow progress during this time is inexplicable, however, since the French had clearly lost the initiative, the new forts were unnecessary, and winter was rapidly approaching.

Amherst now stopped to construct a flotilla of his own for use on Lake Champlain, including two large ships, the *Duke of Cumberland* and the *Boscawen*. The French did in fact have several vessels operating on the lake which threatened to create havoc with the British advance, and Amherst eventually succeeded in trapping three of these vessels and forcing their abandonment. By the time he was able to start down the lake, however, it was 11 October, and he was quickly stalled by cold and windy weather. On the 18th, he received news of the fall of Quebec a month earlier, and decided to return to Crown Point. The season had passed, Quebec had been taken, but the French still held Montreal and another campaign would be necessary. It is clear that Amherst had not taken full advantage of his opportunities that summer, particularly considering that William Johnson, who had replaced the dead Prideaux (who was accidentally killed by one of his men), had captured Niagara. Still, the victories achieved by British and colonial troops were of international significance as part of a chain of British victories around the world.

Predictably, Pitt's orders for 1760 identified Montreal as the principal objective. The plans consisted of a three-pronged attack: James Murray moving up the St. Lawrence with the Quebec garrison; Brigadier General William Haviland moving from Crown Point up Lake Champlain; and Amherst himself moving down the St. Lawrence from Lake Ontario. The French would thus have to divide their limited forces and could not retreat into the interior as they had after the Plains of Abraham defeat. In preparation for this ambitious undertaking, Amherst again requisitioned large forces from the colonies, and spent the winter engaged in extensive logistical planning and preparation. On 9 July, he

arrived in Oswego, and on 10 August, he began the move against Montreal with approximately 11,000 regulars, provincials, and Indians. On 25 August, the British captured Fort Lévis, the major barrier to Montreal. On 6 September, the army landed at Lachine, on the island of Montreal, and encamped before the city. Haviland was by now on the south shore of the St. Lawrence opposite Montreal, and Murray was just below the city. The French, of course, were in an impossible situation. The militia had deserted, and Governor Pierre de Rigaud de Vaudreuil and General François Gaston de Lévis had scarcely more than 2,000 men left to face 17,000 British troops. They had no alternative but surrender. As at Louisbourg, Amherst refused the French the honors of war, citing their Indian atrocities; the French battalions burned their colors rather than give them up, and the garrison surrendered on 8 September 1760. Amherst subsequently organized expeditions against Dominica and Martinique in 1761 and 1762, and recovered St. John's, Newfoundland, in 1762.

Almost as soon as news of the European peace came in early 1763, however, Amherst began to hear of difficulties with the American Indians. His dislike of and contempt for the Indians are well known; he often boasted of his power over them. He was slow to recognize the seriousness of the outbreak, underestimating the military capacity of the Indians. But perhaps more important was his official disapproval of the customary gift-giving in negotiations, a stand which fostered considerable Indian resentment. He also imposed limitations on gifts of gunpowder, which the Indians desperately relied upon for hunting. On 21 June, Amherst was notified of the blockade of Detroit by Pontiac; he suggested to Colonel Henry Bouquet that smallpox might be induced among the Indians, and Bouquet offered to try to do so with blankets. And indeed the attempt was made. Amherst also sent Bouquet on a relief expedition to Fort Pitt after he learned that a British detachment had been routed at Point Pelee on Lake Erie; with this news, in fact, he began to take the uprising much more seriously. But after a British victory at Bushy Run and a defeat at Niagara, the French finally convinced the Indians that the war was indeed over and that they would receive no further support. A conference in November 1763 ended all hostilities. In 1764, Amherst left for England, never again to return to America.

In 1759, Amherst had been given the sinecure post of governor of Virginia, and he had garnered several other military appointments. By 1762, he was a lieutenant general and a Knight of the Bath. In 1763, he built a new country house named Montreal on the family estate. In 1768, when the crown decided it wanted an active governor in Virginia, Amherst resigned rather than reside in the colony. Though he accepted an annuity in compensation, he seems to have taken offense and resigned all his colonelcies, though he was shortly reappointed to them. In 1770, he was made governor of Guernsey, and in 1772, lieutenant general of the ordnance, a position which made him in essence the king's chief military adviser, since there was no commander in chief at the time. He also sought unsuccessfully to obtain a grant of the confiscated Jesuit's estates in Canada, though his heirs were granted an annuity of £3,000 for the lands he never received. Amherst declined an offer from the king in January 1775 to take command of the troops in America, and refused a like offer in 1778, though he was that year appointed commander in chief. In 1776, he was made Lord Amherst. In June 1780, he restored order in London after the Gordon Riots. He was dismissed as commander when North's ministry went out of power in 1782; but in 1793, at 76 years of age, he was again appointed commander in chief with a Cabinet seat. He received his last honor in July 1796, when he was appointed field marshal.

Jeffery Amherst was a person of grave, formal, even cold manners, a solid rather than a brilliant soldier who never conducted a battle; the siege of Louisbourg was the closest he came to actual leadership in combat. He was, however, a strong organizer who left nothing to chance, and this perhaps was what Britain needed most in its confrontation with France.

Ronald P. Dufour

References

Lawrence Henry Gipson, *The Great War for Empire: The Victorious Years, 1758–1760* (1949); Bernard Knollenberg, "General Amherst and Germ Warfare," *Mississippi Valley Historical Review*, LXI (1954–1955):489–494; Douglas Edward Leach, *Arms for Empire: A Military History of the British Colonies in North America, 1607–1763* (1973).

Lee Sullivan McCollester, "Jeffery Amherst," *Dictionary of American Biography*, Vol. 1 (1928); Lawrence S. Mayo, *Jeffery Amherst: A Biography* (1916); C.P. Stacey, "Jeffery Amherst," *Dictionary of Canadian Biography*, 12 vols. (1966–1990), IV; J.C. Webster, ed., *Journal of William Amherst in America, 1758–1760* (1927).

See also BOUQUET, HENRY; GAGE, THOMAS; LOUISBOURG, SIEGE OF (1758); MONTREAL, ATTACK ON; PONTIAC'S WAR; FORT TICONDEROGA (NEW YORK)

Ammunition
Discussions about powder, lead, and shot may appear mundane next to the excitement of battles and the fascination with great leaders, but without these essential supplies battles could not be fought, and great leaders could not command. Sir William Phips suffered a fatal delay in sailing for Quebec in 1690 because he waited in vain for a supply of powder from England. Provincial artillery fire against Louisbourg in 1745 had to be curtailed due to low powder supplies, and the following year Fort Massachusetts surrendered to a French–Native American force when the powder supply was reduced to four pounds. For those living in the New World, whether French, English, or Indians, the subject of powder, lead, and shot was neither mundane nor obscure; it represented a logistical nightmare.

Gunpowder (or black powder in modern terms) was made by mixing saltpeter (potassium nitrate), sulphur, and charcoal with water, alcohol, or urine, forming the mixture into a cake, and allowing it to dry. The cake was then pulverized, breaking it into tiny grains or "corns." The powder was sifted through a series of sieves, separating the grains into several sizes. The large grains were used for artillery, the smallest for pistols or priming. By 1700 the British, French, and Dutch produced the best powder. Spain, hampered by a lack of industrial development, preferred to import most of its powder from the early seventeenth century on. The British and French used slightly different proportions in making powder (the former mixed saltpeter, sulphur, and charcoal 75:10:15, the French 75:12.5:12.5), but both worked equally well. France got some of its saltpeter from domestic sources, but imported most of it from India (thus it became another reason for colonial rivalry). Sulphur was imported from Sicily, and charcoal made from domestic trees.

The English colonies attempted to produce their own powder in the seventeenth century. In 1642, Massachusetts began to produce its own saltpeter and established powder mills in 1666, and later and more successfully in 1675, but demand far exceeded the supply. The most important source of powder in the English colonies was a duty on shipping tonnage to be paid in gunpowder. The duty was assessed on all ships not owned by residents of the colony, and without it, according to Governor Joseph Dudley, "the Province would be undone for want of powder, being no waies able to supply themselves." However, the powder received from the duty only covered normal levels of activity. In the end, supplies of munitions had to come directly from England.

The repeated requests by the government of Massachusetts for powder and shot during the early years of King William's War seriously hampered the negotiations for a new charter. Increase Mather wrote from London that the constant call for aid "was, in effect, to pray for a [Royal] Governor. They could not be so weak as to think the King would send one without the other." Increase Mather's analysis of the situation was apparently astute. According to historian Richard R. Johnson, the entreaties for powder and other war materials throughout the early French wars led to much closer ties with the government in London.

In addition to promoting closer ties, requests for powder took far too long to process. The request had to be sent across the Atlantic, make its way through the formidable bureaucracy of the British government, be collected by the Board of Ordnance, and shipped safely across the ocean. In October 1707, the New Hampshire assembly voted to request additional powder from London. It finally arrived in port two years later.

The arrival of supplies from England did not end the logistical problems connected with munitions, for distribution caused as many headaches as acquisition. Stored in barrels generally containing about 100 pounds, powder had to be transported from the coast to individual towns or sent along with military forces where eventually it would be used to fill powder horns, bandoleers, or cartridges. In 1666, Virginia provided for a store of powder and appointed a "Powder Receiver." The "Powder Master" actually accompanied the powder and filled each powder horn or flask.

Lead was also in short supply in the colonies. New France relied on lead mines on the Mississippi, but once again, the English colonies relied on England. Lead came to the colonies in the form of bars, sheets, or precast into balls which were separated into small kegs according to caliber. The variety of calibers used by provincial soldiers made the distribution of lead most difficult. Kegs of pre-cast balls were broached and the men chose bullets closest to their calibers. Otherwise the balls had to be melted down again and recast with individual molds (molds were often sold with the guns). In the early seventeenth century lead was so scarce that musket balls were used for currency.

While supplies of powder and lead proved difficult for French and English colonists, Native Americans found it far worse. They were totally dependent on Europeans for powder and shot. During the attack on York, Maine, in January 1692, survivors observed Indians ripping the lead glazing out of windows and taking pewter plates to be melted down into musket balls. Provincial soldiers were not unaware of this. They realized that any battle or skirmish with the Indians, even if not a tactical success, could result in a strategic victory by forcing the Indians to use up their precious supplies of ammunition, resulting in at least a truce while they replenished their stock from the French, or even English traders.

Flints caused fewer problems for the Indians because they retained the expertise to knap flint. With the widespread adoption of flint ignition weapons in the mid-seventeenth century, the art of flint knapping resurfaced in Europe. Flints were chipped into long blades, broken into small sizes, and knapped into shape. Flint quarrying centers in France included Loire et Cher and Yonne, while the British mined flint in Mindenhall, Sarenham, Tuddenham, and Brandon (still supplying flints today). French or continental flints had a rounded heel and varied in color from gray to yellow. British flints had a square heel and ran from dark gray to black.

Flints were imported into the colonies in half-casks weighing around 70 pounds and containing anywhere from 2,000 to 4,000 flints, depending on the size of the flints (they would be sized for pistol, carbine, or musket). The flints needed a wrapping of lead or leather to hold them in the jaws of the cock. British army flints were prewrapped in lead for easy changing in the field, otherwise one strip of leather or lead would have to serve many flints. Most flints averaged around 30 strikes before they had to be re-sharpened, or "re-knapped." This could be accomplished by gently tapping the striking face with a metal object to carefully flake the flint away, or by turning the flint over to allow the action of striking the hammer to chip the flint away. Every flint was different, however. Some bore 50, 60, or 70 strikes without re-knapping, while others shattered after a few blows. In combat situations there was no time to fool around with re-knapping and flints were replaced as soon as they began to fail.

The militia acts in the English colonies often required company members to provide "one pound of good powder, twenty bullets fit for his gun, and twelve flints," and governments ordered individual communities to keep a common stock of powder and shot—usually a barrel of powder, 200 pounds of balls, and 300 flints for every 60 soldiers on their rolls. This supply of powder, lead, and flints had to come from outside sources because there were no domestic supplies. Although the logistical support of armies in the eighteenth century was difficult at best, the protectionist or mercantile policies of Great Britain, which denied the colonies an industrial base necessary for the support of warfare in the age of gunpowder, handicapped the colonies in their military operations. Lacking sufficient powder mills and a domestic supply of lead and flints, English and French colonists were forced to rely on their mother countries for war supplies, a reliance which would, in turn, promote closer ties with those European governments. If French or British regulars were involved in a campaign, such supplies were easy to come by, otherwise, tactical and strategic plans could be impeded by delays in procurements. As for the Indians, their dependence was the most acute of all.

Steven C. Eames

References

M.L. Brown, *Firearms in Colonial America: The Impact on History and Technology, 1492–1792* (1980); Harold L. Peterson, *Arms and Armor in Colonial America, 1526–1783* (1956).

See also ARTILLERY; WEAPONS, FIREARMS; WEAPONS, NAVAL

Fort Amsterdam (New York)

Fort Amsterdam was created in order to protect Dutch West India Company interests in the fur trade in New Netherland and became the headquarters of the Dutch colony. It was built on the southernmost point of Manhattan Island in 1626 after Director General Peter Minuit brought the first New Netherland colonists there from their scattered homes on the Delaware and Connecticut Rivers, Governor's Island, and at Fort Orange. This new settlement came to be known as New Amsterdam.

The fort had to be scaled down from the original plan because Director Minuit drafted the company engineer, Cryn Fredricksen, and his materials to build much needed houses for the colonists. When completed, Fort Amsterdam was little more than a stone warehouse, which also served as company store, surrounded by a palisade of sod and timber. Throughout its history, the fort offered protection from Indian attacks to the Dutch settlers who had settled nearby.

In 1633, Director General Wouter van Twiller arrived with instructions to rebuild the fort in order to provide a better defense against European intruders. That task was begun by Luycas Jansen Sprangh, a Dutch bricklayer. His job was to build a quadrangle fort, making one bastion of stone in order to withstand naval gunfire. The rest were to be made of earth and timber. The operation was interrupted when van Twiller drafted the workmen to military service, and Sprangh returned home to the Netherlands. The fort was finished after two years, but required the labor of company slaves imported from the West Indies. When completed, the fort measured 250 feet by 300 feet and cost close to 4,500 guilders to build—extremely expensive by Dutch West India Company standards. It still contained the stone storehouse, but now included two or three frame houses for the director and other company employees. Regardless of the apparent commitment of the Dutch West India Company to create a more permanent defensive structure, the largely earthen fort remained a poor substitute for a stone work and demanded constant improvement, which it rarely received.

After five years the fort began to suffer from decay. A report to the company board of directors issued in 1638 stated that it, as well as the storehouse, was deteriorating to the point that citizens of New Amsterdam could enter the fort at almost any place in the walls; furthermore, the guns were unmanned and in disrepair. This condition was never improved in any significant way, as reports made in 1643 and 1645 suggest. When Director General Petrus (Peter) Stuyvesant first arrived in New Netherland in 1647, he found Fort Amsterdam "resembling more a mole-hill than a fortress, without gates, the walls and bastions trodden under foot by men and cattle." Although Stuyvesant had orders from the Dutch West India Company to repair the fort and made an effort to do so, he was disadvantaged by insufficient funds, poor building materials (the sod available was very sandy and given to rapid deterioration), and lack of cooperation from both soldiers and citizens to make the necessary and proper repairs.

Consequently, when four English ships with 300 soldiers arrived in New Amsterdam's harbor in the late summer of 1664, Fort Amsterdam could not provide necessary defense for the town or colony. Although it was then garrisoned with approximately 150 to 180 troops and armed with 24 cannon, it was in dilapidated condition and not readily defendable. Furthermore, Colonel Richard Nicolls, commander of the English invasion force, had made arrangements with the English militia on Long Island to assist if needed in an assault on New Amsterdam. Stuyvesant had little other choice but to surrender, and on 8 September, the fort, along with the rest of New Netherland, passed into the hands of the English and was renamed Fort James.

Paul Otto

References

Edmund B. O'Callaghan, *History of New Netherland, or New York Under the Dutch,* 2d ed., 2 vols. (1855); Edmund B. O'Callaghan and Berthold Fernow, eds., *Documents Relative to the Colonial History of the State of New York,* Vols. I, II, XIII (1856–1887); Oliver Rink, *Holland on the Hudson: An Economic and Social History of Dutch New York* (1986); Robert C. Ritchie, *The Duke's Province: A Study of New York Politics and Society, 1664–1691* (1977).

See also MINUIT, PETER; NEW NETHERLAND, SURRENDER OF (1664); STUYVESANT, PETRUS

Ancient and Honorable Artillery Company of Massachusetts

The Ancient and Honorable Artillery Company of Massachusetts (AHAC) was the first for-

mally recognized military unit in North America. Formed in Boston in 1637 and chartered by Governor John Winthrop the following year, its original name was "The Military Company of Massachusetts." Many of its founding members, including its first commander, Captain Robert Keayne, had belonged to the Honorable Artillery Company of London. A close association existed between the two units, and the Boston company assumed its present name in the mid-1700s.

The AHAC never actually fought as a military unit per se; rather it provided the officer cadre for many other Massachusetts militia and national guard units. When the Massachusetts Militia was formed in 1644, 27 of the 37 officers came from the AHAC. Members of the AHAC served in key officer positions in a wide number of the military actions of the colonial period, including King Philip's War, Phips' 1690 expedition against Canada, the 1745 siege of Louisbourg, and the Crown Point expeditions. During the Revolution, about 10 percent of the Company's members remained loyal to the Crown.

The AHAC exists today as the third oldest military unit in the world; behind its parent unit, the London HAC (1537), and the Vatican's Swiss Guard (1506). Although the AHAC is a unit of the Massachusetts state militia, it is not recognized as a national guard unit by the U.S. Defense Department's National Guard Bureau.

David T. Zabecki

References

Oliver Ayer Roberts, *History of the Military Company of Massachusetts Now Called the Ancient and Honorable Artillery Company of Massachusetts, 1637–1888* (1895).

Andros, Sir Edmund (1637–1714)

Edmund Andros (pronounced "Andrews") was an archetypical English colonial administrator of the late seventeenth and early eighteenth centuries. He is best known for his tempestuous administration as governor of the Dominion of New England from 1686 to 1689. The majority of his colonial service, however, came as governor of New York (1674–1681) and Virginia (1693–1698).

Andros was born into an aristocratic family on Guernsey, one of the Channel Islands. His close association with the Stuart monarchs (his father served as bailiff of Guernsey and in the royal household) proved a liability as the English civil war unfolded. As a result, he fled to Europe during the interregnum and entered Dutch military service. He soldiered under Prince Henry of Nassau and distinguished himself in battle.

Andros was poised for success after the Stuart restoration in 1660. His aristocratic and military background had instilled in him a world view akin to that of the Stuart kings: authoritarian, arch-royalist, and imperialist. Additionally, he befriended important people, particularly James Stuart, duke of York, the king's brother and heir apparent. These connections brought Andros a commission as major of the Barbados Regiment (1672) and an appointment to replace his father as a bailiff of Guernsey (1674). In every endeavor he displayed a single-minded devotion to duty and to the Stuarts that ensured his continued advancement.

A major promotion came in 1674 when the duke of York, the New York proprietor, appointed Andros governor of the colony. (Technically, Andros was lieutenant governor under James; however, since the duke never trekked to America, Andros had powers equivalent to a royal governor's.) James was hopeful that Andros would resolve the difficult problems that had beset the colony since the English had conquered it in 1664.

Once in New York, Andros's greatest challenge was dealing with tensions rooted in ethnic diversity. Roughly three-quarters of the people were Dutch (New York had been New Netherland formerly), who, of course, did not wish to be ruled by an English governor. Andros adopted conciliatory policies—civil and religious liberties, exemption from military service against Holland, reconfirmation of Dutch land titles and legal decisions, and continuance of the Dutch-controlled Albany fur trade—but resentment and suspicion toward the governor were never eliminated entirely.

The remainder of the population, mostly transplanted Puritans living on Long Island, also chafed at the New York government. Accustomed to the New England style of self-rule, they clamored for a representative assembly that Andros neither favored nor had the power to convene. They were intolerant of other religions, particularly Catholicism (the duke of York's preference) and Anglicanism, the state-sponsored religion of England. They resented navigation acts that restricted trade with their New England brethren, and resisted paying duties, quitrents, and other New York levies.

Andros's fiery temperament was ill-suited to the delicate political balance within the colony. He was harsh and overbearing when it came to protecting the proprietor's interests; in one notorious episode, he imprisoned the governor of East Jersey, Philip Carteret, for exercising authority in an area claimed by New York. If Andros could inflict such indignities on a fellow governor, New Yorkers hardly could expect better treatment.

In contrast to the domestic upheavals of his administration, Andros skillfully managed relations with the Indians. He recognized the importance of spreading English influence among the powerful Iroquois nations that separated New Yorkers from the French in Canada. He also wished to spare the colony from depredations like those inflicted on New England in 1675–1676 by the Indian chief King Philip. Through tenacious diplomacy he concluded a treaty in 1677 known as the "Covenant Chain," which bound the Iroquois to the English for most of the colonial era.

Andros's next administration, his most important, was in the Dominion of New England. Since the Stuart restoration in 1660, the crown had been slowly consolidating its grip on the far-flung colonial empire. New England, because of its flagrant violations of the navigation acts and its proximity to the French and hostile Indians, became the focus of the consolidation scheme. The crown annulled colonial charters, dissolved legislatures, and altered boundaries. At first the dominion included only Massachusetts, New Hampshire, and Maine; by 1688 it also had incorporated New York, the three Jersies, Connecticut, Rhode Island, and Plymouth.

Perfectly suited to the task of authoritarian government, Andros undertook a thorough reconstitution of New England society. He was determined to stamp out the parochialism and autonomy which had undermined imperial authority. He acted decisively, but underestimated the opposition that his policies would generate in the tight-knit Puritan society.

In place of the legislative assemblies, Andros and his council ruled despotically, at least in the eyes of the people. They made law by fiat and without explanation. They censored the press, curtailed legal rights, and restricted local autonomy. The governor distributed his patronage liberally to secure the loyalty of powerful colonists and officials, many of them Anglicans and native Londoners. Royal officials enriched themselves at public expense through fees and perquisites for routine administrative actions. Perhaps most odious was the company of regulars stationed in Boston, which provided daily reminder of the consequences of resistance.

According high priority to establishing revenue, he imposed direct and indirect taxes in early 1687. Though some historians have argued that they were not onerous, these imposts brought an angry response from colonists who decried taxation without representation. The governor made an example out of a few who dared challenge the legality of the taxes; in the end the colonists grudgingly paid.

The governor's next task was land reform. Declaring that the annulment of the colonial charters had invalidated previously issued land patents, he ordered them reissued under the authority of the crown—instead of the townships—and enforced the payment of quitrents to the king. Despite the usual grumbling and procrastination, the colonists submitted to the new arrangement.

Andros pressed religious toleration on the Puritan society by taking measures that threatened to disestablish Congregationalism as the colonial religion. He forbade the use of public funds to support local ministers. He secured the appointment of Anglicans to the council and other important positions. More than anything else, the governor's assault on congregationalist norms poisoned relations with the Puritan majority and ensured his downfall.

Although from the crown's perspective Andros had performed admirably in raising revenue and restoring imperial authority, his "success" cost him popular support. Colonial tension culminated in April 1689, when New Englanders received word of the fall of King James II. The Glorious Revolution in England put Andros's authority in question, and colonists lost no time in exploiting the situation. Local leaders imprisoned him for nearly a year as they negotiated (successfully) with the new monarchs, William and Mary, for reestablishment of their charters. Andros eventually stood trial in England for abusing his power, but imperial judges acquitted him.

Andros's career rebounded under William and Mary despite his stormy administrations in New York and the Dominion of New England. In 1693, he received a royal appointment as governor of Virginia, the most lucrative post in English America. His commission owed to his reputation for honesty and vigor in pursuing royal interests and to his 11 years of experience in imperial administration.

Perhaps remembering the ordeal of popular revolt and imprisonment in New England, Andros balanced competing interests more adroitly in Virginia. He showed uncharacteristic flexibility in managing provincial issues, particularly land distribution and economic diversification. His aristocratic air made him popular with the planter elite, who modeled themselves after the English gentry. He supported imperial interests by contributing more than £1,000 to New York and the New England colonies, which bore the brunt of King William's War against France.

Though generally effective in administering the affairs of Virginia, a feud with commissary James Blair led to Andros's retirement. Blair, the bishop of London's representative in the colony, struggled to found the College of William and Mary. For political and personal reasons, Andros gave him only reluctant support, which prompted Blair to rally his allies in London to remove the governor. Andros obliged them: elderly, ill, and demoralized by the intrigues against him, he resigned in 1698. Except for a brief and uneventful term as governor of Guernsey, he refrained from further public office.

Andros's 30-year career as a colonial administrator reflected important trends in the English empire of the late seventeenth and early eighteenth centuries. First was the reliance of the crown on professional army officers to manage the outposts of empire. English monarchs deemed military experience so crucial to successful governing that between 1660 and 1727 almost 90 percent of royal governors were career officers. Second, Andros's experience reflected the European mercantilist mindset. Colonies, the argument went, were established to enrich the mother country at the expense of imperial competitors; Andros's constant struggle to raise revenues, however, suggested the underlying weakness of the system. Finally, the Andros administrations revealed the growing tension between the authoritarian, centralized government of the empire and the representative, decentralized rule preferred by the colonists. The latent consequences of this conflict became obvious after 1763, when Americans challenged openly the bonds of empire.

Lance A. Betros

References

Richard R. Johnson, *Adjustment to Empire: The New England Colonies, 1675–1715* (1981); Michael Kammen, *Colonial New York: A History* (1975); Richard L. Morton, *Colonial Virginia*, 2 vols. (1960); Robert C. Ritchie, *The Duke's Province: A Study of New York Politics and Society, 1664–1691* (1977); Stephen S. Webb, *The Governors-General: The English Army and the Definition of the Empire, 1569–1681* (1979).

See also DOMINION OF NEW ENGLAND; ENGLISH REVOLUTION; NEW YORK; PURITANS

Anglo-Dutch War, First (1652–1654)

Years of tension caused by competition at sea led to a series of naval wars between the Netherlands and England in the seventeenth century. When Oliver Cromwell assumed power of England in 1648, he sought a way to improve his country's commercial interests around the world by limiting the Netherlands' ability to compete. His solution was to institute a navigation act, which cut into the Netherlands' most lucrative business, the carrying trade. According to the act, only English ships or ships of the country of origin were allowed to transport goods to England. Dutch success at sea depended on the principle of *mare liberum*—the freedom to trade anywhere without penalty. Cromwell was intent on imposing the principle of *mare clausum*—the right to monopolize trade in areas of proprietary interest.

By the time the United Provinces of the Netherlands had achieved their independence from Spain in 1648, it had become the greatest trading nation in Europe, if not the world. In the Baltic region alone, Dutch ships carried three-quarters of the grain and timber, and one-half of Swedish metals. Conversely, three-quarters of French and Portuguese salt destined to the Baltic was carried by the Dutch. Cromwell's Navigation Act was designed to reduce such Dutch advantages at sea.

One of the points of the act that upset Dutch skippers most was the English claim of dominion over the so-called Narrow Seas (the English and Irish Channels). In these waters the Navigation Act required that foreign ships acknowledge English supremacy by lowering their topsails and striking their colors. This emotional issue soon led to violence.

The major personalities in the coming struggle were the Dutch admirals Marten Harpertsz Tromp, Witte de With, and Michiel Adriaansz de Ruyter; on the English side Robert Blake, William Penn, and George Monk. On 29 May 1652, Tromp and Blake met in the Strait of Dover, appropriately called the bottleneck of Europe. Tromp's refusal to strike his colors according to the newly instituted Navigation Act resulted in a brief gun duel during which two small Dutch ships were lost. The Battle of the Downs was followed by more than a month of negotiations. War was finally declared on 8 July 1652. Denmark promptly concluded a treaty with the Netherlands, closing the Sound (also known as Oresund, the body of water between Zealand, Denmark, and Sweden) to English shipping. The Baltic trade was closed to England for the duration of the war.

English strategy was simple: by concentrating the fleet in the Strait of Dover, the navy could protect both the English Channel and the North Sea while also effectively blockading Amsterdam and disrupting the Dutch overseas trade. De With and de Ruyter with 72 ships met Blake and Penn with 68 ships off Kentish Knock near the mouth of the Thames on 8 October. The ensuing fight, although indecisive, was disheartening to the Dutch because of an impressive demonstration of superior firepower by the English. However, the center only held for a month. Tromp and De Ruyter with 81 ships escorted a convoy of more than 300 outbound merchant ships through the Channel on 10 October after defeating Blake at the Strait of Dungeness. Tromp was not so fortunate the following year. When he attempted to escort an inbound merchant convoy of 200 ships, he was met by the combined forces of Blake, Penn, and Monk. The Three Days' Running Battle began off Portland on 1 March and ended near Calais on the 3rd. The Dutch lost 17 warships and more than 55 merchant ships in the encounter. The English had gained control of the Channel, forcing the Dutch to convoy *achterom*, i.e., north around Scotland. Successes in the Channel were countered by a significant defeat in the Mediterranean. In March 1653, an English fleet lost six ships in an unsuccessful attempt at rescuing a convoy of merchant ships trapped by the Dutch at Livorno, Italy. This engagement drove the English from the Mediterranean and excluded them from the Levant trade for the remainder of the war.

Tromp, de With, and de Ruyter attempted to break the blockade in June 1653. Monk and Blake with 100 ships engaged the Dutch north of Dover near the North Foreland. Although the Dutch had an equal number of ships, as usual they carried significantly inferior firepower. For the first time the English employed the new naval tactic of line-ahead formation with devastating results. Rather than engaging at close quarters, maneuvering to board and capture opposing vessels, the English ships followed their commander in a line. Instead of closing with the Dutch fleet, the English were able to bombard the Dutch with their heavier guns at a relatively safe distance. Tromp lost 19 ships and was forced back to the Netherlands where he was blockaded once again. However, on 9 August, Tromp ventured out with 80 ships and encountered the English fleet under Monk near Scheveningen. The 12-hour battle was so fierce that the Dutch lost 1,500 men and 14 ships, as well as Marten Tromp, who was shot through the head by a musket ball. The English were so battered that they withdrew for repairs. The blockade was lifted, allowing 400 Dutch outbound merchant ships to leave Texel. This proved to be the final major naval engagement of the war.

Hostilities threatened to spill over into the North American colonies. In April 1653, a delegation from New England visited Director General Petrus Stuyvesant at New Amsterdam. The New Englanders accused the Dutch of stirring up the Indians to attack settlements in Connecticut. When Stuyvesant denied the accusations, the delegation left abruptly, threatening war. Stuyvesant took the threats seriously and immediately began to strengthen his defenses. He arranged to have a defensive wall built along the northern edge of New Amsterdam from the East River to the Hudson; issued orders for strengthening Fort Orange on the upper Hudson; and strengthened Fort Amsterdam by stripping troops and supplies from Fort Casimir on the Delaware River. However, the New Englanders were unable to unify against the Dutch. At a conference in Boston, the colony of Massachusetts refused to supply troops for an operation against New Netherland. Rumors of war and pirate raids against Long Island from Connecticut were deftly countered by Stuyvesant. He put a stop to the raids against remote farmsteads by forming a mobile strike force on Long Island, which was drilled to move and concentrate quickly according to prearranged warning signals. The most damaging effect of the war in Europe was the English blockade of the Netherlands, which greatly reduced transatlantic shipping. More potentially damaging for New Netherland, however, was the English decision in 1654 to dispatch Major Robert Sedgwick to New England with four ships. His instructions were to coordinate and lead an attack against New Netherland. Before the operation was begun, news reached North America of the conclusion of the war by the first Treaty of Westminster, signed on 15 April 1654.

At Westminster, the Dutch agreed to recognize the Navigation Act, including English dominion in the Channel; they also agreed to pay for fishing rights in English waters, and compensate for English losses in the East Indies. Ostensibly the Dutch had lost the war by failing to defeat proprietary interest in the Channel; however, the English had been excluded from the Baltic, and driven from the Mediterranean and the Far East. Although the Dutch had lost more than 1,200 ships, mostly fly boats (small, fast-sailing boats used in the coastal trade) and herring busses (two- or three-masted ships used for herring fishing) seized in English ports at the beginning of the war, the Dutch had captured more than 400 English ships, mostly merchantmen. The root cause—struggle for commercial supremacy at sea—had not been resolved, and in a decade would again explode into war.

Charles Gehring

References

C.R. Boxer, *The Dutch Seaborne Empire 1600–1800* (1965); Jonathan I. Israel, *Dutch Primacy in World Trade 1585–1740* (1989); Clark G. Reynolds, *Command of the Sea: The History and Strategy of Maritime Empires* (1974); J.G. van Dillen, *Van Rijkdom en Regenten: Handboek tot de Econo-mische en Sociale Geschiedenis van Nederland tijdens de Republiek* (1970).

Anglo-Dutch War, Second (1664–1667)

Much had changed since the first Anglo-Dutch War—Cromwell was dead, and Charles II had been restored as king of England in 1660. However, commercial competition between the Dutch Republic and England had not changed; it had only intensified. When Charles II formed the Royal Africa Company in 1660, it was clear that its main competition was the Dutch trade along the Guinea coast of Africa (also called, from west to east, the Silver, Gold, and Slave coasts, respectively).

In 1664, Robert Holmes of the Royal Africa Company, supposedly without royal approval, captured Dutch posts in the Cape Verde Islands and along the Guinea coast. The only stronghold left in Dutch hands was Elmina Castle (in present-day Ghana). In the same year, Charles granted his brother James, duke of York and Albany, extensive territories in North America, which included the Dutch colony of New Netherland. James was also granted £8,000 to take possession of his overseas holdings. In September, a naval force under the command of Richard Nicolls captured New Netherland, which was renamed New York. The Dutch were understandably upset since both hostile actions had taken place without a declaration of war.

The Dutch government openly protested these warlike acts in a time of peace, but secretly sent instructions to Admiral Michiel Adriaansz de Ruyter to reclaim what had been lost. De Ruyter left Cádiz on 5 October 1664 with 13 ships. After retaking Dutch possessions in the Cape Verde Islands and capturing eight English merchant ships, he headed for the Guinea coast where he retook all the former Dutch posts but one, and captured the English stronghold at Cormantine, including the Royal Africa Company's store of merchandise and five of their ships. De Ruyter then crossed the Atlantic to the Caribbean Sea. His attempt to take Barbados was repelled with some damage to his fleet. The need to repair and refit forced him to head for Newfoundland, bypassing New Netherland. De Ruyter arrived back in the Netherlands in August, in time to participate in the second Anglo-Dutch War.

In addition to de Ruyter, Dutch naval leaders included Wassenaer van Obdam, Cornelis Tromp (son of Marten Tromp), and Jan Evertsen. The English could call on the duke of York, the duke of Albemarle (Monk), William Penn, Prince Rupert, and the earl of Sandwich. After the Dutch Levant convoy was attacked in the Strait of Gibraltar, and the duke of York had seized about 100 Dutch ships, the Netherlands declared war on 4 March 1665. As in the first Anglo-Dutch War, the English strategy was to control the Strait of Dover and disrupt the Dutch convoys.

The first major encounter occurred at Lowestoft on 3 June, where Obdam with 103 ships met the duke of York's 109 ships. The Dutch were in a confused state because the fleet had been divided into seven squadrons. Matters became worse when Obdam himself was killed. During a fierce duel with the duke of York aboard the *Royal Charles*, Obdam's ship, *de Endracht*, carrying 500 men, exploded; there were only five survivors. Tromp and Evertsen covered the retreat. When the earl of Sandwich pursued the East India convoy into Bergen, Norway, he was repulsed by Dutch ships and Danish shore batteries. The English had been deceived into thinking Denmark was about to align with them. Instead, the Danes declared war against England, sealed the Sound, and closed the Baltic to English ships. France joined Denmark and sided with the Dutch Republic in January 1666.

The threat of a French fleet to the south of the Channel put pressure on the English strategy of holding the center. Toward the end of May, Prince Rupert was sent south with 24 ships to intercept a French fleet, which had been reported heading for the Channel. On 1 June, while separated from Rupert, the duke of Albemarle made contact with a large Dutch fleet commanded by de Ruyter. The Four Days' Battle is often called the bloodiest naval engagement in history. The duke of Albemarle was only saved when Rupert returned from the south on the third day. The English fleet finally retreated to the Thames estuary for repairs after suffering 5,000 killed, 3,000 captured, with eight ships sunk and nine captured; the Dutch fared a little better, with four admirals and 2,000 men killed, and eight ships lost.

The English remained blockaded until 4 August when Albemarle and Rupert broke out with 81 ships. They met de Ruyter, Evertsen, and Tromp off the North Foreland. In the St. James' Day Fight (25 July according to the English Old Style calendar) the Dutch again suffered from a divided command. During the encounter Evertsen was killed and 20 Dutch ships were sunk. De Ruyter was forced to take cover in the Scheldt River, leaving the convoy at the island of Vlie unprotected. With the help of a traitor named Laurens Heemskerck, Robert Holmes was able to make his way into the sheltered assembly area between the islands of Vlieland and Terschelling on 8 August. He found 150 merchant ships protected by only two warships. On the next day he sent in fireships to begin a conflagration that was celebrated in

London as Holmes's bonfire; only a few ships managed to escape. Not content with the destruction of the convoy, Holmes put soldiers onto the island who proceeded to burn storehouses and many private dwellings. Several weeks later the outbreak of the Great Fire of London prompted the Dutch to proclaim the tragedy as divine retribution for Holmes's bad behavior at Terschelling.

Although peace negotiations were underway in Breda, two military actions of note occurred in 1667. On 26 February 1667, Abraham Crijnsen, commanding a Zeeland fleet, captured the English sugar colony of Surinam on the Guiana coast of South America. Dutch rights to this territory were eventually exchanged for English rights to New York. Then, a little more than a month before the treaty was signed, de Ruyter sailed into the Medway, an arm of the Thames estuary, where the English had put up their fleet in anticipation of peace. On 17 June, de Ruyter broke the chain protecting access to several large warships. The Dutch burned three men-of-war and towed the flagship *Royal Charles* back to the Dutch Republic. When the English negotiators at Breda heard of this embarrassing incident, they were prepared to break off the talks and return to England. However, the Great Fire, the outbreak of plague in London, and the humiliating defeat in the Medway made peace imperative. The Treaty of Breda was signed on 25 July.

As a result of the treaty, both countries retained their previously captured territories: for England, New Netherland; for the Dutch Republic, Surinam, the former English possession on the Guinea coast of Africa, and Pulu Run in Indonesia. The English modified the Navigation Act so that Germany was considered a hinterland of the Netherlands, making it legal for Dutch merchants to carry German merchandise to England. Finally, Dutch ships were only required to salute English ships in the Channel.

Charles Gehring

References

C.R. Boxer, *The Dutch Seaborne Empire 1600–1800* (1965); Jonathan I. Israel, *Dutch Primacy in World Trade 1585–1740* (1989); Clark G. Reynolds, *Command of the Sea: The History and Strategy of Maritime Empires* (1974);.J.G. van Dillen, *Van Rijkdom en Regenten: Handboek tot de Econo-mische en Sociale Geschiedenis van Nederland tijdens de Republiek* (1970).

See also NEW NETHERLAND, SURRENDER OF (1664)

Anglo-Dutch War, Third (1672–1674)

Within less than two decades the Dutch Republic and England were engaged in hostilities for the third time. However, now there was a difference. On 7 April 1672, both England and France declared war on the republic; this time it was threatened from both land and sea by two powerful countries.

Louis XIV invaded the Dutch Republic in May 1672 with 120,000 men, quickly overrunning the provinces of Overijssel, Gelderland, and Utrecht. English and French naval forces were moving to form a combined fleet in the Channel. The objectives were simple: destroy Dutch military capabilities on both land and sea, and divide up the Dutch Republic and its commercial empire.

At first it appeared that the combined forces of England and France would succeed where Spain had failed (seven northern provinces of the Netherlands conducted a successful revolt against Spain, 1568–1648). On land, the armies of Louis XIV were only stopped when the Dutch used their ultimate defensive weapon. By opening a series of dikes and flooding the land, the French offensive was stalled within sight of Amsterdam. Meanwhile, other European powers were upset at Louis XIV's aggression; not out of sympathy for the Dutch Republic, but out of fear of a stronger France and England. French military forces had to be diverted from the Dutch front when Spain, the Austrian Empire, and Brandenburg-Prussia formed a coalition and declared war against France. At sea, the Dutch also called on another ultimate weapon: Michiel Adriaansz de Ruyter, now 65 years old.

On 7 June 1672, de Ruyter, with admirals Adriaan van Trapen Bankert and Willem van Ghent, attacked the combined English and French fleet at Solebay, north of the Thames. The Dutch fleet of 78 ships faced 84 ships and 30,000 men commanded by the duke of York, the earl of Sandwich, and the French commander, Jean d'Estrées. It was a hotly contested battle. Of the 33 naval engagements de Ruyter had been in throughout his career, he claimed that it was the most terrible he had ever witnessed. The Dutch lost one ship sunk, one captured, and one damaged; the English one sunk, nine damaged, and 1,600 men lost, including the earl of Sandwich. The Dutch lost the services of Admiral van Ghent, who was also killed in action. The fight was so intense that both fleets were forced to withdraw because their ammunition was running low. The allies withdrew to the Thames estuary, while the Dutch anchored off Walcheren in Zeeland. The combined allied fleet was so battered that it was unable to contest the passage of the outbound East India convoy through the Channel. Although in a similar distressed state, the Dutch considered the Battle of Solebay a victory because the allied forces were unable to land troops in the Dutch Republic in support of Louis XIV's armies.

On 14 June 1673, another attempt by the combined French and English naval forces to destroy the Dutch fleet and land troops in Holland was again countered by de Ruyter off the Scheldt. Prince Rupert was now in command, as the duke of York had been removed by virtue of the Test Act when he converted to Catholicism. After a sharp firefight, the allies were again forced to withdraw to the Thames and Medway for repairs without accomplishing their mission. Another indecisive battle was fought off Texel on 21 August 1673. Because of the inaction of the French, suspicions arose that Louis XIV's strategy was to have the English and Dutch destroy one another. Once again, de Ruyter had succeeded in defending his coastal waters; again the allies were unable to contest the passage of an inbound East India convoy through the Channel. Dissension in the allied command led to the withdrawal of the French fleet from the Thames on 28 September 1673 and its return to France. This first attempt at Anglo-French cooperation had lasted hardly two years.

De Ruyter's successful defense of the home country was complemented by several initiatives overseas. In the spring 1673, a squadron of Zeeland ships under the command of Cornelis Evertsen de Jonge sailed west with instructions to take the island of St. Helena in the South Atlantic in order to harass the English East India convoys. If unable to do so, he was to proceed to the Caribbean and the coast of North America where he was to do as much damage to French and English shipping as possible. After aborting plans to take St. Helena, Evertsen combined with an Amsterdam squadron commanded by Jacob Binckes at the island of Martinique. This unified fleet in turn recaptured St. Eustatius, which had been seized by the English the preceding year, entered the James River in Virginia where it badly damaged the English tobacco fleet, and with 19 ships, including prizes captured in the James River and the Caribbean, sailed into New York harbor. Evertsen and Binckes were able to retake the former colony of New Netherland with as much ease as it had been taken by the English nine years earlier. In addition to these overseas activities, Dutch privateers took more than 700 French and English ships as prizes during the period from 1672 to 1674.

After extensive peace negotiations begun during the winter, the Dutch and English concluded the third Treaty of Westminster on 6 March 1674. The most positive gain for the Dutch was the breakup of the Anglo-French alliance; for the English it was the restoration of New Netherland as New York. Although the Dutch again conceded to salute English ships in "British waters," the English recognized Dutch supremacy in the East Indies.

Charles Gehring

References
C.R. Boxer, *The Dutch Seaborne Empire 1600–1800* (1965); Jonathan I. Israel, *Dutch Primacy in World Trade 1585–1740* (1989); Clark G. Reynolds, *Command of the Sea: The History and Strategy of Maritime Empires* (1974); Donald G. Shomette and Robert D. Haslach, *Raid on America: The Dutch Naval Campaign of 1672–1674* (1988); J.G. van Dillen, *Van Rijkdom en Regenten: Handboek tot de Economische en Sociale Geschiedenis van Nederland tijdens de Republiek* (1970).

See also NEW YORK, DUTCH CAPTURE OF (1673)

Anglo-Indian Relations
"Spanish civilization," wrote Francis Parkman, "crushed the Indian; English civilization scorned and neglected him; French civilization embraced him." Parkman's often quoted dictum is simplistic and misleading. The English in North America may have been scornful of Indian culture, but they could not and did not neglect the Indian, whose services as a trading partner and military ally were often essential to

the survival of the fledgling British settlements. Anglo-Indian relations in the colonial era were complex, and cannot be characterized in a succinct phrase. Great Britain never established a coordinated, enforceable Indian policy. Disagreements within and among both English colonies and Native American tribes over trade regulations, land ownership, and military alliances resulted in a succession of Anglo-Indian wars and a steady escalation of intergroup violence in Indian America. Moreover, the frontiers of the British colonies were in a constant state of flux, as the pressure of immigration from Britain and Europe undermined earlier Anglo-Indian accommodations and led to renewed conflict.

Despite their inconsistent behavior, the English in North America generally shared certain fundamental assumptions about the role of the Indian in colonial life. Regarding North America as England's Canaan and themselves as God's new Chosen People, they believed that Englishmen had a divine mandate to occupy, subdue, civilize, and Christianize lands occupied by "savage" peoples. They invoked both legal arguments (such as the concept of *vacuum domicilium*, whereby Indians were denied their "natural" rights to land that they did not "use" by cultivation or habitation) and Old Testament analogies to deny Indian claims to jurisdiction over uncultivated lands. (Roger Williams in Rhode Island and William Penn in Pennsylvania were exceptions. Both recognized Indian sovereignty in principle. Their successors were less enlightened.) English colonists also usually dismissed Indian culture as not only "savage" but diabolical, and believed the Indians worshipped the devil. They were, therefore, profoundly distrustful of Indians, and were much inclined to overreact to rumors of Indian conspiracies. Although the English declared that the conversion of the Indian to Christianity was a primary objective of colonization, their missionary efforts were modest both in scope and outcome.

The founders of the English colonies, initially being in need of Indian assistance, established close ties with their Native American neighbors, who supplied food, trade goods, and military protection. The Virginia colony's accommodation with the Powhatan Confederacy (1608–1622) made possible its survival after the "Starving Time." Plymouth's military alliance with Massasoit, sachem of the Wampanoag in 1621, was no less essential to that colony's welfare. In all of the colonies, Englishmen and Indians in the early years of contact entered into close economic and military relationships. While the English were greatly outnumbered, they had no choice but to follow moderate and pragmatic policies which recognized Indian autonomy. In many instances, the Indian fur trade for some years provided the only substantial source of export income.

Native American conceptions of their early relationships with the English are difficult to reconstruct. However, English reports of early contact suggest that the Indians at first believed the English were either supernatural beings or possessed of supernatural power. Thomas Hariot (1588) wrote that the Roanoke Indians were persuaded that English compasses, magnets, telescopes, and guns were either "the workes of gods" or had been "taught us of the gods." They also thought the English had the power to kill people in distant villages "by shooting invisible bullets into them," and therefore asked them to use their power against an enemy village. The determination to enlist the English as powerful military allies underlies Powhatan's accommodation with the Jamestown settlers in the following century, and is a recurrent theme in Indian diplomacy throughout the colonial era. Even more persistent was the determination to gain and control trade in European manufactured goods. Early seventeenth-century observers related that Indians believed certain English trade goods, such as glass beads and bright colored cloth, possessed *manitou,* that is, supernatural power. Indian demand for European goods reflected not only appreciation of their practical utility, but belief in their miraculous origin and potency. Indians believed the possession of metal implements and firearms, in particular, would provide an advantage over adversaries that was not only material but supernatural. Access to European trade was thus essential to tribal security. The struggle to control trade transformed the nature of Indian warfare and sharply increased intergroup violence. It also constituted a powerful obstacle to efforts of pan-Indian leaders such as Pontiac who sought to mount intertribal resistance movements.

Despite the advantages enjoyed by those tribes which gained access to English trade goods, the overall impact of the English occupation of North America on Native American society was calamitous. Contact with Europeans exposed Indians to infectious diseases for which they had no natural immunity. Epidemics decimated coastal populations. Fatality rates in the first decade often reached or exceeded 90 percent. As traders and missionaries moved into the interior, they spread disease and death across the continent. The resulting depopulation demoralized the survivors, disrupted their social institutions, and undermined their capacity to resist. While the incorporation of Native Americans into European-directed world trade networks brought some immediate benefits through the adaptation of European technology to agriculture, hunting, and warfare, it ultimately led to the total loss of both economic and political autonomy. Demand for furs to exchange for European commodities soon resulted in the extermination of coastal sources of peltry and to intertribal "trade wars," such as the Iroquois-Huron "Beaver Wars" (1640s) over control of the interior trade. The gradual displacement of Indian tools, utensils, and weapons by imported manufactured products led to the deterioration of Indian skills and to an even greater dependency on European trade. While some European products may have enhanced the quality of Indian life, the introduction of alcohol among peoples unaccustomed to its use led to widespread suffering. Alarmed by the high incidence of alcohol-related violence and fatalities from alcohol poisoning, both English officials and Indian leaders throughout the colonial era called for prohibition of the trade in rum. They were generally unable to control unscrupulous traders who used alcohol, along with fraudulent weights and measures, to cheat their Indian clients.

Comparison of Indian relations in Spanish America and French Canada with the patterns of interracial interaction which developed in British North America discloses that the British, in contrast to their competitors, were less successful in their efforts to develop and enforce a consistent and rational Indian policy. The individual colonies competed and squabbled among themselves over control of trade and land, and often disregarded the crown's sporadic efforts to regulate trade and diplomatic relations with the tribes. The individual colonies, moreover, were unable to control the traders and squatters whose behavior on the frontier often provoked Indian retaliation. Opechancanough's Rebellion in Virginia (1622), which resulted in the death of one-third of the English population, was in part a response to the murder of several Powhatan tribesmen, including a prominent sha-

man. In Bacon's Rebellion (1675), Virginia settlers opposed to Governor William Berkeley's Indian policy embarked on an unauthorized genocidal war against tribes at peace with the colony. In South Carolina, the unauthorized Westo War (1680–1683) was instigated by colonists resentful of the colony's proprietors' monopoly of the Indian slave trade. The dissidents paid a band of migrating Shawnees to exterminate the proprietors' Indian clients. The subsequent Tuscarora (1711–1713) and Yamasee (1715–1717) Wars were both the product of trade abuses which neither the colonial government nor London were able to curb. The colonial governments, moreover, did not always honor their own commitments to their Indian allies. The failure of South Carolina in 1748 to abide by treaty provisions obligating the colony to aid the Cherokees, who had been attacked by the Creek, was a prime factor in the dissolution of the Anglo-Cherokee alliance and the subsequent war with that confederacy.

The inconsistencies in the treatment of Native Americans in the English colonies were only in part the result of political decentralization. A more fundamental reason was the lack of agreement on the place of the Indian in British colonial society. To the French, the Indian was a trading partner, military ally, and potential convert. In the Spanish mainland colonies, the Indian populations provided the basic source of labor for hacienda and mine. But in the British colonies, while Native Americans were valued as trading partners in the early years of colonization, the growth of a substantial English agricultural population combined with the decline of the fur trade soon rendered the Indian economically marginal, and also created demands for access to Indian land which led to serious conflicts.

Native American and English concepts of land ownership and usage were incompatible. The eastern woodland Indian economy was based on hunting and fishing, as well as horticulture, and required the maintenance of substantial hunting preserves. The English were willing to recognize Indian ownership only of lands they actually cultivated; the remainder, including hunting territory, they regarded as "vacant" and available for their occupation. While Indian groups were often willing to "sell" land to Englishmen, such sales were regarded by Indians as limited term leases which did not negate their residual right to use the land for hunting. The English concept of individual and

A

absolute land ownership was alien to the Native American conception of man's relationship to the earth. Conflicts over hunting rights on lands presumably sold to the English were endemic throughout the colonies. Opechacanough's Rebellion in Virginia in 1622, and King Philip's War in New England in 1675, both serious challenges to England's foothold in North America, were in part the product of Indian fear of dispossession, as were Pontiac's War and Lord Dunmore's War in the following century.

While changes in the English colonial economy in the coastal areas resulted in the marginalization of Native American people, the international competition for control of the interior in the eighteenth century made it essential that Indians be recruited and supported as English allies. Following the founding of South Carolina, the proprietors' agents had successfully used Indians to terrorize the Spanish colonial frontier in Alabama and Georgia and drive the Spaniards back into Florida. In New York, the English used the Iroquois against the French in Canada. After 1700, the expansion of French settlement in Louisiana and the Mississippi Valley, and their enlistment as allies of powerful Indian groups such as the Choctaw, made the cultivation of rival Indian groups essential to the security of the English colonies. In the eighteenth century, the powerful Indian confederacies of the interior, no longer naive about European intentions, very astutely played a balance of power game with the European rivals in order to preserve and enhance their own independence. Thus the Iroquois, who had lost at least half of their warriors in the seventeenth-century "Beaver Wars" against the French and their Indian allies, made peace with France in 1701, declared their neutrality, and placated the English by ceding to England western territories which they had invaded during the previous century but could no longer hold. The Iroquois remained essentially neutral until the English victory in the French and Indian War was clearly imminent, at which time they joined the victorious side. The Cherokee, traditionally British allies in the upper south, received French envoys and were divided between a pro-French and pro-English faction. Their more astute leaders carefully played the two powers off against each other. The Creek Confederacy of the lower south, hostile to the English in the early years of the century, under the leadership of Brims very skillfully exploited ties with the English, the French, and the Spanish.

In the competition for Indian support, the English were hampered by their inability to control behavior on the frontier. The best efforts of colonial diplomats were all too frequently undone by unscrupulous traders and squatters who defrauded or even murdered members of tribes previously friendly to England. The crown's efforts to eliminate abuses through instructions to governors, and later through the establishment of two Indian superintendancies (in the south, under Edmond Atkin and later John Stuart, in the north under Sir William Johnson) were not entirely without result, but ultimately failed either to eliminate intercolonial rivalry or enforce trade regulations. Nonetheless, English colonial officials in competing with their French counterparts did possess one advantage which proved decisive. English trade goods were more plentiful, cheaper, and of higher quality than the commodities which the French offered their allies. The English were also willing and able to offer more bountiful gifts to friendly tribes to "brighten the chain of friendship." Hence, in the decisive French and Indian War for the control of North America, the French were not able to win or hold the undivided loyalty of the Indians. With Indian assistance, England won control of Canada, the Mississippi Valley, and the eastern Gulf coast. The elimination of French power in North America paved the way for the subjugation of all Native Americans and the total loss of Indian autonomy.

Alfred A. Cave

References

John R. Alden, *John Stuart and the Southern Colonial Frontier* (1944); James Axtell, *The Invasion Within: The Contest of Cultures in Colonial North America* (1985); Alfred A. Cave, "Canaanites in a Promised Land: The American Indian and the Providential Theory of Empire," *American Indian Quarterly,* XII (1988); David H. Corkran, *The Cherokee Frontier: Conflict and Survival, 1740–62* (1962); ———, *The Creek Frontier, 1540–1783* (1967); Verner W. Crane, *The Southern Frontier, 1670–1732* (1929).

Wilber R. Jacobs, *Wilderness Politics and Indian Gifts: The Northern Colonial Frontier, 1748–1763* (1950); Francis Jennings, *The Ambiguous Iroquois Empire: The Covenant Chain Confederation of Indian Tribes with English Colonies from its begin-*

nings to the Lancaster Treaty of 1744 (1984); ———, *The Invasion of America: Indians, Colonialism, and the Cant of Conquest* (1975); ———, *Empire of Fortune: Crowns, Colonies and Tribes in the Seven Years War in America* (1988); Yasuhide Kawashima, *Puritan Justice and the Indian: White Man's Law in Massachusetts, 1630–1763* (1986); Karen G. Kupperman, *Settling with the Indians: The Meeting of English and Indian Cultures in America, 1580–1640* (1980).

James H. Merrill, *The Indians' New World: Catawbas and their Neighbors from European Contact through the Era of Removal* (1989); Christopher L. Miller and George R. Hamell, "A New Perspective on Indian-White Contact: Cultural Symbols and Colonial Trade," *The Journal of American History,* 73 (1986):311–328; Kenneth M. Morrison, *The Embattled Northeast: The Elusive Ideal of Alliance in Abenaki-Euramercian Relations* (1984); Gary B. Nash, *Red, White, and Black: The Peoples of Early North America* (1982); Francis Parkman, *England and France in North America* (1851–1892) 7 vols. in 2 vols., rpt. 1983; Neal Salisbury, *Manitou and Providence: Indians, Europeans, and the Making of New England, 1500–1643* (1982).

Bernard Sheehan, *Savagism and Civility: Indians and Englishmen in Colonial Virginia* (1980); Jack Sosin, *Whitehall and the Wilderness: The Middle West in British Colonial Policy, 1760–1775* (1961); Alden T. Vaughan, *New England Frontier: Puritans and Indians 1620–1675* (1979); Wilcomb E. Washburn, *The Governor and the Rebel: A History of Bacon's Rebellion in Virginia* (1957).

See also ATKIN, EDMOND; FRONTIER; FRONTIER, NORTHERN; FRONTIER, SOUTHERN; INDIAN WARFARE, EUROPEAN ACCULTURATION OF; JOHNSON, WILLIAM; STUART, JOHN; WAR AND SOCIETY IN COLONIAL AMERICA

Anglo-Spanish War (1718–1721)

A brief war fought primarily in Europe as an extension of hostilities begun during the War of the Spanish Succession (1702–1713), between Spain on one side and France, Great Britain, and Austria on the other. The declaration of war in January 1719 was anticlimactic as the decisive battle had already occurred with the destruction of the Spanish fleet at Cape Passaro at the island of Sicily by the British navy in 1718.

Ironically, the border between Spanish Florida and the British colonies to the north and French colonies to the west remained quiet during the years of declared warfare, 1718–1721. A planned Spanish naval expedition against South Carolina and the Bahamas never materialized, although French forces did occupy Pensacola for a brief period. In 1722, however, after European hostilities had ceased, open warfare on the frontier nearly erupted between the forces of Spain and Great Britain. At issue was the establishment of a British fort in 1721, Fort King George, on the north bank of the Altamaha River in present-day Georgia. Spanish emissaries to South Carolina argued the fort had been erected in violation of a treaty signed between the two nations in 1670. The Carolinians countered the Spanish charge with the complaint that fugitive British slaves were being harbored in Spanish Florida under sanctuary provisions. Spanish policy vacillated between belligerency on one hand and a willingness to negotiate a peaceful settlement to the crisis on the other. For its part, Great Britain remained stubbornly adamant in its refusal to withdraw the offending structure. While diplomatic maneuvering took place in European capitals, on the other side of the Atlantic, both sides prepared for war.

The end to the threatened hostilities was as anticlimactic as the war which preceded them. In winter 1725, unbeknownst to the Spanish administration in St. Augustine, the fort burned to the ground and the British troops withdrew to the safety and comfort of Port Royal.

Sherry Johnson

References
Verner W. Crane, *The Southern Frontier, 1670–1732* (1929); Alfred T. Mahan, *The Influence of Sea Power upon History, 1660–1783,* 12th ed. (1918); John Jay TePaske, *The Governorship of Spanish Florida, 1700–1763* (1964).

See also FLORIDA; FORT KING GEORGE (GEORGIA); PENSACOLA IN THE WAR OF THE QUADRANGLE ALLIANCE

Anglo-Spanish War (1739–1744)

An Anglo-Spanish conflict fought over the control of commerce rather than for territory, the Anglo-Spanish War merged with the War of the Austrian Succession when France joined the hostilities in 1744. Historians often refer to the contest as the War of Jenkins' Ear for the 1731 severing of the ear of British navy master Robert Jenkins by the commander of a Spanish coast guard *(guardacosta)* vessel. In 1739 Jenkins appeared before the British Parliament to display a preserved ear in a calculated act of jingoism.

The episode over Jenkins' ear was, however, only one inflammatory event in the escalating struggle among European colonial powers over commercial ascendancy in the New World. British merchants wished to expand their West Indian trade and found Spanish colonial markets especially appealing. But British interests were prohibited to trade with Spanish colonies by the Treaty of Utrecht. The British South Seas Company was permitted limited trade in Spanish West Indian trade fairs, restricted to a single ship of 500 tons. The annual ship proved to be an effective wedge into a sizable illicit commerce. In response, Spanish ships stopped and searched every British vessel they encountered, frequently seizing the cargo. These provocative actions became a major precipitant of hostilities.

British and Spanish diplomats held talks to avert war which were finally concluded in the winter of 1738–1739 with the Convention of El Pardo. The agreement required Spain to pay £95,000 as compensation for British losses. The Spanish countered with grievances against the South Seas Company and never paid. This nonpayment became the proximate cause of the ensuing war. British strategy for success in the Americas included capitalizing on the discontent of Spain's New World subjects among both Creole and Indian groups. Tight control by the Spanish crown and its bureaus hampered trade in the Spanish Indies and increased the price of imported British goods. British strategists intended to take advantage of the dissatisfaction that Spain's American subjects expressed concerning the availability of material goods. The British hoped restive Creoles would seize the opportunity presented by the presence of the British navy in major Spanish ports to rebel against Spanish rule and become independent republics, which would subsequently be good clients for British merchandise. The idea was premature. Great Britain mistakenly assumed Spanish Creole discontent would translate into disloyalty; British designs were not able to co-opt Spanish subjects.

British forces struck first and with brilliant success under Admiral Edward Vernon in November 1739 at Porto Bello, the conduit on the Isthmus of Panama for goods from the Spanish Pacific and also the terminus of Peruvian commerce. The Anglo-Spanish War of 1739–1744 was the first time troops identified as British Americans were dispatched to fight on territory other than their own, and the first time they were sent into battle as marines. Three thousand men departed from the British American colonies to serve under Admiral Vernon in the attack on Cartagena in 1741.

The war was a popular conflict in both Europe and the American colonies; it provided a legitimate basis for privateering, attracting influential and affluent members of British North American society. Likewise, Spanish privateers imperiled British shipping along the Carolina coasts. In the early years of the war, the Chesapeake sea lanes were hard hit, as well. Spanish Florida's port of St. Augustine became a center of privateering, ranking second to Havana. The northern British colonies were spared the Spanish privateering raids that plagued the southern coasts, and France, remaining aloof from the war until 1774, sent no privateers from its North American colonies.

Although a war that was largely fought at sea, it took on the characteristics of a land war in the lower American Southeast with both sides courting the support of Native American groups. In May 1740, British troops from South Carolina and Georgia under James Oglethorpe struck at Spanish Florida in hopes of gaining control of the Bahama Channel and ridding the southern British colonies of the threat of both Spanish privateers and the asylum provided for runaway British slaves in Florida. At St. Augustine, Spanish and British forces exchanged artillery fire for more than three weeks in June and July 1740. The main confrontation took place 26 June (New Style) when 300 Spanish fighting men—European, African, Native American—overcame 142 British troops camped at the free-black town of Fort Mose, two miles north of St. Augustine. To avenge the siege of St. Augustine, Cuban governor Juan Güemes y Horcasitas assembled men and equipment to strike at British Georgia. Under the command of Florida governor Manuel de Montiano, a Spanish force outnumbering the

Georgia defenders appeared off the coast of St. Simons Island on 4 July 1742. Although Spanish firepower was initially successful in silencing the guns of Fort Frederica, a British ambush subsequently routed the advance Spanish guard at the Battle of Bloody Marsh. Montiano departed, deceived by a spurious dispatch and in fear of his ships and men being trapped by British men-of-war known to be en route. In September 1742, Spanish cannonfire and bad weather dispatched British warships from their threatening positions off the bars of St. Augustine and Matanzas. The following spring, Georgia militiamen and their Native American allies killed about 40 Spaniards at Fort San Diego, 20 miles north of St. Augustine, in a raid that marked the end of 73 years of major border conflict in the Southeast.

The steadfastness of Spanish rule in the Southeast after the War of Jenkins' Ear frustrated Anglo-American expansion and denied Great Britain control of the entire Atlantic coast and the Caribbean sea routes. In addition, the long international rivalries permitted Native American groups within the southern region to realize a level of influence and territorial control they could not have achieved against the unilateral power of a single European state.

Susan R. Parker

References
Carl E. Swanson, *Predators and Prizes: American Privateering and Imperial Warfare, 1739–1748* (1991); John Jay TePaske, *The Governorship of Spanish Florida, 1700–1763* (1964); J. Leitch Wright, Jr., *Anglo-Spanish Rivalry in North America* (1971).

See also BLOODY MARSH, BATTLE OF; CARTAGENA, EXPEDITION AGAINST; FLORIDA, BRITISH INVASION OF; FORT FREDERICA (GEORGIA); MONTIANO, MANUEL DE; OGLETHORPE, JAMES EDWARD; PORTO BELLO, ATTACK ON; ST. AUGUSTINE, ATTACK ON; VERNON, EDWARD

Fort Ann (Massachusetts)
See FORT WILLIAM (MASSACHUSETTS)

Fort Anne (New York; also known as Queen's Fort, Fort Schuyler, Mud Fort)
Fort Anne's site, which is strategically placed on the Hudson-Champlain route, has been occupied since at least 1690. In 1692, Fitz-John Winthrop built the first in a series of fortifications, a simple earthwork known as the "Old Stone Fort." Colonel Francis Nicholson, on a mission to take Montreal, rebuilt the fortification at the northernmost tip of the invasion route. Then known as Queen's Fort or Fort Schuyler, the rebuilt fort contained a 140-foot square surrounded by palisades which were filled with dirt on the inside for support and to create an armament platform. Within the square were two garrisons with 20-foot bastions at each corner. The construction was financed by Queen Anne and the province of New York. Nicolson destroyed the fort before he retreated, then returned in 1711 to rebuild it.

Fort Anne fell into disrepair, but during the French and Indian War another fort, with an arsenal and powder house, was erected on the site. In 1777, Fort Anne was again used as a base for a patriotic force, which later destroyed the fort before retreating. After the Battle of Saratoga, the patriots returned and built the final fort on the site; in 1780 it, too, was burned down.

Elizabeth Gossman

References
T. Wood Clarke, *The Bloody Mohawk* (1968); Michael Kammen, *Colonial New York: A History* (1975).

See also WINTHROP, JOHN (FITZ-JOHN).

Apalachee
The Apalachee Indians controlled the territory in the vicinity of Tallahassee, Florida, between the Aucilla and Ochlockonee Rivers and the Georgia border and the Gulf of Mexico. The productiveness of that territory's clay and loam soils supported the heaviest, most concentrated population in the state. When Apalachee's wealth of food drew Hernando de Soto to winter there in 1539–1540, its natives harassed his forces tirelessly. By the start of the seventeenth century, however, the Apalachee sought friendly contact with the Spanish. In 1608, in the wake of a friar's visit to arrange peace between the Apalachee and their eastern neighbors, the Timucua, the Apalachee first gave obedience to Spain's monarch. The first permanent Spanish missions were established among them in 1633.

At the start of the mission era, Apalachee consisted of more than 40 villages, ten of which were principal villages whose chiefs had jurisdiction over the rest. The first Spanish soldiers went to Apalachee in 1638, apparently as commercial agents for the governor, as Apalachee's potential for meeting St. Augustine's need for foodstuffs was a major motive for the launching of the mission effort there. The first deputy governor was stationed in the province in 1645. During the 1630s, under Spanish influence, the Apalachee made peace with the rest of their neighbors with whom they had been warring, inaugurating a 40-year era of peace between the Apalachee and their neighbors, broken only by a 1647 revolt against the Spanish. The Spaniards' expanded presence and the demands for cultural change and labor which it brought led a substantial element of Apalachee society to expel Spanish influence in a violent revolt. But the movement was suppressed quickly by Apalachee who remained loyal to Spain and who were aided by a small force of Spanish and Timucua. So complete was the collapse of the rebellion that in 1651 the friars convinced an interim governor to withdraw the five or six soldiers. Later in the decade the next governor returned soldiers to Apalachee, expanding the garrison to 12 in 1657 and ordering the building of a blockhouse at San Luis de Talimali, which was to be the residence of the deputy governor.

In 1675, Apalachee contained more than three-fourths of Spanish Florida's Christianized natives. By then, Apalachee had become an important source of provisions for St. Augustine and Havana, shipping them products such as maize, beans, hogs, chickens, hams, lard, and tallow. It was the most important source of labor for the building of the castillo at St. Augustine, which was then in progress. During the ensuing quarter-century ranching expanded rapidly in the province.

The era of peace ended in the mid-1670s as unidentified natives began to capture women and children in nighttime raids to sell as slaves to Charles Town. After identifying the raiders as Chisca in 1677, Apalachee destroyed the Chisca's settlement on the Choctawhatchee River, which also housed Chacato and Pansacola. A 1677 pirate attack on Apalachee's port of St. Marks led to construction of a wooden fort there by 1680. The fort was destroyed in a second attack in 1682.

The English presence in South Carolina soon led to more serious tension and hostility between the Apalachee and the Apalachicola, or Creek, which would lead in 1704 to the destruction of Apalachee and dispersal of its people. Rising tension began in 1679 and 1681 when the Creek head chief at Coweta blocked establishment of a mission at Savacola on the Chattahoochee. Tension turned into hostilities as the Creek protected English traders who began to appear in their villages in 1685, thereby reversing their allegiance to Spain's king since the 1640s. The Spanish garrison was expanded to 45. Between 1685 and 1689, five expeditions composed of Apalachee and a few Spanish futilely attempted to capture the English traders. During the second expedition, Apalachee's deputy governor burned four Creek towns whose leaders refused to pledge not to receive English traders. In 1689, the governor deferred work he had ordered in 1688 on a larger blockhouse at San Luis to divert the Apalachee carpenters for construction of an ephemeral fort on the Chattahoochee in the heart of the Creek country as a check on English activity. Many of the Creek then moved to the Ocmulgee, and in 1691, the Spanish governor ordered the fort's largely Apalachee garrison to dismantle it and withdraw.

Work was begun anew on the larger San Luis blockhouse in October 1695 and completed by mid-1697 at a cost of 302 pesos to the crown, most of that for hardware, as the natives donated their labor. In 1702 a disastrous rout suffered by a largely Apalachee force on the banks of the Flint River led to construction of outworks to convert the new blockhouse into a proper stockaded fort surrounded by a dry moat and with its stockade backed by a banquette terreplein (a raised platform from which soldiers could fire at an approaching enemy).

As the Carolinians viewed the Apalachee and the Spanish presence among them as a serious obstacle to their planned expansion to the Mississippi and the Gulf, they gave high priority to destruction of the Apalachee missions before the French entrenched themselves on the Gulf and forged an alliance with the Spanish. The English were encouraged as well by reports of the discontent of many Apalachee over their treatment by the Spanish. As a consequence, a joint Anglo-Creek expedition led by Carolina governor James Moore, which was joined by rebellious Apalachee, devastated the province early in 1704, eliminating all but five of the missions. In mid-1704, a Creek force eliminated three more missions, capturing the people of two of them. Aware that a third attack force was headed for Apalachee, the surviving Spaniards and Apalachee abandoned the province, destroying the fort at San Luis, which had not come under attack, before their departure.

John H. Hann

References

Herbert E. Bolton, "Spanish Resistance to the Carolina Traders in Western Georgia, 1680–1704," *Georgia Historical Quarterly,* 9 (1925):115–130; Mark F. Boyd, Hale G. Smith, and John W. Griffin, *Here They Once Stood, the Tragic End of the Apalachee Missions* (1951); John H. Hann, *Apalachee: The Land between the Rivers* (1988).

See also Apalachee Revolt; Ayubale; Spanish Mission System–Southeast

Apalachee Revolt

A little more than 13 years after two Franciscan friars established a Spanish presence among the Apalachee Indians of the Tallahassee, Florida, region, a serious revolt briefly eliminated the Spanish presence. By 1647, the Spanish presence had grown to eight friars, five or six soldiers, and a deputy governor and his family. The rebels consisted mainly of non-Christianized Apalachee, allies drawn from neighboring Chisca, and some recently Christianized Apalachee. The revolt began on 19 February at the frontier mission of San Antonio de Bacuqua. Three friars and the governor's deputy and his family, who were attending a celebration at that mission, were killed by the rebels. Although the rebels soon torched all but one of the eight mission complexes, the five other friars escaped because of assistance from Christian natives. The five soldiers escaped as well because they were in neighboring Timucua territory, working on wheat plantings on a ranch owned by the governor.

The revolt was, in part, a nativist movement sparked by the increasingly successful friars' demands for the curbing or abolition of traditional native practices and, in part, a reaction against increasing labor demands placed on the natives by the growing Spanish presence. A particular irritant was the governor's establishment of a wheat and cattle operation on Apalachee's eastern border at Asile, on lands belonging to the chief of the Timucua.

Spanish authorities responded to the revolt by hastily dispatching 30 soldiers, who recruited 500 Timucua warriors as allies. A rebel force, allegedly 8,000 strong, engaged the relief force in a day-long battle before that force had reached Apalachee. At five in the afternoon the rebels broke off the action and retreated. The Spaniards, having nearly exhausted their ammunition in firing 2,700 balls from their 30 muskets, made no attempt at pursuit and returned to St. Augustine. The Spaniards believed that reinforcements from Cuba would be needed to regain the province and a permanent garrison of 30 to 40 soldiers would be necessary to hold it.

While plans were being formulated for retaking Apalachee, a royal official hastened back to western Timucua to do what he could in conjunction with loyal Timucua to prevent further Apalachee forays into Timucua territory. On reaching the frontier, the official learned the rebels were in disarray, disheartened by the losses they had suffered in the battle and the rapidity of the Spanish response. The rebels had chosen that time for their revolt, counting on the labor demands of planting time to hinder Spanish recruitment of allies among the Timucua, having the time to consolidate support among Christian Apalachee, and to establish alliances with other non-Christian provinces to resist reassertion of Spanish control. Emboldened by this intelligence, the official crossed into Apalachee secretly with 21 soldiers and 60 Timucua. With support from loyal Christian Apalachee, within a month he persuaded the rebels, both Christian and non-Christian, to surrender and hand over the revolt's leaders for trial. Twelve of the rebels considered to be most guilty were executed in Apalachee and 26 others were sentenced to forced labor in the royal works. The rest received a general pardon in return for the province's acceptance for the first time of the obligation to provide quotas of laborers for employment on a rotating basis on Spanish building projects and the farms of soldiers with families.

Spanish records reveal nothing specific about the mechanisms used to overcome rebel resistance, the identity of the native protagonists, or the interests they represented. In their postmortems, Spaniards mentioned no single incident or cause that served as a trigger as had happened in the 1597 Guale revolt. Friars blamed labor demands made by royal officials and soldiers, and fears aroused by the beginning of Spanish settlement and farming activity. Royal officials and soldiers blamed similar labor demands by friars and spoke also of abusive treatment of the natives by some of the friars and indicted the friars for outlawing native practices such as the ball game, dances, and recourse to the shaman for healing. The burning of the churches and killing of the friars suggests a nativist reaction. That some Apalachee remained loyal suggests that, in addition to the hold of the new religion, there were natives who had benefited from trade with the Spanish. Apalachee's most prestigious chief, "he of Ivitachuco," is most likely to have been the leader of that element loyal to the Spanish.

If Spanish officials are to be believed, support for the rebellion collapsed as quickly as it had arisen. Its collapse, they noted, had rekindled Christian fervor among the faithful and moved many non-Christians to seek baptism. The officials remarked that the people now were raising crosses everywhere with the same joy and enthusiasm with which they had burned them shortly before. The change of heart seems to have been real. Three years later the friars convinced an interim governor to withdraw his deputy and his few soldiers from the province. Although the arbitrary orders of a new governor precipitated revolt in nearby Timucua and strong sentiment for revolt in Apalachee, peace was maintained there.

John H. Hann

References
    John H. Hann, *Apalachee: The Land between the Rivers* (1988).

See also APALACHEE

Fort Among the Apalachicolas (Alabama)
By mid-1685, English traders from Charles Town led by Henry Woodward reached the Chattahoochee River towns of the Muscogulges, known to the Spaniards as Apalachicolas and later to the English as the Lower Creek. In an effort to protect their commercial interests, a force of Spaniards and Indians from Apalachee Province in Florida drove away the English, who soon returned and resumed their trade for deerskins. After several additional forays by Spanish troops and the burning of four unrepentant Indian villages failed to discourage the English interlopers and their Apalachicolas trade partners, Florida's Governor Don Diego Quiroga y Lossada sent soldiers late in 1689 to garrison a fort along the Chattahoochee River.

In two months 100 Apalachee laborers constructed a rectangular palisade measuring about 62 by 53 feet, with a sentry box at each corner, surrounded by an earthen parapet and a dry moat (five feet deep and 11 feet wide). A wattle-and-daub building filled most of the cramped fort interior. The garrison consisted of a lieutenant, a corporal, 19 Spanish soldiers—armed with flintlock and matchlock muskets—and 20 Apalachee warriors.

Instead of strengthening Spanish control over the region, construction of a fort led many Apalachicolas to abandon their settlements in the Chattahoochee Valley and migrate eastward in mid-1690 to the upper Ocmulgee River, which became a major English trade center. The isolated garrison now served no function and withdrew in the summer of 1691, after burning the blockhouse and palisade and filling the moat to prevent reuse of the fort by the English.

Gregory A. Waselkov

References
    Herbert E. Bolton and Mary Ross, *The Debatable Land: A Sketch of the Anglo-Spanish Contest for the Georgia Country* (1925); Verner W. Crane, *The Southern Frontier: 1670–1732*, with an Introduction by Peter H. Wood (1981); Mark E. Fretwell, ed., "Two Early Letters from Alabama," *Alabama Review,* 9 (1956): 54–65.
    John H. Hann, *Apalachee: The Land between the Rivers* (1988); Edward B. Kurjack and Fred L. Pearson, Jr., "Special Investigation of 1RU101, The Spanish Fort Site," in *Archaeological Salvage in the Walter F. George Basin of the Chattahoochee River in Alabama*, by David L. DeJarnette (1975): 199–222.

See also WOODWARD, HENRY

Appomattock
The Appomattock, who in 1607 inhabited the countryside along Virginia's Appomattox River, were termed by the English as a strong, warlike people that had an estimated 60 warriors. They were under the sway of the paramount chief, Powhatan, when the first colonists arrived, and were among the petty chiefdoms he had inherited from his parents. In 1611, Sir Thomas Dale drove the Appomattock from their village at the mouth of the Appomattox River, where he established a settlement he called Bermuda Hundred.

The Appomattock, who later were subservient to Opechancanough, Powhatan's successor, participated in the 22 March 1622 uprising during which the natives attempted to expel the colonists from their homeland. In July 1627, when the settlers undertook an expedition against the Indians of Virginia's coastal plain, the Appomattock were among the native groups targeted for attack. It is likely the Appomattock participated in the 1644 uprising, which was also led by Opechancanough. Fort Henry, a trading post and military garrison, was erected in 1646 in the heart of what had been the Appomattock's territory.

In August 1650, when Abraham Wood and a party of explorers set out toward the head of the Appomattox River, Pyancha, an Appomattock, served as their guide. Twenty-one years later, Perecuta, the Appomattock king, led European explorers Nathaniell Batts and Robert Fallom on their westerly expedition. In 1665 the Appomattock reportedly were living in Charles City County, the boundaries of which then extended southward beyond the James River and west to the Appomattox River. According to a 1669 census of the colony's native inhabitants, the Appomattock had 50 bowmen.

The Appomattock were not invited to sign the 29 May 1677 Treaty of Middle Plantation because some of their people then stood accused of murder. Three years later, when the treaty was expanded to include several more native groups, the Appomattock king signed on his people's behalf. In 1705, the Appomattock reportedly were residing in Colonel William Byrd's pasture in Charles City County, most likely the southerly portion, which later became Prince George County. Afterward, the Appomattock seemingly faded from view. A copper badge labeled "King of Appomattock," which was recovered in Dinwiddie County during the early twentieth century, may have been one of the identification ornaments given to Virginia's tributary tribes in 1662 and/or 1711.

Martha W. McCartney

References

Robert Beverley, *History of the Present State of Virginia (1705)*, ed. by Louis B. Wright (1947); William W. Hening, ed., *The Statutes At Large: Being a Collection of All the Laws of Virginia*, 13 vols. (1809–1823); Helen C. Rountree, *Pocahontas's People: The Powhatan Indians of Virginia Through Four Centuries* (1990); Alexander S. Salley, *Narratives of Early Carolina, 1650–1708* (1911); John Smith, *Travels and Works of Captain John Smith, President of Virginia and Admiral of New England, 1580–1631*, ed. by Edward Arber, 2 vols. (1910).

See also POWHATAN; VIRGINIA-INDIAN WAR (1622–1632)

Arellano, Tristan de Luna y

See LUNA Y ARRELLANO, TRISTAN DE

Arkansas

See QUAPAW (ARKANSAS)

Arkansas Post

Various temporary fortifications were established on the Arkansas River by the French in the late seventeenth and early eighteenth centuries. These posts were little more than trading stations; not until 1734 did the French make a substantial effort to keep a military garrison at the so-called Arkansas Post.

The exact location of the pre-1752 structure is unknown, but all of the posts were located near the mouth of the Arkansas River. The post was an important site for maintaining trade and good relations with the Arkansas Indians and other indigenous peoples of the region. The Arkansas were important allies to the French, as they assisted them on several expeditions against French enemies, particularly the Chickasaw.

Alan Gallay

Army, France

The first French commercial establishments, settlements, and missions in North America were defended by soldiers in the private employ of governors, commercial companies, and the Jesuits; the main burden of defense rested on amateur civilians who took up arms in times of danger. Settlers in Canada, however, could not adequately defend themselves against annual large-scale incursions by the Iroquois, and the Indians almost forced the colonists to abandon their settlements in the early 1660s.

Direct royal government was established in Canada in 1663, and in 1665, Louis XIV dispatched the 1,200-strong Régiment de Carignan-Salières to deal with the Iroquois. This professional unit, organized in 24 companies, burned Iroquois villages and crops and obliged the confederacy to open peace negotiations. Although part of the regiment returned to France in 1667–1668, the government persuaded more than 400 soldiers and several officers to settle in the colony, making a substantial addition to Canada's population and seigneurial class. During the following decades the government maintained a small and fluctuating garrison in the colony. In order to improve local defense, a militia was organized in 1669 comprising all able-bodied males between the ages of 16 and 60. The militia was divided into companies, each with a captain of militia chosen by the governor from among the more notable citizens.

In 1683, the Ministry of Marine, responsible for the navy and the colonies, sent the first of the *Compagnies franches de la Marine,* or Independent Companies of the Marine, to Canada. Two years later, companies were stationed in Acadia and Newfoundland, and troops were sent to Louisiana in 1703. The *troupes de la Marine,* or colonial regulars (they had no connection with the navy), were always recruited in France and wore a uniform of grey-white cloth with blue cuffs, collar, and vest. They resembled line regiments in appearance and armament, but since the corps was trained in irregular as well as conventional tactics, they also adopted a practical field uniform consisting of a short hooded coat, leather leggings, and moccasins, and temporarily replaced their swords with tomahawks and knives. Very early on, detachments of colonial regulars were trained as gunners, and official units of *cannoniers-bombardiers* were established at Louisbourg (on Cape Breton Island) in 1743, in Canada in 1750, and in Louisiana in 1759. These elite gunners also served as grenadiers and wore a blue coat with red cuffs and vest. Companies of colonial regulars garrisoned the main towns and were stationed at forts far into the interior of the continent. They formed the core of every raiding party, and customarily fought in combination with militia and Indians. In Canada, local seigneurial families eventually almost monopolized the officer corps, but in other colonies most officers came from France and returned home when they completed their service. The sons of Canadian seigneurs so coveted officer commissions that they served as common soldiers until vacancies were available, bearing the rank of cadet, which was created for them in 1731. Fort commanders in the west often made considerable fortunes from the fur trade, and officers vigorously competed for appointments to these posts. Since there were no units larger than a company, none of the officers held an official rank higher than captain.

In 1699, there were 840 colonial regulars in Canada, organized in 28 companies of 50 men. The official establishment was fixed at 1,500 troops in 1750, and a final strength of 2,600 men in 40 companies of 65 soldiers was reached in 1757. Louisbourg's garrison rose from six to 24 companies between 1713 and 1749, and Louisiana had up to 16 companies. The shortage of troops capable of meeting the British regulars on the conventional battlefield led to the consolidation of several companies to form a colonial regular battalion in 1757, and a second battalion in early 1760. Lieutenant General Louis-Joseph de Montcalm, marquis de Montcalm (1712–1759), and his officers considered the Canadian officers brave, but unable to cope with the increasingly complex conventional warfare on the continent. This led to some tensions between the two officer corps. Relations between French line troops, colonial regulars, and Canadian soldiers tended to be much better. After the capitulation in 1760, 647 of the colonial regulars returned to France and were incorporated into line regiments. The rest, several hundred line troops, opted to settle in Canada and endure British rule.

In 1723, the Ministry of Marine obtained the Régiment Suisse de Karrer, a Swiss unit raised by the army in 1719, for garrison duty overseas. A depot company was stationed at the French port of Rochefort, and other companies garrisoned Louisbourg, New Orleans, Mobile, Martinique, and Saint-Domingue (Haiti). The soldiers of this regiment, which was renamed Hallwyl when a new colonel purchased the unit in 1752, wore a red coat like other Swiss troops, and blue cuffs, vest, breeches, and stockings. The disciplined Swiss distinguished themselves against the Louisiana Indians and during the first siege of Louisbourg, but were disbanded in 1763.

With the exception of the Régiment de Carignan-Salières, no line regiment of the French army served in North America until the mid-eighteenth century. Four line regiments and some French provincial militia briefly stopped at the future site of Halifax during Lieutenant General Jean-Baptiste Louis Fréderic de La Rochefoucauld de Roye, duc d'Anville's (1709–1746), disastrous expedition to retake Louisbourg in 1746, but during the Seven Years' War numerous line regiments arrived in North America. They were temporarily placed under the authority of the minister of marine, and the commanding general was subject to the strategic decisions of the governor general of New France. Four thousand three hundred men belonging to the second battalions of the regiments of La Reine, Languedoc, Guyenne, Béarn, Royal Roussillon, and La Sarre, and the second and third battalions of Berry served with Major General Baron Jean-Armand de Dieskau (1701–1767) and Montcalm in Canada. With them were gunners and engineers from their respective corps, and a few German and Irish troops sent to attract deserters from the British army. The second battalions of the regiments of Artois, Bourgogne, Cambis, and Volontaires Étrangers served at Louisbourg during the war, and in 1762–1763 a battalion of the Régiment d'Angoumois was stationed in Louisiana. They all wore the grey-white uniforms of the line army with the distinctive facings of individual regiments.

Each line battalion in Canada in 1755 had 12 companies of fusiliers and one company of grenadiers, amounting to an average of 31 officers and 525 other ranks. By the last years of the war, however, each battalion had fallen to two-thirds or even half strength. The desperate shortage of conventional infantry was first met by consolidating the companies of colonial regulars into battalions; then, in 1759, by drafting militiamen into line battalions, which helped to throw Montcalm's columns at the Battle of the Plains of Abraham into confusion; and finally, in 1760, by attaching militia companies under French officers to each regular battalion to serve as light infantry. The latter solution proved to be highly effective at the Battle of Sainte-Foy.

During the Seven Years' War, drafts of unpaid militiamen were organized in five-company brigades, usually strengthened by colonial regular noncommissioned officers and soldiers. The militia officers were *habitants* with limited military experience and authority, and they were customarily placed under the command of professional officers from the colonial regulars and sometimes the line regiments. The lack of experienced officers and the annual raising of militia units made it difficult to turn this body of civilians into an effective fighting force. Nevertheless, the militiamen possessed a strong military tradition and willingly performed valuable service as transport troops and irregulars, patiently enduring miserable conditions and illness because they habitually lacked tents, clothing, and nutritious food. The militia performed best when supported by regular troops. Canadian soldiers saw nothing wrong with destroying American settlements and killing armed civilians, but refrained from scalping the dead and attempted to discourage atrocities by their native allies.

In the seventeenth century, the French government committed small numbers of troops to North America in order to defend Canada against the Indians, but after 1700, they pursued a more aggressive strategy to contain American agricultural settlements behind the Appalachians. A string of garrisons between New Orleans and Quebec held a large number of Indian nations economically and politically in the French orbit, and in wartime the Indians and Canadians kept the enemy on the defensive. The Atlantic fortress of Louisbourg was designed to protect the fisheries, but without naval support it was unable to defend the fishing fleets or withstand a lengthy siege. During the Seven Years' War, the French government ordered its generals in Canada to tie down the British army for as long as possible while the French army made gains in Germany. The generals faithfully carried out their orders and managed to hold out for six years.

Martin L. Nicolai

References

René Chartrand, *The French Soldier in Colonial America* (1984); Edward P. Hamilton, *The French Army in America & The Musketry Drill of 1755* (1967); Martin L. Nicolai, "A Different Kind of Courage: The French Military and the Canadian Irregular Soldier during the Seven Years' War," *Canadian Historical Review,* 70 (1989):53–75; M. Pétard and René Chartrand, "L'homme de 1690: l'infanterie des colonies en Nouvelle-France," *Gazette des uniformes,* no. 28 (1975); George F.G. Stanley, *Canada's Soldiers: The Military History of an Unmilitary People* (1960).

See also ARTILLERY, FRANCE; FRANCE; FRANCE-CANADIAN RELATIONS; NAVY, FRANCE; WEAPONS, FIREARMS

Army, Great Britain (1688–1763)

The British army's history before 1763 dates from the seminal event in modern British history: the Glorious Revolution of 1688. Before the end of the seventeenth century, land forces were limited to "guards and garrisons," with expeditionary forces being raised to meet specific emergencies. The New Model Army arose from the civil wars, but with the Restoration (1660), England returned to traditional military policies. The army's disjointed history was a consequence of important aspects of British history and geography. The respect which all Englishmen professed for crown and common law meant that after the medieval civil wars, and unlike on the continent, neither the king nor the nobility sought to defend their rights through armed force. The confusion with which both sides began the civil wars demonstrated England's unmilitary nature by the seventeenth century. Being an island, Britain was less susceptible than continental powers to foreign invasion. The inevitable result was the predominant position of the Royal Navy in British strategic and popular thought, and the parallel obscurity of the land forces.

The Glorious Revolution changed this situation. As stadtholder of the Dutch Republic and husband to the Protestant heir to the English throne, William of Orange saw an opportunity to unite Dutch and British resources in the struggle against Louis XIV's France. To facilitate this, the military required a legal existence within the Constitution. As "guards and garrisons," land forces were raised specifically to guard the royal family, or to garrison important fortifications. These were not "national" forces, but men paid out of crown revenue. The Bill of Rights (1689) gave Parliament control of military expenditures and, with the annual Mutiny Act, made standing armies illegal in peacetime without parliamentary consent. As an attempt to restrict the crown's military power, these measures would have proven effective had not the nation been in an almost constant state of war from 1689 to 1714. Thus, while military finance was in the hands of an institution historically suspicious of the army, the international situation ensured the development of an effective military administration. Additionally, William III and the duke of Marlborough gave the army a centralized leadership it had not had since Oliver Cromwell, while the length of this era of war created a force of able rankers led by professional officers of long and varied experience.

The pernicious influence of almost 30 years of peace on the army after 1714 was mitigated by the House of Hanover. Reforms such as annual reviews and tactical regulations, instituted as a result of George I's keen Germanic interest in English military matters, were consolidated and

extended in the aftermath of the valiant disasters of Fontenoy (1745) and Rocoux (1746) by George II and the duke of Cumberland. The Hanoverian emphasis on military discipline often conflicted with the individualistic English temperament, but it also ensured that the army could ultimately defeat the last Jacobite bid for the throne in 1745–1746, and win an empire in 1763.

Administrative Structure

While Parliament controlled its finance, the organization and discipline of the army remained a royal prerogative. Though the commander in chief or captain general was to administer military matters, this post was but intermittently filled in the eighteenth century. The king, therefore, effectively ruled the army. When appointed, the commander in chief had little direct control of theater commanders, who answered directly to the king or his ministers. More permanent officials were the adjutant and quartermaster generals, the first seeing to the issue of official regulations, the second to the issue of army necessities. Both were represented by deputies within theater commands, as was the judge advocate general, the army's civilian legal officer. The Board of General Officers from 1706 formed an effective advisory board consisting of the army's most senior generals, while after 1716 the reviewing generals ensured that regiments were inspected by officers of experience and dedication. None of these officers had direct authority in Ireland, the Irish establishment possessing its own staff under the lord lieutenant.

Important civil offices governed the army as well. The secretary at war originated as a personal military secretary of Charles II but, under the Hanoverians, became an M.P. with access to the Closet and head of the War Office, though not a member of the Cabinet. His duties included preparing annual estimates of army size and expense, the issue of royal orders at home and abroad, and, in the absence of commander in chief, the presentation of promotions to the king. The deployment of the army in war and peace was the responsibility not of the War Office, but the secretaries of state for the northern and the southern departments. Though preparing estimates, army pay was not distributed by the War Office but by the Treasury and paymaster general. Finally, the storage and issue of camp equipage, weapons, and ammunition was the task the Board of Ordnance, and sea transport that of the Admiralty. The issue of weapons or the shipping of troops necessitated the secretary at war applying to a secretary of state for the issue of appropriate orders to either the master general of ordnance, or the Navy Board.

As the army was brigaded only in wartime or for specific training exercises, the regiment was the most important formation by which discipline, training, and general fitness was maintained. The household consisted of horse, royal horse, horse grenadier guards, and foot guards. The Line consisted of horse, dragoon guard, dragoon and light dragoon regiments, and foot regiments. The Board of Ordnance was responsible for the artillery and engineers. All regiments were alike in the authority of their colonel, who owned his regiment. As most colonels also served as general officers, the issue of regimental clothing, arms, and pay was administered by a civilian agent, while in camp or billets the regiment was usually in the hands of a lieutenant colonel or major. Captains, too, had a proprietary relationship to their companies, with similar responsibilities for the care of their men. Indeed, the wide dispersal of regiments in peacetime into small pockets of company strength or less often meant captains and subalterns had more responsibilities and real power than did their superiors. By placing so much on officers' shoulders, this system relieved the government of much responsibility. Though peculation was possible, the amounts involved were generally so small, and graft so easily detected in the physical condition of a regiment when annually reviewed, that on the whole the system and the army functioned adequately.

Officers and Men

Given the importance of regiments, regimental officers played a particularly important role in shaping the army's character. More than half of the colonels and generals of the army were nobility or landed gentry. Regimental officers were predominantly lesser gentry, "without the advantage of birth or friends," foreign nationals, experienced rankers, or gentlemen volunteers who served in the ranks until a commission was available. For these men, service was long and often hard. In 1740, lieutenant colonels served on average 40 years from first commission. This was at the end of Walpole's peace, but by 1754, after one bloody war and at the beginning of another, the average was 28 years for the horse, 22 for the foot. In 1759, officers expected to serve ten years before making lieutenant, and 17 before making captain. The purchase system served two important purposes in the eighteenth century. Lacking pensions, the sale of commissions guaranteed officers a small retirement fund. More important in a society which valued property ownership almost to the exclusion of all else, ownership of a commission conferred on officers of humble origin the all-important quality of social status.

The ranks of the army were filled almost completely by volunteers. The army did use the press, as well as the "sweepings" of prisons, but these were extreme measures implemented in wartime. For the most part, men volunteered for life. Men enlisted in wartime, however, were mostly discharged at peace, with the result that at the next war's outbreak the army consisted of a large number of raw recruits. Service for a soldier was often hard; medical services were minimal, and discipline inflicted at the whim of regimental officers. However, a noticeable degree of amity existed between officers and men. Though not denying their social and economic superiority, most officers demonstrated deep concern for the condition of their men; in return, soldiers respected and, as with James Wolfe or Viscount Howe, greatly admired their officers. The army was not without its internal conflicts, though more between officers than they and their men, and while its record was chequered with both glorious victories and ignominious defeats, it deserved its reputation for prowess, bravery, and loyalty as much as did its great rival for the nation's affection, the Royal Navy.

Adam Norman Lynde

References

Correlli Barnett, *Britain and Her Army, 1509–1970: A Military, Political and Social History* (1970); John Childs, *The Army, James II, and the Glorious Revolution* (1970); Alan J. Guy, *Economy and Discipline: Officership and Administration in the British Army, 1714–1763* (1985); J.A. Houlding, *Fit for Service: The Training of the British Army, 1715–1795* (1981); Lois G. Schwoerer, *"No Standing Armies!": The Antiarmy Ideology in Seventeenth-Century England* (1974).

See also ARTILLERY, GREAT BRITAIN; CONTRACTORS, ARMY; DESERTION, ARMY; DISCIPLINE, ARMY: IMPRESSMENT, ARMY; INFANTRY; LIGHT INFANTRY; MARINES; MEDICAL SERVICES; MILITARY MANUALS; MUTINY, REGULAR ARMY; NAVY, GREAT BRITAIN; RANGERS; RECRUITMENT; REQUISITION SYSTEM; STRATEGY; SUPPLIES, IMPRESSMENT OF; SUPPLY; TACTICS, INFANTRY; WEAPONS, FIREARMS

Army, Spain

From the first years of the conquest and colonization of the northern territories of the Spanish empire in America, the presidio, with its combination of civilians, military men, and Indian villages was the fundamental solution used by Spain for securing its frontiers against hostile Europeans and Indians. The presidio supported the Catholic mission villages. What the Spanish crown created was a sequence of advanced military posts manned by garrison companies in charge of their defense, which would be the germ of the future American regular army. Each post acquired its own characteristics depending on the place in which it was located and the peculiar needs of the local population. Not until well into the eighteenth century could one talk of a Spanish regular army operating on Spain's North American frontier.

The founding of St. Augustine, Florida, in 1565 meant the beginning of the garrison regime in the American Southeast: at this time, Pedro Menéndez de Avilés pushed out the French settlers at Fort Caroline and founded the St. Augustine presidio. He also established fortified positions in Santa Elena and San Mateo (South Carolina). Florida had great strategic value as it controlled the pass to the Bahamas Channel through which the Spanish fleet carried its cargoes of treasure and merchandise on its return route to the Iberian Peninsula and, with time, Florida's importance increased as a barrier against possible foreign invasions in the Gulf of Mexico. Its founding as a military presidio made up a large measure of the character of the settlement and the major composition of its villages. There were 300 active places in the garrison during a good part of the seventeenth century, but in practice the number of effectives rarely reached this number due to the fact that many of the places were occupied by sick soldiers, the disabled, or widows and orphans of military men. The inhabitants tended to view "the Indias defense" as "the defense of their personal properties, their country, their religion and their happiness." On the other hand, the absence of regular envoys of reinforced troops in Florida before the 1730s contributed to a continuity in the defensive formation of the villages of St. Augustine. The founding by the British of Jamestown (1607) and especially Charles Town (1670), and also the French settlements in Louisiana at the end of the seventeenth century, forced the Spanish to secure their position in Florida by the construction of the Castillo de San Marcos in St. Augustine, and in the founding of Pensacola. After the attack on Florida in the beginning of the eighteenth century by Carolina led by Governor James Moore, some of the garrison soldiers were placed outside of the military enclosure: small fortifications at Fort Matanzas (some 20 miles south of St. Augustine), San Diego Fort (20 miles to the north), a fort house crossing St. Johns River and, after 1718, a small stone fort at San Marcos de Apalachee, close to Tallahassee. Provisions in the 1730s were increased, thanks to important reinforcement that arrived in the colony soon after the English founding of Georgia.

The thousands of troops that served in Florida reflected a large ethnic diversity: whites, peninsulares, Creoles, half-castes, and an important group of black militiamen who had escaped the English plantations of Carolina and Georgia. The founding of the town of Mose for free blacks in 1738, a short distance to the north of St. Augustine, helped in the integration of this ethnic group in the defense of the garrison.

In the territories situated to the north of the viceroyalty of New Spain, military affairs had similar characteristics to those of Florida. From the middle of the sixteenth century, a series of presidios were strategically situated to allow troops a place where they could organize for defense of the region. With the passing of time, some garrisons were converted into new villages; meanwhile, others were established in places already populated to help with defense. Initially, garrisons held only six men, but this was expanded in the eighteenth century to upwards of 100 soldiers, the bulk of whom were natives of the region. A lack of coordination was constant in these garrisons, especially in the event of an unforeseen attack. They had antiquated equipment, which was poorly distributed; recruiting and the training of troops was difficult; economic resources were scarce and arrived on an irregular basis. In spite of these problems, the garrisons managed to maintain the advance line of occupation in the northern territory of New Spain.

In the last quarter of the seventeenth century, the presence of French colonies on the coast of the Gulf of Mexico and their settlement in the Mississippi Valley, united with the constant danger the Spanish posts were exposed to from the various Indian villages that inhabited this area—Yumas, Pimas, Apaches, Comanches, and others—forced Spain to reinforce its military position as much in Texas and New Mexico as in Florida. After the Pueblo Indian revolt of 1680, the garrisons of El Paso and Santa Fe became fundamental links in the Spanish line of defense, making New Mexico an important bastion against the pressure of the Plains Indians. In 1716, the Spanish secured Texas against French encroachment by garrisoning San Antonio de Béjar, Espíritu Santo Bay, and Los Adaes. From the middle of the eighteenth century a large part of New Spain's northern defense forces were concentrated in central and east Texas. Because of this, until 1763, a line of garrisons spread through the now north Mexican states. Together with the aforementioned, Altar, Tubac, Pitic (now Hermosillo, in Sonora), Janos, El Presidio del Norte, Monclova, and San Luis de las Amarillas, among others, were erected at vital points for territorial defense.

In conclusion, until well into the beginning of the eighteenth century, no overall Spanish defense plan for the northern North American frontier existed. Instead, each small isolated contingent, made up of poorly trained and poorly supported troops, defended itself.

Alberto Bernardez-Alvarez

References

Antonio Acosta and Juan Marchena, eds., *La influencia de España en el Caribe, La Florida y La Luisiana* (1983); John Francis Bannon, *The Spanish Borderlands Frontier, 1513–1821* (1970); Woodrow Boorah, ed., *El gobierno provincial en la Nueva España, 1570–1787* (1985); Verne E. Chatelain, *The Defenses of Spanish Florida, 1565 to 1763* (1941).

Juan Marchena, "Guarniciones y población militar en Florida Oriental (1700–1820)," *Revista de Indias* (1981):91–142; ———, *Oficiales y soldados en el Ejército de América* (1983); Allan R. Millet and Peter Maslowski, *For the Common Defense: A Military History of the United States of America* (1984); John Jay TePaske, *The Governorship of Spanish Florida, 1700–1763* (1964).

See also AGUAYO EXPEDITION OF 1720–1722; BLACK AND INDIAN MILITIAS; FLORIDA; FRANCE-SPAIN RELATIONS; GREAT BRITAIN–SPAIN RELATIONS; NEW MEXICO; PRESIDIO; SPANISH MISSION SYSTEM–SOUTHEAST; SPANISH MISSION SYSTEM–SOUTHWEST; WEAPONS, FIREARMS

Artillery, France

The vast majority of artillerymen who served in French America were colonial troops. In 1697, an unofficial artillery detachment formed at Quebec actually functioned as a school to train other troops in the use of guns and mortars. Artillery detachments of a similar nature were also raised in Acadia in 1707, Louisbourg in 1735, and Mobile, Louisiana in 1744.

The first formal colonial artillery unit, a company of canonniers-bombardiers, was formed in 1743 and assigned to Louisbourg. Two additional companies were raised for Saint-Domingue (Haiti) in 1745; one for the Windward Islands in 1747; two in Canada in 1750 and 1757; a second company for Louisbourg in 1758; and a company in Louisiana in 1759. Soldiers in the canonniers-bombardiers companies were considered elite troops. When not employed as artillerymen they served as grenadiers. These companies disappeared as the French lost their possessions in North America. In 1766, the two surviving companies on Saint-Domingue were absorbed by the regular Corps Royal d'Artillerie.

Several small detachments of the Corps Royal d'Artillerie served in North America, but never enough to make a difference. The French also sent only their most obsolete guns to their American forts. In 1757 a 20-man Royal Artillerie detachment went to Louisbourg. The following year a 40-man detachment went to Quebec in response to Montcalm's plea for more artillery support. During Wolfe's siege of Quebec, the small number of qualified gunners and low stores of powder prevented the French from effectively returning British cannon fire. When the French met the British on the Plains of Abraham, Montcalm asked his artillery commander for the support of 25 field pieces. He got three.

David T. Zabecki

References

René Chartrand, *The French Soldier in Colonial America* (1984); Colonel G.W. Nicholson, *The Gunners of Canada* (1967).

See also ARMY, FRANCE; ARTILLERY, GREAT BRITAIN; NAVY, FRANCE

Artillery, Great Britain

The first cannons in North America arrived with the Spanish in the sixteenth century. These weapons were little different from the black powder, smoothbore, muzzle-loading behemoths that would remain in general use for almost the next 300 years. These old guns had very limited mobility and slow rates of fire. The larger, heavier guns fired as few as 30 rounds per day, while lighter guns had maximum rates of fire up to eight rounds per hour. Maximum ranges seldom reached beyond 2,000 yards, and actual effective ranges were more like 500 yards. The old guns were dangerous to handle as they had a nasty habit of occasionally exploding, killing the gunners and anyone else who happened to be around.

Up until the early 1700s gunners were not even regular soldiers. They were highly skilled specialists who belonged to secretive guilds, and they contracted themselves and their guns to the highest bidder in time of war. Even after artillerymen became regular members of most military establishments, they still were considered a breed apart—clannish practitioners of a black art (an attitude which survives in many armies to this day). In most colonial-era armies, artillery officers had a secondary status which prohibited them from commanding line troops. As specialists, however, they generally received higher pay than line officers of the same rank.

By the start of the eighteenth century, the various types of cannon fell into three broad categories, based on construction and ballistic characteristics. The gun, the most widely used artillery piece, was long in relationship to the size of its bore. It fired a solid projectile at a high velocity and flat trajectory. Guns were especially useful in battering fortifications. The mortar, a short stubby weapon that fired a large exploding projectile at high angles, could shoot over intermediate obstructions at targets on the other side. The howitzer, which first appeared in the early 1700s, fell in-between the gun and the mortar. Howitzers generally had shorter barrels and larger bores than guns and could fire at higher angles, but not as high as mortars. Howitzers had greater ranges than mortars and could shoot a larger projectile than guns of the same tube weight. Modern artillery is still classified into these three basic groups.

Artillery was also classified by its function. Garrison pieces were heavy, relatively immobile, and used to defend fixed fortifications. Siege pieces were used for the opposite function, attacking fortifications. Here too, weapon mobility was not an important factor, since the intended targets rarely moved. Field pieces, on the other hand, had to be lighter to move with the army.

Up until the start of the eighteenth century, size classification of artillery was based on a bewildering array of special names that were unique to each army. In the early 1700s, most armies started size-classifying guns by the weight of the iron ball they fired. Howitzers and mortars were size-classified by the diameters of their bores. In 1736, the British adopted the Armstrong system of artillery. By the end of the Seven Years' War, British guns in America were a mix of Armstrong system and earlier designs. The most common British guns were the three-, six-, nine-, and 12-pounders. The most commonly used mortars and howitzers were the eight- and ten-inchers.

The French had two parallel systems of artillery; land artillery which came under the Ministry of War, and marine artillery controlled by the Ministry of Marine. In addition to warships, marine artillery was used in coastal fortifications and in the colonies. The vast majority of French cannon in North America, therefore, were the heavier marine designs. In 1732, France adopted the Valliere system for land artillery. In 1767 they introduced the famous Gribeauval system. The few French land guns in North America were a mixture of Valliere and older designs. The most common French guns were the four-, six-, eight-, and 12-pounders; and the most commonly used mortars were eight- and 12-inchers. The French did not adopt the howitzer until about 1770.

Iron and brass were the two primary cannon construction materials. "Brass" actually was the general term used in most of the contemporary references to describe a wide variety of different copper-based alloys. Most of these alloys contained some portion of tin, which technically would make them bronze by modern definition. Iron tubes were stronger and could take larger powder charges, which produced greater ranges. Brass cannon, on the other hand, were lighter and more mobile, and therefore preferred for field pieces. Brass was also less susceptible to casting defects. With the correct powder charge, a brass tube rarely burst. Such accidents were far more common with iron tubes.

Artillery ammunition fell into two broad categories: exploding and non-exploding. Solid shot, essentially a cast-iron sphere, was the basic non-exploding round for the gun. Chain shot, crossbar shot, and jointed cross bar shot were variations of solid shot, designed to cut up a ship's rigging or tear wide gaps in ranks of troops. Sometimes, solid shot was heated to a red-hot state before firing to produce an incendiary effect against inflammable targets, such as wooden buildings or ammunition. A slightly more sophisticated form of incendiary round was called carcass; a hollow iron ball filled with pitch or other material that burned with an intense heat for five to ten minutes.

Scatterable shot was another type of nonexploding ammunition. Used almost exclusively against personnel targets, its basic effect was like a huge shotgun. One form was canister, consisting of musket balls, nails, rocks, or just about anything, packed into a tin cylinder and fired (usually point-blank) into advancing troops. The other form was grapeshot, a group of iron balls (larger than canister) tied around a central wooden spindle and base. Grape had a greater effective range than canister, but only about half that of ball shot.

Exploding projectiles, called shells (or bombs), were hollow iron balls filled with a charge and triggered by a tapered wooden fuse packed with a quick-burning substance. Mortars fired only shells, while guns fired only nonexploding ammunition. Howitzers fired shells principally, but in a pinch they could fire scatterable forms of shot at the lower angles of elevation. Early in the colonial period the standard technique for firing shells required the crew to place the round in the tube (fuse away from the propellant), light the fuse, and then quickly fire the cannon—praying for no misfire. This risky practice was called "firing at two strokes." Later in the period gunners discovered that hot gases from firing the cannon would seep around to the front of the projectile and light the fuse. The much safer "firing at one stroke" became the standard practice thereafter.

Black powder, a physical mixture of saltpeter (potassium nitrate), charcoal, and sulphur, was the basic propellant for all firearms. By the early 1700s the standard recipe for war powder was a 7:1.25:1 mix. In the early years of the colonial period, gunners fed powder into the barrel using a ladle on a long pole. Around the start of the eighteenth century, prepackaged powder cartridges appeared. When both the projectile and the powder cartridge were packaged as a single unit, it was called fixed ammunition. Cartridges were made of either paper or flannel. Most gunners preferred the more expensive flannel because it burned more evenly and rarely left a smoldering residue in the tube.

In any event, gun crews always had to swab out the tube with a wet sponge after each shot to prevent any hot residue from prematurely setting off the next round.

Artillery gunnery in those days was far more of an art than the exact science it is today. Sighting was accomplished by visually aligning a notch on the muzzle of the tube with one on the breech. Indirect fire techniques would not appear until almost the start of the twentieth century, and the colonial gunner could only aim at what he could see. High-angle fire at hidden targets with a mortar or a howitzer was not really aimed fire, and appropriately called "firing at random." Although experience and "feel" were major factors in a gunner's accuracy, crude elevation and range tables did exist. When time permitted, the gunner could set a desired angle of elevation by laying a device called a gunner's quadrant along the line of the bore. Modern artillerymen still use a gunner's quadrant, which in principle is the same instrument.

During the colonial period, artillery was used primarily for attacking or defending fortifications rather than in support of armies in the field. In the East in particular, the rough terrain made it almost impossible to move the guns, and the thick forests severely limited the effects of cannon fire. Both Hernando de Soto and Francisco Vásquez de Coronado dragged bronze guns on their expeditions, but found little use for them. The first war use of artillery in America came in 1565, when French Huguenots in Florida used cannon to defend Fort Caroline against the Spanish fleet of Pedro Menéndez de Avilés.

British and French ordnance spread through North America as both countries expanded their network of colonies in the seventeenth century. In 1609, Jamestown had an inventory of 24 pieces of ordnance. In 1628, Samuel Sharpe became the master gunner of Massachusetts Bay Colony at a salary of ten pounds per year. Ten years later, the Ancient and Honorable Artillery Company of Boston emerged as the first native-grown artillery guild in the New World. As the competition for North America intensified, both countries built major fortifications and armed them with artillery. Powerful Fort William in Boston harbor had 18 large 32-pounders, and 18 massive 42-pounders. The French built and armed fortresses at Louisbourg and Quebec, and built Forts Duquesne and Carillon in the interior.

The two Louisbourg sieges were the major artillery actions of the colonial period.

During the 1745 siege, militia artillery units from New England fired 9,000 rounds of solid shot and 600 rounds of shell into the French positions. When the British besieged Louisbourg again in 1758, units from the Royal Artillery fired 13,700 rounds of shot and 4,300 shells.

The widespread use of field artillery in North America did not occur until the Revolution; but the last of the French wars saw the first attempts to use mobile guns in the field. General Edward Braddock took ten guns on his ill-fated 1755 expedition. His entire artillery train consisted of 26 heavy wagons and carts, which made it almost impossible for his column to move through the wilderness with any speed. All the guns were lost when Braddock was ambushed on the Monongahela River. During James Wolfe's 1759 attack on Quebec, his artillerymen hauled two light 6-pounders up the cliffs to the Plains of Abraham and outshot the three field pieces supporting Montcalm's forces.

David T. Zabecki

References

B.P. Hughes, *Open Fire: Artillery Tactics from Marlborough to Wellington* (1983); Albert Mauncy, *Artillery Through the Ages* (1949); John Muller, *Treatise of Artillery* (1780), rpt. 1977; Harold L. Peterson, *Round Shot and Rammers* (1969).

See also AMMUNITION; ARTILLERY, FRANCE; ROYAL REGIMENT OF ARTILLERY; WEAPONS, FIREARMS; WEAPONS, NAVY

Fort Ascension (Illinois)
See FORT MASSAC (ILLINOIS)

Atkin, Edmond (1697–1761)
Native Englishman Edmond Atkin made a career in trade and politics in South Carolina, and was the first superintendent of Indian affairs in the southern colonies during the French and Indian War. A dedicated servant of British imperialism, Atkin was an early proponent of a centralized bureaucracy that would control Indians, and an outspoken critic of colonial governments' factionalized and self-serving Indian diplomacy. Atkin had established himself as an Indian trader in Charles Town in the 1730s. He was appointed to the Council, or upper house

of assembly in South Carolina, in 1738, and fiercely defended the Council's rights and privileges as an appointed British body.

Atkin's championship of the Council's powers peaked in 1750, when he headed a committee of inquiry into the claims of two Indian traders that they encouraged the Choctaw Indians to revolt against the French and ally with the English and the pro-English Chickasaws in the Mississippi Valley. James Adair and Matthew Roche claimed to have had the support of Governor James Glen and wanted monetary compensation for their patriotic services. The Council's committee denied their petitions; neither man was clearly responsible for the revolt, which in any case had ended disastrously—the Choctaw had returned to the French, and British authorities had frowned on the revolt. The decision was upheld in the Commons House of Assembly, which nevertheless avoided accusing Glen of any foolish actions.

The committee in Council then tried to reopen the investigation, despite two obstacles: the provincial records of the revolt were missing (Glen claimed his own copies were laid away at his country estate), and the assembly had adjourned on 31 May. Three committee members (a quorum) maintained that one house of assembly could sit though the other was not in session, a decision Glen believed was unconstitutional. He tried to monitor their meetings and was rebuffed; though the Council adjourned on 6 June (leaving open the question of the Choctaw revolt), no colonial governor ever again tried to attend Council meetings in South Carolina.

Atkin removed to England later in 1750, and wrote two long reports on Indian affairs: his "Historical Account of the Revolt of the Choctaw Indians in the Late War from the French to the British Alliance and of Their Return Since to That of the French" (1753), and his "Indians of the Southern Colonial Frontier" (1755). Atkin preached the wisdom of Britain creating a centralized Indian policy which would unite all pro-British Indians into one force that would be of military consequence against the French and Spanish (a conclusion also reached by both the Albany Conference of 1754 and Britain's Board of Trade).

Establishing himself as an expert on Indians, Atkin was a logical candidate for superintendency of southern Indian affairs when the Board of Trade established this position in 1756. But several British officials—notably

John Campbell, earl of Loudoun—distrusted Atkin, and the new superintendent struggled to receive payment and learn his orders, a prolonged process that delayed his arrival in South Carolina until 1758. Atkin was further handicapped by lack of cooperative colonial governors and houses of assembly (a situation familiar to him), and was especially frustrated by his inability to get sole power to license and regulate Indian traders, a power local officials believed should be manipulated to suit local needs. Georgia's governor, Henry Ellis, for example, believed the way to maintain control over Indians was to keep them so preoccupied with fighting each other that they would be unable to attack English settlers—just the policy Atkin felt was disastrous for imperial security.

Atkin eventually toured several western portions of the south, patching over relations with the Cherokee in Virginia in 1757, signing a peace treaty with the Choctaw in 1758, renewing an alliance with the Creek nation in 1759, and making a treaty with the Catawba in 1760. He had much less success as an agent of peace in the east, where the Cherokee–South Carolina alliance was disintegrating, partly because of friction between bellicose Virginia settlers and disgruntled Cherokee warriors recruited by General John Forbes to attack Fort Duquesne in 1758. Cherokees raided English settlements along the Yadkin and Catawba Rivers in April 1759. South Carolina, after desultory attempts to seek peace, entered the Cherokee War, an episode within the French and Indian War that would not conclude until December 1761.

During this time, South Carolina Governor William Henry Lyttleton and Lieutenant Governor William Bull, Jr., took little advice from Atkin, pursuing the war as a local dispute rather than regarding its imperial consequences. Accustomed to conflict with governors, Atkin only gave up when his own South Carolina Council, as well, ignored him. He then resigned, and died on 8 October 1761, several months before peace with the Cherokee would be declared. He had, however, laid a solid foundation for his successor, John Stuart, and pioneered a consistent yet coercive plan for regulating aboriginal inhabitants in the British Empire.

Joyce E. Chaplin

References

Wilbur R. Jacobs, ed., *The Appalachian Indian Frontier: The Edmond Atkin Report and Plan of 1755* (1967); M. Eugene Sirmans, *Colonial South Carolina: A Political History, 1663–1763* (1966).

Attakullakulla (also known as Little Carpenter, c. 1710–1780)

Attakullakulla was perhaps the best known peace chief of the Cherokees in the eighteenth century. His English name, Little Carpenter, was probably derived from his diminutive size and his great skill at building. He first came to prominence in 1730 as one of the seven Cherokees who accompanied Alexander Cuming to London, a group which signed "Articles of Peace and Friendship" with the crown. About ten years later, French Indians, the Ottawas, captured him and he remained a prisoner until 1748. After returning home he sought unsuccessfully to break the South Carolina Cherokee trade monopoly by establishing commercial ties with Virginia. However, Little Carpenter did successfully improve trading conditions. By the early 1750s he was recognized as the tribe's "second greatest warrior" (next to Connecorte, or Old Hop). Always trying to live in harmony with the white man and thus avoid bloodshed, Little Carpenter was the leading signatory in a 1755 land cession to England of more than 40 million acres between the Wateree and Santee Rivers in South Carolina. The cession included an agreement to build a fort in the Overhill towns, Little Carpenter's tribal region.

Although normally loyal to the British, he courted the French to insure good treatment. When the French and Indian War broke out, Virginia desperately needed the aid of the Cherokees. The Virginians agreed to build the Overhills fort promised by South Carolina but not yet constructed, and open trade with the Cherokees in return. The fort they built was quickly thrown up, poorly constructed, and never manned as promised. Although the Cherokees aided Virginia, frontiersmen murdered about 17 or 18, supposedly mistaking them for enemy Indians. In 1759, the Cherokees under Salouee sought revenge, attacking the Carolina frontier and killing 24 settlers. Governor William Henry Lyttleton responded rashly by seizing a delegation of peace chiefs hostage, which he agreed to exchange for 24 of the murderers. At Fort Prince George, Little Carpenter persuaded Lyttleton to release some of the hostages. In an attempt to release the others, Oconostota (Great Warrior) attacked Fort Prince George, which caused the murder of the remaining hostages. The result was the bloody Cherokee War of 1759–1761.

During the war Fort Loudoun in the Overhills country surrendered and the officers were killed, except for John Stuart (later superintendent of Indians in the south), whom Little Carpenter saved and personally escorted to Virginia. When the war was over, Little Carpenter was the chief negotiator of the peace.

In the years that followed, whites continued their rapid encroachment of Cherokee lands. In an attempt to prevent another war between Cherokees and whites, Little Carpenter played a major role in the purchase by Richard Henderson of a large tract of land comprising most of the modern state of Kentucky and middle Tennessee. Little Carpenter's son, Dragging Canoe, was outraged at the land sale and led the young warriors in attacks on American colonists during the American Revolution. Little Carpenter, who died toward the end of the war, was described by his white contemporaries as "a man of superior abilities" and as the "Solon of his day."

William L. Anderson

References
    John P. Brown, *Old Frontiers: The Story of the Cherokee Indians from Earliest Times to the Date of their Removal to the West, 1838* (1938); David H. Corkran, *The Cherokee Frontier: Conflict and Survival, 1740–62* (1962); J. Norman Heard, *Handbook of the American Frontier: Four Centuries of Indian-White Relationships* (1987); James C. Kelly, "Notable Persons in Cherokee History: Attakullakulla," *Journal of Cherokee Studies,* III (1978):2–34; Grace Steele Woodward, *The Cherokees* (1963).

See also CHEROKEE WAR; FORT LOUDOUN (TENNESSEE); FORT PRINCE GEORGE–KEOWEE (SOUTH CAROLINA); OCONOSTOTA

Augusta

Augusta was established by order of James Edward Oglethorpe, 14 June 1736. The town was to be laid out at the head of navigation of the Savannah River in a pattern of 40 lots around a square, similar to the plan of Savannah. The name honored Augusta of Saxe-Gotha, the recent bride of Frederick, Prince of Wales, and the future mother of King George III. Carolina trad-

ers began moving across the river to take up residence even before the surveys were made in 1737. Georgia licenses were required of all who traded west of the Savannah and the use of rum was forbidden. Although the Indians permitted settlement only as far as the tidewater, they regarded upriver Augusta as their base of supplies and frequented the town on the paths that crossed the river at the fall line. A band of Chickasaw Indians settled just below Augusta at a place called New Savannah.

Captain Richard Kent commanded the garrison at Fort Augusta and acted as conservator, or justice of the peace. After he returned to England in 1749, several Augusta residents were named magistrates. The little town prospered; the inhabitants, mostly storekeepers and traders, ignored the Georgia trustees' restrictions on rum, land ownership, and slavery. In 1751, a church was built and a minister appointed to St. Paul Parish.

During the Great War for Empire, Augusta was a place of refuge for people fleeing from Cherokee war parties. Creek Indians and the New Savannah Chickasaws helped defend the town.

Augusta was the site of a major Indian congress in 1763. Around 900 Creeks, Cherokees, Chickasaws, Catawbas, and Choctaws sat down with the royal governors of Virginia, North Carolina, South Carolina, and Georgia. The Indians agreed to open the backcountry to settlement as far as the Little River to the north and the Ogeechee to the west. The cession was rapidly populated and acts of violence between the settlers and Indians increased. In 1773, the Indians were called to Augusta and asked to sign away more land in return for the cancellation of their debts. Creeks who opposed the Treaty of 1773 terrorized the frontier during the winter of 1773–1774, and Augusta again was a place of refuge.

During the American Revolution, Augusta was the seat of government while Savannah was under British rule. Augusta was occupied by the British for two weeks in February 1779, and for a year from June 1780 to June 1781. Elijah Clarke's raid on Augusta in September 1780 led to the Battle of Kings Mountain. Lieutenant Colonel Henry (Light Horse Harry) Lee defeated the British commander, Lieutenant Colonel Thomas Brown, after a two-week siege ending 5 June 1781. Even though Savannah remained in British hands for another year, Augusta's fall assured

Georgia's claim to independence at the peace negotiations in Paris.

Edward J. Cashin

Augusta, Congress of (1763)

The Treaty of Augusta (1763) marked an important watershed in the history of the southern colonial frontier. It signaled the transition between the traders' frontier and the farmers' frontier as Indians for the first time consented to white settlement west of the Savannah River and above the tidewater.

During the same year the Great War for Empire came to a close. The French presence at Mobile and Fort Toulouse at the forks of the Alabama River had been a constant source of annoyance and danger to the British traders operating out of Charles Town and Augusta. During the height of the late war, the great William Pitt seriously considered launching a land and sea invasion against Mobile and Fort Toulouse. In 1763, the French gave up their vast claims from Quebec to Louisiana in the Treaty of Paris.

The British prime minister in 1763, George Grenville, faced with the problem of governing the interior, needed time to sort out the conflicting land claims of the provinces and balance them against the rights of the Indians who occupied the interior. Georgia's western boundary was put at the Mississippi River by the Treaty of Paris. However, by their treaty with James Oglethorpe in 1739, the Creek Indians defined the Savannah River as their boundary. White settlement was limited to a narrow strip of tidewater land between the Savannah and Altamaha. On 7 October 1763, King George III published a proclamation forbidding white migration beyond the Appalachian Mountains. The effect of the proclamation was to divert restless pioneers toward the South Carolina and Georgia backcountries. Although the situation demanded a renegotiation of the Savannah River boundary, it was not the official reason for summoning the Indians to Augusta in 1763.

The initiative in convoking a congress of Indians at Augusta apparently lay with Henry Ellis, who had resigned the governorship of Georgia in 1760. A document attributed to Ellis advised the ministry that Indians believed the French propaganda that English intended to occupy French forts and enslave the Indians as they had earlier in the century. Ellis urged calling the Indians to Augusta and reassuring them

that the forts, if retained, would be for trade purposes only. Past misdeeds would be forgotten and fair trading regulations would be followed. Grenville's minister for the colonies, Lord Egremont, took the suggestion and directed the governors of Virginia, North Carolina, South Carolina, and Georgia to meet representatives from the Creek, Cherokee, Choctaw, Chickasaw, and Catawba nations at Augusta for the purpose of announcing that the French and Spanish had been banished for their lies and general bad conduct. Significantly, there was no mention in Egremont's instructions about obtaining new land cessions. Valuable presents were dispatched to Augusta as an incentive for the Indians to come to the congress.

For John Stuart, whose appointment as Indian superintendent dated from 5 January 1762, the Augusta meeting was the first major undertaking. It was his job to coordinate the conference and distribute the presents. Although he knew the Cherokees well, he was handicapped by a lack of familiarity with the Indians of the west, the Creeks, Chickasaws, and Choctaws. However, he could count on the advice of experienced Indian traders at Augusta. Stuart realized the new situation would affect the Georgia trade. Georgia enjoyed primacy in the Creek trade because of proximity to that nation. The profits to be made had attracted men of character and ability, men who were an asset to England in its contest with the French and Spanish. Now, with French Mobile and Spanish Pensacola in English hands, Augusta would have competition for control of the trade. There was the danger of a glut of traders and less reason for them to treat the Indians fairly. Stuart asked General Jeffrey Amherst for authority to grant licenses and limit the number of traders. The general's answer reflected a misguided idealism, "I have always considered everything of that kind as inconsistent with the freedom and liberty that ought to be indulged to every British subject. . . ." Unfortunately, with the two new provinces in Florida, there would be six southern governors in the licensing business, and Stuart would be helpless either to limit the number or to prevent abuses.

Considering the circumstances, it is surprising the Augusta Congress took place at all. The French, with their American empire on the verge of dissolution, were still capable of bedeviling the English. Pontiac did their work in the north. The Upper Creek chief called the Mortar was their agent in the south. At least both the French and the English were convinced the Mortar was under the influence of the French, and perhaps he was. On 5 April 1763, he sent a strong talk to Governor James Wright stating that the Savannah River was the right and proper boundary between the English and the Indians. The whites were trespassing on the Creek hunting grounds and as a result there were no deer, bear, or buffalo to hunt. He demanded that the governor remove these intruders, whom he called "Virginians." The Mortar's warning was echoed by another powerful chief, the Gun Merchant, who told Governor Wright he had heard that the English intended to take their lands and reminded the governor "it made their hearts cross to see their Lands taken without their Liberty." They loved their land, he said, "the wood is our fire, and the grass is our bed."

A more serious impediment was the sudden rash of killings. In October, on the eve of the Augusta meeting, three traders were killed. South Carolina governor Thomas Boone favored stern retaliatory measures, but Georgia's James Wright preferred Ellis's earlier policy of blaming an errant few, not the whole nation. The Mortar warned the other chiefs not to go to Augusta; the English would take them hostage as they had done to the Cherokees in the recent war. As a result the principal headmen among the Upper Creeks stayed away from Augusta.

The factionalism among the Indians had a counterpart in the bickering among the governors, who were as jealous of their prerogatives as any Indian chief. On 4 October 1763, Francis Fauquier of Virginia, Arthur Dobbs of North Carolina, and Thomas Boone of South Carolina met together in Charles Town and decided they would rather not go to Augusta. Besides all the inconveniences of getting there, they could not put the Indians under guard in "so straggling and ill-settled a place as Augusta."

Governor Wright took umbrage at this slight to Georgia's second town. Although not as elegant as Charles Town, Augusta "affords sufficient houses, plenty of provisions and accommodations of every kind," he said. Perhaps they had been misinformed about Augusta, answered the three governors. Even so, they did not want to go there. Besides, they argued, Wright was overly concerned about the Creeks. The governors doubted that the Creeks would dare show their faces at the conference. Wright's reply betrayed a growing testiness. He was concerned about the Creeks for the good and sufficient reason that Georgia would be devastated if those people went on the warpath, a prospect the other governors did not face. Given the mood of the Creeks, Wright doubted that they could be made to go to Charles Town, and, if they would not, he would meet them in Augusta, even if he had to go there alone. The reluctant trio said that the Creeks might not like to follow orders, but they should not be indulged. The debate ended when John Stuart informed the governors that the Upper Creeks had indeed come to Augusta and they were adamant they would not go one step farther. Their reason was they much preferred a straggling town in which they were safe to a comfortable one in which they would be put under guard. The Indians were annoyed that the governors were not at Augusta and said they would give them ten days to get there.

The governors had no choice but to go to Augusta. Although they had no reason to expect to gain anything by a conference, they did not want to be held responsible by London for causing the failure. They sent a conciliatory message through John Stuart. He was to assure them that the governors had no thought of taking any land from the Indians: "No such intention is harboured in the breast of any of us," they said.

The Augusta traders acted as hosts to the Indian visitors. George Galphin, who had lived for years at Coweta town, invited the Lower Creek headmen to be guests at his plantation at Silver Bluff on the Carolina side of the river below Augusta, while waiting for the congress to start. On 20 October, Governor Wright and a number of gentlemen left Savannah, escorted by Captain Lachlan McGillivray's mounted militia. They reached Augusta two days later. McGillivray was as influential among the Upper Creeks, having lived at Little Tallassee on the Coosa River, as Galphin was among the Lower Creeks. McGillivray maintained a trading house at Augusta and entertained his old friends there. The most important delegate, in the absence of the suspicious older chiefs, was Emistisiguo, a headman of McGillivray's former village, Little Tallassee. For Emistisiguo, as for John Stuart, the Augusta Congress was a debut upon the stage of diplomacy. Because the laggard dignitaries did not reach Augusta until 3 November 1763, the traders had ten days to confer with the Indian visitors at Galphin's and McGillivray's. The most important business of the Augusta Congress was accomplished in these comfortable sessions marked by pipe-smoking, rum drinking, and interminable talks of the sort the Indians loved, the traders understood, and the governors found tedious.

By 3 November 1763, when the three governors finally reached Augusta, there was a throng of nearly 900 Indians in town, of whom about 700 were men. With due solemnity and to the discharge of Fort Augusta's cannon, the governors announced that the talks would begin. They were astonished when the Upper Creeks asked for a delay of one day while they consulted with the Lower Creeks. The governors could not imagine why; the Indians were merely supposed to listen to a routine ritual of platitudes.

John Stuart's opening talk on behalf of the governors on 5 November was rich with the usual rhetoric. The French and Spanish were bad people and had been made to leave the country. Past offenses were buried in oblivion, he said, thus giving away a negotiating point if he had negotiations in mind. The former French forts would be occupied only for the convenience of the Indians, not for oppressing them. Point by point, Stuart followed Egremont's suggestions. After Chickasaw chief Paya Mataha made a modest request to limit the number of traders in his country, Lower Creek chief Telletcher rose to speak. His announcement must have come as a surprise to the governors. He said that the Creeks were willing to give away a huge tract of their hunting ground. He then proceeded to describe in detail where the new boundaries would be: along the Little River, a specified line to the Ogeechee, down the Ogeechee, and another line to the Altamaha. The boundary line at Pensacola would follow the tidewater. What did the Creeks want in return for this major concession? Only that past misdeeds would be forgiven and the trade be conducted as before. Stuart had already agreed to that, without a *quid pro quo*. The governors asked for a day off to consider the dramatic proposal.

It is clear the agreement was reached before the governors arrived and probably without John Stuart's mediation. The Indians were well briefed on the exact location of the convoluted boundary line. Stuart asked them twice if they knew where the line was to be drawn and twice they assured him that they did. They did not negotiate with Stuart; they handed him a *fait accompli*. The real work of the conference had been carried on by the chiefs and the white men

whom they trusted and who knew the country as well as they did. The conclusion is inescapable that Lachlan McGillivray and George Galphin were the effective parties of the second part of the agreement. Emistisiguo later referred to McGillivray's discussions of the boundary line. When the line was actually marked, McGillivray and Galphin accompanied the surveying team in order to assure the Indians that the line ran true.

The pedantry of the official language of the final treaty conceals the satisfaction the governors must have felt in being handed an unexpected bonus by the Creeks. Other boundaries were quickly agreed to by the Cherokees and Catawbas. The two nervous Choctaw delegates were promised a supply of goods. The Chickasaws were told to keep unwelcome traders out of their country; the governors could not. The treaty was signed and the guns of the fort fired a salute of celebration.

The satisfaction of the governors was tempered by a nagging doubt that the absent Upper Creek would go along with the terms of the agreement. Emistisiguo and the Upper Creek chiefs present at Augusta had declined to sign until they secured the consent of their great men. After the governors left Augusta, John Stuart distributed presents to 312 Cherokees, 305 Creeks, 45 Upper Chickasaws, 113 Lower Chickasaws, 69 Catawbas, and two Choctaws for a total of 846. Among the goods distributed were strouds (a heavy wool cloth), duffles, vermilion, shirts, guns, powder, balls, calico, hoes, hatchets, brass pans, great coats, gun flints, belts, looking glasses, garters, trunks, gunlocks, saddles, bridles, stirrup leather, and cutlery. The Indians left Augusta "with all the marks of contentment and good humor," as Stuart put it.

Some Creeks who had lived in the Cherokee country tried to spoil the treaty by attacking whites in the Long Cane region of South Carolina. Again Wright persuaded Boone of South Carolina to avoid retaliation. His patience was rewarded when the Upper Creeks held their conference on 10 April 1764, with British traders present. It was a mark of Emistisiguo's growing influence that he was the spokesman for the nation and not the Mortar or the Gun Merchant. All the headmen were now present, said the chief, and he wanted the governors to know they would abide by the Augusta treaty "providing you keep your slaves and your cattle within those bounds."

Emistisiguo must be regarded as one of the major architects of the Augusta agreement. His influence increased because of his determination to abide by the treaty; the Mortar's influence declined with the removal of the French. Governor Wright and John Stuart played important roles at Augusta, the other three governors added little but dignity to the occasion. The intervention of the traders, especially Lachlan McGillivray and George Galphin, was of crucial importance in bringing the Creeks to terms.

Unfortunately, the seeds of disruption were sown in 1763. The trade was opened to an influx of unscrupulous newcomers. The new cession was occupied by settlers, many of whom, Governor Wright complained, were more savage than the Indians. They had in common a determination to possess the land and a fierce hostility toward the Indians. Because the Indians continued to use their traditional trails to Augusta, there were numerous instances of violence between the whites and the Indians. The newcomers were angry at traders who sold weapons to Indians and increasingly impatient with a government that protected the Indian trade. In the years that followed, the British government would be torn between the interests of the Indian traders who favored preserving the Indians' hunting grounds and those of the growing number of pioneer farmers who were convinced they needed the land more than the Indians did. The reason why many in the backcountry finally turned against the king was their perception that the royal government was partial to the traders and their Indian clients.

Edward J. Cashin

References

John Richard Alden, *John Stuart and the Southern Colonial Frontier* (1966); Edward J. Cashin, ed., *Colonial Augusta "Key of the Indian Countrey"* (1986); Kenneth Coleman, *Colonial Georgia: A History* (1976); David H. Corkran, *The Creek Frontier, 1540–1783* (1967); *Journal of the Congress of the Four Southern Governors and the Superintendent of that District with the Nations of Indians at Augusta 1763* (1764).

See also AUGUSTA; EMISTISIGUO; MORTAR OF OKCHAI; STUART, JOHN

Fort Augusta (Georgia)

James Edward Oglethorpe gave orders to surveyor Noble Jones on 14 June 1736 to lay out a town under the supervision of Roger Lacy. Lacy was instructed to build a fort to protect the settlement. The name Augusta was chosen to honor the bride of Frederick, Prince of Wales.

Oglethorpe's reason for establishing the town and fort of Augusta was that he intended to gain control of the Indian trade. During the first few months after his arrival in Georgia, he learned from the Indians that the Carolina traders were antagonizing the western Indians by the excessive use of rum and by fraudulent weights and measures. There was a danger the Indians would turn to the French at Mobile and New Orleans for their trade goods. Returning to England, he and his fellow trustees of Georgia sponsored two pieces of legislation. The first gave Georgia authority to license Indian traders west of the Savannah River, and the second forbade the use of rum in Georgia.

Before Roger Lacy could build the fort at Augusta, he had to notify the traders in the Cherokee country about the new regulations. It was not until May 1737 that Lacy, as captain of a company of 15 rangers, began work on the fort. By then, the Carolina traders had begun to set up their storehouses on Kenyon's Bluff, near the site of the fort.

Lacy died in 1738, before the construction was complete. The work on the fort was completed by Lacy's successor, Lieutenant Richard Kent. When Oglethorpe visited Fort Augusta in September 1739, he was so pleased with Kent's management of Augusta that he promoted him to captain and made him conservator of the peace with jurisdiction over the far-reaching Indian country. Oglethorpe commented to the trustees that Augusta was "Key of the Indian Countrey." By regulating the trade, he believed he had averted a possible Creek war and secured the allegiance of that nation.

Fort Augusta, repaired in 1759, was a refuge for settlers fleeing from the Cherokees in 1760. After the return of peace in 1763, Fort Augusta was garrisoned by a company of Royal Americans. The military authorities complained to Georgia's Governor James Wright that the soldiers were not provided with food or proper barracks facilities. Finally, in 1768, the Royal Americans were recalled northward and Fort Augusta was allowed to deteriorate.

During the Revolutionary War, the British constructed Fort Cornwallis on the site of Fort

Augusta. Fort Cornwallis fell to the patriot army under Lieutenant Colonel Henry (Light-Horse Harry) Lee in June 1781, after a two-week siege.

Edward J. Cashin

See also AUGUSTA

Fort Augusta (Maine)

Built in 1718 as a defense against hostile Indians for the fishing village at Small Point Harbor (present-day Phippsburg), Fort Augusta was commissioned and erected by Doctor Oliver Noyes, the principle director of the settlement. The fort was constructed of stone and was approximately 100 feet square. Originally it was garrisoned by a detachment of soldiers provided by the Massachusetts government. However, these troops were later withdrawn to serve elsewhere.

David L. Whitesell

Fort Augusta (Pennsylvania)

Designed to accommodate 400 soldiers, Fort Augusta was easily the largest and most elaborate fort in eastern Pennsylvania. It stood at the confluence of the north and west branches of the Susquehanna River, near the trading town of Shamokin, and by virtue of that location could guard the Susquehanna Valley against attacks from either the French forts on the Allegheny River or from Iroquois country to the north. Fort Augusta was designed by Captain Harry Gordon and Lieutenant Elias Meyer, both accomplished army engineers, and was built under the command of Colonel William Clapham. The fort was laid out in a large square with bastions at each corner, each side of the square 204 feet long and 25 and a half feet high. An outer stockade enclosed the whole fort in a broad arc that ran all the way to the riverbank on each side. Within the fort, six buildings laid out in a square served as barracks, storehouse, and magazine. Though most of the construction was completed in the summer of 1756, work on the surrounding ramparts and parapets continued throughout the following year, and was finally completed in February 1758.

Fort Augusta was the only outpost in the string of forts built in 1756 designed to support offensive as well as defensive operations. It was garrisoned by the third battalion of the Pennsylvania Regiment under the command of Colonel Clapham. Like the other forts on the north-

eastern frontier of Pennsylvania, it saw relatively limited military activity. On 18 October 1756, Clapham was informed by the Iroquois scout Ogagradarisha that a party of 1,000 Indian warriors under French leadership was preparing an expedition against the fort; but instead of taking on Fort Augusta directly, that force broke up into smaller bodies and attacked the colony's outlying settlements. In November, Clapham retaliated by instructing Captain John Hambright to lead a company of 38 men against several Indian towns on the west branch of the Susquehanna, including Chincklacamoose and Great Island. After 1756, however, it was clear the colony's principal line of defense had shifted to the Cumberland Valley, and thereafter Fort Augusta served principally as a base of operations for the Pennsylvania Regiment, a way station for messengers, and a center for Indian negotiations.

By the summer of 1757, Fort Augusta was suffering from the normal difficulties of fort life. In August, Captain Joseph Shippen wrote that, of the 380 soldiers in the garrison, "60 are now ill with bad Fevers which have reduced many of them to meer Skeletons." The winter of 1757–1758 saw numerous desertions in the face of inadequate clothing, supply, and pay. By March, Shippen reported "great Dissatisfaction" among his troops, who had not been paid for six months. Nevertheless, the colony managed to garrison Fort Augusta continuously until 13 June 1765, making it the last provincial fort in Pennsylvania used for military purposes.

The contrast between Fort Augusta's impressive design and construction and its relative lack of usefulness in the war effort is, in part, a reflection of the paradox of military preparedness on Pennsylvania's frontiers. The fort was designed for European-style engagements, and as a defensive stronghold securing a strategic site it was well-conceived. Rather than directing their attacks against such a site, the Indians and their French allies, who harassed the Pennsylvania frontier in the early years of the war, chose to target individual farms and villages. Against such attacks, a single defensive stronghold offered little protection.

Eric Hinderaker

References
C. Hale Sipe, *The Indian Wars of Pennsylvania* (1929); Charles Morse Stotz, *Outposts of the War for Empire: The French and English in Western Pennsylvania; Their*

Armies, Their Forts, Their Peoples, 1749–
1764 (1985).

See also FORT HALIFAX (PENNSYLVANIA);
FORT HUNTER (PENNSYLVANIA)

Ayllón, Lucas Vázquez de (c. 1480–1526)

Lucas Vázquez de Ayllón was the Spanish licentiate in law who, in 1526, established San Miguel de Gualdape, the first documented European colony in the continental United States. A wealthy planter and an influential judge on the island of Española, he backed several Indian slaving expeditions to neighboring islands in the Caribbean. One of these incursions, which reached portions of the East Coast of North America in 1521, moved him to obtain a royal charter from the Spanish crown to explore and colonize that territory. In 1525, he sent two caravels to reconnoiter the Atlantic coast and to select a safe port for landing. The following year, he led six ships carrying ample supplies and about 600 persons, including black slaves and Spanish women, to the Winyah Bay area in South Carolina. Deeming the place unsuitable to sustain a colony, he moved south, probably as far as Sapelo Sound south of present-day Savannah, Georgia, where, in September 1526, he established the town of San Miguel. Cold, hunger due to the loss at sea of most of his provisions, and subsequent diseases decimated the settlers. After Lucas Vázquez died the following 18 October, dissension among the survivors caused the colony to disintegrate and most of its inhabitants to return to Española by November.

Vázquez was survived by his wife, Ana Bezerra, and their five children. One of them, Juan, who later changed his name to Lucas, tried to establish another colony in North America in 1564, but was unable to reach the continent from Spain.

José Ignacio Avallaneda

References
Paul E. Hoffman, A New Andalusia and a Way to the Orient: The American Southeast During the Sixteenth Century (1990); Enrique Otte, Las perlas del Caribe: Nueva Cádiz de Cubagua (1977).

See also SANTA ELENA; SOUTH CAROLINA

Ayubale (Florida)

The Spanish mission of Our Lady of the Conception of Ayubale in eastern Apalachee Province, Jefferson County, Florida, was the first target of Carolina governor James Moore's attack on the Apalachee missions early in 1704. Moore arrived with about 50 Englishmen and 1,000 Indians. Ayubale was the only mission Moore took by storm, killing 24 Apalachee and capturing 84 men, women, and children. His Indian allies captured a like number. The next morning, Moore defeated a relief force from Fort San Luis, killing five or six Spaniards and about 200 Apalachee, and capturing eight Spaniards. Moore lost five Englishmen in the two encounters and had 14 wounded in his attack on the church.

John H. Hann

See also APALACHEE

B

Bacon, Nathaniel (1646–1676)

Nathaniel Bacon was born at Friston Hall in Suffolk, England, and attended the University of Cambridge and Gray's Inn in London. In 1670, he married Elizabeth Duke over the strenuous objections of her father, Sir Edward Duke, who disinherited his daughter. For the next few years Bacon lived beyond his modest means and became involved in serious legal difficulties involving fraud. His father packed him off to Virginia in 1674. In the Old Dominion, the young gentleman was received with open arms by his cousin, also named Nathaniel Bacon, who was a prosperous tobacco planter and a member of the provincial Council. The elder Bacon helped the newcomer purchase Curles, a plantation located within a loop of the James River in Henrico County about 50 miles above Jamestown. The elder Bacon also prevailed upon the governor, Sir William Berkeley, to appoint his young kinsman to the Council, an extraordinary honor for one so recently arrived in the colony. Bacon took little interest in governmental matters, however, and busied himself developing his plantation and seeking out additional sources of income. He joined with William Byrd and other neighboring planters in a trading venture with the Indians. In 1675 the Susquehannock Indians raided the northwestern frontier of the colony. Many frontier residents, including Bacon, were exasperated by the governor's limited response to the Susquehannock incursion and his continuing conciliatory policy toward Indians in general.

In 1676, for reasons which are not clear, Bacon assumed leadership of a protest movement against Berkeley's Indian policy which rapidly swelled into a violent uprising against Berkeley himself. This confused affair is known as Bacon's Rebellion. Though Bacon had nei- ther military rank nor military experience, he grandly styled himself "General by Consent of the People" and led unauthorized, poorly-managed expeditions against the friendly Occaneechee and Pamunkey Indians. On 16 September Bacon's rebels defeated Berkeley's loyalists in a skirmish near Jamestown. Berkeley withdrew across Chesapeake Bay to the Eastern Shore. With the governor temporarily unseated, Bacon and his followers burned Jamestown and engaged in widespread looting and vandalism. The uprising petered out after Bacon died of dysentery on 26 October in Gloucester County.

William L. Shea

References

Wilcomb E. Washburn, *The Governor and the Rebel: A History of Bacon's Rebellion in Virginia* (1957); Thomas J. Wertenbaker, *Torchbearer of the Revolution: The Story of Bacon's Rebellion and Its Leader* (1940).

See also BACON'S REBELLION; BERKELEY, WILLIAM

Bacon's Rebellion (1675–1677)

In the second half of the seventeenth century, the two Chesapeake Bay colonies, Virginia and Maryland, experienced a severe economic depression caused by falling tobacco prices. In Virginia, the misery produced by the economic downturn was exacerbated by growing dissatisfaction with the political situation. Governor Sir William Berkeley and a small coterie of friends had dominated the provincial government for three decades and had enriched themselves at public expense. Other prominent and aspiring planters, the great mass of yeoman farmers, and the horde of free laborers and indentured servants, all suffering from the near collapse of the tobacco market, viewed this privileged aristocracy with mounting envy and anger. Several local uprisings over various issues in the early 1670s indicated social and political tensions were rising in the colony. Virginia was primed for an explosion.

In July 1675, a party of Doeg Indians killed a settler near the Potomac River in the northern part of the colony. The local militia set out in pursuit and killed 11 of the raiders, but also killed 14 friendly Susquehannocks by accident. The Susquehannocks struck back by sniping at settlers along the frontier. In response, the militias of Maryland and Virginia engaged in an extremely rare joint operation and laid siege to a fortified Susquehannock compound on Piscataway Creek in Maryland. The operation ended in utter failure after seven weeks when the Susquehannocks escaped. For the next few months, the outraged Indians raided the northwestern frontier of Virginia and killed at least several dozen colonists.

Governor Berkeley was old and infirm by this time and did not respond to the incursions with the aggressiveness he had shown earlier in his career. He ordered the mobilization of a strong militia force, then, without explanation, canceled the order and referred the problem to the next assembly as if it were a routine matter of business. By the time the assembly met in March 1676, the colony was in an uproar, but the legislators were dominated by the aging governor and did his bidding. The assembly forbade anyone to attack Indians without permission from the governor and authorized the construction of nine small forts scattered along the frontier. This impractical and expensive plan was extremely unpopular and was only partially implemented. As expected, the six or seven forts which were erected failed to protect the settlements. Discontent flamed into anger as Indian attacks continued without letup through the spring.

In late March or early April, the inhabitants of Henrico and Charles City counties along the James River in southwestern Virginia were alarmed by baseless rumors of an impending Indian attack. The colonists petitioned Berkeley for permission to carry out a preemptive strike of their own. When Berkeley refused, several hundred colonists decided to march against the Indians on their own.

They chose a young Henrico County planter named Nathaniel Bacon, a member of the provincial Council, as their leader and set out to defend themselves. Bacon's little army failed to find any threatening Indians hovering about the frontier and wandered aimlessly off to the southwest. After several days the insurgents encountered the Occaneechees, a friendly tribe that lived along the Roanoke River. Following a brief battle in which perhaps 50 Occaneechees and a dozen colonists were killed, Bacon led his men back to Henrico County bragging of his accomplishments. Bacon's treachery in attacking a friendly Indian nation was largely ignored. The fact he had taken the initiative and killed Indians—any Indians—made him a hero to many frightened and exasperated Virginians.

Berkeley, meanwhile, became alarmed by the ugly mood of the colonists and called another meeting of the assembly to come up with a more effective plan for securing the colony's borders. The residents of Henrico County impudently elected Bacon as their representative, despite the fact the governor had declared him to be a rebel. When Bacon arrived at Jamestown, he was arrested, but after meeting with Berkeley and admitting the error of his ways, he was pardoned and released. The crisis seemed to have passed. Bacon, however, soon slipped away to Henrico County. A few days later he returned to Jamestown at the head of 500 armed men. He demanded authority to lead an army of militiamen against the Indians. "God damme my Blood," he shouted, "I came for a commission, and a commission I will have before I goe." Berkeley and the members of the assembly were cowed by this show of force and named Bacon "generall and commander in chiefe" of the militia. Bacon quickly left Jamestown and began preparations for what he promised would be a major campaign against the Indians.

Up to this point the insurgency had been essentially a test of will between Berkeley and Bacon over the proper role of the colony's paramilitary forces. Now it degenerated into a test of strength between the two men and their followers for control of Virginia. Berkeley once again proclaimed Bacon to be a rebel and attempted to raise an army of his own, but could find only a small number of colonists who would support him against Bacon. Bitterly disappointed, Berkeley abandoned the mainland (and his responsibilities as governor in the midst of an Indian war) and sailed across Chesapeake Bay to the tiny sliver of Virginia known as the

Eastern Shore. Bacon was furious at what he considered to be Berkeley's treachery. At Middle Plantation (now Williamsburg), he assembled a larger number of colonists and convinced them to support him against the governor. Many Virginians were shocked at Berkeley's behavior, particularly his attempt to undercut Bacon while the latter was preparing to march against the Indians. They acceded to Bacon's demand that they sign an oath to obey him and oppose the governor until King Charles II could be informed of the situation.

Bacon had gained effective control of Virginia but now it was his turn to act in an inexplicable fashion. Instead of heading toward the frontier where the real problem lay, Bacon attacked the Pamunkey Indians, a once-powerful tribe that had been decisively defeated in 1646 and had remained friendly to the English ever since. Bacon's army of about 1,000 men plunged into Dragon Swamp along the upper Piankatank River and pursued the fleeing Pamunkeys for about three weeks. By the end of that time they had managed to kill or capture only ten Pamunkeys, seven of them women and children. Bacon dismissed most of the militiamen and pressed on with about 150 stalwart followers. Shortly afterward, they stumbled across a Pamunkey camp and killed or captured 53 Indians, again mostly women and children. This wretched affair was Bacon's second and final "victory" over the Indians of Virginia. During his two brief, ill-managed campaigns he had failed to engage a single hostile native or relieve pressure on the beleaguered frontier.

Bacon emerged from Dragon Swamp to learn that Berkeley had returned to Jamestown and again was attempting to raise a force to suppress him. Bacon marched at once toward Jamestown and besieged the little town. On 16 September, a small party of Berkeley loyalists sallied out from Jamestown and made a half-hearted attack on Bacon's fortified position. The loyalists were easily repulsed and suffered 12 casualties. After this debacle, Berkeley and his demoralized supporters sailed back to the Eastern Shore. Bacon now badly overplayed his hand. On 18 October, he ordered Jamestown burned to the ground.

The destruction of Jamestown—the oldest English settlement in America—was a great shock to the mass of Virginians, who now began to question the wisdom of blindly following the increasingly erratic and unpredictable Bacon. An even greater shock was felt when Bacon began recruiting indentured servants and slaves into the ranks of his little army, thereby eroding the foundation of Virginia society. Bacon died, possibly of dysentery, on 26 October, and was succeeded by an obscure newcomer to Virginia named Joseph Ingram. After Bacon's death, popular support continued to ebb and the directionless rebels forgot about the Indians and turned their attention to looting and vandalism. Instead of making peace with Berkeley, Ingram kept up the struggle and made the critical error of dispersing the rebels along the banks of the broad rivers that laced tidewater Virginia.

Berkeley and his loyalists were small in number but they controlled the entrance to Chesapeake Bay. They commandeered several heavily armed merchant vessels as they arrived from England, and began to carry out raids and amphibious operations against the mainland. Near the end of 1676, a flotilla commanded by Robert Morris, captain of the merchantman *Young Prince,* sailed up and down the James River, capturing or dispersing one rebel garrison after another and linking up with colonists who had decided their loyalty belonged to Berkeley after all. The governor himself led a second flotilla up the York River. Resistance grew more intense as Berkeley approached the main rebel stronghold at West Point, and the governor decided to try another tack. He appointed Thomas Grantham, captain of the merchantman *Concord,* to negotiate a surrender of the remaining rebel bands. During the first weeks of January 1677, Grantham successfully convinced about 700 freemen, servants, and slaves to give themselves up, and the rebellion sputtered to a close.

Little is known about the conflict along the frontier after the insurrection got under way, except that the Susquehannocks seem to have departed sometime in mid-1676. A general peace treaty between Virginia and various Indian nations was concluded at Middle Plantation in the spring of 1677. Charles II responded to news of the uproar in Virginia by recalling Berkeley and dispatching Sir Herbert Jeffreys and more 1,000 soldiers, the first regulars to be stationed, however briefly, in the Old Dominion. The insurrection was over by the time the soldiers arrived, and most returned to England; two companies remained in Virginia, but eventually were disbanded. Bacon's Rebellion, like the conflict with the Susquehannocks that ignited it, was a spontaneous local affair caused by an unfortunate combination of circumstances, events, and actions. It lacked ideological foundations and was in no way a precursor of the American Revolution.

William L. Shea

References

William L. Shea, *The Virginia Militia in the Seventeenth Century* (1983); Wilcomb E. Washburn, *The Governor and the Rebel: A History of Bacon's Rebellion in Virginia* (1957); Thomas J. Wertenbaker, *Torchbearer of the Revolution: The Story of Bacon's Rebellion and Its Leader* (1940).

See also BACON, NATHANIEL; BERKELEY, WILLIAM; PAMUNKEY; SUSQUEHANNOCK; VIRGINIA

Balize Post (Louisiana)

Balize was the name for a fort and a post at the northeast mouth of the Mississippi River, from the French word for buoy or channel marker. Built between 1721 and 1723, it consisted of eight barracks, a warehouse, forge, bakery, kitchen, and church. A 96-foot levee protected the post from floods and tides, and a 14-gun battery commanded the head of the island. A road and channel markers complemented the post, from which pilots and lighters were available to assist vessels in traveling upriver. Erected in response to the establishment of New Orleans in 1718, the post served the commercial as well as defense needs of the colony, and was an important factor in the decision to move the capital from Mobile to New Orleans in 1722. Chronic health problems and flooding plagued the garrison. Spanish governor Francisco de Carondelet built a second post, named St. Carlos and sometimes referred to as New Balize, on the southeastern mouth; later, a blockhouse with two cannons was added. The Balize served more to facilitate communication than to provide any credible defense for the colony. Pilots continued to work from the Balize until after the Louisiana Purchase.

Michael James Foret

References

Carl A. Brasseaux, "The French Presence Along the Mississippi River Below New Orleans, 1699–1731," *Southern Studies,* 22 (1983):417–426; H. Mortimer Favrot, "Colonial Forts of Louisiana," *Louisiana Historical Quarterly,* 26 (1943):722–754; Thomas

Hutchins, *An Historical Narrative and Topographical Description of Louisiana and West Florida,* ed. by Joseph G. Tregle, Jr. (1784), rpt. 1968; James Alexander Robertson, ed., *Louisiana Under the Rule of Spain, France, and the United States, 1785–1807,* 2 vols. (1910–1911).

Fort Barnwell (North Carolina)

Fort Barnwell was built by John Barnwell in April 1712 to serve as his headquarters in the Tuscarora War (1711–1713). It was used for the same purpose later in the war by James Moore. The fort was built on the site of the abandoned Indian village of Core Town and was located on the Neuse River, 20 miles northwest of New Bern, and seven miles from (Tuscarora chief) Hancock's Fort. The triangular Fort Barnwell was about 180 feet on a side.

Jim Sumner

See also BARNWELL, JOHN; TUSCARORA WAR

Barnwell, John (c. 1671–1724)

John Barnwell emigrated to South Carolina from his native Ireland in 1701. During the next decade, he served the colony as deputy secretary, Council clerk, and comptroller, and participated in Queen Anne's War against the Spanish and French. When South Carolina in October 1711 received from North Carolina an appeal for aid against the Tuscarora Indians, the assembly voted £4,000 for the purpose. John Barnwell was directed on 3 November to raise a force of friendly Indians and, with 30 white officers, to march to North Carolina's assistance.

Barnwell went into the South Carolina backcountry and recruited a force of Yamasee, Congaree, Waxhaw, Saraw, and other tribes amounting to about 500 men. He then moved northwest into North Carolina, reaching and crossing the Neuse River into Tuscarora territory on 28 January 1712.

Barnwell had been informed before leaving Charles Town that the war in North Carolina was being waged by "the whole Nation of the Tuscarora (though some of them may not yet be actors)." In fact, however, only the six lower towns of the Tuscarora, mostly on Catechna Creek, a northern arm of the Neuse, were involved. The seven upper towns remained neutral.

The first town attacked by Barnwell was Torhunta, a neutral village in what is now Wayne County. Barnwell won a quick victory here, though the defenders of an Indian fort he attacked appear to have been only women and old men. Information obtained there by Barnwell was sufficient for him to have ascertained the Tuscarora division, but he appears to have ignored it.

Pressing on northeastward toward Bath Town at the mouth of Pamlico River, he fought a series of engagements with bands of Tuscarora, all of them apparently allied with the neutrals. He reached Bath Town on 9 February, having conducted every step of his 12-day march through neutral Tuscarora territory. Fortunately, however, Chief Tom Blunt's upper towns maintained their neutrality and the war did not spread.

Barnwell, reinforced by 200 North Carolinians, now marched from Bath Town southeastward to the seat of Chief Hancock's militants, Fort Hancock on Catechna Creek. Arriving there on 5 March, he laid siege to the fort, but at length arranged a pact with Hancock involving the release of white and black hostages and other terms, including the removal of his force from Tuscarora territory. The treaty infuriated North Carolina colonial leaders, who felt he had surrendered a chance to destroy the Tuscarora fighting strength.

Preparing, however, to leave for Charles Town, Barnwell concluded that he and his men were entitled to some Indian prisoners to sell in South Carolina as slaves. Accordingly, he invited the formerly militant tribes to a rendezvous, ostensibly to present them gifts for the safe release of hostages. When the Indians arrived, Barnwell's men set upon them, killing 40 to 50 men and seizing some 200 women and children. With these he left promptly for South Carolina, the war breaking out anew as he did so. His march had resulted in the destruction of only a handful of militants at the price of goading the upper towns to intervene and renewing the war with greater ferocity. It required a second South Carolina expedition under Colonel James Moore to break the fighting strength of the Tuscarora.

Barnwell, however, returned home in triumph, soon dubbed "Tuscarora Jack" for his victories at Torhunta and other neutral towns. He fought against the Yamasee in 1715, was sent to London in 1720 as colonial agent, and returned in 1721. In that year he built a strong-hold on the Altamaha River called Fort King George. Considered an expert on military affairs, he commanded troops on South Carolina's southern frontier and was a member of a committee of correspondence to confer with agents on colonial matters. His wife was Anne Berners, reputedly the sister of an English merchant at Charles Town.

T.C. Parramore

References
Edmund K. Alden, "John Barnwell," in Allen Johnson, Dumas Malone, et al., eds., *Dictionary of American Biography,* 22 vols. (1928–1958), I:639–640; John Barnwell, "Journal of John Barnwell," *Virginia Magazine of History and Biography,* V (1898), Part 1:391–402, VI (1898), Part 2:42–55; T.C. Parramore, "With Tuscarora Jack on the Back Path to Bath," *North Carolina Historical Review,* LXIV (1987):115–138.

See also FORT BARNWELL (NORTH CAROLINA); BARNWELL TOWNSHIP SYSTEM; FORT KING GEORGE (GEORGIA); TUSCARORA WAR; YAMASEE WAR

Barnwell Township System

The Barnwell Township system was a plan suggested by John Barnwell for the defense of South Carolina's southern and western frontiers. South Carolina had relied on the Yamasee and other indigenous peoples to protect their borders from the encroachments of hostile Europeans and aboriginal enemies. The Yamasee War effectively removed the southern buffer in 1715 and reduced western defenses as well. Barnwell proposed establishing a ring of forts with new settlements—European instead of Indian—to protect the valuable low country plantation region. The idea was probably influenced by New Englanders already familiar with this method of frontier defense. Governor Robert Johnson pursued the plan in 1730 with the added objective of securing the colony from internal dangers: a growing slave population led British officials to step up efforts for maintaining a police power and to prevent African Americans from establishing potentially dangerous alliances with the colony's indigenous neighbors; a ring of forts would help hem in the slaves.

The Board of Trade approved Johnson's proposals for establishing 11 townships, including two on the Altamaha River in modern-day Georgia, perilously close to Spanish Florida.

A settlement fund was established to bring impoverished Protestants to the colony and to settle them in the townships, but the fund was much depleted to pay off the colony's debts. Initially, the only successful township established was Purrysburg, settled by Swiss on the Savannah River in 1732, with other attempts made at Amelia, Orangeburg, Saxe-Gotha, the Congarees, Williamsburg, and elsewhere. The failure, however, to provide adequate protection to the colony's southern border played a significant role in the crown's decision to permit the Trustees of Georgia to establish the Georgia colony, another defensive buffer to be manned by impoverished Protestants.

Alan Gallay

References
   Robert L. Merriwether, *The Expansion of South Carolina 1729–1765* (1940).

See also BARNWELL, JOHN

Fort Barrington (Georgia)

Fort Barrington was built on a low bluff on the Altamaha River's left bank about 12 miles northwest of Darien, Georgia, and just above the head of Buffalo Swamp. It guarded the river crossing of one of the major colonial land routes between British Georgia and South Carolina and Spanish Florida. Even before the colonial powers began to use the route in their conflicts it was an important north-south Indian trail. Although the site of Fort Barrington may have been occupied on earlier occasions, the first record of a permanent fortification dates from 1751. The first fort was built in response to a petition by the citizens of Darien by Lieutenant Robert Baillie. It was named in honor of Lieutenant Colonel Josiah Barrington, a military colleague of James Oglethorpe, the founder of Georgia. The original Fort Barrington could not have been very impressive since Lieutenant Baillie only received £18 for its construction. By 1762, the fort had been rebuilt and was described as a "square fort about 75 ft. each way with a caponiere in it and Barracks." From this description it seems doubtful that William Gerard De Brahm's well-known plan and drawing of Fort Barrington had ever been executed as he intended. The garrison played an impor-

tant role in maintaining reasonably peaceful relations with the Creek Indians through the 1760s. When he visited in the autumn of 1765, Philadelphia naturalist John Bartram described Fort Barrington as built of wood, "about 20 foot square with 4 guns mounted in ye chamber, one on each side." In 1773, with the Georgia rangers disbanded, the fort was reported as "now going fast to decay." During the Revolution, Fort Barrington was rebuilt and renamed Fort Howe. For a period it bore the distinction of being military headquarters for the patriots' southern department of operations.

Louis De Vorsey, Jr.

Bateau

During the Seven Years' War, the bateau proved to be an extremely useful vehicle for transporting supplies over inland waters in the various campaigns launched out of the Albany-Schenectady area by the Anglo-American forces. One of the somewhat ugly flat-bottomed boats could be built in only two days by a six-man construction crew. Approximately 25 feet long, three feet in breadth, and two feet deep, the bateau was tapered at each end. It could carry a load of about 1,400 to 1,500 pounds and was usually manned by two men with poles or oars. Freight was the usual cargo, since whaleboats were preferred for the transportation of troops. On the open waters of the Great Lakes, whaleboats and small sailing vessels were usually employed. The bateauxmen's undisciplined behavior made them anathema to many British officers, but with proper leadership, they and their vessels were crucial in delivering provisions to military outposts such as Oswego on Lake Ontario in 1755 and 1756.

William G. Godfrey

Beaufort Fort (South Carolina; also known as Port Royal Fort)

In April 1715, the Yamasee Indians began an offensive that drove settlers from the southwestern part of South Carolina. Because it was possible for Indians to travel by canoe on what is now the Intracoastal Waterway and launch surprise attacks on settlements, a small militia force built a fort on Port Royal Island. They stayed there for the remainder of 1715. In March 1716, two scout boats were placed at the fort to prevent Indian attacks by water. By that spring the Yamasee War was largely over, but the garrison remained to guard against potential Indian or Spanish threats.

Beaufort Fort, also known as Port Royal Fort, was probably constructed south of Beaufort either at Spanish Point or slightly farther south at the site of the present U.S. Navy hospital in Beaufort County. Rebuilt in 1724, the fort most likely contained earthen walls surrounded by a palisade. Between 1721 and 1722, and also in 1727, the Independent Company of Foot, a regular British infantry unit, was stationed there. Within a few years, the fort's condition had deteriorated, and in 1734 it was replaced by Fort Prince Frederick.

Gregory D. Massey

References

Larry E. Ivers, *Colonial Forts of South Carolina 1670–1775* (1970); Robert B. Roberts, *Encyclopedia of Historic Forts: The Military, Pioneer, and Trading Posts of the United States* (1988).

See also FORT FREDERICK (SOUTH CAROLINA); PORT ROYAL (SOUTH CAROLINA)

Fort Beauharnois (Minnesota)

One of several French forts that extended the fur trade into modern-day Wisconsin, Minnesota, and South Dakota, Fort Beauharnois was specifically designed for the maintenance of trade with the Sioux. Built in 1727 on Lake Pepin and abandoned and rebuilt several times, the fort and surrounding area was home to soldiers, *coureurs de bois* (French woodsmen), and missionaries. It was permanently abandoned by the French in 1756 during the Seven Years' War.

Alan Gallay

References

Robert B. Roberts, *Encyclopedia of Historic Forts: The Military, Pioneer, and Trading Posts of the United States* (1988).

See also COUREURS DE BOIS

Fort Beauséjour (Nova Scotia, Canada)

Fort Beauséjour was built in the spring and summer of 1751 in response to the erection of the British Fort Lawrence. The two forts stood on opposite sides of the Missaquash River, Beauséjour to the west. It was a pentagonal,

palisaded structure located on a hill, with a ditch around the walls. In addition to its military function, the fort was also the focal point of abortive French attempts to convince Acadians to migrate to the immediate surrounding region and points further west, away from British control. By 1754, the garrison contained 66 French officers and soldiers of the regular army and 400 Indians; the French could also assemble as many as 1,500 Acadians from surrounding villages. Though the defenses had been strengthened, planned improvements were still incomplete. The buildings were in poor condition, and their tops projected above the walls. In 1755, the fort was the object of a combined expedition of New England and Nova Scotian troops led by John Winslow and Robert Monckton. This British effort was part of a larger plan conceived by Governor Charles Lawrence of Nova Scotia and Governor William Shirley of Massachusetts, who hoped to drive the French back to the St. Lawrence. In May 1755, Lawrence received backing for his plan from the Lords of Trade, who sent a warship with arms and provisions.

On 2 June, the invasion fleet sailed from Boston to Halifax, and thence to Fort Lawrence; the expedition consisted of 2,000 provincials and 250 British regulars. The British plans had been informed by details of the fort's defenses secreted out by a spy within Beauséjour itself, one Thomas Pichon. The offensive began on 4 June, when Monckton's column crossed the Missaquash River several miles upstream. Approximately 450 Acadians and Indians, in prepared positions, were waiting to resist the crossing, but the British succeeded in throwing over a crude bridge and quickly reaching the other side. The French set the buildings they had occupied on fire and fled to Beauséjour within an hour. The British followed quickly and camped a short distance above the fort. The two sides engaged in several skirmishes over the next few days, and the British began to dig approach trenches in anticipation of the siege. By 5 June, they were a mile from Beauséjour; by 8 June, they were entrenched on heights one-half mile away. On 14 June, their mortars opened fire, and on 17 June, the defenders surrendered. The British took 450 prisoners; about one-third were French regulars.

The reasons for the sudden collapse of the heavily-fortified French fort are not terribly mysterious. The French commander, Captain Louis Du Pont Duchambon de Vergor, had not

B

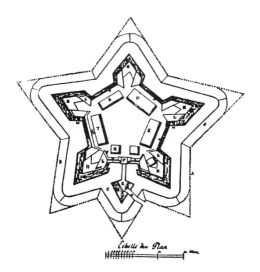

Fig. 3

Fig. 2

1. Ground plan
    A. Palisade of pickets
    B. Glacis
    C. Fosse
    D. Drawbridge
    E. Demi-lune
    F. Entrance
    G. Parapet
    H. Elevated platform,
       an open battery
    L. Flank platforms

    M. Embrasures
    N. Banquette
    Q. Guard house
    R. Small powder magazine
    S. Soldiers' barracks
    T. Officers' quarters
    U. New barracks
    X. Storehouse

2. Profile section through
    a bastion

3. Profile section through
    a curtain
    a. Palisade of pickets
    b. Glacis
    c. Fosse
    d. Sodded surface
    e. Palisade embedded
       in the earth
    f. Subterranean casemate
    g. Rampart
    h. Hand-rail

Plan of Fort Beauséjour in 1752.

expected a major British effort against Acadia that year. When the British appeared, he sent out a call for the Acadians, and they indeed came to the fort, but they asked for—and received—a written order requiring them to bear arms under pain of death; if captured, they could then claim coercion. Finally, Ver-gor failed to receive assistance from Louisbourg. Under such circumstances, the garrison quickly became demoralized and surrender became inevitable on 16 June when a British bomb demolished a casement, killing all of its occupants. The men lost their will to fight; most of the Acadians, in fact, had disappeared back into the countryside before the surrender. Ironically, the capitulation articles stipulated that Acadians who had taken up arms

under pain of death would be pardoned, but Governor Lawrence meant only they would not be put to death. Monckton, knowing this, deliberately duped them, intending to use their labor before removing them from the peninsula in the famed "great displacement" of Acadia.

Ronald P. Dufour

References

Guy Frégault, *Canada: The War of the Conquest*, trans., Margaret M. Cameron (1969); Dominick Graham, "The Planning of the Beauséjour Operation and the Approaches to War in 1755," *New England Quarterly*, XLI (1968): 551–566; George F.G. Stanley, *New France: The Last Phase, 1744–1760* (1968); John Clarence

Webster, *The Forts of Chignecto: A Study of the Eighteenth-Century Conflict between France and Great Britain in Acadia* (1930).

See also CHIGNECTO ISTHMUS; FORT GASPEREAU (NOVA SCOTIA, CANADA); FORT LAWRENCE (NOVA SCOTIA, CANADA); MONCKTON, ROBERT; WINSLOW, JOHN

Beaver Wars
See IROQUOIS WARS (1641–1701)

Fort Bedford (Pennsylvania)
Built by order of General John Forbes in the summer of 1758, Fort Bedford stood at a strategic point on the Old Trader's Path, the route which became the Forbes Road. It guarded the gap through Tussey Mountain and stood along the Warrior's Path between Wills Creek and Standing Stone. The structure was a stockade, pentagonally shaped with bastioned points, enclosing five buildings. Protected on two sides by natural elevation, it had a gallery that extended over a stream, assuring a water supply. It was never assaulted. During the Forbes expedition, 6,000 troops and auxiliaries waited and trained in the vicinity for an assault on Fort Duquesne. From 1759 to 1765, it was garrisoned by a detachment of Royal Americans under Capain Lewis Ourry, Colonel Henry Bouquet's subordinate and friend. The post served as a depot, a checkpoint to control white movement in and out of the western region, and a shelter for settlers during the Pontiac period. In 1764–1765, Ourry seized liquor cargoes intended for the Indians. The Black Boys' leader James Smith stated he took the fort by stealth in 1769 to free frontiersmen held there for terrorizing Indian traders. The fort was abandoned by 1771, although temporarily occupied by settlers as late as 1782 when Indian attacks threatened.

Louis M. Waddell

References
    James Smith, *A Treatise, on the Mode and Manner of Indian War . . .* (1812); Charles Morse Stotz, *Outposts of the War for Empire: The French and English in Western Pennsylvania; Their Armies, Their Forts, Their People, 1749–1764.* (1985).

See also FORT DUQUESNE (PENNSYLVANIA): FORBES CAMPAIGN OF 1758

Berkeley, Sir William (1606–1677)
William Berkeley was the son of Maurice Berkeley of Bruton, Somerset, England, and brother of John, Lord Berkeley of Stratton. He attended the University of Oxford and received both a B.A. and an M.A. In London he served in the Privy Council and earned a reputation as a playwright. Berkeley became a favorite of Charles I, who knighted him in 1639, and appointed him governor of Virginia in 1642. He arrived in Jamestown as the truce ending the First Virginia-Indian War (1622–1632) between the English and the Powhatan Indian empire was breaking down. Berkeley immediately set about revitalizing the provincial militia which had deteriorated during the years of peace. Before much could be done, the Indians initiated the Second Virginia-Indian War (1644–1646) with a surprise attack that killed more than 500 colonists. Berkeley organized defensive measures and laid plans for a counteroffensive. He then set sail for England, where for several months he fought with Charles I in the English civil war and unsuccessfully lobbied the king for men, arms, and ammunition to defend Virginia. Returning to Jamestown empty-handed, Berkeley found that the Virginians had wrested the initiative away from the Indians during his absence.

In 1646, he personally led a small force of horsemen on a daring raid beyond the western frontier and captured Opechancanough, the elderly Pamunkey Indian leader. Indian resistance quickly collapsed. The brief but costly war established English military supremacy in the Chesapeake Bay area. It also convinced Berkeley that the colony's defenses had to be strengthened. During his long tenure as governor (1642–1652, 1660–1677), he pressed the provincial assembly to improve the militia. Training was intensified, county militia companies were organized into regional regiments, and special paramilitary units were established: rangers, dragoons, minute companies, and long-service garrisons. Unreliable and potentially dangerous elements, such as slaves and indentured servants, were excluded from the ranks. Fortifications were erected along the coast and the frontier. Virginia's enhanced defenses were tested during the Anglo-Dutch Wars.

In 1667, and again in 1673, Dutch flotillas entered Chesapeake Bay and plundered English shipping. Berkeley mobilized the militia and harassed the Dutch raiders, but was unable to prevent them from destroying a considerable number of merchant vessels. A more serious challenge came in 1675 when Susquehannock Indians killed numerous settlers along the northwestern frontier. Berkeley, elderly and somewhat infirm, did not respond aggressively enough to suit many frontier inhabitants and the result was Bacon's Rebellion. Nathaniel Bacon and several hundred western militiamen took matters into their own hands, attacked friendly Indians without permission, and then rebelled against Berkeley's authority. Berkeley underestimated the degree of disaffection in the colony and lost control over the militia, which either sided with Bacon or remained neutral. Berkeley and a small number of loyalists were defeated in a skirmish near Jamestown on 16 September 1676, and fled across Chesapeake Bay to the Eastern Shore. After Bacon's death on 26 October, Berkeley initiated a series of effective waterborne raids along the James and York Rivers which quickly brought an end to the uprising. Having reestablished royal authority in Virginia, Berkeley sailed to England to explain the rebellion to Charles II. He died there on 9 July.

William L. Shea

References
    Wilcomb E. Washburn, *The Governor and the Rebel: A History of Bacon's Rebellion in Virginia* (1957).

See also BACON, NATHANIEL; BACON'S REBELLION; OPECHANCANOUGH; PAMUNKEY

Black and Indian Militias (Florida)

Demographic imperatives compelled Spain to enlist non-Spaniards in the defense of their extended empire. There were too few Spaniards to hold Spain's vast territories against foreign encroachment. The garrison at St. Augustine was allotted a troop complement of between 300 and 350 men, but most review lists show less than 200 men fit for battle. Unable to be sure of timely reinforcements from Cuba, Mexico, or Spain, the governors of Florida (as did many of their counterparts in the Caribbean Rim) often made up deficits with black and Indian militias. The earliest recorded black militia in Florida dates to 1683, and was a unit consisting of 63 men commanded by men of color. Their legal status is unknown. Slave militias served in the defense of St. Augustine during the Palmer raid of 1728 and a free black militia was created in 1738 at the town of Gracia Real de

Santa Teresa de Mose. This cavalry unit provided critical frontier reconnaissance for the Spanish forces during the Oglethorpe invasion and siege of 1740, as well as offensive and defensive support. It also participated in the Spanish counterattacks on Georgia in 1742. Indian militias were also important to the Spanish, who kept close count of the number of men at arms at each village. Individual Indians, such as Juan Ignacio and Geronimo, served the Spaniards as spies throughout the Southeast, traveling to Charles Town, Apalachee, and even Cuba to provide critical intelligence about the British enemy. Captains of the Indian militias were elected by the other chiefs, or *caciques*. In 1758, Captain Bernardo Lachiche commanded a unit of 28 men. All served without pay, although their arms and munitions were provided by the Spaniards.

Jane Landers

References
    Herbert S. Klein, "The Colored Militia of Cuba: 1568–1868," *Caribbean Studies*, 6 (1966):17–27; Jane Landers, "Gracia Real de Santa Teresa de Mose: A Free Black Town in Spanish Florida," *American Historical Review*, 95 (1990):9–30; Kenneth Wiggins Porter, *The Negro on the American Frontier* (1971).

See also AFRICAN AMERICANS; MENÉNDEZ, FRANCISCO

Bloody Brook Massacre (1675)

A contemporary called it "that most fatal day, the saddest that ever befel New-England." The day was 18 September 1675. The reason was the deaths of more than 60 Englishmen, victims of a massive Indian ambush. The place was a little stream some five miles south of the village of Pocumtuck, or Deerfield, an isolated post at the tip of the knife's edge of English settlements up the Connecticut Valley in Massachusetts. What brought the clash, and the deaths, was King Philip's War.

Although King Philip's War had begun in June 1675 in southeastern Massachusetts as a local uprising involving local Indians, it quickly spread. By autumn, war had struck central and western Massachusetts. To the English colonists it may have seemed like an inexplicable, unpredictable nightmare. A careful look at native actions in the west, however, reveals the Indians had put together a highly effective strategy. Essentially, between early August and the beginning of November, Philip's forces pushed the frontier back some 25 miles. Bloody Brook, while the most dramatic of the battles in the west, was only one in a series of Indian victories.

The natives first made their presence known in the west when they attacked and destroyed Brookfield, or Quaboag, some 40 miles southeast of Pocumtuck and 20 miles east of Springfield, in early August. The Connecticut Valley's link to the east was now severed. Next, the Indians moved north and west, toward the infant settlement of Northfield, or Squakeag, some 15 miles up the Connecticut River from Pocumtuck. A series of raids there during early September resulted in similar devastation.

Next was Pocumtuck, now the most exposed and isolated town in the region. To the north, east, and west lay no English neighbors at all. Only to the south was there support, and the closest settlement, the hamlet of Swampfield (later Sunderland), had already disappeared amid the fighting. It was a good ten miles south to the next towns of Hadley and Hatfield. Continuing their strategy of reducing the frontier line town by town, the Indians moved on Pocumtuck. On 1 September, 60 Indians struck, killing one garrison soldier who was out "looking after his horse," and then attacking the town. Although the settlers all fled safely into the town's two fortified houses, the natives burned 17 of the outlying houses and barns.

In the face of this attack and the destruction of Northfield, Pocumtuck sent its women and children to safety in the valley towns below. The town's men and the assigned garrison troops, some 50 in all, tried to hold on. But their grasp slipped. The Indians struck again on 12 September, this time killing one more, burning one of the two garrison homes, killing a number of horses, and carting away "horse-loads of beef and pork."

Although Pocumtuck was in desperate straits, the English tried to hold on. For one thing, they doubtless did not want to lose another settlement and see the line of settlement pushed back further. For another, Pocumtuck held what was a vital, perhaps even critical, resource. In stacks in the Pocumtuck meadows stood more than 3,000 bushels of corn. With the valley under siege—indeed, with the General Court within a month of declaring the "great danger of a famine"—Pocumtuck's corn was vital to English survival in the valley.

With this in mind, the military decided to bring Pocumtuck's corn south to greater safety. Captain Thomas Lathrop took his company up to the town and, aided by the remaining townsmen, loaded the grain onto carts. On Saturday morning, 18 September, while Captain Samuel Moseley and his Pocumtuck garrison sent out scouts, Lathrop and about 50 soldiers, plus 15 "teamsters"—Pocumtuck men recruited to help drive the caravan—headed south. As Deerfield's nineteenth-century chronicler George Sheldon tells the story, "Southward along the narrow Pocumtuck path, through the primeval woods, moved Lathrop and his men—brave, fearless, foolish. Confident in their numbers, scorning danger, not even a van-guard or a flanker was thrown out."

That error soon proved fatal. About five miles south of town, the convoy slowed to cross a small, muddy brook. At that moment the muddy brook became Bloody Brook. Hundreds of Indians—Wampanoags, Nipmucks, Pocumtucks—charged Lathrop's bewildered and outnumbered forces. By the time Mosely's militia reached the site, they could do little more than drive off the scalpers. More than 60 men lay dead, including 14 of the 15 Pocumtuck men. It was a disaster, as bad a defeat as the English suffered in the entire war. In the face of such a defeat, Pocumtuck could not survive. Within a few days the region's authorities had ordered Pocumtuck abandoned, and the Indians soon burned the remaining buildings.

The English disaster at Bloody Brook has considerable significance. First, it caused the English line of settlement to be driven back still further; it shows the success of Indian strategy in the west during 1675. In fact, it was a high point of the war for Philip's forces. After Bloody Brook, the English in the Connecticut Valley fought just to survive through the rest of the year. Not until spring of 1676 did the war in the valley begin to turn.

The final significance of Bloody Brook was spiritual. The defeat was so terrible for the English that the "black and fatal day," as Increase Mather put it, became symbolic. Why had "the Lord himself seemeth to be against us, to cast us off, to put us to shame?" The answer lay in "the sinful *Degenerate Estate* of the *present Generation in New-England*." Turning this war around would take great introspection as well as better fighting.

Richard I. Melvoin

References
    Francis Jennings, *The Invasion of America: Indians, Colonialism, and the Cant of Conquest* (1975); Douglas E. Leach, *Flintlock and Tomahawk: New England in King Philip's War* (1958); Richard I. Melvoin, *New England Outpost: War and Society in Colonial Deerfield* (1989).

See also DEERFIELD; KING PHILIP'S WAR; NIPMUCK; WAMPANOAG

Bloody Marsh, Battle of (1742)

The colony of Georgia was founded primarily as a military buffer to protect English territorial claims in the Southeast. Although Spain had relatively few soldiers in Florida, the Spanish had gained a significant number of Indian allies after the Yamasee War (1715–1717), and Indian warriors made sporadic forays along the southern frontier even after James Oglethorpe settled Georgia in 1733.

Because of the proximity of the Spanish, English colonists lived in constant fear of an invasion. One year after the War of Jenkins' Ear began, Oglethorpe led an ill-fated invasion of Florida to destroy the presidio at St. Augustine. This effort failed because neither the Indian warriors Oglethorpe expected nor the promised forces from Carolina arrived to reinforce his troops.

In the summer of 1742, Oglethorpe had his revenge when a decisive confrontation between English and Spanish forces occurred at Bloody Marsh on the southeastern coast of St. Simons Island. Florida's Governor Manuel de Montiano had launched a combined sea and land attack against the English from St. Augustine on 20 June. The Spanish army numbered almost 2,000 men, most of them from Cuba, and a fleet of more than 50 vessels.

Montiano's plans were hampered from the start by storms which separated the smaller Spanish vessels from the main fleet. After a series of skirmishes on Cumberland Island, Montiano's forces headed to St. Simons. Between the 5th and 7th of July, 652 colonists, rangers, indentured servants, and Indian warriors routed the Spanish. The Battle of Bloody Marsh on 7 July was the turning point in this confrontation. Montaino began his retreat to Florida on 13 July, putting colonial fears of imminent invasion temporarily to rest.

Doris B. Fisher

References
    Allen D. Candler, ed., *Colonial Records of Georgia,* 26 vols. (1904–1916); Colonial Office Papers, Series 5, Public Record Office of Great Britain; David H. Corkran, *The Carolina Indian Frontier* (1970); Larry E. Ivers, *British Drums on the Southern Frontier: The Military Colonization of Georgia, 1733–1749* (1974); "A Ranger's Report," Stowe Manuscripts, British Museum.

See also FORT FREDERICA (GEORGIA); GEORGIA; MONTIANO, MANUEL DE; OGLETHORPE, JAMES EDWARD; FORT ST. SIMONS (GEORGIA)

Board of Trade (The Lords Commissioners of Trade and Plantations)

Created by royal order 15 May 1696, the Board of Trade consisted of eight active, paid members chiefly representing merchant interests, and seven high officials. Not having executive powers, the Board of Trade nevertheless influenced policy decisions and was the principal agency in investigating colonial affairs, recommending allowance or disallowance of colonial laws, and maintaining communication with the governors, including the drawing up of their instructions. The board adhered to mercantilist views, and also sought opportunities for greater royalization of the colonies. Its effectiveness fluctuated, achieving a potent role 1696–1715, but afterward falling into lethargy, with its functions largely usurped by the secretary of state for the southern department, the Treasury, and the Admiralty. The board's vitality returned during the presidency of George Dunk, earl of Halifax, 1748–1761. A Privy Council order of 11 March 1752 gave the board the authority to nominate all officials in the colonies, except those responsible to the Treasury and the Admiralty, and the board recovered its powers relating to the governors. The board's determination to establish a more stringent imperialist system was put in abeyance because of the Seven Years' War. Though its plans for tightening the mercantilist relationship between the colonies and Great Britain were adopted after the war, most of the board's authority, including that of patronage, reverted to the secretary of state for the southern department after 1761.

Harry M. Ward

References

Charles M. Andrews, *The Colonial Period of American History,* Vol. 4, *England's Commercial and Colonial Policy* (1938); Oliver M. Dickerson, *American Colonial Government, 1696–1765: A Study of the British Board of Trade in Its Relation to the American Colonies, Political, Industrial, Administrative* (1912), rpt. 1962; Leonard W. Labaree, *Royal Government in America: A Study of the British Colonial System Before 1783* (1930), rpt. 1958.

Bougainville, Louis-Antoine de, Comte de (1729–1811)

Born in Paris on 12 November 1729, Bougainville was the son of Pierre Yves de Bougainville, a king's councilor and notary, and Marie-Françoise d'Arboulin. His family, which originated in Picardy, claimed a noble lineage which went back to the fourteenth century, but his father only "revived" the family's standing when he received a patent of nobility in 1741. Bougainville studied at the University of Paris and distinguished himself in ancient languages, mathematics, and the sciences. Reluctantly following his family's wishes, he entered the Parlement of Paris as a lawyer, but continued to study mathematics under Alexis Clairaut and Jean Le Rond d'Alembert and published a *Traité de calcul intégral* in two volumes in 1754 and 1756. Meanwhile, Bougainville pursued another interest by entering the elite Mousquetaires Noirs in 1750, obtaining an appointment as adjutant in the Régiment de Picardie three years later. He spent from October 1754 to February 1755 in London as secretary to the ambassador, Marshal Gaston-Charles-Pierre de Lévis-Mirepoix, duc de Lévis-Mirepoix (1699–1757), and was well received by the intellectual community, with the result he was elected to the Royal Society of London in early 1756. Resuming his place as aide-de-camp to Lieutenant General François de Chevert (1695–1769), Bougainville was promoted to lieutenant in 1755, and captain a year later.

On 3 April 1756, Bougainville sailed for Canada as the senior aide-de-camp of Major General Louis-Joseph de Montcalm, marquis de Montcalm (1712–1759). He took part in the attack on Oswego, New York, in July and August 1756, and impressed Montcalm with his bravery and excellent staff work. In September he led a reconnaissance of the Anglo-American positions in the Lake Champlain area, and in August 1757 took part in the operations which led to the surrender of Fort William Henry on Lake George, New York. Bougainville was wounded during the Battle of Carillon (Ticonderoga) on 8 July 1758, when the British and American troops under Major General James Abercromby (1706–1781) were repulsed with heavy losses. In September of that year, Montcalm and Canadian-born Governor General Pierre de Rigaud de Vaudreuil de Cavagnial, marquis de Vaudreuil (1698–1778), agreed to send Bougainville to France to explain the colony's grave situation and obtain reinforcements. Because the commander and governor had quarreled over tactics and strategy, however, and Bougainville supported Montcalm, Vaudreuil also sent one of his Canadian colonial regular officers, Major Michel-Jean-Hugues Péan (1723–1782). Bougainville reached France in January 1759 and submitted a number of memoirs to the minister of marine. He argued the colony would be overwhelmed by enemy armies attacking Canada from three sides unless reinforcements or a diversion were provided, and proposed sending some troops to the Carolinas to raise a rebellion among the German settlers. Mme. de Pompadour threw her support behind this plan, but since the king's ministers considered the campaign in Germany a priority and feared that reinforcements sent to North America would be captured at sea, Montcalm was ordered to hold out until a peace treaty was signed. Only 300 recruits and a few supply ships were dispatched.

Bougainville, now a colonel and a knight of the Order of Saint-Louis, arrived back at Quebec on 10 May 1759. Quebec was soon besieged by Major General James Wolfe (1727–1759), and Bougainville was placed in charge of the French camp at Beauport, where Montcalm had his headquarters. In July, Bougainville was given command of the grenadier companies and selected Canadian militia to guard the riverbank upstream from Quebec to ensure communications with Montreal remained open. Following British vessels up and down the river, his force repelled four minor landings during August. On 13 September 1759, however, Wolfe's army seized a position just west of the city between Bougainville's 1,200 men strung out along the river and Montcalm's main army at Beauport.

Montcalm failed to get any messages to Bougainville, who in any case was unable to concentrate his troops, some of whom were nearly a day's march away, before Montcalm engaged the British at 10:00 in the morning. The French general was later criticized by his own officers for attacking before Bougainville's elite troops could be brought into action.

During the following winter, Bougainville led a force which harassed the British troops around Quebec. In March 1760, Vaudreuil placed him in charge of the fort on Isle-aux-Noix in the Richelieu River, a position which the British on Lake Champlain had to capture in order to reach Montreal. The garrison repelled an attack by Brigadier General William Haviland (1718–1784) on 22 August, but on the night of 27 August 1760, Bougainville evacuated the fort and withdrew to Montreal, which by now was nearly surrounded. Bougainville, whose knowledge of English had made him very useful for parleys and the interrogation of prisoners, assisted in the negotiations which led to the capitulation of Canada on 8 September 1760.

Bougainville was not an outstanding military commander, but he was an enthusiastic and competent staff officer, performing best when under the direct command of a superior. Like most French regular officers, he recognized the importance of irregular warfare in achieving French military objectives, but was skeptical that traditional raiding parties could deal with the increasingly well-trained light infantry regiments and more conventional troops attacking Canada. Nevertheless, he showed more interest in irregular tactics than his superior, the marquis de Montcalm.

After his return to France, Bougainville accompanied the minister of war, Major General Étienne-François de Choiseul, comte de Stainville (1719–1785), to Germany as an aide-de-camp, and distinguished himself during the brief 1761 campaign. In 1763, Bougainville was given the rank of captain in the French navy so he could lead an expedition to claim and colonize the Îles Malouines (Falkland Islands). He landed in the Malouines on 3 February 1764, accomplishing his mission, but the Spanish were so outraged by this action that the French soon agreed to cede the islands back to Spain. From 1766 to 1769, Bougainville led a successful voyage of discovery around the world, and his relatively balanced description and analysis of Tahitian culture attracted special attention in literary circles, providing fuel for the debate about the "noble savage."

Bougainville continued his naval career, and in 1779 joined Vice Admiral Charles-Henri-Jean-Baptiste d'Estaing. Comte d'Estaing's (1729–1794) squadron, which crossed to Newport, Rhode Island, attacked Granada in the West Indies, and then unsuccessfully besieged Savannah. Bougainville was promoted to rear admiral on 8 December 1779, and married a Breton noblewoman, Marie-Joséphine de Longchamps Montendre, in Brest on 27 January 1781; they had four children. In 1781 and 1782, he served with Lieutenant General François-Joseph-Paul de Grasse, comte de Grasse (1722–1788), and took part in the Battle of Chesapeake Bay, the capture of St. Christopher (Saint Kitts), and the disastrous Battle of the Saintes. Although he had done no worse than any other French naval officer present at the Saintes, Bougainville was reprimanded at a court-martial held in 1784. As a former army officer in the navy, Bougainville was considered an intruder by many of his colleagues, and they did not hesitate to single him out as a scapegoat. This episode did not affect Bougainville's standing in the eyes of the minister of marine, however, and he was actively employed on many projects of naval and scientific interest. He was named a member of the Académie des Sciences in February 1789. Bougainville was appointed to command the Brest squadron in October of the following year. Despite his reputation for taking care of his crewmen, he had mixed success in imposing discipline on the mutinous revolutionary sailors and soon resigned his command. On 22 February 1792, shortly after his promotion to vice admiral, he resigned from the navy. He lived in retirement at his home in Coutances, Normandy, teaching at a local school, and was briefly imprisoned during the Terror. Under the Directory, Bougainville belonged to various scientific commissions and the Institut de France, and Napoleon made him a senator and a count. He died in Paris on 20 August 1811 and was buried in the Panthéon.

During his diverse career, Bougainville distinguished himself as an army and navy officer, navigator, mathematician, and ethnographer. Admired for his many talents, outstanding intellectual abilities, social graces, and a cheerful, generous disposition, his contemporaries recognized him as one of the leading men of their time.

Martin L. Nicolai

References

Louis-Antoine de Bougainville, *Voyage autour du monde, par la frégate du roi la "Boudeuse", et la flûte "l'Étoile" en 1766, 1767, 1768 & 1769* (1771); Edward P. Hamilton, ed., *Adventure in the Wilderness: The American Journals of Louis Antoine de Bougainville, 1756–1760* (1964); René de Kerallain, "Bougainville à l'escadre du comte d'Estaing, Guerre d'Amérique 1778–1779" and "Bougainville à l'armée du comte de Grasse, Guerre d'Amérique, 1781–1782," in *Journal de la Société des Américanistes de Paris* 19 (1927):155–206 and 20 (1928):1–70; ———, *Les français au Canada: la jeunesse de Bougainville et la guerre de Sept Ans* (1896); Étienne Taillemite, *Bougainville et ses compagnons autour du monde* (1977).

See also ISLE-AUX-NOIX; MONTREAL, ATTACK ON; QUEBEC, SIEGE OF (1759); TICONDEROGA, BATTLE OF

Fort de la Boulaye (Louisiana)

Pierre Le Moyne d'Iberville established this post, also known as Fort Mississippi, in February 1700 to secure the mouth of the Mississippi River after learning of the confrontation of his brother, Jean-Baptiste Le Moyne de Bienville, and Captain William Lewis Bond who was leading a group of British colonists under the patronage of Daniel Coxe, the proprietor of the failed colony of Carolana. The fort was located on the east bank of the river 30 miles south of the present site of New Orleans and approximately 45 miles north of the then mouth of the river. The fort consisted of a wood and mud two-story blockhouse surrounded by a log palisade and a 12-foot-wide moat, and mounted four-pound cannon. Situated too far inland to be of much utility and never very well constructed, manned, or supplied, the fort suffered from a multitude of problems ranging from inadequate fresh water supplies to periodic flooding. The fort was abandoned in 1706, but the site continued to be used for a variety of purposes and showed up on maps for decades thereafter.

Michael James Foret

References

Carl A. Brasseaux, "The French Presence Along the Mississippi River Below New Orleans, 1699–1731," *Southern Studies* 22 (1983):417–426; Marice Ries, et al., "The Mississippi Fort, Called Fort de la Boulaye, (1700–1715)," *Louisiana Historical Quarterly* 19 (1936):829–899.

Bouquet, Henry (1719–1765)

Henry Bouquet was born in Rolle, in the Swiss canton of Berne, to a family that for several generations had maintained a prosperous inn there. His military career began as a cadet in the Regiment of Constant, which was in Dutch service. Transferring to another Swiss mercenary regiment, he served in the army of the king of Sardinia during the War of the Austrian Succession and distinguished himself at the Battle of Madonna del Ormo in September and October 1744.

After the Treaty of Aix-la-Chapelle, he returned to Dutch service. In 1755, a wealthy adventurer, James Prevost, began recruiting Swiss and German officers for a four-battalion regiment he was raising to augment the British army in North America. Bouquet and other officers in Dutch service obtained commissions in this Royal American Regiment (numbered the 62nd Foot; renumbered the 60th Foot in 1757) for service "in America only," at the highest rank for which each man could bargain. The regiment began arriving in New York in the summer of 1756, and with as many American colonists as could be recruited, moved to a camp at Saratoga, New York. From the start it was deficient in strength and quality. The four battalions were assigned to separate commands, and often the battalions and companies were subdivided. Bouquet was the lieutenant colonel of the First Battalion, under Colonel John Stanwix, but he was in full command when the unit was sent to Philadelphia in October 1756. The Pennsylvania authorities denied his request for adequate quarters and a smallpox hospital. In June 1757, Bouquet took half the battalion and several companies of the 77th Highlanders Battalion to Charles Town, South Carolina. Officials there proved as heedless of the requirements of Bouquet's men as those in Philadelphia. With other Swiss officers, Bouquet became privately active in purchasing South Carolina rice-growing land.

Bouquet and his five companies of the First Battalion were brought back to Philadelphia in May 1758 to become part of Brigadier John Forbes's expedition to oust the French from the upper Ohio Valley. Forbes's ill health prevented him from directing troops in the advanced areas and many decisions fell upon Bouquet. Forbes made the critical decision to cut a road due west from Bedford to the forks of the Ohio, rather than to move south from Bedford to Fort Cumberland and then use the road Braddock cut in 1755. Although Bouquet was involved in opening a shortcut through the Laurel Ridge at Rhor's Gap in the final days of July, he was also responsible for underestimating the time needed to assemble enough forces before Fort Duquesne. The point at issue was whether the British expedition could accomplish its mission before wintery weather sapped its vitality. To try to close the time gap Bouquet condoned Major James Grant's precipitous night attack on Fort Duquesne, 13 and 14 September, which was a humiliating defeat. The subsequent French decision to abandon and destroy Fort Duquesne allowed Forbes's army to occupy the forks of the Ohio. Bouquet commanded forces in western Pennsylvania from 1759 to April 1765.

The French menace evaporated in western Pennsylvania by 1760. From 1759 to 1763, Bouquet was employed in administering garrisons and organizing new fortified posts. Sandusky Bay, Presque Isle, and Fort Burd were the outer limits of his command. Bouquet tried to uphold promises made to the Indians that settlers and hunters would not be allowed west of the Allegheny Mountains, although several way stations and supply points were authorized for operational reasons. On 30 and 31 October 1761, Bouquet issued a proclamation against white hunters and settlers west of the Alleghanies, and the governors of Maryland and Virginia stated they were in agreement with his policy.

Bouquet experienced many personal disappointments during these years. Regimental money stored in his personal quarters at Fort Pitt was stolen on 31 July 1761 and it was years before he was cleared of responsibility. His interest in South Carolina rice land was lost because the plantations were mismanaged by their Swiss agent. Choice lands to which he sought title in Pennsylvania were denied him by the whim of the Penn family proprietors. His personal integrity led him to reject a large grant of wilderness land offered as a bribe by the Ohio Company of Virginia. In January 1762, Fort Pitt experienced a flood so damaging as to render it indefensible for several weeks. The following month, the woman he intended to marry, Anne Willing of Philadelphia, married Virginian Tench Francis, throwing Bouquet into

such despair that he lost much of his motivation. Then, on an uncharacteristic evening drinking spree, he suffered accidental injuries that required weeks of recuperation. The progress of Longmeadow, his plantation near present-day Williamsport, Maryland, seemed to be his only personal triumph, and he was seeking a new career when the Native American upheaval associated with Ottawa chief Pontiac called him back, once more, to martial leadership.

In May 1763, while awaiting approval to sail on leave to England, Bouquet was stationed in Philadelphia and corresponding with Captain Simeon Ecuyer, a Swiss Royal American officer commanding Fort Pitt. Signs of hostility on the part of the Shawnees, Mingoes, and Delawares were surfacing when the momentum of the Pontiac-inspired movement struck at the end of May. Delawares massacred the plantation of the provincial colonel, William Clapham, near Fort Pitt on 28 May, and by 2 June, the fort was entirely surrounded. The commander in chief, Major General Jeffery Amherst, ordered an emergency expedition to march from New York City, consisting of Highland light infantry companies still suffering from malaria acquired on the Caribbean campaign. Amherst's general attitude throughout the crisis was to minimize the military capacity of the Native Americans. It was mid-June before Amherst and Bouquet received the grim news of Pontiac's successes in the west. In Bouquet's area only Forts Ligonier, Bedford, and Pitt held out. He was especially vexed that the Presque Isle blockhouse had been surrendered because he had personally supervised its construction. To make matters worse, the provisions at Fort Pitt had been inaccurately overstated. By late June it was clear the only way to save Fort Pitt was to march the emergency force westward with a supply train of flour and force the way into the fort. At the end of July, a four-day assault on Fort Pitt by Delawares, Shawnees, Wyandots, and Mingoes had failed, and on 1 August they moved into a position to ambush Bouquet's column. With about 400 Royal Americans and Highlanders, and a train of packhorses bearing flour, he approached Fort Pitt by way of Bushy Run, where there had been a small army way station. The ambush was sprung there on 5 August, and in the ensuing two-day struggle Bouquet vanquished the attackers, although suffering heavy losses. His column entered Fort Pitt on 10 August.

At the height of the Indian threat, Amherst had recommended infecting the Indians with smallpox by giving them blankets from the sick ward at Fort Pitt. Ecuyer did so. Although this policy has been attributed to Bouquet, documentation rests solely on an undated note by Amherst inserted in his letter of 16 July to Bouquet: "You will be well to try to innoculate the Indians by means of Blankets, as well as every other method, that can serve to extirpate this execrable race." Fairly evaluated, however, the extant evidence points to no source for the smallpox suggestion other than the Indian-hating Amherst.

On 4 April 1764, Major General Thomas Gage, who had replaced Amherst as commander in chief in North America, appointed Bouquet to command the forces "in the Southern Department." In the first week of July, Bouquet began to organize a punitive expedition against the Indian strongholds in central Ohio. At the same time, Colonel John Bradstreet left Niagara with an amphibious force meant to attack the western nations via the Great Lakes. He also had orders to create a diversion for Bouquet's land march into central Ohio by approaching the Ohio plains on the Sandusky River. In addition to Royal Americans and a section of the 42nd Regiment of Foot (Royal Highlanders, "the Black Watch"), Bouquet's expedition had a battalion of Pennsylvania provincial soldiers and a battalion of Virginia volunteers. Desertion, always a problem in Bouquet's area of command, became widespread in 1764, both among the regulars and the provincials. With Gage's approval, Bouquet finally ordered the execution of two redcoat deserters.

Bouquet marched from Fort Pitt on 1 October with about 1,500 soldiers, a packhorse train, and livestock to provide meat rations. Good defensive positions were chosen for each successive encampment as he moved west, and he planned to use the same locations for safe withdrawal if necessary. The absence of summer foliage made ambush less likely. On 12 August, Bradstreet had completed an unauthorized treaty at Presque Isle with Indians representing themselves as emissaries for the many nations of central Ohio. Gage repudiated the treaty on 2 September, but paradoxically, Bouquet would charge the Indians with violating its provisions when he negotiated with them in October and November. A letter from Bradstreet reached Bouquet on 28 October saying the diversion from Sandusky Bay was im-

possible. Instead, Bradstreet had gone on to Detroit.

On 13 October, the expedition camped near Tuscarawas, a Delaware village (site of present-day Bolivar, Ohio), and remained there until the 22nd. On the 25th, the force took a position at the forks of the Muskingum, which placed it within striking distance of a number of surrounding Indian villages, and it remained there until 14 November. Long negotiations took place at both of these sites, at which the Indians agreed to: 1) cease raiding frontier settlements, 2) surrender all white prisoners, yielding hostages from their own ranks to assure compliance, 3) accept Bouquet's view that they had started the war, and 4) send delegates to New York to make a formal treaty with Sir William Johnson, His Majesty's Indian superintendent. These terms were accepted by the Delawares, Shawnees, and Ohio Iroquois (who were also termed Mingos), although the Shawnees were late to come to terms and only grudgingly cooperative. Bouquet was back at Fort Pitt on 28 November, having brought along some of the prisoners, some of the hostages, and some of the delegates. Members of these three groups had, however, run back to Ohio.

The upper Ohio Valley region remained Bouquet's responsibility until April 1765. Eventually he was naturalized by act of Parliament. On 17 April, he received Gage's orders promoting him to brigadier and placing him in command of forces in East and West Florida. When he was rowed ashore at Pensacola on 1 September, he was ill, either from an epidemic of fever then raging among the soldiers, or from malaria contracted at Cape May where his ship had been becalmed. He died on 3 September.

Military historians have attributed to Bouquet a role, shared with Thomas Gage, in developing British light infantry tactics. This rests on a traditional belief that Bouquet had a system in mind when he commanded at Bushy Run. A book published anonymously in 1765 in Philadelphia, now attributed to Provost William Smith, *Historical Account of Bouquet's Expedition Against the Ohio Indians in 1764,* perpetuated this interpretation by surrounding Bouquet's achievements with suggestions for far-reaching reforms in Indian fighting tactics. Smith knew Bouquet, and Thomas Hutchins, Bouquet's subordinate, had some part in the publication, but many of the tactical suggestions were impractical. Bouquet never abandoned the importance of volley firing, nor did

B

he advocate complete concealment or the imitation of Indian stealth. In fact, he learned that woodlands Indians would usually yield to a shoulder-to-shoulder bayonet charge. The importance of advancing along a series of fortified bases was another concept Bouquet embraced, anchored in accepted European military theory. Because of the episode with smallpox blankets, he has been unfairly accused of plotting Indian genocide. His true attitude toward Native Americans was akin to that of Swiss philosopher Emerich Vattel, who held that food gatherers must inevitably yield to agricultural societies.

Louis M. Waddell

References

Niles Anderson, "Bushy Run: Decisive Battle in the Wilderness," *Western Pennsylvania Historical Magazine,* XLVI (1963):211–245; D.H. Kent, A.L. Leonard, S.K. Stevens, J.L. Tottenham, and L.M. Waddell, eds., *The Papers of Henry Bouquet,* 5 vols. to date (1951–); Bernhard Knollenberg, "General Amherst and Germ Warfare," *Mississippi Valley Historical Review,* XLI (1954):489–494; Howard H. Peckham, *Pontiac and the Indian Uprising* (1947); William Smith, *Historical Account of Bouquet's Expedition Against the Ohio Indians in 1764* (1765), rpt. 1907.

See also AMHERST, JEFFREY; BUSHY RUN, BATTLE OF; ECUYER, SIMEON; FORBES CAMPAIGN OF 1758; PONTIAC'S WAR

Bourlamaque, François-Charles de (c. 1719–1763)

Little precise information is known of François-Charles de Bourlamaque's early life and career. In 1739, he entered the Dauphin infantry regiment and fought in the Flanders and Rhine campaigns from 1742–1744. He took part in the battles of Fontenoy and Raucox, and in the sieges of Tournai, Oudenard, and Brussels. In 1756, when the contingent of French regulars sailed for Canada, Colonel Bourlamaque was third in command after Maréchal-de-camp Montcalm and Brigadier François-Gaston de Lévis. During the first campaign of the newly arrived French troops against Fort Oswego (Chouaguen), Bourlamaque was criticized by fellow officers for some poor decisions in conducting the siege against the weakly defended fort. The following year he evidently redeemed himself in the Battle of Fort William Henry since the correspondence of his earlier critics indicates a liking and esteem for this officer.

At the Battle of Ticonderoga in 1758, Bourlamaque commanded the left to Montcalm's center and Lévis's right. This was a stunning victory for 3,500 troops, mostly French, against some 20,000 British. It was during this engagement that Bourlamaque was gravely wounded, but eyewitness accounts enter into no further details. After the breakup of the camp at Ticonderoga in the autumn, Bourlamaque, with three battalions of regulars and 1,000 Canadians, was ordered to return the following spring to the site, hold the position if he could, but fall back to the Isle-aux-Noix if the enemy force were too strong to withstand. He withdrew to the island in July when General Jeffrey Amherst attacked him at Ticonderoga. Even when the threat to Quebec via the St. Lawrence became apparent in the summer, and the bulk of the defenders repaired to the city and its environs, Montcalm ordered Bourlamaque to remain at the Isle-aux-Noix where he stayed until March 1760 with no further assaults by the British.

In early 1759, Bourlamaque had been advanced in rank to brigadier (Louis XV compensated his officers with decorations and promotions instead of sending them more reinforcements). At the death of Montcalm during the battle of Quebec, Bourlamaque then became second in command to the Maréchal de Lévis. After the unsuccessful attempt to retake Quebec in May 1760, during which Bourlamaque had part of a calf shot away, Lévis ordered Bourlamaque's forces to Sorel to follow the movement of Brigadier James Murray's 2,500 men coming from Quebec as one of the three British prongs converging to attack Montreal. Bourlamaque then fell back to the island-city with his numbers much reduced by widespread desertions. The military and civilian authorities, seeing that further fighting was useless, surrendered to the British on 7 September 1760.

On his return to France, Bourlamaque was made commander in the coveted military Order of Saint-Louis, then sent to Malta, along with other officers from the Canadian campaign, to assist the Grand Knight of the Order of St. John with the defense of the island against the Ottoman Turks. He was made maréchal-de-camp and governor of Guadeloupe in 1762, where he died the following year.

Mary Kimbrough

References

René de Kerallain, *La Jeunesse de Bougainville at la guerre de Sept Ans* (1896); Maréchal François-Gaston de Lévis, *Collection des manuscrits;* "Lettres de M. de Bourlamaque au maréchal de Lévis," ed., H.R. Casgrain (1891); Pierre-Georges Roy, ed., *Rapport de l'Archiviste de la Province de Québec pour 1923–24* (1924):204–293.

See also ISLE-AUX-NOIX; MONTREAL, ATTACK ON; TICONDEROGA, BATTLE OF; FORT WILLIAM HENRY, SIEGE OF

Bow and Arrow

The construction, composition, and length of bows and arrows varied by tribe, location, and time, but the "self-bow," made from a single piece of wood, was most popular east of the Rocky Mountains. Arrowheads made of iron replaced those made of stone, bone, antler, etc., after the arrival of the Europeans. These projectile points were often loosely fastened to war arrows so that they continued to induce bleeding after the shaft was removed. The bow and arrow remained the weapon of choice for many Native Americans for a number of years, even after the Europeans introduced firearms. Although the earliest guns offered an initial psychological and technological advantage, they were also undependable and inaccurate. While accounts of proficiency with the bow and arrow were often exaggerated, the weapon did function effectively at close range.

Raymond E. Hauser

References

Harold E. Driver, *Indians of North America* (1961); Gerard Fowke and William H. Holmes, "Arrowheads," in *Handbook of American Indians North of Mexico*, ed. by Frederick Webb Hodge (1968):90–91; Otis T. Mason, "Arrows, Bows, Quivers," in *Handbook of American Indians North of Mexico*, ed. by Frederick Webb Hodge (1968):91–94.

See also INDIAN WARFARE

Brackett's Wood, Battle of (1689)

On 20 September 1689, Benjamin Church sailed to Casco Bay with a mixed force of Provincial soldiers and Plymouth Indians to begin a raid along the coast of Maine. Arriving around 3:00 in the afternoon, he found a small Dutch merchant ship with a redeemed woman captive on board, who related the intelligence that a large band of French-led Indians was poised to attack the settlement at Casco (now Portland, Maine). Church landed and told the inhabitants and provincial officers of the threat. He found the town in poor condition to defend itself, but promised to do all in his power to help. Waiting until nightfall to conceal his plans, Church disembarked his troops and hid them in Fort Loyal, warning them to be ready an hour before dawn.

Shortly before dawn he placed most of his men in some thick brush, and while they sent out scouts, he returned to the fort to both prepare the rest of his force (some of his Plymouth Indians still had no powder and shot, having sold their supply in Boston) and grab some breakfast. Shots rang out indicating the attack had begun. As Church ordered out a company of inhabitants to where the shots were fired, one of Captain Anthony Brackett's sons came running toward the fort. Brackett said his father had been captured and the Indians were all around his farm.

In the midst of this crisis, a messenger reported that the casks of bullets brought on shore were all musket caliber and thus too large for most of the firearms carried by his men. Rushing back to the town, he ordered all casks brought on shore. The oversized balls were turned out on the ground and the inhabitants began hammering them into slugs (reducing their diameter by flattening or elongating them). Church scooped up all the smaller rounds he could find, what slugs were available, a bag of powder, and rushed out to his companies, now hotly engaged with the enemy. Arriving at the river, he found the tide had risen, preventing his crossing, but one of his Indian captains managed to wade the river and bring the ammunition to his men.

Church heard firing to his right and discovered two of his companies, one English, the other Indian, were firing across the deepening river in support of their comrades already engaged. Realizing this blind firing had little effect, Church asked one of the inhabitants, an Irishman "whom he could hardly understand," if there was a way across the river. Church shouted to his troops across the river that he planned to turn the enemy's flank, then followed the Irishman to a bridge three-quarters of a mile upriver, his men "shouting as they marched" to make as big a show as possible. At the bridge they saw a hasty breastwork of logs and brush on the other side. Church gathered his companies together and led a wild charge across the bridge, only to discover that the enemy had fled. Leaving six Indians at the bridge to warn him of enemy attempts to cross, he ordered the English company to follow the riverbank and support the other forces, while he led the Indian company through the woods.

As they came to a burned-over area thick with new growth shrubs, one of his men shouted that the enemy was running westward around them to cross the bridge. Hearing no more shots from the river, and observing running figures in the distance, Church and his Indians retraced their steps to the bridge. The six Indians left there told him the enemy had crossed farther up the river and were heading to the town. Church ordered a pursuit, telling his Indians to "scatter, run very thin, to preserve themselves and be better able to make a discovery of the enemy." As they approached the town with no sign of the enemy, Church concluded the six bridge watchers had made up the story, and once again returned to the bridge. Suddenly, cannon shots from the town seemed to indicate they were under attack, so Church dispatched his Indians toward the town, while he rejoined the other forces across the river. From them he learned the enemy had left about the time Church had reached the burned-over area, probably because of his threat to their rear.

When word reached him that the town was not under attack, Church ordered a pursuit, but found most of his men were out of usable ammunition. In fact, most had been forced to hammer their own slugs in the heat of battle. There was nothing left to do but gather up the wounded and dead and return to the town. The total of killed and wounded varies, according to sources, from 12 to 21. Church claimed his own forces suffered one mortally wounded and "several more badly wounded, but recovered." The number of enemy casualties is unknown.

There is no doubt the timely arrival of Benjamin Church saved the community at Casco, but the respite was only temporary. The following summer the fort came under siege by a large force of French and Indians, and when it fell, most of the inhabitants were killed. The Portland campus of the University of Southern Maine now occupies the site where part of the Battle of Brackett's Wood took place.

Steven C. Eames

References

Thomas Church, *The History of the Great Indian War of 1675 and 1676 Commonly Called Philip's War, also, The Old French and Indian Wars, from 1689 to 1704* (1716).

See also CASCO BAY; CHURCH, BENJAMIN; FORT LOYAL (MAINE)

Braddock, Edward (1694–1755)

Edward Braddock was born in London in December 1694. His father, Edward Braddock (c. 1665–1725), an officer in the Coldstream Guards, saw extensive action in the War of the League of Augsburg and the War of the Spanish Succession, and rose to the rank of major general. Through his father's purchase, the younger Braddock gained an ensigncy in the Coldstreams in October 1710, and was promoted to lieutenant (1716), captain lieutenant (1734), second major, with army rank of colonel (1743), first major (1745), and lieutenant colonel (1745). Although the regiment was actively engaged in several major battles on the Continent, 1742–1748, Braddock cannot be placed at any of them. He did, however, capably handle administrative duties associated with several expeditions. Appointed colonel of the 14th Foot in February 1753, he spent most of that year and 1754 with the regiment at Gibraltar, where he served as governor. He was promoted to major general in April 1754.

In September 1754, after receiving news that a French contingent had pushed deep into the Ohio Valley, constructing Fort Duquesne on the forks of the Ohio, the British government determined to sweep the French from that region and establish British hegemony there. On Cumberland's recommendation, Braddock was chosen to lead the expedition and, in addition, designated commander in chief in North America, with sweeping powers to direct military affairs there. Why Braddock was given such an assignment, after a career that was scarcely distinguished and had not seen him serve as commander in a theater of war, much less on a battlefield, remains a matter for conjecture. Cumberland, who knew him fairly well, may have believed that organizing the war effort in America and consolidating any potential gains of territory suggested the appointment of a military man with a proven record as an administrator, and Braddock, particularly in the light of his recent career at Gibraltar, seemed to have that. In any case, the government, although concerned by French moves in the Ohio Valley, did not consider the matter to be a very high priority. The appointment that Braddock received was not a great plum.

Despite the immensity of Braddock's assignment, he was given a rather small force to work with, primarily just two regular regiments, the 44th and 48th, both of questionable quality and undermanned as well. Beyond this, he was expected to build an army through recruitment in America and through coordinating the enlargement and improvement of the provincial component. But Braddock was nothing if not diligent. Almost immediately after landing at Hampton, Virginia, 20 February 1755, after a two-month voyage from Cork that he described as "very fatiguing," he initiated contact with colonial governors, seeking their assistance. On 20 March, however, he reported to the prime minister, "What Effect His Majesty's Directions to His several Governors upon occasion of the present Expedition may have in the Colonies under their Command, I know not; I cannot say as yet they have shewn the Regard to 'em that might have been expected." Nevertheless, at a meeting with five governors and other notables on 15 April at Alexandria, he was able to win their approval for expeditions against the French strongholds at Chignecto, Crown Point, and Niagara, with the efforts to be mounted mainly by provincial forces. The governors impressed on Braddock the importance of winning Iroquois support, and he agreed to a major gift-giving initiative to this end, while also asking assistance in recruiting Indians to serve in his own expedition. Perhaps the most telling point at the conference, however, was the governors' refusal to establish a common fund to finance the war. They explained that their assemblies would be reluctant to support the plan. Moving on to Wills Creek, whence the army had marched from Alexandria, Braddock found more cause for frustration. Some promised supplies had not arrived, and much of the meat delivered was spoiled. Contractors, taking advantage of his situation, raised their prices and spoke of additional delays. The supply problem eased only in early June, when Benjamin Franklin arrived in camp with wagons—also in short supply—laden with provisions. Another of Braddock's problems lay in the area of Indian recruitment. Because of hostility among the tribes that were approached

for aid, plus the direct interference of the governor of South Carolina, James Glen, who personally stepped in to prevent a contingent of Catawbas and Cherokees from joining Braddock, only eight Indians marched with the army from Wills Creek. Braddock was likewise disappointed by the quality of his American recruits. As late as 8 June he wrote the adjutant general, "the whole of the Forces are now assembled, making about two thousand Effectives, the greatest part Virginians, very indifferent Men, this Country affording no better; it has cost infinite pains and labor to bring them to any sort of Regularity and Discipline: Their Officers very little better." Despite these problems, Braddock evinced optimism as the army marched from Wills Creek on 10 June.

The slowness of the march, coupled with his fears that delay might allow the French to reinforce Fort Duquesne—an eventuality that did in fact occur and proved decisive—caused Braddock to order a division of his army on 16 June at the Little Meadows. Leaving behind about one-third of his men and most of his wagons with Colonel Thomas Dunbar, he pushed on ahead. By early afternoon of 9 July, he was within ten miles of Fort Duquesne with plans to invest it the following day, when his army was confronted by an 800-man enemy force composed mainly of Indians that had moved out from the fort that morning intent on intercepting the British as they forded the Monongahela. The French and Indians reacted quickly and attacked Braddock's vanguard on both flanks, while the British force entirely lost its cohesion, a disintegration caused by the telescoping of units and apparently prompted by panic, as well. Braddock, who was with the main body at the onset of action, sent forward a large detachment, but it collided with the retreating vanguard, compounding the disorder. Braddock seems to have done his best to rally the troops and get them to form, but to no avail. He was in the heat of action throughout, and at least four horses were shot from under him. It was only late in the action that he himself was hit, receiving a serious chest wound. Later, at least two men who claimed to have served in his army asserted independently they had shot him since he would not order a retreat, but neither claim can be substantiated. In the wake of his wounding, Braddock, distraught at the turn of events, may have contemplated suicide. Instead, he was removed with the retreating remnant of his force. He reached Dunbar's camp on 11 July.

The following day, on his order, the British destroyed much of their store of supplies and ammunition, lest it fall into the hands of the enemy. On 13 July he resigned his command in favor of Dunbar, and that evening he died. When he was buried, men and carts passed over the grave to obscure it and protect it from desecration. Braddock's bones were unearthed in 1820, then reinterred, except for a hand, which was sent to the Peale Museum in Philadelphia. A granite monument was erected by his grave in 1913.

During his brief time in America, and even more in the wake of his defeat and death, Braddock acquired a negative reputation that has endured to the present. Most common have been two charges: that he was a martinet; that he blundered in the Ohio Expedition of 1755. The first complaint reflects primarily the fact that Americans saw, in the British army that Braddock personified, a mode of military discipline which was far more harsh than what they, with their militia background, were accustomed to. Still, it should be noted some English observers also regarded Braddock as being an excessively strict disciplinarian, and Horace Walpole, working on hearsay, described him as being "a very Iroquois in disposition." The accusations hurled at him relative to his management of the Battle of the Monongahela are several. First, it has been asserted he may have been complacent on the day of battle, and that in any case he had few scouts out, increasing the possibility his army could successfully be ambushed. Second, both contemporaries and historians have argued that he blundered by trying to fight a European-style battle in an American woodland setting, against a predominantly irregular force. On the issue of complacency, it may be said he displayed caution until almost the hour of battle, as he did, for example, when he ordered a double fording of the Monongahela in order to avoid a dangerous stretch. The quality of his intelligence was certainly weakened by his lack of Indian scouts, but the blame for this shortage would more properly sit with Glen than with Braddock. As for Braddock's tactics, it does appear he held to standard practice during the battle, and this was what his regulars were, in fact, trained for. It is probable that if he had been able to restore order, a bayonet charge, rather than irregular tactics, would have been the tactic most likely to break through and scatter the enemy.

At his death Braddock left behind a legion of critics. The officer corps in his army had been driven by factionalism long before the battle, and in the wake of the action several officers took the opportunity to attack him in letters to their superiors. The press, particularly in America, also became the sounding board for much criticism of him for the debacle of 9 July, some coming from participants in the battle, some being based on hearsay. For fully a century, Braddock's reputation was extremely negative, and the stigma has never entirely been removed.

Paul E. Kopperman

References

Paul E. Kopperman, *Braddock at the Monongahela* (1977); Lee McCardell, *Ill-Starred General: Braddock of the Coldstream Guards* (1958); Winthrop Sargent, *The History of an Expedition against Fort Du Quesne in 1755* (Pennsylvania Historical Society, *Memoirs, 5*) (1855).

See also FORT DUQUESNE (PENNSYLVANIA); MONONGAHELA RIVER; OHIO EXPEDITION OF 1755; SEVEN YEARS' WAR; WASHINGTON, GEORGE

Braddock's Defeat
See OHIO EXPEDITION OF 1755

Bradstreet, John (1714–1774)
Sometimes labeled an American, and on other occasions assumed to be English-born, the enigmatic John Bradstreet was actually an Anglo-Irish-Acadian who attempted to straddle the Anglo-American worlds of the mid-eighteenth century. Born on 21 December 1714 at Annapolis Royal, Nova Scotia, Jean-Baptiste Bradstreet, as he was baptized, was the son of an Anglo-Irish military officer stationed in Nova Scotia, Edward Bradstreet, and of Agathe de Saint-Etienne de LaTour, a member of one of the most prominent Acadian families in the region. John Bradstreet would carefully conceal his Acadian background as he relentlessly pursued profit and preferment through a military career in the British army which peaked during the Seven Years' War and eventually earned him the regular rank of major general, a rank achieved by few other colonials.

After service as a volunteer in Richard Philipps's regiment (40th Foot), in 1735, Bradsteet received an ensign's rank. The young officer was stationed at Canso, Nova Scotia, in the late

1730s and early 1740s, and he acquired an excellent firsthand knowledge of the French fortress Louisbourg as a result of his frequent illegal trading visits. When the French captured Canso and its garrison in May 1744, Bradstreet received preferred treatment and served as the message bearer between Louisbourg and Boston. Once the garrison was released, he was among those submitting plans for a Louisbourg attack to Massachusetts Governor William Shirley, leading Shirley to claim that it was because of Bradstreet's "Intelligence and advice . . . that I set the Expedition on foot." While disappointed that he was not placed in command of the 1745 expedition, Bradstreet served as lieutenant colonel of the 1st Massachusetts Regiment and contributed to Louisbourg's capture. He was rewarded with an appointment as lieutenant governor of St. John's, Newfoundland, and after a quarrel with Charles Knowles, governor of Cape Breton, about his profiteering in rum and fuel at the expense of the Louisbourg garrison, Bradstreet departed to take up the Newfoundland appointment in August 1747. In the fall of 1751, he journeyed to England and over the next few years acquired the "Easie Access" to friends and patrons that would serve him so well when he returned to the colonies. Charles Gould emerged as his most active friend and advocate along with Sir Richard Lyttleton, an intimate of William Pitt, while individuals such as Charles Townshend and Lord Baltimore were other possible champions.

When Bradstreet returned to America in 1755 with Major General Edward Braddock's expedition, he held rank as a captain in William Pepperrell Jr.'s newly raised 51st Foot. His old friend William Shirley pressed him into service in his campaign against Niagara. In the spring of 1755, under orders from Shirley, Bradstreet busied himself with improving Oswego's defenses on Lake Ontario and preparing it as a base for the proposed assault on Niagara. When this was abandoned in September 1755, Shirley made it clear Bradstreet had done his work well, and assigned him command of the first priority in the 1756 campaign, an attack on Fort Frontenac. By now, Bradstreet's abilities as a speedy constructor of bateaux and mover of men and materials had become quite apparent. Consequently, in March 1756, he was entrusted with all aspects of the movement of troops and supplies to the now beleaguered Oswego garrison. Despite enemy attacks, Bradstreet reopened the

Oswego supply lines, leading substantial relief convoys to Lake Ontario in May and early July. After battling his way back to Albany in July, Bradstreet warned of the imminent French threat to Oswego. However, through a change in command, Shirley had been replaced by Lord Loudoun, and the slow movement of reinforcements left Oswego the easy victim of a French attack in mid-August.

Warned by his friends in England about Shirley's demise, the resourceful Bradstreet moved quickly to endear himself to Loudoun—and succeeded. He secured a captaincy in the Royal Americans (60th Foot) and became virtual quartermaster and aide-de-camp at times to Loudoun. Active in organizing supplies and transports in the spring of 1757 for Loudoun's abortive Louisbourg campaign, Bradstreet also bombarded his friends in England with grand plans for winning the war in America. In September 1757, he sent Lyttleton an elaborate outline of a three-pronged assault against Louisbourg and then Quebec, on Ticonderoga and Crown Point, and out of Oswego across Lake Ontario against Montreal. "Charmed with the Spirit and Enterprizing Genius" of Bradstreet, Lyttleton passed his ideas along to Pitt and Lord Ligonier. His suggestions did bear a striking resemblance to the basic plan followed by Pitt and his generals. With some satisfaction Lyttleton reported to Charles Gould on 1 January 1758 that "I have Obtained for our Friend Bradstreet the rank of *Lt. Col. in the Kings Service* as Deputy Quartermaster General for America." Meanwhile, Loudoun employed Bradstreet in the construction of bateaux and approved the proposal he made for a strike at Fort Frontenac, which he was to lead in the early spring.

Loudoun's replacement by James Abercromby shelved the Frontenac plan once again, but Bradstreet continued to play a major role under his new commander, constructing bateaux and moving men and provisions up the Hudson River. In Abercromby's attack on Ticonderoga, Bradstreet served with distinction when the retreat to the boats threatened to turn into a disorderly rout, taking command at the landing place and preserving an orderly embarkation. A few days after this disaster, Bradstreet resurrected his Frontenac proposal and secured Abercromby's approval. Moving his troops down to Schenectady and then up the Mohawk River, by 21 August 1758, Bradstreet's approximately 3,000 largely colonial force reached Oswego on Lake Ontario. His whaleboats and bateaux moved quickly across Lake Ontario, and by the evening of 28 August, he had completed the capture, destruction, and plunder of Fort Frontenac. Bradstreet's victory severely weakened the French hold on the Great Lakes: their provisioning lifeline was cut, their Lake Ontario naval flotilla was destroyed, their Indian alliances were badly shaken, and the way was cleared for the Anglo-American capture of other French posts in the interior, such as Fort Duquesne. Immediately promoted to colonel, backdated to 20 August 1758, Bradstreet's military reputation was at its peak.

As the victorious war years dawned, Bradstreet found himself relegated to quartermaster duties rather than entrusted with the more adventurous tasks for which he yearned. Under his new commander, Jeffery Amherst, he served as deputy quartermaster general at Albany, earning Amherst's respect for the conscientious performance of his duties. These duties were financially rewarding; indeed, some suspected Bradstreet of considerable profiteering, and he acquired a measure of political and economic importance in the Albany area. Nonetheless, as the war ended, letter after letter flowed back to England bemoaning the British government's failure to adequately honor and reward his contributions. By now, with Pitt out of power and Lyttleton no longer in England, it seemed little would be done for the hero of Fort Frontenac.

In late 1763, Bradstreet did receive word of a possible lieutenant governorship in Quebec, but declined such an opportunity in favor of an active military command offered him by Amherst. An Indian uprising was underway and Bradstreet was to lead a northern force from Niagara to Detroit against the Delawares and Shawnees. It was early August 1764 before Bradstreet moved out of Niagara and by then he was disappointed at the delays and the size of his force, which consisted of 1,500 regulars and provincials, along with 400 Indians. He then embarked quite deliberately on peacemaking activities rather than launching attacks on hostile Indian nations. Possible trading activities and claims to Indian lands were very much on the ever enterprising Bradstreet's mind. His expedition reached and relieved Detroit on 27 August 1764. The North American commander, Thomas Gage, who had replaced Jeffery Amherst, openly criticized Bradstreet's failure to properly execute his orders. The original

strategy had been for Bradstreet to attack from the north, while Henry Bouquet led a southern army from Fort Pitt toward the Muskingum River (Ohio). Instead, Bradstreet had failed to intimidate the Indians and negotiated what Gage believed were worthless treaties which he immediately disavowed. He ordered Bradstreet to launch an overland attack but, on his return journey across Lake Erie, Bradstreet continued to feel his forces were too weak for such an undertaking and contented himself with remaining at Sandusky from mid-September to mid-October, thus offering only a potential threat to the Indians and indirect aid to Bouquet. Resuming his journey, Bradstreet's Lake Erie crossing disintegrated into a nightmarish rout because of storms and lack of supplies. Remnants of his command finally drifted into Niagara in early November. His military record and reputation were badly tarnished.

Bradstreet resumed acting deputy quartermaster service at Albany, but Gage cut to the bone his departmental expenditures and responsibilities and often thwarted his efforts at advancement. Bradstreet prospered financially through land speculation and other dealings but his military career stagnated. However, as a result of a general promotion of colonels appointed before the end of 1762, he was promoted to the rank of major general in late 1772. Various schemes, both military and civil, continued to be addressed to patrons and government officials in England, and the faithful Charles Gould continued to lobby on Bradstreet's behalf. Considerable time was spent advocating the establishment of a new western colony centered at Detroit, with Bradstreet as governor, and even as the Quebec Act was passed in 1774 precluding this, Bradstreet remained hopeful and Gould continued to make the case. On 25 September 1774, Bradstreet died in New York City, leaving an estate worth £15,000 sterling along with at least 15,000 acres of land he had accumulated. He was a somewhat irregular regular, but at certain times his unique abilities and insights made a valuable contribution to the Anglo-American military effort.

William G. Godfrey

References

W.G. Godfrey, "John Bradstreet," in F.G. Halpenny, ed., *Dictionary of Canadian Biography*, Vol. IV (1979):83–87; ———, *Pursuit of Profit and Preferment in Colonial North America: John Bradstreet's Quest* (1982).

See also ABERCROMBY, JAMES; AMHERST, JAMES; CAMPBELL, JOHN; FORT FRONTENAC (ONTARIO, CANADA); FORT OSWEGO (NEW YORK); PEPPERRELL, WILLIAM, JR.; SHIRLEY, WILLIAM; FORT STANWIX (NEW YORK)

Brims of Coweta (?–c. 1730)

Popularly known as the "Emperor Brims," this Creek was the *mico* (headman) of Coweta, the most significant town of the Lower Creek. Brims rose to prominence during the period of Queen Anne's War. Brims's early years are a mystery. Brims's war fame and position as spokesman for the Lower Creek lead Europeans to assume he was "emperor" of the Creek, a notion that Brims and his clan did little to dispel. More properly, he was the Great Beloved Man, a title bestowed upon individuals of outstanding merit.

While the record does not mention Brims by name, there can be little doubt that he played a significant role in the Creek-Apalachee clashes which took place just prior to, and as an offshoot of, Queen Anne's War. In 1702, a Spanish-supplied Apalachee army moved against the Lower Creek towns which had recently established trade ties with the English in South Carolina. The Apalachee, fooled by a Creek ruse, were routed. By the middle of the following year, a combined force of Lower Creek and Carolinians attacked St. Augustine. In 1704, James Moore of South Carolina directed raids against Spain's Apalachee missions. One thousand Creek reportedly assisted Moore, and the leading warriors of Coweta were among them. This undoubtedly proved a training ground for Brims, who acquired Apalachee slaves, horses, cattle, and silver goblets. His wealth and prestige enabled him to support two wives, one a highborn Apalachee woman, variously known as Qua or Goa.

Brims's first real appearance in the historic record comes in 1711 when he led a Creek army of 1,300 Lower Creek against French-armed Choctaw. Brims's role in the Yamasee War of 1715 is unclear. Among the Creek, the war officially began with a massacre of all the English traders. It is unlikely this could have taken place without the foreknowledge—and acquiescence—of Coweta's leading man. Chigelley, Brims's brother and the head warrior of Coweta, did lead a Creek war party against South Carolina in August 1715, but with little success. The Creek then attempted to draw the Cherokee into the war in their effort to bolster the native position. Carolina, to prevent such an occurrence, sent Colonel James Moore and Colonel George Chicken into the Cherokee towns. Carolina's initiative worked, and in January 1716, the Cherokee assassinated visiting Creek emissaries and openly cooperated with Carolina against an assembled Creek force. This debacle ended Creek hostilities against the English, but led to a Creek-Cherokee war.

Dispirited, the Creek reached a negotiated peace with South Carolina, began to cultivate ties with the French out of Mobile, and forged new links to the Spanish at Pensacola and St. Augustine. With Creek blessings, the French established Fort Toulouse in the heart of the Upper Creek country in 1717. The Creek also withdrew from village sites that had been established along the Ocmulgee River prior to the Yamasee War. In the years following, Brims of Coweta, now the leading spokesman for the Creek people, advocated a policy of neutrality and non-alliance with the competing European colonizers around the Creek periphery.

Carolina-Creek relations remained unsteady due to Creek friendship with bands of Yamasee Indians who were protected and armed by the Spanish at St. Augustine, and the continuing Cherokee War. When Yamasee killed Brims's favorite son (or nephew), Ouletta, Brims abandoned his staunch pro-Yamasee position. He did not formally break with them until December 1728, when British forces destroyed the Yamasee settlements in Spanish Florida. Carolina arranged peace between the Upper Creek and Cherokee in 1727, but Brims and the Lower Creek refused to comply with the treaty. The Lower Creek continued fighting the Cherokee sporadically for several more years, despite a Carolina trade embargo designed to force them into compliance. Brims died sometime between 1730 and 1733. In the absence of an heir of suitable age, his brother Chigelley became the *mico* of Coweta.

There is much confusion over the Brims lineage or "dynasty." Europeans assumed the younger men whom Brims sent as spokesmen for him were his sons, and historians have repeatedly concluded that Brims's successors were his natural sons. However, given the workings of the Creek matrilineal clan system, it is more likely they were his sisters' sons. The Brims line, one of the better documented families among the Creek, can be loosely traced through the end of the colonial period. Among Brims's more

B

important relatives are Mary Musgrove Bosomworth (Coosaponokeesa), the daughter of Brims's sister, and Malatchi, who served as the spokesman for Coweta until 1756.

Kathryn E. Holland Braund

References
David H. Corkran, *The Creek Frontier, 1540–1783* (1967); Verner W. Crane, *The Southern Frontier, 1670–1732* (1929).

See also CREEK-CHEROKEE WARS; MUSGROVE, MARY

Fort Buade (Michigan)

Jesuit missionaries resettled the Huron and Ottawa at St. Ignace on the Straits of Mackinac in 1671. The strategic location at the crossroads of the Great Lakes attracted fur traders and Fort Buade was established around 1680. The palisaded fort was given the family name of the governor, Count Frontenac, and was used by both a small garrison and the fur traders. While Antoine de Lamothe Cadillac was commandant (1694–98), he developed the idea of establishing a new post at Detroit. When the straits were reoccupied (c. 1715), the new fort, known as Michilimackinac, was located on the south shore.

Russell M. Magnaghi

See also FORT MICHILIMACKINAC (MICHIGAN)

Buffalo Creek, Shawnee Attack on (1754)

During James Glen's tenure as governor of South Carolina, a major concern was maintaining stable relations with the Cherokee Indians. In 1753, Glen led an expedition into the Cherokee lower towns and built Fort Prince George on the east bank of the Keowee River. He hoped the fort would protect the Cherokees from attacks by Indians allied with France, and preserve peace between the Cherokee and Carolina traders.

A party of Shawnee Indians, who were French allies, attacked the home of John Guttery at Buffalo Creek near the North and South Carolina border in September 1754. The Shawnee killed 16 people, including Guttery and his family, as well as several travelers and some guests who were awaiting the return of a couple who had traveled more than 40 miles to be married. The Indians slaughtered livestock and piled the carcasses on top of the dead settlers. They left with at least four captives. The newlywed couple, who had anticipated a festive reception, discovered the bodies.

In response, the South Carolina Commons House of Assembly provided for a body of rangers to patrol the frontier and authorized a bounty for any white or friendly Indian who brought in the scalp of an Indian committing acts of violence. The assembly blamed the Buffalo Creek attack on "our Insidious Friends the Cherokees." Governor Glen approved the establishment of the troop of rangers, but advised against the award for scalps, noting it would only exacerbate tensions and lead to further violence. Moreover, he requested evidence that the Cherokee were guilty of the murders. In his opinion, it was imperative that the colony continue amicable relations with the Cherokee and they not be driven into an alliance with the French.

Though Glen's words calmed tempers, the difficulties with the Cherokee and the French-allied Indians persisted, and culminated in 1757 with the construction of Fort Loudoun in the Overhill towns of the Cherokee nation.

Gregory D. Massey

References
Robert L. Merriwether, *The Expansion of South Carolina, 1729–1765* (1940).

See also GLEN, JAMES; FORT LOUDOUN (TENNESSEE); SHAWNEE

Fort Bull (New York)

In early spring 1756, Fort Bull was one of a series of vital links through which men and supplies flowed to the Anglo-American forces based on Lake Ontario. Moving provisions from Schenectady to Oswego required use of rivers, lakes, and creeks, as well as carrying places such as the one between the Mohawk River and Wood Creek on which the supply depot, Fort Bull, had been erected. William Shirley hoped sufficient troops and supplies could be moved over this difficult route to guarantee Oswego's defense and to facilitate the launch of a major Great Lakes offensive.

In late March 1756, Canadian Gaspard-Joseph Chaussegros De Lery commanded a party of 360 Indians, Canadians, and French regulars with orders to cut the Schenectady-Oswego line of communication. Fort Bull was garrisoned by a 60–80 man force and it quickly fell to Chaussegros De Lery's force when attacked on 27 March 1756. Very few defenders survived the onslaught. Great quantities of munitions and provisions earmarked for Oswego were destroyed and, after the magazine was set on fire, the entire fort was blown up by the withdrawing attackers. From the French vantage point, the attack on Fort Bull had been a complete success. Heavy casualties had been inflicted, substantial and badly needed supplies had been destroyed, and William Shirley's plan for an offensive out of Oswego had been badly disrupted. Almost immediately the French noose tightened around the already beleaguered and vulnerable Anglo-American forces at Oswego.

William G. Godfrey

References
    Francis Jennings, *Empire of Fortune: Crowns, Colonies, and Tribes in the Seven Years War in America* (1988); George F.G. Stanley, *New France: The Last Phase, 1744–1760* (1968); F.J. Thorpe, "Gaspard-Joseph Chaussegros De Lery," in F.G. Halpenny, ed., *Dictionary of Canadian Biography*, 12 vols. (1979).

See also FORT OSWEGO (NEW YORK)

Bulman, Alexander (1702–1745)
Dr. Alexander Bulman of York, Maine was one of the few colonial military doctors. Born in 1702, the son of a Boston baker, at the start of Dummer's War, Bulman came to Maine as surgeon to the provincial forces under Thomas Westbrook in 1722, administering to the sick at Forts Richmond and Menaskoux, and accompanying some raiding parties. Bulman apparently impressed the inhabitants of Maine, for the town of York voted £100 to have him settle in the town for the rest of his life. Bulman purchased a home near the meetinghouse in the center of town and continued his practice in York.

He and his wife, Mary, became close friends of William, Jr. and Mary Pepperrell, of Kittery. When the Louisbourg expedition was proposed in early 1745, Bulman showed keen interest and support, but tied his own participation to the actions of his friend, William Pepperrell, Jr. When Pepperrell accepted the commission as overall commander, Alexander Bulman was named as surgeon to Pepperrell's regiment, and personal physician to the commander in chief. In early September, after weeks of tending the growing number of sick soldiers, Bulman fell ill himself and died on 11 September.

Steven C. Eames

References
    Charles Edward Banks, *History of York, Maine*, 2 vols. (1931–1935); Steven C. Eames, "Rustic Warriors: Warfare and the Provincial Soldier on the Northern Frontier, 1689–1748," Ph.D. Dissertation, University of New Hampshire (1989).

See also DUMMER'S WAR; PEPPERRELL, WILLIAM, JR.

Fort Burd (Pennsylvania)
Fort Burd was named for James Burd, a Philadelphia merchant who served in the Pennsylvania Regiment as a specialist in building roads and forts. In October 1759, Burd and Colonel Joseph Shippen built a fortified storehouse on the Monongahela River to serve as a transshipment point between Forts Cumberland and Pitt. The result was Fort Burd, a large structure atop Rich Hill at the mouth of Nemacolin's Creek, a mile above the mouth of the Redstone River, and overlooking the Monongahela. The fort was a square, the curtains between the bastions 97 and a half feet long, the flanks of the bastions 16 feet, and the faces of the bastions 12 feet. Within the walls stood a magazine 39 feet square that could also house local inhabitants in case of attack.

Eric Hinderaker

References
    Charles Morse Stotz, *Outposts of the War for Empire: The French and English in Western Pennsylvania; Their Armies, Their Forts, Their People, 1749–1764* (1985).

See also BURD, JAMES

Burd, James (? –1793)
James Burd was a major during the French and Indian War. He was from Pennsylvania and the son-in-law of Edward Shippen. He led 2,500 men to Loyalhanna Creek in 1758 and laid the foundation for what would later become Fort Ligonier. In October 1758, he organized a suc-

cessful defense of the British encampment at Loyalhanna against an attack by the French. Initially, the men under Burd's direction were overwhelmed by the superior numbers of French and Indian fighters. However, once the British troops retreated behind their prepared defenses, they withstood the advances of their attackers. This was not only an important military victory for Burd and his men, but a psychological victory as well. Due to the high number of casualties at Loyalhanna and in other battles, the French began to lose the support of Indians living in the upper Ohio.

Michael W. Nagle

See also FORT BURD (PENNSYLVANIA); FORT LIGONIER (PENNSYLVANIA)

Fort Burke (Massachusetts)

Fort Burke was part of a series of forts erected in 1744 and 1745 to defend the northern frontier of Massachusetts during King George's War. It was located in Falltown, now known as Bernardston. The fort was erected after the Massachusetts General Court in 1743 granted each town £100 to pay for self-fortification. Major John Burke constructed a fort consisting of palisades ten- to 12-feet high enclosing a blockhouse and eight barracks. Incorporated into each corner were elevated watchtowers. Major Burke was subsequently wounded in 1747 during an attack on the fort by Indians. During the French and Indian War it was used frequently as a refuge for nearby settlers.

David L. Whitesell

Burlington Island Fort (New Jersey)

Originally, a Dutch settlement occupied Burlington Island; the fort was situated in the Delaware River opposite the present town of Burlington. In 1624, a group of three or four Walloon families and eight single men were placed on the island by Captain Cornelis Jacobsen May. They proceeded to build a palisaded fort which enclosed their rudimentary huts. This settlement was known to the Dutch as Verhulsten Island, meaning "high island" or "beautiful island." The island was also referred to as Matinicunk Island, which translates as "island of pines." The settlement was under the sponsorship of the Dutch West India Company. In the fall of 1626, the island was abandoned in an effort to consolidate

New Netherland, and the settlers were brought to New Amsterdam by Governor General Peter Minuit. The island later became the personal property and homestead of Vice Governor Alexander d'Hinoyossa in 1659. In 1677, the town of Burlington was founded there as a settlement for Quakers.

David L. Whitesell

Burnet, William (1688–1729)

Born into a wealthy and influential family, William Burnet was the son of Gilbert Burnet, the bishop of Salisbury, and Mary Scott. He also was the godson of King William and Queen Mary, and his family had many other influential friends. Through these connections, he was appointed governor of New York in April 1720. New York was a key to the fur trade because of its geographical position. It received shipments of European goods which could be transported inland for trade with Indians in exchange for furs. However, Indians in the Mohawk Valley were trading with the French instead of the English. This allowed the French to gain much influence in the area. Burnet discovered that the French actually obtained the goods they traded with the Indians from merchants in New York. This was profitable for the small number of New York merchants involved in the trade, but might have been a disaster in the long run for the colony. Burnet was determined to end this trade with the French.

Shortly after his tenure as governor began, he proposed a law making it illegal for English colonists to trade with the French in Montreal. Eventually, the law was approved. This angered many of New York's influential families and they were at odds with the governor for the remainder of his term.

In 1722, Burnet also established trading posts at Tirondequot and Onondaga. This helped New York gain a larger control over the trade in the region and reduced some of the French influence in the region. However, the governor's critics continued to oppose his actions. A network of illegal trade did develop, but Burnet's programs were still successful.

By 1727, his critics had grown in number, and he was denounced by New York's assembly. He was transferred to Massachusetts in 1728, but was not in Boston long. He died in that colony after a fight with the assembly concerning his salary.

Michael W. Nagle

Bushy Run, Battle of (1763)

The Battle of Bushy Run, 5 and 6 August 1763, was the only field engagement in the upper Ohio Valley during Pontiac's War. The victorious British commander, Colonel Henry Bouquet, referred to it as the Battle of Edge Hill, the name of the height on which the second day's combat occurred. This was one mile southeast of Bushy Run, a tributary of Brush Creek. Bouquet led an emergency expedition of about 400 regulars, accompanied by between ten and 30 backwoods scouts under Captain Lemuel Barrett who had been recruited at Fort Cumberland, and 340 to 400 packhorses with their drivers. The redcoats included two light infantry companies from the 42nd Foot, one from the 77th Foot (both Highland units), and eight companies of regulars of the 77th, the 42nd, and the 60th Foot (the Royal Americans). Many of the Highlanders had recently survived a Caribbean campaign and showed symptoms of malaria. A detachment of grenadiers operated as a unit during the fighting; Royal Artillery personnel may have been present. Some of the officers recently had been dropped from active status and were present as volunteers. Ambushing this force at 1:00 P.M. on 5 August was a consortium of Delawares, Shawnees, Mingoes, and Wyandots whose total strength is uncertain. This was part of a force that had invested Fort Pitt in June and failed to take the post in a five-day assault that ended on 1 August.

The expedition had been conceived by General Jeffrey Amherst in New York on 6 June, when he assembled light infantry companies on Staten Island for a relief march. It was believed Fort Pitt's garrison would be starved into surrender unless relieved. By the time Bouquet had moved an augmented force west of Carlisle, Amherst was also scheduling the expedition to continue north from Fort Pitt and reoccupy Presque Isle on Lake Erie. On 16 July, he wrote lecturing Bouquet on the necessity of punitive offensive strikes against the western Indians. In the same envelope he included a note suggesting that blankets infected with smallpox be given as gifts to the Indians who habitually demanded presents from the garrison at Fort Pitt. Bouquet detached a party to rush to Fort Cumberland on 19 July and return with musket balls, which were essential for his force. He instructed the commander of the party to charge directly at any Indian groups his soldiers encountered, a foretaste of the tactics for which the Bushy Run engagement became famous.

After following the route to Fort Ligonier used in 1758 by General John Forbes, Bouquet took a shortcut toward Fort Pitt that passed by a small wayside station near Bushy Run maintained by Sergeant Andrew Byerly, a Swiss veteran of the Royal American Regiment. Bouquet scheduled arrival for midday so he would reach the narrow crossing at Turtle Creek Valley at dark. That way, he hoped to avoid repeating General Braddock's calamity. After encountering the Indian ambush east of Bushy Run on the afternoon of the 5th, Bouquet's force repeatedly charged groups of Indians, but the enemy constantly retreated and reformed elsewhere faster than the soldiers could follow. At dusk, Bouquet moved his seriously injured force down from the hill that lay west of Edge Hill and up to the top of Edge Hill for security. Sacks of flour that the horses had been carrying were unloaded and arranged in a circular defensive barrier around the hilltop, with the wounded sheltered within.

At dawn on the 6th, Indians appeared to completely encircle the force and attacked at several points of the circumference. Now Bouquet worked the ruse that turned the day into victory. On the western slope, two light infantry companies and the grenadiers and scouts were pulled back and moved to a concealed area behind a spur of the hill that projected southeastward from the hilltop. Assuming the expedition was fleeing, the Indians pressed forward in full force on the west slope. From the spur charged Highlanders, grenadiers, and scouts, striking the unsuspecting Indians on the right flank and driving them into musket fire from other units hiding in shrubbery on the northwest slope of the hill. The survivors fled in panic, chased by the soldiers for about two miles.

A tradition arose that British light infantry tactics were developed in this battle. Although Bouquet referred to close-in fighting, the documents do not clarify which of the possible alternatives was primarily relied on by his charging force: individual musket fire, clubbed muskets, or bayonets. Furthermore, it is not clear whether the Highlanders were carrying claymores. Also, the accounts do not clarify whether the force firing from the bushes did so in volleys. In basic outline, the battle had been an Indian ambush followed by what the cartographer, Lieutenant Thomas Hutchins, described as an ambush by Bouquet's force. Shoulder to shoulder charges by spirited regulars into groups of warriors were now recognized as tactically effective. The necessity of forcing Indians to remain in place long enough so weapons could be brought to bear on them was now accepted, and one way of bringing that about had been devised.

The expedition suffered 50 killed and 60 wounded. So many packhorses were killed that the flour had to be destroyed and the remaining animals used to transport the wounded to Fort Pitt, 26 miles to the west. The little unit arrived there on 10 August. Reliable figures were never produced for the Indian force, or for the casualties it suffered. Sir William Johnson reported Bouquet had 600 men facing only 95 Indians. The vast circumference of the Indian circle around Edge Hill casts doubt on the 95 figure, but some historians have repeated it. Although Indian war parties from Ohio returned to Pennsylvania in 1764, their defeat on 6 August 1763 had led them to respect forces commanded by Bouquet, and may have convinced their leaders it was futile to try to recapture western Pennsylvania territory without the assistance of a European power. It also convinced colonial leaders that field engagements with the Indians could be won, that political authorities had not entirely neglected frontier protection, and that regulars were worth their price in government expenditures.

Louis M. Waddell

References

Sir Jeffery Amherst Papers, Public Record Office, Kew, U.K. War Office Series 34/40, 34/41; Niles Anderson, "Bushy Run: Decisive Battle in the Wilderness," *Western Pennsylvania Historical Magazine,* 46 (1963):211–245; Edmund B. O'Callaghan, ed., *Documents Relating to the Colonial History of the State of New-York,* Vol. VII (1856).

See also BOUQUET, HENRY; CARLISLE, CAMP NEAR (PENNSYLVANIA); PONTIAC'S WAR

C

Caddoes

Caddoes is a term applied to an agricultural group of tribes sharing the Caddo language and organized in three confederacies and a few independent tribes in east Texas, southwestern Arkansas, and western Louisiana. Of the three confederacies, the largest was the Hasinai, which included eight to ten tribes in the Trinity, Neches, and Angelina River Valleys in east Texas. It was this confederacy which gave Texas its name, a Spanish corruption of the Caddo word *Taysha*, meaning ally or friend. On the big bend of the Red River, in northeast Texas and southwestern Arkansas, lived the four or five tribes that made up the Kadohadacho Confederacy. In western Louisiana, between the Red and Sabine Rivers, lived the Natchitoches, the smallest of the confederacies, made up of the Lower Natchitoches and one or two wayward tribes which joined it in the eighteenth century.

Although linguistically associated with the Pawnee, Wichita, and Kitsay, the Caddoes were culturally similar to the Southeast culture area groups—Creek, Cherokee, Natchez, and the like. From archeological evidence, it appears that at some point in the remote past the Caddoes were mound builders, but by historic times they had a simpler agricultural culture which, nonetheless, made them the most technically advanced of Texas Indians. The Caddoes lived in hamlets and villages that included temples and meetinghouses. The Caddoes were known for their sophisticated pottery, basketry, and bows, trading these items over long distances.

First contact between the Caddoes and Europeans took place in 1541, when the Hernando de Soto expedition crossed western Louisiana into east Texas and battled Hasinai villag-ers. In the 1680s and 1690s, both the French and Spanish made contact with the Caddoes, and in 1701, the French established permanent trading relations with the Natchitoches, where a post was founded in 1713. In the period 1716–1722, a number of Franciscan missions were established by the Spanish among the Hasinai, and one for the independent Adaes, near present Robeline, Louisiana. While the Caddoes were not hostile to the Spanish, most showed a great degree of indifference toward Christianization, leading to the eventual failure of the east Texas mission fields. The Caddoes did serve as allies of the French and Spanish against other Indian enemies, including the Natchez, Osage, Tonkawa, and Apache. Never more than a few thousand, the Caddoes were reduced, mostly through epidemic disease, to a few hundred by the early nineteenth century. The last 300 or so were rescued from massacre by Texans in 1859 and settled in Oklahoma, where they were given a reservation.

Jesús F. de la Teja

References

Elizabeth A.H. John, *Storms Brewed in Other Men's Worlds: The Confrontation of Indians, Spanish, and French in the Southwest, 1540–1795* (1975); W.W. Newcomb, Jr., *The Indians of Texas: From Prehistoric to Modern Times* (1961).

Caesar

Caesar, a Cherokee chief of the lower towns, was captured by enemy Indians and sold to a Savannah planter as a slave. He was rescued by Flint, another Cherokee, around 1713. The following year, urged on by Indian traders, the two made their own slave raid on the Yuchi Indians.

A few years later, when the Yamasee War erupted, Caesar agreed to supply a number of Cherokee to help fight the Creek. When Caesar did not keep his rendezvous, South Carolina troops under Maurice Moore went to Tugaloo to persuade him to aid them. A Creek delegation arrived and proposed war against the English and Caesar probably led the group of Cherokee that murdered the Creek in the town house. This dramatic and unprecedented event united the Cherokee nation and "guaranteed the eventual victory of South Carolina over her Indian enemies" and the survival of British rule in South Carolina.

William L. Anderson

References

David H. Corkran, *The Cherokee Frontier: Conflict and Survival, 1740–62* (1963); J. Norman Heard, *Handbook of the American Frontier: Four Centuries of Indian-White Relationships* (1987); John Phillip Reid, *A Better Kind of Hatchet: Law, Trade, and Diplomacy in the Cherokee Nation during the Early Years of European Contact* (1976).

See also CREEK-CHEROKEE WAR; YAMASEE WAR

Cahokia-Fox Raid (1752)

An exceptionally large Fox raiding party, which included warriors from allied tribes, attacked a Cahokia and Michigamea Illinois village on 1 June 1752. Because of the size and composition of the expedition, this assault represents an adaptation of the raiding tradition. The motive for this assault was the Fox desire for revenge on the Cahokia, who had captured six or seven Fox and Sioux in 1751 and tortured all but one of them to death; a Fox prisoner escaped to alert his relatives, who resided in present-day central Wisconsin. The Michigamea offered sanctuary to the Cahokia in their village located on the Mississippi River just north of Fort de Chartres; both the Michigamea and Cahokia anticipated and feared a retaliatory raid.

The Fox enlisted the Sioux, Sauk, Kickapoo, Potawatomi, Winnebago, and Menominee in their raid. The Fox deliberately concealed their attack from the French because they knew the Europeans would have halted the expedition in order to protect valuable allies. Estimates of the size of the expedition range from 400 or 500 participants in 60 canoes to 1,000 warriors in 180 canoes. The approximate size of the Cahokia-Michigamea village may be calculated at less than 400, and the number of warriors at between 90 and 130. In order to reduce the target population to the desirable raiding advantage, the Fox planned their attack for a day when many Illinois were absent from the village because of a Roman Catholic religious observance at Fort de Chartres. The attackers were able to advance undetected to within a few yards of the Illinois village because of the proximity of woods and a ravine.

The Fox began the attack with a ruse which sent a dozen warriors rushing into the Michigamea village. After discharging their weapons at those Illinois they encountered, this decoy party quickly withdrew. The enraged Illinois immediately raced after the retreating Fox and into an ambush laid by the main raiding force. Concealed by tall grass, the Fox and their allies fired their guns at the advancing Illinois, killing 28. The raiders then charged the Michigamea village in order to burn it and kill or capture as many men, women, and children as possible. After withdrawing, the invaders tortured three or four prisoners to death and used the others as insurance against Illinois retaliation. The French estimated the raiders took 30 scalps while killing or capturing between 70 and 80 Illinois, but suffered only four losses themselves, including a Sioux chief. After this attack, the French initiated negotiations for the return of the captives, and various Illinois subtribes fearfully petitioned the French for protection.

Although this Fox raid was much larger than would have been expected as part of a traditional raid, the size and intertribal composition of the 1752 expedition reflected the changes brought by experience with colonial military operations. This raid also illustrates the irony of French-Indian relations late in the colonial period: while the various western tribes grew in population (including the Fox, whom the French earlier had targeted for extermination), the Illinois (a tribe closely allied with the French) suffered a disastrous population decline.

Raymond E. Hauser

References

Emily J. Blasingham, "The Depopulation of the Illinois Indians," *Ethnohistory,* (1956):193–224, 361–412; Jean-Bernard Bossu, *Travels in the Interior of North*

America, 1751–1752, ed. by Seymour Feiler (1962); Joseph Jablow, "A Study of Indian Tribes in . . . Illinois and Indiana, 1640–1832," in *Indians of Illinois and Indiana: Illinois, Kickapoo, and Potawatomi Indians* (1974):37–436.

Macarty Mactigue to the Marquis de Vaudreuil, Kaskaskia, 2 September 1752, in *Illinois on the eve of the Seven Years' War, 1747–1755,* Theodore Calvin Pease and Ernestine Jenison, eds., *Collections of the Illinois State Historical Library,* Vol. 29 (1940):654–699.

See also Fox; Illinois

California

Although the Spanish presence in Mesoamerica was immense, in California it was relatively late and limited. Several early Spanish forays of the 1530s ranged as far north as Baja, California, charting the coastline and searching for the Northwest Passage. In 1542, an expedition led by Juan Rodriguez Cabrillo, under orders from the viceroy of Mexico, traveled as far north as present-day southern Oregon, naming various bays. After several months of seeking signs of the Northwest Passage, Cabrillo sailed south, only to die of complications from a broken arm and an infection in an old wound that had re-opened.

Cabrillo's fate was emblematic in many ways of Spain's view of the north Pacific shoreline for the next two centuries—it yielded too little and was too dangerous for the efforts involved. Despite various rumors of a Northwest Passage and a short-lived British foray into the Pacific by Englishman Francis Drake in the late 1570s, Spanish and other European ships found no passage, no great riches. As a consequence, California remained little more than faint lines on European maps. Spain concentrated on its Manila trade routes, and other European nations were slow to move into the Pacific.

In the interim, the indigenous peoples of the region began to feel the presence of Europeans in shifting relations on their peripheries. Diseases swept into the Southwest and filtered into California beginning in the 1520s and 1530s, and horses from Spanish stocks increasingly spread into northern Mexico and up through central California in the first half of the eighteenth century. The Southwest, especially the Rio Grande drainage, was more affected by

these new factors; but trade networks between California and that region signaled changes.

The aftermath of the Seven Years' War (1754–1763) and the slow, steady movement of Russian trade into Kamchatka and Alaska prompted Spain to carve out a defensive borderland north of Mexico and west of New Mexico. The first move into California came in 1769 with the establishment of Mission San Diego. By 1776, Spanish colonists had reached as far north as San Francisco. Spain's presidios, missions, and settlements, small and tentative as they might have been, served as a line of outposts stretching from San Francisco to St. Louis.

Spain's occupation of California, though, amounted to far-flung sites along a narrow strip of the California coastline. Soldiers' misconduct, the coercion of Native American labor, and the spread of disease prompted Native Americans to resist the Spanish. At San Gabriel in 1771, for example, when Spanish soldiers abused native Californian women, Indians rose in arms. As at San Gabriel, many of the conflicts were localized and responses to immediate mistreatment.

Other cases, such as that of the Yuma in the southwest corner of present-day California, reveal a different source of conflict. Beginning in the late seventeenth century and continuing through the eighteenth, the Spanish made sporadic contacts with the Yumas. During those years, the two sides assisted each other and engaged in ritual gift-giving to secure diplomatic relations. In the 1770s, Spanish officials contemplated establishing a supply route along the Gila-Colorado River corridor from Sonora to coastal California across Yuma territory. The Yuma had approached the officials about the crossing as early as 1773. The supply route through their territory promised the Yuma significant trade advantages over other peoples in the region. The Spanish, for their part, courted the Yuma as an ally against the Apache who regularly relieved the Spanish of their horses through raids, and because the Yuma controlled the area on the edge of the desert crossing to coastal California.

Finally, in 1779, Spanish officials ordered the establishment, not of full-fledged pueblos or missions, but of two military towns with small churches. Friars at the churches attempted to redistribute Yuma lands, and Spanish livestock decimated Yuma crops and disrupted other important subsistence patterns. Furthermore, the Yuma gained no particular trade or diplomatic advantage by the establishment of such outposts. In summer 1780, the Yuma fell upon the outposts and a contingent of Spanish readying for the crossing of the desert, killing all the men, including Governor Fernando de Rivera y Moncada (who was in the party bound for coastal California), four missionaries, and more than 30 soldiers. The Yuma ransomed captured Spanish women and children, and turned back the investigative and punitive force sent to the region. With this incident, the Yuma asserted control over their territory and effectively cut California off from Mexico along a corridor formed by the Colorado and Gila Rivers.

Between 1780 and the turn of the century, California was not a thriving economic holding for Spain, but it did grow slowly. That increase in Spanish presence came at a horrific cost in native lives. Diseases introduced by the Spanish, complicated by the additional problems of health, hygiene, and treatment at the missions, cut the Indian population in the area between San Francisco and San Diego at the beginning of the mission period from approximately 72,000 to an estimated 18,000 in the early nineteenth century. As in other portions of North America, epidemics severely hindered Native American responses to European advances on their territories.

As Spain nominally gained control of coastal California below San Francisco, it began a second move northward to meet Russian expansion and a renewed British presence in present-day Oregon, Washington, and British Columbia. In 1789, Estéban Martínez took formal possession of Nootka Sound on Vancouver Island in the name of Spain and seized English vessels. Spain and England nearly went to war over the "violation" of British property, but Spain conceded to allow English trade and by the end of the decade withdrew back to California. There, Spanish settlements suffered under rumors of French, British, and Russian attacks, but none materialized.

Between about 1800 and 1820, California became increasingly isolated from Spanish Mexico as a series of wars erupted there. Loyalist Californios ("Mexican" and "Spanish" residents of the area of Spanish, Mestizo, and Indio ancestry) suffered occasional attacks from Mexican revolutionary ships. For the most part, Californios survived by conducting a growing black-market trade with American and British ships in hides, tallow, and provisions. By 1822, news of Mexican independence reached Califor-

nia, and Governor Pablo Vicente de Solá and other officials swore allegiance to the new government.

The first several years of the new Mexican government were uncertain at best, and administration of California lapsed. In that context, the beating of a Native American by a soldier at the mission at Santa Inés led to an attack on the mission. Natives burned the mission and killed four non-Indians. For a month they held control of the mission. Inspired by the success of the insurgents at Santa Inés, Indians at Mission Santa Barbara rose up as well, but failed to take full control. Afterward, many of the mission residents escaped into the hills. The California governor launched a heavily armed force of 100 soldiers and was able to recapture most of the rebellious Santa Barbara Indians, but only after pursuing them far into the interior.

While the expeditions to recapture the Santa Barbarans signaled an immediate victory for the Californios, native peoples in the interior still controlled those territories. The Yokuts, in particular, as well as other central California peoples, engaged in a lucrative trade of stolen Californio horses and other livestock to American fur trappers and New Mexico residents (themselves Mexican citizens). Yokuts relied on extensive trade networks to the east and on former neophyte guides to lead raids in the west in Mexican territory. By the 1840s, on the eve of the Mexican-American War (1846–1848) in which the United States wrested California and much of the Southwest from Mexico, those raids threatened to virtually wipe out Californio livestock.

The Mexican-American War and the Treaty of Guadalupe Hidalgo (1848) put an end to Mexican rule in California and marked the beginning of U.S. control over the region. The treaty marked the transfer of the region to the United States after the briefest of military encounters and was the beginning of a new era of relationships with extra-regional political and financial entities some scholars perceive as colonial, but one that was clearly different than Spanish or Mexican control. In all, California's occupation by Spain, and then Mexico, engendered no huge, global wars as had the competition for empire between Spain, France, and Britain in the eastern portions of North America. There were outbursts of rebellion and resistance among Native Americans in California that included the wars over territory, as among the Yuma, raids on Californio livestock, as among the Yokuts, and rebellions at the missions against ill-treatment, as at Santa Barbara. The most deadly warfare in California was biological, as diseases swept away huge portions of the indigenous population over approximately a century of sustained European presence in the region before U.S. acquisition.

Chris Friday

References

John W. Caughey and Norris Hundley, Jr., *California: History of a Remarkable State,* 4th ed. (1982); Warren L. Cook, *Floodtide of Empire: Spain and the Pacific Northwest, 1543–1819* (1973); Henry F. Dobyns, "Indians in the Colonial Spanish Borderlands," in *Indians in American History: An Introduction,* ed. by Frederick E. Hoxie (1988):67–93; David J. Weber, *The Mexican Frontier, 1821–1846* (1982); Richard White, *"It's Your Misfortune and None of My Own": A New History of the American West* (1991).

Calusa

The Calusa were an indigenous group who inhabited the southwestern Gulf coast of the Florida peninsula in an area stretching from Charlotte Harbor south to the Florida Keys.

At the time of European contact in the early sixteenth century, the Calusa lived in 56 towns and were organized into a confederation under one very powerful chief. Scholars disagree whether the Calusa were of Muskogean linguistic stock or whether they were related to the Taino of Cuba or other Antillean tribes. They received tribute from surrounding groups like the Mayami living as far away as Lake Okeechobee and maintained contact—perhaps tribal and kin relationships—with other tribes, the Ais, the Jeaga, and the Tequesta, of the peninsula's eastern coast. They exploited the littoral region for marine products, hunted the plentiful fauna, and gathered native plants for subsistence. Their dugout canoes held more than 80 men and roamed the seas, venturing far into the Caribbean and the Gulf of Mexico. Villagers lived in wattle-and-daub structures, and reports of shipwrecked Spanish sailors relate that the house of the Calusa chief seated more than 2,000 persons comfortably.

Although the Calusa probably had previous contact with Europeans, as evidenced by their gold and silver ornaments, the tribe officially was visited for the first time by Juan Ponce de Leon in 1513, on a trading and slave-raiding expedition. When he returned in 1521, Indian-Spanish relations had turned hostile, the Calusa attacked, and Ponce de Leon subsequently died of his wounds. Shipwrecked people often were rescued by the Calusa only to be sacrificed or made into slaves. The captivity narrative of Hernando Escalante de Fontaneda (1551–1566) relates that at least one European captive per year was sacrificed and says the name Calusa meant "fierce people."

The first permanent European settlement in Calusa territory was attempted in 1566 by Pedro Menéndez de Avilés, who established friendly relations with the chief, Carlos. Menéndez accepted the sister of Carlos, Doña Antonia, as his "wife" and returned to Havana with her and 12 shipwreck survivors. Before leaving, Menéndez established a military/mission post, San Antonio de Carlos. Jesuit missionary Father Juan Rogel, a veteran of missionizing to the northern tribes of La Florida, arrived in 1567 to begin large-scale conversion efforts.

Spanish missions and military garrisons had little success among the Calusa, and Mission San Antonio de Carlos lasted only three years. The semisedentary Calusa were not amenable to reduction into villages like the Timucua and the Guale who lived in the northern part of the peninsula. As late as 1675, the bishop of Santiago de Cuba, Gabriel Díaz Vara Calderón, in a letter to Queen Mariana of Spain reported that no Spanish missions existed in the southern portion of the peninsula. Between 1680 and 1700, Spanish officials and Franciscan missionaries sought to remedy the situation with several unsuccessful missionizing attempts. Although the Calusa were unwilling to be missionized and reduced into agricultural settlements, throughout the seventeenth century groups of Calusa warriors carried on a lively trade with Havana, a trade which included amber, salt, and songbirds, usually cardinals, which were used as pets and decorations.

The population of the Calusa began to diminish during the seventeenth century from the effects of European diseases, internecine warfare, and population pressures caused by the emigration of northern tribal groups fleeing the border wars after 1670. All of Florida's indigenous groups were particularly vulnerable to raids by Lower Creek, Yuchi, and Yamasee, who were provided with guns by their British allies. During Queen Anne's War (1702–1713), many Calusa sought Spanish protection and were incorporated into resettlement villages near St. Augustine. By 1761, Spanish official Juan José Eligio de la Puente reported that invading tribes of Creek origin had destroyed Calusa towns and the remnants of the most powerful tribe of south Florida, along with other south Florida natives, were voluntarily removed to Cuba in 1763.

Sherry Johnson

References

John H. Hann, ed. and trans., *Missions to the Calusa* (1991); Eugene Lyon, *The Enterprise of Florida: Pedro Menéndez de Avilés and the Spanish Conquest of 1565–1568* (1976); John R. Swanton, *The Indians of the Southeastern United States,* Smithsonian Institution Bureau of American Ethnology Bulletin 137 (1946); David Hurst Thomas, ed., *Spanish Borderlands Sourcebooks,* 27 vols. (1991–1995); J. Leitch Wright, Jr., *The Only Land They Knew: The Tragic Story of the American Indians in the Old South* (1981).

See also MENÉNDEZ DE AVILÉS, PEDRO; SPANISH MISSION SYSTEM–SOUTHEAST; TEQUESTA

Campbell, John, Lord Loudoun (1705–1782)

John Campbell, the fourth earl of Loudoun, enlisted in the army in 1727 and later saw action against the Jacobites in 1745. In 1755, he was appointed colonel in chief of the 60th Foot (the Royal Americans) and in 1756, he was appointed captain general and governor in chief of Virginia. He was appointed commander of the British forces in America on 20 March 1756.

When Campbell made his journey to America, he did so in grand style. His personal baggage, which included his private stock of wine, took up the entire hold of one ship. Also accompanying him on his voyage to America were seventeen servants, his mistress, three coaches, and 19 horses. Finally, on 23 July 1756, Campbell reached New York to take command.

He was met by William Shirley, the man he was to replace as commander. Shirley immediately briefed Campbell on his plans for the campaign in 1756. These plans were very detailed and entailed a movement against the French strongholds at Forts Niagara and Frontenac.

Shirley pushed Campbell to implement these plans immediately. This was exactly the wrong move for Shirley to make. Lord Loudoun had no intention of simply implementing the plans of another. This started the relationship between Campbell and Shirley off badly. The new commander abandoned Shirley's plan and aimed for Fort Carillon instead.

Six days after reaching America, Campbell arrived in Albany. In and around Albany, Campbell had approximately 10,000 soldiers. He was briefed by the famous ranger Major Robert Rogers on his arrival. This intelligence indicated the construction of Fort Carillon was only partially complete and its garrison about half the size of Campbell's forces. The time to attack Fort Carillon was then, but Campbell was in no hurry and the only military move he made was to reinforce Fort Oswego.

Campbell was a capable and meticulous soldier, but tended to over-immerse himself in paperwork. However, he did accomplish a great deal in 1756. His successes were primarily in the areas of administration, logistics, and training. Although important, this was not the kind of work that showed progress to his superiors in England: it involved no battles and gave no indication he was winning the war, or even fighting one.

With up to 75 percent of his army being colonial inserts, he set out to first create an army and then train it. Campbell realized the typical style of European warfare could not be executed in America. Therefore, he decided to implement a training program before taking to the field. He introduced some important innovations into the training of soldiers. After training them in traditional British procedures, he instituted firing from the prone and the use of flanking parties. He also taught his soldiers to fight from behind trees rather than in typical British line formations.

Campbell's plans for 1757 were to fortify the northern route to Quebec. This was the area along the Lake George-Lake Champlain-Richelieu River line. However, William Pitt vetoed the plan and insisted that an expedition be launched to recapture the French strongpoint at Louisbourg. Campbell departed for Cape Breton with most of the British and colonial soldiers on the continent. This left only a small force to guard the frontier from French and Indian raids. Campbell was to be met by additional troops and an ample fleet from England at Cape Breton.

Campbell's expedition to Louisbourg turned out to be a complete failure. There were many reasons for this, most of which were not attributable to Campbell. First, the naval force and troops from England arrived late due to bad weather. They did not land in Halifax until July. Campbell, who was to wait at New York, had already left and landed about the same time as the navy. Second, the bad weather continued and held the fleet at sea, further delaying his attack. Finally, the French used this time to increase their defenses at Louisbourg. Campbell then made the decision to return the expedition to New York without an attempt to take the citadel. The expedition was termed the "Cabbage Planting Expedition." This was because while in Halifax awaiting the attack, his soldiers planted vegetables. Campbell's idea was to have fresh vegetables available for the soldiers to avoid scurvy. According to Pitt, this was all the expedition accomplished.

Campbell not only failed to take Louisbourg, he also failed to accomplish anything in America. He made several attempts to push forward on the offensive to capture Fort Carillon. However, increased French attacks due to the absence of most of his forces at Louisbourg caused him to remain on the defensive. This was particularly true after the capture and destruction of Fort Oswego and Fort William Henry by the French. These were two more setbacks for Lord Loudoun and major failures in the eyes of Pitt.

Campbell was relieved of his command and replaced by Jeffrey Amherst. This was due in part to his failures, but was also politically influenced. Campbell, who was a protégé of the duke of Cumberland, was not well liked by Pitt even before his exploits in America. Lord Loudoun returned to England and was placed second in command of the British forces in Portugal in 1762. He is often overlooked as a good commander because of his failures at Louisbourg, Fort William Henry, and Oswego. However, his contributions in bringing the colonies together and developing a well-trained army helped obtain eventual success for the British in America.

John M. Keefe

References
    Oscar Theodore Barck, *Colonial America* (1958); Donald Chidsey, *French and Indian War* (1969); Allan W. Eckert, *Wilderness Empire* (1969); Edward P. Hamilton,

The French and Indian Wars (1962); Maurice Matloff, *American Military History* (1985).

See also AMHERST, JEFFREY; LOUISBOURG; OSWEGO, BATTLE OF; ROGERS, ROBERT; SHIRLEY, WILLIAM; FORT WILLIAM HENRY, SIEGE OF

C

Canada, British Expedition Against (1709)
The ill-fated 1709 British invasion of Canada was designed to be a cooperative effort between regular British troops and colonials recruited from across New England. Encouraged and accompanied by the French, Indian bands had attacked Haverhill near Boston in August of 1708. Four years earlier, a similar attack on Deerfield, Massachusetts, had resulted in 40 deaths. Not only did the Franco-Indian frontier attacks increase alarm among the colonists, the constant threat also disrupted the economic life of New England settlers and convinced some colonials they needed to provide for their own security. New Englanders were further convinced that New Yorkers did not share their concern for self-protection. These events helped to unify colonial opinion that the best defense would be an assault on Quebec—thus removing the immediate French threat—but the colonists needed British backing.

In 1708, the missing element in invasion plans appeared in the person of Samuel Vetch, a colonial merchant who helped to convince the Board of Trade in England with his "Canada Surveyed," a revision of the 1690 plan to invade Montreal by way of Lake Champlain, and Quebec by the St. Lawrence. Vetch had knowledge of these regions of Canada and was well connected through his marriage to the daughter of Robert Livingston of the Albany Livingstons. Vetch's plan was quickly adopted, as the Privy Council lent their support before the crown. For his role, Vetch was promised the governorship of Canada and commissioned as a colonel. By December 1708, plans for the invasion of Canada became a reality, and Vetch sailed for Boston in April 1709 with the promise of regular British forces.

Vetch's plan was for a two-force invasion, one to be led by Colonel Francis Nicholson, who accompanied Vetch to Boston, and the other by Vetch, who would lead colonial and British troops. Nicholson had previously held colonial administrative positions in New York and as governor in Virginia, thus he too was cognizant of French aggression in the area. Nicholson's force would consist of colonials from New England and New York, about 1,500 men. New York had resisted earlier attempts at colonial military cooperation, but had few options now that the project had crown backing. The Boston contingent would include 1,200 men recruited from the rest of New England, potentially 4,000 British regulars, and six warships. The plan called for this group to approach Quebec and Port Royal by sea, while Nicholson's force would follow Lake Champlain in an attack from the south. In early summer, the Albany force under Nicholson was joined by four Iroquois tribes, thereby exceeding the 1,500 goal. Indian scouts provided valuable logistical information and estimates of French strength at Montreal and Quebec. As summer began, Nicholson's force advanced using a wagon road they built north from Albany. Outposts for supply were established until most of the troops were camped at Wood Creek at the south end of Lake Champlain. They struggled with supply and communication problems, but were still without opposition. Disease proved to be a greater enemy, and morale waned as summer grew into September. There is also evidence of intercolonial jealousies; difficulties with regulars, militia, and volunteers, most without military training; problems with the Indian troops; and the loss of local manpower to the expedition. One historian labeled this aspect of the campaign a catastrophe in the wilderness.

In Boston, the force under Vetch had exceeded the planned 1,200 men, and the campaign took on the stance of a crusade, but the British were yet to arrive. As troops trained and ships were readied, the expectations of Royal Navy arrival also began to dim, and a disgruntled attitude set in among the colonials. In addition, trade was at a standstill, and the gathered troops had to be supported.

By early fall, the leaders of the two gathered forces realized a campaign in 1709 had no chance for success. The impending danger of the Canadian winter was upon them and a naval approach on the St. Lawrence was out of the question. Yet the armies were maintained in hopes of using them for a less perilous and geographically closer objective. But in October, official word arrived in Boston that the operation had been canceled. The primary reason for abandoning the 1709 campaign was the potential for peace between the two warring powers, but the war in Europe was of greater importance to England. The British refused to support an offensive designed to take territory when a settlement would return any captured lands. The crown also saw the Canadian invasion as potentially dangerous and definitely expensive, but the decision, which had been reached in early July, was especially rankling to the colonies that had suffered the costs in manpower and assembling two considerable armies. The forces disbanded, and the Albany contingent even destroyed the structures they had built to supply a northern expedition.

Despite the dismal failure of the 1709 invasion of Canada, its significance should not be lost on history. The fact the British proposed to support an invasion force with 4,000 regular troops is the first instance of a crown army joining with a colonial force. In addition, the heretofore reluctance of the New York colony to aid a New England operation was overcome with backing from the British. It did, however, leave a sour taste in the colonies and proved to be a difficult decision for the disgruntled American leaders to grasp. Yet, they also learned another valuable lesson—to keep an agent at the English court to guard their interests and provide prompt transmission of royal decisions. The invasion of Canada was then planned for the following year and, finally, again in 1711, when the disastrous British loss of more than 800 men on the treacherous St. Lawrence occurred.

Boyd Childress

References
Wesley Frank Craven, *The Colonies in Transition, 1660–1713* (1968); Douglas Edward Leach, *Arms for Empire: A Military History of the British Colonies in North America, 1607–1763* (1973); Bruce T. McCully, "Catastrophe in the Wilderness: New Light on the Canada Expedition of 1709," *William and Mary Quarterly,* 3rd series, 11 (1954):441–456; Howard Henry Peckham, *The Colonial Wars, 1689–1762* (1964); Samuel Vetch, "Canada Survey'd," in *Calendar of State Papers, Colonial Series, America and the West Indies, June 1708–1709,* Vol. 24, no. 60, (1922):44–51; George Macgregor Waller, *Samuel Vetch: Colonial Enterpriser* (1960).

See also ACADIA, BRITISH CONQUEST OF (1710); CANADA, BRITISH EXPEDITION AGAINST (1711); NICHOLSON, FRANCIS; QUEEN ANNE'S WAR; VETCH, SAMUEL

Canada, British Expedition Against (1711)
Following the successful capture of Port Royal in 1710, Colonel Francis Nicholson sailed for England to promote another attempt to capture New France entirely. The English crown had agreed to such a plan in 1709, and soldiers and supplies had been raised in New England, but the British diverted their forces elsewhere at the last moment. Utilizing his success at Port Royal, Nicholson was able to persuade the crown to try for Canada once again. Recent developments in England and Europe, including a Tory victory in 1710 and the opening of secret peace talks with France, had lessened English military commitments on the Continent, but the New World remained a prime opportunity for a final victory and perhaps territorial expansion. For these reasons, the British crown provided unprecedented support for the expedition.

Nicholson arrived in Boston in early June and immediately informed the various governors involved. The plan called for the classic two-pronged assault first used by the colonies in 1690. Nicholson would lead a force of mainly New York and New Jersey troops, with Iroquois support, against Montreal from Albany. Quebec would be assaulted from the sea, involving a British fleet, regular troops, and New England provincials. Overall command of the Quebec force went to Sir Hovenden Walker, with Brigadier John Hill commanding the land troops.

Walker's fleet arrived in Boston on 24 June, and the size and obvious power of the force amazed the New Englanders. Walker had 15 men-of-war, mounting almost 900 guns, and manned by 5,000 seamen. In addition, 40 transport ships carried seven battalions of regular infantry, one battalion of marines, and a train of artillery, including horses. The soldiers disembarked and established a camp on Noodles Island in the harbor, and became a tourist attraction for the locals.

However, immediate friction erupted between British officers and Massachusetts authorities. The unexpected early arrival of the fleet had caught Massachusetts unprepared and, therefore, no provisions were waiting to feed the British soldiers and sailors. For the third year in a row, the people of Massachusetts were being asked to provide foodstuffs for a major expedition, and they had reached their limits, especially in terms of preserved foods. The British quartermaster general, Richard King, had little concern for the plight of New

England farmers. He had thousands of mouths to feed and had been led to expect provisions. King had storehouses and ships in the harbor searched for grain, and he cajoled and threatened Massachusetts authorities until local communities began sending in fresh provisions, mostly on the hoof. Actually, New York had promised to supply provisions, but refused to send the store ships until the British provided an armed escort. The warships were sent to New York and the provisions arrived in mid-July.

Beyond the problem of provisions, the British officers accused Bostonians of encouraging soldiers and sailors to desert. Admiral Walker threatened to impress locals to make up the losses, but Governor Joseph Dudley persuaded him against it. Laws were quickly passed imposing fines on anyone harboring a deserter.

In addition to fencing with British egos, Dudley had to raise two regiments of provincial soldiers, gather supplies for them, and arrange for transports. The assembly issued £40,000 in bills of credit to pay for the provincial contribution, and the two regiments, about 750 men each, were placed under the commands of Samuel Vetch and Shadrach Walton.

Finally, the huge fleet, increased now by the addition of provincial transports and store ships, set sail on 30 July. Adverse winds forced Walker to pause at Gaspé on 18 August. Two days later they sailed again, and on the 22nd found themselves in the St. Lawrence River enveloped in a thick fog. What happened next is somewhat controversial. Walker had no idea where the banks of the river were and believed the fleet lay closer to the south shore. He ordered all ships to heave to, pointing south, and retired for the night. The admiral was soon informed that land had been sighted. Neglecting to ask in which direction, he assumed it was the south shore and ordered the fleet to reverse direction and sail north.

Unfortunately, the fleet was actually quite near the north shore. A panicked infantry officer awoke Walker to tell him breakers had been seen, and Walker haughtily dismissed the landlubber. The officer tried again and Walker arrived on deck in dressing gown and slippers to find his flagship almost surrounded by breakers. The flag captain had ordered the anchor dropped, but Walker realized the error, ordered the anchor cable cut and all sails set, and thus brought the flagship out of danger. Signal guns were fired to alert the rest of the fleet. While most of the ships avoided destruction, eight

British transports did ground and break up on the coast. One provincial ship also went aground, but with no loss of life.

When dawn arrived, Walker ordered a search for survivors, and approximately 500 were rescued. But almost 900 had drowned. The numbers vary according to source. Francis Parkman provided the specific figures of 29 officers, 676 other ranks, and 35 regimental women, taken from army returns. No specific count of sailors lost exists, but Parkman estimated somewhat less than 200.

Although the majority of the fleet survived and Walker still had more than 6,000 soldiers available for duty, the loss of the transports discouraged the British officers, and Walker ordered a withdrawal. The New England transports sailed to Boston, where the news that such an enormous fleet and army had failed to even reach Quebec shocked the colonies. According to legend, when Francis Nicholson, preparing his army to march toward Montreal, heard of Walker's withdrawal and the end of all his plans, he snatched the wig off his head and threw it on the ground in a rage.

The loss of so many soldiers and the ignominious end of such an expensive expedition would normally have led to formal inquiries and investigations. The British government did order the pilots to England, but they were never questioned. With the war ending and the peace treaty under formal negotiation, the crown wanted the embarrassment of the Walker expedition simply to go away. As for Admiral Hovenden Walker, a week after his arrival in Portsmouth, England, his flagship exploded with the loss of most of his personal papers and journals, including Sir William Phips's journal of the 1690 Quebec expedition, and 400 sailors. Walker would publish his account of the expedition in 1720. According to Parkman, Walker was removed from command and stricken from the half-pay list. He later moved to South Carolina, and then to Barbados, where he died.

Steven C. Eames

References

Samuel Adams Drake, *The Border Wars of New England, Commonly Called King William's and Queen Anne's Wars* (1897), rpt. 1973; Francis Parkman, *A Half-Century of Conflict in France and England in North America* (1983); Samuel Penhallow, *The History of the Wars of New England with the Eastern Indians* (1726), rpt. 1973.

See also ACADIA, BRITISH CONQUEST OF (1710); CANADA, BRITISH EXPEDITION AGAINST (1709); NICHOLSON, FRANCIS; QUEEN ANNE'S WAR

Canada, British Expedition Against (1746–1747)

The capture of Louisbourg in 1745 revived memories of campaigns of earlier wars and inspired the British to plan a two-pronged assault against Quebec by a force proceeding up the St. Lawrence River in concert with another moving down Lake Champlain. American colonists were eager "to pursue their darling project, the reduction of Canada," but Cabinet politics and the military balance in the Low Countries had more to do with the planning of the expedition and its eventual cancellation than did American desires. In early 1746, as the threat of Bonnie Prince Charlie receded, the leaders of the British Cabinet, the duke of Newcastle, secretary of state for the southern department, his brother Henry Pelham, the prime minister, and Philip Yorke, Lord Chancellor Hardwicke, obliged King George II to divorce himself from his favorite and their rival, Lord Granville. Newcastle, Pelham, and Hardwicke required the allegiance of the duke of Bedford and William Pitt, and the price of their support was greater activity in America. In April 1746, the government agreed to a Canadian expedition. Admiral Sir Richard Lestock with 20 warships and Lieutenant General James St. Clair commanding eight regiments of regulars (5,600 troops) would sail up the St. Lawrence. Six of the regiments would be from England; two, William Shirley's and William Pepperrell, Jr.'s, were new American regiments stationed at Louisbourg. New England volunteers would augment the British troops and garrison Louisbourg. Colonies south of New England would raise a second detachment to advance from Albany under the command of Governor William Gooch of Virginia.

The duke of Newcastle announced the expedition 9 April 1746. The American response was very good considering recent drains on manpower. New York, Pennsylvania-Delaware, Maryland, and Virginia recruited 2,500 men who rendezvoused at Albany in August and September. The New England colonies raised 4,600, more than half from Massachusetts.

By May 1746, St. Clair and Lestock were ready to sail from Spithead, but delay after delay intervened: first, a series of contrary winds, then, the menace of the French fleet of the duc d'Anville, and finally, it was too late in the season. In August, the expedition was postponed until 1747, but on 12 January 1747, it was canceled. Despite worries about dampening the "ardour of our American colonies," the troops were needed to guard against a French invasion of Britain, and Admiral Peter Warren advised that the allocated forces could never capture Quebec.

American recruits experienced frustration or worse. The soldiers at Albany were inactive, bored, and without a proper commander (Gooch declined to serve because of ill health, and his replacement never arrived); sickness ravaged the camp, and many deserted before all were discharged late in the summer of 1747. Most of the New England troops never left their provinces; a few went on garrison service in Nova Scotia.

Cancellation of the expedition disappointed Americans. However, had it proceeded, we may presume it would have failed, for conquering Canada in 1759–1760 required a far bigger effort than was planned in 1746.

Joseph A. Devine, Jr.

References

Arthur H. Buffinton, "The Canada Expedition of 1746: Its Relation to British Politics," *American Historical Review,* XLV (1940):552–580; Thomas Hutchinson, *The History of the Colony and Province of Massachusetts Bay,* ed. by Lawrence S. Mayo, 3 vols. (1938); Herbert L. Osgood, *The American Colonies in the Eighteenth Century,* Vol. III (1924); John A. Schutz, *William Shirley: King's Governor of Massachusetts* (1961).

See also KING GEORGE'S WAR; LOUISBOURG, SIEGE OF (1745); PEPPERRELL, WILLIAM, JR.; SHIRLEY, WILLIAM

Canada, New England Expedition Against (1690)

The twin expeditions against French Canada launched from New England in the summer of 1690 were a direct outcome of the Glorious Revolution of 1688–1689 in England and America. The revolution, in which William of Orange and his wife, Mary, toppled Mary's father, James II, from the English throne, touched off open warfare between England and France

on both sides of the Atlantic. In Massachusetts, the old charter government that had been restored to power after the overthrow of James's Dominion of New England, struggled to defend the colony's eastern frontier against what it perceived as French-inspired Indian attacks. In New York, a revolutionary regime led by Jacob Leisler, a local militia captain, sought to extend its influence north toward Albany and maintain the vital English alliance with the powerful Iroquois Confederacy. Both governments came to see a direct attack on French Canada as a way to break out of an exhausting defensive stalemate and bolster their reputations at home and in London.

By the fall of 1689, plans occasionally advanced in earlier years for an expedition by land or sea against Canada were once more under discussion. The final impetus came from three concerted French and Indian raids early in 1690 that devastated the town of Schenectady, as well as several settlements in Maine. A seaborne expedition from Massachusetts commanded by Sir William Phips retaliated by plundering the French settlement of Port Royal in Acadia. On 1 May 1690, commissioners from New York, Massachusetts, Connecticut, and Plymouth met in New York and agreed to raise a force of some 850 men to reinforce Albany and attack Canada overland. A month later, encouraged by the deceptively easy success of its Port Royal venture, Massachusetts began to organize its own naval expedition against Quebec. Here were the seeds of the strategy of a two-pronged, land/sea assault on Canada that would be tried several times until its final success in 1759.

In 1690, however, the campaign was poorly planned and coordinated. The Connecticut government could not decide whether the land expedition was to be a feint or a full-scale attack. New York furnished less than half its quota of 400 men; Maryland supplied none of those it had promised, while the forces pledged from Massachusetts were diverted to the naval expedition and the defense of Maine. Further confusion attended the appointment of a commander for the land expedition: eventually, to preserve a semblance of cooperation with New England, Jacob Leisler accepted the appointment of Fitz-John Winthrop of Connecticut, a man of high social status but distinctly limited military talents. Winthrop reached Albany in July to find, he told Connecticut, "all in confusion and not now to be recovered." The assembled troops were plagued by smallpox and food poisoning caused by supplies of rotten pork, no arrangements had been made to cooperate with the Iroquois, and only a few of the canoes needed to transport the expedition once it reached Lake Champlain were ready. With some 500 men from New York, Albany, and Connecticut, Winthrop advanced 100 miles north of Albany, reaching Wood Creek on 7 August. There he found no more than a token contingent of Iroquois warriors ready to join the expedition. Despondent and demoralized, Winthrop and his officers resolved to abandon the enterprise, leaving behind a small force of 29 colonists and 120 Iroquois under Captain John Schuyler of Albany with instructions to raid the region around Montreal. Schuyler reached Canada early in September and laid waste several settlements south of the St. Lawrence River. By 21 August, however, Winthrop and the main force had made their way back to Albany to face the recriminations of those who had dispatched them.

The seaborne expedition, meanwhile, had grown into a formidable force of more than 30 vessels carrying 2,300 men from Massachusetts and Plymouth Colony under the command of Sir William Phips, the victor of Port Royal. Phips's flagship was the 44-gun *Six Friends*. But the fleet waited for weeks in Boston harbor in the vain hope of receiving a much needed supply of ammunition from England. It left port on 9 August—just as Winthrop and his forces were deciding to retreat—and arrived below the walls of Quebec only on 6 October (16 October by the New Style dating used by the French). It was too late to attempt anything more than a quick assault before the St. Lawrence River began to freeze over for the winter. By then, too, the element of surprise had been lost and the collapse of the land expedition's threat to Montreal had allowed the governor of French Canada, Louis de Buade de Frontenac, to concentrate all his forces in Quebec, outnumbering the besiegers. The town's fortifications were still rudimentary compared with those built in later years, consisting of wooden palisades augmented by several batteries of cannon. However, its rocky site commanding the river was naturally strong, and its garrison of professional soldiers was supported by a civilian population far more disciplined and experienced in the rigors of warfare than the farmers and fishermen of New England.

The New Englanders began their assault by sending a single envoy, Major Thomas Sav-age, with a demand for Quebec's surrender, an ultimatum curtly rejected by Frontenac and his assembled officers. The next day, 8 October, some 1,200 men were landed on the beaches two miles downstream and north of the town under the command of Major John Walley of Plymouth Colony. This force, it was hoped, would press an attack across the St. Charles River, a tributary of the St. Lawrence that guarded the northern flank of Quebec's Upper Town. Simultaneously, the fleet, led by Phips, would land a smaller force of 200 men in the Lower Town beneath the French fortification.

From the beginning, however, the main assault was inadequately coordinated and badly led. Soaked by their landing, buffeted by rainstorms, lacking blankets and adequate provisions, and harassed by skirmishing parties sent out by the French, the New England troops milled around in the swampy woods north of the St. Charles for four interminable days and three bone-chilling nights. None came close to pressing an attack upon the town. In the eyes of one trenchant observer, John Wise, a minister who accompanied the landing, the fault lay with Major Walley's leadership, his "Dismal downness of . . . Countenance & Spirit" and an irresolution that could only be attributed to "the Invincible Arrest of fear." To Wise's reproach that the troops were losing their opportunity, Walley replied simply and pathetically, "I cannot rule them." From Walley's perspective, as set out in his subsequent self-defense, the fault lay with the failure of Phips's fleet to support the land forces with provisions and with boats for their assault across the St. Charles. Instead, its warships sailed upriver to exhaust their limited supplies of ammunition in a fruitless bombardment of Quebec's cliffs and fortifications. Twenty-six cannonballs that landed in the gardens of the Hotel Dieu were gathered up by the convent's nuns and delivered to the French batteries for dispatch back at the invaders.

After two days ashore, Walley and his officers already despaired of their position and urged a return to the ships, only to find themselves unable to organize even a retreat in good order. One attempt, on the night of the third day, had to be abandoned because of the press of men on the beach struggling to reembark; a second, at dusk on 11 October, succeeded, but at the cost of leaving behind five of the six small cannon landed and a store of ammunition. Walley was among the first to take to the boats.

Back on board, the expedition's leaders debated what course to pursue. Some favored a new landing at a different spot or a ravaging of the countryside. But the troops were demoralized and exhausted, supplies low, and smallpox was spreading rapidly through the fleet. On 15 October, the expedition began a retreat downriver, pausing for an exchange of captives the following day. It had suffered only a handful of casualties—perhaps 30 men—on the battlefield, but many more died on the voyage home, of smallpox, dysentery, and frostbite. Stormy weather wrecked one vessel on Anticosti Island at the mouth of the St. Lawrence (from which a handful of survivors escaped to New England the following spring), and drove several others as far south as the Caribbean. Final estimates by contemporaries of the expedition's human cost, not counting those colonists back in New England who died from the diseases brought back by the fleet, ranged between 200 and 500 men. The toll was especially heavy among the Indian troops recruited from Plymouth Colony. Financially and politically, the failure of the two expeditions plunged the New England colonies into a morass of public debt and internal dissension that brought government to a virtual standstill. What one contemporary described as "the awfull Frowne of God in the disappointment of that chargable and hazardous Enterprize" played a key role in persuading Massachusetts and Plymouth to accept the reimposition of direct royal rule in the form of the Massachusetts charter of 1691.

Militarily, the expedition's only chance of success lay in coordination and surprise. Had the English fleet arrived earlier in the summer while Frontenac was still distracted by the overland threat against Montreal, then (as French leaders acknowledged) Quebec might have succumbed to a quick assault by superior numbers. By the time the fleet actually appeared, however, not even a more resolute performance than that offered by Phips, Walley, and their men could have offset the French advantage in numbers, leadership, training, and position. Plainly, Quebec remained the key obstacle to English America's conquest of its far smaller neighbor. Not until another 70 years had passed would a professional European siege force, an entire summer, and far better fortune succeed in cracking this nut of French resistance.

Richard R. Johnson

References
W.J. Eccles, *Frontenac: The Courtier Governor* (1959); Ernest Myrand, *Sir William Phips Devant Québec: Histoire d'un Siège* (1893); C.P. Stacey, ed., *Introduction to the Study of Military History for Canadian Students,* 5th ed. (1956); Walter K. Watkins, "The Expedition to Canada in 1690 under Sir William Phips," *Yearbook of the Society of Colonial Wars in the Commonwealth of Massachusetts for 1898,* no. 4 (1898):111–232; John Winthrop's letters in Massachusetts Historical Society, *Collections,* 5th ser., VIII (1882): 303–324; John Wise's narrative in ibid., *Proceedings,* 2nd ser., XV (1902):282–303.

See also FRONTENAC, LOUIS DE BUADE DE; KING WILLIAM'S WAR; LEISLER, JACOB; PHIPS, WILLIAM; WALLEY, JOHN; WINTHROP, JOHN (FITZ-JOHN)

C

Fort Canajoharie (New York)

Fort Canajoharie (Fort Cannatchoeri) was built by William Johnson in 1756 on the southern side of the Mohawk River, across from the mouth of East Canada Creek. Originally it served as a barracks and a fortified depot along the supply route to Oswego. The fort consisted of a square, four-bastioned, 15-foot-high stockade armed with swivel guns. The fort was most likely abandoned in 1764.

Elizabeth Gossman

See also JOHNSON, WILLIAM; FORT OSWEGO (NEW YORK)

Fort Canaseraga (New York)

Fort Canaseraga was located south of the confluence of Black Creek and Chittenago Creek. Originally on Oneida land, the site was first occupied by a Tuscaroran village. Some believe the fort was built by the Tuscarora to imitate the fortifications built by white settlers, but in fact, the Tuscarora had built many forts in North Carolina before moving to New York. A two-story blockhouse and a large gate were added to the fort in 1756 by Jacob Vroomen. Fort Canaseraga was taken on 23 October 1780 by an American force led by Captain Walter Vroomen. The fort was later lost in a surprise attack by a detachment of Butler's Rangers.

Elizabeth Gossman

Canso, Battle of (1744)

Canso was a fortified English fishing station established at the strait separating Cape Breton Island from the Nova Scotian peninsula. When war was declared between France and England in March 1744, Louisbourg's commandant received the news a month before authorities in Boston. This provided an opportunity to launch a surprise attack on Canso's unprepared garrison.

An expedition was mounted from Louisbourg under the command of François Joseph DuPont Duvivier, an untested, opportunistic garrison officer in the *Compagnies franches*. The volunteer French force consisted of 22 officers, 80 French soldiers, 37 Swiss of the Karrer Regiment, and 218 sailors. Resembling more a privateering venture conducted by amateurs than a military campaign, the expedition set sail for Canso in the privateer schooner *Succès* and a fleet of 14 fishing boats.

The sudden French appearance at Canso met no resistance from the English garrison commanded by Captain Patrick Heron, or from the sloop of war guardship, commanded by Lieutenant George Ryall, stationed in the harbor. The fortifications, allowed to lapse into a deplorable state of disrepair, were not defensible. The garrison (five companies of 31 men each) capitulated on 24 May 1744.

The burden of feeding the men, women, and children captives was avoided by paroling the military personnel provided they not bear arms against France for a period of one year. Released in September, the military captives were encouraged to repudiate their paroles, which were felt to have been extracted under duress, especially since their services would be needed for an anticipated expedition against Louisbourg.

The promise of shares in the booty from Canso had prompted recruitment of volunteers from Louisbourg's garrison, but the expedition's officers made off with the lion's share of the plunder before it could be turned over to a prize court. The inequality of the distribution became one of the flagrant injustices cited as a cause for the mutiny of Louisbourg's garrison later that year.

Unmolested further, the English reoccupied and fortified Canso early in the spring and used it as a staging base from which to launch their expedition against Louisbourg in April 1745.

John D. Hamilton

References

Boston Gazette, May 6, 1745; Allan Greer, *The Soldiers of Isle Royale, 1720–45*, Bulletin 28 History & Archeology, Parks Canada (1979):44–45; J.S. McLennan, *Louisbourg from Its Foundation to Its Fall, 1713–1758* (1918).

See also KING GEORGE'S WAR; LOUISBOURG, SIEGE OF (1745)

Captivity, European

From the earliest days of European settlement in North America, Europeans feared and wrote about their capture and the capture of their friends, family, and compatriots in a genre which became known as the captivity narrative. But in the history of Indian-white relations in the Americas, Europeans participated in the process of capturing indigenous peoples first by rounding up native people of the Americas and bringing them back to Europe as showpieces, and then in the notorious practice of capturing Africans by the millions and bringing them to both North and South America.

Beginning with Columbus's first voyage, Europeans took native peoples from the Western Hemisphere as prisoners, enslaved them, and took them home to display in markets and circuses. When Englishmen sailed the North Atlantic in the early 1600s, Indians were frequently abducted and carried to England for future use as guides and interpreters. Squanto of Plymouth was kidnapped to be sold into slavery in Spain. His English was learned on board ship and in England. Pocahontas was kidnapped by the early Virginia colonists. Even after European settlement, capture persisted as a practice of war.

Before the capture of Native Americans or Africans, Europe had a history of capture to acquire labor within Europe. In early modern Europe, people of the Mediterranean islands were captured and brought to the Iberian Peninsula, the Azores, and Madeira to plant and harvest rice. In the Caribbean, after the death of indigenous peoples as a result of infectious disease and overwork, a new labor force was captured out of West Africa. The major European players in the colonization who participated in the slave trade participated in the capture of indigenous people in the Americas. In the Southeast and Southwest of what is today the United States, the Spanish and French kidnapped natives in the sixteenth century. Spanish explorers forcibly took more than 1,000 southeastern Indians to the West Indies. Early French attempts at abduction also began in the sixteenth century. Participants included Giovanni da Verrazano (1524), Jacques Cartier (1534 and 1535), and Jean Ribault (1524). In the early eighteenth century, the French encouraged the capture of indigenous women in Canada for the settlements downriver in Louisiana. According to Peter H. Wood, by 1708 "there were at least 80 Indian slaves in the province, most of them young women" many of whom "soon died after enslavement."

Following Hernando Cortés's conquest of Mexico, what is today the American Southwest became the northern Spanish frontier. There the capture and enslavement of Indians was a common practice indeed. Slaving expeditions were practiced by Nuño de Guzman (1530s), the first governor of Mexico, who took 20 Acoma captives and sentenced them to servitude. Even though by 1526 slavery was illegal under Spanish law, raids were made against Plains Indian groups north of the Spanish borderlands, and orphans were used as forced labor on Spanish building projects. Governor Juan de Eulate (1618–1625) first sold Indians into slavery by shipping them to New Spain, but was then fined and had to release them and return them to Mexico.

After the Pequot War (1636–1637) in southern New England, the British enslaved 48 women and children in the Massachusetts Bay Colony and also exchanged Pequot warriors for African slaves in the West Indies. In 1675–1676, during King Philip's War, Richard Waldron of Dover captured 400 Abenakis and sold them into slavery. Occasionally, colonists bought Indian captives from other Indians.

In Virginia's Bacon's Rebellion (1675), Indians were also sold into slavery. In the Southeast during the early eighteenth century, British settlers arriving from the West Indies in Carolina made slaves of Indians captured in wars with the Coosas, Stonos, and Westos tribes. British colonists raided the Yamasee, Apalachee, and Timucua of northern Florida. Wood finds that the 1,400 Indians captured "became about a quarter of the slave population," while other captives were shipped off to other colonies, including New England and the West Indies. Thus in the Southeast, "numerous slave children were born of Black-Indian union." During the Tuscarora War (1711–1713), more than 400 Indian slaves were sold by the colonial government of North Carolina; in the Yamasee War that followed, South Carolina became a leader in Indian slaving.

Although the lore of Indian-white relations stresses Indians capturing hapless white victims, the record shows when war or profit were involved, this kind of "savagery" was not limited by color or culture.

June Namias

References

James Axtell, *The European and the Indian: Essays in the Ethnohistory of Colonial North America* (1981); ———, *The Invasion Within: The Conquest of Cultures in Colonial America* (1985); John Donald Duncan, "Indian Slavery," in *Race Relations in British North America, 1607–1783*, ed. by Bruce A. Glasrud and Alan M. Smith (1983); Carolyn Thomas Foreman, *Indians Abroad 1493–1938* (1943); Robert F. Heizer, "Indian Servitude in California," in *Handbook of North American Indians*, Vol. 4, *History of Indian-White Relations*, ed. by Wilcomb E. Washburn (1988): 414–416.

Yasuhide Kawashima, "Indian Servitude in the Northeast," in *Handbook of North American Indians*, Vol. 4, *History of Indian-White Relations*, ed. by Wilcomb E. Washburn (1988):404–406; Neal Salisbury, *Manitou and Providence: Indians, Europeans, and the Making of New England, 1500–1643* (1982); Albert H. Schroeder and Omer Stewart, "Indian Servitude in the Southwest," in *Handbook of North American Indians*, Vol. 4, *History of Indian-White Relations*, ed. by Wilcomb E. Washburn (1988):410–413.

Charles Verlinden, *The Beginnings of Modern Colonization: Eleven Essays*, trans. by Yvonne Freccero (1970); Peter H. Wood, "Indian Servitude in the Southeast," in *Handbook of North American Indians*, Vol. 4, *History of Indian-White Relations*, ed. by Wilcomb E. Washburn (1988):407–409.

Captivity, Indian

See INDIAN WARFARE, CAPTIVITY

Captivity Narratives

"On the tenth of *February,* 1675 came the *Indians* with great numbers upon *Lancaster.*" With these opening lines began the first narrative of North American captivity in the English language, *The Sovereignty and Goodness of God* (1682). In her description of the attack on the frontier town of Lancaster, Massachusetts, Mary White Rowlandson constructed a spiritual autobiography of her 13 weeks among the Narragansetts and Wampanoags in late winter and early spring of 1675 during King Philip's War. It became a best seller of its day. First printed simultaneously in London, England, and Cambridge, Massachusetts, often published under the title *A True History of the Captivity & Restoration of Mrs. Mary Rowlandson,* and revived as a popular piece during the American Revolution, the narrative has appeared in more than 30 editions.

In 1704, during Queen Anne's War, Abenaki and French forces attacked frontier settlements in southern Maine, New Hampshire, and central Massachusetts. Thirty-eight residents of Deerfield, Massachusetts, were killed, and more than 100 captured and taken to Canada. Most, but not all, returned after peace negotiations with the French and Canadian Indians. Eunice Williams, the young daughter of Deerfield's Congregational minister, John Williams, did not. She later married and lived the rest of her life with the Catholic Caughnawagas (Mohawks and Oneidas) near Montreal. On his return to Massachusetts, Williams wrote *The Redeemed Captive Returning to Zion* (1707), which sold more than100,000 copies in its first year and has been reissued under various titles in multiple editions down to the present day.

While attacks and captures by Indians were not everyday experiences along the Atlantic and Appalachian frontiers, they were not uncommon. In New England between 1675 and 1763, an estimated 1,641 white captives were taken. Although Indian capture was a central piece in the indigenous system of making war used earlier on native people by other indigenous enemies, New England Puritans like Cotton Mather viewed the experience as an act of providence sent down upon them by an angry God as punishment for the sins of the new Zion gone astray in the wilderness. Built, then, upon actual events during the colonial Indian wars of the seventeenth and early eighteenth centuries, Puritan writings of ministers and captives evolved from religious experience pieces into nineteenth- and twentieth-century works of ethnography, propaganda, and popular culture.

At the same time, some narratives contained fairly accurate ethnographic content. As politics and history, the hundreds of narratives which were written provide early windows on to Anglo-American, Indian, and French interaction in North America. The narratives of Mary Jemison, Colonel James Smith, John Dunn Hunter, and John Tanner depict Euro-Americans of the late eighteenth and early nineteenth centuries captured in war, all of whom lived at length with Indians, were sympathetic and objective enough to offer up to Anglo-American readers information about the native societies in which they lived.

One important function of the narratives from their inception was their propaganda use. The story of Anglo-American settlement and conquest was one of high drama. It pitted white men and women against the natural elements, but was also a drama that scripted white actors against a field of native, in Mather's term, "tawney," inhabitants. Propagandistic and racist elements appeared in narratives from the outset, with New England natives being called "savages," "wolves," and "furious Tawnies"; Indians were often cast as barbarous devils and contrasted with "civilized" whites. Their use of capture, attack, and torture were justifications for Euro-American warfare, expropriation of land, and extermination. Historian Richard Slotkin found mythic power in these narratives exerted first on the frontier, then on a migrating and industrializing culture. He suggested them as the prototypes for American violence.

Although the Puritan narratives were high on biblical citation and didacticism, the captivity narrative itself evolved into the eighteenth and early nineteenth century as a form of patriotic gore, folklore, and wild fiction. By 1800, besides Rowlandson and Williams, Captain John Smith, Father Isaac Jogues, Hannah Duston, Eunice Williams, Mary Jemison, Daniel Boone, and his daughter, Jemima, all became well-known subjects of captivity literature. From history and folklore themes the narratives became further exaggerated and modified into fictional works such as *The Last of the Mohicans* (1824), and dime novels like Ann Sophia Stephens's *Malaeska, The Indian Wife of the White Hunter* (1860), the story of an Indian woman who turned out to be a white captive.

Besides making historical and literary best sellers, captivity themes became a staple of American art and popular culture. In the nineteenth century they were used in the creation of many popular works of art by such American artists as John Vanderlyn, Asher Durand,

Erastus Dow Palmer, and Charles (Carl) Wimar. In the mid- to late-twentieth century, popular films such as *The Searchers, The Emerald Forest, Dances with Wolves,* and *The Last of the Mohicans* portray white men, women, and children captured in war and transformed into Indians.

Unifying the power of captivity materials of all forms and eras was the gendered nature of the roles of men and women they portrayed. Narratives, drawing, sculpture, and film all showed Anglo-American men and women on foreign ground, and tested the notions of gender and sexuality across cultural boundaries. Thus the colonial Indian-white encounter through the captivity narrative left a formidable print on American history, politics, notions of gender, race, the arts, and popular culture.

June Namias

References

Annette Kolodny, *The Land Before Her: Fantasy and Experience of the American Frontiers, 1630–1860* (1984); James Levernier and Hennig Cohen, eds., *The Indians and Their Captives* (1977); June Namias, *White Captives: Gender and Ethnicity on the American Frontier* (1993); Roy Harvey Pearce, "The Significances of the Captivity Narrative," *American Literature* 19 (1947): 1–20; James E. Seaver, *A Narrative of the Life of Mrs. Mary Jemison* (1824), ed. by June Namias (1992).

Richard Slotkin, *Regeneration through Violence: The Mythology of the American Frontier, 1600–1860* (1973); Richard VanDerBeets, ed., *Held Captive by Indians: Selective Narratives: 1642–1836* (1973); Alden T. Vaughan, *Narratives of North American Indian Captivity: A Selective Bibliography* (1983).

Alden T. Vaughan and Edward W. Clark, eds., *Puritans among the Indians: Accounts of Captivity and Redemption 1676–1724* (1981); Wilcomb E. Washburn, ed., *The Garland Library of Narratives of North American Indian Captivities,* 111 vols. (1976–1983).

See also DUSTON, HANNAH; INDIAN WARFARE, CAPTIVITY; JEMISON, MARY

Fort Carillon (New York)
See FORT TICONDEROGA (NEW YORK)

Carlisle, Camp Near (Pennsylvania)

Lying 18 miles west of the Susquehanna River in the Cumberland Valley, Carlisle was the eastern terminus of Forbes's Road to the forks of the Ohio. In spring 1758, the northern half of General John Forbes's army gathered there for his expedition to the Ohio country. In 1757, Colonel John Stanwix arrived in Carlisle with five companies of men to construct a large camp which could accommodate Forbes's forces. The result was an enormous earthworks enclosure of mounds and ditches, 630 feet by 375 feet in size. It was intended to accommodate an encampment of as many as 1,500 soldiers; it also enclosed livestock pens and storage areas for supply wagons and artillery. A series of storage sheds stood along one side of the encampment, while its central space was occupied by rows of tents for the soldiers.

The Carlisle camp was the staging ground for one of the most significant expeditions of the Seven Years' War in America. Second in command to General Forbes at Carlisle in the spring of 1758 was Colonel Henry Bouquet, commander of the Royal Americans, of which a division of the first battalion—perhaps 365 soldiers—participated in the Forbes campaign. The Royal Americans were recruited in the colonies and consisted mostly of non-English speakers, particularly Pennsylvania Germans; its officers came mostly from other Protestant European nations (Bouquet was Swiss). Third in command for the Forbes expedition was Colonel John Armstrong, commander of the First Pennsylvania Battalion. In all, about 2,200 members of the Pennsylvania militia gathered at Carlisle. The final component of Forbes's northern force was a battalion of Scottish Highlanders numbering nearly 1,300 under the command of Colonel Archibald Montgomery.

The earthworks at Carlisle were almost in ruins by 1762, but with the outbreak of Pontiac's War in the following year, Carlisle once again became a staging ground for a western campaign.

Eric Hinderaker

References

C. Hale Sipe, *Fort Ligonier and Its Times* (1932); Charles Morse Stotz, *Outposts of the War for Empire: The French and English in Western Pennsylvania; Their Armies, Their Forts, Their People, 1749–1764* (1985).

See also FORBES EXPEDITION OF 1758; FORT LIGONIER (PENNSYLVANIA); FORT LOUDOUN (PENNSYLVANIA); PONTIAC'S WAR

Fort Caroline (Florida)

Fort Caroline was founded in 1564 by René Laudonnière. He served under Jean Ribault, leader of an expedition of French Huguenots to colonize Florida. Until that time Florida had been exclusively claimed by the Spanish. On 25 June 1564, Laudonnière established his base, naming it La Caroline after Charles IX, king of France. Although the expedition was predominantly Protestant, it included some Catholics.

Fort Caroline was located on the south bank of the St. Johns River, near St. Johns Bluff, about ten miles east of modern-day Jacksonville. Placed on a flat plain to the west of the bluff, the fortifications were in the form of the letter "A," with the base toward the river. The settlers dug moats on the sides of the fort, with a palisade toward the river. The most impressive part was a stone gateway on the south side. A great deal of detail is known of the fortifications because an artist, Jacques Le Moyne, accompanied the group and made numerous drawings.

Shortly after the establishment of Fort Caroline, Ribault returned to France for supplies. By summer 1565, the situation was becoming serious; the fort was running out of supplies. On 3 August 1565, British privateer John Hawkins stopped and left a few provisions. The situation in the colony had become so severe that Laudonnière was preparing to return his group to France. By mid-August, with preparations to abandon the fort fully underway, word came that Ribault had returned with reinforcements. Although Ribault had been commissioned to replace Laudonnière, he left the latter in command of Caroline.

Shortly after Ribault returned, the Spaniards arrived to retake the land settled by the French. The Spanish expedition was led by Pedro Menéndez de Avilés. The two opponents first met on 4 September at sea. The French fled from the Spanish and eventually returned to Fort Caroline. On 8 September 1565, Menéndez landed at St. Augustine.

At Caroline, Laudonnière fell ill and was unable to be moved. The other captains resolved to mass all of their forces and attack the Spanish while they unloaded their ships at St. Augustine. Barely 120–140 men were left at Caroline, under the command of Laudonnière

and the Sieur de Lys. Menéndez was able to get his flagship launched when the French were first sighted. The French then gave him chase. At that point, a storm drove the French much further to the south. Menéndez returned to St. Augustine and planned a counterattack on Fort Caroline, which he reasoned was poorly protected since most of the French forces already had been dispatched. Using what would later be called the Matanzas River, he crossed overland to the lower St. Johns River, thereby approaching Fort Caroline from its poorly defended rear. At daybreak on 20 September 1565, the Spaniards attacked. Records indicate 132 Frenchmen were killed or executed, and 45 escaped. The women and children were captured and eventually returned to France. As the remainder of the French straggled back, they were captured by the Spanish and put to the sword, thus giving the Matanzas (Slaughter) River its name.

Menéndez captured the French cannon and munitions. He also gained their strongbox, which contained the legal documentation of the settlement. On 23 September, Menéndez left, having renamed the fort San Mateo, leaving it under the command of Gonzalo de Villaroel.

John F. Schwaller

References

Charles E. Bennett, *Laudonnière and Fort Caroline, History and Documents* (1964); ———, compiler, *The Settlement of Florida* (1968); Rene Goulaine de Laudonnière, *Three Voyages*, trans. by Charles E. Bennett (1975); Jean Ribault, *The Whole and True Discoverye of Terra Florida* (1563) facsimile ed. 1964.

See also LAUDONNIÈRE, RENE; MENÉNDEZ DE AVILÉS, PEDRO; RIBAULT, JEAN; FORT SAN MATEO (FLORIDA)

Cartagena, Expedition Against (1741)

For Britain, an expedition "to take and hold" a flourishing port in the Spanish Caribbean was a natural beginning to the War of Jenkins' Ear. Britain went to war because of Spain's restraints on foreigners trading to her West Indian empire, and Vice Admiral Edward Vernon's November 1739 raid on Porto Bello, in the Isthmus of Panama, had demonstrated Spain's weakness in the Caribbean, an area where France might not intervene to protect Spanish possessions.

An expedition was planned to arrive in the Caribbean before the 1741 rainy season. Command arrangements, bad from the start, were worsened by deaths and clashing personalities. The navy and army had independent commanders. The able, strong-willed Admiral Vernon, a national hero, headed the navy; Lord Cathcart, a respected veteran of Marlborough's wars, was to command the army; and another of Marlborough's men, Alexander Spotswood, former governor of Virginia, was to be colonel of an American regiment and second-ranking army commander. But Cathcart and Spotswood died before reaching the Caribbean. The inexperienced Brigadier General Thomas Wentworth replaced Cathcart, while the governor of Virginia, William Gooch, took charge of the Americans. Vernon and Wentworth soon quarreled, and within the land forces, Wentworth nourished suspicions that Gooch was a rival for top command.

The duke of Newcastle, the secretary of state in charge of the war, anticipated that "the very great Number of very good men" in British North America would flesh out the 5,800 soldiers coming from England. In January 1740, Newcastle invited American governors from New England to North Carolina (South Carolina was preoccupied with St. Augustine) to recruit troops. American response was enthusiastic. The British had planned for 3,000, but more than 3,700 were recruited. Although Virginia drafted vagrants, and many from Pennsylvania (which supplied the biggest group of 700) were fleeing indentured service, most were enthusiastic volunteers seeking adventure, plunder, pay, and conquered land. Middle- and upper-class Americans like Lawrence Washington of Virginia, a North Carolina councilor, and sons of two New York governors received officer's commissions. Each 100-man company had an American captain, second lieutenant, and ensign, but the field grade officers, first lieutenants, and a leavening of noncoms were Englishmen.

The most tempting Spanish target was Havana; but Cartagena, on the coast of what is now Colombia, seemed more vulnerable. In January 1741, the largest military force yet seen in the Caribbean—37 warships and an army of 5,800 British, 3,600 Americans, and 500 Jamaicans—left Jamaica for Cartagena. Enroute, three precious weeks were lost as Vernon fruitlessly sought a menacing French fleet. When the expedition arrived off Cartagena on 5 March, the rainy season was perilously close. At first

Spanish resistance seemed slight, but the expedition had internal problems. Vernon and Wentworth began bickering and soon despised each other. Governor Gooch and his Americans were unhappy that most Americans were retained aboard their transports long after the British were landed, and that some Americans were used as sailors. Only 200 Americans, under Captain Lawrence Washington, helped take outlying posts.

By the end of March, only a single fort, Fort St. Lazarus, was left defending the city. Vernon sent optimistic dispatches home, causing premature rejoicing at the defeat of the Spaniards. But siege preparations before St. Lazarus did not frighten Don Blas de Lesos and his garrison into surrendering. Heavy rains began, and the attackers began succumbing to diseases that are well described in Tobias Smollett's novel, *Roderick Random*. Wentworth decided that before all his men died he had to risk everything on a predawn assault. On 9 April, Wentworth sent two columns of his best solders, about 1,500 British, supported by 150 Americans carrying scaling ladders, against two sides of the fort. The Spanish were ready. The British were flattened, the Americans ran away, and Cartagena was safe.

The expedition returned to Jamaica, but only after Vernon spent three weeks demolishing fortifications while sickening colonial and British soldiers languished aboard transports as vultures and sharks devoured the dead tossed overboard. The mortality rate was horrendous. Of 5,800 British soldiers and 3,700 Americans, only 3,200 and 2,700, respectively, reached Jamaica in May, and most of these died within a year. Before the expedition was disbanded in December 1742, abortive attempts were made against Santiago, Cuba, and Panama City, and Rattan was occupied. Only about 10 percent of the Americans returned home.

Americans and British serving on this expedition were conscious of their different backgrounds, and some historians think the awareness extended to a recognition of different nationality. Americans remembered a series of horrible experiences, the worst being disease and Spanish bullets. Americans may have resented not being placed in the front of battle; they certainly resented receiving fewer battlefield commissions than Englishmen, but surviving American officers were cheered when, after an initial refusal, they received half-pay pensions for life. Vernon, Wentworth, and Prime

C

Minister Robert Walpole all had their reputations damaged by this expedition, but Vernon's name was immortalized because an admiring American officer bestowed it on the plantation later inherited by his famous half-brother.

Joseph A. Devine, Jr.

References

Albert Harkness, Jr., "Americanism and Jenkins' Ear," *Mississippi Valley Historical Review,* XXXVII (1950):61–90; E. Alfred Jones, "The American Regiment in the Carthagena Expedition," *Virginia Magazine of History and Biography,* XXX (1922):1–20; Charles E. Nowell, "The Defense of Cartagena," *The Hispanic American Historical Review,* XLII (1962):478–501; Herbert W. Richmond, *The Navy in the War of 1739–48,* 3 vols. (1920); *The Vernon Papers,* B. McL. Ranft, ed., *Publications of the Navy Records Society,* XCIX (1958).

See also ANGLO-SPANISH WAR (1739–1744); PORTO BELLO, ATTACK ON; ROBERTSON, JAMES; VERNON, EDWARD

Casco Bay

Casco Bay, stretching 18 miles at its mouth between Cape Elizabeth on the west and Cape Small on the east, is one of the major features of the Maine coast, most remarkable for its 136 officially-cataloged islands.

Its main significance during the colonial wars was as the site of Fort Loyal on Falmouth Neck near the center of modern-day Portland. Not only did the fort and its immediate surroundings figure in several important military encounters, but its location near the contested frontier between New England and Acadia made it an obvious meeting place for negotiations between foes.

"Casco," or "Casco Bay," thus became the designated site for several councils and the name attached to three treaties between New England authorities and various combinations of Indians—the first ending the northeastern version of King Philip's War in 1678; the second a pledge of mutual peace, soon broken, between Governor Joseph Dudley of Massachusetts and the Maine Indians in 1702; and the third a treaty of peace in 1726 ending the three-year period of hostilities known as "Dummer's War."

Charles E. Clark

See also BRACKETT'S WOODS, BATTLE OF; DUMMER'S TREATY; DUMMER'S WAR; FALMOUTH, BATTLE OF; FORT LOYAL (MAINE); FORT NEW CASCO (MAINE)

Fort Casimer (Delaware)

Founded on 19 July 1651 by Dutch settlers from New Amsterdam, Fort Casimer was situated on the Delaware River between Swedish Forts Christina (approximately seven miles below at New Castle, Delaware) and Elfsborg. Its purpose was to control some of the water routes to New Sweden because the Swedes had rendered the Dutch Fort Nassau in New Jersey useless by the control of water routes to it. Fort Casimer could effectively control the Delaware River and was a very real threat to the survival of New Sweden. Petrus (Peter) Stuyvesant, the governor of New Netherland, acted on his own authority in this instance without orders from his superiors in New Amsterdam.

Fort Casimer was constructed in a short time by 200 Dutch soldiers. It was 210 feet long and 105 feet wide. Its earthen ramparts were mounted with 12 cannon, some of which were taken from the now abandoned Fort Nassau in New Jersey. Several Dutch families, some of whom came from Fort Nassau, settled there to secure the Dutch claim to the area. Twenty-two houses were constructed in the vicinity of the fort.

Johan Classon Rising attacked and captured Fort Casimer on 5 November 1651. This was not difficult to do because, despite the importance of this fort, the Dutch garrison consisted of only nine men, none of whom had gunpowder. Rising renamed the fort Trinity to commemorate the day—Trinity Sunday—on which it was captured. The Dutch settlers were given the option of leaving their lands or swearing an oath of loyalty to the Swedish crown. Most of the settlers decided to stay. In 1655, the Swedes improved the defenses of the fort by building a rampart and two bastions close by the river.

Petrus Stuyvesant retook Fort Casimer on 26 September 1655 during his campaign against New Sweden. For 15 years the Dutch West India Company's North American colony was engaged in a war with Sweden's colony. For this effort the Dutch West India Company was granted a sizable portion of New Sweden. Thus, in 1655, Fort Casimer became the seat of Dutch authority in New Jersey and Delaware. Its ramparts were improved and a large garrison was stationed there.

In 1657, the site was given to New Amsterdam, and on 21 April, 160 Dutch settlers from that city settled in the vicinity of the fort under the leadership of Jacob Alrichs. The area was renamed New Amstel. Alrichs was replaced in 1659 by Alexander d'Hinoyossa. The community surrendered to the English in 1664.

Anthony P. Inguanzo

References

Charles M. Andrews, *The Colonial Period of American History,* 4 vols. (1934–1938); Oliver Perry Chitwood, *A History of Colonial America* (1961); James F. Jameson, ed., *Narratives of New Netherland 1609–1664* (1909); Arthur M. Schlesinger, Jr., ed., *The Almanac of American History* (1983); Louis B. Wright, *The Atlantic Frontier: Colonial American Civilization 1607–1763* (1947).

See also FORT ELFSBORG (NEW JERSEY); FORT NASSAU (NEW JERSEY); NEW SWEDEN; STUYVESANT, PETRUS

Catawba

The Catawba were the largest of a number of eastern Siouan tribes that lived in the Carolina backcountry in the historic period. During this time, they occupied a gradually decreasing area in South Carolina and North Carolina, near the river that bears their name.

The Catawba had some contact with early Spanish explorers, including Hernando de Soto and Juan Pardo. In the last quarter of the seventeenth century, they developed increasingly strong ties with Virginia traders. Located on the well-traveled Occaneechee trading path, the Catawba were confederated with nearby tribes such as the Waxhaw and the Sugeree and had an extensive communication network throughout the piedmont into the mountains. They were perfectly situated to act as middlemen in the colonial trading nexus. During the eighteenth century, South Carolina traders gradually gained trade primacy in the Catawba region and increasingly used the tribe as military allies, especially as a bulwark against the Cherokee. The colony of North Carolina was not heavily involved in trade with the tribe.

With the exception of the Yamasee War of 1715, the Catawba had relatively harmonious relationships with colonial governments. They were traditional enemies of the eastern North Carolina Tuscarora, the five nations of the Iroquois Confederacy, and the Shawnee. King Hagler, the last noted Catawba chief, was killed by a Shawnee raiding party in 1763. The Catawba fought alongside the English in the Cherokee War of the late 1750s and early 1760s.

Like other Carolina tribes, the Catawba suffered terribly from imported diseases, particularly smallpox epidemics in 1718, 1738, and 1759. The last, which occurred during the Cherokee War, reduced their population by more than half. They also suffered from the almost constant skirmishing with hostile Iroquian tribes. The Catawba survived by absorbing many of the smaller, related tribes, whose populations had likewise been decimated by disease and conflict. In the early 1740s, trader James Adair counted 20 "dialects," spoken in the Catawba nation, direct evidence of this assimilation. These included Wateree, Yamasee, Eno, and Congaree. Adair estimated there were 400 Catawba fighting men in 1743. By the end of the Cherokee War, however, the number of Catawba warriors had dropped to about 100.

White settlers reached the Catawba territory in increasing numbers in the middle of the eighteenth century, creating conflicts over land, trade, wildlife, and livestock. The rate of settlement accelerated after the conclusion of the Cherokee War. At the Augusta Congress of 1763, the Catawba were granted a reservation of 15 square miles near present-day Rock Hill, South Carolina. Their descendants still live in the area.

Jim Sumner

References

Douglas S. Brown, *The Catawba Indians: The People of the River* (1966); Charles M. Hudson, *The Catawba Nation* (1970); James H. Merrell, *The Indians' New World: Catawbas and Their Neighbors from European Contact through the Era of Removal* (1989).

See also AUGUSTA, CONGRESS OF; SCHENCKINGH'S FORT (SOUTH CAROLINA); YAMASEE WAR

Caughnawaga (Kahnawaké since 1980)

An Iroquois reserve near Montreal, which originated as a Jesuit refuge, was organized by Father Raffeix in 1667 on Prairie de la Madeleine seigneury for Oneida converts. Here the Jesuits sent their catechumens, especially Mohawks, to complete their religious instruction before baptism. The soil was allegedly unsuitable to growing corn, so the native settlement was moved in 1676 to Sault St. Louis seigneury at the Lachine River rapids granted conjointly to the missionaries and the "domiciled natives." The seigneury was enlarged in 1680 by letters patent granted by Louis XIV stipulating that the land would revert to the crown if the Indians abandoned it.

The mission lived under the threat of attack as the Five Nations entered into the Covenant Chain agreement with the English. Canadian Governor Joseph-Antoine Le Febvre de La Barre's ill-fated expedition against them in 1684, and Jacques-René de Brisay de Denonville's retaliatory raid against the Seneca in 1687, were followed by a devastating Iroquois raid on Lachine in 1689 which forced the inhabitants of the reserve to take refuge within the walls of Montreal. In 1690, and again in 1696, when Louis de Buade de Frontenac dealt a crippling blow to the Onondaga and Oneida, the settlement was moved a short distance upstream. The Treaty of Montreal (1701) ended the Iroquois Wars and opened the way for the domiciled natives to engage in trade with Albany and New York, much of it illicit and in the interest of Montreal merchants. They joined with Canadian militiamen in raids on Massachusetts in 1704 and 1707.

In 1716, the settlement began moving to its present site because of soil exhaustion and scarcity of wood, and also to isolate it from the evil influences of the colonists, especially intoxicants, banned since 1669. The population was augmented by captive Pawnee, Illinois, Chickasaws, and even English adopted into the community. In the Seven Years' War, the Mohawks joined the Anglo-American invaders and the Kahnawaké people remained loyal to France. The capitulation of Montreal guaranteed their status quo, but under British rule they began petitioning for title to Kahnawaké. General Thomas Gage in 1762 was prepared to accede to their demands, but changed his mind after examining the original documents. The land reverted to the British crown with all the Jesuits estates in 1800 upon the death of the last Jesuit survivor, and Kahnawaké was officially designated a reserve and its inhabitants an Indian band.

Cornelius J. Jaenen

References
Henri Béchard, *The Original Caughnawaga Indians* (1976); E.J. Devine, *Historic Caughnawaga* (1922); R.A. Goldstein, *French-Iroquois Diplomatic and Military Relations, 1609–1701* (1969); Cornelius J. Jaenen, *The French Relationship with the Native Peoples of New France* (1984).

See also COVENANT CHAIN; IROQUOIS; IROQUOIS TREATIES OF 1700 AND 1701; IROQUOIS WARS; JESUITS; ONEIDA

Cayuga
The Cayuga nation was one of the Younger Brothers of the League of the Iroquois, located between the Onondagas and the Senecas on the west side of the longhouse. In the seventeenth century their warriors numbered 300, about twice the number of the Oneida, the other Younger Brother of the League with whom the Cayugas sat in the councils of the league. Their population was approximately equal to the Mohawk's and the Onondaga's and a quarter to a third of the Seneca's.

The Cayugas lived in an area between Cayuga and Owasco Lakes, now part of Cayuga County in New York state. They hunted a considerably larger area, including the territory around both these lakes, extending north to Lake Ontario and south toward the Susquehanna River. The area around their three principal villages, Oiogouen, Thiohero, and Onontaré, abounded in deer; consequently, the Cayugas relied more on hunting than did other Iroquois tribes. Also plentiful in the area were various fish and birds.

In 1653, after the Iroquois had defeated the Hurons, Petuns, and Neutrals, the Cayugas joined in the Five Nations' peace with the French, which resulted in a brief visit by the Jesuit, René Ménard, in the fall of 1656. During the Susquehannock War, a Cayuga chief led a Cayuga and Onondaga delegation to Montreal in 1661 and gained peace with the French. Another Jesuit, Simon Le Moyne, visited the Cayugas in the winter of 1661–1662. Some Cayugas traveled to Quebec asking for missionaries in 1664, but Alexander de Prouville de Tracy's 1666 attack on the Mohawks prevented the Jesuits from sending one. Waging war with the Susquehannocks during the 1660s pushed the Cayugas closer to the French, and in 1668 both the Sulpicians and Jesuits established missions in Cayuga villages. After the Susque-hannocks were defeated, the need for close re-lations with the French declined, and in 1682 a Jesuit missionary was forced to leave.

Relations between the Five Nations and the French worsened in the late 1680s and 1690s, with French expeditions burning Iro-quois villages in 1687, 1693, and 1696. Louis de Buade de Frontenac had planned to attack the Cayugas in 1696, but after destroying Onondaga and Oneida villages, he decided to leave the Cayuga alone. Thus, the Cayuga was the only nation in the league to escape French attack in the years preceding the 1701 peace between the Iroquois and French.

The Cayugas enjoyed the league's general neutrality regarding European conflicts during the first half of the eighteenth century. The Cayugas continued to trade with the French and British. Peace at home allowed the Cayugas to spread their villages and homes. During this period, Cayugas built villages on the west side of Cayuga Lake and to the south toward the Susquehanna River, but their principal village remained on the east side of the lake.

The year before the French and Indian War began, the Tutelo and Saponi, Siouan speakers originally from Virginia, settled on Cayuga land following their adoption by the Cayuga.

Cayugas tried to remain neutral when the Revolutionary War began, but then they joined the British. Two detachments from General John Sullivan's expedition, which were to de-stroy the Seneca, leveled Cayuga villages on both the east and west sides of Cayuga Lake in 1779. After the American Revolution, many Cayuga moved to the Six Nations Reserve in Canada. Cayugas remaining in New York even-tually sold their land to the state of New York and moved to live with the Sandusky Senecas in Ohio.

Sean O'Neill

See also FRONTENAC, LOUIS DE BUADE DE; IROQUOIS; IROQUOIS TREATIES OF 1700 AND 1701; JESUITS

Chabert de Joncaire, Louis-Thomas (known as Sononchiez by the Iroquois, c. 1670–1739)

Born in France, Louis-Thomas Chabert de Jon-caire came to Canada at about age 20 as a ser-geant in the colonial troops. Soon after, he was lucky to survive the adventure which became

the foundation for the considerable influence he wielded in later years. Captured by the Senecas, he faced the possibility of torture and death, but instead was officially adopted into that nation. He graduated from prisoner to official hostage to two-way spokesman, of the mold made fa-mous by T.E. Lawrence. To the Indians, he was a French trader with a permanent post near Geneva, New York. At Montreal, where he also had a home, he seemed ersatz Seneca, familiar with the language and key personalities, with a wife and words that had weight on both sides.

During 1700–1701, Joncaire took a leading part in the complicated negotiations by which Canada brokered a general peace between its traditional Indian allies and the previously hos-tile Iroquois, and bound the Iroquois to neutral-ity in future British-French disputes. In 1709, he led a conspiracy to murder British Indian agent Louis Montour and prevent disruption of the Canadian trading network in the Great Lakes. In 1717, he "presented" his 10-year-old son from Montreal to the Senecas; young Philippe-Tho-mas had an Iroquois upbringing from that time, groomed to follow in dad's footsteps.

Reaching the peak of his influence among the Western Iroquois, in 1720 Joncaire won permission to establish a trading post at the strategic lower end of the portage around Nia-gara Falls. By 1723 it had expanded into a for-tified position capable of taking a 300-soldier garrison. This was a significant victory for French policy, which aimed to dominate traffic through Lake Ontario with a string of forts along the northern margin. He commanded there with the rank of lieutenant in the colonial troops until 1726, remained an active agent of Canadian empire through the 1730s, and died at Niagara when that empire—of which his unusual bicultural career was both a product and a key support—was at its peak.

Malcolm MacLeod

References

E.B. O'Callaghan, ed., *Documents Rela-tive to the Colonial History of the State of New York*, 15 vols. (1853–1887) 4, 5, 9; *Dic-tionary of Canadian Biography*, 12 vols. (1966–1982) 2; F.H. Severance, *An Old Fron-tier of France* (1917); Peter Wraxall, *An Abridgement of the Indian Affairs . . .* (1915).

See also CHABERT DE JONCAIRE, PHILIPPE-THOMAS; CHABERT DE JONCAIRE DE CLAUSONNE, DANIEL-MARIE; SENECA

Chabert de Joncaire, Philippe-Thomas (1707–c. 1766)

From the 1690s until 1759, a member of the Joncaire family—fully versed in Seneca language and culture and usually dwelling among that nation—was the accredited agent of French Canada among the Western Iroquois. This was the role which Philippe-Thomas, after growing up in Seneca country and becoming an officer in the colonial regular troops, inherited from his father, Louis-Thomas, at the age of 28. After 1735, it was his responsibility to prevent Iroquois hostility and inhibit nations further west from entering into trade relations with New York. He was successful enough in this interchange of bluster, bluff, and intrigue that the British put a price on his head, dead or alive. He resigned this mission in 1748, but a growing crisis facing Canada's empire in the west was too great to permit a leader of Joncaire's special attributes to remain long free of military/diplomatic responsibilities. In 1749, he accompanied the expedition that laid claim to the Ohio Valley for New France, then was stationed with a small squad at Ambridge, Pennsylvania. The next summer he made a tour of principal Iroquois villages in the interests of Canadian diplomacy, recalling the Six Nations to their obligations under the important Treaty of Neutrality which had followed a similar tour by his father 51 years earlier. After four more winters on Ohio headwaters, he returned to Seneca country in 1755, had to withdraw to Fort Niagara in 1759 when Sir William Johnson's invasion force appeared, and was with the garrison there when it surrendered. When the war was over, he went to France briefly, was awarded the Order of Saint-Louis, returned to Canada, and died at age 59.

In June 1759, he had been at the traditional Joncaire trading post at Geneva, New York, when a party of Mohawks intent on collecting the old bounty on his head came in through one window as he dove out another. He had a son-in-law with him at the time, presumably being prepared to continue the tradition of someone in the Joncaire connection filling the role of official hostage and go-between for Canada. The collapse of the French western empire, however, put an end to that challenging career full of cultural richness and sharp risk.

Malcolm MacLeod

References

Dictionary of Canadian Biography, 12 vols. (1966–1982) 2; Lawrence Henry Gipson, *The British Empire Before the American Revolution,* 7 vols. (1930–1954); William A. Hunter, *Forts on the Pennsylvania Frontier, 1753–1758* (1960); E.B. O'Callaghan, ed., *Documents Relative to the Colonial History of the State of New York,* 15 vols. (1853–1857) 6–10.

See also CHABERT DE JONCAIRE, LOUIS-THOMAS; CHABERT DE JONCAIRE DE CLAUSONNE, DANIEL MARIE; FORT MACHAULT (PENNSYLVANIA)

Chabert de Joncaire de Clausonne, Daniel-Marie (1714–1771)

Daniel-Marie Chabert de Joncaire de Clausonne spent part of his boyhood among the Senecas, as the men in his family tended to do. As a young man he was sent to several other nations as well, charged to "cultivate friendship," try to break any links there might be with the British-American enemy, and "dispel plots." At age 34, promoted ensign in the colonial regular troops, he succeeded his older brother, Philippe-Thomas, as principal agent for New France among the Iroquois. Over the previous half-century, his father and brother had good success in gaining either active support or passive neutrality. The geopolitical situation kept changing, however, and Canada's relative advantage was continually undermined by growing American population and ambitions.

The signs were good during the first several years. Mobilizing sufficient support to overcome opposition to the idea, Joncaire built a new fort/trading post ("Little Niagara") at the upper end of the portage around the great waterfall. His monopoly control of traffic served both the Canadian empire and his private pocketbook. Over this route during 1753–1757 went all the logistics that made possible Canada's military occupation and defense of the upper Ohio Valley. When a Canadian expedition in 1756 utterly destroyed the British post at Oswego—the southeastern corner of Lake Ontario in the heart of Iroquois country—it was a tribute to Canada's strength and Joncaire's diplomacy that no Indian protests were made.

From 1758, the whole Canadian posture in the Ohio and Great Lakes collapsed. An early signal was a request from anti-French elements among the Seneca for the services of a British gunsmith. By the twentieth century we are quite familiar with the idea of wars won or lost by the weight of spare parts. This was an early example of diplomacy closely linked to technology. Whoever mends the musket chooses the target. Joncaire left Montreal that spring with diplomatic presents to distribute, and a dozen blacksmiths to be dropped off in various Indian villages to repair firearms. Nevertheless, no Iroquois warned the French when Colonel John Bradstreet's expedition moved across Lake Ontario to destroy Fort Frontenac later that summer; and in 1759, the Iroquois permitted a large British force to undertake the siege of Niagara. Joncaire withdrew from the little fort and was with the main garrison when it fell.

He went to France in 1761 to press an account upon the government in Paris, claiming he had advanced more than one and a half million *livres* of his own goods trying to shore up Indian loyalty. Versailles was not impressed. Joncaire spent 1762 in the Bastille along with other Canadian officers and officials accused of fraud and profiteering. Back in Canada by 1765 with a large consignment of trade goods, for two years he was prohibited from going west for fear of anti-British propaganda or plots he might foment. After 1767, Joncaire was among a specified group of French Canadians authorized by the new government to travel among the Indians. Unable to have his claim to any part of the Niagara portage route recognized, he found a less-crowded frontier at Detroit, and died there at age 57.

Malcolm MacLeod

References

H.R. Casgrain, ed., *Collection des Manuscrits du Marechal de Lévis*, 7 vols. (1889–1895) 7; *Dictionary of Canadian Biography*, 12 vols. (1966–1982) 4; Guy Frégault, *Canada: The War of the Conquest*, trans. by Margaret M. Cameron (1969); E.B. O'Callaghan, ed., *Documents Relative to the Colonial History of the State of New York*, 15 vols. (1853–1887) 6–10; F.H. Severance, *An Old Frontier of France* (1917).

See also CHABERT DE JONCAIRE, LOUIS-THOMAS; CHABERT DE JONCAIRE, PHILLIPE-THOMAS; LITTLE FORT NIAGARA (NEW YORK); SENECA

Chacato Troubles (1674–1675)

Among the Chacato Indians of the Marianna, Florida region, trouble arose from culture conflict several months after two Franciscans established the missions of San Carlos and San Nicolas among them in mid-1674. The overzealous pressure tactics of the friars led three feared warriors, one of them a former chief, to protest being pressed to become Christians against their wills and to threaten the Christian chiefs of the two villages with trouble from friends of a nearby Chisca settlement, some of whom then lived in the two mission villages. To restore calm, the Spanish deputy governor in Apalachee brought a few soldiers and 25 harquebus-armed Apalachee. During their eight-day stay the three recalcitrants and more than 50 other Chacato became Christians (nominally, at least), and the Chisca were expelled from the two missions.

The show of force did not resolve the conflict between the new Christian mores and traditional native ways. Trouble reappeared in less than a year as the friars made it understood that nominal conversion would not suffice. During the summer of 1675, a friar's reprimands for departures from Christian sexual mores led three noted warriors to form a conspiracy to murder the troublesome friar. The nominal leader of the conspirators was Juan Fernandez de Diocsale, the 80-year-old former chief involved in the trouble of 1674. He was half Chisca and enjoyed a considerable following among that nation of feared warriors. The crisis erupted when the friar had three of the old chief's four wives removed from the chief's house and publicly reprimanded one of the other warriors for adultery and punished the warrior's paramour. The two younger warriors and several others recruited followers and actively solicited contributions of two deerskins from various Chacato to be used as gifts to the killers of the friars and to secure allies outside the tribe and refuge from Spanish retaliation. From the beginning the conspirators planned to abandon their homeland once the targeted friars had been killed. They used the Chacato's fear of the numerous Chisca, threatening those who refused to join them with death at the hands of the Chisca. To Christian Chacato leaders, the conspirators spoke solely of expelling the lone friar then working among them. Those leaders responded by posting a round-the-clock guard for the friar. The friar sent a loyal Indian leader to Apalachee to ask for armed support.

To secure support and a refuge, the conspirators dispatched gifts to the Tawasa living near Montgomery, Alabama, and to the Apalachicola/Creek in the vicinity of Columbus,

Georgia. Although the Creek rejected their request, the conspirators falsely claimed to have pledges of support from them. There is no evidence even for significant Chisca involvement at the time these claims were made, although Chisca became involved later after Diocsale's imprisonment. The conspirators used psychological warfare to erode support for the friar's defenders.

A report the conspirators circulated that they had already killed the friar at a nearby Savacola mission on the Apalachicola River, and Chisca were headed for San Carlos to kill the friar and his defenders, precipitated the friar's flight toward Apalachee. Surprisingly, no Chacato warriors accompanied the fleeing friar. A Chacato leader, who had joined the conspirators secretly, assigned two young men to serve as the friar's guides and instructed them to kill the friar soon after they left San Carlos mission. Although one of the guides knocked the friar to the ground with hatchet blows to head and face, the friar killed his assailant with his flintlock. The second guide fled to advise the conspirators of the failure of their plan. The wounded friar reached the security of the Savacola mission a little before the arrival there of a relief force from Apalachee.

This incident led to dispersal of the Chacato from their Marianna-region homeland. Most took refuge among the Tawasa and some with the Chisca. A Christian element, who remained loyal to the Spanish, settled in Apalachee initially on lands under the jurisdiction of the chief of San Luis de Talimali, but later they appropriated the abandoned Savacola mission site. An envoy sent to Tawasa by San Luis's pastor with the backing of the deputy governor, bearing a promise of amnesty for most and something less than the usual death penalty for the leaders, persuaded some of the fugitives, including Diocsale, to return to San Carlos. Diocsale was sentenced to permanent exile in St. Augustine, but was remanded later to Mexico when he was proved to have been responsible for subsequent Chisca raids against Christian Indians. Two other leading Indians who returned were sentenced to four years of labor in the royal works at St. Augustine, the first year without pay.

John H. Hann

References

John H. Hann, "Florida's Terra Incognita: West Florida's Natives in the Sixteenth and Seventeenth Century," *The Florida Anthropologist*, 41 (1988):61–107; ———, "Father Juan de Paiva, Prototype of Colonial Florida's Spanish Friar," in *Spanish Pathways in Florida* (in press); ———, "Translation of the Chacato Revolt Inquiry," *Florida Archaeology* (in press); John R. Swanton, *Early History of the Creek Indians and Their Neighbors* (1922).

See also SPANISH MISSION SYSTEM–SOUTHEAST

Fort Chambly (Quebec, Canada)

In 1665, the first palisaded Fort Chambly was erected by troops of the Carignan-Salières Regiment at the foot of the rapids stretching along the Richelieu River from Fort Saint-Jean to the south. At Chambly the river widens into a basin from which navigation north to Sorel on the St. Lawrence River is quite easy. This water route, Chambly-Sorel, was the one used almost exclusively for transport to and from Montreal.

At first the fort served as an outpost from which raids could be launched in an effort to pacify the Iroquois to the south. Chambly's location also served as a point from which to interdict French fur trade with the British at Albany, who offered better prices and superior goods in exchange for pelts. The eighteenth century saw increased hostilities between New France and the English colonies to the south, largely the North American extension of European conflicts involving the two countries. By the early eighteenth century, French officials realized the palisaded fort would no longer suffice against the British with their more traditional fighting methods and artillery.

The stone fort was erected in 1709 to replace the wooden one that had burned. The new construction was a square with 111-foot curtain walls, with a bastion at each angle. Theoretically, the fort could house 500 men, but it seems that the regular garrison never exceeded more than 150 men in time of war, and as few as seven when little danger threatened. One of the principal uses of Fort Chambly was as a forward depot to supply the more southerly outposts at Saint-Jean and Fort St. Frédéric on Lake Champlain. Chambly also sheltered and supplied troops on their way to or from Quebec and Montreal.

Fort Chambly was never designed to be a fortress in the Vauban style because the French believed the British could bring nothing heavier than four-pounder artillery pieces against it, the difficulties of transport from the south precluding larger pieces. Chambly was never the site of a battle during the War of Conquest, and at the time of the surrender to the British at Montreal, the fort held only 71 men.

The Americans captured Fort Chambly in October 1775 during their otherwise unsuccessful attempt to expel the British from Canada. After occupying the fort during the winter, the Americans retreated the following spring, and that was the last military action Chambly witnessed. The fort was abandoned in 1851, fell into ruin, but was restored in 1883. At present, Fort Chambly is one of the Canadian National Park sites, and is open to the public.

Mary Kimbrough

References
Cyrille Gélinas, *Le Rôle du fort de Chambly dans le développement de la Nouvelle France de 1665 à 1760* (1983); Marc Lafrance, "Art Militaire et technique de guerre: le fort de Chambly de 1710–1711," *Revue d'Histoire le l'Amérique française*, Vol. 37 (1983):21–49.

See also LA PRAIRIE, BATTLE OF (1691); FORT ST. FRÉDÉRIC (NEW YORK); SAINTE THÉRÈSA, BATTLE OF

Fort Charity (Virginia)
See HENRICO FORTS (VIRGINIA)

Fort Charles (Virginia)
Built in 1610 at the mouth of Hampton Creek in Elizabeth City (modern-day Hampton), Virginia, Fort Charles stood about two miles from the larger Fort Algernon on Old Point Comfort. Along with Fort Henry, another small fort built on the other side of the creek, Fort Charles was erected by Sir Thomas Gates after he drove out the Kecoughtan Indians in retaliation for the killing of one of the garrison of Fort Algernon. Designed as havens for seafarers entering the colony, as well as for protection from Indians, each of the two small forts contained garrisons of 15 men and mounted no cannon.

Abandoned soon after their construction, the two forts were reoccupied after the arrival of Sir Thomas Dale in Virginia in May 1611, and men from the garrisons of the three lower peninsula forts were set to clearing and planting the fields around Fort Henry. The two forts were abandoned by the 1630s and the land granted to private individuals.

Thomas Costa

References
Richard P. Weinhart and Colonel Robert Arthur, *Defender of the Chesapeake: The Story of Fort Monroe*, 3rd ed. (1989).

See also FORT ALGERNON (VIRGINIA); FORT HENRY (VIRGINIA)

Charlesfort (South Carolina)
Gaspard de Coligny, the admiral of France, viewed the southeastern coast of North America as a potential source of tropical products and as a haven for French Huguenots to escape persecution. Realizing the area could provide bases for Spanish vessels, Coligny commissioned Jean Ribault to establish a colony.

In 1562, Ribault led a band of Huguenots first to the St. Johns River near present-day St. Augustine, Florida. He continued northward until he entered a large sound, which he named Portus Regalis (Port Royal). The Huguenots built a small fort, Charlesfort, either on an island or the bordering mainland, between the Broad and Port Royal Rivers. Constructed of earth and logs, the fort was named in honor of Charles IX of France.

Leaving behind a small party of volunteers to man the fortification, Ribault returned to France to obtain reinforcements and supplies. During his absence, the men mutinied and chose a new commander. After building a crude vessel, they sailed for France. On the arduous voyage home they resorted to cannibalism in order to survive.

It is still unclear where Charlesfort was located. Though a monument to Ribault and the Huguenots is located on Parris Island, the site of a later Spanish settlement called Santa Elena, several archaeologists contend the French built the fort on the Broad River in the Pigeon Point area of Beaufort.

Gregory D. Massey

References
Robert B. Roberts, *Encyclopedia of Historic Forts: The Military, Pioneer, and Trading Posts of the United States* (1988).

See also PORT ROYAL (SOUTH CAROLINA); RIBAULT, JEAN; SANTA ELENA

Charles Town, Attack on (1706)

During Queen Anne's War, Spain and France decided to link their forces for an attack on South Carolina. Offensive operations would alleviate English pressure against Florida, which combined English and aboriginal forces had attacked on several occasions in the previous few years; France was worried about its nascent settlements in Louisiana and thus looked to weaken England in the Southeast as well. Rumors of an invasion led South Carolina's Governor Nathaniel Johnson to strengthen fortifications.

Jacques Lefebvre, a French captain, obtained men and ships in Cuba, and additional supplies and men in St. Augustine, for an attack he led in early September 1706. Five of his vessels arrived at Charles Town harbor on 7 September, but the city was warned by smoke signals sent by men stationed at Sullivan's Island. Despite a yellow fever epidemic in the town, militiamen from the countryside entered Charles Town to prepare a defense. Lefebvre demanded a surrender, which was refused.

On James Island, a Spanish raiding party was turned back by a combined force of militia and Indians. A larger party of 160 Spaniards easily destroyed two small boats and a small building on a spit of land between the Wando River and the Atlantic. The Spanish celebrated and rested overnight, expecting an easy victory the next day. However, the Carolina militia disrupted the celebration by surprising the invaders. Sixty were captured, 12 killed, and a handful drowned. A few days later, Johnson sent seven small boats, including a fireship, against the French fleet, and Lefebvre called off the invasion.

Soon after the fleet's departure another French ship, *La Brilliante,* arrived with 200 soldiers. This ship had become separated from the main fleet before arrival at Charles Town, and the men were eager for a fight. The ship also carried General Arbousset, who was supposed to have commanded the landing forces. Arbousset determined to fight and landed his men east of the town, intending a march into Charles Town. Governor Johnson repulsed the attackers with militia, and another group captured *La Brilliante.* The campaign ended with more than 320 of the invaders captured and approximately 30 killed.

Alan Gallay

References
Verner W. Crane, *The Southern Frontier, 1670–1732* (1929); John Jay TePaske, *The Governorship of Spanish Florida 1700–1763* (1964).

See also QUEEN ANNE'S WAR

Fort de Chartres (Illinois)

A succession of Forts de Chartres, all of them in the general vicinity of what is now southwestern Illinois, was constructed between 1719 and the end of the French regime in Louisiana (1763). The first of these forts was not built as a pioneering outpost of the fur trade, but rather was erected well after permanent settlements had been established at Cahokia (1699) and Kaskaskia (1703).

In 1717, the French regency government directed by Philippe, duc d'Orleans, reorganized its North American colonies. The Illinois country, including the lower valleys of the Ohio and Missouri Rivers, as well as the middle Mississippi Valley, was removed from Canadian jurisdiction and became the upper part of the colony of Louisiana. Henceforth, the appellations Illinois country and upper Louisiana were, for all intents and purposes, synonymous. At the same time, the concession for economic development of Louisiana was taken from Antoine Crozat and turned over to the French Company of the Indies. Lastly, the French settlements in Louisiana were given a new provincial capital at New Orleans (named in honor of the regent of France) in 1718. These, then, were the developments that formed the backdrop to the building of the first Fort de Chartres in the Illinois country. This fort was to aid and abet the economic development of Louisiana, which in turn would bolster the finances of the French state.

Shortly after the founding of New Orleans, a convoy of *bateaux* left the new capital to ascend the Mississippi River to the Illinois country. This company included French military officers as well as representatives of the Company of the Indies. The commander of the convoy was Pierre Dugué, sieur de Boisbriant, a Canadian-born member of the French lesser aristocracy. Taking the usual six months' time to ascend the river, the convoy arrived at Kaskaskia early in 1719, and Boisbriant immediately began the task of locating a site on which to build a fort. This fort was to serve as a military outpost, a local seat of government, and a headquarters for the Company of the Indies, and was part of the 1717–1719 restructuring of Louisiana.

Rather surprisingly, Boisbriant selected a fort site that was removed from the major concentrations of population at Cahokia and Kaskaskia, choosing instead to locate between the two communities on the eastern bank of the Mississippi. This site may have been chosen because of its central location and its access to the lead mines on the western side of the Mississippi. During 1719–1720, the first Fort de Chartres (named after a prince of the royal blood, duc de Chartres) was built by the troops who made up the military contingent of Boisbriant's expedition. The fort was a wooded palisaded structure, one arpent (an arpent equals approximately 192 feet) square, with two bastions from which the four curtain walls could be covered. Inside the perimeter of the fort several structures were built, including a barracks and an office building for the Company of the Indies. The small garrison at the fort was composed entirely of detached marines, for the entire colony of Louisiana fell within the jurisdiction of the French Ministry of the Marine.

In the vicinity of the fort, farms, villages, and a religious structure developed. The village of Chartres grew near the fort, to the north was the village of St. Philippe, and to the south the village of Prairie du Rocher (still extant). To serve the religious needs of this new population center, the parish of St. Anne was created, the third canonical parish in the Illinois country. The region's economy was based largely on agriculture, and the French *habitants* practiced a system of open-field cultivation reminiscent of medieval France.

Within a few years after the completion of the first fort, a new structure was begun not far away. Precisely why this occurred as soon as the first fort was completed is not known. Perhaps the flooding Mississippi threatened the first one, or perhaps a more substantial structure was required because of hostile Fox Indians. Much of what happened in the Illinois country during the late 1720s was influenced by the very serious threat presented by the Fox. This threat was not eliminated until the French and their Indian allies massacred, somewhere in central Illinois, many Fox men, women, and children in 1730. This massacre was hardly a noble achievement for French arms, but it did prepare the way for further expansion of the French settlements in the Illinois country.

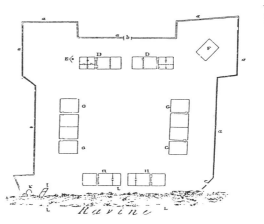

Fort de Chartres. a,a,a, murailles extérieures (1447 pieds); B, porte principale; C, petite porte; D,D, logements du commandant et du commissaire, 96x30 pieds chacun; E, puits; F, magasin; G,G, casernes, 135-36 pieds; H,H, magasin des vivres et corps de garde, 90x24 pieds; I, petit magasin; K, fourneau; L,L, ravin

In 1731, the charter of the Indies company was revoked, and all of Louisiana became a royal crown colony. As a consequence of this transfer, an inventory was made that included a detailed description of Fort de Chartres. It described the second fort as a bit smaller than the first, but substantially stronger, having a double palisaded wall and four bastions. Inside the palisade were a number of buildings, including officers' quarters, an enlisted men's barracks, a storehouse for the Company of the Indies, and a chapel.

Despite the change in organization that occurred in Louisiana during 1731–1732, there was no rebuilding of Fort de Chartres at that time. Throughout the 1730s and 1740s, French colonial officials engaged in much discussion concerning forts in Illinois country. At one time, serious consideration was given to abandoning Fort de Chartres altogether, and a substantial fort was begun atop the bluffs overlooking Kaskaskia. This project was never completed, however, and in the early 1750s, a decision was made to entirely rebuild Fort de Chartres. Given the increased tensions between Great Britain and France at that time, the French government decided to invest a considerable sum in this last rebuilding of the fort, and for the first time, Fort de Chartres was to be built in stone.

Begun in 1752, the stone version of Fort de Chartres progressed slowly during the course of the French and Indian War. It was a limestone quadrilateral, with 15-foot walls, four bastions, several small cannons, and numerous buildings inside the curtain walls. Although no shot was ever fired in anger at this structure, by the end of the French and Indian War it had become one of the strongest military outposts in North America. This site is now a state historic site, and the state of Illinois is rebuilding the fort on its original foundations.

Ceded to Great Britain as part of the Illinois country following the French and Indian War, Fort de Chartres became home to a British garrison beginning in 1765. The British renamed it Fort Cavendish, but the new name did not stick. When the Mississippi River began to undermine the southwestern bastions by 1772, the British moved their garrison to Kaskaskia before finally recalling all of their regulars from their western frontier in 1774 as issues heated up in the thirteen colonies.

Carl J. Ekberg

References

Clarence W. Alvord, *The Illinois Country: 1673–1818* (1920); Natalia M. Belting, *Kaskaskia Under the French Regime* (1948); Margaret K. Brown and Lawrie C. Dean, eds., *The Village of Chartres in Colonial Times* (1977); Edward B. Jelks, Carl J. Ekberg, and Terrance J. Martin, *Excavations at the Laurens Site* (1989); Anna Price, "The Three Lives of Fort de Chartres: French Outpost on the Mississippi," *Historic Illinois, 3* (1980):1–4.

See also Fox; Louisiana

Cherokee

For more than ten centuries the Native American peoples known as the Cherokee lived in the river valleys which cut through the southern Appalachian Mountains. Indeed, the long-term presence of these agricultural peoples continues to be affirmed by twentieth-century archaeological research.

Visitors who reached the Cherokee homelands in the eighteenth century found the Cherokee towns divided into four groups: Overhills, Lowers, Middles, and Valleys. Wherever the Cherokee located, their villages, such as the sacred town of Chota on the banks of the Little Tennessee River, lay beside the waters of a mountain stream. Depending on the width and length of the valley, settlements might number anywhere from 50 to several hundred persons, especially before 1700. In narrow valleys a village might be elongated, stretching for some distance beside the stream. Cherokee dwellings would be clustered near a council house, whose size depended upon the population of the village and the relative influence of the town. When British traveler Henry Timberlake reached the important Lower Cherokee town of Keowee in 1761, he described a large ceremonial building shaped on the outside like a sugar loaf. Timberlake estimated that the interior, however smoky and dark it might be, could seat more than 500 people.

Outside the limits of the villages lay the cultivated fields of these mountain horticulturalists. The most prominent of the crops grown was corn (*zea mays*); the successful cultivation of maize meant a dependable food supply throughout the year because corn could be stored for use prior to the next harvest. By the late eighteenth century, when military expeditions reached the Overhill Cherokee villages, one commander reported the destruction of more than 50,000 bushels of corn in the Overhill towns alone. Next in importance to corn was the cultivation of beans, probably ancestors of modern kidney and lima beans. Not only were the beans grown in the same fields with the corn, but they were often cooked together, producing a chemical reaction which increased the protein yield of the food. In addition to corn and beans, Cherokee farmers raised a variety of plants from the family of squashes and gourds. Along the edges of the fields, sunflowers were planted, giving the native peoples an important oilseed for their diet. One other cultigen raised by the Cherokee, not for food, but for ceremonial purposes, was North American tobacco. Fundamental to the welcome ceremony involving the pipe of greeting, tobacco was grown in small patches sufficient to supply this social need.

Supplementary to the basic diet of vegetables was the game supplied by the Cherokee hunters. Primary among the animals pursued by the Cherokee was the Virginia white-tailed deer. By carefully observing the religious rituals of the hunt, Cherokee hunters were able to find deer during most seasons. Periodic burning of the woodland underbrush by native American hunters also helped maintain the deer population by renewing the forest floor browse the deer preferred.

Second in desirability to the deer was the native bear, sought more for its grease and fat than for meat. The plentiful turkey also fell to Cherokee hunters. Although other small game, such as rabbits and squirrels, were sometimes hunted, the return on a deer was far more fruitful because of the meat and the useful byproducts from both its skin and skeleton. Unfortunately, after the arrival of the Europeans and the rise of the deerskin trade, the ecology of the southeastern forests suffered some decline in deer population as hunters stripped the skins and left the carcasses to rot, acts contrary to forest economy and to Cherokee spiritual values.

The dwellings of the Cherokee villages were log structures somewhat similar to the log cabin later developed by the European settler. A single hole in the roof meant that most of the smoke hung within the cabin's dark interior. Near the dwelling there was often a smaller house used in winter because it was easier to heat; Europeans called these "hot houses." Before the arrival of trade goods, simple tools of wood, bone, and stone, along with white oak or reed baskets, hung on the cabin posts or were stored under the sleeping benches.

Prior to the seventeenth century, the population of the Cherokee villages probably numbered about 30,000 persons living in approximately 60 settlements. By 1715, however, the impact of foreign diseases had reduced that population to fewer than 11,000 in 53 towns. The combined effect of foreign diseases, warfare, and slow reproduction patterns reduced the number of Cherokee from approximately 30,000 in 1685 to fewer than 7,500 in 1785.

First encounters between the Cherokee and Europeans cannot be dated with absolute certainty. Even if the Hernando de Soto *entrada* of the early 1540s did not encounter the Cherokee, European diseases may have been introduced into the region at that time. Certainly, the Cherokee learned of the strange newcomers through the existing Native American trade network. That same communication exchange also may have brought the first manufactured goods, such as glass beads, iron axes, and hawk's bells. By the end of the seventeenth century, however, the commodity most desired was the gun, highly prized as a status symbol, a weapon of war, and a tool for hunting. When traders from South Carolina and Virginia reached the Cherokee towns in the 1690s, guns, powder, and lead were eagerly sought. Visionaries such as Thomas Nairne, South Carolina's provincial Indian

agent, and Charles Craven, the colony's energetic governor, understood the enormous profits possible in the trade. From the traders the Cherokee first acquired the horse, which they sought initially as a symbol of status and then as a beast of burden; by the early eighteenth century, packtrains of horses replaced files of Cherokee women carrying bundles of deerskins to and bales of goods from market.

As trade rapidly followed contact, Cherokee material culture changed dramatically. In its initial phase, at least, this new economic relationship involved the offering of European manufactured goods such as guns, tools, cloth, and unfortunately, rum, for deerskins and slaves. Guns were so highly prized that warriors sought them eagerly, in the process not only abandoning the bow and arrow, but also depleting the native deer herds. At the same time, Cherokee women found cloth easier to work with than animal hides; soon the inventories of traders and trading houses listed several types of cloth woven in British knitting mills.

Perhaps the most destructive item introduced by the traders was rum, the demonic beverage for which Indian peoples developed great fondness but little tolerance. Alcohol became the means by which many traders cheated hunters of their hard-won skins or promoters won larger land cessions. On the other hand, another invasive byproduct of the trade was the arrival of traders as residents in the Cherokee villages early in the seventeenth century. Their marriages to Cherokee women eventually resulted in the adoption of European names and the presence of mixed-blood tribal leaders by the late-eighteenth century.

The women of Cherokee culture held a special place, enhanced not only by their economic contributions from farming, but also because theirs was a matrilineal society, wherein descent from generation to generation, usage of traditional fields, and clan membership were determined by the mother's genealogical line. Women of specific accomplishments and influence might receive the honorific title "Beloved Woman." A Cherokee woman who took up her fallen husband's weapon in battle might become known as a "War Woman." One of the best known of these individuals was Nanye'hi, also known by her Anglicized name, Nancy Ward. When her first husband fell in battle against the Creeks, Nanye'hi took up his weapons and joined in driving away the enemy.

C

While women's direct involvement in warfare was never the norm, war and its "little brother," hunting, dominated the lives of boys and men. Gender roles were fixed early in life, as young Cherokee males played at both the hunting game and the war game. Passage to manhood, moreover, was marked by participation in a raiding party, usually about the age of 12 or 13. If the venture was successful, the new warrior would be identified with the other fighting men of the village, thus gaining adult responsibilities both in the protection and the governance of his town.

Also introduced to the Cherokees by the Europeans were diseases against which they had no resistance. Most devastating seemed to be smallpox, which dramatically reduced the populations of the Cherokee villages, sometimes by 50 percent, according to contemporary accounts. Depopulation often was exacerbated as weakened survivors of major contagions fell victim to ordinary, but no less deadly, illnesses as the result of lowered resistance. Loss of population also was connected to relocation of villages, especially when a town's inhabitants no longer were sufficient in number to work its fields or defend its exposed locale.

The first recorded outbreak of smallpox in the Cherokee towns occurred in 1697, possibly following initial contacts with traders; this pandemic may have reduced the population by as much as one-half to three-quarters. During the next century there were at least three more documented devastations, in 1738, 1760, and 1783. Although the eighteenth-century eruptions may not have reached the proportions of the 1697–1698 catastrophe, population loss was still high. The Cherokee became so fearful of smallpox that on one occasion diplomats traveling eastward for negotiations turned back toward the Cherokee towns when they learned of an outbreak on the coast.

Another new and powerful force impacting Cherokee society was military conflict with the Europeans. Although warfare had been a part of Cherokee life, the nature of that armed strife, such as the historic cycle of warfare between the Cherokees and their Creek neighbors, had been ritualized in terms of social needs and retaliations in kind. As often as the two tribes had been at war, neither sought the total annihilation of the other. If raiders from a Cherokee town attacked a Creek town, a counter-raid could be expected in order to maintain face. Europeans, on the other hand, thought in terms of eliminating the Indian enemy entirely, or at least destroying so many villages and caches of food that the Native American opponents had little or no will to resist or respond.

As the British fought the French (and sometimes the Spanish) for political and economic control of eastern North America in the seventeenth and eighteenth centuries, forest diplomacy included forging alliances and enlisting Native American warriors as auxiliary troops. Cherokee warriors were recruited by South Carolina as part of a plan for defense against an attack from Spanish Florida. On the Cherokee-Creek frontier, one of the openly pro-British Cherokee leaders was Caesar of Echota, who was more than willing to engage his warriors against their traditional Creek foes. Fear of retaliatory actions by Francophile Creeks eventually prompted South Carolina to order troops under Colonels James Moore and George Chicken temporarily stationed in the Cherokee towns.

One rather unusual form of forest diplomacy was fulfilled by a promoter named Alexander Cuming, a professional eccentric whose travels happened to bring him to South Carolina and then to the mountain homelands of the Cherokee in 1730. In a series of theatrical appearances throughout the Cherokee villages, he not only attempted to impress the Cherokee with his own importance, but with that of his king as well. As confirmation of England's greatness, he invited a delegation of Cherokee to accompany him back to England. Among them was an obscure warrior named Attakullakulla, who would later remember this voyage when he was known to his tribe as the "Little Carpenter."

As the European contest for empire intensified, the Cherokee found themselves wooed by both the French and the English. The overall French policy, aimed at limiting British expansion, resulted in the construction of a string of forts stretching from Niagara to Mobile. One of the beads on this strand was the outpost known as Fort Toulouse, near the confluence of the Coosa and the Tallapoosa Rivers. From this outpost, in present-day Alabama, French agents could operate, either to cultivate trade and alliances with the Cherokee, or failing that, support Creek raids against the Cherokee villages, as well as the frontier settlements of South Carolina. There was even discussion by the French of building a fort in the Overhill Cherokee country.

Adding to the uneasiness on the part of officials in South Carolina and Georgia was the presence in the Cherokee country of an educated visionary named Christian Priber. A university graduate with a doctorate from Erfurt, Priber had found his way to Georgia as a potential settler in 1736. In that same year he relocated to the Cherokee town of Tellico, where he began to advocate a utopian society, open to anyone. General James Oglethorpe (himself no stranger to reformist philanthropy, but an Englishman nonetheless) later wrote that Priber was organizing a "Kingdom of Paradise" which would be a home for "fugitive English, French, Germans & Negroes," as well as an asylum for "debtors, Transport Felons, Servants & Negro Slaves in the two Carolinas & Virginia." Whatever Priber's actual intentions, he was most troubling to the trade since he tried to prevent the traders from cheating the Indians, as well as help the Cherokee understand the value of their lands. When unhappy South Carolina authorities commissioned a party to arrest Priber, the Cherokee protected him. Later, when Priber attempted a journey west toward the French outpost at Fort Toulouse, he was captured by pro-British traders and Indians who returned him to imprisonment at Frederica, Georgia. Although many colonial officials assumed he was a French agent, there is no confirmation of this, nor did Priber ever fully clarify his intentions or motives before his death in prison after 1744.

In reaction to these actions and implied threats by the French, as well as the puzzling activities of Priber on the Cherokee frontier, the English responded by establishing Forts Loudoun (1757), Prince George (1753), and Ninety-Six (1759). Loudoun was located in the heart of the Overhill Cherokee country, just down the Little Tennessee River from the sacred town of Chota. The necessity of these countermeasures was underscored when the British discovered one source of the vocal French party among the Overhills. The activist was a young French officer named Louis de Lantagnac, at one time reportedly a deserter (1745) from Fort Toulouse who had fled to South Carolina, established himself as a trader at the Cherokee town of Great Tellico about 1750, and then returned to his former post in 1754. Thereafter he worked untiringly to encourage the French faction among the Overhill Cherokee.

Cherokee life and politics were further complicated during this period by the British policy of seeking Indian allies. While governors of South Carolina such as James Glen (1743–1755) and William Henry Lyttleton (1755–1759) sought immediate protection for their colonial frontier, others in the British imperial military establishment obtained the aid of Cherokee warriors in an attempt to dislodge the French from Fort Duquesne.

The alliance soured when Cherokee warriors returning from the Pennsylvania frontier stole horses as they passed through Bedford County, Virginia, which lay on the eastern edge of the major north-south trail known as the Great Warrior Path. Attempts on the part of South Carolina officials to punish the guilty Cherokee escalated into warfare, which forced the garrison at Fort Loudoun to take refuge inside the post. After an initial attempt to rescue the garrison failed, the troops were more isolated than ever, since the relief effort had generated increased hostile feelings between the Cherokee and their British neighbors. Ultimately, the fort would surrender under terms allowing the garrison's retreat to either Virginia or South Carolina. Soon after the soldiers evacuated the fort, the Cherokee attacked, killing a number of persons and capturing several dozen others, including John Stuart, who later became the British Indian superintendent for the southern district in North America.

Not until 1761 would a successful expedition be launched to punish the Cherokee and force them to terms. The leading Cherokee negotiator was the long-time pro-British chief Attakullakulla, or the Little Carpenter, who had visited England in 1729–1730 and had been instrumental in rescuing John Stuart and ransoming many other prisoners in the aftermath of Fort Loudoun's fall. Cherokee loss of life during the Cherokee War of 1759–1761 was not extraordinarily high, since village inhabitants fled before the army approached, and parties of warriors attacked only under the best of circumstances and refused to be cornered. Although the total number killed in battles might not have exceeded 100, another devastating smallpox outbreak had been carried into the Cherokee country by the intruders. The combined impact of war, invasion, and disease further reduced the population of the Cherokee, as well as reducing their ability to resist encroachments by settlers from Virginia, the Carolinas, and Georgia.

During the 15 years after the Cherokee War, the Cherokee sought to restore their lives, al-

C

though under further altered circumstances. The British victory over France left the English in complete control of eastern North America. As a step toward settling some of the tensions between native peoples such as the Cherokee and the ever westward-moving settlers, the British government attempted to institute a policy of control in the trade and to establish surveyed boundaries between tribal lands and territories claimed either by the crown or by the colonies. This initiative meant a new official with whom to deal, the British Indian superintendent for the southern district of North America. For some of the Cherokee, the appointment of John Stuart, whom they knew from his assignment to Fort Loudoun and his captivity among them, seemed to promise a period of improved diplomatic communication. Perhaps Superintendent Stuart would be able to curb the unscrupulous traders and halt the ever aggressive land speculators.

Stuart did take steps toward implementation of Britain's new western policies. First, he invited delegates from the southern tribes to a great congress at Augusta, Georgia, in the fall of 1763. Delegations of Cherokee and Creek leaders, although not necessarily representative of all tribal factions, attended, along with representative Chickasaw diplomats and two Choctaw chiefs, plus Governors Thomas Boone (South Carolina), Arthur Dobbs (North Carolina), and Francis Fauquier (Virginia). Principal spokesmen for the Cherokee in attendance were Attakullakulla, the "Prince" of Chota, and Saluy. Noticeably absent was Oconostota, the "Great Warrior," whose earlier pro-British loyalties had been reversed during the Cherokee War. In the negotiations which followed, Attakullakulla pointed out the major points of contention: inadequate trade, and encroachments on lands claimed by the Cherokee.

During the 12 years after this conference, John Stuart sought to improve trade through the use of his good offices, since he had no real power to regulate or enforce. With regard to land matters, he was guided by the intention of the royal government in attempting to survey a boundary between each of the southern tribes and colonies involved.

The participation of the Cherokee and their leaders in the boundary process stemmed from their desire to hold the settlers as far away from their villages and homelands as possible. Despite all their efforts and cooperation with Stuart and other officials, the Cherokee found themselves threatened by the arrival of settlers west of the mountains between 1769 and 1775. Recent estimates suggest some 2,000 of these folk had crossed into Cherokee territory by 1775; that nothing seemed to daunt them is reflected by the first federal census which registered more than 31,000 non-Indians populating the five counties of eastern Tennessee in 1790.

The combined pressures of aggression by growing numbers of settlers and the failure of frontier diplomacy by 1776 prompted the Cherokee once more to attempt to defend themselves by driving away the troublesome settlers. Anxious to protect their lands and hopeful they could take advantage of the rift between Britain and its North American colonies, Cherokee warriors attacked the western settlements of Georgia, the Carolinas, and Virginia in early summer 1775. Almost predictably, this action ultimately better served the interests of their adversaries than those of the Cherokee. While some settlers were killed and others withdrew to safety, the immediate result was a retaliatory expedition against the Cherokee. During late summer and early fall 1776, a joint expedition was undertaken by the Continental Congress and the four states involved; several thousand troops marched into the Cherokee heartlands. Although the actual loss of life was not high because most of the Cherokee people withdrew before the enemy arrived, the invaders destroyed thousands of bushels of foodstuffs along with the dwellings in many villages. This scorched earth policy would leave the Cherokee weakened and exposed, unable adequately to defend or care for themselves.

The long-term result of the Cherokee War of 1776 was even more ominous for the Cherokee, since it placed them, at least in the minds of the United States, in the camp of the British enemy. Once the war was over, the winners could claim the spoils of war, which in the case of the Cherokee was their land. Indeed, the Cherokee understood this. At a conference to restore peace in 1777, a chief known as the Corn Tassel cut through the diplomatic hyperbole: "But Brothers, do you remember that the difference is about our land?"

As Corn Tassel and his fellow Cherokee leaders knew from experience, their adversaries would never let them rest until no land remained in Cherokee hands. Between 1777 and 1789, the Cherokee again and again were called to negotiations ostensibly aimed at a settlement of disputes or differences; for the most part these were ruses designed as a means to request more land. Despite all the Cherokee attempts to accommodate and acculturate after the American Revolution, they would never be accepted on any equal footing, or even on a live-and-let-live basis. The "Trail of Tears" over which they walked in the nineteenth century had its origins in the eighteenth century, when the settlers first began invading Cherokee territory in search of new lands.

James H. O'Donnell

References

David Corkran, *The Cherokee Frontier: Conflict and Survival, 1740–1762* (1962); Verner W. Crane, *The Southern Frontier, 1670–1732* (1929); Charles Hudson, *The Southeastern Indians* (1976); John Philip Reid, *A Law of Blood: Primitive Law of the Cherokee Nation* (1970); Robert Weir, *Colonial South Carolina: A History* (1983); Samuel C. Williams, ed., *Lieut. Henry Timberlake's Memoirs* (1972).

See also ATTAKULLAKULLA; AUGUSTA CONGRESS; CAESAR; CHEROKEE WAR; CREEK; CREEK-CHEROKEE WAR; CUMING, ALEXANDER; FORT LOUDOUN (TENNESSEE); LYTTLETON, WILLIAM HENRY; FORT MASSAC (ILLINOIS); OCONOSTATA; FORT PRINCE GEORGE–KEOWEE (SOUTH CAROLINA); STUART, JOHN

Cherokee War (1759–1761)

At the beginning of the French and Indian War, Virginia requested the Cherokees send a number of warriors to attack the Indian allies of the French. The tribe honored this request, but were ill-treated by their English allies and lost their supplies. On their return home, several Cherokees seized some stray horses and food as compensation for their own losses while protecting Virginia. In retaliation, Virginia frontiersmen killed a number of Cherokees. They later claimed they mistook the Indians for enemies, but they sold their scalps at a premium. This action led to Cherokee reprisals in May 1759 when warriors from Settico killed a number of settlers on the Yadkin and Catawba Rivers.

About the same time, Lieutenant Richard Coytmore (who succeeded the well-liked Lachlan McIntosh as commander of Fort Prince George) and an Ensign Bell went on two drunken sprees, mistreating Cherokee women while the men were away. Supposedly, the warriors intended to seek revenge for these insults by attacking the Virginians who had murdered their tribesmen. Instead, they attacked along the closer Carolina frontier, killing more than 20 settlers. Charles Town immediately embargoed Cherokee trade.

In an attempt to keep peace and restore needed trade, a delegation of Cherokee chiefs went to Charles Town. Already determined on war, Governor William Henry Lyttleton, supported by the South Carolina Council, took the peace delegation hostage to Fort Prince George with 1,300 soldiers. At the fort, Lyttleton presented his demand: 24 warriors involved in the killings on the Carolina frontier had to be turned in before the hostages would be released and trade restored. Eventually, Cherokee leader Attakullakulla (Little Carpenter) turned in two warriors and persuaded Lyttleton that he should not hold more hostages than he was asking to be surrendered. After several unsuccessful attempts to free the remaining innocent hostages, Oconostota (the "Great Warrior") lured Coytmore out of the fort. When the Englishman appeared, Oconostota gave a signal; Coytmore was mortally wounded and the fort attacked. As a result, the garrison killed the remaining hostages.

In response to a request by Governor Lyttleton, General Jeffrey Amherst, commander in chief of British forces in America, sent Colonel Archibald Montgomery and 1,600 men to attack the Cherokees. Burning the Lower Cherokee towns of Keowee and Estatoe, Montgomery was able to relieve Fort Prince George. Montgomery then sent a message to Little Carpenter requesting a meeting. A few days later Montgomery marched north where he was ambushed by Oconostota south of Etchoe (about six miles south of Franklin, North Carolina). Montgomery suffered 20 men killed and 70 wounded, among the latter was Montgomery himself. After the Indians withdrew, Montgomery continued as far as Etchoe, which he burned. Believing he had sufficiently chastised the Cherokees, he returned to Fort Prince George, harassed all the way by the Cherokees. From Fort Prince George he returned to Charles Town to embark on a new assignment.

Montgomery's expedition temporarily freed Britain's southern frontier from Cherokee attack. But in the Overhill Cherokee country a siege of Fort Loudoun had begun. Little Car-

Cherokee war.

penter managed to have women slip some food into the fort. Still, the garrison was forced to surrender and the commanding officer, Captain Paul Demeré, signed the articles of capitulation on 7 August 1760. The garrison was told they could march to Fort Prince George, but were attacked the following morning, supposedly because they had violated the peace by burying some gunpowder. The Cherokees killed Demeré and 23 of his men—a total equal to the number of hostages killed. John Stuart, the only officer spared, was later ransomed by Little Carpenter and taken to Virginia. (A few years later the crown appointed Stuart superintendent of the Indians in the southern district.) The remaining captives were either tortured, ransomed by Virginia and South Carolina, or chose to remain with the Cherokees.

In early 1761, South Carolina took advantage of Cherokee needs and sent a large quantity of nonmilitary goods to Fort Prince George to be exchanged for the many white captives held by the Indians. By the end of May, the freedom of 115 prisoners had been gained in this manner. At the same time, however, the South Carolinians prepared to strike a decisive blow against the Cherokees. Lieutenant Colonel James Grant, who was part of Montgomery's Highland Regiment, was now given command of more than 2,400 men for the attack. Little Carpenter, who had returned 12 Fort Loudoun survivors, met with Grant in May 1761 and asked for peace. Grant refused to make peace until the Cherokees were punished, and he marched toward the Cherokee towns. About two miles south of where Montgomery was ambushed in 1760, Grant's scouts detected another Cherokee ambush. After nearly six hours of fighting the Cherokees ran out of ammunition and retreated. Grant proceeded to destroy the Middle Cherokee towns, which had never been invaded by whites before. Lieutenant Francis Marion (later known as "the Swamp Fox") deplored the destruction and wrote that he "saw everywhere around the footsteps of little Indian children, where they had lately played under the shade of their rustling corn. When we are gone, thought I, they will return and peeping through the weeks with tearful eyes, will mark the ghastly ruin where they had so often played. 'Who did this?' they will ask their mothers and the reply will be, 'The white people did it—the Christians did it.'"

Grant's expedition destroyed 15 towns, 15,000 acres of crops, and drove 5,000 Cherokees into remote mountains to starve. Grant returned to Fort Prince George in early June and sent word he was ready to discuss peace. In August, Little Carpenter, Ostenaco (Judd's Friend), and many other chiefs met with Grant. When the terms for peace included that four Cherokees be executed, Little Carpenter refused and requested permission to go to Charles Town to confer with the governor. Lieutenant Governor William Bull agreed to drop this demand and a preliminary peace was signed with South Carolina on 23 September 1761.

William L. Anderson

References

John Richard Alden, *John Stuart and the Southern Colonial Frontier* (1966); John P. Brown, *Old Frontiers: The Story of the Cherokee Indians from Earliest Times to the Date of Their Removal to the West, 1838* (1938); E. Lawrence Lee, *Indian Wars in North Carolina: 1663–1763* (1963); Duane H. King and E. Raymond Evans, eds., "Memoirs of the Grant Expedition Against the Cherokees in 1761," *Journal of Cherokee Studies* II (1977):271–336; Grace Steele Woodward, *The Cherokees* (1963).

See also ATTAKULLAKULLA; CHEROKEE; FORT DOBBS (NORTH CAROLINA); FORT LOUDOUN (TENNESSEE); LYTTLETON, WILLIAM HENRY; FORT PRINCE GEORGE–KEOWEE (SOUTH CAROLINA); STUART, JOHN

C

Chickahominy

The Chickahominy, a populous Algonquian-speaking native group, had several villages within the Chickahominy River basin when the Virginia colonists arrived in 1607. Although the vast coastal territory within which the Chickahominy resided was controlled by the paramount chief, Powhatan, they had managed to retain their autonomy, thanks to their superior strength. The Chickahominy, unlike the other native groups then under Powhatan's sway, were governed by a council of eight elders. During November and December 1607, Captain John Smith and his men made exploratory visits to the Chickahominy River where they bartered for corn and noted that the Chickahominy had an estimated 200 warriors.

Although the April 1614 marriage of Powhatan's daughter to John Rolfe ushered in a period of generally peaceful relations between Virginia's natives and colonists, the Chickahominy secured an independent peace treaty with the English later that year. In 1616, when a food shortage impelled 100 armed settlers to seize corn from the Chickahominy, who also were experiencing hunger, their relationship with the English was strained beyond the breaking point. Shortly thereafter, the Chickahominy joined forces with Powhatan and the tribes under his sway, but they continued to be governed internally by a council of elders.

On 22 March 1622, the Chickahominy were among the native groups that participated in the major uprising that claimed nearly 350 settlers' lives. Later, their villages were attacked by bands of armed colonists embarking on a series of retaliatory raids. In 1632, the Chickahominy and the Pamunkey made a tenuous treaty with the English. In the wake of the 18 April 1644 Indian uprising, a massacre in which the Chickahominy participated, a fortified military outpost called Fort James was built on the Chickahominy River at Moysenac, in the heart of the natives' territory. After the colonists, by virtue of the 1646 treaty, gained exclusive control of the James-York peninsula, the Chickahominy withdrew to the Mattaponi River basin, where they were still residing in 1677 when a new treaty was signed with the colonial government. Although Cockacoeske, the Pamunkey queen, attempted to relegate the Chickahominy to a subservient position, they were steadfast in maintaining their independence and their old mode of leadership. They continued to live along the banks of the Mattaponi River during the first quarter of the eighteenth century.

Martha W. McCartney

References

William W. Hening, ed., *The Statutes At Large: Being a Collection of All the Laws of Virginia,* 13 vols. (1809–1823); H.R. McIlwaine, ed., *Minutes of Council and General Court of Colonial Virginia* (1934); Nell M. Nugent, *Cavaliers and Pioneers: Abstracts of Virginia Land Patents and Grants,* 3 vols. (1969–1979); Helen C. Rountree, *Pocahontas's People: The Powhatan Indians of Virginia Through Four Centuries* (1990); John Smith, *Travels and Works of Captain John Smith, President of Virginia and Admiral of New England, 1580–1631,* ed. by Edward Arber, 2 vols. (1910).

See also COCKACOESKE; POWHATAN; SMITH, JOHN; VIRGINIA-INDIAN WAR (1622–1632); VIRGINIA-INDIAN WAR (1644–1646)

Chickasaw

During the colonial era, the Chickasaw could claim to be the most successful southeastern Indian nation—they were the only unconquered nation by the end of the American Revolution. Their success was due to their skillful, though debilitating, policy of alliance with the English and maintenance of a certain amount of intertribal peace in their native region, the upper Mississippi Valley; they thus repelled invasions of the nearby French, and attempted to minimize martial relations with neighboring Indians. They nevertheless suffered serious losses in war over the course of the eighteenth century, and were not innocent of making war on other tribes to gain slaves or further support from the English.

The Chickasaw were, like most southeastern Indians, descendants of the Moundbuilders. This Indian civilization—named for the enormous ceremonial mounds its members built—had flourished in the Mississippi region, declining around 500 C.E., possibly as a result of warfare or climatic changes that lessened agricultural productivity. Around 700 C.E., the Mississippian culture began to expand over the ruins of Moundbuilder societies. Like the Moundbuilders, the Mississippian civilization fostered building of mounds and an urban life centered in towns that encouraged elaborate crafts and extensive regional trade. Mississippian culture flourished around 900 C.E., then collapsed suddenly. In turn, the woodland Indian cultures that would be in place when Europeans arrived in the New World began to emerge. These societies drew on the heritage of Mississippian culture (especially the characteristic of town-dwelling), and it is possible the societal conflict involved in the collapse of the Mississippian civilization imbedded limited warfare into woodland lineages as a sporadic but permanent activity.

A woodland culture of the Southeast, the Chickasaw belonged to the Muskogean language group, which included the Creeks and Choctaws. They shared kinship with the Choctaw; both groups had a myth of origin that implied their common ancestors had emerged near the Atlantic coast and migrated across the Appalachian Mountains in the distant past. The Chickasaw and Choctaw divided once they settled in the Mississippi Valley. The Chickasaw dwelled in the north, mostly in what is now western Tennessee and northern Mississippi, though they claimed lands in Kentucky and Alabama as well. In the pre-Columbian era, their population numbered 3,500–4,500 divided among several towns. Their population would always remain small, especially after European contact (bringing war and disease). The Chickasaw adopted captives to increase their numbers; the English noted Chickasaw tendencies to adopt and intermarry by calling members of the nation "breeds."

Pre-Columbian Chickasaw society was organized by non-totemic clans divided into exogamous groups; matrilineal descent was the rule. Nearly all of the population lived in towns (six or seven would be in place during the era of European exploration), each centered around a "square," and surrounded by agricultural fields. As was the rule in woodland societies, women tended the fields while men hunted, each within her or his own kinship group. The towns were concentrated in the center of the nation at Chikasahha or the Chickasaw Fields, near the present-day city of Memphis. Governance was communal; leaders were elected. Each town had its own permanent civil chief, and its own temporary war chief whenever a need for him arose. Pre-Columbian warfare existed for two reasons: blood revenge and slave raiding. The former activity allowed Chickasaw to wage limited war on another Indian group to obtain justice (through wartime casualties) for deaths this external group had inflicted on Chickasaw. The latter enabled them to seek captives for trade or to incorporate into their own society.

Some new needs for war arose with European contact. Hernando de Soto was first to explore the Southeast; he and his troops traipsed through Chickasaw territory in December 1540. Relations with the Spanish remained fairly peaceful until they demanded that Chickasaw bearers assist them on their further marches through North America. In March 1541, the Chickasaw attacked the town where Soto had bivouacked, and pursued the Spaniards after they had fled to another settlement—the first sortie would begin to establish the Chickasaw reputation for fierce and canny fighting.

The Spanish would not be permanent neighbors of the Chickasaw, who had instead to consider the virtues and vices of the French against those of the English. The French would settle north of the Chickasaw in Illinois, and south in Mobile and New Orleans. The English had already settled at Charles Town in Carolina in the 1660s, and sent Indian traders across the Appalachians by the 1690s (they would cross the Mississippi by 1700) to open traffic with the Chickasaw. As in other portions of North America, the Indian trade focused on exchange of animal pelts and Indian captives for European manufactured goods—especially guns, which Indians could use to gain more pelts and captives. The trade thus built on pre-Columbian activities of hunting and making war, but tended to disrupt the balance among activities in Native American society: it encouraged Indians to overhunt their environment, aggrandized the role of the male hunter/warrior, and increased the possibility of intertribal warfare—all of which would eventually increase Indian

dependence on European guns to continue the cycle of trade and destruction.

Compared to other Indian groups, the Chickasaw were wary customers, preferring not to declare themselves exclusive allies (and therefore pawns) either of the French or English, a policy followed by their southern cousins, the Choctaw. Trade goods filtered over from Carolina and up from Louisiana, but neither the English nor French could truthfully claim dominance over the region, and the trade did not seriously erode the Choctaw and Chickasaw nations. In the early 1700s, both Indian groups tended to make limited war on their neighbors (the Chickasaw repelled the Shawnee in 1715), and tried not to let Europeans make them permanent enemies of each other. Each nation raided the other for slaves, and the English sponsored a Chickasaw raid on the Choctaw in 1711, but that did not prevent the Chickasaw from sheltering Choctaw who had killed English settlers during the Yamasee War (1715–1717).

From the 1690s to 1729, the Chickasaw maintained a tricky balancing act between French and English, and among neighboring Indian towns. This strategy required considerable effort—as early as 1700, the English had tried to create a Choctaw-Chickasaw feud to gain slaves and thwart French expansion, but despite episodes of severe war (c. 1690–1702, 1719, 1723), neither Indian group had played into their hands. Alliance with the English, in fact, had sometimes served Chickasaw interests while embarrassing the Charles Town government; acting independently, a group of Cherokee and Chickasaw attacked a Lower Creek town in 1726, parading a drum and flag that had been presented to them by the Carolinians. Nor were the English, for their part, consistent in a policy that favored the Chickasaw—a South Carolina act of 1725 had tried to encourage trade with the Choctaw.

This shifting series of balances among powers ended suddenly when the Natchez struck at the French Forts Rosalie and St. Peter (near present-day Natchez) in November 1729, killing or enslaving most of the inhabitants. Though both Chickasaw and Choctaw had helped the Natchez, the Choctaw would break faith with them. The French demanded that other Indians assist in subduing the Natchez, but the Chickasaw instead sheltered the fleeing Natchez. The French, from this point forward, favored alliance with the Choctaw in order to

C

wear down the Chickasaw and the English who provided them with arms.

Especially after the Natchez War, European influence strengthened in the Mississippi Valley. Threatened by French aggression, the Chickasaw stepped up the frequency of trade with the English in order to gain more arms and ammunition. They felt the English influence in other ways as well. The English evidently taught the Chickasaw how to fortify their towns, a tactic that helped them resist every invasion they would face in the eighteenth century; because the English did not build their own forts in the Chickasaw nation, fortifications at Chikasahha served their interests as well. The Chickasaw also moved toward a system of inherited rather than elected chiefdoms, something that smacked of European innovation, though such chiefs were inherited (in Chickasaw fashion) matrilineally—a chief gave his position to his brother or nephew rather than his son.

In the meantime, the neighboring Choctaw (undergoing similar European influence) began to chafe under the demand that they be the exclusive allies of the French. During the 1730s, English privateering and continental warfare lessened Louisiana's ability to deliver trade goods to the Choctaw. A Choctaw chief named Red Shoe (Shulush Humma), who might have had marriage connections with the Chickasaw, began to solicit English support in 1734, strengthening ties between his people and the Chickasaw. Fearful of the erosion of Indian support, the French decided to strike at the Chickasaw using Choctaw warriors, tactics intended to weaken the former nation while implicating the latter in French military activities.

In 1735, Jean-Baptist Le Moyne, sieur de Bienville, governor of Louisiana, organized an invasion of Chikasahha. In February 1736, he led French and Indian troops up the Tombigbee River, where he had arranged to meet troops from Illinois led by Pierre d'Artaguette. The Chickasaw, sheltered within their fortifications, easily brushed off the French invaders; Artaguette attacked first and was repelled at the town of Hashuk-humma, and Bienville was forced to retreat in disarray. Bienville's new policy of attacking any Chickasaw without first attempting alliance through peace was evident in his siege of the town of Ackia, whose chief had been pro-French.

Bienville then determined to destroy the Chickasaw with a sizable and Choctaw-filled force. He called out troops from Illinois and Canada, organized soldiers in Mobile and New Orleans, and asked for French regular troops, as well as unprecedented amounts of ammunition. The northern force assembled across the Mississippi in the present-day state of Arkansas. Bienville chose a route along the Mississippi rather than risk another defeat along the Tombigbee. Disease, lack of provisions, and other delays prevented him from striking quickly, and by January 1740, the assembled troops were in poor condition. Bienville refused to retreat or regroup, but a provincial council of war that convened in February ordered him to fall back.

As the bulk of the French force descended the Mississippi, Pierre-Joseph Celeron de Blainville, leader of the Canadian troops, marched on to Chikasahha with a smaller force. The Chickasaw evidently believed Celeron was merely the first force to advance (as Artaguette had been in 1736). They might have attacked Celeron's troops, or even the fatigued force slipping back down river. They pursued a path of peace, however, perhaps hoping to build on the recent (though inconclusive) defection of Choctaw villages to their side. Overtaking Bienville, a Chickasaw delegation managed to extract conditions of peace, but Bienville refused to include the Choctaw nation in the negotiations. Therefore, the Choctaw were free to continue warring on the Chickasaw, while receiving French rewards for Chickasaw scalps—a strategic attempt to continue weakening pro-British Indians, and an exploitation of the system of blood revenge among southeastern Indian groups to serve European needs.

The French had made clear that they had a strict division between allied Indians and enemies, and regarded a semipermanent war as a necessity, regardless of Native American preference for weaker alliances and limited warfare. When King George's War (1744–1748) again disrupted French shipments of Indian trading goods, Red Shoe again struck out at the French, killing three Louisiana traders in November 1746. He made peace with the Chickasaw and sent a peace delegation to Charles Town. In April 1747, Governor James Glen signed a treaty with the Choctaw, though he subsequently proved unable to deliver arms to support their fight against the French. In 1747, a French agent assassinated Red Shoe; by 1749, 22 Choctaw towns made renewed promises of loyalty to France.

Louisiana's new governor, Pierre de Rigaud de Vaudreuil, like Bienville before him, seized on the first signs of renewed Choctaw enmity toward the Chickasaw to attack the latter nation, which had been weakened by smallpox in 1749. Vaudreuil sent two forces against the Chickasaw, under Benoist in 1752, and under Reggio in 1753. Both sorties failed—the Chickasaw were, as usual, well fortified and armed. Chickasaw victory ended British suggestions (begun in the 1720s) that the nation move eastward, something the French had long hoped for.

Triumphant, though battered in their struggles with the French, Chickasaw good fortune would continue beyond 1753. They saw little action during the French and Indian War (1754–1763), and would feel themselves honored and protected by the Proclamation Line of 1763 that forbade further white settlement beyond the Appalachians. At the end of the war they would thus enjoy special status as Britain's long faithful and never-defeated allies, and would finally make a lasting peace with the Choctaw in 1763. The British had, nonetheless, begun to take more direct control over all Indian allies, starting with the creation of a superintendency for southern Indians in 1756. Traders and Indians who had European ancestry took more power in Chickasaw affairs, working increasingly closely with British officials.

The Chickasaw fought against the colonists during the American Revolution, but managed to make peace with the new nation, starting with a treaty signed with Virginia in 1783. The Chickasaw would also ally with the Spanish, then would come under United States control because of the Louisiana Purchase. After this time, Chickasaw fortunes declined and they would be forced to accompany the Creek, Cherokee, Seminole, and Choctaw nations on the "Trail of Tears" to Oklahoma as a result of the Indian Removal Act of 1830.

The success the Chickasaw had in avoiding this catastrophe until the nineteenth century was due as much to their diplomacy as their method of making war. They were a comparatively small nation, and military strength would not have solved all their problems had they not been strategic in their foreign relations as well. The key to their success lay in their policy of keeping their European friends at a distance and their enemies in plain sight, a paradoxical stance that allowed them to avoid entangling relations with whites who pretended to be too friendly. Being trapped between two French settlements only made them wary of nearby Europeans—a wise policy. Indians who had

been near English settlements always suffered exploitation, whether they had been allies or not; Indians were displaced as soon as their military functions were no longer needed but their lands were. Sheltered in the Mississippi Valley, far from the expanding English population and distrustful of the French, the Chickasaw managed to avoid being displaced until the nineteenth century.

Joyce E. Chaplin

References
John Richard Alden, *John Stuart and the Southern Colonial Frontier* (1944); Verner W. Crane, *The Southern Frontier, 1670–1732* (1929); H.B. Cushman, *History of the Choctaw, Chickasaw and Natchez Indians* (1899); Patricia K. Galloway, "Choctaw Factionalism and Civil War, 1746–1750," in Carolyn Keller Reeves, ed., *The Choctaw before Removal* (1985).

James H. Malone, *The Chickasaw Nation: A Short Sketch of a Noble People* (1922); Gary B. Nash, *Red, White, and Black: The Peoples of Early America* (1974); M. Eugene Sirmans, *Colonial South Carolina: A Political History, 1663–1763* (1966); John R. Swanton, *The Indians of the Southeastern United States* (1946).

See also ACKIA, BATTLE OF; LE MOYNE DE BIENVILLE, JEAN-BAPTISTE; CHICKASAW WARS; CHOCTAW; CHOCTAW-CHICKASAW WAR; FRONTIER, SOUTHERN; LOUISIANA; NATCHEZ WAR; OGOULA TCHETOKA, BATTLE OF; RED SHOE

Chickasaw Wars (1736, 1739–1740)

The Chickasaw Wars were episodes in European-Indian relations that not only demonstrated the ability of the Chickasaw to resist one European power, the French, but also their inability to free themselves from a European-sponsored and debilitating enmity between their nation and that of the Choctaw. The wars resulted from factionalism within southeastern Indian nations and from the growing fears of French colonial officials that they would lose their dominance in the Mississippi Valley.

The Chickasaw had long tried to detach local tribes from direct alliance with the French. Since the 1690s, they had managed to maintain a tricky balancing act between the French and English, and among the neighboring Choctaw and Natchez towns. This balance ended abruptly when the Natchez attacked the French Forts Rosalie and St. Peter (near present-day Natchez) in November 1729, killing or taking captive most of the inhabitants. The French demanded other Indians assist in subduing the Natchez, which the Chickasaw refused to do, sheltering the fleeting Natchez instead. From this point forward, the French favored alliance with the Choctaw, using them to wear down the Chickasaw nation and discourage the English from expanding their trade and influence into the Mississippi Valley via the Chickasaw.

Alliance between the French and the Choctaw Indians began to weaken during the 1730s. English privateering and continental warfare lessened Louisiana's ability to deliver trade goods and treaty gifts to the Choctaw. A chief named Red Shoe (Shulush Humma) began to solicit English support in 1734; he might also have had marriage ties with the Chickasaw that overrode any pro-French sentiment. To prevent further erosion of Indian support, the French decided to strike at the Chickasaw using Choctaw warriors, a strategy that would weaken the former nation while implicating the latter in French military activities.

In 1735, Jean-Baptiste Le Moyne, sieur de Bienville (founder of New Orleans and Mobile, and governor of the French colony) organized an invasion of the Chickasaw nation at their center in Chikasahha near the present city of Memphis, Tennessee. He led a force of 500 Frenchmen and a number of Choctaw up the Tombigbee River in February 1736 toward the new Fort Tombecbé (250 miles above present-day Mobile), arranging to meet troops from France's Illinois territory, led by Pierre d'Artaguette. The Chickasaw easily brushed off the French invaders; Artaguette's forces attacked first and were repelled by 500 Chickasaw and 30 Englishmen at the town of Hashuk-humma. Bienville was also forced to retreat—on 29 May his troops fled in embarrassing disarray, and the Chickasaw captured prisoners and materiel. Bienville's new policy of attacking any Chickasaw without attempting to gain alliance through peace was evident in his attack on the town of Ackia, whose chief had been pro-French.

Understandably wary of French intentions toward any Indians, the Choctaw moved further toward the English and Chickasaw in the late 1730s. By this time, Red Shoe led a Choctaw faction of ten villages (out of 42) to accept English gifts, pledge military alliance with the provincial governments based in Charles Town and Savannah, and promise the English they would not raid Chickasaw villages. At the end of 1739, however, Red Shoe suddenly changed his stance; after returning from a disappointing visit to Georgia, he declared himself in favor of the French, burning three English trading warehouses and leading warriors against the Chickasaw.

In the atmosphere of worsening imperial tensions that would end in the Anglo-Spanish War (1739–1744), the Choctaw's shaky relations with the French took on heightened meaning. Encouraged by the sudden shoring-up of Choctaw-French relations in 1739, Bienville was determined to destroy the Chickasaw and called in not only troops from Louisiana, Illinois, and Canada, but from France as well. Troops from Illinois and Canada assembled across the Mississippi in what is now the state of Arkansas, and Bienville led a force of 1,200 French soldiers and 2,400 Indian allies up the Mississippi River in the spring of 1739, fearing the Tombigbee route would fail as it had done in 1736. A new post at Fort Assumption was the base for Bienville's operations.

Disease, delays, faulty attempts at exploring the region, and lack of provisions all prevented a sudden attack on Chikasahha. By January 1740, the assembled troops were in poor condition and, despite Bienville's reluctance to retreat or regroup, a provincial council of war that convened in February ordered him to fall back. As the body of troops descended the Mississippi, Pierre-Joseph Céleron de Blainville, leader of the men from Canada, marched on Chikasahha with 100 whites and 500 Indian soldiers. The Chickasaw had been aware of the size of the force initially arrayed against them, and evidently believed Celeron was the vanguard of the entire army. They sent an embassy to treat with Celeron, who accepted their terms and told them to pursue Bienville and present their case to him.

At this point, the Chickasaw underestimated the strength of their position. They might have attacked Celeron's troops, or even the fatigued force slipping back down the Mississippi. They pursued a path of peace, however, perhaps expecting too much from the recent, though inconclusive, defection of Choctaw villages to their side. Overtaking Bienville on his way back to New Orleans, the Chickasaw delegation managed to extract propositions of peace from him, but Bienville refused to include the Choctaw nation in the negotiations. The Choctaw were thus encouraged to continue warring on the Chickasaw, and received French rewards for Chickasaw scalps.

Bienville's conditions reflected not only a strategic attempt to continue weakening any Indians allied with Great Britain, but also an exploitation of the southeastern Indian system of blood revenge. Blood revenge had meant that Indians of one nation could seek justice for deaths through limited warfare on any members of the nation that had inflicted the deaths. The French, by fostering enmity between Choctaw and Chickasaw, demanded that the Choctaw seek vengeance for French deaths inflicted by English or Chickasaw by killing other Chickasaw—a policy that indirectly attacked the Chickasaw nation that had successfully repelled any direct French attack.

Joyce E. Chaplin

References

H.B. Cushman, *History of the Choctaw, Chickasaw and Natchez Indians* (1899); Patricia K. Galloway, "Choctaw Factionalism and Civil War, 1746–1750," in Carolyn Keller Reeves, ed., *The Choctaw before Removal* (1985); James H. Malone, *The Chickasaw Nation: a Short Sketch of A Noble People* (1922); M. Eugene Sirmans, *Colonial South Carolina: A Political History, 1663–1763* (1966).

See also ACKIA, BATTLE OF; LE MOYNE DE BIENVILLE, JEAN-BAPTISTE; CHICKASAW; OGOULA TCHETOKA, BATTLE OF; RED SHOE; FORT TOMBECBÉ (ALABAMA)

Chignecto Isthmus

At the head of Chignecto Bay lay Chignecto Isthmus, a strategically crucial strip of land that linked the Nova Scotia peninsula to the mainland. The isthmus was laced with rivers and marshes (the name, of Micmac origin, means "the great marsh district") quickly crossed by portage. To the north lay Baie Verte, to the south Beaubassin Bay, an arm of Chignecto Bay proper, which itself opened into the Bay of Fundy. The isthmus's central location was thus crucial, a crossroads to the St. John River, Ile Saint-Jean (Prince Edward Island), and Ile Royale. The whole network was linked with Canada by a recently opened road between Lake Temiscouata

and the Rivière du Loup. The area thus played a crucial part in France's Acadian strategy, designed to convince Acadians and Indians to raid the British settlements there.

The isthmus was the site of several significant military confrontations. During the winter of 1746–1747, French Captain Jean-Baptiste-Nicholas-Roch de Ramezay spent several months at Beaubassin in a strong fort, while the British wintered nearby with a force of 500 men at the Acadian village of Grande Pré. In the autumn of 1749, the chevalier Louis-Luc de la Corne was assigned the job of blocking the isthmus. During spring and summer 1750, he encountered a British detachment of about 400 men under Major Charles Lawrence; little of military import followed, and the confrontation was a standoff. As a result, though, the British constructed Fort Lawrence, the French, Forts Beauséjour and Gaspereau.

Most significant, of course, was the 1755 campaign in which a British/colonial force under Robert Monckton and John Winslow captured Fort Beauséjour and Fort Gaspereau, giving the British unchallenged control of Nova Scotia.

Ronald P. Dufour

See also FORT BEAUSÉJOUR (NOVA SCOTIA, CANADA); FORT GASPEREAU (NOVA SCOTIA, CANADA); GRAND PRÉ, BATTLE OF; FORT LAWRENCE (NOVA SCOTIA, CANADA); MONCKTON, ROBERT; WINSLOW, JOHN

Chippewa
See OJIBWA

Fort Chiswell (Virginia)
Erected in 1760, about eight miles east of the present town of Wytheville, in Wythe County, Virginia, Fort Chiswell was named for Colonel John Chiswell, owner of the nearby lead mines. Colonel William Byrd had the fort constructed to serve as winter quarters for his troops marching to relieve Fort Loudoun in Tennessee.

Later, Colonel Adam Stephen, who relieved Byrd (who had resigned after failing to reach Fort Loudoun), negotiated a treaty with the Cherokee at Fort Chiswell. The fort remained a military post, arsenal, and supply depot until 1790. Today the site of Fort Chiswell is a Virginia historic landmark.

Thomas Costa

References

Lewis Preston Summers, *History of Southwest Virginia, 1746–1786, and Washington County, 1777–1870* (1903).

Choctaw

The first mention of the historic Choctaws by name, as a large and formidable group of Indians somewhere to the west of the Apalachees, appears in Bishop Gabriel Díaz Vara Calderón's 1675 report on his journey to the Spanish missions of Florida. The Choctaws had probably emerged as a multiethnic confederacy sometime after Hernando de Soto passed through the Mississippi-Alabama region in 1540–1541 because Soto heard of no such group; they probably included people related to Soto's Mabila Indians (who had staged a huge battle with his forces) and the Pafalaya Indians of the Alabama-Tombigbee River region (who had abandoned their villages and taken their food supplies in advance of his arrival), together with eastern cousins of the ancestors of the Natchez living on the lower Pearl River. Clearly, only the western element of the confederacy on the headwaters of the Pearl River had been long resident in the region, for the rest of the historic Choctaw homeland of east central Mississippi was unpopulated in late prehistoric times.

Because the Choctaws came together as a confederacy during the long hiatus in European contact that followed the earliest Spanish explorations, the Europeans who first met them as an entity were Englishmen and Frenchmen. Although French explorer René-Robert Cavelier de La Salle did not meet with Choctaws in 1682, the establishment of a trading post on the Arkansas River in 1686 by his lieutenant, Henri de Tonti, aroused the British to block the French on the Mississippi by establishing contact with the Chickasaws and Quapaws in the 1690s. Soon afterward, a demand for slaves in the Carolinas led to British support of such Indian allies in making slave raids on other tribes, especially the Choctaws.

The Choctaws would continue to be important to the imperial strategies of the French and British throughout the colonial period. The reason for this is easy to see on a map. The Choctaws were so numerous—some 20,000 in 1700—that their neighbors tended to make alliance rather than war. If Choctaws allied with Chickasaws to the north and Mobilians, Tohomes, and Naniabas to the south, the combined tribes formed a north-south barrier lined up just west of the Tombigbee-Mobile River system that blocked the southern overland route to the Mississippi from the east.

During the first period of extended European contact, the British tried to use their influence with the Chickasaws to decimate the Choctaws and discourage the French from uniting their colonial ventures in the Illinois country and on the Gulf of Mexico. By the time the French were prepared to establish a colony on the Gulf coast, the Choctaws had lost more than 800 people to British-sponsored slave raids, not counting those who were killed defending their villages. Led by Pierre Le Moyne d'Iberville, the French landed on the Mississippi Gulf coast in 1699. Information given by the coastal tribes soon made the French aware of the size and power of the Choctaw nation, as well as its predicament at the hands of slave raiders. Iberville immediately recognized the buffer function the Choctaws could perform against the English if they could be armed, and their desperate need would guarantee loyalty. In 1702, as the War of the Spanish Succession broke out between the English and the French, the latter were preparing to make a permanent settlement at the north end of Mobile Bay, Tonti was called in by Iberville to serve as his ambassador to the Choctaws and Chickasaws.

The Choctaws recognized the advantages of an alliance with this new group of Europeans, who showed no signs of encroaching on Choctaw lands and offered the guns they needed to defend themselves. They returned with Tonti to the coast, providing safe-conduct as well for Chickasaw ambassadors who might make a treaty expelling the British slavers from their villages. The young French colony began to depend on the Choctaws not only for common defense, but when crops failed and supplies from France ran short, the French ate Choctaw food, and at times even accepted the hospitality of the Choctaw villages. In return, the Choctaws obtained firearms and other goods. The new French alliance held perils as well as benefits for the Choctaws. European diseases reduced their population from some 20,000 in 1700 to 15,000 within ten or 15 years.

When Europeans began to settle and take a place in the political world of the region, former patterns of friendship, alliance, and enmity shifted. The period of slave raiding, which partly coincided with and extended the conflict of the War of the Spanish Succession (1702–1713), simply expanded on early slaving efforts to encompass schemes for massive attacks on the Choctaws in 1708 and 1712. British alliances with the Chickasaws and Alabamas to carry out these projects made peaceful Choctaw relationships with these tribes impossible. On the other hand, the coastal and Mobile Bay tribes became even more closely linked with the Choctaws because they were similarly persecuted. During the course of the century these relationships changed. After the slaving period had passed and the British realized that annihilation of the Choctaws was not possible, their goal became to win them over through mediation of the Chickasaws. To the French, the Choctaw alliance always remained indispensable, so they would continue fairly consistently to promote war with the Chickasaws.

Alliances depended heavily on exchanges of goods and services that were seen to be profitable by both sides. The French used gifts in an attempt to control the Choctaws, while the British strategy was to win them over by commerce. In 1708, the French artificially set up a single Choctaw "Great Chief" through whom they tried to funnel all the gifts to the tribe. Over the years the natural power structure within the tribe caused it to become elaborated, so eventually one man was honored as supreme chief of the nation, while four other men were honored as "medal chiefs." The village chiefs and "honored men" (probably older men who served as advisors to the chiefs) also received gifts according to their rank. This system of gifts, which also included the gratis services of French gunsmiths for the maintenance of firearms, was in some ways misguided and unwieldy. Individual Choctaws, like the war chief Red Shoe, were able to take advantage of it to build loyal factions. And it cut both ways, when supplies failed to arrive on time from France, the chiefs were forced to seek another source of supply—the British—to maintain the influence they had built with their presents. Ambitious men not included in the system might do the same. But because the British were not willing to continue presents without commerce, the Choctaws never fully severed their relationship with the French.

During the early years of the French colony (1700–1717) colonists numbered only a few hundred, and were concentrated on the Mississippi Sound coast and the upper and lower ends of Mobile Bay. As communications with and supplies from France were cut off during the war, particularly in 1707 and again in 1708–1711, settlers were frankly dependent upon the Choctaws for help and sometimes for mere survival. Guided by the fine Indian diplomatist, Jean-Baptiste Le Moyne de Bienville, the colony held on to its small settlements and forged strong Choctaw loyalty as Bienville led French soldiers to defend against the British-led slave raids on the Choctaws and Frenchmen lost their lives in the Indians' defense.

At the close of the War of the Spanish Succession, the French crown found Louisiana an expensive luxury, and farmed it out to financier Antoine Crozat. Crozat and his governor, Antoine de Lamothe Cadillac, tried to milk the colony of every penny it could yield. This made trading terms with the French less and less favorable for the Choctaws and other Indians allied with the French at a time when the British were prosecuting an aggressive trading policy. The Choctaw-French alliance was saved by the greediness of the British traders, which led to the outbreak of the Yamasee War and the temporary withdrawal of many British traders from the interior in 1715–1717.

In addition, the French colony's operation was taken over by John Law and the Company of the West, which began to pump considerable investment into it. Bienville, who had been serving as a post commandant, was commissioned as governor in 1717. Although Bienville proceeded to capitalize on the results of the Yamasee War by establishing several new French posts, no trade house or outpost was placed among the Choctaws except for the small stocks kept in some villages by itinerant traders.

Under John Law the population of the Louisiana colony increased rapidly during the 1719–1722 period, but there was still no pressure on the Choctaw lands of east central Mississippi because the center of the colony shifted west to Biloxi and then to New Orleans. With this shift, most settlement pressure was exerted on the Natchez, whose eventual rebellion in 1729 brought the Choctaws into action as allies of the French. In the Natchez War of 1730–1731, the Choctaws served first in a party attacking the Natchez forts at Natchez, then attacking a refuge on the Red River. The young chiefs Red Shoe and Alibamon Mingo both distinguished themselves in the process.

In 1728, a Choctaw mission had been established in the village of Chickasawhay by Jesuit father Mathurin Le Petit. During the year of the Natchez rebellion, Governor Etienne Périer, who had replaced Bienville in 1723, had at last sent a young officer, Guillaume Régis du Roullet, to make a study for the establishment of a government-controlled trading house in the Choctaw nation. With the assistance of Le Petit's replacement, Father Michel Baudouin, Régis and another officer, Jean-Christophe de Lusser, explored a good deal of the Choctaw homeland. Ultimately, Régis established his trading post in the southernmost Choctaw town of Yowani on the Chickasawhay River because it was handy to both Mobile by land and New Orleans by river. The new interest evidenced by this exploration also resulted in the first attempt at a comprehensive mapping of the Choctaw towns; the famous 1733 map made on the basis of Régis' and de Lusser's reports by the commandant at Mobile, the baron de Crenay. This map would remain the best source for the location of the Choctaw towns until the remapping in the early 1770s by Bernard Romans.

After the Natchez War, the Natchez survivors fled to the Chickasaws, who had never completely given up allegiance to the English and had probably been involved in the Natchez-Yazoo conspiracy. In spite of the fact the revolt did ultimately fail, Governor Périer was blamed—probably justifiably—for having allowed such an uprising to take place at all. Once more, Bienville returned to take over as governor, charged with destroying the Natchez once and for all, subduing the Chickasaws and forcing them to give up their alliance with the English. The Choctaws were a fundamental element in his plans.

As a start, Bienville encouraged the Choctaws to make raids on the Chickasaws and paid a bounty for each Chickasaw killed, hoping that this tactic would force the Chickasaws to hand over the Natchez living among them and trade only with the French. It soon became apparent this plan would not work. It would, therefore, be necessary to undertake a major war against the Chickasaws, which Bienville did in 1736. He and his Choctaw allies came up the Tombigbee River—incidentally establishing the Tombecbé fort that the Choctaws had been requesting for years—with the intention of attacking the Chickasaws from the south, while a party of Frenchmen with Illinois Indian allies attacked from the north. The northern group, however, attacked too soon, and many of the Frenchmen in the party were captured and killed by the Chickasaws, whose English military advisors

found the campaign plans in the French commander's pocket. When the French and Choctaws attacked several days later, the Chickasaws were ready for them, and thus Bienville lost the famous Battle of Ackia in the vicinity of modern Tupelo, Mississippi.

His Choctaw allies had acquitted themselves well, however, and in this war Red Shoe earned the French medal that made it possible for him to begin to build a power base within the tribe. Alibamon Mingo also received a French medal for his part in the Natchez War. These two men were eventually to become the most influential leaders of the tribe.

Bienville's failure at Ackia meant he had to mount another expedition to assert French supremacy in the area and remove the Chickasaw (and British) threat to Mississippi River traffic. This expedition was to include massive numbers of French troops sent to Louisiana specifically for this purpose. While preparations were taking place, however, two Choctaws, a man and his wife, were murdered by two young men from Mobile. The Choctaws asked that justice be done. Bienville, realizing the risk of losing Choctaw allies, saw that the young men were tried and executed in front of Choctaw witnesses, thus establishing a precedent for equal justice for Indian allies.

Bienville's second Chickasaw War (1739–1740) was a logistical nightmare as the French attempted to mount a campaign overland from the Chickasaw Bluffs. It ended in a half-hearted and face-saving peace negotiated after a single attack made by a Canadian contingent and its Indian allies. The Choctaw contingent had long since gone home in disgust, Bienville was recalled to France, and Louisiana lost its wisest Indian diplomatist, being replaced by the marquis de Vaudreuil.

From 1740–1744, the Choctaws were involved in sporadic attacks on the Chickasaws in revenge for the murder of a peace embassy in 1740. In 1744, however, another war broke out in Europe, with France and England on opposite sides. The success of English sea power in enforcing blockades meant that it soon became impossible for the French in Louisiana to obtain the trade goods Choctaws wanted. A whole generation of Choctaws had become used to a steady supply of European trade goods, so during the middle 1740s, Alibamon Mingo joined Red Shoe in making peace with the Chickasaws and inviting English traders into the nation.

This move was strongly resented by the French, although the Choctaw intention seems to have been merely to take a neutral course as the Alabamas had done all along; but the French feared what might happen to their powerful Choctaw alliance, which was, in fact, soon in grave danger. For various reasons, including some undue attentions paid to Red Shoe's wife, a young officer from Fort Tombecbé and two traders who lived in the nation were killed. This happened apparently at the command of Red Shoe, but also with the cooperation of the two chiefs in whose villages the two traders were located. No one had forgotten that two young Frenchmen had murdered two Choctaws in 1738 and had been executed for it. So, to the French, it seemed eminently reasonable that they should demand the same kind of justice from the Choctaws. But Choctaw custom required when a murder occurred within the nation, only the family of the victim was entitled to carry out the execution of the murderer. Though it was an ally whose men had been murdered, any Choctaw who tried to avenge the murders would then put himself or his family in jeopardy. At first the Choctaws responded by killing Chickasaws and Englishmen, the common enemies of Frenchmen and Choctaw.

The French continued to insist that the guilty men or the chiefs who had ordered the murder should be killed by the Choctaws themselves, and threatened to withhold trade merchandise that the Choctaws needed. Their allies, however, no longer included the whole of the Choctaw tribe. Red Shoe had cleverly used presents and profits from both French and English to build a party for himself within the nation, predominantly located in the western division towns, and this party followed Red Shoe in going over entirely to the English. By the same token, Alibamon Mingo had built a similar faction in the eastern division, and this faction remained loyal to the French. Both factions killed French and Englishmen, respectively, to satisfy their European allies. Such proxy murders went on back and forth for many months until finally a Choctaw escort of one of the English trading convoys was killed by accident.

Now there was cause for the intratribal retaliation mechanism to come into play as the Choctaws were now divided in their allegiances and pressured by their European allies. The reasons why this single death escalated rapidly into civil war are complex, but the main outlines are clear. In spite of the fact the pro-British faction enjoyed numerical superiority, the English line of supply was too long and it was difficult to provide the war materials they needed. In the end, the proximity of the French to their allies told in their favor. More than 400 Choctaws were killed, and the sixtowns division was savagely split apart before the war ended in 1750 with a treaty that provided for a more regular settlement of murders between French and Choctaws.

There is no doubt, however, that the social structure of the Choctaw nation was seriously damaged by this civil war, which pitted the formerly cohesive constituent groups against each other. The Choctaws, who up until the war had notably resisted any serious adoption of European custom, were much more culturally vulnerable in the aftermath.

The years following the Choctaw civil war appear to have been quiet ones for the tribe, as French and British clashes shifted further east. At the conclusion of the French and Indian War with the Treaty of Paris in 1763, the French handed over their lands east of the Mississippi River to the English, who insisted for the first time on formal land grants from the Choctaws. In 1780, the British succumbed to the Spaniards, who had been wooing the Choctaws for years. The Spaniards then reestablished the abandoned Fort Tombecbé as Fort Confederation and supplied the Choctaws liberally with trade goods through Panton, Leslie, and Company in Pensacola.

Patricia Galloway

References
Verner W. Crane, *The Southern Frontier, 1670–1732* (1929); Patricia Galloway, "Choctaw Factionalism and Civil War, 1746–1750," *Journal of Mississippi History* 44 (1982):289–327; ———, "Confederacy as a Solution to Chiefdom Dissolution: Historical Evidence in the Choctaw Case," in Charles Hudson and Carmen McClendon, eds., *Spanish Explorers and Indian Chiefdoms: The Southeastern United States in the Sixteenth and Seventeenth Centuries* (1991). Clara Sue Kidwell and Charles Roberts, *The Choctaws: A Critical Bibliography* (1980); Dunbar Rowland and A.G. Sanders, eds. and trans., *Mississippi Provincial Archives: French Dominion*, Vols. I–III (1927–1932); Dunbar Rowland, A.G. Sanders, and Patricia Galloway, eds. and trans., *Mississippi Provincial Archives: French Dominion*, Vols.

IV and V (1984); John R. Swanton, *Sources for the Social and Ceremonial Life of the Choctaw Indians,* Bureau of American Ethnology Bulletin 103 (1931); Richard White, *The Roots of Dependency: Subsistence, Environment, and Social Change among the Choctaws, Pawnees, and Navajos* (1983).

See also CHICKASAW; CHICKASAW WARS; CHOCTAW-CHICKASAW WARS; CHOCTAW CIVIL WAR; CREEK; CREEK-CHOCTAW WARS; FRONTIER, SOUTHERN; LE MOYNE DE BIENVILLE, JEAN-BAPTISTE; LOUISIANA; NATCHEZ WAR; RED SHOE

Choctaw-Chickasaw War (1752)

The failed French and Choctaw assault on the Chickasaw nation in 1752 was the culmination of a half-century of conflict in the Mississippi Valley, the last in a series of unsuccessful French campaigns which preceded that nation's loss of authority in the region after 1763, and the capstone of successful diplomacy and warfare on the part of the Chickasaw.

The 1752 raid had been preceded by two earlier assaults in 1736 and during the winter of 1739–1740, and grew out of repeated attempts on the part of the Choctaw, sometime allies of the French, to disengage themselves from France. While encouraged to make war on the pro-English Chickasaw, the Choctaw had long suspected they might gain more from an alliance with their aboriginal neighbors, who tended to follow through on their promises of military alliance (with the assistance of English traders) more often than the French. A Choctaw faction led by Red Shoe had been courting the English as potential allies; Red Shoe had first declared himself in alliance with Great Britain in the mid-1730s, then had gone back on this threat in 1739. During King George's War and the disruptions in shipping it entailed, Louisiana received few shipments of trade goods that they could use to placate Choctaw allies. Red Shoe became dissatisfied with the French—he killed three French traders in November 1746, made peace with the Chickasaw, and sent a delegation to Charles Town led by his brother, the Little King.

On 18 April 1747, South Carolina Governor James Glen signed a treaty with the Choctaw, giving them arms in exchange for attacking French settlements. Glen intended his strategy to support Britain's efforts in the war against France, but his promises to reward the Choctaw for their military alliance far exceeded his effective delivery of trade goods and gifts to them. Soon, civil war raged between pro-English and pro-French towns in the Choctaw nation. In the meantime, a French agent assassinated Red Shoe in 1747, and the Little King died two years later. By 1749, 22 out of the 46 towns in the Choctaw nation made renewed promises of loyalty to France, and the other towns seemed to be leaning toward this stance. Glen continued to bungle attempts to deliver guns and ammunition to the Choctaw, and the British government would not support his strategy against the French. When King George's War ended in 1748, the Carolina-Choctaw experiment in alliance had amounted to nothing.

The experiment had made the French nervous, on the other hand. Louisiana's governor, Pierre de Rigaud de Vaudreuil, waited for the Choctaw towns to return to the French alliance, then planned a 1752 raid—using 700 French soldiers and a large force of Indians—on the Chickasaw nation, which had been weakened by smallpox in 1749. His efforts paralleled Anglo-French squabbles along the Miami River (1752) and in the Ohio Valley (1753). But two military ventures against the Chickasaw—under Benoist in 1752 and under Reggio in 1753—failed. As with every other attempt to invade the nation, the sorties were botched failures. Chickasaw victory ended British suggestions that the nation remove eastward, an action the French had hoped for because it would remove a hostile Indian group that lay between the French colonies in Louisiana and Illinois. This sore point would be moot after Britain's victory over France in the French and Indian War (1754–1763): Britain would gain control of the Mississippi Valley and the Chickasaw would enjoy special status as long-faithful and never-conquered allies.

Joyce E. Chaplin

References

H.B. Cushman, *History of the Choctaw, Chickasaw and Natchez Indians* (1899); Patricia K. Galloway, "Choctaw Factionalism and Civil War, 1746–1750," in Carolyn Keller Reeves, ed., *The Choctaw before Removal* (1985); James H. Malone, *The Chickasaw Nation: A Short Sketch of a Noble People* (1922); M. Eugene Sirmans, *Colonial South Carolina: A Political History, 1663–1763* (1966).

See also CHICKASAW; CHOCTAW; LOUISIANA

Choctaw Civil War (1746–1750)

The Choctaw Civil War, which lasted from 1746 to 1750, resulted from the attempt by the red (war) chief Shulashumastabé, also known as Red Shoe and Soulier Rouge, to establish an English alliance, and Louisiana's success in blocking it. Red Shoe, who rose to prominence fighting the Chickasaws during the 1720s and 1730s, hoped to emulate the Creeks, who had an alliance and trading relationship with both the British and the French. The Creeks and the French were both against an Anglo-Choctaw alliance in order to keep the British from gaining too much influence in the region. Red Shoe could only open trade by way of the Chickasaws, who, despite several decades of endemic conflict with the Choctaws, were anxious to facilitate the Anglo-Choctaw relationship that would enhance their role as middlemen. Louisiana's inability to adequately supply the Choctaws gave Red Shoe the leverage he needed to convince a significant portion of the nation, initially mostly from the western division, to follow him.

In 1738, South Carolina recognized Red Shoe as "King of the Choctaws," but it took until April 1747 to conclude a formal Anglo-Choctaw alliance. South Carolina Governor James Glen attempted to grant a monopoly of the Choctaw trade to a company in which he was a silent partner; the company badly mishandled the trade, never providing Red Shoe or his followers with the goods or ammunition they needed to counter French-sponsored diplomacy and war. Louisiana curtailed Red Shoe's influence during the colony's war with the Chickasaws (1736–1740), but in its aftermath attempted to forestall the alliance by encouraging its partisans to kill Chickasaws and British traders operating in the nation; Red Shoe's partisans killed three Frenchmen in 1746 to satisfy the English for the deaths of their traders.

In January 1747, Louisiana Governor Pierre de Rigaud de Vaudreuil demanded the deaths of Red Shoe and two lieutenants; the Choctaws resisted because in their culture the aggrieved party was responsible for extracting retributive justice, and there was no mechanism for a sanctioned murder, i.e., every death required clan retaliation. French partisans, mostly from the eastern division of the Choctaws, attempted to satisfy the French with the deaths of Englishmen and Chickasaws, but because the Choctaws were so dependent on French trade and presents, they reluctantly agreed to French demands, and Red Shoe was killed by unknown assassins in June 1747. Red Shoe's partisans took the war to French settlements near Mobile, on the "German Coast" upriver from New Orleans, and to Natchez, as well as to their fellow Choctaws in 1747 and 1748. Although the eastern division was basically pro-French, and the western division pro-English, the escalating chain of attacks led to an ever-increasing spiral of killings which split each of the divisions, including the generally neutral central division. Although by November 1748 the Choctaws had fulfilled the original French demand for three chiefs' heads, Vaudreuil then demanded satisfaction for deaths on the German Coast.

By March 1749, inability to resolve the crisis had disrupted the fabric of Choctaw society to such a point that Seneacha village split into French and British factions that made war on each other. By mid-1750, Louisiana officials realized that the Choctaw nation would destroy itself if the war was not resolved definitively; in September 1750, Fort Tombecbé commandant Joseph Louis Boucher de Grand Pré led a party of French soldiers and eastern division warriors in an attack on the western villages of Cushtusha and Caffetalaya that resulted in the destruction of the villages and the death of many Choctaws. Afterwards, the Choctaws agreed they would avenge the deaths of any Frenchmen; British traders and their Choctaw sponsors would be killed with no retaliation; the western division would destroy their forts and give up their prisoners; and the Choctaws would take up war with the Chickasaws once more. More than 400 Choctaws died in the civil war; adding to the disruption of Choctaw society was a smallpox epidemic that at the same time took more than 1,200 lives.

Michael James Foret

References

James Adair, *Adair's History of the American Indians,* ed. by Samuel Cole Williams (1930); Edmond Atkin, "Historical Account of the Revolt of the Chactaw Indians in the late War from the French to the British Alliance, and of their Return Since to that of the French . . . ," Lansdowne Manuscripts, Vol. 809, folios 1–32, British Museum, copy located in the Mississippi Department of Archives and History, Jackson, Mississippi; Michael James Foret, "On the Marchlands of

Empire: Trade, Diplomacy, and War on the Southeastern Frontier, 1733–1763," Ph.D. Dissertation, College of William and Mary (1990).

Patricia Galloway, "Choctaw Factionalism and Civil War, 1746–1750," in Carolyn Keller Reeves, ed., *The Choctaw before Removal* (1985):120–156; Charles W. Paape, "The Choctaw Revolt: A Chapter in the Intercolonial Rivalry in the Old Southwest," Ph.D. Dissertation, University of Illinois (1946).

See also ADAIR, JAMES; CHICKASAW WARS; CHOCTAW; GLEN, JAMES; RED SHOE

Fort Christanna (Virginia)

Located in Brunswick County, Virginia, adjacent to the Meherrin River, Fort Christanna was built in 1714 by Governor Alexander Spotswood, who wished to provide defense against the western Indians and reform the Indian trade. Following the Tuscarora War (1711–1713), Spotswood desired that tribes living on the south side of the James River form a buffer against the more hostile Indians of North Carolina. His policy also included sending children of friendly tribes as hostages to be educated at the College of William and Mary.

Named for Christ and Queen Anne, Fort Christanna stood on a six-square-mile tract which included settlements for friendly Indians. Each of the fort's five sides were about 100 feet long. The walls were formed by five large log houses as bastions connected by a wooden palisade backed with earth. Each house contained a large gun weighing 1,400 pounds, and the garrison numbered 12 men and an officer.

In conjunction with the building of Fort Christanna and adjacent Indian settlements, Spotswood organized the Virginia Indian Company, granting it a 20-year monopoly of the Indian trade south of the James River. In return for this monopoly, after two years the company would take over maintenance of the fort and its garrison. Spotswood's subsequent attempts to get funds for the Indian Company's expenditures for the fort provoked protests from Virginia burgesses.

In 1717, the Iroquois attacked a number of friendly Indians at Christanna, and the Virginia Council debated dismantling the fort. The following year the House of Burgesses voted to abandon Fort Christanna and disband the In-

dian Company. The settlements remained inhabited during the 1720s, but as English settlers moved into the area, the Indians relocated. By the 1730s the fort had fallen into disuse, and by 1752 it was reported abandoned.

Thomas Costa

References
David K. Hazard and Martha W. McCartney, "Fort Christanna," *Archaeological Reconaissance Survey* (1979).

See also SPOTSWOOD, ALEXANDER; TUSCARORA WAR

Fort Christina (Delaware)

Fort Christina, constructed at the junction of two rivers on the site of present-day Wilmington, Delaware, was well situated for defense since it was partially surrounded by swamps, and also could load and unload ships. The plan of Christina was that of a typical seventeenth-century fort: a square with projecting corners in the shape of arrowheads. The two corners that faced the river, along with the northeast corner, were mounted with cannons taken from the *Kalmar Nyckel*, the ship that brought over the first colonists. Christina consisted of earthen ramparts and a palisade of wooden posts sharpened at one end. The initial size of the garrison was 25 men. At this time, two log houses were built within the confines of Christina's walls. Fort Christina was primarily a trading post.

By 1640, the walls of the fort had collapsed in three places due to neglect. They were repaired, but the Swedish colonists continued their neglectful ways so that in 1644 the fort needed a complete overhaul. Ten years later the fort had to be rebuilt once again and the work was not yet complete when the Dutch captured it in 1655.

The size of the different garrisons that manned the fort and the number of civilians residing in or near the fort varied over the years, but growth was slow. In 1644, 34 people, only three of whom were regular soldiers, resided here. On the eve of the Dutch conquest of New Sweden, 100 people, only a few of whom were soldiers, lived in and around Fort Christina.

In 1655, during the general campaign against New Sweden, Petrus Stuyvesant, at the head of 300 Dutch soldiers and seven ships, captured Fort Christina without firing a shot. The Dutch renamed it Altena.

Anthony P. Inguanzo

References

Israel Acrelius, *A History of New Sweden: or, The Settlements on the River Delaware* (1874); Amandus Johnson, *Swedish Settlements on the Delaware, 1638–1664* (1911); John A. Munroe, *Colonial Delaware: A History* (1978); Albert Cook Myers, ed., *Narratives of Early Pennsylvania, West New Jersey and Delaware, 1630–1707* (1912); Louis B. Wright, *The Atlantic Frontier: Colonial American Civilization, 1607–1763* (1947).

See also NEW SWEDEN; STUYVESANT, PETRUS

Chubb, Pasco (?–1698)

Perhaps no provincial officer had more contempt heaped upon him by contemporaries than Pasco Chubb. A citizen of Andover, Massachusetts, Chubb had served on the Maine frontier in the early part of King William's War, leading patrol and raiding parties before ordered to relieve John March as commander of Fort William Henry at Pemaquid. In February 1696, several prominent Indian chiefs approached the fort to parley for the exchange of prisoners. During the meeting, Chubb and his men attacked the chiefs, killing four and capturing one. Later that summer, Fort William Henry was invested by several hundred French and Indians, with naval support and artillery, led by Pierre Le Moyne d'Iberville. Chubb initially put up a brave front, replying to a surrender request that he would not yield the fort though "the sea was covered by French vessels, and the land with Indians." But fearing what the Indians would do to him and his command because of the incident in February, Chubb surrendered the fort after one day of bombardment.

On his return to Boston, Chubb was thrown in jail to await court-martial. Although he petitioned the government to either bring him to trial or set him free, Chubb was not released, and sat in jail through the winter. In March 1697, a vote taken in the assembly acknowledged the imprisonment of this *persona non grata*. Chubb's court-martial never took place, and he was released that spring to live quietly in Andover. Less than a year later, in February 1696, the Indians killed both Chubb and his wife, apparently in revenge for his treachery two years before.

Steven C. Eames

References

Steven C. Eames, "Rustic Warriors: Warfare and the Provincial Soldier on the Northern Frontier, 1689–1748," Ph.D. Dissertation, University of New Hampshire (1989); Cotton Mather, *Decennium Luctuosum* (1699), rpt. in Charles H. Lincoln, ed., *Narratives of the Indian Wars, 1675–1699* (1913).

See also MARCH, JOHN; FORT WILLIAM HENRY (MAINE)

Church, Benjamin (1639–1718)

It can be stated with little exaggeration that Benjamin Church was the first English provincial to learn and adopt the ways of *la petite guerre*—guerrilla warfare including small groups of men who live off the land as they gather intelligence and strike quickly at enemy targets. He blazed a trail that others such as John Lovewell, Johnson Harmon, John Goffe, and Robert Rogers would follow. Born in Duxbury, Plymouth Colony, in 1639, Church learned the carpentry trade from his father. But in 1674, he gave up carpentry for a less sure but more exciting existence on the frontier. He settled in what would become Little Compton, Rhode Island, partners with a group of speculators interested in the Plymouth-Rhode Island border. Church apparently did not contribute money; he was the front man, serving as a connection with the local Indian tribes. Church developed a relationship with the local female sachem (his wife had not accompanied him to the frontier) which would serve him well in King Philip's War.

From the beginning Church showed no reluctance to deal with the native population on an equal basis. He regularly used Indians in his commands, listening and learning from them the secrets of their warfare. This affinity for pagan Indians, his inclination to live on the edge of the frightening wilderness, and his less than fervent church affiliation created stormy relations with the political powers of both Massachusetts Bay and Plymouth colonies. They saw in Benjamin Church an effective military leader, but certainly no Puritan.

Church was drafted by Plymouth authorities at the start of King Philip's War to serve as a guide or "pilot." He participated in numerous skirmishes and the Great Swamp Fight. According to his entertaining memoirs, he promoted the use of mixed native/white forces, but the

Puritan leadership initially rejected such a blasphemous thought. They finally relented in the summer of 1676 and allowed Church the independence to employ his own methods. His success culminated in the death of King Philip and the capture of Philip's chief officer, Annawon.

King William's War greatly expanded the area of battle for New England. Rather than fighting an enemy within the geographic limits of the English holdings, the provincials had to mount attacks against long-distance targets in Maine and the maritimes. The exploits of Benjamin Church provided an exception to the rather bleak record of offensive scouts during that first French war. Church was one of the few veterans of King Philip's War able to utilize his previous experience and adapt to the new, larger kind of conflict. Using his usual mixed force of Indians and whites, Church participated in four major raids. The first, in 1689, consisted principally of his arrival "in the nick of time" to help drive away an enemy force attacking the settlement at Casco Bay, an engagement known as the Battle of Brackett's Woods. During the second raid in the fall of 1690, Church landed at Macquoit (Freeport, Maine), marched to the abandoned Fort Andros at Pejepscot, and then up the Androscoggin River to an Indian fort where he killed several Indians, captured some important Indian women, and destroyed the structure. At a council of war, his officers convinced him to end the raid, so they returned to Macquoit and sailed to Casco Bay, now deserted after the French capture of Fort Loyal earlier that summer.

While at Casco Bay, he allowed his Indians to sleep on shore, where they were attacked by a force of French Indians. Church disembarked the rest of his command and drove the attackers away, but not without one scary, and in hindsight only, amusing moment. Hugging the bank along the shore, the Plymouth Indians held off the enemy until Church could land his provincial soldiers. Church, assisted by James Converse, passed the word he would give three shouts as a signal for attack, and then, having shouted three times, he and Converse launched themselves up the bank toward the enemy. However, Church's valiant charge ended abruptly when Converse yelled that no one else had followed them. The two officers hastily retreated back to the bank under heavy fire where they organized another assault and, this time followed by their men, drove the enemy away.

On returning to Portsmouth, he wanted to enlist more soldiers and continue the raid, but the Massachusetts Bay government, shocked at the debts incurred over the Quebec expedition, begged poverty and disbanded his command. In fact, the government could not afford to pay either Church or Converse for their services. Church related how the two officers met in a tavern and could not come up with enough money between them for a parting glass. Church's brother had to send him a horse so he could get home.

The third raid, in 1692, attempted ambushes around Penobscot Bay, and then proceeded up the Kennebec River to Teconnet. The Indians burned their village at his approach, but he did manage to destroy considerable stores of corn. Four years later, his fourth raid went along the coast of Maine and into the Bay of Fundy, where he plundered and burned some French settlements. Superseded in command by a Lieutenant Colonel Hathorne, Church wanted to raid the principal Indian village at Norridgewock, but Hathorne refused. The raid ended with a half-hearted attempt to take a small French fort and truck house on the St. John River.

Church's last raid occurred at the beginning of Queen Anne's War. Before going on the raid, Church drew up a list of recommendations for the Massachusetts Bay government concerning this raiding party and long-range scouts, in general, which provides some insight into his methods. He suggested that all whaleboats be fitted with leather loops and poles so they could be lifted over rocks, that two brass kettles be sent with every boat to cook food, and that all soldiers wear "Indian shoes" to protect the whaleboats and canoes. Church further suggested that leather, hemp, and wax be brought along to replace worn-out shoes. The raiding party should also take hatchets or light axes, "made pretty broad," to widen carrying places for the whaleboats. Church felt that whalemen should be hired to run the boats, as long as they could be released for whaling in the fall. Samuel Penhallow reported that it was the custom of the men under Church's command "to rest in the Day, and row in the Night; and never fire at an Indian if they could reach him with a Hatchet, for fear of alarming them." On this occasion Church again raided along the Maine coast and into the Bay of Fundy, the principle damage being the burning of Grand Pré, destruction of the dikes in that area, and the capture of French settlers to exchange for English prisoners. During one chase, the now elderly and overweight warrior had a sergeant assigned to boost him over fallen trees.

In one action, Church ordered his men to pull down a bark house where some people were holed up and to "knock them in the head, never asking whether they were French or Indians; they being all enemies alike to me." They were French, as it turned out, and the Massachusetts authorities, who, of course, were not present in the action, had a different view of the matter. Church came under a cloud for ordering the deaths of French prisoners. As Samuel Penhallow observed, "notwithstanding the Fatigue that this worthy Gentleman had undergone, and the Dangers he had run; the Spoil he had done, and the victories he had won, yet he could not escape the Censures of many." After much debate, the Massachusetts General Court finally voted him thanks and paid him 15 pounds.

Although he retired under a cloud, Benjamin Church's expertise in warfare was not forgotten. Samuel Vetch consulted him in preparing for his aborted expedition against Quebec in 1709. Church extolled the virtues of whaleboats so well that Vetch ordered 35 of the craft. Church's memoirs, *The Entertaining History of King Philip's War,* prepared by his son, Thomas, were published in 1716. Two years later he died on 17 January, and was buried in Little Compton, Rhode Island.

Steven C. Eames

References

Thomas Church, *The History of Philip's War* (1829); Richard Slotkin, *Regeneration Through Violence: The Mythology of the American Frontier, 1600–1860* (1973).

See also BRACKETT'S WOOD, BATTLE OF; CONVERSE, JAMES; FALMOUTH, BATTLE OF; KING WILLIAM'S WAR; QUEEN ANN'S WAR; RANGER; SCOUT

Fort Clinton (New York)

See FORT SARATOGA (NEW YORK)

Cockacoeske, Queen of the Pamunkey (?–1686)

Cockacoeske, who in 1656 became queen of the Pamunkey, was a descendant of Opechanca-nough (brother of the paramount chief, Powhatan) and successor of her late husband, Totopotomoy, who led the Pamunkey from c. 1649 to 1656. The Pamunkey, like other native subscribers to the Virginia-Indian treaty of 1646, were tributaries to the English crown. Thus, by the time Cockacoeske commenced her rule, the ancient Powhatan chiefdom had disintegrated and the Indians of Virginia's coastal plain no longer were subordinate to a paramount native leader.

At the onset of 1676, Cockacoeske was summoned to Jamestown, where members of the Governor's Council asked her for warriors to oppose the hostile tribes that lived on the colony's frontier. The Pamunkey queen, who "entered the chamber with a comportment graceful to admiration," tearfully reminded the council it was in just such circumstances that her husband, Totopotomoy, and a hundred of his warriors had lost their lives. At length, however, she agreed to lend 12 warriors to the colonists' campaign, although she was rumored to have 150 under her command.

In March 1676, the Pamunkey signed a peace treaty with Virginia Governor William Berkeley, just as the popular uprising known as Bacon's Rebellion had gotten underway. Even so, Nathaniel Bacon and his followers made two unprovoked attacks upon the Pamunkey, during which they took both prisoners and plunder and drove the Indians from their village. Later, Cockacoeske, as a tributary leader, petitioned the colonial government for the restoration of her people and personal belongings. In 1677, when King Charles II's commissioners arrived in Virginia to investigate the cause of Bacon's Rebellion, they concluded that Cockacoeske was "a faithfull friend to and lover of the English" and asked that she, in recognition of her loyalty, be sent a cornet and regal attire.

That Cockacoeske was a leader of considerable influence and political acumen is evidenced by the fact that in May 1677, when the Virginia government signed a major treaty with the Indians of the coastal plain, "severall nations [were] now reunited" under her subjugation. But some of the tribes who had been free of domination by the Pamunkey since 1646 stubbornly refused to resume their old subservient roles. Cockacoeske, though unsuccessful in her attempt to recapture the chiefly dominance enjoyed by her people's leaders during the first half of the seventeenth century, ruled the Pamunkey until her death in 1686.

Martha W. McCartney

References

Charles M. Andrews, *Narratives of the Insurrections, 1675–1690* (1915); Peter Force, *Tracts and Other Papers Relating Principally to the Origin, Settlement, and Progress of the Colonies in North America*, 4 vols. (1836); William W. Hening, ed., *The Statutes at Large: Being a Collection of All the Laws of Virginia*, 13 vols. (1809–1823).

Martha W. McCartney, "Cockacoeske, Queen of Pamunkey: Diplomat and Suzeraine," in Peter H. Wood, et al., eds., *Powhatan's Mantle: Indians in the Colonial Southeast* (1989); Wilcomb E. Washburn, *The Governor and the Rebel: A History of Bacon's Rebellion in Virginia* (1957).

See also BACON'S REBELLION; PAMUNKEY; VIRGINIA-INDIAN TREATY (1646)

Fort Condé (Alabama)

The French built fortifications on the Mobile River to help guard the mouth of the Mississippi as early as 1702. From the start, flooding pestered the French, who had moved their fortifications to the modern site of Mobile, Alabama, by 1711. First named Fort Louis de la Mobile and then renamed Fort Condé, this fort, with its stone and brick foundation, was an important statement of French military power in the southeast.

The actual value of the fort under potential attack was questionable. The locally-made bricks were of inferior value and the fort's buildings were of timber—in fact, the entire structure faced the repeated threat of collapse. Moreover, the soldiers assigned to the fort were usually too few and of poor health and military skills. Fortunately for the French, the British did not test the fort and its soldiery.

Alan Gallay

References

Marcel Giraud, *A History of French Louisiana*. Vol. V: *The Company of the Indies, 1723–1731*, trans. Brian Pearce (1987).

See also FORT LOUIS (ALABAMA)

Conferences

FOR SPECIFIC CONFERENCES, SEE UNDER INDIVIDUAL NAMES

Congresses

FOR SPECIFIC CONGRESSES, SEE UNDER INDIVIDUAL NAMES

Connecticut

Massachusetts' residents traveled to Connecticut in the 1630s in search of the fertile soil they had heard of in the Connecticut River Valley. By March 1636, the core of the Connecticut colony of three towns and 250 settlers had been established. Colonists settled in Connecticut for many years without a charter from the English government, leaving them independent in their governing. In 1662, they received a charter that allowed them to continue in their tradition of autonomous governing. They cherished this charter above all else and strongly defended it throughout the colonial years.

In its first decade, Connecticut did not organize militarily, but did prohibit colonists from bartering guns with Indians, as leaders were wary of the natives, who exhibited superior military skills. After several outbreaks of violence with the Pequot Indians, Connecticut residents set up a militia system requiring men over 16 to take part in training.

In 1636, the Pequot War began when Massachusetts attacked Indians on Block Island. This quickly escalated into a full scale war with Pequot attacks upon Connecticut. The New England colonies responded powerfully, and with their Indian allies, the Mohegans and the Narragansetts, a quick and decisive victory was attained. The victory was so complete that Connecticut, in comparison to other colonies, had relatively little military problem with Native Americans in the following decades. But Connecticut also became dependent on its Amerindian allies for security and did not develop adequate military skills to defend itself. One consequence of its increased dependence on the leader of the Mohegans, Uncas, was his easy manipulation of the colony to meet his own ends. This caused extra military problems for Connecticut, especially in its relations with the Narragansetts, the Mohegans' competitor. To meet the perceived threats, Connecticut found allies outside of its borders by joining the New England

Confederation, an alliance of New Haven, Massachusetts, and Plymouth in 1643.

The Dutch, who preceded the English colonists in Connecticut, were also of concern. Settled at Fort Good Hope, the Dutch warned away with no success the first English expedition led by William Holmes in 1633. Shortly after the establishment of English settlement, a Dutch force of 70 confronted the newcomers at the Windsor trading house, attempting again to scare them away. The English responded by reinforcing their position. Dutch access to the sea was then cut off by an independent group of English who built Fort Saybrook at the mouth of the Connecticut River. Growing numbers of English increasingly isolated the Dutch. Tensions continued over the next two decades as both competed for trade with Indians. When war broke out between the English and the Netherlands in the 1650s, Connecticut authorities seized Fort Good Hope.

Diplomatic relations with American Indians after the Pequot War through 1675 were uneasy, but the exchange of furs, wampum, and European goods tied people together. Also, there was little pressure placed on the Indians for their land in the 1640s and 1650s. In the 1660s, the native-settler coexistence deteriorated as the local fur supply diminished, wampum was discontinued as the colonial currency, and English land hunger increased.

The last great Indian threat to Connecticut erupted in 1675 due to the Plymouth Colony's increased pressure on King Philip and his people, the Wampanoag. The chief convinced several tribes to join him in an attempt to rid the region of all English colonists. Soon all of New England was embroiled in the worst warfare between Indians and American colonists in the seventeenth century. Connecticut's frontier was concerned with the threat of surprise attack. Most towns initiated a watch and many built additional fortifications for added protection. Connecticut authorities held that the colonists' best defense was to conduct fair relations with local Indians, which would allow the colony to focus its resources against hostile forces. Most tribes did not join with King Philip, and believed it in their best interests to ally with the colonists. Unlike the Pequot War, the colonists were unable to deliver a quick and decisive blow to end the conflict. Instead, outbreaks of violence continued for many months, and the colonists took the opportunity to nearly annihilate both the Narragansetts and the Nipmucks. At the end of the war, great numbers of Indians surrendered to the English. Though victorious, the colonies suffered financially and diplomatically as the United Colonies was greatly weakened because of the constant bickering and disagreements among its members. King Philip's War did give Connecticut experience useful in meeting the challenge of future French encroachments on its frontier.

With the failure of united colonial efforts in King Philip's War, Connecticut was especially horrified by the threat to its charter by the Dominion of New England. The English crown took advantage of the weak state New England colonies were in after King Philip's War to gain more power in the region. Edmund Andros was sent over to the colonies as governor of the dominion, which eventually combined New York and the New England colonies into one political entity. In July 1675, he attempted to take over Fort Saybrook and the surrounding territory, but was unsuccessful. However, a decade later, Connecticut surrendered into the dominion. Andros took over Connecticut's government in October 1687, but was unable to seize the colony's charter. He had a great deal of trouble raising both troops and money for the Anglo-French conflict because the governing apparatus of Connecticut had been superseded by his takeover. The dominion collapsed in April 1689 when William of Orange replaced King James II, and Connecticut leaders remained forever soured on imperial military colonial unions.

The colonists' enemies were in large part determined by England's enemies, as was evident in the series of Anglo-French wars from the late seventeenth century through the 1750s. At stake in King William's War, lasting from 1689 to 1697, was control of the Northwestern Atlantic fisheries, the continental fur trade, and ultimately control of North America. Connecticut was involved with both the unsuccessful expedition in 1690 to seize Quebec and the occupation of the French fortress of Port Royal in Acadia. Connecticut was able to prevent direct attacks by French raiders on its own soil by successfully defending western Massachusetts. The crown believed Connecticut's resources inadequate to defeat Canada, and appointed a royal governor to supervise defense efforts. Fearing for its charter, the colony's leaders determined Connecticut's immediate safety was not at stake in this conflict with the French, so they refused to turn over their military resources to imperial control. Connecticut was so success-ful at keeping English authorities at bay that it would soon have to find a way to placate them. With the lack of imminent danger, Connecticut also found its military system, based on popu-lar consent and voluntary participation, to be ineffective.

With imperial authorities angry at Con-necticut for its isolating tactics, the colony found involvement in Queen Anne's War (1702–1713) necessary to demonstrate loyalty. With the de-struction of nearby Deerfield, Massachusetts, in 1704, Connecticut towns were instructed to for-tify, and with its own borders readied, authori-ties sent soldiers to help defend western Massa-chusetts. By 1709, colonists had decided that the best way to rid themselves of the border menace was to cut it off at the source, so campaigns were planned to make several attacks in Canada. Con-necticut contributed to all three efforts, although only one was a success. Because of the expense of the 1709, 1710, and 1711 expeditions, Con-necticut's financial structure was reorganized and its first paper money was distributed. The distant fighting also required adaptation from a frontier militia system. Connecticut authorities turned to the use of bounties to stir enlistment, since col-lective self-defense pleas were not effective.

The augmentation of the bounty system pointed toward a shift in Connecticut society from war as a security issue to an economic activity. During Connecticut's involvement in the border wars between Massachusetts and Maine's Indians in the 1720s, and again in 1740 in England's campaign in the West Indies, the poor were offered financial incentives to enlist; Connecticut's participation in military affairs outside of its borders was a way to improve ties with other colonies and an illustration of loy-alty to the empire.

King George's War (1744–1748) consisted mainly of raids along New England and Cana-dian borders. The colonists' most ambitious action was their capture of the French base, Louisbourg. Though Louisbourg was returned to France in the postwar settlement, the victory gave colonists confidence for a generation and created a war fever which, when combined with economic incentives, raised hundreds of men for war.

The addition of French Canada to the Brit-ish Empire and the opening of areas to the west to British colonization was the outcome of the final French and Indian war lasting from 1754 to 1763. The colonists did not win this battle alone. The mother country contributed both men and financial support because by 1758, colonies like Connecticut could no longer afford to pay for the war. The colonists' military role shifted to a supporting one as thousands of British troops were shipped to the front lines. The immense pride in and for the Empire in the aftermath of the great victory replaced the mili-tary threat of the French and their Indian allies. But pride was soon superseded by distrust as Connecticut's charter seemed at risk as the Empire's authorities moved to control colonial activities more closely. On 20 April 1775, Con-necticut sent Israel Putnam to lead its troops to the siege of Boston to fight in the last colonial war to defend and preserve the autonomous government it coveted.

Leslie Miller

References
Harold E. Selesky, *War and Society in Colonial Connecticut* (1990); Robert J. Tay-lor, *Colonial Connecticut: A History* (1979).

See also DOMINION OF NEW ENGLAND; FORT GOOD HOPE (CONNECTICUT); KING PHILIP'S WAR; MOHEGAN; NEW ENGLAND CONFED-ERATION; NIPMUCK; PEQUOT; PEQUOT WAR; PURITANS; FORT SAYBROOK (CONNECTICUT); WAMPANOAG; UNCAS; WINDSOR BLOCK-HOUSE (CONNECTICUT)

Fort Conti (New York; also known as Old Fort Niagara, Fort Denonville)

Fort Conti was a French fortification used throughout the French and Indian War, espe-cially in defense against the Seneca. The site is on a triangular area of land where the Niagara River empties into Lake Ontario. Fort Conti was constructed in January 1679 by French explorer René-Robert Cavelier, sieur de La Salle. The site, on rock bluffs reaching 25–50 feet high from the eastern shore of the river, was proclaimed highly defensible by the French, as it gave sweeping views from the bluffs across the river and the southern prairie.

On its completion, La Salle assigned 12 men to the fort, adding another squad under a Sergeant Le Fleur in November. Later, the French fled, destroying the fort, possibly in re-sponse to an assault by the Seneca.

Jacques-René de Brisay de Denonville be-came governor in 1684 and was ordered by the king to begin a campaign to destroy the Iroquois nation in 1687. Denonville rebuilt Fort Conti, naming the new fort after himself. Fort Denonville was to serve as a strategic French post for the communication lines that ran into New France. It was fortified with palisades and four bastions, housing 120 men under the command of the chevalier de Troyes. Equipped for an eight-month period, the fort's deployment was to guard against British raids. However, due to the severe winter, food spoilage, disease, and starvation, Troyes and 80 of his men died long before spring thaw. In March, Father Jean de Lamberville and three soldiers made their way into the fort and buried Troyes and his men. They erected an 18-foot cross in the square in honor of the dead men. By August, Denonville ordered the Niagara and Frontenac forts abandoned. The Senecas subsequently burned Fort Denonville.

Not until 1725–1727 was the first fort named Niagara built. The structure was built with Iroquois permission and was also known as the House of Peace and the French Castle. The masonry house was actually more of a fortress, built with four-foot-thick walls to withstand cannonfire. It stood 48 feet by 96 feet and had two stories, including an attic used to store armaments.

Because of its strategic location, the site was a point of contention between the French and the English. Under French control, the fort prevented westward invasion by the British; if it fell to the British, it would divide New France in two and destroy intercommunications.

Elizabeth Gossman

References

Robert West Howard, *Thundergate: The Forts of Niagara* (1968); William Smith, Jr., and Michael Kammen, eds., *The History of the Province of New York,* 2 vols. (1972).

See also DENONVILLE, JACQUES-RENÉ DE BRISAY; FORT NIAGARA (NEW YORK); SENECA

Contractors, Army

Contractors who supplied food and equipment to provincial and British armies were enmeshed in a web of imperial and colonial politics in their pursuit of profit. The following examples suggest quarrels that developed over war contracts.

First, the drive for profits strained the relationship between British officials and Ameri-

can colonials. During the joint New England-British expedition against Canada in 1711, British commanders accused Boston merchants of hoarding, refusing to sell supplies on credit, and manipulating the rate of exchange between sterling and Massachusetts paper money to drive up the cost of goods.

Second, competition for contracts among colonials caused conflict. In 1755–1756, Massachusetts Governor William Shirley negotiated a supply contract with merchants who were at odds with Lieutenant Governor James DeLancey of New York. By using his London connections, DeLancey had Shirley and his contractors ousted and replaced by a British firm for whom the New Yorker was the American agent.

Third, colonial politicians used quarrels over contracts to make other political points. Brigadier General John Forbes had troubles with Pennsylvania farmers and teamsters with whom he had contracted to carry supplies to the forks of the Ohio River in 1758. Those troubles fueled the struggle for power between the Pennsylvania assembly and the colony's proprietors. The Quaker party championed the farmers' cause, and the Penns took the side of the British army.

The loyalty of American contractors and politicians to the British crown did not depend solely on the bottom line, but economic machinations did stir up Anglo-American politics.

Alan Rogers

References

Fred Anderson, *A People's Army: Massachusetts Soldiers and Society in the Seven Years' War* (1984); Douglas Edward Leach, *Roots of Conflict: British Armed Forces and Colonial Americans, 1677–1763* (1986); Alan Rogers, *Empire and Liberty: American Resistance to British Authority, 1755–1763* (1974); John A. Schutz, *William Shirley: King's Governor of Massachusetts* (1961).

See also SUTLER

Converse, James (1645–1706)

James Converse proved himself one of the few effective military leaders for the New England colonies during King William's War (1689–1697). In particular, his command in the defense of the Storer garrison probably saved that post and what remained of the Maine frontier. He was a popular leader and never forgot the sol-

C

diers who served under him. Several letters survive in which he assisted wounded veterans in their attempts to gain compensation or pensions from the government.

James Converse was born in Woburn, Massachusetts, on 16 November 1645. Little is known at this time of his public service before 1689, but at the beginning of King William's War, Converse was serving on the Maine frontier with the provincial rank of captain. In July 1690, he recovered the bodies of those slain in the fight at Wheelwright Pond (Lee, New Hampshire), and later that fall served as second in command during Benjamin Church's raid into Maine. In June 1691, Converse was at the Storer garrison in Wells, Maine, when 200 warriors from Norridgewock attacked and were repulsed. One year later, several hundred French-led Indians made a more serious attempt to destroy the Storer garrison. At this time, Converse commanded 15 provincial soldiers and an undetermined number of inhabitants. During the 48-hour siege, the Indians, under the direction of French officers, tried several strategies to burn the garrison and force a surrender. At one point, when a defender lost nerve and suggested a surrender, Converse declared he would shoot the next person who brought the subject up, then ordered them to open fire. During this particular firefight, Converse moved around the palisade, personally directing the fire of the defenders. The French and Indians finally moved off.

With the destruction of York, Maine, the previous winter, if the Storer garrison had fallen, it is conceivable all of the Maine frontier would have been abandoned, pushing the frontier closer to the older communities to the south. The Massachusetts government was certainly aware of this, and rewarded Converse with a promotion to the provincial rank of major in overall command of Massachusetts forces on the northern frontier. The following year he led a raid into Maine as far north as present-day Waterville. Although England and France ended hostilities in Europe in 1697 through the Treaty of Ryswick, King William's War continued along the northern frontier. In 1698, Converse was appointed one of three commissioners to negotiate a peace treaty with the eastern Indians at Casco Bay. This treaty, signed on 7 January 1699, finally ended the war.

Converse served in the assembly as a representative from Woburn during the years 1695–1699 and 1701–1705. His military success led to political appointments as well, as lieutenant colonel of militia, and in 1699, 1702, and 1703, as Speaker of the Massachusetts House of Representatives. With the outbreak of Queen Anne's War, Governor Joseph Dudley named Converse commander of all forces in the field. Elected to another term in the assembly in 1706, James Converse died unexpectedly on 8 July.

Steven C. Eames

References

Edward E. Bourne, *The History of Wells and Kennebunk* (1875); Steven C. Eames, "Rustic Warriors: Warfare and the Provincial Soldier on the Northern Frontier, 1689–1748," Ph.D. Dissertation, University of New Hampshire (1989); Cotton Mather, *Decennium Luctuosum* (1699), rpt. in Charles H. Lincoln, ed., *Narratives of the Indian Wars, 1675–1699* (1913).

See also CHURCH, BENJAMIN; KING WILLIAM'S WAR; SCOUT; WELLS (MAINE)

Fort Corchaug (New York)

A palisaded fort was constructed during or shortly after the Pequot War by the Corchaug Indians on the west bank of Downs Creek near Peconic Bay in Suffolk County, Long Island. Fort Corchaug, excavated by Ralph Solecki between 1936 and 1948, was oblong in shape, with walls 210 feet in length running north to south and 160 feet east and west. It was designed primarily as a refuge in time of danger, and did not include a permanent village within the stockade. Archaeological evidence, however, indicates it was also used as a center for wampum production. The Corchaug Indians in the first half of the seventeenth century occupied the north fork of Long Island from Orient Point to the Wading River. They were loosely affiliated with other eastern Long Island groups through a confederacy of four sachems, said to be blood brothers, headed by the sachem at Montauk. In the early 1630s, the Indians of eastern Long Island, including the Corchaug, paid tribute to the Pequots. After the Pequots' defeat at Ft. Mystic in 1637, the eastern Long Island sachems hastened to offer tribute to the English, and as a token of their intention to subordinate themselves to Boston power, killed 60 Pequot refugees and sent their heads to Lieutenant Lion Gardener at Fort Saybrook. In response to a subsequent Narragansett effort to establish tributary control over them, the Long Islanders declared they must send their wampum to the English, or "they will come and kill all of us as they did the Pequits." With the establishment of English settlement on Long Island, the indigenous inhabitants gradually lost their sovereignty. The sale of their land to the English in 1648–1649 marked the effective end of Corchaug autonomy, for the English thereafter refused to recognize the authority of the Corchaug sachem. In the latter seventeenth century, a number of Corchaug were subsequently enslaved in punishment for violations of various English laws. Fort Corchaug was abandoned around 1660.

Alfred A. Cave

References

Lynn Ceci, "The Effect of European Contact and Trade on the Settlement Pattern of Indians in Coastal New York, 1524–1665: The Archaeological and Documentary Evidence," Ph.D. Dissertation, City University of New York (1977); Lion Gardener, *Leift Lion Gardener his relation of the Pequot warres,* in *Massachusetts Historical Society Collections,* 3rd Series, 3 (1833):131–160; Ralph Solecki, "The Archeological Position of Fort Corchaug," *Archaeological Society of Connecticut Bulletin* 21 (1950):3–40; Lorraine E. Williams, "Fort Shantok and Fort Corchaug: A Comparative Study of Seventeenth-Century Culture Contact in the Long Island Sound Area,": Ph.D. Dissertation, New York University (1972).

See also PEQUOT WAR

Coronado, Francisco Vázquez de (c. 1510–1554)

After the promising news brought back by previous explorers of fabulous treasures to be found at Cíbola, or Tusayan, and the legendary Seven Cities, in February 1540, Francisco Vázquez de Coronado led out of Compostela, Mexico, a group of around 336 European men including several priests, wives and children of a few soldiers, plus several hundred Indian servants, hundreds of horses and mules loaded with supplies, a flock of sheep, and a herd of pigs. Vázquez and his companions covered thousands of miles, from the Gulf of California to south-central Kansas, where the rich Quivira was said to exist, and from Compostela in western Mexico to the Indian Pueblos at Zuñi, Hopi, Acoma, Tiguex, Taos, and Pecos, in today's Arizona and New Mexico. For the first time, Europeans admired the wonders of the Colorado Grand Canyon, the confluence of the Colorado into the Gulf of California, the Rio Grande Valley, the Llano Estacado, and the western plains teeming with buffalo.

Almost two years after his departure from Mexico, Vázquez was seriously hurt in an equestrian accident. His failing health and the disillusionment of not having found any visible treasures, or a northern passage to the Orient, nor any docile and wealthy natives, moved him to return to Mexico. He had failed to establish any colonies in the northern territory. He left behind only two priests who wished to indoctrinate the Indians, and a few persons to stay with them. On his return, he was appointed governor of New Galicia, Mexico. During the fall of 1542, he traveled to its future capital, Guadalajara, with his wife and family. Later, they moved to Mexico City, where Vázquez died on 22 September 1554.

José Ignacio Avallaneda

References

Herbert E. Bolton, *Coronado, Knight of Pueblos and Plains* (1949); George P. Hammond, *Narratives of the Coronado Expedition 1540—1542* (1940).

See also NEW MEXICO

Coulon de Villiers, Louis (1710–1757)

Louis Coulon de Villiers, captain in the French colonial regular army and chevalier of Saint-Louis, commanded the detachment from Fort Duquesne in July 1754 which forced the young Lieutenant Colonel George Washington to surrender the primitive Fort Necessity (at Great Meadows near present-day Farmington, Pennsylvania) and retreat across the Alleghenies.

One of six Coulon de Villiers brothers in the military, Louis Coulon was born at Verchères 10 August 1710 and began service as a cadet under his father, Nicolas-Antoine Coulon de Villiers. He was wounded in 1733 and his father and one of his brothers killed in battle with the Fox tribe near present-day Green Bay, Wisconsin. Commissioned a second ensign at 24, in 1739 he served with his younger brother, Joseph Coulon de Villiers, sieur de Jumonville, under Pierre-Joseph Céleron de Blainville in the campaign against the Chickasaw. During King George's War, he joined the garrison of Fort St. Frédéric (now Crown Point, New York) on Lake Champlain and was promoted to lieutenant in 1748. He was given command of Fort des Miamis near present-day Fort Wayne, Indiana, in 1750 with the assignment of breaking Miami attachment to English fur traders. Despite his poor success in this endeavor, he was promoted to captain when recalled to Montreal in 1753, where he married Marie-Amable Prud'homme in December of that year.

Louis Coulon was at the Chautauqua portage in early June 1754, preparing to lead reinforcements to Fort Duquesne as part of the French buildup in the Ohio Valley region, when he learned that his brother, Jumonville, had been killed in a skirmish with a Virginia militia unit under George Washington somewhere southeast of Fort Duquesne. Jumonville commanded a 30-man scouting party trying to find Washington and order him out of French-claimed territory when he was surprised by the Virginians; Jumonville and nine others were killed and all but one of the remainder made prisoner. Joining a detachment which left Chautauqua on 16 June 1754 bearing supplies, Coulon reached the fort on 26 June. There he discovered the garrison's commander, Captain Claude-Pierre Pécaudy de Contrecoeur, organizing an expedition to expel the Americans. Contrecoeur immediately acceded to Coulon's demand that he command the force, numbering some 500 Canadians and 200 Indians, because of his rank, experience, and obvious interest in revenge.

On 28 June 1754, Coulon set off up the Monongahela River in search of Washington, who, informed of Contrecoeur's reinforcements, was retreating toward Fort Necessity with considerably less than 500 men. On the rainy morning of 3 July, Coulon passed the site of his brother's death and observed a number of unburied corpses still scattered around. Around 11:00 a.m., as he approached Great Meadows from the northwest, Coulon discovered Washington's men advancing in the open ground in front of the fort's entrenchments and had to expose his own force to a brief flanking fire from two swivel guns mounted inside the fort in order to meet the Americans head to head. Expecting the French to attack across the clearing, Washington held his fire and then, when he saw Coulon's force remain in the cover of the woods, retreated to the poor shelter of two hastily-thrown up entrenchments and the tiny stockade which hardly merited the designation of fort. Immediately, Coulon dispersed his men around the fort and began a steady musket fire through heavy rain into the American position. By nightfall, Coulon had lost only three men killed and 17 wounded while he inflicted more than 100 casualties on Washington's force. Still, Coulon was short of ammunition and his Indians were threatening to leave, so he summoned the defenders to parley and offered quite generous surrender terms to Washington. The capitulation specified that the prisoners taken when Washington attacked Jumonville must be returned to Fort Duquesne within two and a half months, that the English would stay out of the Ohio region for a year and a day, that they could retire east of the Alleghenies with their arms, and that two hostages be turned over to Coulon to guarantee adherence. Coulon also inserted a statement by which Washington, who knew no French, admitted the "assassination" of Jumonville.

The next morning, panic seized Washington's men as they began to file out of the fort; they abandoned most of their baggage, including Washington's journal of the campaign, and fled homeward. Louis Coulon returned to Fort Duquesne to the plaudits of Captain Contrecoeur, who praised his handling of the affair in reporting to Governor Duquesne. Duquesne, in turn, recommended Coulon for a cross of the military Order of Saint-Louis in his account to the French minister of war, a recommendation repeated by Duquesne's successor, Pierre de Rigaud de Vaudreuil, the following year.

Coulon served in the campaign to preserve French holdings in the Ohio region in 1755, but was not present at the battle ignominiously known as Braddock's Defeat. In 1756, he gained further fame by commanding the party that took Fort Granville (near Lewistown, Pennsylvania) on 3 August, and later in the year was present at the capture of Fort Oswego. Then in 1757, his final campaign, Louis Coulon de Villiers participated in the conquest of Fort William Henry. Tragically, he came down with smallpox only a few days after his elevation to the status of chevalier of Saint-Louis and died on 2 November 1757.

Ronald Martin

References
W.J. Eccles, "Louis Coulon de Villiers," *Dictionary of Canadian Biography,* 3:148–

149; Lawrence Henry Gipson, *The British Empire Before the American Revolution*, Vol. 4, *The Great War for the Empire: The Years of Defeat, 1754–1757* (1946); Amédée Gosselin, "Notes sur la famille Coulon de Villiers," *Bulletin des Recherches historiques*, 12 (1906):161–290.

Fernand Grenier, ed., *Papiers Contrecoeur et autres documents concernant le conflit anglo-français sur l'Ohio de 1745 à 1756* (1952); Ronald Martin, "Confrontation at the Monongahela: Climax of the French Drive into the Upper Ohio Region," *Pennsylvania History*, 37 (1970):133–150; Walter O'Meara, *Guns at the Forks* (1965).

See also COULON DE VILLIERS, JOSEPH; FORT DUQUESNE (PENNSYLVANIA); FORT NECESSITY (PENNSYLVANIA); PÉCAUDY DE CONTRECOEUR, CLAUDE-PIERRE; WASHINGTON, GEORGE

Coulon de Villiers de Jumonville, Joseph (1718–1754)

Joseph Coulon de Villiers, sieur de Jumonville, ensign in the French colonial regular army, was killed along with nine of his soldiers on 28 May 1754 while commanding a 30-man scouting party from Fort Duquesne, which was surprised by a slightly larger force led by Lieutenant Colonel George Washington near present-day Farmington, Pennsylvania. Jumonville and his men may well be considered the first casualties of the Seven Years' War.

Born at Verchères 8 September 1718, one of six Coulon de Villiers brothers in army service, Jumonville entered the military as a cadet at the age of 15 in 1733, the year his father and one of his brothers were killed in a battle against the Fox tribe near present-day Green Bay, Wisconsin. He married Marie-Anne-Marguerite Soumande on 11 October 1745. In 1739 he participated under Pierre-Joseph Céloron de Blainville in the campaign against the Chickasaw and, during the War of the Austrian Succession, received a commission as second ensign in 1743. During the course of that struggle he served with little notice on the frontiers of Nova Scotia and New York.

Jumonville next appeared in 1754 as an ensign on the staff of Captain Claude-Pierre Pécaudy de Contrecoeur, commander of the newly-constructed Fort Duquesne located where the Allegheny and Monongahela Rivers come together to form the Ohio. Increasing British interest in the Ohio Valley, personified by rambunctious fur traders and openly manifested by British colonial land speculators' operations, had led the French in 1753 to begin building a series of forts to secure long-standing claims to the region. The young George Washington, sent by the governor of Virginia in the late fall of 1753 to demand French evacuation of the area, received only a formal rejection. Contrecoeur arrived with 500 men at the forks of the Ohio in April 1754 under orders to construct a fort in the vicinity. Selecting the strategic but not particularly defensible junction, Contrecoeur began building the fort named in honor of the French governor of Canada, Ange de Menneville, marquis de Duquesne, on the site later occupied by Fort Pitt and modern-day Pittsburgh, Pennsylvania.

Contrecoeur soon received reports that a large British force under Washington was on its way to dispute his possession of the forks. Under ambivalent orders not to fire first, but to defend his position, Contrecoeur sent Jumonville and about 30 men on 23 May 1754 to find Washington, inform the fort of his location, and deliver a message ordering him out of French territory. On 27 May, Washington, who was camped at Great Meadows (later the site of Fort Necessity), heard from one of his scouts that 50 French soldiers were nearby; that same evening the Indian leader Half King reported that the French party's trail was merely six miles away. With only 40 men at his immediate disposal, Washington decided to take the initiative rather than wait to be attacked, and marched through the night to join the Indians in a dawn assault on Jumonville's position.

Washington achieved total tactical success in a surprise attack on Jumonville's camp the rainy morning of 28 June 1754. After a firefight of less than 15 minutes, the surviving French laid down their arms; only one soldier, a Canadian named Monceau, escaped to bear word to Contrecoeur. Washington reported ten enemy dead, including Jumonville, one wounded, and 21 prisoners. However, Monceau told Contrecoeur that Jumonville had been shot while attempting to read his message to the English and the French quickly charged that Washington's first military success was a barbaric assassination of a peaceful diplomatic emissary. The whole story will never be known, but Jumonville was in an ambiguous situation. He had more soldiers than necessary simply to deliver a summons to Washington, while far fewer than required for any offensive action had the English been in the numbers the French feared.

Ronald Martin

References

W.J. Eccles, "Joseph Coulon de Villiers de Jumonville," *Dictionary of Canadian Biography*, 3:150–151; Amédée Gosselin, "Notes sur la famille Coulon de Villiers." *Bulletin des Recherches historiques*, 12 (1906):161–290; Fernand Grenier, ed., *Papiers Contrecoeur et autres documents concernant le conflit anglo-français sur l'Ohio de 1745 à 1756* (1952); Walter O'Meara, *Guns at the Forks* (1965).

See also FORT DUQUESNE (PENNSYLVANIA); WASHINGTON, GEORGE

Council of the Indies

Officially known as the Royal and Supreme Council of the Indies (Consejo Real y Supremo de las Indias), this was the highest administrative body which dealt with the Spanish possessions overseas. The council was an outgrowth of the older Council of Castille, which had jurisdiction over all the kingdom of Castille and León. The Council of the Indies was officially created in 1524, by order of Charles V, king of Spain and Holy Roman Emperor. The council had a dual role. It acted as the highest court of appeals for cases coming from the Spanish Indies. It also advised the monarch on administrative matters, proposed candidates for civil and ecclesiastical offices in the New World, and drafted legislation for the government of the colonies. Until 1555, the council traveled with the monarch. In this year the court was formally established in Madrid, where the council thereafter had its seat. The membership of the council initially consisted of nine to 12 trained lawyers (*letrados*). In the early seventeenth century, several gentlemen (*caballeros de capa y espada*) councilors were added. All were appointed by the monarch. The chief officer of the court was the president, who usually was a close advisor of the king. After about 1600, military affairs of the Indies were handled by the *Junta de Guerra de Indias*, a committee made up of the president and two members of the Council of the Indies and the president and two members of the Council of War. Similarly financial matters were handled by the *Junta de Hacienda de Indias*, composed of members of the Councils of Indies and Treasury. Operating partially under the control of the Council of the Indies was the *Casa de Contratación* (House of Trade) located in Seville. The *Casa* regulated the trade between the Old World and the New.

John F. Schwaller

Coureurs de bois

Coureurs de bois, runners of the woods, lived between colonial French and Indian societies. Samuel de Champlain, during New France's first years, had sent young men to live among Indians and become interpreters and traders. Through the seventeenth century, young Frenchmen were attracted to life among Algonquian and Iroquoian speakers. Although life among Indians offered the attraction of escaping the restraints of Christian French colonial society, living with Algonquians or Hurons but being without social standing was dangerous, especially for wealthy, defenseless individuals, so *coureurs de bois* were forced to establish personal ties with the people with whom they traded. At times the interests of the *coureurs de bois* and French conflicted with those of their hosts, and the Frenchmen suffered as a result. Etienne Brûlé was murdered by his Huron hosts because they suspected him of trying to negotiate a trading relationship with the Seneca. *Coureurs de bois* angered western Indians by trading arms to the Sioux; in retaliation these Indians withheld their support of Louis de Buade de Frontenac's 1696 invasion of Onondaga and Oneida lands. Initially, French leaders encouraged men to infiltrate native societies and marry their women, but late in the seventeenth century, missionaries and government officials began to fear the French would become Indians, while Indians continued to resist French ways, so they tried to control the traders.

Coureurs de bois embody romantic, heroic qualities in Canadian mythology, but, while they adopted significant elements of native cultures such as clothes, diets, languages, and social and political customs, few *coureurs de bois* early in the seventeenth century "became" Indians, preferring instead to exploit trade opportunities and return to colonial society. Later in the century, *coureurs de bois* advanced westward, spreading French claims and commerce west of the Great Lakes and far into the Mississippi Valley. Some of these *coureurs de bois* stayed among the Indians and founded the métis nation. First encounters between Frenchmen and natives were more likely to be between *coureurs de bois* and Indians than between missionaries and Indians. Although they were not always controllable, *coureurs de bois* were essential to the economic survival and political expansion of the French colony.

Efforts by government officials to control free-spirited *coureurs de bois* appear to have sped the metamorphosis of men into *sauvages,* beyond the grasp of French officials. A consequence of the government's efforts was the loss of the men's loyalties. Médard Chouart Des Groseilliers and Pierre-Esprit Radisson opened the Hudson Bay area to French trade, but when the French mistreated them, they switched to helping the English. New York Governor Thomas Dongan successfully attracted French *coureurs de bois* to help lead a trading expedition from Albany to Michilimackinac in 1685. If the English had succeeded in opening regular trade with western Indians at Michilimackinac, the French colony would have been economically crippled and soon destroyed. The governor of Canada, Jacques-René Brisay de Denonville, knew this and was able to capture the English expeditions in 1686. The French traders were also captured and executed as traitors in Quebec.

Most *coureurs de bois* remained loyal to the French government and were crucial in helping the colony's military exploits. *Coureurs de bois* shared their knowledge of geography and Indian cultures, helped raise armies, and gained Indian alliances, including occasional commitments of warriors. It was *coureurs de bois* and Indian allies who captured and brought to Quebec Dongan's trading expeditions to Michilimackinac. *Coureurs de bois,* with Indian allies from the west, supported then Canadian Governor Joseph-Antoine Le Febvre de La Barre's dismal attempt in 1684 to establish French hegemony over the Five Nations. *Coureurs de bois* also helped Denonville when he ransacked the Seneca villages in 1687. In the eighteenth century, *coureurs de bois* assisted the French by harassing both Englishmen and their Indian allies.

Sean O'Neill

Covenant Chain

The Covenant Chain was a multilateral alliance between the five (and after 1720, six) Iroquois nations, other Indian nations, and various English colonies, most notably New York. The most integral partners in the alliance and the ones who initiated it were the Mohawk/Iroquois nation and the colony of New York. This was an outgrowth of previous alliances between the Mohawks and the Dutch of New Netherland, which Mohawk orators had described as a "rope" between them. When the Dutch colony was taken by the English in 1664, relations between the new administration and the influential Mohawks continued in close alliance, and the chain metaphor, from the Mohawk language, was continued and elaborated. In Iroquois languages, the word for chain translates roughly as "arms linked together," a positive connotation of solidarity. The Dutch/Mohawk relationship was metaphorically upgraded in the 1640s from a "rope" to an iron chain. The first recorded mention of the "Covenant Chain" made of silver came in 1677 at a bicultural meeting in Albany. The Mohawk orator described this alliance relationship as now extending to not just the New Yorkers, but to several other English colonies whose representatives were present.

In accordance with Iroquois political/cultural tradition, the chain had to be "polished" or "greased" periodically to prevent the build-up of dirt or rust; periodic meetings of alliance members had to take place to symbolically reaffirm the commitment of each member to the alliance, as well as to renegotiate its terms. By the end of the seventeenth century, English colonial officials had mastered the concepts of perpetual renewal involving oratory and other features of forest diplomacy. The diplomatic protocol of the Covenant Chain became a bicultural phenomenon respected and adhered to by both sides. At that point, it operated mostly as an alliance for aggrandizement and aggression by the five Iroquois nations and New York, mainly to counter the economic and diplomatic inroads made by the French into the interior of North America.

The membership of the Covenant Chain varied at different times in the late seventeenth and eighteenth centuries. The Iroquois Confederacy claimed various smaller groups of Indians as "tributaries" and included some of them as members: the Schagticokes of the upper Hudson River, various bands of the Delawares and Shawnees, the Susquehannocks, Tutelos, Saponis, Nanticokes, etc. An important incentive for some of the English colonies, such as Massachusetts and Virginia, to belong to the alliance was to prevent Iroquois attacks on their habitations. Another motivation, notably for Pennsylvania and New York, was to be able to claim Iroquois territory and the territory traditionally held by Iroquois "tributary" tribes (such as the Susquehanna Valley—traditional Susquehannock land) as their own. New York was known to claim, far from the forest diplomacy council fires, that their alliance with the Iroquois was in fact a relationship of conquest, giving them control of Iroquoia. Yet they would also speak, at the council fires of forest diplomacy, of their Covenant Chain as an alliance between equals. (In fact, no member of the alliance gave up its sovereignty, and all decisions were made by consultation and treaty.)

Similar political machinations took place among the Iroquois. The English colonies assumed the alliance was an exclusionary one prohibiting separate dealings with enemy powers, such as the French. Yet the Iroquois made a private peace agreement with the French in 1699–1701, straining the Covenant Chain relationship with New York, whose officials thought they should have been involved in any negotiations between a member of their alliance and the French. The Iroquois took full advantage of the Covenant Chain and its benefits while not allowing themselves to be limited in dealings with other powers. At times the New Yorkers had also breached the terms of the alliance as well by not coming to the aid of Iroquois villages attacked by French troops.

The Covenant Chain took on a different character after the end of French rule in 1763 and never regained its bicultural, balanced relationships. However, the tradition of this formidable alliance played a significant role in the decision of most Iroquois to side with the British in the Revolutionary War.

Gretchen L. Green

References

Wilbur Jacobs, "British Indian Policies to 1783," in *Handbook of North American Indians, History of Indian-White Relations,* Vol. 4 (1988); Francis Jennings, *The Ambiguous Iroquois Empire: The Covenant Chain Confederation of Indian Tribes with English Colonies from its beginnings to the Lancaster Treaty of 1744* (1988); Francis Jennings, et al., eds., *The History and Culture of Iroquois Diplomacy* (1985).

See also IROQUOIS

Craven, Charles (1682–1754)

Charles Craven, brother of one of the Lords Proprietors of South Carolina, was appointed governor of that colony at a time of great strife. North Carolina was gripped by an ongoing Indian war, and South Carolinians were in constant fear of a surprise attack. Craven, appointed in February 1711 (New Style), assumed the office in early 1712, immediately attempting to assuage such fears by strengthening defensive positions and improving relations with the local Indian tribes. Most colonists followed Craven's urgings and avoided controversy with the tribes, but several merchants were less interested in the good of the colony than in the good of their pocketbooks and continued the abusive and deleterious practices that Craven sought to halt.

As relations between colonists and aborigines worsened, in 1715, Craven sent Agent for Indian Affairs Thomas Nairne to the Yamasee to attempt to settle differences and to make recompense for past wrongs. As the party approached, the natives launched a surprise attack, killing all but one. Word of the attack spread rapidly and with it the terror of an Indian war.

Governor Craven responded to the threat immediately and decisively. He proclaimed martial law, encouraged settlers to seek safety within Charles Town's defenses, and began organizing militia companies to avenge the deaths of the peace commissioners. The governor dispersed the companies throughout the colony to strongpoints where they could meet local threats.

One such body Craven led personally. He led his 240 men toward Yamasee Town to face the main Yamasee force. The colonists camped along the Combahee River, some 16 miles below Yamasee Town. That evening, the Indians launched a full-scale attack which caught Craven's band completely by surprise. Craven rallied his men and fought an excellent defensive in which the colonists killed many of the Indian leaders and dispersed the rest, while losing only one dead and a few wounded.

Craven then turned his attention to defending the colony as a whole. He returned to Charles Town where he coordinated militia activities and asked the governors of North Carolina and Virginia to send reinforcements. He also requested that the proprietors send British troops to secure the colony. Such requests were in vain. The colonies to the north were reticent, fearing the Creeks and Cherokees would enter the fray and decimate their populations; the proprietors were likewise unwilling to secure substantive aid, preferring to allow the colony to fend for itself because the expense of fighting a war would be too great.

Governor Craven, against all odds, succeeded in dissuading the Cherokees and defeating the Yamasees. He moved quickly and decisively to thwart the Indian onslaught. By February 1716, hostilities had ground to a halt, the Yamasees had fled to Spanish Florida, and South Carolina's borders were secure.

The war, though a stunning victory for the colonists, had cost them dearly. Vast stretches of property were laid waste, the settlers having fled to safety in Charles Town. Plantation owners and merchants alike were bankrupted, and the colony had to be built anew. But, for a time, the colony was secure. The settlers were free to develop economically and socially, and it was a generation before the Indians again rose up against the colonists.

Richard Dukes

See also NAIRNE, THOMAS; YAMASEE WAR

Creek

The origins of the Creek Confederacy remain obscure, as does much of their internal political and diplomatic history in the protohistoric and historic periods. The English first used the name "Creek" to refer to a number of Native American peoples to the south and southwest of their Carolina settlements in the late seventeenth century. The English tended to divide this loose association of peoples into "Lower" and "Upper" Creeks, the latter generally residing to the west of the former along the riverways of present central Alabama, and the former in present central and southwest Georgia. The French, at this time, did not use the designation Creek, but instead tended to refer to individual ethnic, tribal, or town names, usually focusing on the larger groups, such as the Alabama, Abihkas, and Cowetas, to name a few. The French had much more interaction with the Upper Creek than with the Lower, while the reverse was true for the Spanish in Florida. The confederacy appeared amorphous in European eyes, and some scholars have questioned the usefulness of referring to the Creek as a political entity in the colonial period. On the other hand, it is clear some sort of political association did exist among the numerous peoples of the region, an association that grew in impor-

tance in the eighteenth century; this association was a direct response to the military and political changes taking place in the colonial Southeast.

Recently, archaeologist Marvin T. Smith suggested that the spread of European diseases, which decimated many of the complex chiefdoms of the sixteenth-century Southeast, left in their wake "small societies that banded together by the early eighteenth century." Admittedly, Smith concedes the archaeological record is weak in providing conclusive evidence for population decline, but the historical record suggests as much. Population decline, however, cannot explain why such diverse groups opted to confederate. Smith argues that what tied these transforming societies together were the "armed incursions of northern native groups and pressure from European slave traders in the middle to late seventeenth century."

The newness of the Creek Confederacy helps to explain why the association of these diverse peoples remained so amorphous and ill-defined. Responding to dramatically changing circumstances, notably the influx of Europeans and their trade goods, and the introduction of new aboriginal groups to the region, the peoples who became known as the Creek associated together when the situation demanded. Initially, they created alliances of convenience. Muscogulge peoples comprised a major component of this loose confederacy, but as J. Leitch Wright noted, most Creek Indians did not speak the Muskogee language, or spoke a Muskogean language unintelligible to the aforementioned group. The Hitchiti, Tuchebatchee, Alabama, and Yuchi comprised major political groups in the confederacy despite their language differences from each other and the dominant Muskogee speakers. Additionally, the Creek assimilated other diverse aboriginal peoples, including Natchez, Yamasee, Apalachee, and perhaps individuals from dozens of other aboriginal groups who had migrated from every direction.

What ultimately forced stronger bonds of alliance among these Indians residing along the Coosa, Tallapoosa, and Chattahoochee Rivers was encirclement by hostile enemies. Westos armed by Virginia traders pushed the Creek from the northeast, while Choctaw pressured from the west. The Spanish moving north from the Florida peninsula pressured the Creek to enter their sphere of influence as they hoped to continue expansion of their mission system. The entry of England into Carolina, however, provided the Creek with impetus to resist the Spanish and counter the Westo. British trade goods flooded into the Lower Creek towns and several groups moved eastward to the Ocmulgee River. Emboldened by English aid, the Creek began raiding the Spanish missions, forcing their contraction. Missions in modern-day Georgia and west Florida collapsed under the Spanish inability to protect their Indian allies and priests. The weakening of the Westos by Carolina further reduced pressure on the Creek, who then increased their offensive activities—only now they were in pursuit of Indians to sell as slaves to the English Carolinians. The Upper Creek raided the Choctaw, while the Lower Creek ravaged the Apalachee and other Florida Native Americans. By 1704, Creek forces in league with the Carolinians had decimated the Apalachee, setting the Spanish in Florida into a permanent state of military decline. The Creek then turned on the newborn French settlements at Mobile, limiting French expansion and establishing themselves as the dominant power in the region.

The Alabama, who apparently operated at times independently and at other times in conjunction with the Creek, forged a peace with the French that opened the way for improved relations between the French and the Creek. This came on the eve of the Yamasee War in 1715. The Creek supported the Yamasee against the English for reasons that remain unclear, though the most probable cause seems to have been Creek resentment of abuses by English traders. The Yamasee were forced to retreat to Florida and join their erstwhile enemies, the Spanish, while the Creek attempted to induce the Cherokee to join them against the English. The English countered by sending a large force to the Cherokee, hoping to lure them into alliance. The Cherokee needed little convincing. They took advantage of the opportunity to forge closer relations with the English, which would benefit them against the Creek. When the Creek sent a party of 18 chiefs to the Cherokee to conclude an alliance, their hosts murdered them. This led the Creek to steadily reduce hostilities with the English and form closer bonds with the French and Spanish; the Lower Creek towns moved from the Ocmulgee to the Chattahoochee and Flint Rivers to put more space between themselves and the English and Cherokee, and to place themselves into closer proximity to the rest of the confederacy. Additionally, the Creek would not forgive the Cherokee

for their duplicity, and relations remained hostile for more than a century. More important, however, was that the Creek followed a new strategy that guided them through the eighteenth century: no entangling alliances. Peace was made with the English, and English traders were invited to return to Creek towns, while the French were invited to build Fort Toulouse among the Upper Creek. Relations were also improved with the Spanish. French and British influence were used to counter each other, and the Creek then had available multiple lines of European trade. The Creek learned to play the European powers against one another, collecting presents from each and not allowing any to become powerful close to their domain.

The Creek position steadily improved over the next few decades. The southern flank remained secure as the Spanish struggled to maintain themselves in the face of growing English power. The French were preoccupied to the west with expansion, maintenance of their nascent settlements, and severe hostilities in the 1730s and 1740s with the Natchez and the Chickasaw. Moreover, the French had constant tension with their allies, the Choctaw, with whom the Creek were often at odds. The French viewed Creek pressure on the Choctaw eastern flank as a salubrious way to keep their Choctaw allies in line. The French maintained their presence among the Creek and relations between the two generally were good: trade flowed between the two (the French had an advantage over the British in their propinquity and ability to provide gunpowder), and both parties had no need to disrupt the relationship. French trade goods, however, were never enough to supply all Creek needs—but they were enough to prevent the English from establishing a position of dominance.

The British settlement of Georgia in 1733 below the Savannah River on Creek territory actually improved Creek relations with the English. Trade between the Creek and English increased and hostility declined. James Oglethorpe diligently smoothed relations between the English and Creek in order to allow the new settlers a chance for peace—which would be impossible without Creek acquiescence. Yet Oglethorpe failed to forge an alliance that would insure active Creek assistance against the Spanish in Florida. Small parties of Creek warriors occasionally joined Oglethorpe against the Spanish, particularly in the invasion of Florida in 1740 and again in 1743. But the Creek, as a whole, remained out of the British-Spanish dispute.

In the 1740s, many Creek towns favored a stronger relationship with the English, while others leaned toward the French or continued neutrality. Pro-English Creek worked to wean the Choctaw from the French—British traders promised the Choctaw sufficient trade to allow such a break to occur—but traditional Creek-Choctaw hostilities prevented any strong bond from forming between the two; the British also failed to supply the Choctaw with the promised goods: the Choctaw wound up in a brutal civil war in the mid-1740s, one that allowed the Creek additional breathing space on their western flank so they could focus their attention on the Cherokee to the north. In 1744, the English established a brief peace in the intermittent hostilities between the Creek and Cherokee, but the Upper Creek soon renewed attacks.

During King George's War (1744–1748), both the French and English tried to enlist the Creek against the other. Growing Creek discontent with English traders and growing English power might have led to a rupture, but the Creek recognized French inability to supply them with all of their trade needs, especially enough supplies for continued warfare with the Cherokee. Relations with the English remained strained for the rest of the colonial period, but the English and the Creek kept the peace and often worked together out of mutual interests. The Creek towns allowed the English to mediate a peace with the Cherokee in 1749, particularly to convince the Cherokee not to allow Indians from the north (Iroquois) to pass through their territory to attack Creek towns. The peace soon fell apart. Grievances on both sides were too deep to disappear overnight and the Creek again warred with the Cherokee in the early 1750s. This time, the Upper Creek and Upper Cherokee tended to refrain from the conflict, and it was the lower towns of both groups that conducted hostilities. The great Lower Creek military leader, Malatchi, had stunning success against the Lower Cherokee, forcing the latter to consider abandonment of their settlements and to move westward to join the Overhill Cherokee. The Lower Creek also improved relations with the French until Mary Musgrove, a half-Creek, half-English trader mediated to improve Creek-English relations. After much wrangling and numerous false starts, a Creek-Cherokee peace was made in 1753 that would last through the colonial period—but as peace was made with the Cherokee, war broke out with the Choctaw, and the latter were faced with the prospect of a Creek-Cherokee-Chickasaw alliance against them. The Creek, however, again grew disgusted with English traders and patched things up with the Choctaw and French, but with the Creek-Cherokee peace remaining intact. The 1750s might be thus characterized as a decade of great tension for the Creek, but with minimal military engagements.

Georgia increasingly replaced South Carolina as the important source of English trade and negotiation of English interests in the Creek confederacy, particularly after Henry Ellis's arrival as Georgia governor in 1757. Declining French and Spanish power tied the Creek ever closer to the English with the necessity of keeping open lines of trade. Creek military power was the greatest military threat faced by Georgia and the government worked hard to prevent warfare. White settlers moving into the Georgia backcountry encroached on Creek land, heightening tension and leading the Creek to demand that Georgia control its settlers. When the government proved unwilling, the Creek attacked, and in 1761, 14 settlers were killed on the Carolina-Georgia border above Augusta.

Intermittent hostilities continued, but neither the Creek nor Georgia desired war. In 1763, a congress at Augusta temporarily settled outstanding differences and resulted in a Creek cession of land. With the French removal from Louisiana at the conclusion of the Seven Years' War, the traditional Creek policy of entangling alliances with none was coming apart. The British were too weak militarily to "conquer" the Creek, but they could threaten to close trade to force concessions—which became the chief English negotiating weapon for the remainder of the colonial period. Thus, from 1763–1775, the Creek-Georgia frontier was characterized by constant tension and intermittent hostilities, which, however, did not lead to the outbreak of war. The Georgia government tried to limit illegal settlements on Creek land, but further cessions were pushed. John Stuart became Indian superintendent and worked to maintain the peace, while promoting Creek hostilities with the Choctaw at the end of the 1760s. For the remainder of the colonial period the Creek looked for alternative sources of trade to keep expanding English power in check. The American Revolution would leave the Creek to face the most aggressive power yet: a new state of Georgia that had no respect for Creek rights to their land.

Alan Gallay

References

Edward J. Cashin, *Lachlan McGillivray, Indian Trader: The Shaping of the Georgia Colonial Frontier* (1992); David H. Corkran, *The Creek Frontier 1540–1783* (1967); Alan Gallay, "The Search for an Alternate Source of Trade: The Creek Indians and Jonathan Bryan," *Georgia Historical Quarterly,* 73 (1989):209–230.

Marvin T. Smith, *Archaeology of Aboriginal Culture Change in the Interior Southeast: Depopulation During the Early Historic Period* (1987); John R. Swanton, *Early History of the Creek Indians and Their Neighbors* (1922); J. Leitch Wright, Jr., *Creeks and Seminoles: The Destruction and Regeneration of the Muscogulge People* (1986).

See also BRIMS, EMPEROR; CHOCTAW; CREEK-CHEROKEE WARS; CREEK-CHOCTAW WARS; EMISTISIGUO; FRONTIER, SOUTHERN; GUN MERCHANT; MORTAR; MUSGROVE, MARY; OGLETHORPE, JAMES EDWARD; STUART, JOHN; YAMASEE WAR

Creek-Cherokee Wars (c. 1716–1754)

Creek-Cherokee relations during the eighteenth century were marred by two major conflicts. The first Creek-Cherokee conflict arose in 1716 during the Yamasee War, when Cherokees assassinated Creek deputies who had come into the Lower Cherokee towns to sound out support for the war against South Carolina. A Cherokee party led by Carolinians then attacked a force of Creek warriors who were awaiting word from their deputies. During the ensuing struggle, Cherokees raided Abeika (Upper Creek) towns on numerous occasions. South Carolina supported the Cherokee war effort as a check on Creek aggression. In early 1726, 40 Lower Creek Cussitas waylaid a combined force of 500 Cherokees and Chickasaw. The Creek killed 60 of the enemy before they withdrew. After this Creek success, Charles Town negotiated an end to the conflict in January 1727.

War between the tribes broke out again in 1740 when Upper Creek warriors assaulted a Cherokee war party traveling through their territory. European intrigues lay at the heart of this incident, as the English-supplied Cherokee were en route to attack the French-backed Choctaw. The Cherokees had counted on Creek-Choctaw animosity to ensure their safe passage. But the Creeks, already strained by war with the Choctaw, were anxious to make peace with that tribe and feared retaliation for allowing a hostile party to pass through their territory. This Creek-Cherokee war was a disaster for the English as neither the Creek nor Cherokee were able to spare warriors for the English campaigns against Spain during the War of Jenkins' Ear (1739–1744).

Governor James Glen of South Carolina negotiated an end to the Creek-Cherokee conflict in 1745. Intertribal tensions were exacerbated by incursions of northern Indians, primarily Seneca and Iroquois, who used the Cherokee country as a base for attacks on the Creek. Continued attacks by both Cherokee and warriors from northern tribes led to a quick renewal of combat in spite of Glen's efforts. By the winter of 1748–1749, both tribes sent word asking Glen to help arrange a truce. The French feared a Creek-Cherokee rapprochement and French agents, acting from Fort Toulouse, commissioned a Creek headman, the Acorn Whistler, to attack a number of Cherokee in order to thwart the peace process. Though the Acorn Whistler did kill and scalp two Cherokee, the tribes still exchanged peace tokens and were able to establish a boundary dividing their hunting territories. In 1749, both tribes sent emissaries to Charles Town, where under Glen's auspices, the Cherokee pledged to stop northern war parties bound for Creek towns and both sides agreed that should one tribe break the peace, South Carolina would punish the aggressor with a trade embargo.

French rumors and more attacks from northern tribes quickly spoiled the 1749 agreement. South Carolina, citing Cherokee cooperation with the northern tribes, refused to levy a trade embargo against the belligerent Creeks. The Upper Creek towns quickly came to an understanding with the Cherokee and reestablished peaceful relations. However, for the Lower Creek towns, the entire character of the war changed. No longer content simply to seek retribution for attacks against their people, the leading Lower Creek towns of Coweta and Cussita determined upon a war of conquest aimed at acquiring valuable hunting territory from the Lower Cherokee, one of the four Cherokee divisions. In April 1750, Malatchi of Coweta led 500 Creek warriors against the Lower Cherokee towns of Echoi and Estatoe. The Cherokee suffered heavy casualties and the Creek victors looted and burned the villages.

Several border incidents resulted in a brief South Carolina trade embargo against the Cherokee in 1751. While their enemies were suffering from a shortage of guns and ammunition, the Creeks stepped up their attacks. In 1752, Creek parties attacked several major Cherokee villages, including Hiwassee. Keowee, Tugaloo, and most other Lower Cherokee towns were destroyed, leaving numerous casualties and creating a refugee problem for the Overhill and Middle Cherokee villages.

In the spring of 1752, the Acorn Whistler, who was visiting Charles Town, conspired with other Creeks to kill Cherokees who had sought refuge in that town. Indignant, Governor Glen threatened the Creek with a trade embargo. After considerable pressure, leading Creeks secretly executed the Acorn Whistler, and in May 1753, traveled to Charles Town to confirm a peace settlement with Glen and the Cherokee. Despite several minor incidents, the tribes exchanged envoys, and in April 1754, Cherokee deputies visited Coweta to participate in peace ceremonies that formally closed the 14-year conflict and established a lasting peace between the two tribes.

While colonial documents regarding the war provide only sketchy details, one of the most significant results of the protracted war between the Lower Creek and Lower Cherokee after 1749 was the conquest of valuable hunting land by the Lower Creek. The land in question lay between the Little and Broad Rivers on the south side of the Savannah River above Augusta, Georgia. Widely acknowledged to be Creek territory by both the Cherokee and English by right of conquest, Georgia ultimately gained control of the valuable parcel as part of the 1773 New Purchase, by which the trade debts of both the Cherokee and Creek were canceled in return for the land cession. The devastation and humiliation of the Lower Cherokee towns by the Creek during the war also made that tribe more amenable to the construction of a British fort in the heart of their territory. This fort, Fort Prince George, was erected with the hope of reestablishing the deerskin trade following the war, as well as protecting the lower towns from the incursions of both northern tribes and Creek, and providing protection for the white settlements along the border. The fort soon became the center of controversy and contributing factor to the Anglo-Cherokee war of 1760.

Kathryn E. Holland Braund

References

John R. Alden, *John Stuart and the Southern Colonial Frontier* (1944); David H. Corkran, *The Cherokee Frontier: Conflict and Survival, 1740–62* (1962); ———, *The Creek Frontier, 1540–1783* (1967); Verner W. Crane, *The Southern Frontier, 1670–1732* (1929).

See also CHEROKEE; CREEK; FRONTIER, SOUTHERN; GLEN, JAMES

Creek-Choctaw Wars (c. 1702–1776)

Hostilities between the Creek and Choctaw Indians, two of the most populous tribes of the Southeast, most likely predate European exploration and settlement. But conflict between these distantly-related tribes became more frequent, more violent, and more prolonged as a result of the European presence. The earliest recorded campaigns were really slaving raids, carried out by English-armed Creek warriors and South Carolina traders. Seeking aid against these assaults, the Choctaw turned to the French in Louisiana for supplies and support against Anglo-Creek aggression. One of the earliest and most devastating slave raids against the Choctaw took place in 1711 when more than 1,000 Creek marched against the French-armed Choctaw during Queen Anne's War. Though the market for Indian slaves in South Carolina disappeared after 1715, Creek-Choctaw hostility did not. As auxiliaries to Britain and France, the two tribes engaged in intermittent skirmishes until the withdrawal of the French from eastern North America following the Seven Years' War.

The most devastating Creek-Choctaw war began in 1763, independent of European machinations. In 1763, Britain called a general congress of all the southern tribes at Augusta, Georgia, to establish better relations in the wake of French withdrawal from North America. The Creek, alarmed that their ancient enemies would now be supplied with adequate weapons by British traders at newly-won Mobile or from Georgia, attempted to thwart an Anglo-Choctaw rapprochement. The Creek stymied Choctaw participation at the congress by threatening to kill any Choctaw emissary traveling through their country. Only one Choctaw, the pro-British headman Red Shoe, traveling among the Chickasaw, managed to reach Augusta. To ensure his safety, the British sent him back to Mobile on a naval vessel. When it seemed clear that the British and the Choctaw intended to establish peace and conduct trade, Creek warriors instigated hostilities to disrupt this budding commercial relationship and to protect Creek claims to disputed hunting territory, particularly land on the east side of the Tombigbee River. The ploy backfired, and Britain profited from the ensuing carnage, actively supplying both belligerents. Many West Floridians and Georgians welcomed and encouraged the intertribal war due to their belief that, if Indians were busily engaged fighting each other, they would be less likely to attack white settlements.

During the Creek-Choctaw War of 1763–1776, there were substantial casualties on both sides, including a number of prominent headmen. Both tribes suffered in other ways as well, particularly due to the disruption of winter hunts, which resulted in fewer deerskins to barter for European goods. During certain periods of the conflict, Britain distributed liberal amounts of free ammunition to the Choctaw as a hedge against Anglo-Creek hostilities. On the other hand, the Creek had to acquire their munitions through deerskin trade and relied heavily on credit to obtain arms. As a result, the Creek ran up enormous debts that they were ultimately forced to clear by ceding land to Georgia in 1773. Indirectly, Britain's willingness to supply the Choctaw both alienated the Creek and helped promote Anglo-Choctaw friendship. With the onset of the American Revolution, British policy makers decided to honor Creek-Choctaw requests to negotiate an end to the conflict. The war officially ended in October 1776 at Pensacola under the auspices of the British Indian superintendent, John Stuart.

Kathryn E. Holland Braund

References

John R. Alden, *John Stuart and the Southern Colonial Frontier* (1944); David H. Corkran, *The Creek Frontier, 1540–1783* (1967); Verner W. Crane, *The Southern Frontier, 1670–1732* (1929).

See also Augusta, Congress of; Choctaw; Creek; Stuart, John

Fort Crevecoeur (Illinois)
This small fort, built in early 1680 by René-Robert Cavelier de La Salle and his lieutenant, Henri de Tonti, was the first French fort erected in the Illinois country. It was a wooden stockade structure located on the southeastern bank of the Illinois River just below Lake Peoria, about where the small town of Crevecoeur, Illinois, is now situated. The name, meaning "broken heart" in French, is not related to the doleful fate of the fort; rather, the name was probably taken from the village of Crevecoeur in La Salle's native Normandy.

Although occupied only briefly (several months at most), Fort Crevecoeur has gained some historical reputation as La Salle's first attempt to establish a permanent outpost for his envisioned fur-trading empire in the Illinois country. The structure was built on and around a small knoll, which was shaped and buttressed with timbers. Ravines surrounding the knoll were employed as natural ditches and a palisade was erected around the entire complex. Interior structures were minimal, and no ordnance of any kind was available to be mounted.

While La Salle and Tonti were absent in the spring of 1680, the small garrison at Crevecoeur apparently abandoned and burned the fort, leaving a cryptic message scrawled in charcoal: "We are all savages." Although long since abandoned, Fort Crevecoeur was shown on the famous Coronelli map of North America drawn in 1688, and on many later maps as well. Repeated attempts by archeologists to locate the remains of this fort have proved futile, although local enthusiasts have built a wooden palisade fort in the town of Crevecoeur, Illinois.

Carl J. Ekberg

References

Clarence W. Alvord, *The Illinois Country: 1673–1818* (1920); Arthur Lagron, "Fort Crevecoeur," *Journal of the Illinois State Historical Society,* 5 (1913):451–457; Pierre Margry, ed., *Decouvertes et etablissements des francais dans l'ouest et dans le sud de l'Amerique Septentrionale, 1614–1698,* Vols. 1 and 2 (1876, 1879); Francis Parkman, *La Salle and the Discovery of the Great West* (1908).

Croghan, George (?–1782)
A native of Ireland, George Croghan emigrated to North America in 1741 where he flourished as a frontier diplomat and land speculator for 40 years. There is no recorded information about his family or education. Given his untrained handwriting and spelling, his instruction appears minimal. In 1742 he associated with

Peter Tostee, an Indian trader in the Ohio country. Croghan later based his independent operations at the mouth of the Cuyahoga River where he impressed customers with his fairness, conviviality, and willingness to take risks. Since the Indian trade was conducted on credit, the persuasive Croghan borrowed such sizable sums that he soon compiled a £3,000 debt. His speculative zeal, combined with the eruption of international conflict, brought insolvency in 1751. Undaunted, he promised in 1754 to deliver thousands of barrels of flour to George Washington, but he had neither flour nor the horses to deliver it. Washington, subsequently, was suspicious of Croghan's schemes and later refused to buy land from him. During 1754, George Croghan's trading empire collapsed, with estimated losses of £16,000, plus 52 employees killed or captured by the French. Despite his shortcomings, Pennsylvania asked Croghan to serve as agent to the Ohio tribes. One responsibility would be to secure allies for British military expeditions. His charisma is reflected in his ability to impress leaders like General Edward Braddock, who hired Croghan as a conductor of Indians. Although the scouts departed before the battle, George Croghan ingratiated himself with General Thomas Gage of Braddock's staff. After Braddock's defeat, Croghan blamed British policy for the absence of Indian scouts. Despite his failures, Pennsylvania so desperately needed his expertise that they appointed him to an Indian commission and passed legislation protecting him from arrest for debt for ten years. Then, when they objected to his spending, he resigned, went to New York for a conference with Sir William Johnson, became Johnson's senior deputy, and returned to Pennsylvania to investigate the colony's frontier Indian problems. During his visits with Johnson he met the daughter of a Mohawk leader; their daughter, Catharine, later married Joseph Brant. Evidently he had been married earlier to an unidentified colonial woman; their daughter, Susannah, later married the younger Augustine Prevost. As Johnson's deputy, he was instrumental in the successful treaty at Easton, Pennsylvania, in 1758. None of his skills, however, could forestall Pontiac's alliance. Late in 1763, Croghan sailed for England, where he hoped to introduce new ideas for trade regulation to the Board of Trade and obtain compensation for his wartime losses. Back in Philadelphia in 1764, he constructed an expensive home (on credit of course), promoted Illinois land speculation, and planned a trip west. Early in 1765 he parleyed with the tribes at Fort Pitt, descended the Ohio, and then moved through the Illinois country, negotiating with tribal representatives as he went. Back in New York he conferred with General Gage (now British commander in chief). On a second trip in 1766 he contracted malaria, which forced him to sail downstream to New Orleans and then by sea to New York. Croghan's continued land speculation efforts included thousands of acres near Lake Otsego and a proposed new western colony of Vandalia. Although the coming of the American Revolution curtailed his land speculation, he supported the patriot cause, even though he was not appointed an Indian agent by the Continental Congress. His deteriorating health left him bedridden much of the time, interrupted by an occasional trip to Warm Springs, Virginia, in search of relief. The collapse of his ventures left him dependent on the charity of friends in the months before his death on 31 August 1782.

James H. O'Donnell

References
    Albert T. Volwiler, *George Croghan and the Westward Movement, 1741–1782* (1926); Nicholas B. Wainwright, *George Croghan: Wilderness Diplomat* (1959).

See also EASTON CONFERENCE OF 1758; JOHNSON, WILLIAM; LOGSTOWN, TREATY OF (1752)

Crown Point (New York)

Crown Point, a French military post and village about 90 miles from Albany, New York, in present-day Essex County, was strategically located in the eighteenth century at the southwestern end of Lake Champlain in order to control the natural waterway connections with Lake George. Fort St. Frédéric at Crown Point was built in 1731 and improved and enlarged in the 1750s as the crisis over empire developed between France and Great Britain. Fort St. Frédéric and Fort Vaudreuil at Ticonderoga were intended to control the passage of any invasion from Albany. Made of stone, perched high on a rocky point, and surrounded by a ditch and walls 25 feet high, Fort St. Frédéric was an impressive post which was supplied with heavy cannon and had housing for 4,000 troops.

Crown Point was regarded as a severe threat to British American safety. Its location was challenged by the British and the Iroquois Indians, but William Johnson, in several moves against the fortress, the most serious in 1755, failed to penetrate the dense forest near the fort and suffered a surprise attack similar to General Edward Braddock's. Though painfully wounded himself, Johnson captured the French leader, Jean-Armand de Dieskau, and was knighted for his bravery. Another military thrust in 1758 was equally indecisive, but ruined the reputation of General James Abercromby. General Jeffery Amherst, with a large British army, moved cautiously up Lake George to Lake Champlain in 1759, and the French in retreat hastily destroyed both forts and abandoned the waterway. The British, in the fall of 1760, captured Montreal and Quebec and claimed Canada. Once captured in 1759, the forts at Crown Point and Ticonderoga were partially repaired and used from time to time as frontier posts in the years before the American Revolution.

John A. Schutz

References

Christopher Ward, *The War of the American Revolution*, 2 vols. (1952); J. Clarence Webster, ed., *The Journal of Jeffery Amherst: Recording the Military Career of General Amherst in America from 1758–1763* (1931).

See also ABERCROMBY, JAMES; JOHNSON, WILLIAM; LAKE CHAMPLAIN; LAKE GEORGE; FORT ST. FRÉDÉRIC (NEW YORK); FORT TICONDEROGA (NEW YORK)

Fort Cumberland (Maryland)

At a spot where Wills Creek empties into the north branch of the upper Potomac River stands a hill once known as Mount Pleasant. There at age 22, George Washington began his military career in a log cabin that served as his headquarters when he marched west with his small command to take control of the western territory at the forks of the Ohio River. He built Fort Necessity about 60 miles north of his Wills Creek headquarters, and was subsequently forced back to Wills Creek by the French. Fort Cumberland was constructed on the site of Washington's Wills Creek headquarters about a year later, in 1755, at the order of General Edward Braddock. Braddock's plans were to

defeat the French and Indians in a three-pronged attack from Crown Point, Niagara, and Wills Creek.

Braddock and Washington met in Frederick, Maryland, and proceeded west to Wills Creek, which Braddock renamed Fort Cumberland after the duke of Cumberland, who was commander in chief of all British forces. From Fort Cumberland, which Braddock decided was the most important point in his plan of attack, a combined force of British and American troops set out on 10 June 1755, to engage the French forces at Fort Duquesne. Along the way, they cut out the road that eventually became the National Road, or U.S. Route 40. When Braddock's forces were routed by the French less than a month later, with Braddock dead and Washington in nominal command, the bedraggled survivors fled back to Fort Cumberland, as did many of the frontier settlers seeking protection from Indian attacks.

Washington's log cabin headquarters was enlarged in September 1754 to include a 120-square-foot stockade. Colonel James Innes with a small army had been ordered to the Wills Creek site after Washington's defeat at Fort Necessity, and it was these troops that built the first enlarged wooden fortification. Maryland's Governor Horatio Sharpe believed the fortifications were too small and called for construction of a larger bastion. Once more the fort was expanded and 18-foot-long palisades embedded six feet deep were erected forming a wall 400 feet long by 160 feet wide, with the main gate facing west. Additional gates were located on the north and south sides, and two water gates opening in trenches, lead to the creek. Inside the fort there were quarters for 200 men and officers, and two tunnels were constructed that also led down to the creek. Those tunnels were used for fetching water and as possible escape routes. As part of the tunnel closest to the Potomac River, a small room was constructed for storing ammunition. The second tunnel emanated from the officers' quarters. A parade and drill ground was located outside the fort.

For the remainder of its life, Fort Cumberland, as it was now named, was basically a wooden stockade. Fort Cumberland's career was short-lived, however, for once Washington and Forbes defeated the French at Fort Dusquesne, and the battles moved farther afield, Fort Cumberland was no longer needed for military purposes other than as a staging and supply area. Fort Cumberland was garrisoned until 1765, when the British returned the fort to Maryland. Later in his career, as president and commander in chief, Washington returned to Fort Cumberland during the Whiskey Rebellion in 1794, to review his troops for the last time, which was also the last time the fort served a military purpose.

By 1818, the town of Cumberland, Maryland, was growing rapidly and Emmanuel Parish built its first brick structure on the site of the fort. Today, Emmanuel Episcopal Church and the Masonic Temple are located on the site of Fort Cumberland, and the Cumberland public library and courthouse are situated on the old parade grounds. Washington's log cabin headquarters building is preserved in Riverside Park.

Debra R. Boender

References
Niles Anderson, "The General Chooses a Road: The Forbes Campaign of 1758 to Capture Fort Dusquesne," *The Western Pennsylvania Historical Magazine,* 42 (1959):109–138; Kenneth P. Bailey, *The Ohio Company of Virginia and the Westward Movement, 1748–1792: A Chapter in the History of the Colonial Frontier* (1939); "History of Fort Cumberland and Emmanuel Episcopal Church, Cumberland, Maryland," Fort Cumberland, Maryland Vertical File, Maryland Room, Enoch Pratt Free Library, Baltimore, Maryland.

J. William Joynes, "Cumberland: Washington's Military Birthplace," *The Baltimore American* (4 July 1954); Charles Schaeffer, "Fort Cumberland Gave Washington Big Start On Military Career," *Evening Sun* (20 May 1955); Thomas J.C. Williams, *History of Washington County, Maryland, from the Earliest Settlements to the Present Time* (1968).

See also BRADDOCK, EDWARD; FORT NECESSITY (PENNSYLVANIA); OHIO EXPEDITION OF 1755; WASHINGTON, GEORGE

Cuming, Alexander (c. 1690–1775)

Alexander Cuming was a Scottish baronet who wanted to be appointed governor of the Bermuda Islands, where he thought he could participate in the education of the American Indians. Unfortunately that position was not available. Later, his wife had a dream about going to the American wilderness and shortly afterward he took an unauthorized trip to the New World, arriving in Charles Town in December 1729. He got involved in land schemes and stock financing before he began his journey to Cherokee country in March 1730. En route, some other Scots joined him. Cuming met with the Cherokee at Keowee near Clemson, South Carolina, and later at Nequasse near Franklin, North Carolina. He persuaded the Indians to recognize Moytoy, chief of Tellico, as the "emperor of the Cherokees" and in doing so he changed the Cherokee political system by establishing a title later tribal members would vie for. Cuming also persuaded the Cherokee to swear loyalty to King George.

Realizing that British officials would not believe his story, Cuming persuaded seven Cherokee to return with him to London. One of these seven was Attakullakulla (Little Carpenter), whose reputation was enhanced by the trip and who later became the major peace chief during the eighteenth century. In England, the Board of Trade negotiated a commercial treaty with the Cherokee, while Cuming offered to live with the Cherokee for 13 years to promote loyalty and service to England. Later, Cuming suggested schemes to pay off the British national debt and establish a homeland for 300,000 Jews in Cherokee territory.

Most of Cuming's later life was spent in debtors prison, although in 1762 he acted as interpreter for a new group of Cherokee who appeared in London under the auspices of Lieutenant Henry Timberlake. Cuming died in poverty in 1775.

William L. Anderson

References
J. Norman Heard, *Handbook of the American Frontier: Four Centuries of Indian-White Relationships* (1987); James C. Kelly, "Notable Persons in Cherokee History: Attakullakulla," *Journal of Cherokee Studies,* III (1978):2–34; Samuel Cole Williams, ed., *Early Travels in the Tennessee Country, 1540–1800* (1928); Grace Steele Woodward, *The Cherokees* (1963).

See also ATTAKULLAKULLA

D

Dakota

See OJIBWA-DAKOTA CONFLICT

Fort Darby (Massachusetts)

Fort Darby was erected sometime between 1629 and 1632 to provide fortifications for Marblehead. It was constructed due to fears of pirate raids and possible foreign invasion. The fort was situated on Naugas Head at the northwest corner of the peninsula. The local settlers constructed the fort under the direction of Acting Governor John Endicott. Its name is derived from a similar point in Derby, England.

David L. Whitesell

De Brahm, William Gerard (1718–1799)

A brilliant but eccentric military engineer/cartographer, De Brahm played a major role as a designer and builder of fortifications in the colonial Southeast. After establishing an apparently successful career in the imperial army of Charles VII, and rising to the rank of "captain engineer," De Brahm renounced the Roman Catholic faith and was forced to resign his army commission.

At the age of 30, with a newly acquired wife, he found himself nearly destitute in the troubled and fragmented Germany of the mid-eighteenth century. Possessed of a good education, gained while growing up in the Koblenz where his father served as a court musician to the elector of Triers, De Brahm was soon recognized by a leader in an effort designed to settle displaced German Protestants in Georgia. In 1751, he was placed in charge of a party of 156 "Salzburger" Germans being transported to Georgia. In recognition of this service, the Trustees for Establishing the Colony of Georgia granted him 500 acres of land.

Soon after arriving in Georgia De Brahm began conducting surveys and preparing maps of the colony. A devastating hurricane and storm surge "totally demolish'd" the already dilapidated fortifications of Charles Town, South Carolina, in September 1752, and De Brahm was summoned from Georgia to design and oversee their replacement. He lost no time in surveying the city, and on 24 November 1752, presented a report and colored manuscript, "Plan of a Project to Fortifie Charlestowne Done by Desire of His Excellency the Governour in Council by William De Brahm Captain Ingineer in the Service of his Late Imp: Maj.: Charles VII." The plan was as elaborate as its title was long and would have cost the staggering amount of £294,140 by De Brahm's estimate! Eventually a greatly simplified and far less expensive system of conventional defensive works was begun under De Brahm's supervision in 1755.

While De Brahm was residing in South Carolina the colony's surveyor general of lands died and De Brahm was appointed to temporarily assume this important post until a permanent replacement was sent from England. The year before, he had received a royal appointment to the similar post in the newly formed royal government of Georgia. Georgia, like neighboring South Carolina, began to feel vulnerable to attack during this period. In response to a request from the colony's first royal governor, John Reynolds, De Brahm prepared a plan for the defense of Georgia. Unlike his first grandiose South Carolina scheme, De Brahm made allowances for Georgia's small population and stressed the most economic use of both troops and resources in his plan. He proposed the fortification of a small number of strategic locations that would provide great flexibility in the defense of Georgia's Indian frontier. Governor Reynolds forwarded De Brahm's detailed "Representation of the Forts and Garrisons Necessary for the Defense of Georgia . . ." to London in January 1756.

In the spring of that year, South Carolina moved to cement the Cherokee Indians to the British cause by promising to build a fort amid their Overhill towns in what is now eastern Tennessee. Dean of frontier historians Dale Van Every termed Fort Loudoun "the first English lodgement west of the mountain barrier anywhere along the colonies' long western frontier stretching from the Mohawk to Florida." South Carolina's governor ordered De Brahm to proceed to the Indian country and begin construction on Fort Loudoun overlooking the Little Tennessee River close to the Cherokee town of Little Tomothly (Tomately).

Captain Raymond Demeré, the garrison commander, was bitterly critical of both De Brahm's site and design for Fort Loudoun. He observed that the German engineer built his fort "as if the River was navigable for Men of War" when in fact it was suitable for little more than canoes. As the summer of 1756 lengthened into winter, disagreement between Demere and De Brahm settled into a raging feud that threatened the security of the frontier outpost in the midst of an increasingly disaffected Cherokee nation.

Rather than reassuring the Cherokees and cementing them to the British imperial cause, Fort Loudoun soon came to represent one more despised British encroachment on the Indians' jealously guarded territory. Leaving the still unfinished Fort Loudoun in late December 1756, De Brahm returned to Georgia and directed the fortifying of Savannah and Ebenezer for Governor Henry Ellis. In 1761, fears of a French-Spanish alliance caused Georgia's governor to undertake the defense of the entrance to the Savannah River. To fill this need De Brahm built the work known as Fort George on the eastern end of Cockspur Island. De Brahm also prepared a well-known map and plan for Fort Barrington on the Altamaha River.

In 1764, De Brahm was appointed surveyor general for the southern district of North America, a newly created British imperial office with responsibility for conducting detailed geographic surveys and economic assessments for the region stretching from the Potomac River to the Florida Keys. In addition to his imperial title, De Brahm was also appointed as surveyor general for the new British colony of East Florida. Early in 1765, De Brahm and his family took up residence in St. Augustine, which was to serve as his base until 1771. In those six years he accomplished the detailed mapping of most of the eastern and southern coastal zone of the Florida peninsula. As a result of a bitter feud with East Florida's governor, he was forced to break off his Florida surveys and return to England for an administrative hearing. Exonerated, he returned to America equipped with the armed ship *Cherokee* to continue the interrupted surveys. On the voyage he conducted detailed studies of Atlantic surface currents and atmospheric conditions.

Shortly after arriving at Charles Town in 1775, the *Cherokee* was commandeered for more urgent military business and De Brahm was made a prisoner-at-large by the revolutionaries. He was allowed to return to London via a neutral port in the autumn 1777. For the next several years, dogged by ill health, he dropped from sight in England. Finally, in 1789, he quit the British Isles and made his way to Philadelphia, where he lived out the last decade of his life.

Louis De Vorsey, Jr.

References

Ralph H. Brown, "The De Brahm Charts of the Atlantic Ocean, 1772–1776," *Geographical Review,* 28 (1938):124–132; Louis De Vorsey, Jr., "William Gerard De Brahm, Eccentric Genius of Southeastern Geography," *Southeastern Geographer,* 10 (1970): 21–29; ———, *De Brahm's Report of the General Survey in the Southern District of North America* (1971); ———, "William Gerard De Brahm, 1718–1799," *Geographers Bibliographical Studies,* 10 (1986): 41–47.

See also FORT BARRINGTON (GEORGIA); FORT LOUDOUN (TENNESSEE)

Decanisora (?–1720s)

Decanisora (Teganissorens to the French), a powerful Onondaga orator and diplomat, participated extensively in negotiations between the Five Nations and the French and British during the late seventeenth and early eighteenth centuries. Impressed by Decanisora's talents,

Cadwallader Colden testified, "He was grown old when I saw him, and heard him speak; he had a great Fluency in speaking, and a graceful Elocution, that would have pleased in any Part of the World."

In 1682, while the western Iroquois fought the Illinois and Miamis, Decanisora persuaded Governor General Louis de Buade de Frontenac that the Iroquois had no inclination to interfere with the French, thus keeping them out of the conflict. He was back in Quebec the next year to convince Governor Joseph-Antoine Le Febvre de La Barre that the Iroquois wanted to keep the peace with New France despite their war with the Illinois. Senecas undermined his efforts by attacking the French Fort Saint Louis at Starved Rock, but La Barre responded with a brief and ineffective campaign.

Decanisora likely was involved in the efforts of Governor General Jacques-René de Brisay, marquis de Denonville, to achieve a cease-fire following his ravaging of Seneca villages in 1687. Conflict revived in 1689 when France and England declared war in Europe, and the Iroquois attacked the French at Lachine. Frontenac returned to New France in 1689; in 1694 he specifically requested Decanisora's participation in peace negotiations. Decanisora went to Quebec to offer peace on Iroquois terms in the spring 1694, demanding that the English colonies be included in a general peace settlement. Probably, Decanisora was just delaying war while dividing the French strength, as the next year Iroquois warriors returned to attack Montreal. The French and English ended their war in Europe in 1697, and before they started the next one four years later, the Iroquois negotiated the peace treaty of 1701, which ended, for a time, the intermittent fighting between the Five Nations and Canada.

When Frontenac had first proposed peace talks in 1694, the Iroquois were strong, but when the war ended in Europe in 1697, and New York withdrew its support for the Five Nations, the French had recovered their strength while the Iroquois had been worn down by fighting. New France was in a position to demand that their allies be included in the negotiations and that Jesuit missionaries be established in Iroquois villages. Negotiations were slowed by Decanisora's desire to absent himself while mourning the death of his wife in 1700, by New York's efforts to disrupt the negotiations, and by the difficult issue of exchanging prisoners. A peace treaty was finally ratified in

August 1701; when the War of the Spanish Succession broke out, the Iroquois remained neutral.

Decanisora continued in his role as spokesman and peacemaker. In 1703 he proposed that New York and New France agree to maintain neutrality. When New France used the neutrality to attack New England, the Iroquois protested. Then, when the British prepared a major assault on Canada, Decanisora sent a messenger to warn then Governor General Pierre de Rigaud de Vaudreuil.

Decanisora informed the Albany commissioners in 1719 that the French had taken advantage of the Senecas' granting to Louis-Thomas Chabert de Joncaire permission to build a trading post by constructing a fort at Niagara. That the Seneca were not strong enough to stop the French from building the fort, and that the Five Nations decided to maintain a balance of powers by allowing the English to build a fort at Oswego illustrate the changing circumstances for the Five Nations, Canada, and New York during Decanisora's lifetime. The dates of his birth and death are not recorded, yet in 1727 Cadwallader Colden wrote of him in the past tense. Decanisora appears to have been a major figure among the Five Nations and a commanding person in Albany and Quebec as well.

Sean O'Neill

See also IROQUOIS; IROQUOIS TREATIES OF 1700 AND 1701; ONONDAGA; FORT ST. LOUIS AT STARVED ROCK (ILLINOIS); SENECA, FRENCH ATTACK ON THE

Deerfield (Massachusetts)

Although today a tranquil, pristine, rural historic village, Deerfield's colonial history was dramatic and violent. First settled in 1670, for almost half a century Deerfield stood on the frontier, on the northwestern edge of English settlement in New England. During those 50 years the town endured more than 30 attacks; the town was destroyed in 1675; an attempt to rebuild was quickly snuffed out in 1677; and rebuilding which brought the town's population to almost 300 was undone by the most famous of attacks, the so-called "Deerfield Massacre" of 1704. Not until the 1720s and the establishment of new towns to the north and west did Deerfield become safer. Still, attacks on the town came as late as 1746, and another within ten miles of the 1760s.

The town's history is even richer than this, for the wars which swept over it were not just between Native Americans and Europeans, but also between Indians and Indians. Before Deerfield was an English town, it was an Indian village. The village was called Pocumtuck, named for its inhabitants, the Pocumtuck Indians, one of several Algonkian bands in the upper Connecticut Valley of Massachusetts. Pocumtuck was a prime site for settlement: a central plateau roughly a mile long by half a mile wide, falling away to the rich bottomlands of the Deerfield River on three sides, the river just beyond, with a rise of gentle Berkshires to the east.

It would seem strange, then, that when English explorers from the town of Dedham, southwest of Boston, visited the site in 1665, they found it empty. The reason was that 1664 had seen the destruction of the Pocumtucks by their rivals, the Mohawks. These easternmost Iroquois had been fighting intermittently with the Indians of New England throughout the seventeenth century. When the Pocumtucks insolently killed a Mohawk prince, Saheda, who had visited Pocumtuck on a peace mission, the Mohawks responded in kind. Their massed attack on the Pocumtuck fort destroyed the settlement and splintered the survivors. Thus did the land open up to the English.

The land did not lie open for long. By 1670, English settlers were encamped on the land; by 1675, the town, incorporated in 1673, held more than 200 people. The English, too, called the place Pocumtuck.

But now another war struck. Although King Philip's War began in southeastern Massachusetts more than 100 miles away in June, by July it had spread west; by August it had hit the Connecticut Valley; and by September it had come to Pocumtuck. A two-day siege in early August destroyed Brookfield, some 40 miles southeast of Pocumtuck; next came attacks on the infant settlement of Northfield, the only town to the north of Pocumtuck, which soon forced abandonment of that hamlet. Pocumtuck was next. A series of strikes starting on 1 September put the town in peril and caused the women and children to be sent to safer valley towns below, while the men and a troop of regular Massachusetts soldiers tried to hang on. They could not. On 18 September 1675, a troop of soldiers, plus 15 Pocumtuck men, slowly started south out of town. They were protecting a convoy of carts which carried some 3,000 bushels of corn that had been standing in Poc-

umtuck's fields. The grain was considered crucial in feeding the valley through the coming winter, and this is why the valley's military commanders had ordered it driven south. Some five miles south of town, the convoy slowed to cross a muddy brook. At that moment hundreds of Indians—Wampanoags, Nipmucks, Pocumtucks—struck and annihilated the surprised and outnumbered English at a site that soon became known as Bloody Brook. Soon more than 60 English lay dead, including 14 of the Pocumtuck men—nearly one-third of all the adult males in the town. One contemporary called it "that most fatal day, the saddest that ever befel New England." After Bloody Brook there was little hope of holding on to Pocumtuck. Within days the English abandoned the town, and the Indians burned it soon after.

Even after King Philip's War ended, Pocumtuck's luck did not improve. An attempt to rebuild the town in 1677 was quickly quashed by yet another Indian attack, and the town lay abandoned for five years.

But the English did return. A series of meetings and efforts bore fruit in the early 1680s, and the new town, now called Deerfield, grew quickly. Still, war intervened again. King William's War began in Europe as the War of the League of Augsburg, or the Nine Year's War, but as England and France went to battle in 1688, so did New England and New France. As the northernmost town in a valley that was now looking north toward its enemy, Deerfield fell victim yet again. Although this war did not destroy the town, it certainly damaged it. Of 13 attacks which struck the Connecticut Valley, seven hit Deerfield. Predictably, Deerfield's losses were the highest of any valley town: 12 dead, five wounded, and five captured (out of total valley losses of 37, six, and ten, respectively.

Although the Treaty of Ryswick stopped the fighting in 1697, the agreement was more an armistice than a real commitment to peace. When Charles II of Spain died in 1702 and his will handed control of the Spanish empire over to Louis XIV of France, the English quickly moved again to war. The War of the Spanish Succession came to America as Queen Anne's War, and Queen Anne's War soon came to Deerfield.

Fighting broke out in the summer of 1703 on the eastern end of the New England frontier, near Wells and Saco in southern Maine. The threat of war spread quickly. Reports through the spring and summer of 1703 warned that

Deerfield might be next. All stayed quiet, however, until October, when two Deerfield men in the fields north of town were captured. The threat heightened, then died as the weeks passed, for wars were not generally fought in the dead of winter. This winter proved different, though. While the people of Deerfield strengthened their town's defenses, aided by soldiers and funds from the General Court, a troop of between 200 and 300 French and allied Indians was making its way south from Montreal. Traveling more than 200 miles across frozen lakes and rivers, they reached their destination on the afternoon of 28 February 1704. The next morning, two hours before dawn on that fatal leap year day of 29 February, they struck. With the town's watch failing in his duty, the French and Indians quickly got into the town. The surprise was total and the attack devastating. By the time the forces had pulled back, three-fifths of the town's population was dead or captured: of 291 people, 56 were dead and 109 captured. In addition, 17 of the town's 41 houses had been burned. Although Deerfield was not abandoned this time—the region's military commander would not allow it—the town was barely alive.

Queen Anne's War was not yet done with Deerfield. Although both townspeople and English authorities tried by negotiation to get the captives back, they were only partly successful. Of the 109 captured, 88 survived their march up to Canada. Of these 88, 59 eventually returned, but 29 never did. They were the young: all under 20, most under 14. The town took more blows, too. By the time this war ended in 1712, Deerfield had borne ten attacks, including the two largest strikes in the valley, in 1704 and 1709. Although the town survived, it had paid a huge price.

When peace finally came, Deerfield began to grow and prosper. The growth was never dramatic—by the Revolution the town held only about 750 people—but the rich farmlands of the town did yield steady dividends. Even so, war continued to influence Deerfield's life. While Dummer's War of the 1720s was never a significant threat to the colonial balance of power or to the Connecticut Valley, it still brought more times of tension to Deerfield. Between 1722 and 1725 a series of strikes around the valley kept Deerfield on edge. While the town suffered a couple of small raids, resulting in three men being wounded and another captured, Deerfield escaped without any major attacks.

By the 1730s, Deerfield was more secure. No longer was it the region's outpost: new towns and forts to the north and west now flanked the village. Warfare which swept down from the French and allied Indians now was deflected away. Although Deerfield citizen/soldiers were involved, the town itself was safe.

There were tradeoffs to that safety. Interestingly, the dangers of the frontier had helped forge a town that was strikingly egalitarian in its local government; that had, in its shared poverty, a highly interdependent barter economy; that held an unusually open church; that was without a dominant elite; that was, in essence, a commune. It was only with the passing of the frontier that Deerfield took on characteristics that Frederick Jackson Turner ascribed to the frontier: individualism, contention, and democracy.

Richard I. Melvoin

References
Richard I. Melvoin, *New England Outpost: War and Society in Colonial Deerfield* (1989); George Sheldon, *A History of Deerfield, Massachusetts,* 2 vols. (1895–1896), rpt. 1972; John Williams, *The Redeemed Captive Returning to Zion* (1707), rpt. 1976.

See also BLOODY BROOK MASSACRE; DEERFIELD, ATTACK ON

Deerfield, Attack on (1704)

In the early eighteenth century, war between European powers often spurred war between the colonies of those powers as well. Thus it was that 1703 saw the carryover of European war to America. The European War of the Spanish Succession became known as Queen Anne's War, the second of the four so-called "French and Indian Wars" in America between 1688 and 1763.

Although fighting broke out in the summer 1703 along the Maine frontier, more than 100 miles to the west the people of Deerfield felt the threat as well. That threat was soon realized. In October, Indians struck the Connecticut Valley at Deerfield, capturing two men. The village hurried to shore up its defenses, with considerable assistance from the General Court.

With the onset of winter, though, efforts eased, for wars in the early eighteenth century generally were not fought in the dead of winter. Still, Deerfield took precautions. Although three-quarters of the town's houses stood outside the palisade that encircled the middle of town, all residents slept inside the fort each night. With 20 soldiers sent out by Boston to help protect the town, 291 people crowded into the ten or 12 houses inside the fort as darkness settled on the night of 28 February 1704. While the townspeople slept, a sentry patrolled the village.

But while Deerfield slept, the enemy watched. A force of between 200 and 300 French and allied Indians had journeyed more than 200 miles south from Canada across frozen lakes and rivers to attack the village. The French included both regular army men and *coureurs de bois*. The Indians included two groups: Caughnawagas, or French Mohawks, and Abenakis. The group was led by a French officer, Jean-Baptiste Hertel de Rouville. Now they waited, and what they saw gave them promise of success. For one thing, the snows of late winter had drifted up against the palisades, and that ten- or 12-foot-high wall could now be breached. For another, and more important: there was no sentry. To use the evocative description later penned by the town's minister, John Williams, the watch had proven "unfaithful."

Two hours before dawn on that leap year morning of 29 February, the French and Indians struck, coming down on the town, as Williams said, "like a flood upon us." Although the townspeople fought back valiantly, they were overwhelmed. The attackers killed many outright and captured even more, taking them to a site outside the town where they readied for a quick retreat. Other attackers set fire to many of the buildings. A couple of the fortified houses held on amid fierce fighting that lasted perhaps three hours. At that point, with English resistance ebbing, a force of 30 men from Hadley and Hatfield charged into the town on horseback: young Deerfielder John Sheldon had escaped at the beginning of the attack and, covering his feet with strips of cloth, had rushed southward for help. The reinforcements succeeded in driving the remaining Indians out of town toward the north; in their zeal, however, they overextended themselves and ran into an ambush set by the other French and Indians.

Once the English force retreated back to the town, the survivors began to measure their losses. They were staggering. Fifty-six people had been killed: 44 townspeople, five soldiers, and seven men from Hatfield and Hadley; 109 had been captured. In all, the town had lost three-fifths of its population. Seventeen of 41 houses had been burned. While the French and Indians reportedly lost as many as 40 men, the raid was still enormously successful from the French and Indian side. And when bad weather, plus a lack of snowshoes, made pursuit impossible, the French and Indian triumph was complete.

Why attack Deerfield? Francis Parkman called it an "unoffending hamlet." But it was more. Perched on the northwest tip of English settlement, it was perhaps the "closest" English town in New England for the French and Indians to attack. But why attack at all? The reasons are many. Foremost is the fact that the French wanted to dictate the terms of this war. By striking on the New England frontier, they hoped to establish that in this war the battles would be fought in New England, not in New France. Yet the attack was also important in terms of French-Indian relations. The French were anxious to firm up their newly established alliance with the Abenakis and to show all their Indian allies that they could be counted on. They also wanted to keep the Iroquois, for decades English allies, in their new position of neutrality. The raid on Deerfield accomplished all this.

Was the attack, then, a success? On one level the answer is clearly yes. In military terms, the actual strike was enormously successful; it served its aims in cementing alliances as well. Yet it also backfired. The "Deerfield Massacre," as it became known, was such a huge disaster for the English that it accomplished what no talk or letters or cries had previously done: it united the English colonies. Within weeks New England's galvanized colonies sent out a war party of 700 men against French posts on the Atlantic. Frontier towns received more aid and redoubled their defense efforts, for no one could forget the horror of Deerfield. Meanwhile, the town clung to life, and as authorities worked to redeem the captives (88 of 109 survived the march to Canada, and 59 eventually came home), the war slipped into stalemate.

Richard I. Melvoin

References

Richard I. Melvoin, *New England Outpost: War and Society in Colonial Deerfield* (1989); Francis Parkman, *Half-Century of Conflict* (1902); George Sheldon, *A History of Deerfield, Massachusetts* (1895–1896), rpt. 1972; John Williams, *The Redeemed Captive Returning to Zion* (1707), rpt. 1976.

See also DEERFIELD

Delaware (Lenni Lenape)

The Lenni Lenape, meaning "original or real people," were of the Algonkian linguistic family. At the time of European contact, they were located in the present states of Delaware, New Jersey, southeastern Pennsylvania (between the Susquehanna and Delaware Rivers), and southeastern New York (west of the Hudson River). They came to be identified as the "Delaware" when the bay and river they lived near was renamed in honor of the third lord de la Warr, Thomas West, governor of the Jamestown, Virginia, colony in 1610.

Historically the Delaware have been divided geographically into three subtribes. The Munsee (people of the stony country; the wolf totem) were located from the headwaters of the Delaware to the Lehigh Valley. The Unami (people downriver; the turtle totem) lived on the east bank of the Delaware from the Lehigh Valley southward. The Unalachtigo (people near the ocean; the turkey totem) lived on the west bank and were centered near present-day Wilmington, Delaware. Of the three groups, the Unami claimed to hold precedence over the others. More recently the Lenape have been divided into two groups, the northern Munsee-speaking and southern Unami-speaking peoples.

Each subtribe of the Lenape was divided into independent communities with its own chief, or sachem. The Delaware were a matrilineal society, with an individual of royal blood being selected by the outgoing chief as successor. The chief exercised authority over the recognized hunting and fishing territory.

Early in the seventeenth century, the Lenape were in a defensive war with the Minquas, their Iroquoian neighbors to the north and west. The Minquas frequently invaded the Lenape by using the Delaware River tributaries, Appoquinimink Creek and Minquas Kill. Dutch trader David Pietersz DeVries' journals of 1633 recorded Minquas raids on Delaware villages near Big Timber Creek and near Trenton. Farther north, members of the Five Nations had begun to encroach on Delaware territory.

The Dutch were the first group of Europeans to actively travel and trade with the Lenape on the Delaware River. They were not initially interested in settlement. However, in 1624, a small plot of land was purchased from the Delaware for a trading post to be named Fort Nassau (Big Timber Creek, New Jersey).

In 1629 the first recorded land purchases between the Dutch and the Delaware took place. For a quantity of duffel, axes, adzes, and beads, a strip of land 32 miles long and one-half mile wide was purchased and named Swanendael (near Lewes, Delaware). Dutch patrons placed 34 men at Swanendael to cultivate tobacco and grain, and to establish a whaling community. Within the first year the Delaware Indians had murdered the entire colony over what seems to be a misunderstanding. A Delaware chief had taken a piece of tin painted with the Dutch coat of arms to make tobacco pipes. He was killed and vengeance for his death followed. Swanendael was not resettled, but the Dutch did continue to trade for fur at Fort Nassau.

When the Swedes came to the Delaware River in 1638, they found no European colonists. Land was purchased on the west side of the river from five Delaware sachems on 29 March 1638. The Swedes erected a fort at Minquas Kill, naming it Fort Christina (Wilmington, Delaware). The Delaware Indians did not, at this time, believe they were ceding the land permanently, but rather sharing the use of it with the Swedes.

Over the next 17 years, the Delaware, Swedes, and Finns at the New Sweden colony for the most part lived together peacefully, but not without incident. The Indians were a great source of furs, corn, and other food items for the colonists. As small numbers of new colonists came, additional land was purchased from the Delaware on both sides of the river. The Swedish crown had instructed New Sweden's Governor Johan Printz to treat the Indians with respect, but to take every opportunity to Christianize them. To this end, the first Lutheran minister of New Sweden, Reverend Johan Campanius Holm, became well versed in the Delaware dialect. Holm compiled their vocabulary into a written record and translated Luther's catechism for them.

The Dutch gained control of the Delaware River from 1655 to 1664. European colonists from Holland, Sweden, and England began to settle in increased numbers on the river and bay. Cleared land holdings for agriculture and settlement purposes infringed more and more on former Delaware hunting territory. In addition, the Delaware had become increasingly dependent on commodities traded by the Europeans. Guns, shot, and powder had rapidly begun to replace the bow and arrow. Regulations and

D

restrictions on fur trade, along with differing rates of exchange, were difficult for the Delaware to understand. Outbreaks of smallpox, measles, and other diseases, alcohol consumption, and continuing raids from the northern Five Nations decimated the Delaware. By June 1660, Dutch records indicate, some of the Delaware left their ancestral homelands to move west toward the Susquehanna River and into Minquas territory. Estimates in 1671 of the total population of Delaware Indians on both sides of the river were 1,000 warriors.

A new European power claimed Delaware lands by right of conquest over the Dutch in 1664. The duke of York was granted title to the Delaware River Valley. New laws, new trade regulations, and another new language further confused the Delaware. Friction between the English and Delaware continued when English cattle strayed into Indian villages, destroying corn fields. Members of both cultures initiated acts of murder, theft, and arson.

In 1674, the duke of York sent Edmund Andros to govern the colony. Andros inherited not only the Delaware problems but those of other Iroquoian tribes to the north. At a treaty conference at New Castle in 1675, Andros declared his desire for peaceful relations with the Delaware. It was during Andros's years from 1674 to 1682 that many of the Delaware dispossessed themselves, by treaty, of their homelands. The western bank of the river became colonized by Swedish, Finnish, Dutch, and English families from the Schuylkill River on the north to the colony of Lewes at the south. A great many of the southern Delaware moved north into Shackamaxton (Philadelphia) along with some of their former enemies turned allies, the Minquas.

It is also during the Andros years that the Delaware assumed the status of "women"— becoming mediators or peacemakers between the Iroquois and the Algonquin nations. Francis Jenning remarks that reluctantly, and under pressure from Andros, the Delaware also became "tributaries" of the Five Nations. This relationship appears not to have involved subjugation, but rather acceptance of political spokesmanship for them by the Five Nations (particularly the Mohawks) when dealing with colonial governments (at this time mainly in New York). It did not include any claim to Delaware territory by the Five Nations, and the Delaware continued to speak for themselves in treaties involving their lands.

When William Penn claimed lands granted to him by Charles II in 1682, they included the western shore of the Delaware River westward 5 degrees longitude and north to the 43rd parallel. Most of the remaining Delaware Indian population was placed within these bounds under Penn's jurisdiction. Penn promised the Indians fair treatment and assured them payment for their land, with clearly defined boundaries. He stated they would have redress for their grievances and, above all, there would be peace.

Over the next few years land purchases from the Delaware were made by Penn or his officials. The Delaware now understood that they were permanently terminating all rights and claims to the land. With Penn's approval, two reservations were established—Okehocking (between Newtown Square and West Chester) and Queonemysing (on the Brandywine).

Deerskin became the main trade item when early in the eighteenth century beaver pelts were no longer in demand in Europe. In response, the Delaware traveled further and for longer periods of time to hunt. They were now congregated into three main areas. The first was the valley called Tulpehocken (between the South and Blue Mountains), with small villages scattered along the Tulpehocken Creek. Sassoonan was made "king" of these Delaware by the Pennsylvania government. The second area was in the Valley of the Brandywine. Checochinican was the spokesman for this group. The third area was from the Lehigh River (where the Delaware joined it, also known as the Forks) extending to the Blue Mountains. Nutimus was considered the head of these people by the Pennsylvania authorities.

After William Penn died in 1718, his three sons inherited their father's lands in America. Unfortunately, they did not share their father's peaceful intentions toward the Delaware. Sassoonan was pressured into selling the land in the Tulpehocken Valley, and together with the Brandywine Delaware, was forced to move to land along the Susquehanna River. The Forks Delaware were the recipients of the fraudulent "Walking Purchase" of 1737. When they refused to leave the Lehigh Valley, they were told to by Canasatego, the Six Nations spokesman. The Delaware were given the choice of removing to Shamokin (Sunbury) or Wyoming (Wilkes-Barre), both on the Susquehanna River. There the Delaware would join or be joined by displaced Shawnee, Conoy, Nanticoke, Mahican, Tutelo, Minquas, and Twightwee. All would be under the watchful eye of the Six Nations authority, Shickellamy. The Delaware were soon to realize they were no longer in possession of any Delaware Valley land.

Though the loss of land was a factor in deteriorating relations between the Delaware and the British, an even worse insult was the British self-serving reinforcement of the Six Nations power over them. The Six Nations named Sassoonan, who by now was old, feeble, and a chronic alcoholic, as spokesman for all the Delaware.

Some of the young and dissatisfied Delaware left the Susquehanna to found a village on the Allegheny River known as Kittanning. Others settled on the upper Susquehanna, and another group traveled farther to settle on the Ohio at a place called Chininqué, or Logstown. In all these places, the Six Nations claimed suzerainty and placed two Indian supervisors, Tanaghrisson (Half-King) and Scarouady, over the Delaware.

In the Ohio country, the Delaware found themselves confronted with two advancing empires, the British and the French. Both wanted to gain Delaware tribal allegiance and military strength. The British were especially concerned that the Ohio Delaware and Shawnee would join with the French. In truth, the Delaware were less likely to be pro-French than they were to be pro-Delaware. Nevertheless, the provincial government of Pennsylvania and Virginia sent word to Sassoonan (through the Onondaga Council) to bring the Ohio Delaware back to the Susquehanna. There they could be watched. The Delaware at Logstown and Kittanning refused. The provincial powers then deemed it necessary to choose a new spokesman for the Delaware. At the Treaty of Logstown in 1752, Shingas was named king of the Delaware by the Six Nations.

On the Susquehanna, Moravian missionaries had founded an Indian mission called Gnadenhütten (Lehightown). It was there that another Delaware chief named Teedyuscung lived. When a group of Connecticut businessmen began to survey and map the area for the Susquehanna Company, Teedyuscung decided to leave. He took with him a mixed group of Indians to settle at Wyoming, away from white intrusion.

The French continued to move steadily southward into the Ohio country from the Great Lakes region, hoping to link Louisiana with French Canada. At the same time the British claimed the Ohio country as property of Virginia. The Ohio Delaware were caught in between. The French were sent warning from both the Six Nations and Virginia's Governor Robert Dinwiddie to leave the Ohio country. Their trade practices and the erection of forts all contributed to Delaware discontent. When an Indian council meeting was held at Logstown in 1753, George Washington was present. As a representative of Virginia, Washington promised full support for the Ohio Indians in disposing of the French. The Delaware remained skeptical.

When Washington surrendered Fort Necessity on 4 July 1754, it brought the Ohio Delaware closer to the French. Though they had initially resented French intrusion, they realized the French had the supplies and manpower to oppose the English. The Delaware saw no choice but to turn to the French for their economic survival when the English traders left the Ohio country.

On the Susquehanna in 1754 the Susquehanna Company, through chicanery, obtained rights to the land at the Delaware settlements of Wyoming and Shamokin. When the Connecticut people came to look at their new lands, the Delaware were surprised, and protested to their overlords, the Six Nations. Through Shickellamy, the Delaware informed the Pennsylvania authorities that further white intrusion would ensure first the killing of colonists' cattle, then of the colonists themselves.

The Ohio Delaware were said to have taken a neutral position when British General Edward Braddock was defeated on the Monongahela in July 1755. According to the Delaware chief, Shingas, Braddock had asked for his warriors' assistance in the battle. When Shingas asked what the Delaware status would be in regard to the land after a British victory, Braddock replied "that no Savage Shoud Inherit the land." With Braddock's defeat there followed total alienation of the Ohio Delaware and Shawnee toward the British.

The Susquehanna Delaware were called by the Oneida in September 1755 to assist them in an attack on the French. The Shamokin and Wyoming Delaware had experienced a summer of drought that left them without crops or fish. They refused to leave their starving families to go to war, and requested aid from the Pennsylvania government. No help was to come in the form of food, nor would a fort be built to protect the Indians from French attacks from the north. It was at this point that Shingas, in the Ohio country, felt the Susquehanna Delaware needed assistance. He allied the Ohio Delaware with the French, and requested the Susquehanna Delaware to do likewise. The Susquehanna Delaware still wished to remain neutral.

In October 1755 Shingas's war captains and warriors started what would be a rampage of attacks against settlers in Pennsylvania, Virginia, and Maryland. By the end of November 1755, C.A. Weslager wrote, the "Pennsylvania frontier from the Maryland border to the Delaware Water Gap was aflame." The Susquehanna Delaware entered the fray in November 1755 with an attack on Gnadenhütten, followed by raids in the Tulpehocken Valley, and settlements north of the Kittatinnies. There seems to have been no one incident that set the Delaware on the warpath. A series of British broken promises, fraudulent land purchases, the introduction of alcohol, smallpox, and other diseases, plus the continued acknowledgment of Six Nations domination over the Delaware had been accumulating and festering since the Europeans' arrival.

Pennsylvania Governor Robert Hunter Morris declared war on the Delaware nation on 14 April 1756, offering scalp bounties and cash for Indian prisoners. The assembly voted funds to establish a string of forts and blockhouses to be erected and garrisoned on the frontier. When Colonel John Armstrong lead an attack on the Delaware village at Kittanning on 8 September 1756, he set fire to 30 houses and destroyed a French arsenal held there. Shingas and the Ohio Delaware were not ready to surrender.

Temporary peace was made with the Susquehanna Delaware after a series of meetings were held at Easton during July and August 1757. Teedyuscung assumed leadership for the Susquehanna Delaware and declared them independent of the Six Nations. When Teedyuscung asked for the return of title to lands at Wyoming, the Pennsylvania government refused to acquiesce. They did not want to jeopardize their position with the Six Nations.

In the Ohio country the French were unable to supply the Delaware with the goods they needed. Their loyalty began to waver in their own self-interest. Chief Shingas passed his role of leadership to his brother, Beaver, so that peaceful negotiations with the British could resume. On 9 July 1759, the Ohio Delaware, led by Beaver, and a Shawnee delegation entered into a peace treaty with George Crog-

han. The British promised the Delaware that following the French withdrawal from the Ohio, the English would also depart to leave the land for the Indians. But at the same time, the Ohio Company was making preparations for settlement on the same lands. In addition the Pennsylvania assembly passed a law to concentrate Indian trade at two forts, Fort Augusta and Fort Pitt. Trade goods at both forts would soon be in short supply for the Ohio Indians.

The end of the war between Britain and France in 1763 seemed to trigger the Delaware, Shawnee, and other Iroquois Indians in a war of liberation against Britain. It was not until 8 May 1765 that a peace treaty was signed by representatives from both the Ohio and Susquehanna Delaware and the British. In effect the Delaware were placed in the position of a vanquished enemy. Of the 12 articles contained in that treaty, by far the most damaging to the Delaware was the one which stated the "Delaware forfeited all land rights until the English and Six Nations decided where they might live and hunt."

Linda M. Thorstad

References

Daniel G. Brinton, *The Lenâpé And Their Legends With the Complete Text and Symbols of the Walam Olum* (1884); Francis Jennings, *Empire of Fortune: Crowns, Colonies, and Tribes in the Seven Years War in America* (1988); Amandus Johnson, ed. and trans., *Instruction for Johan Printz* (1930); Herbert C. Kraft, *The Lenape, Archaeology, History, and Ethnography* (1986).

John A. Munroe, *Colonial Delaware, A History* (1978); Albert Myers, ed., *Narratives of Early Pennsylvania, West New Jersey, and Delaware* (1912); Daniel K. Richter and James H. Merrell, *Beyond the Covenant Chain: The Iroquois and Their Neighbors in Indian North America, 1600–1800* (1987); C.A. Weslager, *The Delaware Indians: A History* (1972).

See also ANDROS, EDMUND; EASTON CONFERENCE (1758); FINNS; HALF-KING; IROQUOIS; KITTANNING, BATTLE OF; LOGSTOWN, TREATY OF; FORT NASSAU (NEW JERSEY); FORT NECESSITY (PENNSYLVANIA); NEW SWEDEN; PENNSYLVANIA; PONTIAC'S WAR; FORT SWANENDAEL (DELAWARE); SWEDES; TEEDYUSCUNG; WASHINGTON, GEORGE

Fort Denonville (New York)
See FORT CONTI (NEW YORK)

Denonville, Jacques-René de Brisay, Marquis de (1637–1710)

Jacques-René de Brisay, marquis de Denonville, acquired extensive military experience before being appointed governor general of New France to replace Joseph-Antoine Le Febvre de La Barre. Denonville entered the army while still young and in 1663 was a captain in the Régiment Royal. He fought Algerians in North Africa and served throughout the Dutch war; he was commissioned in the Queen's Dragoons in 1675, appointed inspector general in 1681, and promoted to brigadier in 1683.

Commissioned governor by Louis XIV on 1 January 1685, Denonville sailed months afterward from La Rochelle, arriving in Quebec on 1 August. The governor shared Colbert's old belief in strengthening the colony by centralizing the French population and requiring that the Indian traders come to them. The governor made a reconnaissance of the colony within weeks of his arrival, traveling from Quebec to Fort Frontenac; he was not impressed. The habitants were too dispersed and indefensible; they were too much like Indians, he believed. Although they were fine physical specimens, they seemed debauched, undisciplined, and lacking in respect for authority. He took action to reduce drunkenness and the liquor trade with Indians. He also attempted to limit the fur trade by granting fewer *congés* (trading licenses), and registering *voyageurs* (fur company employees who carried the trading goods). Denonville was governor during a time when Louis XIV was interested in strengthening France's presence in America. The marquis de Seignelay, minister of marine, had ordered 500 reinforcements for the regular troops in the colony, but many had died of typhus or scurvy on the voyage. Many troops already in the colony had succumbed to influenza the year before, so Denonville's forces were never enough.

Denonville's primary responsibility, considering his predecessor's failure, was to remove the Iroquois threat. The French colony also perceived an English threat from Hudson Bay in the north and New York in the south. An expedition sent out under Pierre de Troyes from Montreal unexpectedly succeeded in removing the northern threat by capturing three English posts. To the south, Thomas Dongan, the governor of New York, sent some Albany fur traders to trade with the Ottawas at Michilimackinac. If Dongan were successful in directing the Ottawas' furs to Albany and away from Montreal, as the Iroquois had long been encouraging the Ottawas to do, the French colony would have been ruined.

The Iroquois were far too strong and in control of their environment for Denonville to conquer in a single campaign; nevertheless, he covertly prepared to attack the strongest and furthest west of the Five Nations, the Seneca, while overtly accepting the Onondagas' proposal for a conference at Fort Frontenac to reconcile differences. Denonville used Father Jean de Lamberville, a Jesuit missionary, to arrange the conference, keeping him ignorant of the governor's plans to use it to ambush the leaders and initiate his war on the Seneca.

Denonville's expedition left Montreal on 13 June 1687 with only a little more than 2,000 colonial regulars, Canadian militia, and Indian allies, which limited his expectations. As the French made their way up the St. Lawrence River, they captured Iroquois and sent them to Montreal to serve as hostages. Denonville's war on the Senecas included no major battles, for the Seneca fled after the first skirmish. As a result, immediate casualties were slight, but the French pushed on, destroying Seneca villages and food supplies, which produced a strain on the Five Nations' ability to provide for themselves. Denonville continued to Niagara, building a blockhouse at the mouth of the river and leaving 100 men under the sieur de Troyes before returning to Montreal.

One consequence of the war was that Denonville, following orders, shipped 36 Iroquois prisoners to France to row in the royal galleys. Only 13 eventually returned, following a peace settlement. Another was that Denonville realized that forcing the Iroquois to submit would require a much larger military commitment from France. He even suggested that capturing New York would be an easier way to gain the Five Nations' submission than conquering all their towns. The Iroquois responded with sporadic attacks on Canadians; Forts Niagara and Frontenac were made prisons by Iroquois raiding parties. At the same time, more than 1,000 French colonists were succumbing to disease. Therefore, Denonville was forced to pursue peace with the Five Nations, but he refused to abandon France's Indian allies, as his predecessor, La Barre, had done in 1684.

Before both parties ratified the treaty, however, France and England went to war, and Iroquois warriors surprised the French with an attack at Lachine on 5 August 1689. This renewed war lasted another ten years, but under a different governor. With Iroquois war parties ranging throughout the French colony, making supply efforts too dangerous, the governor decided to abandon Forts Niagara and Frontenac. Weeks after disposing of Fort Frontenac, Denonville's successor, Louis de Buade, comte de Frontenac, returned to Canada.

Sean O'Neill

See also FORT CONTI (NEW YORK); FORT FRONTENAC (NEW YORK); FORT NIAGARA (NEW YORK); SENECA; KING WILLIAM'S WAR

Desertion, Army

Under military law, a deserter is an individual who leaves his unit or post without permission and thus abandons the service.

The prevention of desertion was a prime objective of all armies and the rigid control over the movements of the rank and file imposed by military discipline was intended to decrease the possibility of desertion. The absence of a system of barracks and the quartering of troops in inns and the houses of civilians, however, made control over the movements of soldiers difficult. British military law severely limited furloughs for soldiers and defined desertion rather rigidly. Any soldier found more than one mile away from camp was considered a deserter. The government rewarded those who captured deserters, while the concealment of a deserter carried severe punishment.

Desertion was punishable by death, but frequently deserters faced instead the prospect of flogging of up to 1,000 lashes or running the gauntlet of their regiment up to 16 times. The sometimes thousands of lashes received from rods or halberds in the process of running the gauntlet often constituted a *de facto* death sentence until the use of the gauntlet was discontinued around 1740. Acquittal rates were extremely low, less than 10 percent for the British army in the Seven Years' War, while about one-third received the death penalty. Between 1756 and 1763, the annual desertion rate for the British army as a whole hovered around 5 percent per year, or 4,000 men, higher in North America and Canada, but lower in Europe. Almost 30 percent of all deserters caught in-

sisted they had not wanted to desert at all but had gotten drunk and left behind by their regiment. About 10 percent argued their desertion was caused by fear of punishment, while another 7 percent testified they had been kidnapped by Indians or had been taken prisoners by enemy forces. The rest cited various grievances with military life, such as not receiving promised pay, or that the time of their enlistment was up and they were held against their will.

Such testimonies reveal much about the reasons why men deserted in the seventeenth and eighteenth centuries. Desertions occurred frequently on the spur of a moment, when the soldier was fortified with drink. But recruiting sergeants and officers made promises they knew could not be kept, and illiterate soldiers often signed documents that contained clauses they did not understand. The strictness of military discipline, with its ferocious punishments even for minor offenses, actually encouraged desertion, and the soldiers were often afraid they would find little sympathy from their officers. The limitations on mobility and the strictness of furloughs even for important family matters almost forced soldiers to take unauthorized absences despite the risks involved.

The British government tried to prevent desertion by an elaborate system of control and punishment, but the system proved ineffectual in the long run. The frequent proclamation of general pardons, which permitted deserters to return within a specified time period without fear of punishment, provided a way out of the dilemma both for the deserter and for a government facing the necessity of keeping the armed forces at full strength.

Robert A. Selig

References
Sylvia R. Frey, "The Common British Soldier in the Late Eighteenth Century: a Profile," *Societas* 5 (1975):117–132; Arthur N. Gilbert, "Why Men Deserted from the Eighteenth-Century British Army," *Armed Forces and Society* 6 (1980):553–567.

Desertion, Navy

Desertion was a chronic problem for the Royal Navy. The roots of the problem were twofold. Many seamen were there involuntarily, having been pressed from the merchant marine, the fisheries, or right off the streets of their native towns; and the deplorable conditions of the service itself: poor and infrequent pay, bad food, crowding, and iron discipline.

So endemic was the urge to desert that captains had at times to run their ships virtually like floating prisons. Newly pressed men were confined below decks until the ship had sailed. Despite the fact that a deserter lost his accumulated pay and was subject to draconian punishment if caught, thousands deserted by slipping away from parties sent ashore to handle stores or assist in repairs to the ship, by dropping into a passing boat, or merely by swimming ashore when in harbor. To inhibit this, at times a captain ordered to take his ship into dockyard would transfer his untrustworthy seamen to ships remaining at anchor in the roads, picking them up again on leaving the harbor. Many times the sailing of a ship under orders had to be delayed because the captain dared not send large working parties ashore to complete his stores lest he lose some of the men through desertion.

In the Seven Years' War there were times when desertion was greater than the influx of sailors from recruitment and the press gangs. Cited as a progressive and humane undertaking, the building of large naval hospitals was in fact a way of limiting desertion by confining sick and injured seamen under close naval supervision. The quartering of these men in private homes ("sick quarters") before the 1740s had led to desertion on the order of 8 to 10 percent per annum.

Nor did service abroad curtail desertion. While few seamen deserted in the Mediterranean where disease was rampant and enslavement was still a possibility, the West Indies and North America presented an open invitation to reluctant sailors of the Royal Navy. Merchant shipping bound for England always needed a few more hands and premium pay was offered as a further inducement for prime seamen to desert. In 1747, Captain Charles Knowles, RN, established the prize ship *Bien Aimé* at Nantasket as a holding ship for seamen while their ships were in Boston harbor, as well as a storeship.

Until conditions for enlisted personnel could be improved to the point where an all-volunteer force became a possibility, the Royal Navy would continue to suffer from desertion.

John F. Battick

De Soto, Hernando

See SOTO, HERNANDO DE

Detroit

The trade routes/warpaths of the Great Lakes heartland were, in the seventeenth and eighteenth centuries, necessarily water routes. Portages, straits, and waterway junctions were of prime strategic significance. The Detroit River was one such route by which peoples south of the lakes (Iroquois Five Nations, New Yorkers) might have access to the rich interlake beaver grounds, or conversely, by which northern peoples (Hurons, Ottawas, and other Algonkians) might have access to the fur mart of Albany as an alternative to bartering with Montreal traders. In 1687, the governor of Canada, Jacques-René Brisay de Denonville, marquis de Denonville, ordered Fort St. Joseph to be built on the Detroit River near its connection with Lake Huron. He wished to ensure that the route was in French hands to control its Indian allies and the hunting grounds. He also saw Detroit as opening the route to a further trade in the Illinois country.

Around 1680, a Quebec merchant, Claude Charron de La Barre, had proposed that a Canadian colony be established at Detroit to bring order and focus to the French presence in the west, which then consisted of a few troops at palisaded posts and a large number of *coureurs de bois,* a law unto themselves. Two decades later, on 24 July 1701, a permanent Canadian settlement was established at Detroit by Antoine Laumet, alias Lamothe Cadillac. Convinced by Laumet's arguments and his own necessities, Jérôme Phélypeaux Maurepas, comte de Pontchartrain, minister of marine, believed this single post would give France the authority in the interior that it would need in the impending War of the Spanish Succession and at the same time not contribute to the oversupply of beaver that had led to the abandonment of all the other inland posts in 1696. In accord with Laumet's plan, Hurons, Ottawas, Miamis, and other French allies, even the dubious Fox, were encouraged to settle in their own stockades along the river outside Fort Pontchartrain. Laumet, as commandant (1701–1710), controlled the trade. A few Canadian settlers took up residence.

While Canadian officials saw some merit in securing the Detroit River, they resented Laumet's *de facto* monopoly and feared that the post would be an affront to the Senecas, that the western allies would be brought too close to the Iroquois-New York trading zone and would be suborned by the competition, and that, living

D

side by side, the allies would fight among themselves. All of their fears were realized.

After 1712, when all the old western posts rose again from their ashes, Detroit remained the inland depot of the Canadian southern trade. In 1727, its trade passed from the hands of its commandant into those of licensed traders from Montreal. Its Canadian colony of traders and provisioners increased, and many of its Indian inhabitants remained. Fort Pontchartrain was abandoned by French troops on 29 November 1760. Its role in the Canadian fur trade continued under the British regime, but the scattering of the Indian nations and the westward movement of the American frontier had ruined the trade by the time of Great Britain's surrender of the western posts to the United States in 1796.

Dale Miquelon

References

Jean Delanglez, "The Genesis and Building of Detroit"; "Cadillac at Detroit," *Mid-America*, 30 (1948):75–104, 152–156; W.J. Eccles, *The Canadian Frontier, 1534–1760* (1974); Dale Miquelon, *New France, 1701–1744: "A Supplement to Europe"* (1987).

See also Fort Pontchartrain de Detroit (Michigan)

Fort Detroit (Michigan)

See Fort Pontchartrain de Detroit (Michigan)

Fort Dickenson (Virginia)

Located on the Cowpasture River, about four miles below the present town of Millboro in Bath County, Virginia, Fort Dickenson was constructed sometime after the first white colonists settled in the area in 1749. Named for John Dickenson, one of the earliest local landowners, the fort probably consisted of a stockade of logs enclosing a blockhouse. A council of war held at Staunton in 1756 designated it as one of a line of strongholds to protect the Virginia frontier and fixed its garrison at 40 men.

Thomas Costa

References

Louis K. Koontz, *The Virginia Frontier, 1754–1763* (1925).

Dieskau, Jean-Armand, Baron de (1701–1767)

Jean-Armand Dieskau, baron de Dieskau, born a Saxon, went to France in 1720 as an aide-de-camp to Maréchel de Saxe, where he served in various campaigns during the 1730s and early 1740s, rising through the French ranks to become a major general and military governor of Brest in 1747. In 1755, he was appointed commander of the French regulars going to Canada to counter the British forces sent with General Edward Braddock. Dieskau arrived in Quebec in June along with his superior, the new governor general, Pierre de Rigaud de Vaudreuil, a Canadian.

Braddock's defeat at the Monongahela River and the French possession of papers revealing the British military strategy gave Dieskau a clear advantage. Initially, Vaudreuil sent Dieskau to take Oswego on the south shore of Lake Ontario, disrupting the British plans for a Great Lakes campaign, but when he learned of Colonel William Johnson's progress against Fort St. Frédéric (Crown Point) in August 1755, Vaudreuil recalled Dieskau from his preparations at Fort Frontenac and sent him down the Richelieu River. The French were past Ticonderoga, almost to the head of South Bay, when Johnson learned of their presence. Johnson attempted to warn his men at Fort Edward of Dieskau's approach; then he sent a force against Dieskau before improvising a fort at the head of Lac St. Sacrament (which he renamed Lake George).

Dieskau decided to move quickly against the supposedly weak Fort Edward when a prisoner mislead him about Johnson's forces being split, saying that most of them had returned to Albany. After leaving some of his regular troops at Fort Frontenac, Dieskau now left 1,300 regulars and 400 militia at Fort Carillon, taking only 200 regulars, 600 militia, and about 700 Indians—mostly Christian Mohawks from Caughnawaga and Abenaki. Vaudreuil had specifically ordered Dieskau not to divide his forces and would blame his defeat and capture on disobeying those orders.

Dieskau's Indian allies recommended that he not attempt an attack on Fort Edward because it was fortified with cannons. Meanwhile, he learned from another prisoner that Johnson's army was near, so he turned to attack Johnson's position at the head of Lake George, which was less entrenched and had fewer cannons. On 8 September, Dieskau discovered 1,000 reinforcements, including Mohawks led by Theyanoguin (Hendrick), which Johnson had sent to Fort Edward. The French had time to prepare an ambush much like the one used against Braddock but failed to execute it effectively. Dieskau claimed the Christian Mohawks spoiled the plan by alerting their kin. Although Theyanoguin and the militia leader, Colonel Ephraim Williams, died in the ambush, many of their men successfully retreated to Lake George. Johnson had improvised a fortification there, so when Dieskau reached it, he was faced with leading a frontal assault on a prepared position. This was the circumstance which Dieskau's critics say required a larger force of disciplined regulars. After hours of fighting, the battle ended in a stalemate with the French retreating. Dieskau, who had been wounded early in the assault, refused to move from where he had propped himself up against a tree and was captured there.

Although little was achieved by either side in the battle, the British claimed a victory and made Johnson a hero for capturing the French colony's second-in-command. The French constructed Fort Carillon at Ticonderoga and the British built Fort William Henry at Lake George (which the French would capture before the war was over). Louis-Joseph, marquis de Montcalm, succeeded Dieskau as commander of the French regular troops in Canada. The British took their high-ranking prisoner to New York and then to London, where Dieskau sat out the war recuperating from his wounds, finally being repatriated to France in 1763.

Sean O'Neill

See also FORT EDWARD (NEW YORK); JOHNSON, WILLIAM; LAKE GEORGE, BATTLE OF

Fort Dinwiddie (Virginia)

Located five miles west of the present town of Warm Springs in Bath County, Virginia, Fort Dinwiddie was an important stronghold during the French and Indian War. Built in 1755 around the house of William Warwick, about 20 miles west of Fort Dickenson, and named for Virginia Lieutenant Governor Robert Dinwiddie, the fort was variously known as Warwick's Fort, Byrd's Fort, and Hog's Fort. Captain Peter Hog commanded its garrison of between 60 and 100 men in 1756. One interesting feature of the fort was a log-covered passageway leading from the blockhouse to a spring within the fort. Fort Dinwiddie served as a frontier military outpost until 1789.

Thomas Costa

References

Louis K. Koontz, *The Virginia Frontier, 1754–1763* (1925).

Dinwiddie, Robert (1692–1770)

Robert Dinwiddie, merchant, royal placeman, and lieutenant governor of Virginia, was born at Germiston, near Glasgow, one of nine children of Robert Dinwiddie, a merchant, and Elizabeth Cumming Dinwiddie. After graduation from the University of Glasgow in 1711, he quickly acquired wealth as a merchant and made influential friends in government. Dinwiddie married Rebecca Affleck, and they had two daughters, Elizabeth and Rebecca.

In 1721 Dinwiddie was appointed agent for the Admiralty in Bermuda. From 1727–1738 he was collector of customs for Bermuda and sat on that colony's council. As surveyor general of customs for the southern district of America (the mainland colonies from Pennsylvania southward and Jamaica) from 1738–1749, Dinwiddie, as was his privilege, took a seat in the Virginia Council, though not permitted to act in a legislative and judicial capacity. From 1743–1749 he also held the office of inspector general of customs. Resigning his posts in 1749, Dinwiddie left Virginia and returned to trade in England. On 20 July 1751, he was appointed lieutenant governor of Virginia (the governor, William Keppel, earl of Albemarle, as was customary, stayed in England and collected half of the governor's salary). Dinwiddie arrived in Virginia on 20 November 1751.

Like many of his predecessors, Dinwiddie staunchly defended the royal prerogative and had difficulties with the Virginia legislature, which was bent on exercising control over appropriations and expenditures. An enterprising businessman himself, Dinwiddie aroused the ire of George Washington and other military officers for his close review of details regarding disbursement of funds. Dinwiddie's reports to home officials were thorough and incisive in comment.

A foremost concern of Dinwiddie was westward expansion. He arranged the Logstown Conference in spring 1752, which resulted in a treaty that confirmed the earlier cession (Lancaster Treaty of 1744) by the Iroquois of lands

D

from the Alleghenies to the Ohio River—favoring the interests of the Ohio Company. Dinwiddie steadfastly promoted the career of George Washington, sending the young Virginian as emissary to the French posts in western Pennsylvania, commissioning him head of the Virginia Regiment (on the death of Colonel Fry in 1754), and trying to get legislative support for Washington's little army. Dinwiddie joined General Edward Braddock, Commodore Augustus Keppel, and the governors of Maryland, Pennsylvania, New York, and Massachusetts at the Alexandria Conference in early 1755 that planned the northern military operations. After Braddock's defeat, Dinwiddie pursued a defensive policy. He set up ranger companies of militia for the Virginia frontier settlements and had a string of forts (about 25 in all) built, at 20–30 mile intervals, from the northern Shenandoah Valley southward to present Patrick County, along the east slope of the Alleghenies. Dinwiddie vigorously supported Virginia participation in the Forbes expedition (the colony contributing 2,000 troops), which resulted in the taking of Fort Duquesne on 25 November 1758.

Dinwiddie and the House of Burgesses engaged in a bitter dispute—the pistole fee controversy. The governor, immediately after proroguing the legislature in April 1752, ordered the payment of one pistole (a Spanish coin equal to £4/5) on land patents bearing the governor's seal and signature. Exceptions were allowed for grants of less than 100 acres, headrights, and lands filed for surveys before 22 April 1752. In response, the House of Burgesses drew up a protest document, appealed to the crown, sent attorney general Peyton Randolph to England as a special agent, and refused to pass appropriation bills until the governor acquiesced in paying Randolph's salary as agent, and also reinstating Randolph as attorney general (Dinwiddie having relieved Randolph of this position). On the advice of the Board of Trade, Dinwiddie gave Randolph back his post and also abandoned the pistole fee (1756). The dispute over the fee, nevertheless, had engendered a strong rhetorical defense against "no taxation without representation" by the legislature and Virginia leaders, several of whom wrote tracts on the subject.

Dinwiddie, an imperialist and expansionist, had great interest in the external relations of the colonies. Among reforms that he recommended were: 1) establishment of metallic currency for the colonies; 2) prevention of aiding the enemy by requiring certain provisions to be sent from the North American colonies only to Great Britain; 3) substitution of royal for the proprietary governors; 4) a poll tax levied by Parliament on the colonists to defray frontier defense and military expenses; 5) creation of two confederacies for the colonies—northern and southern; 6) extensive building of forts on the frontier; 7) naming a board of commissioners for each colony to supervise Indian trade; and 8) creation of a new colony beyond the Appalachian divide, to be settled by European Protestants.

Being replaced as the resident governor of Virginia, Dinwiddie returned to England, arriving there 17 February 1758. While living in London he kept in contact with Virginians. During a visit to the Baths of Clifton in Bristol, he died at his lodgings there on 17 July 1770. He was buried at the Clifton parish church in Bristol. One of few merchants who governed a royal colony, Robert Dinwiddie diligently led Virginians in the defeat of the French along the western frontier and aided in the development of the western part of the colony.

Harry M. Ward

References
John R. Alden, *Robert Dinwiddie: Servant of the Crown* (1973); R.A. Brock, ed., *The Official Records of Robert Dinwiddie*, 2 vols. (1883); Louis K. Koontz, *Robert Dinwiddie: His Career in American Colonial Government and Westward Expansion* (1941); Richard L. Morton, *Colonial Virginia*, 2 vols. (1960); Paul R. Shrock, "Maintaining the Prerogative: Three Royal Governors in Virginia as a Case Study, 1710–1758," Ph.D. Dissertation, University of North Carolina (1981).

See also LOGSTOWN, TREATY OF; OHIO COMPANY; FORT TRENT (PENNSYLVANIA); WASHINGTON, GEORGE

Discipline, Army
Military discipline is determined by military manuals and the laws of war issued for the guidance of all military personnel and all military action. It embraces conduct in both peace and war, and governs the daily lives of the soldiers.

The earliest existing set of rules for war in England dates to the year 1642 and was issued by Charles I. Beginning in 1673, and then in the

Articles of War of 1685, military discipline was to be enforced by two types of courts: regimental courts to try misdemeanors and to mete out corporal punishment, and general courts as appellate courts in all felony cases with the power to impose capital punishment and all other punishment they considered appropriate. Until 1753, military law made no provision for bail for offenders, but beginning in 1716, all soldiers had to be given minimal instruction in military law. After 1718, the Articles of War had to be read bimonthly to the soldiers as a fixed principle, and after 1718, all members of a military court and all witnesses had to testify under oath.

Given the prevailing attitude toward the soldier and the principles of waging war, military discipline in the eyes of the eighteenth century had to be as harsh as possible. Yet when seen in the context of the times, military discipline with its reliance on physical punishment was no worse than civilian law enforcement. While the rules of warfare of 1642 knew no less than 21 capital crimes, their number was reduced periodically until 1753, when only plunder, mutiny, aid to the enemy, and desertion remained as capital offenses. Between 1666 and 1782, some 512 men were executed in the British army for various offenses.

The great majority of crimes were punished by flogging, yet as late as 1722, the Articles of War authorized military courts to order mutilation or maiming for misdemeanors such as drunkenness or the sending or accepting of a challenge to a duel, even though the Bill of Rights of 1689 had prohibited cruel and unusual punishment. Moral transgressions such as blasphemy, swearing, or willful absence from divine services, a relic of the religious wars of the seventeenth century, were still carried as crimes as late as 1790, punishable with the cat-o'-nine-tails. Until 1832, there were no limitations on the number of lashes that could be meted out, and in severe cases courts ordered up to 1,000 lashes, which were administered over the course of several weeks.

Military discipline and the punishment used to enforce it reflected the general attitude of the times toward offenders. Throughout the seventeenth century those punishments were extremely harsh, but the eighteenth century saw a gradual humanization of military law as the character and composition of the British army changed from mercenaries and conscripts to genuine volunteers.

Robert A. Selig

References
Sylvia R. Frey, "Courts and Cats: British Military Discipline in the Eighteenth Century," *Military Affairs* 43 (1979): 5–11; Arthur N. Gilbert, "The Regimental Courts Martial in the Eighteenth Century British Army," *Albion* 8 (1976):50–66.

Discipline, Navy

Prior to 1645, naval discipline appears to have been governed solely by tradition. In that year, the Long Parliament issued "An Ordinance and Articles of Martial Law for the Government of the Navy," that authorized the holding of courts-martial by admirals and vessel commanders. In 1660, the restoration of the monarchy automatically annulled this ordinance and the year following the Cavalier Parliament authorized the Lord High Admiral to issue commissions to officers to hold courts-martial (13 Charles II, c. 9). A formal, universal, and permanent code of naval discipline was not promulgated for the Royal Navy until 1731. In that year, *King's Regulations and Admiralty Instructions* were issued by the Admiralty. In 1749, at the instigation of Admiral George Anson, Parliament consolidated all previous regulations and statutes in the *Naval Discipline Act* (22 George II), the basis of all later disciplinary codes of the Royal Navy.

Major crimes such as desertion, disobedience, mutiny, and murder were tried by courts-martial consisting of the officers of a vessel or of a fleet and were punished by hanging or by flogging, but the authority of a vessel's commander also included summary judgment for lesser crimes and misdemeanors, the punishments for which ran a gamut from mastheading to flogging. "White-collar crimes" committed by officers usually resulted in confinement to quarters, standing double watches, etc. or, for more serious offenses, dismissal from the service with or without forfeiture of pay, hence social disgrace, but for other ranks, physical punishment was the norm.

"Mastheading" was normally reserved for midshipmen guilty of minor lapses and consisted of spending a period of time high in the rigging, usually tied in place. More serious defaults by "young gentlemen" were punished by caning while bent over a gun ("kissing the gunner's daughter"). For talking back, gagging was the usual penalty, an iron or wooden object being tied, like a horse bit, in the mouth, and the miscreant, hands bound behind the back, lashed to a mast. To penalize laggardness, "starting," or striking the back or buttocks with a rope end, was administered extrajudicially. Theft from another person was punished by "running the gauntlet," wherein the perpetrator was bound hand and foot, seated on a tub placed on a grating which was dragged round the deck while the assembled crew struck the miscreant on the back with rope's ends, the bosun and his mates striking with their cat-o'-nine-tails. Older punishments such as tieing men to the capstan, confinement by the bilboes, a long iron bar with shackles attached to the ankles, ducking from the yardarm, and keel-hauling were seldom inflicted after the seventeenth century.

The most general and painful punishment administered was flogging with the cat-o'-nine-tails. Most sentences consisted of one or two dozen lashes; but for desertion, the punishment seems to have increased from 50 lashes to 500 over the course of the eighteenth century. The instrument was a whip composed of a heavy rope handle to which nine lengths of small rope about 18 inches long were attached, with knots tied in the ends. The victim was stripped to the waist, trussed up vertically to a ladder or grating and, before the assembled ship's company, given the specified number of strokes by the bosun and/or his mates. The effect was brutal, the skin of the back being lacerated and contused. Sentences of 500 lashes ("flogging round the fleet") were usually fatal but justified on the grounds that desertion threatened the very existence of the navy.

Hanging, the penalty for murder, mutiny (which could include disobedience to orders), and cowardice, was carried out by hauling the victim to a yardarm by the neck rather than by the drop so that he very probably strangled to death. The body was normally exposed for a while at the yardarm. In the case of officers, execution was by firing squad.

Some officers were notorious punishers, tyrannical, and even sadistic, while others were able to maintain discipline without recourse to physical punishment. The harshness of naval justice, however, should be measured against contemporary standards. It was a brutal age wherein deterrence, even for petty offenses, was held to be the only solution to crime.

John F. Battick

Fort Dobbs (North Carolina)

The short-lived Fort Dobbs was built in 1756 at the urging of Provincial Governor Arthur Dobbs, for whom it was named. Located about four miles north of Statesville, Fort Dobbs was designed to protect the North Carolina backcountry from attack by the Shawnee and other Indian tribes allied with the French during the early years of the French and Indian War. It was primarily used, however, against the Cherokee, who turned toward the French in the late 1750s.

Fort Dobbs served sporadically as a garrison for provincial troops on the frontier and as a refuge for the region's widely scattered settlers. It was attacked only once. On 27 February 1760, a group of about 70 Cherokee braves, responding to the recent massacre of captured Cherokee at Fort Prince George, surrounded the fort. Provincial troops under the command of Hugh Waddell drove them off after a brief but sharp fight. At least ten Cherokee and one defender were killed.

The fort was abandoned after the end of the Cherokee War. In 1764 the fort's remaining supplies were transferred to Salisbury and it was allowed to fall into ruins. The only contemporary description of Fort Dobbs describes it as a "good and Substantial" building, three stories high, 53 feet by 40 feet, with oak walls 24 and one-half feet in height.

Jim Sumner

References
Jerry C. Cashion and Stephen E. Massengill, *Fort Dobbs* (1976).

See also CHEROKEE WAR

Dominion of New England (1686–1689)

The Dominion of New England, a short-lived political consolidation of the northern English colonies in America, was the culmination of the Stuart monarchy's policy of bringing colonial America into closer dependence on the crown. From the 1660s onwards, London's attempts to regulate colonial trade and intervene on behalf of dissidents within New England met with bitter resistance from a Massachusetts determined to preserve its Puritan orthodoxy from external contamination. After prolonged negotiations, Boston's refusal to accept any revision of its 1629 charter of government precipitated the charter's total nullification by legal action in

October 1684. Buoyed by a resurgent royalism within England, crown officials now pressed beyond their original plan of sending a royal governor to oversee the various New England colonies. Instead, all were to be brought within a single government—the Dominion of New England—ruled without an elected legislative assembly. This shift in policy reflected the authoritarian militarism of the new king, James II (1685–1689). Long distrustful of representative government, James also knew from his years as proprietor of New York of the difficulties faced by the fragmented northern English colonies in meeting the threat of French and Indian attack.

Initially, as established in May 1686, the Dominion of New England consisted of a president, Joseph Dudley, and a crown-appointed council ruling over a union of Massachusetts, Plymouth, Maine, New Hampshire, and part of Rhode Island. Following the arrival in December of Sir Edmund Andros, an experienced English soldier, to serve as governor, the dominion's bounds were extended to include Connecticut, the rest of Rhode Island, and finally, in 1688, New York and New Jersey, creating a single government stretching from Maine to the Delaware River. With Andros came 60 regular soldiers, the first English redcoats seen in New England.

Dudley, a native New Englander, had proceeded cautiously; Andros's brusque ways soon threatened the cornerstones of New England's way of life. He levied taxes without representative consent, forbade town meetings, challenged existing land titles, and displaced Puritan Congregationalism from its privileged legal position in favor of a policy of religious toleration. Scorning local advice, Andros governed his overextended state through a clique of intimates drawn mostly from New York. Opponents were fined and imprisoned: "Either you are Subjects," the governor told one dissenter, "or you are Rebels."

Widely unpopular, the dominion finally collapsed in the face of frontier conflict at home and revolution in England. Early in 1689, as Andros directed a punitive expedition against the eastern Indians, word began to reach Boston of an invasion of England by William of Orange that promised a restoration of liberties on both sides of the Atlantic. Thus encouraged, the militia around Boston rose in revolt on 18 April, captured Andros and his leading supporters in a bloodless coup, and shipped them back to England. Stripped of leadership, the dominion disintegrated into its component parts.

The fate of the dominion, and popular memories of it as the epitome of Stuart tyranny, discredited the crown's experiment of governing without elected assemblies. Yet royal government in more moderate form soon returned to Massachusetts and New York, and crown officials continued to search for solutions to the military disunity that the dominion had been designed to solve, as by appointing governors with authority over neighboring militias.

Richard R. Johnson

References

Viola F. Barnes, *The Dominion of New England: A Study in British Colonial Policy* (1923); Richard R. Johnson, *Adjustment to Empire: The New England Colonies, 1675–1715* (1981); William H. Whitmore, ed., *The Andros Tracts*, 3 vols. (1868–1874).

See also ANDROS, EDMUND

Dongan, Thomas, Second Earl of Limerick (1634–1715)

Thomas Dongan was lieutenant governor of New York from 1682 to 1685, during which time James Stuart, duke of York, was the proprietor. On James's accession to the English throne in February 1685, New York became a royal colony and Dongan the governor general. He was recalled in April 1688, concurrent with New York's incorporation into the Dominion of New England.

Dongan was born into a prominent Irish-Catholic family intensely loyal to the Stuart monarchs. On the fall of King Charles I to parliamentary forces in the English civil war, the Dongans fled to France to avoid persecution. Like many of the landless expatriates during the interregnum, Thomas joined the French army, rising eventually to the rank of colonel and commander of the Régiment d'Irlandais. He returned to England in 1678 at the behest of King Charles II, who had been restored to the throne in 1660.

In exchange for a promising French army career, Dongan received in 1679 an appointment as lieutenant governor of Tangier and a commission as lieutenant colonel of the Tangier Regiment. His tour was cut short after a few months, however, because of Parliament's concern over Dongan's Catholicism. Stripped of civil and military authority, he remained out of office until the duke of York (also a Catholic) appointed him as New York's lieutenant governor.

Arriving in August 1683, Dongan acted quickly to redress the colonists' discontent over authoritarian government. In accordance with proprietary instructions, he convened New York's first representative assembly in October. He approved the Charter of Liberties and Privileges, a surprisingly liberal document that reflected the colonists' demand for the full range of English political and civil rights. Though both the assembly and charter were short-lived (James dissolved them soon after acceding to the throne), they served as models for representative government throughout the colonial era.

Besides his work with the assembly, Dongan settled boundaries with adjacent colonies, promoted settlement through land distribution (a large amount went to himself and political allies), and approved city charters for New York and Albany.

Dongan's greatest achievement was the formulation of an aggressive diplomacy vis-à-vis the French in Canada. Prior to his arrival, the French had expanded their influence over the interior of North America through exploration, Jesuit missions, and trade; meanwhile, the English had clung to the coast, forsaking the wilderness behind them. Dongan recognized the consequences of inaction for the future of the English empire and labored to reverse the situation. In pursuit of economic and territorial sovereignty, he secured a military alliance with the powerful Iroquois nations. He discredited the work of French missionaries, who for years had been active along the New York-Canadian frontier, and pressured allied Indians to expel them. Finally, he dispatched trading parties to the "far Indians" of the Great Lakes, a region claimed by France.

Subsequent to a French invasion of Iroquois territory in July 1687, Dongan received King James's unequivocal support in pursuing aggressive policies toward New France. The following winter he organized a joint English-Iroquois defense force at Albany in response to rumors of a second invasion. In the spring he directed the Iroquois in a series of retaliatory raids that inspired panic among the French and won from them important concessions. Periods of fighting continued intermittently long after Dongan's departure, but the significant beginnings of Anglo-French rivalry for the interior, which lasted until the expulsion of the French from North America in 1763, must be traced to the Dongan administration.

Lance A. Betros

References

Lance A. Betros, "A Glimpse of Empire: New York Governor Thomas Dongan and the Evolution of English Imperial Policy, 1683–1688," Ph.D. Dissertation, University of North Carolina (1988); David Ellis, et al., *A History of New York State* (1967); Michael Kammen, *Colonial New York: A History* (1975); Lawrence H. Leder, *Robert Livingston, 1654–1728, and the Politics of Colonial New York* (1961); Robert C. Ritchie, *The Duke's Province: A Study of New York Politics and Society, 1664–1691* (1977).

See also SENECA, FRENCH ATTACK ON THE

Fort Dorchester (South Carolina)

Between 1757 and 1760, at the height of the Great War for Empire, South Carolinians built a fort to protect the community of Dorchester, a trading post and port located 25 miles northwest of Charles Town along the Ashley River. Located 50 feet from and 15 feet above the river, the fort's walls were constructed of tabby, a mixture of oyster shell and lime cement. The structure was designed as a squared breastwork with half-bastions at each angle.

Gregory D. Massey

References

Robert B. Roberts, *Encyclopedia of Historic Forts: The Military, Pioneer, and Trading Posts of the United States* (1988).

Dover, Attack on (1689)

England's Glorious Revolution of 1688 was felt in New England when Governor Edmund Andros of Massachusetts was given jurisdiction over the duke of York's land grant in Maine. Almost immediately, Andros broke the peace by attacking St. Castin's French trading post on the lower Penobscot River. Baron Jean-Vincent d'Abbadie de St. Castin, the son-in-law of the Penobscot chief, Modockawando, had considerable influence with the Indians. Soon retaliatory raids were planned on New England frontier settlements.

Dover, New Hampshire, known as Cochecho, or Quochech, by the Indians, was one of the first English settlements targeted by the French and Indians. Dover was the home of Major Richard Waldron, who had settled there about 1635 as a young man. He became a trader with the Indians but gained a reputation among them as a great cheat. He went to Pemaquid to trade with the Indians regularly. In 1664 Waldron built a fine Boston-style house, probably the finest home in Dover. Ten years later, fearing attacks by the Indians he had cheated, he added a tall stockade around his yard. On 6 September 1676, at the end of King Philip's War, Waldron contrived to induce 400 eastern Indians to his stockade for trading and a sham battle marking the end of hostilities. At a signal, Indians and soldiers were to fire their guns into the air. At the signal the Indians fired and found themselves surrounded by armed soldiers. They knew that they had no alternative but to surrender. About half the Indians were sent to Boston where they were hanged. Most of the others were jailed or sold as slaves. The Indians never forgave Waldron for this treacherous act.

On 27 June 1689, two Indian women arrived at Waldron's stockade and said that the next day a large group of Indians would arrive with furs to trade. They received permission to sleep by the fire within the stockade. During the night the squaws noted how the gates were locked and counted the number of soldiers sleeping in each apartment. Then the gates were opened. The Indian "traders" were signaled by a bird call, stealthily came in, were directed to the soldier's quarters, and quickly killed their adversaries. Waldron, who rushed out of his apartment bravely brandishing a sword, was soon surrounded by Indians, struck down with a tomahawk, carried out, and tortured. Twenty-three people were killed, 29 taken prisoner, four or five houses burned, and others looted before the Indians retired.

Nicholas N. Smith

References
Samuel Drake, "The Remarkable Escape of the Widow Elizabeth Heard Also Taken at the Destruction of Major Waldron's Garrison in Dover," in *Indian Captivities or Life in the Wigwam* (1857):68–70; John Gyles, *Memoirs of Odd Adventures, Strange Deliverances, etc. In the Captivity of John Gyles, Esq.* (1736) [Many reprints]; E. Hoyt, *Antiquarian Researches: Comprising a History of the Indian Wars in the Country Bordering Connecticut*

River and Parts Adjacent, and Other Interesting Events, From the First Landing of the Pilgrims, to the Conquest of Canada by the English in 1760 . . . (1824); John Scales, *History of Dover, New Hampshire* (1923); Robinson V. Smith, "New Hampshire Remembers the Indians," *Historical New Hampshire* 8 (1952): 1–36.

See also KING WILLIAM'S WAR; NEW HAMPSHIRE

Drake, Sir Francis (c. 1540–1596)

Born in Crowdale, Devonshire, Francis Drake joined the commercial navy under the guidance of the Hawkins family who had adopted him. His military successes against the Spanish fleets and ports of Europe and America gave him fame and won him the recognition and trust of Queen Elizabeth. His circumnavigation of the world (1577–1580), his position as vice admiral of the English fleet, and his victory over the Spanish Armada in 1588 were the highlights of his naval career.

Between his travels and activities, one can point out two episodes in which Drake had contact with territory now part of the United States: his exploration of the coast of California (1579), and the overthrow and burning of the Spanish settlement of St. Augustine, Florida (1586).

Toward the end of 1577, Drake led a small royal expedition with the object of reaching the Isles of "Las Especias" in the Pacific Ocean. After crossing the Strait of Magellan, in the spring of 1579 he reached the coast of California north of the Spanish domain boundaries, landing on 17 June in what is now Drake's Bay and taking possession of this territory in the name of Queen Elizabeth I. There he established a fortified camp close to the coast while he finished careening the boat in which he was traveling, departing for the Isles of "Las Especias" on 23 July.

In September 1585, Drake set sail from the British Isles at the head of a powerful fleet that had as its visible objective the attack of the western Spanish Indies and as a secret mission the reinforcement of the recently created Roanoke colony on the North American coast. After overthrowing important Spanish ports in the Caribbean, he headed toward the Spanish military post at St. Augustine, arriving on 6 June. But the attack was expected by the governor, who hid all the provisions and money and evacuated the majority of the people, and then offered a symbolic resistance, thereby avoiding the complete annihilation of the village's inhabitants. The village itself was overthrown and completely burned by its attackers. A few days later the fleet arrived at a secret anchorage off Roanoke in Virginia, where the English colony was suffering from serious problems due to lack of provisions. The arrival of Drake signified a strengthening of the settlement, but bad weather dispersed the fleet, so he decided to begin his return voyage.

The last years of Drake's career were marked by failure. He died, a victim of dysentery, on 26 January 1596, close to the Island of "Escudo de Veragua" in what is now Panama during an expedition to the Caribbean.

Felipe del Pozo-Redondo

References
Verne E. Chatelaine, *The Defenses of Spanish Florida 1565 to 1763* (1941); Robert F. Heizer, *Francis Drake and the California Indians, 1579* (1947); Christopher Lloyd, *Drake, Corsario y Almirante* (1958).

See also ROANOKE; ST. AUGUSTINE

Dry Docks

Dry docks were artificial basins constructed of timber or stone and fitted with floodgates into which ships entered at high tide. The gates were then closed and the water removed by gravity or chain pumps. The absence of water made it possible to repair or clean the vessel's hull below the waterline.

During the age of sail, wooden ships required constant attention. Barnacles, marine crustaceans that adhered to vessels below the waterline, fouled bottoms and had to be removed or they would impair the vessel's sailing ability. *Teredo navalis,* a marine mollusk commonly referred to as the shipworm, was another threat to wooden ships, especially in warm waters like the Caribbean. Before copper sheathing was introduced in the 1770s, it was necessary to scrape and burn off (bream) the worm to prevent serious structural damage. The best place to perform this maintenance was in dry dock. The Royal Navy's standing orders in the mid-eighteenth century called for cruisers in home waters to be docked, if possible, every six weeks; ships of

the line were normally cleaned in dry dock three or four times a year.

In the colonies, the absence of dry docks posed considerable problems. The normal method of cleaning ships in America was careening, a laborious process in which the vessel was hove down to expose first one side of the hull for cleaning, and then the other. Careening wharves were built for this purpose, and all the leading colonial ports maintained such facilities for merchantmen. The Royal Navy used these wharves in North America and maintained its own at its Caribbean stations in Jamaica and Antigua.

Carl E. Swanson

References
Daniel A. Baugh, *British Naval Administration in the Age of Walpole* (1965); J.G. Coad, *Historic Architecture of the Royal Navy: An Introduction* (1983); Philip MacDougall, *Royal Dockyards* (1982); N.A.M. Rodger, *Wooden World: An Anatomy of the Georgian Navy* (1986).

Fort Dummer (Vermont)

In 1723, the Massachusetts legislature voted to build a blockhouse on the Connecticut River to protect its settlements from Grey Lock's Abenaki raiders. The garrison was to consist of 40 men, both English and Indians, and was to send out scouts in an effort to provide early warning of enemy war parties.

The wooden blockhouse was built near Brattleboro, Vermont, by carpenters from Northfield, Massachusetts, and named Fort Dummer. Captain Timothy Dwight's original garrison of 55 men contained a dozen Indians, mainly from Hudson River tribes, and Indians continued to serve at the fort in subsequent years.

Fort Dummer became the major base of operations for scouting and retaliatory expeditions northward into Abenaki country, but Indian war parties regularly slipped past the garrison to strike settlements further south. Throughout Dummer's War (1722–1727), the fort was the scene of frequent skirmishes between English soldiers and Abenaki raiders, and the garrison occasionally had to fend off Indian attack.

The fort functioned as more than just a military outpost. A trading post was established here in 1728 and Captain Joseph Kellogg was appointed truckmaster. In 1735, Massachusetts appointed a minister to the fort to cater to the Indians who regularly came downriver to trade.

At the beginning of King George's War (1744–1748), the king ordered that Fort Dummer be properly garrisoned and maintained, but jurisdictional disputes between Massachusetts and New Hampshire, and New Hampshire's reluctance to finance the fort, hindered the work. Fort at Number Four, farther upriver at Charlestown, New Hampshire, bore the brunt of enemy attacks and, by the end of the war, Fort Dummer and Fort at Number Four were the only English settlements left in the upper Connecticut Valley.

As the frontier of English settlement pushed north, Fort Dummer became less important as a bastion against French and Indian raids and it was abandoned in 1760.

Colin G. Calloway

References

"Papers Relating to Fort Dummer," *Collections of the New Hampshire Historical Society,* Vol. 1, 143–147; Egbert C. Smyth, ed., "Papers relating to the construction and first occupancy of Fort Dummer," *Proceedings of the Massachusetts Historical Society,* 2nd series, 6 (1891):359–371; Myron O. Stachiw, *Massachusetts Officers and Soldiers 1723–1743: Dummer's War to the War of Jenkins' Ear (1979);* Josiah Temple and George Sheldon, *History of the Town of Northfield, Massachusetts* (1875).

See also DUMMER'S WAR; FORT AT NUMBER FOUR (NEW HAMPSHIRE)

Dummer's Treaty (1727)

Dummer's Treaty is probably the most important treaty that the Indians of Maine and the Maritime Provinces made with Massachusetts. In 1724, both Indians and whites suffered terrible losses in their wars. Both sides were ready for a truce. Although there had been several earlier treaties made with the Wabanaki Indians and the English, the Indians realized that this treaty must provide guarantees for both English and Indians. The Dummer Treaty negotiations begun in 1725 were not ratified until 1727 when Sauguaaram (alias Loron), the head spokesman for the Indians, was assured that the treaty provided the rights that the Indians needed. These Indians, who had negotiated their first land deed in 1625, had become famil-

iar with European methods of transacting business. Early in 1725, Sauguaaram met with the English to assure them that the Penobscot had no part in the recent Indian raids and would negotiate a treaty. As head chief, Sauguaaram was determined that the treaty include Indian rights. The Dummer Treaty guaranteed the Indians specific lands, a priest of their religion (Catholic), hunting, fishing, fowling, and land use rights forever. To assure himself that the treaty contained all that he wished, he returned to Boston in 1727 and signed another treaty providing the Indians with the same guarantees.

Dummer's Treaty became the model for Treaty No. 239 between England and the Maliseet and the Treaty of 1749 between England and the Maliseet and Micmac. In recent years it has been used in court successfully for Indian rights cases.

Nicholas N. Smith

References

Peter A. Cumming and Neil H. Mickenberg, *Native Rights in Canada,* 2nd ed. (1972); *Dummer Treaty,* Original Copy, Office of the Secretary of Massachusetts, Statehouse, Boston, Massachusetts; Edward Goddard, "Journal of Edward Goddard, 1726," *The Colonial Society of Massachusetts* 20: 128–147; William Williamson, *The History of the State of Maine* (1832); Justin Winsor, ed., *Narrative and Critical History of America* (1884):432.

See also DUMMER'S WAR

Dummer's War (1722–1727)

The Treaty of Utrecht (1713), which ended Queen Anne's War, initiated 40 years of uneasy peace between New England and New France. That same year, France's Abenaki allies made peace with the English with the Treaty of Portsmouth. The treaties, however, did not remove the fundamental issues of conflict on the northern New England frontier and in less than a decade the Abenakis were at war with New England once more, while the French, New York, and the Iroquois watched anxiously from the sidelines.

Population growth in the English colonies following Queen Anne's War pushed the frontier eastward along the coast of Maine, north up the Merrimack and Connecticut Valley, and westward into the Berkshires and northwest-

D

ern Connecticut. The Abenakis became increasingly angry over English encroachment on their lands, the dishonest practices of English traders, and the construction of English forts. Treaties with the Abenakis in 1717 and 1719 failed to redress their concerns and tensions continued to escalate. In 1722, Governor Samuel Shute of Massachusetts declared war on the Abenakis of Maine, declaring "the said *Eastern Indians,* with their Confederates, to be Robbers, Traitors and Enemies to his Majesty King George."

The conflict did not develop into a full-scale "French and Indian war." Massachusetts and New Hampshire bore the brunt of the fighting. New York supplied sympathy and intelligence but kept out of the fighting, and the Iroquois Confederacy resisted Massachusetts's offer of scalp bounties and other inducements to serve as allies. The French encouraged the Abenaki war effort and prompted other tribes to support them, but they likewise refused to get involved.

Known variously as Dummer's War, Grey Lock's War, Father Rasle's War, and Lovewell's War, the conflict followed a characteristic pattern of guerrilla warfare, with Abenaki war parties raiding frontier settlements, and English retaliatory expeditions penetrating Indian country on search and destroy missions.

The English regarded the Jesuit missionary, Father Sebastien Rasle, as a sinister force who corrupted the Abenakis with Catholic teachings and incited them to raid English settlements. After several attempts, English troops finally killed Rasle in 1724 when Captain Jeremiah Moulton destroyed his mission village at Norridgewock. The following spring, the English claimed another victory when Captain John Lovewell and his men fought a famous but costly skirmish with the Pigwackets in the White Mountains. English troops also burned the Indian village at Penobscot. Many Abenakis fled to French missions in Canada or took refuge in the northern reaches of their territory until the war was over.

Farther west, the English fared less well. In the Green Mountains of what is now Vermont, chief Grey Lock led Missisquoi Abenakis from the Champlain Valley in a series of devastating raids on the Massachusetts frontier. Time after time, he struck without warning and eluded hastily assembled English pursuits. Massachusetts constructed Fort Dummer in an effort to protect settlements farther down the Connecticut River but Grey Lock continued to harass the frontier and "Grey Lock's War" continued long after the eastern Abenaki tribes made peace.

The war came to a close with Dummer's Treaty, negotiated at a series of conferences between 1725 and 1727. The Penobscots played a significant role in inducing other Abenakis to make peace and one by one the Abenaki tribes fell in line with the treaty, although Grey Lock and the Missisquoi Abenakis never did make peace. The English made Dummer's Treaty the basis of their diplomatic relations with the Abenakis and the peace held until the outbreak of King George's War.

Many of the Abenaki tribes were divided and dispirited by the end of Dummer's War and their efforts did little to halt the progress of English expansion. Nevertheless, the war demonstrated that the Abenakis were not simply the pliant auxiliaries of the French. They went to war without their French allies and fought it for their own reasons. The war also revealed a lack of cooperation among the English colonies, as Massachusetts and New Hampshire suffered considerable distress in a war they felt should have been a common endeavor.

Colin G. Calloway

References
James Phinney Baxter, *The Pioneers of New France in New England* (1894); Colin G. Calloway, "Gray Lock's War," *Vermont History,* 55 (1987):212–227; Fanny Hardy Eckstorm, "The Attack at Norridgewock, 1724," *New England Quarterly,* 7 (1934):541–578; David L. Ghere, "Mistranslation and Misinformation: Diplomacy on the Maine Frontier, 1725–1755," *American Indian Culture and Research Journal,* 8 (1984):3–26; Kenneth Morrison, "Sabastien Rasle and Norridgewock, 1724: The Eckstorm Thesis Reconsidered," *Maine Historical Quarterly,* 14 (1974):76–97.

See also ABENAKI; DUMMER'S TREATY; LOVEWELL, THOMAS; LOVEWELL'S FIGHT; MOULTON, JEREMIAH; NORRIDGEWOCK, BATTLE OF; RALE (RASLE), SEBASTIEN; FORT ST. GEORGE'S (MAINE); WESTBROOK, THOMAS

Fort du Portage (New York)
See LITTLE FORT NIAGARA (NEW YORK)

Fort Dupui (Pennsylvania)

Fort Dupui was one of the easternmost posts in the string of forts that stretched along the Blue Mountains on Pennsylvania's northeastern frontier. It was built on the Delaware River, on the property of a Huguenot settler named Samuel Dupui. It was one of three forts constructed in the heart of traditional Munsee lands, but, like the rest of these eastern posts, it saw very little military activity during the war. On 25 March 1757, however, Sergeant Leonard Den was killed by an Indian war party within two miles of the fort.

Eric Hinderaker

See also FORT ALLEN (PENNSYLVANIA); FORT HENRY (PENNSYLVANIA); FORT LEBANON (PENNSYLVANIA); FORT NORRIS (PENNSYLVANIA)

Fort Duquesne (Pennsylvania)

Fort Duquesne, named after Ange de Menneville, marquis de Duquesne, governor general of Canada (1752–1755), was constructed at the junction of the Allegheny and Monongahela Rivers (present-day Pittsburgh, Pennsylvania) in the spring of 1754 and demolished by the retreating French in November 1758. As the French headquarters for the Ohio region it was the largest of the four forts in the area. It was built of wood in a square with a 10–12 foot deep ditch and bastions at each corner covering a total area of around 150 feet square. Beyond the ditch on the two landward sides ravelins provided further defense. The fort mounted some 15 guns, six of which were six-pounders and the remainder two- or three-pounders. Later buildings on the northeast side were enclosed with protective works and referred to by the English as the "second fort." Fort Duquesne sustained a permanent garrison of 200–300 men; during the summer months, reinforcements from Canada occasionally raised the number to around 1,500.

In 1753, under Governor Duquesne, the French initiated a major effort to secure control of the Ohio Valley, which was being infiltrated by English trappers and traders. A force of some 2,300 men constructed Fort de la Presque Isle (Erie, Pennsylvania) and Fort Le Boeuf (Waterford, Pennsylvania) opening the portage from Lake Erie to the Allegheny tributary of French Creek. In January 1754, Duquesne officially appointed Captain Claude-Pierre Pécaudy de Contrecoeur, to command in the Ohio region and ordered him to erect at Logstown (Ambridge, Pennsylvania) a major fortification to be named after the governor. If the forks in the Ohio, supposedly some 20 miles upstream, provided a better position to block the English, Contrecoeur could build there instead.

Arriving at the forks with some 600 men on 16 April 1754, Contrecoeur encountered a 42-man party of Virginia militia in the process of constructing a wooden stockade on the site. The British militiamen could do little else than surrender the position and withdraw eastward. Contrecoeur immediately decided to build the French fort in the same location; over the next two months his men, working under the direction of the expedition's engineer, Captain François Le Mercier, laid out the basic plan of the fortification, dug the ditch, threw up log and earthen walls on the two landward sides, erected wooden palisades on the river sides, and completed the four bastions. As manpower availability permitted over the next two years, Contrecoeur added two ravelins and cleared the glacis outside the ditch.

The construction of Fort Duquesne brought French and British rivalry over the Ohio region to a head. George Washington's failure in 1754 to regain control of the site and his surrender at Fort Necessity led directly to the British decision to send Major General Edward Braddock with regular forces in 1755 to establish British dominion over the entire area, beginning with an attack on Fort Duquesne itself. Braddock's surprising and complete defeat on 9 July 1755 a few miles up the Monongahela from the fort was the last serious British threat to French ascendancy on the Ohio until 1758. Braddock's defeat itself served as the trigger for the formal declaration of what became known as the Seven Years' War in Europe and as the French and Indian War in the English colonies. The French victory and the plunder associated with it greatly impressed the Indians of the area who participated with the French in a series of raids against New York and Pennsylvania settlements directed from and supplied by Fort Duquesne over the next three years. The deliberate campaign by Brigadier John Forbes in 1758 made the position untenable and in the face of overwhelming British forces, on 24 November 1758, the last French commander, Captain François-Marie Le Marchand, sieur de Lignery, blew up the fort with about 50 or 60 barrels of gunpowder after burning everything flammable.

Ronald Martin

References

Fernand Grenier, ed., *Papiers Contre-coeur et autres documents concernant le conflit anglo-français sur l'Ohio de 1745 à 1756* (1952); William A. Hunter, *Forts on the Pennsylvania Frontier, 1753–1758* (1960); Alfred Procter James, *Drums in the Forest* (1958).

See also FORT BEDFORD (PENNSYLVANIA); BRADDOCK, EDWARD; FORBES CAMPAIGN OF 1758; FORT LE BOEUF (PENNSYLVANIA); MONONGAHELA RIVER; OHIO EXPEDITION OF 1755; PÉCAUDY DE CONTRECOEUR, CLAUDE PIERRE; FORT DE LA PRESQUE ISLE (PENNSYLVANIA); WASHINGTON, GEORGE

Durham (New Hampshire)

See OYSTER RIVER (NEW HAMPSHIRE)

Duston, Hannah (1658–c. 1730)

When the town of Haverhill, Massachusetts, was attacked on 15 March 1697, the 39-year-old Hannah Duston lay in bed recuperating from giving birth to her twelfth child six days previous. Her husband, Thomas, made the painful choice of leaving his bedridden wife and infant child in order to save the remaining seven children (four children had previously died). As he herded the children to the nearest garrison house, the raiders captured Hannah, her infant, and her midwife, Mary Neff. The infant was killed within the hour and the two women taken with other captives north into New Hampshire.

The raiding party divided, with Duston, Neff, and a 14-year-old boy named Samuel Leonardson taken by a group of Indians which included two warriors, their wives, seven children, and an elderly woman. On 30 March, as they camped on an island at the confluence of the Contoocook and Merrimack Rivers (in present-day Boscawen, New Hampshire), Hannah Duston, Mary Neff, and the Leonardson boy killed most of their captors with hatchets as they slept. The elderly woman escaped with a head wound, and the youngest Indian, a six-year-old boy they spared in order to bring back, also escaped into the woods. Hannah then proceeded to scalp the dead and the party returned to Massachusetts.

Hannah was hailed as a heroine. Thomas Duston petitioned for a special scalp bounty for his wife and the others, and the General Court obliged, awarding £25 to Hannah, and £12/10 each to Neff and Leonardson. Hannah and Thomas had one more child in 1698, and lived out their lives in relative obscurity.

Steven C. Eames

References

Cotton Mather, *Decennium Luctuosum* (1699), rpt. in Charles H. Lincoln, ed., *Narratives of the Indian Wars, 1675–1699* (1913); Laurel Thatcher Ulrich, *Good Wives: Image and Reality in the Lives of Women in Northern New England, 1650–1750* (1982).

See also CAPTIVITY NARRATIVES; HAVERHILL (MASSACHUSETTS); INDIAN WARFARE, CAPTIVITY

Dutch-Mohawk Treaty (1643)

This was the first alliance of the Mohawk (*Kaniengehaga*) with all the Dutch of New Netherland. Several formal treaties of friendship had earlier been made with the traders at Fort Orange (later Albany), but this agreement ensured that the special relationship with the Mohawk was official policy. The text of the treaty has not been found. However, later references are sufficient to identify its existence and to establish it as something more than a nonaggression treaty: it was a mutual assistance pact.

By 1643, the Mohawk were about 1,500 warriors, responsible for the relations of the Five Nations with their neighbors to the east, that is, Algonquin tribes and European colonies. In New Netherland this meant acting as intermediaries for the Dutch in the fur traffic with more distant tribes. By 1643, the Mohawk needed increased quantities of arms. The French were building Fort Richelieu and had formed a settlement on Montreal Island in order to protect their own native allies against Mohawk depredations. This threatened Mohawk subsistence.

A mutual assistance pact also served Dutch purposes. The role of the Mohawk in the so-called Esopus Wars of the 1650s and 1660s shows them willing to pressure a subservient tribe (the Esopus) into agreeing to peaceful negotiations with Petrus Stuyvesant. Earlier they had acted as negotiators between the Esopus and Director-General Willem Kieft. There is a remarkable parallel in these events: just as the Dutch authorities at New Amsterdam looked upon the settlers at Wiltwijck (later Kingston) as insubordinate for not living peacefully with the Esopus natives, so the Mohawk chiefs were angry with the Esopus for following violent policies, independent of their wishes.

The treaty of 1643 endured without violation until the seizure of New Netherland by the English in 1664. Then it became a relationship on which the English immediately built a powerful political alliance. Francis Jennings has argued in *The Ambiguous Iroquois Empire* (1984) that in Mohawk tradition the pact of 1643 was an "iron chain," meaning an alliance of far greater significance than a nonaggression pact. However, it was only under the English that the term "a covenant chain" came into use.

Donna Merwick

References

Francis Jennings, *The Ambiguous Iroquois Empire: The Covenant Chain Confederation of Indian Tribes with English Colonies from its beginnings to the Lancaster Treaty of 1744* (1984); Edmund B. O'Callaghan and Berthold Fernow, eds., *Documents Relative to the Colonial History of the State of New York,* 15 vols. (1856–1887):1–2; Daniel K. Richter, "Rediscovering Links in the Covenant Chain: Previously Unpublished Transcripts of New York Treaty Minutes, 1677–1691," *Proceedings of the American Antiquarian Society,* 92 (Pt. 1, 1982):45–85; Allen W. Trelease, *Indian Affairs in Colonial New York: The Seventeenth Century* (1960).

See also COVENANT CHAIN; ESOPUS WARS; KIEFT, WILLEM; MOHAWK; STUYVESANT, PETRUS

D

E

East Fort (New York)
See FORT ONTARIO (NEW YORK)

Easton Conference (1758)
The conference held at Easton, Pennsylvania, from 7 to 26 October 1758, was the fourth negotiating session between the province and Indian groups at that location. These were called treaties under an obsolete definition: treaty meaning a negotiation for the purpose of reaching an agreement. The Treaty of 1758 was provoked by the Delawares' war on the English colonies and the belligerence of the usurper leader of the Susquehanna Delawares, Teedyuscung. Although supported by the Quakers' powerful Friendly Association for the Gaining and Preserving Peace with the Indians by Pacific Measures, Teedyuscung was maneuvered into yielding on almost all points because of his drunken behavior and poor judgment. Also represented at the conference were the Six Nations, the Ohio Delawares, and several smaller eastern Pennsylvania and New Jersey Indian nations, as well as the governors of Pennsylvania and New Jersey, and Sir William Johnson's deputy, George Croghan. Teedyuscung made peace with Pennsylvania, accepted Iroquois control over Delaware affairs (symbolically expressed as woman's status), and withdrew his claim that the Walking Purchase of 1737 was a fraud. His plea for a deed to protect Delaware occupation of the Wyoming Valley was rebuffed, and the Six Nations denied that the Delawares owned any land anywhere. Also, Teedyuscung received no significant assistance in imposing European culture on the Native Americans, a principle for which he stood. However, the Delawares and Six Nations both benefited from Pennsylvania's repudiation of part of the Albany Purchase of 1754. By the terms of this arrangement, Pennsylvania and the English government guaranteed the Six Nations that land west of the Allegheny Mountains would not be occupied by white transients or settlers. When news of the treaty reached Indians in the upper Ohio Valley they began to abandon their alliance with the French, clearing the way for the success of General John Forbes's expedition in late 1758.

Louis M. Waddell

References

Minutes of Conferences Held at Easton in October, 1758, with the Chief Sachems and Warriors . . . (1759); Anthony F.C. Wallace, *King of the Delawares: Teedyuscung, 1700–1763* (1949).

See also CROGHAN, GEORGE; DELAWARE; FORBES, JOHN; IROQUOIS; TEEDYUSCUNG; WALKING PURCHASE

Fort Ebenezer (Georgia)
Ebenezer was the main settlement for the several hundred German-speaking Lutheran families who came to Georgia during the colonial period. Known as "Salzburgers," their town was located about 30 miles upstream from Savannah on an elevation known as Red Bluff. Ebenezer was first fortified against Indian attack by William Gerard De Brahm in 1761. Far more substantial were the fortifications constructed by British officer Lieutenant Colonel Archibald Campbell in 1779, when he made Ebenezer the main logistical base for his march up the Savannah River to Augusta. In a private

letter to Lord Germaine dated 20 January 1779, Campbell mentioned that he was "constructing some Redoubts to shut up the Gorge between the two Swamps" that flanked Ebenezer to the east and west. Some of these earthworks are still visible in the pine woods now covering the site of historic Ebenezer.

Louis DeVorsey, Jr.

Ecuyer, Simeon (?–?)

A Swiss professional soldier in the Royal Americans, Captain Ecuyer commanded Fort Pitt (Pittsburgh) from 1761 to 1763. It was from Ecuyer's reports that General Jeffery Amherst, in New York, first learned of the assaults that began what is now known as "Pontiac's War."

Ecuyer's most noted act was to present two Delaware Indians with blankets and handkerchiefs from Fort Pitt's smallpox hospital in a deliberate effort to destroy them with disease. Historians long knew that both Amherst and Colonel Henry Bouquet, then in eastern Pennsylvania, had considered such action, but some, including Francis Parkman, expressed doubts that any officer had actually carried out what Parkman called the "detestable suggestion." Such doubts lingered among some scholars even after the publication of the trader William Trent's Fort Pitt journal, which established that someone at Fort Pitt had given the blankets to Turtle Heart and another Delaware chief. Ecuyer and the soldiers were not yet directly implicated. Other scholars, notably Howard H. Peckham, saw Ecuyer behind the act. Historian Donald H. Kent ended the controversy in 1955, pointing to a banal smoking gun: a bill, acknowledged by both Ecuyer and, later, General Thomas Gage, corroborating Trent's journal. The account, to be paid to Levy, Trent and Company, was for two blankets and two handkerchiefs "taken from people in the Hospital to Convey the Small-pox to the Indians." Evidence from released captives and the disappearance from the record of well-known Delaware individuals indicate that smallpox indeed decimated the Delawares during the war. It is unknown whether or not the disease broke out as a result of Ecuyer's "detestable" deed.

In July, Delawares and Shawnees attacked Fort Pitt. Ecuyer sustained an arrow wound in his leg, but successfully defended his post until Bouquet arrived with some 400 troops to assume command on 10 August 1763.

Gregory E. Dowd

References

Francis Jennings, *Empire of Fortune: Crowns, Colonies, and Tribes in the Seven Years War in America* (1988); Donald H. Kent and Bernard Knollenberg, "Communications," and Bernard Knollenberg, "General Amherst and Germ Warfare," *Mississippi Valley Historical Review* 41 (1954–1955):454–489, 762–763; Albert T. Volwiler, "William Trent's Journal at Fort Pitt, 1763," ibid. 11 (1924):400; Francis Parkman, *The Conspiracy of Pontiac* (1850); Howard H. Peckham, *Pontiac and the Indian Uprising* (1947).

See also BOUQUET, HENRY; FORT PITT (PENNSYLVANIA); PONTIAC'S WAR

Fort Edisto (South Carolina)

During the Yamasee War, this fort was built at the plantation of James Rawlings on the east bank of the Edisto River near present-day Givhan's Ferry State Park in Dorchester County. The fort protected Savannah Path, the strategic western passage into South Carolina's settlements. Between May 1715 and December 1716, an army unit, supplemented by river boats, manned the fort.

Gregory D. Massey

References

Larry E. Ivers, *Colonial Forts of South Carolina 1670–1775* (1970).

Fort Edward (New York; also known as Fort Nicholson, Fort Lyman, "The Great Carrying Place," Fort Lydius)

The structure on this site was known variously as the "First," "Long," and "Great Carrying Place" fort. Located on the upper Hudson River, it was the first post along the water route leading to the southern end of Lake Champlain.

The first fortifications were constructed in 1709 when British General Francis Nicholson built a stockade during his attempt to invade Canada. It was rebuilt in 1731 to protect John Henry Lydius's trading post located on the site. This rebuild was known as Fort Lydius until it was destroyed in 1745 by the French and their Indian allies. Later, General Phineas Lyman began construction of another fort on the site. The structure was completed by British engineer Captain William Eyre. After the Battle of Lake

George, Major General William Johnson renamed the fort "Edward" in honor of Prince Edward, duke of York.

In 1755, Johnson, his provincial army, and his loyal Indians used the site as a base of operations for assaults on the French. During this time, Johnson oversaw the construction of a 14-mile road leading from the fort northwest to the near end of Lake George, where he began construction of another fortification.

The fortifications at Fort Edward were downgraded, and in 1756, the barracks caught fire. They were destroyed, but the powder magazine was saved. After the fire, Governor William Shirley enlisted engineer Harry Gordon to inspect and report on the state of the fort. His report in 1756 described the fort as consisting of four bastions, with one side facing the Hudson River, one side containing a gate which faced a rivulet, and a main gate standing nearest the great plain. The fort had a palisaded ditch running along the northern and eastern sides, an eight- to ten-foot parapet of sand (which was also palisaded but not faced), and a magazine covered by logs located on the eastern side. Gordon announced the fort as underfortified and in disrepair; he suggested strengthening the fort with a 14- to 16-foot facing, raising the eastern and southern ramparts, building casements under them, and adding two more covered magazines. By 1760, evidence indicates the fort had been refurbished and could house 600 men.

In 1766, the site was abandoned and dismantled by settlers who used the fort's material for their new homes. The Americans destroyed the fort's ruins in 1775 to prevent British occupation of the site. Between 1775 and 1777, the Americans used the site as a supply depot and as General Philip Schuyler's headquarters until it was surrendered to General John Burgoyne's army. In 1777, Fort Edward was the site of the "Jane McCrea Atrocity," later used in patriot propaganda. After the victory at Saratoga, Fort Edward was used as a way station along the Hudson-Champlain route until the end of the Revolution.

Elizabeth Gossman

References

Mark Boatner, *Landmarks of the American Revolution* (1973); T. Wood Clarke, *The Bloody Mohawk* (1968); James Thomas Flexner, *Mohawk Baronet: Sir William Johnson of New York* (1957); Michael Kammen, *Colonial New York: A History* (1975).

See also LAKE CHAMPLAIN

Fort Elfsborg (New Jersey; also known as Fort Elsinburg, Fort Myggenborgh, Mosquito Fort)

Constructed by Governor Johan Printz of New Sweden during the summer of 1643, the fort was named after Fort Elfsborg near Gothenburg, Sweden. It was the first Swedish fort built on the east shore of the Delaware River, on land purchased from the Delaware Indians in 1641. Its location was south of Mill Creek on an island of upland near the present-day town of Salem, New Jersey. The fort was designed as an earthwork redoubt with three angles facing the river. Garrisoned with 12–14 soldiers and officers, it was amply fortified with four brass and four iron 12-pound guns, and one mortar.

Fort Elfsborg was built with two purposes in mind, one of which was to watch the activities of an English settlement which had been established in 1641 on Varken's Kill, a few miles north of the fort. The second purpose was to control trade and traffic on the Delaware River north of Delaware Bay; particularly to neutralize the Dutch trading post, Fort Nassau, located on Big Timber Creek (near present-day Gloucester City, New Jersey). Accordingly, all ships were required by Governor Printz's command to lower their flags on approaching Fort Elfsborg, to weigh anchor, and to be boarded by soldiers before proceeding upriver. The New Sweden Company claimed it was the only rightful owner of the land along both sides of the Delaware, a claim disputed by both the Dutch and English.

To its detriment, the marshes surrounding Fort Elfsborg bred vast swarms of gnats and mosquitoes. The insect stings and bites caused the soldiers and nearby colonists to be "so swollen, that they appeared as if they had been affected with some horrible disease. Therefore they called this Fort Myggenborgh (Mosquito Fort)."

Factors leading to the abandonment of Fort Elfsborg in 1651 were: (1) the hostile environment plagued with insects, and (2) the movement of the Dutch Fort Nassau's garrison, guns, and stores downriver to a new stronghold named Fort Casimir (New Castle, Delaware), across the Delaware River. By 1655, when the

E

Dutch under Petrus (Peter) Stuyvesant gained control of the Delaware River, the fort lay in ruins. Its remains now lie beneath the river.

Linda M. Thorstad

References
Amandus Johnson, *Swedish Settlements on the Delaware, 1638–1664* (1911).

See also FORT CASIMIR (DELAWARE); FORT NASSAU (NEW JERSEY); NEW SWEDEN

Emistisiguo (c. 1718–1782)

Emistisiguo became the principal leader of the Upper Creek towns between 1763 and the Revolutionary War. Although he gained some prestige through family connections, he owed his rise to power chiefly to his firm alliance with the British. Creeks had long maintained relative independence by playing the British off against the French. With the departure of the French, the deterioration of the Indian trade, and the Choctaw War in the 1760s, however, the Creeks had to depend on British connections more than ever before. Nevertheless, Emistisiguo also gained prominence among his own people because he opposed colonial and British actions that he deemed contrary to his people's interests.

The Creek leader's first major diplomatic effort occurred in the aftermath of the 1763 Augusta Congress. Lower Creek townsmen at the congress had approved a major land cession to Georgia. Since the Upper Creek had kept a low profile at the congress, however, the British Indian superintendent, John Stuart, urged Emistisiguo to gain Upper Creek ratification of the cession. As usual, Emistisiguo both complied with this request and used it as an opportunity to bargain with the British. In 1764, at his hometown of Little Tallassee, Emistisiguo and other Upper Creek leaders confirmed the Treaty of Augusta. At the same time, however, Emistisiguo emphasized that, in return, British authorities should prevent white settlers, with their cattle and slaves, from crossing the new boundary line. Furthermore, Emistisiguo and other Creeks at Little Tallassee insisted that the British prohibit a West Florida-based Indian trade. Clearly, Emistisiguo realized that the Creeks could maintain their independence only if their contacts with whites were limited and controlled.

In the years after Stuart made Emistisiguo and four other Upper Creeks great medal chiefs at the Pensacola Congress of 1765, this "staunchest ally" of the British continued to complain to British officials about white demands for Indian land and about traders' flagrant violations of British trade regulations. In 1768, Emistisiguo even organized an attack on illicit traders and their goods. In the early 1770s, furthermore, he scorned merchants' offers of lower trade prices in exchange for a major land cession. On the other hand, when he believed that his people might make war needlessly on the colonists in 1767 and again in 1774, he supported the decision of British officials to cut off the Creeks' trade lifeline temporarily.

With the coming of the Revolutionary War, Emistisiguo continued to follow his policy of realpolitik, believing that a cautious British alliance best served his people's interests. Certainly, Stuart and his administration seemed better than colonists, who could offer the Creeks neither goods nor protection against boundary violations and trade abuses. True to his conviction, Emistisiguo led his fellow Creeks on military expeditions against the revolutionaries as far away as Kentucky and South Carolina. "The brave, gallant Emistisiguo," as Stuart's successor called him, died attempting to defend Savannah against General Anthony Wayne's attack in 1782. By acting according to British assumptions about Creek tribal unity, Emistisiguo helped unify a loose confederation of towns and paved the way for his successor, Alexander McGillivray.

J. Russell Snapp

References
Edward J. Cashin, *The King's Ranger: Thomas Brown and the American Revolution on the Southern Frontier* (1989); ———, *Lachlan McGillivray, Indian Trader: The Shaping of the Southern Colonial Frontier* (1992); David H. Corkran, *The Creek Frontier, 1540–1783* (1967); J. Leitch Wright, Jr., *Creeks and Seminoles: The Destruction and Regeneration of the Muscogulge People* (1986).

See also AUGUSTA, CONGRESS OF; CREEK

Endicott Expedition (1636)

In July 1636, John Gallop found John Oldham's pinnace under the control of a handful of Block Island Indians. After a short fight, in which 10–

11 Indians drowned, Gallop found Oldham's corpse below deck. This incident seriously strained relations between the English, Narragansett, and Pequot Indians. Block Island was an extension of Narragansett territory, and the ensuing Massachusetts investigation concluded that several Narragansett sachems planned the attack on Oldham because he traded with the Pequot. In August 1636, the Massachusetts government sent a team to investigate the Narragansett's fidelity toward the English. The investigators returned, reassuring Massachusetts officials that the two major Narragansett sachems—Canonicus and Miantonomo—were loyal and willing to punish those behind Oldham's death. Massachusetts Governor Henry Vane then selected John Endicott to lead some 90–120 Massachusetts volunteers to "do justice upon the Indians for the death of Mr. Oldham." Assisted by Captain John Underhill, Captain Nathan Turner, Captain William Jenningson, and an Ensign Davenport, the Endicott expedition set sail for Block Island on 24 August 1636.

Governor Vane provided Endicott with a set of clear-cut objectives. On landing, Endicott's force was to put all the men of Block Island to death. They should spare the women and children, but only to bring them back as slaves. In the process, Endicott would take possession of the island. Surprisingly, Vane then ordered Endicott's force to sail to Pequot territory and demand the murderers of John Stone (d. 1633), and 1,000 fathoms of wampum. In addition, to make sure that the Pequot remained peaceful, Endicott was to demand a number of Pequot children as hostages. If the Pequot refused any of these demands, Endicott was to obtain the objectives by force.

Endicott, however, found the ends of the mission difficult to achieve. A small force of Block Islanders contested Endicott's landing as his men struggled to make shore against a difficult surf, though none of Endicott's men were disabled. Once the landing force made the beach, the Block Islanders fled. Scouring the island, Endicott found two Indian villages, but the inhabitants had already fled to the swamps for protection. Unable to inflict physical revenge on the Indians, Endicott decided to burn and pillage what he could find. After raiding the island for two days and inflicting 1–14 Indian deaths, the expeditionary force returned to the ships to implement the next phase of its mission.

Before engaging the Pequot, Endicott sailed to Fort Saybrook where he met a staunch critic of the expedition in Lieutenant Lion Gardener. Trained in the military arts in the Netherlands, Gardener moved to New England in 1633–1634. Having built Fort Saybrook from the ground up, he realized the desperate condition of the English in the region. Gardener warned Endicott that war was like a three-footed stool. Success depended on men, food, and munitions. Lacking any one of these three, the whole matter falls. Therefore, Gardener asked Endicott to wage a war against "Capt. Hunger" before stirring the Pequot "wasp's nest." Gardener also wondered aloud why the Massachusetts leaders were more concerned about the death of a Virginian (John Stone), three years past, than the safety and well-being of their own subjects at Saybrook. Gardener resigned in the end "as they came without acquainting any of us in the River with it (Endicott's strategy), so they went against our will."

As Endicott's fleet of five ships arrived at the intended location, the Pequot came to the shore inquiring of the force's intentions. On the first day Endicott remained on board and refused to answer. The next morning the Pequot sent an elderly ambassador on board to get some answers. It was then that Endicott informed the ambassador that he came to "demand the heads of those persons" who had killed Stone. The ambassador then reminded Endicott of the Dutch's execution of Wopigwooit, noting that the Pequot did not differentiate between Europeans when seeking revenge. Unsatisfied with the Pequot answer, Endicott reasserted his demands. As the ambassador took his leave to get further instructions, Endicott ordered his force to assume battle positions on shore. The Pequot asked for patience, since the major sachems were on Long Island, but Endicott dismissed the request as a ruse to buy time for preparations. After several hours of delay, the Pequot finally asked the English to meet with their sachems unarmed. Perceiving this latest request as an attempt to gain English firearms, Endicott decided to "beat up the drum and bid them battle." As on Block Island, Endicott's force could not find a Pequot army to engage so they fell back on burning and plundering the villages. After two days of destroying Pequot villages, Endicott set sail for Massachusetts Bay having achieved none of his objectives.

In the end Lieutenant Gardener was correct. Describing Endicott's action among the Pequot, Gardener wrote, "and thus began the

E

war between the Indians and us in these parts." After Endicott returned to the bay colony, the Pequot began a guerrilla campaign against the English settlers in Connecticut that shortly erupted into the Pequot War.

Richard C. Goode

References

Lion Gardener, *Lieft Lion Gardener his relation of the Pequot Warres,* in *Collections of the Massachusetts Historical Society,* 3rd Ser., 3 (1833):131–160; John Underhill, *News from America,* in *Massachusetts Historical Society,* 3rd ser., 6 (1837): 1–18; John Winthrop, *Winthrop's Journal: "History of New England," 1630–1649,* James Kendall Hosmer, ed., 2 vols. (1908).

See also MIANTONOMO; NARRAGANSETT; PEQUOT WAR

English Bend (Louisiana)

At the time of the French and Indian War, the most heavily fortified place in French Louisiana was the English Bend (Detour de l'Anglois), located on the Mississippi River about fifteen miles below New Orleans. This curious name for a fortified location in a French colony derived from an encounter on the lower Mississippi between the French and the English in 1699. Jean-Baptiste Le Moyne de Bienville, who later became the first governor of Louisiana, encountered an English war vessel commanded by Captain William Lewis Bond and apparently persuaded the Englishman to leave the area in the face of a superior French presence. In any case, despite the name, Great Britain never occupied or fortified the English Bend.

The strategic importance of the English Bend, where sailing ships had difficulty ascending the Mississippi, was obvious, and French authorities in Louisiana considered fortifying the area almost as soon as New Orleans was founded in 1718. It was the chronic warfare of the 1740s, however, that finally prompted action. In 1746, the governor of Louisiana, Pierre de Rigaud de Vaudreuil, developed a plan for placing batteries of heavy guns on both banks of the Mississippi at the English Bend. A few years later, batteries of 18-pound guns were placed behind earthworks contained by revetments of wattle and fascines. Vaudreuil advocated masonry facings for the earthworks, but the French royal gov-

ernment never allocated the necessary funds. The fort on the right bank of the river became known as Fort St. Leon, and the one on the left bank as Fort Ste. Marie.

With the Peace of Aix-la-Chapelle in 1748, the forts at the English Bend had their garrisons withdrawn and their cannons placed in storage. It soon became apparent, however, that peace between Great Britain and France was merely temporary, and by 1751, Governor Vaudreuil regarrisoned the forts at the bend and built new quarters for the officers. By 1753 the fortifications contained 30 18-pound guns, and four each of eights, sixes, and fours. The heavier pieces were intended to sweep the river and the lighter ones to defend the landward perimeters of the forts. Muster rolls from 1759 show the forts at the bend each to have had garrisons consisting of three officers, two noncoms, and 20 to 25 enlisted men.

Although the British never attempted to invade French Louisiana during the Seven Years' War, it was at that time that the forts at the English Bend reached their highest stage of development and strategic importance. After France ceded Louisiana to Spain (1762), the artillery from the forts was shipped back to France and the forts fell into desuetude. Between 1807 and 1813, the American government built the first masonry fortifications at the English Bend and, although these fortifications never saw action, their garrisons participated in Andrew Jackson's defense of New Orleans in 1815.

Carl J. Ekberg

References

Henry P. Dart and Edith Dart Price, eds. and trans., "Inventaire of the Estate of Sieur Jean Baptiste Prevost, Deceased Agent of the Company of the Indies, July 13, 1769," *Louisiana Historical Quarterly* 9 (1926):411–498; Carl J. Ekberg, "The English Bend: Forgotten Gateway to New Orleans," in Patricia K. Galloway, ed., *La Salle and His Legacy: Frenchmen and Indians in the Lower Mississippi Valley,* (1982):211–230; Samuel Wilson, Jr., "Colonial Fortifications and Military Architecture in the Mississippi Valley," in John F. McDermott, ed., *The French in the Mississippi Valley* (1965):103–122.

See also LE MOYNE DE BIENVILLE, JEAN-BAPTISTE ; RIGAUD DE VAUDREUIL DE CAVAGNAIL, PIERRE DE

English Revolution of 1688–1689

The revolution of 1688–1689 has had a checkered historiographical career. Praised at one time by whiggishly-inclined historians as the "Glorious Revolution" that safeguarded the rights of freeborn Englishmen, it has been analyzed more critically by recent scholars who have identified its role in promoting bloody religious conflicts. In the English colonies in North America, the revolution was welcomed by those who opposed existing colonial regimes and those who wished greater freedom in waging war on native and French rivals. However the revolution's pretensions may be appraised, there is no doubt that it represented a crucial turning point in the military affairs of both Europe and North America.

The revolution's origins lay in the accession to the throne of England in 1685 of James, duke of York, as James II. The former king, Charles II, had shifted English foreign policy away from its traditional hostility toward France. In the secret clauses of the Treaty of Dover, signed with France in 1670, he had committed England to join with France in a war on their common commercial foe, the Netherlands. He had also promised that he would convert to Catholicism, although speculation that he did so on his deathbed is inconclusive. Charles II's brother, the duke of York, was openly Catholic and pro-French. His accession, in the same year as the expulsion of the French Huguenots, implied that England would now become even more closely identified with an aggressively Catholic France. Among the first fruits of the new regime was the Treaty of Whitehall (1686) in which England and France entered into a series of agreements regarding their mutual security in the Americas. Its clauses included renunciation of illegal trade or fishing within the bounds of one another's colonies, and an agreement that even in the event of a European war the colonies would remain neutral. The Treaty of Neutrality, as it was also known, was a statement of intent that provided no instant solution for the many frictions between the French and English in North America. Nevertheless, it did provide a framework within which the colonial administrators of both powers could work to minimize outright conflict.

Events in England would soon sweep away even the Treaty of Whitehall's fragile restraints. By the early summer of 1688, James II had succeeded in eroding the crucial supports of the Stuart monarchy: the Church of England, and the Tory majority in the House of Commons. By moving toward the establishment of civil rights for all dissenters from the established church, including Catholics, and by using his personal authority to appoint Catholic officers to the army and navy, the king aroused vehement opposition. It ranged from seven Church of England bishops charged for seditious libel for resisting the royal policy of ending religious discrimination, to the popular anti-Catholic demonstrations in London that greeted the bishops' acquittal. These events coincided within three weeks with the birth of the king's son, which implied that there would now be a Catholic successor. Up to that time, the heir to the throne had been James's Protestant daughter, Mary, the wife of Prince William of Orange. William, captain general of the Dutch Republic, had good reason for concern over the growing English affinity with France. When disaffected English political leaders now invited him to intervene, he did so without delay. The invasion force that reached England in early November met no significant resistance. By year's end, James II had fled to France, and on 13 February 1689 (Old Style) William and Mary were offered the crown as joint monarchs. In Europe, the English revolution significantly affected the military balance of power. Already, in 1686, William of Orange had taken a leading role in the formation of the League of Augsburg, a combination of states formed to resist the encroachments of France. The revolution meant that England would become an adherent of the league, and that France was opposed by every other significant European power. The Dutch declaration of war on France came in February 1689, and was followed by that of England in May.

The revolution had already begun to affect North America. The governor of the Dominion of New England, Sir Edmund Andros, heard of James II's flight in March 1689 while at the northeastern outpost of Pemaquid seeking a negotiated end to the English-Abenaki hostilities that had persisted since the preceding fall. The Dominion of New England had arisen from a lengthy constitutional struggle between the colony of Massachusetts and the English government, culminating in 1684 with the destruction of the Massachusetts charter. The dominion, instituted in 1685, had originally included Massachusetts, Maine, New Hampshire, and the Narragansett country. Subsequent additions by 1688 had extended it to cover all of New

England, New York, and East and West Jersey. The establishment of the dominion had brought fundamental changes to government structures in these areas, including the abolition of representative assemblies. It had also aroused opposition from those who had been displaced and who now had a strong vested interest in using the English revolution as an instrument of reaction.

The dominion quickly disintegrated in the spring of 1689. The return of Andros to Boston was followed in mid-April by a number of his troops from Pemaquid, who had mutinied and left their post. On 18 April, Andros was besieged by a hostile crowd, and agreed the following day to surrender power to a council of safety headed by the last governor of the colony under the old charter, Simon Bradstreet. Pending a permanent settlement by William and Mary, government reverted to its pre-dominion form. Other New England colonies that had lost their charters followed a similar course. In New York, officials of the dominion managed to cling to their authority for a few more weeks before a provisional government took control, headed by a merchant and militia captain, Jacob Leisler. Here there was a significant difference, in that the establishment of the dominion in New York had proceeded with the cooperation of the province's established mercantile elite. Leisler's seizure of power thus had a narrower power base than was true in the New England colonies. The contrast was dramatically illustrated in the settlements that finally proceeded from England. Generally favorable treatment of the demands of the New England colonies was symbolized by the Massachusetts charter of October 1691, which established a system of royal government and also a representative assembly. Leisler's fate was public execution in May of the same year. The revolution also had implications elsewhere in the English colonies. In Maryland, the successful rebellion of a "Protestant Association" headed by John Coode paved the way for the replacement of the existing proprietary government by a new royal structure. The neighboring proprietary colony of Pennsylvania retained its existing form of government, as did the royal colony of Virginia, although the rhetoric of the English revolution was not absent from either. Social unrest in the colonies, while contemporaneous with the revolution and its aftermath, drew more on internal tensions than on external influences from England or elsewhere.

Militarily, the effects of the English revolution in North America were twofold. First, the resulting political upheavals rendered the English colonies less able to manage existing tensions and hostilities. This was especially true on the northern frontiers where English claims were resisted by native forces or contested by France. The Dominion of New England, whatever its political faults, could fairly lay claim to a degree of military professionalism. The same was not necessarily true of the governments that overthrew it, and the results were quickly seen in the disputed territory known to the English as northern New England. Andros, while committed to preserving the English claim to rule as far northeast as the St. Croix River, was flexible enough to combine armed force against any French encroachment in this area with a more conciliatory approach to the Abenaki. Though fundamentally no more sympathetic to native interests than any other English colonial administrator, he had learned from experience to respect the Abenaki's military skill. In late 1688, Andros had not hesitated to denounce the seizure of 20 Saco Abenaki captives that had prompted the outbreak of hostilities. His sojourn in the Northeast in early 1689 even prompted rumors among New Englanders that the governor was planning a pro-Catholic conspiracy in conjunction with the Abenaki and the French. The overthrow of the Dominion brought to power in Boston a group incapable of sustaining negotiations with the Abenaki, or indeed of understanding the persistent native desire for accommodation if it could be reached on acceptable terms. At the same time, the depletion of English forces in the Northeast through desertion, and the general confusion of military command engendered by the change of government, led to reverses that included the fall of Pemaquid to Abenaki forces in August 1689. In the same month, a group of prominent citizens of Albany, New York, proclaimed an organization to be known as a "convention." In opposition to Leisler's rule, though recognizing William and Mary, the convention aimed to organize a firm defense against possible French attack. The ensuing quarrel had just the opposite effect, as the destruction of Schenectady by *Canadien* and Iroquois forces showed in February 1690.

The Schenectady raid, quickly followed by others at Salmon Falls, New Hampshire, and Casco, Maine, was also symptomatic of the second and more general military consequence of the English revolution. With the upsetting of the fragile balance that had previously kept the peace between English and French, both native and non-native populations in northeastern North America were embroiled in what would prove to be an extended period of destructive warfare. Native peoples who had hitherto pursued their resistance to either the English or the French without formal European assistance could now intensify their efforts. The Iroquois raid on the Canadian settlement of Lachine in August 1689 was undertaken in the knowledge that English support could now be expected. A military alliance between French and Abenaki quickly followed the fall of Pemaquid to the Abenaki in the same month. Not that either native people was gratuitously aggressive, as was shown by Abenaki efforts to secure peace at various points in the 1690s, and by the French-Iroquois agreement of 1701. But the availability of European alliances had created new military opportunities. The breach between France and England also brought about a harsh new climate for relationships between the North American colonists of the two powers. The bitterness created by the land raids launched on New England from Canada was reflected in language used in the commission issued to the commander of the 1690 expedition against French Acadia: Sir William Phips was to "attack take pursue spoyle kill and destroy the . . . Common Enemy ffrench and Indians both by Sea and Land." This was also the era of strategic plans evolved by both French and English to conquer the other's colonies. French schemes to attack New York from the Hudson Valley and Boston by sea corresponded to English notions of thrusting at Montreal from Lake Champlain and taking Quebec by naval assault. Whether either of these plans would come even partly to fruition remained to be seen in 1690. Already, by the early months of that year, however, it was clear that the English revolution had unleashed strong conflicting forces. Whether "Glorious" or not in its political implications, the revolution would leave to North America a bloody legacy.

John G. Reid

References

Viola Florence Barnes, *The Dominion of New England: A Study in British Colonial Policy* (1923); W.J. Eccles, *Canada Under Louis XIV, 1663–1701* (1964); David S. Lovejoy, *The Glorious Revolution in America* (1972); Kenneth M. Morrison, *The Embattled Northeast: The Elusive Ideal of Alliance in Abenaki-Euramercian Relations* (1984); John G. Reid, *Acadia, Maine, and New Scotland: Marginal Colonies in the Seventeenth Century* (1981).

See also ANDROS, EDMUND; DOMINION OF NEW ENGLAND; KING WILLIAM'S WAR; LEISLER, JACOB; LEISLER'S REBELLION

English Turn (Mississippi)

See ENGLISH BEND (MISSISSIPPI)

Esopus

The Esopus Indians comprised at least two bands of Munsee-speaking Lenni Lenape called the Waoranecks and Warranawankongs. They held farming and settlement lands on the west side of the Hudson River, midway between New Amsterdam and Fort Orange, just south of the Catskill Mountains, and hunted in the hinterland to the west of their settlements. They acted in military and diplomatic conjunction with the other Munsee speakers to the south and west of them, and were involved in three hostilities with the Dutch, most notably the Esopus Wars (1659–1660, 1663–1664), in which they came into conflict with Dutch farmers who settled on their land.

The diplomatic relations of the Esopus also extended beyond their fellow Munsee speakers. Records left by the Dutch show the involvement of both Mohawks and Mahicans in the affairs between the Dutch and Esopus Indians, especially during the Esopus Wars. While the nature of these diplomatic connections and the reasons for them remain vague, it is likely that the Esopus, like many of the tribes of the Northeast, formed a buffer zone that protected the Mohawk and other Iroquois nations from outside forces and also provided a trading link to those outside peoples. This had gone on among Native Americans for some time, but after 1480, the trade included Europeans as well. The Esopus and Iroquois remained relatively at peace with one another, due most likely to the trade connection the Esopus made between the Iroquois and the Indians further downstream who manufactured wampum, a commodity valued by the Iroquois for its powerful religious and ceremonial significance.

After the Esopus Wars with the Dutch, the Esopus Indians gave up their land to the Europeans and moved west, settling with the linguistically related Minisinks. With them, the Esopus moved across Pennsylvania in the eighteenth century to join the other Lenni Lenape, who were then known as Delawares.

Paul Otto

References

Ives Goddard, "Delaware," in *Handbook of North American Indians,* Vol. 15, *Northeast,* ed. by Bruce G. Trigger (1978):213–239; ———, "The Ethnohistorical Implications of Early Delaware Linguistic Materials," in *Neighbors and Intruders: An Ethnohistorical Exploration of the Indians of Hudson's River,* ed. by Laurence M. Hauptman and Jack Campisi (1978): 88–102; Daniel K. Richter, *The Ordeal of the Longhouse: The Peoples of the Iroquois League in the Era of European Colonization* (1992); Allen Trelease, *Indian Affairs in Colonial New York: The Seventeenth Century* (1960).

See also ESOPUS WARS

Esopus Wars (1659–1660, 1663–1664)

The third Dutch-Indian war took place around the Dutch settlement of Wiltwyck (Kingston, New York), located halfway between New York and Albany. As early as 1652, many Dutch families came to settle and farm in the fertile lands along the Rondout and Esopus Creeks which empty into the Hudson River. They purchased land from a group of Esopus Indians who had long ago discovered the rich agricultural potential of the land and still lived in the region. While relations began peacefully enough, they soon deteriorated, leading to two major outbreaks of hostility between the years 1659 and 1664.

Friction first developed between the Dutch settlers and the young tribesmen, who were becoming increasingly dependent on alcohol, which they purchased from traders operating illegally near Fort Orange. The tribal leaders, who desired to keep peace between the two peoples, did what they could to maintain normal relations with the Dutch, but they could not prevent the occasional flare-ups which occurred. In spring 1658, after one particularly grievous attack in which a young Esopus warrior killed a Dutch settler and burned a farm, Director General Petrus (Peter) Stuyvesant trav-

eled to the Esopus region to secure peace and arrange for the protection of the settlers. He met with the Indians and demanded that they make reparations for attacks on the settlers. Furthermore, he extracted a promise from the Indians to sell more of their land to the colonists. Stuyvesant then made it clear to the settlers that they could not properly defend themselves if they continued to live far apart from one another. They agreed to concentrate their settlement and he and his soldiers helped them build a small fort. After garrisoning the new defensive structure with a squad of soldiers, Stuyvesant returned to New Amsterdam.

Over the next year, relations between the Dutch and the Esopus Indians remained relatively quiet. Once, when the threat of Indian violence appeared imminent, Stuyvesant returned and reinforced the garrison. Nevertheless, the Indians remained restless and some complained that the Dutch had not paid them for the land they had ceded. Frustrated with the continued threat of Indian attack, the agitated settlers finally took matters into their own hands. On September 21, 1659 they ambushed a group of young Indian men who had been drinking brandy in the woods near the Dutch settlement. One Esopus tribesman was killed, and on the following day, several Indians attacked a group of settlers in retaliation. All the Dutch were either killed or taken prisoner and these events precipitated open warfare. The Dutch settlers soon found themselves besieged in their small fort by 500 Esopus warriors.

When Stuyvesant arrived with reinforcements on 10 October 1659, he found the siege recently lifted, and after furnishing the village with some of his regular soldiers and a few supplies, returned to New Amsterdam. Although a state of war existed, the Dutch were in no position to launch an attack on the Indians. Instead, Vice-Director Johannes La Montagne, in charge at Fort Orange, pursued peace through diplomatic channels. With the help of the neighboring Mohawks, Mahicans, and Catskill Indians, La Montagne arranged for the release of two captives and a temporary cease-fire. Although isolated hostile actions continued to be committed on both sides, farming and trade with the Indians resumed under the protection of armed soldiers.

In the spring of 1660, Ensign Dirck Smith, in charge of the troops at Wiltyck, made several attempts to attack the Indians with varying degrees of success. Around 17 March, he led 40 soldiers against an Indian camp of about 60 men. Alerted to the Dutch presence, the Esopus fled, but the Dutch troops managed to kill three or four of them, and took 12 prisoners as well. They then burned the provisions they found in the village. On 4 April, Smith led an ambush a few hundred yards outside the fort against several Indian warriors who had been harassing and taunting the Dutch during the day. When the Indians discovered the ambush, a skirmish broke out and the Dutch shot five Indians, killing three and wounding two, taking no losses themselves. Ensign Smith led his soldiers in their final foray on 29 and 30 May against an Esopus village located in the hinterlands. Their travel was twice restricted by high water and they were detected on their approach. The second day, however, they did come across a very old Indian man, who was in fact, the oldest sachem of the Esopus tribe, but too feeble to escape with the rest. The Dutch killed him, ostensibly because he threatened them with a gun and talked abusively to them.

It was through the efforts of other Indian tribes, however, that the Esopus finally agreed to a peace settlement. Besides the diplomatic efforts of the Mohawks, Mahicans, and Catskills, the Susquehannas, Wappingers, and Hackensacks also became involved, and through their influence, a meeting between Director General Stuyvesant and the Esopus sachems was arranged for 14 July 1660. A formal peace was signed the following day which required that the Esopus make reparations by paying back the ransom previously paid for the release of prisoners and by giving up a large portion of their land along the creeks and moving elsewhere.

Although the treaty served to reduce hostilities, it did not permanently put an end to the war. A number of factors contributed to the continuation of the conflict. First, several Esopus men planned a new attack on the village to avenge their kin who had been captured by the Dutch during the war and sent to Curaçao by Director General Stuyvesant for safekeeping. This attack never came, but along with the continued public abuse of alcohol by many of the young Esopus men, it led to increased tensions at Wiltwyck. Furthermore, the European population in the area increased and a second village, Nieuwdorp (New Village), was founded near Wiltwyck, but against the Indians' expressed wishes. This only increased the frustration of the Esopus sachems, who frequently requested Stuyvesant to make good his offers to provide gifts to the Esopus people in recompense for the land they had already surrendered, and to seal the previous peace treaty. In fact, a meeting between Stuyvesant and the Esopus chiefs had been arranged for 5 June 1663 to discuss these matters, but it was apparently never held.

Then, on 7 June, the Esopus Indians made surprise attacks on Wiltwyck and Nieuwdorp beginning the so-called Second Esopus War. Waiting until most of the men had left the settlements to tend the fields, secretly-armed Indians entered and quickly spread throughout both villages with the excuse that they had come to trade. Nieuwdorp was attacked first, and was completely burned to the ground. Most of its inhabitants were taken prisoner or killed. The attack at Wiltwyck came soon after when several Dutch horsemen rode into town shouting the news of the other attack. The Indians in the town drew their firearms and hatchets and began the attack, while reinforcements from behind the settlement opened fire as well. The Indians quickly gained command of the streets and soon set fire to the buildings while taking women and children hostages and sniping at the men as they entered the village. But the tide of the battle turned when several Dutchmen made it back to the settlement at the same time the wind changed direction and the fires began to die out. Captain Thomas Chambers quickly took charge and the inhabitants repelled the Indians and secured the gates. By the end of the day, about 45 of the Dutch settlers had been captured, at least 20 more killed, and 69 survivors, including some from Nieuwdorp, remained in Wiltyck and prepared for a siege.

The siege never came, but skirmishes continued outside the fort for the next few weeks. Stuyvesant soon made his arrival at Wiltwyck and by the end of June, he had reinforced the town with 60 troops whom he placed under the command of Martin Cregier. Before launching an attack, however, the Dutch attempted to negotiate for the release of prisoners. Through the help of the Mohawks and others, a female prisoner was released who had been taken to the Esopus's fortified village. A few weeks later, Cregier also arranged for the return of five other captives.

By the end of July, though, Cregier was ready to launch his first expedition. Armed with the information provided by the released female captive, Cregier led a force of 210 soldiers, settlers, slaves, and Indian allies to attack the Esopus fortress. Armed with two cannons and wagons, the company slowly made its way over terrain that was alternately mountainous and swampy, only to find on their arrival that the fort had been deserted two days before. The Dutch occupied the site, sent out a smaller force to pursue the Indians, and set about the task of destroying what appeared to be the Esopus Indians' major food reserves. After the smaller expedition returned empty-handed and their work at the Indian village was done, Cregier and his men burned the stockade and returned to Wiltwyck.

By the end of August, when only a few more hostages had been recovered and the Indian allies were threatening to leave, Cregier received word that the Esopus were fortifying another site. He quickly assembled a company of 55 soldiers and, with the aid of a Wappinger guide, made a two-day march to arrive at the site of the new Indian stronghold on 5 September. Finding the Indians outside their uncompleted hilltop fortress, the Dutch split into two groups and began to quietly surround them. Although an Indian woman spotted one of the platoons and gave warning, the soldiers still had the element of surprise and caught the Indians largely unarmed. The Indians fled through the fort picking up what arms they could with the Dutch close behind. The soldiers chased the Indians down the hill and across a creek where the warriors chose to stand their ground and fight. They quickly gave up when a small force of soldiers came across the creek and broke their resistance. The Dutch troops then destroyed the guns and other supplies left by the Indians, but did not take the time to burn their crops. Cregier could count this battle a success, his soldiers having killed or captured more than 30 Indians, while only six of their own were wounded and three others killed. In addition, they recovered 23 Dutch prisoners.

In October, three more smaller expeditions were conducted, but accomplished little except the destruction of more Indian crops and food supplies. As in the previous war, however, it was not only the military actions which pressured the Esopus Indians to ask for terms. Throughout the summer and fall, Stuyvesant and his officials at Fort Orange had been busy meeting with representatives of the Mohawks, Nyacks, Hackensacks, and Wappingers, through whom they hoped to secure the release of the prisoners and arrange a peace settlement. It soon became evident that the Esopus did not hold all the prisoners in one place and, in fact, other bands such as the Catskills, and perhaps the Wappingers themselves, also held some Dutch captives. During the winter of 1663–1664, however, the rest of the captives had been returned a few at a time. Then, in May 1664, three Esopus sachems came to New Amsterdam to negotiate a peace agreement with the Dutch.

Stuyvesant dictated fairly strict terms. He insisted that the Esopus cede all their territory from the Hudson River up to the sites of the two destroyed forts. Any trade to be conducted with the Dutch settlers was restricted to a single spot along the creek near Wiltwyck, and the Indians were only allowed to come in small numbers and under a flag of truce. Furthermore, all disputes between the Indians and Dutch were to be handled in Dutch courts. To ensure compliance with this treaty by all the Esopus peoples, it was to be ratified within a month by the rest of the tribal leaders and renewed yearly at Fort Amsterdam.

Paul Otto

References

Edmund B. O'Callaghan and Berthold Fernow, eds., *Documents Relative to the Colonial History of the State of New York*, 15 vols. (1856–1887): Vols. I, XII, XIII; Edmund B. O'Callaghan, ed., *The Documentary History of the State of New York*, Vol. IV (1851); ———, *History of New Netherland; or, New York under the Dutch*, Vol. 2 (1848); Allen W. Trelease, *Indian Affairs in Colonial New York: The Seventeenth Century* (1960).

See also ESOPUS; KIEFT'S WAR; PEACH WAR; STUYVESANT, PETRUS

F

Falls Fight (1676)

The Falls Fight of 19 May 1676 was a turning point of King Philip's War. This successful predawn English attack took place at a site the Indians called Peskeompscut, on the Connecticut River some ten miles north of Hadley, the northernmost English settlement still inhabited in the Connecticut Valley. The English called this place the Great Falls, both for its size and for the abundant shad and salmon found there. After Captain William Turner led his attack, the place became known, as it is today, as Turner's Falls. What the English saw as a successful raid was to the Indians a shocking, demoralizing disaster. By the time the battle was over, the Indians' final defeat was not far off.

The year 1675 had seen major success for the Indians, especially in the Connecticut Valley, the war's western front. Once the war had broken out of southeastern Massachusetts, the English had lost control. Indian attacks from August through October devastated the Connecticut Valley. By winter, four of nine English settlements in the Connecticut Valley of Massachusetts had been destroyed: Brookfield, Northfield, Pocumtuck (Deerfield), and Swampfield (later Sunderland). Philip's forces then headed north and west, for comfort and safety, to winter near the Hoosic River.

But spring of 1676 saw a different war in the west. Major Indian attacks on surviving English towns failed: the colonists were better prepared and had adopted better tactics. In addition, there were signs that all was not well among the Indians. By May, contemporary William Hubbard wrote, "many . . . were destroyed by fevers and fluxes" and there was "some Quarrel amongst themselves," with warriors "now strangely divided and separated the one from the other."

Still, the result through March and April was stalemate, not defeat, for the Indians. In fact, as of early May, the Indians felt secure in settling into their traditional site on the Connecticut River at Peskeompscut. In addition, while larger attacks on local towns had failed, the Indians continued to make successful smaller forays. One of these took place in the Hatfield meadows, where on 12 May the Indians stampeded some 70 head of cattle and drove them into the woods.

This time the English responded. Outraged by this theft, and learning that the Indians had become careless about sending scouts or posting guards, between 15 and 18 May, Captain William Turner gathered an English troop at Hatfield. The troop was unusual in that it included largely local citizen/soldiers, not regular Massachusetts militia. On the night of 18 May, Turner's force of more than 150 men headed north, past the ruins of Pocumtuck and across the Deerfield River, and looped up above the Indians at the falls. Then, with no Indian guards posted, just before daybreak the soldiers crept into the sleeping camp. As Increase Mather reported it, "our Souldiers came and put their Guns into their Wigwams . . . and made a great and notable slaughter amongst them." Many Indians were killed in the first few seconds of the attack as they lay asleep in their tents. Others died before they could offer resistance. Still others ran to the river, leaping into canoes or headlong into the waters; a vast number of these died as they hurtled over the falls. More were chased to the river bank and shot there. In all, the colonists killed outright some 100 Indians; roughly 140 more died trying to escape via the river. Notable also is that the assault was carried out largely against "old men and women"; there were reportedly only "69 or 70 fighting-men" at Peskeompscut. Although nearby Indians rushed to the scene and routed and scattered Turner's forces, killing the captain and 37 others, the Indian losses were staggering.

Looking at the overall story of King Philip's War, this incident has fourfold significance. First, the attack marked the first true English victory in the west, a result dramatically different from any of 1675. Second, it devastated an Indian force that was already showing signs of splintering: the effect on Indian morale was profound. Third, in terms of the path of the war, it drove Philip's forces out of the Connecticut Valley, where they had had such notable success, back toward the south and east where they would meet their end within just three months. Finally, that move south and east had enormous implications for other forces in the war—Indian forces. When the English routed the Indians at the falls, the survivors certainly had options other than heading south and east, which was, of course, where greater colonial strength lay. Yet they went. The reason appears to be that Philip's forces feared other Indians as well as the English: they feared the Mohawks. Through the winter of 1675–1676, the English in Boston, Governor Edmund Andros in New York, and Philip himself all had tried to get these powerful eastern Iroquois onto their side. The English in Boston had no success; Andros claimed some; and Philip lost badly in his bid. The truth is that the Mohawks were working for themselves, continuing their decades-old conflict with some of New England's bands, and a series of Mohawk strikes between February and June drove Philip's forces south and east. In fact, although Turner's raid was an independent English action, Indians ran from their tents reportedly crying "Mohawks! Mohawks!" Thus, while the raid was an unusual show of English military success, it also fits into a larger and more complex swirl of forces that were spinning around the Great Falls, forces that included not only the English and Philip's allies, but other Indians as well. When new English success was coupled with Mohawk pressure to form a two-front war, Philip's forces could not hold.

Richard I. Melvoin

References

George Madison Bodge, *Soldiers in King Philip's War* (1906); William Hubbard, *A Narrative of the Indian Wars . . . to 1677* (1677), rpt. 1903; Douglas E. Leach, *Flintlock and Tomahawk: New England in King Philip's War* (1958); Richard I. Melvoin, *New England Outpost: War and Society in Colonial Deerfield* (1989).

See also KING PHILIP'S WAR

Falmouth, Battle of (1690)

The term "Battle of Falmouth" refers most properly to the five-day struggle, 16–20 May 1690, during which a French and Abenaki force overwhelmed and destroyed the English fort and settlement at Falmouth (now Portland), Maine. More generally, the term might be expanded to include both the climactic event of 1690 and a preliminary encounter on 21 September 1689, when a French and Indian attack was repelled. After the fall of Falmouth, all the English settlements between there and Wells were abandoned until the end of King William's War.

At the outbreak of the war in 1689, the settlement at Falmouth consisted of something more than 80 families. A palisaded fortification called Fort Loyal (also called Casco fort), built under Massachusetts authority about 1680, overlooked the harbor and Casco Bay from the shore of Falmouth Neck. No English settlement or fortification stood between there and New England's remotest outpost at Pemaquid, more than 40 miles eastward.

Early in the war, the rather easy Indian capture of Pemaquid had been followed by destructive raids on settlements in southern Maine and New Hampshire, but the timely arrival at Casco Bay of a force under Major Benjamin Church of Plymouth Colony—on 20 September 1689—saved Falmouth from the same fate. Church led a coordinated defense by his own troops, friendly Indians from southern New England, and Falmouth men to drive off a force of 300 or 400 attackers in a six-hour engagement the next day.

Early in 1690, Canadian Governor Louis de Buade de Frontenac sent three French and Indian expeditions against various English targets. One of the three set out against the Maine settlements from Quebec City in January under Pierre Robinau de Portneuf. Joined at the Kennebec River in May by Indian reinforcements, Portneuf led a force now totaling 400 or 500 men against Falmouth.

Although four fortified houses had recently been built to supplement Fort Loyal, the garrison had been depleted when the commander of the fort and his troops were ordered to join the campaign against Port Royal. Captain Sylvanus Davis, the principal local landowner and militia leader, was left in charge of the fort and the fewer than 100 local militiamen who were left to defend the town.

During Portneuf's five-day siege, all of the houses in the settlement were burned and more than half of Davis's militiamen killed or wounded. Davis surrendered in the afternoon of 20 May on condition that the surviving soldiers and their families be given safe passage to the nearest English town. Instead, all were either killed or taken captive to Canada. Davis himself was among those taken to Quebec, where he was entertained by Frontenac, but even more memorable was the captivity of Hannah Swarton, whose narrative was among those made famous by Cotton Mather.

Charles E. Clark

References
William Willis, *The History of Portland,* 2nd ed. (1865).

See also CASCO BAY; CHURCH, BENJAMIN; KING WILLIAM'S WAR; FORT LOYAL (MAINE)

Father Rale's War
See DUMMER'S WAR

Finns
The first Finns to arrive in America in 1640 came from Sweden. They came to Fort Christina on the Delaware River, which had been established in 1638 by the New Sweden Company. Many of the Finns were of Savo-Karelian origin. Most had been coerced into leaving the forested areas of Sweden due to their slash-and-burn techniques of land clearing. These activities had run them afoul of the Swedish government and earned them the title of "forest-destroyer Finns." For this and other offenses, such as poaching, army desertion, and unpaid debts, they were captured and imprisoned, or deported.

When the New Sweden Company found it difficult to secure immigrants for the new colony in America, the Finns became part of the solution. Finnish criminals had the options of a new life in America, hanging, or languishing in prison. Most chose the first.

In New Sweden the Finns were in their element. They quickly set about clearing land,

building the first log cabins and split-rail fences, planting crops, and breeding cattle. They were skilled in hunting, made articles from birchbark (including shoes), and constructed steam bathhouses called saunas. Two early agricultural settlements arose in New Sweden that contained both Finnish and Swedish farmers; Finland (near Marcus Hook, Pennsylvania) and Upland (Chester, Pennsylvania). The two colonies lived at peace with, and without fortification from, the Delaware Indians. Later, on the east bank of the Delaware, a predominantly Finnish settlement developed near Finns Point (Churchtown, New Jersey). Two other settlements of Finnish and Swedish colonists combined were established at Raccoon (Swedesboro, New Jersey) and Repaupo.

Between 1643 and 1653, the governor of New Sweden was Johan Printz. Printz thought the Finns to be a lazy lot, and reports indicate his harsh treatment of them. In 1649, Printz charged Anders "The Finn" Jönsson with treason. Jönsson was the leader of a group of 22 Finns who had defied Printz's orders and traded independently with the Indians and the Dutch freemen. Printz had Jönsson tried and executed by hanging to set an example. In addition, Printz had "Karin the Finnish Woman" and "Lasse the Finn" separated from the main colony and imprisoned for practicing witchcraft, because in Sweden, the Finns were seen as "masters in the art of witchcraft and sorcery."

The Dutch took control of the Delaware in 1655, and at that time approximately 200 Swedish and Finnish colonists lived at Upland and Finland. After Governor Rising signed capitulation papers signifying the end of New Sweden, only 37 people chose to leave the colony for their homeland. The remaining pledged their allegiance to the Dutch. Accordingly, they were allowed to continue farming, to practice their religion, and for the most part, to govern themselves.

When more than 100 more Finnish and Swedish colonists arrived in 1656 shortly after the Dutch takeover of the Delaware, they were allowed to disembark and settle peacefully. Even though the Dutch were ever fearful of an uprising (they were by now outnumbered by the Finns and Swedes), none happened while they controlled the Delaware.

Finns and Swedes continued to immigrate to the Delaware Valley even after the English took possession in 1664. By William Penn's arrival in 1681, he noted the Finns remarkably large and sturdy families and acknowledged the improvements they had made in the Delaware Valley.

Linda M. Thorstad

References
Amandus Johnson, *The Swedish Settlement on the Delaware 1638–1655*, 2 vols. (1911); Terry G. Jordan and Matti Kaups, *The American Backwoods Frontier* (1989); Peter Lindeström, *Geographia Americae*, trans. by Amandus Johnson (1925); Christopher Ward, *The Dutch and the Swedes on the Delaware 1609–64* (1930); ———, *New Sweden on the Delaware* (1938).

See also New Sweden

Florida

The peninsula located in the southeast of the North American subcontinent makes up one of the actual states of the country. However, Florida's territory today has no direct relation with the vague government which was situated in the north of the peninsula and the Gulf of Mexico, owned by the Spanish crown, with some interruptions in its sovereignty, until its sale to the United States.

Upon arrival of the Spanish, Florida was populated by the Arawac Indians in the southwest, Yuchi and Timucuans in the center and north, and the Apalachee in the northwest. The Spanish viewed Florida as including all of the present southeastern United States, including the territories of the Chickasaw, Choctaw, Cherokee, Creek, and Alabamas. All these tribes played an important part in the territorial disputes between the three European powers established in the area in the colonial era: Spain, France, and Great Britain.

Although the coast of the Florida peninsula was possibly explored before, as can be deduced from its appearance in maps before these dates, it was officially discovered in 1512 by Juan Ponce de Leon, whose expedition, consisting of three ships, traveled the east coast and part of the western. He christened it Florida because it was sighted on the feast of the Resurrection of Christ, popularly called "Pascua Florida."

Many attempts were made in the sixteenth century to conquer Florida, all of which ended in disaster. In 1519, the officer Alfonso Alvarez de Pineda was sent by Francisco de Garay, governor of Jamaica, who discovered the north coast of the Gulf of Mexico showing that Florida was a peninsula and not an island, and the impossibility of discovering a route through to northeastern Asia. They did not dare try to base themselves in Florida after they lost so many people on the expedition, but they did find a very large river which they named El Espíritu Santo (Mississippi). They also discovered that in the interior of this area the Indian population was very large and culturally more developed than those of Florida. The next attempt was led by Lucas Vázquez de Ayllón in 1526, who had left the island of Santo Domingo with three large ships, arriving to exchange some products with the Indians. This conqueror carried out the second landing with more than 200 men, who died unsuspectingly at the hands of the Indians after the welcome they had received on their arrival at the Indian village, attacking afterwards those who had been left to guard the boats.

Pánfilo de Narváez left Sanlúcar de Barrameda (Spain) with five vessels and 600 men, some of whom stopped off in La Española. Only four of the boats survived a storm and, after being repaired, they arrived at the Bay of Santa Cruz (Florida) in 1528. The expedition headed toward Apalachee, but on seeing that there were no riches, they returned and put to sea in barges. This ended in complete disaster with only three of its group surviving, who, after wandering among the Charruas, Abaraes, Malicones, Cibolas, Tagos, and other Indians, arrived at San Miguel in Mexico in 1536. One of the survivors, Alvar Núñez Cabeza de Vaca, recounted these tough adventures in his work *Los Naufragios,* which stirred Spanish interest to return to the region.

After a few aborted attempts, the next major Spanish thrust into the Southeast was led by Hernando de Soto. His expedition consisted of more than 1,000 men and traveled a good part of the southeastern United States between 1539 and 1542, ending with his death after an Indian attack.

Due to the lack of success in conquering Florida, the Spanish tried to develop a different model of colonization, sending in 1549 an expedition headed by Friar Luis de Cáncer to convert the Indian population to the Christian faith and to submit them to the sovereignty of His Catholic Majesty (the king of Spain). This project was again a disaster and the friars died at the hands of the Indians.

Tristán de Luna was sent as the viceroy's new envoy of New Spain, with 1,500 settlers to Ichuse (Pensacola Bay) in 1559. Meanwhile, the following year, his substitute, Angel de Villafañe, tried to establish himself in Santa Elena (South Carolina).

In 1561, due to the difficulty of its possession, King Philip II ordered this project abandoned, but changed his mind after the establishment of French Huguenot colonies in the area led by Jean Ribault and René de Laudonnière in 1562 and 1564, respectively.

After these French attempts to take possession of Florida, the expedition was organized with 1,000 men transported in four ships which would be under the command of Pedro Menéndez de Avilés. In 1565, Menéndez destroyed the French settlements exterminating the population of Fort Caroline and 200 Huguenots who had been shipwrecked in a cove, from which it acquired the name "Matanzas." This was the same place where later he killed Ribault and the rest of his expedition. In the same year Pedro Menéndez founded the presidio of San Augustin (the first European city established in United States territory); a short time after its founding it was the object of a fruitless French attack. Soon afterwards, the forts and villages of San Antonio in the Bay of Carlos, Tocobaga in the Bay of Tampa, Tequesta in the southeast, Guale in Georgia, and Santa Elena in South Carolina were built, although some of them lasted but a short time. To convert the natives the conqueror sent in the Jesuits who, in 1570, founded a mission in what is now Virginia before their failure and death at the hands of the Indians, and Franciscans who, in 1573, spread up the coasts reaching what is now Georgia.

The Spanish settlements in Florida were constantly beset by military threats from Europeans and Indians. St. Augustine suffered numerous attacks in the colonial period, beginning with a raid by Francis Drake, which plundered the garrison and left it in flames.

In 1597, there was an Indian uprising by the Guale and other tribes that destroyed and forced the missions to be abandoned, but this type of colonization began anew after the settlement of the English in 1607 at Jamestown, in Chesapeake Bay, Virginia.

By 1609, an expedition was organized against Jamestown headed by Captain Pérez de Ecija, but instead of attacking they set the Indians against the British. In 1611, another attempt was made but failed mainly because of the opposition of their own King Philip III. In the area of rebellious natives, between the colonized territory and the land occupied by the English, Friar Luis de Oré settled new missions in 1612, quickly expanding into 20 settlements over Florida and 44 by 1634, with a large converted native population. In 1633, the Apalachee missions were being built toward the northwest part of the peninsula, with its center in Saint Louis. By the middle of the century, there were eight of these missions located in the region, some of them up to 120 miles from the Atlantic coast. These missions were abandoned in the second half of the century due to an Apalachee uprising.

The extension of British colonization toward the south with the first settlements in North Carolina in 1653 and in South Carolina in 1670 again fomented the occupation of territories in Georgia by missions and increased the border fighting between the British and Spanish.

In 1665, a new attack was brought about directed at St. Augustine, with the consequent burning of the village at the hands of buccaneers led by Captain Robert Searles.

Due to the continual frontier tensions, an expedition was organized against Carolina in 1670, but it could not break through the coastal barriers due to bad weather—so the Spanish built a fort at Santa Elena, while also maintaining the occupation of Santa Catalina Island. In 1683, the evacuation of Santa Elena was carried out although later on it again was reestablished.

At this time the threat of the French increased due to their attempts to establish themselves on the Gulf of Mexico. The Spanish used galleons to keep the French out of Pensacola in 1698 and Biloxi in 1699, and then Mobile in 1702. These actions and the construction of the San Marcos castle in St. Augustine made the most of the few years of tranquillity that followed the signing in 1697 of the Treaty of Ryswick.

During the War of the Spanish Succession, relations with the French eased but there were confrontations with the British settlements. In 1702, South Carolina and its allied natives, 2,000 men under the command of Governor James Moore, razed to the ground the Apalachee missions and dwellings and besieged and burned St. Augustine. The inhabitants saved themselves by taking refuge in the castle. In retaliation, the Spanish-French allies organized a strong attack on Charles Town in 1706, failing in the attempt because they were unable to sur-

F

prise the British due to being delayed a day in crossing the coastal barrier and having to land on Sullivan's Island. The signing of the Treaty of Utrecht put an end to the war. Meanwhile, in the abandoned Apalachee territory the English made some settlements which became the foundation for the building of Georgia in 1733.

In 1715, the Yamasee War began, when the Indians from the north Florida border advanced on the British colonies, believed by the British to have been instigated by the Spanish. The Spanish provided refuge for the Yamasee and many escaped slaves from South Carolina: both groups remained thorns to the English settlements.

The Spanish occupation of Sardinia and Sicily during the War of the Quadruple Alliance (1718–1721) led the governor of Cuba to prepare an expedition against New Orleans, Biloxi, and Mobile. The French, foreseeing this, surrounded Pensacola on 14 March 1719 with mixed naval and native military forces under the command of Captain Joseph Le Moyne de Sérigny. They forced the Spanish to surrender; but on 29 July Pensacola fell again into Spanish hands after the arrival of a powerful expedition from Cuba. Following these attempts, the Spanish attacked New Orleans and Mobile, but Spanish artillery had little impact on the French forts; meanwhile five French ships approached from Guarico in New Orleans's defense and managed to achieve the surrender of the Spanish expedition on 17 September. Due to French attacks, Pensacola fell again under French rule, although with the Treaty of Madrid, 27 March 1721, France returned it to Spain.

Simultaneous to the Spanish-French hostilities on the Gulf coast, united Anglo-French forces attacked the east coast and temporarily took possession of St. Catherines Island. Also, frequent attacks were made by the British-allied Indians against the Spanish-allied Indians. In 1719, an expedition against New Providence was prepared and from there continued to Charles Town, but a storm broke up the flotilla.

The peace signed in 1721 put off a new expedition planned to attack Charles Town and St. George; but as a delegation went to South Carolina to confirm the armistice, they discovered the building of a fort at the mouth of the Altamaha River. A protest was presented in London and the Spanish and British tried to fix the limits between both colonies, as had been signed in the Treaty of 1670 (Treaty of Madrid), but to no avail.

In 1728, the English again attacked St. Augustine, at the same time that the Yuchi and Yamasee Indians rebelled at St. Marcos in Apalachee, devastating Spanish Florida's northern frontier. Due to Spain's tenuous situation and the unrest of the garrisons and the slowness of their colonial administration, Spain signed the Treaty of Seville, in which newly stipulated boundaries were made between the Spanish and British in the Southeast, but these were disregarded by the British with the creation of the British colony of Georgia in 1732 under Governor James E. Oglethorpe.

In 1736, an agreement was signed between the governor of Florida, Francisco del Moral Sánchez, and Oglethorpe's agent, Captain Charles Dempsey, in which the English promised to evacuate the islands of "San Jorge y San Juan," demolish its fortress, and leave the St. Johns River as the provisional frontier between both. King Philip V did not accept the agreement, as he had no previous information in regard to it. Spain reasserted its sovereignty to all territories that belonged to it, including Georgia, and a naval expedition was ordered in 1737 to secure Spanish claims. The expedition was suspended but the forces were used instead to reinforce the garrisons in Florida. Toward the end of 1739 conventions were held in London and El Pardo (Spain).

On hearing in America of a new confrontation between Britain and Spain—the War of the Austrian Succession—the governors of Florida and Georgia prepared to do battle. Oglethorpe, with more than 1,000 soldiers and 1,200 Indians, attacked St. Augustine in 1740 where all the Floridians had taken refuge. Governor Montiano left the fort and attacked the British on 26 June with new forces sent from Havana, taking 39 prisoners and leaving more than 100 dead. Oglethorpe withdrew his forces shortly thereafter.

In 1742, the governor of Florida received information that Oglethorpe was preparing a new attack, therefore 35 vessels with troops prepared a counterattack. Governor Montiano landed at St. Simon and took the village of Frederica, but soon thereafter the Spanish were forced to withdraw. Hostilities between the British and the Spanish in Florida steadily receded. Finally, Florida was handed over to the English according to a clause in the Treaty of Paris (1763) ending the Seven Years' War.

During the colonial period, Florida was considered a border area, a fundamental point of the colonial system because of its strategic position in the Caribbean, its importance to the communications system of the empire, and its position as a defensive barrier against other European positions. Above all, the scarce population that developed had some very specific characteristics, being fundamentally of a military character. The major foundation made in this territory was St. Augustine, which, before being a city or nucleus of civil population, was a military presidio that had as appendixes other strategically placed forts, like those of San Marcos of Apalachee and Matanzas. This grew with the founding in 1738 of the first free Negro village of North America, "Gracia Real de Santa Teresa de Mose," a short distance to the north of St. Augustine, serving as a defensive barrier against the British settlements as well as attracting slaves who had run away from their plantations.

There was no civil power that existed equal to the military power in Florida and from the colony's establishment the position of a person on the military roll list was what determined his social level and esteem. Economic development of the colony was retarded by the defensive nature of the colony, its lack of financial support from the mother country, the failure to attract civilian settlers, and the small number of reinforcements sent by Spain.

In conclusion, we can see that the historical evolution of Florida was largely based on the ability of Spanish military power to defend the colony, and the health of the missions. European and Indian attacks kept Florida on the defensive; without adequate support from home the colony entered a steady state of decline from the mid-seventeenth century onward. The French settlement of Louisiana completely separated Mexico from Florida, restricting Florida's western border, while the northern borders were constantly pressured and steadily pushed south by the British and the Amerindians of the region. The home government had little interest in developing the territory's resources, particularly due to the lack of Indian workers; yet Florida's strategic location for the security of the Caribbean and the Bahamas Channel forced the Spanish to maintain their position. For this reason above all, during the reign of Philip V, each international treaty signed upheld the possession and the integrity of Floridian territory, although because of their feebleness the Spanish could do little to establish a strong position.

Due to its expansive frontier, and its military and defensive character, Florida was totally dependent on the mother country for support; economically, administratively, and ecclesiastically, its support came from outside its borders. For that reason it developed little beyond being an outpost of Cuba, another of its territories.

Juan I. Arnaud-Rabinal

References

Antonio Acosta and Juan Marchena, eds., *La influencia de España en el Caribe, la Florida y la Luisiana, 1500–1800* (1983); Elizabeth Alexander, et al., *Fuentes para la Historia Social de la Florida Española (1600–1763)* (1988); Fernando de Armas Medina, *Luisiana y Florida en el reinado de Carlos III* (1960).

John Francis Bannon, *The Spanish Borderlands Frontier 1513–1821* (1970); Antonio de Bethancourt, "Felipe V y la Florida," *Anuario de Estudios Americanos* (1950):95–123; Amy Bushnell, *The King's Coffer: Proprietors of the Spanish Florida Treasury, 1565–1702* (1981); Gabriel de Cárdenas y Cano, *Ensayo cronológico para la historia general de la Florida* (1723); Verne E. Chatelaine, *The Defenses of Spanish Florida 1565 to 1763* (1941).

Hidalgo de Elvas, *Expedición de Hernando de Soto a Florida* (1965); Juan Marchena, "Guarniciones y población militar en Florida Oriental (1700–1820)," *Revista de Indias* (1981):91–142; P. Fr. Jerónimo de Oré, *Relación histórica de la Florida, escrita en el siglo XVII* (1931); Eugenio Ruidíaz y Caravia, *La Florida, su conquista y colonización por Pedro Menéndez de Avilés* (1893); John J. Tepaske, *The Governorship of Spanish Florida 1700–1763* (1964).

See also ANGLO-SPANISH WAR (1718–1721); ANGLO-SPANISH WAR (1739–1744); APALACHEE REVOLT; BLACK AND INDIAN MILITIAS; CHACATO TROUBLES; DRAKE, SIR FRANCIS; FLORIDA, BRITISH INVASION OF (1740); GEORGIA; GUALE; MENÉNDEZ DE AVILÉS, PEDRO; MONTIANO, MANUEL DE; MORAL SÁNCHEZ, FRANCISCO DE; NARVÁEZ, PANFILO DE; OGLETHORPE, JAMES EDWARD; PENSACOLA; ST. AUGUSTINE; SAN MARCOS, CASTILLO DE; SOTO, HERNANDO DE; SPANISH MISSION SYSTEM–SOUTHEAST; TIMUCUAN REVOLT

F

Florida, British Invasion of (1740)

By the time of the War of Jenkins' Ear/King George's War (1739–1748) the colony of St. Augustine in Florida had served Spanish interests for more than 200 years. One of its purposes was to prevent other European powers from colonizing southeastern North America. The nearest European settlement was South Carolina, 150 miles to the north, established in 1670. The land between the rival colonies was basically unoccupied after about 1680. However, Britain suddenly occupied the area in 1733 by establishing the colony of Georgia. Under James Edward Oglethorpe (1696–1785) the colony quickly expanded and developed into a British military colony. In 1737, Oglethorpe received a general's commission and command of the 42nd Regiment of Foot, a British infantry battalion, which was sent to Georgia the following year.

The British presence in Georgia was naturally considered a threat by Spain. Negotiations regarding the colony were initiated between the two powers, but the issue was not settled. In late September 1739, General Oglethorpe received orders from England to mobilize his forces and to harass the Spaniards. He immediately requested that South Carolina assist him in laying siege to the town of St. Augustine in Florida.

The Spaniards struck the first blow. On 13 November 1739, a war party of their Yamasee Indian allies ambushed and killed two Scottish militiamen on Amelia Island, not far north of Florida. Two weeks later Yamasee again penetrated Georgia defenses and harassed the British. On 1 December 1739, General Oglethorpe personally led a 200-man waterborne reconnaissance force of British regulars, rangers, scouts, militia, and Yamacraw Indians down the Inland Passage (the modern Intracoastal Waterway) into northern Florida. For three weeks they reconnoitered the terrain, while the Spaniards kept their distance.

Meanwhile, the South Carolina assembly had been slowly debating General Oglethorpe's request for assistance in attacking St. Augustine. In late December he sent an officer to Charles Town with another request for soldiers, laborers, artillery, and boats. The governor and assembly continued their deliberations.

General Oglethorpe led another force of 180 men into Florida on 1 January 1740, with the object of capturing Fort San Francisco de Pupo on the west bank of the St. Johns River. The fort lay astride the road that connected St. Augustine and the Spanish settlement of Apalachee in northwest Florida. A week later the fort fell. General Oglethorpe placed more than 80 men in garrison and then returned to Georgia.

In late January General Oglethorpe sent an expanded request for assistance to South Carolina. The debate within the assembly continued. About two weeks later, Spaniards ambushed a detachment of British regulars and scouts in Georgia, killing two men.

During the last week in March 1740, General Oglethorpe visited the assembly in Charles Town and gave his personal guarantee of a successful invasion. He was accompanied by Commodore Vincent Pearse, of the Royal Navy, who commanded the British ships assigned to the project. Two weeks later the assembly passed a law that provided a levy of men, equipment, and supplies for the proposed invasion. During the ensuing month, troops were recruited and equipment and supplies were gathered in both South Carolina and Georgia.

The town of St. Augustine was protected by Fort San Marcos, one of the strongest fortifications in North America. Nevertheless, St. Augustine's defensive situation was not good. There were only a few hundred regular Spanish troops, scattered across north Florida. There were few armed boats or vessels. The British garrison at Fort San Francisco de Pupo had cut off most communication from the outposts in western Florida. Supplies were limited because British men-of-war had blockaded St. Augustine from outside help. However, during April 1740, the Spanish governor of Cuba dispatched more than 200 soldiers, provisions, two armed sloops, and six armed half-galleys to St. Augustine. Just before their arrival, the British warship *Tarter* abandoned its blockade station and sailed north to South Carolina, three days before it was due to be relieved by another warship. During that three-day period the Spanish reinforcements sailed unopposed into St. Augustine. The Cuban half-galleys would prove to be very dangerous to the British.

The British invasion force began moving into northeast Florida in the first week of May 1740. Included were the 42nd Regiment of Foot; the newly raised South Carolina Regiment of Foot; the understrength English Troop of Rangers and the Highland Troop of Rangers from Georgia; the Carolina Troop of Rangers, also understrength; the Highland Company of Foot from Darien in Georgia; about 100 scouts

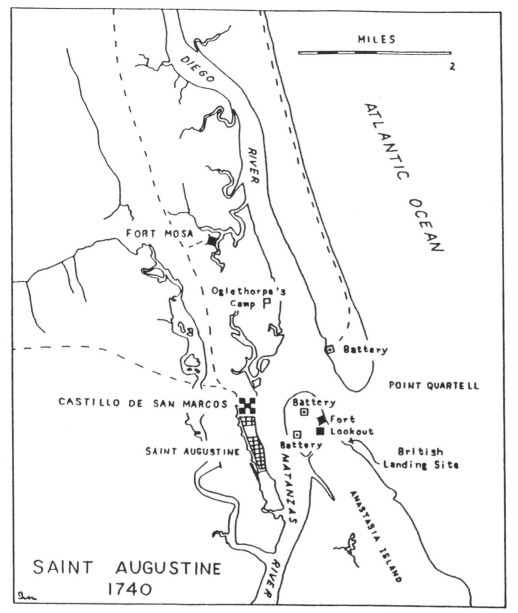

MILES

2

ATLANTIC OCEAN

DIEGO RIVER

FORT MOSA

Oglethorpe's Camp P

Battery

POINT QUARTELL

CASTILLO DE SAN MARCOS

Battery
Fort
Lookout

SAINT AUGUSTINE

Battery

British
Landing Site

MATANZAS

ANASTASIA ISLAND

SAINT AUGUSTINE
1740

MATANZAS RIVER

Reproduced from Larry E. Ivers, British Drums On The Southern Frontier: The Military Colonization of Georgia, 1733–1749 *(Chapel Hill, 1974) by permission of the University of North Carolina Press.*

from Georgia, with their scoutboats; and a party of workmen. General Oglethorpe had hoped for a large number of Creek Indians to take part in the invasion. However, both the Upper and the Lower Creek nations preferred to maintain neutrality in the War of Jenkins' Ear/King George's War. Only a few Creek, Yamacraw, and Chickasaw Indians served the British in Florida.

On 12 May 1740, a company-sized Spanish garrison at Fort San Diego north of St. Augustine fell to the British. On 19 May, General Oglethorpe and Commodore Pearse met and finalized their tactical plans. Their information regarding the Spanish defenses was incomplete; nevertheless, they agreed to press ahead. Oglethorpe planned to march his troops from their encampment on the south bank of the St. Johns

FLORIDA, BRITISH INVASION OF 209

River south to St. Augustine. Pearse planned to continue his blockade of the harbor, supply Oglethorpe's troops by sea, and transport the heavy siege artillery to batteries that would be constructed near the harbor. St. Augustine would then be assaulted by land from the north and across the harbor from the east. After the town was taken, they planned to bombard Fort San Marcos until its garrison surrendered.

The British land force arrived near St. Augustine on 1 June 1740. General Oglethorpe tried to entice the Spaniards out of the heavily fortified town, but Governor Manuel de Montiano had no intention of meeting the British in open combat on their terms. Instead, the Cuban half-galleys drove a British detachment from its outpost on Point Quartell, across the harbor from the town.

Four days later, Commodore Pearse warned General Oglethorpe that because of the approaching hurricane season, his ships would have to leave the area on 5 July—in one month. He recommended that Oglethorpe establish a long-term siege of St. Augustine until after the hurricane season. He offered to help build batteries of heavy cannon on Anastasia Island, at the harbor's entrance, to blockade the town from resupply. Commodore Pearse's proposed change of plans was not very practical. The presence of the Cuban half-galleys would endanger any force on Anastasia Island. In addition, without help from the ships of the Royal Navy, General Oglethorpe could not prevent the Spaniards from resupplying the town from the south via the Matanzas River. Therefore, General Oglethorpe held to his plan to assault the town as soon as possible. He did agree to the establishment of batteries on Anastasia Island so that the planned assault would have adequate fire support. He also insisted that the Cuban half-galleys must be destroyed in any case. The 42nd Regiment and the South Carolina Regiment were quickly landed on Anastasia Island and Point Quartell and construction of batteries was initiated. A detachment of 137 provincials and regulars were ordered to act as a "flying party" and patrol the north side of St. Augustine until the 42nd Regiment returned for the assault on the town.

Morale within St. Augustine was badly in need of a boost. A battery on Point Quartell had begun lobbing shells into the town. Although that initial bombardment apparently had little affect, the citizens of the town were terrified. Governor Montiano had been waiting and watching for an opportunity to strike the British invasion force. The flying party gave him that opportunity. The small force of Georgia and South Carolina rangers, Highland infantry, a file of regulars, and a few Creek Indians established themselves to the north of the town. They made their camp at Fort Mose, a partially demolished, mud-walled fortification. Some patrolling was accomplished, but mostly for the purpose of capturing Spanish horses. The flying party remained camped for five days in and around the old fort, instead of camping in a different place each night as General Oglethorpe had instructed them. The Georgia and South Carolina leaders of the flying party began bickering among themselves regarding who was in command and what tactics should be used.

On 14 June, Captain Antonio Salgado assembled 300 Spanish regulars, militia, and Yamasee Indian allies in Fort San Marcos. Just before midnight they quietly began moving toward Fort Mose. After reconnoitering the British defenses Captain Salgado placed his men in position for the attack. They were undetected. At first light the Spaniards began assaulting from three directions. Most of the British were wakened by the initial noise of battle, and were thrown into confusion. Despite a hard fight they were quickly overrun. More than half of the flying party were killed or taken prisoner. The rest escaped across the Diego River to Point Quartell. Morale among the British invasion force began sinking.

Colonel Alexander Vanderdussen, an experienced soldier who commanded the South Carolina Regiment of Foot, believed that the invasion plans were still workable. He attempted to convince General Oglethorpe and Commodore Pearse that the batteries of cannon should be quickly completed, the Cuban half-galleys should be destroyed, and the town should then be assaulted from both land and sea. However, Commodore Pearse was apparently afraid of the half-galleys. He refused to lend boats and crews to attack them. So long as the half-galleys were operational, a British assault was impractical. Colonel Vanderdussen was convinced that the army should at least remain in siege positions until the Royal Navy's return at the end of the hurricane season. General Oglethorpe agreed, but he wanted the assistance of the 200 seamen who were manning the batteries on Anastasia Island. Commodore Pearse refused to leave some of his seamen in Florida.

On 3 July, Spanish supply boats from Cuba evaded the Royal Navy blockade and delivered badly needed food to St. Augustine via the Matanzas River. All but two of the British men-of-war left Florida on 5 July. The army began retreating on 9 July. A week later, after the army had assembled on the south bank of the St. Johns River, a letter arrived from Charles Town informing Oglethorpe that more help was on the way from South Carolina. He quickly decided to march south again and place St. Augustine under siege. However, the regular troops of the 42nd Regiment were not of like mind; they wanted to return to Georgia. On 20 July, when part of the regiment was near mutiny, Oglethorpe abandoned all hope and continued the retreat. By 26 July 1740, all British soldiers had left Florida soil. Britain lost about 152 men killed, captured, or deserted. General Oglethorpe had badly underestimated the strength of Fort San Marcos and the courage of the Spanish settlers and troops.

Larry E. Ivers

References

J.H. Easterby, ed., *The Journal of the Commons House of Assembly, May 18, 1741–July 10, 1742. The Colonial Records of South Carolina* (1953); Larry E. Ivers, *British Drums on the Southern Frontierr: The Military Colonization of Georgia, 1733–1749* (1974).

See also FLORIDA; MONTIANO, MANUEL DE; OGLETHORPE, JAMES EDWARD; ST. AUGUSTINE; FORT SAN FRANCISCO DE PUPO (FLORIDA); SAN MARCOS, CASTILLO DE

Forbes, John (1710–1759)

John Forbes organized and led the 1758 expedition which resulted in the reoccupation of the forks of the Ohio during the French and Indian War.

He was born in Pittencrieff, Dunfermline, Scotland, the son of Colonel John Forbes. Originally a medical student, the son opted in 1735 to pursue a military career. He first purchased a commission as cornet in the 2nd Royal North British Dragoons (commonly called the Scots Greys), and went with his regiment to the Low Countries when the War of the Austrian Succession erupted. There he distinguished himself as a staff officer, particularly as aide-de-camp to Colonel Sir James Campbell in the Fontenoy campaign, and as a deputy quartermaster general in the closing months of the war. Under the British system of commission by purchase he rose in rank to lieutenant colonel of his regi-

ment in 1750 and to colonel of the 17th Regiment of Foot in February 1757, just before it was ordered to Halifax, Nova Scotia.

In North America, his skills as a staff officer resulted in appointment as an adjutant general under Lord Loudoun, followed by appointment as a brigadier, in America only, in December 1757. His skills in management and diplomacy recommended him as an officer capable of dealing with the complexities posed by provincial politicians and militia officers and, together with his close ties to the Campbells, probably account for the decision to give him command of the expedition against Fort Duquesne in 1758.

During the campaign, General Forbes achieved his major objectives. He successfully assembled a mixed force of regulars and militia, engaged in Indian negotiations, obtained supplies and funding from colonial sources, constructed a military road (commonly called Forbes Road) across western Pennsylvania, and brought his forces and supplies successfully across the mountains. His advance eventually compelled the French garrison to abandon and destroy Fort Duquesne in late November 1758.

After leaving a small garrison to begin the construction of Fort Pitt, Forbes returned east. During the campaign he had contracted a severe dysentery, commonly called the "bloody flux," of which he died on 11 March 1759. He was buried, with full military honors, in Christ Church in Philadelphia.

George Geib

References

Alfred P. James, ed., *Writings of General John Forbes Relating to His Service in North America* (1938).

See also FORBES CAMPAIGN OF 1758

Forbes Campaign of 1758

The Forbes campaign was one of three prongs of an English offensive directed against French forces in North America in 1758. The objective of the Forbes campaign was to capture Fort Duquesne at the forks of the Ohio, and to secure the allegiance or neutrality of the Indian tribes of that area. It was conceived by Prime Minister William Pitt to complement planned assaults on Louisbourg and on the French positions on Lakes George and Champlain.

Forbes planned the details of the expedition in Philadelphia. Because his objective in-

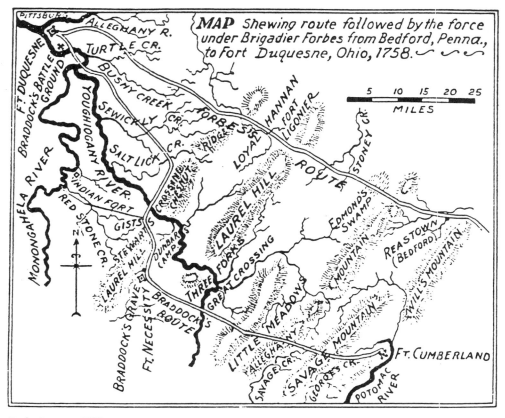

MAP Shewing route followed by the force under Brigadier Forbes from Bedford, Penna., to Fort Duquesne, Ohio, 1758.

Forbes's route, 1758.

cluded territory claimed by both Virginia and Pennsylvania, he expected those two colonies to contribute substantial forces to accompany a strong nucleus of British troops. Much of his planning involved balancing the conflicting ambitions of the two colonies, particularly with regard to the routes to be followed to the west. Virginia preferred a route using the path of Braddock's Road, approaching the forks from Fort Cumberland and the southeast. Pennsylvania preferred to create a new route from Philadelphia, guarded by new forts, and passing directly over the mountains from east to west. Each colony recognized that, if successful, the military route would become a valuable path for commerce and settlement.

Forbes eventually decided in favor of the Pennsylvania alternative, although allowing Virginia forces to use Fort Cumberland as a staging area. His resulting path, commonly called Forbes Road, proceeded from Carlisle and Shippensburg. It led to the construction of Forts Loudoun and Lyttleton as supply depots,

and eventually arrived at Raystown (modern Bedford).

Forbes assembled his forces from three sources. The first was British regular troops, totaling about 1,600 effectives, including 13 companies from the Highland Regiment under Lieutenant Colonel John Montgomery, and four companies from the Royal American Regiment under Colonel Henry Bouquet. The second source was two regiments of Virginia militia, totaling about 2,500 men. The third source was Pennsylvania militia, perhaps 2,700 in number. With the addition of civilian wagoners and sutlers, the total strength of his force was about 7,000 men. Bouquet, the ranking regular officer, was named second in command of the expedition, and was responsible for the operational details of the move westward.

Forbes arrived in Philadelphia in April 1758, but the expedition did not march until the fall. Several factors contributed to the delay. First, he became involved in the complicated politics of Pennsylvania as he sought support for his expedition. The assembly, from which Quaker members had withdrawn, wished to tie its support to the question of the taxation of proprietary lands, and was slow in voting funds. Second, the general sought without success to obtain substantial support from North Carolina and Maryland. Third, he found that the actual collection of supplies and transport proved extremely time-consuming and frustrating. And finally, he devoted substantial effort to obtaining support from Indian tribes.

Efforts with the Indians took two forms. First, Forbes sought to obtain scouts and auxiliaries from friendly tribes, notably the Catawba and Cherokee. Second, he sought through diplomacy to secure the alliance of the Delaware and Shawnee at an Easton conference which dragged on into the autumn before producing an inconclusive agreement.

The actual expedition moved west in August and September. Apart from the usual complaints about supply and militia indiscipline, the march was uneventful until it left Raystown and arrived at Loyalhanna, about 50 miles east of Duquesne. There, as fortifications were being erected, a period of skirmish warfare ensued.

The most important resulting British initiative was an unsuccessful assault upon the outworks of Fort Duquesne by Major James Grant and a mixed force of about 800 regulars and militia on 14 September. The assault burned some buildings, but saw the attackers become separated in pre-dawn darkness, opening them to counterattack by a strong Indian and French force that killed or captured nearly 300 of Grant's men.

The most important French initiatives were raids on Loyalhanna on 12 October and 12 November, each designed to scatter livestock and draw British detachments into forest ambush. The raids were ineffective in material terms, although they may have affected the morale of some troops.

Fort Duquesne was not in good condition in 1758. Its fortifications had been damaged by flood, it was short of supplies, and its commander was having great difficulty maintaining the presence of substantial Indian auxiliaries. These conditions became known to Forbes from an English-speaking prisoner taken during the pursuit of the 12 November raiding party, and led to the decision to launch a fast final assault upon the fort. Three col-umns of men, one each from the regular, Pennsylvania, and Virginia troops was organized, commanded respectively by Colonel Bouquet, Colonel Archibald Montgomery of Pennsylvania, and Colonel George Washington of Virginia.

The approach of the British columns served to activate orders which Captain François-Marie Le Marchand de Lignery, commander of Fort Duquesne, had received to evacuate and destroy his post. The fort was a smoking ruin when Forbes's troops arrived on 25 November and celebrated the successful completion of his expedition.

George Geib

References
Douglas Edward Leach, *Arms for Empire: A Military History of the British Colonies in North America, 1607–1763* (1973); S.K. Stevens, D.H. Hunt, A.L. Leonard, eds., *The Papers of Henry Bouquet, Volume II: The Forbes Expedition* (1951).

See also BOUQUET, HENRY; CARLISLE, CAMP NEAR (PENNSYLVANIA); FORT CUMBERLAND (MARYLAND); FORT DUQUESNE (PENNSYLVANIA); FORBES, JOHN; FORKS OF THE OHIO; FORT LOUDOUN (PENNSYLVANIA); FORT LYTTLETON (PENNSYLVANIA); WASHINGTON, GEORGE

Forks of the Ohio
The Forks of the Ohio was the conjunction of the Allegheny and the Monongahela Rivers that formed the Ohio River. This site on the western slopes of the Appalachian Mountains became important in the 1740s and 1750s as France and England vied for control of the Mississippi River watershed. Successive forts constructed at the site after 1753 became the objective of a number of military campaigns.

The actual fortress site between the rivers was described by contemporaries as a rise of ground, 20 to 30 feet above the waters of the slow-moving Monongahela, flowing from the southeast, and the faster and more turbulent Allegheny, coming from the northeast. Nearby lands were described as well timbered, with level stretches suitable for pasture. A small Indian village, Shannopin's Town, was found there, although the primary Indian town of the area, called Logstown by the English, was some 20 miles downriver. The principal tribes encountered in the area were Mingo, Delaware, and Shawnee.

The site was easy of access by either water or Indian trail from any of the three colonies that served as staging areas for imperial ambition, New France, Pennsylvania, and Virginia. It was claimed by the imperial powers on a variety of grounds, including exploration, royal charters and instructions, and Indian treaties. The claims reflected desire for the site as a basis to protect trade routes, control Indian trade, and validate land title. Pennsylvania was represented in the area by a number of traders, including George Croghan and Conrad Weiser. Virginia was represented after 1748 by its Ohio Company, including Christopher Gist and George Washington. France was represented by various traders and officials, including the expedition of Captain Pierre-Joseph Céloron de Blainville in 1749.

In 1753, both the French government and the Virginia Company decided to erect a fort at the Forks. From then until Pontiac's War in 1763, the site was a focus of military ambition by English, French, colonist, and Indian. Four major military efforts, in 1754, 1755, 1758, and 1763, were directed against it.

The first effort witnessed the arrival of forces sent by the Ohio Company of Virginia, their expulsion by a superior French force under Captain Claude-Pierre Pécaudy de Contrecoeur, and the subsequent engagements associated with George Washington and Fort Necessity. The fort erected by the French, Fort Duquesne, then became the target of the unsuccessful Braddock expedition of 1755. Three years later the Forbes expedition forced the withdrawal of the French garrison and the destruction of the fort.

Under British occupation a redesigned fortification, Fort Pitt, and its neighboring village of Pittsburgh, were then built. The site remained a focus for rival claims, including those of Indian leaders who resented the British presence. Fort Pitt was besieged during Pontiac's War in 1763, and relieved by Bouquet's expedition after the Battle of Bushy Run.

George Geib

References

Randolph C. Downes, *Council Fires on the Upper Ohio* (1940); Walter O'Meara, *Guns at the Forks* (1965).

See also BRADDOCK, EDWARD; CROGHAN, GEORGE; FORT DUQUESNE (PENNSYLVANIA); FORBES EXPEDITION OF 1758; GIST, CHRISTOPHER; FORT MACHAULT (PENNSYLVANIA); MONONGAHELA RIVER; OHIO COMPANY; OHIO EXPEDITION OF 1755; PÉCAUDY, CLAUDE PIERRE, DE CONTRECOEUR; FORT PITT (PENNSYLVANIA); WASHINGTON, GEORGE; WEISER, CONRAD

Forts

FOR PARTICULAR FORTS, SEE UNDER INDIVIDUAL NAMES

Forts, Provincial

Throughout the French war period, the English colonial governments built numerous forts on their frontier line. These forts symbolized a permanent military presence, not only in providing a strong defensive structure, but in serving as headquarters for the provincial forces in the area, and as barracks for scouting parties. To the native tribes, these forts embodied the power and the presence of the English government by providing a site for the negotiation and signing of treaties and, when built on their major invasion routes, by disrupting their normal operations in time of war. Both the symbolic and very real threat posed by English forts made them special targets for French and Indian raiding parties and expeditions, especially after the expansion of the frontier line and the accelerated fort building program during the 1720s and 1730s. Because of the special attention focused by the larger enemy raiding forces on the frontier forts, it could be said they became magnets, drawing the fury of the enemy on themselves and away from the exposed communities.

As the French wars began, only a few forts existed on the northern frontier. When Governor Edmund Andros took his small army into Maine during the fall of 1688, he constructed several small forts to house his soldiers during the winter; however, the majority of these structures were quickly abandoned during the subsequent Glorious Revolution the following spring. In 1689, the principal forts on the New England frontier line included one at Pemaquid, Fort Loyal at Falmouth in Casco Bay, a fort on the Merrimack River at the "upper plantations," and another fort similarly situated on the Connecticut River. Of those four major forts, two, Pemaquid and Fort Loyal, were destroyed by the fall of 1690. During the course of King William's War numerous small forts, like Fort Mary at Saco, Maine, in 1693 and a small fort at Newcastle, New Hampshire, at the mouth of the Piscataqua, were built to protect the surrounding regions. In 1692, Governor William Phips replaced the destroyed fort at Pemaquid with a substantial and expensive stone structure which he named William Henry, but this fort was subsequently captured by a French expedition and destroyed in 1696.

By the beginning of Queen Anne's War, and during the course of that conflict, several forts were added to the defenses of New England. The English military engineer for the colonies, Wolfgang W. Romer, rebuilt the fort at Falmouth, Maine, and in New Hampshire, Fort William and Mary which was first proposed in 1697 as a replacement for the small fort protecting Portsmouth harbor, gradually took form under Romer's supervision. The building and maintenance of this fort would be a constant source of controversy throughout the history of provincial New Hampshire. Under the administration of Governor Joseph Dudley, the Massachusetts Bay government completed work on Castle William in Boston harbor, erected fortifications around the trading house at Dunstable, and replaced Fort Mary at Saco, considered to be "ill-placed and ill-built," with a fort at Winter Harbor. Fortifications also existed at Marblehead and Salem.

At the conclusion of Queen Anne's War, the frontier in Maine began to push eastward, and with it the need for protection. The Company of Pejepscot Proprietors, using land at the mouth of the Sagadahoc River which had been purchased from the Indians as well as the heirs of the settlers who had abandoned the region in 1689, established the towns of Brunswick and Topsham in 1715. As part of that settlement the company refurbished and enlarged one of the abandoned Andros forts, calling it Fort George. Four years later they sponsored the construction of Fort Richmond a few miles up the Kennebec to further protect their new settlements. At the same time, the Bay government constructed Fort St. George in present-day Thomaston, adjacent to Penobscot Bay.

The extended period of peace after Dummer's War encouraged the continued expansion of the frontier line and, with it, a virtual boom in the building of forts. In the 1730s, the government of Massachusetts attempted to block the northern invasion route in its growing western frontier by constructing two forts along the Connecticut River, Fort Dummer in present-day Brattleboro, Vermont and a fort at Number Four, and in the 1740s covered the western approaches with Forts Shirley, Pelham, and Massachusetts. Number Four was the most northern post and Massachusetts, situated on the Hoosic River which flowed into the Hudson River above Albany, the most exposed to the west. During King George's War, New Hampshire forces also constructed a fort, called Atkinson after their commander, on Lake Winnipesaukee. Throughout this period, numerous small forts built by communities or other interests were erected along the northern frontier, including Lovewell's fort built on Ossipee Lake, the defensive structure built by Scotch-Irish settlers at Penacook, New Hampshire, and a small fort built at Gorham, Maine.

The provincial forts presented almost a myriad of designs and sizes. Most used wood as their main construction element, but some forts, especially those near the coast, were substantial structures made of stone. Fort George in Brunswick and Fort Mary in Saco were stone forts, as was Fort William Henry at Pemaquid. William Henry had an outside circumference of 737 feet and the wall fronting the sea was 22 feet high and six feet thick at the gun ports. A round tower near the western side stood 29 feet. The fort had 28 gun ports and 18 guns mounted, including six 18-pounders, and usually had a garrison of 60 to 100.

Forts built in the interior, such as the fort at Number Four and Fort Massachusetts, used logs as their main defense. The structure at Number Four had large, connecting buildings of horizontal hewn logs built almost in a square shape. A palisade of upright logs extended around most of the fort. Palisades built in this manner often did not have the logs touching each other with firing platforms as our folklore commonly depicts, but were actually planted several inches apart. In this case the palisade only kept the enemy at a distance, while the defenders fired from the buildings within. The palisade of Fort Massachusetts had logs laid horizontally over a foundation of stone, the northeast angle protected by a watch tower. Inside the fort a large log house and several smaller structures served both as barracks and blockhouses.

Similar in construction, the fortification at Gorham, Maine, typifies the small community

F

fort. Built on the highest point of land, the principal structure was a building 50 feet long made of hewn logs surrounded by a palisade of timber with two flankers or watch towers. An excellent description of the palisade was provided in 1757 when the proprietors of the town voted to have it repaired. "Voted money, per foot for stockading the fort where the walls are defective, supposed to be one hundred feet, and to be done with spruce, pine, or hemlock timber, and the bark peeled off, and to be thirteen feet long and ten inches in diameter, to stand three feet in the ground and ten above, where the rocks will admit of digging three feet; and to be lined with six inch stuff, peeled as the other timber." The difference in appearance between these small forts and the larger garrisons was very small, distinguished only by the fact that garrisons were privately owned, and the forts belonged to the community or the province. As the French wars progressed, and the frontier began to expand, it became the practice of the proprietors of new communities and the provincial governments to build a fort for the protection, not to mention the encouragement, of the settlers.

The cost of construction of frontier forts, as well as the maintenance, could amount to a considerable burden. When the Pejepscot Company proposed to settle the communities of Brunswick and Topsham, Maine, they were ordered by the government not only to provide a fort for the safety of the settlers, but a road for communication and the movement of troops. Arrangements for building the road and fort would be made by the proprietors, and the cost would be borne by the Bay government. However, despite the fact the shell of a stone fort built by Andros in 1688 remained, the proprietors understood the Bay government wanted "a Wooden Fort on account of the cheapness of it." The directors of the Pejepscot Company estimated the cost of a wooden fort, based on a similar one built a few years earlier at Winter Harbor, to be £500. The proprietors suggested the government kick in the £500, send 15 soldiers for laborers, and they would pay for the rest to restore the stone fort. The fort, to be named "George," would be 50 feet square with four bastions or blockhouses, two made of wood "at our own charge," and barracks to house the garrison. The proprietors only asked that £300 be advanced to pay for materials.

The General Court agreed to this proposal and worked commenced on the fort. The final costs included: labor charges for masons, carpenters, smiths, laborers (mostly the 15 provincial soldiers), and "Mr. Watts Boy cooking the pot"; materials such as shell lime, stone lime, more than 10,000 feet of boards, pine plank, oak plank, glass casements, hinges, and a "large lock for the Gate"; provisions and drink; the hiring of sloops to transport materials; and "small expenses" including "1 horse lost," "loss and wear of tools," and £30 "allowed Mr. Watts his trouble." The total cost for the completion of Fort George came to £688/9/4, of which the government of Massachusetts contributed £500 for the fort and £12/2 for the subsistence of the soldiers.

Of course, Fort George was only a small installation, the cost of the larger provincial forts caused even more controversy, pitting colonies against the British government and against each other. After the close of King William's War, the British government insisted Massachusetts replace Fort William Henry at Pemaquid, which had been destroyed by the French in 1696. They believed the presence of a fort at Pemaquid helped to reassert the British claim to disputed territory and would discourage Indian incursions by covering the Kennebec, Damariscotta, and Sheepscot Rivers. The fort would thus become another strategic and political card in their dealings with the French. The Bay government balked at this order, however, as they felt the site offered little strategic advantage to justify the frightful cost involved.

Fort William and Mary in Portsmouth harbor caused similar friction between governors and assemblies. When Governor Bellomont urged the building of a fort on Great Island in 1697, the New Hampshire assembly agreed to listen to proposals, but they were astonished when the engineer Romer presented his construction estimate of £6000. The assembly pleaded poverty and with the death of Bellomont, the project was put on a back burner until the commencement of Queen Anne's War.

At that time the assembly voted £500 in grain and other supplies, and £500 in labor provided by inhabitants pressed on a rotating basis who worked for their subsistence only. Unfortunately, the grain did not realize the price originally thought, and so the contribution was devalued to £450. In addition, Romer reported that the labor provided consumed far more than they worked. Though reported completed in 1705, the fort required constant repair and became a continuing source of friction concerning its maintenance costs. In July 1708, George Vaughn, agent for New Hampshire, reported that the fort had never really been completed and was decaying because the province could not afford to pay for its upkeep.

The controversies and arguments over the support of William and Mary would continue throughout the French wars. At one point, the British government attempted to have Massachusetts pay part of the cost for William and Mary, but the Bay government flatly refused, citing New Hampshire's failure to support the defense of other areas. The controversy here concerned the upkeep of another frontier fort, Fort Dummer on the Connecticut River. Built in a disputed area between New Hampshire and Massachusetts, Dummer was found to be in New Hampshire territory when the border was finally settled, so the Bay government naturally felt New Hampshire should pay for the fort. However, the New Hampshire assembly refused, pointing out, with some justice, that Dummer gave very little protection to their communities and, in fact, was designed to cover the Massachusetts towns to the south. In the end Massachusetts had to garrison and maintain both Fort Dummer and Number Four to its north.

The provincial governments kept soldiers posted in their forts even in times of peace, although in most cases this involved only a token force. Some forts became important trading posts, or "truck houses," which required the presence of men to handle the lucrative Indian trade. Of course, during declared wars the number of soldiers at provincial forts increased substantially, and often included not only the garrison, but men assigned to patrols and raiding parties.

The normal tour of duty in a provincial fort was one year. Any longer and the government would begin to receive complaints and petitions from the soldiers, their families, or their communities demanding their release. But other soldiers became long-term residents of the fort and even permanent members of the local community. For most who stayed, however, the lure was less spectacular. Their extended tour was simply the natural consequence of their chosen profession or particular assignment. The commanders, interpreters, gunsmiths, blacksmiths, and even chaplains all had the potential for extended service at frontier forts—to become, as gunsmith Ebenezer Nutting did while stationed at Casco Bay, Maine, during Dummer's War, a "resident of Falmouth in the King's service."

The presence of families in provincial forts was not unusual. Although certainly not an extensive practice, it was not uncommon for soldiers to bring their wives and children when posted at frontier forts. Women and children were present at Fort William Henry when it fell in 1696 and at Fort Massachusetts in 1746. In assessing the disaster at Fort William Henry, Francis Parkman concluded that concern for the safety of the families led to the fort's quick capitulation. However, although it certainly entered into the garrison's discussions, the failure of both William Henry and Massachusetts to withstand a siege involved far more compelling reasons than the presence of families.

In addition to easing the pain of separation and reducing the problems of subsistence for poorer families while the husband was serving on the frontier, wives and children may have helped the soldiers endure garrison life which consisted mainly of fatigue duty, watches, and boredom. The most constant chore, and the most dangerous, was the cutting and hauling of firewood from the surrounding forest. Other chores proved less dangerous and more mundane. Repairs, digging wells and latrines, planting gardens, standing watch, and patrols filled the hours, as well as such diversions as wrestling and drinking.

Soldiers at forts near population centers could moonlight, or take jobs in the community to supplement their income and fill the time. Usually these were odd jobs, cutting firewood or splitting shingles and clapboards, but soldiers with specific skills, such as gunsmiths or cordwainers, could employ them for the benefit of the community and their own pocketbooks. For the forts removed from frontier communities, there was no chance for moonlighting, and for them, time could weigh very heavy. Long tours of duty and the inevitable boredom of garrison life always made desertion a problem for post commanders.

The forts could not stop all the raids on the frontier, but then no defense could totally stop the small Indian raiding parties. The provincial forts on the northern frontier provided a military presence and represented the authority of the English government, and thus provided an obvious political target for the French and Indians. They also threatened the line of retreat for larger raiding parties, especially those built on major invasion routes. As a result, the

F

French and Indians began sending their larger raiding forces against the provincial forts rather than the frontier communities. Thus, though expensive to build and maintain, even in defeat and destruction the provincial forts were magnets that drew the fury of large enemy raiding forces away from the frontier towns.

Steven C. Eames

References

Henry E. Dunnack, *Maine Forts* (1924); Steven C. Eames, "Rustic Warriors: Warfare and the Provincial Soldier on the Northern Frontier, 1689–1748," Ph.D. Dissertation, University of New Hampshire (1989).

See also GARRISON HOUSES

Fox

The Fox Indians (Mesquakies or Red Earth People; Renards; Outagamis) were living in eastern Wisconsin at the time of their first contacts with the French around 1670. The Fox unsuccessfully sought to establish themselves as middlemen between the French and the Sioux, one of their two traditional enemies, the other being the Ojibwas (Chippewas) in northern Wisconsin.

In 1697, the western posts were closed as a result of the termination by Louis XIV of the fur trade west of Montreal. In 1701, Antoine de Lamothe Cadillac established Fort Pontchartrain at Detroit in order to provide a more accessible trading location than Montreal for the western tribes. By 1711, a large number of Fox and Mascoutens had joined the volatile mix of tribes at Detroit, now commanded by Jacques-Charles Renaud Dubuisson. Intending to dominate the post, the Fox and their allies lost no time in harassing and insulting not only the Ottawas and Miamis near Detroit, but the French settlement as well. The latter two tribes joined with the Potawatomis and the Illinois in a campaign to wipe out the Foxes and their allies, the Mascoutens and Kickapoos.

In 1712, the Fox built a fort within easy gunshot range of Fort Pontchartrain de Detroit and began to besiege the outnumbered Detroit French and Hurons. The arrival of 600 allied warriors under Ottawa war chief Saguima and Potawatomi chief Makisabé reversed the situation, with the besiegers now the besieged. The Fox under Pemoussa resisted heroically for 19 days before slipping away during a rainstorm

on the night of 30 May 1712. The pursuing French and their allies cornered the Fox, and all but 100 of the Fox warriors were slaughtered. The French reported the Fox and Mascouten dead at 1,000.

The Wisconsin Fox, aided by their Mascouten and Kickapoo allies, now wrought havoc along the French trade routes. In 1716, an expedition of 800 Frenchmen and allied Indians reached and besieged the fortified Fox village at the Butte des Morts on the Fox River. After three days, the Fox negotiated a peace treaty with the French commander which held for several years.

By 1718, the Kickapoos and Mascoutens were raiding the Illinois country which, to the dismay of the Canadians, had just been made part of the Louisiana colony, together with its fur trade. Despite the efforts of the Fox peace faction headed by Chief Ouchala, the Fox were drawn into the warfare, encouraged and supplied by the commanders of the upper country posts, trade rivals of the upper Louisiana (Illinois) French. By 1725, the year in which the aged Governor General Philippe de Rigaud de Vaudreuil died, the Illinois fur trade was totally paralyzed. The acting governor general succeeded in achieving peace in 1726, the year in which the new governor general, Charles de Beauharnois de La Boische, arrived in New France.

In 1727, Beauharnois planned for the following year a major, secret pre-emptive strike against the Fox villages in Wisconsin. When the French and Indian army descended upon the Fox villages just west of Lake Winnebago, they found that their quarry had fled. The French burned the Fox villages, forts, and cornfields as well as those of the Foxes' nearby allies, the Winnebagos. Within the next few months, the Sauks, Mascoutens, Kickapoos, and Winnebagos abandoned the Fox and joined the French alliance while the Sioux and the Iowas refused the Fox sanctuary. In 1729, and again in early 1730, the French-allied Ottawas, Menominees, Chippewas, and Winnebagos attacked the Fox villages, killing 500 men, women, and children.

Most of the 900 remaining Fox decided to seek refuge en masse among the Iroquois, and Fox envoys negotiated safe passage for them from the Ouiatanons (Weas) to cross the Wabash River. In August 1730, cornered by French-allied Indians on the Illinois plains some 100 miles southeast of Starved Rock, the 360 Fox warriors and their families built a remarkable fort in which they withstood a one-month siege by more than 1,400 allied French and Indians from several midwestern posts before slipping away. But on 9 September 1730, their pursuers caught them and, by the end of the day, over 400 of the Fox men, women, and children had been killed outright or burned to death. Only about 60 warriors succeeded in escaping back to the handful of Fox who had remained in Wisconsin. The captives were distributed as slaves among the Indian allies.

In 1731, the remaining Fox sent two of their new chiefs to Montreal to beg mercy from Beauharnois. Beauharnois granted them conditional peace, with a definitive treaty to be concluded in September 1732. However, as soon as the 1731 agreement was recorded, he approved a sneak winter attack on the Wisconsin lodges where some 300 Fox, who had been released by their captors after the 1730 defeat, were living. Two hundred sixteen were killed on the spot or shortly thereafter, and another 92 were taken to Detroit where they were killed by the Hurons on the urging of the French second in command.

Beauharnois, in reporting this achievement, stated that he hoped "for the total destruction" of the remaining Fox. He sent an officer to Green Bay to bring in all the survivors, who had been granted sanctuary by the Sauks, to be dispersed among the domiciled tribes or to have the French-allied tribes kill them "so as not to leave one of the race alive." But Beauharnois's planned genocide failed when the Sauks and Fox resisted, killing or wounding 28 French officers and men and 17 allied Indians. The Sauks and Fox fled to Iowa where, in 1735, a French-led punitive expedition failed to exact vengeance, returning to Montreal in humiliation.

The western Indian nations, aware since 1732 of Beauharnois's duplicity and attempted genocide of the Fox, increasingly flocked to their support. Fearing the defection of the upper country tribes, Beauharnois finally granted a general pardon to the Sauks and Fox in 1737. Formalizing the pardon in 1738, he sent an officer to live among the Fox, who from that point on were counted among the "children of Onontio (the governor general of New France)."

Joseph L. Peyser

References

Charles Callender, "Fox," in *Handbook of North American Indians,* Vol. 15, *Northeast,* ed. by Bruce G. Trigger (1978); "Glossary of Indian Tribal Names," *Dictionary of Canadian Biography,* Vol. 2, 1701 to 1740 (1969); Louise Phelps Kellogg, "The Fox Indians During the French Regime," in *Proceedings of the State Historical Society of Wisconsin at Its Fifty-fifth Annual Meeting* (1908); Joseph L. Peyser, "The Fate of the Fox Survivors: A Dark Chapter in the History of the French in the Upper Country, 1726–1737," *Wisconsin Magazine of History,* 73 (1989–1990):82–110.

See also CAHOKIA-FOX RAID; FOX FORT (ILLINOIS) AND SIEGE; ILLINOIS; KICKAPOO; OJIBWA; FORT PONCHARTRAIN DE DETROIT (MICHIGAN)

Fox Fort (Illinois) and Siege (1730)

In the summer of 1730 nearly 1,000 Fox Indians, including some 360 warriors, fled their Wisconsin homeland in an effort to take refuge among the Iroquois to the east. Closely pursued and harried in the Illinois country by 200 French-allied Kickapoos, Mascoutens, Illinois, and Potawatomis, the Foxes were obliged to stop and make a last stand. Near the end of July, about 100 miles to the southeast of Starved Rock on a vast, treeless prairie somewhere between the Illinois and Wabash Rivers, the Fox fought off their pursuers in a day-long encounter. The Fox took possession of a grove of trees on a rise on the northwest bank of a small river and proceeded to fortify the site. Their assailants dug in nearby to cut off the most likely escape routes, and sent runners to request reinforcements from the French at Fort de Chartres in the Illinois country, Fort St. Joseph (Niles, Michigan), and the Ouiatanon post (West Lafayette, Indiana).

On 17 August, Lieutenant Robert Groston de Saint-Ange arrived at the siege from Fort de Chartres with 100 Frenchmen and 500 Illinois and Missouri Indians. On 21 August, Lieutenant Nicolas-Antoine Coulon de Villiers, senior officer present and commander in chief of the allies, arrived from Fort St. Joseph with about 30 Frenchmen and 300 Potawatomis, Miamis, Sauks, Kickapoos, and Mascoutens. Also on 21 August, as many as 400 Ouiatanons and Piankeshaws arrived from the ungarrisoned Ouiatanon post led by the resident trader Simon Réaume, accompanied by two dozen Frenchmen. On 1 September, Lieutenant Nicolas-Joseph de Noyelles arrived from the Miami post with ten Frenchmen and 200 Miamis, bringing

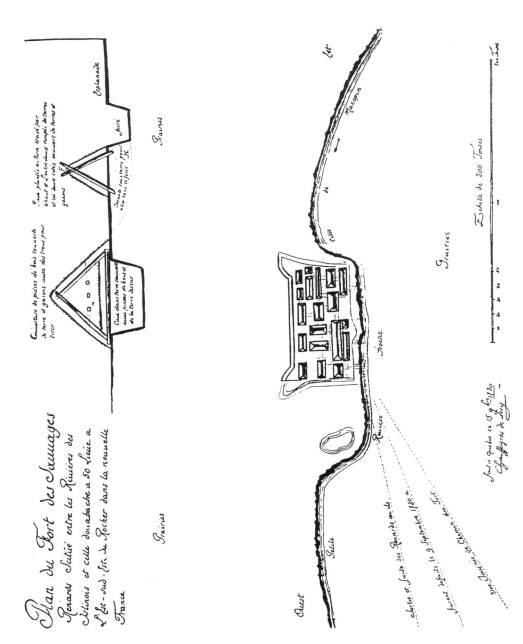

Plan du Fort des Sauuages

Renards Scitué entre les Riuières des
Scilinois et celle douabache a 50 lieüe a
l'Est-Sud-Est du Rocher dans la nouuelle
France

Prairies

Prairies

Esplanade

Couuerture de pièces de bois couuerte
de terre et gasons auec des trous pour
tirer

Caux dans Nerre Couuerte
auec pieux de bout
de la terre dessus

Une palisade en bois croisé par
le bas et l'intervalle rempli de terre
et les deux cotés arrousont de terre et
gazon

Toise

Fossé

Fossé

Même lin terre pour
rire dans le fossé FH

Ouest

Petite

Riuiere

Cuite

de

Roche

Macapin

Est

Prairies

chûtes et suite des Renards au 11 ....
furent défaits le 9 Septembre 1730 a . . . .
que Jacques de Charnis été Fort. . . . .

Echelle de 200 Toises

Fait à quebec ce 15 9 bre 1730
Gaultier de Levy

Fox Fort.

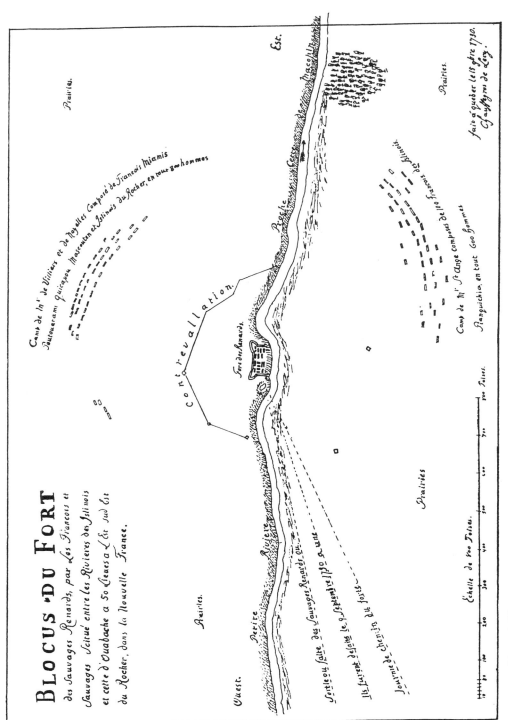

F

Fox Fort and Siege, 1730.

the total number of besiegers to around 1,600 men.

Before the arrival of the allied reinforcements the Fox had had the time to build ingenious defenses, taking advantage of the natural features of the site they had selected. The fort was situated on a slope originally covered by a grove of trees on the northwest bank of a small river. The Foxes also occupied and fortified a hill less than 200 feet to the west of the fort which it overlooked. They built an underground passageway linking the top of this position with the interior of their fort.

The men felled many of the trees at the main fort site to construct a palisade about 12- to 14-feet high on the three sides not protected by the steep river bank. The palisade walls were constructed of two rows of stakes planted at an angle in the ground about six feet apart and crossed near the top. The wall interior was filled with earth and the exterior was covered with earth and sod as protection against fire. The earth was taken from a ditch or trench dug outside the walls which ran around the fort. This ditch was six feet wide and five feet deep, and access to it from inside the fort was provided by underground passageways. The Fox farsightedly left standing within the fort enough trees to provide shade to protect themselves from the blazing sun. Outside the ditch, the land had been cleared to provide the defenders with a clear line of fire. The river side was protected only by two rows of stakes atop the 15-foot embankment, and underground passages were constructed from within the fort to the river to provide the besieged with protected access to water.

Inside the fort, the Fox had dug numerous fortified positions with sloping wooden walls and roofs all covered with sod and with holes for defensive firing in the event the enemy gained entry into the fort. Each position was dug seven or eight feet into the ground and all were interconnected with underground passages. The fort compound was estimated to be from about one to three acres in size, with its river side about 500 feet in length.

Without mortars or cannon, the besiegers were unable to breach the walls. The French built two gun towers (*caveliers*) which prevented Fox sorties and then had a zig-zag attack trench opened on the north side through which they unsuccessfully attempted to set fire to the wooden defenses. This well-designed fortification was to resist successfully for a month the

attacks of an army outnumbering the defenders by four to one. On the night of 8 September, the starving Fox abandoned their fort, only to be tracked down one day later. During and after the ensuing battle, only 50 or 60 Fox warriors escaped, while about 500 Fox men, women, and children were killed. About 350 Fox were taken by the allied tribes as slaves. This defeat marked the end of the Fox military threat to the French in the Midwest. Despite numerous attempts to identify the fort site, it has not been definitively located.

Joseph L. Peyser

References

Joseph L. Peyser, "The 1730 Fox Fort: A Recently Discovered Map Throws New Light on Its Siege and Location," *Journal of the Illinois State Historical Society*, LXXIII (1980):201–213; ———, "The 1730 Siege of the Foxes: Two Maps by Canadian Participants Provide Additional Information on the Fort and Its Location," *Illinois Historical Journal*, LXXX (1987):147–154.
———, "The Fate of the Fox Survivors: A Dark Chapter in the History of the French in the Upper Country, 1726–1737," *Wisconsin Magazine of History*, 73 (1989–1990): 91–93, 102–110; "1730: Victory over the Foxes," *Collections of the State Historical Society of Wisconsin*, 17 (1906): 109–118; J.F. Steward, "Conflicting Accounts Found in Early Illinois History," *Transactions of the Illinois State Historical Society*, 13 (1908):251–258.

See also FORT DE CHARTRES (ILLINOIS); FOX; KICKAPOO

France

French attitude toward its overseas possessions was at best ambivalent and at worst indifferent. France's rulers could never decide whether to exploit and plunder the New World, or to colonize and Christianize it. In trying to do both, they succeeded in doing neither. With little apparent advantage to be gained overseas, France's primary effort centered on the dynastic ambitions, economic competition, and military opportunities in Europe. War and society in the New World remained on the periphery of French interest.

As long as Frenchmen were content to raid Spanish treasure fleets or trade with Atlantic coastal tribes, colonial conflict was primarily a fight for booty. Permanent settlements in 1609 and subsequent expansion into the interior, however, led to a century-long war with the Iroquois Confederacy for territory and trade. Finally, confrontation with expanding English colonies after 1689 meant a 70-year struggle for control of the continent.

Despite the shift in opponents and issues over three centuries, certain patterns persisted. With French attention centered on Europe, New France adopted an aggressive defense to keep its enemies from mobilizing their superior manpower and resources. Privateers waging *guerre de course* and wilderness raiders fighting *petite guerre* attacked isolated targets, disrupted communications and kept the enemy off-balance.

Within a decade of Columbus's first voyage, Frenchmen were gathering Newfoundland cod, trading for northern furs and Brazilian logwood, and raiding the Spanish Caribbean. Royal interest soon followed. Cortez's conquests and Magellan's explorations encouraged Francis I to send Giovanni da Verrazano in 1524 to survey and claim the Atlantic coast from Florida to Maine. But neither Verrazano, nor subsequent voyages by Jacques Cartier between 1534 and 1541, found either a new route to Asia to challenge Magellan or Indian kingdoms to rival those of Cortez.

The Iberians might allow France to explore the frozen wastes of Canada, but activity further south met with a harsh response. Huguenot expeditions by Villegaignon to Brazil in 1555, and by Laudonniere and Ribault along the Carolina and Florida coast a decade later, were destroyed by the Portuguese (vs. Villegaignon) and then the Spanish (vs. Laudonniere). It would not be until 1598, with peace in Europe and a religious truce at home, that France would again look overseas. Even then it took a decade of false starts before a permanent trade post was established at Quebec by Samuel de Champlain in 1608.

In effect, Champlain anticipated the colony's strategic and diplomatic development over the next century and a half. The natural defenses at Quebec were improved to command the St. Lawrence, the island of Montreal was surveyed as a logical base for further expansion, and a compact agricultural colony was proposed. A skilled explorer and cartographer, Champlain extended French knowledge and influence south along the Richelieu to the lake he named for himself in 1609, and west to the Great Lakes in 1615.

Champlain's legacy also included enmity with Canada's Iroquois and English neighbors. Trade with the western Hurons and Algonquins secured the colony's economy; but as the French soon discovered, economic ties meant political alliances, and Champlain inherited his trading partners' conflict with the Five Nations. French settlements soon attracted the attention of his English neighbors as well. Port Royal was devastated by Virginian Samuel Argall in 1613. At Quebec and Acadia, where trade monopolists did little to promote either colonization or agricultural development, there were fewer than 100 inhabitants when the colony was captured by the Kirke brothers during the English wars of 1628–1632.

Yet, colonization was inherent in French claims to the New World. Francis I and his successors challenged Papal grants of new lands to the Iberians on the principle of prior discovery and formal possession. Because France thus must occupy any territory it wished to claim, trade comptoirs (factories) gradually evolved into settler colonies. Coastal fishing stations and trading posts were fortified and manned year around; missionaries wanted a formal European colony as a model to promote Indian acculturation and conversion; the need to organize France's growing commitments brought administrative centers. By the time of Richelieu's ministry, colonization was an established fact.

Permanent settlements meant permanent defenses. For security the colony relied on geographic advantage, political centralization, and Indian alliances. Military and political authority was concentrated on the colonial governor, who commanded a small but permanent garrison of French regulars after 1665. Reorganized in 1690 as the troupes de la marine, the force became increasingly "Canadianized" as its officers, if not its men, were appointed from within the colony. From the colony's strategic center at Quebec, interior lines of communication extending along the St. Lawrence and its connecting waterways allowed for a coordinated strategy over half a continent.

Militia units formed the numerical bulk of Canada's defense force. While its population remained minuscule compared to its English neighbors, all able-bodied men between 16 to 60 were enrolled into unpaid companies organized at the parish level. Militia, buttressed by *coureurs de bois,* proved effective guerrilla fighters; but military service drew civilian sol-

F

diers from essential agricultural and economic activities. The same was true for Indian society, where war diverted warriors from hunting and trapping. Thus, Franco-Indian campaigns were necessarily short and often conducted during the winter season.

Canada's outer line of defense rested on its Indian allies. Abenaki, Micmac, and Maliseet villages formed a wilderness screen for Acadia and supplied raiders against New England. Villages of mission Iroquois and Abenaki, resettled along the St. Lawrence, offered an additional striking force and formed a strategic reserve. In the west, French traders and missionaries secured alliances with the Hurons and Algonquins; but they also generated competition and opposition with Albany and the Five Nations. In 1649, a devastating Iroquois assault destroyed Huronia, threatened Canada's links to the interior, and kept Montreal virtually under siege for a decade. Now it was Canada which suffered the effects of guerrilla war.

France was also expanding in the Indies. During Richelieu's ministry the Lesser Antilles, Guadeloupe, and Martinique were occupied, while he and Mazarin encouraged colonization of Guiana. As in Canada, French expansion generated native opposition and a bitter war ensued with the Caribs during the 1650s in the islands and on the mainland. At mid-century, France was on the defensive throughout the Americas. Mazarin's concern with the Fronde until 1654, and war with Spain until 1659, left the 10,000 French in the Caribbean and the 2,500 Canadians along the St. Lawrence to fend for themselves.

Within a decade, however, Louis XIV and the ministry of Jean-Baptiste Colbert opened a new colonial era. France's fleet was revitalized, new trading companies were chartered, while immigration swelled Canada's population and that of the Indies. Experienced military men were appointed colonial governors and civilian intendents served as fiscal and administrative watchdogs. In Canada, the 1,200-man Carignan-Salières Regiment was sent to punish the Mohawk villages and show the Five Nations that their homeland was not inviolable; an illusive enemy, a terrible winter campaign, and almost impossible logistics also proved how difficult it would be to mount large-scale wilderness operations by French regulars.

Colbert, as had Champlain, wanted an economically diverse, compact colony along the St. Lawrence. But Canada's grain competed with that of France, and its naval stores proved too costly. Dependent on furs and Indian alliances, French influence was extended through Wisconsin by Louis Jolliet and Jacques Marquette in 1673, and by René-Robert Cavelier de La Salle to the Gulf coast a decade later.

Outflanked by the French along the upper lakes, the Iroquois drove resident Algonquians from southern Ontario and lower Michigan. When the Five Nations moved into Illinois in 1680, Iroquois and French expansionist streams again collided. For the next 20 years, France and its allies hounded the confederacy until the league accepted an enforced truce. Peace with the Iroquois in 1701 would secure Canada's western flank to mid-century.

After 1689, wilderness conflict merged with the larger European war. From the English perspective, it appeared that France had encircled and hemmed in the seaboard colonies. Despite an island empire which extended some 4,000 miles from the St. Lawrence to the Gulf, however, it was Canada which felt surrounded and on the defensive. English ships were on Hudson Bay, traders from Carolina penetrated the lower Mississippi Valley, while New Englanders were pressing the Atlantic fisheries and expanding on Acadia from Maine. Outnumbered 20 to one, Canada's heartland along the St. Lawrence and its flanks were vulnerable.

The French fell back on their inner defenses. Canada's core along the St. Lawrence was anchored by the natural fortress at Quebec City and by the fortified settlements at Montreal and Three Rivers, while its extremities were secured by a network of strong points placed along major access routes. Acadia and the Atlantic approaches were guarded by Port Royal and satellite posts along the Bay of Fundy. In the continental interior, fortified settlements controlled communications bottlenecks and major trade routes from Biloxi and Mobile on the Gulf and lower Mississippi to Detroit and Fort Frontenac on the Great Lakes. A similar series of outposts extended south along the Richelieu River-Lake Champlain route toward the Iroquois homeland and New York.

Canada's defensive network paralleled the system of mutually supporting fortresses created by Sébastien Le Prestre de Vauban to defend France's vulnerable frontiers in Europe. From the Netherlands to the Pyrennes, strategically placed defenses delayed enemy penetration and allowed reinforcements time to respond. Once the attack was contained, strong points then provided a staging area for a counter-assault against the invading force or an invasion of enemy home territory. By the end of the century, Vauban's line of fortresses formed a strategic frontier which offered the opportunity for both defensive and offensive operations.

So apparently did North American forts. They, too, were defensive "trip-wires" to warn of attack, and they provided bases for offensive action by privateers or guerrilla raiders. There was, however, a crucial difference. Vauban's system assumed that fortresses only need withstand a short siege before the defenders would be relieved. But in America, distance and the lack of a mobile reserve meant there would be no assistance; nor could aid from France arrive in time.

Unless the colony's Indian allies could keep attackers at a distance, its outposts must surely fall to a determined enemy as they did at Quebec in 1628, Port Royal in 1710, Louisbourg in 1745 and 1758, and at virtually every wilderness fort attacked during the Seven Years' War. Canada's best defense was to prevent its opponents from mobilizing their superior manpower and resources. But material shortages and difficult terrain meant that campaigns against the seaboard colonies after 1689 were primarily low-intensity operations.

Even had Canada been capable of supporting a major offensive, there was no strategic center to attack. As Britain would discover after 1775, the seaboard colonies had no target comparable to Quebec, whose loss could determine the course of a war. Despite its demographic and economic weakness, Canada had no choice but to fight a protracted guerrilla action to divert enemy attention until fighting in Europe decided the larger conflict.

Although Versailles urged an attack on New York in 1689, the colony was reeling from attacks by the Iroquois on Lachine and by the English on Port Royal. Governor Louis de Buade de Frontenac instead launched a series of spoiling raids against frontier settlements in New Hampshire (Salmon Falls), Maine (Falmouth), and New York (Schenectedy). Canada's ability to attack such widely separated targets in turn forced each colony to ignore its neighbor and concentrate on home defense. The failure of the Atlantic seaboard colonies to develop a common strategy, or to create a coordinated defense, was thus as much a product of French tactics as it was a result of English disunity.

For New England this was a new kind of war. In place of local opposition from Pequots or Wampanoags against which they could mobilize their superior strength, they now faced a more distant enemy backed by European power; this demanded greater organization, resources, and outside aid. Rather than dissipate their energy against the outer screen of Indian villages and French forts, Anglo-Americans would concentrate on the centers of French strength along the St. Lawrence.

In 1690, an amphibious attack by Sir William Phips on Quebec was combined with an overland assault against Montreal. English strategy was thus more direct—and more decisive. It was also complex. Land and naval forces from England had to be combined with those gathered from several colonies, and then coordinated into a two-pronged assault with one wing moving by sea and the other operating 200 miles inland from upper New York. Not surprisingly, assaults by Phips in 1690 and by Sir Hovenden Walker in 1711 fell victim to ineffective leadership, poor logistics, or just bad luck. In 1759, Jeffrey Amherst and James Wolfe were more efficient and more fortunate.

The *guerre de course* at sea mirrored *la petite guerre* on land. While the naval defeat at La Hogue in 1692 did not destroy French sea power, it did mark a change in mood and strategy. The cost of maintaining a battle fleet became an expensive luxury as long as a continental, rather than a colonial, strategy dominated French planning. On both sides privateers, often in combination with warships, attacked commerce or raided coastal settlements.

In the Indies, renegade buccaneers comparable to Canada's *coureurs de bois* provided an undisciplined and often ruthless raiding force which destroyed plantations, stole slaves, and waged economic war on the sugar industry. And the British retaliated in kind. For the most part, inhabitants on both sides were content to retreat to mountain refuges and simply wait until boredom, greed, or disease drove off their attackers; thus war brought a major disruption of trade and destruction of property, but there was limited loss of life among the civilian population.

The Treaty of Utrecht in 1713 ended a generation of rather desultory and inconclusive colonial fighting. It was not that the issues were unimportant. English penetration of the North American interior threatened to flank Canada and open the road to Mexico. Conversely, with the Bourbon Family Compact after 1702, that same road might be open to France. When that became impossible, territory in New France was sacrificed to maintain French interests in Europe. The loss of Acadia, Hudson Bay, Newfoundland, and St. Kitts was serious but not fatal. And France was more than compensated with St. Domingue in 1697.

For the next 30 years, France and Britain waged a diplomatic and commercial cold war that on occasion turned hot. When English traders, land companies, and forts at Oswego and Halifax threatened Canada's flanks, the French strengthened their outer defenses and built the massive fortress of Louisbourg to guard the St. Lawrence; and when England and France began the last round of colonial wars in 1744, Louisbourg promptly fell to a combined New England-imperial attack. Few strongpoints could withstand a prolonged siege and Louisbourg was simply too isolated, and French sea power too weak to provide relief. Although Louisbourg was returned by the Treaty of Aix-la-Chapelle in 1748, in the wilderness interior, France was losing the battle for Indian trade and alliances.

Although New York and the Iroquois frontier remained quiet, after 1713, traders from Pennsylvania and Virginia penetrated the Appalachian barrier. Forced on the defensive, the French became increasingly bellicose. When a show of force by Pierre-Joseph Céleron de Blainville against English traders was rebuffed by tribes along the Ohio in 1750, French raiders destroyed the pro-English village of Pickawillany and its chief, La Demoiselle. Versailles then built a chain of forts south from Lake Erie to drive the English from the Ohio country. When first Virginia and then London challenged the French move in 1754, it triggered the last colonial war.

For 60 years, the English colonies had been kept divided and on the defensive. Now London moved to provide strategic unity, Major General Edward Braddock was appointed commander in chief, William Johnson was named superintendent of Indian Affairs, and 1,000 regulars were sent to North America. The French population of Acadia was deported, and a fleet was ordered to intercept French reinforcements for Canada. France responded by sending Jean-Armand, Baron de Dieskau and 3,000 regulars, most of whom escaped the blockade. For both sides, the colonial dispute had become an imperial war.

Once again, Franco-Indian *la petite guerre* stymied the English. Braddock's force was routed near modern Pittsburgh and the general was killed. For the next three years, the backcountry reeled under a series of devastating attacks as Canada remained secure behind its screen of Indian allies and wilderness outposts. Unfortunately for Canada, French strategy was too effective. For France, war in the colonies was always a secondary theater where disproportionate English resources might be tied down while the major issues were being decided in Europe. After 1757, William Pitt accepted the challenge.

When Pitt committed the bulk of Britain's navy and 20,000 regulars to the colonies, Canada was overmatched. Attacked in detail, Forts Duquesne at the Ohio, Niagara and Frontenac on the Great Lakes, Ticonderoga and Crown Point along the Champlain-Richelieu system, and Louisbourg at the Atlantic gateway each fell. Already on the defensive, Canada was torn by a bitter controversy over grand strategy. Canadian-born Governor Vaudreuil demanded greater use of Canadian militia and Indians for *la petite guerre*, while French General Louis-Joseph de Montcalm denigrated the use of irregulars and relied on his French *troupes de terre*. The tradition of English disunity and of French centralized command had been reversed at a decisive moment.

England made full use of its sea power to blockade the St. Lawrence and concentrate superior forces on land. Material shortages and loss of the western forts in turn led to the defection or isolation of France's Indian allies. Within a year, Canada's outer defense of forts and Indian allies was breached and Britain was free to concentrate on the St. Lawrence. Well before Montcalm and Wolfe met at Quebec in 1759, the result in North America had been decided.

Over the course of three centuries, war in the New World evolved from a series of plundering expeditions into a struggle for continental dominance. As the value of northern fur and fish declined relative to the sugar, slaves, and tobacco of the Indies, French North America became a strategic rather than an economic possession. Its primary functions were to contain the English colonies and distract Britain from the main center of French interest in Europe. By mid-century, Canada had clearly failed in its first mission—to keep the Anglo-Americans behind the Appalachian barrier. Ironically, after 1754, it succeeded all too well in its second task of diverting London's attention toward North America. By 1763, with no longer any significant strategic role to play in imperial policy, Canada was expendable.

David R. Farrell

References

P.W. Bamford, *Forests and French Seapower, 1661–1789* (1956); Andre Corvisier, "La Societe militaire francaise au temps de la nouvelle france," *Histoire Sociale/Social History* (1977):219–227; Charles Cole, *French Mercantilism, 1683–1700* (1965); Louise Dechene, ed., *La Correspondence de Vauban Relative au Canada* (1968); William J. Eccles, "The Social, Economic, and Political Significance of the Military Establishment in New France," *Canadian Historical Review*, LII (1971): 1–22; ———, *France in America* (1990).

Robert Goldstein, *French-Iroquois Diplomatic and Military Relations, 1609–1701* (1969); Gerald Graham, *Empire of the North Atlantic: the Maritime Struggle for North America* (1958); Cornelius Jaenen, *Friend and Foe: Aspects of French-Amerindian Cultural Contact in the Sixteenth and Seventeenth Centuries* (1976).

Francis Jennings, *The Ambiguous Iroquois Empire: The Covenant Chain Confederation of Indian Tribes with English Colonies from its Beginnings to the Lancaster Treaty of 1744* (1984); Jean Lunn, "Agriculture and War in Canada, 1740–60," *Canadian Historical Review*, XVI (1935):123–136; Christopher Moore, *Louisbourg Portraits: Life in an Eighteenth-Century Garrison Town* (1982).

Richard Pares, *War and Trade in the West Indies, 1739–63* (1963); J.H. Parry, *Trade and Dominion: European Overseas Empires in the Eighteenth Century* (1971); Donald Pilgrim, "France and New France: Two Perspectives on Colonial Security," *Canadian Historical Review*, LV (1974): 381–408; Herbert Priestley, *France Overseas Through the Old Regime* (1939).

George Stanley, *Canada's Soldiers, 1604–1754* (1954); Ian K. Steele, *Guerrillas and Grenadiers: The Struggle for Canada, 1689–1760* (1969); Geoffrey Symcox, *Crisis of French Seapower, 1688–1697: From guerre d'escadre to guerre de course* (1974).

See also ARMY, FRANCE; FRANCE-CANADIAN RELATIONS; FRANCE-INDIAN RELATIONS; FRANCE-LOUISIANA RELATIONS; FRANCE-SPAIN RELATIONS; FRONTENAC, LOUIS DE BUADE DE; GREAT BRITAIN–FRANCE RELATIONS; LE MOYNE DE BIENVILLE, JEAN-BAPTISTE; LE MOYNE D'IBERVILLE, PIERRE; IROQUOIS TREATIES OF 1701; KING GEORGE'S WAR; KING WILLIAM'S WAR; KIRKE BORTHERS; LAUDONNIÈRE, RENÉ GOULAINE DE; LOUISBOURG; LOUISIANA; NAVY, FRANCE; QUEBEC; QUEEN ANNE'S WAR; RIBAULT, JEAN; RIGAUD DE VAUDREUIL DE CAVAGNIAL, PIERRE DE; SEVEN YEARS' WAR

France-Canadian Relations

Prior to 1755, there had been few occasions for metropolitan-colonial friction in Canada. The colonial elite were firmly bound to the metropolis, and French administrators from the Ministry of Marine were familiar with Canadian conditions and sympathetic to colonial aspirations. The garrison of Canada was composed of independent companies of infantry administered by the Ministry of Marine and led by Canadian officers.

During the Seven Years' War, this garrison was reinforced by several battalions of the French army. Although the French regulars significantly strengthened the forces available for the defense of Canada, French and Canadian officers quickly formed themselves into distinct and mutually antagonistic factions, led and personified by Pierre de Rigaud de Vaudreuil, governor general of New France and commander in chief of the French armed forces in North America, and Louis-Joseph de Montcalm, marquis de Montcalm, the commander of the metropolitan battalions.

Montcalm consistently questioned Vaudreuil's orders, feared failure and sought to place the blame for apprehended disaster on his superior, and ignored orders to exploit victories at Forts William Henry and Carillon. While promoting himself as a future governor general of Canada, Montcalm filled his correspondence with savage criticisms of Vaudreuil and the Canadians, and accused the governor general of conspiring against him. A confirmed defeatist, Montcalm set the tone for a largely unhappy and querulous officer corps.

Training and experience had prepared Montcalm's officers for war in Europe. Instead, they found themselves, often against their will, waging war along the waterways of the interior of North America. Compelled to serve in the vast distances and empty spaces of the New World, and to cope with the unfamiliar technology and procedures of amphibious warfare, their judgment was often poor, their reaction to Canada and Canadians hostile, and their outlook pessimistic.

The Canadians, on the other hand, were the heirs of a long tradition of victory against the British in North America, were accustomed to coping with the problems posed by North American war and transportation, and were disposed to be activist, aggressive, and optimistic. The difference in outlook between the two groups was summed up in 1756 by a French engineer who observed that "It is notable, that all of the Canadian officers, without exception, see the capture of Oswego as the easiest thing in the world. None of them notice the innumerable difficulties that we [the French] all see."

There were, however, officers who bridged the gap between colonials and metropolitans. The most prominent of these was François-Gaston de Lévis, a brilliant French officer who made every effort to maintain good relations with the colonials and remained confident in the outcome of the war. After Montcalm's death in 1759, he was replaced by Lévis, who quickly established harmony between metropolitans and colonials, and led them to the last French victory of the war at Sainte-Foy in 1760.

The actual impact of French-Canadian discord on the outcome of the war which should not be confused with problems caused by Montcalm's failings as a commander, proved to be limited. French operations were hindered rather than paralyzed. Membership in rival organizations did not prevent metropolitan and colonial officers from working together in campaign after campaign. As governor general, Vaudreuil was endowed by the French colonial system with the authority to compel Montcalm to follow his general plans of action, which produced an unbroken series of victories until 1759. Adherence by Montcalm to Vaudreuil's orders to follow up on victories might have prolonged the war and allowed the French to hold out until fighting ended in Europe. Greater confidence in Vaudreuil by the lieutenant colonels of the French battalions might have enabled the governor general to rally the survivors of the French army after the Battle of the Plains of Abraham and prevented the subsequent surrender of Quebec.

At the level of the private soldier, French-Canadian relations were much calmer, if occasionally strained. In the absence of barracks, French troops were billeted in Canadian homes, which led to generally cordial relations with their hosts and a significant number of marriages between Canadian women and French soldiers.

D. Peter MacLeod

References

Jean Delmas, ed., *Conflits de sociétés au Canada français pendant la guerre de sept ans et leur influence sur les operations* (1978); W.J. Eccles, "Louis-Joseph de Montcalm, Marquis de Montcalm," in F.G. Halpenny, ed., *Dictionary of Canadian Biography, Vol. III, 1741 to 1770* (1974); ———, "Pierre de Rigaud de Vaudreuil de Cavagnial, Marquis de Vaudreuil," in F.G. Halpenny, ed., *Dictionary of Canadian Biography, Vol. IV, 1771 to 1800* (1979):662–674; ———, *Essays on New France* (1987).

Guy Frégault, *Canada: The War of the Conquest*, trans., Margaret M. Cameron (1969); D. Peter MacLeod, "The Canadians against the French: The Struggle for Control of the Expedition to Oswego in 1756," *Ontario History*, LXXX (1988): 144–157.

See also COUREURS DE BOIS; FRANCE; FRONTENAC, LOUIS DE BUADE DE; LÉVIS, FRANÇOIS-GASTON DE; RIGAUD DE VAUDREUIL DE CAVAGNIAL, PIERRE DE

France–Great Britain Relations
See GREAT BRITAIN–FRANCE RELATIONS

France-Indian Relations
Breton and Norman fishermen were in contact with Native Americans as early as 1504, and the first Indians were brought as captives to France in 1508–1509. Giovanni da Verrazano in 1524 and Jacques Cartier on his first voyage in 1534 noted that the coastal peoples were anxious to barter furs for ornaments, metal goods, and red cloth. These early bartering contacts inaugurated an economic exchange which was not without its moments of violence, according to the travel literature.

In the sixteenth century, the French were intent on establishing their sovereignty over northeastern North America, the lands "not possessed by any other Christian prince," and justified by the occupation of supposedly vacant or uncultivated lands, by the imposition of "Christian dominion," and if need be, by the right of conquest. But in the seventeenth century, as the fur trade developed and as missionary work progressed, a policy of peaceful coexistence replaced the earlier aggressive intrusion. Royal instructions to the colonial governor of New France in 1665, warned against any acts of violence against the original inhabitants, adding that no one should dare "take the lands on which they are living under pretext that it would be better and more suitable if they were French." There was no need to displace the original inhabitants to make way for European settlement because the St. Lawrence Valley since at least 1580 no longer contained Laurentian Iroquois. Likewise, French settlement along the Bay of Fundy, the original Acadia, required no displacement of Micmacs.

Under Samuel de Champlain's administration (1608–1635), the French established their alliance with the Algonkians and Hurons against the Iroquois Confederacy, introduced missionaries into the Great Lakes basin, and enunciated a policy of racial intermarriage, or *métissage*. In Acadia, the Micmacs began accepting baptism as a sign of their alliance with the French. Missionary work in the "upper country" of Canada (present-day Ontario) suffered serious reverses as a result of the Iroquois dispersal of the Hurons (1649–1650) and their attempts to establish themselves as middlemen in the fur trade between the western tribes and the French colony.

When the policy of *métissage* proved no more successful than the educational efforts of the Ursuline nuns and the Jesuit priests in assimilating the Indians, the Paraguayan model of the *réduction* was introduced where Indians were brought together for religious instruction under the tutelage of a missionary, and contact with the outside was limited. This later developed into the *réserve,* where Indians had to restrict their residence to a single locale. These seigneuries were granted by the Crown to the missionaries for the sedentarization, evangelization, and transformation of Indians into French-style farmers and artisans living under strict Christian discipline. They bore some resemblance to the "praying towns" of New England, but unlike the British reserves, they were never created to restrict Indian habitation to make way for European settlement. On the contrary,

they represented a voluntary relocation of native peoples to formerly uninhabited lands within the restricted Laurentian Valley zone of French settlement.

There were eventually two reserves near Quebec, two near Trois-Rivières, two near Montreal, and two on the upper St. Lawrence. Proximity to Quebec and Montreal proved disruptive to maintaining order and sobriety, so the missionaries sometimes removed these *réductions* farther away from immediate contact with the French settlements. An institution conceived as an agency of integration was becoming an instrument of segregation. The Hurons at Lorette near Quebec were refugees from the Iroquois War, while the Abenakis near Trois Rivières were refugees from New England encroachment on their lands. The Iroquois at Sault St. Louis (Caughnawaga) and the Algonkians, Nipissings, and Iroquois at Lake of the Two Mountains (Oka/Kanesatake) near Montreal were attracted there because these were havens for persecuted Christian converts and locations affording economic opportunities to engage in trade, participate in French military expeditions, and provide the townspeople with local produce and crafts. The reserves at St. Regis (Cornwall/Akwesasene) and La Présentation (Ogdensburg) were later creations as frontier buffers on the upper St. Lawrence with New York. These "domiciled natives," as they were called, never became thoroughly francisized, wholly given to agriculture, or completely converted, but they were staunchly loyal to France in the colonial wars.

France spent large sums of money for the annual distribution of the "king's presents" to the allied tribes. In the 1730s, the cost had mounted so much that cutbacks were ordered by Versailles, but the officers commanding at interior posts and the administrators at Quebec insisted that the practice must continue to ensure peace and tranquillity on the frontier. In addition, the crown issued clothing, weapons, and ammunition to native warriors who fought as independent auxiliary units alongside the French against the Anglo-Americans or hostile tribes. The French not only paid these warriors for their services, but also maintained their families during hostilities. The natives were judged invaluable for guiding, scouting, and surprise raiding parties. Their war aims and practices, including scalping and torture, were rarely interfered with because their support was often crucial to success. In the hour of final defeat, the French remembered them and, in the terms of the capitulation of Montreal (1760), they obtained the promise they would be treated as soldiers under arms, not brute savages, that "they be maintained in the lands they inhabit," and that they enjoy freedom of religion and be permitted to retain their missionaries.

In the eighteenth century, *métissage* took on new characteristics. Voyageurs and canoemen engaged in the fur trade of the Great Lakes basin acquired the services of native women to make and break camp, cook, carry baggage, and serve as mistresses. Many of these unions became long-lasting and were recognized locally as legitimate *à la façon du pays* (in the manner of the country). Canon law forbade the marriage of Catholics with pagans, so missionaries often had to instruct and baptize adults then regularize such unions canonically. In 1735 Louis XV forbade such mixed marriages, but the practice continued and gave rise to distinct métis communities, especially along Lake Superior.

Three aspects of relations with the French had devastating consequences for the Indians. First, there was the introduction of microbes, notably smallpox and respiratory diseases. Even the common European childhood ailments reached epidemic proportions in Indian villages and encampments. These plagues, or "virgin soil epidemics," carried off at least one-third, often more, of the native population in the first wave of infection. The young and elderly were especially vulnerable, so besides depopulation, demoralization set in as the revered elders and the upcoming generations were wiped out.

Secondly, the introduction of intoxicants had such disruptive effects on health and traditional social conventions that even the French traders recognized the evil effects of brandy trafficking. In a consultative assembly of colonial notables held in 1678, the nefarious traffic was condemned, yet held to be necessary to compete with "Protestant rum" from New York. The drunken bouts which characterized bartering sessions should not be confused with the later development of alcoholism in native communities.

Thirdly, French intrusion resulted in intensified intertribal warfare. From the day Champlain joined an Algonkian-Huron attack on the Mohawks in 1609, to native participation at the side of the French army in the battles of the Seven Years' War, Indians became involved more frequently, in greater numbers, and with increasing devastation and casualties in warfare. The Canadian militia quickly adopted native guerrilla tactics, while the Indians began to fight for nontraditional objectives. Northern warriors joined in expeditions against the Chickasaws, for example, in the lower Mississippi region. In an effort to maintain the alliance of the interior tribes, a Three Fires Confederacy was organized, but it never succeeded in uniting all the Great Lakes basin peoples into unfaltering support of French trade and arms. Pontiac's War in 1763 was a manifestation of the attachment to the French cause and of the fear of Anglo-American intrusion.

Finally, it is necessary to correct an erroneous view that constantly appears in the historical literature. It is reported that the French never recognized aboriginal rights. Beginning with the royal instructions of 1665, there are countless official pronouncements making it clear that the French recognized native possessory and territorial rights in North America. These statements contain such phrases as "these nations govern themselves alone" and "they must be deemed free everywhere on their lands." Ministry of War directives in 1755 were even clearer: "The natives are jealous of their liberty, and one could not without committing an injustice take away from them the *primitive right of property* to the Lands on which Providence has given them birth and located them." While it is true that France proclaimed its sovereignty over this vast colony, it asserted these rights not over native rights, but through recognition of native self-government and territorial possession. Recognition of "native nationhood" was the means of extending French sovereignty against the claims of Britain and Spain. The various tribes always maintained their independence while sharing land and resources with the French on the understanding that they had entered into a kinship relation. An Abenaki chief affirmed, "We are entirely free; we are allies of the King of France from whom we have received the Faith and all kinds of assistance in our needs; we love that Monarch, and we remain strongly attached to his interests."

Cornelius J. Jaenen

References
Cornelius J. Jaenen, *The French Relationship with the Native Peoples of New France* (1984).

See also ABENAKI; COUREURS DE BOIS; FRANCE; FRANCE-LOUISIANA RELATIONS; HURON; IROQUOIS; IROQUOIS TREATIES OF 1701; JESUITS

France-Louisiana Relations

French activity in the lower Mississippi Valley dates from the explorations of Jacques Marquette and Louis Jolliet in 1673, and of René-Robert Cavelier de La Salle a decade later. Although La Salle built a short-lived outpost at Matagorda Bay in 1685, formal French occupation of the Gulf coast did not come until 1699 with the expeditions of Pierre Le Moyne d'Iberville.

While Marquette and La Salle came by canoe from Canada, Iberville was sent by sea from Versailles. The difference in focus was crucial. La Salle's vision of a French empire on the lower Mississippi would encourage expansionists for the next 80 years. However, it would be French interests in Europe, not those of North America, which would determine Louisiana's future.

Iberville's primary mission was to secure a base for the protection, and perhaps expansion, of French influence during the Spanish succession crisis. Minister of the Marine Jérôme Phélypeaux de Pontchartrain was particularly concerned by rumors of Carolina traders on the Mississippi, and by reports that Englishman Daniel Coxe was planning a Huguenot colony on the Gulf. In 1699, Iberville established Fort Maurepas at Biloxi, and in 1702, his brother, Jean-Baptiste Le Moyne de Bienville, built the more elaborate Fort Louis at Mobile. The Spanish, alarmed by the English and by their erstwhile Bourbon allies, countered with a post at Pensacola.

The Huguenot settlers were effectively deterred by Iberville's arrival; but the Carolinians continued to control the trade, and hence the politics, of the local tribes. Isolated from Europe during the decade of war after 1702 and virtually driven from the wilderness, the Bourbon defensive perimeter fell back on Pensacola, Mobile, and Biloxi. Louisiana would remain on the diplomatic and economic defensive until after the return of peace in 1713.

In Louisiana, as with Canada a century earlier, France tried to promote colonization through private enterprise. A monopoly of the colony's trade given to financier Antoine Crozat in 1712, however, was surrendered after four years. An even more generous grant to John

Law in 1717 brought growth and a flurry of settlers, many from the prisons and alleys of France; it ended in the financial disaster of the South Sea Bubble in 1720. Although Louisiana's economy languished, its population had doubled and New Orleans was established as the colony's commercial and administrative center in 1718.

As Louisiana's center of gravity shifted to the Mississippi delta, Forts Rosalie at Natchez, Toulouse on the Alabama, and Natchitoches on the Red River were established to form a defensive arc surrounding the colony's core in lower Louisiana. Eventually, the search for mines, an expanding fur trade, and military security opened a secondary hinterland in upper Louisiana which extended into Illinois, Minnesota, and Ohio.

Louisiana's primary defensive strength, and its greatest danger, came from its Indian neighbors. France not only inherited their allies' rivalries, the colony soon generated conflicts of its own. A dispute with the Natchez in 1729 led to the destruction of Fort Rosalie and its surrounding community, while almost perpetual warfare with the pro-English Chickasaw was intensified by that tribe's traditional hostility with France's Choctaw allies. A generation of peace in Europe after 1713 was thus punctuated by bitter Indian wars fought to protect France's economic and military alliances in America.

Following a major defeat in 1736, the French and their allies conducted an elaborate campaign against the Chickasaw on the Mobile River. Militarily inconclusive and horrendously expensive, it did show French willingness to wage full-scale wilderness war and finally brought peace through mutual exhaustion. Louisiana, however, was simply too remote from the strategic centers of conflict to be a factor in the last 20 years of colonial warfare after 1744. Distance and Indian opposition would eventually delay British occupation of the Mississippi Valley until 1765.

Louisiana was a garrison colony whose functions were essentially negative and defensive. There was little economic development because it was a military, not a commercial enterprise. The colony provided flank protection for Caribbean sugar colonies and guarded the "back door" to Canada; it slowed English expansion from the Carolinas and Georgia; and it helped maintain French economic and military influence among the western tribes. Versailles asked little from Louisiana; it got what it expected.

David R. Farrell

References

Verner Crane, *The Southern Frontier, 1670–1732* (1929); William Dunn, *Spanish and French Rivalry in the Gulf Region of the United States, 1678–1702* (1917); Guy Frégault, *Le Grand Marquis: Pierre de Rigaud de Vaudreuil et la Louisiane* (1952); Patricia K. Galloway, ed., *La Salle and His Legacy* (1982); Patricia Woods, *French-Indian Relations on the Southern Frontier, 1699–1762* (1980).

See also CHICKASAW; CHOCTAW; FRANCE; LE MOYNE DE BIENVILLE, JEAN-BAPTISTE; LE MOYNE D'IBERVILLE, PIERRE; LOUISIANA

France-Spain Relations

For much of the late seventeenth and eighteenth centuries, Spain, France, and Great Britain engaged in a struggle for empire in North America. The three powers, their Indian allies, and their settlers, soldiers, and missionaries tried to advance claims to the continent through warfare, trade, colonization, and conversion. Spain tried to protect its vast, underpopulated North American empire against French and British encroachment and in the eighteenth century intensified its efforts to ward off European rivals. Defining possession of a colony as based on actual occupation and settlement, other European nations refused to recognize provisions of a papal bull (1493) and the Treaty of Tordesillas (1494) that divided the New World between Spain and Portugal. Even though it considered British colonization along the lower Atlantic seaboard and French settlement in Louisiana illegal, the Spanish crown was unable or unwilling to do much about it. Establishment of these colonies in North America created new sources of tension and conflict between Spain, France, and Britain, a rivalry mainly manifest in the Caribbean and the region that today encompasses the southeastern United States.

Intercolonial conflicts between Spain and France in North America were rare before the end of the seventeenth century. France mainly attempted to disrupt Spain's commerce with its colonies—accomplished with inexpensive, lucrative pirate enclaves from which French corsairs conducted raids on Spanish treasure fleets—rather than to build permanent settlements, or even trading posts. The exceptions were Charlesfort, established in 1562 by French Huguenots on an island in the strategic bay of Santa Elena and Fort Caroline, also constructed by French Protestants two years later near the mouth of the St. Johns River. These incursions, as well as the need to protect the Spain-bound silver fleets that hugged the Florida coastline before pushing off across the Atlantic, prompted the crown to establish a defense and supply base at St. Augustine, 40 miles south of the French Fort Caroline. In September 1565, Pedro Menéndez de Avilés took possession of Florida for Spain, quickly destroyed the French settlements, and began building St. Augustine and other forts in Florida. The French posed no further threat on the Atlantic coast.

French interest in colonization near Spanish territory was reawakened, however, in the last decades of the seventeenth century. In 1682, René-Robert Cavelier, sieur de la Salle, claimed possession of the Mississippi River, its tributaries, and all the lands drained by these waters in the name of Louis XIV, king of France, which territory was also claimed by Spain. Prior to France's exploration and settlement of Louisiana, competition between the two European powers was confined to the Caribbean and was in part settled by the Treaty of Ryswick (1697), in which Spain gave the western half of the island of Hispaniola to France (present-day Haiti). More than a century and a half before La Salle, several Spanish *entradas* entered the Mississippi Valley region. After Hernando de Soto's expedition in the 1540s, however, most explorers turned elsewhere to look for the precious metals, fertile soils, and docile native laborers they desired.

French explorers rekindled an interest in the Mississippi Valley and Gulf coast region. Like the Spaniards who came before them, they hoped to find hidden and instant wealth in the area. In addition, they sought a westward waterway to link Canada with the Pacific Ocean and the Orient. Although this dream of an east-west water route across North America was quickly dispelled, French King Louis XIV encouraged exploration of the Mississippi River in order to enlarge his empire and halt Britain's and Spain's expansion. Expansion, commerce, and settlement in the Americas increased under Louis XIV and his minister, Jean-Baptiste Colbert. Colbert's goal was to make France the richest industrial and commercial nation in Europe, and he needed colonies to do it. The French crown envisioned a giant arc of settlement stretching from Canada through the middle of the continent and into its Caribbean islands, an arc that would provide France access to and keep Britain away from New Spain's silver mines. La Salle enticed the French crown with a map that showed the Mississippi emptying into the Gulf far west of where its actual mouth was and very near to Spanish mines. Involvement in the War of the League of Augsburg, however, delayed further French exploration until the turn of the century.

With the permanent settlement of Louisiana in 1699 France succeeded in driving a wedge between Spanish Florida and New Spain on the Gulf coast. The French probably would have taken more of Florida if the Spanish had not founded Pensacola just one year earlier in 1698; French forces briefly seized Pensacola in 1719 during the War of the Quadruple Alliance. Faced with this French threat, the Spanish crown also moved quickly to defend the eastern boundary of northern New Spain and repel the westward march of French colonists. In response to La Salle's expeditions of 1682 and 1684, Spain despatched exploratory parties to intercept La Salle and sent missionaries and soldiers to occupy eastern Texas. Spain hoped to convert Native American allies and use them against the French, but hostile Hasinai Indians forced Franciscan missionaries to retreat back to the Rio Grande River in 1693. Twenty years later, renewed French colonization at the post of Natchitoches on the Red River spurred Spanish reoccupation of east Texas missions and presidios, including San Miguel de los Adaes, 12 miles west of Natchitoches.

During the eighteenth century there was a seeming contradiction between France's foreign policy, which cultivated a Spanish alliance, and its colonial policy, which antagonized the Spanish. Although the War of the Spanish Succession (1702–1713) and the First (1733), Second (1743), and Third (1761) Family Compacts united the Bourbon rulers of France and Spain, Louis XIV and his regent successor aggressively pursued colonial expansion at the expense of Spain in the early 1700s, as evidenced in Louisiana. In addition, France's rising commercial and maritime strength threatened Spanish mercantilism, given new life by Bourbon reformers. France and Spain also competed for the friendship of Indian allies, although both usually lost to superior British trade goods. In most of southern North America, where whites were scarce, European powers relied on Native Americans—and Africans—to fight for them, as well as to provide food and furs.

Outside the realm of crown politics, however, relations between the Spanish in Texas and Florida and the French in Louisiana were amicable and mutually beneficial. Early French settlements at Mobile and Natchitoches depended on contraband trade with Pensacola, Cuba, and Texas in order to survive; often ignored by their European mother countries and considered marginal outposts, Gulf coast colonials found cooperation indispensable. French Governor Antoine de Lamothe, sieur de Cadillac (1713–1716) promoted trade with Louisiana's Spanish neighbors as key to the colony's prosperity, and subsequent officials continued to incorporate Louisiana into a Caribbean contraband network that was intended to break Spain's mercantilistic hold on the region and channel some of its mineral wealth into French coffers. French colonists sold foodstuffs to the Spanish garrison at Pensacola, and merchants used ports at Mobile and New Orleans to smuggle French goods into Spanish colonies, and vice versa.

The Seven Years' War (1754–1763) drastically altered French and Spanish rivalry in North America. In this struggle fought primarily between England, France, and their American colonies, Spain entered late (1762) and on the side of France. Spain's King Carlos III, who assumed the throne in 1759, pursued a pro-French foreign policy and entered into the Family Compact of 1761, in which Spain agreed to declare war on Britain if that nation and France had not signed a peace agreement by May 1762. Unable to rejuvenate France's war effort, Spain suffered a quick defeat. According to the Treaty of Paris (1763), victorious England acquired French Canada, Spanish Florida, and that part of French Louisiana east of the Mississippi (minus the "Isle of Orleans"). France compensated Spain with the western half of Louisiana and New Orleans, and Britain returned Havana in exchange for Florida. Although it remained a rival of Spain in the Caribbean, France thus withdrew from its colonial empire in North America, leaving Spain to contend directly with England, and then the United States, for control of the region.

Kimberly S. Hanger

References

Henry Folmer, *Franco-Spanish Rivalry in North America, 1524–1763* (1953); Elizabeth A.H. Johns, *Storms Brewed in Other Men's Worlds: The Confrontation of Indians, Spanish, and French in the Southwest, 1540–1795* (1975); Daniel H. Usner, Jr., *Indians, Settlers, and Slaves in a Frontier Exchange Economy: The Lower Mississippi Valley Before 1783* (1992).

David J. Weber, *The Spanish Frontier in North America* (1992); Robert S. Weddle, *Spanish Sea: The Gulf of Mexico in North American Discovery, 1500–1685* (1985); Glyndwr Williams, *The Expansion of Europe in the Eighteenth Century: Overseas Rivalry, Discovery, and Exploitation* (1966).

See also AGUAYO EXPEDITION; FORT CAROLINE (FLORIDA); CHARLESFORT (SOUTH CAROLINA); FLORIDA; FRANCE; PENSACOLA; PENSACOLA AND THE WAR OF THE QUADRUPLE ALLIANCE; PRESIDIO NUESTRA SEÑORA DEL PILAR DE LOS ADAES (LOUISIANA); RYSWICK, TREATY OF; SAINT DENIS, LOUIS JUCHEREAU DE; SANTA ELENA; VILLASUR, PEDRO DE

Franciscan

A missionary order founded by St. Francis of Assisi in 1209 and dedicated to the ideal of poverty, the Franciscans arrived in Florida in 1574 to Christianize and indoctrinate Native American tribes.

Spanish colonization policy throughout the North American borderlands combined military and mission settlements. With the foundation of a Spanish fort came members of the religious orders, who established *doctrines,* primary mission centers from which friars proseletyzed and catechized the native peoples. The friars represented an advance guard who mediated between royal officials, the military, and the native populations. On the southeastern Spanish borderlands, Franciscans were sent to replace the Jesuits, who had accompanied the first permanent Spanish settlers to La Florida in 1565.

From St. Augustine, Franciscan friars went out into the countryside, but their early efforts were only moderately successful. They encountered many obstacles, including the hostility of native populations and a lack of royal support. In the wake of the Tolomato Uprising of 1597, which wiped out established missions north of the St. Marys River, Franciscan accomplish-

ments in La Florida were nearly abandoned. However, the Franciscans were loath to abandon their successes, which by 1610 numbered 6,000 converted Indians, and their arguments persuaded the king of Spain, Philip III, to change his mind.

After 1595, the Franciscans embarked upon a large-scale campaign to win over the Indians of La Florida. Their efforts were successful, and the seventeenth century became known as the "Golden Age" of the Florida missions. Concentrating on the mostly sedentary Timucua, Guale, and Apalachee tribes in the northern portion of the peninsula, Franciscan missionizing proceeded in a westwardly-moving line, establishing a chain of missions extending from St. Augustine to Apalachee Bay, ultimately reaching the Flint River frontier. At the height of their success in the mid-seventeenth century, Franciscan friars could count more than 26,000 faithful in 38 villages. At the center of the mission system was San Luis, near modern-day Tallahassee, in the heart of the Apalachee region. Yet in spite of their successes in north Florida, the Franciscans never succeeded in Christianizing the semisedentary tribes on the southern peninsula.

Tensions ran high between the friars and the military establishment, who coexisted alongside each other. Unlike Franciscans in other areas, the brothers assigned to La Florida were dependent upon royal subsidies, not on local charity. Both the military and religious groups vied for the precious funds allotted by the Spanish crown for the colony's maintenance and for an ever-diminishing supply of Indian labor. Not surprisingly, their antagonism was spurred on by jealousy and provoked mutual criticism. Friars often interceded between the military and the native people, and to the monarch they argued that they were more successful in influencing and controlling the Indians than were their rivals. Paradoxically, the tension between the religious and the soldiers was exacerbated by their mutual dependence. The Franciscans needed military protection to extend their mission frontier; the military needed the Franciscans to continue religious indoctrination to keep the indigenes pacified.

In 1670, Great Britain challenged Spain's dominance in the Southeast and founded Charles Town, South Carolina. Beginning by trading with the interior tribes, the British soon turned a contest for the economic allegiance of native peoples into a contest between the two European powers for territorial control of the borderlands. Between 1702 and 1708, South Carolina Governor James Moore raided Spanish territory and destroyed most of the missions in Apalachee, carrying off nearly 12,000 Christianized Indians as slaves. During the subsequent border wars, the Franciscans won the allegiance of 161 villages for the Spanish. For the next 25 years, disastrous raids by British forces combined with a continued diminuition of indigenous populations and internal bickering spelled doom for the mission system. By the 1730s, the mission system on the Florida frontier was destroyed and the Franciscans were reduced to ministering to a few small churches clustered around St. Augustine.

Sherry Johnson

References

Mark F. Boyd, Hale G. Smith, and John W. Griffin, *Here They Once Stood: The Tragic End of the Apalachee Missions* (1951); Michael V. Gannon, *The Cross in the Sand: The Early Catholic Church in Florida, 1513–1870,* 2nd ed. (1983); Maynard J. Geiger, *The Franciscan Conquest of Florida (1573–1618)* (1937); John H. Hann, *Apalachee: The Land Between the Rivers* (1988); ———, ed. and trans., *Missions to the Calusa* (1991).

See also APALACHEE; CALUSA; FLORIDA; JESUITS; NEW MEXICO; SPANISH MISSION SYSTEM–SOUTHEAST; SPANISH MISSION SYSTEM–SOUTHWEST; TEXAS; TIMUCUA; TOLOMATO PRESIDIO

Franklin, Benjamin (1706–1790)

A virtuoso and a dilettante, yet a man of practicality and common sense, Benjamin Franklin exemplified the aspirations and character of the "new American." Honored in Europe and America, Franklin made his mark as scientist, printer, publisher, essayist, businessman, philologist, politician, public servant, statesman, and diplomat. As a self-made man, Franklin early gained recognition for his *Pennsylvania Gazette* and *Poor Richard's Almanack* (which he published from 1733–1758). Franklin was a major founder of the Library Company of Philadelphia, the College of Philadelphia (later the University of Pennsylvania), American Philosophical Society, Union Fire Company, the Philadelphia police, and the Philadelphia Hospital. His scientific experiments, approached from the view of pure science but having utilitarian objectives, brought him wide fame. His many humorous and satirical writings mocked hypocrisy. As agent in London representing Pennsylvania beginning in 1757 and later for other colonies, as commissioner and then as minister to France during the Revolution, and as a negotiator of the peace treaty ending the war, Franklin made eight Atlantic voyages and became more at home in the European capitals than in Philadelphia. On the provincial level, Franklin served in the Pennsylvania assembly, the Pennsylvania executive council, and as an Indian commissioner. In the 1750s and 1760s, he led the popular party versus proprietary control of Pennsylvania. Franklin's reputation in public life rested largely on his role as a conciliator. Franklin was the principal author of the Albany Plan of Union. During the French and Indian War, unofficially as "general," Franklin commanded militia for a brief duration in defense of the northeastern Pennsylvania frontier. In 1764, he single-handedly persuaded the "Paxton Boys," a rough-hewn mob intending to seek redress by arms, to desist in their march on Philadelphia. From 1753–1774, Franklin was one of the two deputy postmaster generals for the colonies, which position he used to promote road improvements and also to stir interest in colonial union. Ostensibly the reason given by British authorities for his dismissal was his prolonged absences from America. In his writings Franklin constantly called attention to the future destiny of America, especially the capability for self-reliance and productivity. Franklin served in the early Continental Congress and as a delegate to the Constitutional Convention of 1787. From both sides of the Atlantic, Franklin was judged by his contemporaries as the greatest living American.

Harry M. Ward

References

Ruth L. Butler, *Doctor Franklin: Postmaster General* (1928); Ronald W. Clark, *Benjamin Franklin: A Biography* (1983); Bernard Fay, *Franklin, the Apostle of Modern Times* (1929); J. Bennett Nolan, *General Benjamin Franklin: the Military Career of a Philosopher* (1936); Carl Van Doren, *Benjamin Franklin* (1938); Esmond Wright, *Franklin of Philadelphia* (1986).

See also ALBANY CONFERENCE; PAXTON BOYS

F

Fort Frederica (Georgia)

Fort Frederica was built by British settlers in 1736 on St. Simons Island by the order of James Oglethorpe. One of several forts guarding Georgia's southern flank, it was located along the Altamaha River, which let into the inland passage. The site, surrounded by marshes and thick forests, was 20 miles south of the mainland settlement of Darien and six miles north of two other forts on the island, Fort Delegal and Fort St. Simons. Fort Frederica was square in shape and measuring 124 feet by 125 feet on the inside with a regular bastion at each corner. It also had a spur battery jutting beyond the fort on the river side.

It, as well as the adjacent town of Frederica, were never completed. Oglethorpe headquartered his regiment, the Forty-Second Regiment of Foot, at the fort in 1738 and rotated the troops between there and Fort St. Simons. He considered Frederica his home from 1738 until his departure from Georgia in 1743.

During July 1742, Spanish invasion forces numbering between 3,000 and 5,000 men landed on St. Simons Island and occupied Fort St. Simons. Oglethorpe evacuated his troops to Fort Frederica. His forces numbered 700 to 800 men, including regular army, colonial militia, volunteers and Yamacraw, Creek, and Chickasaw warriors.

On 7 July, a Spanish reconnoitering party came within one and one-half miles of the fort and was repulsed. Later that day the Spanish were defeated at the Battle of Bloody Marsh. On 9 July they attempted to sail up to the fort, but were turned back by cannon.

Fort Frederica declined once the threat of Spanish invasion eased in 1748. The Forty-Second Regiment of Foot was stationed there until 1749, when it was deactivated. Military stores and cannon were retrieved from the fort by the Whig government in 1776.

Leslie Hall

References

Kenneth Coleman, *Colonial Georgia: A History* (1989); Larry E. Ivers, *British Drums Along the Southern Frontier: The Military Colonization of Georgia, 1733–1749* (1974); Phinizy Spalding, *Oglethorpe in America* (1977).

See also BLOODY MARSH, BATTLE OF; OGLETHORPE, JAMES EDWARD; FORT ST. SIMONS (GEORGIA)

Fort Frederick (Maine)

See FORT WILLIAM HENRY (MAINE)

Fort Frederick (Maryland)

After General Edward Braddock's forces suffered disastrous defeat at Fort Duquesne during the French and Indian War, it was feared the war would advance, endangering the lives and property of settlers on Maryland's frontiers. Only Fort Cumberland, a wooden stockade and blockhouse constructed for Indian trade and situated more than 60 miles west of the Maryland frontier, stood between the colony and hostile French and Indian forces. Maryland's governor, Horatio Sharpe, feared further attacks reaching into Maryland and noted the unwillingness of residents in the eastern portion of the colony to become involved in the frontier settlers' predicament. Sharpe, therefore, repeatedly petitioned the Maryland Assembly to provide funds for construction of a fort, and in May 1756, the assembly met his requests. A total of £40,000 was set aside to construct a fort with no more than four barracks on the western frontier, to raise, pay, arm, and support a garrison of 200 men there, to defray expenses of two commissioners to raise assistance among southern Indians, to pay bounties for scalps of hostile Indians, and to carry out any expeditions from Maryland on the king's service.

A site for Fort Frederick, named after the current proprietor of Maryland, Frederick Calvert, was selected on North Mountain about 100 feet above the Potomac River and one-quarter-mile distant. Learning from the experiences of Pennsylvania and Virginia, whose wooden stockade forts were burned by French and Indian forces, Maryland constructed the new fort of native stone set in cement, with walls more than three feet thick and 20 feet high. It was laid out in a 240-foot square with bastions at each corner, and a recessed opening on the south side facing the river. Two wells were dug inside the fort and barracks were erected to accommodate 200 men as a regular force and double that number in emergencies.

After its completion in late 1756, troops from Maryland, Pennsylvania, and Virginia rendezvoused at Fort Frederick, and it became the base of operations in the campaign against Fort Duquesne. George Washington visited the fort and met with Governor Sharpe during its construction, and was there again during the Forbes expedition of 1758. And, in April

1757, chief Wahachy and some 60 Cherokee warriors camped outside the fort preparatory to joining forces with the English against the French.

When Fort Duquesne fell to combined British forces in 1758, Fort Frederick fell into a period of slack use until Pontiac's War revived it a few years later. During Pontiac's War, more than 700 settlers from the surrounding frontiers fled to the fort for safety. After Pontiac's confederation of Indians was defeated, the frontier overtook Fort Frederick, moving rapidly father west. Once again, the fort was abandoned.

Then, during the Revolutionary War, Fort Frederick was used once again when it served as a prisoner of war camp for captured British and German soldiers. Prisoners from the Battle of Yorktown were the last to arrive there. After the war ended, Fort Frederick was abandoned and sold at public auction in 1791. For a brief period during the Civil War until 1862, the fort served to guard the Baltimore and Ohio Railroad and the Chesapeake and Ohio Canal against Confederate attack, then again reverted to private ownership until Maryland repurchased the property in 1922. Restored in the twentieth century, Fort Frederick is one of only a few pre-Revolutionary stone forts to survive in the United States.

Debra R. Boender

References

Niles Anderson, "The General Chooses a Road: The Forbes Campaign of 1758 to Capture Fort Duquesne," *The Western Pennsylvania Historical Magazine* 42 (1959):109–138; Kenneth P. Bailey, *The Ohio Company of Virginia and the Westward Movement, 1748–1792: A Chapter in the History of the Colonial Frontier* (1939); Gilbert Crandall, "Fort Frederick: Bastion of the American Frontier," *Valleys of History* 4 (1968):4–7.

"Data on Fort Frederick, in Washington County, MD," Fort Frederick, Maryland Vertical File, Maryland Room, Enoch Pratt Free Library, Baltimore, MD; Mary Vernon Mish, "Fort Frederick," *Daughters of the American Revolution Magazine*, 90 (1956):123–124; Mary Warren, "On the Western Frontier," *Maryland Conservationist* (1967):15–17.

See also FORT CUMBERLAND (MARYLAND)

Fort Frederick (South Carolina)

This fort was constructed between 1731 and 1734 at the site of the present U.S. Navy Hospital, three miles south of Beaufort. Built as a replacement for Beaufort Fort, the small structure was 125 by 75 feet, with four-foot high tabby walls on three sides. A battery of cannons on the eastern wall commanded Port Royal River. Over the next 20 years the fort was garrisoned periodically by British regulars and provincial troops. By 1757, the fort was dilapidated, and the Commons House of Assembly appropriated funds to construct a replacement, Fort Lyttleton, which was begun in 1758.

Gregory D. Massey

References

Larry E. Ivers, *Colonial Forts of South Carolina 1670–1775* (1970).

See also BEAUFORT FORT (SOUTH CAROLINA); FORT LYTTLETON (SOUTH CAROLINA); PORT ROYAL (SOUTH CAROLINA); FORT PRINCE FREDERICK (SOUTH CAROLINA)

French and Indian War

See SEVEN YEARS' WAR

Fort Frey (New York)

Fort Frey's site on the northern side of the Mohawk River opposite the city of Canajoharie was settled in 1689 by a Swiss immigrant named Heinrich Frey. Frey bought 300 acres from the Mohawks and built his cabin at a site 40 miles west of Schenectady.

Frey's cabin was fortified during the years 1702 and 1713 when the British palisaded it for use in Queen Anne's War. The fort was in continual use as a British military post until well after that war.

Another stone house was constructed on the site by Frey's son in 1739. The house was probably not used as a fort although the British did occupy both the military post and the house during the French and Indian War, 1754–1763. The structure was one and one-half stories high and had a gabled roof. It is still standing and is in good condition.

Elizabeth Gossman

References

T. Wood Clarke, *The Bloody Mohawk* (1968); Robert B. Roberts, *New York's Forts in the Revolution* (1980).

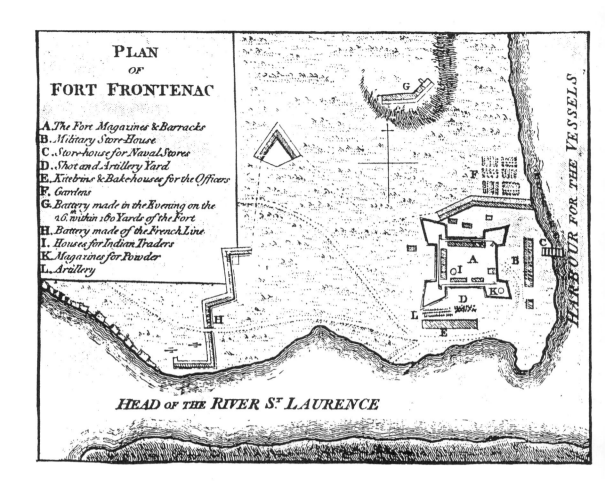

PLAN
OF
FORT FRONTENAC

A. *The Fort Magazines & Barracks*
B. *Military Store-House*
C. *Store-house for Naval Stores*
D. *Shot and Artillery Yard*
E. *Kitchins & Bakehouses for the Officers*
F. *Gardens*
G. *Battery made in the Evening on the 16. within 160 Yards of the Fort*
H. *Battery made of the French Line*
I. *Houses for Indian Traders*
K. *Magazines for Powder*
L. *Artillery*

HEAD OF THE RIVER St LAURENCE

HARBOUR FOR THE VESSELS

Fort Frontenac (Ontario, Canada)

Fort Frontenac was established in July 1673 by New France's governor, Louis de Buade de Frontenac. Situated at the head of Lake Ontario, on the Cadaraqui River, it was a fur-trading outpost which also protected French missionaries and served as a gathering and resting place for various French trading and military excursions to and from the upper lakes. As a military fort it was considerably neglected, although in the 1741 to 1748 period, some repairs were launched because of the safe harbor and warehouse for goods and furs moving east or west that it provided. With the outbreak of the Seven Years' War it was the French post closest to the Anglo-American forts at Oswego and, as a result, was the obvious marshaling point for any French attack across Lake Ontario, as well as a vital link in the French line of communication with forts further up the Great Lakes and in the western interior.

In the spring of 1756, Massachusetts Governor William Shirley had commissioned John Bradstreet to lead an attack on Frontenac once Oswego's defenses were stabilized. Before this could be accomplished the French employed Frontenac as the base for a successful attack on Oswego in August 1756 led by Louis-Joseph de Montcalm. Relying on the small naval flotilla based at Frontenac to preserve control of Lake Ontario, the French did little to strengthen the weak fort. Bradstreet, for one, remained aware of the post's importance and its vulnerability to a quick strike, and by late January 1758, had persuaded his new commander, Lord Loudoun, to allow him to raise 800 men at his own expense to attack Fort Frontenac. If the assault was successful, or if it had to be canceled, he would be reimbursed for his expenses. While Loudoun approved the Frontenac proposal, scheduled for the early spring, Bradstreet first had to supervise the construction of *bateaux* in the Schenectady-Albany area needed for the next campaign. When Loudoun was relieved of his command by William Pitt in March 1758, and replaced by James Abercromby, the Frontenac attack had to be abandoned to focus total attention on Abercromby's thrust against Ticonderoga (Fort Carillon). This campaign ended in a shattering British defeat and retreat down Lake George in July 1758. Bradstreet was then quick to resurrect a possible Frontenac strike.

Abercromby was desperate for a victory of some sort and, with approval by a 13 July council of war, authorized Bradstreet to lead substantial reinforcements to John Stanwix at the Great Carrying Place on the Mohawk River route to the now destroyed Fort Oswego. If after joining Stanwix it was clear that there was no imminent threat of a French thrust down the Mohawk, Bradstreet could then lead a 3,600 man force against Frontenac. On 14 July 1758, Bradstreet began moving troops out of the Fort William Henry camp, one regiment per day. Within ten days they all had arrived at Schenectady and commenced movement up the Mohawk River, a route well-known to Bradstreet since he had directed *bateaux* convoys over it in 1755 and 1756 in relief of Oswego. By 10 August, all the forces had reached the Great Carrying Place and Stanwix formally assigned Bradstreet approximately 3,000 men for a Frontenac expedition. Given the regulars' often-expressed contempt for the military abilities of the American provincials, it was an unusual army in that it was overwhelmingly colonial and commanded by an Anglo-Irish-Acadian, John Bradstreet. Only 150 British regulars were involved, while there were 2,520 American provincials, 300 *bateaux*-men, and about 40 Indians. New Yorkers were the largest colonial contingent, numbering more than 1,000, while other provincials were drawn from Massachusetts, New Jersey, and Rhode Island units. Since many of the troops had just come through the harrowing experience of Ticonderoga, sickness and desertion were major problems. Nonetheless, Bradstreet drove his force, heavily laden *bateaux* and all, across rivers, lakes, creeks, and carrying places and arrived at Oswego and Lake Ontario on 21 August. One setback occurred when a scouting party was attacked by French Indians near Oswego and information about the strength of the expedition was quickly relayed to the commander of Frontenac, Pierre-Jacques Payen de Noyan et de Chavoy.

Wasting no time, on 22 August, Bradstreet's force set out on Lake Ontario in 123 *bateaux* and 95 whaleboats and was within sight of Fort Frontenac on 25 August. In 1755, the defenses of the fort had been in such a state of deterioration that "when one of the guns . . . is discharged the whole fort shakes," and little improvement had been made. With a defending garrison of only 110 men, the French obviously were not expecting an attack and the fort was in no position to withstand a siege. Even the French naval power was virtually useless. Only two of the vessels were armed, while four or five others were not even rigged. Landing his troops on 25 August, and artillery the next day, Bradstreet's forces quickly occupied an old breastwork 250 yards south of the fort and another position 150 yards west of Frontenac's walls. French firing was sporadic and ineffective, while Anglo-American shells were more damaging, one landing near Fort Frontenac's magazine and setting off "a quantity of gun-powder." On the morning of 27 August 1758, Noyan recognized his impossible situation and surrendered, the very day that a French relief force left Lachine. The prisoners were allowed to return to Montreal while vessels, provisions, goods, and fortifications were set afire or otherwise destroyed; provisions and goods destroyed were worth at least 800,000 livres, or £35,000 sterling, if Bradstreet's estimate was correct. The remaining plunder, and there was considerable, was loaded on a captured brig and schooner as well as on the *bateaux* and by 30 August, the force had safely reached Oswego and began to retrace its steps down the route away from Lake Ontario.

With this one bold stroke Bradstreet became, briefly at least, the toast of London, praised by the likes of William Pitt, Lord Halifax, and Lord Barrington, while honored in America as the effective leader of a courageous colonial force. In the Great Lakes theater of war, the victory was a turning point in terms of paving the way for further British victories. The lifeline of the Great Lakes empire of the French had been severed and, before this rupture could be repaired completely, Fort Duquesne would fall. The demolition of Fort Frontenac, the capture of French provisions and the destruction of their vessels significantly weakened the morale of the western Indian allies of the French and stopped the drift of the Six Nations. The capture and destruction of Fort Frontenac had generously contributed to the final defeat of New France.

William G. Godfrey

References

W.G. Godfrey, *Pursuit of Profit and Pre-ferment in Colonial North America: John Bradstreet's Quest* (1982); Francis Jennings, *Empire of Fortune: Crowns, Colonies, and Tribes in the Seven Years War in America* (1988); R.A. Preston and L. Lamontagne, eds., *Royal Fort Frontenac* (1958); George F.G. Stanley, *New France: The Last Phase, 1744–1760* (1968).

See also BRADSTREET, JOHN; FORT OSWEGO (NEW YORK)

Frontenac, Louis de Buade de, Comte de Frontenac et de Pallau (1622–1698)

Louis de Buade de Frontenac was the only son of Henri de Buade, comte de Frontenac. He was baptized in 1634 and King Louis XIII served as his godfather. The Buades were a family of warriors, members of the nobility of the sword in France. Only the basic outlines of Frontenac's early career are established. He served in the Thirty Years' War and his right arm was crippled from a wound he received in 1646; in compensation for this, he was made a maréchal-de-camp (equivalent of brigadier general). Married in 1648, he and his wife proceeded to run up a host of debts from gambling and extravagant living notable even in the court of Louis XIV! In addition to being a spendthrift, Frontenac was a cheat; he refused to pay his creditors in 1668, even after they had given him a four-year reprieve. He saved himself from financial ruin in the manner of his time; he joined a French-Venetian campaign against the Turks in 1669, but he quarreled with his superiors and was dismissed the same year.

In light of these events, it is surprising that Frontenac was appointed the governor of New France in 1672. It appears likely that two things aided him in securing the appointment: his standing as the leading member of a distinguished family and his personal charm, which could, when he chose to use it, be effective. Since the appointment gave him a certain immunity from his creditors, it was vital to his fortune.

Frontenac arrived at Quebec in the fall of 1672. He soon irritated and then exasperated several constituencies within French Canada: the Conseil Souverain, the merchants of Montreal, the intendant of the colony, and the religious orders. Frontenac attempted to inject himself as the chairman of the Conseil, and he expanded the fur trade by building Cataracoui (later named Fort Frontenac), which took trade away from Montreal. Frontenac also countenanced the selling of brandy to the Indians in the fur trade; the clergy of the colony took offense at this and used every opportunity to speak against Frontenac at the court of Versailles. Frontenac also disputed the authority of the new intendant of the colony, Jacques Duchesneau. When one considers the amount of dissension that existed within the colony, it is remarkable that Frontenac's first term as governor (1672–1682) lasted as long as it did.

Frustrated by Frontenac's intemperate behavior, Louis XIV and Colbert recalled the governor in 1682. Frontenac returned to France and continued to fight to stave off his creditors, all the while seeking some sort of suitable appointment for a man in his financial situation. While he was in France, two successive governors (La Barre and Denonville) struggled against the growing power of the Iroquois nations, which had become subjects of King Charles II (at least on paper), and who were determined to prevent a possible domination of the fur trade by the French in Canada. The Iroquois made open war on Canada in 1689 and terrorized the colony.

In April 1689, Frontenac was again named as the governor of New France. His appointment came at the start of King William's War (1689–1697) between France and England. King Louis XIV charged Frontenac with carrying out an ambitious plan to attack and seize Albany and New York City and thus dominate the fur trade entirely. Knowing the limits of his resources, Frontenac sent out three war parties of French Canadians and Indians to attack the English frontier in the winter of 1689–1690. The war parties attacked Schenectady, New York (which they burned), Fort Loyal, Maine, and Salmon Falls, New Hampshire. The raids lifted the morale of the French Canadians and boosted Frontenac's prestige within the colony. Frontenac wrongly judged that there was little danger of retaliation from the English colonists, who, to his mind, were adept only at trade, never at warfare.

Frontenac's raids, however successful in the short term, turned much of Puritan New England against French Canada. In the spring of 1690, Sir William Phips led a Puritan fleet north from Boston and captured Port Royal, Acadia (present-day Annapolis Royal, Nova

Scotia). Phips and his men brought back booty from the conquest which encouraged the Bostonians to attempt a much greater project—an all-out attack on Quebec City, the heart and soul of New France. Although the risks were daunting, the potential prize was enormous. On 9 August 1690, a fleet of 32 ships carrying 2,200 men sailed from Boston and headed toward French Canada.

Although he prided himself on his foresight and diligence, Frontenac was completely unaware of this major threat to Quebec. The governor was in Montreal in order to repulse a possible land assault from Albany. At nearly the last possible moment, Frontenac was alerted that a great enemy fleet had passed by Maine. He made all speed to reach Quebec and arrived there three days before the fleet of Phips sailed into view on the St. Lawrence River on 16 October 1690. Fortunately, Major Prevost had hastily built fortifications and the town was reasonably well prepared for this assault by the "Bostonnais," a term which the French Canadians would use to describe all future assailants of Quebec (those in 1711, 1759, and 1775).

Phips had taken too long on his voyage; if he had arrived even a week sooner, Quebec would surely have fallen into his hands. Once Frontenac was within the city's walls, he became the rallying point for the city's defense. The townspeople, whom he had infuriated in the past, now saw him as their protector and, in this role as soldier fighting on the defensive, he was proficient. Phips sent an envoy, Thomas Savage, ashore under a white flag. Savage was blindfolded and brought up the streets of the lower town to the Château St. Louis where he was met by Frontenac and his military aides. When the Bostonian emissary demanded the town's surrender within one hour, Frontenac responded with a diatribe which concluded with his famous words,

> I will answer your general only through the mouths of my cannon, that he may learn that a man like me is not to be summoned after this fashion. Let him do his best, and I will do mine.

Thomas Savage was again blindfolded and then returned to the lower town and to his boat. Frontenac had played his dramatic role superbly.

The French also enjoyed several tangible, tactical advantages. Winter was rapidly approaching and Phips needed to act at once if he was to have any chance of taking the city. Also, Frontenac's defenders now outnumbered the "Bostonnais," who were trying to seize one of the natural strongholds of North America. Phips landed soldiers on the north bank of the St. Charles River, but these men had only small supplies of food and gunpowder. While his men on shore were still debating how to cross the St. Charles River, Phips made a cardinal error; he brought his ships close to the lower town and tried to subdue the city through a cannonade. The Puritan ships were outgunned in this contest; the New England gunners could not properly elevate their cannons, while the French gunners hit the enemy's ships time and again. The Puritan ships sustained heavy damages; therefore, Frontenac's boast was vindicated. Meanwhile, the Puritan soldiers were suffering from both cold and hunger. Phips embarked his men and sailed down the St. Lawrence on his way home. The Puritan armada ran into storms and a good number of the New Englanders died from smallpox and shipwreck on the return voyage (others died from wounds suffered during a skirmish along the St. Charles River). The result was a military and economic fiasco for New England and a narrow, defensive victory for the French. Frontenac and New France exulted over the victory; a medal was struck to commemorate the event and the chapel, Notre Dame de la Victoire (in the lower town), was dedicated as a memorial to the defense of Quebec.

Frontenac found, to his frustration, that he was unable to repay the attack in kind. During the next six years, he petitioned the French court to send warships to collaborate with him in an attack on Boston, but the hoped-for ships never came. Therefore, Frontenac's two offensives came by land. In 1696, a French-Canadian and Indian war party captured the English stone fort at Pemaquid, Maine, which Phips had built in 1692. Frontenac led an army into the Iroquois territory (in present-day New York state) and burned both crops and villages. The procession through the Indian territory was more symbolic than substantive, as the Iroquois maintained their alliance with the English colonists. However, the two campaigns of Pemaquid (1696) and the Iroquois country (1697) allowed Frontenac to end King William's War with some measure of success. In 1698, Frontenac learned that the war was over. He died at Quebec the same year.

Frontenac's legacy is a divided one. It can be said with some certainty that he remains the most visible and the most well-known of the governors of New France—both to French readers and to English ones—particularly because of the writings of Francis Parkman. Frontenac's first term as governor was disastrous from the standpoint of the smooth functioning of the civil government. In his second term, he was occupied with both King William's War and the continued expansion of the fur trade. There is little that can be said in Frontenac's defense as regards his public relations; he was indeed arrogant, vain, and impetuous in many of his actions. Usually, historians have followed the lead of Francis Parkman and forgiven Frontenac, since in his second term as governor, "Of the immensity of his services to the colony there can be no doubt. He found it, under Denonville, in humiliation and terror; and he left it in honor, and almost in triumph." This view has been sharply disputed by Frontenac's modern biographer, W.J. Eccles. Eccles points out that time and again Frontenac misjudged and underestimated his opponents, whether they were administrators, the Iroquois Indians, or the Puritan New Englanders.

Eccles maintains that the war parties of 1689–1690 succeeded mostly in provoking the Bostonians into attacking Canada. Frontenac also has been criticized by several writers for being too cautious in his defense of Quebec; they maintain that he could have done great harm to Phips's soldiers before they were embarked. Eccles concludes that the offensive against the Iroquois in 1697 was largely "the actions of his subordinates; the men who deserve most of the credit for the final victory over the Iroquois were Callieres, Vaudreuil, Champigny, the officers' corps of the Troupes de la Marine, and the Canadian habitants." Certainly, Frontenac has usually been accorded greater credit for his actions than was necessary; the "great man" concept of history almost guaranteed this. As a governor and as a man, Frontenac had many weaknesses and failings. His historical reputation has fared well, due in part to his colorful personality and also to his memorable response to Phips's demand for the surrender of Quebec. "Only through the mouths of my cannon," or "Par la bouche de mes cannons," has lasted in the memory of historians and to some degree in the mind of the general public. Of course, if Frontenac had lost Quebec to Phips, the phrase would not be memorable at all.

Samuel Willard Crompton

References
Remi Chenier, *Quebec: A French Colonial Town in America, 1660 to 1690* (1991); W.J. Eccles, *Frontenac: The Courtier Governor* (1959); Gerard Filteau, *Par La Bouche De Mes Cannons!: La ville de Quebec Face a l'Ennemi* (1990); William Kingsford, *The History of Canada, Vol. II, 1679–1725* (1885); Francis Parkman, *Count Frontenac and New France under Louis XIV* (1877).

See also CANADA, NEW ENGLAND EXPEDITION AGAINST (1690); KING WILLIAM'S WAR

Frontier

Over the past century, no historical concept has generated more interest and argument than the "frontier." In 1893, when Frederick Jackson Turner published his remarkably influential article on "The Significance of the Frontier in American History," he defined a central issue for a whole generation of scholars. In Turner's eyes, American history could largely be explained by the recurring process of westward movement toward the "free land" of the frontier. Movement toward the west also implied a "steady movement away from the influence of Europe," allowing the American people to "escape from the bondage of the past" and "escape to the free conditions of the frontier." Thus it was, Turner argued, that the frontier encouraged the development of social and political democracy and, more generally, the emergence of a distinctly American culture.

This "frontier thesis" attracted a large number of scholars to the "Turner school" of historical writing, but it also created a sizable share of skeptics. In the first half of the twentieth century, many historians challenged Turner's emphasis on the frontier as the single most significant source of American civilization. They pointed to other important factors—industrialization, urbanization, and immigration, for instance—and they questioned the extent to which westward movement did indeed offer the openness and opportunity Turner and his followers found. More recently, historians have raised serious questions about Turner's very definition of the term "frontier" itself. Turner had described the frontier as "the outer edge of the wave—the meeting point between savagery and civilization." Clearly, such a distinction between supposed Indian "savagery" and Euro-American "civilization" implied a strong ethnocentric bias. Moreover, the notion that the frontier formed "the outer edge of the wave" of westward movement likewise privileged the perspective of Euro-Americans. To the extent that "frontier" still carries such assumptions of cultural and racial superiority, some historians are now reluctant to use the term at all.

Yet rather than discarding it altogether, other historians are seeking to redefine "frontier" in ways that avoid the earlier Eurocentric bias. Instead of portraying the frontier as the outer edge of Euro-American (or, more commonly, Anglo-American) advance, for instance, they now describe it as the "contact zone" or "middle ground" between cultures, an area of intercultural interaction that ran both ways. The emphasis is not just on the conquest of Native Americans by Euro-American invaders, but also on various forms of cooperation and cultural exchange; the main point is that contact affected *both* cultures. The concept of cultural exchange helps strip away the stereotypes of "savage" and "civilized" and promotes a better appreciation of distinct peoples as active participants in a mutually transforming process. Moreover, the notion of frontier as contact zone helps broaden the focus beyond two-dimensional relationships between Native Americans and Euro-Americans to encompass more complex connections among various Indian groups and European colonizers.

That, in fact, is the most important point for the period under consideration in this volume: during the era of European colonization, Europeans and Indians did not form two competing cultural monoliths. There was no single, westward-moving line to define the frontier, nor was there a single frontier experience. Rather, there were several contact zones defined by different relationships among different peoples at different times. The main European colonizers—the English, French, and Spanish—all operated (and often overlapped) in different regions of North America, and they shaped their economic and military strategies to suit the particular circumstances of time and place. So did the major Indian groups they encountered—the Iroquois Confederacy, the Abenaki, Cherokee, Creek, Choctaw, and others in the eastern woodlands; the Pawnee and Pueblo in the plains and desert regions farther west. Over the course of two centuries, these groups formed many complex patterns of economic, diplomatic, and military alliance, with each group playing off the others in the pursuit of its particular self-interest.

In the long run, the Europeans (or their Euro-American descendants) prevailed in their conquest of the continent. One of the great ironies of American history, in fact, is that they could not have done so without Indian assistance. Yet in the more immediate context of the colonial era, when the ultimate outcome was still quite uncertain, Europeans and Indians interacted with each other in ways that defied simple assumptions of superiority. In a sense, by confronting each other as significant actors, whether adversaries or allies, they also had to confront each other as equals.

One tragic factor made Europeans and Indians more equal in numbers: disease. Even before Europeans arrived in North America on a large scale, deadly pathogens preceded them, brought over by the comparative handful of fishermen and explorers who first made contact with native inhabitants. Indians had no natural or acquired immunity against these imported illnesses—especially smallpox, diphtheria, and the measles—and they died by the tens of thousands. Along the eastern seaboard of North America, where the Europeans established most of their first permanent settlements, the native population had already been devastated by disease, suffering a loss of as much as 90 percent in some regions. This demographic catastrophe was the first significant result of contact, and in the short run certainly the most critical.

In the two centuries that followed this initial period of contact, the increasing presence of European trappers, traders, and settlers on the North American landscape created a complex pattern of interaction with native peoples. Indians responded to the European influx not just with armed resistance but also with conditional acceptance. No less than the Europeans, Indians had their own economic and diplomatic agendas, and they often saw Europeans as useful trading partners and military allies. Both peoples used the other to promote their own interests, and sometimes the relationship worked out to be mutually beneficial—at least for a while.

The fur trade is a case in point. Long before the arrival of Europeans, Indians had been accustomed to intergroup trade. Trade was a means whereby one group could exchange something it had in abundance for another group's surplus—say, shellfish for furs. Moreover, trade was not just an exercise in exchange but an expression of friendship; it often took the form of elaborate gift-giving, a ceremonial sealing of diplomatic relations between two groups in which goods added to the weight of words. When Europeans arrived on the scene, Indians readily engaged in trade, offering them baskets and other handmade items, exotic plants, and, above all, deerskins and beaver pelts. Furs were comparatively easy to get, and therefore easy to let go. In turn, they valued the commodities the Europeans had in abundance—glass beads, mirrors, colored cloth, metal pots, hatchets, knives, guns, and liquor. Both parties, then, stood to make a good bargain.

What the Indians did not bargain for, however, was the effect this trade would ultimately have on their culture. In some respects, European trade goods revolutionized the Indians' ways of life. The most dramatic example was the acquisition of Spanish horses by the nomadic groups of the Great Plains, who became more mobile as hunters and warriors. By the nineteenth century, when the expanding United States began to encroach on their territory, the Plains Indians were a powerful military force of skilled horsemen. Similarly, guns increased the Indians' killing power in hunting and war and became a kind of status symbol. As one Englishman in seventeenth-century Virginia observed, "they think themselves undrest and not fit to walk abroad, unless they have their gun on their shoulder, and their shot-bag by their side." Metal tools and cooking utensils were also important acquisitions as labor-saving devices that made it easier to clear fields, raise crops, and cook food; once an Indian had used a metal axe, there was little desire to go back to a stone one.

But just as there were obvious advantages to the new trade goods and technology, so were there disadvantages, albeit less immediately apparent. In general, the more Indians came to rely on European goods, the less they were able to rely on themselves; where once they had been essentially self-sufficient, they became increasingly dependent. Liquor, for instance, was an important lubricant in commercial relations with Indians. Indians often incorporated European liquor into their religious ceremonies, drinking it to hasten or heighten their sense of spiritual possession. Unfortunately, once the liquor had been consumed, they needed more, and the only place to get the best beverage was from a European trader. The same was true with guns. Indians could make minor repairs to wooden stocks or replace ramrods, but they could not cast more complex metal parts or make gunpowder. Even so-called consumer

durables—knives, tools, cooking utensils, and so forth—created another sort of dependency; when Indians could trade for such items, they gave up making them themselves. Handicraft skills did not suddenly collapse, but they declined over time, further increasing the gap between Indian products and European imports. Thus trade often gave Europeans a means of leverage and even control over native peoples without having to resort to military means.

Contact almost invariably led to conflict, however, and frontier regions were almost always the scenes of raids and skirmishes. More important, in the seemingly unending series of European wars for empire in the seventeenth and eighteenth centuries, the competition for control of the continent made North American frontier regions both the battleground and the prize. The fact that many of the major wars discussed in this volume had different names on different sides of the Atlantic—e.g., the War of the Spanish Succession, or Queen Anne's War (1702–1713); the War of the Austrian Succession, or King George's War (1744-1748); the Seven Years' War, or the French and Indian War (1754–1763)—underscores the two-front nature of the conflict, with fighting in both Europe and America. In America, in fact, they were usually *two-frontier* wars, with separate theaters in the north and south.

The complexities of Euro-American war and diplomacy were further exacerbated by the equally complex interests of Native American people, who also competed, both with Euro-Americans and with each other, for territory and trade. Indians played a critical role in each of the major European wars in North America, whether as active combatants or as interested neutrals. Indeed, given the small number of European soldiers or armed settlers on the North American frontier, European officials found it impossible to pursue their imperial policies over such a vast expanse of territory without the assistance of Indian allies. In some European-led campaigns Indians made up well over half the fighting force. That is not to say, however, that Indians became mere cannon fodder in these frontier conflicts. They entered into alliances with Europeans to pursue their own goals, especially to gain an advantage over their traditional Indian enemies. Moreover, Indians initiated hostilities on their own, sometimes just when war-weary Europeans thought they had resolved their imperial conflicts. Two such Indian uprisings, the Yamasee War (1715–1717) and Pontiac's War (1763), made Euro-Americans painfully aware that treaties negotiated by the great powers on the other side of the Atlantic could not guarantee peace on the American frontier.

Even in periods of relative peace, in fact, Euro-American officials had difficulty maintaining control over their own people. Long before any colonial government could establish firm authority over contested territory, independent settlers often began moving into frontier regions to make their own claims to the land. They lived off the land with little concern for legal title or proper surveys, and thus they stood in the way of orderly settlement, proper administration, and profitable land sales. In the eyes of government officials, elite landowners, and other promoters of proper settlement, these squatters were a blight on the landscape, lazy louts who survived in a semi-savage state and symbolized human sloth and social disorder. They were commonly disdained, in commonly-used eighteenth-century epithets, as "scum," "banditti," and "white Indians." Moreover, their constant encroachment on the lands of real Indians often stirred up trouble just when government officials wanted to maintain peace.

The problem of squatters and other unauthorized settlers became especially acute for Anglo-American authorities at the end of the Seven Years' War, with the outbreak of Pontiac's War. Although the British army had emerged victorious in this last round of imperial warfare, government officials had no assurance that peace would be permanent. They knew, though, that they had to avoid creating unnecessary unrest in the northwest, and that depended, they reasoned, on keeping their own colonists out of the region. Accordingly, in October 1763, in the face of the sudden Indian uprisings that threatened the army's very existence in the northwest, the British government issued a proclamation that prohibited Anglo-American settlers from living west of the Appalachian Mountains. In effect, the authorities in London drew a line on the map running down the Appalachian ridgeline from Maine to Georgia, thus creating two separate zones of settlement: the western part would be Indian territory regulated by the British army; all other British subjects would be limited to the eastern part.

What seemed like sensible regulation in London seemed more like restrictive confinement in the colonies. Land-hungry Anglo-Americans felt that they had fought effectively in the late war, and now they deserved to reap the benefits of the peace. No prize looked more appealing than the land across the mountains. And no official proclamation could deter them from claiming that prize. The British army was virtually powerless to stop squatters, and they pushed through the proclamation line with impunity. In the decade after the conclusion of the Seven Years' War, tens of thousands of Anglo-American colonists took up land in the trans-Appalachian frontier. To those officials who called them "scum" or "banditti," they remained a resentful and potentially resistant force on the frontier. Indeed, by the 1770s, they would add their resentment to the more widespread unrest that was pushing the Anglo-American colonies toward revolution. The British government, like the other colonial powers that had struggled to conquer the North American continent for two centuries, would learn again the fundamental lesson of the frontier: no nation could truly claim control of the land or of the people living on it.

Gregory H. Nobles

References

Verner W. Crane, *The Southern Frontier, 1670–1732* (1929); Francis Jennings, *The Invasion of America: Indians, Colonialism, and the Cant of Conquest* (1975); Gregory H. Nobles, "Breaking into the Backcountry: New Approaches to the Early American Frontier," *William and Mary Quarterly,* 3rd ser., 46 (1989):641–670; Walter Stitt Robinson, *The Southern Colonial Frontier, 1607–1763* (1979).

Frederick Jackson Turner, *The Frontier in History* (1920); David J. Weber, *The Spanish Frontier in North America* (1992); Richard White, *The Middle Ground: Indians, Empires, and Republics in the Great Lakes Region, 1650–1815* (1991).

See also CHURCH, BENJAMIN; COUREURS DE BOIS; FORTS, PROVINCIAL; FRONTIER, NORTHERN; FRONTIER, SOUTHERN; GARRISON HOUSES; PROCLAMATION LINE OF 1763; RANGERS; WAR AND SOCIETY IN COLONIAL AMERICA

Frontier, Northern

The northern frontier comprised the region north and west of colonial Virginia. Penetrating inland, via the river systems and valleys of the region, were the British and French North American settlements. Opposing this thrust were the Indian groups comprising the northeastern woodlands culture. The frontier emerged where these competing cultures met. Over time, the northern frontier of the colonial period stretched from the confluence of the Ohio and Mississippi Rivers to the mouth of the St. Lawrence River and Newfoundland. The region was populated by indigenous and colonial peoples of the northeastern United States and southeastern Canada. Such a definition of the northern frontier is not made arbitrarily. When British officials created an Indian superintendency system, they gave the northern superintendent the same geographic parameters.

The northern frontier was characterized by several specific biotic and geographic zones. New England is characterized by two distinct ecological zones alone. While New England's soil was nutrient poor, the bottomlands of New York's river systems comprised rich alluvial flatlands. The black soil was four to six feet deep and required little manure to maintain its productivity. To the south, the piedmont region provided ideal conditions for tobacco production. Fur-bearing animals abounded throughout the northern region.

Both Indians and colonists made use of these resources. Historically, the Indians had managed the region's environmental resources for community survival. European contact changed traditional Indian relationships with their environment. Colonists viewed the New World in terms of "commodities." This attitude allowed them to begin the ecological transformation of the region. Meadows provided forage for animals and, in the minds of the colonists, potential planting fields. Forests provided firewood and ample timber for naval supplies. When Native Americans began hunting animals to exchange for European trade goods, the hunter transformed his role within the ecosystem. In some regions the result was over-hunting. When coupled with the introduction of new animals to the environment, Indian homelands were altered profoundly. Over the course of the colonial period, the transformation of the environment along the frontier led to a declining standard of living for the Indians.

The environmental transition from forest to European-style farmland helps define the frontier. Colonial settlement in a region did not mean the expulsion of the Indians. In some areas of the northern frontier, Native American and colonial communities lived within easy distance of each other. In New York, colonial settlements in the Mohawk Valley did not drive the Mohawks away. The residents of Caughnawaga Castle, Fort Hunter, and Mount Johnson lived in close contact during the mid-eighteenth century. Along the Pennsylvania frontier, Indian and colonial migrations westward created a series of heterogenous communities. Shawnee, Delaware, Iroquois, and colonial traders lived together in towns such as Great Island, Logstown, Kittanning, and Kuskuski. Here they conducted business and forged personal relationships that led to personal alliances. In this respect, the northern frontier bears little resemblance to the one described by Frederick Jackson Turner.

Four time periods distinguish the political and military history of the northern frontier. The first era dates from European contact to 1650. The second division involves the years from 1650 to 1700. The next phase of frontier history is from 1700 to 1744. The last era is from 1744 to 1763. Although arbitrary, these dates correspond to the changing nature of Indian-colonist relationships along the northern frontier. The first delineation corresponds with the early history of colonist-Indian relations. During this time period both sides tried to understand each other within existing conceptual frameworks. The second phase of frontier history concerns the struggle of colonists and Native Americans to come to grips with the other side. The early- to mid-eighteenth century represents an era of tremendous fluidity along the frontier. Both cultures struggled to adjust to the other's presence in North America. The final period evidenced the great struggles for empire among colonial powers. British victory in 1763 resulted in a change in Indian-colonist relations along the frontier.

Europeans had been in contact with the coastal Indians of North America since roughly 1497. Drawn by the fisheries off the coasts of northern North America, the sailors also found time to trade manufactured items for furs. Within two generations of the failed Roanoke colony, Europeans had established settlements from Jamestown to New Amsterdam to Boston. These isolated communities developed along different economic, social, and religious paths.

Initially, both Indian and colonist viewed the other as a useful tool. Powhatan, leader of the Powhatan Confederacy in 1607, and his subordinate chiefs hoped the exchange of corn with the colonists would incorporate the for-

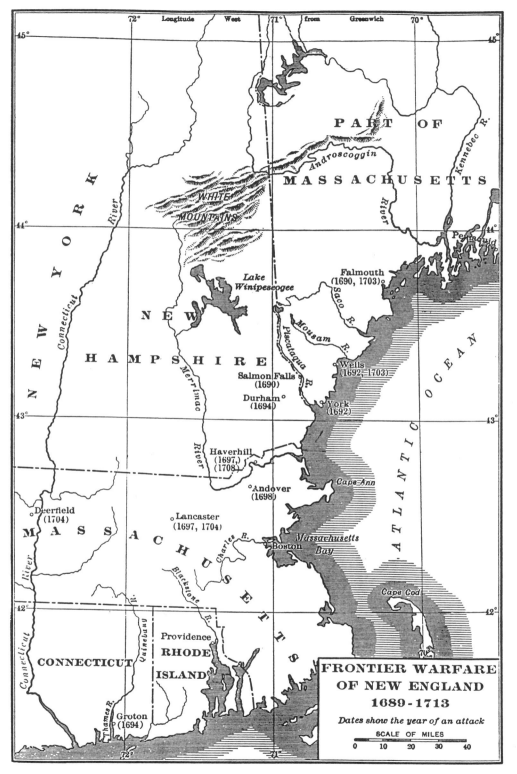

F

45°   72°   Longitude   West   71°   from   Greenwich   70°   45°

PART OF

MASSACHUSETTS

Androscoggin

Kennebec R.

NEW YORK

Connecticut River

WHITE MOUNTAINS

44°   Pemaquid   44°

River

Lake Winipeseogee

Falmouth
(1690, 1703)

NEW

Saco R.

Mousam R.

Piscataqua R.

HAMPSHIRE

Wells
(1692, 1703)

Merrimac

Salmon Falls
(1690)

Durham
(1694)

York
(1692)

ATLANTIC OCEAN

43°   43°

River

Haverhill
(1697,)
(1708)

Cape Ann

Andover
(1698)

Deerfield
(1704)

Lancaster
(1697, 1704)

Charles R.

MASSACHUSETTS

Boston

Massachusetts Bay

River

Cape Cod

42°   42°

Quinebaug

Providence

RHODE

ISLAND

CONNECTICUT

Blackstone R.

Connecticut

Thames R.

Groton
(1694)

72°   71°

FRONTIER WARFARE
OF NEW ENGLAND
1689 - 1713

Dates show the year of an attack

SCALE OF MILES

0   10   20   30   40

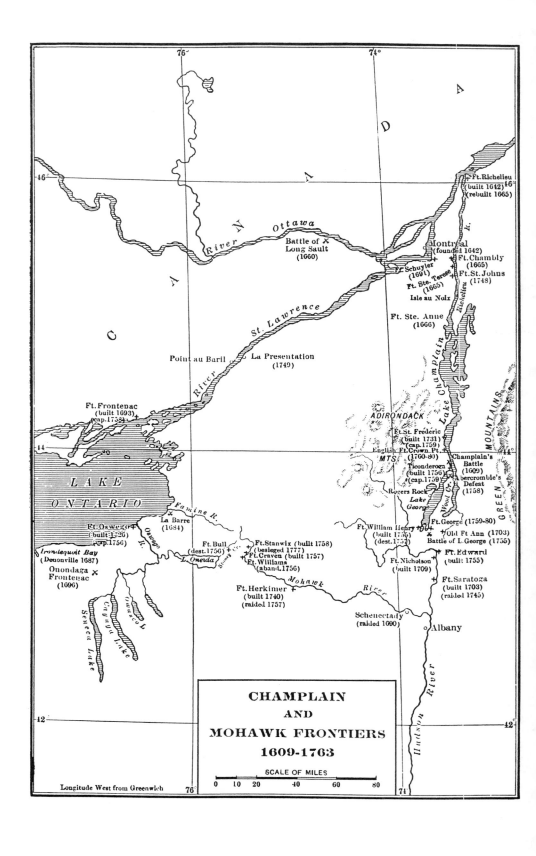

CHAMPLAIN
AND
MOHAWK FRONTIERS
1609-1763

SCALE OF MILES

0 10 20   40   60   80

Longitude West from Greenwich

eigners into an existing system of exchange and tribute. John Smith had his own objectives when trading with Powhatan. The de facto leader of the starving colony hoped to impress his Indian neighbors with the European's superiority. Both sought control of the other via trade. Powhatan used corn and Smith used copper to secure the advantage. This struggle for domination, when coupled with the search for new tobacco lands, led to wars in 1622 and 1644.

Like Virginia colonists, the New England settlers fought with their Indian neighbors in the early 1640s. The "Great Migration" forced Puritan New England to find land for nearly 20,000 immigrants between 1630 and 1642. Fortunately for the settlers, nearly 80,000 Indians had died since 1616. Still, Indian depopulation did not open enough land for colonial settlement. In 1643, the Puritans used force against the Narragansetts to expand their frontier settlements. This Puritan conquest was an underlying cause of the conflict that erupted in New England during the late seventeenth century.

Before 1650, the Iroquois Confederacy waged a series of "beaver wars" against the Huron, Erie, and Neutral nations. These wars made the Iroquois middlemen in the fur trade issuing from the Ohio and Illinois Valleys. In the century to come, the Five Nations would claim territorial rights to the entire region because of their victories. The Iroquois's action was an important event along the northern frontier. Their conquest, when coupled with Britain's need to maintain the confederacy as allies, influenced how colonial westward expansion developed. The periphery of Iroquoia became the avenues of colonial expansion along the frontier. Iroquois sovereignty gave the lines demarcating the frontier its peculiar "bulge" pattern.

The years 1650 to 1700 witnessed some momentous events along the northern frontier. Three events deserve special mention: the creation of the "Covenant Chain," Metacom's War (King Philip's War), and Bacon's Rebellion. A period of tremendous tension, these years saw the emergence of new relationships along the edges of colonial America. Following the bloody 1670s, both Indians and colonists worked to arrange a policy of coexistence. By 1700, an uneasy acceptance of each other had occurred.

The "Covenant Chain" was a metaphor used to describe a political alliance between the British and the Iroquois Confederacy. In the alliance, New York emerged as the center of colonial activity when it came to British dealings with the Indians. Metaphorically, the chain that emerged between New York and the Iroquois was made of "silver." This silver chain replaced an earlier chain of "iron" that had united the Mohawks and Dutch of Fort Orange (Albany). The basis of this united alliance was trade, and the "new" chain was forged between the years 1675 and 1677. A Seneca speaker gave the chain its "silver" hue in a 1684 speech. Credit for the Covenant Chain is usually given to either New York Governor Edmund Andros or the Onondaga leader Garakontié. Initially, Andros and other British officials viewed the chain as means of confronting unrest on New York's eastern and southern borders. Both Metacom's War and Bacon's Rebellion had created problems along New York's borders. The Covenant Chain greatly altered the frontier situation. The chain gave New York and the Five Nations a preeminent place in colonial-Indian relations along the northern frontier.

While New York and the Iroquois worked to establish the Covenant Chain, Metacom's War exploded in New England. This war illustrated the Puritans' weakness along the frontier. Only after Andros asked the Mohawks to drive Metacom back into New England were the Puritans able to take the initiative in the war. The Mohawks accepted Andros's request because they had their own political score to settle with the New England Indians. The Mohawks' decision to enter the struggle illustrates how preexisting Indian-Indian issues remained the basic determinant of their actions during the seventeenth century. The Puritans defeated Metacom and his allies with Mohawk assistance. The Puritans then forced the defeated Wampanoags, Nipmucks, and Narragansetts out of New England or onto proto-reservations. Those who moved west took up residences in the Susquehanna and Delaware Valleys. From these new locations they worked to limit future colonial expansion.

The Chesapeake Bay region experienced its own frontier conflict: Bacon's Rebellion. Begun by frontiersmen to revenge the death of a colonial overseer by Doeg Indians—themselves the victims of abuse by the overseer's employer—the frontiersmen ultimately turned against the government of Virginia. Like their

F

New England counterparts, Virginians did not differentiate between friendly and hostile Indian neighbors during the conflict. The Indians were the enemy. Although they claimed only to be reacting to Indian provocation, the frontiersmen also showed a keen interest in the Indians' land. They were especially drawn to lands already cleared for planting. Only the death of Nathaniel Bacon and the arrival of imperial commissioners brought an end to the conflict. In 1677, imperial commissioners and tidewater Indian groups signed an agreement known as the Treaty of Middle Plantation which ushered in a new period of peaceful relations between tidewater Indian groups and the colony of Virginia.

Throughout the seventeenth century, British officials told colonists that friendly Indians on the frontier were their best defense against attack by hostile Indians in the interior. In addition to military protection, Indian informants kept the colonists abreast of French actions. During the eighteenth century, imperial officials increasingly worried that colonists moving westward were moving beyond governmental control. Beyond the reach of colonial and imperial government, these frontiersmen produced conflict with neighboring Indian groups.

Colonial expansion coincided with the erection of European trading posts. Designed for the fur trade, lying beyond the lines demarcating Indian and colonial territories, these blockhouses also served military strategy. They allowed traders, both French and British, to observe not only the actions of their enemies but also neighboring Indians. In addition to trade advantages, the blockhouses showed the colonists' renewed commitment for western lands. Unlike earlier territorial acquisitions, trade was the driving force behind territorial acquisition in the early eighteenth century.

By the early eighteenth century, an unofficial boundary line ran along the northern frontier. Beginning in Virginia and following the Shenandoah Mountains, the frontier stretched northward to the Susquehanna and Delaware Valleys and into New York. From New York the frontier moved eastward along the Mohawk River and then in a northeasterly direction into New England. By 1720, the Kennebec River marked the frontier's eastern extremity. During the third phase of colonial expansion colonists would gaze longingly at the lands west of the mountains. Colonial interest in these western lands helps explain the growing antagonisms along the Pennsylvania and Virginia frontier.

Between 1700 and 1740, the French and British colonial governments systematically built a series of permanent forts in Indian territory. These outposts provided Europeans a permanent place in the North American interior. These trading posts had two purposes: to capture more of the Indian trade, and to provide military defense in time of war. The construction of Forts Niagara and Oswego illustrate these points. The French established a wooden outpost at Niagara during the 1670s. To create a more permanent presence in the region, the French built a fort out of stone in 1726. The French hoped that Fort Niagara would allow them to intercept furs headed east toward Albany. Responding to the French threat, New York's Governor William Burnet convinced the Mohawks to grant his colony the right to build a rival trading post. The result was Fort Oswego, completed in 1727. Oswego effectively excluded Pennsylvania traders from the beaver trade. After Oswego's construction, Pennsylvania traders put their energy into developing a deerskin trade in the Ohio Valley. This placed new pressures on the Ohio Valley frontier.

From the Indian perspective, the British construction of blockhouses led to the settlement of the lands surrounding the post. Where colonists or crown built blockhouses, change followed. Married soldiers might bring their wives and discharged veterans might take up farming in the adjacent land. The soldiers stationed at these outposts brought cattle and swine with them. The livestock roamed outside the gates of the compound and competed with indigenous fauna for food. The resulting environmental change often displaced traditional animals to new areas, forcing Indian hunters into new regions. The Ohio Valley was one region settled by refugees and hunters searching for new lands. As groups such as the Delaware moved west, colonists pushed into the lands recently vacated by the Indians. Yet the gradual movements of Indians westward did not proceed fast enough for most colonists. The quest for western lands led to the Anglo-Franco clashes of the mid-eighteenth century.

Through natural reproduction and immigration, the colonies continued to grow. Many immigrants and the sons of original community settlers sought cheap land on the frontier. By 1718, the Delawares and William Penn's commissioners had completed a series of treaties defining the lands held by colonist and Indian in Pennsylvania. These treaties left the lands lying between the Susquehanna and Delaware Rivers, as far as Tohickon Creek, free of Indian encumbrance. By the time King George's War began in 1744, Pennsylvania politicians had already fraudulently extended the boundaries of Pennsylvania. The politicians desire for more land culminated in the "Walking Purchase," which embittered the Delawares and helps explain their decision to "take up the hatchet" against the colony during the wars for empire and Pontiac's War.

Not all Indians aligned themselves with the Ottawa warrior. As was the case during Metacom's War, Indian-Indian politics influenced which groups joined the uprising. Mohawk and Onondaga warriors helped the colonial and imperial soldiers defeat the western Shawnee and Delaware attacks. This time, however, British and Mohawk policy objectives now coincided. Mohawk warriors were helping colonists because they were dependent on British aid to support their claims of preeminence among the Indians. By the 1760s the Ohio Indians' strength challenged Six Nations prestige with the British. Colonial expansion was predicated on the manipulation of existing Indian-Indian struggles throughout the colonial period.

During the years 1744 to 1763, the northern frontier changed dramatically. A generation of almost constant warfare weakened the Indian communities of the region. Their ability to resist renewed colonial expansion had been dissipated. Although the European powers enjoyed a six-year peace during this period, some Indian groups were not so fortunate. While colonial frontiersmen were regrouping, the Six Nations and Cherokee continued their long-standing conflict. An outbreak of smallpox and influenza during the late 1750s and early 1760s along the northern frontier further weakened the Indians' ability to withstand colonial pressures.

These tensions led to an interesting scenario along the northern frontier. During these years, war chiefs emerged among Indian polities whose power rivaled civil leaders. Civil leaders on both side of the cultural divide were unable to enforce agreements on their followers, and the frontier became the site of numerous clashes. The war called Pontiac's is the most famous of the post-1761 conflicts.

At the same time Native American war chiefs were coming to the fore of Indian politics, British officials moved from a policy of accommodation to domination. Making such a policy change required British officials to deal with the Indians in a different manner after 1763. To accomplish this task, imperial officials put together a "comprehensive treaty system" that changed the very nature of the northern frontier. After 1763, both colonist and Indian struggled to define a boundary that would separate them. Indeed, by 1763, a paradigm had emerged that dictated how diplomacy along the northern frontier operated.

By the time of Pontiac's War, colonial settlement of the frontier had assumed the characteristics of an ocean tide. Settlers moved west and north, only to be driven back by the Indians. Settlers moved in again—this time a little farther—but once again the Indians drove the settlers back, only not as far as before. In this manner, the northern frontier assumed the attributes of a tide. Rather than thinking of the frontier as a constant push westward, it is more accurate to think of it as a series of victories and defeats for all groups living in the region in question. As Pontiac's War made clear, and Britain's response to it suggested, it was not absolutely foreordained that the colonists occupy lands west of the Shenandoah Mountains. The colonists' possession of their territory is the story of the American War for Independence.

Michael J. Mullin

References

William Cronon, *Changes in the Land: Indians, Colonists, and the Ecology of New England* (1983); Laurence M. Hauptman, "Refugee Havens: The Iroquois Villages of the Eighteenth Century," in *American Indian Environments: Ecological Issues in Native American History,* ed. by Christopher Vecsey and Robert W. Venables (1980); Francis Jennings, *The Ambiguous Iroquois Empire: The Covenant Chain Confederation of Indian Tribes with English Colonies from its beginnings to the Lancaster Treaty of 1744* (1984); Dorothy V. Jones, *License for Empire: Colonialism by Treaty in Early America* (1982).

Michael N. McConnell, "Peoples 'In Between': The Iroquois and the Ohio Indians, 1720–1768," in *Beyond the Covenant Chain: The Iroquois and Their Neighbors in Indian North America, 1600–1800,* ed. by Daniel K. Richter and James H. Merrell (1987):93–112; Stephen R. Potter, "Early English Effects on Virginia Algonquian Exchange and Tribute in the Tidewater Potomac," in *Powhatan's Mantle: Indians in the Colonial Southeast,* ed. by Peter H. Wood, et al. (1989): 151–172; Frederick Jackson Turner, *The Frontier in American History* (1986); Stephen Saunders Webb, *1676: The End of American Independence* (1985).

See also BACON'S REBELLION; CHURCH, BENJAMIN; COUREURS DE BOIS; COVENANT CHAIN; DUMMER'S WAR; FORTS, PROVINCIAL; FRONTIER; FUR TRADE; GARRISON HOUSES; IROQUOIS; IROQUOIS WARS; KING GEORGE'S WAR; KING WILLIAM'S WAR; PONTIAC'S WAR; PROCLAMATION LINE OF 1763; QUEEN ANNE'S WAR; RANGERS; WALKING PURCHASE

Frontier, Southern

Frontiers are the peripheral locales of societies where the ordinary institutional structures of societal life are weak or non-existent. As opposed to a wilderness, where the number of inhabitants by definition is small and the connection to settled areas minimal at best, frontiers often display a significant amount of human activity and have important relations with more established areas. Because the frontiers of one society often adjoin or overlap the frontiers of other societies, there is often a great deal of intersocietal interaction. This interaction takes various forms, including trade, intermarriage, warfare, and cultural exchange.

The colonial south possessed one of the most fascinating frontiers in terms of the diversity of human inhabitants. Dozens of Native American peoples interacted in myriad ways with diverse peoples from Africa and Europe. The settled areas of the south below Virginia tended to hug the Atlantic and Gulf coasts (in the case of the Europeans) and a few significant inland waterways (in the case of the aborigines), such as the Mississippi, Tennessee, Chattahoochee, and Flint Rivers. In between the settled areas were the vast expanses of land where hunters, traders, soldiers, a few farmers, refugees, and ne'er-do-wells could be found.

On the southern frontier the inhabitants, whether of Amerindian, African, or European descent, lived a relatively insecure existence, as military threats hailed from numerous directions. Those who chose to live on the frontier did so out of desperation, adventure, or the search for profits. Whites frequently chose frontier life because of the availability of inexpen-

sive or free land, sometimes taken by squatting. Indians who inhabited the frontier often had been pushed out of their traditional lands, and they found both land and employment on the periphery of other societies. Runaway slaves often sought refuge in indigenous, European, or Maroon communities, and banditti from all of the South's cultures found the frontier a relatively safe haven from which to ply their trade.

Europeans and aborigines in the settled areas devoted much of their resources, manpower, and diplomatic efforts to securing their frontiers, which they recognized as a first line of defense for their communities. The European powers—the Spanish, British, and French—all persuaded indigenous groups to relocate their towns to the purlieus of their settlements to provide a buffer against the incursions of hostile aborigines and Europeans and to keep their own subjects, particularly soldiers and slaves, from deserting or escaping. The French described these Indian allies as the *"petite nations,"* and the British used the term "settlement Indians." Often these relatively small groups agreed to relocation because their proximity to European settlements allowed them help for defense and easy access to trade goods. Many also found employment in frontier enterprises as guides, trackers, and hunters, or in providing agricultural goods in exchange for European manufactures. The Spanish differed from the French and British in that they built a mission system as a buffer to house Indians on their frontier, and the Indians who inhabited the missions hailed from both large and small nations. The destruction of the missions in the late seventeenth and early eighteenth centuries forced the Spanish to adopt the British and French method of having Indian buffers reside in non-mission towns on their frontier.

The larger Indian nations of the Southeast secured their frontiers in various ways. The Creek Confederacy, for instance, incorporated many small groups, refugees from other frontiers, thus building their military power. Relocation was another option. During the Yamasee War, the Creek moved their villages hundreds of miles from South Carolina, thus using vast expanses of land to protect themselves. Distance provided one of the best methods of security for southern aborigines, as they recognized the weakness of European armies in their ability to pursue them in the interior continent.

The Chickasaw, lacking Creek numbers, had to work doubly hard to secure their fron-

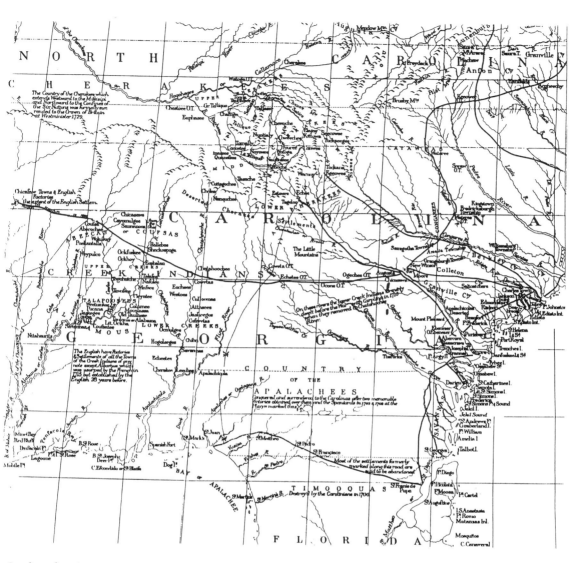

Southern frontier.

tiers. They erected impenetrable forts in difficult to find locations that successfully turned away numerous French and Choctaw invasions. During the Natchez War, large numbers of Natchez refugees joined the Chickasaw and built their own forts. The Chickasaw, of course, had to leave their forts to hunt, and sometimes fell prey to aborigines as distant as the Iroquois, who traveled all the way to modern-day southwest Tennessee from New York in search of scalps. The Chickasaw, however, were able to use their reputation as great warriors to forestall attacks from their neighbors, particularly when they traveled through dangerous frontier areas. Thomas

Nairne, a trader and agent from South Carolina, noted that when traversing frontiers Indians used stealth so as not to alert their enemies. However, the Chickasaw used a different tactic. They publicized their presence by dancing around huge bonfires to dare their enemies to attack; they believed their reputation and their bravado would protect them. If not, they remained ever on the alert—for as soon as their enemies would attack, they would flee from the bonfire with their weapons, turn, and fire at the bonfire, having trapped their enemies by the light.

Although warfare occurred frequently on the southern frontier, diplomacy was the most common resort of frontier peoples. European and aboriginal representatives negotiated military alliances, trade relations, and nonaggression agreements. For example, despite decades of enmity between the French and the Choctaw, and between the British and the Creek, these parties rarely experienced large outbreaks of violence in their relationships, as they worked out their differences and contained enmities from swelling into war. (The Choctaw civil war and the Yamasee War are important exceptions to the above.)

As alluded to earlier, offensive actions on the southern frontier were a most difficult proposition, no matter whether the party was aboriginal or European, though the latter had especial trouble because of the great difficulty in moving large forces over difficult terrain. The French had a miserable time trying to reach the Chickasaw on several occasions, and were not able to transport their artillery through Chickasaw country. The British likewise had several failed invasions of Spanish Florida, and the Spanish fared no better when taking the warpath to the north. Raiding the frontier was more easily accomplished than full-scale invasions, but casualties inflicted were relatively small and property destruction minimal. (An important exception to this were the raids carried out by various Indian and Carolinian groups against the indigenous population of Florida.) The spread of terror, however, was one outcome of raiding, though it did not grip the Southeast's inhabitants as it did those who lived on the New England frontier, for raiding was not as sustained or as common a tool of war as it was in the Northeast.

Communication played a great role in ameliorating hostilities on the southern frontier. Before the European arrival, sign language was used as a means of communication between Indian groups, and though after the European arrival its used continued, trade languages took on great importance. In the old Southwest, Mobilien, a combination of several southeastern languages was employed, and there is evidence that Shawnee was employed in the east. To foster effective communication, aboriginal groups had trained orators to deliver speeches, which translators then translated. The French relied on soldiers, traders, priests, and Indians to translate, though some of their political leaders, like Jean-Baptise Le Moyne de Bienville, were adept in aboriginal languages and customs. The British tended to rely on white traders, though sometimes Africans who had learned aboriginal languages through involvement in the Indian trade or on plantations were employed. Government agents, who often had worked as traders, also translated.

Frontier diplomacy between natives and Europeans was often conducted on aboriginal terms. Europeans learned that participation in native ceremonies, such as smoking the calumet and drinking black drink (*Ilex vomitoria*) were essential to conducting negotiations. The exchange of presents accompanied most negotiations and were critical to the maintenance of positive relations. For the Europeans, supplying presents often involved a considerable outlay of material goods; in return, aborigines exchanged goods and services. Noncompliance with ceremonies and presents could have dire consequences, as when French Governor Antoine de Lamothe Cadillac passed hastily through nations along the Mississippi, who concluded from his actions that hostility with the French was soon to ensue.

Diplomacy remained important to southern peoples because of the inability to secure frontiers. The Spanish grew weaker in the eighteenth century with their settlements steadily contracting; French weakness fell into full-scale decline with the Natchez War of 1729; the British, on the other hand, expanded into Georgia in 1733, in part to provide a new frontier buffer to protect South Carolina, but Georgia's weakness, the Stono Rebellion in 1739, and the failed British invasion of Florida in 1740 left the entire region below Charles Town unsecured. Not until French removal from Louisiana after the Seven Years' War did the British grow more confident, and even then, most British policymakers recognized the weakness of their frontier and preferred diplomacy to warfare with their aboriginal neighbors. Additionally, Parliament poured large sums of money into the defense of Georgia, which helped support rangers who ably augmented the colony's defense. For the southeastern Indians, the weakness of the European powers provided some breathing room, but the British steadily encroached on Indian frontiers. After the Seven Years' War, the British were able to threaten aborigines with the closing of trade to induce land concessions that pushed the frontier to the west and the south. Not until the early nineteenth century, however, were white Americans in a position to drive indigenous inhabitants from their borders and remove them from the south.

Alan Gallay

References

David H. Corkran, *The Creek Frontier, 1540–1783* (1967); Verner W. Crane, *The Southern Frontier, 1670–1732* (1929); Alan Gallay, *The Formation of a Planter Elite: Jonathan Bryan and the Southern Colonial Frontier* (1989); John H. Hann, *Apalachee: The Land Between the Rivers* (1988); Alexander Moore, ed., *Nairnes's Muskhogean Journals: The 1708 Expedition to the Mississippi River* (1988); Daniel H. Usner, Jr., *Indians, Settlers, and Slaves in a Frontier Exchange Economy: The Lower Mississippi Valley before 1783* (1992).

F

See also ATKIN, EDMOND; ATTAKULLAKULLA; AUGUSTA, CONFERENCE OF; BRIMS, EMPEROR; CHEROKEE; CHEROKEE WAR; CHICKASAW; CHOCTAW; CREEK; CREEK-CHEROKEE WARS; GEORGIA; LOUISIANA; NAIRNE, THOMAS; NATCHEZ WAR; PROCLAMATION LINE OF 1763; RANGERS; RED SHOE; SOUTH CAROLINA; STUART, JOHN; TUSCARORA WAR; WESTO; YAMASEE WAR

G

Gage, Thomas (1719/20–1787)

Thomas Gage was born in 1719 or early 1720, his birthplace unknown, but possibly Highmeadow, Gloucestershire, where he was raised. His father, first viscount Gage (Irish peerage)—Thomas, a second son, did not inherit the title—and mother, both Catholics by upbringing, were by the time of his birth converts to Anglicanism. Although they later returned to their ancestral faith, Thomas Gage was raised an Anglican, a fact that made his military career possible. After attending Westminster School, Gage entered the army, acquiring his first commission, probably an ensigncy, sometime in the late 1730s. He purchased a lieutenancy in January 1741 and, after joining an Irish corps, he advanced to the rank of captain within two years. While his regiment was involved in the War of the Austrian Succession, Gage spent much of the war as an aide-de-camp to the duke of Albemarle. He was present at Fontenoy, and also participated in the Culloden campaign under the duke of Cumberland, but it is not certain that he personally saw action. Joining the 55th (soon renumbered the 44th) Foot in 1748, he was stationed in Ireland until late 1754. The purchase of a lieutenant colonelcy in the regiment (March 1751) made him second-in-command.

The 44th sailed for North America in late 1754, a central component in General Edward Braddock's army. Gage does not appear to have played an important role in the management of the subsequent expedition into western Pennsylvania, but on 9 July 1755, when the army was confronted by a small French and Indian force, he was in command of the advance guard. In the hours before battle, and during the early action, Gage was guilty of several major blunders. First, whereas early in the day he was given charge of two small field pieces, he left them behind after his men had forded the Monongahela, a decision that prevented them from being used in the first moments of battle. Second, he failed to secure a hill to the right of the line of march, and early in the battle it was taken by the enemy, who used it as a vantage point from which to fire on the British. When the advance guard was attacked, Gage seems to have failed to send a messenger to inform Braddock (who was to the rear, with the main body) of what was happening. Nor does he appear to have attempted to reinforce the flanking parties. These errors probably did not cause the defeat of Braddock's army, but they speak poorly of Gage as a leader in the field. Sir Peter Halkett, colonel of the 44th, was killed in the battle, and although Gage was unsuccessful in his campaign for the vacant colonelcy, he in fact commanded the regiment for several years. In early 1758, he raised a light infantry regiment, the 80th, and as colonel led it in the abortive assault at Fort Carillon (July 1758), an engagement in which he was slightly wounded. Despite his association with two major disasters, he continued to win favor at home, and was promoted to brigadier general during the fall of 1758. Hitherto he had not commanded an army on an expedition or in battle, although he had held important subordinate positions. In July 1759, however, Jeffrey Amherst ordered him to lead an army against the French outpost of La Galette and then march toward Montreal. Gage moved cautiously, in the end deciding not to advance against either objective, his timidity bringing down Amherst's wrath. When Amherst himself led the expedition against Montreal in 1760, Gage was relegated to commanding the rear guard.

In September 1760, Amherst appointed Gage military governor of Montreal, and the following year he was promoted to major general. Despite his enhanced stature, and the fact that he was senior in rank to the governors of Quebec and of Three Rivers, he did not attempt to enforce his will over the province at large. Within the region of Montreal, however, he instituted impressive reforms, especially in commerce and in the judiciary.

When Amherst resigned his command in 1763, Gage took his place, assuming the position of commander in chief in November and being confirmed in that appointment in 1764. Gage inherited a number of problems from his predecessor, chief among them being the prosecution of a war effort against Pontiac's confederation. During his first six months in command he also faced a series of mutinies over pay. In both cases he proceeded vigorously and successfully, although it was subordinates rather than himself who faced the challenges directly.

Gage's early career in America scarcely suggests that he had much ability as a battlefield commander, but in fact he did not again participate in an engagement after Fort Carillon. His abortive La Galette expedition shows him to have been a cautious and indecisive commander, but the practical impact may have been reduced by the fact that after 1760 he was more an administrator than a general. Indeed, except for Pontiac's War and the mutiny in 1763–1764, and the far more serious crises of the 1770s that led into the War of Independence, Gage's time as commander in chief was dominated by routine matters. This played to his strong suit, for Gage had real strengths as an administrator. Working with civilians as he had in Montreal, he was able to convey an air of impartiality. His management of the army was also of a high order. At least when working on a regimental level, he demonstrated rare ability; he took the 44th, shattered in Braddock's defeat, and by 1757 molded it into a unit that Lord Loudoun regarded as one of the two best in his army. No less impressive was his work with the 80th, a regiment that from the beginning reflected his belief that it was necessary for the British to have units that could handle both regular and irregular styles of combat. Gage may not have been the best of the string of officers who served as commander in chief in North America during the period 1755–1783, but he was far from being the worst.

By mid-1775, Gage was engulfed by the political crisis in Massachusetts, where he was serving as governor in addition to his place as commander in chief. Shortly after George Germain suggested that he was "in a situation of too great importance for his talents" he was recalled, and in early 1776, he was stripped of his command. Thereafter, his military functions were minor, although he was promoted to general in 1782. He died in London, 2 April 1787.

Paul E. Kopperman

References

John R. Alden, *General Gage in America* (1948); Paul E. Kopperman, *Braddock at the Monongahela* (1977); ———, "The Stoppages Mutiny of 1763," *Western Pennsylvania Historical Magazine*, 69 (1986):241–254; John Shy, *Toward Lexington: The Role of the British Army in the Coming of the American Revolution* (1965).

See also AMHERST, JEFFREY; BRADDOCK, EDWARD; OHIO EXPEDITION OF 1755; PONTIAC'S WAR

Fort Garrison (Maryland) and the Maryland Rangers

Prior to the outbreak of King William's War in 1693, Maryland colonists grew fearful of increased Indian attacks along their northern and western frontiers. When a large contingent of Indians allied with the French under the leadership of Baron Jean-Vincent d'Abbadie de St. Castin reportedly appeared near the head of the Chesapeake Bay, at Colonel Augustine Herman's property, Bohemia Manor (a rumor later discovered to be false, although the baron's wife was at the manor), the Maryland council took steps to provide protection for the colony's frontiers. In March 1692, the council levied an assessment of 50,000 pounds of tobacco on Maryland residents for the purpose of constructing and manning three forts located in Charles County, Anne Arundel County (then including Howard County), and in Baltimore County near the falls of the Patapsco River and toward the Susquehanna River. These forts were necessary to protect outlying settlements from the sporadic Indian raids that had plagued them for several decades, first by Susquehannocks, then Senecas (the generic designation for several Iroquois tribes), and finally by western tribes from the Ohio Valley who were allied with the French. Each fort was designed to house a contingent of one captain and nine rangers whose job was to patrol the outlying settlements and generally make their presence known to the Indians.

Of these three forts, Fort Garrison in Baltimore County is the only one to survive and to give its name to a section of the county. Fort Garrison was built of stone on a knoll that provided a clear view of the surrounding countryside to the edge of the nearby forest. Its walls were two feet thick, 50 feet long, and 20 feet wide, pierced by a series of six musket ports or embrasures. Doors were three feet off the ground, the oversized chimney was constructed inside the building to prevent Indians from entering through that structure, and the steep-pitched roof was originally made of stone to prevent its being set on fire during an attack. Later, undated but early structural alterations added a second floor and changed the configuration and material of the roof. And, in addition to the stone fortification, a cabin next door housed four friendly Nanticoke or Piscataway Indians who assisted the rangers in scouting and other activities.

In 1696, Captain John Oulton, commander of "the Garrison," reported to Maryland's Governor Francis Nicholson, giving an account of the roads the rangers made behind and between the scattered cabins of settlers, that extended about 50 miles, but connected only about four cabins with the fort. Along this track the rangers patrolled weekly. Similar activities occurred at the other two forts, the one in Charles County under the command of Captain John Addison, and the one in Anne Arundel County under the command of Colonel Nicholas Greenbury.

Fort Garrison was particularly important in protecting Elkridge Landing, a major tobacco shipping site, and the various rolling roads along which Maryland's hogsheads of tobacco were rolled to the landing. In addition, the fort protected settlers on their move westward along the Indian trails that served as Maryland's only highways west in the early years. Rangers at the fort were specifically instructed to spend as much time as possible in the open, stopping travelers and questioning suspicious passersby, and chopping wood in addition to their regular activity of scouting for Indians. These functions of the fort persisted into the eighteenth century, and as late as 1755, Fort Garrison served to protect Marylanders during the French and Indian War.

Within four days of General Edward Braddock's defeat at the Monongahela, near Fort Duquesne, messengers bearing the news arrived and spread the word in Maryland and the surrounding colonies. Marylanders became fearful that an attack was imminent, and the women and children north and northwest of Fort Garrison feared to leave their dwellings. Men were heavily armed while following their daily activities and during travel. A report spread that a force of French and Indians were within 30 miles of Baltimore Town, and a group of the county militia was hastily assembled and installed at Fort Garrison under the command of Captain John Risteau, then Baltimore County sheriff. Parishioners of St. Thomas's, near Fort Garrison armed themselves, carrying their guns into the church pews on Sundays, lest an attack come during their worship. Activity of this sort occurred in and around Fort Garrison throughout the summer and autumn of 1755.

Soon after the outbreak of the French and Indian War, however, when fear of attack ceased, the Maryland frontier passed far beyond the reach of the militia at Fort Garrison and the fort fell into disuse. It did, however, survive, and remains today as the oldest stone fort in Maryland, and the only surviving Maryland fort from the seventeenth century.

Debra R. Boender

References

Baltimore County Historical Society Pamphlet, *Fort Garrison,* Maryland Vertical File, Maryland Room, Baltimore, Maryland; Isobel Davidson, ed., *Real Stories from Baltimore County History* (1967): 60–63; Charles L. Shipley, "The Old Garrison Forest Fort," *Maryland Monthly Magazine,* 2 (1907):3–8.

See also SENECA; SUSQUEHANNOCK

Garrison Houses

Garrison houses provided the first line of defense for frontier communities. These ubiquitous structures, whose numbers varied from town to town, were usually owned by local officials, officers of the militia and ministers, or simply occupied a strategic location. In addition to being the center of military activity, garrison houses often served as public houses and taverns as well. Some of these structures were simply a single house built of squared logs laid horizontally on top of each other. Sometimes the second floor projected out over the first, and the windows and doors were strengthened as well. As the French and Indian wars progressed, it became common to turn these fortified houses into small forts by erecting a palisade or outer wall of upright logs set into the ground. There was a fortified gate and flankers, or log towers, built at opposite corners of the palisade that could serve as watch towers and cover the outer walls in case of attack. These larger garrisons had smaller houses built either within the palisade or around the outside to accommodate the other families seeking shelter.

Families within the community were assigned to the nearest garrison, and the numbers involved, combined with the length of stay, could create intolerable living conditions. Garrisons, depending on their size and situation, regularly housed one to 14 families and averaged 25 to 30 individuals, although the larger structures could house anywhere from 60 to more than 100.

Added to this cramped, uncomfortable "heap" of humanity were the provincial soldiers assigned to bolster the defenses of the frontier towns. Normally, 20 to 30 soldiers were assigned to the exposed towns, with one to four being posted in individual garrisons. Whether specifically raised for garrison duty or assigned when their "scout" (partrol) or expedition outlived its usefulness, the soldiers operated under the dual command of the provincial officers and the militia officer who commanded the garrison, although the provincial officers took precedence. The men were ordered to obey the commands of the masters of the garrisons where they were posted and not absent themselves without official leave, and their principal duties were to guard the inhabitants as they performed their daily labors and add their weight to the defense of the garrison if attacked. The overlapping command situation could create difficulty if protocol and diplomacy were not observed.

The issues of military protocol and the effects of close quarters, as well as other irritants such as differences in religion, could lead to animosity between the inhabitants and the provincial soldiers. Another reason for this animosity often grew out of the fact that while the soldiers represented a degree of safety for the frontier communities, they also were a very real strain on their limited supplies of provisions and clothing. The destruction of crops and livestock by Indian raiding parties and the obvious physical dangers involved in the further cultivation of their fields diminished the amount of food available on the frontier, and the restriction of all business activity, agricultural or otherwise, hampered trade for essential goods, especially clothing. The presence of provincial soldiers only aggravated this situation.

The inhabitants provided for the soldiers, and themselves, as best they could, working their own fields under the protection of provincial guards, or land in the immediate area of the garrisons allotted to the families living there. The government informed the owners of these garrisons that they were compensated for this by the increased defense offered by the presence of these other families. All contributions by the inhabitants to the maintenance of the provincial soldiers was to be indemnified by the provincial governments, although this compensation could be delayed, which only increased the level of animosity.

The friction between inhabitants and the provincial soldiers went beyond the problems of cramped quarters and minimal supplies; the inhabitants were not always impressed with their defenders. Unfortunately, the caliber of soldier posted in garrisons along the frontier was not high because provincial officers retained their best men, the most physically fit and the most enthusiastic volunteers, for scouting and raids, and posted those incapable of marching and the pressed men in garrisons. When provincial forces were reduced after a campaign, it was the pressed or hired men who were left behind in garrison, men whose enthusiasm for the service of their country was less than could be desired, at least as far as the inhabitants of the frontier were concerned.

In two respects, one negative and one positive, the garrisons proved to be more a psychological defense than an actual military strongpoint. The proximity of the garrison houses and the presence of the provincial soldiers, no matter what their quality, led to overconfidence. The strength of the building itself seemed to be a sufficient safeguard so that in many cases, sentries and watches were not posted. Such carelessness often led to death or captivity. In addition, despite laws requiring all persons to abide in their assigned garrisons or be fined, the inhabitants needed to get on with living, planting, milling, masting—all the work which was to be protected by the provincial soldiers posted in the town. But when this work became extensive, tired men neglected simple precautions.

The negligence and laxity on the part of the inhabitants of frontier communities emanating from this false sense of security represented in part by the garrison houses and the soldiers assigned created nothing but anxiety and aggravation for the provincial officers assigned to protect them. As Colonel Thomas Westbrook, commander of the Maine frontier during Dummer's War, observed, "the people generally preach up peace to themselves if the Indians do not knock some in the head in six or seven days."

However, in addition to the negative aspect of false security, the garrisons could provide positive benefits from a purely psychological standpoint by deterring some Indian attacks and saving the lives of people who had no actual defensive capabilities. Numerous instances are recorded where women or individual men used the apparent strength of the garrison to bluff their attackers. Shouting to imaginary defenders, changing hats and firing out of different windows sometimes convinced the Indians that the garrison was well-guarded. In each of these cases, the apparent strength of the buildings and outworks provided a psychological defense where no real military deterrent existed.

Of course, when called to, and prepared, larger garrisons could prove quite adequate for defense against a determined attack. Perhaps the most famous incident occurred at the Storer garrison in Wells, Maine, 9–11 June 1692. The Storer garrison had a palisade and flankers with small shacks outside for local families, and sat on a small rise just above Wells harbor. The garrison was commanded by Captain James Converse, who had 15 provincial soldiers and an unknown, but apparently small, number of inhabitants. In addition, there were 15 men on board two sloops anchored close to the garrison in the harbor. On the morning of 9 June, a force of 500 Indians under French command stepped out of the woods, brandishing their weapons, hurling shouts of defiance and firing musket balls at the garrison. For two days the garrison withstood attack, including a fire raft sent against the sloops. But, in the end, the French and the Indians withdrew.

This siege represents the ultimate example of the military effectiveness of garrison houses. They were a necessary component of frontier defensive strategy, a first line of defense used by both the English and the French. In some re-spects the garrison houses were a dubious blessing. Beyond the diffusion of manpower, the effectiveness of the garrison system, like all the endeavors of mankind, depended much on the human factor. Garrisons defended by individuals with the fortitude of a James Converse could withstand enemy attacks, and quick-witted individuals in seemingly hopeless situations could use the obvious strength of the garrison to bluff the Indian attackers, but the presence of the garrisons could also lead to a false sense of security and result in carelessness, negligence, and ultimately death or captivity.

Steven C. Eames

References

Edward Emerson Bourne, "Garrison Houses, York County," in *Collections of the Maine Historical Society,* Vol. VII (1876):112–113; Robbins Paxson Gilman, *The Old Logg House by the Bridge* (1985).

See also CONVERSE, JAMES; FORTS, PROVINCIAL; FRONTIER; RANGERS; WELLS

Fort Gaspereau (Nova Scotia, Canada)

The French Fort Gaspereau was constructed in 1751 on the north, or Baie Verte, side of the Chignecto Isthmus at the same time as Fort Beauséjour; the two forts were approximately 15 miles apart. Gaspereau was constructed on level ground near the shore, just below the mouth of the Gaspereau River. A 114-foot square, it was framed by a two-story blockhouse at each corner, with small cannon in the upper stories. It contained only six buildings and no water supply. The fort was intended to help secure the French line of communications between Cape Breton and the St. John River, and to serve as a depot for supplies shipped directly from Quebec to Fort Beauséjour during the summer. In 1755, it was manned by only 25 men, and its capture during that campaign was almost an afterthought and a fore-ordained certainty. The French commander in charge, Benjamin Rouer de Villeroy, could perhaps have burned rather than surrender the fort, but he seems to have acted more from a lack of military intelligence than any absence of courage. Regardless of his decision, the fort could not have withstood a siege and bombardment and lacked adequate personnel for an extended defense. It surrendered on 18 June 1755.

Ronald P. Dufour

Fig. 1

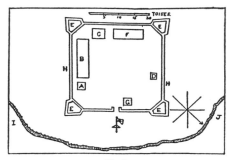

Fig. 2

1. External view of fort
2. Ground plan
   A. Guard house for storehouse
   B. Storehouse for goods
   C. Commandant's quarters
   D. Powder magazine
   E. Corner blockhouses
   F. Projected barracks for soldiers
   G. Projected guard house near entrance
   H. Palisaded curtain joining blockhouses
   I. Baye Verte
   J. Gaspereau river

Fort Gaspereau.

References

Guy Frégault, *Canada: The War of the Conquest,* trans., Margaret M. Cameron (1969); Francis Jennings, *Empire of Fortune: Crowns, Colonies, and Tribes in the Seven Years War in America* (1988); John Clarence Webster, *The Forts of Chignecto* (1930).

See also CHIGNECTO ISTHMUS; FORT BEAUSÉJOUR (NOVA SCOTIA, CANADA)

Fort George (Rhode Island)
See FORT ANNE (RHODE ISLAND)

Fort George at the Battery (New York)
See FORT JAMES (NEW YORK)

Georgia
Georgia was founded for three reasons: to give a new start to England's "worthy poor," to pro-vide England with commodities (silk, for example) that were not obtainable within its empire, and to guard the southern frontier of the British North American colonies. Of the three, the latter, the military objective, did the most to define the early history of Georgia.

In the wake of the 1715 Yamasee War, imperial planners in both South Carolina and in England urged that a military presence south of the Savannah was necessary to protect the southern flank of Britain's North American colonies from the Spanish in Florida and the French at Fort Toulouse. Sir Robert Montgomery's plan for the "Margravate of Azilia," a colony he hoped to plant in the region, had this as an objective, and though his scheme was never realized, his idea of "one continuous fortress" of citizen/soldiers generated some enthusiasm. South Carolinian John Barnwell convinced the British in 1720 to supply a company of regulars to assist in building a screen of forts to guard the frontier, though only one was actually constructed—Fort King George at the mouth of the Altamaha. Carolina remained concerned and Governor Robert Johnson's 1730 plan for townships settled by Protestant refugees was also prompted by defensive concerns. It might have become the model for frontier settlement if the Georgia venture had not been born.

Even before colonists set sail, Georgia's trustees were acknowledging that the colony would serve as a barrier to enemy interests, and as the "Georgia Plan" began to take shape, military goals were incorporated into the design. By the time colonists were enlisted and the expedition mounted, it was accepted that a principle reason for the settlement was the defense of the frontier. Moreover, the presence of James Oglethorpe in the first transport guaranteed that military considerations would hold sway. His own experience and inclinations all but mandated this, and under his guidance Georgia would become a military colony.

While the "Georgia Plan" did not emerge fully until the colony was a few years old, from the beginning it was obvious that defense was a critical concern. The idea of small landholdings forming a defensive perimeter was incorporated into the scheme as was tail-male inheritance, which guaranteed that an able-bodied male would be on the land to defend it. Equally important was the prohibition of slaves, for it was feared that if war erupted potential soldiers would have to guard them or they would join the enemy against their masters. All of this was the enemy against their masters. All of this was impressed on the settlers as soon as they arrived in February 1733. Savannah's plan, devised by Oglethorpe, organized town lots so units of ten men could quickly form on the adjacent town square and deploy for defense. While he was doing this, Oglethorpe was also negotiating with local Indians and laying out forts on the perimeter of the town. By the time he returned to England the following year, the military character of the colony was established and Oglethorpe was ready to move in a new direction.

Back in England, Oglethorpe personally lobbied for the establishment of 880 men in 20 forts along the Altamaha River, to hold and defend the land before the Spanish could move into the area. Though this idea did not bear full fruit, efforts to recruit soldiers from the Highlands of Scotland did, and in October 1735, more than 170 people embarked for Georgia. Arriving at Tybee in January 1736, they continued the journey down the coast to the mouth of the Altamaha, where they built the town of Darien. These were not "worthy poor" but soldiers recruited for this very purpose.

In December 1735, Oglethorpe left England with a flotilla that looked very much like a military expedition. Most of the more than 250 colonists on two ships were not destined for the Savannah area but for St. Simons Island, below Darien, where Oglethorpe proposed to build a fort. By February they were in Georgia. Oglethorpe then went south, outlined the plan for Fort Frederica, visited Darien, then returned for the settlers. Once they arrived on St. Simons, colonists began work on the fort, while Oglethorpe scouted the inland passage farther south and planted an outpost on the northwest side of Cumberland Island. He then continued on as far as the St. Johns River before returning to oversee the construction of Frederica.

To no one's surprise, Oglethorpe's venture heightened existing tensions in the area, and it was rumored that the governor of Florida, Francisco del Moral Sánchez, was preparing to attack Darien. Though Oglethorpe was convinced that the land he occupied was rightfully England's (and was not opposed to the idea of eventually taking Florida), he wrote Moral that his goal was to prevent Creek war parties from moving into Florida. Moral was not satisfied, but when the Independent Company of Foot was transferred to Frederica from South Carolina, the governor became convinced that Florida was too weak to defend itself and agreed to

negotiations. Talks were held, but no solution was reached.

Meanwhile, Oglethorpe was under pressure from Britain, funds were cut, and the Georgia trustees ordered him to withdraw from Darien and Frederica to a point above the Ogechee River. Oglethorpe chose to disregard the instructions and to continue to build and supply the two settlements, a decision the trustees later reluctantly accepted. From this point until the early 1740s, Frederica gradually became Georgia's major city, and Savannah suffered as a result.

At this same time, Oglethorpe turned his attention to the western frontier, where the French threat was very real. As early as 1736 he had ordered a fort to be built at the falls of the Savannah River. After delays, Fort Augusta was finally completed in the summer 1737. It would be the key to the backcountry—a center for the Indian trade and a source of military intelligence for the southern colonies.

His work well advanced, James Oglethorpe left for England in November 1736 and arrived just as the new year began. He returned home with one goal in mind—obtaining the men, money, and authority necessary to defend the colony. Believing (correctly) that Spain was getting ready to invade, he argued that British regulars were needed to supplement the roughly 300 militiamen in Georgia. British Prime Minister Sir Robert Walpole was concerned that stationing British soldiers on the frontier would further upset the Spanish, but word of Spanish invasion preparations overcame his reservations. Oglethorpe was commissioned as "General & Commander in Chief of the Forces in South Carolina and Georgia" and was promised at least some of the regulars he requested. A short time later he was commissioned a colonel of a regiment to be raised for Georgia service and the process of recruiting began.

During the following months men were raised, troops were transferred, and the expedition outfitted. By March 1738, they were ready, and by May, the regiment, consisting of more than 600 men and officers, was in Georgia. Fort Frederica again became the focus of Oglethorpe's concern, and Savannah slowly became secondary. Money and supplies went south, in some cases not even stopping at Tybee, and soon Savannah colonists complained of the neglect. In time, there were many Georgians who saw the settlement on St. Simons as a cause for the colony's decline, not its salvation.

After settling the troops at Frederica, on 8 July 1739, Oglethorpe set out for the western frontier, to bring the Creek nation to the British side. In part he was successful, for the Creeks would remain neutral in the upcoming struggle, but he had hoped that they would be active allies instead. His attention quickly turned to other matters. Returning to Augusta, the rumor reached him that England and Spain were at war. This was followed with news of the slave rebellion on the Stono River in South Carolina, an event that local whites linked to Spanish intrigues. Arriving in Savannah at the end of September he received a letter from King George II, with news that a negotiated settlement with Spain had fallen through, and that he was to take his regiment and "annoy the Subjects of Spain, and to put the Colonies of Carolina and Georgia in the best posture of defense." Immediately, he relayed the news to Governor William Bull of South Carolina and asked for that colony's help in attacking St. Augustine. He also sent messages to the Indian nations asking for help and urging them to attack Florida. After settling things in Savannah, he left for Frederica. On the Georgia frontier, the "War of Jenkins' Ear" was about to begin.

Events began to move quickly. In mid-November, a band of Spain's Yamasee allies attacked a British post on Amelia Island and massacred the small garrison. Oglethorpe responded with a raiding party which burned houses, killed cattle, and generally created havoc in the area south and east of the St. Johns River. He then reestablished the garrison at the mouth of the St. Johns and made plans to capture Fort Pupo, due east of St. Augustine, on the St. Johns and at the juncture of two major overland trails. With 180 men and four small cannon, Oglethorpe attacked the fort, and after a brief exchange, the Spanish surrendered. The general then returned to Frederica to plan the next phase of the conflict.

In Oglethorpe's mind, St. Augustine had always been the goal, and since that opinion was shared by leaders in South Carolina, he immediately pushed for assistance in capturing the Spanish city. Time was of the essence, for if there was to be a siege, it would have to begin soon. A small British fleet under Commodore Vincent Pearse was available to help, but only until hurricane season, which would not give them much time once the South Carolina forces arrived. Moreover, the support that Georgia's sister colony offered was less than Oglethorpe

had hoped and he personally went to Charles Town to ask for more. His proposal was for an attack on St. Augustine, which was poorly defended and ill supplied. Convinced that the town would fall and the Castillo de San Marcos would be unable to hold the refugees, General Oglethorpe reasoned that the objective could be taken without a siege and before hurricane season began. South Carolina leaders finally agreed and on 5 April the assembly authorized men and material for the expedition.

As work went forward, St. Augustine received reinforcements and supplies from Cuba, and the prospects for holding out against an attack were vastly improved. Meanwhile, Oglethorpe waited at Frederica. On 3 May 1740, things were finally prepared, and the army began to move south to join forces that had been sent ahead. Slowly they pushed closer to St. Augustine and finally, on the night of 31 May, everything seemed ready. Even with the objective in sight, grumbling began in the ranks. Some South Carolina gentry began to complain of Oglethorpe's tactics and of what they felt was an unwarranted delay in mounting the attack. This was accentuated by Commodore Pearse's warning that he could stay no longer than 5 July. Despite his critics, Oglethorpe set up batteries that could bombard the town and moved troops into place for an assault. By mid-June he felt his army was ready.

Then things began to come apart. Spanish galleys and shallow water prevented Oglethorpe from landing troops on Anastasia Island, opposite the city, so the only alternative was to cut off communication between the Spanish and supporters outside St. Augustine, and settle down for a siege. But the Spanish leader was not content to watch and wait. On the night of 15 June, Governor Manuel de Montiano sent a force out to attack some of Oglethorpe's men at Fort Mose, an outpost they occupied when Spanish troops retreated. The Georgia unit lost about 50 men (half of whom were captured), while the attackers lost twice that number. But Fort Mose was taken, contact between St. Augustine and the backcountry was reestablished, and the grumbling in the British ranks increased.

Oglethorpe's options were becoming increasingly narrow. He could not take St. Augustine; the British fleet could stay only a few weeks more; and his troops were sickly and desertions were increasing. Realizing that the effort had failed, he ordered the siege raised on 20 July 1740, and began the withdrawal. The

Spanish let him go, and by the first of August, his army was back at Frederica.

The blame for the failure fell on Oglethorpe, and South Carolina troops were especially critical. To some degree they were right, for the commander undertook the venture without sufficient knowledge of conditions in and around St. Augustine and without adequate preparation for the heat of the season. On the other hand, the blame must be shared by South Carolina, which did not provide the long-range artillery it promised and on the navy for not cooperating more fully, so in the final analysis, what they believed would be a joint success ended as a joint failure.

Spain lacked the resources to follow up its "victory," so Oglethorpe had time to regroup his forces and prepare for the expected offensive against Frederica. But a year passed and it was into the fall of 1741 before Spanish officials in Cuba received royal orders to move against the Georgia garrison. Preparations were made through the winter, and in May 1742, an expedition of more than 50 vessels and some 7,000 men left Cuba for St. Augustine. Delayed by a storm, the force did not actually move against St. Simons until June, thus Oglethorpe learned of their coming and had time to assemble more troops and prepare for the coming assault. In late June, some 3,000 Spanish troops landed on the south end of the island, and on 7 July, they moved against Fort Frederica and Oglethorpe's force of less than 700.

The engagement that followed has come down through Georgia history as the Battle of Bloody Marsh. It was, in reality, several battles—a day of attack and counterattack that ended with the Spanish retreating but not driven from the island. Another attempt by the Spanish to take Frederica failed, and Spanish officers began to argue over the strength of the enemy they faced. Fearing British reinforcements were about to arrive (a fear encouraged by a letter Oglethorpe planted on a released prisoner), Spanish leaders concluded that the time had come to leave, and by 15 July 1741, the invaders were gone.

Oglethorpe attempted to follow the retreat, but was able only to hurry them along. St. Augustine remained out of his reach, as an abortive attempt to take the city in early 1743 was to prove. Nevertheless, the victory enhanced the Georgia commander's reputation and salved an ego hurt by earlier failures. Most observers saw it as a significant accomplishment, for it ended

the immediate Spanish threat. What they could not foresee at the time was that the invasion of St. Simons represented the high-water mark for Spanish efforts on the southern frontier. The Battle of Bloody Marsh had guaranteed that Georgia would remain a British colony.

Oglethorpe's military career in Georgia was almost over. Though promoted to the rank of brigadier, his victory had so reduced the need for troops in Georgia that little was done to strengthen the garrison at Frederica. In July 1743, the general left Georgia, never to return, and with him went much of the military orientation that had so shaped the colony's first decade. Yet the result of his emphasis on defense (and offense) was evident. At his leaving, Frederica, his headquarters, was Georgia's principle town, while Savannah, away from the frontier and from the general's watchful eye, had become something of a backwater. It is hardly surprising, given the way Georgia's first city was neglected by Oglethorpe, that it became a hotbed for "malcontents" who wanted to undo the trustee system.

The War of Jenkins' Ear, which evolved into King George's War, ended in 1748, with a treaty (Aix-la-Chapelle) that did little to clearly define the Georgia-Florida border, but that was not to be a serious issue again. Instead, the colony's military concerns refocused on the Indians on the frontier, and colonial defenses fell more and more to local militia units. Fortunately, these were not severely tested, for though there were rumors of Indian unrest (some well-founded), the general Indian war that some feared never materialized. Much of the credit for this should go to the men who governed the colony after it became a royal province in 1752. In particular, Governors Henry Ellis (1757–1760) and James Wright (1760–1776), worked successfully to keep the Creeks from joining the French who remained British rivals in the west.

As a result (in part at least) of the efforts of Ellis and Wright, there was no fighting in Georgia during the French and Indian War (1756–1763), though the colony stayed on its guard most of the time. With the peace that followed the conflict, the military became even less significant, for the treaty made Florida a British province and expelled France from North America. Now the Indians had no one else to whom they could turn, and Governor Wright was able to conclude treaties that kept the frontier peaceful. Nevertheless, as immigration into the upcountry increased, tensions increased as well. But these problems would not be resolved during the colonial era, and much of the early history of the "state" of Georgia focuses on frontier conflicts.

In the final analysis, the colonial wars, and in particular the War of Jenkins' Ear, had a major impact on the development of colonial Georgia. Spain's threat to the frontier influenced the thinking of the trustees, and the imprint of their thought was seen in the town plan of Savannah, the location of frontier forts and villages, and the eventual founding of Fort Frederica. Military considerations also influenced the choice of colonists, where they were settled, and the way in which they were supported. But the most significant way in which military concerns shaped the growth of early Georgia was the manner in which the center of power shifted away from Savannah and to Frederica. Once that outpost became Oglethorpe's headquarters, Savannah languished, and it was not until after the war that Georgia's first settlement began to regain its authority.

It is also significant to note the impact the de-emphasis of the military had on the colony. Once the war was over and money for defense was no longer flowing into the colony, Frederica (and other military settlements—like Darien) went into a decline. As their influence waned, Savannah's rose, and with it the influence of leaders whose concerns were land and the labor to put it into production. At peace at last, civilian concerns took precedence, and Georgia began to follow the lead of its more prosperous neighbor, South Carolina. Georgia had served well in its role as a buffer colony; it was time to turn to other things.

Harvey H. Jackson

References

William W. Abbot, *The Royal Governors of Georgia, 1754–1775* (1959); Kenneth Coleman, *Colonial Georgia: A History* (1976); Larry E. Ivers, *British Drums on the Southern Frontier: The Military Colonization of Georgia, 1733–1749* (1974); Harvey H. Jackson and Phinizy Spalding, eds., *Forty Years of Diversity: Essays on Colonial Georgia* (1984); John Tate Lanning, ed., *The St. Augustine Expedition of 1740: A Report to the South Carolina General Assembly* (1954); Phinizy Spalding, *Oglethorpe in America* (1977); Clarence L. Ver Steeg, *Origins of a Southern Mosaic* (1975).

See also ANGLO-SPANISH WAR (1739–1744); AUGUSTA; BARNWELL TOWNSHIP SYSTEM; BLOODY MARSH, BATTLE OF; CREEK; FORT FREDERICA (GEORGIA); FRONTIER, SOUTHERN; MONTIANO, MANUEL DE; MORAL SÁNCHEZ, FRANCISCO DEL; OGLETHORPE, JAMES EDWARD

German Flats, Battle of (1757)

In 1757 the British lost both Forts Oswego and William Henry. This, combined with the failure of the British to retaliate for either loss, lowered the opinion of the British in the eyes of the Iroquois. In mid-1757, William Johnson realized that the loss of support of the Iroquois would severely hamper the British war effort. He decided something must be done to make the Indians regain faith in the British. This was a problem for Johnson because Lord Loudoun had taken most of the British army in America on his expedition against Louisbourg. This left Johnson with no other choice but to personally lead a raid into the French area.

Johnson accomplished this raid against the French. However, at the same time he enraged the French and Indians aligned with them. In retaliation, the French and Indians raided central New York, destroying many small settlements. The most notable was the raid on German Flats.

In the early hours of the morning on 12 November, approximately 300 men raided German Flats. This force consisted of Indians and Canadian colonial regulars under Captain François-Marie Picoté de Belêtre. They moved into the village which was located just upriver from Fort Johnson and completely destroyed the settlement. The several small picket forts of the area had been taken one by one and then burned. In all, 60 homes had been destroyed. The 40 or 50 male inhabitants were killed and scalped. The remaining women and children were marched off as captives. German Flats had virtually ceased to exist as a village. Only Fort Johnson remained on the Mohawk River above Schenectady. The end of 1757 found the French at the height of their power in North America.

John M. Keefe

References

Oscar Theodore Barck, *Colonial America* (1958); Donald Chidsey, *French and Indian War* (1969); Allan W. Eckert, *Wilderness Empire: A Narrative* (1969); Edward P.

Hamilton, *The French and Indian Wars: The Story of Battles and Forts in the Wilderness* (1962); Maurice Matloff, *American Military History* (1985).

Fort Germanna (Virginia)

Located on the south bank of the Rapidan River in Orange County, Virginia, Fort Germanna was one of the two forts built in 1714 by Lieutenant Governor Alexander Spotswood to regulate Indian activity in the aftermath of the Tuscarora War. Like Fort Christanna, Fort Germanna was to include Indian settlements, but when local Indians declined to settle there, a group of German immigrants occupied the site. The German settlers eventually developed a prosperous iron industry. After leaving the office of lieutenant governor, Spotswood himself settled nearby and built a substantial brick mansion.

Thomas Costa

References

Warren Billings, John Selby, and Thad Tate, *Colonial Virginia: A History* (1986).

See also Fort Christanna (Virginia)

Gist, Christopher (c. 1706–1759)

Christopher Gist was an influential surveyor and speculator on the trans-Appalachian frontier before and during the French and Indian War.

He was born in Maryland, the son of a prominent surveyor who had been responsible for plotting the town of Baltimore. The younger Gist pursued his father's career, traveling extensively in the southern backcountry.

About 1750, he became associated with the Ohio Company of Virginia, a group of speculative land developers interested in the upper Ohio River valley. Acting on behalf of the company, he visited much of that valley in the next two years, traveling from Shannopin's Town at the forks of the Ohio as far west as the Scioto River. He thus helped to establish the basis of the Virginia claim to the area, and contributed to French concerns about English ambition in the Mississippi watershed. He was an active participant in negotiations which led to the Treaty of Logstown between the Virginia Company and Indian leaders of the Ohio Valley. He then scouted south of the Ohio River

from the Monongahela to the Kanawha Valleys, and in 1753 he established a home, Gist's Plantation, usually considered the first white settlement in the Monongahela region.

Gist's association with the Ohio Company put him in contact with another leader and western representative of that group, George Washington. In 1753, Gist traveled with Washington on his trip to the French posts in the interior. In 1754, Gist was present during the Fort Necessity campaign, and suffered the loss of his settlement after the French victory. In 1755, he was a guide for General Edward Braddock's expedition, and thereafter was captain of a company of the Virginia Regiment. Termed a scout in many accounts, he might better be portrayed as an adviser whose extensive reconnaissance of the western country and concern for the affairs of the Ohio Company made him a valuable advance agent of colonial expansion.

In 1756, he shifted his interests to the Cherokee areas of east Tennessee, and the following year he was appointed deputy superintendent of Indian affairs for the southern colonies. He died of smallpox in the southern backcountry in 1759.

George Geib

References

Kenneth P. Bailey, *Christopher Gist* (1976).

See also Logstown, Treaty of; Ohio Company; Washington, George

Glen, James (1701–1777)

James Glen was born at Linlithgow, Scotland. After studying at the University of Leyden, he practiced law in Scotland, holding various posts such as magistrate, high sheriff, and inspector of seignories in Scotland. In 1722, Glen inherited from his father two estates in Scotland, Bonnington and Loncroft, making the latter his home. With backing from friends in high places, including Lords Dalhousie and Willington, Glen was appointed the royal governor of South Carolina on 23 December 1738, but did not arrive in the colony until 19 December 1743.

While viewed as too complaisant toward the colony's legislature by British authorities, Glen carefully studied the constitutional system in South Carolina, urging reforms to enhance the powers of the governor, which had been steadily eroded in the past by the council and

Commons House of Assembly. In this he was unsuccessful. Though at times in confrontation with the council and lower house, Glen was able to obtain financial support for his programs.

Glen almost single-handedly had charge of Indian relations in the southern colonies, 1744–1756. He may be regarded as the most influential person of his time in colonial Indian affairs, with the exception of William Johnson among the Iroquois. Glen met frequently with the Indians and journeyed into the backcountry. He was the only colonial governor with a definite Indian policy. With his insistence on humane treatment of the Indians, there was no war between the Indians and the southern colonists during his administration. Glen persuaded the South Carolina legislature to fix prices in the Indian trade, but interlopers into the Cherokee trade from Virginia and Georgia undermined this policy. Glen was criticized by other governors and home officials for narrowly pursuing the interest of South Carolina. He withheld Indian assistance for General Edward Braddock's expedition on grounds of the priority of South Carolina frontier defense. He squabbled with Governor Robert Dinwiddie of Virginia over financial aid in the French and Indian War, frontier defense, and jurisdiction over Indian tribes. Among Glen's recommendations were the creating of a league among all the Indians and sending military expeditions against the Spaniards in Florida and French in Louisiana.

Glen's record in Indian affairs was indeed impressive. He brought about the end of the Creek-Cherokee War, and for awhile had an effective alliance with the Choctaw against the French in Louisiana (which friendship was largely negated by the shortcomings of McNair and Company, a firm that Glen had given a monopoly of the Choctaw trade). In 1753, Glen visited the Overhill towns of the Cherokee and personally supervised the building of Fort Prince George near the Indian town of Keowee on the east slope of the Appalachians. Glen boasted of his success among the Cherokee, claiming that now the Indians spoke of the English government as "father" rather than as "brother." In 1755, Glen concluded a treaty with the Cherokee whereby the Indians sold 40 million acres (Glen used £600 of his own personal wealth), though the Indians later insisted the treaty was only one of friendship and any land cession was in the vicinity of Fort Prince George.

A major reason for Glen's lack of support for military operations at the outset of the French and Indian War was that he considered the Ohio country a public domain belonging to all the colonies and not to be preempted by Virginia. He had his own plan for securing the Ohio Valley—by building a series of forts west of the Appalachian Mountains.

Increasingly under censure from the home government for compromising the royal prerogative, Glen was recalled in 1756, being replaced by William Henry Lyttleton. In the same year the crown established the northern and southern Indian superintendencies—a scheme to which in the south, Glen, by his actions, had made a substantial contribution. Three years after his departure, the Cherokee War engulfed the frontiers of the Carolinas. Glen died in England (Middlesex County). His wife had died previously, and there were no children mentioned in his will.

Harry M. Ward

References
Mary F. Carter, "James Glen, Governor of Colonial South Carolina: A Study in British Administrative Policies," Ph.D. Dissertation, University of California, Los Angeles (1951); Edward McCrady, *The History of South Carolina under the Royal Government, 1719–1776* (1901); Robert L. Meriwether, *The Expansion of South Carolina, 1729–1765* (1940); M. Eugene Sirmans, *Colonial South Carolina: A Political History, 1663–1763* (1966); Robert M. Weir, *Colonial South Carolina: A History* (1983).

See also CREEK-CHEROKEE WARS; FORT PRINCE GEORGE–KEOWEE (SOUTH CAROLINA)

Glorious Revolution
See ENGLISH REVOLUTION OF 1688–1689

Fort Gloucester (Massachusetts)
Fort Gloucester was located on the bluff Stage Head overlooking Gloucester Harbor. Since no official title was given to the fort, it was known under the various names of Fort Gloucester, Stage Fort, Fort Eastern Point, and Fort Point. The first defenses consisted of simple breastworks and were erected in 1703 during Queen Anne's War. In 1743, prior to King George's War, the breastworks were improved and eight

12-pounder cannon were installed. During the French and Indian War the fortifications were reactivated and refurbished. In October 1775, new fortified breastworks were built to further upgrade the defenses.

David L. Whitesell

Gloucester Fort (Virginia)

Gloucester Fort was one of several fortifications noted by Virginia Lieutenant Governor Robert Dinwiddie in a 1756 letter to the Lords of Trade. Located at Gloucester Point (also known as Tindall's Point) to guard the north side of the entrance to the York River, Virginia, the fortification dated back to the 1680s, but suffered from chronic disrepair. A visitor noted a battery and parapet there in 1732, but asserted the fort was used mainly for storage. By 1756, Dinwiddie found the fort's cannon corroded and useless and attributed its poor condition to the lack of skilled engineers among the Virginians.

Thomas Costa

References

Governor Dinwiddie to the Lords of Trade, 23 February 1756, in *The Official Records of Robert Dinwiddie*, 2 vols. (1883–1884), rpt. 1977: 2.

Goffe, John (1701–1786)

John Goffe was born in Boston on 16 March 1701. His father later moved the family with Scotch-Irish settlers to the Merrimack River above Dunstable, Massachusetts, in what would become Londonderry, New Hampshire. Goffe began his military career in a spectacular fashion by joining with John Lovewell in his last scout to Pequawket in 1725. Goffe was selected to stay at the makeshift fort with a sick soldier (Benjamin Kidder, a close friend of Goffe's and his future brother-in-law), thus he missed the actual battle in which Lovewell was killed.

After Dummer's War, John Goffe moved farther north along the Merrimack in the area that would become Manchester, New Hampshire. In 1738, he took interest in land to the west of the Merrimack. King George's War interrupted his plans, however. As an avid hunter and woodsman, Goffe was a natural to be offered a command of a company of provincial soldiers to patrol the area around the Merrimack River, and he conducted several scouts

and patrols. In 1746, he served in the New Hampshire regiment raised for a possible attack on Quebec. When the plan fell through, the regiment built a fort on Lake Winnipesaukee where it spent the winter of 1746–1747.

After the war, Goffe settled in the area west of the Merrimack, a settlement that soon became known as Goffstown. When the last French war broke out in 1754, Goffe once again found himself commanding scouts and patrols. In 1755, he commanded a company in the New Hampshire regiment raised for William Johnson's campaign against Crown Point (Robert Rogers commanded another company). The regiment began work on Fort Edward and therefore did not take part in Johnson's battle.

The following year, Goffe, now promoted to major, served with the New Hampshire regiment as it continued work on Fort Edward. In 1757 the New Hampshire men were at Fort William Henry during the fateful siege and massacre. Goffe, promoted once more to lieutenant colonel, was one of the officers who signed the letter to Colonel George Monro urging surrender. The New Hampshire regiment left the camp last on the massacre march, losing 80 men.

During 1758 and 1759, John Goffe continued to field with the New Hampshire regiment. They would arrive too late to take part in Abercromby's attack on Ticonderoga, and see little action in Jeffrey Amherst's advance on Crown Point the following year. In 1760, Goffe commanded the New Hampshire regiment as a full colonel. The regiment performed its most famous work by finishing the military road between the settlement of Number Four and Crown Point. Once connected with the army, they participated in the campaign against Montreal.

John Goffe's military career had thrust him into prominence in New Hampshire, and he would continue public service. With the exception of one year, he served in the assembly from 1762–1777, was appointed judge of the probate court for the county of Hillsborough from 1771–1775, as well as being colonel of the county militia regiment. In his seventies he actively supported the War for Independence, especially in the local committee of safety, and in recruiting. Goffe died on 20 October 1786 and is buried in Bedford, New Hampshire.

Steven C. Eames

References

William Howard Brown, *Colonel John Goffe: Eighteenth Century New Hampshire* (1950).

See also CROWN POINT; FORT EDWARD (NEW YORK); FORT AT NUMBER FOUR (NEW HAMPSHIRE); JOHNSON, WILLIAM; SCOUT

Fort Good Hope (Connecticut)

With the appearance of the English along the Connecticut River in the 1630s, the Dutch felt the need to attempt permanent establishment. In 1633, the Dutch bought land from the Pequots at present-day Dutch Point in Hartford's harbor on the Connecticut River and built a fortified trading post, naming it Het Huys de Hope (House of Hope). They hoped to keep the English from ascending the river and to create a free trading zone to break the Pequot's trade monopoly. The English outmaneuvered the Dutch by settling the mouth of the Connecticut River and building Fort Saybrook, preventing Dutch sea access to their own fort. The Dutch abandoned Fort Good Hope in 1654.

Leslie Miller

References

Bruce Grant, *American Forts Yesterday and Today* (1965); Robert B. Roberts, *Encyclopedia of Historical Forts: The Military, Pioneer, and Trading Posts of the United States* (1988).

See also FORT SAYBROOK (CONNECTICUT)

Grand Pré, Battle of (1747)

Failing in an attack on Annapolis Royal in the fall of 1746, French forces under Jean-Baptiste-Nicholas-Roch de Ramezay withdrew to winter quarters at Beaubassin. Reinforcements for Annapolis arrived from Massachusetts in December under the command of Colonel Arthur Noble. The new arrivals were quartered on the Grand Pré Acadians while engaged in building blockhouses there.

It was feared in Quebec that an English base at Grand Pré would cut off contact with Acadians in the Port Royal (Annapolis) region and afford the British an unmolested opportunity to expand in Nova Scotia. To counter and remove this incursion, Ramezay dispatched a force of 300 Canadians and Indians under the command of Captain Antoine Coulon de Villiers with orders to route the New Englanders. The attackers set out from Beaubassin on 23 January, making a rugged snowshoe march to Grand Pré, arriving there during a raging blizzard at 3 a.m. on 11 February.

Reconnoitering Noble's dispositions and learning that the English were quartered in ten separate buildings, Villiers divided his force to stage ten simultaneous attacks. With the element of surprise in their favor, the Canadians carried all buildings except one stone house where cannon were manned. In the attack, Noble was killed along with 130 other Bostonians (including six officers), 34 were wounded, and 53 made prisoner. Canadian losses were light with six killed and 14 wounded (including Villiers). The English command devolved on Benjamin Goldthwait, who capitulated 12 hours later.

Except for those wounded or already taken prisoner, Goldthwait was allowed to return his remaining 330 men to Annapolis provided they not bear arms "at the head of the Bay of Fundy for a period of six months." Entitled to the honors of war, Goldthwait nonetheless had to parade his men through two lines of victorious Canadians. Although England had been handed a humiliating setback, Villiers and his men returned to Beaubassin in the spring, having accomplished little toward reestablishing French power in Acadia.

John D. Hamilton

References

Edward B. O'Callaghan, ed., *Documents Relative to the Colonial History of the State of New York; Procured in Holland, England, and France,* Vol. VI, London Documents and Vol. XI, Paris Documents (1858).

See also CHIGNECTO ISTHMUS; KING GEORGE'S WAR

Fort Granville (North Carolina)

Fort Granville was located near the present-day town of Portsmouth, adjacent to Ocracoke Inlet on the Atlantic Ocean. Although authorized in 1748, serious construction began in 1755, at the behest of Governor Arthur Dobbs. The fort was garrisoned sporadically during the French and Indian War, but was never involved in hostilities. The garrison was removed in 1764. The fort was described as "a fascine Battery, secured by piles, with 2 faces."

Jim Sumner

Fort Granville (Pennsylvania)

Fort Granville stood on the Juniata River about a mile west of the mouth of Kishacoquillas Creek. It was built shortly after General Edward Braddock's defeat in the fall of 1755, one in a line of forts west of the Susquehanna. Commanding a narrow pass where the Juniata falls through a mountain ridge, the site was chosen because it appeared defensible by a small garrison against even a large body of attackers. Lying at the far northeastern edge of Pennsylvania's frontier, the fort was a prominent target of the raids by French-allied Indians in 1756. Late in the summer of that year, while the fort was garrisoned by a small force commanded by Lieutenant Edward Armstrong, it was besieged by a party of Ohio Indians under the direction of the Delaware chief, Captain Jacobs. Following a long siege, a party of attackers approached the fort through a deep ravine along the river and managed to set a fire at its base that burned a hole through the log wall. Firing through the hole, the attackers killed Lieutenant Armstrong, among others, and demanded the surrender of the fort. The gates were opened to the attackers and they took as prisoners 22 men, three women, and a number of children.

The prisoners were taken to the town of Kittanning, on the Allegheny River, where John Turner, the man who opened the fort's gates to the attackers, was tortured and killed. The rest of the group remained as prisoners, though in the weeks that followed parties escaped captivity and returned to the colonies.

The fall of Fort Granville led most of the colonists inhabiting the immediate area to abandon their farms and move back toward Fort Augusta, Carlisle, or Shippensburg.

Eric Hinderaker

References

Thomas L. Montgomery, ed., *Report of the Commission to Locate the Site of the Frontier Forts of Pennsylvania*, 2nd ed., 2 vol. (1916).

See also KITTANNING, BATTLE OF; FORT LYTTLETON (PENNSYLVANIA); FORT SHIRLEY (PENNSYLVANIA)

Great Britain

Despite inclinations which led them in other directions, English (and later British) imperial administrations found themselves involved in major wars in North America from the 1680s to the 1760s: in 1688–1697, 1702–1713, 1739–1748, and 1755–1763. Much of this occurred in the absence of a settled colonial policy for America, something not developed until the 1740s. For many decades North American affairs attracted no sustained concern by any important English interest group. No American enthusiasts were found in any inner council, until the duke of Bedford, the earl of Sandwich, and William Pitt became converted in 1745–1746 to the idea of an aggressive naval and military policy there. The acquisition of Louisbourg in 1745, a deep embarrassment to the ministry then bent on peace negotiations, was the first occasion when an American event captured English public opinion. Such prolonged myopia by politicians and bureaucrats in London, which arose from their enduring ignorance of America, stimulated in part by their lack of personal experience of the New World, and the seriously inadequate information supplied them by their colonial governors, has been characterized by some scholars as salutary or benign neglect. When compared, for instance, to the range and variety of reports ordered by and supplied to the French court even before 1700 on the potential of North America, the English government remained largely uninformed. The independent and widely scattered military successes in the colonies, such as in New Netherlands in 1664 or in Acadia in 1710, failed to ignite in any English government an aggressive imperial policy of expansion. Not until the 1750s was the principal object of British foreign policy—the defense of the realm—in any serious or sustained way influenced by events in North America. Naval or military forces sent, or public funds spent, were often as not resented by the English political nation. North American events constituted very much a sideshow for successive British administrations until the mid-eighteenth century. In America, at least, Britain was an imperial power until the 1740s of very slight importance. Throughout this long period, no review of American colonial defense problems was ever undertaken. Instead military decisions for America were invariably formulated by the demands of English politics.

Newfoundland, where settlement was expressly forbidden, was the one exception owing to its abundant fisheries and the rhetoric annually repeated about its value not only for cod, largely sold in Portugal and the Caribbean, but as a nursery for seamen. That great rock, in the eyes of English ministers, was much more an extension of the British Isles than part of a North American colonial empire.

Two principal factors spawned a change in American policy. The first was a continuous and increasing military and naval involvement in America from 1745 onward, largely in response to perceived French initiatives which threatened to limit English settlements to a long, narrow coastal enclave. The second was the growing understanding by the 1740s that America, whose population in the eighteenth century was growing more rapidly than any other part of the Atlantic world, from earlier insignificance was becoming an important element in the Atlantic economy, especially for British exports and re-exports. What might have otherwise activated British imperial interest in America, such as the eroding by colonial lower houses of the power of governors and the authority of the metropolis itself, was still unfocused and ignored by England's politicians, despite repeated warnings for a half century before the 1760s.

If, for many decades after first permanent English settlements had been established in America, English troops on a long-term basis in America were few, the colonial governors were almost invariably professional officers of extensive military experience. For defense they relied on colonial militias and whatever vessels the colonial legislatures paid to arm and man. Thus, when Schenectady was overrun in 1690, the response was a seaborne attack on Quebec by sea, entirely a colonial undertaking. Indeed, throughout King William's War (1689–1697), except for the 1697 expeditionary force of 510 men sent to recapture St. John's and other Newfoundland harbors, the colonists depended on their own military resources. Later, when Charles Town was attacked by a French and Spanish force in 1706, defense was in the hands of the colonists. When the French on Cape Breton continued after 1713 to use Canso as a fishing station, Massachusetts troops, with the help of a Royal Navy frigate, drove them away and destroyed their property. When the French at Louisbourg invaded peninsular Nova Scotia, seized Canso and invested the small fort at Annapolis Royal in 1744, Massachusetts sent reinforcements, unaided by British arms.

An insignificant part of the English army, which from the 1680s in peacetime rarely numbered more than 20,000 and rose in wartime to perhaps 50,000 all ranks, was stationed in the American colonies before the 1745 conquest of Louisbourg. American colonials first encountered imperial troops in 1651–1652, when royalist Virginia was overawed by the Puritan Commonwealth. A second bloodless intervention occurred when Richard Nicolls secured the surrender of New Amsterdam with 400 regulars carried on two warships. These few regular troops were organized as independent infantry companies. Much later scattered artillery batteries were based in America. In 1677, after the collapse of Bacon's Rebellion, a regiment of 1,130 officers and men arrived in Virginia. From these, two companies of 100 regulars each were established in Virginia by 1679, but they were disbanded in 1682 because of their cost to the crown. In 1686, when Edmund Andros assumed the governorship of the newly fashioned Dominion of New England, he was accompanied to Boston by 100 regulars. Similarly, English regulars were sent in 1691 to wrest imperial control of New York from Jacob Leisler. As in Virginia earlier, a number of these troops, organized into four independent companies of 100 men each, remained in the colony until disbanded in 1763. Used principally for defense, they were stationed in the Mohawk Valley no farther west than Fort Hunter. The system was extended to Fort William, Newfoundland, in 1697 (easily overpowered in the French attack in 1705), to Annapolis Royal, Nova Scotia, in 1710, and to South Carolina in 1721, where one independent company garrisoned Fort King George (near Darien, Georgia) on the Altamaha River. The Carolina company consisted entirely of men discharged from active service because of age or infirmity. When Georgia was established as a colony in 1733, this company was sent to Savannah. Three other independent companies were allocated to South Carolina in 1743, and soon after were stationed on the Upper Congaree River. They were disbanded only in 1764. None of these companies were subject to any active supervision; and men were kept on the rolls long after they had become unfit for duty. Their historian has called them "ineffective, inefficient, expensive."

Not until 1710–1711 was any attempt undertaken by Britain to carry the war to the enemy. Then it was done in direct response to American appeals. This unusually ambitious new policy focused first on Acadia, where in 1710, a British naval force with some 400 marines, aided by New England militiamen, easily seized the unimpressive earthen defenses of Port Royal (earlier seized without orders by Robert Sedgwick with a colonial force in 1654 and held until 1667). The next year the prize became Quebec itself, last subjected to attack by William Phips in 1690, and whose greatest protection was not its ramparts, but its distance from the sea up the hazardous St. Lawrence River with its tide, powerful currents, mists, and fogs. A force of 5,300 soldiers in seven regiments, with artillery and 6,000 seamen and marines, was sent to Boston where some 2,200 colonials were embarked for the campaign. On the north shore of the great river, several transports ran aground, with great loss of life. The expedition was abandoned as a humiliating fiasco. Only in 1746 was a second attempt planned, when more than 4,000 troops with an artillery train were embarked at Portsmouth, with 4,300 seamen and marines. When contrary winds prevented the squadron from even getting into the English Channel, the costly scheme was abandoned.

From 1711 until the mid-1750s, except for the temporary ambitions of 1746, British policy in America remained essentially defensive. After Nova Scotia was incorporated into the British Empire by the terms of the 1713 Treaty of Utrecht, a modest increase in the number of regulars stationed in America was the only change in policy. The independent companies in Newfoundland and Nova Scotia became the 40th Foot Regiment in 1718. This did not end the serious neglect to which they were habitually subjected. Tested at Canso, where the French appeared upon the outbreak of war in 1744, they surrendered at the first volley. In 1737, to support the new colony of Georgia established to protect the South Carolina frontier, the 500-man 42nd Regiment was raised by James Oglethorpe. It participated in the failed 1740 siege of St. Augustine, and was disbanded in 1748. When Louisbourg fell in 1745, two regiments (65th and 66th) were raised from among the colonials, which, with two Gibraltar regiments (they wisely had wintered in 1745–1746 in Virginia), garrisoned the fortress from 1746 to 1749, William Shirley's and William Pepperrell, Jr's regiments were disbanded in 1748. The others were dispatched to Halifax for the defense of Nova Scotia, when Halifax was built in 1749. In 1750, a third regiment joined them there.

This first indication of an important new phase in British thinking about America emerged when Edward Braddock's two regiments (44th and 48th) of regulars were dispatched from Ireland to Virginia early in 1755, and Shirley's and Pepperrell's regiments were newly raised, as the 50th and 51st Foot, from colonial volunteers. Under the unified command of a professional officer who not only directed military operations but negotiated with colonial governments for supplies and troops, this small force now extended to the Ohio Valley the challenge to French ambition in North America first begun at Louisbourg in the 1740s. The panic and demoralization which had immediately engulfed colonial leaders when General Edward Braddock died in ambush on the Monongahela in July 1755 cast a long shadow thereafter over both the behavior of British and colonial troops in wooded areas and British North American strategy. The 1,470 British troops suffered 980 casualties, while the French force of less than 900, three-quarters of whom were aboriginals, lost only 20 killed and as many wounded.

Hostilities, it immediately became clear in London, could not be confined to the frontier. Rather, the war would be directed against Canada itself, as had earlier been intended in 1690, 1711, and 1746. To do this, regular troops in large numbers were deployed in America, which, for the first time, became the main British theater of war until after 1760. The war was primarily a matter for the infantry, with no cavalry units serving there, and by 1758, one-third of all British artillery companies were in America. By 1758–1759, some 32 regular infantry battalions, numbering almost 30,000 men, were serving in America, when only six served in Germany. By war's end, many who served in the ranks were American recruits; and the 60th Foot (Royal American Regiment) had four battalions, all raised in the colonies. As with the navy, so too with the army. Where before 1745 few British officers had any experience in America, by 1760 only a minority did not. From being an unpopular and unfamiliar place to serve, America, through the exingencies of prolonged campaigning, became central to the experience of such professionals.

If, in 1755, war against France was still undeclared, decisions to conduct war were taken in London. The war was to have two main theaters. New York became the strategic center for operations against the French on the frontier. The towns of Albany and New York became the principal logistical centers. Halifax became an auxiliary base to Portsmouth, England, for operations in the Gulf of St. Lawrence region. Only in 1758 did the Admiralty belatedly and very reluctantly agree to build at Halifax the first British naval base in North America. The strategy of 1746 was resurrected. It embraced a two-pronged attack by forces concentrated at Albany, through the Lake Champlain corridor (to Jennings, the Mahican Channel) to the St. Lawrence Valley, westward along the Mokawk Valley to Lake Ontario, and then eastward into the upper St. Lawrence. Success there depended on a new and powerful siege of Louisbourg, as bypassing Cape Breton was rejected as too risky. With the fortress reduced, an expeditionary force would proceed into the Gulf to seize Quebec. Although provincial levies were raised, and colonies were compensated by the British taxpayers for the bulk of their costs, the principal burden of fighting rested with British regulars. The Americans supplied as well nine ranger companies, at the expense of the crown. Each such company contained some Native Americans; one was composed entirely of Mahicans.

The first step taken, after Braddock's defeat, was to oust the French from the Bay of Fundy. This was accomplished by the successful attack on Fort Beauséjour (near Sackville, New Brunswick) and nearby Fort Gaspereau, by 2,000 Massachusetts troops, authorized and paid from England, and perhaps 300 redcoats. There were about 450 defenders at Beauséjour, two-thirds of them Acadians. The success led directly to the deportation of the bulk of the Acadian inhabitants and the utter destruction of their settlements, a long-advocated proposal finally taken locally by British officials in Halifax. By such intemperate action, the British laid waste one of the few advanced agricultural settlements in America and set the tone of brutal destruction of property which characterized the British on Cape Breton Island, along the lower St. Lawrence in 1758, the following year in the Quebec region, and elsewhere.

There is much evidence from this war to support those who believe that, if in any war British arms are to prevail, it must be a long one, for it invariably took them years to discover how to fight it. The inevitability of French defeat, seen so clearly by modern historians of New France, remains a modern myth, and was believed in the eighteenth century by no one

except, ironically, General Louis-Joseph de Montcalm. The Bay of Fundy campaign remained an isolated success, as the strategy on the New York frontier under the direction of William Shirley, Braddock's militarily innocent successor, collapsed under the strain of inept commanders, political intrigue, and uncooperative colonial units unused to the wilderness and inexperienced in military affairs. Shirley's plans against Fort St. Frédéric (Crown Point, New York), Fort Niagara (near Youngstown, New York), and Fort Frontenac (Kingston, Ontario) evaporated. A tactical success was achieved at Fort William Henry (Lake George, New York) in September 1755, when 300 French regulars were stopped in their intemperate frontal assault by 3,000 provincials and natives under William Johnson, who was rewarded by Parliament with £5,000 and by the king with a baronetcy. Never in the annals of eighteenth-century American warfare was a more insignificant engagement more richly rewarded! In August 1756, with war between Britain and France at length declared, Fort Oswego (Oswego, New York) and two others nearby, with their united garrison of 1,660 Americans recruited into the 50th and 51st Foot, were captured by a French force of 3,040, of whom only 30 were slain. The year 1757 brought no comfort to British arms. Fort William Henry was surrendered in August 1757, while an impressive French naval force in Louisbourg harbor utterly frustrated the British, who had concentrated an even larger expeditionary force at Halifax in the summer 1757. Montreal seemed as safe from British attack in 1758 as it had been earlier, when 6,400 British regulars and 9,000 provincials under Abercromby were stymied in their bloody frontal assault at Fort Carillon (Ticonderoga, New York) in July 1758, and where more than 1,600 British and Americans were killed or wounded.

These were the last British reversals at the hands of the French. Fortress Louisbourg capitulated in August 1758, when 13,140 troops (of whom about 500 were provincials) and 14,000 seamen and marines were concentrated there. There were about 800 French and 560 British casualties in the seven-week siege. The same month Fort Frontenac on Lake Ontario was taken and burned. Defended by about 50 French against an attacking force that numbered more than 3,000, the fort contained 400 tons of supplies, all of which were seized. In November, the British with a force of 7,000, of whom less than 1,300 were regulars, took from

300 defenders Fort Duquesne (rebuilt as Fort Pitt), hitherto the symbol of French hegemony in the upper Ohio Valley. In 1759, the masonry Fort Niagara, emblematic of French control of the Great Lakes and defended by 490 men, was taken by 1,500 regulars and 500 provincials in July. Victory was attained only after a bloody battle fought nearby at La Belle Famille, where some 500 of a French relief force of 600 were killed. Johnson, who commanded after the death of Brigadier John Prideaux, at length earned the baronetcy he had been awarded in 1755! Both Crown Point and Ticonderoga were also taken in 1759, almost without loss, by Jeffrey Amherst, who came with overwhelming numbers. Finally, with defeat staring at them after a summer of discouraging setbacks at Quebec, the British outfought the French forces, who fled the field and the battered town in mid-September. British casualties numbered almost 1,500.

The remnants of this victorious British force came within an ace, in the spring 1760, of being beaten by the considerable French forces still undefeated in New France. By spring, death had reduced the British to less than 4,000, many of whom were sick. When Brigadier General James Murray gave battle outside the walls of the city in April, he had 3,875 effectives, 1,100 of whom became casualties at Sainte-Foy in a battle he need not have fought. The British situation at Quebec was rescued by the surprisingly early arrival of British naval units in the St. Lawrence. The victory on the Plains of Abraham the previous autumn was now secure, and the surrender of Montreal seemed certain. Some 11,000 troops, of whom 5,500 were regulars, fought their way eastward from Lake Ontario. Another 3,400 (1,750 of them regulars) pushed up the Richelieu River to join Murray's force from Quebec in the encirclement of this last Canadian stronghold, defended by 3,500.

With Montreal's surrender, the British army in America soon shrank in size. In 1761, Amherst sent 2,000 to occupy Dominica and 7,000 to attack Martinique; in 1762, every spare man was dispatched to the Havana expedition. Thus weakened, the British were twice embarrassed by the French in 1762 in the Gulf of St. Lawrence. A small French naval force from Bordeaux entered Restigouche Bay in July. The 400 troops on board rallied some 2,000 Acadians in the region. Earlier in May the British had been greatly embarrassed by a sudden descent on St. John's, Newfoundland, by a na-

val force from Brest. Defended by only 80 soldiers, some 800 French took Fort William and held it for four months. Hundreds of British fishing vessels were seized with their catches. It took months to assemble a British counterattack. The expeditionary force, numbering about 1,560 regulars and provincials, sailed from New York in mid-August via Halifax and Placentia, before retaking the town in mid-September 1762. The raids were of no strategic importance, for France ceded all of Canada to Great Britain.

To become dominant in Canada, a place then of little perceived value beyond the fur trade, the British had expended by their own estimate some £80 million. This outrageous cost stemmed largely from a strategy which, instead of blockading the St. Lawrence and attempting to starve Canada into submission, focused on a wasting frontier war. For such folly, the disciplined ranks of the British regulars in the foot regiments could hardly be responsible. Political myopia in America and England, professional military ignorance of America occasioned by a colonial policy of relative neglect, combined with an excessive regard for the martial skills of the French soldier, and genuine fear of the Canadian militia and their aboriginal allies, were at the root of British difficulties. Their ignorance and hence their fear of Native Americans the English military came by honestly. From the outset of colonization, war against the Amerindians was largely carried forward by the English settlers unaided either by British troops or finances. This is clear from the opening hostilities in Virginia in 1622 and 1644, through the devastating wars against the Pequots in 1637 and the Wampanoags and Narragansetts in 1675–1676, inhabiting lands disputed by New Englanders, to equally ruinous raids against the Apalachees on the Florida frontier of South Carolina between 1704 and 1710, and the general uprising in South Carolina in 1715 led by the Yamasee. In North Carolina, when the Tuscaroras, aided most importantly by the Corees and Pamlicos, rose up in 1711, again the colonials alone defended themselves. The Abenakis and Pennacooks remained hostile to Anglo-American settlers of the Northeast from the 1680s until virtually destroyed by colonial forces in Dummer's War from 1722–1727.

Regular troops became heavily involved against the aboriginals only in the mid-eighteenth century. The first occasion was in Nova

Scotia in 1750 and involved the Micmac, where the 40th, 45th, and the 47th Regiments proved singularly ineffective against them. When General Edward Braddock was defeated more by Indians than by French regulars and Canadian militiamen in 1754, colonists everywhere along the frontier, except the Carolinas, found themselves under attack and poorly placed to defend themselves. Historians have counted 177 raids between 1754 and 1758 alone along the frontier from the Holston to the Monongahela Rivers in the Ohio country. In eastern Pennsylvania and Maryland, aboriginal war parties boldly harassed military convoys and attacked isolated settlements.

The success of British arms against the French in America led to the direct confrontation with aboriginals by British regulars. The policy was first directed against the Cherokee, traditionally favoring the Anglo-Americans, but who, with the establishment of Fort Prince George and Fort Loudoun in their territories in the 1750s, turned hostile. In 1759, the Cherokee took Fort Loudoun and attacked settlements on the upper Yadkin and Catawba Rivers in Rowan County, North Carolina. In response, some 1,200 regulars were sent to South Carolina in 1760 to contain the Cherokee, but were defeated at Little Tassantee. Only when the remnants were reinforced by a new infusion of regulars, some of whom remained there until 1768, were the Cherokee thrown onto the defensive.

The more important commitment of British troops occurred when Pontiac rallied the western tribes in 1763. Within two months, every British fortification west of the Alleghenies, except Detroit and Fort Pitt, was taken. Some 400 soldiers and 2,000 settlers are estimated to have been slain. Relief columns of regulars eventually reached the besieged settlements, but peace terms were never dictated to the warring tribes as they had been earlier to French garrisons. Instead of the musket and cold steel and a radically new trade policy, as Amherst had preferred, a different policy emerged. His successor, Thomas Gage, in the face of severe postwar spending constraints, adopted the French policy of diplomacy, control of land speculators, a regulated fur trade, and payment for services rendered as constituting the only path likely toward accommodation.

That Pontiac's allies had 400 soldiers west of the Alleghenies says much about postwar military realities in British America. Without a conscious decision, an army of about 8,000 regulars remained in America, principally to overawe the newly-conquered *habitants* of Quebec, where about 3,500 regulars were stationed. Another 1,700 were in Nova Scotia, a battalion each in Halifax and at Louisbourg, whose fortifications had been systematically demolished in the summer of 1760. All the forts in the Lake Champlain corridor were garrisoned, as well as those in the Mohawk Valley to Oswego, which required 1,250 men. At the New York City headquarters, some 700 found employment. The rest were scattered in two dozen other places, some in forts specified for the conduct of trade with aboriginals, and as far west as La Baye in the Illinois territory and Michilimackinac and St. Joseph in the Michigan territory. Moreover, the colonies of East and West Florida, newly ceded by Spain, where barracks were erected, needed to be garrisoned. That the British postwar army was larger than was strictly needed, and some of it was kept in America had far more to do with retaining places for deserving officers than with a desire to police colonials. How infantry, brutalized by discipline, were to act effectively in support of the custom service or to prevent illegal acquisition of native land, no one in England, where the decision was made, tried to explain. John Shy, among others, has explained the consequences for 13 of the colonies in British America.

Julian Gwyn

References
John Richard Alden, *Robert Dinwiddie, Servant of the Crown* (1973); Fred Anderson, *A People's Army: Massachusetts Soldiers and Society in the Seven Years' War* (1984); Daniel J. Beattie, "The Adaption of the British Army to Wilderness Warfare, 1755–1763," in Maarten Ultee, ed., *Adapting to Conditions: War and Society in the Eighteenth Century* (1986); John Bartlet Brebner, *New England's Outpost: Acadia before the Conquest of Canada* (1927); Gillian Cell, *English Enterprise in Newfoundland* (1969); J.C.D. Clark, *Revolution and Rebellion: State and Society in England in the Seventeenth and Eighteenth Centuries* (1986); David H. Corkran, *The Cherokee Frontier: Conflict and Survival, 1740–1762* (1962).

W.J. Eccles and Susan L. Laskin, "The Seven Years' War," *Historical Atlas of Canada: From the Beginnings to 1800*

(1988), Plate 42; John E. Ferling, *A Wilderness of Miseries: War and Warriors in Early America* (1980); ———, *Struggle for a Continent: The Wars of Early America* (1993); William A. Foote, "The American Independent Companies of the British Army in America, 1664–1764," Ph.D. Dissertation, UCLA (1966); Guy Frégault, *Canada: The War of the Conquest*, trans., Margaret M. Cameron (1969).

Lawrence Henry Gipson, *The Great War for Empire. The Victorious Years, 1758–1760* (1949); William G. Godfrey, *Pursuit of Profit and Preferment in Colonial North America: John Bradstreet's Quest* (1982); Gary C. Goodwin, *Cherokees in Transition: A Study in Changing Culture and Environment Prior to 1775* (1977); Gerald S. Graham, ed., *The Walker Expedition to Quebec, 1711* (1953); Julian Gwyn, ed., *The Royal Navy and North America: The Warren Papers, 1736–1752* (1973); ———, "British Government Spending and the North American Colonies, 1740–1775," *Journal of Imperial and Commonwealth History*, 8 (1980):74–84; ———, "The Use of Naval Power at the Two Sieges of Louisbourg: 1745 and 1758," *Nova Scotia Historical Review*, 10 (1990):63–93; Julian Gwyn and Christopher Moore, eds., *La Siege de Louisbourg . . . 1745* (1978).

Philip S. Haffenden, *New England in the English Nation 1689–1713* (1974); Edward P. Hamilton, *The French and Indian Wars: The Story of Battles and Forts in the Wilderness* (1962); Milton W. Hamilton, *Sir William Johnson: Colonial American, 1715–1763* (1976); James A. Henretta, *"Salutary Neglect": Colonial Administration under the Duke of Newcastle* (1972); Dallas Irvine, "The First British Regulars in North America," *Military Affairs*, 9 (1945):337–354; Larry E. Ivers, *British Drums on the Southern Frontier: The Military Colonization of Georgia, 1733–1749* (1974).

Francis Jennings, *The Invasion of America: Indians, Colonialism, and the Cant of Conquest* (1975); ———, *The Ambiguous Iroquois Empire: The Covenant Chain Confederation of Indian Tribes with English Colonies from its beginnings to the Lancaster Treaty of 1744* (1984); ———, *Empire of Fortune: Crowns, Colonies, and Tribes in the Seven Years War in America* (1988); Paul E. Kopperman, *Braddock at the Monongahela* (1977).

Paul Langford, *Modern British Foreign Policy: The Eighteenth Century 1688–1815* (1976); John Tate Lanning, ed., *The St. Augustine Expedition of 1740: A Report to the South Carolina General Assembly* (1954); M.E.S. Laws, *Battery Records of the Royal Artillery* (1952); Douglas Edward Leach, *Flintlock and Tomahawk: New England in King Philip's War* (1958); ———, *Arms for Empire: A Military History of the British Colonies in North America, 1607–1763* (1973).

Lee S. McCardell, *Ill-Starred General: Braddock of the Coldstream Guards* (1986); Michael N. McConnell, *A Country Between: The Upper Ohio Valley and Its Peoples, 1724–1774* (1992); John S. McLennan, *Louisbourg from Its Foundation to Its Fall, 1713–1758* (1918); Richard Middleton, *The Bells of Victory: The Pitt-Newcastle Ministry and the Conduct of the Seven Years' War, 1757–1762* (1985).

Stanley Pargellis, "The Four Independent Companies of New York," *Essays in Colonial American History Presented to Charles McLean Andrews by His Students* (1931):96–123; ———, *Lord Loudoun in North America* (1933); ———, ed., *Military Affairs in North America, 1748–1765; Selected Documents from the Cumberland Papers in Windsor Castle* (1936); Howard H. Peckham, *The Colonial Wars 1689–1762* (1964); William Pencak, *War, Politics and Revolution in Provincial Massachusetts* (1981).

George A. Rawlyk, *Yankees at Louisbourg* (1967); Trevor R. Reese, "Britain's Military Support of Georgia in the War of 1739–1748," *Georgia Historical Quarterly*, 43 (1959):1–10; Jerome R. Reich, *Leisler's Rebellion: A Study in Democracy in New York* (1953); Robert C. Ritchie, *The Duke's Province: A Study of New York Politics and Society, 1664–1691* (1977); W. Stitt Robinson, *The Southern Colonial Frontier, 1607–1763* (1979); Peter E. Russell, "Redcoats in the Wilderness: British Officers and Irregular Warfare in Europe and America, 1740 to 1760," *William and Mary Quarterly*, 35 (1978):629–652.

John A. Schutz, *William Shirley, King's Governor of Massachusetts* (1961); R.E. Scouller, *The Armies of Queen Anne* (1966); Harold E. Selesky, *War and Society in Colonial Connecticut* (1990); John Shy, *Toward Lexington: The Role of the British Army in*

G

the *Coming of the American Revolution*
(1965); C.P. Stacey, *Quebec, 1759: The Siege
and the Battle* (1959); ———, "The British
Forces in North America during the Seven
Years' War," *Dictionary of Canadian Biogra-
phy*, 12 vols. (1966–1974) 3:xxiv–xxx;
George F.G. Stanley, *New France: The Last
Phase, 1744–1760* (1968); Ian K. Steele,
*Grenadiers and Guerillas: The Struggle for
Canada, 1689–1760* (1969); ———, *Betray-
als: Fort William Henry and the "Massacre"*
(1990).

Ricardo Torres-Reyes, *The British Siege
of St. Augustine in 1740 . . .* (1972); Leslie
F.S. Upton, *Micmacs and Colonists: Indian-
White Relations in the Maritime Provinces,
1713–1867* (1979); G.M. Waller, *Samuel
Vetch, Colonial Enterpriser* (1960); Stephen
Saunders Webb, *The Governors General: The
English Army and the Definition of Empire,
1569–1681* (1979); ———, *1676: The End
of American Independence* (1984).

See also ACADIA; ANGLO-INDIAN RELATIONS;
FRONTIER, NORTHERN; FRONTIER, SOUTH-
ERN; GEORGIA; GREAT BRITAIN–FRANCE
RELATIONS; GREAT BRITAIN–SPAIN RELA-
TIONS; KING GEORGE'S WAR; KING
WILLIAM'S WAR; MASSACHUSETTS; NEW
YORK; OHIO COUNTRY; PONTIAC'S WAR;
QUEEN ANNE'S WAR; SEVEN YEARS' WAR;
SOUTH CAROLINA

Great Britain–France Relations

In the sixteenth century, France and England
were preoccupied, not with each other, but with
Spain and Portugal, countries that monopolized
the colonial world. Throughout the century,
their pirates and privateers preyed on Spanish
shipping. In the 1590s, both countries were at
war with Spain. When they became involved in
exploration, however, both were careful to keep
well north of Iberian claims. The result of
Jacques Cartier's voyage west in 1534 was to
focus French activity on securing the St. Lawrence River as a potential route to the Orient.
Beginning with Martin Frobisher's voyage of
1576, the English concentrated on finding a
northwest passage. Everything exotic and precious was the goal of these explorations: spices,
gold and silver, new Eldorados.

England and France began the seventeenth
century in alliance (1603). Both envied the new
colossus of colonial trade, the Dutch Republic,
which was building a vast wealth from its trade
in South America, the Caribbean, but most
particularly in India and the East Indies. England fought two wars against Holland (1652–
1654, 1664–1667) and in 1672 joined France
in a third (England to 1674; France to 1678).
The Dutch wars reveal that trade was a national
concern and rivals in trade were considered
national enemies. If trade was to be a national
monopoly, so too were colonies, established in
the hope of developing trade. The more successful France and England were in developing colonial empires, the more obvious it became that
in doing so they were on a collision course.
Trade rivalry was grafted into the older rivalry
of political dominance in Europe. It was difficult, then as now, to sort out whether a particular call to arms resulted from purely dynastic or
continental reasons or because of considerations of trade and empire.

Both France and England participated in
the Newfoundland/Grand Banks fishery in the
sixteenth century and both laid claim to Newfoundland (England in 1583, France in 1624).
In the first half of the seventeenth century, small
settlements and trading posts were established
in North America by private, chartered companies given limited rights to govern under the
French and English crowns: Port Royal in 1605,
Jamestown in 1607, Quebec in 1608, Plymouth
in 1620, and so on. The Acadian peninsula,
located at the frontier between French and English areas of interest and in the heart of the
fishery, had particular strategic value. Anglo-
French hostilities in North America were initiated by Sir Samuel Argall, who, acting as admiral of Virginia, destroyed French settlements at
Saint-Sauveur and Port Royal. In 1621, the
Nova Scotia grant created a Scottish claim to
Acadia, further complicating the history of the
region. The first major colonizing expedition to
Canada, sent by Cardinal Richelieu's Company
of One Hundred Associates, set sail at a time of
Anglo-French war and was captured (1628) as
was Quebec (1629). By that time, a few Scots
had been settled among the French remnant at
Port Royal. Both ramshackle colonies were returned to France in 1632. Inspired by Dutch
example, both the French and English would
make use of chartered companies as instruments of imperial development.

Newfoundland and the fishing banks, the
Gulf of St. Lawrence and the wilderness shores
that surrounded it, and Acadia constituted a
separate, maritime zone of Anglo-French inter-

est and rivalry. New England, too, was cut off from the interior and looked to the sea and the North American coast that extended to the north and east. In 1655, while France and England were at peace, a New England expedition burned Port Royal and seized Acadia. Pursuant to the Treaty of Breda (1667), Acadia was restored to France in 1670. The Acadians, marginal to both empires, traded with New England merchants in time of peace and fell prey to New England pirates in time of war.

Canada remained remote and difficult to access, but increasingly was seen by English colonials as a threat as it developed Indian trade alliances on their northern and western flanks and served as a base of operations against them in time of war. Elements of the geography of North America, which would have a profound effect on Anglo-French rivalry, were beginning to become apparent. Both the St. Lawrence and the Hudson, explored for the Dutch by Henry Hudson in 1609, were highways to the Great Lakes heartland, the locus of the fur trade, well-peopled by Indian tribes that were potential military allies and trading partners. Hudson Bay, discovered by Hudson for the English in 1610, gave access to a more distant fur hinterland and, through James Bay, was a back door to the Great Lakes region. The creation of the Hudson's Bay Company in 1672 inaugurated English competition from this route. When England captured the colony of New Netherland in 1664, it then held two of the three competitive routes to the same treasure of men and furs. "The King of England did graspe at all America," was the Canadian governor's comment.

While the English were making the more significant *settlements* in North America, the French had the advantage in *penetration* of the continent by way of the fur trade. The dispersal of their first allies, the Hurons, by the Five Nations Iroquois in 1648, did not stop the elaboration of Franco-Indian trading alliances. On the New York side, imperialist drive came not from Albany merchants, who were content to trade behind their Iroquois barrier, but from English governors such as Thomas Dongan, who sent New York traders inland and claimed the Iroquois as subjects.

The potential for conflict on a continental scale increased exponentially when the Canadian navigator, Louis Jolliet, and the Jesuit missionary, Jacques Marquette, discovered the Mississippi River (1672–1674) and its close connection to the Great Lakes system by portage routes (Chicago-Illinois, Fox-Wisconsin Rivers). Trading alliances in the Illinois and Mississippi Valleys extended French influence in the interior, west of the American seaboard colonies. The game board on which Anglo-French rivalry was being played out was increased to mind-boggling size.

The Glorious Revolution in England and the exile of the Stuarts (1688) marked a watershed. William III brought England into a gathering alliance against France, beginning what has been called the Second Hundred Years' War. This was a period of Anglo-French rivalry both for influence in Europe and increasingly for colonial dominance, marked by intermittent wars—1689–1697, 1702–1713, 1744–1748, 1754–1763, 1778–1783, 1793–1801, 1803–1814, 1815—that were divided by mere breathing spaces and, for the lucky generation of 1713–1744, by an Anglo-French alliance of convenience.

An Iroquois attack on Lachine, near Montreal, opened the long wars in North America. The form that developed became standard. Guerrilla raids from Canada goaded New Englanders and New Yorkers into joint action in the form of a two-pronged attack: overland via Lake Champlain against Montreal, by sea against Quebec. Hapless Port Royal suffered attack. Micmacs, Maliseets, and Abenakis protected the French eastern flank; Iroquois protected the English western flank.

This first phase of the Second Hundred Years' War was brought to a close by the Treaty of Ryswick (1697). The Iroquois Five Nations subsequently consented by the Treaty of Montreal (1700; ratified 1701) to be neutral in Anglo-French contests. In the years that followed, the Iroquois, with great skill, played the French and English off one another, preserving in large measure their own independence. As New Yorker Peter Wraxall observed, "The great ruling principle of the modern Indian politics" was "to preserve the balance between us and the French."

It seemed for a time that the French, saddled with a glutted, valueless fur trade, would abandon the west and be content to let Indians bring furs to the Canadians, emulating in this the traders of Albany. But when Louis XIV's grandson ascended the throne of Spain (1701) against the opposition of England and much of Europe, it seemed to the French the best policy was to maintain some control of the interior to hold the

G

American colonies in check—especially to prevent them from proceeding overland to seize the silver mines of Mexico and New Mexico. Such was the rationale for the foundation of Detroit and for the development of Louisiana. The War of the Spanish Succession thus had its North American phase, marked by the usual border raids, the definitive New England capture of Port Royal (1710), and another failed pincers campaign against Canada (1711). By the Treaty of Utrecht (1713), Great Britain garnered in Hudson Bay, Newfoundland, and Acadia, as well as the *asiento,* the contract to supply slaves to Spanish America. The French were desperate to preserve (and did preserve) what they saw as essential: the fishery, a great source of wealth and the nursery of seamen, and Canada, which they valued as controlling the Great Lakes and thereby the continent.

The next phase of Anglo-French rivalry unfolded, surprisingly, under the umbrella of an Anglo-French alliance (1716–1733). The ministries of both kingdoms feared succession crises and were doubtful of their old allies. Thus it was France and Great Britain that maintained the status quo by diplomacy, congresses, even preventive war. Still, the period of alliance, and inertial abstinence from war to 1744, was not so much a period of Anglo-French peace as of competition with only covert violence. In North America there were preparations for war, diplomatic struggles by Indian council fires, and proxy wars in which Indians fired the guns. Across the Atlantic, an Anglo-French commission on North American questions met in earnest in 1720 and, again, as diplomatic showmanship in 1751.

In France, the regency government (1715–1723) authorized the building of Louisbourg at enormous expense (1718) to control the fishery, the entrance to Canada, and the Micmacs. It established numerous forts in the Great Lakes region and in Louisiana, including New Orleans (1718). The recovery of the fur trade from the 1720s made it possible to pursue this expansionist policy with greater confidence. With some misgivings as to cost, Jean-Frédéric de Maurepas, Louis XV's minister of marine (1723–1749), pursued expansion and a French *cordon sanitaire* came to separate the English from the west.

The Board of Trade in London, established in 1696 to advise on trade and colonies, understood that the considerable demographic and economic strength of the colonies was not being translated into political and military strength because of the lack of a single policy or single authority among colonies "crumbled into little governments." Much advice was forthcoming, but the ministries and, indeed, many colonial assemblies that held the purse strings were reluctant to loosen them. What British policy there was regarding the interior was the policy of New York and South Carolina. New York officials met annually with the Iroquois at Albany to renew their "Covenant Chain" of alliance. South Carolina, center of the deerskin trade, maintained alliances with a number of peoples including the Cherokee, who, in that sense, were the Iroquois of the south.

In 1726, New York challenged Canada by building Oswego in Iroquois country, whereupon the Iroquois gave the Canadian governor permission to build a fort at Niagara. By the 1730s, land speculators were active in the backcountry of all the English colonies. With this in view, a New York governor, George Clarke (1737–1746), attempted to build a British-Indian alliance by the device of extending the Covenant Chain to include colonies and tribes to the south, but he met with indifferent success. Louisiana was unable to mount an Indian policy as successful as that of Canada. In the south, Indians were an obstacle to the development of a plantation economy, whereas in the north they were the Canadians' economic partners. The suspicious, uncooperative Natchez were destroyed outright (1729). The Choctaws were kept busy in wars against the anglophile Chickasaws. Canadian allies were deflected from attacks on the Iroquois by being encouraged to go south to fight "flatheads" (Cherokees, Catawbas). Canada itself joined in these Louisiana campaigns (1736, 1739). In the Northeast, New England's desire for land led to Dummer's War (1722–1727) against the Abenakis, who were covertly supplied with arms by the French. All of this activity in Indian country north and south was undertaken while Great Britain and France were either allies or, at least, were committed to peace.

The first British colony in North America founded as an act of policy was Georgia (1732), which was intended to hold the British frontier primarily against Spain and only to a lesser extent against France. When war finally did break out in the colonial theater, it was an Anglo-Spanish War (War of Jenkins' Ear,

1739)—Great Britain's war for the trade of the Spanish colonies. France held aloof from the war until its interests were threatened by Britain's intervention in Germany. This reluctance to throw down the gauntlet for trade and empire reveals a baffling French myopia as to where France's true interests lay.

The colonial world was swept into the vortex of war in 1744, with surprisingly little in the way of permanent result. New England's conquest of Louisbourg (1745) was annulled at the peace table. As a result of wartime experience, it became clear to the French whatever promise Canada held as a market and as a supplier within a mercantilistic empire, its role as anchor of the barrier against the English colonies would be foremost. A reorientation of the Canadian economy, away from hope-laden exports of provisions and merchant ships to the import of French flour and war materiel and the building of warships, had already begun during the war. Everyone understood the next few years were to be a period, not of peace, but of preparation for war. In 1749, Great Britain again founded a colony, the naval and military base of Halifax, that would counter the fortress of Louisbourg.

The challenge that led to war was the movement of settlers from Virginia and Pennsylvania into the trans-Appalachian west. The French secured the Ohio Valley by a road and a number of forts, including Fort Duquesne (1754) at the strategic headwaters of the Ohio River. It was the ambush of the army of General Edward Braddock, sent against the fort, that touched off the nine years of warfare Lawrence Henry Gipson has called "The Great War for the Empire." Five years later, Quebec was lost at the Battle of the Plains of Abraham (1759), and the following spring, Canada was surrendered.

The French foreign minister, the duc de Choiseul, decided not to use his much-depleted forces to attempt to regain Canada, reasoning that if the French incubus were lifted from the backs of the American colonies, they, no longer needing Great Britain, would rebel against it. His attempt to reverse French fortunes in the West Indies by bringing Spain into the war was a complete failure. Spain proved a reed to lean upon and soon lost Havana to the British. A complicated set of exchanges was agreed to: France giving Louisiana east of the Mississippi to Great Britain and the western part (which included the actual French settlements) to

Spain; Spain ceding Florida to Great Britain; Great Britain returning Havana to Spain. The end result, then, of the Treaty of Paris (1763) was that France was completely excluded from North America, although it retained its place in the North Atlantic fishery based on possession of the islands of St. Pierre and Miquelon and the exclusive use of the "French Shore" of Newfoundland.

A further chapter in Anglo-French rivalry in North America was yet to unfold. The revolution Choiseul had predicted began in 1776. France joined the United States in their War of Independence to ensure the British Empire would indeed be sundered. Curiously, however, the French foreign minister, the comte de Vergennes, intended that Canada remain in British hands to give Great Britain the whiphand over the new United States that France had once enjoyed over the thirteen colonies. With the Treaty of 1783, the real rivalry of France and England in North America came to an end.

The Second Hundred Years' War had begun from European causes. In the eighteenth century, colonial causes had become more prominent and, between 1754 and 1763, paramount. With the wars of the French Revolution and of Napoleon, the primary causes were once again continental, although with colonial implications, even in North America.

Dale Miquelon

References

Philip P. Boucher, *The Shaping of the French Colonial Empire: A Bio-Bibliography of the Careers of Richelieu, Fouquet, and Colbert* (1985); Frances Gardiner Davenport, ed., *European Treaties Bearing on the History of the United States and Its Dependencies,* 4 vols. (1917–1937), rpt. 1967; W.J. Eccles, *France in America* (1990); Dale Miquelon, *New France, 1701–1744: "A Supplement to Europe"* (1987).

See also ABENAKI; ACADIA; CHOCTAW; COVENANT CHAIN; FRONTIER, NORTHERN; IROQUOIS; IROQUOIS TREATIES OF 1700 AND 1701; KING GEORGE'S WAR; KING WILLIAM'S WAR; OHIO COUNTRY; QUEEN ANNE'S WAR; SEVEN YEARS' WAR

Great Britain–Indian Relations
See ANGLO-INDIAN RELATIONS

Great Britain–Spain Relations

Great Britain emerged as Spain's most formidable rival in North America during the late seventeenth and eighteenth centuries, a period when transatlantic colonies and commerce began to play a major role in European politics. For most of the two centuries following Columbus's encounter with the New World, Spain claimed all territory in the Western Hemisphere—except Portuguese Brazil—and no European power offered a serious challenge to this claim. Engrossed by the prospect of riches in Mexico and South America, the Spanish crown and colonists viewed North America as a strategic region that had to be defended, but which was not economically attractive, an area that absorbed rather than produced money and people. Great Britain (and France), on the other hand, saw in North America and the Caribbean its primary opportunity to obtain New World colonies. After warding off threats made by British privateers to its sea lanes along the Florida coast in the 1500s, Spain mainly ignored British settlement in the New World as long as it remained far north in North America and far east in the Caribbean. British expansion southward into the Carolinas and Georgia and westward across the Appalachians, however, rekindled Spain's missionary, defensive, and commercial efforts in North America and created a contest for empire that peaked with the Seven Years' War (1754–1763).

Once Spanish expeditions in the early 1500s indicated the southern part of North America possessed no easily exploitable mineral wealth or native laborers, Spain focused on its profitable colonial kingdoms of New Spain and Peru. Only when British and French privateers operating from bases in the Caribbean successfully began to attack silver-laden Spanish ships as they made their way up Florida's Atlantic coast did the crown send Pedro Menéndez de Avilés in 1565 to establish St. Augustine and other Spanish strongholds in the area. Spanish soldiers and missionaries ventured northward to plant settlements on Chesapeake Bay in the 1560s and 1570s but failed, as did most of Spain's early endeavors in Florida. By the mid-1570s, only two viable communities remained in Florida—Santa Elena and St. Augustine—and in 1587, colonists were further consolidated at St. Augustine in response to attacks made by British privateer Francis Drake. Spain almost elected to abandon Florida, but the founding of Jamestown by English colonists in 1607 contributed to the crown's decision to stay. Through the middle of the seventeenth century, Spain succeeded in securing the Bahama Channel (a key passageway between Florida and Cuba), in providing a base for shipwreck victims at St. Augustine, and in establishing a series of Franciscan missions along the Atlantic coast and into the Florida interior.

Great Britain once again challenged Spanish hegemony in southeastern North America by establishing the colonies of Carolina in 1670 and Georgia in 1733. Finding no gold and silver, the British in Carolina turned to competing with Spaniards for furs and hides and for the loyalty of the Native American nations who supplied these desired staples. In order to alienate Spain's Indian allies, English forces began attacking Spanish missions in northern Florida in the 1680s and selling mission Indians into slavery. A Spanish fort at San Luis de Apalachee, built in the 1670s, did little to protect the missions, and once again Spain almost resolved to withdraw from Florida. British assaults during the War of the Spanish Succession (1702–1713) destroyed the Apalachee missionary province, forcing the Franciscans to abandon all missions except those in the vicinity of St. Augustine.

In addition to attacking Spanish missions, the British succeeded in gaining powerful Indian allies by offering them armaments, liquor, and trade goods. England's factories produced superior trade goods at lower cost and in greater quantities than Spain could obtain. Native Americans astutely recognized that competition between Great Britain, France, and Spain presented them with alternatives: they could bargain for the best deal. When British forces entered Spanish territory, many mission Indians seized the opportunity to rebel against their Spanish wardens and side with the invaders. Unlike Spaniards, most British colonists merely wanted to trade with Native Americans and occasionally use them to fight other European powers and their Indian allies; they generally did not try to alter native religions and cultures, and had few qualms about giving Indians guns and ammunition. Great Britain's strategy did not always work, however, as evidenced by the Yamasee War (1715–1717), when Yamasees and Creeks turned against abusive British slave traders and in defeat sought sanctuary among the Spanish in Florida.

Nevertheless, following the War of the Spanish Succession, Spain adopted Great Britain's technique of trying to win native allies with material goods rather than spiritual salvation. Spanish colonists tried to provide better protection and win allegiance of such nations as the Creeks by reestablishing Fort San Luis de Apalachee in 1718 as a military and trading post. A weakened Spain, however, was unable to protect its Indian allies or supply them with the quality and quantity of goods that Britain could. Great Britain extended its empire even further south with the establishment of Georgia in 1733 to serve as a buffer between the Carolinas and Florida. Around St. Augustine, Spain began to rely more heavily on African American defenders, offering sanctuary to runaway slaves from the Anglo colonies and putting them to work building and defending a walled fort just north of St. Augustine, named Gracia Real de Santa Teresa de Mose.

The bitter struggle between England and France for overseas supremacy in the eighteenth century embroiled Spain mainly because of its close ties to France. The War of the Spanish Succession placed a French Bourbon on the Spanish throne (Felipe V, grandson of Louis XIV), and a series of Family Compacts (1733, 1743, and 1761) reinforced Spain's alliance with France. Spain, however, awarded its *asiento* (a contract to supply African slaves) to England after the War of the Spanish Succession; France previously held the *asiento*. Unlike Spain, Great Britain had the manufacturing and commercial capacity to meet the needs not only of its own colonists, but also those of other nations. Spain used much of the wealth extracted from Spanish America to purchase manufactured goods from England in an increasingly dependent relationship.

An attempt by Spain to strengthen its mercantilistic policies and dislodge British trade from its American colonies in the 1730s marred the fairly peaceful association forged between these two countries after the War of the Spanish Succession and resulted in the War of Jenkins' Ear (1739). Spain placed tighter restrictions on trade in the Caribbean, increased its defensive activity with the use of *guardacostas* (coast guard vessels), and suspended the *asiento* when the South Sea Company refused to pay for its contract. British officials, in turn, felt compelled to protect their mercantile interests in the New World. Although the War of Jenkins' Ear began as a colonial conflict, it escalated into the War of the Austrian Succession (1740–1748), which pitted Great Britain and Austria against Prussia, France, and Spain. British forces under James Oglethorpe invaded Florida in 1740,

captured several posts around St. Augustine, and lay siege to Fort San Marcos, where Spaniards, Indians, and blacks had taken refuge. Spanish soldiers and black militia retook Fort Mose and inflicted heavy casualties on the British. When Cuban reinforcements arrived, Oglethorpe withdrew. Spanish troops staged a counteroffensive into Georgia in 1742, but soon retreated.

For most of the 1740s and into the 1750s, Spanish and British rivalry along the Florida-Georgia border was calm. Florida's sparse population posed little threat to the English colonies, and its lack of easily exploitable resources offered few enticements. On the European front, England was more concerned with rising French naval power than with Spanish imperial designs. Relations between Britain and Spain were strained by the treaty that ended the War of the Austrian Succession, the Treaty of Aix-la-Chapelle (1748), whose provisions canceled British trading privileges in Spanish America, including the *asiento*.

Britain and Spain maintained their amicable relationship during the early part of the Seven Years' War. What began as the French and Indian War in 1754 between French and British colonists in North America merged into a larger imperial conflict between England and France. Spain tried to remain neutral. When Carlos III assumed the Spanish throne in 1759, however, he adopted a strong pro-French policy, signed the Third Family Compact in 1761, and one year later entered the Seven Years' War on the side of France. Spain suffered a quick, humiliating defeat. In the peace negotiations that resulted in the Treaty of Paris (1763), Spain had to give Florida to Britain in order to retrieve Havana, seized by British forces in 1762. To compensate Spain for its late assistance, France ceded Louisiana west of the Mississippi River and New Orleans to Carlos III and gave the eastern half and Canada to England.

With the Seven Years' War one phase of the contest for empire ended and another began. Britain emerged from the Seven Years' War as the dominant imperial power; it acquired vast territories and established primacy on the seas. The war left Spain and Britain as the two major competitors for North American territory and trade. Although frontier conflict between Florida and Georgia evaporated when Britain took over both colonies, Spain had a new, more difficult border to defend: Louisiana along the Mississippi River. Spain could no longer depend on France to pro-

G

vide a protective buffer between the silver mines of New Spain and the aggressive, expansive designs of Anglo colonists.

Kimberly S. Hanger

References

Jane Landers, "Gracia Real de Santa Teresa de Mose: A Free Black Town in Spanish Colonial Florida," *American Historical Review* 95 (1990):9–30; John Jay TePaske, "The Fugitive Slave in Intercolonial Rivalry and Spanish Slave Policy, 1687–1764," in *Eighteenth-Century Florida and Its Borderlands,* ed. by Samuel Proctor (1975):1–12.

David J. Weber, *The Spanish Frontier in North America* (1992); Glyndwr Williams, *The Expansion of Europe in the Eighteenth Century: Overseas Rivalry, Discovery, and Exploitation* (1966); J. Leitch Wright, Jr., *Anglo-Spanish Rivalry in North America* (1971).

See also AIX-LA-CHAPELLE, TREATY OF; ANGLO-SPANISH WAR (1718–1721); ANGLO-SPANISH WAR (1739–1744); CARTAGENA, EXPEDITION AGAINST; FLORIDA; GEORGIA; MONTIANO, MANUEL DE; OGLETHORPE, JAMES EDWARD; PARIS, TREATY OF; PORTO BELLO, ATTACK ON; ST. AUGUSTINE; SOUTH CAROLINA; SPANISH MISSION SYSTEM—SOUTHEAST

Great Carrying Place (New York)

See FORT EDWARD (NEW YORK)

Great Swamp Fight (1675)

The Great Swamp Fight was the bloodiest battle of King Philip's War (1675–1676), for Englishmen and Indians alike. When Philip (Metacomet) led the Wampanoag into war with the English settlers in June 1675, the neighboring Narragansetts of Rhode Island held aloof. But as the war spread, colonial leaders became alarmed at reports that the Narragansetts intended to join Philip in the spring. It was also clear the Narragansetts intended to ignore treaty promises to deliver up the many enemy Indians who had sought refuge among them.

To intimidate the Narragansetts, the largest tribe in New England, in December 1675, the United Colonies (Plymouth, Connecticut, and Massachusetts Bay) sent an army of more than 1,000 men into their country. The army, commanded by Governor Josiah Winslow of Plymouth, was accompanied by 150 Mohegan and Pequot allies. As the army concentrated at tiny Wickford, on the western shore of Narragansett Bay, a series of skirmishes indicated the Narragansetts would not yield. But the English had taken a Narragansett prisoner, called Peter, who offered to lead them to a secret fortress where the tribe had gathered. This fortification proved to be an unusually elaborate palisaded village, built on a piece of higher ground in the middle of the Great Swamp, north of Worden's Pond and about 15 miles from Wickford. The log defensive wall was strengthened by blockhouses and protected by a dense hedge of brush. Closely packed within the wall were hundreds of bark-covered wigwams.

The army set out on 18 December, marching through deep snow and intense cold. Early the next afternoon the Great Swamp was reached, and the leading companies pushed into it in pursuit of sentries who had fired on them. The mire, which normally would have been almost impassable, was frozen hard. As the fortress came into view, the soldiers saw directly before them a small gap in the uncompleted wall. Rushing forward they forced their way through this opening, only to be driven out again by heavy musket fire. Reinforced by fresh companies coming up, the soldiers rallied and reentered the village as the defenders began to flee into the surrounding swamp.

With the consent of Governor Winslow, soldiers now began to set fire to the highly flammable wigwams. Hundreds of Indians, many of them women and children, died in the resulting inferno. Indian testimony taken after the massacre suggests that more than 300 warriors died in the fighting and in the fire (some estimates were much higher). With an unknown number of women and children added, it seems likely that at least 1,000 Indians perished. The Narragansett population at this time was probably between 5,000 and 8,000.

English losses, though much smaller, still illustrate how deadly warriors equipped with firearms had become. About 20 soldiers were shot dead and more than 200 others wounded, some 20 percent of the army. More died of wounds and exposure in the retreat that night to Wickford, and the dead eventually passed 80. In a similar incident during the Pequot War in 1637, when an English force stormed a Pequot fort defended by warriors armed only with bows, just two Englishmen had been killed.

That fort was also burned by the attackers, perhaps a precedent.

After this terrible blow the Narragansetts abandoned their country and fled north into the icy wilderness. Today a historical monument, near West Kingston, Rhode Island, marks the site of the Great Swamp Fight.

Bert M. Mutersbaugh

References

Douglas Edward Leach, *Flintlock and Tomahawk: New England in King Philip's War* (1958); Richard Slotkin and James K. Folsom, eds., *So Dreadfull a Judgment: Puritan Responses to King Philip's War, 1676–1677* (1978).

See also KING PHILIP'S WAR; NARRAGANSETT; NEW ENGLAND CONFEDERATION; PHILIP

Grenadier

Originally, grenadiers were soldiers trained to throw a grenade and were frequently used during the last decade of the seventeenth century when campaigns consisted largely of siege operations. However, with the unreliability of the hand-thrown grenade, the role of the grenadier gradually changed so that eventually the military term "grenadier" referred to an elite company of men in a battalion who were clothed differently from the rest of the battalion by wearing a "high cap."

The term "grenadier" was first used in France in 1667 when four or five such soldiers were allocated to each company in a regiment. The grenadiers were usually recruited from the "tallest and stoutest" men, the term "stoutest" in this context meaning physically strong and agile.

The French army withdrew grenadiers from the foot companies in 1670 and formed them into grenadier companies. The formation of such companies began in the British army in 1685, and at that time one company was added to each regiment of foot guards and troop of household cavalry. The establishments of the regiments of foot were later changed to include a company of grenadiers who were used for special tasks. In General Richard Kane's book, *A system of camp-discipline, military honours, garrison duty, and other regulations for the land forces . . .*, published in 1757, the grenadier company in a regiment of foot is shown parading on the left of the regiment, and when forming a hollow square, the grenadier company is divided to form a guard on each of the four corners.

A commanding general could, when necessary, withdraw all the grenadier companies from the regiments of foot under his command and form them into a grenadier battalion. General James Wolfe formed the regiment of "Louisbourg Grenadiers" in 1759 from the grenadier companies garrisoned at Louisbourg.

Grenadiers wore a distinctive cap with no brim, initially so as to allow free movement of the arm when throwing a grenade and, although the role was changed, this distinctive headdress remained. The front of the cap was of the same color as the regimental facing and also carried the regimental device.

Alan Harfield

References

Charles James, *New and Enlarged Military Dictionary* (1805); Bernard Lens, *The Grenadiers Exercise of the Grenade, 1735* (1967).

Grey Lock's War

See DUMMER'S WAR

Gridley, Richard (1711–1796)

Richard Gridley was the first American-born military engineer and artillery officer of any significance. He was the brother of Jeremiah Gridley, the lawyer who argued the legality of the Writs of Assistance in 1761. Richard Gridley made his start in life as an apprentice to a wholesale merchant, but a talent for mathematics drew him into surveying and civil engineering. As a colonial militiaman, Gridley learned the fundamentals of gunnery and military engineering under the tutelage of John Henry Bastide, a British officer.

During King George's War, Gridley commanded the artillery train in Colonel William Pepperrell, Jr.'s 1745 expedition against the French fortress at Louisbourg. For his services in the successful siege, Gridley received a captain's commission in Governor William Shirley's regiment, and was assigned the task of improving the fortifications in Boston harbor against an expected French attack. In 1752, Gridley accompanied Shirley's expedition up the Kennebec River, where he built Fort Western and Fort Halifax.

During the French and Indian War, Gridley served as a colonel in the Massachusetts regiment raised for Sir William Johnson's unsuccessful 1755 expedition to seize the French fort at Crown Point. In 1759, General Jeffery Amherst placed Gridley in overall command of the provincial artillery. Gridley commanded the guns during General James Wolfe's attack on Quebec. When Wolfe's troops made their daring night climb up the 300-foot rock cliffs. Gridley's gunners hauled two fieldpieces to the top. Firing grapeshot, these guns achieved deadly effect against General Louis-Joseph de Montcalm's infantry. When the war ended, England rewarded Gridley with the Magdalen Isles in the Gulf of St. Lawrence, which included a valuable seal and cod fishery. Gridley also received a half-pay colonel's pension of £91 per year. In 1773, the governor of New Hampshire awarded him 3,000 acres of land.

Gridley served in the Continental army in the early years of the Revolution. After the state of Massachusetts agreed to assume his British pension, Gridley commanded the state's artillery regiment at Bunker Hill. Although Gridley himself fought bravely, almost all of his green troops abandoned their guns. Two of Gridley's sons, Samuel and Scarborough, were officers in the regiment, and were later sacked for their conduct during the battle. Despite the debacle at Bunker Hill, the Continental Congress appointed Gridley chief of Continental artillery in September 1775. Washington, however, quickly replaced him with the younger and more energetic Henry Knox. Gridley continued to serve as the chief engineer in the eastern department until his retirement in 1780.

David T. Zabecki

References

Boston City Council, *A Memorial of the American Patriots Who Fell at the Battle of Bunker Hill, June 17, 1775* (1889); Aubrey Parkman, *Army Engineers in New England* (1978); State of Massachusetts, *Massachusetts Soldiers and Sailors of the Revolutionary War: A Compilation from the Archives* (1899).

See also ARTILLERY; LOUISBOURG EXPEDITION (1745)

Fort Griswold (Connecticut)

See LITCHFIELD FORTS (CONNECTICUT)

Guale

Prior to the arrival of the first Spanish explorers in the sixteenth century, the Southeast was inhabited by a wide variety of Indian tribes. Most of the inland tribes had become sedentary, agricultural societies, but the Guales, who inhabited the coastal regions of Georgia, were exclusively hunter-gatherers in the precontact period. Although they depended on fish as their primary source of protein, middens show that mollusks, crustaceans, deer, rabbit, otter, and possum were also a significant part of their diet.

The Indians of the Southeast developed different economies in response to their specific environments, but they were interconnected through a widespread trade network which encompassed tribes from the Atlantic and Gulf coast to the Mississippi River. The Guales' main contributions to the southeastern trade network were most likely shark teeth and shells.

When the Spanish established a mission system along the Florida coast and on the Sea Islands of Georgia, the Guales met the Europeans for the first time. The Santa Catalina mission on Saint Catherines Island was founded in 1568 by Jesuits in the heart of Guale country. The Guales were not willing to accept Christianity and were erratic in their dealings with the Spanish. Two years later the Jesuits withdrew in frustration, abandoning Santa Catalina.

In 1577, the Guales massacred a boatload of Spaniards who were headed toward Santa Elena. Four years later, Franciscan friars arrived on St. Catherines to reopen the mission, and they remained despite undisguised hostility by the Indians. A concerted effort to convert the Guales in 1595 resulted in the establishment of five new missions. Two years later, the Guales revolted and murdered four friars and a lay brother before Spanish soldiers stopped the rebellion at Cumberland Island.

The Spanish responded to the Indian uprising by burning all villages, granaries, and fields in Guale territory. Retaliatory raids by the Spanish in 1598 and 1601 finally forced the Indians to surrender. The Guales and the other coastal tribes remained under Spanish rule for the next 75 years.

These subject tribes were finally dispersed at the end of the seventeenth century by English-armed Indians on slave raids for Charles Town traders. In all probability the Guale survivors were incorporated into the growing Creek Confederacy in the latter decades of the seventeenth century.

Although the Guales most likely spoke a Hitchiti dialect common to the coastal regions, if they were absorbed into the Muskogean Creek nation they eventually lost their language as well as their tribal identity. By the early eighteenth century, any surviving Guales were no longer known by their ancient tribal name, but instead were identified by the towns in which they lived.

Doris B. Fisher

References

Herbert E. Bolton and Mary Ross, *The Debatable Land: A Sketch of the Anglo-Spanish Contest for the Georgia Country* (1925); *Colonial Records of Spanish Florida,* ed. by Jeannette Thurber Connor (1925); John Tate Lanning, *The Spanish Missions of Georgia* (1935); Lewis H. Larson, *Aboriginal Subsistence Technology on the Southeastern Coastal Plain during the Late Historic Period* (1980).

Jerald T. Milanich and Susan Milbrath, eds., *First Encounters: Spanish Exploration in the Caribbean and the United States, 1492–1570* (1989); J. Leitch Wright, *Creeks and Seminoles: The Destruction and Regeneration of the Muscogulge People* (1986).

See also SANTA ELENA; SPANISH MISSION SYSTEM–SOUTHEAST; TOLOMATO PRESIDIO (GEORGIA).

Gun Merchant of Okchai (?–late 1770s)

Enochtanachee of the Okchai was one of the most influential Creek Indian headmen of the late colonial period. His official position in Creek government was as a *henihi* or second man, traditionally an adviser to the town's chief or *mico*. His English appellation, the Gun Merchant, suggests he acquired prestige through his procurement and protection of English traders for his town. A skillful politician and talented diplomat, he was ultimately recognized as the *mico* of Okchai. He was sometimes referred to as the Oakehoy (Okchai) king by the English and also appears in the records as Mico Lucko. In later life, he was named as the Head Beloved Man of the Abeikas, reflecting his influence among all the Abeika villages, one of the three main divisions of the Upper Creek Indians. His brother-in-law was the Mortar of the Okchai, the town's leading warrior.

The Gun Merchant's first major role as a diplomat came in the fall of 1746 when he and several other Creek headmen visited Charles Town, South Carolina. There, Governor James Glen pushed for a Creek offensive against Fort Toulouse, a French fort in the heart of the Upper Creek territory. Glen also proposed establishing a British fort among the Creek to promote trade and counteract French influence. The Gun Merchant opposed both moves. Ostensibly, he espoused neutrality in the European wars. In reality, he was forced to court the British colonies due to the inability of the French to supply the Creek with trade goods.

During the protracted Creek-Cherokee War of 1740–1754, the Gun Merchant was successful in negotiating a truce between the Upper Creeks and the Upper Cherokee during the later phases of the war. After 1749, though the Lower Creeks still warred on the Lower Cherokee, parties of Upper Creek, led by the Gun Merchant, hunted and mingled peacefully with the Upper Cherokee in their territory. While there, visiting Creeks learned that the exchange rates set for Cherokee deerskins by South Carolina were more favorable than those established for the Creek trade. Upper Creeks immediately began demanding comparable trade terms for the Creek towns. After the war, the Gun Merchant gained widespread respect among his people for his determined efforts to obtain lower Creek trade prices with Georgia and South Carolina. He won concessions from South Carolina in 1753, but the Creeks failed to ratify the treaty because it called for an English fort to be built in Upper Creek territory. During the Anglo-Cherokee War (1759–1761), the Gun Merchant headed the neutralist faction and was instrumental in keeping the Creek out of that conflict.

In recognition of the Gun Merchant's prestige among the Upper Creeks and his support of strong Creek-Anglo relations, the British presented him with a Great Medal at the 1765 Congress of Pensacola. He was one of five Upper Creek headmen so honored. In addition, he was given a Small Medal to present to a headman of his choice, a singular occurrence and one that signifies the respect with which the British establishment viewed the aging headman. The Gun Merchant's efforts to reduce Creek trade prices were finally rewarded in 1767 when Creek traders agreed to an abatement in prices for European trade goods. He supported the 1773 New Purchase cession to Georgia to clear the collective Creek trade debt, noting that the affair was a Lower Creek matter since the land in question belonged to the lower towns. The Gun Merchant disappears from the historic record during the early years of the American Revolution, and it is presumed he died during the war. After the death of the Mortar and the Gun Merchant, the center of power among the Upper Creek shifted to Okfuskee, a Tallapoosa village.

Kathryn E. Holland Braund

References
    John R. Alden, *John Stuart and the Southern Colonial Frontier* (1944); David H. Corkran, *The Cherokee Frontier: Conflict and Survival, 1740–1762* (1962); ———, *The Creek Frontier, 1540–1783* (1967).

See also CREEK-CHEROKEE WARS; GLEN, JOHN; MORTAR OF OKACHAI

Gyles, John (c. 1674–1735)

John Gyles was captured as a teenager during the raid on Pemaquid, Maine, in August 1689. Kept among the eastern Indians for the rest of King William's War, Gyles became an expert on Indian languages and culture. This experience led him into public service. From 1700–1706, he was posted at the provincial fort in Falmouth, Maine, as chief interpreter for the government of Massachusetts. In 1714, he directed the construction of Fort George in Brunswick, Maine, and commanded there until 1725, when he was given command of Fort St. George's in Thomaston, Maine, where he played a major role in negotiating the treaty that ended Dummer's War.

Steven C. Eames

References
    Steven C. Eames, "Rustic Warriors: Warfare and the Provincial Soldier on the Northern Frontier, 1689–1748," Ph.D. Dissertation, University of New Hampshire (1989); John Gyles, *Memoirs of Odd Adventures, Strange Deliverances, etc. In the Captivity of John Gyles, Esq.* (1736); Stuart Trueman, *The Ordeal of John Gyles* (1966).

See also FORT ST. GEORGES (MAINE)

H

Half-King (also known as Tanaghrisson, ?–1754)

Known to the English as "Half-King," Tanaghrisson (or Tanacharison) was an adopted Seneca who gained fame as a leader among Indians of the Ohio country just prior to the French and Indian War.

Born a Catawba, the young Tanaghrisson was captured by the Senecas, who adopted and raised him as one of their own. Sometime in the late 1730s or early 1740s, Tanaghrisson accompanied fellow Senecas westward to settle in the Ohio country, probably along the Cuyahoga River. There, these Ohio Iroquois came to be known as Mingos.

Tanaghrisson's first appearance in historical records came in 1747, when he was listed as one of five Mingo chiefs requesting aid from the Pennsylvania government. The following year, Pennsylvania officials dispatched Conrad Weiser to the Ohio Indian village at Logstown (located on the Ohio River about 18 miles below present-day Pittsburgh) to develop relations with the Ohio Indians represented by Tanaghrisson and the Mingos.

Tanaghrisson emerged from the Logstown conference recognized by the English as the "Half-King" chief of the Ohio Indians. His actual relationship to the Ohio tribes, not to mention the Iroquois Confederacy (whom he allegedly represented in the Ohio country), is difficult to determine. More clear is the role played by Tanaghrisson in Indian-white relations in Ohio.

At the Logstown Conference, the newly-appointed Half-King helped establish direct communications between the Ohio tribes and the Pennsylvania government, successfully bypassing the Iroquois League Council at Onondaga. In 1752, at another conference in Logstown, Half-King further strengthened the Ohio tribes' ties to Pennsylvania and reaffirmed the Mingos' position as Pennsylvania's most-favored Indian nation in the Ohio country. This role enabled Half-King and the Mingos to serve as diplomatic brokers in negotiations between Ohio Indians and the Pennsylvania colonial government.

In 1752, Tanaghrisson met with commissioners from Virginia who hoped to secure claims to the Ohio country by building a trading post near the source of the Ohio River. After considerable bargaining and backroom dealing, Half-King finally agreed to their demands. His role in the proceedings undermined his credibility with many Ohio Indians, such as the Delawares and Shawnees, who were determined to keep the English off their lands.

By 1753, Half-King was trapped between the jaws of the European powers. Wedded to British interests, Tanaghrisson now had to contend with growing French power on the banks of the Ohio. In July 1753, French troops under Captain Pierre-Paul de La Malgue, sieur de Marin established a post on French Creek. Tanaghrisson led a party of Mingos to Presque Isle to warn the French to turn back, but Marin dismissed the Mingos' empty threats. Later that year Tanaghrisson accompanied George Washington on a similar mission; but again the French refused to retreat.

Half-King helped a party of Virginians build a small outpost at the juncture of the Allegheny and Monogahela Rivers in 1754. After the French seized the post, Tanaghrisson joined George Washington's forces to attack the French. When the Virginians retreated to the hastily-built Fort Necessity at Great Meadows,

Tanaghrisson, realizing that Washington's post was indefensible, fled with his Mingos. Half-King proved to be correct when the Virginians were forced to surrender on 3 July. A few months later, Tanaghrisson died of pneumonia.

Tanaghrisson's brief but important career tells us a great deal about the diplomatic and military strategies employed by Indians and whites on the Ohio frontier. Like other Ohio Iroquois, Half-King was willing to use his familial ties to the Iroquois Confederacy to further his personal interests, as well as those of the Mingos. Tanaghrisson and the Mingos improved their position by becoming diplomatic middlemen between the Ohio tribes and the English. The Delawares, Shawnees, Miamis, Wyandots, and other Ohio Indians were willing to rely on Tanaghrisson and the Mingos, as long as they retained their own sovereignty and received economic and political benefits from the English.

Half-King's rise to a leadership position also reflects the English strategy for dealing with Ohio tribes. Officials in Pennsylvania and Virginia were willing to recognize Tanaghrisson as the "Half-King" chief of the Ohio tribes because his cooperation would allow the English to win over the Ohio Indians as trading partners and allies against New France.

Tanaghrisson's successes and failures were determined by the delicate webs of frontier diplomacy spun by both Indians and whites. His political machinations reveal the importance of Indian factionalism on the Ohio frontier and show how Indian leaders played a significant role in the settlement of the Ohio country. His actions helped promote English expansion into Ohio and ultimately contributed to the coming of the French and Indian War.

Tanaghrisson's career provides evidence that Indians were not just passive victims of aggressive white pioneers, nor were they simply reactors to white initiatives. Indian leaders like Half-King were active participants who played important roles in American colonial history.

Richard Aquila

References
Richard Aquila, *The Iroquois Restoration: Iroquois Diplomacy on the Colonial Frontier, 1701–1754* (1983); Randolph C. Downes, *Council Fires on the Upper Ohio* (1940); Francis Jennings, *Empire of Fortune: Crowns, Colonies, and Tribes in the Seven Years War in America* (1988); Daniel K. Richter and James Merrell, eds., *Beyond the Covenant Chain: the Iroquois and Their Neighbors in Indian North America, 1600–1800* (1987); Paul A.W. Wallace, *Indians in Pennsylvania* (1961).

See also DELAWARE; LOGSTOWN, TREATY OF; MINGO

Fort Half-Moon (New York; also known as Camp Van Schaick)

Located on Van Schaick Island in the Mohawk River, the site held a succession of camps beginning as early as 1692. However, it was generally unoccupied except in times of war and unrest. In 1698, chief British engineer Colonel Wolfgang Romer recommended the fortifications, which were in a state of disrepair, be reconstructed as a palisaded stone redoubt accommodating 20 or 30 men. The rebuild was completed in 1703.

Anthony Van Schaick constructed a mansion on the island, which later served as headquarters for Sir William Johnson, General James Abercromby, and General Jeffrey Amherst during the French and Indian War. The fortification was rebuilt during this war.

During the Revolution, General Philip Schuyler rebuilt the fort again in 1777, adding a stockade, blockhouse, barracks, and entrenchments. The site served as a ferry point across the river, and as headquarters for Generals Philip Schuyler and Horatio Gates.

Elizabeth Gossman

References
Robert B. Roberts, *New York Forts in the Revolution* (1980).

Fort Halifax (Maine)

Located in the town of Winslow at a strategically important site overlooking the convergence of the Kennebec and Sebasticook Rivers, Fort Halifax was built from 1754 to 1755 on orders of Governor William Shirley as a barrier to the French. The plans were designed by Major General John Winslow and called for a massive fort to house 400 men. However, the design was altered during construction and a simpler structure was erected. The fort included blockhouses, barracks, and a storehouse. It was named in honor of the earl of Halifax, who was then serving as secretary of state. No direct attacks against the fort are recorded, but a number of skirmishes occurred in the area. After the French and Indian War, it served as a popular trading post. By the American Revolution, the fort had become dilapidated. However, it was used in 1775 as a stopping point by Colonel Benedict Arnold and his army of 1,100 men on the way to their unsuccessful invasion of Canada.

David L. Whitesell

Fort Halifax (Pennsylvania)

Located at the mouth of Armstrong Creek on the Susquehanna River 17 miles above Harris's Ferry, Fort Halifax was constructed to serve as a depot and auxiliary base for Fort Augusta. Its site was chosen because it lay on high ground about halfway between the ferry crossing and the proposed location of Fort Augusta and would, therefore, be a useful way station for troops and supplies. Colonel William Clapham's regiment stopped on their way to the site of Fort Augusta and built this intermediate post in June 1756. On 1 July, Clapham continued northward with the main body of his regiment, but he left a Captain Miles in command of a detachment of 30 men to occupy the fort and complete the construction of a barracks and storehouse within its walls.

The following summer, inhabitants of Paxton petitioned the provincial council to object to the fact that Fort Hunter, near their settlement, was evacuated in favor of Fort Halifax, which neither offered protection to settlers nor even provided a good way station for *bateaux* on the river. No one lived nearby and Fort Halifax did not successfully command the river's channel. In October 1757, perhaps in response to these criticisms, Fort Halifax was evacuated, and in 1763, the fort itself was dismantled.

Eric Hinderaker

References
Thomas L. Montgomery, ed., *Report of the Commission to Locate the Frontier Forts of Pennsylvania*, 2nd ed., 2 vols. (1916); Charles Morse Stotz, *Outposts of the War for Empire: The French and English in Western Pennsylvania; Their Armies, Their Forts, Their People, 1749–1764* (1985).

See also FORT AUGUSTA (PENNSYLVANIA); FORT HUNTER (PENNSYLVANIA)

Hardy, Charles (1716?–1780)

Admiral Sir Charles Hardy was the son of Vice Admiral Sir Charles Hardy. He entered the Royal Navy as a volunteer on board the *Salisbury* in 1730–1731. Promoted rapidly, by 1741 Hardy commanded the *Rye*, a 24-gun ship patrolling off the coastline of the Carolinas and Georgia to protect commerce from Spanish privateers.

In 1744, Captain Hardy received command of a convoy to Newfoundland, and after some of the vessels were captured on the return trip, Hardy was court-martialed, but acquitted of blame. After further service against the French in the 1740s, Hardy became governor of New York in 1755. Appointed rear admiral the following year, he commanded a convoy of transports bound for the siege of Louisbourg, and was named second-in-command of the fleet sent out from England to support the attack. After the failure of his attempt to capture Louisbourg, Hardy resigned his governorship and sailed to England.

He returned to American waters in 1758, commanding a vessel in the blockade of the harbor during the successful siege of Louisbourg that year. The following year, Hardy found himself second-in-command to Admiral Sir Edward Hawke in the Battle of Quiberon Bay, in which the British decisively defeated the French fleet. He later served as governor of Greenwich Hospital, member of Parliament for the borough of Portsmouth, and came out of retirement in 1779 to take command of the Channel fleet on the death of Admiral Augustus, Viscount Keppel. Hardy died the following year.

Thomas Costa

References
Piers Mackesy, *The War for America, 1775–1783* (1965).

Fort Hardy (New York)

See FORT SARATOGA (NEW YORK)

Harmon, Johnson (1680–c. 1750)

A native of York, Maine, Harmon's involvement in the French wars, beyond experiencing the attacks on York, began in Queen Anne's War when he was captured in October 1710 and exchanged the following year. During Dummer's War, Johnson, promoted to captain, would command a company of provincial soldiers under Colonel Thomas Westbrook and lead numerous scouts, where he became very adept at the tactics of *la petite guerre*. Harmon would be senior captain in command of the attack on Noridgewock in August 1724. Johnson continued his military activity in command of a company of snow shoe men, and in 1727 he was elected representative to the General Court. In 1745, the old soldier sent a touching appeal to William Pepperrell, Jr., to allow him to serve in the Louisbourg expedition, as "their is something yet for me to do . . . before I leave the world." The records are unclear about the answer and his participation.

Steven C. Eames

References

Charles Edward Banks, *History of York, Maine*, 2 vols. (1931–1935); Steven C. Eames, "Rustic Warriors: Warfare and the Provincial Soldier on the Northern Frontier, 1689–1748," Ph.D. Dissertation, University of New Hampshire (1989).

See also CHURCH, BENJAMIN; NORRIDGE-WOCK, BATTLE OF; SCOUT; WESTBROOK, THOMAS

Hartford Treaty (1650)

By the terms of this settlement, the authorities of New Netherland and New England agreed on a mutual boundary. A line was to be run on Long Island from the westernmost point of Oyster Bay in a direct line to the sea, thus dividing the island, the English occupying the eastern half and the Dutch the western portion. On the mainland, the boundary line began just west of Greenwich Bay and ran north for 20 miles. In the future it would be extended in a mutually satisfactory way, but not come within ten miles of the Hudson River. While the Dutch retained Fort Good Hope at Hartford, they effectively surrendered all claims to the Connecticut River valley. The treaty would have been the diplomatic coup that Director General Petrus Stuyvesant hoped for had the English not continued to encroach upon Dutch lands and press claims for their own legitimate possession of them.

The treaty was a much needed agreement and had been a direct concern of Stuyvesant since 1647. He was aware of English incursions on the lands of New Netherland and increasingly hostile relations with the New England Confederation, especially with New Haven. There Governor Theophilus Eaton had put faith in complaints about the Dutch selling arms to natives and charging high duties on cargoes at New Amsterdam. In 1649, he threatened to put force behind English claims along the Delaware River, then settled under Dutch authority. In 1650, Stuyvesant's persistence in arranging a treaty was supported by the directors of the West India Company. They advised that a favorable boundary be procured subject to a future agreement between the two powers in Europe. He traveled to Hartford and was instrumental in the plan to turn the negotiations over to four arbitrators.

The treaty was unpopular in New Amsterdam as being too conciliatory, and its conditions were soon ignored by the English. Nevertheless, it is significant for having allayed a potentially violent encounter over territories and for illustrating the peaceful diplomacy that Stuyvesant strove for during his administration.

Donna Merwick

References

John J. Chiodo, *The Foreign Policy of Peter Stuyvesant: Dutch Diplomacy in North America, 1647 to 1664* (1974); Franklin B. Dexter, "The Early Relations Between New Netherland and New England," *New Haven Colony Historical Society, Papers*, III (1882):443–469; Richard S. Dunn, *Puritans and Yankees: The Winthrop Dynasty of New England, 1603–1717* (1962).

Edmund B. O'Callaghan and Berthold Fernow, eds., *Documents Relative to the Colonial History of the State of New York*, 15 vols. (1856–1887), Vol. 14; Philip J. Schwarz, *The Jarring Interests: New York's Boundary Makers, 1664–1776* (1979).

See also FORT GOOD HOPE (CONNECTICUT); STUYVESANT, PETRUS

Hatfield Fort (Massachusetts)

The defenses for Hatfield, a settlement along the Connecticut River, were constructed by the inhabitants directly after the outbreak of King Philip's War in 1675. The fortifications consisted of a ten- to twelve-foot-high stockade which enclosed the houses of Hatfield. On 19 October 1675, Hatfield was assaulted by a large number of hostile Indians. This resulted in a protracted battle that produced heavy losses for both sides. However, the settlement was well defended by troops under the command of Captain Samuel Moseley and the Indians were forced to retreat from the vicinity. This victory helped to restore the confidence of the English after the previous disaster at Springfield. A large group of 600 to 700 Indians attacked the town on 30 May 1676. They proceeded to set fire to 12 buildings outside the stockade and drove off or killed a number of cattle and sheep. On 19 September 1677, the town was raided by a remnant of 20 hostile Indians en route to Canada led by a war chief named Ashpelon. The raiding party killed 12 settlers and succeeded in taking 17 of the inhabitants to Quebec, some of whom were later ransomed. This attack was the final end to the violence associated with King Philip's War in southern New England.

David L. Whitesell

See also KING PHILIP'S WAR; SPRINGFIELD, BURNING OF

Havana (Cuba)

The primary city on the island of Cuba located on the north coast, Havana became known as the "Key to the New World" because of its strategic position guarding the sea lanes that exited the Caribbean.

Originally established in 1511 on the southern coast of the island, the site of San Cristóbal de la Habana was relocated to its present site in 1519. Taking advantage of a magnificent natural harbor and the Gulf Stream, which flowed through the Florida Straits, ships laden with treasure left mainland ports Nombre de Dios (Panama), and Vera Cruz (Mexico), revictualled in Havana, and set out on their return journey to Spain. Until the mid-sixteenth century, Havana's economy was based on cattle raising, hide exports, and ship provisioning and refitting. The city's defenses depended upon ill-led and ill-paid local militias, and except for a poorly-located fortification on the western side of the city, the town was virtually unguarded.

Changes in European political alliances in mid-century sent French, English, and Dutch "raiders, traders, and invaders" to the Caribbean to challenge Spain's hegemony. In 1555, French corsair Jacques Soares (Sores) sacked Havana, prompting the Spanish crown to institute widespread reforms in its defense policy. The Spanish navy was assigned to the area to protect trade and treasure routes, and a royal order mandating group sailings (*flota*) was issued in 1561. From Havana, Pedro Menéndez de Avilés set off to expel foreign interlopers from Spanish territories and to establish settlements on the North American mainland at St. Augustine and Santa Elena to protect the homebound treasure fleet. As royal governor of the island, Menéndez ordered construction to begin on Havana's famed fortifications, efforts which accelerated in the 1590s under the direction of engineer Juan Bautista Antonelli. After 1570, subsidies to pay for the increased defense spending arrived from Mexico. Although costly, such reforms were successful. The city was bypassed by English corsair Francis Drake in 1586 in favor of more easily attained prizes in Nombre de Dios and Cartagena, and for nearly two centuries afterward, Havana was considered impregnable by its enemies.

The quickening pace of the eighteenth-century economy and shifting political alliances in Europe brought changes to the Caribbean. Havana became the center of the royal tobacco monopoly and the only official port of disembarkation for slaves supplied by the British South Seas Company, whose monopoly was gained in 1713 under the terms of the Treaty of Utrecht, which ended the War of Spanish Succession (1702–1714). After 1733, Spain entered into a political and military alliance with its Bourbon cousins in France, and Great Britain once again became its enemy. During subsequent conflicts of 1739–1741 and 1743–1748, British navies avoided the city; but in 1762, during the Seven Years' War (French and Indian War), Havana was occupied by British forces. At war's end, the city was ransomed back at the cost of ceding the entire province of La Florida to Great Britain.

Sherry Johnson

References

Paul S. Hoffman, *The Spanish Crown and the Defense of the Caribbean, 1535–1585: Precedent, Patrimonialism, and Royal Parsimony* (1980); Richard Pares, *War and Trade in the West Indies, 1739–1763* (1963).

See also COUNCIL OF THE INDIES; NAVY, SPAIN (1492–1699); NAVY, SPAIN (1700–1763)

Haverhill (Massachusetts)

Situated on the Merrimack River northwest of Boston, the town of Haverhill formed part of the frontier line in eastern Massachusetts. Haverhill in particular seemed to attract enemy raiding parties coming south from New Hampshire, and many of its citizens found death or captivity at the hands of small groups of Indians. In addition to these numerous scattered incidents, Haverhill suffered larger attacks on at least three occasions through King William's and Queen Anne's Wars.

On 15 March 1697, a large raiding party descended on the 30-odd structures scattered along the Merrimack. In the end, several buildings were burned, and 27 inhabitants killed and 13 captured. Among the latter were Hannah Duston and her midwife, Mary Neff, who achieved fame by the remarkable and bloody way in which they made their escape. During Queen Anne's War, the attacks continued. On 8 February 1705, a small enemy scouting force noticed a garrison house with no sentinel and the door wide open. Rushing in, the small raiding party quickly killed or captured all those within.

Finally, on Sunday, 29 August 1708, Haverhill suffered its last major attack. The Indian raiding party apparently chose Sunday deliberately, and their surprise was complete. With no alarm being given, they rapidly slipped into town through the garrison on the outskirts and attacked several buildings at once, killing or capturing 30 to 40 inhabitants. Hearing drums and musket shots from a distance, and knowing a pursuit force was approaching, the raiding party gathered up their prisoners and plunder. But they delayed too long and the pursuit force caught them. After a sharp fight in which several were killed on both sides and several captives managed their escape, the raiding party withdrew, leaving their packs and plunder.

Steven C. Eames

See also DUSTON, HANNAH

Henrico Forts (Virginia)

In the fall of 1611, Sir Thomas Dale established the town of Henrico, named for a son of King James I, on the site of an Indian village on the James River about ten miles south of the present city of Richmond, Virginia. Intended to serve as the new capital of the colony, Henrico represented the first important expansion from James-town. Working his men harshly, Dale palisaded seven acres of land on a peninsula formed by a bend in the river. Within this area, the colonists built a five-sided walled city, with a bastion at each corner. Nearby, to guard against attack from across the river, Dale erected five forts: Fort Charity, Fort Hope in Faith, Mount Melado (a sick house), Elizabeth Fort, and Fort Patience.

Henrico City eventually included a tract set aside for a university, and a school for Indians was planned. Chief Opechancanough's attack of 1622 destroyed the town and its forts, and the colonists abandoned the settlement.

Thomas Costa

References

Alexander Brown, *The Genesis of the United States*, 2 vols. (1891).

Fort Henry (Pennsylvania)

Fort Henry was one in the line of forts built by the colony of Pennsylvania along the ridge of the Blue Mountains in early 1756, after the first outbreak of fighting on the colony's frontiers. It has been called the most important outpost between the Susquehanna and Lehigh Rivers: it was located about midway between them; it stood on the main road to the trading town of Shamokin; and it protected the township of Tulpehocken and its environs, the most populous part of the region. Although it is often described as standing at the Tolihaio Gap where Swatara Creek cuts a pass through the Blue Mountains, in fact it was located 14 miles east of the pass, on the road leading to it. Fort Swatara stood at the pass itself.

Built in February 1756, Fort Henry offered protection to an area of settlement that was severely victimized by Indian attacks beginning in November and December 1755. In response to the attacks, many of the area's settlers fled temporarily. During the summer of 1756, the fort's most important function was to make an elaborate set of arrangements for sending guard parties to nearby plantations to permit the area's farmers to harvest their crops. The only casualties near Fort Henry during the harvest season of 1756 occurred in October, when two women and a 14-year-old boy were killed by a war party, two children were wounded, and two captured. Similar attacks, however, victimized other small parties along the Blue Mountain ridge throughout Berks and Lebanon Counties in the late summer and fall.

Like the rest of the forts in the Blue Mountain line, Fort Henry was manned by the Pennsylvania Regiment, and was commanded by Captain Christian Busse. It was a particularly sound and well-run fortification. The fort itself saw little military activity, but the garrison's guard and patrol parties were in high demand among the local inhabitants.

Eric Hinderaker

References

Thomas L. Montgomery, ed., *Report of the Commission to Locate the Frontier Forts of Pennsylvania,* 2nd ed., 2 vols. (1916); C. Hale Sipe, *The Indian Wars of Pennsylvania* (1929).

See also FORT ALLEN (PENNSYLVANIA); FORT DUPUI (PENNSYLVANIA); FORT LEBANON (PENNSYLVANIA); FORT NORRIS (PENNSYLVANIA)

Fort Henry (Virginia)

During the Virginia-Indian War (1622–1632), the Virginia colonists erected a palisade across the narrow waist of the peninsula between the James and York Rivers in order to secure their settlements from Indian incursions. When another Virginia-Indian War (1644–1646) erupted a generation later, the colonists again turned to fortifications to protect their exposed western frontier. In 1645, they established Fort Royal at the head of the York River (now West Point), Fort Charles at the falls of the James River (now Richmond), and Fort James about midway between the other two outposts. A year later the colonists added Fort Henry at the falls of the Appomattox River (now Petersburg). Fort Henry consisted of a blockhouse, assorted barracks, and storehouses surrounded by a palisade, and a garrison of 50 militiamen. Colonel Abraham Wood, commander of the combined Charles City County and Henrico County militia, was in charge of the post. No engagements or significant military operations took place at Fort Henry. After the Second Tidewater War, the fort gradually changed from a military outpost to a successful commercial establishment under Wood's astute guidance. As the westernmost outpost in the colony, it became a notable frontier trading post and the primary jumping-off point for explorers and traders seeking new lands and new customers in the rolling hills stretching away to the west and southwest.

Wood led an exploring party out from Fort Henry in 1671, which reached the Allegheny Mountains in present-day West Virginia. Two years later he dispatched another party under the direction of James Needham, which crossed the Appalachian Mountains and made contact with Cherokee settlements in what is now Tennessee. In 1676, Nathaniel Bacon led his rebel army away from the fort toward the Roanoke River and a violent encounter with the Occaneechee Indians. Wood died in 1680 after a notable career as militia officer, entrepreneur, and explorer. By the end of the seventeenth century, the advancing frontier had bypassed Fort Henry. The site of the military outpost and trading post was obliterated by a clutter of shops, homes, wharves, and warehouses marking the embryonic town of Petersburg. No trace remains today.

William L. Shea

References

Clarence W. Alvord and Lee Bidgood, *The First Explorations of the Trans-Allegheny Region by the Virginians, 1650–1674* (1912).

See also BACON'S REBELLION

Fort Herkimer (New York; also known as Fort Dayton, Herkimer Church Fort, Fort Kouri)

The original structure, a log house, was erected in 1723 by Johann Yost Herscheimer (Herkimer) and his eldest son, General Nicholas Herkimer. In 1740 "Jan Jost" constructed a stone dwelling next to the log house where he ran a store and trading post, dealing with both Indians and Dutchmen. After William Johnson fortified it, the English called it Fort Herkimer. The Indians continued to call it Fort Kouri ("bear") after Jan Jost's "bear-like" strength.

The house was 40 feet by 70 feet and two stories high. Surrounding it, at a distance of 30 feet, was a six- by seven-foot ditch along which palisades were placed. Behind these was a square firing platform with small bastions on each side. Next to the platform stood the barracks, which was separate from the larger structure. Fort Herkimer was destroyed, but later replaced in 1776–1777 by a new post called Fort Dayton. The new Fort Herkimer was built around the Herkimer Dutch Reformed Church. The stockaded church and blockhouse were encircled by a ditch with palisaded firing parapet.

H

Herkimer Church Fort, as it was then called, was refortified in the beginning of the Revolution with more palisades and earthworks. The site was visited by Benedict Arnold in 1777 and General George Washington in 1783 as he inspected the Mohawk Valley. The fort was refurbished in 1812 with an added second story, pitched roof, and cupola. It was destroyed in 1819 with the completion of the Barge Canal.

Elizabeth Gossman

References
Mark Boatner, *Landmarks of the American Revolution* (1973); T. Wood Clarke, *The Bloody Mohawk* (1968); Howard Peckham, *The Colonial Wars, 1689–1762* (1964).

Fort Hill (Maine)
See FORT MARY (MAINE)

Hilton, Winthrop (1671–1710)
Descended from John Winthrop and Samuel Dudley, Winthrop Hilton lived in Exeter, New Hampshire, and had a successful masting business. In 1704, he contributed to the New England war effort by being the first to lead a winter raid. After this, winter raids became quite common and frontier communities eventually established companies of "snowshoe men" who were available for service at any time of year. In addition to the first in 1704, Hilton led major winter raids in 1705, 1707, and 1708. In the summer of 1707, Hilton commanded one of two provincial regiments in the aborted attempt to capture Port Royal. Hilton was nominated to the New Hampshire Governor's Council. Before this could be confirmed, he was ambushed and killed by Indians (23 June 1710) while his masting party worked near present-day Epping, New Hampshire.

Steven C. Eames

References
Jeremy Belknap, *The History of New Hampshire* (1831), rpt. 1970.

See also ACADIA, NEW ENGLAND ATTACK ON (1707); SCOUT

Fort Hoarkill (Delaware)
See FORT SWANENDAEL (DELAWARE)

Hudson River
Henry Hudson discovered the river the Dutch called "'t noordt rivier" in 1609. Based on his voyaging, they laid claim to New Netherland and proceeded to map this remarkable riverine system. Navigable for about 120 miles, it allowed the Dutch to establish a permanent trading post in 1624 at Fort Orange (later Albany). After 1626, its use was restricted by passes issued at Fort New Amsterdam on Manhattan Island. Hydrographic mapping in the early 1630s immediately made it a valuable vehicle for the fur trade. By 1664, when the English seized New Netherland, traders using skows from Fort Orange could make a round trip to Manhattan Island in as little as nine days and, during the summer trading season, find available transport on the average of two days a week. The river was never used by the Dutch for purposes of warfare. However, the English used it as the main artery for getting ordinance and personnel to Albany in repeated military engagements against the French of Canada.

Donna Merwick

References
Donna Merwick, *Possessing Albany: 1630–1710: The Dutch and English Experiences* (1990); Isaac Newton Phelps Stokes, *The Iconography of Manhattan Island, 1498–1909*, 6 vols. (1918), 1–3; Paul Wilstach, *Hudson River Landings* (1969).

See also NEW NETHERLAND

Fort Hunter (New York)
In 1709, Queen Anne sent a delegation to meet with the Mohawk Indians and negotiate a deal for land along the junction of the Schoorie (Schoharie) River. The Mohawks gave the delegation the land to be used in the settlement of Palatine German Protestants displaced by the French wars of religion. Fort Hunter was subsequently built in 1711–1712 between the southern side of the Mohawk River and the eastern side of the Schoharie River. It was to serve multiple purposes: to defend the frontier; to protect the Five Nations; and to protect the Palatines. The fort was named after Governor Robert Hunter, who had brought the Palatines to America in 1709.

The first commandant of the fort was Captain John Scott, who had 20 men serving under him. The structure was 150 feet square, made with one-foot-thick logs, and stood 12 feet high. On each corner stood a two-storied blockhouse, standing 17 feet high. These were 24 feet square, housed 20 men each, and were armed with seven- and nine-pounder cannon. Around the inside curtain stretched a five-foot-wide parapet.

In 1733, Captain Walter Butler, then commander of the fort, met with a delegation of Mohawk Indians. By giving them rum, blankets, and knives, he obtained 86,000 acres of Mohawk land around the fort site, thus extending British control.

The fort fell into disrepair and was torn down at the beginning of the Revolution and a new fort replaced it. At the center of this fort stood Queen Anne's Chapel, built specifically for "her Mohawks." The chapel was a one-story structure of limestone, 24 feet square, and contained an attic. Underneath the chapel was a 15-foot lined cellar used as a powder magazine. The chapel was garrisoned and used for barracks for the Oneida Indians. Within the fort's walls were 30 cabins specifically to house Mohawks. A stone parsonage added to the site in 1734, used as one of William Johnson's free schools, was later fortified, palisaded, and garrisoned during the Revolution.

Elizabeth Gossman

References
    T. Wood Clarke, *The Bloody Mohawk* (1968); James Thomas Flexner, *Mohawk Baronet: Sir William Johnson of New York* (1959); Robert West Howard, *Thundergate: The Forts of Niagara* (1968); William Smith, Jr. and Michael Kammen, eds., *The History of the Province of New York*, 2 vols. (1972).

Fort Hunter (Pennsylvania)

Fort Hunter was located on the Susquehanna River just below the mouth of Fishing Creek, and only six miles north of the fort at Harris's Ferry. Despite its proximity to Fort Harris, the site of Fort Hunter was deemed important both because it protected the town of Paxton, and because it commanded the point at which the Blue Hills crossed the Susquehanna River—an obvious landing spot for any war parties coming from the north. Its origins are unknown, but historians have speculated that construction was begun by local residents in November 1755, and completed by soldiers of the Pennsylvania Regiment in January 1756. It was manned briefly by a detachment from Captain Adam Read's company before Captain Thomas McKee was stationed there in command of a company of 30 men.

When Fort Halifax was built 11 miles upriver in the summer of 1756, Fort Hunter appeared redundant to Governor William Denny and Lord Loudoun, and in March 1757, Fort Hunter was ordered abandoned and demolished. The inhabitants of Paxton objected, arguing that Fort Hunter was a more useful and strategically sited post than Fort Halifax. In response to their petition, the governor reversed his earlier order. Fort Halifax was abandoned in the fall of 1757, and Fort Hunter was strengthened. For several months thereafter its garrison was active as war parties made periodic attacks in the neighboring country. However, after early 1758, the fighting shifted away from the Susquehanna and the fort saw very little military activity.

Eric Hinderaker

References
    Thomas L. Montgomery, ed., *Report of the Commission to Locate the Frontier Forts of Pennsylvania*, 2nd ed., 2 vols. (1916).

See also FORT HALIFAX (PENNSYLVANIA)

Huron

The Huron collectively called themselves Ouendat (Wendat). After 1650, they were known to the French as the Tionontai (Khionontaternon or Petun), Tionontati Huron, or simply as the Huron. The English called them the Wyandot. In 1600, they were located in Huronia between Georgian Bay and Lake Ontario, Ontario. Their economy was based on hunting, gathering, farming, and trading.

Samuel de Champlain first visited them in 1615 and noted that they were waging war with the Iroquois. Récollet missionaries began to work with them in 1615–1616, but it was not until the arrival of the Jesuits in 1626 that the missions expanded. Their alliance with the French caused wars with the Iroquois to continue until 1648–1650, when the remaining Huron were forced westward. They would never be the warriors they were prior to this time.

Their migration took them to Green Bay and eventually to northern Wisconsin where the Jesuit, Claude Allouez, established the mission of La Pointe du Saint Esprit in 1665 at Chequamegon. They remained there for five years until Sioux hostility and Iroquois peace sent them to the Straits of Mackinac. At St. Ignace they established a settlement and were ministered to by the Jesuits and traded at Fort Buade. Tensions with their Ottawa neighbors continued and in 1702, they migrated to the newly established French settlement, Fort Pontchartrain de Detroit.

Throughout their sojourn in Michigan, they maintained good commercial and military relations with the French and formed alliances with other Indians, who they dominated. In the Detroit area, they migrated across the Detroit River to Sandwich, Ontario, and in 1745, a large party under the leadership of Orontony (Nicholas) settled at Sandusky Bay, Ohio. Soon after, British agents and French hostility provoked Nicholas to unite a number of tribes in an ill-fated anti-French conspiracy. The plot was revealed and a struggle ensued, but by 1748, the coalition dissolved.

After this struggle, the Wyandot, as they came to be known, returned to Detroit and Sandusky and dominated Ohio's Indians. After the War of 1812, they remained in Ohio, but in 1842, they migrated to the northeast corner of Oklahoma. Another small group of Huron settled at Lorette, Quebec (1660s). Descendants of the Wyandot remain in both locations today.

Russell M. Magnaghi

References
Conrad E. Heidenreich, *Huronia: A History and Geography of the Huron Indians, 1600–1650* (1971); Louise P. Kellogg, *The French Régime in Wisconsin and the Northwest* (1925), rpt. 1968; Bruce Trigger, *The Children of Aataentsic: A History of the Huron People to 1660*, 2 vols. (1976).

See also ORONTONY; FORT PONCHARTRAIN DE DETROIT (MICHIGAN); SANDUSKY BAY

Fort Hyde (North Carolina)
This fort was established in the early part of the Tuscarora War. It was located on the Pamlico River, near the town of Bath, and was designed to protect that town. It was garrisoned by 30 men and was never attacked.

Jim Sumner

I

Illinois

The Illinois (Illini, Illiniwek) Indians entered the historic period in 1673 when Jacques Marquette and Louis Jolliet arrived in their Illinois country. Although they became closely allied with the French and played a pivotal role in the French colonial effort, dramatic population losses reduced their value to the Europeans. Of the numerous subtribes extant at contact, the Cahokia, Kaskaskia, Michigamea, Moingwena, Peoria, and Tamaroa survived to control a strategic location centering around the present states of Illinois, eastern Missouri, and eastern Iowa. According to Charles Callender, "During the early postcontact period the Illinois retracted into a much smaller area, with one concentration on the upper Illinois and another in the American Bottom along the [east bank of the] Mississippi between the Illinois and Kaskaskia rivers."

Traditional Illinois conceptions of offensive military action during the late prehistoric period involved the small raiding party. A continuous state of war existed between the Illinois and seven or eight neighboring tribes, including the Sauk, Fox, and Sioux. The arrival of European trade goods in the upper Mississippi Valley before the appearance of the French themselves encouraged the Illinois to expand raiding operations into communal warfare by at least the mid-1660s. A few firearms allowed them to exploit a technological and psychological advantage over tribes located to the south, such as the Chickasaw and Shawnee, and over tribes to the southwest along the Missouri River, such as the Pawnee, Quapaw, Wichita, Osage, and Missouri.

From the beginning of the historic period, the Illinois became important to the French because of their strategic location along the Illinois and Mississippi Rivers. The tribe offered protec-tion for France's lines of communication and transportation between the colonies of New France and Louisiana. The Illinois enlisted in French military expeditions in order to battle France's colonial enemies. Frequently operating in small raiding parties attached to large invasion forces, they often frustrated their European sponsors because the Indian conception of war did not include European discipline, the time required to attack distant targets, protracted sieges, and coordinated attacks. In the larger raiding parties of the historic era, the Illinois did march against such Indian enemies of the French as the Iroquois to the east, the Chickasaw to the south, and Fox to the north.

By 1763, it was apparent, noted Helen Hornbeck Tanner, that the "tragedy of the French Era in the western Great Lakes was the population loss of the Illinois." The Illinois maintained a total population of about 12,000 in 1680, including approximately 2,900 adult males. By 1763, they numbered just 1,900, of whom approximately 460 were men. The population decline resulted from the Illinois decision to improve their condition by aligning themselves closely with the French. The Europeans did not deliberately destroy the Illinois, but they did intentionally make the Illinois Indians dependent on them. This dependency made the Native Americans more vulnerable to such depopulation influences as warfare, disease, alcoholism, etc. It is significant the French were unable to exterminate their Fox enemies or to protect their Illinois allies. The heavy price the Illinois paid for their pro-French policy was an erosion of traditional culture, a constriction of territory to the American Bottom, and a population loss of more than 80 percent.

Raymond E. Hauser

References

Emily J. Blassingham, "The Depopulation of the Illinois Indians," *Ethnohistory*, III (1956):193–224, 361–412; Charles Callender, "Illinois," in *Handbook of North American Indians*, Vol. 15, *Northeast*, ed. by Bruce G. Trigger (1978):673–680; Raymond E. Hauser, "The Illinois Indian Tribe," *Journal of the Illinois State Historical Society*, LXIX (1976):127–138; ———, "Warfare and the Illinois Indian Tribe During the Seventeenth Century," *The Old Northwest*, 10 (19841985):367–387; Helen Hornbeck Tanner, ed., *Atlas of Great Lakes Indian History* (1987).

See also CAHOKIA-FOX RAID; FOX

Impressment, Army

Using impressment to fill the ranks of the British army was a means to which the government only occasionally resorted. Animosity to impressment had deep roots within British political culture. As early as 1648, during a debate over the future of the New Model army, gentry and radicals alike opposed the creation of a standing army outside the control of Parliament or unrestricted by the "Law of this Land." Specifically, it was said that the Petition of Rights protected a man from being pressed into the army except in time of invasion.

In 1695–1696, during King William's War, Parliament passed a carefully restricted press law that permitted imprisoned debtors to be conscripted into the army. Unemployed, able-bodied men were added to the pool of unwilling recruits in 1704 during Queen Anne's War. Thousands of Englishmen were impressed under this law despite popular opposition and the lack of cooperation by local authorities, including the courts.

Intense opposition to the use of impressment resurfaced in Britain and America in 1756–1757. William Pitt, the popular war minister, barely succeeded in pushing through Parliament a law allowing unemployed or "notoriously idle" men to be impressed without an amendment that would have extended the right of habeas corpus to pressed men. The opposition argued it was wrong to condemn a man to military service without recourse to legal action.

Army impressment ended in 1780 during the American Revolution.

Alan Rogers

References

Sylvia R. Frey, *The British Soldier in America: A Social History of Military Life in the Revolutionary Period* (1981); Arthur N. Gilbert, "Army Impressment During the War of the Spanish Succession," *The Historian*, XXXVIII (1976):689–708; H.C.B. Rogers, *The British Army of the Eighteenth Century* (1977); Lois G. Schwoerer, "*No Standing Armies!*": The Antiarmy Ideology in Seventeenth-Century England* (1974).

See also ARMY, GREAT BRITAIN; RECRUITMENT

Impressment, Navy

Throughout the seventeenth and eighteenth centuries, the British Empire faced chronic shortages of experienced seamen during wartime. To secure full complements on naval vessels, the Royal Navy had to compete with the merchant marine, privateers, and (in America) colonial coast guard vessels. For a large variety of reasons, most British sailors shunned naval service whenever possible. Because the navy was unable to obtain sufficient volunteers, it relied on impressment—the physical coercion of mariners into the service.

Naval service was notoriously unpopular throughout the 1600s and 1700s, especially in America. The low levels of pay, which remained static from 1653 to 1797, were far lower than wage rates in the merchant service, while privateering offered seamen the allure of Spanish gold and Caribbean plunder. The risks of battle were another disincentive for naval service. Combat was not the only threat to a sailor's physical well-being, however. Naval discipline was rigorous and relied heavily on corporal punishment, including floggings with the cat-o'-nine-tails, beatings from the boatswain's rattan, and capital punishment for a myriad of offenses. In addition, shore leave was extremely rare because it was thought to increase desertion. Moreover, the navy frequently delayed payment of wages, sometimes for years on end, to deter desertion. For all these reasons, the Royal Navy relied on impressment instead of voluntary enlistments.

Press-gangs comprised of seamen or local toughs and commanded by naval lieutenants sought mariners at sea and ashore. Contrary to much romantic literature on the subject, impressment was confined almost entirely to seamen and shipyard workers, though mistakes were not unknown. Pressing at sea was more productive than on land because seamen could easily be found with few opportunities for escape or evasion. The navy followed the general rule of pressing men only from inbound vessels; outward bound merchantmen were theoretically off limits. Commerce dictated this policy because outward bound vessels denuded of mariners might be incapable of completing their voyages, and trade would suffer. Ashore, press-gangs concentrated on the waterfront districts most frequented by sailors, especially taverns.

Mariners often resisted impressment in Britain and the colonies. Riots were frequent, and pitched battles broke out between inward bound merchantmen and naval press-gangs. In America, anti-impressment riots erupted in Boston, Newport, New York, and Charles Town at various times during Queen Anne's War (1702–1713), King George's War (1739–1748), and the French and Indian War (1755–1763). In Boston and Charles Town, several mariners were killed. Tempers flared so violently in the 1740s that on one occasion the governor of Massachusetts had to dissuade the colony's council from ordering the province's battery from firing on Royal Navy vessels; on another, a British admiral threatened to bombard Boston.

The Royal Navy relied on impressment throughout the seventeenth and eighteenth centuries. Although press-gangs were universally hated in Britain and America, imperial officials could see no alternative. Because governments were incapable or unwilling to devise an effective method to increase the supply of trained sailors, the navy resorted to impressment to alleviate manpower shortages during wartime.

Carl E. Swanson

References

Daniel A. Baugh, *British Naval Administration in the Age of Walpole* (1965); Jesse Lemisch, "Jack Tar in the Streets: Merchant Seamen in the Politics of Revolutionary America," *William and Mary Quarterly,* 3rd Ser., XXV (1968):371–407; Richard Pares, "Manning the Navy in the West Indies, 1702–03," Royal Historical Society, *Transactions,* 4th Ser., XX (1937):31–60.

Marcus Rediker, *Between the Devil and the Deep Blue Sea: Merchant Seamen, Pirates, and the Anglo-American Maritime World, 1700–1750* (1987); Carl E. Swanson, *Predators and Prizes: American Privateering and Imperial Warfare, 1739–1748* (1991).

See also MASSACHUSETTS

I

Indian Presents

Throughout the colonial period, presents to the Indians often represented a colonial government's largest expenditure. Indian presents were an important aspect of introducing European society to the Indian nations of North America. These presents were also used to solidify alliances and enlarge trading networks. For Europeans, presents to the Indians provided entree into the world of Native Americans. The presentation of such presents was used to symbolically manifest special allegiances among friends. Often, Indian presents were given as part of a gift-giving ceremony, an indigenous practice that colonists adopted as a matter of policy. Both the French and the English found Indian presents an unavoidable part of conducting diplomatic relations with Native Americans. England's ability to provide presents for its Indian allies throughout the Seven Years' War helps explain its victory in North America over the French.

The French and English differed in how they handled Indian presents. The French system was characterized by centralization and bureaucracy. In New France, the governor general directed the Indian presents operation. Annual shipments of cloth, arms, medals, flags, and brandy were shipped from France. After arriving in Montreal, Quebec, or New Orleans, the goods were dispatched to commanders stationed in the North American interior. The French commanders then presented the neighboring Indians with presents in the name of the French "father." The term "father" had its own symbolic significance within the exchange. Jesuit priests working in New France also distributed presents to the Indians on behalf of the French government. With the government, military, and church working together, the French gave the impression their Indian system was uniform. The system allowed the various segments of the French colonial system to speak with one voice.

Recognizing the importance of renewal in Indian culture, French commanders used the gifts to reaffirm Indian goodwill and loyalty. Despite the bureaucratic inefficiency New France is sometimes noted for, the French system worked until midway through the Seven Years' War. At that time, England's navy was able to prevent Indian presents from reaching the French governor and therefore his Indian allies. By the time Montreal fell to the English in 1760, longtime Indian allies such as the Ottawa, Huron, Miami, and Wyandot had switched to the Anglo-American side. Britain's ability to provide them with presents was an important factor in their decision to switch.

While the French Indian system was centralized and highly regulated, the English colonies' Indian system was not. Competing colonial entities sought to influence the Indians through the use of Indian gifts. The colonies maintained their own Indian commissioners. Land speculators throughout the colonies used Indian presents to curry favors from the Indians. Colonial assemblies and royal governors often fought over who was going to present the Indians with that year's gift. This competition abated somewhat after 1755, when the British crown tried to systematize Indian affairs by creating an Indian superintendency system.

The superintendents attempted to bring uniformity to British gift-giving practices. They were charged with the task of giving Indian presents in the name of the king, not individual colonies. Unfortunately, the superintendents were never successful in preventing other groups from providing the Indians presents without governmental consent. Until the Seven Years' War, British presents to the Indians followed no consistent policy. Indian presents often secured specific policy objectives, cemented alliances, and continued friendships. William Johnson, superintendent of the northern colonies, frequently used presents to renew acquaintances and reaffirm Indian loyalty to the British.

The types of presents the Indians received varied and depended on one's social standing, sex, and age. Indian agents and fort commanders received detailed lists containing information about how much lead, shot, linen, combs, and jewelry each Indian should receive. These lists differentiated between chiefs and followers, men and women, young adults and children. Gifts for males above the age of 16 might include lead, shot, gunpowder, flints, vermilion, ribbon, ear bobs, and shoes. A leading warrior, chief, or sachem might also receive arm bands, broaches, and hardware. A leading matron among the Indians might receive cloth, ribbon, broaches, a blanket, a hat, and a lace handkerchief. Children received blankets as gifts. During times of unrest, promised gifts of lead, powder, and shot were conveniently forgotten. Native Americans believed such failures gave

them a legitimate reason to switch sides in Anglo-French conflicts.

The distribution of Indian presents took place in a variety of ways. Sometimes the colonial governments invited the Indians to specific locations to receive their gifts. Both the French and English used this method. Some of the locations chosen for this purpose were Montreal, Charles Town, Philadelphia, Mount Johnson, and Albany. Another method was the distribution of presents at the conclusion of formal conferences between natives and colonists. This type of distribution was particularly popular after the British government created the Indian superintendency system.

The importance of Indian presents in European-Indian relations was so critical that both European governments sent presents directly to the Indians. These presents often accompanied the arrival of new governors in North America. Without presents, colonial-Indian relations would have been far more difficult. Indian presents were a decisive factor in colonial diplomacy.

Michael J. Mullin

References

Edmond Atkin, *The Appalachian Indian Frontier: The Edmond Atkin Report and Plan of 1755*, ed. by Wilbur R. Jacobs (1954) rpt. 1967; James Axtell, *The Invasion Within: The Contest of Cultures in Colonial North America* (1985); Wilbur R. Jacobs, *Wilderness Politics and Indian Gifts: The Northern Colonial Frontier, 1748–1763* (1966); ———, *Dispossessing the American Indian: Indians and Whites on the Colonial Frontier*, 2nd rev. ed. (1985); Bruce G. Trigger, *The Huron: Farmers of the North*, 2nd ed. (1990).

Indian-France Relations
See FRANCE-INDIAN RELATIONS

Indian–Great Britain Relations
See ANGLO-INDIAN RELATIONS

Indian Trade
Indian trade predates Indian-European contact. Pre-Columbian trade routes ran both north-south and east-west. The north-south route often concerned the exchange of furs for food stuffs and sea products. The east-west route

might involve the exchange of wampum produced along the New England coast for copper from the Great Lakes. These early trade routes help explain the presence of copper in regions where such deposits did not exist. Indian-European trade also predates European colonization. Sailors fishing along the coast of North America traded mirrors, knives, and cloth for indigenous products: skins, meat, and in some instances, slaves.

Initially, Europeans considered trade in furs as an adjunct to their fishing enterprises. It was not until the early seventeenth century that Europeans pursued the Indian trade as a stand-alone business venture. For the Indians, European trade almost immediately assumed importance. Contemporary reports tell of the Powhatan Indians having thousands of beaver pelts ready for trade at the time of Jamestown's settlement. When French, Dutch, English, Spanish, and Swedish colonizers settled the Atlantic seaboard, they often tapped the preexisting trade networks for survival, and then economic opportunity.

Following coastal contact, North American river systems provided the first point of entry for colonial trade with the Indians. The St. Lawrence, Hudson, Susquehanna, Savannah, and many other rivers allowed the various colonial entities to begin trading with interior peoples. Yet even before Europeans had penetrated inland, the Indian trade had unleashed changes. The Europeans' demand for furs and the Indians' appetite for European articles produced Indian-Indian conflicts. The Iroquois "Beaver Wars" are an example of Indian-Indian conflict resulting from a changing world brought about by European contact. For some Indian groups, the fur trade stimulated the political centralization already underway. Often, this centralization was accomplished before the Indians had seen a foreign trader. In other cases, the Indian trade led to the dispersal of Indian groups from traditional homelands and into new regions.

The colonial Indian trade was predicated on the exchange of animal furs. This trade differed from the nineteenth-century trade. Whereas white trappers hunted the animals in the nineteenth century, the Indians did the hunting and trapping in the seventeenth and eighteenth centuries. In the northern colonies, the Indians often brought the furs and skins either to Indian towns or European trading posts. At these centers, which often doubled as military forts, co-lonial traders bought the pelts. As the trade developed, Indian societies began to alter their traditional perceptions. The spiritual relationship between man and animal gave way to the animal as commodity. In some regions the result was the regional extinction of particular fur-bearing animals. This exploitation then led to unforeseen environmental changes.

Wherever the fur trade developed, the Indians exchanged beaver, raccoon, marten, otter, deer, and other pelts for European items. In exchange for pelts the Indians received cloth, duffles, strouds, ironware, jewelry, rum, or brandy (depending on the ethnic origin of the trader), axes, hoes, guns, powder, and ammunition. East of the Mississippi River, deerskins were the major skin traded by 1763. Price lists of the period used deerskins as the basis for rates of exchange. Around the Hudson's Bay region, beaver pelts were the basis for rates of exchange.

Throughout the colonial period Native Americans and colonists perceived trade differently. Colonists and military officers viewed trade as directly related to issues of war and peace, land purchases, and prisoner exchanges. The Indians separated trade from these other issues. Sir Jeffrey Amherst, commander in chief of the British military in North America, typified the Anglo-American viewpoint. Following the fall of Canada, Amherst ordered the curtailment of trade with the Delawares and Shawnees, hoping to force the Indians into returning prisoners taken during the war. Delaware and Shawnee spokesmen argued that trade and a return of the prisoners were separate issues. Amherst's intransigence on the issue of trade helps explain the Shawnees' decision to take part in Pontiac's War.

Trade, or access to it, was a crucial factor in colonial-Indian relations. European policy makers saw disloyalty in any Indian attempt to trade with another country's traders. From the Indian perspective, dealing with other nations' traders was good business in that it allowed them to obtain items generally not available to them. Even after France surrendered Canada to the British, imperial Indian agents worried about the influence of French Indian traders on the Indians. For both colonist and Indian, trade was driven by self-interest. Both sides sought what served their group's best interests. Sometimes this led to conflict; other times it led to alliance. The relationship between trade and war was typified by Pontiac's War. When asked why they went to war against the English, many Indians responded by citing trade abuses and the curtailment of trade credit.

By the mid-eighteenth century, Indians east of the Mississippi River had come to regard trade goods as necessary items of daily life. Warriors needed guns and ammunition to hunt and fight, and native women gardened with iron hoes. Both groups demanded the services of blacksmiths to maintain their way of life. Despite their preference for European manufactured goods, Indian peoples continued to maintain some of their traditional skills. In many ways they had integrated trade goods into their society on their own terms. New gifts entered into personal relations and kinship networks. However, the Indians' ability to sustain long-term wars against the colonists was now dependent on their access to trade items of European origin. The Indian trade brought Native Americans into contact with the emerging merchant capitalist system of Europe. By 1763, the Indian trade had transformed native life in ways neither the Indians nor the early traders could have imagined a century earlier.

Michael J. Mullin

References

George Croghan, "An Account of the Price Goods, as agreed upon to be sold to the Indians at Sunduskee [sic]," in Croghan Papers, February 5, 1761, Box 1, Folder 7, Historical Society of Pennsylvania; William Cronon and Richard White, "Ecological Change and Indian-White Relations," in *Handbook of North American Indians,* Vol. 4, *History of Indian-White Relations,* ed. by Wilcomb E. Washburn (1988):417–429.

William J. Eccles, "The Fur Trade in the Colonial Northeast," in *Handbook of North American Indians,* Vol. 4, *History of Indian-White Relations,* ed. by Wilcomb E. Washburn (1988):324–334; Charles Hudson, *The Southeastern Indians* (1976); Arthur J. Ray, *Indians in the Fur Trade: their role as trappers, hunters, and middlemen in the lands southwest of Hudson Bay, 1660–1870* (1974).

Neal Salisbury, *Manitou and Providence: Indians, Europeans, and the Making of New England, 1500–1643* (1982); Bruce G. Trigger, *Natives and Newcomers: Canada's "Heroic Age" Reconsidered* (1985).

See also IROQUOIS WARS

Indian Uprising of 1747

See UPRISING OF 1747

Indian Warfare

The theory and practice of war among the eastern woodland Indian tribes was quite different from that practiced by the European settlers in the seventeenth century. The difference grew from the alternative purposes and objectives that most eastern tribes ascribed to warfare. Because the Indians were largely indifferent to the accumulation of material possessions, and because they normally possessed adequate amounts of land, their intertribal conflicts tended to be of a more limited nature than the wars waged in Europe. The Indians customarily were drawn into combat to seek vengeance for isolated depredations or as a result of personal feuds between chieftains. On occasion, boundary disputes precipitated conflicts, and it was not unheard of for a tribe to seek to humble a burgeoning foe. Frequently, tribes went to war in quest of captives who might be incorporated into the group to serve as surrogates for deceased spouses or children. War, therefore, was not waged from land hunger or in the hope of plundering a neighbor. Normally, the aim of the combatants was to achieve symbolic dominion over a neighbor rather than to effect the actual subjugation of a rival.

Indian warfare was less well organized than the management of conflicts in Europe. In some tribes war could only begin when sanctioned by the sachem, or chief; in some instances, the chieftain's decision required the endorsement of his council and military leaders. Among some southern tribes war could begin upon the exhortation of the "war captain" or the "Big Warrior." Among other peoples, however, a demand for hostilities by a few tribesmen was sufficient to inaugurate conflict. There were instances, too, when warfare erupted as a manifestation of a tribal rite, a symbol of the coming of age of the young male generation, a collective endeavor designed to exalt the values and ethos of the people's culture.

The rank and file of the Indian fighting forces normally was raised by voluntarism; those who took up arms often did so only after a careful evaluation of the necessity to enter into war. Frequently, those who had initially agreed to participate grew disinclined to fight and returned home, never completing the march against the adversary.

The scope of the wars between tribes was slight when compared to the wars waged between European nations. It was not uncommon for the contending forces to agree in advance to spare all women and children. The conflicts that followed were waged with primitive weapons, including bows and arrows, clubs, spears, knives, and hatchets, often with the contending warriors separated by great distances. In addition, the engagements usually occurred in dense wilderness environments, which only contributed to the inaccuracy of the weaponry. The result was a meager casualty rate by the standards of Europe. Seldom more than a score of warriors perished; many colonists testified the Indians shrank in horror when only ten or 12 of their number fell in battle.

Limited casualties notwithstanding, most Indian war parties were led by experienced commanders. The Indian warriors, moreover, usually had undergone some martial training. Hurrying into battle in their garish war paint, chanting and howling in a hair-raising manner, the Indians presented a terrifying spectacle. Many colonists testified to the courage and endurance of these Indian adversaries. Lieutenant Lion Gardner, a professional soldier employed by the first Puritan immigrants to Massachusetts, even judged the Indians to be better soldiers than the Spaniards against whom he had fought.

There was a plan to most Indian engagements. Surprise attack was the desired objective. While the fighting was chaotic, each side sought to surround its foe, inflict some damage and seize a few captives. Once these objectives were realized, or when it became apparent the plan had been foiled, the battle ended and the two sides withdrew. There was no concept among the Indians of making a death-defying stand.

The final stage of war often involved the ritualistic torture of those unfortunate souls taken captive during the conflict. These prisoners were treated with a barbarism that would have taxed the sadistic ingenuity of Europe's most ruthless despots.

The arrival of the European settlers resulted in important alterations in Indian warfare. Of course, much that was traditional in their fighting persisted. For instance, ambushes and guerrilla tactics were hardly discarded. But significant changes did occur. Once the Indians overcame their initial panic on first experiencing European firearms, they sought to equip themselves with such weapons. While they did not discover the secrets of manufacturing muskets, some tribes did learn how to make musket balls; ultimately, many Native American craftsmen grew proficient in the repair of defective European weapons. The presence of the ever-expanding English settlements often forced tribes into alliances with traditional rivals or into the pursuit of assistance from the European rivals of the British. Moreover, while the eastern Indians initially were aghast at the nature of European warfare, arguing it resulted in too many deaths, they, too, eventually resorted to all-out warfare, preying on civilians and extirpating entire villages. To go to war with the settlers, they soon realized, was to commit themselves to a fight to the death.

John E. Ferling

References

Adam J. Hirsch, "The Collision of Military Cultures in Seventeenth-Century New England," *The Journal of American History* 74 (1988):1187–1212; Francis Jennings, *The Invasion of America: Indians, Colonialism, and the Cant of Conquest* (1975); Douglas E. Leach, *Arms for Empire: A Military History of the British Colonies in North America, 1607–1763* (1973); Alden T. Vaughan, *New England Frontier: Puritans and Indians, 1620–1675* (1965).

See also INDIAN WARFARE, CAPTIVITY; INDIAN WARFARE, EUROPEAN ACCULTURATION OF; RAIDING PARTY

Indian Warfare, Captivity

Capture was a widely used tactic of warfare in North, South, and Central America before European contact in 1492. Although first written about by the Spaniards to justify their own conquest of Mexico, the frequent use by Aztecs of captives as slaves and religious sacrifices made them so hated and feared that it lead to the demise of Aztec society.

In the Northeast, death, torture, adoption, or ransom were the possibilities after capture for native men in wartime from approximately 1550 through the American Revolution. From colonial times, accounts by British, French, and American survivors testify to white comrades and native enemies alike being beaten, tortured, burned to death, and alternatively accepted as members of indigenous societies. Father Isaac Jogues's account (1643–1646) was one of many

Jesuit Relations depicting the capture and torture of Huron captives among the Iroquois. Similar accounts can be found dealing with Southwest and Northwest societies in the early nineteenth century. Adoption was commonly related to capture among Indians east of the Mississippi from Hurons and Iroquois in the Northeast to Cherokees in the Southeast and among Great Lakes Ojibwa and Santee Sioux.

In the seventeenth- and eighteenth-century Northeast, native women were powerful determinants of the fate of war captives. Among the Iroquois, female elders decided whether men would go to war as the taking of captives to assuage the loss of kin was an accepted reason for warfare. A wife or mother who had lost a son, husband, or daughter in war chose a captive man or woman to adopt into her family. Either sex was a possible substitute for a lost relative. So common was this practice in the eighteenth century that Lewis Henry Morgan claims the Iroquois would have died out without taking captives into their midst. Often children were among the largest number of those adopted, their easy acculturation obviously recognized by their captors. Even as prisoners were brought into the village, or during and after the ordeal of the gauntlet, a choice of a new family member was made. The scene described by Captain John Smith of Pocahontas saving him in early Virginia (1607) was probably a cultural misreading of the accepted powers of leading women to save prisoners.

The sex and age of the victim was important in determining treatment as a prisoner of war. Among many indigenous nations of the Northeast (and well into Canada), men went to war knowing that if captured a trial including torture and possible death was likely. Adoption was possible if the man could endure his trials, but this meant becoming one with the enemy. Terror frequently accompanied the arrival of a male captive at the village of his captors. In native groups from the Southeast into eastern Canada and the Great Lakes region, captured male warriors were greeted by members of a grieving and angry village. Men, women, and children of all ages lined the entry to the village armed with sticks and stones poised to assault the incoming enemy, thereby avenging their own dead, lost, or captured kin. Men ran this gauntlet attempting as best as possible to avoid attack. Writing on the fate of male captives among the Northeast Iroquois, Lewis Henry Morgan wrote, "adoption or torture were the alternative chances of the captive" as a test of "their powers of endurance." The "ordeal" pointed them to their future home. If the victim made it through "this long avenue of whips" running naked to the waist, he would be "treated with the utmost affection and kindness." Those who did not pass the test were "led away to torture, and to death."

Native women and small children, although at times psychologically terrorized and frequently traumatized by the death or scenes of torture inflicted on parents, relatives, and friends, might be treated gently in preparation for their ultimate integration into the enemy tribal, village, and family life. Mary Jemison was one such captive. She was captured by French and Shawnees in 1758 during the Seven Years' War in southwestern Pennsylvania. She was adopted and married into Seneca society and refused repatriation to white society. In other cases, captured Huron women committed suicide rather than become Iroquois.

In Iroquois ways of war, the taking of captives was central to the waging of war and included in all stages of war-making ritual. According to Daniel K. Richter, such "considerations set native warfare strikingly apart from Euroamerican military experience. 'We are not like you Christians for when you have taken Prisoners of one another you send them home, by such means as you can never rout one another,' one early eighteenth-century Onondaga explained." For many indigenous people before 1800, neither the taking of territory nor killing the enemy were the signs of success in war. Without captives, there was no victory.

June Namias

References

James Axtell, *The European and the Indian: Essays in the Ethnohistory of Colonial North America* (1981); ———, *The Invasion Within: The Conquest of Cultures in Colonial America* (1985); A. Irving Hallowell, "American Indians, White and Black: The Phenomenon of Transculturalization," in *Contributions to Anthropology: Selected Papers of A. Irving Hallowell* (1976):498–529; Lewis H. Morgan, *League of the Ho-dé-no-sau-nee or Iroquois,* ed. by Herbert M. Lloyd, 2 vols. (1904); June Namias, *White Captives: Gender and Ethnicity on the American Frontier* (1993).

Daniel K. Richter, *The Ordeal of the Longhouse: The Peoples of the Iroquois*

League in the Era of European Colonization (1992); Reuben G. Thwaites, ed., *The Jesuit Relations and Allied Documents: Travel and Explorations of the Jesuit Missionaries in New France, 1610–1791; the Original French, Latin, and Italian Texts, with English Translations and Notes*, 73 vols. (1896–1901), rpt. 1959; Bruce G. Trigger, *The Children of Aataentsic: A History of the Huron People to 1660* (1976); Richard White, *The Middle Ground: Indians, Empires, and Republics in the Great Lakes Region, 1650–1815* (1991).

See also CAPTIVITY NARRATIVES; INDIAN WARFARE; JEMISON, MARY

Indian Warfare, European Acculturation of

The earliest English settlers in America were both bemused and horrified by the manner of Indian warfare. The undisciplined behavior of Native Americans during combat was derided by English commentators. It was incomprehensible to them that the Indians would proceed toward their enemies in an undisciplined state, oblivious to the need to march in a formation or to be subject to the commands of their superiors. Their style of fighting appeared to be foolish to the professional English soldiers. One commentator noted the Indians charged about in a pell-mell fashion, firing their arrows indiscriminately. Another observer scoffed at how the Indians discharged an arrow, then stood immobilized watching to see if the weapon struck its object.

An English soldier employed by the first Puritan settlers in New England observed with disbelief that Indians seemed to fight for the sport of it, not for the purpose of conquest. The natives' tendency to retreat following the first casualties and their tactics of hiding behind trees rather than fighting in the open were ridiculed by English commentators. To the initial English settlers, the Indians were ineffectual warriors who were not likely to pose a serious threat to Europe's professional soldiers.

Some Indian practices outraged the English. Colonial spokesmen condemned the ritualistic torture of captives as well as the natives' habit of scalping their victims. Not privy to the European manuals of warfare, the Native Americans fought in a manner that the English often characterized as "irregular." They struck from ambush, relied on skullduggery, and used the American wilderness as an ally. The English looked upon the Indians as cowards for their utilization of such tactics. It was not a manly way to fight, the early Anglo-Americans often said, and they frequently equated what they regarded as the Indians' treachery with the behavior of wolves, the beast of the wilderness most despised by this farming society.

Gradually, however, the utility of employing some Indian tactics became apparent to many colonial leaders. As early as King Philip's War in 1676, Colonel Benjamin Church on occasion ordered his Massachusetts soldiers to dress as Indians and crawl stealthily through the forest, hoping to surprise and overwhelm his Indian adversary. In the wars of the eighteenth century, colonial forces often sought to ambush their foes. Some colonies even encouraged the Indian practice of scalping.

When the last of the intercolonial wars erupted in 1754, many colonial leaders had come to embrace a style of warfare that often was called the "American Way of Fighting." The news of General Edward Braddock's debacle on the Monongahela in July 1755 validated the wisdom of augmenting the most prudent martial tactics of Europe with those best suited for the American environment. Throughout America, Braddock was condemned for not understanding that America's wilderness demanded American tactics, many of which were precisely those which the Indians had employed against the first English settlers. Confirmation of the new wisdom came from diverse sources. Braddock's successor as commander of the British forces in America, John Campbell, the earl of Loudoun, announced his intention of relying more thoroughly on ranger units in the course of waging what he called the "Bush Fight." Young George Washington, who had fought beside Braddock, also endorsed the merits of irregular warfare. The members of the Virginia Regiment had performed more ably than the professional British soldiers, he subsequently remarked. They had taken to the forests and grappled with the Indians in the now conventional American way of warfare. Many Virginians had perished, he added, but they had "behav'd like Men and died like Soldiers."

John E. Ferling

References

John E. Ferling, *A Wilderness of Miseries: War and Warriors in Early America* (1981); ———, "The New England Soldier: A Study in Changing Perceptions," *American*

Quarterly , 33 (1981):26–45; Peter E. Russell, "Redcoats in the Wilderness: British Officers and Irregular Warfare in Europe and America, 1740–1760," *William and Mary Quarterly,* 35 (1978):629–652.

See also CHURCH, BENJAMIN; INDIAN WARFARE; SCALP BOUNTIES; SCALPING

Infantry

Soldiers who fight on foot, even though they may be transported to the battlefield by other means, are called infantry. The term is derived from Spanish *infante* i.e. a youth, a foot soldier. Infantry has existed since the beginning of organized warfare and has always constituted the largest single element of field armies. Their objective is to seize and hold ground and, when necessary, to occupy enemy territory.

The development of the modern infantry is intricately connected with the rise of the absolutist state and the concept of the standing army. The demise of the mercenary and the creation of a permanent military establishment proved an expensive but indispensable component of absolutist rule as monarchs tried to concentrate all power in their hands and enforce an arms monopoly for the state. Beginning in the middle of the seventeenth century, standing armies served as a means to bind the nobility to the state through their integration in the officer corps, as an ever-present tool to enforce the will of the ruler at home, and as a means of power politics in foreign affairs. The concurrent standardization of arms, drill, and organization in companies, battalions, and regiments reflected the will of the absolutist monarch for order and clarity, which determined the organization of society as a whole as well.

The introduction of firearms resulted in the division of infantry into pikemen, armed with the pike, and soldiers armed with guns, called *musketiere* in Germany and *fusiliers* in France. In the seventeenth century, grenadiers were added as a specialized form of infantryman. With the introduction of the flintlock and the fixed bayonet, the pikemen disappeared from the armies of Europe. Concurrent changes in infantry tactics resulted in the development of line or heavy infantry for close combat purposes, which in turn necessitated the formation of light infantry for irregular warfare. Levied from among the lowest social classes, forced into military service as an alternative to punish-

ment or recruited from prisoners of war, the standing armies of Europe more often than not were held together by brutal force and blind drill. Too great an investment to be risked lightly in battle and liable to desert, line infantry was most efficient in a pitched battle over open ground, where superior drill, volume of fire, and sheer numbers often decided the outcome of battles. Any kind of individual action by line infantry was neither possible nor welcome. Light infantry found its justification in its ability to perform tasks and assignments that the line could no longer cover, a point driven home to the British by their experiences in the French and Indian Wars.

Robert A. Selig

References
John I. Alger, *Definitions and Doctrine of the Military Art* (1985).

See also ARMY, FRANCE; ARMY, GREAT BRITAIN; GRENADIER; LIGHT INFANTRY

Intercolonial Relations

Intercolonial relations during the wars of the eighteenth century were shaped largely by the determination of each colony's legislative assembly to be autonomous and by the long period of "salutary neglect" of the American colonies by British policy makers. When America became a prize sought by England and France in their quest for world power and wealth, some British ministers and a few Americans proposed the formation of a colonial union. These proposals generated little enthusiasm in America or in Britain, except among British officers attempting to organize military operations. However, the danger posed by the French and Indians in Canada and the Ohio Valley and the promise of royal support caused some colonies to cooperate with each other temporarily.

During Queen Anne's War (1702–1713), an Anglo-American force consisting of a few ships, a regiment of Royal Marines and several thousand New England soldiers drove the French from Port Royal in October 1710. The following year, New England leaders hatched an ambitious plan to conquer Canada. The previous year's display of cooperation collapsed. Rhode Island unilaterally reduced its assigned quota of troops; Boston merchants refused to extend credit to British commissary officers; New England naval pilots had to be forced to sail with the British fleet; and, when the expedition failed, New York merchants, who were said to be illegally trading with the French, were blamed.

Mistrust and dissension also characterized the military operations of the southern colonies. In 1740, Governor James Oglethorpe of Georgia led a small intercolonial army against the Spanish at St. Augustine, Florida. When the attack failed, the South Carolina legislature blasted Oglethorpe and his Georgians and heaped praise on the Carolinians. A defender of Governor Oglethorpe argued that the general had been "betrayed and neglected by the mean Carolina regiment."

Faced with the possibility of another war with France in the 1750s. Anglo-American leaders revived the idea of an intercolonial union. The Board of Trade proposed a political "Union between ye Royal, Proprietary, and Charter Governments" and the appointment of a high-ranking military officer as governor general of all the colonies. Governor William Shirley of Massachusetts suggested a plan for a mutual defense alliance, financed by proportionate assessments of each colony. In Pennsylvania, Benjamin Franklin published a woodcut depicting a snake cut into 13 parts with the motto "Join or Die."

The crown proposed simply that the northern colonies send delegates to a conference with the Six Nations Indians, whose friendship was considered indispensable in the event of war. Shortly after the conference began, however, the delegates brushed aside their restrictive instructions and resolved unanimously to debate the matter of an intercolonial union. The Albany "Plan of Union" was designed primarily by Franklin. It was proposed that each colony send delegates to a "Grand Council" presided over by a royal governor general. The assembly was empowered to negotiate Indian treaties, create new settlements, provide for colonial defense, and "everything that shall be found necessary for the . . . support of the Colonies in General."

The Albany Plan was rejected by the colonies and the crown. Most colonial legislatures feared the proposal would lead to greater British control. The Massachusetts house of representatives, for example, opposed any intercolonial union on the grounds it would be "subversive of the most valuable rights and Liberties of the several Colonies. . . ." In Britain, the duke of Newcastle warned that "Uniting too closely the Northern Colonies" might lead to a dangerous movement for "an independency from this Country."

In fact, the American colonies seemed incapable of burying their mutual hostilities and rivalries. "The strength of our colonies . . . is divided," wrote one American during the Great War for Empire (1754–1763). In every colony, the struggle between the legislature and the executive continued unabated throughout the war years. Together with their hostility toward arrogant British commanders, this meant each assembly appropriated only as much money as it saw fit and insisted on full control of its troops.

The American colonies made significant contributions to their defense and took important political steps in the process during the wars of the eighteenth century, but in 1763, an intercolonial union seemed highly unlikely.

Alan Rogers

References
Lawrence H. Gipson, *The Great War for the Empire: The Years of Defeat, 1754–1757* (1946); Douglas Edward Leach, *Roots of Conflict: British Armed Forces and Colonial Americans, 1677–1763* (1986); Alan Rogers, *Empire and Liberty: American Resistance to British Authority, 1755–1763* (1974); John Schutz, *William Shirley: King's Governor of Massachusetts* (1961).

See also ALBANY CONGRESS; BOARD OF TRADE; DOMINION OF NEW ENGLAND; NEW ENGLAND CONFEDERATION; OGLETHORPE, JAMES EDWARD; SHIRLEY, WILLIAM

Inspector General
The inspector general was a special staff officer, named by the commander in chief, to audit all requisition accounts before they were approved by the commanding general and paid by the British Treasury. Lieutenant Colonel James Robertson acted as inspector general to General Jeffrey Amherst, the commanding officer of British forces in America from 1758 to 1763.

Given the thousands of pounds sterling French and Indian War cost the British Treasury, the inspector general played an especially important role in the system of checks designed to keep expenses within reasonable bounds. An experienced quartermaster general, Robertson had gained the trust of General Amherst, who would be held responsible if the Treasury Department raised questions about military expenses. In short, Robertson, as inspector general, supervised the accounts of other quartermasters, commissaries, ordnance officers, and engineers. General Amherst would not approve such accounts unless Robertson accepted their legitimacy.

Ronald W. Howard

References

Edward Pierce Hamilton, *The French and Indian Wars: The Story of Battles and Forts in the Wilderness* (1962); Milton M. Klein and Ronald W. Howard, eds., *The Twilight of British Rule in Revolutionary America: The New York Letter Book of General James Robertson, 1780–1783* (1983); Stanley M. Pargellis, ed., *Military Affairs in North America, 1748–1765* (1936); John Shy, *Toward Lexington: The Role of the British Army in the Coming of the American Revolution* (1965).

See also ROBERTSON, JAMES

Iroquois

The Iroquois League, also referred to as the Iroquois Confederacy, originally encompassed speakers of five closely related languages whose homelands stretched through the portion of what is now upstate New York between the Mohawk and Genesee River valleys. From east to west, the Five Nations were the Mohawks or *Ganienkeh* (the French called them *Agniers* and the Dutch *Maquas*), the Oneidas (in French *Onneiouts*), the Onondagas (*Onontagués*), the Cayugas (*Oiogouens*), and the Senecas (*Tsonnontouans*). In the mid-1720s, the league expanded and became the Six Nations, as it added the Tuscaroras, who emigrated a decade earlier from what is now North Carolina.

In the seventeenth and eighteenth centuries, only the French regularly called these peoples *Iroquois,* a word of uncertain definition derived from one of the languages of the Algonkian family. The English simply called them the Five or Six Nations, or employed the words *Mohawks, Maquas,* or *Senecas* for them all. Native neighbors used labels that have come down in English as *Naudoways, Menkwes, Maquas,* or *Mingos.* Within the league, the preferred collective self-descriptions were terms that meant "the extended house," "the whole house," or "the longhouse," metaphorical usages that were based on the peoples' characteristic form of communal dwelling. In the Mohawk language the word was *Kanosoni;* in Seneca *Haudenosaunee,* a term preferred by many Six Nations people today.

Throughout the colonial period, but particularly in the early seventeenth century, the People of the Longhouse seldom dealt with outsiders as a unified diplomatic or political entity. The Iroquois League existed primarily to suppress warfare among its constituent groups rather than to coordinate interactions with outsiders, and within it the individual village rather than the nation was the largest effective political unit. Each major village was home to between a few hundred and 2,000 people, organized into from three to nine clans. The total precontact population of the league is a matter of scholarly controversy, but seems to have been well over 20,000. From the 1630s, after the initial ravages of European diseases, until the era of the American Revolution, population fluctuated in a range slightly under 10,000. In the face of repeated epidemics, that figure was maintained by massive adoptions of native refugee peoples and, particularly in the seventeenth century, of war captives.

An appreciation both of the significance of those captives and of the decentralized nature of the Iroquois League depends upon an understanding of the role of warfare in Iroquois culture. The People of the Longhouse were, of course, no more "warlike" than Europeans, but organized violence served functions in their culture that were quite distinct from those familiar to the colonizers. In patterns they shared widely with their eastern North American neighbors, the Five Nations used war captives to replace the dead, either literally through adoption or symbolically through ceremonial executions; thus warfare was, in many respects, an integral part of culturally defined mourning practices. Because prisoners filled the demographic and emotional void left by death, demands for small- or large-scale campaigns to secure them flowed upward from the women of matrilineal kin groups to villages and perhaps larger groupings, rather than downward from centralized political structures. Almost by definition, then, neither the league nor a nation nor, in many respects, a village could exclusively govern war and peace.

By the first half of the seventeenth century, two products of the European invasion of North America—trade goods and disease—

transformed these apparently ancient patterns of conflict. By the mid-sixteenth century, although none of the Five Nations was yet in direct contact with European fishers and explorers, exotic iron, glass, and brass objects were already finding their way to Iroquoia through native channels of exchange. Initially, such goods appear to have been prized primarily for their symbolic and aesthetic significance. By the turn of the seventeenth century, however, metal items began to arrive in larger numbers, and they assumed more mundane, but no less significant, roles as tools, household items, and weapons.

As trade goods increased in military and economic importance, the inland geographic position of Iroquoia placed the Five Nations at a severe disadvantage in comparison to native groups nearer the coastal sources of European trade. The dilemma was particularly acute for the Mohawks, the easternmost Iroquois nation; in the 1610s, most of their warriors were still fighting with brass arrowheads and iron axes with stone counterparts. As a result, the looting of metal items gradually seems to have become a major determinant of the timing and location of Iroquois mourning-war campaigns. Most of the recorded early seventeenth-century fighting between Mohawks and their northern neighbors therefore occurred in the uninhabited region surrounding the junction of the Richelieu and St. Lawrence Rivers, where warriors could waylay Huron and Algonquin traders bringing home goods purchased from the French at Quebec.

In the late 1610s, the Mohawks eased their assaults on Indians leaving the Quebec markets, primarily because Dutch traders on the upper Hudson were by that time providing them with a more plentiful source of European goods. Access to that source was hardly secure, however, for it depended upon the willingness of the Mohawks' Mahican neighbors to allow them to pass through their country to Fort Orange (present-day Albany). In 1623 and 1624, Dutch officials at that post began to court trade with the Mahicans' Algonquin allies to the north, who had access to furs of higher quality than those available south of the Great Lakes. Mohawks could well have found themselves cut off from direct commerce with Europeans. To avoid that fate, Mohawk warriors battled the Mahicans for four years, until in 1628 the latter abandoned all their lands on the west side of the Hudson River and allowed the Iroquois unobstructed access to Fort Orange.

By the early 1630s Mohawks again were sporadically blockading the St. Lawrence and pillaging native traders. Fighters from the other four Iroquois nations soon joined them and began conducting their own expeditions that mixed economic and mourning-war motives. The raiders now focused primarily on traffic moving downriver with furs rather than on canoes paddling upriver with French wares, for the Iroquois faced a scarcity of pelts that they could profitably barter for the readily available Fort Orange trade goods. A large proportion of the mid-seventeenth-century furs that Iroquois sold at Fort Orange were probably hijacked in these expeditions.

But the Iroquois' wars with their native neighbors cannot be explained solely in terms of fur-trade piracy. Shortly after economic motives began to play a large role in the Five Nations' conflicts with their neighbors, the mourning functions of warfare also assumed vastly increased significance. Like Native Americans throughout the hemisphere, Iroquois possessed no immunities to the major endemic viral diseases of Europe—smallpox, measles, influenza, and others. The earliest documented epidemics in Iroquoia were massive smallpox outbreaks that struck the Mohawks and probably other nations in 1633, and the Senecas and perhaps additional Iroquois in 1640–1641. Some scholars have argued for a much earlier onset of imported diseases, but whatever the case, by the early 1640s, the plagues had more than halved the population of the Five Nations; Mohawk numbers alone may have plunged by as much as 75 percent. As disease continued to levy a grim toll throughout the next few decades, the thousands of deaths inspired survivors to seize ever more captives to replace the dead. War parties that might earlier have settled for a handful of potential adoptees now sought massive numbers of prisoners.

The explosive new mixture first appeared in 1634, when first Senecas, and later Oneidas, Onondagas, and Cayugas, intensified attacks on their old enemies, the Iroquoian-speaking nations of the Huron Confederacy. By the 1640s, wars that mixed demographic and economic motives had achieved an apparently unprecedented scale, duration, and persistence. A turning point came in 1642, when Senecas and probably warriors from other western Iroquois nations attacked a geographically exposed Huron village and secured in one major stroke a large supply of furs, trade goods, and captives.

From 1643 to 1647, the Senecas, Cayugas, and Onondagas engaged in annual battles with the Hurons that cost each side dearly in lives. Meanwhile, the Mohawks and Oneidas abandoned their former practice of sporadic raids on the St. Lawrence in favor of annual, systematically organized, summer-long blockades that yielded a steady stream of captives and furs. During 1648 and 1649, the blockades temporarily ceased, as warriors from all five Iroquois nations united their forces in a systematic campaign to pick off Huron villages. In the end, all those who survived fled their homes. For most of the next decade, warriors from the Five Nations pursued the Huron refugees relentlessly and overran in turn each of the neighboring Iroquoian-speaking peoples that sheltered bands of them: the Petuns were dispersed by 1650, the Neutrals by 1651, the Eries by 1657. The battles in the Great Lakes region soon merged with raids on the St. Lawrence in a single conflict that pitted the Five Nations against virtually every Indian people in the Northeast.

These campaigns—which scholars focusing solely on their economic motivations have labeled the "Beaver Wars"—assumed an additionally deadly character when the combatants began to use firearms. Mohawks were among the earliest native peoples of the Northeast to acquire significant numbers of muskets; by the mid-1640s, they wielded an estimated 400 of them. As Mohawk musketeers gained experience and western Iroquois also amassed arsenals, warriors of the Five Nations developed skills the European manufacturers of guns could barely have imagined; they learned far sooner than Europeans how to aim cumbersome firearms accurately at individual targets and insisted on flintlocks in an era when most colonists still settled for matchlock models. Temporarily, plentiful supplies and dexterous use of guns gave the Iroquois a considerable advantage over their Indian enemies, particularly the less well-armed Hurons and poorly arsenalled Neutrals, Petuns, and Eries.

For all the Iroquois' military advantages, however, the mid-century Beaver Wars hardly constituted a clear-cut series of triumphs. Instead, the conflicts traced a devastating cycle: economic demands led villagers of the Five Nations into battles with their native neighbors; epidemics produced deadlier mourning wars fought with firearms; the need for guns increased the demand for pelts to trade for them;

the quest for furs demanded expanded raids. At each stage, fresh economic and demographic motives fed the spiral. The Beaver Wars increasingly became desperate struggles to acquire sufficient peltries for the trade in European goods and sufficient captives to replace huge population losses.

Almost inevitably, the colony of New France fell ever more deeply into the Indian conflicts because of its trading ties to enemies of the Five Nations. In the early 1640s, Mohawks killed or took prisoner several French traveling with the natives they attacked. Such incidents, combined with economic disruptions caused by blockades of the St. Lawrence trade route, produced on-again, off-again warfare between New France and the Iroquois from 1647 through the early 1660s. During that period, the small string of French outposts on the St. Lawrence posed only a slight military threat to the Five Nations, and at times the colonists believed their very existence was imperiled. Although there is little evidence the Iroquois regarded the colonists as much more than troublesome interlopers, French officialdom took the Iroquois threat very seriously; in 1663, the crown revoked the charter of the Company of New France and assumed direct control of the colony. In the summer of 1665, Daniel de Rémy de Courcelles and Alexander Prouville, seigneur de Tracy, arrived in America as, respectively, the new governor and royal viceroy, and brought with them a thousand royal troops.

This highly visible show of force helped to convince Seneca, Cayuga, Onondaga, and Oneida leaders to agree to a comprehensive treaty with the French and their Indian allies in December 1665; the pact was reconfirmed with great ceremony the next year. Just as important, however, in explaining Iroquois willingness to make peace was the collapse of their long-standing trading ties to New Netherland. In the late 1650s and early 1660s, the trade had been disrupted by the difficulties of Hudson River Dutch traders. The final blow came in 1664, when English forces seized New Netherland. With both transatlantic and European-Indian trading relationships thus disrupted in what was now called New York, at least some Iroquois who made peace with New France were more eager to gain access to St. Lawrence markets than they were afraid of French military might. Others hoped that, once an alliance was formed, New France might be convinced to aid them in their war against their principal native foes, the Susquehannocks of present-day south-central Pennsylvania.

Despite all these factors, most Mohawks remained aloof from the negotiations. Close enough to Albany to be assured of some supply of trade goods and embittered by decades of more intense conflict with New France than other Iroquois had experienced, many in that nation deeply distrusted the colonizers of the St. Lawrence. More importantly, their principal antagonists were not the Susquehannocks—whom the French might be convinced to war upon—but eastern and northern Algonkian-speaking peoples long tied economically to New France. In January 1666, with the bulk of the nation's village headmen refusing to come to terms, Tracy and Courcelles embarked with more than 500 men for the Mohawk country. Frostbitten, starving, and inadequately guided, the army stumbled not to the native towns but, apparently accidentally, to just outside Schenectady, from which they soon retreated. In September, however, Tracy returned with more than a thousand French and native troops, who burned the Mohawks' villages and food stores. The inhabitants had sufficient warning to flee the destruction, but their leaders, struggling to rebuild their homes, bereft of secure economic ties to the Hudson, and intimidated by rumors of renewed military preparations, had little choice but to make peace at Quebec in June 1667.

For most of the next decade, the Five Nations became part of the expanding web of native peoples who professed allegiance to New France. Meanwhile, the wars of the Oneidas, Onondagas, Cayugas, and Senecas with the Susquehannocks, along with a renewed conflict of the Mohawks with the Mahicans and a number of southern New England Algonquin peoples, continued the cycle of violence characteristic of the Beaver Wars. French dominance in this difficult period was marked in the Five Nations by the growth of trade with the St. Lawrence, by the susceptibility of many to the religion preached by resident French Jesuit missionaries, by the emigration of many Christians to mission villages such as Kahnawake (Caughnawaga) near Montreal, and by the growth of cohesive francophile political factions.

Beginning with the return of New York to English control in 1674, the provincial government of Sir Edmund Andros systematically cultivated ties with disgruntled Iroquois leaders and provided a focus for anti-French sentiment.

Early in his tenure, Andros struck a partnership with Mohawk military leaders and encouraged them to intervene against New England Algonquians in Metacom's ("King Philip's") War; their attack on Metacom's winter encampment in 1675–1676 was a turning point in the conflict. Simultaneously, Andros and his agents at Albany worked to end Iroquois conflicts with the Mahicans and the Susquehannocks. By 1680, both wars were over with results highly favorable to the Iroquois, who emerged not only as the principal Indian power in the Northeast, but as protectors of large groups of refugees from their former enemies whom Andros resettled near Iroquoia. In these military and diplomatic developments lay the origins of the set of English-Indian alliances known as the "Covenant Chain."

Buttressed by their new alliances and peace on the eastern and southern flanks of Iroquoia, anglophile factions in each of the Five Nations eclipsed the francophiles, expelled the French Jesuit missionaries from their villages, and challenged the interests of New France in the Great Lakes region. In the late 1670s and early 1680s, fighters from the Five Nations did battle with a host of western native foes, including Miamis, Illinois, Ojibwas, Fox, and some bands of Shawnees, Wyandots, and Ottawas (other groups of those peoples remained at peace). In the same period, warriors from Iroquoia began to raid Conoys, Piscataways, Catawbas, and other Indian neighbors of Maryland, Virginia, and the Carolinas. As a result of victories in both the west and the south, captives flowed into Iroquoia in numbers unseen since the 1640s. Meanwhile, some western Indians—in particular several hundred Eries who had earlier sought refuge in the Ohio Valley—voluntarily relocated in Iroquoia to avoid forced adoption. Despite these gains, however, between 1679 and 1685, the population of the Five Nations apparently declined by several hundred. In the 1680s, just as in earlier decades, epidemics, mourning wars, and economic considerations produced a dangerous spiral of conflict in which the Five Nations could barely hold their own.

Meanwhile, in the Great Lakes region to the west of the Five Nations, Iroquois and French aims inevitably came into conflict. A series of embarrassments for New France led Governor Joseph-Antoine Le Febvre de La Barre to attempt an invasion of the Seneca country in 1684. At La Famine on Lake Ontario, a delegation of Onondagas, Cayugas, and Oneidas met his army, which was too short of supplies and too weakened by disease to travel any further, and La Barre had to come to terms. Subsequently, Iroquois raiders and traders, encouraged by the English of New York, redoubled their western offensives. By 1687, their activities provoked a successful French invasion of the Seneca country under the leadership of new Governor Jacques-René de Brisay de Denonville, who supervised the burning and looting of that nation's towns, which the inhabitants had abandoned on the army's approach.

In retaliation, for the next two years, Iroquois forces relentlessly pounded the settlements and outposts of New France. Meantime, the Glorious Revolution of 1688–1689 brought England openly into the conflict on the side of the Five Nations, as an adjunct to the struggle known in Europe as the War of the League of Augsburg. During what Anglo-Americans called "King William's War," however, the offensive contribution of New York and its fellow colonies was limited to ill-conceived attempts to invade New France in 1690 and 1691. By the middle of the 1690s, the lack of any serious English military support helped to turn the tide of battle against the Five Nations, as native foes to the north and west combined forces with New France against them. In January 1693, more than 600 French regulars, Canadian militia, and Indian allies surprised and mastered the three Mohawk towns. Three years later, an army of 2,000 French and natives burned the principal villages of the Onondagas and Oneidas. For the rest of the 1690s, the Iroquois took a severe pounding from western and northern foes. In retaliation, the Five Nations could mount only a few ineffective counterattacks.

Peace came to Euro-Americans, but not to Iroquois, with the Treaty of Ryswick in 1697. Because both New France and New York claimed the Five Nations as subjects, both alternatively insisted the Indians could neither be subsumed by the European pact nor negotiate as independent agents. The pounding the Five Nations took from Indian foes in the last years of the century eventually led Iroquois diplomats to come to terms with their French and Indian enemies in the 1700 and 1701 treaties of Montreal, in which they accepted the principle of neutrality between the European empires.

To one degree or another, that neutrality guided Iroquois interactions with their European and native neighbors throughout the first half of the eighteenth century. Six Nations diplomacy, however, continued to operate within a framework of localism and factional politics that seldom saw the league operate as a unified diplomatic entity. Anglophiles (particularly among the Mohawks) and francophiles (particularly among the Senecas) continued to cultivate unilateral ties to Albany or Quebec, and on occasion, groups of Iroquois warriors would join one or another imperial power as military allies. Substantial numbers from all Five Nations, for instance, joined ambitious English attempts to conquer Canada in 1709 and 1711 during the War of the Spanish Succession (Queen Anne's War, 1702–1713); many Mohawks enlisted with New Yorker William Johnson to battle the French in the War of the Austrian Succession (King George's War, 1744–1748); and fighters from most Iroquois nations sided with the English again in the Seven Years' War of 1754 to 1763. On the other side of the equation, many Iroquois seriously threatened war on the English during the first decade of the eighteenth century; throughout the period warriors from the Five Nations participated in French-encouraged raids on the Natives allied with the southern English colonies; and many Onondagas and Senecas fought beside the French in the Seven Years' War. But on the whole, even these occasional lapses often served to increase Iroquois bargaining power with the two opposing empires.

Despite the importance of diplomacy with Europeans, the Six Nations' wars in the first half of the eighteenth century—like those of the first three quarters of the seventeenth century—focused primarily on native, rather than Euro-American foes. That focus, however, shifted abruptly southward, away from the Great Lakes Indian allies of New France with whom peace had been established in 1701. Cherokees, Choctaws, and, most significantly, Catawbas provided the principal targets for long-distance raids and counter-raids that, in many respects, returned to the limited and largely symbolic mourning-war patterns of more than a century earlier. The brutal experiences of the seventeenth century had taught the Iroquois to abandon, for all intents and purposes, warfare as a means of achieving economic ends—apart, perhaps, from the limited benefits of arms and ammunition that French and occasionally English agents distributed to encourage the southern campaigns. The demographic demands that had fueled the seventeenth-century wars also eased somewhat, as the epidemiological situation reached a plateau and the peaceful absorption of refugee peoples fleeing the advancing frontiers of English Pennsylvania, Virginia, and the Carolinas reinforced an indigenous population that continued gradually to decline.

The outcome of the Seven Years' War, however, destroyed the delicately balanced system of neutrality between the empires that made both the southern campaigns and the continuation of Iroquois political independence possible. When English forces—aided by Iroquois allies—conquered Quebec and Montreal in 1761 and dispossessed the French of nearly all their North American possessions in the Treaty of Paris of 1763, the native diplomacy of balanced neutrality became irrelevant. The cluster of Indian uprisings against British hegemony that historians traditionally lump together as "Pontiac's War" of 1763 marked the beginning of a 50-year period in which the Six Nations, like all the surviving native groups of the Great Lakes region, fought bitterly among themselves and with first the British and then the newly independent Americans to preserve their lands and political autonomy.

In "Pontiac's War," only a portion of the Senecas actively took up arms; most other Iroquois saw their best chance in an ever-closer political alliance with British officialdom. That strategy—building on the now hoary tradition of Iroquois diplomatic dominance within the English Covenant Chain of alliances—served them well for a little over a decade until the cataclysm of the Revolutionary War, in which, with the exception of many Oneidas and Tuscaroras, the vast majority of the Six Nations took up arms on behalf of the British. No matter which side they chose, the Iroquois were able to cling to only a small fraction of their ancestral lands after the American victory, and the league split into groups divided by the border between Canada and the United States. In the wars in the Northwest Territory that followed the Revolution, the fragmented Six Nations would play only a minor role.

Daniel K. Richter

References

Richard Aquila, *The Iroquois Restoration: Iroquois Diplomacy on the Colonial Frontier, 1701–1754* (1983); Denys Delâge, *Le pays renversé: Amérindiens et européens en Amérique du nord-est, 1600–1664* (1985); Leroy V. Eid, "The Ojibwa-Iroquois War: The War the Five Nations Did Not Win," *Ethnohistory* 24 (1979):297–324; Michael K. Foster, et al., eds., *Extending the Rafters: Interdisciplinary Approaches to Iroquoian Studies* (1984); Barbara Graymont, *The Iroquois in the American Revolution* (1972).

Richard L. Haan, "The Problem of Iroquois Neutrality: Suggestions for Revision," *Ethnohistory* 27 (1980):317–330; Francis Jennings, *The Ambiguous Iroquois Empire: The Covenant Chain Confederation of Indian Tribes with English Colonies from its beginnings to the Lancaster Treaty of 1744* (1984); ———, *Empire of Fortune: Crowns, Colonies, and Tribes in the Seven Years War in America* (1988); ———, et al., eds., *The History and Culture of Iroquois Diplomacy: An Interdisciplinary Guide to the Treaties of the Six Nations and Their League* (1985).

Keith F. Otterbein, "Why the Iroquois Won: An Analysis of Iroquois Military Tactics," *Ethnohistory* 11 (1964):56–63; Daniel K. Richter and James H. Merrell, eds., *Beyond the Covenant Chain: The Iroquois and Their Neighbors in Indian North America, 1600–1800* (1987); Daniel K. Richter, *The Ordeal of the Longhouse: The Peoples of the Iroquois League in the Era of European Colonization* (1992).

Marian W. Smith, "American Indian Warfare," New York Academy of Sciences, *Transactions*, 2nd ser., 13 (1951):348–365; George S. Snyderman, "Behind the Tree of Peace: A Sociological Analysis of Iroquois Warfare," *Pennsylvania Archaeologist* 18, nos. 3–4 (1948):2–93; Bruce G. Trigger, *Natives and Newcomers: Canada's "Heroic Age" Reconsidered* (1985); Anthony F.C. Wallace, *The Death and Rebirth of the Seneca* (1969).

See also CAUGHNAWAGA; CAYUGA; COVENANT CHAIN; DECANISORA; DELAWARE; IROQUOIS TREATIES OF 1700 AND 1701; IROQUOIS WARS; JOHNSON, WILLIAM; MINGO; MOHAWK; ONEIDA; ONONDAGA; SENECA; TUSCARORA

Iroquois Treaties of 1700 and 1701 (with New York and New France)

Two sets of simultaneous treaty conferences at Montreal and Albany in September 1700 and in August 1701 ended the Native American phase of what Europeans called the War of the League of Augsburg and English colonials named King William's War. More broadly, the agreements, sometimes labeled "the Grand Settlement of 1701," terminated nearly 70 years of conflict between the Five Nations Iroquois (the Mohawks, Oneidas, Onondagas, Cayugas, and Senecas) and the Great Lakes Indian peoples allied to New France (chief among them the Miamis, Ottawas, Ojibwas, and Wyandots). The treaties also inaugurated the "play-off" system of eighteenth-century intercultural diplomacy, in which most Iroquois leaders pursued a policy of aggressive neutrality between the French and British empires.

From an Iroquois perspective, the War of the League of Augsburg merely brought the French and English colonies openly into a contest between the Five Nations and Indian groups of the St. Lawrence River valley and the Great Lakes region that had prevailed for nearly a century. Since 1687, native opponents of the Iroquois had been under the aggressive leadership of New France, which had organized invasions of Iroquoia in that year, in 1693, and in 1696. Beginning with England's entry into the War of the League of Augsburg in 1689, the Five Nations had been militarily allied with New York. Apart from unsuccessful invasions of Canada in 1690 and 1691, however, English support consisted primarily of arms and ammunition. Neither was a match for the overwhelming military force that New France and its native allies were able to field.

As a result, by the mid-1690s, the fortunes of war had turned dramatically against the Iroquois. Even after the 1697 Treaty of Ryswick declared a truce between the European powers, the Indian war continued as New York Governor Richard Coote, earl of Bellomont, attempted to prevent direct peace negotiations between the Five Nations and the French in order to strengthen English claims to hegemony over them. French Governor Louis-Hector de Callière encouraged his native allies to fight until the Iroquois defied the English ban. In spring 1700, as the Five Nations' military situation worsened, a minority of headmen who had long maintained ties to the French seized control of Iroquois councils, made peace at the Onondaga town with a visiting delegation from several western Indian villages, and dispatched emissaries to New France to capitulate to the governor.

Those actions promised to end the Five Nations' war with both the French and the Great Lakes nations. In the localistic and multi-headed world of Indian diplomacy, they were only a first step, for the majority of both Iroquois and western natives were not yet a part of the process. In the extended period of consensus-building that followed, the initiative passed away from headmen identified with the French to a group whose most prominent spokesman was the Onondaga Teganissorens (Decanisora). In a protracted set of informal negotiations, and in the public treaty conferences at Montreal and Albany in 1700 and 1701, their apparent objectives were to preserve their peoples' political independence by threading a middle course between the French and English empires, and to secure their economic survival through peaceful guarantees of hunting rights in the Great Lakes region.

In pursuance of these aims, the groups of headmen who attended the September 1700 treaty conferences at Montreal and Albany followed parallel agendas. At Montreal, Teganissorens convinced Callière to reopen to the Iroquois trade at French western posts (thus guaranteeing access to the Great Lakes trading network), and to pledge redress of future Iroquois grievances against the natives who controlled the western hunting territories. At Albany, meanwhile, the Iroquois delegation embraced Bellomont's suggestion that the Five Nations encourage Great Lakes Indians to trade on the Hudson, but also demanded that the English and French crowns settle their differences regarding claims to the lands and commerce of the west.

The primary function of the treaties of the next August was to secure further guarantees from the two European colonial powers and to build a native consensus in favor of the arrangements shaped in 1700. In the interim, actions by both colonial governments greatly strengthened the political position of the Teganissorens faction: Bellomont pushed plans to build forts in the Five Nations and to bypass Iroquois mediators in the Great Lakes trade, while Callière's representatives forcibly rounded up captives who preferred to stay with their Iroquois adoptive families and encouraged Great Lakes Indians to relocate from Michilimackinac to Detroit, where they threatened to exclude the Iroquois from the western hunting territories.

Against this background occurred the August 1701 councils at Montreal and Albany. On the banks of the St. Lawrence, 38 native leaders from the Five Nations and headmen of the 700 to 800 Indian allies of the French present—Ottawas, Wyandots, Miamis, Sauks, Potawatomis, Fox, Mascoutens, Menominees, Ojibwas, Winnebagos, Nipissings, and Algonquins, as well as Eastern and Western Abenakis and Iroquois from Canadian mission villages—affixed their marks to a multi-party treaty of peace. In separate bilateral proceedings, the Iroquois confirmed their agreements with Callière regarding access to Great Lakes hunting lands and French western trading posts and, in exchange, confirmed a prior capitulation to the governor's demand of neutrality in future imperial wars.

The Iroquois headmen who almost simultaneously negotiated at Albany never explicitly mentioned the neutrality pledged at Montreal, but a close listener would have detected significant gaps in their discussions of military obligations to the English. Such subtleties were lost, however, in light of a surprise announcement that the Five Nations intended to deed to the English crown a vast hunting territory stretching roughly from present-day Erie, Pennsylvania, to Chicago, to Michilimackinac. The purpose does not seem to have been the transfer of literal ownership of the land, to which the Iroquois lacked a clear title. To the contrary, the area was controlled by their victorious Indian and French enemies; it was the same region to which the Montreal treaty guaranteed them access. And those French guarantees were the keys to the transaction at Albany. The Five Nations' leaders—who futilely insisted New York Indian Affairs Secretary Robert Livingston personally deliver the document to England—expected the king to use the deed in European negotiations over boundaries in North America, and thus deny the French the suzerainty that the Montreal treaties seemed to acknowledge. Although the English failed to follow through, such a strategy of playing one European power against the other became a recurrent theme in eighteenth-century intercultural diplomacy, and helped to preserve Iroquois economic and political independence for more than half a century.

Daniel K. Richter

References

Richard Aquila, *The Iroquois Restoration: Iroquois Diplomacy on the Colonial Frontier, 1701–1754* (1983); Bacqueville de la Potherie, [Claude Charles Le Roy], *Histoire de l'Amerique Septentrionale,* Vol. 4 (1722); Francis Jennings, *The Ambiguous Iroquois Empire: The Covenant Chain Confederation of Indian Tribes with English Colonies from its beginnings to the Lancaster Treaty of 1744* (1984).

Daniel K. Richter, *The Ordeal of the Longhouse: The Peoples of the Iroquois League in the Era of European Colonization* (1992); Anthony F.C. Wallace, "Origins of Iroquois Neutrality: The Grand Settlement of 1701," *Pennsylvania History,* 24 (1957):223–235.

See also DECANISORA; IROQUOIS, IROQUOIS WARS

Iroquois Wars (1641–1701)

The Five Nations Iroquois in the last half of the seventeenth century engaged in a series of wars against the French and their Indian allies. During these so-called "Beaver Wars," the Iroquois hemmed in New France, spectacularly destroyed entire Indian tribes, ground other tribes into submission after long periods of confrontation, and generally earned a reputation among historians as the "Romans" of the eastern woodlands. By the late 1680s, however, Iroquoia itself was under intense attack and the Five Nations were reeling from the combined onslaughts of several French armies, numerous Indian small-scale raiding parties, and combinations of what can only be described as Indian armies. With relief, the Iroquois accepted a treaty with France in 1701 that allowed them the respite of neutrality.

Because the wars of the Iroquois have so many participants with so many conflicting motives, and because of a paucity of historical documentation in some areas, many conflicting historiographical views have evolved. The general English and American historiography tends toward a belief in a Five Nations Iroquoian empire built on conquest. The general French view emphasizes heroic defenses of New France and devastating French attacks on Iroquoia itself as the key part of the story. French Canadian historians emphasize the day-by-day centrality of the generally anonymous *habitants,* voyageurs, and *coureurs de bois.* Indian oral tradition of many tribes portray Indians as the main actors. Today's social historians stress the lethalness of epidemics that devastated parts of the Iroquois Confederacy. What is incontrovertibly certain is, by 1700, the Five Nations were no larger in influence and territory than they were in 1640. Also incontrovertibly, during that entire time, the Five Nations Iroquois had shown a strategic expertise, a wide variety of tactical maneuvers on numerous battlefields, and unfailingly heroic actions by their soldiers.

By 1641, and after a number of years of being on the defensive, the Five Nations Iroquois acquired guns from the Dutch and increased pressure on gun-poor Iroquoian and Algonquian tribes north of Lake Ontario to enter into alliance with the Five Nations Iroquois to unify control over the fur trade. The Five Nations realized early the importance of being the middlemen, the brokers, between the interior tribes and the Europeans. In particular, they attacked the traditional Iroquoian traders of the area, the Hurons, on the St. Lawrence and Ottawa Rivers. Follow-up attacks on Huronia south of Georgian Bay in 1648 and 1649, and the "loathsome fever" that struck the following winter, combined to destroy completely the power of the Hurons, whose people fled in every direction. Some moved to Quebec to form the Lorette community; captive Hurons set up the separate village of Gandougarae in Seneca territory; and others fled to areas in Georgian Bay, or even to Chequamegon Bay in western Lake Superior. More than any other event in the Beaver Wars, the suddenness and completeness of Huronia's collapse electrified the entire Northeast and gave the Five Nations Iroquois military apparatus its enduring juggernaut image. Other tribes that refused to join the Iroquoian new order, such as the Tionontati (Tobacco or Petun nation), the Neutral Confederacy, and the Nipissing, were driven from Ontario almost as easily. The Iroquois, in the winter of 1651–1652, moved south and overwhelmed a group known only as the Atrakwaeronons. By 1656, another Iroquoian nation, the Erie, or Cat nation, of the southeast corner of Lake Erie, completely disappeared after well-executed, large-scale Five Nations attacks overcame spirited resistance. Many survivors from these various defeated groups accepted the Five Nations' option to join them. The Iroquois then aggressively traveled 600–800 miles to harry further the remnants of the Hurons and their allies who would not accept Five Nations leadership.

Nevertheless, attacks against pro-French tribes in the late 1650s failed to win decisively in the Ohio and Illinois countries or in the western Great Lakes waterways. Indeed, around 1662, the Iroquois received a major setback at "Iroquois Point" on Lake Superior. In this battle, the very large backwoods tribe (or group of tribelets) known as the Ojibwa, or Chippewa, revealed for the first time why in the next century they would be able to expand in three directions against three different enemies. The Iroquois, in short, found the French did not have to succumb because they had numerous Indians ready to replace the Hurons as middlemen to tribes even farther in the interior of the continent. Shortly afterwards, the Iroquois attacked both an old ally of the Hurons, the well-armed Susquehannocks, or Andastes, of the lower Susquehanna Valley, as well as the Mahicans (and their local allies) of the Hudson River area of New York, and the Sokokis of the upper Connecticut Valley. In time the Iroquois prevailed, but in all three cases it took decades and only after punishing warfare. In 1680, the Iroquois won some easy early victories over the Illinois Indians, but offensives into that region in 1684 against Fort St. Louis and 1687 south of Chicago did not achieve much. The Illinois had acquired guns and allies.

The tide had turned. The Algonquin and French armies now began to counterattack against Iroquoia. In 1687 the French destroyed four Seneca villages. The outbreak of King William's War in 1689 prevented an Iroquois-French truce. Even though the Iroquois desperately attacked New France and caused great losses, French armies began to pound Iroquoia. In 1693, the French destroyed the Mohawk villages and captured hundreds, and in 1696, the French burned the village of Onondaga and its crops. The Missisauga Ojibwa and their allies at the same time were doing more than attacking buildings and crops: they began to move east and south into the eastern Lake Ontario area devastated in the opening decades of the Beaver Wars. Traditional oral accounts describe the small skirmishes and the large decisive clashes that accompanied this Algonquin seizure of lands so recently won by Five Nations Iroquois armies. Indian casualties on both sides were quite high.

The physical displacement of the Iroquois by their Algonquin enemies, French control of the Niagara portage, and the large glut of furs on the world market caused by the opening of the trade routes from the west illustrate how little in control of the Great Lakes the Iroquois were by the end of the century. With great relief, the Iroquois signed a 1701 treaty with France which, by allowing them to follow a neutrality policy in the French-English struggles, gave the Five Nations the illusory hope that—through diplomacy—they would finally achieve the hegemony not won by 60 years of war. Diplomatic maneuvering, in fact, succeeded to the degree that the Five Nations weathered the defeats of the seventeenth century and continued to be treated by the English as important spokespersons for all Indians.

Leroy V. Eid

References

Robert A. Goldstein, *French-Iroquois Diplomatic and Military Relations, 1609–1701* (1969); George T. Hunt, *The Wars of the Iroquois: A Study in Intertribal Trade Relations* (1940); Francis Jennings, *The Ambiguous Iroquois Empire: The Covenant Chain Confederation of Indian Tribes with English Colonies from its beginnings to the Lancaster Treaty of 1744* (1984); Helen H. Tanner, ed., *Atlas of Great Lakes Indian History* (1987); Bruce Trigger, ed., *Handbook of North American Indians: Vol. 15, Northeast* (1978).

See also HURON; IROQUOIS; IROQUOIS TREATIES OF 1700 AND 1701; MOHAWK-MAHICAN WAR; SENECA, FRENCH ATTACK ON; SUSQUEHANNOCK

Isle-aux-Noix

Isle-aux-Noix was one of the forts in the series along the Richelieu River-Lake Champlain-Lake George water route designed to guard the approach to Montreal, 25 miles distant. Located where the Richelieu exits north of Lake Champlain, the island is approximately 1,475 meters long by 290 meters wide. It is less than 200 meters from the eastern bank of the river, and less than 300 meters from the western bank.

Had the island been properly fortified and garrisoned by the French-Canadians, it would have represented a threat to a British advance to attack Montreal via the waterway. During the summer 1759 campaign of the French and Indian War, Brigadier François-Charles de Bourlamaque, with three battalions, fell back to the Isle-aux-Noix from Fort Ticonderoga, and there began the difficult work of erecting a palisade without enough log cutters or carpenters to do the work properly. Although he had some 100 cannon on the island, Bourlamaque must have taken most of the artillery with him on his transfer, for his replacement, Colonel Louis-Antoine de Bougainville, complained of having only ten or 12 poor pieces with which to defend his command.

In August 1760, the British, under Brigadier General William Haviland, outflanked the barriers running from each side of the island to the shore, began to shell the French from the rear, forcing their flotilla of small boats to scatter and ground, thus destroying the French transport. Seeing that further resistance was futile, Bougainville and his 1,300 men quietly slipped away from the island, wading through the swamps during the night of 27 August and eventually returning to Montreal. Left behind was a contingent of 40 men, mostly wounded, who kept up sporadic fire until they surrendered the next afternoon according to their commander's instructions.

Mary Kimbrough

References

Edward P. Hamilton, ed. and trans., *Adventures in the Wilderness: The American Journals of Louis-Antoine de Bougainville 1756–1760* (1964); René de Kerallain, *La Jeunesse de Bougainville et la guerre de Sept Ans* (1896); "Lettres de M. de Bourlamaque au maréchal de Lévis," ed. by H.R. Casgrain; Francis Parkman, *Montcalm and Wolfe,* 2 vols. (1884).

See also BOUGAINVILLE, LOUIS-ANTOINE DE; BOURLAMAQUE, FRANÇOIS-CHARLES DE; LAKE CHAMPLAIN; MONTREAL

J

Fort James (New York; also known as Fort Amsterdam, Fort George at the Battery)
The first structure on the Fort James site was built in 1626; there have since been many rebuilds and subsequent name changes. The first building named Fort James was a 1664 rebuild of Fort George at the Battery. The fort was built to protect the surrounding city of New York. By 1665, the stone and earthwork structures, including barracks, chapel, and officer housing, had fallen into disrepair. The surrounding palisades were destroyed by the wild hogs that ran loose through the city. The fort was captured by the British under the command of Mathias Nicolls in 1665. To refortify the structure, Nicolls, then governor of New York, was forced to ask the citizens to finance the repairs.

A special city tax was levied in 1670 to pay for the repairs, but the tax became the symbolic focus of the unrest between the townsmen and city merchants. The townsmen bore the brunt of the tax, yet the fort was actually too distant to serve as real protection for any except the merchants (who paid little of the repair costs). The townsmen also felt the fort's garrison to be a potential threat to their civil liberties.

In 1673, while the fort remained in disrepair, Dutch troops attacked it. It was an opportune moment for an assault; Governor Frances Lovelace was away and the fort was under the command of Captain John Manning, who was recuperating from a serious injury. The small British force, about 60 men, was overwhelmed by the Dutch assault. When the Dutch landed 600 men, Manning was forced to surrender and abandon the fort.

Ten years later, in 1683, Fort James was the site for New York's first legislative assembly.

Elizabeth Gossman

References
Michael Kammen, *Colonial New York: A History* (1975); Robert C. Ritchie, *The Duke's Province: A Study of New York Politics and Society, 1664–1691* (1977); Robert B. Roberts, *New York Forts in the Revolution* (1980).

Fort James (Virginia)
Fort James was the first English-built fort in Virginia. Situated on a marshy peninsula some 45 miles up the James River from its mouth at the Chesapeake Bay, Fort James (Jamestown) was constructed in 1607 as the first permanent English settlement in America.

The initial fortification consisted of a half-moon structure made of tree limbs. It soon became apparent that a stronger fort was necessary, and the colonists built a triangular palisade, consisting of logs placed vertically in the ground, reaching a height of about 14 feet. Completed about one month after the landing, the fort had a 420-foot base along the James River, with its two other sides meeting 300 feet inland. There was a bulwark at each corner, on each of which the colonists mounted several cannon, probably demi-culverins firing a nine-pound ball. In 1610, there were a reported 24 pieces of heavy ordnance in the fort.

The main entrance to the fort stood in the wall facing the river, and there were gates in each corner, in front of which stood a cannon. Within the fort, the colonists hastily threw up a storehouse, church, and living quarters. Outside the wall, adjacent to the west bulwark, the colonists cleared a parade ground, where they practiced military exercises. In 1611, a munition house, a powder house, fish house, and stable were added to the fort's interior.

During the winter of 1609–1610, Indian warriors under chief Powhatan sealed off the fort, and its inhabitants suffered terribly from disease and hunger. More than half of the 200 colonists died before the siege ended in May 1610. Only the timely arrival of a relief expedition in June prevented the colonists from abandoning their settlement.

But the English remained at Jamestown, and as they eventually constructed houses outside the fort's walls, the triangular palisade became the inner stronghold of an expanded town. As settlement spread along the James River, Jamestown declined in importance, but remained capital of the Virginia colony throughout most of the seventeenth century. In 1616, the garrison at Jamestown comprised 50 men, most of them farmers, but the fort itself seems to have fallen into disuse by the 1620s. During the 1622 Indian attack, Jamestown inhabitants were forewarned and may have escaped slaughter by taking refuge inside the fort's walls.

In 1652, Governor William Berkeley fortified Jamestown against an expedition of parliamentary forces from England, an indication the fort itself was no longer usable. During the Anglo-Dutch War of 1664, Berkeley again began to fortify Jamestown, but the work was transferred to Old Point Comfort to provide better defense for the lower James River. When the capital of the colony moved to nearby Williamsburg in 1692, Jamestown had been a backwater for a number of years, its fort long abandoned.

Thomas Costa

References

Warren Billings, John Selby, and Thad Tate, *Colonial Virginia: A History* (1986).

See also JAMESTOWN

Jamestown

On 13 May 1607, representatives of the Virginia Company of London, led by Christopher Newport and Edward Maria Wingfield, established a settlement on a small peninsula that jutted out of the northern bank of the James River in tidewater Virginia. In deference to their king, the adventurers named the site Jamestown. Surrounded by marshes, brackish water, and hostile Indians, Jamestown afforded its colonists few strategic advantages. After early encounters with the nearby Paspehegh tribe, the settlers erected a triangular palisaded fort with

"three Bulwarkes at every corner like a halfe moone." Gripped by incessant quarreling among the leadership, a devastating fire, and an omnipresent shortage of competent labor, the colony faced almost certain failure when John Smith assumed its leadership in 1608. Smith solved the labor problem and reinforced the community's defenses by placing Jamestown under quasi-military rule. Sluggish resupply efforts and rumors of a reorganization by the Virginia Company, however, placed the colony in disarray by the time Smith was injured in a gunpowder explosion that forced his return to England in October 1609.

Smith's departure placed the already unstable colony in a precarious position. The winter of 1609–1610, known infamously as the "starving time," nearly bested the settlers. But resupply efforts in the spring of 1610 and strict regulation under the *Lawes Divine, Morall, and Martiall* (1611), brought a measure of stability to the settlement. Between 1611 and 1613, John Rolfe's experiments with tobacco gave the settlers a cash crop to exploit; however, the discovery of the staple did not bring riches to the Virginia Company of London. In a desperate attempt to revive the colony's fortunes, the company reorganized in 1618 under the "Grand Charter," which allowed Virginians to elect a general assembly and instituted the "headright" system that sought to attract new settlers. Following the passage of the Grand Charter, Jamestown became the site of the first general assembly in British North America in 1619. That year also marked the appearance of a Dutch man-of-war, which deposited a cargo of 20 Africans.

From 1607 to 1699, Jamestown served as the seat of government for the Virginia Colony. During that time, Jamestown survived three severe fires, one of which was set by Virginians in 1676 during Bacon's Rebellion; several company and royal reorganizations; five law revisals; the English civil war; Indian and Dutch raids; and 40 leadership changes.

Despite rigorous efforts on the part of Virginia's governors, especially Samuel Argall (1617–1619), Sir John Harvey (1630–1635), and Sir William Berkeley (1642–1652, 1660–1677), Jamestown failed to become a thriving enterprise. After 1699, Jamestown became a private farm, its bucolic existence interrupted only briefly in the Revolutionary War when American and French commanders used it for a landing base for supplies and troops prior to the siege of Yorktown.

Although Jamestown failed to become a thriving polity, its measured success gave the English a toehold in the New World. From those fragile beginnings, the British launched their colonial empire in North America.

Mark F. Fernandez

See also BACON'S REBELLION; BERKELEY, WILLIAM; FORT JAMES (VIRGINIA); VIRGINIA

Jemison, Mary (1742 or 1743–1833)

Mary Jemison, daughter of Thomas Jemison and Jane Erwin, a Protestant couple of Scottish-Irish background, was born in 1742 or 1743 on shipboard en route to colonial Pennsylvania from Ireland. On 5 April 1758, the Jemison family and visiting friends were attacked by Shawnee and French forces on their farm in western Pennsylvania during the Seven Years' War. Only she and the friends' young boy were spared. The Shawnee carried her down the Ohio River to Fort Duquesne (Fort Pitt) where she was given to two Seneca women. In their Seneca camp near the Sciota River, she became their sister by means of a ritual adoption.

In 1760, she married Sheninjee, a Delaware. Her first child died, but Thomas, her second, lived. She returned with her sisters and brother to Genishau, a large Seneca town on the Genesee River, traveling 600 miles through Ohio and into west-central New York. Shenenjee died that year. Within a year of her arrival in Seneca country (c. 1762–1763), she married Hiokatoo, a Seneca warrior with whom she had six children.

During the Revolution, Jemison saw the War for Independence from the Seneca side of the frontier, noting its impact as John Sullivan's expedition came through Iroquois country burning corn fields and towns in reprisal for British and Iroquois raids along the Pennsylvania and New York frontiers.

Following the Revolution at the Treaty of Big Tree in Geneseo, 15 September 1797, through negotiations and with the help of her brother, Kau-jises-tau-ge-au (Black Coals), Jemison was given the Gardow Tract, which consisted of 17,927 acres of prime river property along the Genesee near present-day Castile. Jemison lived on the Gardow Flats until, between being cheated and selling her land, she moved with her daughters to the Indian community at Buffalo Creek in the mid-1820s. She died there in 1833 at the age of 90.

Known as "the White Woman of the Genesee," Jemison's story, as written by Dr. James E. Seaver in *A Narrative of the Life of Mrs. Mary Jemison* (1824), became one of the most popular captivity narratives in American history going into more than 20 editions in its first 100 years. Jemison was one of a number of captives who chose not to return to white society. Although other captives stayed with Indians, Jemison became a popular folk heroine. Seneca and Iroquois also claim her, seeing her life as a symbol of Iroquois resilience.

June Namias

References

Dawn Lander Gherman, "From Parlour to Tepee: The White Squaw on the American Frontier," Ph.D. Dissertation, University of Massachusetts (1975); June Namias, *White Captives: Gender and Ethnicity on the American Frontier* (1993); Daniel K. Richter, *The Ordeal of the Longhouse: The Peoples of the Iroquois League in the Era of European Colonization* (1992); James E. Seaver, *A Narrative of the Life of Mary Jemison: The White Woman of the Genesee*, ed. by Rev. Charles Delamater Vail (1925); ———, *A Narrative of the Life of Mrs. Mary Jemison*, ed. by June Namias (1992); Anthony F.C. Wallace, *The Death and Rebirth of the Seneca* (1972); Susan Walsh, "'With Them Was My Home': Native American Autobiography and *A Narrative of the Life of Mrs. Mary Jemison*," *American Quarterly* 64 (1992):49–70.

See also CAPTIVITY NARRATIVES; INDIAN WARFARE, CAPTIVITY

Jesuits

The Society of Jesus was founded in Paris in 1534 by Ignatius Loyola, a Spanish soldier who experienced a profound religious conversion and devoted his life to converting Protestants and pagans. Authorized by Pope Paul III in 1540, the Jesuits, as they became known, embarked on worldwide missionary work. They arrived in Acadia (Nova Scotia) in 1611 to work briefly among the Micmacs, and in Canada (Quebec) in 1625 to work among Algonkian nomadic hunting bands and sedentary agricultural Hurons near Georgian Bay. In Maryland, a few English Jesuits arrived in 1633, acquired land from a local chieftain, but saw their mission closed by Cromwellian forces in 1644.

In 1635, they organized a college in Quebec, the oldest institution of higher learning on the continent. Two years later, they organized the first Indian reserve at Sillery with the intention of attracting nomadic hunting bands to take up sedentary agricultural parish life in the proximity of French colonists who could serve as models of European husbandry and industry. This assimilationist policy earned them generous land grants and royal subsidies, but their political activities brought stern warnings from Versailles to curb their influence. In 1639, the Jesuits reorganized their Huron mission on the Paraguayan model, with a central fortified headquarters at Sainte-Marie from which pairs of evangelical workers visited the missions in the surrounding villages. The mission disappeared when the Mohawks and Senecas dispersed the Huron in 1649–1650.

The French Jesuits remained the chief missionaries to the Indians in the seventeenth century, sending out 174 religious aided by scores of voluntary workers called *donnés,* salaried servants, soldiers, and slaves. They operated mission stations at Tadoussac for the Saguenay region, on Cape Breton and Ile Mingan, at Ville-Marie until 1657, six missions among the Five Nations Iroquois, and itinerant missions to the Abenakis and Great Lakes tribes. Several suffered martyrdom: six priests at the hands of the Iroquois, one among the Algonkians, also one brother and one *donné.* Two priests had their hands mutilated and one was assassinated at James Bay.

The eighteenth century saw further expansion of missions into the Illinois and Mississippi regions, and among the Abenakis, Sioux, and Cree. But recruits and financial support from France declined in the competition with the Oriental missions. Among the French colonists they continued to offer vocational and theological training, to serve as spiritual directors to women's religious communities, and to direct five Indian "reserves"—one for the Hurons near Quebec, two for the Abenakis south of Trois Rivières, and two for the Iroquois along the St. Lawrence River above Montreal. Income from their seigneurial estates in the colony made them less dependent on royal subsidies and metropolitan bequests.

Their evangelical labors were much publicized, earning them financial backing, but also attracting criticism. The missionaries in the field compiled annual reports of their activities which were edited by the superior at Quebec, then sent on to the provincial in Paris. From 1632 to 1672, when suppressed by Louis XIV, these reports were published as *Relations des Jésuites* by Sebastien Cramoisy. In the eighteenth century, some letters from the missions of New France appeared in *Lettres édifiantes et curieuses* published in Paris from 1702–1776.

Cornelius J. Jaenen

References

Henry Warner Bowden, *American Indians and Christian Missions* (1981); John Webster Grant, *Moon of Wintertime: Missionaries and the Indians of Canada in Encounter since 1534* (1984); Cornelius J. Jaenen, *The Role of the Church in New France* (1976); J.H. Kennedy, *Jesuit and Savage in New France* (1950); Reuben G. Thwaites, ed., *The Jesuit Relations and Allied Documents: Travels and Explorations of the Jesuit Missionaries in New France, 1610–1791,* 73 vols. (1896–1901).

See also CAUGHNAWAGA

Fort Johns (New Jersey; also known as Fort Shapanack)

Constructed in 1756 to provide a sanctuary for settlers in the immediate area, Ft. Johns was located in Walpack Township, Sussex, on an elevation overlooking the Delaware River. The fort consisted of a palisaded structure 120 feet square with 15-foot-square bastions at three of its angles. The fourth angle incorporated a 15- by 20-foot log cabin. The palisades enclosed a wooden blockhouse and stone building. It was designed to protect against hostile encroachments at the beginning of the French and Indian War and housed 100 soldiers. It was used as a military fort until the end of the American Revolution.

David L. Whitesell

Fort Johnson (New York; also known as Mount Johnson)

In 1748, construction began on Sir William Johnson's residence: Mount Johnson. The site was located on the Mohawk River about three miles west of Amsterdam. The structure was made of fieldstone, had two stories, an attic, portholes, and a lead roof. It was not occupied until 1750, and continued to be known as Mount Johnson until it was palisaded in 1755.

A stockade and cannon were added in 1756 in an effort to protect against French invasion of the area, and to aid Governor William Shirley's defense of the Sacandaga River.

From 1754 to 1760, many important Indian councils were held at Fort Johnson. These councils were a British attempt to garner favor and support of the many Indian nations, including the Mohawk, Seneca, Cayuga, and Onondaga. In 1758, two blockhouses, able to hold 40 men, were built at either end of the site. The fort also had a heavy swinging gate that was plated in iron; a one-story covered walkway ran along the western wall and was protected by crossfire from the other blockhouses. Another smaller blockhouse was built and served mostly as a lookout post.

Sir William lived on the site until 1763, when he moved to the newly constructed Johnson Hall on the western border of Johnstown, a village he founded; he left Fort Johnson to his son, John Johnson. The fort was confiscated and stripped during the Revolutionary War by patriots, who used the lead and iron for bullets.

Elizabeth Gossman

References

T. Wood Clarke, *The Bloody Mohawk* (1968); James Thomas Flexner, *Mohawk Baronet: Sir William Johnson of New York* (1959).

See also JOHNSON, WILLIAM

Fort Johnson (South Carolina)

Fort Johnson, or Johnson's fort, stood at Windmill Point on James Island overlooking the southeastern side of Charles Town harbor, two miles below the town. It was erected in 1708, during the administration of proprietary governor Sir Nathaniel Johnson (1703–1709), as a response to a combined French and Spanish invasion two years earlier. Constructed of mud, pine saplings, and oyster shells, it was triangular in shape, with three bastions or demi-bastions and a lower battery of heavy cannons along the waterfront. Its inland defenses included a gate protected by a ravelin, a dry moat with palisades implanted in the bottom, two drawbridges, and a glacis. The fort was armed with approximately 30 cannons. A dozen or more 24-, 18-, and 12-pound guns were mounted in platforms in the lower battery, while smaller six- and nine-pound pieces were positioned throughout the upper works.

Fort Johnson was originally to be garrisoned by a commander, a sergeant, and a guard of six men. In times of distress, this force was to be augmented by the militia of James Island. Eventually, barracks were constructed to house 50 men, though the garrison was never that large. Except in wartime, the fort seems to have been manned by a half dozen men or less, the captain or commander, a gunner, and the quarter-gunners. After 1730, the commander of the fort held a royal commission.

In a state of disrepair almost from the beginning, by mid-century Fort Johnson was deemed obsolete and badly situated by military engineers Peter Henry Bruce and William De Brahm, and considered a tremendous, unnecessary drain on the provincial treasury by governor James Glen. However, the Commons House clung tenaciously to the little fort, looking upon it "as the Key to Charles-town, our Metropolis." Ultimately, the assembly prevailed. Repairs began in earnest after the complete devastation of Charles Town and its fortifications by the hurricane of 1752 and with the commencement of the French and Indian War four years later. However, by war's end, the fort was again in an "indifferent" state of defense. As one contemporary declared "it was not looked upon as a place of defence, but to stop infected shipping to preserve [the] health of the inhabitants."

Never attacked by an enemy during the colonial period, Fort Johnson fought a losing battle against wind and waves (it was devastated by hurricanes in 1713, 1728, and 1752), and the neglect of its commanders and the colonial government. The only shots fired by its cannon were as signals to shipping, in celebration and commemoration of state and public events, and on one occasion at a customs cutter and royal naval vessel.

James Hill

References

Larry E. Ivers, *Colonial Forts of South Carolina 1670–1775* (1970); H. Roy Merrens, ed., *The Colonial South Carolina Scene: Contemporary Views 1697–1774* (1977); Harry S. Mustard, "On the Building of Fort Johnson," *South Carolina Historical Magazine,* 64 (1963):129–135; Robert M. Weir, *Colonial South Carolina: A History* (1983).

See also DE BRAHM, WILLIAM

Johnson, Sir William (1715–1774)

Both to the Iroquois peoples of the Mohawk River valley and to his political rivals and economic competitors in colonial New York, William Johnson more than fulfilled the nickname given to him by the Iroquois: Warraghiyagey, "He Who Does Big Business." Born in County Meath, Ireland, in 1715, at the age of 23 he emigrated in search of greater opportunity to the British North American colony of New York. He undertook this journey across the Atlantic at the invitation of his uncle, Peter Warren.

As a British naval captain stationed in North America, Warren had profited handsomely from prizes captured in the Anglo-French wars; to this fortune he added the dowry brought by his marriage to a member of New York's wealthy DeLancey family. Anxious to expand his role as a part of the colonial landed aristocracy, he purchased 14,000 acres in western New York at the confluence of the Schoharie and Mohawk Rivers. Such an estate demanded the attention of a trustworthy manager, which in the eighteenth century meant a member of one's family. Accordingly, Warren invited his maternal nephew, William Johnson, to join him in America. Before coming across the Atlantic, Johnson was instructed to recruit several farming families who could aid him in the settlement of the district, which would become known as Warrenbush.

Soon after his arrival, the ambitious newcomer lost no time in establishing his own role in the economic life of the New York frontier. By 1739, he had purchased land on the north side of the Mohawk River and opened a small trading house for selling provisions to the local farmers and trade goods to the Indians.

Within five years after his arrival, not only had he successfully settled tenants on his uncle's lands, but he also expanded his own holdings. Sales of grains from his farms to the West India markets yielded sufficient profit for him to build the first of several substantial stone houses.

In his role as landed squire, he included service as a patron of the Church of England. With his support, an Anglican chapel was built near Fort Hunter. From this location, not only could the needs of the area farmers be served, but also those of interested Mohawks. Johnson encouraged Anglican missionary activities and sponsored several Mohawks who showed educational promise; the young Joseph Brant was so favored. Rather latitudinarian in his outlook,

William Johnson was even willing to tolerate clergy other than those of the Church of England, as long as they did not meddle excessively in frontier politics.

While he secured his membership in the colonial planter gentry, Johnson did not neglect the political side of his life. As the approximate colonial equivalent of an English country squire, he fulfilled the role of military leader by assuming command of a local militia unit, manned by tenants from both his own and his uncle's estates. Throughout British North America, membership and participation in the militia was an important ingredient in the mixture necessary for success. Many young gentlemen manqué turned militia service into political, social, and economic advantage. A leadership role in the militia gained the attention of one's peers, as well as one's superiors; demonstrated political loyalty to crown and colony; and, often as not in the days of the Anglo-French wars, it could be translated into grants of land as a reward from grateful monarchs or colonial governors and assemblies.

As if his roles as planter/developer and militia officer were insufficient to keep him busy, William Johnson added to his list of official responsibilities a commission from Governor George Clinton as colonel of the Six Nations of Indians. Through his expanding trading activities, Johnson had won the allegiance of the powerful Iroquois peoples. The occasion for this appointment took place in August 1746 as Clinton sought to meet the Indians in conference at Albany. With an Anglo-French war looming once more, the governor wished to improve the colony's western defenses and cement the friendship of the Six Nations by recruiting Iroquois auxiliaries. William Johnson reportedly surprised the entire official gathering by entering the meeting as a painted Mohawk war chief leading a party of warriors.

Johnson's symbolic regalia no doubt indicated his willingness not only to recruit the Mohawks for service with the crown, but also his intention to take up Indian affairs as an ongoing responsibility. His new office would work to his advantage by benefiting his Indian trading operations.

From the financial perspective, however, it might be observed that in his capacities as landed aristocrat, militia officer, church patron, and Indian official, he was likely to need a substantial amount of credit. By 1748, he had advanced funds, for various reasons, amounting to £7,000, which was a small fortune for the time whether reckoned in New York currency or sterling.

Despite the fiscal and physical burdens of carrying so many offices, William Johnson continued all his activities, even expanding his military duties to include command of all the militia drawn from the entire Mohawk Valley area. As a result, he was given Governor Clinton's commission as colonel of the Second battalion of the western district in the Albany County militia. Likewise, through the governor's influence, he was appointed to the privy council of New York; he was named surveyor of the woods for the colony; and after the eruption of yet another war in 1754, the crown appointed him superintendent of the British northern Indian department and he received commission as major general of the Crown Point expedition. On that military undertaking Johnson was wounded, forcing him to turn over the active command to General Phineas Lyman, of Connecticut who actually carried the day.

Despite Johnson's absence from the field, he later reported the battle in official correspondence as if he had commanded and won. Since Crown Point was the only British victory in America during 1756, Johnson parleyed his success into a monetary reward of £5,000 and an Ulster baronetcy. Three years later, Johnson added to his military luster by intercepting a French relief column headed toward Fort Niagara. The British capture of this French unit sealed Niagara's fate and once more piled glory on the head of Sir William Johnson.

In the same year that he became the hero of Niagara, William Johnson took two other important steps. First, he was completing the handsome stone dwelling which would become known as Johnson Hall; then he brought to his new estate house an Iroquois companion named Molly Brant. Because of her influential clan connections, she would be extremely helpful to Johnson in maintaining the support of the Mohawks and other members of the Iroquois confederation. Molly Brant's influence was such that no frontier diplomat dared ignore her. William Johnson's understanding of Iroquois politics had taught him such a marriage alliance would be of unequaled assistance.

Even if the close of the war with France reduced Johnson's military responsibilities, it did not lessen his concern for Indian affairs. His representatives among the western tribes notified him that Indian peoples living near Lake Erie were unhappy about the French withdrawal and concerned about new British policies involving land and trade. Although official warfare against the French had ceased, Superintendent Johnson's administrative and organizational skills would be tested in 1763 and 1764. By spring 1763, there was an expanding Indian war being carried out by the Ohio Indian peoples against the remaining British posts in the west. Through the adroit use of forest diplomacy, Johnson persuaded the Iroquois that the Ottawas under Pontiac and the other members of the western Indian confederation were fighting the wrong war at the wrong time against the wrong enemy. Johnson's advice seemed doubly prophetic when the efforts of the western tribes collapsed in 1764.

As Sir William Johnson clearly understood, two of the issues which had precipitated the western Indian war were land boundaries and the scarcity of trade goods. About the latter, Johnson probably could make some difference in restoring trading activity once the dislocations of war had ceased. The matter of fixed boundaries for tribal lands, however, would require extensive diplomacy. In London, royal officials had proposed an official dividing line running along the watershed of the Appalachians, thus separating the settled colonists east of that line from the Indian country to the west. No such simplistic solution, however, was available.

An imperial administrator, land speculator, and ally of the Iroquois, William Johnson both clearly perceived and, to some extent, personified the forces at work on the frontier. Instead of the somewhat ambiguous line along the mountain summits, Johnson knew that only a clearly defined and properly surveyed line would be satisfactory. Accordingly, he met with the representatives of the tribes in 1768 near Fort Stanwix on the New York frontier. The delegates agreed upon a line which would be surveyed southward from Oneida Lake to the upper Susquehanna River westward to the Ohio River at Kittanning, and subsequently follow the Ohio to its confluence with the Mississippi. The land-wise Johnson realized that by delineating the Ohio as the boundary, the treaty opened to settlement the lush bluegrass lands south of the Ohio.

Although most of William Johnson's energies were devoted to his responsibilities on the frontier, he was not ignorant about the developing political crisis between many of the colonial politicians and the mother country. Nevertheless, despite urgings from the officials in the east that he become involved, he refused to do so in any direct way. By the late 1760s, he may have begun to feel the effects of more than 30 years of service on the frontier.

Nevertheless, as visitors made their way to Johnson Hall during the decade after the Treaty of Paris, they found the lord of the manor overseeing a multitude of activities. All the while he exercised the diplomatic skills necessary to maintain some semblance of order in all his many interests.

By 1774, however, distant events were intruding into his councils with the Iroquois. A war had erupted in the Ohio country pitting the Shawnees and their allies against the land-hungry Virginians under Governor Lord Dunmore. The precipitating events had occurred along the Ohio River in spring 1774, when the last members of Logan's family were killed by bands of frontiersmen. Logan or Tachnechdorus, the son of the western Iroquois sachem known as Shilleckamy, urged the western Iroquois, the Delawares, and the Shawnees to stop the Virginia Long Knives before they crossed the Ohio River and seized still more Indian lands. Consequently, the Shawnees had sent a war belt to the Iroquois Council at Onondaga, asking for help. Superintendent Johnson's advice to the Iroquois was as potent as the black belt of war was powerful: the western quarrel is not in the best interest of the Iroquois; remain neutral toward the Ohio wars, even as you did in the days of Pontiac. He urged the assemblage at Onondaga to return the war belt with a message that the Iroquois would remain outside the conflict.

This would be Superintendent William Johnson's last council meeting at Onondaga and his final bit of advice to the Iroquois. Although he had been ill frequently since 1769, each time previously he had recovered. In July 1774, he would not do so; on 12 July the Iroquois mourned the death of their long-time friend. His absence would be felt not only by the Iroquois peoples, but also by the British colonial establishment in a time of intensifying crisis.

During his three decades in North America, William Johnson had acquired property, power, and prosperity, as well as political success. As superintendent of the British northern Indian department, and as a military hero of the French and Indian War, Johnson had enjoyed both fame and a substantial amount of influence. No other Indian official in North America could rival him. Without a doubt, he had fulfilled his Iroquois name, for he had indeed done "big business."

James H. O'Donnell

References

James Thomas Flexner, *Mohawk Baronet: Sir William Johnson of New York* (1959); Milton W. Hamilton, *Sir William Johnson, Colonial American, 1715–1763* (1976).

See also IROQUOIS; FORT JOHNSON (NEW YORK); FORT KANADESOGA (NEW YORK); FORT NIAGARA (NEW YORK)

Just War

Since antiquity, writers and leaders have pondered the concept of the "just war," the notion that only some wars could be considered to be legitimate. Greek and Roman writers often defended as "just" those conflicts that were waged for reasons of race, wars with peoples deemed to be barbarians, struggles conducted in self-defense, or hostilities likely to result in domestic and foreign peace. Early Christians believed Jesus' message amounted to a denunciation of war, but by the fourth century church leaders in the West defended wars mounted in defense of Christianity or in pursuit of peace. The hand of god often was seen as a causative factor in the outbreak of warfare. At the moment the English colonization of North America commenced, the principal study of justifiable warfare was *De Jure Belli ac Pacis* (1625), authored by Hugo Grotius, a Dutch businessman. Grotius recognized three kinds of "just wars": wars of self-defense; wars to recover lost property or territory; and wars of revenge. While Grotius was not regarded by articulate Americans as the only authority, he remained the most respected writer on the subject through the end of the colonial period.

John E. Ferling

See also WAR AND SOCIETY IN COLONIAL AMERICA

K

Fort Kanadesoga (New York)

Fort Kanadesoga was erected in 1756 by order of Sir William Johnson. The site was located at the foot of Seneca Lake in the Indian village of Kanadesoga, which was the capitol of the Seneca nation. The 100-foot square was surrounded by 15-foot-high palisades and had two 20-foot-square blockhouses at diagonal corners. It was used by the British throughout the French and Indian War. Fort Kanadesoga was later destroyed in 1779 during the Sullivan-Clinton expedition.

Elizabeth Gossman

References

Robert B. Roberts, *New York Forts in the Revolution* (1980).

Karankawa

Karankawa is a term applied to a handful of coastal Texas tribes inhabiting the region between western Galveston Bay and north of Corpus Christi Bay. The Cocos and Hans were the most northern of the bands; the Kohanis and Karankawa proper occupied the region around Matagorda Bay; and the Copanos lived in the area of St. Joseph's Island and Copano Bay. Some of the groups ranged as far as 100 miles inland.

The Karankawa were non-sedentary bands whose territory provided them with a diet of seafood, prickly pear, pecan, and game animals. Although they did not have permanent dwellings, they returned to seasonal campsites on an annual basis. Shelters were little more than windbreaks composed of long, slender willow poles covered with thatch or animal skins. They made pottery vessels and baskets and fashioned milling stones to grind seeds and nuts. The Karankawa were considered expert at constructing dugout canoes and bows and arrows. The size of bands being small, their political organization was simple, with leadership being won and held on merit.

First contact between Karankawans and Europeans came with the shipwreck of the Pánfilo de Narváez expedition on the Texas coast in 1528. Alvar Núñez Cabeza de Vaca and four companions, the sole survivors to make it to New Spain, were held captive by Karankawans for a considerable time. In 1689, the Karankawa were responsible for killing the last French settlers left by René Robert Cavelier, sieur de La Salle, at Fort St. Louis near Matagorda Bay. During the eighteenth century, the various Karankawa groups had missions established for them by the Spanish, but they proved highly resistant to accommodation. The historical and archaeological evidence suggests they became adept at using the missions as one more resource stop during their annual movements. Primarily because of their behavior toward castaways, the Spanish considered them fierce warriors, cannibals, and treacherous. Never many in number and ravaged by epidemic diseases, the Karankawa proved no match for Anglo-American settlers in the 1820s and 1830s. Defeated in a number of skirmishes, forced to retreat southward beyond the line of settlement, and warred upon by the Mexicans as well, the Karankawa ultimately disappeared in the 1840s.

Jesús F. de la Teja

References

Elizabeth A.H. John, *Storms Brewed in Other Men's Worlds: The Confrontation of*

Indians, Spanish, and French in the Southwest, 1540–1795 (1975); W.W. Newcomb, Jr., *The Indians of Texas: From Prehistoric to Modern Times* (1961).

See also FORT ST. LOUIS (TEXAS)

Kickapoo

The Kickapoo Indians were first encountered in the 1630s in the area of Green Bay and the Fox River, with hunting grounds south to the Illinois River. One of a number of tribes speaking an Algonquian dialect, they enjoyed a reputation for being culturally aloof and unusually resistant to the acculturation to European trading practices common in the Great Lakes region.

Kickapoo policy was directed primarily toward defending the tribe's farming villages and hunting grounds against intrusions from other tribes of the region. Only when the needs of defense became particularly urgent were the Kickapoo drawn into the larger diplomatic arrangements forged by the French.

The first significant recorded period of war involving the Kickapoo occurred in the 1680s when the tribe was attacked by both the Iroquois from the east and the Sioux from the west. Three years of assaults greatly weakened tribal authority, shifting power to the leaders of several war bands. These bands acted in cooperation with the Fox and Mascouten to carry the war back to both east and west in 1684. By the late 1680s, the Kickapoo had earned a reputation as effective fighters, and by the 1690s, they were allied with French forces attacking the Iroquois heartland.

Military cooperation did not, however, imply friendship for the French. Kickapoo leaders appear to have resented the French for counseling passive defense in the 1680s and for not providing adequate supplies of weapons and food. By the 1690s, French traders and missionaries in the west had become targets of small Kickapoo raiding parties, a situation that continued until 1712.

In that year, antagonism escalated into war after fighting erupted at Detroit between a Fox and Mascouten band on the one hand, and the French with allied bands of Potawatomi, Ottawa, Osage, Missouri, and Illinois on the other. After defeat of the Fox and Mascouten, the French attacked surviving Mascouten villages to the west. They treated the Kickapoo as Mascouten allies, beginning with the capture and execution of a hunting party on the Miami River. The Kickapoo promptly counterattacked the French and their allies, disrupting the western fur trade for nearly three years. Only a counterattack by a strong French column in the winter of 1715–1716 resulted in a shaky peace settlement.

The Kickapoo then shifted their enmity to the tribes of the Illinois River area, driving them south and permitting the Kickapoo to migrate into the valleys of the Illinois and Wabash Rivers. Those settling along the Illinois and Sangamon became known as the Prairie band; those along the Vermilion and Wabash as the Vermilion band. Attacks on French traders also continued, prompting the French to attack the new Kickapoo villages in 1726, taking hostages and briefly driving the bands west of the Mississippi River.

In this period, the French were also faced with strong resistance from the Fox. The latter, overeager to draw Kickapoo into their activities, apparently offended their traditional allies and set in motion a great reversal of Kickapoo policy. By 1730, the Kickapoo had returned to their villages east of the Mississippi and were active French allies, remaining so for the next four decades. The primary contribution of the Kickapoo to this new alliance was a series of campaigns against the Chickasaw designed to safeguard the Ohio and Mississippi perimeter of the French empire. Even the defeat of the French in the late 1750s did not quickly disrupt Kickapoo resistance to the British and their allied tribes. The Kickapoo took an active role in Pontiac's War, particularly at Forts Miami and Ouiatenon.

George Geib

See also FOX; PONTIAC'S WAR

Kieft's War (1639–1645; also known as Governor Kieft's War, Willem Kieft's War)

The first of three Dutch-Indian wars in New Netherland, Kieft's War was actually a series of violent clashes and intermittent truces which took place in the region of New Amsterdam (Manhattan Island), where the Dutch West India Company had established Fort Amsterdam, its headquarters for the colony. Participants included Dutch soldiers and settlers and several groups of Munsee-speaking Lenni Lenape people (Delawares), including Navasinks, Raritans, Hackensacks, Tappans, Haverstraws, Canarsees,

Wappingers, Wecquaesgeeks, Tanitekes, Rock-aways, and the Mantinecocks (non-Munsee speakers living on Long Island, but who were closely related in culture). The name of the war comes from the disastrous handling of the affair by the administration of Director General Willem Kieft, whose opinion that local Indians ought to be exterminated led to acts which caused and later intensified the war. However, other events also led to tension between the Dutch and their Indian neighbors, including confusion over concepts of land ownership, conflicting agricultural practices, and pressures the fur trade placed on Native American society.

The war began after Director General Kieft passed a resolution to tax the Indian groups in the vicinity of New Amsterdam in the fall 1639. The following spring, a brutal confrontation erupted between the Raritans and the Dutch, which was resolved with a peace treaty in 1641. During the next two years, several Dutch settlers were killed by members of the Wacquaesgeek and Hackensack bands in separate incidents. In each of these cases, attempts were made by members of both Indian and Dutch societies to resolve matters, but Kieft's stubborn refusal to accommodate the Indians' methods of diplomacy blocked any significant advances toward peace. As a result, the murders remained unresolved, and though tensions grew, hostilities did not escalate for the time being.

By 1643, however, tensions were reaching critical levels. Director Kieft and several other New Amsterdam residents were especially anxious to settle matters militarily with the local Indians. Their opportunity came when many Wecquaesgeeks and other Indians made two camps near the fort while seeking refuge from their Indian enemies. Kieft dispatched soldiers to attack one camp and gave permission to several settlers to attack the other. This nighttime assault resulted in the slaughter of 100 Indians and the eruption of all-out warfare between the other Munsee-speaking groups of the region and the Dutch. Although Director Kieft made peace with the Hackensacks and Rockaways during the two months following the massacre, this did not last long and soon individual farms and houses were burned by Hackensacks and others throughout lower New Netherland. In September 1643, all the farms in the private colony of Pavonia were burned. In addition, the Wappingers began attacking Dutch boats and trading vessels on the Hudson River above New Amsterdam.

The Dutch administration reacted by recruiting an army of Dutch and English mercenaries. At first, they were unable to wage a war against the Indians, who practiced a form of guerrilla warfare unfamiliar to European soldiers, and the Dutch colonists continued to suffer attacks that destroyed isolated houses and farms. No place outside Fort Amsterdam was safe. It was so severe that almost all the farms on and around the lower Hudson were destroyed or abandoned. Even at the fort it was too dangerous to collect firewood without protection.

In early 1644, however, the Dutch troops claimed several victories. Most notable of these was the Poundridge Massacre. Under the command of English Captain John Underhill (who had previously led an English force against the Pequots at Mystic Fort), 130 soldiers landed at Greenwich and marched north to an Indian fortress near present-day Poundridge, New York. There, the soldiers surrounded the fortified village and opened fire. When the Indians refused to come out and fight, Underhill ordered the village set on fire. More than 500 Indians died; only eight escaped. Most perished in the flames, choosing a fiery death over slaughter at the hands of Underhill and his men, who lost only one of their members.

These attacks did not end the hostilities, however. Although the Mantinecocks made peace in April, other bands remained on the warpath through the following year. In the meantime, Kieft's council, eight leading citizens of New Amsterdam whom he called together to advise him during the war, wrote letters to the directors of the colony requesting aid and complaining about Kieft's handling of the affair. As a result, the directors recalled Kieft and appointed a new commander, Petrus (Peter) Stuyvesant. The change in leadership did not occur until 1647, however, by which time the war was over.

In spring 1645, warfare slackened and several groups of Indians made peace in April. The great loss in numbers which the Indians had suffered and perhaps pressure from other Indian tribes, especially the Mohawks who lived to the north, compelled the warring tribesmen to make peace. The war came to a final end that summer when the remaining Indian groups appeared at Fort Amsterdam seeking peace. On 30 August 1645, the Dutch and their Munsee neighbors signed an official peace treaty putting an end to the hostilities of the previous six years.

K

By war's end, much had changed in New Amsterdam. Almost all the Munsee-speaking Indians in lower New Netherland had been involved in the war. Farms and houses across the countryside had been destroyed and most Europeans had fled to Fort Amsterdam for safety or left the colony altogether. By the end of the war, more than 1,000 Delawares had died and the European population in the area dropped dramatically (mostly due to emigration), and those who remained faced immediate food shortages. Financially, the war had been a drain on the Dutch West India Company, which had to borrow money to cover military expenses; it was a boon to the merchants who benefited from increased prices the colonists paid for supplies and provisions, while the prices the merchants paid for furs decreased. Other results included the replacement of Director General Kieft, and the increased opportunity for the ever-spreading population of New England to encroach on New Netherland's now poorly defended eastern frontier.

Paul Otto

References

J. Franklin Jameson, ed., *Narratives of New Netherland, 1609–1664* (1909); Edmund B. O'Callaghan, *History of New Netherland, or New York Under the Dutch,* 2nd ed., 2 vols. (1855); —— and Bertold Fernow, eds., *Documents Relative to the Colonial History of the State of New York,* Vols. I and XIII (1856–1887); Oliver Rink, *Holland on the Hudson: An Economic and Social History of Dutch New York* (1986); Allen W. Trelease, *Indian Affairs in Colonial New York: The Seventeenth Century* (1960).

See also KIEFT, WILLEM

Kieft, Willem (?–1647)

Willem Kieft served the Dutch West India Company as director general of New Netherland from 1638 until 1647. He was headquartered at Fort Amsterdam on Manhattan Island.

Kieft faced two major challenges while serving as director general. On the colony's eastern frontier, the English settlers in the Connecticut Valley and New Haven threatened the Dutch West India Company's claim to the region. Close to home, the stability of the colony was shaken by a disastrous encounter with the Munsee-speaking Indians who lived in the vicinity of Fort Amsterdam. Unfortunately for the colony, Kieft could not consistently provide the necessary leadership these situations required.

Willem Kieft was born in Amsterdam to a merchant of La Rochelle, France. He succeeded his father in that business, only to face bankruptcy in 1633. Later, he went to work for an accountant in the same city, but was arrested for embezzlement. After being tried and convicted, he fled and appeared in Amsterdam. Although it is not clear why the directors of the Dutch West India Company appointed him to the post of director general in 1638, it was not their practice to waste qualified men on posts which were of less importance to them, and New Netherland's significance paled in comparison with other West India Company outposts such as those in Brazil. Although Kieft had the experience of a merchant to guide him in his command of a trading outpost, he apparently lacked other qualities necessary to succeed as an administrator. Contemporary observers have noted his arrogance, belligerence, ignorance, selfishness, and imprudence.

Nevertheless, Kieft was obviously educated and could rely on his knowledge of Latin to pursue his diplomatic responsibility with the English. And yet his reliance on Latin pointed to a significant deficiency—he could not communicate in English. Lacking a knowledge of the language of Dutch West India Company's competitors in North America, and the experience to deal with delicate diplomatic matters, Kieft was unable to stem the tide of English migration into the Connecticut River valley. Kieft did evict several groups of English who tried to settle in the Delaware Bay region and on the shores of Long Island Sound. However, the overwhelming numbers of English moving into Connecticut, coupled with the lack of support in arms and troops from the Dutch West India Company, made it impossible for him to maintain Dutch territorial claims in Connecticut.

Although Kieft was familiar with some of the contemporary literature regarding the native inhabitants of North America, he lacked the practical understanding that would enable him to adequately administer Indian affairs in New Netherland. Combined with his apparent hatred of the Indians and desire to exterminate them, this inability to handle Indian affairs appropriately led to the war which bears his name. While other factors may have been involved, Kieft clearly played a role in inflaming the Indians with acts of stubbornness and injustice.

Once the war began, Kieft's lack of judgment and inability to properly treat the Indians prolonged it. The cause of the war was not lost on the Dutch West India Company who recalled Kieft and replaced him with the more qualified Petrus (Peter) Stuyvesant.

Paul Otto

References

Michael Kammen, *Colonial New York: A History* (1975); Charles McKew Parr, *The Voyages of David De Vries* (1969); Oliver Rink, *Holland on the Hudson: An Economic and Social History of Dutch New York* (1986); George L. Smith, *Religion and Trade in New Netherland: Dutch Origins and American Development* (1973); Allen W. Trelease, *Indian Affairs in Colonial New York: The Seventeenth Century* (1960).

See also KIEFT'S WAR; LONG ISLAND

Fort Kilburn (Connecticut)

See LITCHFIELD FORTS (CONNECTICUT)

Fort King George (Georgia)

By the beginning of the eighteenth century, the British colony of South Carolina had established a system of defense against Indian attack that consisted of a protective screen of friendly Indian sentry towns. The system collapsed in spring 1715 when the Indians of the sentry towns and other tribes suddenly attacked the frontier settlements. After a short period of total war, the South Carolinians drove the Indians from their frontiers. However, their plantations lay in ruins and the colony remained open to future attacks. Several requests for military aid were submitted to the British government, but most were too impractical for serious consideration. In 1720, John Barnwell, an experienced South Carolina frontiersman, visited the government in London and proposed that Britain build and garrison forts at strategic locations on the southern frontier. The government agreed to his plan, but Fort King George was the only fort built and garrisoned.

During 1721, Barnwell and a party of South Carolina scouts and Indian slaves constructed Fort King George, named for the British sovereign, on the north bank of the Altamaha River near present-day Darien, Georgia. It was intended to be a temporary structure until a stronger fortification could be constructed. The principal part of the fort was a large blockhouse, 26 feet square, constructed of thick planks. It had three floors and mounted several small cannon. Barnwell's blockhouse included a very unusual feature: it was designed to be taken apart and moved to another site for continued use after a permanent fort was constructed. The blockhouse was surrounded by outworks. On the land side a moat was dug and the dirt was used to build an earthen wall with a diamond-shaped bastion. A palisade wall of upright logs was planted the length of the moat as a further impediment to attackers. Another palisade protected the river and marsh side of the fort.

South Carolina colonial troops were initially stationed at the fort, but during 1722, the Independent Company of Foot, a regular infantry unit from England, was placed in garrison. Fort King George was a very unpopular station. It was located in an otherwise uninhabited area, more than 80 straight-line miles from the nearest South Carolina settlement. The area was swampy, and sickness and death were common.

The fort burned during the winter 1725–1726. Although it was soon rebuilt, the living conditions did not improve. Not long afterward, several soldiers deserted for Spanish St. Augustine. Finally, in late 1727, the British garrison was withdrawn to Beaufort in South Carolina. South Carolina then placed two colonial soldiers at the fort as lookouts. They remained in garrison until the founding of Georgia in 1733.

Larry E. Ivers

References

Verner W. Crane, *The Southern Frontier, 1670–1732* (1929).

See also ANGLO-SPANISH WAR (1718–1721); BARNWELL, JOHN

King George's War (1744–1748)

The War of the Austrian Succession in Europe, 1741 to 1748, was known in the British American Colonies as King George's War. This narrower term focused on the conflict between France and England, which began unofficially in June 1743, when King George II, having led an army into Holland to check French ambitions toward the Austrian Netherlands, was attacked by the French at Dehingen and forced to retreat. War was subsequently declared by both sides in March 1744. The European conflict was a typically eighteenth-century affair involving dynastic rivalries, territorial ambitions, shifting alliances, and, particularly in Britain's case, the determination to create a favorable balance of power on the Continent. The military history featured several lusty French land victories, at Fontenoy (1745) and Laffeldt (1746), for example, offset by equally significant English naval successes, most notably by Admiral Edward Hawke off the coast of Brittany in 1747. When the war ended in 1748, it was judged a standoff in both the European and colonial theaters, though most historians agree the North American struggle produced ominous foreshadowings of the more decisive conflict soon to come—the Seven Years' War, 1754–1763.

Indeed, King George's War in America had its own distinct character. For one thing, while British and French navies were involved, along with some metropolitan land troops, the war was largely fought by colonial militias under colonial leaders. It was also fought with colonial concerns, including the brisk illegal trade between French and English colonies, well to the forefront. The origins of this branch of the war go back at least as far as the Treaty of Utrecht in 1713, which ended the last and most costly of Louis XIV's wars. Victorious England had gained a double-barreled triumph over its chief colonial rivals, France and Spain, by acquiring Newfoundland and Acadia from the former, thus obtaining advantages in the Atlantic fisheries, strategic control of the Gulf of St. Lawrence, and negotiating ironclad trading privileges and control of the slave traffic, or *asiento,* to the Spanish colonies. By exploiting these advantages to the hilt, England expected to emerge as Europe's undisputed mercantile power.

For most of the Thirty Years' Peace, 1713 to 1744, France was led by Cardinal André-Hercule de Fleury, Louis XV's chief minister, whose peaceful policies made trade "the darling of the dynasts." By the 1730s, French Atlantic commerce rivaled England's, and the long-serving British prime minister, Sir Horace Walpole, though opposed to risking war, came under strong pressure to promote British interests more militantly. Belligerent action fell first upon Spain and its crumbling colonial empire. During the late 1730s, there were numerous skirmishes and shipboardings in the West Indies

and Caribbean, as well as minor clashes between Britain's southernmost North American colonies, especially Carolina and Spanish Florida. Finally, in 1739, a British navy master named Robert Jenkins, who had lost an ear in a fight with the Spanish, apeared before the English Parliament which chose to regard this as a supreme provocation and declared war on Spain. Through the first years of what was called The War of Jenkins' Ear, France remained neutral, though sympathetic to Spain. By 1743, Cardinal Fleury was dead and the war party was gaining influence at Versailles. Increasingly, the war was portrayed as one of English colonial expansion that France could not longer tolerate.

When news of the English-French declaration of war reached Boston in May 1744, there were powerful economic interests in New England who welcomed it. Indeed, North American historians generally refer to it as a war of "merchants and militias." To quote one: "It was [to be] a struggle . . . of Virginians anxious to secure land; of New Yorkers anxious to take over the fur trade; of New Englanders anxious to control the fisheries; and of Canadians and Acadians resolved to prevent them." Governor William Shirley of Massachusetts, a lawyer/politician representing Bostonian fishing and trading interests, was the leading "war hawk" of his day with a passionate hatred for the "popish" French. Perhaps the most visionary of the American war leaders, he pressed the duke of Newcastle, the secretary of state for the colonies, to provide concrete support commensurate with the notion that victory for New England over New France was of crucial strategic importance to Britain. But Newcastle was not William Pitt and he never regarded the colonial struggle as of greater significance than the war on the Continent. Shirley soon realized it was up to him and like-minded men, such as Governor George Clinton of New York, to take the military initiative.

At Quebec, the capital of New France, the outbreak of hostilities was greeted with less enthusiasm. Charles de Beauharnois de la Boische, the aging governor general, was well aware that the loss of Newfoundland and Acadia in 1713 had given the English a stranglehold on his supply line and communications with France. Construction of the great fortress at Louisbourg, the "Gibraltar of the Atlantic," between 1717 and 1737, had considerably offset this disadvantage, but not enough to change Beauharnois's view that Canada's greatest danger was, as always, from the sea. His first orders, therefore, were to prepare the St. Lawrence River defenses, including fire boats, and erect a wooden palisade below Quebec at the St. Charles River. But New France's leaders were also aware the New York frontier was poorly defended, with a small garrison at Crown Point (Fort St. Frédéric) on Lake Champlain and an even less imposing outpost at Chambly on the Richelieu River. Farther west in the Great Lakes-Illinois region, the French were still in good control with their elaborate network of forts and Indian alliances. However, the activities of New England's fur traders had for some time been a cause for concern and, while Louisiana was not destined to be a factor in the war, there was good reason to worry about continuing English intrigues among the Chickasaw and Natchez tribes farther south. In short, New France's long frontier with New England, extending from the Gulf of St. Lawrence to New Orleans, was vulnerable at several points, and the English, with a population base of one million in 1744, compared to New France's 48,000, were in a much better position to seize the offensive.

New France's military leaders had always depended in wartime on a policy of energetic, small-scale attacks to offset New England's greater strength. When Jean-Baptiste-Louis Le Prévost Duquesnel, the French commander at Louisbourg, got news of the war on 3 May 1745, he took immediate action. In addition to launching an aggressive privateering campaign that netted 28 English ships in the first five months alone, he sent François Du Pont Duvivier, with approximately 350 officers and men, to attack the English fishing post at Canso. The garrison, which consisted of about 120 men, surrendered on 24 May. Given the honors of war, several were transferred to Louisbourg before being sent home to Boston. Their observations on the fortress's defenses and the poor morale of its garrison were to prove invaluable for Governor Shirley. Meanwhile, Duvivier, with roughly 250 soldiers and Indians, moved to Annapolis Royal (Port Royal). He laid siege to the fort, which was defended by approximately 100 men under the command of Paul Mascarene. Duvivier wisely postponed an assault until two ships with expected reinforcements could arrive from Louisbourg. It was not until 19 October that this flotilla was dispatched and, by then, Duvivier had been ordered to fall back. Although the poorly coordi-

nated campaign fell short of its main goal, it had succeeded in spreading fear and consternation throughout New England. Louisbourg was not only a menace to the fisheries and English control of Acadia, but its presence provided the French with the means to secure the allegiance of the region's Indians, especially the Micmac and Abenaki.

Paradoxically, the French aggression in Acadia was a boon to Governor Shirley and his project, already underway, to mount an expedition against Louisbourg. He was also able to exploit the report of Lieutenant John Bradstreet, one of the Canso prisoners taken to Louisbourg, that the fortress was undergunned, short of supplies, and garrisoned by unhappy soldiers, some of whom, Swiss mercenaries, had mutinied the previous winter. Although Shirley failed in his initial attempt to convince the Massachusetts assembly to fund an expedition, virulent representations from merchants and fishermen precipitated a second vote. This time the assembly committed the impressive sum of £50,000.

Shirley had no such difficulty raising a strong volunteer force. Whipped up by anti-French rhetoric and the promise of both pay and plunder, militia joined from Massachusetts, the Maine district, New Hampshire, and Connecticut, while New York, Rhode Island, New Jersey, and even the pacifist Quaker assembly of Pennsylvania, sent some men and provisions. On 4 April 1745, a fleet of 90 transports escorted by privateers carrying 4,300 men set sail under the command of William Pepperrell, Jr., a rich merchant from Kittery, Maine. Shirley had also convinced Newcastle to send a British naval force consisting of four warships under Admiral Peter Warren. The two fleets met near Canso, where the troops trained for several weeks. The attack finally began on 11 May, when American militia disembarked at Gabarus Bay, less than two miles from Louisbourg.

The siege that followed was the major military episode of King George's War in the colonial sphere. It lasted 47 days, during which the English forces, beneficiaries of extraordinary good luck throughout, took swift and decisive advantage of numerous French weaknesses and tactical blunders. The French commander, Louis Dupont, sieur Duchambon, who had succeeded Duquesnel in October 1744, was handicapped from the outset. His garrison of 618 regular troops and perhaps twice as many militia was understrength, poorly housed, and in defeatist spirits. The fortress walls, though of formidable proportions, were badly made and vulnerable to a sustained cannonade. In addition, there were only 116 cannon in the 148 enclosures. With Warren's successful naval blockade of reinforcement by sea, Chambon was forced to make do, and he made do badly. He mounted a belated half-hearted attempt to oppose the English beach landing, and dithered long enough deciding whether or not to abandon the Royal Battery, a key position remote from the fort, to allow the English to restore its cannon quickly and turn them on the French. It was generally a case of too little, too late and, after absorbing 3,000 cannonballs, the defenders surrendered on 27 June. As Shirley informed Newcastle, " . . . all the houses and other buildings within the city (some of which were quite demolished [were] so damaged that but one among them was unhurt. . . . "

The jubilation which swept New England over the capture of Louisbourg marked the high point of wartime unity and confidence. The victory was seen as an exclusively colonial triumph and, as such, gave impetus to the already strong expansionist mood in colonies like Virginia and New York. Americans, the feeling was, were capable of shaping their own destiny. In England, the news was welcomed as a palliative, following the crushing defeat of the English-led coalition at the hands of the Maréchal de Saxe near Fontenoy on, coincidentally, 11 May. At Versailles, on the other hand, the loss of Louisbourg not only dampened the celebrations over Fontenoy, but was so rife with strategic implications for trade, the fisheries, and the Canadian colony that plans were immediately set in motion for its recapture.

But it was May 1746 before a fleet with 7,000 troops on board was assembled under the command of Jean-Baptiste de la Rochefoucauld, duc d'Anville. During its three-month crossing, the fleet encountered every conceivable hazard, including terrible storms that scattered ships in every direction. The remnants limped into Chebucto Bay in September. Soon after, the inexperienced and demoralized Anville suffered a seizure and died. His terrified successor, the chevalier d'Etournelles, having no idea what to do, stabbed himself with his own sword. Command then fell to Jacques-Pierre de Taffanel, the sieur de La Jonquière, a veteran naval officer who carried orders to take over from Governor Beauharnois at Quebec once Louisbourg was taken. With 537 men dead

from smallpox and scurvy, and another 1,500 beyond use, he concluded his only option was to attack Annapolis Royal instead. Setting sail on 22 October, he was immediately enveloped in fog and storms and finally gave up entirely—returning to France. "It was" wrote one commentator "the end of one of the most disastrous expeditions ever undertaken by the French navy—thousands dead and not a single objective attained." Jonquière would try again with a smaller fleet in 1747, only to be defeated and captured after a fierce running fight with a more powerful force under Lord Anson. In the end, it would be up to French diplomats, not the military, to "recapture" Louisbourg.

At Quebec, news of Louisbourg's fall in 1745 had opened a new chapter in the war. Governor Beauharnois came under severe pressure from Versailles, as well as Canada, to take the offensive. The French understood William Shirley well enough by now to know that even if England chose to rest on its laurels, he would not. They were not surprised, therefore, to learn from returning prisoners and the New England gazettes that plans were underway for an attack on Quebec. They could not know, of course, that Shirley would secure Newcastle's pledge to send eight battalions of British regulars, plus Warren's fleet, to assist the 7,500 American militia already being mustered. Nor could they foresee the whole scheme would be undone; first, by the Scottish uprising under the "Young Pretender," Charles Edward Stewart; and second, by Newcastle's last-minute decision to send the promised troops to Europe. Anticipating the worst, and egged on by the frightened Quebec citizens, Beauharnois launched a strong counteroffensive designed not to capture territory, but to defend the colony at its outer limits.

It began in 1746 with the dispatch of a formidable war party consisting of 680 Canadian militia under Jean-Baptiste-Nicholas-Roch de Ramezay to join up with Anville's fleet in Acadia. Despite the naval fiasco, Ramezay succeeded in laying siege to Annapolis Royal. Late that same year, a detachment from his force, under Nicholas-Antoine Coulon de Villiers, captured Grand Pré on the Bay of Fundy from Captain Arthur Noble after a spectacular deep-winter march. The French employed the same guerrilla tactics that had always been their main weapon in wars with New England. Along the vulnerable New York frontier, their fierce, destructive raids were intended to keep the American colonists so busy defending themselves and wondering where the next blow would fall that they would be unable to launch attacks of their own against the French St. Lawrence communities. Between 1746 and 1748, war parties of Canadian militia and French Indians were constantly in the forests of New York, Massachusetts, and Connecticut. They were led by experienced officers like Ramezay, Villiers, Pierre de Rigaud de Vaudreuil, Jean-Baptiste Boucher de Niverville, Jean-Louis de La Corne St. Luc, and Paul Marin de Malgue, who had grown up learning the Indian style of fighting. At times, so many Canadians were involved in the bloody campaign against frontier settlements like Haverhill and Fort Massachusetts, and Saratoga, New York (twice) that New France's manpower was stripped bare and the crops could not be harvested.

Though New England's leaders made plans to strike back, including an ambitious scheme to attack Crown Point in 1747, by and large, "rumours only, crossed the frontier." Governor Clinton, for example, who was as anxious as Shirley to defeat the French, was restrained throughout by two considerations. First, the New York assembly, influenced by merchants who profited from the illegal trade with New France and land speculators who were primarily interested in grabbing the lands of New York's Iroquois allies, refused to vote funds for frontier defense. Second, the Iroquois themselves refused, until September 1746, to take up the hatchet against the French. The Five Nations Confederacy was only a pale shadow of the military power it had been in the seventeenth century and, for some years, it had been pursuing a shrewd balance of power diplomatic strategy with the English and French. Forced to allow more and more fur traders to pass through their cantons, thus jeopardizing their middleman status in the trade, the Iroquois were still strong enough (largely because of this strategy) to control the New York frontier south of the Great Lakes. But a war, no matter who won, would surely weaken them further. Hence they dutifully attended the war assemblies called by Governor Clinton at Albany, accepted his praise and presents, and did nothing. Even when the Mohawks did finally accept the governor's war belt in late 1746, the other four nations temporized. They argued, rather convincingly after the expedition against Crown Point was abandoned in 1747, that the English were asking them to fight a war they wouldn't fight themselves.

Further west, Iroquois neutrality proved to be a mixed blessing for the French. Governor Beauharnois had threatened as early as 1744 to destroy the English post at Oswego, which had been established in 1727, because, in addition to being a notorious illegal trading center and an attraction to the French Indian allies on their way to Montreal, it was poised like a sharp knife over New France's narrow supply route to the Great Lakes posts and beyond. But the Iroquois strongly opposed any attack on Oswego and Beauharnois was well aware that the confederacy was an important buffer against English military attacks in the west. As it stood then, he had only to worry about aggressive New England fur traders.

In the long run, it was the growing influence of these traders, from New York and Pennsylvania especially, that was the most significant new development of King George's War. Governor Clinton's most far-reaching wartime decision was to appoint a trader named William Johnson in charge of Indian affairs. A young, Irish-born nephew of Admiral Warren, who had come to New York originally to oversee his uncle's lands along the Mohawk River, he quickly established his own trading empire and was adopted by the Mohawks, who he lived among. With others, like George Groghan of Pennsylvania, another Irishman who had arrived in the colonies in 1741, he pushed the English trade all the way to the Ohio Valley. Taking full advantage of French supply problems during the war and the fact that Indians had always preferred the price and quality of English goods, the English traders successfully wooed Indian allies. For example, they convinced the Delaware and Seneca tribes, along with some Micmacs from the Illinois country, to relocate close to their Ohio trading center at Pickawillany. In 1747, Paul-Joseph Le Moyne de Longueuil, the French commandant at Detroit, reported formerly loyal local Indians were conspiring with English provocateurs to attack the fort. And in 1748, a gathering of French Indian allies signed an agreement at Logstown welcoming the Pennsylvania traders into their midst. If the French did not find a solution to this problem, they were in danger of losing the Ohio Valley, the Illinois country, and perhaps the whole Southwest.

The final year of the war, 1748, was the least active militarily. New England's fervor had turned into political squabbling over war costs,

K

alarm about the brutal and successful French border raids, and bitterness at the evaporation of concrete British support. A foolish attempt by the navy to press-gang Bostonians into the navy in 1747 had further alienated colonial opinion. Even Louisbourg turned out to be a costly victory, with far more men dying of disease on garrison duty than had been lost in the siege. As for the French, the ruinous losses of Anville's and La Jonquière's fleets had thoroughly blunted the navy's zeal, and the high cost of sustaining so many expeditions in Canada, not to mention provisioning the Indian allies, had ruptured New France's already fragile financial system. The first dispatches from Versailles to Quebec in 1748 ordered a halt to all but the most necessary operations. In North America, as in Europe, the war petered out before it officially ended.

The Treaty of Aix-la-Chapelle was signed on 18 October 1748. Although the news reached Boston before Christmas, the terms were not published until March 1749. Included was the stunning provision for the return of Louisbourg to France in exchange for Madras, India, which had been captured by the French during the war. The American colonists had seen Louisbourg as "their" success, inspired by, led, and fought for New Englanders. In addition, they had lost more than 500 men in combat during the war, and perhaps twice as many to disease and exposure. All this to have the great prize bargained away at the imperial conference table. Who can say what long-term damage this did to the intangible fabric of loyalty between colony and mother country? It is certain, however, that the New England colonies had gained a stronger sense of their own separate interests during the war and responded more warily when, in a few short years, England again declared war on France.

In fact, the broader significance of King George's War was as a precursor to this more decisive struggle to come. In Europe, it had been demonstrated yet again that England, no matter what new alliances it struck, could not defeat France and its allies on the Continent; just as France was always at a strategic disadvantage when confronted by British naval strength. If the European balance of power was ever to shift overwhelmingly in favor of one of these two great states, the decisive blow would have to be struck in the colonies; in North America, to be precise. It was the brilliant French statesman Roland Baron de la Galisonière who first advanced this idea following King George's War. Sent to New France in 1748 as an interim replacement for Beauharnois, he gathered information for the commission established by the peace treaty to iron out the border disputes in Acadia and elsewhere. By 1750, he had concluded that France's North American colonies, though vulnerable militarily and an economic liability, would have to be defended at all costs, for if England should conquer them it would lead to English supremacy in Europe as well. The greatest immediate danger, moreover, arose from the steady advance of English fur traders and land speculators into the far west. It was clear to Galisonière, as it would soon become clear to the European leaders as well, that the French could either fight to defend their western posts and links to Louisiana or they could await certain extinction in the St. Lawrence Valley. By the late 1750s, this struggle would become an imperial fight to the finish.

Donald J. Horton

References
T.A. Crowley, *Louisbourg: Atlantic Fortress and Seaport* (1990); Guy Frégault, *Canada: The War of the Conquest*, trans. by Margaret M. Cameron (1969); Lawrence Henry Gipson, *The British Empire Before the American Revolution*, 15 vols. (1936–1970) Vols. I, II, III; Milton W. Hamilton, *Sir William Johnson, Colonial American, 1715–1764* (1976).

Howard Peckham, *The Colonial Wars, 1689–1762* (1964); William Shirley, *Correspondence of William Shirley, Governor of Massachusetts and Military Commander in America, 1731–1760*, 2 vols., ed. by Charles H. Lincoln (1912); R.C. Simmons, *The American Colonies: From Settlement to Independence* (1976); George F.G. Stanley, *New France: The Last Phase* (1968).

See also AIX-LA-CHAPELLE, TREATY OF; BRADSTREET, JOHN; CANADA, BRITISH EXPEDITION AGAINST (1746); CANSO, BATTLE OF; GRAND PRÉ, BATTLE OF; HAVERHILL (MASSACHUSETTS); IMPRESSMENT, NAVY; JOHNSON, WILLIAM; LOGSTOWN, TREATY OF; LOUISBOURG EXPEDITION; FORT MASSACHUSETTS (MASSACHUSETTS); FORT AT NUMBER FOUR (NEW HAMPSHIRE); SARATOGA, BATTLE OF; SHIRLEY, WILLIAM; WARREN, PETER

King Philip's War (1675–1676)

King Philip's War was the first general war between the English settlers of New England and the native inhabitants. It takes its name from Metacomet, sachem or chief of the Wampanoag, who was called Philip by his English neighbors. In 1675, the Wampanoag (also called the Pokanoket) occupied a much-shrunken territory centered on Mount Hope Neck on Narragansett Bay in present-day Rhode Island. Philip was the son of the sachem Massasoit, famous for befriending the Pilgrims soon after their landing in 1620. The alliance of Plymouth and the Wampanoags had achieved a generation of mutual protection and general peace, but after Massasoit's death (c. 1660–1661), relations between his nation and the English deteriorated. By the late 1660s, rumors were circulating that Philip, the new sachem, was attempting to organize an alliance, to include the Wampanoags' traditional enemies the Narragansetts, to drive the English out.

The underlying cause of the war was doubtless the steady growth of English numbers and power, which threatened eventually to overwhelm the Indian peoples of southern New England. By 1675, repeated epidemics of unfamiliar European diseases had greatly reduced the Indian population of the region, so the approximately 35,000 Englishmen living in the four colonies of Plymouth, Massachusetts Bay, Connecticut, and Rhode Island greatly outnumbered the Indians. On the eve of the war, Philip's counselors complained to English negotiators:

> when the English first came, the king's father [Massasoit] was a great man, and the English as a little child; he constrained other Indians from wronging the English, and gave them corn and showed them how to plant . . . and had let them have a hundred times more land than now the king had for his own people.

Other grievances concerned land titles and boundaries, the sale of liquor to the Indians by unscrupulous traders, and much else. Neither the assurances of colonial authorities nor their efforts to intimidate Philip were effective.

Fighting finally broke out in connection with the murder of John Sassamon, a Christian Wampanoag who at one time had served as Philip's translator and scribe. Sassamon was murdered in January 1675, shortly after he had brought the English fresh warnings of Philip's conspiracy. On testimony of an Indian witness, three Wampanoags were tried and executed (8 June) for the crime at Plymouth. About 20 June, Wampanoag warriors began burning and looting at the village of Swansea in southwestern Plymouth Colony near Mount Hope Neck. Killing began on 23 June and the war rapidly spread.

But if Philip was trying to weld a general alliance of Indian nations, as the evidence suggests, he signally failed. The closely related Pocasset and Sakonnet bands immediately joined him, and a few weeks later the Nipmuck bands of western Massachusetts began their raids. Except for the Narragansett, no other tribe in the region joined him. Others, most importantly the Mohegan, Pequot, Niantic, and many of the Christian or "praying Indians," sided with the English and contributed greatly to their eventual victory. Traditional rivalries among the Indian nations outweighed their common grievances.

Colonial forces assembled to block the entrance to Mount Hope Neck, but Philip escaped the trap, crossing by water to the Pocasset country on the east side of Narragansett Bay. At this time, the Wampanoag were reported to number only about 300 warriors (implying a total population of 1,300 to 1,400 persons), about half of them armed with muskets. Energetic action now might have overwhelmed this small force and ended the war at once, but the English were cautious and ineffective. On 19 July, colonial troops greatly outnumbering Philip's band pursued him into a great cedar swamp, but were unable to pin the Indians down. Advancing through heavy cover, the English pulled back after seven or eight were killed and more wounded. As the Puritan chronicler William Hubbard (c. 1621–1704) put it, "It is ill fighting with a wild Beast in his own Den." On 29 July, Philip escaped from the swamp and crossed the Taunton River, moving north toward Nipmuck country. The failure of the English to stop Philip encouraged other tribes, already disaffected, to go on the attack. On 14 July, Nipmucks attacked Mendon, the first town in Massachusetts Bay Colony to experience war, and Providence was attacked, probably by Narragansetts.

Acting through the New England Confederation (formed 1643), the colonies of Massachusetts Bay, Plymouth, and Connecticut attempted to follow a joint strategy and, on occasion, put a combined army into the field. While Rhode Island assisted in the war effort, it did not take part in these joint operations. The English soldiers were provided by the militia company, the "trainband," that each town was required to maintain and in which every fit man between the ages of 16 and 60 served. When an army was to be assembled, colonial authorities assigned each town its quota. If there were not enough volunteers, town officials selected those who would go. The English were unable at first to deal with the raiding tactics of the Indians, in which English patrols were lured into ambush and overwhelming numbers of warriors could be concentrated against isolated villages, melting away before relief forces arrived. As the war reached into central Massachusetts Bay and the upper Connecticut River, towns like Brookfield, Deerfield, and Squakeag (Northfield) were attacked. On 3 September 1675, Captain Richard Beers and some 36 men, coming to aid in the evacuation of Squakeag, marched into an ambush. More than half, including Beers, were killed. In the "Bloody Brook Massacre" on 18 September, Captain Thomas Lathrop's company was surrounded while assisting in the evacuation of Deerfield. Lathrop and 63 others were slain. This frontier area was turned into a wasteland. But the English were becoming more experienced in wilderness warfare and more careful to make effective use of their Indian allies, large numbers of whom served as soldiers, scouts, and spies.

In December 1675, the bloodiest and most decisive campaign of the war occurred when a united army more than 1,000 strong, including 150 Pequot and Mohegan warriors, invaded the Narragansett country in the eastern part of Rhode Island. The army, commanded by Governor Josiah Winslow (c. 1629–1680) of Plymouth Colony, came to force the Narragansetts to abide by their treaty obligations. By treaty, the Narragansetts were required to deliver to the English any enemy Indians who took refuge among them, but the Narragansetts had allowed many Wampanoag and their allies, including Weetamoo, the squaw sachem of the Pocasset, to find shelter. It was reliably reported as well that the Narragansetts had determined to join the war against the English when spring came. The Narragansetts were variously reported as numbering 1,000 to 2,000 warriors, a total population of 4,000 to as many as 10,000 people. As the English advanced into Narragansett country, fighting a number of minor skirmishes, a Narragansett captive in-

formed them of the location of a fortress in the middle of a swamp where the Narragansetts had concentrated. Guided by the Narragansett turncoat and marching through bitter cold, the army entered the swamp the afternoon of 19 December, now frozen solid, and approached a log-walled village built on several acres of high ground. Directly before the advancing Englishmen was a gap in the still-uncompleted wall, into which the leading companies rushed in the face of intense musket fire. The battle, known ever after as the Great Swamp Fight, was costly. At least 20 Englishmen were killed outright and another 200 wounded (more than 20 percent casualties). A number of the English wounded died later, partly from exposure in the bitter cold and deep snow, so the English dead eventually numbered more than 80. But the Great Swamp Fight was a calamity for the Narragansetts. Reports of the number of warriors killed ranged from about 300 to more than 1,000. In addition, hundreds of women and children perished when the English set fire to the close-set bark wigwams within the walls. More Narragansetts died of wounds and exposure as they fled northward through the snow, abandoning their country and its hoarded food supplies. The Narragansetts fought on, but never recovered from this blow in which perhaps one-third of their people died. Today, a historical monument near West Kingston, Rhode Island, marks the site of the fortress.

As the war continued into the spring of 1676, more English villages were attacked, with steadily mounting loss of life and property. While there is disagreement on the total number of English dead, it has been argued the New England colonies suffered the greatest proportional losses of any war in American history. Probably 800 to 1,000 were killed. At the latter figure, about one adult white man in ten lost his life in New England. A dozen villages were abandoned to the enemy and burned, including Simsbury, Northfield, Deerfield, Lancaster, Groton, Middleborough, Brookfield, Mendon, Wickford, Warwick, and Wrentham. Forty others were more or less heavily damaged, and years were required for rebuilding and economic recovery.

But English superiority in numbers, firepower, and supplies gradually told. Enemy bands were pursued and harried, attacked when they tried to turn to their normal fishing and planting. In the famous narratives of her captivity among the Narragansetts (reprinted in *So*

Dreadfull a Judgment, see References), Mrs. Mary Rowlandson (c. 1635–1678), who was taken prisoner in the attack on Lancaster on 10 February 1676, described the near-starving condition of the Indians at this time. On more than one occasion boiled horse hooves seemed a delicacy. By the summer of 1676, dispirited Indians were surrendering by the hundreds. The war was fading away when Philip himself was tracked down and killed in August.

With the handful of warriors left to him, Philip had slipped back to his home territory near Mount Hope. An angry Wampanoag, whose brother Philip had ordered killed, probably for defeatist counsel, volunteered to lead the English to a swamp where Philip lay hidden. As soldiers pushed through the swamp, Philip stepped out of it into a carefully prepared ambush. The sachem was shot by one of the Indian auxiliaries and his head taken to Plymouth, where for many years it was displayed on a pole. By October 1676, the war was virtually over except in the Maine district, where it dragged on for some months.

Virtually every hostile sachem had been killed, along with several thousand other tribesmen. The power of the Indian nations of southern New England was broken forever. In the course of the war, hundreds of captured Indians had been sold as slaves, mostly in Spain or the West Indies, including Philip's wife and small son. Even those tribes which had aided the English received no long-term benefit. Their numbers continued to shrink from disease, and their lands, like those of the defeated nations, steadily passed into English possession.

Bert M. Mutersbaugh

References

William Hubbard, *A Narrative of the Troubles with the Indians of New England* (1677); Francis Jennings, *The Invasion of America: Indians, Colonialism, and the Cant of Conquest* (1975); Douglas Edward Leach, *Flintlock and Tomahawk: New England in King Philip's War* (1958); Richard Slotkin and James K. Folsom, eds., *So Dreadfull a Judgment: Puritan Responses to King Philip's War, 1676–1677* (1978).

See also BLOODY BROOK MASSACRE; FALLS FIGHT; GREAT SWAMP FIGHT; NARRAGANSETT; NEW ENGLAND CONFEDERATION; PHILIP; PLYMOUTH; SPRINGFIELD, BURNING OF; WAMPANOAG

King William's War (1689–1697; also War of the League of Augsburg, the Nine Years' War: 1688–1697)

The most obvious importance of this war is that it was the first of four contests extending from 1689 to 1763 between England and France for control of North America. More than that, however, the war exhibits patterns military, political, and constitutional that characterize all the colonial wars in British North America.

The first war in this series erupted in Europe in 1688 as an effort by the League of Augsburg, composed of Austria, several German states, Spain, Sweden, Savoy, the Netherlands, and eventually England, to resist French expansion. Mutual exhaustion of the combatants brought the War of the League of Augsburg, or the Nine Years' War, as it was known in Europe, to an inconclusive end in the Treaty of Ryswick, 1697. The treaty settled no outstanding differences among the major combatants, and since King Louis XIV's territorial ambitions remained unfulfilled, the peace following the treaty was merely a prelude to successive struggles of ever greater magnitude and scope.

The European struggle rapidly spread to North America where later historians refer to it as King William's War, after the English monarch at that time. In America, the European war merged with bitter rivalries among Native Americans and between English and French colonists. Long before the European war began, the Iroquois confederacy, consisting of five "nations," the Seneca, Cayuga, Onondaga, Oneida, and Mohawk, tried to expand into the St. Lawrence River valley from their own territory which lay east and south of Lakes Erie and Ontario. The Algonquin residents of the valley joined with the more westerly Hurons to repel this invasion, but the enmity remained deep and persistent. These Native American political realities merged with European competition for control of the region's peoples and their fur trade. The northern Algonquins and Hurons succeeded in persuading the French to aid them against the Iroquois. The Iroquois, in turn, looked to the English at New York for economic and military support. The English were as eager as the Iroquois to cultivate friendly relations. Not only were the Iroquois a valuable source of furs, but they were in the process of expanding their hegemony over tribes to the west in what is now Ohio and Illinois. If successful, the Iroquois would divert the flow of western furs to Albany and the British rather than to Montreal and the French. Such an eventuality would seriously jeopardize Canada's economy, as well as undermine French influence in the interior. In addition to such economic advantages, the English valued the confederacy's military strength and strategic location as protection for New York from its northern enemies. Mutual self-interest brought the Iroquois and the English together at Albany in 1677 to sign an alliance, called the Covenant Chain. Although technically the treaty included all the English colonies from Virginia to Massachusetts, the location of the negotiations, as well as geographical realities, made New York the chief English participant and beneficiary.

While France and England were still at peace in Europe, competition between their respective colonies was rapidly moving toward open war. Both the Iroquois and English traders sought to penetrate the French-controlled western territory to capture control of the fur trade. To protect the Iroquois from French retaliation, New York's governor, Thomas Dongan, went so far as to claim the Iroquois as British subjects and to push British territorial claims as far north as the St. Lawrence River—claims that even the independent-minded Iroquois would dispute.

Canada's governor general, Jacques-René de Brisay, marquis de Denonville (1637–1710), defied Dongan by conducting a punitive expedition into Iroquois country. In 1687, a mixed force of 2,000 French and Indians burned five Seneca villages and destroyed their food supplies. Humiliated by their defeat and feeling deserted by the English, the Iroquois agreed to discuss peace terms with the French that the entire confederacy would ratify the following spring.

Conditions on New England's northeastern frontier were no more stable than in New York. The bitter legacy of King Philip's War still festered among the Abenaki Indians in Massachusetts's eastern dependency, Maine. They resented the failure of provincial authorities to honor the terms of the Treaty of Casco that in 1678 ended the northern phase of King Philip's War. Supplies of corn promised in the treaty were not paid to the Indians nor did the provincial government fulfill its obligation to prevent further encroachment on Indian land. Continued friction with the English forced these eastern Indians—later designated by their riverine locations between the Saco River and Passamaquoddy Bay—to relocate further to the north and east where they increasingly came under French influence.

In the summer and fall of 1688, Indian resentment boiled over in sporadic raids that Massachusetts Governor Sir Edmund Andros (1637–1714) was unable to quell either by military force or by negotiations. Governor Andros himself was partly responsible for the renewed hostilities. In 1688, he led an expedition to Penobscot Bay that looted and destroyed a French trading post owned by baron Jean-Vincent d'Abbadie de St. Castin (1652–1707), a former French army officer who, when his unit was disbanded, became an Indian trader and married the daughter of an important chief, Madockawando. Aided by Indian allies, St. Castin retaliated by destroying a rival English post at Pemaquid (Bristol) along the coast to the west. In Maine, as in New York, competing imperial claims of England and France conflicted and clashed, absorbed and became absorbed, in rivalries among Native Americans before the outbreak of hostilities between England and France in Europe.

These American hostilities merged into one war when England declared war on France in May 1689. England's participation in the anti-French coalition evolved out of the "Glorious Revolution," when English political leaders forced their autocratic Catholic monarch, James II, to flee to France. In February 1689, Parliament bestowed the crown on the Dutch leader, William of Orange (1650–1702) and his wife, Mary. In contrast to James, the new king, William III, promised to rule through Parliament, protect traditional English liberties and the Protestant faith. He also reversed James II's pro-French foreign policy by bringing England into the War of the League of Augsburg.

News of the Glorious Revolution and of probable war with France created a crisis in England's North American colonies. In 1686, James had merged all the colonies from New York northward into a centralized political union called the Dominion of New England. Throughout the dominion, the arbitrary rule of a single governor general, Sir Edmund Andros, replaced colonial institutions of self-government. But rumors of the Glorious Revolution triggered a reaction against James's dominion officials. If James was no longer monarch, commissions based on his authority were no longer valid. Seizing the unexpected opportunity, dissident Puritan leaders in Massachusetts carried out a "coup." On 18 April 1689, they arrested the governor general on his return from campaigning in Maine and eventually sent him back to England. Amid public expressions of loyalty to William and Mary and to English liberties, Massachusetts Puritans resumed their old government in hopes the new sovereigns would confirm their actions by restoring their charter. Following the bay colony's example, the other Dominion colonies quietly resumed their previous forms of self-government as well.

In May and June, New York followed suit. A faction of ambitious malcontents led by merchant Jacob Leisler (1640–1691) forced the dominion's lieutenant governor, Sir Francis Nicholson, to flee to England and seized power themselves. Claiming to save New York from French invasion and from pro-French crypto-Catholic subversives, Leisler and his supporters declared their allegiance to England's new sovereigns and to the Protestant faith. Unlike the New England colonies, however, New York had no charter or pre-dominion form of self-government to fill the constitutional vacuum created by the dominion's collapse. Leisler and his followers desperately needed some form of royal approval to legalize their coup—to make it appear a preservation of liberties, rather than a revolutionary seizure of power by dissidents.

At the very moment a formal war with France appeared a certainty, the northern British American colonies destroyed the Dominion of New England, their one institutional hope for unified action against the enemy. In its place, seven "revolutionary" regimes reappeared claiming to restore English rights of self-government to their colonists. In practical terms this meant the primacy of local provincial interests at the expense of intercolonial and imperial concerns. With no recognized leadership for conducting the war, each English colony hoped the new government in England would sanction their actions and someone else would assume responsibility for fighting the French.

The Iroquois eagerly assumed that role, confident they no longer needed to make peace with the French now that the English were finally at war. At dawn on 4 August 1689, 1,500 Iroquois fell on the unsuspecting community of Lachine, about six miles from Montreal. Their savage surprise was a complete success, for news of the war had not yet reached Canada. Fifty-six farms were destroyed and more than 100 Canadians killed or captured. Throughout the rest of the summer Iroquois war parties ravaged the Canadian frontier, forcing the French to abandon Forts Niagara and Frontenac, which controlled the water routes westward.

At this critical moment, French morale received a considerable boost with the arrival of a new governor general. Louis de Buade, comte de Frontenac (1622–1698), was no stranger to Canada. Having served as governor general from 1672 to 1682, he was recalled to answer charges of maladministration and corruption. Now 70 years old, the crusty old soldier/courtier returned vindicated, with an audacious scheme for a campaign by land and sea to seize New York, bisecting the English colonies and destroying their association with the Iroquois. Insufficient support from home forced Frontenac to discard that plan in favor of one more suitable to his limited resources. He first gained a respite from the Iroquois by requesting peace negotiations in the spring. Meanwhile, to keep the English off balance, he dispatched from Canada three French-Indian raiding parties against Albany, Salmon Falls in New Hampshire, and Falmouth (Portland) in Maine. The French assaults were as devastatingly successful as that of the Iroquois against Lachine the year before. The first blow fell on the village of Schenectady, which the attackers assumed would be an easier victim than more heavily defended Albany. They were right; the little community was deeply divided over Leisler's recent seizure of government, and the inhabitants had gone to bed on the night of 8 February 1690 without setting a guard or securing the gate. The enemy struck about dawn; in the space of two hours the village was in flames, some 60 inhabitants lay dead, and 27 more were being hurried away into captivity with the retreating raiders.

Salmon Falls and Falmouth experienced similar fates. A mixed force of 50 Canadians and Indians surprised the little village of Salmon Falls, several miles inland from Portsmouth, in mid-March. Typical of many New England towns, Salmon Falls was an extended rather than a compact settlement. Except for several fortified garrison houses, the town had no effective means of defense when the enemy struck. The attackers killed 34 residents and carried off more than 50 more after burning their homes and slaughtering the livestock.

In May, it was Falmouth's turn to suffer. A large party of 500 French and Indians, including St. Castin and participants from the raids against Schenectady and Salmon Falls, first destroyed the village of Casco, killing 20 inhabitants. The survivors fled to nearby Fort Loyal at

McIntyre Garrison House, York, Maine, c. 1707. Photograph first published in Robert L. Bradley, Maine's First Buildings: The Architecture of Settlement, 1604–1700 *(Augusta: Maine Historic Preservation Commission, 1978). Reproduction by permission of the Commission.*

Falmouth, to which the enemy laid siege. The outnumbered defenders held on for three days, but on the fourth, their commander made an agreement with his French counterpart to surrender on the promise they be allowed to depart in safety. As soon as the English surrendered, however, the French allowed their Indian allies to seize whomever they thought most valuable and to massacre the rest on the excuse that one need not keep one's word to rebels against their lawful king.

The French and Indians had no monopoly on the brutality of frontier warfare. In a futile effort to intimidate the Maine Indians and to separate them from their French allies, Massachusetts commissioned the portly, aging hero of King Philip's War, Benjamin Church (1639–1718), to lead a series of expeditions composed of English militia and mercenary Indians from southern and eastern New England. Near Brunswick in Maine, Church surprised an Indian fort occupied largely by women and chil-

dren while their men were away fighting. Church's own account states that while he saved several of the more important captives as hostages, the rest of them, women and children, he had "Knock'd on the head." Clearly, neither age nor sex provided any protection in frontier war.

The success of the French and Indians against the extended and vulnerable English frontier convinced the colonial governments they would have to take action against the enemy. Indeed, the colonial revolutionary regimes may have seen a successful campaign as a means to justify their existence and to preclude any future restoration of the dominion by authorities in England. After all, there were only 1,000 French settlers in Acadia still dependent for sustenance on New England, and 10,000 in Canada itself. Such numbers paled into insignificance in contrast to the English, whose North American population in 1690 totaled more than 200,000. New York and Connecticut numbered 3,000 and 4,000 men of military age, respectively; Rhode

Island had more than 800, while New England (Massachusetts, Plymouth, and New Hampshire) had a military potential of 12,000 men. Together, these northerly colonies possessed a military population of 20,000, almost half the total number of adult males in all the English colonies. With the aid of the Iroquois, who could field a force of 2,800 warriors, the English clearly possessed sufficient force to eliminate the French threat once and for all. The problem for the English, besides the major one of intercolonial cooperation, was how to reach the enemy, for the French in Montreal and Quebec had the advantage of highly defensible, compact settlements in the midst of a friendly Indian population. To expel the French from Canada would entail a major expedition, detailed planning, large sums of money, and above all, cooperation.

The prospects for such an expedition appeared favorable when an intercolonial conference met at New York in May 1690 under the auspices of New York's insurgent leader, Jacob Leisler. Only Massachusetts, Plymouth, and Connecticut—which had already dispatched reinforcements to Albany—sent delegates, but Rhode Island and Maryland indicated their support by promising money and men to a cooperative venture. The plan that emerged from the conference laid down a grand strategy that would dominate American-British military thinking in respect to Canada until 1759, and even during the American Revolution. It called for an intercolonial army, accompanied by a force of Iroquois, to proceed overland, cross Lake George and Lake Champlain to the Richelieu River to take Montreal. Meanwhile, an amphibious operation from Massachusetts would lay siege to Quebec. New York offered 400 troops, Connecticut 135, Plymouth 60, and Massachusetts, because it was already engaged in an expedition against Port Royal and would carry the burden of the seaborne attack against Quebec, agreed to furnish only 160 men. It was enough; with 100 troops promised by Maryland, the force totaled 855 English, and the Iroquois were expected to supply at least 1,000 warriors.

The ease with which an expedition from Massachusetts captured the French settlement at Port Royal in Acadia (Nova Scotia) raised expectations that Quebec might fall with equal ease. Leading the expedition was Sir William Phips (1651–1695), a former ship's carpenter from Maine who rose to prominence through a profitable marriage, successful trade, and the

recovery of sunken treasure. With 700 Massachusetts troops, Phips arrived before Port Royal on 19 May 1690. The French governor and his small garrison surrendered almost immediately, but the lack of resistance did not save the town, despite Phips's assurances that it would. When Phips returned in triumph to Boston at the end of the month, he carried with him the French governor, two Catholic priests, and enough plunder to pay the costs of the expedition. The lessons of the expedition were clear: the colonies were capable of mounting their own campaign against Quebec, and it would pay for itself through plunder, especially of Quebec's Catholic churches, which were supposedly crammed with gold and silver ornaments. In short, the enemy would be forced to pay for its own defeat.

Despite such prospects of success, the grand plan to seize New France fell victim to factional distrust, intercolonial rivalries, ineptitude, and simple bad luck. At the very outset, a quarrel ensued over who would command the expedition. Only with ill-grace did Leisler agree to accept Connecticut's candidate, Fitz-John Winthrop, a person of considerable military experience, in place of Leisler's nominee, Jacob Milborne. Well might Leisler comply with Connecticut's demands; that colony alone had met its promised quota of 135 troops; New York managed to raise 150, while Massachusetts, Plymouth, and Maryland sent none. The Iroquois, dismayed by the lack of English enthusiasm and ravaged by smallpox, sent only a token contingent that spread the disease among the English troops gathering at Albany. It was a small, sickly force that finally set out from Albany late in July, only to halt at the lower tip of Lake Champlain. There it waited and then, lacking provisions and the means for transportation, turned back..

The collapse of the overland expedition infuriated Jacob Leisler, who desperately needed a military triumph to quell growing opposition to his administration. He arrested Fitz-John Winthrop, the commander of the expedition, and threw him into jail for deliberately sabotaging the enterprise—but soon released him on vigorous protests from Connecticut. The most Leisler could hope for was to salvage some prestige with both Indians and English from a raid by a mixed force of 150 English and Iroquois led by Captain John Schuyler. As the dispirited troops from the failed expedition straggled back to Albany, Schuyler led his force along the route the expedition had intended to follow. On 23 August, they fell on the village of La Prairie, just across the St. Lawrence from Montreal. As at Lachine, Schenectady, and Salmon Falls, surprise was complete and savage. The raiders killed half a dozen men, destroyed houses, barns, livestock, and haystacks, and returned to Albany by the end of August with 19 prisoners. The destruction of La Prairie again terrorized the Canadian frontier and gained some measure of revenge for the Schenectady massacre, but presented a feeble alternative to the intercolonial expedition. It did not save Leisler, nor did it reassure the Iroquois of English commitment to the war.

The other half of the grand plan turned into an even greater embarrassment. With remarkable exertion, Massachusetts embarked an army of 1,300 militia aboard 32 vessels under the command of the hero of Port Royal, Sir William Phips. To raise and equip such a force took more time than planned, so the expedition did not set out until late August, by which time it was not only late in the season, but the overland expedition from New York was already a failure. Nevertheless, in Massachusetts, optimism ran so high that the General Court raised no money to finance the campaign, expecting plunder from Quebec, as from Port Royal, to pay the costs. The expedition, battling adverse winds and hazardous navigation in the St. Lawrence, reached Quebec in the middle of October with the feel of winter in the air.

Governor General Frontenac, well-informed of the impending attack, reinforced Quebec with troops no longer needed at Montreal to resist the expedition from New York. To defend Quebec, Frontenac now had some 3,000 regulars and militia. With supreme contempt, he dismissed Phips's demand to surrender, calling the English "Hereticks and Traitors to their King" who had "taken up with that Usurper, the Prince of Orange, and had made a Revolution." Quebec was no Port Royal; everything went wrong for the English forces. Twelve hundred militia under Major John Walley, of Plymouth, landed just east of Quebec intending to march along a little tributary called the St. Charles to attack the city from the rear, while the fleet bombarded it from the river. Immediately the landing force ran up against 600 French, who pinned down the invaders in a swampy place where their six field guns sank uselessly into the soft ground. For three days and three freezing nights, the militia expended their ammunition trying to dislodge the French, while the fleet consumed much of its ammunition in a cannonade of the fort. The bombardment did little harm to the fort, but French guns seriously damaged several ships—including the flagship which commander in chief Phips, still a ship's carpenter, helped to repair. Meanwhile, the weather grew colder and stormy, smallpox appeared among the fleet, and morale reached such a low among the land forces that when Walley and Phips decided they should return to the fleet, reembarkment became a rout that left behind most of the cannon.

Low on ammunition, provisions, morale, and military alternatives, Phips acknowledged defeat by ordering the expedition to sail for home on 25 October, little suspecting the return voyage would be far more lethal than the fighting. Thirty New Englanders died in combat, while approximately 60 were wounded. On the way back, however, wintry storms battered and scattered the fleet. Phips reached Boston on 19 November, but many of the remaining vessels were driven far off course; some as far away as the Caribbean, while others were lost at sea, one with all hands. All told, 300 to 400 men died, the vast majority by disease and shipwreck. For example, more than half the men who enlisted from the Massachusetts towns of Dorchester and Braintree died as a result of their service; in Dorchester, 57 more died from the epidemic that followed their return. Little wonder that Phips remained in Boston only long enough to lay blame for the disaster on his commander of the land forces, Major John Walley, and soon set out for England to repair his reputation there. He left behind in Massachusetts a bankrupt government facing a debt of more than £40,000 for the failed expedition, and soldiers verging on mutiny for lack of pay. In desperation, the General Court resorted to the novel expedient of issuing paper currency as legal tender. The paper depreciated rapidly, but it served the needs of the moment and set an irresistible precedent for the future.

Among the victims of the failed expedition were New York's insurgent leaders, Jacob Leisler and his associate, Jacob Milborne. The failure of the overland campaign deprived them of any recognition and legitimacy in London. When the new monarchs belatedly turned their attention to New York, they commissioned as their new royal governor Colonel Henry Sloughter (d. 1691), and renamed as his resident council those who had served under James's appointee, Sir Francis Nicholson—who were also Leisler's inveterate opponents. Leisler was understandably reluctant to surrender his authority when the new governor arrived in March 1691. When he finally yielded, Sloughter immediately arrested Leisler and Milborne. At the urging of his council, Sloughter tried the two insurgents for treason, and on their conviction, executed them at once without allowing any appeal to England. Three years later, the "martyred" leaders and a half-dozen convicted followers received royal pardons, but the factional bitterness polarized New York politics for years to come.

The dismal failure of the joint campaign of 1690 cooled colonial ardor for such military undertakings through the rest of the war. After 1690, the English fought the war defensively without any broader strategy than survival and revenge. In 1693, a British fleet under Sir Francis Wheeler stopped briefly at Boston to provide assistance for a renewed attack on Quebec. The northern colonies, however, were in no condition to resume such an enterprise, even had there been sufficient time for preparation. The fleet, which was returning to England from an unsuccessful campaign in the West Indies, was so riddled with disease that more than half of its sailors and soldiers had died. New England was well rid of its pestilential ally when the fleet resumed its voyage to England without attempting any joint action against the enemy. But failure to renew united efforts against New France had a dampening effect on New York's first line of defense, the Iroquois.

The loyalty of the Iroquois was becoming a matter of increasing concern to New York's governor. The Indians complained bitterly that the English colonies failed to send help and refused to fulfill the obligations of the Covenant Chain against the common enemy. To allay their fears, Governor Sloughter met with the Iroquois chiefs at Albany in spring 1691 to reassure them of English support and commitment to the war. As though to prove it, in the summer 1691, Colonel Peter Schuyler led yet another Anglo-Iroquois party of 400 men into the region of Montreal. Too late he discovered the French had been alerted, and his party succeeded in returning to Albany at the price of 40 dead and only after the most desperate hand-to-hand combat.

Aware of Iroquois discontent with their English allies, Frontenac devised a strategy to neutralize the Indians by a skillful combination of force and negotiations. In February 1693, Frontenac dispatched 400 regulars and militia

with 200 mission Indians to invade Mohawk territory. Catching their enemy by surprise, the raiders destroyed three villages with their winter food supplies and hastily set out for home with 300 prisoners. Vigorous pursuit badly mauled the retreating French and freed most of their prisoners, but the fact remained that the enemy had penetrated to the heart of Iroquois country. The new governor of New York, Colonel Benjamin Fletcher (1639–1718)—Sloughter having died of a guilty conscience, according to supporters of Jacob Leisler—quickly sent reinforcements to the northern frontier and tried to reassure the Mohawks with promises of provisions and protection. At the same time, Fletcher urged the Indians to restore their honor by retaliating against the French. The Iroquois, in turn, reminded the governor that they were in this war together and the enemy might be attacked by sea as well as by land if the colonies would only unite and join with a fleet from England—an embarrassing reminder of the fiasco of 1690 and subsequent colonial disunity.

Try as he might, Fletcher could not persuade the other colonies to assist New York in defending its northern frontier, let alone launch another attack on Canada. The most Fletcher could do was convene another intercolonial conference at Albany in 1694 in a futile effort to dissuade the Iroquois from making peace with the French by a display of colonial cooperation. The Iroquois were not fooled; they were already negotiating a truce with Frontenac for, as one of the Iroquois sachems explained, "The Fat is melted from our Flesh, and fallen on our Neighbours, who grow fat while we grow lean: They flourish while we decay." These were grim days for New York: the Iroquois appeared to be deserting the English cause, other English colonies ignored New York's demands for military assistance, and even New York's own assembly, weary of the cost in defending the frontier and suspicious of Fletcher's honesty, was increasingly reluctant to raise money and troops for its own defense.

The English enjoyed no better success on the northeastern frontier extending from western Massachusetts into eastern Maine. Cotton Mather titled his history of the period *Decennium Luctuosum* (The Sorrowful Decade), and it is a sorry tale of repeated raids by the French and Indians against frontier settlements so small, isolated and extended as to be indefensible. As in King Philip's War, the Connecticut River valley towns were again subjected to raids and ambushes. In the course of the war, Hatfield

K

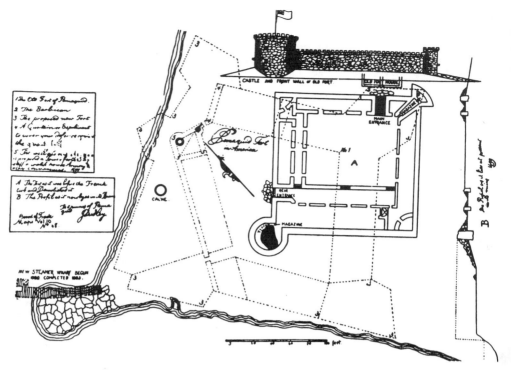

Fort William Henry. Colonel Romer's 1699 sketch of Fort William Henry is in the Public Record Office, Kew, Richmond, Surrey, England. Document reference number: C.O. 700, Maine/4.

suffered two attacks, Hadley and Brookfield one each, and Deerfield, the northernmost, withstood no less than six. As terrible as the experience was for towns of western Massachusetts, the settlements of Maine bore a far costlier burden.

In February 1692, 200–300 local Indians, reinforced with a few French, including St. Castin, surprised the town of York. Although they spared several old women and children in recognition of those saved by Benjamin Church in his massacre at Brunswick, the attackers killed 48, took 73 prisoners, and then burned the town. Had not Massachusetts sent timely relief, the survivors would have abandoned the settlement entirely. In June, the blow fell on the neighboring towns of Wells. Five hundred French and Indians attacked the settlement's five fortified houses, defended only by the residents themselves aided by Captain James Converse and 29 militiamen. Despite the apparent hopelessness of the situation, the English refused demands to surrender. Aided by the presence of two English sloops that arrived to deliver supplies, the small garrison successfully fended off the Indian assaults. The Indians burned the town, killed the

livestock, and tried unsuccessfully to set the sloops on fire with fire arrows and even a burning raft. Perhaps as a final effort to draw the garrison out of its defenses, the Indians brought forth an English captive. Just beyond musket range of the defenders, they stripped their victim, scalped him alive, and after castrating him, slit his body and stuck burning brands into the gashes. Still the garrison held fast, and leaving their victim bleeding and blazing, the enemy withdrew in frustration.

Except for seasonal raids conducted by Converse and Benjamin Church into the countryside to destroy Indian villages and food supplies, the Massachusetts government conducted an entirely defensive sort of warfare. The most impressive manifestation of that mentality was the construction in 1692 of Fort William Henry at Pemaquid, Maine. Since 1625 or so, Pemaquid had been England's easternmost outpost and its tangible claim to the region. But Pemaquid led a precarious existence; in 1677 and 1689, the Indians and French had destroyed the settlement. Now, in 1692, the new royal governor of Massachusetts, none other than Sir William Phips himself, received royal orders to refortify the

Tower of Fort William Henry. Photograph first published in Robert L. Bradley, The Forts of Maine, 1607–1945: An Archaeological and Historical Survey *(Augusta: Maine Historical Preservation Commission, 1981). Reproduction by permission of the Commission.*

place. With assurances of repayment by the crown, the provincial legislature raised £20,000 for an impressive stone fortification. Benjamin Church derided such static defenses as "Nests for Destruction," as he ranged the countryside to protect the builders. Even today, the partially reconstructed fort presents an impressive facade. A menacing stone tower 29 feet high surmounts walls six feet thick and, in some places, 22 feet high that encompass a quadrangle 108 feet square. Eighteen cannon defended the structure, six of them 18-pounders. No wonder Phips boasted his fort was strong enough to resist all the Indians in America.

The construction of Fort William Henry, as well as another new fort across the river from Saco (now Biddeford), deeply concerned eastern Indians, whose plight was analogous to that of the Iroquois. Lacking French aid to destroy the forts, and fearing the English might enlist the Mohawks against them, 13 Abenaki saga-mores representing tribes from Saco to Passamaquoddy came to Fort William Henry in August 1693 to talk peace. They agreed to submit to the English crown, restore captives, resume trade with the English, and to refrain from intercourse with the French.

The French, however, could not allow a cessation of hostilities in Maine that might release English resources against Quebec. Claude-Sebastien, sieur de Villieu (ca. 1690), French commander at Penobscot, and (according to Puritans, at least) French missionaries at Norridgewock, especially Father Sebastien Rale (1657–1724), excited a continuation of hostilities among the Abenaki. Cotton Mather, a leading Puritan preacher, was convinced the French missionaries taught the Abenaki they need not keep their treaty promises with heretics. The Indians themselves were divided over what policy to follow, and while one faction sought peace, others remained unreconciled. In any case, Indian raiding parties struck again at Dover, York, Kittery, and even Groton during the summer of 1694, effectively ending the short-lived peace. The war continued, but by now the Maine Indians were in a badly weakened condition. War had taken a severe toll on their villages, food supplies, and population. Indian efforts to reopen peace negotiations broke down in summer 1695 and also in February 1696 when the commander of Fort William Henry, Captain Pasco Chubb, apparently assuming Puritans need not heed promises to heathens, killed several of the Abenaki peace delegation. So the war dragged on through 1695—as much a stalemate on the northeastern frontier as it had become on New York's frontier.

The stalemate in both areas ended abruptly in summer 1696 when Frontenac regained the initiative for France through several superbly executed expeditions. In July, Frontenac gathered at Montreal a mixed force of 2,000 men who, with the 74-year-old governor general at their head, paddled up the St. Lawrence to Fort Frontenac on Lake Ontario; then, after crossing the lake with artillery, and bearing their feisty governor on a litter, invaded the very heart of Iroquois country from the west. Caught by surprise, the Onondagas fled in terror, leaving their villages in flames. The Oneidas were next, and although they hastily sued for peace, Frontenac put their villages to the torch as well, arguing if they truly wanted peace and safety they would have to move to Canada and end their association with the English. So ponderous a force inflicted little loss of life among the Iroquois, but it testified to French power in contrast to English helplessness.

In a fall conference with New York's Governor Fletcher, the Iroquois again pleaded for a united attack to root the French out of Canada: "We are now down upon one knee, but we are not quite down upon the ground, lett the Great King of England send the great cannoes with seaventy guns each, and let the brethren . . . awake, and we will stand up straight againe upon our feet; our heart is yet stout and good; we doubt not but to destroy the enemy." Fletcher could offer nothing more substantial than condolences and empty promises, but to demonstrate his good faith and concern, he endured a winter at Albany in watchful proximity to the Iroquois. While Frontenac intimidated the Iroquois with his display of French power, another expedition set out from Quebec to end the military impasse in Maine. Three ships carrying two companies of troops under

the command of Pierre Le Moyne d'Iberville (1661–1706) and 200 Indians, along with St. Castin and Sebastien de Villieu, suddenly appeared at Pemaquid in August 1696 equipped for a formal siege of Fort William Henry. Phips's formidable fortification failed the test of battle. Since the fort's water supply was located outside the fort itself, the garrison could not have withstood a long siege in any case. A more pressing problem arose from the clay mortar the builders had used owing to the lack of lime. Even before the attack, Fort William Henry's ramparts were beginning to crumble, and during the engagement, the firing of the fort's cannon caused the walls to shudder and crumble more. Commander Pasco Chubb and his 95-man garrison surrendered after only token resistance. The French managed to prevent a massacre of the garrison, which was allowed safe passage to Boston. There Chubb was court martialed and expelled from the service; he retired to his home in Andover where a year and a half later he died in an Indian raid on the town. The French, meanwhile, dismantled Fort William Henry— apparently not a very arduous task. They were long gone by the time Benjamin Church led his fourth and final expedition into the interior as far as the Bay of Fundy in yet another futile effort to come to grips with the elusive enemy.

After destroying Fort William Henry, Iberville sailed northeast to Newfoundland where he laid waste the most important English fishing settlements, reducing English occupation to a mere foothold. The year following, he led an expedition to Hudson Bay that destroyed three armed ships belonging to the British Hudson's Bay Company and seized Fort Nelson on the west shore of the bay, which controlled a key water route into the interior.

By the time England and France signed the Treaty of Ryswick in September 1697, the French clearly had regained the initiative in the American war. They had forced the Iroquois to seek peace, rolled back the New England frontier until it consisted only of Wells, York, Kittery and Isles of Shoals, seized most of Newfoundland, and controlled a key area of the Hudson Bay region. Yet, the situation was not entirely one-sided. While Iberville was busy in Hudson Bay, a fleet from England regained control of the English fishing villages in Newfoundland, and despite French success at Port Nelson, the English remained in control of St. James Bay. New York and New England may have trembled in fear of a French-Indian invasion, but the enemy never had the resources at its disposal for anything more than raids against isolated objectives.

The terms of the Treaty of Ryswick, by which territories seized during the war reverted to previous owners, rather accurately reflected the military situation in America as well as in Europe. The French retained control of several posts they had seized in Hudson Bay, where the borders remained ill-defined, and regained possession of their posts in Newfoundland. The treaty resolved none of the conflicting territorial claims or rivalries over control of the fur trade that had precipitated the conflict; indeed, by failing to deal with those issues, the war merely accentuated the old tensions.

The end of the war between Europeans did not mean an end to hostilities involving Native Americans. Both the eastern Indians and the Iroquois emphasized their autonomy by their determination to remain independent of the European peace terms. In New England, the Indian raids continued sporadically into summer 1698, and not until the fall of that year were the Indians, ravaged by disease and famine and deserted by the French, willing to discuss peace with the English. At Brunswick in January 1699, the Indians promised to return all prisoners, agreed to submit to the protection of the English government, and declared their allegiance to the English crown. In turn, the Massachusetts commissioners pardoned the Indians for conducting war against the English, thereby accepting the Indians' argument that French intrigue was to blame for the outbreak of hostilities. Here, too, the causes of the war remained unsettled, and it was doubtful if promises of protection and pledges of allegiance were anything more than face-saving expedients.

The Iroquois, like the Abenaki, suffered grievously in the course of the war. Through death, disease, and desertion to Canada, their fighting strength dropped from 2,800 when the war began to 1,250 when it ended. Nonetheless, it took the Iroquois until 1701, the eve of the second great imperial war, to conclude peace with the French and their Indian allies—some of whom, such as the Hurons, Ottowa, Miami, and Potawatomi—still waged war against the western Iroquois. Yet the Iroquois refused to permit the English to include them as dependents in the peace terms of Ryswick, nor would the French accept such a testimony of British hegemony; so Frontenac, and his successor, Louis-Hector, chevalier de Callière (1648–

1703), insisted the Iroquois speak for themselves. When they finally consented to peace at Montreal in 1701, the Iroquois did not abandon outright their old alliance with the English—its economic advantages, if not the military ones, were too valuable for that. Instead, they simply agreed to peace terms with the French Indians, and adopted a position of neutrality between England and France in any future wars. The English of New York thereby lost their most militant allies, yet were not entirely the losers. The neutral Iroquois still served as a buffer for New York's northern frontier that the French were reluctant to disturb. Neutrality served the interests of all three sides so well that, during the first few years of the next struggle, the New York frontier enjoyed unusual tranquility, while New England bore the brunt of the fighting.

Despite the fact France seemed to emerge from the war stronger than before, the French had endured severe hardships. Historian William J. Eccles estimates the war cost French Canada more than 300 dead and so disrupted Canada's economy that the government found it difficult to provide for the swarm of war refugees that fled to Quebec and Montreal from as far away as Newfoundland. Oddly enough, the war's impact on the fur trade did not lessen the supply in Canadian warehouses, but increased it as the French extended their forts westward. Forts served an economic function as well as a military one, and did so to such a degree that they caused a glut of furs not only in Canada, but also in Europe, with a resultant sharp drop in prices.

The war bore unequally on the English; it effected only the northern English colonies, with New England carrying much of the burden. By the time the Maine Indians came to terms, the eastern frontier lay in ruins beyond the little town of Wells, and Indians had raided interior settlements within 20 miles of Boston. Maine's nineteenth-century historian, William Williamson, estimates about 700 settlers were killed or captured—most in Maine itself. As in Canada, refugee families created difficult social and economic problems for the larger towns to which they fled. New England's fragile economy suffered severely through the loss of trade to Newfoundland, and by the destruction of its fishing vessels by French privateers and Indian raiders, as adept at sea as on land. Yet, the war stimulated New England's mast trade and also the risky business of privateering against French shipping. One of the risks involved private vessels commissioned to cruise against the enemy that often turned pirate— New York's governor, Benjamin Fletcher, became notorious for his protection of returning pirates in exchange for a share of the loot. Perhaps the most famous of all was Captain William Kidd, whose career carried him from New York to the Red Sea and eventually to a gibbet at Execution Dock in London.

The psychological burden of the troubled times appears most dramatically in Salem, Massachusetts, where the famous witchcraft trials occurred in 1692. Purely local and particularistic causes for the hysteria surely exist, yet the episode takes place in a provincial society devastated by a sense of sin and God's wrath as revealed in King Philip's War by the loss of the provincial charter, and now King William's War. In his account of this sorrowful decade, *Decennium Luctuosum*, Cotton Mather refers to the outbreak of witchcraft in Salem as a "Prodigious War, made by the Spirits of the Invisible World upon the People of New England," and surmises it might have its origin "among the Indians, whose chief Sagamores are well known unto some of our Captives, to have been horned Sorcerers, and hellish Conjurers and such as Conversed with Daemons." To Mather, war and witchcraft were inextricably linked by the "Great God" who "had further Intentions to Chastise a Sinful People, by those who are not a People."

Against such an enemy bay colony Puritans showed little mercy. They executed 20 people as witches; Indians they hunted down and scalped when this was not their own fate. Hannah Duston won undying fame by the manner of her escape from a band of Indians who burned Haverhill in 1697, dashed out the brains of her newborn child, and carried her into captivity with several other survivors. For the return to Canada, the Indians assigned Duston, another woman, and a young English boy to a small band of a dozen Indians, two warriors, three women, and seven children—a curious sort of war party. On an April night, over a hundred miles en route to Canada, Duston and her two companions quietly picked up their captors' own hatchets and methodically smashed in their skulls while the Indians lay sleeping. Only one old woman and a young boy escaped the slaughter. After scalping their victims, Duston and her companions returned to "civilization" as heroes to claim their reward of £50 in scalp bounties.

Such intensity of spirit did not characterize the provincial administrations responsible for conducting the war. After the failures of 1690, the colonies did not again attempt any unified action against Canada. Instead, they remained on the defensive, dissipating their numerical advantage in quarrels over who should aid whom, when, and how. With the collapse of voluntary intercolonial cooperation came schemes of joint action from England as authorities there sought alternative to the old Dominion of New England. With each colony now autonomous, the problem lay in how to persuade or coerce colonial governments to cooperate militarily without infringing on their rights of self-government. One step was to appoint as royal governors men experienced in military affairs. Sir William Phips, Massachusetts' wartime governor, at least had a reputation for military experience; the royal governors of New York, Colonel Henry Sloughter, and his successor, Colonel Benjamin Fletcher, were both experienced professional soldiers.

The English government expanded the authority of both Phips and Fletcher by authorizing them to call on the military strength of their neighbors to defend their vulnerable and strategic frontiers. Gradually, the Lords of Trade developed the view that New York, because of its proximity to the land route to and from Canada and to the Iroquois, was the military key to North America. Between 1691 and 1694, their lordships acknowledged the importance of New York by sending two companies of troops, paid from the royal treasury, to help in its defense. In addition, the crown expanded the New York governor's commission to include the governorship of Pennsylvania, authority to command the Connecticut militia, and to demand a quota of troops from all the other colonies in case of emergency. The policy failed for three basic reasons. Except for providing a garrison for Albany, the quota system was unworkable even had the other colonies sent the troops when requested. By the time they arrived in New York and were transported upriver to Albany, the emergency had long passed. Short of an all-out invasion of New York by the French, or of Canada by the English, the quota system was simply impractical.

The second reason for failure of the quota system lay in the refusal of the colonies to cooperate. Governor Phips, for example, was furious over royal favoritism shown to New York when Massachusetts had a far longer and more dangerous frontier to defend. He intrigued against Fletcher in England, and espoused Fletcher's political opponents in New York. When Fletcher sent an emissary to demand a quota of troops from Massachusetts for the defense of Albany, the Massachusetts governor fell into such a towering rage the messenger felt it prudent to withdraw. Less dramatically, but just as successfully, other colonies rejected Fletcher's appeals. Both Pennsylvania and Connecticut successfully nullified the extensions of Fletcher's authority. From England, William Penn encouraged his colonists to oppose Fletcher's commission. The obstinate Quakers needed no encouragement; they repeatedly rejected Fletcher's appeals for aid even when he requested nonmilitary assistance for the Iroquois rather than troops and warlike supplies. A similar deadlock occurred when Fletcher tried to exercise his authority to command the Connecticut militia. Civil authorities there stoutly insisted on their charter rights to control their own forces, and they appealed to England to escape Fletcher's jurisdiction. When the New York governor arrived in Connecticut to withdraw a militia quota to help guard Albany, the argument grew so heated the frustrated Fletcher seized one of his antagonists and hurled him down the stairs.

The stalemate in both Pennsylvania and Connecticut ended in 1694 when the English government finally acknowledged colonial complaints over lost charter rights and limited Fletcher's authority to New York. To compensate New York, the Lords of Trade again granted Fletcher power to demand from all colonies quotas to defend New York in case of invasion. To assist New York in providing a permanent garrison for Albany, the crown agreed to send two more companies of royal troops, increasing to 400 the forces raised and maintained at royal expense for defense of New York's borders.

The new imperial arrangement ended Fletcher's difficulties with the colonies of Pennsylvania and Connecticut, and the arrival of royal troops in the spring 1695 eased an awkward controversy between Fletcher and his assembly in New York over his handling of public money voted for defense. But within a year it was clear that nothing had been resolved. Colonial governments were less inclined than ever to send quotas to assist New York, since the crown seemed willing to shoulder more of the burden. Most colonies ignored Fletcher's frantic appeals to counter the French invasion of Iroquois country in 1696, and royal instructions in 1697 insisting colonies honor their assigned quotas had no effect. Soon, desertions among the royal troops at Albany required Fletcher to again appeal to his assembly for money to recruit replacements, reviving the controversy over his use—or misuse—of public funds.

So matters remained until the war ended in 1697, ending the need for quotas and garrisons for Albany. By that time, too, intrigue against Governor Fletcher in England reached a successful climax. King William agreed to replace Fletcher with Richard Coote, earl of Bellomont (1636–1701), who arrived in 1699 not only as governor of New York, but of Massachusetts (vacated by Phips's death) and of New Hampshire as well. In addition, Bellomont was commissioned captain general over the military forces of Connecticut, Rhode Island, and New Jersey. In this manner, the Board of Trade tried to re-create its own version of the old Dominion of New England with its political and military centralization—while at the same time acknowledging colonial self-government.

But herein lies the third essential weakness of the British imperial system that the British government seldom faced, never solved, and which doomed it from the start. This was the fundamental contradiction between a mercantile empire requiring absolute control on the one hand, and the large measure of self-government that the colonists enjoyed as English subjects on the other. This contradiction thwarted English governors at every turn both as soldiers and as politicians. Their tasks were made yet more impossible by the tendency of the British government to compromise its own commands in a futile effort to meet colonial protests. Imperial vacillation only stimulated colonial opposition, while denying royal governors assurances of support from the home government. Rather than confront the problem head-on, English authorities found it more convenient to muddle through each successive war by assuming an ever greater share of the military effort rather than resolving the constitutional contradiction at the heart of the empire. Not until the end of the French and Indian War did imperial officials come face to face with the constitutional problem of autonomous colonies in a mercantile empire, and by then it was too late; imperial reform turned into the American Revolution. Nothing points up this contradiction more clearly than King William's War, and in this lies its ultimate significance.

James S. Leamon

References

Bruce J. Bourque, "Ethnicity on the Maritime Peninsula, 1600–1759," *Ethnohistory*, 36 (summer 1989):257–284; Robert L. Bradley, *Maine's First Buildings: The Architecture of Settlement, 1604–1700* (1978); ———, *The Forts of Maine, 1607–1945: An Archaeological and Historical Survey* (1981).

Benjamin Church, *History of the Eastern Expeditions of 1689, 1690, 1692, 1696 and 1704* (1867); Cadwallader Colden, *The History of the Five Indian Nations: Depending on the Province of New-York in America* (1727), rpt. 1958; Wesley F. Craven, *The American Colonies in Transition, 1660–1713* (1968); W.J. Eccles, *Frontenac: The Courtier-Governor* (1959); ———, *France in America* (1972).

Evarts B. Greene and Virginia D. Harrington, comps., *American Population before the Federal Census of 1790* (1932); Philip S. Haffenden, *New England in the English Nation, 1689–1713* (1974); Thomas Hutchinson, *History of the Colony and Province of Massachusetts Bay*, 3 vols., ed. by Lawrence S. Mayo (1936); Francis Jennings, *The Ambiguous Iroquois Empire: The Covenant Chain Confederation of Indian Tribes with English Colonies from its beginnings to the Lancaster Treaty of 1744* (1984); Richard R. Johnson, *Adjustment to Empire: The New England Colonies, 1675–1715* (1981).

Douglas E. Leach, *The Northern Colonial Frontier, 1607–1763* (1966); James S. Leamon, "War, Finance and Faction in Colonial New York: The Administration of Governor Benjamin Fletcher, 1692–1698," Ph.D. Dissertation, Brown University (1961); Alice Lounsberry, *Sir William Phips* (1941); Cotton Mather, *Decennium Luctuosum* (1699) in *Narratives of the Indian Wars, 1675–1699*, ed. by Charles H. Lincoln (1913); ———, *Magnalia Christi Americana* (1702), ed. by Kenneth B. Murdock (1977).

Herbert L. Osgood, *The American Colonies in the Eighteenth Century*, Vol. 1 (1924); Francis Parkman, *Count Frontenac and New France Under Louis XIV* (1877); Howard H. Peckham, *The Colonial Wars, 1689–1762* (1964); Harry Ward, *"Unite or Die": Intercolonial Relations, 1690–1763* (1971); William D. Williamson, *The History of the State of Maine: from its first discovery, A.D. 1602 to the Separation, A.D. 1820, Inclusive*, 2 vols. (1832).

See also ABENAKI; ACADIA, NEW ENGLAND ATTACK ON (1690); BRACKETT'S WOODS, BATTLE OF; CANADA, NEW ENGLAND EXPEDITION AGAINST (1690); CHUBB, PASCO; CHURCH, BENJAMIN; CONVERSE, JAMES; DOMINION OF NEW ENGLAND; DOVER, ATTACK ON; DUSTON, HANNAH; ENGLISH REVOLUTION; FALMOUTH, BATTLE OF; FRONTENAC, LOUIS DE BUADE DE; LE MOYNE D'IBERVILLE, PIERRE; IROQUOIS; IROQUOIS TREATIES OF 1700 AND 1701; LACHINE, BATTLE OF; LA PRAIRIE, BATTLE OF (1690); LA PRAIRIE, BATTLE OF (1691); LEISLER'S REBELLION; NICHOLSON, FRANCIS; PEMAQUID, ATTACK ON; PHIPS, WILLIAM; RALE, SEBASTIEN; RYSWICK, TREATY OF; SALMON FALLS, BATTLE OF; SCHENECTADY, BATTLE OF; WALLEY, JOHN; WELLS (MAINE); FORT WILLIAM HENRY (MAINE); WINTHROP, JOHN (FITZ-JOHN); YORK (MAINE); YORK, ATTACK ON

Kirke Brothers

The first of five attempts to capture Quebec City (1629, 1690, 1711, 1759, 1775) was undertaken by the Kirke brothers in 1629. Gervase Kirke (1568–1629), an English merchant, lived for many years in Dieppe, France, where his five sons (David, Lewis, Thomas, John, James) and two daughters were born. The Kirkes returned to England in 1616 and were in a position to take advantage of the war that broke out between England and France in 1626. The Merchant Adventurers of London were granted permission to take Nova Scotia and Quebec and create an English fur trade there. Having received a letter of marque from King Charles I, Gervase Kirke gave command of an expedition to his oldest son, David, who sailed for the New World in 1628 with his brothers.

Almost simultaneously, French Cardinal Richelieu and others had organized the Company of One Hundred Associates in order to stimulate greater activity at the settlement that Samuel de Champlain had founded at Quebec. The One Hundred Associates fitted out a large fleet with supplies for Quebec, the largest that France had yet sent to the New World. While the French fleet was at sea, the Kirkes proceeded up the St. Lawrence River as far as Tadoussac. David Kirke sent some Basque fishermen to Quebec to demand Champlain's surrender. The French colonist and soldier refused the summons and dared the Kirkes to do their worst. They did not approach Quebec in 1628, but on their way back to England, the Kirkes met the fleet carrying supplies for Champlain. A battle was engaged off Tadoussac and David Kirke captured 18 French ships and nearly all the supplies intended for the colony. When news of this disaster reached France, the Kirkes were burned in effigy in Paris.

During the winter 1628–1629, Champlain and his men suffered from extreme hunger. The Kirkes, emboldened by their success, left Gravesend, England, in March 1629 (Gregorian calendar) aboard six ships and three pinnaces. Lewis and Thomas Kirke commanded the ships, which arrived off Quebec on 19 July 1629, and called on Champlain to surrender. Faced with both the real danger of starvation and the presence of his foes, Champlain had no choice but to submit. Lewis and Thomas Kirke came ashore to accept his surrender and on 22 July 1629, the English flag was hoisted over Quebec. Under the terms of the surrender agreement, Champlain and his men (less than 100) were sent to England and then repatriated to France.

In the absence of his brothers, who returned to England, Lewis Kirke ran Quebec as an occupied territory for the next three years. The Kirkes and their associates dominated the fur trade and clearly hoped to establish a permanent English presence in Canada. But their claim to Quebec was imperiled by two things: the Treaty of Susa (April 1629) which predated their conquest, and the dowry of Queen Henrietta Maria, half of which was still due King Charles I. Using these circumstances to their advantage, the French diplomats demanded the return of Quebec. After three years of discussions, all of Canada and Nova Scotia were formally returned to France under the Treaty of Saint Germain-en-Laye (29 March 1632). The Frenchman, Emery de Caen, proceeded to Quebec and formally repossessed the area for France; Champlain was not given the initial honor of reclaiming the settlement at Quebec, yet he did return in 1633.

The Kirkes had lost their prize, but the leading member of the family, David Kirke, continued to be active in the New World. Knighted on 16 July 1633 by King Charles I, David Kirke received a charter to be the governor on Newfoundland in 1637. He went to Newfoundland in 1638. Known as an effective and firm governor, he also remained a strong royalist during the English civil war (in fact, he encouraged King Charles I to escape from England and take refuge in Newfoundland). He was recalled by the commonwealth government in 1651, which was suspicious of his entire family (all five Kirke brothers were royalists). Although no charges were ever proven against him, he died in prison near London in 1654. On the opposite side of the contest, Champlain died at Quebec in 1635, secure in his position as the "father" of New France.

The potential significance of the Kirke conquest has often been overlooked. If Quebec had not been returned by the Treaty of Saint Germain-en-Laye, there might well have been no French Canada, no northern intercolonial rivalry, and no series of French and Indian wars. Instead, the Kirke conquest was a rehearsal of things to come, a prelude to the long struggle between English and French colonists in North America. On a lighter note, the conquest by five brothers seeking beaver skins and profits can also be seen as indicative of its period; the Kirke brothers fit into the tradition of the sea dogs and the merchant adventurers of the Elizabethan period. Incidentally, the era and events of the English-French War of 1626–1629 (especially the siege of La Rochelle), have been commemorated in Alexandre Dumas's novel, *The Three Musketeers*.

Samuel Willard Crompton

References

Gerard Filteau, *Par La Bouche De Mes Cannons! La ville de Quebec face a l'ennemi* (1990); Henry Kirke, *The First English Conquest of Canada* (1871); The Publications of the Champlain Society, *The Works of Samuel de Champlain,* Vol. VI, 1629–1632 (1936); Marcel Trudel, *The Beginnings of New France, 1524–1663* (1973).

Kittanning, Battle of (1756)

The Delaware Indian village of Kittanning was the "place on the big river," referred to by the French as "Attiqué." It was located on the east bank of the Allegheny River approximately 40 miles north of its confluence with the Monongahela and Ohio Rivers. Kittanning was founded in the 1720s by the Delaware after having lost their lands in eastern Pennsylvania and after they had been successively moved westward.

From this village two Delaware leaders, Shingas and Captain Jacobs, based raids on frontier settlers of Pennsylvania and British defense points west of the Susquehanna River. The Delaware had aligned themselves with the French for economic and defensive purposes and had subsequently been supplied with arms and ammunition. In 1756, the population of Kittanning was estimated to be 140 Delaware and Shawnee warriors, 100 white captives, and an unknown number of women and children.

During the last two weeks of July 1756, the frontier Fort Granville (near present-day Lewistown) was besieged, captured, and burned to the ground by Delaware warriors led by Jacobs with the aid of a few Frenchmen. Two soldiers were killed and 22 captured. A French flag was left near the fort's ruins and Captain Jacobs boasted he could take any fort that would burn. In effect, Jacobs threatened all the remaining provincial forts since they all were constructed of wood.

At the time of the raid at Fort Granville, Lieutenant Colonel John Armstrong had been commissioned to command the Pennsylvania Regiment's second battalion. His station was the fort at Carlisle and his garrisons were comprised of those west of the Susquehanna. His brother, Lieutenant Edward Armstrong, had been one of the two men killed at Fort Granville in the Delawares' July assault.

An act of retaliation was deemed imperative to counter the Delawares' recent actions. In addition, Armstrong felt that frontier morale needed boosting with a consolidation and fortification of the frontier defenses. It was not surprising when Pennsylvania Governor Robert Morris gave his approval to Lieutenant Colonel John Armstrong for a secret attack on Kittanning in August. The expedition was comprised of seven companies (300 men). Detachments from McDowell's Mill (Markes), Carlisle, Fort Lyttleton, and Fort George (near Mexico, Pennsylvania) were instructed to advance by varied routes to Fort Shirley (Shirleysburg). They would gather there for final preparations. Armstrong and his provincial troops began their march west to Kittanning from Fort Shirley on 30 August.

At about 10 p.m. on 7 September, within six miles of Kittanning, an advance scout for Armstrong's troops came upon a Delaware campsite. Armstrong left 14 men with instructions to lay in wait and attack the small group at sunrise. The main provincial army moved quietly through the woods toward Kittanning. By approximately 3 a.m., Armstrong had reached the Allegheny River. His troops were within 100 rods south of the village, at the edge of a cornfield.

Just before daybreak, Armstrong sent a detachment north along a hill on the east side of the village. At first daylight, Armstrong's party charged through the cornfield and the detachment charged the houses from the east. The Delaware Captain Jacobs sounded an alarm. Women, children, and prisoners fled their shelters, crossing the river to Shingas's settlement and into the woods. Shingas's warriors and a small number of French soldiers who had arrived at Shingas's settlement also heard the alarm.

The center of the battle focused on Captain Jacobs's house. From it many of the Provincial troops (including Armstrong) were wounded by musket balls. Armstrong ordered the village houses, about 30 in all, to be burned. When the stronghold was set afire, Jacobs, his wife, and son ran through the door, and were shot and killed. Jacob's house had been a magazine filled with a sizable supply of ammunition that created a large explosion when the fire found the French gunpowder barrels. The battle lasted for six hours. By noon, Armstrong had destroyed most of the village by fire and withdrew his troops hurriedly, fearing arrival of Shingas's reinforcements.

According to Armstrong's report, 17 men were killed, 13 wounded, and 19 missing. Delaware losses were thought to be comparable. Of the supposed 100 white captives held at Kittanning, only 11 were rescued by Armstrong, and some of those were recaptured by the Delaware in the withdrawal.

The provincial troops who had been left to attack the small group of Delaware outside the village found themselves outnumbered in the light of day. A lieutenant and five soldiers were killed and two were wounded before the Indians heard the explosions at Kittanning and quit firing. Armstrong rejoined the remaining soldiers and quickly returned to Fort Lyttelton without further engagement.

Linda M. Thorstad

References

William A. Hunter, "Victory at Kittanning," *Pennsylvania History,* 23 (1956):376–407.

See also DELAWARE; FORT GRANVILLE (PENNSYLVANIA); MONONGAHELA RIVER

Fort Kouri (New York)
See FORT HERKIMER (NEW YORK)

L

Fort La Bahía (Texas; also known as Nuestra Señora de Loreto)

The foundations of presidio Nuestra Señora de Loreto (also known as presidio La Bahía del Espíritu Santo—a Spanish name for Matagorda Bay) were begun on 6 April 1722, at the precise site of René-Robert Cavelier, sieur de La Salle's Fort St. Louis. The fort's founder, the marqués de San Miguel de Aguayo, also supervised the beginnings of a nearby mission, Nuestra Señora del Espíritu Santo de Zúñiga, for the Coco, Karankawa, and Cujane Indians. The fort was also intended as a defensive outpost against possible incursions by the French at Matagorda Bay. Subsequently, however, unhealthful climate at the site, improved relations with the French, and the intransigence of local Indians combined to prompt a relocation of the presidio and mission (known collectively as La Bahía) to the Guadalupe River in 1726. A second relocation in 1749 to the present-day site at Goliad, Texas, positioned them for the remainder of the colonial era. A reconstructed presidio and mission at Goliad commemorate these frontier outposts.

Donald E. Chipman

References

Donald E. Chipman, *Spanish Texas, 1519–1821* (1994); Robert S. Weddle, *San Juan Bautista: Gateway to Spanish Texas* (1968).

See also AGUAYO EXPEDITION; FORT ST. LOUIS (TEXAS)

La Belle Famille, Battle of (1759)

A defensive action fought by the British besiegers of Fort Niagara against a French relief force, the battle occurred one mile south of Fort Niagara near the center of present-day Youngstown, New York.

On July 6, 1759, a British force of about 2,500 European troops and 1,000 Six Nations warriors landed near Fort Niagara and lay siege to the post. The French commandant, Captain Pierre Pouchot de Maupas, requested assistance from Captain François-Marie Le Marchand de Lignery, who commanded French forces on the Allegheny River. Lignery was poised to attack the British at Pittsburgh. With his supply and communications line to Canada threatened by the attack on Niagara, however, Lignery diverted his army to Niagara to raise the Siege. He was supported by Captain Charles-Philippe Aubry and a contingent of colonial troops and militia from the Illinois. The force that left Presqu' Ile for Niagara numbered about 1,500 French and Indians.

The French army reached the Niagara River near the modern site of Buffalo, New York on 22 July. Lignery and Aubry sent Indians to inform Pouchot of their approach. Pouchot acknowledged their messages in the same fashion and suggested two options for the relief force. If Lignery and Aubry felt their force was powerful enough, they could advance down the Portage Road on the east side of the river and attack the besiegers. If not, they could avoid battle by moving down the west bank and crossing to Fort Niagara. The French leaders, confident of success and knowing the British to be widely scattered between camps and siege works, decided to attack.

News of this threat probably reached Sir William Johnson, who commanded the besiegers, as early as 22 July. On the 23rd, he dispatched 150 men of the light infantry companies of the 44th, 46th, and the fourth battalion of the 60th Regiments of Foot under Captain James Delancey to a place on the Portage Road known as "La Belle Famille." This was about one mile south of Fort Niagara and was judged a suitable location to oppose the French and protect the camps and trenches. Early on the morning of 24 July, the French advanced to within a mile of La Belle Famille and surprised a British party, killing or capturing 11 men. The firing alerted Delancey, who appealed for reinforcements. Within a half-hour, Sir William sent two more detachments from the 44th, 46th, and New York Regiments to La Belle Famille and ordered Lieutenant Colonel Eyre Massey of the 46th to take command. When the French appeared at about 8:00 A.M., Massey had 454 regulars and an undetermined number of Iroquois on the field. Most of the latter, however, expressed no interest in fighting.

The French had been delayed by their own Indians, who demanded to speak with the Iroquois. During a short council, the Iroquois persuaded most of the French Indians to withdraw. Undaunted, Lignery and Aubry pressed on with their soldiers and few remaining Indians, the former by this time numbering about 800. The French advanced confidently in a column of 14 against a British force they probably believed still numbered only 150 men. As they emerged into the cleared land at La Belle Famille, the French perceived the small British force and, in the words of one British officer, advanced "with a very great noise and shouting."

Massey was prepared. The main body of his own 46th Regiment lay in the grass and suffered few casualties from the random French fire. Massey, wounded in the first volley, allowed the French to approach to within about 30 yards before ordering his men to rise and fire. The 46th discharged seven rapid volleys before Massey directed them "to advance by constant firing." The French column, still largely pressed into the road, attempted to deploy into line to their right, but the British fire was too destructive. After a few minutes of fighting, during which many of the French officers were wounded, they broke and retreated. Massey ordered his troops forward in a steady pursuit.

If the Iroquois had earlier expressed no interest in the fight, they joined in with enthusiasm as soon as the French wavered. They "fell on them like so many Butchers," reported one observer. The retreat became a panicked rout with the Iroquois pursuing the French survivors to the

Niagara escarpment, five miles to the south. The British advance bagged a number of prisoners and 17 French officers, including Lignery and Aubry. Total casualties were impossible to determine. The British estimated as many as 500 dead, while one French report admitted a more likely total of 344 killed and captured. British losses were 12 killed and 40 wounded.

When word of the French defeat was carried to Fort Niagara, Pouchot at first refused to believe it. One of the garrison officers was then escorted to view the captured officers. With his last hope for relief dashed, Pouchot requested terms for his exhausted garrison. British troops took possession of Fort Niagara on the morning of 25 July.

The defeat of the French relief force sealed the fate of Fort Niagara. The action at La Belle Famille gained as much contemporary attention as the capture of Niagara and the occupation of Ticonderoga and Crown Point. Most newspapers awarded the laurels to Sir William Johnson (who was not on the field) and to the Iroquois (who did not participate until the action had been decided). Massey and his regulars were largely overlooked, a slight (possibly intentional on Johnson's part) that he bitterly resented. Nor was the action an ambush as some later writers have suggested. The leaders of the relief force overconfidently believed they had the strength to fight their way into Fort Niagara. Lignery and Aubry were mistaken, and the last French army in the west was lost.

Brian Leigh Dunnigan

References

Brian Leigh Dunnigan, "Action at La Belle Famille," *Courier*, VIII (1989):5–10; ———, *Siege—1759: The Campaign Against Niagara* (1986); George Douglas Emerson, *The Niagara Campaign of 1759* (1909); Lawrence Henry Gipson, *The Great War for the Empire: The Victorious Years, 1758–1760* (1949); Franklin B. Hough, ed., *Memoir Upon the Late War in North America,* 2 vols. (1866); Frank H. Severance, *An Old Frontier of France,* 2 vols. (1917).

See also JOHNSON, WILLIAM; NIAGARA, BATTLE OF; POUCHOT DE MAUPAS, PIERRE

Lachine, Battle of (1689)

On 25–26 July 1689 a force of 1,500 Iroquois warriors attacked the small farming community of Lachine, a settlement in New France. Under cover of darkness the warriors moved into the village just as a severe storm broke. By dawn the raid was over, leaving 24 dead and 56 of the village's 77 homes destroyed.

The Lachine raid was followed by several other less successful raids on outlying settlements. Although these raids were small, they left the populace anxious and demoralized. French Governor Louis de Buade de Frontenac had carried earlier retaliatory raids on the Iroquois but with little or no success. Faced with decreased morale from assaults by the Indians and hostilities with the British heating up after the outbreak of King William's War, Frontenac realized his only hope was to ally with the Iroquois and organize a joint force to rival the British. Indeed, the French and Iroquois alliance proved very powerful and succeeded in several bloody assaults on British settlements, including the massacre at Schenectady in the winter of 1690.

Elizabeth Gossman

References

Robert Wise Howard, *Thundergate: The Forts of Niagara* (1968); Douglas E. Leach, *Arms for Empire: A Military History of the British Colonies in North America, 1607–1763* (1973); Howard Peckham, *The Colonial Wars, 1689–1762* (1964).

See also SCHENECTADY, BATTLE OF

Fort La Galette (New York)

See FORT LA PRÉSENTATION (NEW YORK)

Lake Champlain

Lake Champlain forms, for 102 miles of its length, the northern part of the boundary between Vermont and New York, and extends a further five miles into Quebec. Its drainage pattern—northerly, by means of the Richelieu River—makes it part of the St. Lawrence watershed. The southern headwaters, however, provide navigation for small craft to within six to 14 miles (depending upon portage route chosen and the dryness of the season) of Hudson River waters. During the colonial era, when rivers were the principal roads, the Champlain-Richelieu route was the main access between rival settlements of the St. Lawrence Valley and the Atlantic seaboard.

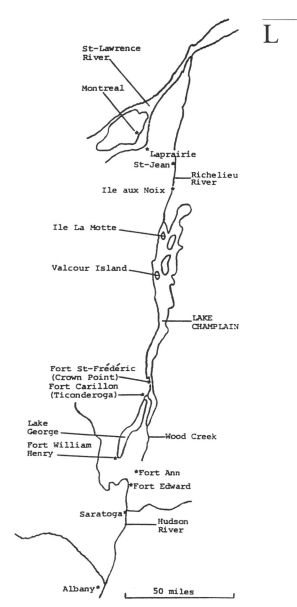

Principal military/strategic locations, Lake Champlain corridor, 1600–1783.

Before that time, presumably, for long eons before the French, Dutch, and English appeared in the region, the Champlain corridor served the canoe traffic of the Iroquois and other native peoples. The coming of the Europeans increased traffic on the lake. Some was for peaceful purposes: trade, smuggling, and visiting between the Iroquois homeland in New York and villages of Christianized colonists that developed near Montreal. Unfortunately, however, a good deal of the interchange during the 1600s and 1700s was warlike, presaged by the 1609 expedition in which Samuel de Champlain and two other Frenchmen came up the lake with a war party of Huron and Algonquin against the Mohawk, whom they put to rout by the first introduction of firearms into the warfare of these nations. Raids and annoyances launched along these waters grew ever more bloody until, by the period 1690–1780, a Lake Champlain campaign was usually the main element in strategical planning for attacks, feints, and full-scale invasions in either direction.

Significant positions on land were fortified as time went by. They represented lines drawn across narrow water, one side or the other, saying to the enemy they might advance this far, but no farther.

The French established a palisade fort in 1666 on Ile La Motte, close to where the international border eventually settled. During the hostilities that culminated in the Treaty of Utrecht, the British built Fort Anne near the south end of the lake, and upgraded the portage trail leading there from the Hudson River to the status of an actual road. In 1730–1731, the French erected a stockade at Pointe à la Chevelure (Crown Point), three-quarters of the distance up the lake, which later evolved into Fort St. Frédéric. The British opened the 1755 campaign with the construction of Fort William Henry at the southern end of Lake George, the most modest "baby step" into the disputed corridor. The enemy countered by advancing the defended frontier of New France an additional 16 miles south. They built the largest, most regular fortification in the whole region at a highly strategic location where its guns would command both the slim width of Lake Champlain and the usual portage route leading around the fractured land where the Lake George outflow drops 200 feet, filling the air with such a racket the new fort was named "Carillon" (clatter, din, bellchime). This was the place that earlier Mohawk, and later Americans, called Ticonderoga.

In 1757, a French/Canadian/Indian force under the not-too-firm command of Louis-Joseph de Montcalm besieged and took Fort William Henry. The following year a similar combination forestalled an attack on Fort Carillon by a huge British-American army. In 1759, however, forces defending Canada had to be withdrawn from Lake Champlain when Que-

bec City was directly menaced. An advance from the south forced the French to abandon both Carillon and St. Frédéric, and build a sort of last-ditch fort on Ile-aux-Noix instead. The final British-American advance along this line during the war of the conquest caused that position to be abandoned as well in August 1760, and an army from Albany finally swept into Montreal.

The conquest of Canada brought all of the Hudson-Champlain-Richelieu corridor within the same political empire. One might expect this should end the hostility between peoples and governments at its two extremes, but it did not. Rivalry and war continued flowing along the same old waterways. Lake Champlain, therefore, reminds us that the lay of the land was a powerful factor helping shape people and their history. What looked like merely the importation into this continent of quarrels from Europe turned out to be actually the expression of rivalry between North American communities asserting their own interests, channeled, naturally, by their own geography.

The Lake Champlain corridor continued to be a major south-north invasion route: for an irregular American rebel army in 1775, which occupied Montreal again before the Declaration of Independence was penned; for the British counterattack in 1776–1777, which penetrated as far as the upper Hudson River but no further; for numerous raids and invasions during the War of 1812–1814; for various smaller excursions associated with the Canadian rebellion of 1837–1838 and the War between the States. The advance in 1870 of 240 Fenians from St. Alban's, Vermont, over the border into Quebec was the last attack.

Recorded history in the Lake Champlain region began less than 400 years ago. For 270 of those years, war parties were common. This seems to bear out the American dictum that "Good fences make good neighbors," since here there is no natural fence. Between Albany and Montreal are 200 miles, more than half an easy passage over lake and river waters, or level roads that run alongside. It makes little difference whether the diplomacy and strategy are Iroquois/Algonquin of the sixteenth century, or Canadian/American of the twenty-first. As long as separate traditions are maintained, communities at either end of the corridor will likely look up or down the lake with suspicion, made edgy by its openness.

Malcolm MacLeod

References

Guy Frégault, *La guerre de la conquête* (1955); Lawrence Henry Gipson, *The British Empire Before the American Revolution*, 15 vols. (1936–1970); Frederic Van de Water, *Lake Champlain and Lake George* (1946).

See also CROWN POINT; LAKE GEORGE; FORT ST. FRÉDÉRIC (NEW YORK); FORT TICONDEROGA (NEW YORK)

Lake George

Lake George, in upper New York about 50 miles north of Albany, in colonial times on a natural highway between Albany and Montreal, Quebec, was given that name by William Johnson in 1755. Formerly called Lake Sacrament, its control was the object of bloody battles in the 1750s. In late summer 1755, Major General Johnson set out to capture Crown Point on Lake Champlain, but encountered the French forces of Baron Jean-Armand de Dieskau. Three engagements occurred—a forest ambush of a British advance party, capture of Dieskau, and wounding of Johnson. Though the British claimed victory, their casualties were double those of the French. The British then constructed a new fort, William Henry, on the southern end of Lake George and met later French assaults in 1755 from behind protected battlements.

Fort William Henry, readied for assault in 1756 by engineer William Eyre, became the outer defense for Fort Edward near Albany. Both were the staging areas in 1757 for a projected attack on Fort Ticonderoga, near the north end of Lake George, by General Daniel Webb. His lack of professional troops, only a few colonials, and less Indians made any offensive attack inadvisable, but he was surprised by the massive assault of Louis-Joseph de Montcalm, marquis de Montcalm whose army of 8,000 men used the heavy forested sides of the lake to provide a major attack. Webb was unable to meet the attack, capitulated his forces and abandoned the fort, and made a withdrawal toward Fort Edward. The French forces at this point could not control their Indian auxiliaries and a serious massacre of British soldiers occurred. Approximately 200 people were killed, even though the French tried to shield the British army.

The capture of and massacre at William Henry caused a brief mobilization of the New England militia and wide fears of an all-out French attack. However, Montcalm did not have horses to carry siege cannon to Fort Edward nor sufficient Indian auxiliaries to provide security in the densely forested area. His great victory frightened the British and Americans and renewed efforts by them to clear the lake of French forces.

In 1758, the British under James Abercromby, with a massive army of colonials and some regulars, moved across Lake George and through the forests toward Fort Ticonderoga. Unfortunately, Lord George Howe, the popular field commander, was killed by exposing himself while leading the troops in the field. His death had a great impact on morale and strategy that weakened Abercromby's command. But the French also brought good generalship into battle, experienced troops, and expert cannonading from the fort, and inflicted heavy losses mostly on the British colonials, who broke in panic. Abercromby made strategic errors in not using a superior battle position, his experienced artillery, and his presence to bolster morale. His retreat was encouraged by his replacement when Jeffrey Amherst arrived from England.

Amherst regrouped the British forces in 1759, increasing the number of regulars, and moved up Lake George early in the year, taking the French forts of Ticonderoga and Crown Point and eventually going into Quebec. Lake George was used as part of the waterway to Canada during the remainder of the Seven Years' War.

John A. Schutz

References

Lawrence Henry Gipson, *The Great War for the Empire: The Years of Defeat 1754–1757; The Victorious Years 1758–1760*, Vols. VI, VII (1946–1949); Ian K. Steele, *Betrayals: Fort William Henry and the "Massacre"* (1990).

See also ABERCROMBY, JAMES; CROWN POINT; DIESKAU, JEAN-ARMAND; FORT EDWARD (NEW YORK); JOHNSON, WILLIAM; LAKE CHAMPLAIN; MONTCALM-GOZON DE SAINT-VERAIN, LOUIS JOSEPH; FORT TICONDEROGA (NEW YORK); TICONDEROGA, BATTLE OF; WEBB, DANIEL; FORT WILLIAM HENRY (NEW YORK)

Lake George, Battle of (1755)

In 1755, Sir William Johnson was the greatest Indian trader in the Mohawk Valley of New York state. Known to the Iroquois Indians he

L

befriended as Warraghiyagey—"He Who Does Much"—Johnson's legendary rapport with the Indians caused him to be named superintendent of Indian affairs. But 1755 was not the most propitious time to win such an appointment. In July of that year, the defeat of British General Edward Braddock had been a disastrous blow to British prestige along the frontier in the eyes of the Indian tribes, for these "savages" were as politically astute in their woodland home as any diplomat in Paris or Vienna. Indeed, at this time, with British power on the verge of extinction in the eastern forests, Johnson was indisputably "the indispensable man."

It would not be long before Sir William's much-vaunted influence among the Indians would be put to the acid test. Following up their victory over Braddock, the French planned an attack down the strategic Lake Champlain water highway that led directly into what is now New York state. At Fort St. Frédéric, a run-down post at Crown Point on the lake, the French under Baron Jean-Armand de Dieskau, a veteran of France's European wars, planned to lead south an invasion army of some 700 French regulars, 1,600 Canadians of the Independent Company of Marines, New France's own "army," and Canadian militiamen, plus about 700 supporting Indians. This foray was prompted by one of the greatest intelligence coups in early America: Dieskau had papers that had been found at the site of Braddock's disaster that pointed to a British attack on Fort St. Fréderic. Thus Dieskau moved swiftly to forestall the attack. It is no wonder French Governor Pierre de Rigaud de Vaudreuil urged Dieskau to "make all haste." It was unfortunate that the commander Dieskau was told to "make all haste" against the resourceful Johnson, who had been ordered to lead the advance on Fort St. Frédéric.

By the end of July—the month of Braddock's debacle along the banks of the Monongahela River in western Pennsylvania—Johnson had already mustered some 3,000 colonial troops from the New England colonies and New York. With the Americans were Johnson's Mohawks under Tiyanoga, or Old Hendrick, as redoubtable a chief who ever fought on the frontier; eventually, the Mohawk contingent would rise to some 300, all wise in the ways of war in the forest. After what seemed inexorably long preparations, Johnson's heterogeneous command reached the body of water the French had dubbed Lac St. Sacrament, whose name

Johnson now patriotically changed. "I have given it the name of Lake George," Johnson wrote to London, "not only in honor of His Majesty, but to ascertain his undoubted dominion here," on 26 August 1755. It was a "dominion" the "Mohawk baronet" would soon have to fight to defend.

Dieskau received word that Johnson's force had constructed a forest citadel, which soon would be known as Fort Edward, from a British prisoner on 4 September. Talking under threat of Indian torture, the man revealed the fort but greatly underestimated the size of Johnson's force, saying it only numbered some 500 men. Dieskau, a true pupil of the great French commander Marshal de Saxe, was anxious to come to grips with Johnson. Accepting the false report of the captive—what would be called "disinformation" in the world of espionage today—the impetuous commander plunged ahead with 216 regulars of Languedoc and La Reine, 684 Canadians, and about 600 Indians. Already, the disinformation was having its effect: the Indians refused to move on Fort Edward. Nevertheless, Dieskau, reassuring them "the more there are, the more we shall kill," got the warriors to attack Johnson's men at Lake George.

On the morning of 8 September, both armies advanced toward each other, much like the fateful first day of Gettysburg in 1863. Against Dieskau's fighters, coming north was a party of 1,000 colonials under Colonel Ephraim Williams of Massachusetts and some 200 Mohawks led by Tiyanoga, still at the head of his braves at 80 years of age. Somehow, Johnson made the fatal mistake of believing Dieskau was retreating, and foolishly dividing his force, sent Williams's combat group to head them off. Showing more tactical wisdom than Sir William, Tiyanoga said of the blocking force, "if they are to be killed, they are too many; if they are to fight, they are too few." Sadly, the advice of this old wilderness warrior fell upon deaf ears.

Dieskau laid a cunning ambush. Holding his regular troops in reserve, he pushed forward his militia and his Indian auxiliaries to surprise the approaching enemy, following the same winning tactics that had crushed Braddock's army only that July. Tiyanoga's keen eye suddenly spotted something in the trees, and a musket rang out—perhaps a warning shot from Dieskau's Indians for their brothers with the British. If so, the alarm was sounded too late. A volley crashed out from Dieskau's men lying in wait and the British and Indians, in Dieskau's apt comment, "doubled up like a pack of cards." Williams was slain by a bullet in the brain and Tiyanoga was bayoneted. Then, reeling from the ambush, the colonials were greeted with a withering volley from the regulars, who appeared as out of nowhere almost directly in their faces. Blasted by the gunfire, the colonials and Mohawks beat a hasty retreat. However, they soon regained their cohesion, and put up a spirited rearguard action against the oncoming French. Seth Pomeroy proudly wrote, "this was the last fire our men gave our enemies, which killed great numbers of them; they were seen to drop as pigeons." One of the felled "pigeons" was Jacques Legardeur de Saint-Pierre, leader of all the Indians and Canadians. The losses the French suffered in this morning skirmish, known as the "bloody morning scout," forced Dieskau to halt his troops, reform them, and raise their trampled morale. It was a pause that was to have terrible consequences.

The gunshots of the "bloody morning scout" alerted Johnson that the French were on the offensive, as did the retreating troops. Dieskau's hesitation gave Sir William time to prepare for the blow to fall, and to plan revenge for the defeat of the morning, which had killed Old Hendrick, grandfather of Johnson's lover Degonwadonti, or Molly Brant. Johnson hurried to throw up a barricade of wagons, overturned boats, and hewn-down trees around his camp before Dieskau arrived. Most important of all, he placed three cannon to greet the attackers.

At midday, Dieskau struck. Pomeroy wrote later, "the regulars came rank and file about six abreast," while "the Canadians and Indians . . . came running with undaunted courage right down the hill upon us, expecting to make us flee." Johnson's artillery did terrible work upon the enemy, but they kept on, giving the besieged colonials, in Pomeroy's description, "the most violent fire perhaps that ever was heard of in this country." Finally, however, Johnson's cannon decided the battle. Dieskau's Indians began to retire, mauled by the great "firesticks." Johnson's men, sensing the turn of the tide, leaped over their defenses and counterattacked with hatchets and gun butts and knives. Those enemies who still remained on the field fled. Severely wounded, Dieskau could do nothing but surrender. The day which had begun so badly for Johnson's troops ended in triumph.

John F. Murphy, Jr.

References
   Allan W. Eckert, *Wilderness Empire: A Narrative* (1969); Edward P. Hamilton, *Fort Ticonderoga: Key to a Continent* (1964); Bruce Lancaster, *Ticonderoga: The Story of a Fort* (1959); Douglas E. Leach, *Arms for Empire: A Military History of the British Colonies in North America, 1607–1763* (1973); Francis Parkman, *Montcalm and Wolfe,* 2 vols. (1884); Seth Pomeroy, *The Journals and Papers of Seth Pomeroy,* ed. by L.E. de Forest (1926); Francis Russell, *The French and Indians Wars* (1962).

See also DIESKAU, JEAN-ARMAND; JOHNSON, WILLIAM; RIGAUD DE VAUDREUIL DE CAVAGNIAL, PIERRE DE

Lake Ontario

Lake Ontario was a key nexus in the riverine transportation network that linked French and British North America, and their western hinterlands. Here, a waterway from Albany and New York intersected another leading from Montreal to French posts in the west. The widening of the rivers into a lake afforded both sides the opportunity to construct small navies to control passage along this channel.

For the British, Lake Ontario offered only opportunities. British North America was not threatened with conquest, so control of invasion routes was not absolutely necessary, and furs from the post at Oswego were not essential to the Anglo-American economy.

The French, however, could maintain their presence neither on the lake itself nor in the west without free passage over Lake Ontario. Forts Niagara, Frontenac, and Toronto could only be supplied by way of the lake, and were thus vulnerable to blockade. The domination of Lake Ontario by the British would sever French communications to the west, and lead directly to the fall of every French outpost west of Montreal, end the western fur trade, disrupt the Franco-Amerindian alliance system, and expose Canada to invasion by way of the upper St. Lawrence.

D. Peter MacLeod

References
   D. Peter MacLeod, "The French Siege of Oswego in 1756: Inland Naval Warfare in North America," *The American Neptune,* XLIX (1989):262–271; George F.G. Stanley, *New France: The Last Phase, 1744–1760* (1968).

See also FORT FRONTENAC (ONTARIO, CANADA); FORT NIAGRA (NEW YORK); OSWEGO, BATTLE OF

Lancaster, Treaty of (1744)

On 22 June 1744, 252 members of the Iroquois Confederacy of Six Nations marched into Lancaster, Pennsylvania. After time was spent welcoming the group by feasting, dancing, and pipe smoking, negotiations were ready to begin. There were 24 chiefs in attendance, lead by Canasatego, a member of the Onondaga council.

Assembled at the courthouse on 26 June were: the lieutenant governor of Pennsylvania, George Thomas; Commissioners William Beverly and Colonel Thomas Lee from Virginia; Commissioners Edmund Jennings and Philip Thomas from Maryland; deputies of the Six Nations (without the Mohawk representatives), and Conrad Weiser, acting as interpreter.

Delegates from Maryland began the negotiations as they had sent the invitation to the Six Nations. The delegates contended the Iroquois had no claim to land that was within Maryland borders, land that had been so for more than 100 years. Canasatego asked, "[W]hat is One Hundred Years in Comparison of the Length of Time since our Claim began? Since we came out of this ground?" According to Francis Jennings, this was the only recorded occasion that the Iroquois claimed actual ancestry in Maryland. The Iroquois had, however, recently claimed by right of conquest over the Delaware, the latter's lands in Maryland and Virginia.

The Virginians and Iroquois accused one another of violating the 1722 Treaty of Albany by crossing the Spottswood line. Virginia Governor Alexander Spottswood had designated a line of demarcation to keep the Iroquois out of Virginia, and to keep Virginia's Indian allies from travelling north to attack the Six Nations. Canasatego claimed the line to be on the mountains closest to Virginia's lowlands. In addition, he argued there was nothing in the treaty which required the Indians to stop their travels through the mountain valleys along this first ridge. The Virginians countered that no article prohibited the colonists from passing through and settling west of the Great Mountains either.

An agreement was finally reached whereby the Iroquois consented to move their warrior paths to the foot of the Great Mountains. The Virginians could have the valleys, but the Iroquois wanted the use of a road—the "Virginia Road." The Six Nations also wanted compensation for the land in Maryland and Virginia. A settlement was drawn for the following sums to be paid to the Iroquois: Maryland, £300 in Pennsylvania currency; Virginia £200 in Pennsylvania currency, plus £300 in gold; and, Pennsylvania, £300 in their own currency.

Confusion on the cession would resurface years later because the members of the Six Nations believed they had ceded only the lands of the Shenandoah Valley. In actuality, the area was vastly larger. They not only renounced their rights and claims to the valley, but recognized the rights and title of the king of Great Britain to "all the lands within the said colony (of Virginia) as it now or hereafter may be peopled and bounded by his Majesty . . . his heirs and successors." They did not realize the Virginia charter limits were a distance of 200 miles north and 200 miles south of Cape Comfort, west and northwest from sea to sea. The territory potentially encompassed a large portion of North America from the Atlantic to the Pacific Ocean.

When negotiations were completed on 4 July, the Iroquois had gained compensation for colonial encroachments, and the right of passage through Virginia for their warriors. But even more satisfying to them was the recognition of their preeminence over all the northern Indians, which had been formally given to them by their English colonial allies. For this, Canasatego had promised to help his English brothers against the French by prohibiting their passage for acts of war through Six Nations lands.

Within weeks of the signing of the Lancaster treaty, petitions were granted for some 300,000 acres of land by Virginia's provincial government. The trans-Appalachian settlement door had been opened.

Linda M. Thorstad

References

Alfred P. James, *The Ohio Company: Its Inner History* (1959); Francis Jennings, *The Ambiguous Iroquois Empire: The Covenant Chain Confederation of Indian Tribes with English Colonies from its beginnings to the Lancaster Treaty of 1744* (1984); Paul A.W. Wallace, *Conrad Weiser, Friend of Colonial and Mohawk* (1971).

See also IROQUOIS; WEISER, CONRAD

Fort La Pointe (Wisconsin)

The French erected Fort La Pointe in 1718 on an easily defensible island (now called Madeline) overlooking Chequamegon Bay on Lake Superior in present-day northern Wisconsin. In the 1650s, the Jesuits had maintained the mission of La Pointe du St. Esprit nearby for Huron and Ottaway Indians until Dakota Indians chased them from the area in 1671. From at least 1680, Chippewa (Ojibwa in the Canadian usage) Indians lived there and used it as a staging area for extending their territory south against the Fox Indians and west against the Dakotas. Fort La Pointe remained important into the nineteenth century because it was midway between the traditional Chippewa home at Sault Ste. Marie and the later central fur depot at Grand Portage-Thunder Bay.

Leroy V. Eid

References

Lyman C. Draper, "Early French Forts in Western Wisconsin," Wisconsin Historical Society, *Collections* 16 (1902); Grace Lee Nute, "Posts in the Minnesota Fur-Trading Area, 1660–1855," *Minnesota History* 11 (1930):353–385; Reuben G. Thwaites, "The Story of Chequamegon Bay," *Wisconsin Historical Collections* 13:397–425.

See also Fox; Ojibwa

La Prairie, Battle of (1690)

By 1690, the English colonists in America were weary of frequent French assaults along the northern frontier that had decimated many towns. It was decided a single bold strike on a French settlement would prevent further assaults by forcing the French to defend their frontier. The colonists, along with their allied Indians, met in Albany to deliberate over a planned invasion expedition into Canada. Sir William Phips was assigned the task of capturing Quebec by an assault from the sea, while a united army of colonists would move up Lake Champlain to Montreal. This force, under the command of John (Fitz-John) Winthrop of Connecticut, was unfortunately beset with problems. Dysentery, starvation, and squabbles over command served only to delay the mission. Finally, after almost a year's delay, Winthrop sent 22-year-old Captain John Schuyler, with a small force, on what was meant to be a decisive raid into Canada. With 29 whites and 120 Indians, Schuyler traveled through Lake Champlain and down the Richelieu River. Along the way they met up with Johannes Glen (a survivor of the earlier massacre at Schenectady), who had 28 whites and five Indians with him. Schuyler enlisted 13 whites and all of the Indians, then continued as far as Chambly before debarking about three miles from the fort located there. On 13 August 1690, the men marched across to La Prairie and took the garrison there by surprise. Schuyler's group slew six men (not 25 women and children as was rumored at the time), took 19 captives, and shot 150 head of cattle. After the assault, Schuyler and his men quickly retreated, but not before they burned down 16 houses with adjacent barns and haystacks.

The attack on the settlement of La Prairie was hardly the strategic battle it was meant to be. A year in the making, delayed by sickness and quarrels, the battle's sole accomplishment was the deaths of six noncombatants and increased tension between the French and English colonists, setting the stage for another battle at La Prairie a year later.

Elizabeth Gossman

References

Michael Kammen, *Colonial New York: A History* (1975); Douglas E. Leach, *Arms for Empire: A Military History of the British Colonies in North America, 1607–1763* (1973); Howard Peckham, *The Colonial Wars, 1689–1762* (1964); William Smith, Jr. and Michael Kammen, eds., *The History of the Province of New York*, 2 vols. (1972).

See also King William's War; La Prairie, Battle of (1691); Schenectady, Battle of; Winthrop, John (Fitz-John)

La Prairie, Battle of (1691)

After the numerous French raids on outlying settlements along the American northern frontier, the colonists decided to fight back. The first such effort was a raid on the Canadian settlement of La Prairie in 1690. This raid was fairly unsuccessful and served little purpose other than to increase tensions between the British and French. A year later it was followed by a second raid on the La Prairie settlement. On 1 August 1691, Major Peter Schuyler, an Albany merchant and commissioner of Indian affairs, led a contingent of several hundred English and Indians, mostly Mohawk, into an attack on La Prairie.

By Schuyler's own account his force was received by approximately 420 Frenchmen. Other sources cite as many as 800, lying in wait outside Fort Chambly. Schuyler's troops made use of a strategically placed ditch that they occupied and engaged the French forces. Suffering severe losses, the French were briefly driven back, but they rallied and once again advanced on Schuyler's men. The French did little damage to Schuyler's force and were repelled a second time. The French rallied yet a third time, moving east to avoid the British entrenchment. Schuyler's men left their ditch and attacked the rear of the French force, meeting the entire French army on open ground. The French were finally forced back into Fort Chambly, losing three men as prisoners to Schuyler's force.

Surprised by the strength of the French forces, Schuyler decided to retreat back to where his troops had left their canoes on the shore of Lake Champlain. Along the way, Schuyler's men encountered another French force. Schuyler later described the fighting as "close and severe;" he claimed to have killed at least 200 French, which were many more casualties than he had men in his force. However, Schuyler's force lost at least 40 men, a fairly high number for such a small force. The French claimed their losses were attributable to a lack of order and leadership, but more likely it was the French's officer's unfamiliarity with the practices of Indian fighting that was the real reason for the French losses.

As a result of the battle, a vital transportation route was opened for the British, but the losses were considerable and the survivors were met with a subdued homecoming in Albany when they returned. The 1691 battle at La Prairie was meant to turn Indian settlements against the French and to stymie French expansion in the area. In reality, the battle made it all too clear that the French and their allied Indians were indeed formidable, and Canadian territory was proving to be a colonial chimera; within the colonist's sight, yet continually beyond their grasp.

Elizabeth Gossman

References

T. Wood Clarke, *The Bloody Mohawk* (1968); Robert West Howard, *Thundergate: The Forts of Niagara* (1968); Michael Kammen, *Colonial New York: A History* (1975); Douglas Edward Leach, *Arms for Empire: A Military History of the British Colonies in North America, 1607–1763* (1973); Howard

Peckham, *The Colonial Wars, 1689–1762* (1964).

See also FORT CHAMBLY (QUEBEC, CANADA); LA PRAIRIE, BATTLE OF (1690); SCHUYLER, PETER

Fort La Présentation (New York)

Fort La Présentation was established at the confluence of the Oswegatchie and St. Lawrence Rivers (Ogdensburg, New York) in 1749 by the French missionary to the Indians, Abbe François Picquet. It controlled the St. Lawrence gateway to the Great Lakes, the supply route for the French forts there. The mission and trading post lured the Onondaga and Oneida Indians away from Colonel William Johnson in central New York. In 1750, Picquet, guided by his Indians, mapped Lake Ontario and made contact with other Iroquois. In May 1751, Bishop Pont Briand arrived to confirm 148 Iroquois Indians who had come to the mission and sworn allegiance to France, the first time a Catholic bishop celebrated a sacrament in New York state. Picquet visited France in 1755, taking with him three Iroquois to impress them with the strength of the French army and the finery of the French court. The fort was a staging area for both Iroquois and Algonquin Indians. In 1755, Picquet led Indians at Fort Duquesne and in the Battle of Lake George; in 1756 at Fort Bull; in 1757 at Oswego; in 1758 at Ticonderoga; and in 1759 in a second attack on Oswego. In 1759, when the Indians saw the French retreating from northern New York, many returned to central New York to realign themselves with the English. The French evacuated La Présentation, going to Fort Lévis, an island several miles downstream, or to other islands in the St. Lawrence. The English found La Présentation deserted and used it as a base for attacks on Fort Lévis, which fell about three weeks later. Picquet and some of his loyal Indians went to Quebec City and took part in the final battle of this war.

Nicholas N. Smith

References

Robert Eastburn, *A Faithful Narrative of the Many Dangers and Sufferings as Well as Wonderful and Surprising Deliverances, of Robert Eastburn, During His Late Captivity Among the Indians* (1758); P.S. Garland, *The History of Ogdensburg* (1927); Auguste

Gosselin, "Le Fondateur de la Presentation (Ogdensburg): L'abbe Picquet," Memoir S.R. Canada (1894); Justin Winsor, ed., *Narrative and Critical History of America . . .*, 8 vols. (1884–1889), 5:3, 4, 489, 571.

See also FORT LÉVIS (NEW YORK); ST. LAWRENCE RIVER

Laudonnière, René Goulaine de (?–c.1572)

René Goulaine de Laudonnière was a French military explorer who led two expeditions of French Protestants with the aim of inhabiting the coast of Florida previously claimed by the Spanish. These attempts at colonization of American regions by the French were a consequence of the religious wars that divided France during the second half of the sixteenth century. Admiral Gaspard de Coligny prepared the first colonizing expedition led by Laudonnière and Jean Ribault, who left Le Havre on 18 February 1562, and reached the North American coast at the end of April, founding the small colony of Port Royal in modern-day South Carolina. It was necessary to have reinforcements in both men and provisions to maintain the new arrivals. However, serious internal French conflicts impeded any type of help, which soon disheartened the colonists, and the population finally disappeared in 1564 owing to the lack of resources.

In April 1564, Laudonnière left France with an even bigger expedition than the previous one, with the aim of helping the inhabitants of deserted Port Royal. When they reached the coast of Florida, they decided to found a new colony on the shores of the St. Johns River, which they named Fort Caroline in honor of King Charles IX of France. History then repeated itself at Fort Caroline, producing various revolts and numerous desertions. When the long-awaited supplies arrived with a third expedition led by Jean Ribault in August 1565, the situation was almost untenable, and Laudonnière began to think of evacuation. Before evacuation could take place, a Spanish fleet under the command of Pedro Menéndez de Avilés reached Florida, and his troops took over and then demolished Fort Caroline (20 September), taking numerous prisoners, most of whom were killed. Laudonnière was among the fortunate few who managed to escape to France. Little more is known about his life, except that he left an account of all these incidents in the

"Histoire notable de la Floride," published in 1586.

Felipe del Pozo-Redondo

References

Eugene Lyon, *The Enterprise of Florida: Pedro Menéndez de Avilés and the Spanish Conquest of 1565–1568* (1976); Jean Parker Watebury, ed., *The Oldest City: St. Augustine, Saga of Survival* (1983); Verne E. Chatelaine, *The Defenses of Spanish Florida 1565 to 1763* (1941).

See also FORT CAROLINE (FLORIDA); MENÉNDEZ DE AVILÉS, PEDRO; RIBAULT, JEAN

Fort Lawrence (Nova Scotia, Canada)

Fort Lawrence was erected in late 1750 by Colonel Charles Lawrence on the ruins of the Acadian village of Beaubassin on the isthmus of Chignecto. The fort was first built as a defensive structure in the face of an opposing French force, and was part of a British scheme to evict the French from Nova Scotia. It sat on the northwest shore of the Missaquash River, soon mirrored on the opposite shore by the French Fort Beauséjour. The British fort was a quadrilateral, palisaded structure with two blockhouses and a pair of platforms for cannon. It is best remembered as the assemblage site for the 1755 British invasion.

Ronald P. Dufour

See also FORT BEAUSÉJOUR (NOVA SCOTIA, CANADA); CHIGNECTO ISTHMUS; FORT GASPEREAU (NOVA SCOTIA, CANADA)

Fort Lebanon (Pennsylvania)

One of the string of forts built by Pennsylvania along the ridge of the Blue Mountains, Fort Lebanon was completed in December 1755 or January 1756 under the direction of Captain Jacob Morgan. It was located at the forks of the Schuylkill River, and guarded the gap cut by that river through the mountain ridge. A large square log stockade, about 100 feet on a side and 14 feet in height, Fort Lebanon was built very shortly after the outbreak of border raids in November and December 1755. Within its walls stood three houses designed to shelter the local inhabitants when they took refuge there periodically. In June 1756, a visitor reported six families were living within the fort, making it "a little too much Crowded on that acc[oun]t."

Although Fort Lebanon did not defend a township, it was located near a recently purchased tract of land where as many as 100 families reportedly depended on its protection.

Like the other forts in the Blue Mountain line, Fort Lebanon was important chiefly as a base of operations for a company of the Pennsylvania Regiment; it was under the command of Captain Morgan, who sent out parties of rangers to scout the area four or five times a week and to guard the local inhabitants while they worked in their fields. In the fall 1756, Indian raids began to claim victims in the area. In addition to Fort Lebanon, Morgan's company was also expected to man the nearby Fort Northkill, a task which Morgan complained was impossible to accomplish effectively for the 53 militiamen under his command. Nevertheless, the fort itself remained an important place of refuge during periods of attack.

In late 1757 or early 1758, the name of Fort Lebanon was changed to Fort William.

Eric Hinderaker

References

Thomas L. Montgomery, ed., *Report of the Commission to Locate the Frontier Forts of Pennsylvania*, 2nd ed., 2 vols. (1916); C. Hale Sipe, *The Indian Wars of Pennsylvania* (1929).

See also FORT ALLEN (PENNSYLVANIA); FORT DUPUI (PENNSYLVANIA); FORT HENRY (PENNSYLVANIA); FORT NORRIS (PENNSYLVANIA)

Fort Le Boeuf (Pennsylvania)

On 11 July 1753, Captain François Le Mercier began construction of the second in a chain of posts connecting Lake Erie with the Allegheny River. Fort Le Boeuf, as the stockade would be called, was placed at the south end of the portage connecting the post of Presque Isle on Lake Erie with the Rivière aux Boeufs (French Creek to the English), a tributary of the Allegheny. From that point, French forces could descend to the forks of the Ohio where the confluence of the Allegheny and the Monongahela formed the Ohio or "La Belle Rivière."

Fort Le Boeuf was intended as little more than a fortified storehouse, but it was nonetheless sufficiently strong to repel Indians or British raiding parties. The post was laid out in the form of a square with a bastion at each corner. The bastions were constructed of pickets with

the rear walls of the log barracks forming the curtain walls. The fort apparently contained nine buildings, including a chapel and powder magazine. Simple stockaded outer works provided an additional secure area for camps and storehouses.

The best known incident in the brief history of Fort Le Boeuf occurred 11–13 December 1753, when George Washington, at the conclusion of his exhausting journey to confront the French intruders into territory also claimed by the British, met at Le Boeuf with its commandant, Captain Jacques Legardeur de St. Pierre. Both made their positions known, and the battle lines were drawn for the French and Indian War in the Ohio Valley and, indeed, all of North America.

Fort Le Boeuf continued in use as a support base for French operations in the Ohio Valley until the summer 1759. In July of that year, Captain François-Marie Le Marchand de Lignery learned of the British siege of Fort Niagara (Youngstown, New York). He diverted his forces from an intended attack on Pittsburgh in an attempt to protect his chief supply base and communications with New France. Fort Le Boeuf was burned as the French army withdrew toward Lake Erie.

When British forces advanced north from Pittsburgh in 1760, they found only the charred ruins of Fort Le Boeuf. They constructed a new post near the site of the French fort to protect their own communications between Pittsburgh and Presqu' Ile. The post was held by a small garrison until 1763. On 18 June of that year, it was attacked and captured by local Indians participating in the general uprising then taking place on the Great Lakes. Fort Le Boeuf was not reestablished by the British.

Brian Leigh Dunnigan

References

Lawrence Henry Gipson, *The Great War for the Empire: The Victorious Years, 1758–1760* (1949); Walter O'Meara, *Guns at the Forks* (1965); Max Schoenfeld, *Fort de la Presqu' Ile* (1989); Charles Morse Stotz, *Drums in the Forest* (1958); ———, *Outposts of the War for Empire: The French and English in Western Pennsylvania; Their Armies, Their Forts, Their People, 1749–1764* (1985); George Washington, *The Journal of Major George Washington, Sent by the Hon. Robert Dinwiddie . . . to the Commandant of the French Forces on the Ohio* (1754), facsimile ed. 1959.

See also NIAGARA, SIEGE OF; PONTIAC'S WAR; WASHINGTON, GEORGE

Leisler, Jacob (1640–1691)

Jacob Leisler was born in Frankfurt-am-Main, Germany, the eldest son of the Rev. Jacob Victorian Leisler, minister of the Frankfurt French Reformed congregation, and Susannah Adelheid Wissenbach. The Leislers were a family of continental jurists who were active in the Calvinist movement. The Rev. Leisler died in 1653, and Jacob subsequently enrolled at a German military academy. In the winter of 1658–1659, he entered the employ of the Amsterdam chamber of the Dutch West India Company. The following year the company gave him a military commission, and in April 1660, named him an officer of the troops being sent to New Netherland aboard the ship *Otter*.

Shortly after his arrival in the New World, Leisler entered into the fur and tobacco trade. With his 1663 marriage to Elsie Tymens, the widow of ship's carpenter Pieter Cornelisen Van der Veen, he emerged as one of the wealthiest merchants in New Netherland. In August 1664, Leisler signed a remonstrance urging Petrus (Peter) Stuyvesant to capitulate to the English. Thereafter, he frequently served as a juror and court-appointed arbitrator in the English legal system. During the 1673–1674 Dutch reconquest, Dutch Governor Anthony Colve appointed Leisler to make a survey of the province's fortifications, named him a tax assessor, and used him in other advisory capacities. In 1677, the Maryland government named him as its New York agent. While on a voyage to Europe the following year, he was captured by Algerians, but was able to swiftly obtain the ransom for his release. In the 1680s, Governor Thomas Dongan appointed Leisler as a commissioner to the Admiralty Court (1683), as foreman to the Court of Sessions (1684), and as a New York City and County justice of the peace (1685). Leisler also served as Suffolk County's agent to the provincial government, and as the agent representing the interests of Huguenot refugees in the province.

Despite his various commissions, Leisler does not appear to have been politically motivated except on the behalf of Calvinist orthodoxy. A member of the New York City Dutch Reformed Church since 1661, he was a deacon by 1670 and a member of the consistory. His religious activism came to the fore in 1676 when Albany minister Rev. Nicholas Van Rensselaer sued him for having declared that Van Rensselaer's preaching did not conform to reformed tenets. The suit rent the province before being ended by command of the governor. In 1685, Leisler left the Dutch church, and it is said he became a founding elder of New York City's first French Reformed congregation.

Under both Dutch and English administrations Leisler served as a militia captain. It was in his militia capacity that, on 27 April 1689, Lieutenant Governor Francis Nicholson appointed him to an expanded council to suppress the unrest inspired by England's Glorious Revolution. With the New York militia's 31 May revolt, Leisler switched his allegiance from Nicholson's government, and on 2 June, he took over the New York fort on behalf of England's new Protestant monarchs, William and Mary. On 28 June, a committee of safety designated him captain of the fort, and on 16 August 1689, as commander in chief of the province. In December 1689, upon the arrival of royal letters addressed to "Francis Nicholson, Esq., or in his absence, to such as for the time being takes care for preserving the peace and administering the laws in His Majesties province of New York," Leisler assumed the title of lieutenant governor.

Leisler's increasingly autocratic government bitterly divided New York, with long-lasting consequences for the colony. His administration came to an end on 19 March 1691, with the arrival of Royal Governor Henry Sloughter. Leisler was arrested, tried for treason, and on 16 May 1691, executed along with his son-in-law, Jacob Milborne. At the instigation of William III, Parliament reversed the New York court's sentences in 1695.

David William Voorhees

References

Edwin R. Purple, *Genealogical Notes Relating to Lieut.-Gov. Jacob Leisler, And His Family Connections in New York* (1877); Robert C. Ritchie, *The Duke's Province: A Study of New York Politics and Society, 1664–1691* (1977); Else Toennies Volhard, *Die Familie Leissler in ihrer Beziehung zu den familien Volhard und Waechter* (1930); David William Voorhees, "Leisler's Pre-1689 Biography and Family Background," *De Halve Maen*, LXII (1989):1–7.

See also DOMINION OF NEW ENGLAND; ENGLISH REVOLUTION; LEISLER'S REBELLION

L

Leisler's Rebellion (1689–1691)

Political unrest became endemic in New York after James II's August 1688 consolidation of the former Dutch West India Company colony, first acquired by the English in 1664, into the mega-colony of the Dominion of New England. New York became an administrative district within the dominion, whose headquarters were in Boston. New York's administration was placed under a military lieutenant governor, career officer Francis Nicholson, and an advisory board of three resident councilors—Nicholas Bayard, Frederick Philipse, and Stephen Van Cortlandt, all of whom were subordinate to Dominion Governor Sir Edmund Andros.

On 3 December 1688, Lieutenant Governor Francis Nicholson learned of a war between England and Holland. When Sir Edmund Andros's 10 January 1689 proclamation to hold the dominion for James II circulated, the war became known throughout the province. On 5 February, definitive news arrived that the Protestant William, prince of Orange, had successfully invaded England. This was followed on 1 March by official word that the Catholic James had attempted to flee the country. Despite Nicholson's efforts to keep it secret, news of the king's attempted flight rapidly spread, causing New Yorkers' resistance to the dominion government to coalesce. On 18 April, Boston rose up and imprisoned Sir Edmund Andros and his council. Boston's overthrow of the dominion government placed Nicholson's government in chaos. In order to maintain control, Nicholson convened a council of the chief civil and military figures in the province on 27 April. Among them was Jacob Leisler.

New York's uprising formally began on 3 May 1689, when the eastern Long Island towns of Suffolk County, following Boston's example, overthrew James's officials. The Suffolk militia then began a march on New York City to take possession of Fort James. By 15 May, when the militia had reached Jamaica, Long Island, Queens, and Westchester counties had also rebelled. To augment the regular army troops in New York City, Nicholson admitted into Fort James several Irish Catholic soldiers fleeing the Boston uprising. Tensions between the New York militia and the regular army, intensified by the arrival of the Catholic soldiers, exploded when Nicholson reprimanded militia captain Hendrick Cuyler for stationing a sentry without his permission on 30 May. The confrontation ended with Nicholson shouting he would rather "sett the town in fyre" than live under the continuing tensions.

Nicholson's words provoked the New York militia to rebel and seize Fort James on 31 May 1689. Five militia captains then agreed to take turns guarding the fort, while, following the Boston model, a committee of safety was called to oversee civil affairs. The following day the captains asked militia colonel and councilor Nicholas Bayard to take command. Bayard's refusal led second-in-command Jacob Leisler to enter the fort on 2 June with 49 men and vow that he would remain until all had joined with him. On 3 June, the captains issued a statement that they would hold the fort until receipt of instructions from the prince of Orange. The next day a ship arrived bearing official papers of Parliament's declaration that James had abdicated and the Protestant William and Mary were to be joint rulers.

Despite the arrival of official word, Nicholson and his council steadfastly refused to publicly declare for the new monarchs, though they made a private declaration upon receipt of William's orders that James's Protestant appointees be retained in office. The council then sent Nicholson to London on 11 June to present their version of the events. Nicholson's arrival in England before any communication from the militia captains, whose initial correspondence was lost to the French, would have dire consequences for the rebels.

On 21 June 1689, Connecticut militia officers Major Nathan Gold and Captain James Fitch arrived in New York City with a militia contingent and a printed proclamation for the Protestant king and queen. Leisler made the proclamation for the New York militia and then attempted to have Stephen Van Cortlandt, in his capacity as New York City mayor, make the civil proclamation. Van Cortlandt's refusal resulted in Leisler's also making that proclamation. Two days later a riot ensued in which Nicholson's councilors were attacked. Bayard and Van Cortlandt fled to Albany, which had separately declared for William and Mary, where they began to organize the opposition to Leisler.

While Leisler strengthened the city's fortifications, on 27 June 1689, a revolutionary committee of representatives from various East Jersey and New York counties began to meet. Under the leadership of Peter Delanoy and Samuel Edsall, the committee appointed Jacob Leisler captain of the fort on 28 June and as provincial military commander on 16 August. Four days later, the committee sent Joost Stol to England to present the rebel's case to the king. Despite William's directive to the contrary, the committee then undertook to obtain those offices held by James II's Protestant appointees by calling for local elections.

By October 1689, all New York counties except Albany, which had its own convention, had sent delegates to the provincial committee. In order to bring the Albanians into line, Leisler sent Jacob Milborne to Albany with 50 militiamen. Milborne, a man of radical principles, divided the Albanians with his rhetoric and further antagonized its leadership. After a month of futile negotiations, Milborne was forced to withdraw when Mohawks friendly to the Albanians threatened to attack him and his men.

In December 1689, both Nicholson's councilors' and Leisler's claims to govern New York seemed upheld by the arrival of William III's long-awaited instructions. The ambiguously addressed royal letters to Nicholson, "or in his absence, to such as for the time being takes care for preserving the peace and administering the laws in His Majesties province of New York" were brought by Captain John Riggs, who also brought the news the obscure Henry Sloughter was to be appointed royal governor. Nicholson's councilors rushed to New York City, where a clash developed as to whom the letters should be delivered. At length Riggs gave the letters to Leisler. With his authority thus legitimized, Leisler assumed the title lieutenant governor, formed a council, and dissolved the provincial committee. He then undertook to destroy his opposition. Nicholas Bayard, William Nicolls, and several other prominent malcontents were imprisoned.

On 8 February 1690, long-standing fears of a Roman Catholic plot seemed confirmed by a bloody French and Indian massacre of the frontier community of Schenectady. The massacre created panic in the province, causing Albany to capitulate to Leisler's government. Leisler then ordered the imprisonment of all Catholics and their sympathizers, called for an assembly to meet in April to raise funds for the frontier's defense, and wrote to the other colonial governments to join him in a congress to deal with the French-Catholic threat. In May 1690, the first intercolonial congress ever held in English America occurred when delegates from Massachusetts, Connecticut, Plymouth, and New York met in New York City. A two-prong plan was devised to attack French Canada by land and by sea. John (Fitz-John) Winthrop of Connecticut was appointed commander of the land forces, and Sir William Phips of Massachusetts the commander of the naval forces.

With the conclusion of the congress, Leisler's power was at its height. At the same time, Joost Stol returned with the news his mission to England had been a disaster and that Nicholson was appointed governor of Virginia. In early June, a riot occurred about taxation and the condition of those imprisoned during which Leisler was physically attacked. Thereafter, Leisler faced growing opposition. Suffolk County, which had long sought to join with Connecticut, withdrew its support. The Canadian expedition was a disaster: smallpox ravaged the united colonies' troops and the promised Indian allies never materialized. Leisler's subsequent imprisonment of Winthrop for the expedition's failure antagonized his New England allies. By the time the assembly sat again in September 1690, centers of opposition had emerged in Westchester and Ulster Counties. In October, Queens County rose in rebellion.

Administrative difficulties delayed Sloughter's departure for New York. It was not until 25 January 1691, that the first of his fleet arrived carrying troops commanded by Captain Richard Ingoldsby. Ingoldsby, without producing a commission, demanded Leisler surrender the fort. Leisler refused, claiming he would surrender only to Sloughter. His refusal, and the bitter contest between pro- and anti-Leislerians for control of the city, exploded into violence on 17 March when several people were killed. The violence cost the Leislerians when Sloughter finally arrived two days later. Leisler and his council were arrested, tried for treason, and sentenced to death. On 16 May 1691, Leisler and Milborne, who had recently become his son-in-law, were hanged and beheaded. Sloughter commuted the other death sentences until the king's pleasure was known.

While in Leisler's execution many found a martyr, his administration had created bitter enmities. As a result, New York hovered on the brink of civil war. Historians have given numerous explanations for the depth of this bitterness, including class, ethnic, and religious tensions. In 1692, the English court ordered a halt to all legal proceedings against Leislerians. At the direction of William III, in 1695 Parliament reversed the New York court's sentence of treason against Leisler and Milborne and returned their attained properties to their heirs. Nonetheless, Leislerian and anti-Leislerian factionalism continued to rend the colony for another two decades.

David William Voorhees

References
    Thomas J. Archdeacon, *New York City, 1664–1710: Conquest and Change* (1976); David S. Lovejoy, *The Glorious Revolution in America* (1972); Charles H. McCormick, *Leisler's Rebellion* (1989); Jerome R. Reich, *Leisler's Rebellion: A Study of Democracy in New York, 1664–1720* (1953); Robert C. Ritchie, *The Duke's Province: A Study of New York Politics and Society, 1664–1691* (1977); David William Voorhees, "'In Behalf of the true Protestants religion': The Glorious Revolution in New York," Ph.D. Dissertation, New York University (1988).

See also DOMINION OF NEW ENGLAND; ENGLISH REVOLUTION; KING WILLIAM'S WAR; LEISLER, JACOB; NICHOLSON, FRANCIS; WINTHROP, JOHN (FITZ-JOHN)

Le Loutre, Abbe Jean Louis (?–?)

Abbe Jean Louis Le Loutre, a militant French missionary sent to Canada in 1737 to attend the Micmac Indians at Schubenacadie, Nova Scotia, foreswore taking an oath of allegiance to England and acted as conduit for the distribution of French money, provisions, and arms to the Micmacs. Under his dynamic leadership, the Micmacs were incited to prevent English settlement south of Chignecto, and to intimidate the Acadian population there into remaining loyal to France. The British offered rewards for his arrest, while the French appointed him vicar-general of Acadia and assigned him to the parish of Beaubassin.

Chevalier Louis–Luc de La Corne's military efforts to fortify the Chignecto Isthmus at Beauséjour were critically delayed by Le Loutre's impressment of the Acadians to build an extensive system of dikes (*aboiteaux*) that would reclaim the Bay of Fundy's tidal marshlands. However, Robert Monckton's campaign against Fort Beauséjour in 1755 caused Le Loutre to threaten the Acadian *habitants* with destruction and Indian massacre if they did not evacuate their homes and enlist in the fort's defense. Against their long-standing neutrality, the Acadians were finally forced to commit themselves to the French cause when La Loutre unleashed the Micmacs against them in a "scorched earth" policy that even included burning his own church at Beaubassin.

Fearing capture at the fall of Beauséjour (16 June 1755), Le Loutre escaped in disguise to Quebec where, with reproaches from his bishop for deserting his flock, he embarked for France. En route, his ship was captured and he was confined on the Isle of Jersey. King George issued specific instructions that incendiary priests like Le Loutre never be allowed to return to Canada. After the Peace of 1763, Le Loutre was released and allowed to return to France and obscurity.

John D. Hamilton

References
    Edward B. O'Callaghan, ed., *Documents Relative to the History of the State of New York; Procured in Holland, England, and France* (1858).

See also FORT BEAUSÉJOUR (NOVA SCOTIA, CANADA); CHIGNECTO ISTHMUS

Le Moyne de Bienville, Jean-Baptiste (1680–1767)

Jean-Baptiste Le Moyne, sieur de Bienville, was born on 23 February 1680 at Ville Marie (Montreal), the twelfth child of Charles Le Moyne de Longueuil et de Châteauquay and Catherine Thierry (Primot). After his father's death in 1685, he was raised in the home of his eldest brother, Charles Le Moyne de Longueuil. When another brother, François Le Moyne de Bienville, was killed in 1691 by the Iroquois, he received his title of de Bienville.

At 12 years of age, Bienville joined the navy in 1692 as a *garde de la marine* (midshipman). During the War of the League of Augsburg (King William's War, 1689–1697), he participated in expeditions commanded by his brother, Pierre Le Moyne d'Iberville, against the English in Hudson Bay, Newfoundland, and off the coast of New England. During one of these engagements, he was seriously wounded in the head.

Because of his success against the English, Iberville was selected to lead an expedition, which left France in October 1698, to find the Mississippi River from the Gulf of Mexico and Bienville accompanied him. Iberville's expedition found the Mississippi River on 2 March

1699. Returning to the Gulf, Iberville and Bienville built Fort Maurepas at Biloxi (Ocean Springs), Mississippi. In May 1699, Iberville returned to France, leaving an Ensign Sauvole as the commander of the newly completed Fort Maurepas, a garrison of 80 men, with Bienville second in command.

On 6 September 1699, Bienville, leading an expedition of two pirogues and six men to explore the Mississippi River, encountered an English frigate under the command of Captain William Lewis Bond, coming up the river. Bienville convinced Captain Bond that the river was held by France, and the Englishmen turned around and sailed back into the Gulf. Bienville named the place, located 18 miles below New Orleans, the English Turn.

When Iberville returned on his second expedition to Louisiana in January 1700, he ordered a second fort to be built about 50 miles from the mouth of the Mississippi: Fort de Mississippi (Fort de la Boulaye). Iberville departed Biloxi at the end of May 1700, and left Bienville in command of Fort de Mississippi.

In August 1701, when yellow fever struck Biloxi killing Sauvole, the commander, Bienville assumed command. He was 21 years of age. Iberville returned on this third and last voyage to the colony in January 1702. Departing in spring 1702, Iberville left Bienville as the governor of the colony of Louisiana. One of the first tasks facing the new governor was to build Fort Louis at Twenty-Seven Mile Bluff on the Mobile River. Work was begun on the fort in January 1702 and completed shortly thereafter. In 1711, Fort Louis was abandoned and a new fort built at Mobile, renamed Fort Condé in 1720.

On Iberville's return to France, he was chosen to lead an expedition against the British West Indies in 1706 and successfully raided and plundered the islands of St. Christopher and Nevis. However, he caught yellow fever and died suddenly in July 1706, probably at Havana, Cuba. In the wake of his death, scandals erupted over his financial handling of the expedition, as well as his use of the king's funds in Louisiana.

The scandal over Iberville's financial mismanagement of the West Indian campaign, and by implication Louisiana, would lead to questions of the honesty and leadership of Bienville and his family in Louisiana, especially from Jérôme Phélypeaux Maurepas, Comte de Pontchartrain, the minister of the marine. Soon accusations arrived from the commissioner of Louisiana, Nicholas La Salle, and the new curate of Mobile, Henry Roulleaux de La Vente, accusing Bienville of a variety of transgressions ranging from financial mismanagement to allowing soldiers and settlers to keep Indian women domestics for "libertine" pleasures to the torture of Indian prisoners. These charges against Bienville and his family convinced Pontchartrain to send a commissioner to investigate Bienville's conduct in the colony.

In 1710, he sent Jean-Baptiste Martin d'Artaguette Diron, who would hold power jointly with La Salle as commissioner and investigate the charges against Bienville. Pontchartrain appointed as governor, instead of Bienville, Nicolas Daneaux, sieur de Muy. However, de Muy died in Havana on his way to Louisiana and Bienville remained the acting governor. Artaguette, after a lengthy investigation, dismissed most of the charges against Bienville as unprovable. What does emerge from the record was a Bienville who was determined to run the colony in his own way, always remaining loyal to his family and supporters, and in turn demanding theirs. The constant charges and countercharges between the three men, Bienville, La Salle, and La Vente, divided the colony into factions and weakened it.

The weakened state of the colony forced Louis XIV, in September 1712, to turn the colony over to Antoine Crozat, king's councilor and financial secretary, who, under the auspices of the Company of Louisiana, agreed to govern the colony and develop it for a 15-year term. Antoine de Lamothe, Sieur de Cadillac, was appointed governor in 1710, but did not arrive in Louisiana until 5 June 1713 to assume the office from Bienville.

Under orders to investigate Bienville, Cadillac dug up old charges against him, which proved to be both painful and humiliating to Bienville. Once again the colony was divided between the majority who supported Bienville and the small minority who supported Cadillac.

Before the arrival of Cadillac, Bienville had proven his skill at Indian diplomacy by leading a successful expedition in the summer of 1704 against the Alabamas, who had killed several Frenchmen. Several years later, in the spring of 1712, Bienville concluded a peace treaty with this formerly pro-English tribe. The Chitimachas, a small tribe located on the Mississippi, had killed a Jesuit missionary, Jean François Buisson de Saint-Cosme, and three other Frenchmen in 1706. Bienville sent an expedition in 1708 which killed and enslaved many of the Chitimachas.

In 1714, Bienville was given a freer hand in dealing with the Indians when he was made, by Pontchartrain, military commander from the Ohio to the Gulf. This provided Bienville the opportunity, in February 1715, to drive the English traders from the colony. He demanded the Choctaw expel the English traders among them and made them deliver to him the heads of the two chiefs who had brought the English into the nation.

As Bienville was having the Choctaw expel the English traders, the excessive greed and slave-trading activities of the English among the Indians of the Southeast helped launch the Yamasee War of 1715. In the wake of this severe reversal to the English, the Alabamas invited the French to build a fort in their nation, and in 1717, Fort Toulouse was built.

Bienville showed some of his outstanding skills in dealing with the Indians in his 1716 expedition against the Natchez. Cadillac gave the task of subduing the Natchez to Bienville with only 49 men against a potential force of 800 warriors. Bienville marched to the Natchez villages, and through intimidation, force, courage, and kidnapping, captured several Natchez chiefs and held them as hostages until the Natchez turned over the murderers of the French. Bienville had the chiefs executed and forced the Natchez to help build a fort among them, Fort Rosalie.

In 1716, Cadillac was removed as governor, and Bienville became the acting head of the colony until the arrival of a new governor, Jean-Michiel, seigneur de Lépinay et de La Longueville. The new governor and Bienville soon clashed; but with the transfer of Louisiana to John Law's Company of the West, soon to be reorganized under the Company of the Indies, the directors appointed Bienville on 20 September 1717 as commandant general, entrusting him with the defense of the colony. Seven days later, on 27 September 1717, Bienville was awarded by the king with the coveted honor of the cross of the Order of Saint-Louis.

Less than a year later, in 1718, at a portage he had explored between Lake Pontchartrain and the Mississippi River, Bienville oversaw the laying out of the town of New Orleans, which would become the capital of the colony in July 1722. While New Orleans was being built, Bienville and his brothers, Joseph Le Moyne, seigneur de Sérigny et de Loiré, and Antoine Le Moyne, chevalier de Chateauqué, participated in the capture and recapture of the Spanish port of Penascola in 1719 during the brief Franco-Spanish War (1719–1722).

Unrest began again among the Natchez in late 1722. Once again, Bienville marched into Natchez country, and in September 1723, was able to suppress the revolt and make peace with the Natchez.

John Law's scheme soon collapsed and, under crown supervision, the Company of the Indies was reorganized. The new royal commissioner, Jacques de La Chaise, soon clashed with Bienville and asked that he be recalled to France. On 15 October 1723, Bienville, along with his brother, Chateauqué, were recalled to confer with the officials of the company. Bienville left the colony in early 1725, arriving in France 20 August 1725, and was replaced as commandant general.

After Bienville's departure, the new commandant general, Etienne Périer, and the French made a series of errors in their relations with the Natchez. This, combined with English and Chickasaw intrigues, lead to the Natchez War of 28 November 1729. Within several days, 145 men, 36 women, and 56 children had been killed and a large number of French women and children taken prisoner. The Natchez revolt convinced the company that its experiment in colonizing had failed and, in December 1730, the company petitioned the king to take back the colony, leaving Louisiana in 1731 once again under the direct administration of the king. On July 25, 1732, the king, realizing Bienville's expertise with the Indians, appointed him as governor, and he arrived in Louisiana on 3 March 1733.

On his return to Louisiana, Bienville found that the Natchez revolt and massacre had severely weakened his old system of alliances with the major tribes. Following French punitive expeditions in 1730 and 1731, many of the Natchez had either been killed, captured, sold into slavery, or had been granted sanctuary by the Chickasaw. The Chickasaw had laid down the gauntlet of war with the French by refusing to turn over the Natchez. The Choctaw, who had helped the French put down the Natchez revolt, were in a state of unrest, with the English making inroads among the Eastern Choctaw.

Almost immediately after he returned to the colony, Bienville incited those Choctaw loyal to the French to begin war against the Chickasaw. However, by 1735, this war had not produced the results Bienville desired, and with English intrigues still occurring among the Choctaw and the efforts of a Choctaw war chief, Red Shoe (Soulouche Oumastabé), to bring English traders into the nation, Bienville decided to launch an expedition against the Chickasaw in 1735.

The first Chickasaw expedition, as conceived by Bienville, called for a French detachment of 600 men to move up the Mobile-Tombigbee route to the Chickasaw, establishing a fort (Fort Tombecbé) along the way, and to go as far as Octibia by water (Amory, Mississippi). There, Bienville's Choctaw allies would meet him and, after a short march overland to the Chickasaw forts, Bienville would link up with Pierre d'Artaguette, the commandant of Fort de Chartres, with his force of 150 Frenchmen and several hundred Indians.

Bienville attacked the Chickasaw fort of Ackia on 26 May 1736, losing 25 dead and 52 wounded, including a high percentage of officers killed or wounded. This expedition did nothing to gain the confidence of the Choctaw and, as in the Natchez War of 1729, once again displayed the military weakness of the French. Bienville soon learned that Artaguette had been defeated before the Chickasaw forts in late March, with the majority of his force killed in the attack or retreat. Artaguette and 19 others were taken prisoner, with 17 of this number tortured and killed.

Determined to revenge his honor and that of France, Bienville began making preparations for a second Chickasaw expedition. The 1739 French expedition was one of the largest expeditions mounted in the colonial history of the Southeast. The combined force would total more than 1,200 men, plus a force of 445 Canadians and Iroquois. The French erected a fort, Fort Assumption (Memphis, Tennessee), as a base camp to attack the Chickasaw forts.

The expedition proved to be a failure, with the French unable to find a road to the Chickasaw forts until very late in the campaign. By early 1740, after some minor French operations against the Chickasaw forces, Bienville signed a peace treaty with the Chickasaw which pledged them to give up several Natchez prisoners and prevent English traders from entering their villages. The Chickasaw agreed to this, but returned few Natchez to the French, and English traders continued to travel to their villages.

Shortly after his return from the campaign, Bienville, now near 60, tired and worn out from his struggles against the Chickasaw, on 18 June 1740 requested permission to return to France in 1742. Due to complications finding a successor, he was unable to leave Louisiana until August 1743, arriving in France in October 1743.

Bienville would live for 24 more years in Paris, pensioned by the king, a man of some means, content with his nephews and their families. He died in Paris on 7 March 1767 at the age of 87.

Any assessment of Bienville must take into account the longevity of his career in Louisiana and his relationship with the Indians of the colony. Bienville's greatest strength, at least in the eyes of his contemporaries, had always been his ability to deal with the Indians, and it is here any assessment of Bienville must concentrate. He spoke Choctaw fluently and perhaps other dialects as well. He had learned the Indian methods of war, their customs and culture. One contemporary source mentions that Bienville was tattooed as were the Indians, and dressed as they did for battle, striped except for a breech cloth. If true, perhaps this helps explain his apparent rapport with them. He was able, by his actions, despite the constant severe shortage of trading goods, to keep the Choctaw in alliance with the French and to suppress the Natchez on two occasions.

His greatest fault militarily and as an Indian diplomat was his inability to defeat the Chickasaw, the staunch allies of the English, in two major campaigns. It is true that Bienville's campaigns and, more importantly, his inciting other tribes, notably the Choctaw, to attack the Chickasaw had so severely weakened them that by 1740, they were no longer a threat to the colony. However, the lack of French military success in the 1736 and 1739 campaigns severely undermined French military prowess and prestige among the Choctaw. His earlier military efforts against the Alabamas and Natchez had been, on the whole, small unit actions in which he had defeated his opponents by guile, ruse, surprise, threats, kidnapping, and intimidation.

On his return to Louisiana in 1733, Bienville was forced to change his tactics. He faced in the Chickasaw a determined opponent, one that would defend its homeland with all the valor its exalted military reputation entailed. He was forced to assault the enemy in its own homeland, in heavily, well entrenched, palisaded forts. The 1736 campaign and the attack on the village of Ackia was a poorly planned operation, strategically and tactically, especially his attempt to link up with Artaguette. The 1739 campaign was a logistical nightmare, which turned into disaster for the French. For the size of the operation and the amount of money invested by the crown, it produced few noteworthy successes—several Natchez prisoners, four English traders, and a promise from the Chickasaw to expel the English, which they did not do.

In conclusion, Bienville's military reputation should be seen for what it was. He was a successful commander during the period 1701–1725, who, through knowledge of his opponents, diplomacy, divided loyalties, intimidation, threats, resourcefulness, and courage, was able to keep the majority of French-Indian allies loyal to the French. After 1733, the assessment of Bienville's military reputation and Indian diplomacy must be considered largely a failure. The failure of the French campaigns of 1736–1739 produced a major loss of respect for the French among the Choctaw. This undermining of French military prestige, lack of French trade goods, and English intrigues would be factors in an attempt by Red Shoe's faction of Choctaw to break with the French by 1746, producing the disastrous Choctaw civil war.

A new generation of French colonial and ethnohistorians must undertake a reexamination of French Louisiana's most puzzling and complex figure, Jean-Baptiste Le Moyne, sieur de Bienville.

Joe Bassette Wilkins

References

Archives Nationales, Paris, C13A, Letters written to the Ministry in France from the Colony in Louisiana, vols. 1–17; Bertet de la Clue, *A Voyage to Dauphin Island in 1720: The Journal of Bertet de la Clue*, trans. and ed. by Frances Escoffier and Jay Higginbotham (1974).

Marcel Giraud, *Histoire de la Louisiane francaise*, 4 vols. (Paris: 1953–1974); ———, *A History of French Louisiana, Vol. One: The Reign of Louis XIV, 1698–1715*, trans. by Joseph C. Lambert (1974); ———, *A History of French Louisiana, Vol. Five: The Company of the Indies, 1723–1731*, trans. by Brian Pearce (1991); Jean-Baptiste Benard de La Harpe, *The Historical Journal of the Establishment of the French in Louisiana*, trans. by Joan Cain and Virginia Koening, ed. by Glenn R. Conrad (1971); Jay Higginbotham, *Old Mobile: Fort Louis de la Louisiane,*
1702–1711 (1977); Jack D.L. Holmes, "Jean Baptiste Le-moyne, Sieur de Bienville," in *The Louisiana Governors: From Iberville to Edwards* (1990):7–13.

Grace King, *Jean Baptiste Le Moyne, Sieur de Bienville* (1892); Charles Edwards O'Neill, *Church and State in French Colonial Louisiana: Policy and Politics to 1732* (1966); ———, "The Death of Bienville," *Louisiana History*, VIII (1967):362–369; ——— ———, "Jean-Baptiste Le Moyne de Bienville," *Dictionary of Canadian Biography*, 11 vols. (1974), 3:379–384; Dunbar Rowland and Albert G. Sanders, eds., *Mississippi Provincial Archives: French Dominion*, Vols. I–III (1927–1932); Dunbar Rowland, Albert G. Sanders, and Patricia K. Galloway, eds., *Mississippi Provincial Archives: French Dominion*, Vol. IV (1984).

Daniel H. Usner, Jr., *Indians, Settlers, & Slaves in A Frontier Exchange Economy: the Lower Mississippi Before 1783* (1992); Joe Wilkins, "Outpost of Empire: The Founding of Fort Tombecbé and De Bienville's Chickasaw Expedition of 1736," *Proceedings of the Twelfth Meeting of the French Colonial Historical Society, Ste. Genevieve, May 1986*, ed. by Philip Boucher and Serge Courville (1988): 133–154; Patricia Dillion Woods, *French-Indian Relations on the Southern Frontier, 1699–1762* (1980).

See also ACKIA, BATTLE OF; CHICKASAW WARS; CHOCTAW; FORT CONDÉ (ALABAMA); ENGLISH BEND (MISSISSIPPI); LE MOYNE D'IBERVILLE, PIERRE; FORT LOUIS (ALABAMA); LOUISIANA; FORT MAUREPAS (MISSISSIPPI); NATCHEZ WAR; FORT TOMBECBÉ (ALABAMA)

Le Moyne d'Iberville, Pierre (1661–1706)

Pierre Le Moyne d'Iberville, one of New France's greatest heroes, was born around 20 July 1661, at Ville-Marie (Montreal). He was the third son of Charles Le Moyne de Longueuil et de Châteauguay and of Catherine Thierry (Primot). Charles Le Moyne had arrived in Canada as an indentured servant to the Jesuits and, by his skill in Indian languages and warfare, combined with a mercantile talent, had risen to be one of the richest men in the colony by the time of his death in 1685. Iberville came from a large family of two sisters and 11 brothers. The elder Le Moyne, as his sons grew up, added to their names titles taken from the surrounding area of his native Dieppe in France. Iberville's title came from a fief held by Charles Le Moyne's family near Dieppe, in the province of Normandy. Many of Charles Le Moyne's sons served with great distinction in the colonial wars in which Canada found itself in the seventeenth and eighteenth centuries. Iberville was accompanied in most of his campaigns by at least one or two of his brothers and relatives.

Iberville began his military career accompanying an expedition lead by Chevalier Pierre de Troyes against the English in the Hudson Bay area in spring 1686. The English had established themselves in the Hudson Bay as early as 1668 when an English ship traded with the natives. By 1670, the Hudson Bay Company was chartered and began to establish posts on the shores of the bay to trade with the various tribes in the area, especially the powerful Cree. These natives had once traded with the French, but now began to trade with the English. The French sought to counter this English move by organizing the Compagnie du Nord in 1682, driving the English from the area. Iberville distinguished himself in these Hudson Bay expeditions and others from 1686–1688 by a series of heroic deeds which helped to establish his military reputation.

It was during Iberville's Hudson Bay expeditions that a paternity suit was lodged against him in 1686 by a girl in Montreal. She claimed Iberville had seduced her under the promise of marriage and he was the father of her expected child. The Sovereign Council found him guilty in 1688, and he was forced to pay for the upbringing of the child until her 15th birthday. In 1693, Iberville married Marie Thérèse Pollet, the daughter of a French army officer stationed in Canada.

Shortly after Iberville's return from the Hudson Bay area in 1688, war officially broke out between France and England, the War of the League of Augsburg (King William's War, 1689–1697). Iberville was placed as second-in-command of an expedition raised by Governor Frontenac (Louis de Buade, comte de Frontenac et de Palluau), who had recently returned as governor, to raid the English colony of New York. Under the joint command of Iberville's brother, Jacques Le Moyne de Sainte–Hélène, and Nicholas d'Ailleboust de Manthet, with another brother, Francois Le Moyne de Bienville, also accompanying them, the expedition of 210 men, 114 Canadians, and 96 natives was given the mission of destroying the English settlement of Corlaer (later Schenectady, New York). Frontenac was determined to revenge the Lachine massacre of August 1689, which saw more than 1,000 Iroquois warriors, in a surprise attack, carry the war to the very gates of Montreal.

The expedition arrived at Corlaer during the early morning hours of 18–19 February 1689. Finding the town unprepared, the Canadian-native force launched a surprise attack before daylight the next morning, massacring more than half of the inhabitants, taking about one-fourth prisoner, burning the settlement to the ground, and returning to Montreal with 50 horses loaded with plunder. This attack was brutal and cold-blooded but typified the warfare of the time. Iberville and his fellow Canadians were products of the environment in which they lived. New France had been carved out of North American wilderness at the expense of blood and hard work and the constant fear of Iroquois attack. To survive, these Canadians adopted the tactics of their enemy, the Iroquois, at times outdoing them in cruelty and ruthlessness, neither accepting nor giving any quarter.

The declaration of war between England and France cleared the way for a series of expeditions by Iberville to the Hudson Bay area between 1690 and 1694. By summer 1694, Iberville and his brother, Joseph Le Moyne de Sérigny, undertook an expedition against Fort York, the English stronghold in the Hudson Bay region. Iberville, with his two ships, blockaded the fort and, with winter setting in, the English surrendered York. Renaming it Fort Bourbon, Iberville left a small garrison to man the post and returned to France by fall 1695. Iberville's capture of the Hudson's Bay Company's greatest asset in the north was short lived, as the fort was retaken by the English in 1696.

Iberville returned to action in 1696 with an expedition against the English-held Fort William Henry on the coast of Maine (Penobscot), which he burned to the ground in August 1696, sailing afterward with his expedition of three ships to the French capital of Newfoundland, Placentia. In a campaign from November 1696 to April 1697, Iberville destroyed 36 settlements, killed 200 people, took 700 prisoners, and captured an enormous amount of cod. Before he could consolidate his gains and finish driving the English completely off the island, his brother, Sérigny, arrived with orders from Jérôme Phélypeaux Maurepas, comte de Pontchartrain, the French minister of the marine, to undertake an expedition to the Hudson Bay area to recapture Fort York.

The expedition of 1697 to recapture Fort York would produce more deeds of valor to enhance the rising military reputation of Iberville. Iberville was placed in command of the *Pélican,* mounting 44 guns, along with five other French ships, which were to proceed to the Hudson Bay region and capture Fort York. In traveling through the straits of Hudson Bay, the *Pélican* became separated from the other French ships and proceeded to the mouth of the Hayes River. On the morning of 4 September 1697, Iberville was attacked by three English warships, the *Hampshire* carrying 56 guns, the *Hudson Bay* of 32 guns, and the *Dering* of 36 guns. In a series of brilliant naval maneuvers, Iberville sank the *Hampshire,* captured the *Hudson Bay,* which soon sank, and forced the *Dering* to flee. The next day, three of the French ships arrived and Iberville began besieging Fort York. By 13 September 1697, Fort York surrendered to Iberville. He left his brother, Sérigny, in command of the French interest in the Hudson Bay and, with his wounded younger brother, Bienville, on board his ship, he arrived in France in November 1697.

Ironically, the Treaty of Ryswick (1697), which ended the war, signed 11 days after the surrender of Fort York, provided that the Hudson Bay territory return to the situation as it existed prior to the beginning of official hostilities. The efforts of Iberville had no effect on the composition of the treaty; although in reality, neither side strictly adhered to the terms of the treaty as it related to the Hudson Bay area.

The Mississippi basin had long interested France and Louis XIV, especially since the expeditions in the 1680s of Robert Cavelier, sieur de La Salle. With the signing of the Treaty of Ryswick, Louis XIV moved to put himself in position to place one of his relatives on the throne of Spain. If the French could establish a colony at the mouth of the Mississippi River, they could link their empire in Canada with a chain of forts, providing a barrier to English expansion by gathering the tribes of the interior into a firm alliance with the French. If the French were successful in placing a Bourbon on the throne of Spain, this would provide a base of operations to keep the English from taking over the Spanish colonies in Florida. If the French were unsuccessful in placing a family member on the throne of Spain, the colony

could be used to attack the Spanish empire in Florida and Mexico. The English also became interested in establishing a colony in the area, largely due to the writings of the renegade priest, Father Louis Hennepin, a former companion of La Salle. Pontchartrain, fearful of a possible English expedition to Louisiana being promoted by Daniel Coxe, a former physician to Charles II, rushed ahead with preparations for an expedition to be lead by Iberville.

After many delays, Iberville's expedition of two ships, the *Badine,* a 32-gun frigate, and the *Marin,* a 38-gun frigate, and two *traversiers* (freighters), the *Pretieuse* and the *Voyageur,* set sail from Brest on 7 October 1698 for the French colony of Saint Domingue (Haiti). Iberville arrived off the north coast of Saint Domingue on 4 December 1698. After a short stay on the island, Iberville sailed for the Florida coast and entered the Gulf of Mexico, arriving at Pensacola Bay in late January 1699. There he found the Spanish already in possession, having beaten Iberville to the Gulf coast by only a couple of weeks.

During the next several weeks, Iberville and his brother, Bienville, explored the coast, sighting Mobile Bay, exploring Massacre Island (Dauphin Island), as well as Ship and Cat Islands, and establishing relations with the natives on the coastal mainland. Iberville decided to build the first establishment at the northeast side of Biloxi Bay (near present-day Ocean Springs), strategically situated between the Mississippi and the Spanish in Pensacola. Work on the fort, to be named Fort Maurepas, was begun in the second week of February 1699. On 27 February 1699, Iberville set out with his brother and 48 men, with two large rowboats and two birch canoes, to find the mouth of the Mississippi. He entered the birdfoot subdelta of the Mississippi, the old East pass (now the North pass), on 2 March 1699, when he broke through an almost inaccessible passage of mud and logs that looked from a distance to be rocks, to reach the Mississippi River. Iberville continued up the course of the river where he encountered the native tribes of the Bayagoulas and Mongulachas (Mugulashas), the latter had a letter left by Henri de Tonty, La Salle's companion, written by Tonty in April 1685. This convinced Iberville this was indeed the Mississippi River which he had been seeking. Sending the main body of men down the river, he discovered two lakes, naming them respectively, Maurepas and Pontchartrain, and a portage to

Ship Island. Leaving an Ensign Sauvole in command at Fort Maurepas, Iberville set sail for France on 3 May 1699.

On Iberville's return to France, he was rewarded with the Cross of Saint-Louis, the first Canadian to be so honored. Despite the pleadings of Iberville for France to commit itself to the colonization of Louisiana, the French were wary to offend their Spanish brethren. Pontchartrain did provide enough men and ships for a second expedition, and Iberville left France in October 1699 for Louisiana, arriving at Fort Maurepas in January 1700. Iberville, seeing that he needed a second fort on the Mississippi, built Fort Boyulaye (Fort Mississippi), located on the west bank of the river. Iberville continued his exploring expeditions, visiting the Natchez and Taensa, taking with him his brother, Bienville, who had acquired a knowledge of the native dialects. In his journals he has left historians a vivid picture of native life at the beginning of the eighteenth century in the Southeast.

Iberville left the colony in May 1700 to return to France. During his 11 months in France—from August 1700 to September 1701—Iberville lobbied the crown for more support for the Louisiana colony. He wanted to establish a major fort and naval base in the Mobile region to counterbalance that of Spain's at Pensacola. He sought also to win support for his Indian policy, that of creating an alliance of the tribes to halt English expansion into the region. With three ships, Iberville left La Rochelle for Louisiana in September 1701. By this time, the once robust warrior was suffering from repeated bouts of malaria. He landed in Pensacola and was allowed by the Spanish to rest on board his ship for two months. Iberville had decided to move the location of the fort to a point 26 leagues up the Mobile River from Massacre Island—at a location called Twenty-Seven Mile Bluff. Here the fort was laid out (Fort Louis de la Louisiana—to be called La Mobile), with Bienville to build it and a naval station to be built at Massacre Island.

Iberville's plan to win over the Indians was, in reality, much like the Canadian plan of which he was familiar. He realized France could not hold this vast territory without the cooperation of the natives, and he sought to win them over. If he could ally the tribes with the French and against the English, he had a chance of succeeding. He wanted missionaries among the Indians to help convert them, as well as to act as observers. This, combined with annual presents to be given to allied tribes to secure their loyalty, and the placing of young boys to live among the Indians to learn their languages, would provide the French with a sound intelligence system among the tribes and aid in controlling them. He sought, before he left, to bring the Chickasaw and Choctaw together in peace; however, this effort failed after his departure. When Iberville departed Louisiana in April 1702, he placed his brother, Bienville, in command.

Iberville would never return to the colony he founded. Recurring bouts of malaria kept him from returning to the colony, although he constantly advised the government on the situation in the colony. With the outbreak of the War of the Spanish Succession (Queen Anne's War), Iberville was assigned an expedition to raid the English held colonies in the Caribbean. He sailed for the West Indies from France in early 1706 with 12 vessels. In April 1706, he attacked the English island of Nevis, capturing the island, taking prisoner more than 1,700 men, women, and children, 6,000 slaves, and capturing 24 ships. When Iberville departed on 22 April 1706, much of the island had been put to the torch and sacked. Iberville's career was cut short soon after this, when he died, probably of yellow fever, in Havana on 9 July 1706. In the wake of his death, scandal erupted over the mismanagement of the expedition.

Any assessment of Iberville must put into perspective his military accomplishments. Despite his many apparent military successes, they amounted to very little as far as the long-term physical boundaries of New France were concerned. His efforts in the Hudson Bay region, where he expended so much effort and blood, were short-lived, as the area was to become English by the Treaty of Utrecht, which ended the War of the Spanish Succession in 1713. Newfoundland and Nevis remained in the hands of Great Britain, and even his planting of the colony of Louisiana, despite the best efforts by his brother, Bienville, and his relations, would become English in 1763. Perhaps Iberville's greatest contribution was in his military style, the style of that of the seventeenth-century Canadian. Canada, outnumbered by the expanding English colonies, relied on men like Iberville and his numerous relations to stop the tide of English expansion. Through the use of ruthless tactics, the tactics of *la petite guerre,* these men held the frontier for France against all odds until overwhelmed in 1763. His abil-

L

ity to deal with the Indians, a method acquired from his Canadian experience and background, he passed on to his brother, Bienville. Yet there was something else associated with Iberville's character that was not as positive. He often mixed his own commercial and trading concerns with those of his military expeditions, whether it was in Hudson Bay, Newfoundland, Louisiana, or the West Indies, Nevis. Future biographers of Iberville and other members of the Le Moyne family, in particular his brother, Bienville, will have to analyze this aspect of the family character more fully. Iberville was a product of his age and environment and, as one of Canada's greatest modern colonial historians has noted, deserves to be ranked in the same group as Cortés and Drake—men of daring, resourcefulness, adventure, and courage; yet utterly ruthless.

Joe Bassette Wilkins

References

Mathé Allain, *"Not Worth A Straw": French Colonial Policy and the Early Years of Louisiana* (1988); Archives des Colonies Series, C13A, Letters Written to the Ministry in France from the Colony in Louisiana, Vol. 1; John Anthony Caruso, *The Southern Frontier* (1963); Nellis Crouse, *Le Moyne d'Iberville: Soldier of New France* (1954); W.J. Eccles, *Canada Under Louis XIV, 1663–1701* (1968).

Alcée Fortier, *Early Explorers and the Domination of the French, 1512–1768,* 2nd ed., 2 vols., ed. by Jo Ann Carrigan (1966); Marcel Giraud, *A History of French Louisiana, Volume One: The Reign of Louis XIV, 1698–1715,* trans. by Joseph C. Lambert (1974); Jean-Baptiste Bénard de La Harpe, *The Historical Journal of the Establishment of the French in Louisiana,* trans. by Joan Cain and Virginia Koening, ed. by Glenn R. Conrad (1971); Jay Higginbotham, *Old Mobile: Fort Louis de la Louisiane, 1702–1711* (1977); Jack D.L. Holmes, "Pierre Lemoyne, Sieur d'Iberville et d'Ardillières," in *The Louisiana Governors: From Iberville to Edwards* (1990): 1–3.

Richebourg Gaillard McWilliams, "Iberville at the Birdfoot Subdelta: Final Discovery of the Mississippi River," in *Frenchmen and French Ways in the Mississippi Valley,* ed. by John Francis McDermott (1961):127–140; ———, "Iberville and the Southern Indians," *Alabama Review,* XX (1967):243–262; ———, trans. and ed., *Fleur de Lys and Calumet: Being the Penicaut Narrative of French Adventure in Louisiana* (1988); ———, trans. and ed, *Iberville's Gulf Journals* (1991).

Charles Edwards O'Neill, *Church and State in French Colonial Louisiana: Policy and Politics to 1732* (1966); Bernard Pothier, "Le Moyne d'Iberville," *Dictionary of Canadian Biography,* 12 vols. (1969), 2:390–401; Paul Du Ru, *Journal of Paul Du Ru* [February 1 to May 8, 1700] *Missionary Priest to Louisiana,* trans. by Ruth Lapham Butler (1934); Daniel H. Usner, Jr., *Indians, Settlers, & Slaves in a Frontier Exchange Economy: The Lower Mississippi Valley Before 1783* (1992).

See also FORT DE LA BOULAYE (LOUISIANA); FRONTENAC, LOUIS DE BUADE DE; KING WILLIAM'S WAR; LE MOYNE DE BIENVILLE, JEAN-BAPTISTE; LOUISIANA; FORT MAUREPAS (MISSISSIPPI); SCHENECTADY, BATTLE OF; FORT WILLIAM HENRY (MAINE)

Lenni Lenape
See DELAWARE

Fort Lévis (New York)
In the summer of 1759, the French selected Isle Royale (now Chimney Island, just east of Ogdensburg, New York), a small, low-lying island at the head of the Galops Rapids as the best site for a fort to command the upper St. Lawrence River. The French engineer, Captain Jean Nicolas Desandroüins (1729–1792), began Fort Lévis in August 1759. After the following March, the work was continued by Captain Pierre Pouchot (1712–1769) of the Régiment de Béarn. Pouchot's six Canadian colonial regular officers and eventual garrison of 330 men—Canadian militia and sailors and a few French colonial regulars—improved the timber-faced earthworks and erected a breastwork around the circumference of the island with an abatis of tree branches extending into the water. Sailors commanded by a Canadian naval militia officer, Captain René-Hypolite Pépin, *dit* Laforce (1728–1802), and colonial regulars manned a dozen 12-pounders and 23 cannon of very small caliber.

An army of 10,000 regulars, provincials, and Indians and 100 siege guns commanded by

Lieutenant General Jeffrey Amherst, First Baron Amherst (1717–1797), left Oswego in 900 boats in early August 1760 and cautiously descended the St. Lawrence toward Montreal. The Canadian sloop *Outaouaise,* commanded by a Captain Labroquerie, engaged the British above La Présentation (Ogdensburg) on 17 August, but the lack of wind allowed the British row galleys to pound the helpless vessel into submission in three hours. Fifteen Canadians were killed or wounded and 100 captured. The following day, British troops occupied the mainland around Fort Lévis and landed on two islands between the north shore and Isle Royale.

Amherst deployed 75 guns on the islands and mainland. On 23 August, when the batteries were ready, he ordered his three sloops and artillery to silence Pouchot's guns, clearing the way for grenadiers and light infantry waiting in *bateaux* below the closest island to storm the fort. The French, however, disabled all of the attacking vessels, and Amherst called off the assault. The British bombarded Fort Lévis for three days and demolished the fort and outlying bastions, set the debris on fire with red-hot shot and fire bombs, and put 48 men, including all of the officers, out of action. On 25 August, when the Canadian gunners ran out of shot and fires threatened to blow up a principal magazine, Pouchot asked for terms.

The British and Americans lost 21 killed and 43 wounded during the siege, and Amherst was obliged to spend nearly two weeks at Fort Lévis; he could only resume his advance on 31 August, but this did not prevent the fall of Montreal on 8 September.

Martin L. Nicolai

References

John Knox, *An Historical Journal of the Campaigns in North America for the Years 1757, 1758, 1759 and 1760* (1769); Pierre Pouchot, *Memoir Upon the Late War in North America Between the French and the English, 1755–60* (1866); John C. Webster, ed., *Journal of William Amherst in America 1758–1760* (1927); ———, *The Journal of Jeffrey Amherst Recording the Military Career of General Amherst in America from 1758 to 1763* (1931).

See also AMHERST, JEFFREY; FORT LA PRÉSENTATION (NEW YORK); MONTREAL, ATTACK ON; POUCHOT DE MAUPAS, PIERRE

Lévis, François-Gaston de, Duc de Lévis (1719–1787)

Lévis, a member of a cadet branch of one of the most ancient and prestigious noble families in France, was born at the Château d'Ajac, near Limoux, Languedoc, on 20 August 1719. His parents were Jean de Lévis, baron d'Ajac, and Jeanne-Marie de Maguelonne. In 1735, the 15-year-old chevalier de Lévis, as he was known, was commissioned a second lieutenant in the Régiment de la Marine. During the War of the Polish Succession (1733–1738), he took part in the Rhine campaign, rising from lieutenant to the rank of captain. Lévis also distinguished himself in the War of the Austrian Succession (1740–1748), serving at Dettingen and in Bohemia, Alsace, southern Germany, and Piedmont. During the latter campaign, he was assistant chief of staff for his influential cousin, Gaston-Charles-Pierre de Lévis-Mirepoix, duc de Lévis-Mirepoix (1699–1757), who later became a marshal of France.

Anxious to advance his career but unable to afford a regiment, Lévis volunteered to accompany Major General Louis-Joseph de Montcalm, marquis de Montcalm (1712–1759), to Canada as his second-in-command with the rank of brigadier. Arriving at Quebec on 31 May 1756, Lévis was immediately given an independent command on the Lake Champlain frontier while Montcalm besieged the forts at Oswego. His order of battle, issued at the beginning of the advance, demonstrated that Lévis was already familiar with the role of light troops in protecting and supporting conventional infantry, and he made excellent use of the Indians, Canadians, and French colonial regulars under his command. Although Lévis and Montcalm had frequently seen irregular troops in action in Bohemia and Piedmont, Lévis made better use of this experience. His great personal charm, intelligence, and interest in irregular tactics made him very popular among the Canadian officers and the governor general, Pierre de Rigaud de Vaudreuil de Cavagnial, marquis de Vaudreuil (1698–1778).

Lévis displayed his military talents during Major François-Pierre de Rigaud de Vaudreuil's (1703–1779) raid on Fort William Henry in early 1757, and during the fort's capture that summer when he commanded the siege train, transport boats, and later the advance guard. In 1758, the marquis de Vaudreuil ordered Lévis to march into the Mohawk villages and coerce this pro-British tribe into joining the French, but

Lévis's mixed force had barely set out when Major General James Abercromby (1706–1781) began his offensive. Lévis was recalled, and he moved quickly to join Montcalm, arriving at Fort Carillon late on 7 July with 400 men. He took up positions covering the exposed right of the French abatis. Fortunately for Montcalm, Abercromby made no attempt to outflank these works during the battle the following day.

Montcalm blamed Vaudreuil for the lack of Canadian and Indian support during the Battle of Carillon or Ticonderoga, and the governor general responded by asking the minister of marine to replace Montcalm with his second-in-command. The minister promoted Lévis to major general, but Montcalm remained at his post. In 1759, Montcalm advocated placing his army on the defensive in and around the fortifications of Quebec, but Lévis realized it would be fatal for the troops to be penned up in the city. He successfully argued that the army be stationed in a strong advanced position by the Montmorency Falls to prevent the British from even approaching Quebec. Lévis sharply repulsed an Anglo-American landing at Montmorency on 31 July using the firepower of Canadian militia supported by a reserve of French regulars.

On 9 August 1759, Montcalm sent Lévis and 800 men to the upper St. Lawrence to counter a feared descent from Lake Ontario. On hearing the news of Montcalm's disaster on the Plains of Abraham on 13 September, however, Lévis rushed back to the main army and found a mob of demoralized officers and men in retreat toward Montreal. He promptly turned the army around and marched to the relief of Quebec. Much to his disgust, he learned that Canadian commander Major Jean-Baptiste-Nicolas-Roch de Ramezay (1708–1777) had surrendered the city on 18 September. Lévis did not hesitate to blame the defeat on his late superior's decision to attack Wolfe's army before the French troops were assembled.

During the winter of 1759–1760, Lévis stationed detachments around Quebec to harass the British while the bulk of the army remained in winter quarters around Montreal. On 20 April 1760, before the river ice melted, Lévis advanced on Quebec with 4,000 regulars and 3,000 militia. With the exception of Captain Louis Legardeur de Repentigny's (1721–1786) Canadian brigade, Lévis had each militia company attached to a French battalion under selected French officers in order to ensure closer cooperation between the line infantry and light troops. This innovation greatly increased the strength and effectiveness of his regular battalions and contributed to his victory at Sainte-Foy on 28 April 1760. Brigadier General James Murray's (1721/22–1794) British infantry suffered heavy losses from the fire of the French regulars and their Canadian light companies, and Lévis's counterattacks forced Murray to order a retreat.

Lévis besieged Quebec with a few field guns, but it was evident the city would only fall if French ships arrived and landed reinforcements and more cannon. When British warships began anchoring by Quebec on 9 May, Lévis had little choice but to raise the siege and retreat to Montreal. When Major General Jeffrey Amherst, First Baron Amherst (1717–1797), negotiated the capitulation of Canada on 7–8 September 1760, he refused to grant Lévis's remaining troops the honors of war, and Lévis requested Vaudreuil's permission to fight rather than surrender. The governor general, however, ordered him to accept the articles of capitulation rather than needlessly destroy the city. After burning their colors, the French surrendered and returned to France on the condition they would not serve again for the duration of the war.

Lévis was promoted to lieutenant general in 1761, and the British, to recognize his brave defense, granted him permission to fight anywhere in Europe. Lévis served with Marshal Charles de Rohan, prince de Soubise (1715–1787), on the lower Rhine in December 1761, and commanded the advance guard of Lieutenant General Louis-Joseph de Bourbon, prince de Condé (1736–1818), the following year, distinguishing himself at the Battle of Nauheim or Johannisberg. He married Gabrielle-Augustine de Danton, daughter of the treasurer general of the artillery and a director of the Compagnie des Indes, in March 1762.

After the end of the Seven Years' War, Lévis left active service. He was appointed governor of Artois in 1765, created a marquis, and then named marshal of France on 13 June 1783. A year later he was elevated to the peerage as duc de Lévis. He died at Arras on 26 November 1787, aged sixty-seven.

François-Gaston de Lévis's military conduct was characterized by clear and innovative planning, decisive action, and an ability to inspire the confidence of soldiers and Indian warriors belonging to different corps and nations.

His use of Canadians as irregulars and then light infantry was particularly impressive. There is little doubt that if Lévis had been in command from the beginning of the war, Canada would have stood a much better chance of surviving the enemy invasions.

Martin L. Nicolai

References

Henri-Raymond Casgrain, ed., *Collection des manuscrits du maréchal de Lévis* (1888–1894); Guy Frégault, *Canada: The War of the Conquest,* trans. by Margaret M. Cameron (1969); Gustave de Hauteclocque, *Le maréchal de Lévis, gouverneur général de l'Artois (1765–1787)* (1901); George F.G. Stanley, *New France: The Last Phase, 1744–1760* (1961).

See also MONTCALM-GOZON DE SAINT-VERAN, LOUIS-JOSEPH; MURRAY, JAMES; QUEBEC, FRENCH ATTEMPT TO RECAPTURE; RIGAUD DE VAUDREUIL DE CAVAGNIAL, PIERRE DE; TICONDEROGA, BATTLE OF; FORT WILLIAM HENRY (NEW YORK)

Fort Lewis (Virginia)

Fort Lewis was one of several forts erected in western Virginia during the French and Indian War. Located near the present town of Salem, in Roanoke County, Virginia, Fort Lewis may also have been called Fort George or Fort Prince George. Originally garrisoned with 30 men, the fort was the jumping-off point for an expedition against the Shawnee Indians living near the Ohio River. In February 1756, a mixed force of Virginia troops and Cherokee Indians under the command of Major Andrew Lewis marched to the Big Sandy River on the present Kentucky-West Virginia border. The expedition proved a failure; they encountered no Indians, and returned to Fort Lewis reduced to near starvation.

Thomas Costa

References

Louis K. Koontz, *The Virginia Frontier, 1754–1763* (1925).

Light Infantry

Highly mobile elite companies of the best trained, most dependable, and ablest men drawn from the various companies of a regiment for the most demanding and dangerous duties.

The origins of light infantry are rooted in southeastern Europe, where the Habsburgs recruited their feared Pandours, and in the steppes of the Ukraine, where the Tsars levied units of Cossacks for use in their wars. From there, the concept of light infantry as irregular troops was introduced by the French into the armies of western Europe during the 1680s as light cavalry in the form of dragoons and hussars. Irregular light troops performed valuable services during the Silesian and Seven Years' Wars, but were always considered unreliable and discharged at the end of war. In the 1740s, this east European concept was supplemented by the central European concept of light infantry, which had been pioneered by Hesse in the Thirty Years' War, where *jäger* had first been raised for military service out of the hunting personnel of the state in 1631. By the mid-eighteenth century, all European states had units of regular light infantry following the Hessian model.

In 1741/1742, light infantry companies became a regular, and elite, feature of British regiments. They were institutionalized in 1771/1772, when each British infantry battalion formed a light company of 44 men. In the American colonies, Colonel Thomas Gage proposed the first independent regiment of light infantry in November 1757. This proposal was based to a large degree on the mistrust in the capabilities of irregular light infantry such as Rogers' Rangers. Gage's regiment was raised in spring 1758 to combine the necessary staying power of the line with the mobility of the rangers. In August 1777, a corps of light infantry was raised for the Continental army as well.

Robert A. Selig

References

Johann Ewald, *Treatise on Partisan Warfare,* trans. and ed. by Robert A. Selig and David C. Skaggs (1991).

See also INFANTRY

Fort Ligonier (Pennsylvania)

Fort Ligonier was the last in a string of outposts along Forbes's Road, constructed as a way station and supply post for General John Forbes's successful campaign against Fort Duquesne in 1758. In July, Major John Armstrong scouted the site, which lay about 45 miles west of Fort Bedford just beyond the Laurel Ridge on the site of an old Delaware town on Loyalhanna Creek.

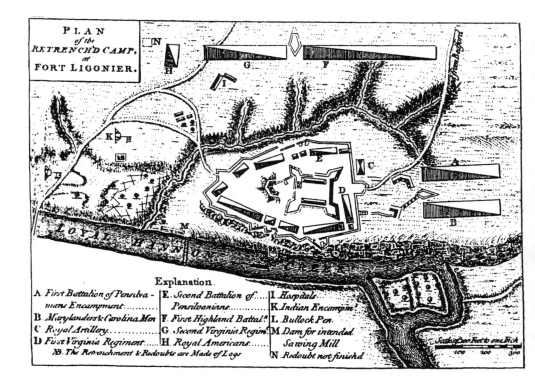

PLAN
of the
RETRENCH'D CAMP,
at
FORT LIGONIER.

Explanation.

A. *First Battalion of Pensilva-* | E. *Second Battalion of* | I *Hospitals.*
mans Encampment. | *Pensiloanians.* | K *Indian Encampm*
B. *Marylanders & Carolina Men* | F. *First Highland Battal.* | L. *Bullock Pen.*
C *Royal Artillery.* | G. *Second Virginia Regim.* | M *Dam for intended*
D *First Virginia Regiment* | H. *Royal Americans.* | *Sawing Mill*
NB. *The Retrenchment & Redoubts are Made of Logs* | | N *Redoubt not finishd*

Armstrong and Colonel James Burd initiated the fort's construction by erecting stockades and digging entrenchments around their camp. When Colonel Henry Bouquet arrived in September, construction resumed and was not completed until the following spring. In its final form, Ligonier consisted of a fort proper, square in shape with bastions at the corners, surrounded by an enormous irregular pentagon of log retrenchments which enclosed the fort and some of the soldiers' encampments. The inner fort was about 200 feet on a side, and its east face, which could be assaulted with cannons, was built of two parallel rows of logs laid horizontally. The rest of the fort was built of picket-style vertical logs. Within the fort were four log buildings: an officers' quarters, a mess, and two storehouses. The surrounding retrenchment consisted of a low log wall 1,700 feet in length that enclosed three and a half acres. The entire complex stood at the crest of a bluff overlooking the Loyalhanna.

In the fall of 1758, 6,200 men massed at Fort Ligonier to prepare for Forbes's assault on Fort Duquesne. Colonel Bouquet arrived in early September along with Forbes's advance guard; the general came two months later. In the mean-

time, Bouquet approved Major James Grant's request to lead a reconnaissance force of nearly 850 Highlanders and colonists to Fort Duquesne. The result was a disastrous rout of Grant's forces; about 500 were killed or taken prisoner. In an effort to take advantage of this reversal, the French commander at Fort Duquesne, François-Marie Le Marchand de Lignery, marched against Fort Ligonier. On 12 October, a force of about 1,200 French soldiers attacked the fort, but suffered a decisive defeat at the hands of Colonel James Burd, commander of the Second Pennsylvania Regiment and temporary acting commander of the fort. Forbes arrived at Fort Ligonier about 1 November, and based on reports of French weakness of Fort Duquesne, determined to march on the fort immediately. Lignery chose to abandon Fort Duquesne rather than fight against Forbes's superior forces. On the night of 24 November, he ordered the magazine and fort burned, and his forces retreated to Fort Machault. Forbes and his army took possession of the site the following morning.

Even after the construction of Fort Pitt on the site of Fort Duquesne, Ligonier continued to be an important outpost for the rest of the war; it was a crucial point in the supply line connecting Pittsburgh with eastern Pennsylvania. In July 1759, the fort was again attacked unsuccessfully by the French, and during Pontiac's uprising in 1763, Fort Ligonier was one of only three British posts that withstood Indian attacks (the others were Fort Pitt and Detroit).

Eric Hinderaker

References
C. Hale Sipe, *Fort Ligonier and Its Times* (1932); Charles Morse Stotz, *Outposts of the War for Empire: The French and English in Western Pennsylvania; Their Armies, Their Forts, Their People, 1749–1764* (1985).

See also BOUQUET, HENRY; BURD, JAMES; CARLISLE, CAMP NEAR (PENNSYLVANIA); FORT DUQUESNE (PENNSYLVANIA); FORBES CAMPAIGN OF 1758; FORT LOUDOUN (PENNSYLVANIA); PONTIAC'S WAR

Litchfield Forts (Connecticut)

Connecticut frontier towns, such as Litchfield, were forced to go on the defensive in reaction to warfare between Massachusetts colonists and Maine Indians that threatened to spread to local Indians in the 1720s. Outbreaks of violence did erupt, as in 1723, when Indians killed a Litchfield resident. The town responded by building four outlying forts: North Fort (also named Fort Kilburn), East Fort, West Fort (also named Fort Griswold), and South Fort. All were built between the years 1723 and 1725.

Leslie Miller

References
Robert B. Roberts, *Encyclopedia of Historic Forts: The Military, Pioneer, and Trading Posts of the United States* (1988).

See also DUMMER'S WAR

Little Fort Niagara (New York; also known as Fort du Portage)

Built in the summer of 1750 by Daniel-Marie Chabert de Joncaire de Clausonne, Little Fort Niagara (Fort du Portage) was located behind the falls on the shore of Cayuga Creek. The site, which earlier was the location of the Griffon shipyard, was a French post during the Seven Years' War.

Elizabeth Gossman

References
Robert West Howard, *Thundergate: The Forts of Niagara* (1968).

See also CHABERT DE JONCAIRE DE CLAUSONNE, DANIEL-MARIE

Logstown, Treaty of (1752)

Logstown, also known as Chininqué, was situated eighteen miles below the forks of the Ohio River, near present-day Ambridge, Pennsylvania. It was a polyglot village composed of Delaware, Shawnee, Wyandot, and other members of the Iroquois league. Logstown was an important trading center on the upper Ohio, and the place of many Indian council meetings. Its site and situation on the river were desired by both the French and British. In addition, provincial representatives of Virginia and Pennsylvania, along with the Ohio Company, hoped to obtain Indian quit claims to the region. They wanted to open settlement west of the Allegheny Mountains.

On 31 May 1752, the commissioners from Virginia, Colonel Joshua Fry, Lunsford Lomax, and Colonel James Patton, and commissioners from Pennsylvania arrived at Logstown with £1,000 worth of gifts. Their objective was to reconfirm title to the land that had been established with the Treaty of Lancaster in 1744. Andrew Montour, a métis of French and Iroquois descent, served multiple roles as interpreter, a member of the Iroquois league, and representative for Virginia and Pennsylvania. George Croghan represented his own interests and those of the Pennsylvania government. Christopher Gist represented the Ohio Company. The representatives would wait almost two weeks for the arrival of the Iroquois "Half-King," Tanaghrisson, along with a sachem of the Onondaga council and his party.

On 10 June, the commissioners from Virginia formally presented the king's gifts. The terms of the Lancaster Treaty were reexplained. In essence, Virginia claimed the lands that are present-day Kentucky, West Virginia, and western Pennsylvania. The commissioners also presented a declaration of intent regarding new settlement to the south and east of the Ohio River. The lands Virginia wanted to make certain of and secure were those near the source of the Ohio (Pittsburgh).

These lands presented a problem for Tanaghrisson, since they were mainly occupied by Delaware Indians. Tanaghrisson knew the Delaware would not agree to new colonial intrusion. Furthermore, the Ohio Delaware already had been recognized by Pennsylvania as individuals able to negotiate for themselves without Iroquois intervention. Tanaghrisson put the representatives off for a short time, claiming the need to consult the full Onondaga council.

When the Virginians complained about attacks on frontier colonists, including the murder of a British woman on the New River, it left a perfect opportunity for Tanaghrisson to seize control. He deftly took the hatchet from the Delaware and Shawnees, and told them they were now to be ruled by him. Tanaghrisson appointed Shingas, in absentia, as the spokesman for the Delaware. Since Shingas was not at the meeting, his brother and proxy, Beaver, was given a gift from the Virginia commissioners. Tanaghrisson thereafter dominated the proceedings.

The commissioners from the beginning of negotiations repeatedly stressed the importance of British-Six Nations friendship and distrust of the French in the Ohio Valley. Only recently under French authorization, the Miami (or Twightwee) village of Pickawillany had been attacked. With this in mind, Tanaghrisson requested a stronghouse be built at the junction of the Monongahela and the Allegheny. He wanted a stockaded trading post and arsenal, but not a settlement. Tanaghrisson felt the new post could supply the Iroquois with powder and lead for defense.

Montour then consulted with the other Iroquois chiefs present in a private meeting. He urged them to see the necessity and advantage of a British settlement for trade and security reasons. After a short time, a treaty was drawn that reversed much of what had been said earlier by the Iroquois.

The treaty signed at Logstown on 13 June 1752 confirmed the 1744 Lancaster land cession. In addition, the Iroquois consented to a settlement or settlements by British colonists to be built south or east of the Ohio River. The settlements would remain unmolested, and even protected by the Iroquois.

Francis Jennings sums up the treaty, ". . . conducted in a welter of cross-purposes and intrigue that almost baffles comprehension; it seems to have had more conspiracies present than people."

Linda M. Thorstad

References

Francis Jennings, *Empire of Fortune: Crowns, Colonies, and Tribes in the Seven Years War in America* (1988); "The Treaty of Logg's Town, 1752," *Virginia Magazine of History and Biography,* Vol. 13 (1905–1906): 148–174; Richard White, *The Middle Ground: Indians, Empires, and Republics in the Great Lakes Region, 1650–1815* (1991).

See also CROGHAN, GEORGE; DELAWARE; GIST, CHRISTOPHER; HALF-KING; MONONGAHELA RIVER

Long Island

The first Dutch families arrived on Long Island in 1636, settling in the Dutch West India Company's colony of New Netherland. Until 1664, when the English took possession of the entire colony, Long Island remained the center of competition between the Dutch and English in New England. The inhabitants on Long Island, however, enjoyed relative peace with the local Native Americans, who seriously attacked the Long Island settlers only once.

Willem Kieft, governor of New Netherland, sparked the war with the local tribes in 1643 by having 80 local Hackensack Indians killed over a trade dispute. The Native Americans sought revenge on the Dutch in New Jersey, New Amsterdam, and on Long Island, and by the time peace was restored in 1645, the Dutch had abandoned most of Long Island. Kieft's replacement, Petrus (Peter) Stuyvesant, struggled to improve relations with the local tribes, but land disputes kept both sides angry into the 1650s. Stuyvesant finally smoothed relations, and when several tribes attacked New Jersey and New Amsterdam in 1655, Long Island remained quiet. Responding to a rumored attack in 1659, Stuyvesant led his private soldiers through the island, reassuring the settlers and encouraging them to return to their farming. Unlike the English, the Dutch did not develop a strong local militia system for defense and therefore relied on the governor's private forces.

The final threat of Indian attack came after the English had taken possession of New Netherland. During King Philip's War (1675–1676) in New England, New York Governor Edmund Andros disarmed the local natives and prepared the island's defenses. No fighting occurred on the island, and after the war, the threat of Indian trouble on Long Island ended.

Competing territorial claims by the English and Dutch caused Long Island to be the object of tense, though bloodless, colonial competition. By 1642, English settlers had established Gravesend, and in 1647, the English tried unsuccessfully to break Dutch control of eastern Long Island. Governor Stuyvesant hoped to improve Anglo-Dutch relations by negotiating a treaty of peace in 1650, but the Anglo-Dutch War of 1652 commenced before the home governments could ratify the treaty. New England leaders began to assemble forces in Connecticut and Long Island to attack New Amsterdam, but the war's end in 1654 prevented the attack.

English encroachment on the island continued, and in 1662, a local English settler, John Scott, tried to carve out a private island domain and there await the expected arrival of an English naval force commanded by James, duke of York. Stuyvesant had company orders to avoid conflict and so continued to urge a settlement by the home governments until September 1664, when Richard Nicolls arrived with English warships. Bowing to the desires of the Dutch inhabitants, Stuyvesant surrendered New Netherland without a fight.

With the English takeover, Long Island ceased to hold an independent place of importance in the colonial conflicts. Despite continued friction between New York and Connecticut over control of the island, which almost led to fighting between Governor Andros's soldiers and several island towns in 1674–1675, Long Island itself was no longer an object of foreign competition. Throughout the imperial colonial wars of 1689–1763, the French were unable to mount a naval threat to the coastal regions of the British colonies and the fighting on the northern frontiers did not spread to the coast. Long Island's part in these wars consisted of supplying militia contributors to the defense of New York's frontier. Long Island, on its own, no longer occupied a place of importance in colonial competition on North America.

Mark V. Kwasny

References

Francis Jennings, *The Invasion of America: Indians, Colonialism, and the Cant of Conquest* (1975); John E. Pomfret, with Floyd M. Shumway, *Founding the American Colonies, 1583–1660* (1970); Ellis Lawrence Raesly, *Portrait of New Netherland* (1945); Allen W. Trelease, *Indian Affairs in Colonial New York: The Seventeenth Century* (1960); Stephen Saunders Webb, *1676: The End of American Independence* (1985).

See also KIEFT, WILLEM; STUYVESANT, PETRUS; UNDERHILL, JOHN

Loudoun, Earl of
See CAMPBELL, JOHN, LORD LOUDOUN

Fort Loudoun (Pennsylvania)
Located on the west branch of Conococheague Creek, Fort Loudoun was originally constructed by Pennsylvania in 1756 to help defend the colony's settlements west of the Susquehanna. Named by Governor William Denny for the earl of Loudoun, commander in chief of British forces in North America at the beginning of the Seven Years' War, the fort was garrisoned by the Pennsylvania Regiment until June 1758, when it was absorbed into the supply line for General Forbes's western campaign. As the first military post on Forbes's Road, Fort Loudoun became the crucial supply base for Forbes's army and the real starting point for the westward march of Forbes's northern forces.

Eric Hinderaker

See also CARLISLE, CAMP NEAR (PENNSYLVANIA); FORT LIGONIER (PENNSYLVANIA)

Fort Loudoun (Tennessee)
The colonial government of South Carolina built Fort Loudoun in 1756 in the Overhill Cherokee territory to protect the southern frontier of the English from the French. For more than a decade, the Cherokees had requested that forts be built among them to protect their women and children while the Indians fought the French. As the French threat grew, the English interest in frontier forts increased, and in 1753, South Carolina built Fort Prince George near Clemson, South Carolina. Although satisfactory to the Lower Cherokees of South Carolina, this fort did not provide any protection for the Overhill towns of Tennessee, which were the closest and most exposed to the French.

Finally agreeing on the necessity of a fort in Overhill country, Virginia Lieutenant Governor Robert Dinwiddie sent £1,000 to South Carolina Governor James Glen, who had estimated the construction cost at £7,000. When South Carolina did not begin construction

L

within a few months, Virginia, which desperately needed Cherokee assistance against the French, proceeded to build a fort near Chota, the Overhill Cherokee capital. This fort was never manned or named, and was eventually burned by the Indians.

After several delays, the new South Carolina governor, William Henry Lyttleton, ordered three companies under the supervision of William Gerard De Brahm to construct the fort. The fort was named for John Campbell, fourth earl of Loudoun, and commander in chief of British troops in North America. It covered two acres and was atypical of other forts on the American frontier in that it was European in style, diamond-shaped, with a bastion protecting at each corner. The garrison consisted of 90 British regulars and 120 South Carolina militiamen. Captain Raymond Demeré commanded the fort until August 1757, when he relinquished command to his younger brother, Paul Demeré.

In 1759, relations broke down between the Cherokees and British on the Virginia frontier, which led to the execution of more than 20 Cherokee chiefs who were being held as hostages at Fort Prince George. By March 1760, the Cherokees laid siege to Fort Loudoun, which finally surrendered in August. The Cherokees agreed to allow the soldiers to march unmolested to Fort Prince George. Perhaps because the English broke their agreement that the "fort, great guns, powder, balls and spare arms be delivered up without any fraud," the Cherokees attacked the retreating garrison and killed Demeré, the junior officers (except John Stuart) and 20 enlisted men—the same number of Cherokees massacred at Fort Prince George. Of the remaining soldiers, some were later tortured and killed, others were ransomed, and a few chose to remain with the Cherokees. Within a year or so, Fort Loudoun was burned by the Indians (perhaps accidentally). Today, the fort has been reconstructed.

William L. Anderson

References
John P. Brown, *Old Frontiers: The Story of the Cherokee Indians from Earliest Times to the Date of Their Removal, 1838* (1938); David H. Corkran, *The Cherokee Frontier: Conflict and Survival, 1740–1762* (1962); P.M. Hammer, "Fort Loudoun in the Cherokee War of 1758–1761," *North Carolina Historical Review* 2 (1925):442–458; Paul Kelley, *Historic Fort Loudoun* (1958); Stuart Stumpf, "James Glen, Cherokee Diplomacy and the Construction of an Overhill Fort," *East Tennessee Historical Society Publications* 50 (1978):21–30.

See also CHEROKEE WAR; DE BRAHM, WILLIAM GERARD; DINWIDDIE, ROBERT; GLEN, JAMES; LYTTLETON, WILLIAM HENRY; FORT PRINCE GEORGE–KEOWEE (SOUTH CAROLINA); STUART, JOHN

Fort Loudoun (Virginia)

Built in the winter of 1756–1757 at Winchester in Frederick County, Virginia, Fort Loudoun stood at the intersection of the north-south Philadelphia wagon road into the Shenandoah Valley of Virginia and Indian trails running to the west. Constructed by order of Colonel George Washington, who had been given command of Virginia forces after the defeat of British General Edward Braddock in 1755, and named for General Lord Loudoun, commander in chief of the British forces in America, Fort Loudoun served as Washington's headquarters during his tenure as Virginia commander. It featured four square bastions and double-palisaded, earthern-core walls. Its batteries mounted 24 guns, and the fort contained barracks for 450 men.

Thomas Costa

References
Louis K. Koontz, *The Virginia Frontier, 1754–1763* (1925).

See also WASHINGTON, GEORGE

Fort Louis (Alabama)

Pierre Le Moyne d'Iberville's colonizing expedition established the first permanent French settlement on the northern Gulf coast in January 1702 on a bluff overlooking the Mobile River, about 25 miles north of Mobile Bay. Iberville's brother, Jean-Baptiste Le Moyne de Bienville, served as commandant of Fort Louis. The Le Moyne brothers selected this location for its proximity to Mobile and Tomeh Indian villages, from which the colonists obtained much of their food and which also afforded some protection from English-inspired raids by Creek Indians living farther inland.

Bastions and curtain walls were constructed in the *pièce-sur-pièce* style, with squared pine logs laid horizontally and dovetailed at the corners. Inside the fort, which was about 120 feet square, stood a guardhouse, the royal storehouse, a chapel, and officers' quarters, where Bienville lived. Palisades surrounded the fort and extended to the riverbank, where a powder magazine and barracks were located. Because wood placed directly on the ground quickly rotted in the humid climate, the collapsing fort had to be rebuilt and enlarged in 1708.

Although the fort was never directly attacked, raids by the French and their Indian allies were launched from there against the Alabama Indians in 1703, 1707, and 1709. The fort also served as the site of conferences with the Choctaws and other visiting Indian delegations, who camped on the open ground to the south.

By 1711, the fort was again decaying. A series of disastrous floods, and political pressure to relocate the town nearer the colony's port on Dauphin Island at the mouth of Mobile Bay, finally led to the abandonment of Fort Louis. A new fort (renamed Fort Condé in 1724) and village were constructed at the head of the bay—the present-day location of Mobile—in May and June, and Old Mobile reverted to forest.

Gregory A. Waselkov

References

Marcel Giraud, *A History of French Louisiana, Vol. I, The Reign of Louis XIV, 1698–1715,* trans. by Joseph C. Lambert (1974); Jay Higginbotham, *Old Mobile: Fort Louis de la Louisiane, 1702–1711* (1977); Richebourg G. McWilliams, ed., *Iberville's Gulf Journals* (1981); ———, ed., *Fleur de Lys and Calumet: Being the Pénicaut Narrative of French Adventure in Louisiana* (1988); Dunbar Rowland and Albert G. Sanders, eds., *Mississippi Provincial Archives, French Dominion,* 3 vols. (1927–1932).

See also FORT CONDÉ (ALABAMA); LE MOYNE DE BIENVILLE, JEAN-BAPTISTE; LE MOYNE D'IBERVILLE, PIERRE

Louisbourg (Nova Scotia, Canada)

Louisbourg, the town and fortress situated near the eastern extreme of Cape Breton Island, was founded in 1713 in an attempt by the French to retain a share of the cod fishery of the Grand Banks. It fell to the British in 1745, again in 1758, was then destroyed, and never mattered much again. During its career, it exasperated French authorities, who developed exalted hopes for its contribution to the French empire in America, and excited the cupidity of New Englanders, who nurtured ambitions for fuller control of the fishery.

Cape Breton Island, known as Ile Royale during the French period, is a poor landscape with thin soils, a harsh climate, and little in the way of natural resources. Although it had timber and coal in 1713, now much depleted, it was an unpromising seat for a new colony. But after the Treaty of Utrecht (1713) assigned Newfoundland to Great Britain, Ile Royale was the closest place the French had to the Grand Banks, aside from two flyspeck islands. The value of the fishery was such that the French crown chose to create a new colony at Ile Royale and erect a huge fortress on a marshy promontory jutting into the Atlantic. The geography of winds, currents, and commerce of the North Atlantic also put Louisbourg in a convenient and potentially important position with respect to sea lanes. Its hinterland was almost worthless, but its connection to the sea endowed Louisbourg with considerable promise.

The colony got off to a slow start, as various obstacles impeded construction, but by the mid-1720s, the population of the town exceeded 1,000, and that of the colony of Ile Royale topped 3,000. At their maximums, Louisbourg's population approached 5,000 and Ile Royale's 10,000 in the 1750s. At all times soldiers accounted for a large share of Louisbourg's population. The rest consisted chiefly of fishermen, although in the interior of Ile Royale a few families tilled the stony soils. Nonetheless, the population of both town and colony were overwhelmingly young, male, and unmarried, a population profile characteristic of many colonial settings. Louisbourg was a healthy place, compared to the French districts whence most of the population had come, and natural increase was high, considering that women were scarce until the 1750s (by which time females still accounted for only about 35–40 percent of the population).

The explicit purpose of the Ile Royale colony was to provide a place from which to prosecute the so-called dry fishery. In the eighteenth century, Europeans both salted and dried cod. The salting could be done on shipboard without a local land base, but drying required much more space and hence land, ideally in a sunny and windy place. The explicit purpose of the fortress of Louisbourg was to protect Ile Royale and the French fishery.

The fortress imitated in design those built along the French frontiers in Europe. It cost huge sums, which its backers justified with illogical claims concerning its defense capabilities. Jean-Frédéric Phélypeaux, comte de Maurepas, the minister of the marine (1723–1749), touted it as a bulwark of all Canada, a role it could not play without a naval squadron. It never was home to a squadron, and in fact, could not even defend itself effectively. Like other fortresses of its type, Louisbourg was designed to withstand siege for two months. Such a fortress made sense in infantry wars in Europe, but not in the context of Louisbourg, where columns of French soldiers could not come to the rescue in time. Louisbourg was attacked twice, in 1745 and 1758, and held out for seven weeks on both occasions. As a fortified naval base, Louisbourg had great potential; a squadron there could have dominated the straits giving access to the St. Lawrence, the chief artery to the interior of North America at the time. But without a squadron, Louisbourg had almost no defensive value for the French in North America. Beyond the range of its cannon, enemies could and did move freely.

The Treaty of Aix-la-Chapelle (1748) returned Louisbourg to France, against the wishes of the New Englanders who had taken it three years before. Thus the town participated in the economic life of the French empire in North America for 42 years (1713–1745 and 1749–1758) before its final destruction, and this is where its real importance lay. In these years it played two cardinal roles for France. The first was as a base for the fishery. Fishermen operating out of Louisbourg provided France with a trade worth about three million *livres* per year, or 20 times the annual budget of the colony of Ile Royale, and one-third the budget of the French navy. The cash value of Louisbourg's fish exceeded that of the Canadian fur trade until the 1750s. The protein value of the Louisbourg fishery was sufficient to meet the needs of about 5 percent of the French population. To the extent that Louisbourg protected the wet fishery as well, it assured France of a business worth about 20 million *livres* per year.

Louisbourg's second contribution to France's empire in North America was commercial. Louisbourg developed into a lively port, but not along lines satisfactory to the French. Maurepas and others hoped it would serve as an *entrepôt* among Quebec, France, and the French Antilles. Its geographic location astride North Atlantic sea lanes suited it for such a role. But eventually, New England dominated the trade of Louisbourg. Quebec never produced consistent surpluses of the things Louisbourg needed; flour above all, but timber, iron and many other items besides. Additionally, Quebec was much further by sail from Louisbourg than Boston. Enterprising New Englanders took advantage of an opportunity thus presented to them. Louisbourg officials condoned this technically illegal trade rather than attempt to stop it. Indeed, some of them participated in it, impervious to complaints registered by French merchants.

New England rose in importance in Louisbourg's commerce when British legislation (the Molasses Act of 1733) outlawed trade between the French Antilles and the British colonies of North America. New England's appetite for rum and molasses exceeded supplies from the British West Indies, so Louisbourg traders sailed to Saint-Domingue and Martinique to buy barrels to sell to Boston merchants. This trade expanded sharply after 1748, partly because New Englanders, who had ventured to Louisbourg for war in 1745, came expressly for rum and molasses when peace prevailed.

Louisbourg traded with France directly, a business controlled by French, not Louisbourg, merchants. A small (technically illegal) trade also existed with the French-speaking, but British subject, population of Acadia. On the whole, Louisbourg's commerce thrived, especially after 1748, providing profits for a handful of families and work for a few hundred sailors and off-season fishermen. But it violated the mercantilist principles held dear in France, and proved a consistent irritant to French officials and merchants.

The fishery at Louisbourg, its original raison d'être, succeeded admirably and alone justified the expense of the Ile Royale colony. Trade worked out well for locals, if not for France. As a military installation, however, Louisbourg was a failure.

After the 1758 siege, the British tore down the fortress, and with the redistribution of colonies following the Treaty of Paris in 1763, the commercial role of the town disappeared. The French lost their dry fishery (except for that based at the islands of St. Pierre and Miquelon), which Newfoundland came to dominate. For 200 years, Louisbourg was a tiny fishing hamlet. In the 1970s, Parks Canada rebuilt the fortress and much of the town, creating one of the most spectacular, and most accurate, reconstructions of colonial life in North America.

John R. McNeill

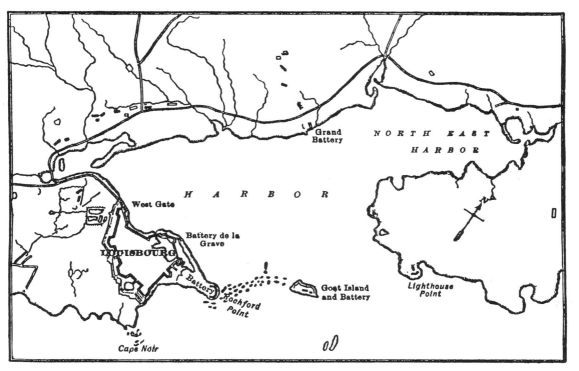

Harbor at Louisbourg.

References

Charles La Morandrière, *Histoire de la pêche française de la morue dans l'Amérique septentrionale*, 2 vols. (1962); John S. McLennan, *Louisbourg: From Its Foundation to Its Fall, 1713–1758* (1918); John R. McNeill, *The Atlantic Empires of France and Spain: Louisbourg and Havana, 1700–1763* (1985); Christopher Moore, *Louisbourg Portraits: Life in an Eighteenth-Century Garrison Town* (1982).

National Museum of Man [Ottawa], *Papers and Abstracts for a Symposium on Ile Royale during the French Regime* (1972); George Rawlyk, *Yankees at Louisbourg* (1967); F.J. Thorpe, *Ramparts lointains: la politique française des travaux publics à Terre-Neuve et à l'Ile Royale, 1695–1758* (1980).

See also AIX-LA-CHAPELLE, TREATY OF; LOUISBOURG EXPEDITION (1745); LOUISBOURG, SIEGE OF (1758); ST. LAWRENCE RIVER

Louisbourg, Siege of 1758

The seaport of Louisbourg was located on a rugged promontory on the east coast of Cape Breton Island, south of a spacious harbor. The harbor was sheltered, three miles long and three-quarters of a mile wide, with a narrow channel about one-half mile wide, bordered by islands and shoals. The town itself was about a half-mile long and a quarter-mile wide, with broad and uniform streets and a number of substantial buildings, including a convent and a hospital. The town depended heavily for its defense on the presence of a large and powerful fleet in port. The fortress and garrison town had been constructed in the early eighteenth century to provide shelter and service for the French navy, and to help defend the Gulf of St. Lawrence. Economically, Louisbourg functioned as an important trade depot for products from both the northlands and the northern British colonies, and as a center for the fishing industry. In addition, it proved over the years to be a fruitful embarkation point for French privateers preying on New England shipping in particular. As such, it was always a highly desirable prize to both the British and the American colonists.

The Americans, particularly Bostonians, harbored bitter memories of the decision by Britain to return the fortress to the French in

1748, after the hard-fought, costly victory of 1745. The Pitt ministry subsequently received a number of proposals for attacks on the city, including one from William Bollan, the Massachusetts agent in London, and another from Brigadier Samuel Waldo, a New Englander who had commanded the land forces during the 1745 siege. When Pitt and the king made it clear after 1757 that England intended to carry the war to the enemy in North America, enthusiasm in Massachusetts was unbounded. Pitt understood that Quebec must be the principal objective this time, and he realized the capture of Louisbourg would be a critical start.

Taking charge of the entire operation, Pitt replaced the earl of Loudoun with General James Abercromby, who was allowed little personal leeway. Loudoun, meanwhile, had organized excellent auxiliary services—transport, commissariat, engineers, artillery—and he had deliberately made his troops independent of the whims of the colonists. In 1758, Pitt adopted the same basic plan that had been floating around for several years, essentially the same plan Loudoun himself had adopted. It proposed a three-pronged attack: General John Forbes would take Fort Duquesne; Abercromby, Ticonderoga, and Crown Point; and Jeffrey Amherst, Louisbourg. Ultimately, the plan called for Amherst to subsequently move to Quebec, join forces with Abercromby, and move through the heartland of New France to the lower Mississippi. Winter curtailed the latter portion of these plans, and Abercromby suffered a disastrous loss at Ticonderoga; but the rest of the campaign was successful. In particular, Louisbourg was the key and its capture was an event of extreme importance.

The French, meanwhile, faced serious difficulties and were forced to take the defensive. They were suffering from shortages of food, arms, munitions, and most importantly, men. General Louis-Joseph de Montcalm did anticipate that the principal effort would be against Louisbourg, so he increased the size of the naval squadron stationed there. Even here, however, delays and shortages proved fatal to the French effort. The British succeeded in blocking the French fleet from leaving the Mediterranean. And while they did not have the same successes in blockading the Atlantic ports, one French fleet arrived too late to be of assistance, and another ship had to turn back because of ice and illness. Overall, the French tried to send 23 ships to relieve the port, including 12 trans-

ports. Only seven warships, two fully armed, made it into port, together with three frigates and various cargo vessels. On land, the garrison was reinforced with two battalions and reasonably well supplied with provisions. At the time of capitulation, there were 2,000 officers and men among the land troops, 1,000 marines, 2,600 seamen, and 400 militiamen. The attacking British fleet, meanwhile, had 1,900 guns, and Amherst led a force of 13,200 officers and men, joined by 1,968 sailors.

The British preparations began in early spring at Philadelphia and Albany. On 19 March, Rear Admiral Charles Hardy arrived at Halifax, and the squadron Pitt had previously ordered to winter there was ready. A naval blockade of Louisbourg was shortly established, though it proved somewhat porous. Abercromby also imposed an embargo on all seaports from Nova Scotia to South Carolina to conceal preparations from the French. The army at Halifax consisted of 14 infantry regiments, four ranger companies, and an artillery detachment, with a total of 13,000 men. The entire force was organized into three brigades commanded by Brigadier General James Wolfe, Charles Lawrence (governor of Nova Scotia), and Brigadier General Edward Whitmore. Colonel John Henry Bastide was the chief engineer. In addition to the land forces, there was a naval force of 39 ships and 14,000 sailors. However, Admiral Edward Boscawen, senior officer for the expedition, did not reach Halifax until 9 May, too late to intercept French naval reinforcements, but early enough to engage in invaluable practice in landing exercises. Finally, on 29 May, Boscawen could not wait any longer for Amherst's expected arrival, and he set sail for Louisbourg, expecting Amherst would join him there. Ironically, Amherst appeared almost immediately after the force left harbor, and he quickly boarded the flagship and assumed command.

Since 1748, the French had regarrisoned Louisbourg, repaired the walls and reconstructed the Island Battery, and it was as formidable as ever. It was now commanded by Governor Augustin de Boschenry de Drucour, a French navy captain. Remembering the 1745 debacle, the French were determined to prevent the British from landing along the north shore of Gabarus Bay. They had now constructed extensive shore defenses there—a system of trenches and gun emplacements overlooking the rocky beaches, with felled trees pointed outward forming an additional barrier. The entire battery was manned by about 2,000 regulars. There was also a battery on Pointe de Rochefort at the tip of the peninsula, and an outwork on the sandbar of the sea pond. Finally, a 36-gun battery was located on the northern harbor shore, and a 30-gun battery on the Island Battery. Land defenses consisted of an incline with an elevation that the defenders could fire from, a covered way beneath it, a moat behind it, and above the moat another parapet. In the center of the wall stood the citadel, with the gates on either side. Only 450 French troops were deployed east of the harbor entrance, since the land approach to the fortress was marked by virtually impassable terrain, alternatively rocky and marshy. To the east, Anse de la Cormorandiere was manned by 1,000 men, one 24-pounder, four six-pounders, and six swivel guns. Somewhat closer, 350 men, one 24-pounder and six six-pounders were situated at White Point. Seventy-five men were placed at Cap Noir, with two 24-pounders. Small flanking parties were located to the west of these beaches, though a landing there was not considered likely. The French viewed Cormorandiere as the most likely landing spot, and they deployed their forces accordingly. But the view to the east was obscured by a rocky point capped by an 80-foot hill and graced by an open sandy space, very narrow but wide enough; the French seemed to have overlooked this spot. Drucour, finally, refused to allow the fleet to leave the harbor; he wanted to prolong the defense as long as possible in order to save Quebec.

On 2 June, Amherst and Wolfe examined the beach defenses more closely. From 3 June through 6 June, bad weather forced the British fleet to lay at anchor off the beaches; but Admiral Jean-Antoine Charry Desgouttes, who commanded the French fleet, overlooked this opportunity to conduct sorties on the transports. Better weather and calmer seas came on 7 June; Amherst sent a regiment in sloops east around Black Point, past the harbor's mouth, to establish a small base at Lorembec. Concurrently, he began making final preparations for the main assault. The plan was relatively simple. Each of the three brigades would embark and assemble off a designated part of the shore—Wolfe off Coromandiere near the western extremity of the French line; Lawrence further east in the center; and Whitmore beyond that near White Point. Support ships would pound the shore defenses with gunfire, in the hope this would spread out the French defenses. Only

Wolfe was to move straight in at first, however, while Lawrence and then Whitmore would slip westward to land in the same area as Wolfe, bringing the entire force together. The beach here was a concave arc confined at each end by low rocky headlands, with the French defenses arranged so as to allow a crossfire on the beach and the area of felled trees. The British landing would obviously be an extremely dangerous effort.

On 8 June at 2 A.M., signal lights from the flagship gave the order to prepare. British soldiers scrambled into waiting boats and proceeded to assembly points on the seaward side of the gunships. The British began shelling around 4 A.M. for about 15 minutes, and the boats then approached the shore. The French had begun their own shelling, however, and Wolfe immediately saw that a frontal landing would be impossible. He signaled the force to draw back. At the same time, three boats inadvertently drifted off to the west, toward the aforementioned rocky headland. They found the small beach there undefended and well shielded from possible French fire, and landed unopposed. Wolfe observed their success and ordered the rest of the division to follow. The rocky shoreline damaged boats and caused several drownings, but most of the force landed successfully. Wolfe and his men now succeeded in advancing on the French flank, taking them completely by surprise. The French commander, Colonel Jean Mascle de Saint–Julhien, hesitated before ordering a grenadier attack, long enough to guarantee defeat. The French broke and fled, joined by the group at Pointe Platte. Lawrence and Whitmore now landed their divisions, and the French were soon in full flight toward Louisbourg. The British stopped their pursuit only when they heard cannon fire from the fortress itself. The fighting was over by 6 A.M., and by 8 A.M. the French forces were safely within the walls of the fortress. The British had lost eight officers and just over 100 men killed or wounded; the French losses numbered about 114, including deserters.

The British now consolidated their positions, placing their advance units about two miles from the walls. Amherst had landed and was now in command. The wind had come up again, however, and it was still not possible to land artillery, though tents and light supplies could be brought ashore. On 11 June, some light artillery was landed and, in the meantime, Boscawen blockaded the port. The French, meanwhile, seemed to be panicking. Within two days, they had abandoned both the Royal and Lighthouse Point batteries without firing a shot. On 12 June, Wolfe established British batteries at Lighthouse Point; the position overlooked the Island Battery and dominated the harbor entrance. Supplies and artillery were easily delivered here from Lorembec, where there was enough shelter for easy landing. The British also established lines outside the west walls of the fortress, bombarded incessantly by French cannon from both the fortress and the harbor. The weather finally broke on 16 June and the British landed their two-pounders. On the night of 19 June, Wolfe's guns opened fire for the first time.

There was, to be sure, a more chivalrous side of the siege. Amherst, for example, sent a pair of pineapples to Madam Drucour, and the governor returned the compliment with some champagne. Wolfe received "sweetmeats" from the French. For the ordinary inhabitants of the garrison, however, there was little more than suffering and horror. Morale began to wane, and Drucour was forced to resort to severe measures against those who sought to evade duty; at one time the British counted 16 men hanging from the walls. The British, meanwhile, were suffering their own trials, as smallpox appeared among the ranks, particularly among the New England carpenters.

By 26 June, Wolfe's artillery had finally succeeded in silencing the Island Battery. Admiral Desgoutes, understanding this would open the harbor to the British navy, scuttled four of his ships in the channel; this left him with only five battleships and a frigate. Amherst, meanwhile, advanced the siege lines, built access roads, extended trenches, and built batteries and redoubts ever closer to the walls. Boscawen patrolled the coast to prevent entry or escape. The French could only respond with continued bombardment. A force of about 725 French troops did raid the British lines from the Black Point area, taking an outpost by surprise, killing the officer in charge and four of his men, and penetrating an important segment of the British line. But they were forced to withdraw with heavy losses. Partisans and Indians also caused some problems for the British in roving attacks behind the lines, but they did not inflict any serious damage.

Then, around noon on 21 July, a lucky shot from a British gun ignited powder on the 74-gun French ship *Entreprenant,* causing an explosion and fire. That ship swung close to the 64-gun *Capricieux,* which then broke out in fire and in turn set the *Celebre* afire. Boats from the town bringing assistance suffered under a constant British barrage. The British, moreover, continued their bombardment of the town with cannon and mortars. On the morning of 22 June, the barracks caught on fire and a large part of the fort was subsequently ruined. Civilians now began to seek refuge outside the walls and in the ditch surrounding them. Only the 74-gun *Prudent* and the 64-gun *Bienfaisant* were keeping Boscawen from entering the harbor unchallenged. Both were close to the town, however, and in a strong defensive position. Boscawen and Amherst then agreed on a daring plan, which they carried out the night of 25 July. Amherst's batteries distracted the French garrison with a heavy bombardment, and British sailors in about 50 boats slipped into the harbor's mouth. Some occupied the ruins of Island Battery, while the rest boarded the *Prudent* and *Bienfaisant.* The British grounded and burned the former, and towed the latter beyond the range of French artillery. They took 152 prisoners, losing only seven killed and nine wounded themselves. Before the British squadron could be sent into the now defenseless harbor, Drucour asked for terms. The surrender was arranged on 26 July and effected the next day. It included all French forces on Cape Breton and Prince Edward Islands. Civilians who had not borne arms were to be shipped to France, while military personnel were made prisoners of war. The French lost the entire garrison, together with 2,400 seamen and several valuable fighting ships. The British victory had been a masterpiece of naval strategy, reflective of both luck and British naval power. Unfortunately for the British, Montcalm's successful defense of Fort Carillon on 8 July, together with the tenacious French defense at Louisbourg, meant the British offensive against Quebec would have to wait for another year.

While British operations continued in the Nova Scotia area, Amherst sailed into Boston harbor on 13 September, receiving a hero's welcome. His troops set up camp on the Common, and he commented that "Thousands of People came to see them and would give them Liquor and make the men Drunk in Spite of all that could be done." The colonists, of course, were fully aware of the immediate economic benefits the capture brought to them. The benefits for England were clear in other ways as well. Insurance rates on cargoes bound for America, for instance, fell from 30 to 12 percent, and England gained control of the Atlantic fisheries. All in all, the fall of Louisbourg is generally accepted as marking the beginning of the end of French rule in North America. The French court was fatalistic in its view of the future; Canada's administrators were advised that they would receive even fewer supplies the next year, when a massive British assault could surely be expected.

The colonists learned other lessons from this siege. They were appalled by the strict, cruel discipline of the British army; the regulars were, in their eyes, mere slaves to the British officers, products of a culture clearly different from their own and perhaps deficient in moral character. The British, moreover, seemed lacking in any sort of religious commitment. New Englanders who garrisoned Louisbourg after 1758, finally, seemed discontent with their lot; mutiny and desertion were common. While the siege produced the very results the British had hoped for, it brought mixed blessings for the American colonists and sowed at least a tiny seed of doubt about the moral commitment of Britain to the cause of Protestantism and political liberty.

Ronald P. Dufour

References

Fred Anderson, *A People's Army: Massachusetts Soldiers and Society in the Seven Years' War* (1984); Guy Frégault, *Canada: The War of Conquest,* trans. by Margaret M. Cameron (1969); Lawrence Henry Gipson, *The Great War for the Empire: The Victorious Years, 1758–1760* (1949); J. Mackay Hitsman, with C.C.J. Bond, "The Assault Landing at Louisbourg, 1758," *Canadian Historical Review,* XXXV (December 1954):314–330; Douglas Edward Leach, *Arms for Empire: A Military History of the British Colonies in North America, 1607–1763* (1973).

See also AMHERST, JEFFREY; HARDY, CHARLES; LOUISBOURG; WOLFE, JAMES

Louisbourg Expedition (1745)

The capture of Louisbourg in 1745 was the greatest triumph of American troops during the colonial period. The stout fortress, built by France after Queen Anne's War to defend the approaches to St. Lawrence Bay, was a base from which the French could attack New England, Nova Scotia, and their fisheries. Before New Englanders knew Britain and France were at war, such a raid occurred in May 1744, when Captain François Du Pont Duvivier and soldiers from Louisbourg overwhelmed fishermen at Canso, Nova Scotia. The raid demonstrated that New England's fisheries and shipping would not be safe until Louisbourg was captured.

In the winter 1744–1745, New Englanders dared to think of reducing the fortress themselves without waiting for troops from England. Governor William Shirley of Massachusetts became enthusiastic about the project. On 9 January 1745, he dramatically swore the General Court to silence and revealed recent intelligence about Louisbourg's weaknesses. William Vaughan, James Gibson, and other traders familiar with Cape Breton thought Louisbourg was vulnerable. Returned prisoners taken from Canso to Louisbourg confirmed its garrison numbered only 700; their pay was in arrears, a fifth of them were disgruntled Swiss mercenaries, and their food supplies were low, thanks to New England privateers and the Massachusetts guardship who, in the summer of 1744, had captured more than 40 French ships, several of them carrying provisions needed at Louisbourg. Shirley was certain he could secure the help of the Royal Navy, and if Massachusetts attacked quickly before reinforcements came from France, 2,000 soldiers would suffice. For two days the legislators debated. All appreciated the desirability of capturing Louisbourg, but many doubted success was possible. By a narrow margin the General Court rejected the idea, but Shirley persisted. He persuaded merchants and fishermen to ask their representatives to reconsider, and on 25 January 1745, the General Court agreed to the expedition. Soon it appropriated money for four months' provisions and pay for 3,000 soldiers. Privates were promised 25 shillings (New Tenor) per month and a share in all plunder.

Inspired by a chance of plunder and a certainty of adventure, infused with patriotism, and assured of a quick return home, volunteers from all levels of society eagerly enlisted to free New England from the menace of the great fortress of Catholic France. With the Great Awakening still ablaze in New England, the expedition was virtually a Calvinist crusade. William Pepperrell, Jr., a wealthy merchant of Kittery, Maine, and president of the Massachusetts Council, was pressed into service by the governor as commander of the expedition. Shirley invited colonies south to Virginia to participate, but only other New England colonies sent men. None of them equaled the zeal of Massachusetts which, in three months, raised 3,300 men, a third of them from Maine. Connecticut, pleased by the appointment of Deputy Governor Roger Wolcott as second-in-command, contributed its provincial guardship and 500 men. New Hampshire also raised 500 men, but asked Massachusetts to pay for 150 of them. The support of Rhode Island, which nursed grievances against Massachusetts, was less than wholehearted, but its guardship did join the siege and Rhode Island soldiers shared garrison duty after the victory. Beyond New England, New Jersey appropriated £2,000 (provincial currency), New Yorkers sent £7,000 and ten 18-pound cannon, Pennsylvania's assembly voted £4,000 to buy bread, meat, and wheat "or other Grain" ("grain" is assumed to have been a Quaker euphemism for gunpowder), and Virginia sent £1,300 worth of food.

The expedition left the Boston area on 24 March 1745 to rendezvous at Canso, Nova Scotia, within 60 miles of Louisbourg, in early April. At Canso, a tedious three-week wait for winter ice to melt from the approaches to Louisbourg was cheered by wonderful news: the Royal Navy was joining the venture. As soon as the expedition had been decided, Shirley had written to the Admiralty and directly to Commodore Peter Warren, then in the West Indies, to secure the vital help of the navy. Warren, who commanded the station ships at Massachusetts in the warm months and took them to the West Indies in the winter, felt obliged to reject Shirley's request unless authorized by the ministry. However, he wrote Shirley on 9 March that he had received orders from the duke of Newcastle, the secretary of state for the southern department, to cooperate with American governors against the French, and therefore he was bringing his ships north immediately. On 23 April Warren arrived at Canso with *Superbe* (60 guns), and by the end of the siege he had a formidable squadron of 12 warships, plus the New England guardships.

On 30 April, the New Englanders overcame French skirmishers and began landing near Louisbourg at Gabarus Bay. Despite the onset of sickness, absence of military regularity, and occasional losses to Indians and Canadians who fell upon wanderers searching for booty, Pepperrell's men began the siege. Under the direction of their artillery commander, Richard Gridley (who in 1775 was to lay out the rebel earthworks at Bunker Hill), they dragged their cannon up and down hills and through mud, to place them before Louisbourg's formidable walls, whose size astounded the colonists and shook their optimism.

The fortunes of war, or as the besiegers believed, the will of God, was with the attackers. They had not brought enough cannon, but on 3 May they acquired 30 guns in the Grand or Royal Battery, a French position located across the harbor and north of the main fort which had been foolishly abandoned by its panicky defenders to be occupied by 14 New Englanders. Working at night and with cover of fog, Pepperrell's men moved the heavy cannon into position and began battering the fort and town. While the land forces fired on the town, Commodore Warren's fleet prevented any reinforcements reaching the besieged. On 19 May, a French 64-gun man of war, *Vigilante,* loaded with ammunition, was intercepted by the English flotilla. *Vigilante's* cargo proved vital to Pepperrell's army, which was running short of gunpowder, and its loss was devastating to Governor Louis Du Pont Duchambon's garrison. The attackers' only failure was a bungled night raid on 26–27 May against the Island Battery, a fort astride the harbor entrance. Three hundred New Englanders who rowed out to attack the island may have been inebriated and certainly were noisy—they actually cheered—and the alerted French defenders got the better of a gun battle. At dawn, survivors who could rowed away, and more than 100 surrendered.

On 15 June, General Pepperrell and Commodore Warren, who had become impatient with the pace of the siege, agreed to attack the fortress from land and sea as soon as the wind would allow the warships to force the harbor entrance. But that evening the French, battered by more than 9,000 cannonballs and 600 mortar shells and low on ammunition, asked for terms. The victors took possession of the town on 17 June, the army entering from the land side and the navy from the harbor. The wonderful news overjoyed Boston on 3 July and delighted London on 20 July. To the disappointment of the colonial troops, the defeated French received honorable terms and no plundering was permitted. Whether Pepperrell or Warren received the keys to the fort, and thus primary credit for the success, was hotly disputed among contemporaries and remains uncertain today. Both the land

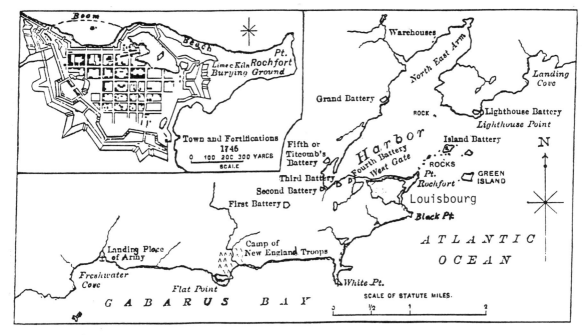

Siege of Louisbourg, 1745.

forces and the navy had been essential to success, but Americans stressed the contributions of Pepperrell's soldiers; while in Britain, the ministry magnified the role of Commodore Warren and his ships at the expense of Pepperrell's men. The victory cost few lives, perhaps 130 attackers and about the same number of French, but during the next few months, while awaiting British regulars who would take over garrison duties, more than 1,400 New Englanders were to die from disease. The regulars did not arrive until the spring of 1746. Until then, it took all the persuasive powers of Pepperrell, Warren, and Governor Shirley to stave off mutiny by homesick (and physically sick) soldiers who had expected to be home to harvest the crops of 1745. Colonial soldiers' spirits were not cheered when they saw one French ship after another sail unawares into Louisbourg harbor to become prizes of the navy. Warren and his sailors shared no prize money with the land forces.

The Treaty of Aix-la-Chapelle that ended the war in 1748 returned the fortress to France, much to the chagrin of New Englanders. Britain did reimburse the colonies' expenses (£183,649 went to Massachusetts alone), but the fort had to be captured again by James Wolfe in the next war.

Joseph A. Devine, Jr.

References

Louis E. de Forest, ed., *Louisbourg Journals, 1745* (1932); Thomas Hutchinson, *The History of the Colony and Province of Massachusetts Bay,* ed. by Lawrence S. Mayo, 3 vols. (1938); John S. McLennan, *Louisbourg from Its Foundation to Its Fall, 1713–1758* (1918); Francis Parkman, *A Half-Century of Conflict,* 2 vols. (1892); *Pepperrell Papers, (Massachusetts Historical Society Collections, 6th ser., Vol. 10)* (1899).

See also AIX-LA-CHAPELLE, TREATY OF; GRIDLEY, RICHARD; KING GEORGE'S WAR; LOUISBOURG; PEPPERRELL, WILLIAM, JR.; SHIRLEY, WILLIAM; WARREN, PETER

Louisiana

French exploration of the lower Mississippi River valley and the northern Gulf of Mexico, the region that would become French colonial Louisiana, began with descents of the Mississippi by Jacques Marquette, Louis Jolliet in 1673, and René-Robert Cavelier de La Salle in 1682. After the failure of La Salle's colonizing attempt on the Texas coast between 1685 and 1687, more than a decade passed before the French moved again to claim the region. In

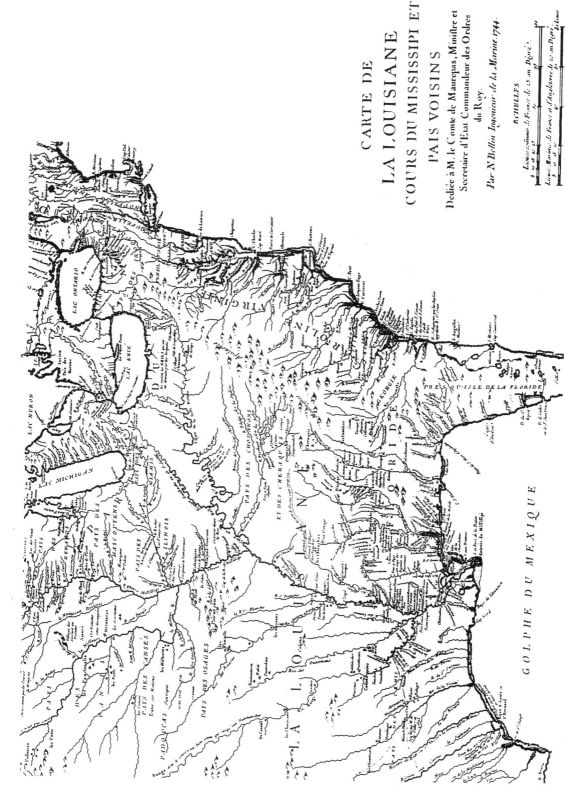

Louisiana, 1744.

1698, Louis XIV and his minister of the marine (which included overseas colonies), Jérôme Phélypeaux de Pontchartrain, sent a colonizing expedition comprised largely of Canadians to the Gulf coast led by Pierre Le Moyne d'Iberville and his brother, Jean-Baptiste Le Moyne de Bienville.

Iberville quickly established military outposts at two strategic points along the Gulf coast (i.e., Fort Maurepas on Biloxi Bay and Fort de la Boulaye near the mouth of the Mississippi River) and began the search for a permanent settlement location. During the winter of 1701–1702, the colonists focused their energies on the construction of Fort Louis and the surrounding town of Mobile atop a bluff overlooking the Mobile River, about 50 miles from the Gulf. Both the fort and town were relocated to the head of Mobile Bay in 1711. From this first capital of the Louisiana colony, the French established a network of forts and settlements throughout the midcontinental region of North America.

By dominating the Mississippi River system, Pontchartrain hoped to contain the rapidly growing English colonies along the Atlantic coastline. The Canadians who founded Louisiana employed proven colonizing methods that had enabled them to control the vastness of sparsely settled New France. From small military posts built along major rivers flowing through the territories of dominant Indian groups, the French managed to maintain a complex alliance of Indian tribes, which helped them hold back the impending surge of English settlers until the surrender of Louisiana in 1763.

Good relations with Indians in Louisiana depended largely on liberal distributions of presents to pro-French tribal factions and providing a market for the deerskin trade. The distribution of presents was the prerogative of the governor, while local military commanders controlled trade directly or by issuing permits to independent French traders at each post. Chronic supply shortages in the colony, however, often prevented officials from either delivering presents in a timely fashion or offering trade goods in sufficient quantities, thereby undermining French influence among the Indians. In order to at least partially overcome the colony's inadequate supply system, officials made particular efforts to provide a few essential commodities, principally gunpowder and lead shot, to their Indian allies. Because each fort could be resupplied by water (using *ba-*

teaux laboriously rowed upstream each summer or fall), French officers and traders were able to transport such bulky and heavy goods more efficiently and offer them at lower prices than could English traders from the Carolinas and Georgia, who had to rely on human bearers or packhorses to carry goods overland.

Another component of French Indian policy in Louisiana—an explicit disinterest in Indian lands—evolved more slowly. Incessant and unreasonable demands by the commandant at Fort Rosalie for lands occupied by a Natchez village directly precipitated the Natchez War of 1729, with disastrous consequences for the colony. Thereafter, French officials carefully avoided even the appearance of coveting the lands of powerful Indian allies, and frequently drew pointed comparisons between their own enlightened attitude and the seemingly insatiable English appetite for Indian lands.

French diplomatic efforts were most successful with tribes close to Mobile and New Orleans, such as the Mobilians, Choctaw, Tunica, and Quapaw. Pro-French factions balanced pro-English factions among the Upper and Lower Creek, which enabled that tribal confederacy to maintain its neutrality in European affairs for almost half a century. Elsewhere, as among the Cherokee and Chickasaw, French influence was fleeting or ineffectual.

In situations where the colony's very existence depended on firm control of the Indian population (which always outnumbered combined white and black population throughout the life of the colony), French policy demanded harsh response to any hostile acts. Frequently (and preferably, from the French perspective) this involved the use of Indian surrogates to punish infractions, such as when the Quapaws, at the instigation of Bienville, destroyed a village of Koroas who had killed the missionary Nicholas Foucault. When more serious situations arose, such as during the Natchez War and ensuing Chickasaw campaigns, officials felt compelled for political reasons to send French soldiers into battle, often with disappointing results.

In general, colonial officials tried to maintain peaceful relations among the many different inhabitants of the vast area claimed for France. One approach involved sending young French boys to live among the various tribes, where they could learn native customs and languages (including the "Mobilian trade jargon," a southeastern pidgin); many later served as

L

official translators or became military officers at the more remote outposts. Another effective measure, instituted by Bienville, was the impartial application of *lex talionis*, the demand that murderers be executed, whether Indian or French; in several instances, Frenchmen were executed for killing Indians. A third important factor in establishing and maintaining peaceful relations between French and Indians, as well as between Indian tribes, was the virtual elimination of Indian slave raiding in the Southeast after the Yamasee War against South Carolina in 1715. English traders in the region either were killed or fled in the aftermath, which suddenly opened the deerskin trade to the French and led them to establish Fort Rosalie (1716) among the Natchez and Fort Toulouse (1717) among the Alabamas. Despite English claims that the French had instigated the war, unjust English trade practices seem to have actually precipitated the uprising; the French simply benefited from English bungling.

With the founding of New Orleans in 1718, the establishment of Fort de Chartres in the Illinois country in 1719, and governmental control passing to the Company of the Indies in the same year, a new era of colonial expansion began. Hundreds of French colonists settled at concessions in the lower Mississippi Valley around Fort Rosalie and at the Yazoo Post, Fort St. Pierre, after 1719. Largely because of the destruction of these settlements during the 1729 Natchez War, which revealed the ineptitude of the company's leadership, the colony reverted to royal control in 1731 and Bienville was appointed governor.

Among the reforms instituted at that time was the military reorganization of the colony. Under the governor, the commanding military officer, lieutenants of the king were stationed at the colony's three administrative centers, from which the outlying posts were supplied and garrisoned. The Mobile commandant was responsible for Fort Toulouse, Fort Tombecbé, and Dauphin Island. The Illinois district included Fort de Chartres, Arkansas Post, and the post at Natchitoches. Garrisons at Balize Post, English Turn, Point Coupée, and Natchez were administered from New Orleans.

Commandants at these far-flung forts were lieutenants, captains, or majors, depending on the post's importance. Since there seldom were more than 1,000 troops in Louisiana, garrison size was usually small, with 20 to 40 soldiers at most posts. These *troupes de la marine* were re-cruited by the minister of the marine for use exclusively in the colony. In addition, one company of Swiss mercenaries was organized in 1732, with half stationed in New Orleans and half in Mobile. All of these colonial soldiers were encouraged to settle after their discharge from service to augment the perennially low population. Troops typically rotated to different posts every few years, except at Fort Toulouse, where desertions to the English became too prevalent. After a mutiny of most of the garrison in 1721, the garrison consisted primarily of permanently stationed troops and, later, soldiers recruited from among the Creoles inhabiting the village that grew up around the fort.

Troops were issued standard uniforms, for which an allowance was deducted from their pay. These consisted of white shirts with collars, breeches, woolen stockings, shoes with double leather soles, a hat, one cravat, a greatcoat, and one blue waistcoat. Differences in lace trim, coat lining color, and button style indicated an individual's rank. In addition to receiving a uniform, each soldier was also issued a number of accouterments and weapons, including a hatchet, socket bayonet and scabbard with belt, powder horn and string, a cartridge box or shoulder pouch, and a flintlock musket. The large, .68 caliber Tulle military musket was standard, but lightweight (.52 and .56 caliber) muskets intended for the Indian trade were also widely employed. Rations of flour and rice were supplemented by purchases of meat and foodstuffs raised by the soldiers. When supplies failed to reach the colony, as happened frequently due to English naval blockades during the numerous wars of the eighteenth century, soldiers went without these standard issues, often for years at a time. In 1723 and 1745, troops in New Orleans mutinied over the lack of supplies and proper barracks.

Fort armament typically included small iron and brass swivel guns with removable breech blocks. These guns were mounted on the stockade at the bastions and could fire one-pound or two-pound solid shot or quantities of lead shot. Larger ordnance, such as iron four-pounder and six-pounder cannons, was mounted on garrison carriages for use on stockade gun platforms or on field carriages in the parade grounds. Even larger cannons were used in the defenses at New Orleans, Mobile, and Fort de Chartres.

Each post had several other assigned individuals: a priest who served as chaplain (and sometimes acted as missionary among nearby

Indian villages), and a *garde-magasin,* or warehouse keeper who was responsible for the disbursement of royal property at the post. The *gardes-magasin* distributed pay, subsistence, uniforms, and weapons to the officers and troops, provided the governor with his annual allocation of presents for the Indians, and kept tabs on post repairs. Because wooden and even masonry structures deteriorated quickly in the hot, humid climate of Louisiana, fort construction and repair costs accounted for a large proportion of annual military expenses.

Military engagements in the Louisiana colony were generally small affairs. The earliest occurred in 1702 and involved five men sent by Bienville from Mobile upriver to obtain corn in trade from the Alabamas. A pro-English faction among the Koasati Alabamas ambushed the Frenchmen, killing three; this action provoked a French response, which resulted in the deaths of two Koasati villagers. Years of skirmishing ensued. A raiding party from Mobile in 1707 captured two Alabamas, a man and a woman, who reportedly were put to death "by slow fire" at the gate of Fort Louis. Two years later, an Alabama war party captured more than 20 women and children from a Mobilian village near French Mobile. The captives were all killed before the raiding party could be overtaken.

Through the influence of English traders living among them, the Alabamas had been drawn into the War of the Spanish Succession, in which France and Spain were allied. When a force of 1,200 Creek Indians (including Alabamas) and some Englishmen besieged Pensacola in 1707, Bienville brought a relief force of 150 French and Indians to the aid of the Spanish garrison. The Spaniards reciprocated in following years by sharing powder and ammunition when the Creek threatened to descend on Mobile. Bienville's diplomacy finally established a lasting peace with the Alabamas in 1712.

When the French-Spanish alliance dissolved and war broke out early in 1719, a seesaw struggle began between the two colonial outposts for control of the northern Gulf of Mexico. Bienville's fleet of 13 ships carrying 500 men captured Pensacola in May, but the town was recaptured by a Spanish fleet in August. After a successful defense of Dauphin Island, at the mouth of Mobile Bay, the French (reinforced on land by the Choctaw) sailed back to Pensacola, and attacked and burned the Spanish fort.

When some Chitimacha in the lower Mississippi Valley murdered a missionary priest, Jean François Buisson de Saint-Cosme, in 1706, Bienville launched the first in a series of wars of annihilation directed against tribes that were considered particularly threatening to French interests. During the next 12 years, French and allied Indian raids decimated the Chitimacha tribe, with many captives sold into slavery in Louisiana and the Caribbean colonies.

An extremely successful attack by the Natchez on French colonists in 1729 provoked several more wars of annihilation. Alarmed that the Natchez uprising would lead to a general revolt against French rule, Governor Etienne Périer sent a force of armed black slaves to destroy the Chaouacha in order to intimidate any tribes that might be wavering in their support of the French and, not incidentally, to generate ill-will between blacks and Indians. The French then methodically began to exterminate the much more numerous and powerful Natchez. With Tunica and Choctaw reinforcements, the French laid siege to the Natchez forts and forced them to release about 250 black slaves and French women and children taken captive during the uprising. The Natchez slipped out of the siege and fled west. When the French relocated their enemies, they managed to capture 450 Natchez, including the paramount chief. They were taken to New Orleans and sold as slaves in Saint-Domingue (Haiti). Remnants of the Natchez continued the war, attacking the Tunica village in 1731, and eventually finding refuge with the Chickasaw.

When the Chickasaw refused to turn out their guests, the French expanded the war. In 1736, Governor Bienville marched a force of 700 Choctaw warriors and 600 soldiers (nine French companies, Karrer's Swiss company, two militia companies, and 140 slaves led by free blacks) against the Chickasaws. He had built Fort Tombecbé the year before as a staging point for the expedition and to interrupt English trade among the Choctaw. Bienville had intended to coordinate his attack with the arrival of a force of French and Indians from Illinois led by Pierre d'Artaguette, commandant at Fort de Chartres. But the northern force arrived first; Artaguette decided to attack the Chickasaw villages alone and was decisively defeated. Bienville's subsequent attack also failed, with the loss of many officers and men killed and wounded. A second campaign in 1740 also ended in a stalemate.

The failure of the French military to defeat the Chickasaw emboldened the pro-English faction of the Choctaw, led by Red Shoe, to defy the French monopoly on the Choctaw trade. England and France were again at war (in the War of the Austrian Succession) so English traders made a concerted effort to supply these potential allies, who lived primarily in the western Choctaw towns. Red Shoe's murder of three French traders, and Canadian Governor Pierre de Rigaud de Vaudreuil's demand for Red Shoe's execution precipitated a bloody civil war among the Choctaw, which finally ended in the defeat of the pro-English faction.

The Seven Years' War in Louisiana was a relatively peaceful period. Diplomatic negotiations with the Indian tribes successfully countered English threats to the more remote forts. And French agents among the Cherokee encouraged that tribe to besiege Forts Loudoun and Prince George. There were no major defeats of French forces in Louisiana during the war, so news of the surrender of the colony to the English in 1763 shocked the French inhabitants and the Indians who had aligned themselves with the French.

Gregory A. Waselkov

References
Bill Barron, *The Vaudreuil Papers* (1975); Philip P. Boucher, *Les Nouvelles Frances: France in America, 1500–1815, An Imperial Perspective* (1989); Norman W. Caldwell, *The French in the Mississippi Valley, 1740–1750* (1941); Verner W. Crane, *The Southern Frontier: 1670–1732*, with an Introduction by Peter H. Wood (1981); Marcel Giraud, *A History of French Louisiana, Vol. I, The Reign of Louis XIV, 1698–1715*, trans. by Joseph C. Lambert (1974).

David Hardcastle, "The Military Organization of French Colonial Louisiana," *Proceedings of the Gulf Coast History and Humanities Conference*, 7 (1978):1–20; Dunbar Rowland, Albert G. Sanders, and Patricia K. Galloway, eds., *Mississippi Provincial Archives, French Dominion*, Vols. 4–5 (1984); Patricia D. Woods, *French-Indian Relations on the Southern Frontier, 1699–1762* (1980).

See also AFRICAN AMERICANS; ARKANSAS POST; ARMY, FRANCE; ARTILLERY, FRANCE; FORT DE CHARTRES (ILLINOIS); CHICKASAW; CHOCTAW; FORT CONDÉ (ALABAMA); ENGLISH BEND (ALABAMA); ILLINOIS; LE MOYNE DE BIENVILLE, JEAN-BAPTISTE; LE MOYNE D'IBERVILLE, PIERRE; FORT LOUIS (ALABAMA); MISSISSIPPI RIVER; NATCHEZ WAR; NEW ORLEANS; RED SHOE; FORT TOMBECBÉ (ALABAMA); FORT TOULOUSE (ALABAMA); TUNICA

Louisiana-France Relations
See FRANCE-LOUISIANA RELATIONS

Lovewell, John (1691–1725)
John Lovewell can be considered the "King of the Scalp Hunters." During Dummer's War when the government of Massachusetts offered a scalp bounty of £100 for soldiers not in the government's pay, scalp hunting became popular among the more adventurous on the frontier. Raising companies mainly from communities along the Merrimack River, including his home town of Dunstable, Massachusetts, Lovewell led three raids into the Winnipesaukee-Ossipee-Pequawket region of New Hampshire. In December 1724, his first raid netted him one scalp and a captive boy, but in February 1725, he and his men took ten scalps and returned in triumph to Dover, New Hampshire, waving the bloody trophies. He left Dunstable on 16 April with another company. On 8 May, they fought a long, intense battle with the Pigwacket Indians in present-day Fryeburg, Maine. Heavy casualties were suffered on both sides and Lovewell was among those killed. Like that other overconfident Indian fighter, George Armstrong Custer, John Lovewell became an even greater hero in death than he had been in life. Eulogies and songs were composed in his honor and for the men who accompanied him. The war itself was often referred to as "Lovewell's War" due to the fame of this slain scalp hunter.

Steven C. Eames

References
Steven C. Eames, "Rustic Warriors: Warfare and the Provincial Soldier on the Northern Frontier, 1689–1748," Ph.D. Dissertation, University of New Hampshire (1989); Samuel Penhallow, *The History of the Wars of New England with the Eastern Indians* (1726).

See also DUMMER'S WAR; INDIAN WARFARE, EUROPEAN ACCULTURATION OF; LOVEWELL'S FIGHT; SCALP BOUNTIES; SCOUT

Lovewell's Fight (1725)

The last major action against the eastern Indians during Dummer's War, this time against the Pigwackets on the upper Saco River, involved the fall of the "King of the Scalp Hunters"—John Lovewell. Lovewell had led two successful raids into the Winnipesaukee-Ossipee-Pequawket region of New Hampshire in December 1724 and February 1725. On 16 April, he left Dunstable, Massachusetts, leading a force of 47 men back to the same area. Three men turned back and another became so sick that Lovewell was forced to build a simple fort at Ossipee Lake where he left the sick man, the doctor, and eight others. Lovewell then pushed on to Pequawket, located near present-day Fryeburg, Maine.

Apparently, Lovewell's earlier successes generated an overconfidence which resulted in an unaccountable neglect of elementary precautions. Hearing the report of a gun, Lovewell's men dropped their knapsacks and went to investigate, but unlike his earlier raids, Lovewell did not post a guard over the knapsacks. A large party of Pequawkets discovered the packs and laid an ambush.

Meanwhile, Lovewell's company found a solitary Indian who was apparently hunting. Lovewell's men shot the Indian, mortally wounding him, but the Pequawket managed to return fire, seriously wounding Lovewell. The Indian was dispatched and the chaplain, Jonathan Frye, scalped him.

Carrying their wounded leader, the company returned to their packs, only to have the waiting Pequawkets, estimated to number around 80, open fire and charge. The English apparently returned fire and charged themselves, despite the fact that Lovewell was hit again, this time mortally, and several others were wounded in the first fire. Benjamin Hassell, a cousin of Lovewell's, became unhinged when he saw Lovewell fall "and heard him Groan." Despite the fact he later could not "Deny but our people were charging the Enemy briskly when he left," Hassell panicked and ran all the way to the temporary fort to report the destruction of the company. Believing the wild-eyed Hassell, and expecting the Pequawkets to attack the fort at any time, the group immediately fled south for the settlements.

But the fight in the woods continued. Seth Wyman's account, published in the *Boston Newsletter* a couple of weeks after the battle, related that:

After the first Fire, the Indians advanc'd with great Fury towards the English, with their Hatchets in their Hands, the English likewise running up to them, till they came within 4 or 5 Yards of the Enemy, and were even mix'd among them, when the Dispute growing too warm for the Indians, they gave back, and endeavour'd to encompass the English, who then retreated to the Pond, in order to have their Rear cover'd.

The English took up position on the edge of the pond, where a stream served to protect one flank. The firefight continued for ten hours, with both sides taunting and yelling. Seth Wyman took over command of the company, yelling encouragement throughout the fight. According to one story, Wyman moved forward during a lull in the action, and discovering the Indians in a group discussing the situation, fired into the crowd, killing a chief.

Another legend from the fight concerns the killing of the chief Paugus. As the story goes, John Chamberlain knew Paugus and the two exchanged insults throughout the battle. Late in the day Chamberlain fell back to the edge of the pond to quickly clean out the powder fouling in his musket barrel. Seeing Paugus doing the same thing nearby, both men began to load as fast as possible. Chamberlain took a shortcut by thumping the butt of his musket on the ground to shake powder from the barrel into the flash pan rather than using his powder horn. This edge allowed Chamberlain to fire a second before Paugus, who was killed in the act of pulling his trigger.

At sunset the Indians withdrew, and the English took stock of their situation. Twenty men were left alive, including 11 wounded. The shattered company pulled itself together and began its retreat to the crude fort. Four of the wounded, Lieutenant Josiah Farwell, the young chaplain, Jonathan Frye, Josiah Jones, and Eleazer Davis, seemed to be too hurt to travel, and were left behind with the promise that help would be sent. The remainder, many of whom were also wounded, split into three parties and made their way home. When they arrived at their fort, they found it abandoned with a note left saying all of Lovewell's company had been killed. Some food had been left and while they refreshed themselves, another wounded man, Solomon Keyes, arrived. Keyes had been wounded three times and had crawled away during the fight after calling out that he was a dead man. However, Keyes found a canoe, crawled into it, and floated to safety.

Meanwhile, the four wounded men left behind, realizing that help would be a long time coming, struggled on as best they could. After his return and partial recovery, Eleazer Davis described his adventure to Samuel Penhallow (See Penhallow, *History of the Wars of New England,* 114–115). "The report he gave me was," wrote Penhallow,

> that Lieut. Farewell, with Mr. Fry their Chaplain, Josiah Jones, and himself, who were all wounded, march'd towards the Fort; but Jones steer'd another way, and after a long fategue and hardship got safe into Saco. Mr. Frye three days after, thro' the extremity of his Wounds, began to faint and languish, and died. . . . Mr. Farewell held out in his return till the eleventh day; during which time he had nothing to eat but Water and a few Roots which he chewed; and by this time the Wounds thro' his Body were so mortified, that the Worms made a thorow Passage. The Same day this Davis caught a Fish which he broil'd, and was greatly refresh'd there with; but the Lieut. was so much spent, that he could not taste a bit. Davis being now alone in a melancholy desolate state, still made toward the Fort, and the next day came to it, where he found some Pork and Bread, by which he was enabled to return as before mentioned.

The impact on the Pigwackets was profound. No accurate account of their casualties is know, but they did lose at least one principal chief and many braves. Penhallow quoted a report that out of 70 Indians involved in the fight, 40 were killed outright and 11 mortally wounded. This is obviously overly optimistic, but there is no question the Indians suffered more casualties than they were used to, and it also put a severe strain on their powder and lead supplies. They broke off the fight and did not return to scalp the dead. Three Indian bodies were found by soldiers sent to collect Lovewell's body, including the chief, Paugus. Historian Charles E. Clark believed the defeat of the Pigwackets during Dummer's War opened the interior of New Hampshire, and the bloody results of Lovewell's fight contributed a great deal to this. Like the Norridgewocks, the Pigwackets

did not disappear, but their military significance diminished greatly after Dummer's War.

The impact on the New England colonies was also profound. The death of John Lovewell and the suffering of his party received much coverage in the newspapers and from the pulpit, overshadowing even the attack on Norridgewock the previous summer. In the retelling of the tale, Lovewell became a folk hero similar to a Daniel Boone or Davy Crockett. Indeed, such was his fame that the war itself was often called "Lovewell's War."

Steven C. Eames

References
Charles E. Clark, *The Eastern Frontier: The Settlement of Northern New England, 1610–1763* (1970); Francis Parkman, *A Half-Century of Conflict,* in *France and England in North America,* 2 vols. (1983); Samuel Penhallow, *The History of the Wars of New England with the Eastern Indians* (1726), rpt. 1969.

See also ABENAKI; DUMMER'S WAR; LOVEWELL, JOHN

Lovewell's War
See DUMMER'S WAR

Fort Loyal (Maine)
Fort Loyal or Loyall was built in 1680 for the defense of the settlement of Falmouth on Casco Bay, present-day Portland. It was intended to provide a safe refuge from Indian attacks for the area's settlers. The fortifications consisted of a palisaded structure which mounted several light guns. During King William's War, 50 Canadian soldiers and 70 Abenakis under Captain Pierre Robinau de Portneuf and Lieutenant Augustin Legardeur de Courtemanche set out from Quebec against English settlements in Maine. These forces were augmented by Captain Joseph-François Hertel de La Fresnière and baron Jean-Vincent d'Abbadie de St. Castin, producing a force of approximately 500 French soldiers and Abenaki Indians. This large force laid siege to Fort Loyal for five days during mid-May 1690. The garrison at the fort was under the command of Captain Sylvanus Davis. After a settler was attacked outside the fort, Lieutenant Thaddeus Clark and 30 volunteers sought to engage the enemy. After being overcome by superior numbers, only four wounded men re-

turned to the fort. The siege of the fort was held off with the help of a number of settlers, including women and children. Captain Davis agreed to negotiate a surrender after most of his men were either dead or wounded and the enemy was preparing to destroy the palisade. The siege was ended by a truce guaranteeing safe conduct to the nearest English town. The terms were violated when most of the soldiers and refugees were massacred by the Indians. Captain Davis and four others were taken as prisoners to Quebec. The fort was subsequently burned and the neighboring settlements destroyed.

David L. Whitesell

See also CASCO BAY; FALMOUTH, BATTLE OF; KING WILLIAM'S WAR; FORT NEW CASCO (MAINE)

Luna Arellano, Tristan de (c. 1505–1573)

In 1559, Luna was chosen by his cousin, the Spanish viceroy in Mexico, to establish colonies at Ochuse (Pensacola Bay) and at Santa Elena on the Carolina coast. These were intended to protect the Atlantic traffic, to Christianize the Indians of La Florida, and to gain Spanish control of land previously explored by Hernando de Soto in 1539–1543. Luna was an experienced soldier who had been active in Mexico since 1530 and who had explored the Southwest with Francisco Vázquez de Coronado.

On 11 June 1559, Luna sailed 11 vessels out of San Juan de Ulua, Mexico, with 1,500 persons and 240 horses on board. Two months later the fleet reunited at Pensacola Bay. There a hurricane struck in September, beaching seven ships, drowning many people, and ruining most of the provisions still on board. In spite of receiving additional supplies from Cuba and Mexico, the two colonies he established north of Pensacola did not take root and Luna's reputation suffered. The viceroy replaced him with Angel de Villafañe, who received orders to establish a colony at Santa Elena, on Parris Island, South Carolina, to prevent the French from settling on the lower Atlantic coast. This colonizing effort also met with failure. Luna went to Spain to answer royal charges, but returned to Mexico City where he died penniless in 1573.

Jose Ignacio Avellaneda

References

Herbert I. Priestley, *The Luna Papers: Documents Relating to the Expedition of*

Don Tristan de Luna y Arellano for the Conquest of La Florida in 1559–1561, 2 vols. (1928); Robert S. Weddle, *Spanish Sea: The Gulf of Mexico in North American Discovery, 1500–1685* (1985).

See also CORONADO, FRANCISCO VÁSQUEZ DE

Fort Lydius (New York)

See FORT EDWARD (NEW YORK)

Fort Lyman (New York)

See FORT EDWARD (NEW YORK)

Fort Lyttleton (Pennsylvania)

Fort Lyttleton was one of four forts built by the colony of Pennsylvania following British General Edward Braddock's disastrous defeat in the summer 1755. Located on upper Aughwick Creek just east of the Sidelong Hill Ridge, the fort's construction was begun by the Indian trader, George Croghan, later in the same year. Croghan had a home at Aughwick, and he was commissioned by the colony to oversee the construction of several forts in the area. The fort consisted simply of a square stockade, about 100 feet on a side, surrounding two or three cabins. It may have had blockhouses at two of its corners, but otherwise it had none of the features of more carefully planned fortifications.

Fort Lyttleton (named by Governor Robert Hunter Morris for George Lyttleton, chancellor of the exchequer in England) was one of the earliest points of refuge for frightened settlers who were fleeing from Indian attacks in late 1755 and early 1756. During this period, the outlying settlements were struck with panic and experienced, in the words of one observer, "the utmost confusion imaginable one flying here & the other there for Safety[.]" Whatever its architectural deficiencies, Fort Lyttleton was an important center of strength and protection in this first phase of the French and Indian War.

Eric Hinderaker

References

Timothy Horsfield to the Governor of Pennsylvania, Nov. 27, 1755, Horsfield Papers vol. 1, American Philosophical Society, Philadelphia; Thomas L. Montgomery, ed., *Report of the Commission to Locate the*

L

Frontier Forts of Pennsylvania, 2nd ed., 2 vols. (1916); Charles Morse Stotz, *Outposts of the War for Empire: The French and English in Western Pennsylvania; Their Armies, Their Forts, Their People, 1749–1764* (1985).

See also FORT GRANVILLE (PENNSYLVANIA); FORT SHIRLEY (PENNSYLVANIA)

Fort Lyttleton (South Carolina)

Port Royal Island and the town of Beaufort were isolated from mainland South Carolina. Strategically located, Port Royal possessed a large harbor that invited easy entry by invaders. Inhabitants of the area constantly feared attacks from the Spanish in Florida, the Indians, and later in the colonial period, from the French.

Fort Frederick was built between 1731 and 1734 at a poor location, with high ground commanding the fort's west side. By the next decade, the fort's condition had deteriorated and the South Carolina Commons House of Assembly received frequent reports that the post needed to be repaired or replaced with a new fort at a better location. In 1757, the assembly appropriated £10,000 to build a new fortification. Realizing that command of the sea was needed to protect the area, the assembly also asked Governor William Henry Lyttleton to request that the crown station at least one 50- or 60-gun ship at Port Royal.

Begun in 1758, Fort Lyttleton, named in honor of the governor, was completed in 1763. It was built at Spanish Point, a mile and a half below Beaufort. Any ship headed to Beaufort would have to pass the fort, but the structure did not command Port Royal Sound. Triangular in shape, the fort's base, along Port Royal River, measured 375 feet and its landward walls were surrounded by a moat. The tabby (a mixture of oyster shells, lime, and water) walls were reinforced with dirt from the moat to provide additional support. At least 15 cannon were mounted. "The fort has two demi-bastions to the river," a visitor observed in 1763, "and one bastion to the land with a gate and ditch; the barracks are very good and will lodge one hundred men with their officers." The province stationed one gunner at the fort, who was supported by militia. Though the fort probably allayed the settler's fears, the area was not truly secure until the Spanish and French threats were removed in 1763.

Gregory D. Massey

References

Larry E. Ivers, *Colonial Forts of South Carolina 1670–1775* (1970); Terry W. Lipscomb, ed., *The Journal of the Commons House of Assembly: November 20, 1755–July 6, 1757* (1989); H. Roy Merrens, ed., *The Colonial South Carolina Scene: Contemporary Views, 1697–1774* (1977); Lawrence S. Rowland, "Eighteenth Century Beaufort: A Study of South Carolina's Southern Parishes to 1800," Ph.D. Dissertation, University of South Carolina (1978); Henry A.M. Smith, "Beaufort—The Original Plan and the Earliest Settlers," *South Carolina Historical and Genealogical Magazine* 9 (1908):141–165.

See also FORT FREDERICK (SOUTH CAROLINA); FORT PRINCE FREDERICK (SOUTH CAROLINA); PORT ROYAL (SOUTH CAROLINA)

Lyttleton, William Henry (1724–1808)

William Henry Lyttleton was born in England and studied at Eaton College and St. Mary's Hall at Oxford, from which he graduated in 1742. He became a member of Parliament representing Bewdley, Worcestershire, in 1748. He vacated his seat upon being appointed governor of South Carolina replacing James Glen. En route to America, French corsairs captured Lyttleton's ship and he remained a prisoner for several months. He returned to England for fresh instructions, which included directions to constrict the colonial assembly's powers in an attempt to bring the colonies under closer control.

Lyttleton arrived in Charles Town just one month before the Seven Years' War broke out with France. The new governor also had been instructed by the Board of Trade to obtain from the assembly an unconditional grant to build a fort among the Overhill Cherokees in present-day Tennessee. The retiring governor, James Glen, already had appropriated money on the assumption it would be refunded by the crown and had begun an expedition to build the fort when Lyttleton arrived and recalled him. Lyttleton's request for money was honored by the assembly and £4,000 was appropriated. The new governor appointed Captain

John Stuart and John Postell to raise two militia companies of 60 men each to serve under Captain Raymond Demeré, who was to oversee construction and command the fort (Fort Loudoun) when it was built.

Aware of the Overhill Cherokee's negotiations with the French in 1757, Lyttleton pointed out to the Cherokees that the English navy would prevent supplies from reaching the French and thus the Cherokees. The governor demanded that the Cherokees send 200 warriors to aid Virginia in fighting the French. In December 1757, four Cherokees from Estatoe were killed and scalped, probably by the English. To add to the growing friction between the tribe and the English, colonists were constantly encroaching on Cherokee land.

The Cherokees who aided Virginia were mistreated by the men they were assisting. Losing all of their supplies, they began their return home, taking food and horses from the colonists for whom they had lost their own. White frontiersmen killed about 17 or 18 Lower and Middle Cherokees, claiming they thought they were enemy Indians, but they promptly sold the scalps at a premium. The governor of Virginia promised to send presents to the families of the victims; but after a year had passed and the presents had not arrived, the Cherokees sought their own revenge. In response, Lyttleton ordered an embargo on supplies to the Cherokees and prepared for war.

When a peace delegation arrived in Charles Town, Lyttleton took them hostage and marched them to Fort Prince George (near present-day Clemson, South Carolina) accompanied by more than 1,300 soldiers. There he demanded 24 of those responsible for the attacks on the North and South Carolina frontiers. Measles, smallpox, and desertion swept through the ranks of the militia. Lyttleton signed a treaty to exchange the hostages for 24 of those responsible for the frontier raid. He then led the remnants of his force back to their homes in what notable Indian trader James Adair called a "wild ridiculous parade."

In February 1760, the Cherokees attacked Fort Prince George, which resulted in the murder of all the hostages. What followed was the Cherokee War of 1760–1761.

Lyttleton requested aid from Jeffrey Amherst, the commander in chief of British forces in America. Amherst sent 12 companies of Highlanders comprising more than 1,300 men under Colonel Archibald Montgomery. Before Montgomery departed for Cherokee country, Lyttleton received an appointment as governor of Jamaica and sailed from South Carolina, leaving that country in the throes of what became known as "Lyttleton's War." Following his Jamaica governorship, Lyttleton served as ambassador to Portugal and later reentered Parliament. Still later he occupied the post of one of the commissioners of the treasury. He resigned that last post in 1782 and died in Worcestershire in 1808.

William L. Anderson

References
John P. Brown, *Old Frontiers: The Story of the Cherokee Indians from Earliest Times to the Date of Their Removal to the West, 1838* (1938); David H. Corkran, *The Cherokee Frontier: Conflict and Survival, 1740–1762* (1962); John W. Raimo, *Biographical Directory of American Colonial and Revolutionary Governors* (1980); M. Eugene Sirmans, *Colonial South Carolina: A Political History, 1663–1763* (1966); Robert M. Weir, *Colonial South Carolina: A History* (1983).

See also ADAIR, JAMES; AMHERST, JEFFREY; CHEROKEE WAR; GLEN, JAMES; FORT LOUDOUN (TENNESSEE); FORT PRINCE GEORGE–KEOWEE (SOUTH CAROLINA); STUART, JOHN

M

Fort Machault (Pennsylvania)

Fort Machault, named after Jean-Baptiste Machault d'Arnouville, French minister of the marine, was erected on the west side of the Allegheny River just below the mouth of French Creek at Venango (present-day Franklin, Pennsylvania) between 1755 and 1757. It was burned to the ground in August 1759 amid the hasty French withdrawal from the area following the fall of Fort Niagara. Located at the junction of the two French supply routes to the Ohio region (the Chautauqua portage from Lake Erie and then down the Allegheny and the Presque Isle portage to French Creek), Fort Machault was intended to protect the Venango supply depot. It was constructed in the form of a small square wooden stockade with bastions at each corner and buildings forming two sides of the square. The garrison's size fluctuated wildly from as few as 15 to as many as 300 men, but rarely numbered more than 40 for any length of time and seldom had more than a single swivel gun in place.

As early as 1753, the French intended to build a fort at Venango and designated it as Fort d'Anjou; however, early difficulties on the portages from Lake Erie and the perceived need for a major fortification further down the Belle Rivière (as the French called both the Allegheny and Ohio Rivers) postponed construction until 1755, a year after the establishment of Fort Duquesne at the site of modern Pittsburgh, Pennsylvania. Still, in 1753, English traders were expelled from Venango and a permanent garrison installed under the command of Captain Philippe-Thomas Chabert de Joncaire. In June 1755, Lieutenant Michel Maray, sieur de La Chauvignerie, arrived to replace Joncaire and the next month began work on a small redoubt now christened Fort Machault. Plagued by shortages of manpower and wood suitable for construction, La Chauvignerie worked sporadically on building and improving the fort until November 1758 when Captain François-Marie Le Marchand de Lignery, after razing Fort Duquesne, fell back on Fort Machault and superseded La Chauvignerie. During the Seven Years' War, Fort Machault served primarily as the last depot on the Fort Duquesne supply route, and secondarily as a launching point for French and Indian raids against Pennsylvania and New York settlements.

Following the evacuation of Fort Duquesne, Captain Lignery made Fort Machault his command post until the British attack on Fort Niagara in the summer 1759. Lignery and La Chauvignerie left only a token force at Fort Machault when they withdrew to participate in the abortive attempt to relieve Fort Niagara, during which Lignery was mortally wounded and La Chauvignerie captured. The fall of Fort Niagara doomed the French enterprise in the Ohio region; consequently, the handful of troops remaining in the area distributed to their Indian allies what supplies they could not remove and burned Fort Machault to the ground in early August 1759.

Ronald Martin

References

Frenand Grenier, ed., *Papiers Contrecoeur et autres documents concernant le conflit anglo-français sur l'Ohio de 1745 à 1756* (1952); William A. Hunter, *Forts on the Pennsylvania Frontier, 1753–1758* (1960); Alfred Procter James, *Drums in the Forest: Decision at the Forks* (1958).

See also CHABERT DE JONCAIRE, PHILIPPE-THOMAS; FORT DUQUESNE (PENNSYLVANIA); VENANGO

Mahican

The Mahicans, an eastern Algonquian tribe, were often called Loups by the French. They should not be confused with the Mohegans of Connecticut. They occupied numerous villages on the upper Hudson River, with their council fire at Schodac on an island near Albany, and had hunting ranges in the Hoosic and Housatonic Valleys and southwestern Vermont. Henry Hudson met them in 1609, at which time Dutch estimates suggested their population was about 4,000.

The Mahicans were active participants in precontact native trade networks, but the introduction of the European fur trade had a dramatic impact on their world. The Dutch built trading posts first at Fort Nassau (1614–1617) and then, in 1624, at Fort Orange near Albany. The Mahicans enjoyed a temporary monopoly, acting as middlemen in trade with other tribes and limiting their neighbors' access to the Dutch posts. Mohawk resentment over the situation led to the Mohawk-Mahican War (1624–1628), at the end of which the Mahicans were forced to evacuate their hunting territories west of the Hudson. Some retreated north and east to escape the Mohawk threat.

The Mahicans retained their villages around Albany and remained a significant power in the region, but disease and war thinned their numbers. Mahican relations with the Mohawks fluctuated and the Mohawks may have relied on the Mahicans to supply them with wampum beads, but there was recurrent conflict between the tribes which continued after the surrender of New Netherland to the English in 1664.

A Mahican community grew up at Schaghticoke on the Hoosic River. During and after King Philip's War (1675–1676), increasing numbers of New England Indians took refuge at Schaghticoke, encouraged by Governor Edmund Andros of New York and his successors, who hoped to establish a protective buffer for the colony. The community retained its Mahican core, but the English often referred to the inhabitants as simply "River Indians." The Mahicans at this time seem to have headed a "River Indian Confederacy" that included the neighboring Wappingers, Wyachtonoks, and Housatonics.

Schaghticoke was vulnerable to attack and the inhabitants frequently complained to the governor of New York for protection during the colonial wars. The Indians gradually abandoned the village for safer locations, and many migrated to the Abenaki mission village at St. Francis on the St. Lawrence River. Other Mahicans moved to the Midwest and took up residence in Ottawa and Miami country, and increasing numbers of Mahicans moved to the Housatonic Valley.

The Mahicans in the Housatonic Valley congregated at Stockbridge, and eventually the Mahican "fireplace" was moved there. In 1734, the Rev. John Sergeant began preaching to the Housatonic Mahicans and their neighbors, and he established a mission village at Stockbridge. Moravian missionaries also began work among the Mahicans around 1740 and some Mahicans moved with them to Pennsylvania and then to Ohio.

The Mahicans played a limited role in King Williams' War and Queen Anne's War, but in the eighteenth century, Stockbridge Mahicans frequently served the English as scouts and auxiliaries against the French and their Indian allies. Stockbridge also furnished soldiers for the Americans during the Revolution. After the Revolution, the depleted Stockbridge Mahicans moved first to Oneida lands in New York, and then with the Oneidas to Wisconsin. Other Mahicans moved to Indiana and new homes beyond the Mississippi.

Colin G. Calloway

References

Ted J. Brasser, *Riding on the Frontier's Crest: Mahican Indian Culture and Culture Change* (1974); ———, "Mahican," in Bruce G. Trigger, ed., *Handbook of North American Indians, Vol. 15: Northeast* (1978):198–212; Allen W. Trelease, *Indian Affairs in Colonial New York: The Seventeenth Century* (1960); Bruce G. Trigger, "The Mohawk-Mahican War, 1624–1628: The Establishment of a Pattern," *Canadian Historical Review* 52 (1971):276–286.

See also MOHAWK; MOHAWK-MAHICAN WAR; FORT NASSAU (NEW YORK); FORT ORANGE (NEW YORK)

Maine

The region of Maine was considered by both England and France to be economically and strategically important. The area offered abundant fishing, fur, and timber resources. For the English settlements of Massachusetts having a northern frontier that was settled offered an important measure of security. Likewise, New France looked to the region for the protection of their settlements on the St. Lawrence. Both nations claimed the region and did not agree on a border. The English set the boundary at the St. Croix River, while the French considered the legitimate border to be the Kennebec River. Consequently, England and France pursued separate strategies to strengthen their respective claims to territory. In 1654, an expedition under Major Robert Sedgwick seized Acadia, but it was given back to the French under the Treaty of Breda in 1668. Thereafter, the strategy of the Massachusetts government was to establish forts at key locations and encourage settlement. This expansion was resented by the Abenaki who inhabited the region. The French used English expansion to gain the friendship and trust of the Abenakis, who helped protect the passes leading northward.

The Abenakis played a key role in the competition between England and France for dominance in Maine. The Abenakis consisted of related tribes of Indians living throughout Maine, New Hampshire, and Vermont. In Maine the largest bands were situated on the Saco, Kennebec, and Penobscot Rivers. There were generally peaceful relations between the Abenakis or "Eastern Indians" and English settlers until 1675. However, concern over English expansion caused the Abenakis to unite with the Indians of Massachusetts during King Philip's War. This resulted in sporadic attacks against English settlers in Maine. After the end of this war, the Abenakis looked increasingly to authorities in New France for assistance. Successful relations between the Indians and New France were often the result of missionary activities. These missionary efforts produced a network of relationships and interdependence between the Abenakis and the French. Furthermore, the French depended on the Abenakis to be a major part of any war effort against the English. French military aid proved successful in preventing the rapid expansion of English settlements and resulted in the active involvement by at least some Abenaki bands on the side of the French in each major conflict.

During King William's War, hostilities erupted throughout Maine involving the English, French, and their Abenaki allies. On 2 August 1689, the English settlement at Pemaquid fell to a war party of 100 Indians under chief Moxus. Consequently, all settlements east of Falmouth were abandoned by the English. Governor Louis de Buade de Frontenac mounted a three-pronged offensive against English settlements in New York, New Hampshire, and Maine. The successful siege of Fort Loyal at Falmouth by French and Indian forces compelled the English to abandon all settlements east of Wells. Major Benjamin Church, commander of the militia in Maine, proceeded to counterattack Abenaki settlements. After the conquest of Port Royal by Sir William Phips, a truce was signed with six Abenaki chiefs in November 1691. However, on 5 February 1692, a war party of 200 to 300 Abenakis attacked York by surprise. They proceeded to burn the town except for the fortified houses, and more than 160 settlers were killed or captured. The settlement at Wells was attacked on 10 June 1692 by 400 Abenakis under chief Moxus. After successful counterattacks under Captain James Converse, the Indians again agreed to a truce in August 1693. However, with the French capture of Fort William Henry at Pemaquid in July 1696, the Abenakis renewed their attacks. These raids continued until a peace treaty was finally concluded with the Abenakis in 1699.

With the outbreak of Queen Anne's War, the government of Massachusetts recognized the importance of peaceful relations with the Abenakis. As a result, Governor Joseph Dudley negotiated a successful peace treaty in June 1703 at Falmouth. However, Governor Philippe de Rigaud de Vaudreuil was able to assemble a war party of 500 French and Abenakis under the command of Lieutenant Alexandre Leneuf de La Vallière de Beaubassin. They were divided into several war parties, and on 10 August 1703, they assaulted the settlements of Wells, Cape Porpoise, Saco, Scarborough, Spurwink, Purpooduck, and Casco. After recovery from this surprise, the English launched an offensive under Colonel Benjamin Church. It succeeded in destroying St. Castin's fort and the settlement at Grand Pré, securing the east Maine coast by 1705. However, this did not completely stop the hit-and-run tactics employed by the Abenakis, whose raids lasted until the end of the war. In July 1713, Governor Dudley concluded a peace treaty with the Abenakis, who broke their political ties with the French and pledged friendship to the English.

The treaty with the Abenakis allowed English settlers to safely reoccupy the region of the lower Kennebec River. However, a resumption of war between Massachusetts and the Abenakis occurred with the outbreak of Dummer's War (1722–1727). The major cause of the conflict was the Abenakis' resentment over advancing English settlements. Along with the Indians, Governor Vaudreuil and Father Sebastien Rale were determined to prevent expansion along the Kennebec River and encouraged the Abenaki war effort. After an unsuccessful attempt to seize Rale, full-scale war broke out in 1722 with raids on Brunswick, Arrowsic, and Merrymeeting Bay. The Massachusetts government proceeded to declare war on the "Eastern Indians." Of particular concern was stopping the activities of Father Rale, who was suspected of influencing the Indian attacks. Therefore, the Abenaki village at Norridgewock was attacked in August 1724, and Father Rale was killed. As a result of this attack, the resistance of the Indians was seriously weakened. During the war, the Massachusetts government set a bounty of £100 for every scalp, which encouraged numerous bands of volunteers to mount expeditions against the Abenakis. The most famous were the expeditions under Captain John Lovewell. On 8 May 1725, Captain Lovewell and 46 volunteers were surprised by a large number of Indians in present-day Fryeburg, Maine. In the protracted skirmish, one-third of their party were killed, including Captain Lovewell. A treaty was reached on 15 December 1725, finally ending the war.

Less dramatic activity occurred during the final phases of the French and English struggle for North America. During King George's War, the Indians east of the St. Croix joined with the French against the English. The resumption of border warfare occurred in July 1745 with the attack on Fort St. George's. Further Indian attacks occurred throughout Maine in 1746 and 1749. However, during this war the French and Indians were not successful in driving away settlers or completely destroying settlements. Although the Treaty of Aix-la-Chapelle ended the war in 1748, the Abenakis continued sporadic raids against Maine until 1751. During the French and Indian War, military activity concentrated primarily on the Ohio Valley and Canada. In Maine there were still tensions and problems along the borders. Consequently, raids and plundering by Abenakis resumed throughout the region. However, by 1758, the English had gained the military advantage and were able to defeat the Abenakis. With the Treaty of Paris in 1763, all of French Canada reverted to British control, ending the struggle for dominance in Maine.

David L. Whitesell

References
Colin G. Calloway, *The Western Abenakis of Vermont, 1600–1800* (1990); Charles E. Clark, *Maine* (1977); Douglas E. Leach, *The Northern Colonial Frontier, 1607–1763* (1966); Howard H. Peckham, *The Colonial Wars, 1689–1762* (1964); J. Marion Smith, *A History of Maine: From Wilderness To Statehood* (1949).

See also ABENAKI; ACADIA; CASCO BAY; CHURCH, BENJAMIN; CONVERSE, JAMES; DUMMER'S TREATY; DUMMER'S WAR; FALMOUTH, BATTLE OF; GRAND PRÉ, BATTLE OF; KING WILLIAM'S WAR; LOVEWELL, JOHN; LOVEWELL'S FIGHT; FORT LOYAL (MAINE); PEMAQUID, ATTACK ON; RALE, SEBASTIEN; RIGAUD DE VAUDREUIL, PHILIPPE DE; SCALPING BOUNTIES; WELLS; FORT WILLIAM HENRY (MAINE)

Fort Manaskin (Virginia)

Fort Manaskin was built by order of Virginia Governor William Berkeley some time after he returned to power in Virginia following the English Restoration of 1660. Situated on the Pamunkey River in New Kent County, the fort was designed to improve the colony's defenses against Indians. The fort was also known as Fort Matuxon, and Indian allies may have formed part of its garrison.

Thomas Costa

References
Philip Alexander Bruce, *Institutional History of Virginia in the Seventeenth Century*, 2 vols. (1910): 2.

Manuals, Military

Military manuals for the training and discipline of the armed forces were issued in Great Britain by a small body of officers, i.e., the adjutant general, who was responsible for the proper drill and discipline of the armed forces, and the Board of General Officers, which had sat permanently since 1706. Together with the commander in chief, they functioned as a general staff under the authority of the crown. Despite occasional tinkering with the manuals by senior officers, this organization guaranteed the necessary uniformity of standards of training in the British army at a time when training exercises beyond the regimental level were rare.

Drill books had been appearing since midway through the reign of Charles II (1642) and laid the foundation for later manuals. Between the publication of *English Military Discipline* (1672) and *The Manual Exercise with Explanations as Ordered by His Majesty* (1778), at least ten different manuals were issued for the training of troops. Frequently reprinted, these manuals generally followed the continental norms, but Prussian manuals in particular exercised great influence on British military thinking and training. In 1754, a translation of Prussian infantry regulations was published; in 1756, the 1st Foot Guards exercised for the first time in Prussian drill; and in 1757, both the Prussian infantry and cavalry regulations were translated.

By the early eighteenth century, drill manuals usually consisted of five parts, i.e., the "manual exercise," the "platoon exercise," the "evolutions," the "firings," and the "manoeuvres." They were extremely detailed, e.g., the "manual exercise" of 1728 consisted of 64 vocal commands and involved 185 separate motions for the soldiers to perform. The purpose of such detailed instructions and their seemingly endless repetition was to acquaint the soldier with the use of his arms, to move in a regulated and machine-like way, and to enforce docile obedience.

Besides these official training manuals, translations of military classics such as Thucydides's *Peloponnesian War,* Caesar's *Gallic War,* and Vegetius's *The Military Institutions of the Romans* supplemented the military manuals of the times and formed an integral part of an officer's education. Of the more contemporary works, Frederick the Great's *Histoire de mon temps,* Guibert's *Essai general de tactique,* Folard's *Découvertes sur la guerre,* Puységur's *Art de la guerre,* and Feuquières's *Memoirs,* as well as Maurice de Saxe's *Mémoires* and *Rêveries* were particularly popular.

Robert A. Selig

References
Ira D. Gruber, "The Education of Sir Henry Clinton," *Bulletin of the John Rylands University Library of Manchester* 72 (1990): 131–153; John A. Houlding, *Fit for Service: The Training of the British Army, 1715–1795* (1981).

See also ARMY, FRANCE; ARMY, GREAT BRITAIN

March, John (1658–c. 1720)

M

John March would have an active career as a provincial soldier on the New England frontier, only to have it end in disgrace when handed a task apparently beyond his capabilities. In 1691, John March and Daniel King led a raid into Maine that was dogged by illness and misfortune, and ended with their force being ambushed as they embarked at Maquoit (Freeport, Maine). Next given command of the new Fort William Henry at Pemaquid, March in 1694 captured some prominent chiefs who came to trade. This led to inconclusive peace talks with eastern Indians. In 1696, March petitioned the General Court to be relieved of duty at William Henry, and was replaced by Pasco Chubb. The following year, Captain March was in command of the eastern frontier, and directed a fight at Damariscotta, Maine, on 9 September 1697.

The start of Queen Anne's War found John March, now a provincial colonel, in command of the fort at Falmouth. He led the defense of the fort, including personal hand-to-hand combat, during a two-day siege that began 10 August 1703 (part of a massive attack on the Maine frontier that began Queen Anne's War). Later that fall he led 350 men on a raid to Pequawket that produced mixed results.

Colonel March was selected to command the provincial attack on Port Royal in 1707. Contending with a recalcitrant British military engineer backed by the English naval officers, and clashes between provincial officers, March withdrew the force. A furious Governor Joseph Dudley ordered him to try again, sending a trio of civilian politicians to oversee his efforts. Reluctantly, March returned to Port Royal, but soon broke down under the strain, turning command over to Francis Wainwright. March never again held provincial command.

Steven C. Eames

References
Steven C. Eames. "Rustic Warriors: Warfare and the Provincial Soldier on the Northern Frontier, 1689–1748," Ph.D. Dissertation, University of New Hampshire (1989).

See also ACADIA, NEW ENGLAND ATTACK ON (1707); FORT NEW CASCO (MAINE); CHUBB, PASCO; FALMOUTH, BATTLE OF; FORT LOYAL (MAINE); FORT WILLIAM HENRY (MAINE)

Marine Forces

The utilization of seaborne infantry is as ancient as seapower itself. Large numbers of ground forces were carried aboard both Greek and Roman war fleets because the standard naval tactics dictated ramming and grappling followed by boarding—the action then being decided by the soldiers much as it would have been done on land. While these troops could not truly be termed "marine forces," their employment by the ancient thalassocracies does represent the genesis of the modern concept of marine forces—a body of specialized infantry employed and administered by the navy in a variety of roles. The Greeks termed these forces *epibatae,* while the Romans called them *classiarii milites.* Both are quite recognizable in vase paintings and mosaics depicting ancient sea battles. The *epibatae* wear light, minimal, body armor—usually only a helmet and a pair of grieves; the *classiarii milites* wear a light bronze helmet and armor made entirely of leather. Both use a shortened version of the javelin or pilum and a short sword. The use of lighter, specialized equipment is both a concession to the crowded fighting conditions aboard a warship and a survival factor, as both the lightly-armored Greek and Roman "marine" had a much greater chance of survival if thrown overboard than did the more heavily armored infantryman. The Roman maritime regiments also carried on their shield what might be considered a regimental badge distinguishing them from the land legions, a fist grasping a trident, symbol of the sea god Neptune. This device affirms their link to the sea and the naval forces, thus setting them apart from the masses of purely seaborne infantry.

During the Middle Ages and early modern periods, infantry continued to serve aboard ships, but no specialized forces such as the *epibatae* or the *classiarii milites* appear until the middle of the seventeenth century. And then it would take more than a century for one of these bodies, the English marine regiments, to achieve true institutionalization as a modern marine force. The Anglo-Dutch wars of the mid-seventeenth century saw the use of seagoing ground forces by both combatants. Large numbers of Cromwellian "redcoats" served aboard republican and protectorate fleets, and a specialized body, the Admiral's Regiment, was raised in 1664 after the Restoration. The regiment was so named because it was commanded by James, duke of York and lord high admiral. Along with other infantry forces, the Admiral's Regiment fought both at sea and on land during the Second Dutch War of 1664–1667. During the Third Dutch War of 1672–1674, the Admiral's Regiment again served at sea and on land; in 1672, after the Battle of Solebay, in a dispatch Lord Arlington's secretary referred to "those marines of whom I soe [sic] oft have wrote you, behaved themselves stoutly." This is the first use of the term "marines," but in all likelihood the writer was referring to all infantry in the fleet, not just the Admiral's Regiment. When the exclusion crisis of 1675–1676 forced James to resign his commission as lord high admiral, the regiment was restyled the Duke's Regiment.

The rather ambiguous nature of the Admiral's Regiment (was it a land or naval force?) is illustrated by the careers of two young officers. John Churchill, later Duke of Marlborough, served with the regiment from 1672 until 1683, when he left as lieutenant colonel and second-in-command to assume command of the Royal Dragoons. He went on to become England's greatest soldier of the early eighteenth century. George Rook, a naval officer, served in the Admiral's Regiment from 1674 until 1688, when he returned to the Royal Navy. Rook would later command the expedition to the Mediterranean in 1704 where the marine forces of that period won the singular battle honor that is today carried on their regimental badge: "Gibraltar." At this time the regiment also appears to have adopted the motto *Per Mare et Terram* [By sea and by land], which was later shortened to the official motto of the modern Royal Marines, *Per Mare per Terram* [By sea by land].

When James became king in 1685, command of his regiment was given to George, prince of Denmark, the husband of his daughter, Princess Anne. Following the Glorious Revolution of 1688–1689, it was thought too dangerous to keep a regiment in existence that had a long history of personal attachment to the deposed king. Accordingly, it was disbanded in February 1689. With the outbreak of war between England and France in 1690, two regiments of marines were raised for service at sea. Designated the 1st and 2nd Marines, they were placed under control and command of the Admiralty. The 1st was commanded by a line officer, Arthur Herber, lord Torrington; the 2nd by Thomas Herbert, lord Pembroke, who was a civilian in charge of the Admiralty. The 1st and 2nd Marines continued the tradition of serving at land and sea throughout the War of the League of Augsburg, but were disbanded shortly after the Treaty of Ryswick ended the conflict of 1697. This period, however, was instrumental in the later evolution of the marine forces.

The 1st and 2nd Marines apparently wore no military uniforms, dressing as seamen and performing seamen's duties. This practice affirmed the link to the naval forces, but at the same time blurred the distinction between marine forces and the sailors. Split up among many ships, paying, regulating, disciplining, and training the marines proved nearly impossible. During this period, the lieutenant colonel of the 2nd Marines, Admiral Sir Cloudesley Shovel, worked very hard to bring some regulation to the marine forces. Just as his efforts were beginning to have some effect, the order for disbandment was issued in October 1697. Between 1697–1699, the 1st and 2nd Marines were merged with three army regiments and the whole designated as marine forces. In May 1699, when the process was nearly complete, an order for general disbanding was issued.

Two years later in November 1701, 15 new regiments were raised, with six being designated marines. The reason for this increment was in preparation for the outbreak of the War of the Spanish Succession, which began the following year. In July 1704, 1,900 English marines and 400 Dutch marines successfully landed on Gibraltar, and after a five-day siege and naval bombardment, the marines and naval forces took possession of the rock. From July through April 1705, the marines and other forces endured the first siege of Gibraltar by Spanish and French forces. The siege was lifted in April 1705. For the tenacity of their defense and their devotion to duty, the marines were allowed to adopt "Gibraltar" for their battle honor. For the remainder of the war, the marine forces continued to serve at sea and on land in the Mediterranean, the Atlantic, South America, and in the American colonies. In 1710, 600 marines were detached to the colonies to take part in an attack on Port Royal, Nova Scotia. Departing from Boston on 8 October 1710, the Anglo-colonial forces landed at Port Royal on 25 November. After a six-day siege, the French capitulated and Port Royal, renamed Annapolis Royal in honor of Queen Anne, was taken. In this operation, the marines, under the command of Major James Redding, cooperated with colonial troops from Massachusetts, Connecticut, Rhode Island, and New Hampshire. In 1713, following the Treaty of Utrecht, which ended the War of the Spanish Succession, the six marine regiments were disbanded.

During the period 1701–1713, the six marine regiments were organized as land forces under the command of army officers. They were known by the names of their colonels. The old troubles which had plagued earlier marine forces soon appeared, and the colonels requested a separate paymaster of marines in December 1702, which was granted. In April 1703, the marine regiments were placed under the jurisdiction of the lord high admiral. Brigadier General Edward Seymour was placed in command of all marine forces in 1703, new orders for the regulation of the forces were issued, and the men were given both military uniforms and sea clothing. Control, command, and utilization of the marines was still clouded, however. Their officers endeavored to keep them a separate military force, while the captains of the ships to which they were deployed attempted to use them as sailors. Marlborough specifically restricted the latter practice, but the mixing of marines and seamen became more widespread due to the necessities of war, and administration was chaotic. With the 1713 disbanding, three of the six regiments, Fox's, Mordaunt's, and Villier's, were incorporated into the British army.

From 1713–1739, the only vestige of the marines were the "Invalid" companies, which were more often a fiction than a fact. With the outbreak of war with Spain in October 1739, marine forces were again needed. In late November 1739, Parliament debated the whole idea of marine forces, their necessity, their jurisdiction, administration, and employment. This remarkable debate brought into sharp focus all of the ambiguities which had so long clouded the nature and administration of Britain's seagoing military forces. Following the debate, Parliament resurrected the basic organization of 1701, creating six marine regiments by drafting from line regiments. When all six regiments had been deployed, four more were raised in England in 1741, bringing the total to ten marine regiments. In addition, four marine forces were ordered raised in the American colonies, the most famous of these being Gooch's—later Spottswood's—Marines raised in Virginia.

The Anglo-Spanish war of 1739 became the general European and global War of the

Austrian Succession in 1740. From 1740–1748, the ten marine regiments saw hard and active service all over the world. Marines, along with colonial forces, in June 1745 successfully assaulted the great French fortress of Louisbourg, which guarded the entrance to the St. Lawrence River. Marines also served with Admiral Edward Vernon in his expeditions to Panama, Cartagena, and Cuba. With Admirals George Anson and Richard Howe, the marines fought in the Atlantic and they were in the expedition of Admiral Edward Boscawen to Pondicherry in India. With the conclusion of the war in October 1748, a now familiar pattern repeated itself: the marines were disbanded. The reasons for the disbanding were not surprising. A lack of centralized administration with clear jurisdiction over the forces had resulted in chaos. In addition, the nature of their duties had made the marines unappealing to potential officers. Commissions in the marines sold for half that of the line. Consequently, the caliber of the officers declined, leading G.M. Trevelyan to conclude:

> It is remarkable how soon they [the marines] acquired two reputations that clung to them for many generations—a reputation for good, honest, modest service and character, and a reputation among snobs of being socially less smart than the army.

Though disbanded in 1748, events were at work which would guarantee this would be the last time the British marine forces were to pass from existence.

In 1755, when fighting between the French and English erupted in America, marine forces were again raised. This time, however, much more planning and forethought were given to the establishment of the marines. Heading the Admiralty was Admiral Lord George Anson, who had seen firsthand the value of the marine forces and the terrible difficulties of properly administering them. Under Anson's prodding, Parliament voted an establishment of 5,000 marines early in 1755. This force was divided into 50 independent companies formed into three grand divisions based at each of Britain's three major naval bases: Portsmouth, Plymouth, and Chatham. And, most importantly, command and administration of the marines was placed completely under the jurisdiction of the Admiralty. The organization of the marines into the three grand divisions remained the basic unit of the British marine forces for nearly two centuries.

In addition to having their identity clarified and established, the marines of the Seven Years' War truly established their reputation for worldwide service at sea and on land. Raised with great haste and very often minimally trained, the marines were at sea very quickly. Many veteran officers from the ten regiments of 1740–1748 returned, as did a large number of the noncommissioned officers who had gone to the line. It was around this nucleus that the new, permanent, marine corps was formed. From 1756–1763, the marines saw service in the Mediterranean; took part in the raids along the French coast; were in the fleets of Admirals Edward Hawke, Boscawen, and Howe in the Atlantic; with Commodore John Moore in the Caribbean; and in 1759, were with Wolfe's forces at Quebec. Major Hector Boisrond commanded a force of marines in a feint that drew the French away from the path up to the Heights of Abraham, allowing Wolfe to land the bulk of his army. Later in 1759, marines from Admiral Charles Saunders's fleet fought at Quebec. Later in the war, marines from Admiral George Pocock's fleet assisted in the capture of Pondicherry in India; two battalions were landed at Havana in 1762, and 270 Marines and 300 seamen captured Manila the same year.

In 1761, the marines participated in the siege and capture of Belle Isle off the French coast. It was here the French referred to the marines as *les petites grenadiers*. The marines wore grenadier caps rather than the standard tricorn hat because the brimless cap made handling the musket easier aboard crowded warships. They did not, however, attain the height of the army grenadiers, resulting in the description of the French—who noted these "little Grenadiers" had been among the toughest troops they had faced. The laurel wreath that surrounds the modern cap badge is believed to have been awarded to the marines for their service on Belle Isle. In a dispatch to William Pitt, Admiral Augustus Kepel said:

> Major-General Hodgson, by his constant approbation of the battalion of marines landed from the ships . . . gives men the pleasing satisfaction of acquainting you . . . of the goodness and spirited behaviour of that corps . . .

During the Seven Years' War, the marines also undertook the specialized task that today characterizes all marine forces—amphibious landings. Because of their being used to the sea and adept at handling boats, the marines were always the first ashore in a landing. First ashore also meant first to fight, another marine reputation.

At the conclusion of the Seven Years' War in 1763, the marine corps was not disbanded. Like the rest of the Royal Navy, it suffered considerably under the scandalous and neglectful administration of the earl of Sandwich. The Seven Years' War, however, had given the marine corps two great gifts: permanence and a reputation for fighting. The next time the marine corps saw action it would be in the American colonies. English marines had first come to America in 1676, when a detachment of the Admiral's Regiment had been sent to Virginia in the wake of Bacon's Rebellion. In the series of wars beginning in 1689 and continuing through 1763, marines often fought alongside colonial forces. In the French and Indian War, the value of the marines had been obvious to American commanders.

On 10 November 1775, little more than six months after British marines and American soldiers had fought one another at Lexington, Concord, and Bunker Hill, Congress authorized the creation of the United States Marine Corps. It served with distinction throughout the Revolutionary War, but in 1783, it was disbanded—a dubious inheritance from its British ancestor. Congress re-created the Marine Corps in 1798, placing it under the jurisdiction of the Navy Department, a much more advantageous legacy. In 1948, Admiral Sir Henry Moore addressed the National Newcomen Luncheon in New York on the common heritage and traditions of the British and American navies. In his address he made note of their marine forces:

> Allied to this tradition [amphibious invasion] we have another great common bond between our navies—the Marine Corps of our two countries. True, their roles have drifted apart. . . . Both however have won a high place in the affections and respect not only of the naval services but of the general public.

Alfred J. Marini

References

Richard Cannon, ed., *Historical Record of the Marine Corps Containing an Account of Their Formation and Services from 1664 to 1748* (ca. 1827—1830); Colonel Cyril Field, *Britain's Sea Soldiers,* 2 vols. (1924);

Admiral Sir Henry Moore, "The British and American Navies: Their Common Heritage and Traditions," *The Newcomen Society of England* (1948); J.L. Moulton, *The Royal Marines* (1972); Paul H. Nicolas, *Historical Records of the Royal Marine Forces,* 2 vols. (1845); G.M. Trevelyan, *England Under Queen Anne,* Vol. 2 (1932).

Fort Mary (Maine)

In 1617, the first English settlement near the mouth of the Saco River was established. It was not necessary to build a fort for the protection of the settlement until 1708, when marauding Indians attacked. Fort Hill, named for John Hill, its commander, was enlarged in 1710 and renamed Fort Mary. It discouraged further attacks.

Nicholas N. Smith

Maryland

Maryland was founded in 1633 as a proprietary colony through a charter Charles I granted to Cecil Calvert, second lord Baltimore. This charter was the second the Calvert family received, the first being for Avalon, a colony in Newfoundland the Calverts retained until 1754. Maryland, situated immediately north of Virginia, was also named for an English queen, Henrietta Maria, wife of Charles I.

Different from all other colonial charters, Maryland's was least restrictive of the proprietor who was granted rights and prerogatives similar to those of the Bishop Palatine of Durham. This amounted to quasi-royal powers second only to the king. In exchange, a yearly rent of two Indian arrowheads and the royal fifth of all gold and silver were deliverable to the king.

Baltimore and his family were Roman Catholics, and in order to protect their own religious preferences and those of others, they opened Maryland to all persons who believed in the Trinity. From the outset, Maryland encouraged religious freedom, even though the Roman Catholic settlers were in the minority. That minority, however, held most of the power and wealth in the colony for many years. Because of the problems generated by his religious preference, Cecil Calvert was forced to remain in England to protect his interests and was never able to visit his colony. Instead, he sent his brother, Leonard, to act as the first colonial governor.

Wary of religious disputes that could disturb the peace of the colony, Baltimore directed the colonists to keep religious disputes to a minimum and make every effort to maintain good relations with everyone they encountered. This injunction included relations with the local Indians.

Two ships, the 300-ton *Arke* and the 50-ton *Dove,* sailed out of Cowes, Isle of Wight, on 22 November 1633, carrying about 200 people bound for Maryland. Soon separated by a severe storm at sea, the ships eventually reunited in January 1634 in Barbados. On 27 February 1634, the colonists arrived in Virginia, where they stopped to deliver a message from Charles I to Sir John Harvey, the royal governor. Proceeding on, the Marylanders reached the mouth of the Potomac River, Maryland's southern boundary, on 5 March. They sailed slowly up the Potomac and landed on St. Clement's Island (later called Blakiston's Island) 25 March 1634, where they ceremoniously constructed a large wooden cross, held Mass, read the king's charter to Baltimore, and read Baltimore's instructions to the colonists.

Even the armed and hostile Indians that met the colonists at the mouth of the Potomac did not deter the Maryland colonists from pursuing the prescribed course of peace. However, the colonists did not refrain from beginning their exploitation of the local tribes. Leonard Calvert and others traveled upriver to establish friendly contact with the various villages of Indians, and to seek permission from the natives to settle in a permanent location. That settlement, called St. Mary's City, was constructed on a plot of land purchased from the Yoacomico Indians, located at the mouth of St. Mary's River. During the first year of settlement, colonists and Indians lived side by side within the same Yoacomico village, intermingling daily. Yet despite the friendly relations with local Indians, the colonists took the precaution of erecting Fort St. Mary's on the same site.

Maryland continued to grow and prosper with few troubles or altercations with local Indians. In fact, the Maryland colonists were in greater danger from Indians outside the colony's borders, primarily the Iroquois and Susquehannocks who lived on the northern border. Local Indians used the colonists for protection against incursions by hostile tribes, including the Susquehannocks, Iroquois, and the Nanticokes on the Eastern Shore. Likewise, the colonists began to use the local Indians as a buffer against sporadic raids by those same "hostile" tribes. For several years, until settlement spread farther afield, the arrangement worked well for both colonists and local tribes. However, by the early 1640s, this situation began to change when freemen of the colony demanded a greater voice in colonial affairs, and Susquehannocks and other Iroquoian tribes began raiding the livestock of outlying settlements. While in themselves these raids were not events that resulted in open warfare, there was an attempt to mount a campaign against the Susquehannocks that failed to materialize.

Of greater significance to Maryland, however, was the outbreak of the English civil war. Leonard Calvert returned to England and appointed Giles Brent as governor in his stead. Shortly thereafter, Richard Ingle, an ardent parliamentarian sea captain from London, arrived in Maryland. Two years of anarchy known as "the plundering time" ensued. Ingle was finally captured, tried four times by juries who reached no verdict, escaped, and continued to do business in Maryland waters.

In autumn 1644, Leonard Calvert returned to Maryland and traveled to Virginia, bearing letters of marque against parliamentary supporters. Ingle obtained similar letters of marque against royalists in 1645, and proceeded to raid in Maryland, attacking and plundering settlements and manors, capturing Jesuit missionaries and several important political leaders in Maryland. These latter prisoners he carted off to England. Various lawsuits instituted in England, but it was obvious that parliamentary forces were gaining the upper hand in England.

Maryland was in chaos. Calvert was still in Virginia, the temporary governor was in England, and a new government and governor were established by the council in an attempt to restore order. Calvert finally returned, ended the interim government, restored order during spring 1647, and then suddenly died in June. Before his death, Calvert appointed Thomas Greene, a staunch royalist, as governor. Then, in mid-1648, Lord Baltimore, who was shifting toward a pro-Parliament stance to preserve his colonial rights, demoted Greene to the council and replaced him with William Stone, a Protestant. By this time, the council was heavily Protestant, contributing to a return to peace in Maryland. Baltimore kept his colony until 1654.

By 1654, tensions had again increased, this time between Puritans and most others in

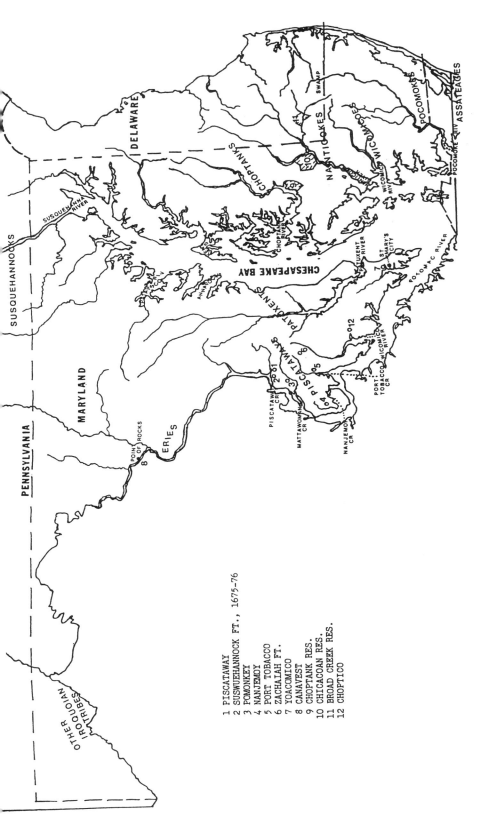

1 PISCATAWAY
2 SUSWUEHANNOCK FT., 1675-76
3 POMONKEY
4 NANJEMOY
5 PORT TOBACCO
6 ZACHAIAH FT.
7 YOACOMICO
8 CANAVEST
9 CHOPTANK RES.
10 CHICACOAN RES.
11 BROAD CREEK RES.
12 CHOPTICO

Maryland. © 1988, *Debra R. Boender.*

Maryland. Internal and external Puritan hostilities caused pro-proprietary forces under Stone to march north, where they engaged a smaller Puritan force near present-day Annapolis on the Severn River. Puritan forces were victorious in what became known as the Battle of the Severn on Sunday, 25 March 1654. Baltimore did not regain full control of his colony again until the Restoration of Charles II in 1660.

Political dissent continued, as did sporadic Indian troubles. By 1675, there were serious and far-reaching changes among Maryland Indians, especially the Susquehannocks. Smallpox swept through the tribe, severely reducing its population and power. Iroquois warfare drove the Susquehannocks to seek aid from Maryland, and eventually saw them resettle near the Potomac River, north of St. Mary's City. There, the Marylanders helped construct an Indian fort similar to European designs and used these Indians as a buffer against Indian attacks coming from the Potomac Valley. However, the next attacks came not from hostile Indians, but from Virginia and Maryland militia.

Iroquoian raids along Virginia's northern frontier that led to Bacon's Rebellion were erroneously blamed on the Susquehannocks in Maryland. A combined force of Virginia and Maryland militiamen surrounded the Susquehannock fort, and when several headmen surrendered as hostages, they were brutally murdered by order of the Virginia commanders. This opened a new front of Indian raiding along the upper Potomac settlements, the brunt of which fell on Virginia colonists. It also served to drive the remaining Susquehannocks into the Iroquois Confederacy.

Meanwhile, events on the Eastern Shore led to open hostilities with the Wicomicoes, a tribe that had been obstinate in refusing to negotiate with Maryland authorities. After Captain John Odber, a local resident, and his servant were killed in retaliation for the murder of a Wicomico woman, the government sentenced five Wicomicoes to death for the crime. When the Wicomicoes, who in the past had crossed Chesapeake Bay to raid colonial settlements, refused to cooperate with the government, war was declared against the tribe. Captain Philemon Lloyd, at the head of Maryland troops, pursued a vigorous but lengthy campaign against the Wicomicoes between 1667–1669. The Maryland force decimated the tribe and sold the survivors they were able to capture into slavery in Barbados. In addition to ridding the colony of a hostile tribe, this action served as a warning to the Nanticokes who lived near the Wicomicoes and witnessed the campaign at close quarters.

Over the next several decades a series of evermore restrictive treaties were signed with the Nanticokes, and in 1698, a reservation at Chicacoan (the main Nanticoke village) was set aside for exclusive Nanticoke use. In 1711, a second Nanticoke reservation was established several miles away at Broad Creek, and the third reservation for the Indian River Indians (a particular group of Nanticokes and other tribal remnants) was established even later. These reservations fell victim to white encroachments, and within several decades were severely reduced in area. Pressures from white settlers combined with rapidly changing intertribal structures until 1742, when the Nanticokes were pushed into preparing for armed hostilities.

In spring and summer 1742, Shawnee emissaries arrived on the Eastern Shore intending to unite tribes there in a general rebellion to drive out the English. This conspiracy was tied to the planned arrival of French ships and troops. Nanticokes and other Eastern Shore tribes gathered at Winnasoccum, a small island in Pocomoke Swamp. However, the conspiracy was uncovered when local whites discovered the Indian towns totally empty and raised the alarm. Hearing of the search for their leaders, the Indians emerged and surrendered their weapons to the vastly superior Maryland forces. Eventually, the Indian leaders were released and the affair was over, albeit at the expense of Nanticoke tribalism. Shortly after, the tribes on the Eastern Shore split apart and many Indians moved north to join the Iroquois in Pennsylvania and beyond.

After 1642, Maryland became more involved with tribes beyond its borders, notably the Iroquois. Maryland paid the Six Nations for lands at the head of the Chesapeake Bay after participating in negotiations at the Lancaster Conference in June and July 1744, which resulted in the Lancaster Treaty, sometimes called the "Grand Treaty."

There were further difficulties with the Nanticokes and other Maryland tribes that moved north, but nothing serious until the French and Indian War. At that time, the Nanticokes and Conoys (as the Piscataways in Pennsylvania were known) joined with the Iroquois to fight for the British. Those tribesmen who remained in Maryland were far removed from the conflict.

After the French and Indian War, the Nanticokes were caught up in the Anglo-American squabbles that erupted into the Revolutionary War. Confused, the tribes at first attempted to stay out of the conflict because Maryland's colonial authorities told them the argument would soon be settled. When warfare began, the Nanticokes, now part of the Iroquois Confederacy, were forced to take sides. For years, the Iroquois complained to Maryland authorities that the Nanticokes still on the Eastern Shore were being held there against their will. Maryland's Council of Safety received the complaints, and Samuel Chase, then delegate to the Continental Congress, urged the Council of Safety to give this matter its immediate attention. Before an investigation could begin, the Iroquois and their allies (or "props" as they were known) joined the side of the British. Nanticokes were engaged in pro-British activities outside of Maryland, most ending up in New York at Otseningo, then in Canada after General John Sullivan's expedition through the Iroquois villages in 1779.

In contrast to the Nanticokes, the Piscataways emigrated from Maryland at a much earlier date. Between 1634 and 1680, the Piscataways were allies of the Maryland colony, but as settlement quickly overtook their territory, the Piscataways suffered a rapid decline. In 1666, a reservation was planned for the Piscataways and was finally established between the heads of Mattawomen and Piscataway Creeks in 1669. A year later, Iroquois raids on the Piscataways increased and the tribe could no longer maintain its defenses on the reservation. Piscataway headmen petitioned Maryland authorities to protect them from being chased out of the colony. At the same time, Piscataways established a short-lived alliance with the Susquehannocks, casting colonial suspicions on the Piscataways and leading to further deterioration of relations between the colony and tribe.

After Bacon's Rebellion and the colonial pursuit of the Iroquois and their allies, including the Susquehannocks, the tribes of Southern Maryland were further reduced. As a rule, the Piscataways and others joined colonial officials in tracking down and capturing hostile Indians. Piscataways also acted as frontier scouts for the colony (some were stationed at Fort Garrison in this capacity). Casualties associated with these endeavors reduced tribal populations in southern Maryland until they were irrevocably weakened.

Because the Piscataways were so weakened after 1675, they requested assistance from the Marylanders in protecting their tribe against the Iroquois warriors who had moved into the old Susquehannock fort at the head of Chesapeake Bay. Rumors were the Iroquois planned to attack the Piscataways from that base. Maryland tried to honor the treaty with the Piscataways, and sent an envoy with a message to the Iroquois to remind them of their treaty obligations. That envoy never delivered the message, however, because the settlers at the head of the bay refused to assist him in crossing the Susquehanna River. Therefore, Maryland officials concocted a plan to transport the Piscataway women and children across the bay to safety on the Nanticoke River. This planned removal, the Marylanders believed, would place the Piscataways beyond Iroquois raiding and remove them from their proximity to the Virginia frontier, thereby ending complaints against them from the Virginia frontiersmen.

Meanwhile, armaments were sent to the Piscataway fort in their main village of Piscataway on Piscataway Creek. Eventually, they decided to remain at Piscataway because the Nanticokes were traditional enemies as much as the Iroquois. Piscataway headmen even ventured to suggest to the Marylanders that all remaining Indians in southern Maryland join them at their fort.

However, the Iroquois were already beginning to attack the Piscataways and had already destroyed most of the Piscataway crops. Maryland officials worried because the Piscataways had no food supplies, and in their reduced straits were incapable of holding off the Iroquois attack. A Piscataway defeat would remove a major colonial frontier buffer. However, the Marylanders did not move quickly enough. By the time they arrived with assistance, most of the siege was over and the Senecas had returned home. Only the Susquehannocks remained, still attacking the Piscataways. Even the Susquehannocks vanished when a colonial force arrived under the command of Captain Randolph Brandt of Charles County.

Once more, in May 1680, the Piscataways appealed for colonial assistance against hostile tribes, but when a large number of "strange Indians" appeared, the Piscataways fled. Their fort and village were abandoned. After this, colonial officials decided to resettle the

Piscataways at Zachaiah fort, a site closer to St. Mary's City. Colonial officials asked the Piscataways to destroy their old fort so hostile tribes could not use it as a base of operations against the colony. Even after most of the Piscataways moved to Zachaiah, they continued to suffer almost daily raids from the Iroquois. Little additional colonial assistance was offered, however, until the Piscataway Indians threatened to surrender to the Iroquois. By this time there was a second Piscataway stronghold at Nanjemoy, which was also under constant attack. To enhance the strength of the Piscataways, the Patuxent Indians living to the north along the Patuxent River on reserved lands were relocated to Zachaiah. Even the colonists were becoming alarmed, as they observed a force of approximately 200 Senecas lurking in the woods near the Piscataway forts.

In 1681, the Iroquois sent a delegation to St. Mary's City, where they boasted they would soon make an end of the Piscataways. Soon after, the Iroquois built a fort within sight of the Zachaiah fort, and they attacked in August 1681. At that time they took 17 prisoners from the Piscataway fort. Captain Brandt was once more sent out to investigate the intertribal conflict at Zachaiah, and he reported seeing a sortie of Senecas attack the Piscataway defenders. Brandt's presence, however, disrupted the attack, and the Senecas fled into the forest. Seven Susquehannocks were also captured about this same time near Zachaiah in a series of related frontier skirmishes.

After the Susquehannocks were captured, the Iroquois released seven Christian prisoners, hoping an equal number of Susquehannocks would also be released. Part of the Iroquois plan was to maintain peace with Maryland as the Albany Treaty of 1677 established between the Five Nations and the Maryland colony. Maryland sent Colonels Henry Coursey and William Stevens to negotiate a settlement with the Iroquois to end raids on the Piscataways and outlying settlements. Senecas, Oneidas, Onondagas, and Cayugas participated in the conference, as did several affiliated tribes. They declared war could not be averted because the Piscataways had recently planned to destroy the Onondagas and had killed several members of the recent Iroquois war party. Talks broke down and the Iroquois abruptly left.

After this aborted conference, Maryland officials feared the Iroquois would now attempt to destroy all remaining southern Maryland tribes, thereby involving colonial frontiersmen and leaving frontier borders unprotected. Captain Brandt was ordered to continue ranging along the frontiers, and he had about 30 Piscataways under his command. At the same time, Maryland troops were assigned to the Zachaiah fort to help protect the elderly, women, and children.

Meanwhile, the proprietary government was overthrown, and Lionel Copley was appointed as the first royal governor. He arranged for a treaty with the Piscataways, which was signed in 1692. That treaty was basically the same as prior treaties. However, royal governors were not as lenient in dealing with Indians as had been the proprietary leaders. Indian movements within the colony were severely restricted, and attempts were made to keep all tribesmen within their respective reservation limits. These attempts were not successful.

Later, Governor Francis Nicholson tried to relocate all southern Maryland tribes at a spot near the Little Falls of the Potomac River. He also interfered in the internal workings of the tribes when he appointed the headman of the Piscataways to the post of chief commander and governor over all the tribes on the western shore. However, before these plans could be enacted, the Piscataways fled into the Virginia mountains and settled at the head of the Occoquan River, where they planted a cornfield on Goose Creek. This relocation was the Indian response to tightening colonial controls and increasing interference. Continuing raids on the frontier were blamed on the Piscataways, and soon after the murder of a young man in Prince George's County, Nicholson ordered all the Piscataways to return to southern Maryland where the colonial authorities could control them. Negotiations ensued, but the Piscataways remained reluctant to return. Nicholson even constructed a fort near Rock Creek (now in Washington, D.C.) hoping to entice the tribe back. After renewed colonial threats, the Piscataways deserted their Occoquan fort and settled on Conoy Island in the Potomac River, near Point of Rocks, Maryland. However, Conoy Island was an Iroquois name (a moniker never used by the Piscataways or in reference to the tribe while they resided in Maryland). The Piscataways built a sizable fort—Canavest, as this settlement was called—on Conoy Island; it boasted only about 100 warriors, a sign of the steady deterioration of the tribe.

When Governor Nathaniel Blakiston assumed leadership of Maryland, Piscataway problems remained unsettled. Some Pamunkey-based Indians returned to southern Maryland and resumed their former residence at the town from which they derived their name. Once more, after negotiations, the Piscataways signed another treaty that failed to differ from previous treaties. A new reservation was surveyed for their use, but the Piscataways never returned to their traditional lands in Maryland. In fact, they applied to Governor William Penn of Pennsylvania for permission to settle there.

Despite efforts to force the tribe back to Maryland and, on the part of Virginia, off Conoy Island, the tribe remained there for another 20 years. During that time, it seems they allied themselves with their former enemies, the Iroquois, as the Nanticokes did about the same time. While on Conoy Island, Virginians accused the Piscataways of harboring Iroquois who engaged in raids on the Virginia frontier. However, in 1704, a smallpox epidemic forced most of the Piscataways to abandon Canavest, leaving their corn in the fields. Some of the displaced tribesmen settled in Conejohola on the west bank of the Susquehannock River in what is now York County, Pennsylvania. Later, in 1722, the Iroquois ordered the remaining Piscataways to leave Conoy Island and settle in Pennsylvania near present-day Bainbridge. In this way, the majority of the Piscataways moved north to settle in Conoy Town and became known as Conoy Indians.

During the French and Indian War, and the American Revolutionary War, the Conoys lived with the Nanticokes and were, for the most part, absorbed by that tribe. Eventually, most Piscataways and Nanticokes became part of the Delawares, Cayugas, and Tuscaroras, moving into Kansas, Oklahoma, and Canada. In 1790, only 50 Conoys remained in the Iroquois Confederacy when they signed a treaty in Detroit. A few Piscataways remained in Maryland, however, just as a few Nanticokes stayed on the Eastern Shore in what had become Delaware. Those remaining Piscataways, perhaps only one or two families, married into the local populations, white and black, in southern Maryland during the eighteenth century. Those who remained, or the few who straggled back into Maryland after the Revolutionary War, were a mixture of southern Maryland tribes, including the Piscataways, Port Tobaccoes, Nanjemoys, Mattawomans, Patuxents, Yoacomicoes, and others. On the Eastern Shore, the same applied to the Nanticokes who, by 1776, included Nanticokes, Assateagues, Choptanks, Wicomicoes, Pocomokes, and others.

Overall, Maryland suffered little real Indian warfare during most of the colonial era. Maryland troops and envoys regularly engaged in Indian warfare and treaty making, primarily in terms of intertribal conflicts. Special forts were established to protect the early colonial frontiers from hostile attacks, and Maryland rangers and Indian allies patrolled the frontiers from the 1670s through the end of the French and Indian War. Other Maryland forts on the far western frontiers, such as Fort Frederick and Fort Cumberland, were primarily used as staging areas for the French and Indian War, and later played a peripheral role in the Revolutionary War. Maryland did, however, encourage the local Indian allies to construct fortifications that helped protect Maryland borders from hostile Indian attacks throughout most of the colonial era. Basically, despite the continued fear of Indian attack, Maryland remained rather peaceful and suffered no major Indian wars or attacks at any time.

Debra R. Boender

References

A Relation of Maryland (1966), facsimile ed., 1635; Matthew Page Andrews, *The Founding of Maryland* (1933); *Archives of Maryland,* ed. by William Hand Browne, 72 vols. (1883):1–61; Debra R. Boender, "Our Fires Have Nearly Gone Out: A History of Indian-White Relations on the Colonial Maryland Frontier, 1633–1776," Ph.D. Dissertation, University of New Mexico (1988); John Leeds Bozman, *The History of Maryland,* 2 vols. (1837).

Donald Marquand Dozier, *Portrait of the Free State: A History of Maryland* (1976); Alice L.L. Ferguson, "The Susquehannock Fort on Piscataway Creek," *Maryland Historical Magazine,* 36 (1941):1–9; ———, *Moyaone and the Piscataway Indians* (1963); ———, *The Piscataway Indians of Southern Maryland* (1960); Clayton Coleman Hall, ed., *Narratives of Early Maryland, 1633–1684* (1925).

John Thomas Scharf, *History of Maryland, from the Earliest Period to the Present Day* (1879), rpt. 1967; Raphael Semmes, *Captains and Mariners of Early Maryland* (1937); Frank G. Speck, *The Nanticoke and Conoy Indians with a Review of Linguistic Material from Manuscript and Living Sources: An His-*

M

torical *Study* (1927); Richard Walsh and William Lloyd Fox, eds., *Maryland—A History, 1632–1974* (1974); Clinton A. Weslager, *The Nanticoke Indians—Past and Present* (1983).

See also BACON'S REBELLION; FORT CUMBERLAND (MARYLAND); FORT FREDERICK (MARYLAND); FORT GARRISON (MARYLAND) AND THE MARYLAND RANGERS; IROQUOIS; LANCASTER, TREATY OF; MARYLAND, INDIAN FORTS IN; MILITIA, THE ARCHAEOLOGICAL RECORD; NICHOLSON, FRANCIS; PAMUNKEY; ST. MARY'S FORT (MARYLAND); SUSQUEHANNOCK

Maryland, Indian Forts in

There were only a few Indian forts in Maryland, although colonial officials often referred to the palisaded Indian towns as "forts." Most of the true Indian forts were built with the assistance of the colonial officials in the hope that resident tribesmen would act as a buffer against hostile Indian attacks. Among the most irritating of these attacks came from the Susquehannocks and later from the various tribes of the Iroquois Confederacy, such as the Senecas and the Eries (who eventually were absorbed into the confederacy).

At the head of the Chesapeake Bay, along and near the Susquehanna River, resided the various villages of Susquehannock Indians. At first a strong and threatening tribe hostile to the English settlers and the other Maryland tribes farther to the south, the Susquehannocks suffered heavy losses from warfare with the Iroquois, combined with a severe smallpox epidemic that swept through the tribe. By 1675, Susquehannock numbers were greatly reduced and they were forced to seek assistance from Maryland colonial officials. At about this time, the Susquehannocks established a fort near the head of the bay, probably on Palmer's Island, but the precise site of the fort has not been definitely located. Apparently this fortification was similar in design to the Maryland forts at St. Mary's and St. Inigoes, as the Susquehannocks requested the colony to install cannons and provide ammunition for them (a request that was denied). It seems, however, the colonists did help design the Susquehannock fort in the northern bay area. This fort was not held for long as continued Iroquois raids made the Susquehannock position untenable, Eventually the weakened tribe decided to join the Iroquois Confederacy as an allied tribe, or "prop."

A second Susquehannock fort was definitely established in about 1675 on the south bank of Piscataway Creek, where the creek empties into the Potomac River, after the Susquehannocks were forced south. This latter fort was clearly described at the time of Bacon's Rebellion, when combined Virginia and Maryland troops attacked the Susquehannocks, murdering several chiefs who had surrendered. This fort, unlike the circular Indian villages, had straight sides that turned at right angles. There were bastions at the corners. Perhaps this fort was one the colonists had built in 1642 and subsequently abandoned, or the Susquehannocks erected it utilizing the knowledge they had acquired from the colonists.

Recent excavations in the twentieth century indicate the Susquehannock fort on Piscataway Creek at one time stood some distance from the creek, but subsequent erosion along the bank has eradicated about half of the remaining posthole mold, leaving only the western and southern lines of the fort still visible. Other archeological evidence indicates the presence of a circular colonial horse corral and a colonial camp, both to the southwest of the Susquehannock fort. This corroborates a map drawn of the fort and the colonial stockade at the time of the attack on the Susquehannocks during Bacon's Rebellion. Although the Susquehannocks were subject to this attack in 1675 by Virginia and Maryland troops, they reinhabited this fort through the remainder of the seventeenth century and into the early eighteenth century. Sometime prior to King George's War in the 1740s, the fort was abandoned.

There was a second Indian "fort" located just a short distance upstream from the Susquehannock fort, also on the south bank of Piscataway Creek, at the Piscataway village known as Piscataway. In actuality, this second fort was really the main Piscataway village which was palisaded in the fashion of most Algonquian tribes of the mid-Atlantic region. Piscataway's fortifications were enhanced, however, with the assistance of officials in Maryland, who used it for many years as the primary buffer between white settlements and the hostile Indians to the west and north, notably the Iroquois. At various times, Maryland officials supplied the friendly Piscataways with weapons and enlisted their aid in scouting the Maryland frontiers in search of hostile Indians.

Second and third Piscataway forts were established by the Maryland authorities at

Zachaiah Swamp and the village of Nanjemoy in 1680. These forts were to replace the more outlying Piscataway fortifications and villages which, by the late 1670s, were suffering from constant Iroquois raids and had become unstable. At Zachaiah Swamp, situated between Port Tobacco Creek and Wicomico River (in southern Maryland) in a marshy region believed to offer greater protection against hostile raids, the Marylanders helped erect a fort intended to house all Piscataways and other remnant tribal groups. The exact appearance of Zachaiah fort is unknown, but was probably a squared, stockaded fortification like all the others the colonists had built. However, not all Indians agreed to move into Zachaiah fort, and an alternate fortification was built or enhanced at Nanjemoy, an Indian village situated on the eastern side of the great bend of Nanjemoy Creek. Nanjemoy was about ten to 15 miles west of Zachaiah fort. Neither fort deterred Iroquois raids on the Piscataways, who continually petitioned the colonial government for further assistance.

During King William's War, the new royal governor of Maryland, Francis Nicholson, ordered the Maryland rangers to build a new fort near the Little Falls of the Potomac. Nicholson then ordered all remaining Indians of southern Maryland to remove to that fortification. Before forced removal could occur, the Piscataways abandoned Zachaiah fort and fled into Virginia. Nicholson's plans were never fulfilled.

Overall, little remains of the colonial Indian forts, either in archeological or archival evidence. Only the Susquehannock fort on Piscataway Creek is fully described. Settlement advanced quite rapidly after 1675, and overran the old Indian villages or "forts," generally obliterating all visible traces of the previous inhabitants. It is also difficult to ascertain from colonial records what constituted an Indian fort; aside from those constructed with colonial assistance, major palisaded villages seem to have occasionally been labeled "forts," thereby confusing the situation. While Maryland attempted to maintain the Piscataways and other friendly tribes in fortified locations on the western borders of the colony, the council and assembly provided inadequate assistance in foodstuffs, firearms, and military assistance in the form of troops for the Indians to maintain their positions. Finally, changes in colonial policy that amounted to forced removal and relocation caused most friendly tribes of the western shore to flee into neighboring colonies, and ultimately into the relative safety of the Iroquois Confederacy. All of the Indian forts were abandoned by the early years of the eighteenth century.

Debra R. Boender

References

Archives of Maryland, ed. by William Hand Browne, 72 vols. (1883):1–3, 5, 7–8, 13, 15, 17, 20, 22–25, 29; Alice L.L. Ferguson, "The Susquehannock Fort on Piscataway Creek," *Maryland Historical Magazine,* 36 (1941):1–9; William B. Marye, "Piscattaway," *Maryland Historical Magazine,* 30 (1920): 194–196; ———, "Former Indian Sites in Maryland as Located by Early Colonial Records," *American Antiquity,* 2 (1936): 40–46.

See also BACON'S REBELLION; KING WILLIAM'S WAR; MARYLAND; NICHOLSON, FRANCIS; SUSQUEHANNOCK

Fort Massac (Illinois)

Fort Massac was on the north bank of the Ohio River, approximately 40 miles above its confluence with the Mississippi River. It was constructed by French forces in early 1757 to help protect their river communications and deter British influence among the western Indian tribes. The wooden stockade was originally named Fort Ascension. Its garrison company successfully withstood attack by a large Cherokee force in the fall 1757. Following later French defeats around the Great Lakes, the fort was rebuilt and strengthened with earthworks in 1759. At that time it was renamed for the marquis de Massiac, the minister of marine. The fort was abandoned after the French ceded the area to Britain in 1763, and soon fell into ruin. Its current spelling is an anglicization adopted when the fort was rebuilt by General Anthony Wayne in the 1790s.

George Geib

Massachusetts

Even though early American historians in the twentieth century have expanded more energy studying colonial Massachusetts's Puritan heritage, town-based social order, and revolutionary prominence, the bay colony's role as the province most involved in warfare deserves equal emphasis. Guardian of the Canadian frontier along with New York and New Hampshire—Maine was part of Massachusetts until

1820—Massachusetts's homogeneous, united, and religiously-inspired population mustered far more zeal on the battlefield than tiny New Hampshire or contentious New York. Massachusetts led its fellow colonies in the Pequot (1636–1637), King Philip's (1675–1676), King William's (1689–1697), Queen Anne's (1702–1713), and King George's (1744–1748) Wars, and made the heaviest colonial contribution to the French and Indian War (1754–1763) in which predominantly British forces finally eliminated the French menace. Furthermore, in addition to military history, Massachusetts's wars profoundly influenced its own political and economic life and decisively shaped Anglo-American relations in general.

Founded in 1629, Massachusetts, like its sister colony, Plymouth, begun nine years earlier, lived in peace with its Native American neighbors until the mid-1630s. At this time, the arrival of the Pequots, a warlike tribe from the upper Hudson River valley, in the area of Narragansett Bay, inspired the smaller tribes to request help from the whites to rid the region of a mutual enemy. A pretext for war appeared when Indians who murdered an English trader on Block Island fled to the Pequots and received sanctuary. Massachusetts then led Connecticut and Plymouth in a war of extermination, culminating in the 25 May 1637, surprise attack on the Pequot's principal settlement on the Mystic River. Encircling the wooden palisade, forces commanded by John Mason infiltrated the perimeter and set fire to the Indian huts. The soldiers then shot down the men, women, and children fleeing the inferno. It "was a fearful sight to see them thus frying in the fire, and the strains of blood quenching the same," wrote contemporary chronicler Nathaniel Morton. New England sold the survivors into slavery in the West Indies and praised God, in Morton's words, for "so speedy victory over so proud, insulting, and blasphemous an enemy."

With the Pequots eliminated, Massachusetts maintained peaceful, yet sometimes strained, relations with the Native Americans for four decades. Realizing their impotence before the rapidly expanding settlements, surviving tribes relocated to North America's first Indian reservations, the "praying towns" established by John Eliot beginning in 1646. In 1675, however, Metacom, chief of the Wampanoags, called King Philip by the English, ended the era of amicable relations begun by his father Massasoit, the Pilgrim's great friend. After futilely attempting to persuade southern New England's remaining Indians to join a confederation, the Wampanoags launched raids against frontier towns in an effort to halt Puritan expansion. Massachusetts's first strategy to combat them failed: armed companies searched for Indians who either ambushed or avoided them.

In response, Captain Benjamin Church developed the first major innovation in frontier warfare in American history. Church organized flying columns comprised jointly of white volunteers and friendly Indians who marched in loose formations, whereas previously "the English always kept in a heap together, that it was easy to hit them as to hit a house." Church's men gave the Indians a taste of their own medicine, burning villages and crops, and killing regardless of sex or age. Teaming up with Connecticut and Plymouth, in November 1675, Massachusetts reprised the tactic that destroyed the Pequots, this time against the main Narragansett settlement near present West Kingston, Rhode Island. The troops killed about 500 Indians, members of a tribe that had refused to aid the whites or surrender to them hostiles seeking sanctuary. Church's men captured and executed Philip himself in August 1676, although pockets of resistance lingered until the following year. The war cost New England at least 500 combatants and an equal number of civilian casualties, Indians destroyed half the towns in Massachusetts, damaged most of the rest, and cost the colony £100,000. Already plagued by divisions between strict Puritans and their assorted critics, Massachusetts's ministers, magistrates, deputies, and merchants blamed each other's military incompetence and moral turpitude for the severe losses. The war increased anxiety in a colony troubled about a less cohesive social order at home and challenges to its virtual independence from royal authority without.

Warfare ceased for a dozen years until May 1689, when Massachusetts learned England's new king, William III, had declared war on a France whose king, Louis XIV, refused to recognize his right to the throne. The two powers instructed their colonies to enter the lists. French Canada, led by the veteran soldier, Louis de Buade de Frontenac, stirred up the Norridgewock and Abenaki Indians to attack settlements Massachusetts had established in Maine as far as 100 miles north of the New Hampshire border. In a few months the Native Americans reduced English control to a few precariously held towns in Maine's southern tip. The provisional government, which in 1689 had overthrown Sir Edmund Andros, the absolute governor sent by William's predecessor James II to rule New England, sent troops. But the men were disgusted at failing to encounter the Indians and even more angry at not being paid. Many soldiers preferred imprisonment to military service, people refused to pay increased taxes needed for future expeditions, and the populace "spoke very insolently to their new masters, crying publicly in the streets: God Bless Sir Edmund Andros, and damn all pumpkin states."

Anxious both to impress King William with its loyalty and to unite a restless people who questioned its legitimacy, Massachusetts's new government prepared a major force to conquer Canada in 1690. That April, the colony's representatives coordinated plans for a joint effort with New York: the bay colony would send a fleet up the St. Lawrence while the Yorkers would strike via Lake Champlain. Sir William Phips, a Massachusetts naval captain noted primarily for recovering sunken treasure in the West Indies, captured Port Royal, France's principal fort in Acadia (Nova Scotia) in May, but came to grief that October before Quebec. He sailed in late August with 34 vessels and 2,200 men. However, smallpox and lack of knowledge of the treacherous and foggy St. Lawrence delayed Phips's arrival near Quebec until October, by which time New York had withdrawn its men. He thus faced the entire force of Canada. Phips landed most of his men at the foot of the cliffs on which Quebec perched. The general squandered his cannon shot in a futile effort to counter the heavy resistance they met. Cold weather set in, the troops suffered from frostbite, and the treacherous currents made it difficult for the soldiers on land even to receive supplies. Faced with the prospect of being trapped in an icy river in enemy territory, Phips retreated to Boston following three weeks of ineffectual skirmishing.

With most of the public's attention and money focused on Phips's campaign, Massachusetts's frontier defenses fell apart. Taxes increased to 30 times the prewar level, and paper money issued to support the Canada expedition depreciated 50 percent. The provisional government told Maine frontiersmen who begged for help "That Jesus Christ was king of earth as well as heaven, and that if Jesus Christ did not help them, they could not." In January 1692, a surprise winter raid destroyed Falmouth, the principal remaining settlement in Maine. The ineffective interim government, in its third year in 1692, implored the king to settle some legitimate authority and help with the war. Three years of disastrous conflict had reduced Puritan Massachusetts, so proud of its autonomy in the 1680s, to pleading for royal protection.

Thanks to Increase Mather's lobbying, William appointed Phips himself as Massachusetts's new governor, a post he held from 1692 until his return to England in 1694. He proved as disastrous an administrator as he was a military commander. Phips refused to assist New York and New Hampshire in frontier defense, although his lieutenant governor, William Stoughton, made an effort in his absence. When the English sent a fleet, which arrived in June 1693 under Sir Francis Wheeler, to attempt another reduction of Canada, Phips refused to raise troops and would not even permit the soldiers and sailors suffering from a smallpox epidemic to mingle with the inhabitants. Phips was recalled to England in 1694 to answer charges of corruption and malfeasance.

Depredations on Massachusetts's frontier continued sporadically until news of the Treaty of Ryswick brought the province's sufferings to an end in November 1697. Indians raided in Maine with impunity by sidestepping immobile garrisons, and in July 1697, a combined French and Indian expedition destroyed an exposed fort at Pemaquid on the Kennebec River that had cost Massachusetts £20,000. To encourage volunteers to pursue Indian raiders, the province offered bounties of £50 for the scalp of every Indian man, woman, or child, a sum equal to Increase Mather's annual salary as president of Harvard College. Laws forbade frontier inhabitants to desert their towns, but hundreds of people left not only the frontier, but Massachusetts itself to avoid heavy taxation and military service.

The five years between King William's and Queen Anne's Wars were more of an uneasy truce than a real peace for Massachusetts and Canada. In the first decade of the eighteenth century, Massachusetts once again suffered severely from Indian raids which reached to Lancaster, 40 miles west of Boston, in 1703, and Haverhill, 30 miles north of the capital, in 1708. The most famous raid occurred 29 February 1704 against Deerfield on the Connecticut River just south of the present Vermont state line. A joint French and Indian force killed 40 settlers, took 111 captives back to Quebec, and destroyed the town. Joseph Dudley, Massachusetts's governor from 1702 to 1715, posted garrisons of 2,000 men in summer and 600 in winter, which cost £40,000 per year.

Massachusetts took the offensive in spring 1704, when old Benjamin Church destroyed a French settlement at Minas on the eastern shore of the Bay of Fundy. However, a more substantial effort in 1706 to seize Port Royal, the principal French settlement in Acadia, ended when the troops inexplicably failed to assault the town. The Massachusetts legislature, although frustrated with years of expensive and futile war, refused to accept the allegations of Dudley's enemies that he and his cronies refrained from attacking to continue profiting from illegal trade with the French.

Massachusetts's hopes lifted in 1709 when the province received word that England planned to send a fleet and 4,000 regulars, to be joined by an intercolonial force, to end French rule in Canada. Massachusetts cheerfully raised an army and then spent the summer and autumn watching "them only eat and drink and run this country into debt" to the sum of £30,000. Peace rumors in Europe had changed the ministry's mind about sending the fleet. When the year continued, the British tried again in 1710: six royal warships transported 3,500 colonials from Boston to Port Royal, which surrendered at once to the overwhelming force. However, the town did not fall until 24 September due to various delays for which the province and the navy blamed each other. An attack on Quebec proved impossible.

Massachusetts joined England for one last try in 1711. It raised 900 men and another £40,000 to join the largest military expedition sent to North America before the French and Indian War. In late June, Admiral Sir Hovenden Walker and General James Hill arrived in Boston with nine warships, 60 transports, and 12,000 soldiers and sailors. Combined with colonials, they should easily have overwhelmed the 2,000 French troops available in Canada. Walker, however, who had gathered three months' food supplies for his huge force, lacked confidence. He was struck "with horror [at being] . . . locked up by adamantine frosts, in a barren and uncultivated region, swollen with high mountains of snow, great numbers of brave men famishing with hunger, and drawing lots who should die to feed the rest." Sailing into the mouth of the St. Lawrence on 23 Au-

gust, Walker's fleet was caught in a dense fog: eight ships crashed on the rocks, and some 900 persons drowned. Walker lost his nerve and returned to Boston. Once again, Massachusetts had nothing to show for its patriotism except a huge debt of £173,000, casualties, and resentment against incompetent British commanders and their men who, when in the province, quarreled and fought with the Bostonians. Little of consequence happened in the last two years of the war in New England.

Historian Douglas Edward Leach refers to the quarter-century following the 1713 Treaty of Utrecht as a "Cold War Eighteenth-Century Style." But things heated up between Massachusetts and Canada from 1720 to 1725, largely due to the missionary zeal of French Jesuit Sebastien Rale and the mutual dislike of the Massachusetts house of representatives and the governor from 1716 to 1722, Samuel Shute. The Norridgewock Indians had become dependent on European trade goods, a fact of which New England merchants took full advantage. During a protracted quarrel over the governor's right to veto the speaker of the house and the nature of Massachusetts's money supply, Indian relations became a pawn in the power struggle since the remote tribe, which lived in the region of the Penobscot River, posed no threat to most of the province. As a result, the legislature refused to approve truck houses suggested by the governor to regulate the corrupt trade with the Indians or to authorize an expeditionary force to seize Rale, even after Indian raiders killed and imprisoned inhabitants as far south as Brunswick and as far west as the upper reaches of the Connecticut River. Instead, the deputies put a reward of £200 on the priest's head as "a constant and notorious fomenter and incendiary to the Indians" and refused to authorize troops until the governor surrendered his command over the armed forces to a legislative committee.

That the Norridgewocks did not pose much of a threat appeared in the ease with which they were defeated once Shute fled the province following an assassination attempt. Lieutenant Governor William Dummer launched what is known as Dummer's War (1722–1727), which consisted primarily of two pitched battles. A surprise attack on the main Norridgewock village by 80 men on 12 August 1724 killed Rale. The following April, a mere 35 Indian hunters (Massachusetts once again had placed bounties on scalps) defeated what was left of the tribe near present Fryeburg, Maine, even though fewer than ten of the colonials escaped death or wounds. Treaties signed in December 1725 and the following two years ended the menace to the Maine frontier for two decades.

The Anglo-Spanish War (1739–1744) involved Massachusetts in 1740, when about 1,000 men, mostly young from the crowded towns of eastern Massachusetts, enlisted in a British expedition against Cartagena in Spanish Central America; fewer than half returned. Further, British naval captains took advantage of the patriotism of Governor William Shirley, Massachusetts's governor from 1741 to 1756, and his council, who allowed them to impress sailors in Boston harbor when fleets from Europe put in for supplies and repairs. Although natives of Massachusetts were supposedly exempt from the press, the navy took some, and Bostonians violently resisted the press gangs throughout the decade. (Similar violence had occurred during the 1690s, during which enraged British mariners beat up two members of the Massachusetts legislature. In 1702, the provincial council had even ordered that a man-o-war be fired upon for impressing men without permission.)

When King George's War broke out between France and England, neither country had great plans for the northern frontier. However, in January 1745, the ambitious Governor Shirley persuaded the legislature, in secret session, to vote £50,000 and raise 3,000 men to capture France's principal fort at the mouth of the St. Lawrence, Louisbourg on Cape Breton Island. The legislature agreed, at least in part because Louisbourg served as a base for privateers wreaking havoc on Massachusetts shipping and fishing. The expedition, commanded by William Pepperrell, Jr., of Maine and supported by an English fleet under Admiral Peter Warren, besieged the town from 29 April until 17 June. While an assault on 26 May proved futile and produced more than 200 casualties, the 10,000 shells lobbed into the fort by the blockading ships destroyed virtually every habitation within, provoking a French surrender. The American colonies reacted with "bonfires, illuminations, and other demonstrations of joy."

But Louisbourg proved to be the only high point in an otherwise dismal war for Massachusetts. As an eager Shirley and Warren planned to conquer Canada in 1746 by way of Crown Point and the Champlain Valley, a Canadian/Indian force destroyed Fort Massachusetts on the Housatonic River. However, outside of the bay colony, colonial legislatures refused to supply men and cash. When Massachusetts men who enlisted for frontier defense found themselves pressed into the Canada expedition by their zealous governor, the provincial house of representatives, protesting that "we have always looked upon the impressing of men even for the defense of their own inhabitants as a method to be made use of in cases of great necessity only," refused to support them. Unwilling to raise the extraordinary expenses of 1745 and 1746 through taxation, Massachusetts issued paper money, which depreciated to one-tenth of sterling and produced a paper debt of nearly £2 million. Even Louisbourg left a bitter aftertaste: the conquerors waited ten months, until April 1746, to be relieved by a promised contingent of British regulars, during which time 900 died from exposure and disease. Nor did the royal treasury make good on a promise to compensate the province for at least some of its exceptional costs until 1749, when a shipment of £183,000 sterling ended most of the province's serious currency problems.

King George's War brought Anglo-American tension in Massachusetts to a level unknown since the 1680s. In addition to taxes, inflation, casualties, and the interruption of trade, anger at naval impressment culminated in November 1747 with Boston's greatest riot before the Stamp Act. A mixed crowd of sailors and Bostonians held the British officers on shore as hostages. They then besieged the governor and council until Shirley promised to plead with the responsible commander, Charles Knowles, for the release of the pressed men. Knowles responded by threatening to blow up the town, although after the mob freed the officers, he at least let the captured Bostonians go. Two weeks after the riot, 25-year-old Samuel Adams and a group of friends launched *The Independent Advertiser,* Massachusetts's first protest newspaper, which attacked the war, accused Shirley and his cronies of profiteering, and justified violent resistance to press-gangs on grounds of natural rights. When England and France agreed to the Treaty of Aix-la-Chapelle in spring 1748, which restored Louisbourg to the French in return for Madras in India, *The Advertiser* expressed Massachusetts's sentiments:

Why is the security of the brave and virtuous given up to purchase some short-lived and precarious advantages for lazy d___d f___ls and idle All__s? The security was purchased with the blood of the former and sacrificed to the indolence of the latter. The first won it by bravery; the latter sacrificed it by Tr–ach–ry and Cow—dice. [Omissions in the original to avoid prosecution for libel.]

Massachusetts did not retain the predominance in the French and Indian War it had demonstrated in the previous three. It launched no major expeditions of its own; nor did fighting center in the New England region, although for two years Governor Shirley succeeded Edward Braddock as commander in chief after the latter's death in 1754. However, in part because of the province's crusading zeal and a large supply of young men anxious for military pay, Massachusetts enlisted far more troops to support the British army and for frontier duty, and spent much more money, than any other colony. Massachusetts enlisted 7,000 men annually from 1755 to 1759; 5,000 in 1760; and 3,000 each year from 1761 until 1763. Massachusetts's tax bill rose to the astronomical sum of £100,000 in 1759 and 1760. To pay off a £500,000 war debt without inflation, the sum rose to nearly £200,000 in 1765 (the year Britain imposed the Stamp Tax, supposedly because the colonies did not support their own defense) and remained at £75,000 or more until 1772. Even Francis Bernard, the province's governor from 1760 to 1769, termed this "an immense sum for such a small state! The burden of which has been grievously felt by all men." England acknowledged Massachusetts's effort by returning £352,000 sterling (of a total colonial reimbursement of nearly £1 million).

But money was only one of Massachusetts's wartime problems. In the winter of 1757, John Campbell, the earl of Loudoun, sought to quarter in Boston the soldiers and sailors who were to participate in that summer's (unsuccessful) expedition to retake Louisbourg. When the province refused, fearing disorderly conduct, he had to threaten to quarter them by force. He thereby compelled the admittance of the troops to empty buildings and Castle William in Boston Harbor. Massachusetts's own troops mutinied at least 11 times in the course of the war, usually over not being paid, being held in service beyond their annual enlistments, being subjected to British rather than their own officers, or being sent to locations for which they had not explicitly enlisted. Impressments continued despite the best

efforts of Massachusetts's governors to persuade the navy to desist. Worst of all, as Boston's economy declined following almost two decades of hostilities, the city became a test case for tighter British customs enforcement. In part provoked by colonial trading with the enemy, the crackdown proved a poor reward for the province which had expended the most men and money in the common cause since 1689. While Massachusetts's war effort was not a direct cause of the American Revolution, Britain's refusal to appreciate it and the determination to make the bay colony bear the brunt of imperial reorganization in the 1760s and 1770s clearly added to its resentment. Even a loyalist, Isaac Royall, personally pleading with his friend Lord Dartmouth to forgive the Bostonians for the Tea Party, argued the connection:

This province, Sir, has always been foremost, even beyond its ability, and notwithstanding the present unhappy disputes would perhaps be so again if there should be the like occasion for it in promoting the honor of the king and nation. Witness their many expensive and heroic efforts against the common enemy.

William Pencak

References
Fred Anderson, *A People's Army: Massachusetts Soldiers in the French and Indian War* (1984); Charles E. Clark, *The Eastern Frontier: The Settlement of Northern New England, 1601–1763* (1970); Philip S. Haffenden, *New England in the English Nation, 1689–1713* (1974); Richard R. Johnson, *Adjustment to Empire: The New England Colonies, 1675–1715* (1981); Everett Kimball, *The Career of Joseph Dudley* (1911); Douglas E. Leach, *Flintlock and Tomahawk: New England in King Philip's War* (1958); ———, *The Northern Colonial Frontier, 1607–1763* (1966).

John G. Palfrey, *A Compendious History of New England*, 5 vols. (1856–1890); William Pencak, *War, Politics, and Revolution in Provincial Massachusetts* (1981); John A. Schutz, *Thomas Pownall: British Defender of American Liberty* (1951); ———, *William Shirley: King's Governor of Massachusetts* (1961); Alden T. Vaughan, *New England Frontier: Puritans and Indians, 1620–1675* (1965).

See also ACADIA, NEW ENGLAND ATTACK ON (1690); ACADIA, NEW ENGLAND ATTACK ON (1707); CANADA, NEW ENGLAND EXPEDITION AGAINST (1690); CARTAGENA, EXPEDITION AGAINST; CHURCH, BENJAMIN; DOMINION OF NEW ENGLAND; DUMMER'S WAR; IMPRESSMENT, NAVY; KING GEORGE'S WAR; KING PHILIP'S WAR; KING WILLIAM'S WAR; MAINE; FORT MASSACHUSETTS (MASSACHUSETTS); NEW ENGLAND CONFEDERATION; PEQUOT WAR; PRAYING INDIANS; PURITANS; QUEEN ANNE'S WAR; SCALP BOUNTIES; SEVEN YEARS' WAR; SHIRLEY, WILLIAM; WINTHROP, JOHN

Fort Massachusetts (Massachusetts)

In 1744, with the outbreak of war between England and France, Massachusetts hastily constructed three simple log forts to protect the province's extreme western settlements in what later became Berkshire County. These were Fort Shirley (at present-day Heath), Fort Pelham (at Rowe), and the largest, Fort Massachusetts, at East Hoosac on the Housatonic River (the present town of Adams), 25 miles east of Albany. Although normally garrisoned by 50 men commanded by Ephraim Williams, future founder of Williams College, the company was reduced to 22 in the summer of 1746. With Massachusetts planning a major expedition to attack the French fort at Crown Point, it did not expect an attack. However, in August, a combined force of French regulars, Canadians, and Abenaki Indians, variously estimated at between 700 and 1,200, moved on the small detachment commanded by Sergeant John Hawks of Deerfield. Although only ten of his men were fit to fight, Hawks held out for 28 hours, killing 16 of the enemy and losing only three men of his own, before negotiating a surrender. Even though he had promised the captives to the Indians, French leader Pierre de Rigaud de Vaudreuil, the major who commanded at Trois Rivières, guaranteed the safety of the prisoners until they could be taken to Canada and exchanged for French captives. Thanks to Vaudreuil's influence, his Indian allies not only left the prisoners in peace, but carried or gave up horses to the sick and wounded. One of the five women (there were also three children) at the fort, Mrs. John Smead, gave birth to a daughter, christened Captivity, on the long trip to Montreal and Quebec. (Both mother and daughter died of disease in Canada.) Vaudreuil's force burned Fort Massachusetts to the ground, killed three men and a boy on the outskirts of Deerfield, and sacked the Dutch settlement at Hoosac in New York before returning to Canada. Massachusetts quickly rebuilt the fort, but it saw no further military action until it was demolished in 1759 with the French demise imminent.

William Pencak

References

Francis Parkman, *A Half-Century of Conflict, 1700–1750* (1892).

See also FORT PELHAM (MASSACHUSETTS); RIGAUD DE VAUDREUIL DE CAVAGNIAL, PIERRE DE; FORT SHIRLEY (MASSACHUSETTS)

Fort Matanzas (Florida)

The location of a blockhouse and garrison constructed on the orders of Pedro Menéndez de Avilés in 1569 to fortify the south entrance to the Matanzas River. The fort's function was to guard against an attack on Menéndez's principal settlement, St. Augustine, 18 miles to the north. Matanzas marked the southernmost boundary of effective Spanish control in the province of La Florida.

The area takes its name (literally, "slaughters") from Menéndez's execution in 1565 of French prisoners who were fleeing from a Spanish attack on Fort Caroline, located at the mouth of the St. Johns River. Acting on the orders of the king of Spain, Philip II, to "use any means" to extirpate French threats to Spain's control of the area, Menéndez executed Protestant soldiers, including the leader of the expedition, Jean Ribault, but spared the lives of those who professed to be Catholic.

Sherry Johnson

References

Verne E. Chatelain, *The Defenses of Spanish Florida 1565 to 1763* (1941); Paul S. Hoffman, *The Spanish Crown and the Defense of the Caribbean, 1535–1585: Precedent, Patrimonialism, and Royal Parsimony* (1980); Eugene Lyon, *The Enterprise of Florida: Pedro Menéndez de Avilés and the Spanish Conquest of 1565–1568* (1976).

See also MENÉNDEZ DE AVILÉS, PEDRO; RIBAULT, JEAN

M

Fort Mattapony (Virginia)

Fort Mattapony was built in 1657 near the present site of Walkerton in King and Queen County. Councilor Edward Digges, who later served as interim governor of the colony, laid out the fort, and Major (later Colonel) Thomas Walker served as its commandant. Named for the Mattapony Indian tribe that still inhabits a reservation near Walkerton, Fort Mattapony was torn down in 1677, and a second fort was built further west near the present town of Milford in Caroline County. This fort was abandoned or destroyed in 1678.

Thomas Costa

References

Philip Alexander Bruce, *Institutional History of Virginia in the Seventeenth Century,* 2 vols. (1910): 2.

Fort Matuxon (Virginia)

See FORT MANASKIN (VIRGINIA)

Fort Maurepas (Mississippi)

Pierre Le Moyne d'Iberville, leader of the French expedition that founded Louisiana, established that colony's first settlement in April 1699, overlooking Biloxi Bay (in modern-day Ocean Springs, Mississippi). Named for the French colonial minister, Fort Maurepas consisted of eight barracks, a warehouse, powder magazine, oven, and forge inside a well-built palisade measuring about 134 feet on a side. Two of the four bastions were constructed, in the *pièce-sur-pièce* style, of squared timbers one-and-a-half-feet thick, laid one on another, and dovetailed at the corners. Inside these two bastions were officers quarters and a chapel. Armament included swivel guns and eight-pounder cannons.

Iberville appointed Ensign Sauvole commandant of the new post and left a garrison of 80 men, including soldiers, sailors, Canadians, indentured servants from France, six cabin boys who were billeted in local Indian villages to learn native languages, and buccaneers who had enlisted with the expedition during its layover in Saint Domingue (Haiti). The colony supported itself by trading for corn and venison from nearby Indian tribes, especially the Mobile Indians. Because no major rivers flowed into Biloxi Bay, however, the garrison had difficulty maintaining contact with the interior tribes they depended upon for provisions, trade, and military alliances.

The fort was intended only as temporary headquarters for the colony until a more suitable town location could be found. After three years of vacillation, Iberville finally settled on a site on the Mobile River for his new town and fort, Fort Louis. Sauvole had died of a fever in August 1701, so his successor—Iberville's brother, Jean-Baptiste Le Moyne de Bienville—directed the dismantling of Fort Maurepas and relocation of the colony in January 1702. The abandoned fort site was briefly reused by the French in the 1720s for the site of the Biloxi concessions.

Gregory A. Waselkov

References

Marcel Giraud, *A History of French Louisiana, Vol. I, The Reign of Louis XIV, 1698–1715,* trans., Joseph C. Lambert (1974); Jay Higginbotham, *Fort Maurepas: The Birth of Louisiana* (1968); Richebourg G. McWilliams, ed., *Iberville's Gulf Journals* (1981); Samuel Wilson, Jr., "Colonial Fortifications and Military Architecture in the Mississippi Valley," in *The French in the Mississippi Valley,* ed. by J.F. McDermott (1965):103–122.

See also LE MOYNE DE BIENVILLE, JEAN-BAPTISTE; LE MOYNE D'IBERVILLE, PIERRE; FORT LOUIS (ALABAMA)

Medical Services

During the eighteenth century, basic medical policy for the British army was set at the War Office, the king's consent usually being pro forma. Working through the secretary at war, the surgeon general and (secondarily) the physician general dominated before 1756, when, in a major restructuring, William Augustus, duke of Cumberland created the position of inspector of regimental infirmaries and gave it to Robert Adair. Until his death in 1790, Adair dominated medical policy and major appointments, his advice being almost automatically accepted. Charm aided him, and so did his promotion of cost-cutting schemes. But he was also able, and he dealt with a vast range of problems.

In theaters of war, the general hospital was the most important medical institution, for both administration and treatment. "Hospital" referred to the institution, facility, and staff alike. Hospital physicians and surgeons were the elite of army medical personnel. Other staff included apothecaries and surgeons' mates (also, prior to 1763, some apothecary's mates). Since any staff member might be detached to serve a remote garrison, responsibility could be heavy. "Servants" included the matron, though she was sometimes classed as staff (e.g., Charlotte Browne, matron in North America, 1755–1763). Nurses, most of whom were soldiers' wives, often served reluctantly, but were nevertheless heavily relied upon. Beyond them, a large number of laborers, artisans, and servants were employed by the hospital at any time.

Regimental medical personnel for foot regiments usually included a surgeon and one mate, but because of the size of regiments, two mates were allowed most regiments serving in America, 1758–1760. In many regiments, a nurse helped maintain the infirmary. Regimental personnel usually handled less serious cases, while patients with more difficult or serious problems were taken to hospital facilities. However, they also handled emergency situations, such as epidemics or battle-related injuries. The army employed two other categories of medical officers. Medical personnel were on establishments for most major garrisons. Expeditionary hospitals were often created for particular enterprises (e.g., those to Guadaloupe and Havana).

The quality of medical facilities was generally poor. Preexisting structures (homes, barns, churches) were often rented or appropriated. For a force that was in camp or on the march, huts or tents were thrown up. Medical writers emphasized hospital sanitation and recommended structures that were spacious, airy, and allowed for the isolation of contagious cases. The institution of the general hospital was criticized by many writers because hospital facilities tended to be crowded, increasing the likelihood of epidemics. In fact, facilities at all levels were often cramped and filthy.

Virtually all medical officers had some legitimate training. Many had served apprenticeships and some had a university background, though an M.D. acquired prior to service was rare. However, the practical experience of medical officers prior to appointment was often limited. Most had not had a private practice and they were generally young: the average for regimental surgeons at appointment was about 23; for mates, 20. Senior hospital staff were typically older, better educated, and more experienced than regimental personnel. There was usually

some inquiry made into the credentials of any would-be medical officer prior to his appointment. Many applicants were examined by the board of the Company of Surgeons (London), and senior hospital staff abroad sometimes reviewed candidates. However, examinations tended to be quick and easy, and few failed.

On all levels, but particularly the regimental and garrison, the advice of medical personnel was often ignored. Patients sometimes refused recommended courses of treatment, especially operations, and they often stopped taking medicines as soon as they were released from a medical facility, thereby prompting a relapse. The relationship of officers to the medical services was pivotal and complex. Many officers (e.g., Forbes) had medical training, and some entered the army as regimental surgeons' mates. Some commanding officers took pride in personally supervising efforts to promote the health of their troops. Officers regularly inspected medical facilities and checked to see what was lacking. Furthermore, commanding officers often translated the advice of medical personnel (e.g., on sanitation, inoculation) into orders, particularly when the advice came from senior hospital staff. However, orders sometimes were not passed down or were not enforced. Many officers, moreover, disparaged regimental staff, ignored their advice, and removed patients from their care, sending serious cases to hospital facilities and forcing men with lesser ailments back on duty, often prematurely.

The health of the mid-eighteenth century British army suffered from a host of man-made problems. Shortages of food, medicines, and other supplies were often avoidable. Despite constant warnings by medical officers and writers, encampments were often sited in unhealthy places, even when no strategic considerations suggested the choice. Camps and barracks were often filthy, and orders to counter this were widely ignored, as were those that encouraged bathing and good grooming. And when troops were being quartered in a town, the health and welfare of troops was often ignored by owners of billets, especially innkeepers. But probably the worst man-made problem was alcohol abuse. Alcoholism was widespread, and although officers condemned excessive drinking, they encouraged it through liquor rations and by using liquor to pay for labor. Poorly distilled or adulterated spirits killed some troops, while lead in liquor caused many health problems (e.g., "Dry Belly-Ache"). Furthermore, although rations were ample and generally provided a better diet for soldiers than was enjoyed by most civilians, this advantage was undone by the fact men often traded rations for liquor. This practice was made easier by the fact messing was not regulated and troops were often scattered among billets, rather than concentrated in barracks.

Prior to the French and Indian War, British medical services in the New World were only on the regimental, garrison, and expeditionary levels. The general hospital in North America was first created in November 1754. From the start, it was dominated by the director, James Napier. It served virtually intact on General Edward Braddock's expedition. Though some medical staff stayed at the fort, most, including Napier, followed Braddock and were present at the climactic battle. After the defeat of Braddock's army and the subsequent retreat to Philadelphia, Napier recommended breaking up the hospital. Instead, he was given greater authority, and in 1756, the hospital gained a central facility at Albany. The size of hospital staff increased steadily from 1756–1760, roughly keeping pace with an increasing commitment of British regulars.

Each of the successive commanders in chief had a major impact on medical services, but not always a positive one. William Shirley created confusion in the hospital through capricious appointments and dismissals. Lord Loudoun promoted the career of his protégé, Richard Huck, installing him as hospital physician, but he also cooperated with Napier in hospital matters. He was quite concerned for the health of his troops and encouraged camp sanitation. James Abercromby generally followed Loudoun's policies, but while Loudoun had encouraged the treatment of provincial troops in British hospital facilities, Abercromby banished them. Jeffrey Amherst reverted to Loudoun's policy on provincials and generally cooperated with hospital staff, especially Napier, but he was cost-conscious and wanted to see the staff used in such a way as to save expense. After the fall of Montreal, staff was divided among many outposts, often serving in lieu of regimental personnel.

Although it was standard practice to disband the hospital at the close of a war, Thomas Gage delayed doing so as long as possible; on several occasions vainly asking the War Office for permission to reestablish the hospital. Failing to persuade his superiors, he retained some personnel on a staff basis. During his early years as commander in chief, much of the army was isolated in frontier garrisons, and regimental and garrison personnel were spread thin. However, large garrisons were well served, and although there were a few major outbreaks of illness, the troops were generally healthy, except in the Floridas.

There has been a tendency among medical historians (there are exceptions) to deprecate pre-nineteenth-century medicine and surgery. This carries over into military/medical history as eighteenth-century army medical personnel are often dismissed as quacks and butchers, whose craft was primitive, if not barbaric. On the contrary, evidence suggests gross incompetence was rare, that senior hospital staff was usually strong, and that medical officers overall were probably somewhat more competent than were the general run of British practitioners. Their advice to officers on ways to prevent disease among the troops (e.g., improving sanitation, reducing alcoholism) tended to be prudent, and they were capable of handling several major diseases. Indeed, during the French and Indian War, medical services in North America enjoyed major successes. The greatest medical triumph was the conquest of scurvy, which was a scourge throughout the French and Indian War, although rarely a problem after 1763 except in siege situations. The cultivation of gardens to provide troops with fresh vegetables, coupled with the use of antiscorbutics, especially spruce beer, accounted for this change. In the same few years, the danger of smallpox was reduced through inoculation, a practice introduced by Loudoun and employed more generally thereafter.

Americans admired British army medical organization, patterned their own on it during the Revolution and afterwards, and also were heavily influenced by British medicine. It is probably fair to say British services were among the finest of the time and they reflected the best in eighteenth-century medicine.

Paul E. Kopperman

References
Paul E. Kopperman, "Medical Services in the British Army, 1742–1783," *Journal of the History of Medicine and Allied Sciences,* 34 (1979):428–455.

See also SICKNESS AND MORTALITY

Menéndez, Francisco (c. 1700–1772)

Francisco Menéndez was captain of the militia which garrisoned the town of Gracia Real de Santa Teresa de Mose, two miles north of St. Augustine. Mose was composed of slaves who had fled the English colonies and been freed in Spanish Florida in return for their conversion to Catholicism. Menéndez was a Mandingo, born in West Africa about 1700. Enslaved and taken to South Carolina, he escaped to join the Yamasee War against the planters in the 1720s. He and other slaves fought for more than three years with the Yamasee before their defeat. Menéndez then joined the Yamasee exodus to Spanish Florida where Governor Antonio de Benavides first appointed him captain of the slave militia in 1726. This militia helped repulse the English invasion led by Colonel John Palmer in 1728. Menéndez was reappointed by each successive Spanish governor and freed by Governor Manuel de Montiano in 1738. In that year, Menéndez became the leader of the newly established town of Mose and captain of its militia. The Mose militia provided reconnaissance for the Spanish during the War of Jenkins' Ear, participated in the battle of "Bloody Mose" in 1740, and in the Spanish counterattack on St. Simons Island, Georgia, in 1742. Menéndez was a literate man who petitioned the king for remuneration for the "loyalty, zeal and love I have always demonstrated in the royal service, in the encounters with the enemy . . . ." Menéndez took a corsairing commission and battled the English on the Atlantic until he was captured, tortured, and sold into slavery in the Bahamas. He somehow managed to return to St. Augustine and resume his command at Mose by at least 1752. Menéndez and his guerrilla forces served on the frontier from that time until the Spanish evacuation of Florida in 1763. After almost 40 years of service to the Spanish crown, Menéndez led his community of freed slaves into exile in Matanzas, Cuba.

Jane Landers

References

Jane Landers, "Gracia Real de Santa Teresa de Mose: A Free Black Town in Spanish Florida," *American Historical Review,* 95 (1990):9–30; Richard Price, ed., *Maroon Societies, Rebel Slave Communities in the Americas* (1976).

See also AFRICAN AMERICANS; BLACK AND INDIAN MILITIAS; FLORIDA; MONTIANO, MANUEL DE; YAMASEE WAR

Menéndez de Avilés, Pedro (1519–1574)

Pedro Menéndez de Avilés was born in 1519 in Avilés, Spain. He came from the ranks of the lower nobility of his home province of Asturias. From his youngest days, he was involved in life at sea. In the early 1540s, he owned his own ship, and by 1548, he was receiving royal commissions to sail against corsairs who infested Spanish coastal waters. His first voyage to the Spanish Indies occurred in 1550. He would come to dominate the Indies trade, known as the *carrera de Indias.* After his first voyage, on his return to Spain, he proposed a method of eliminating the corsair threat from the Indies fleet. The Council of the Indies granted him the rank of captain general of the Indies fleet, giving him a great degree of freedom in organizing operations within the fleet. While the Indies trade was ostensibly controlled by the Seville merchants' guild, the *consulado,* there were a significant number of Asturian and other northern merchants and captains, among whom Menéndez moved easily.

Before Menéndez could act on his commission, he was called into service for Prince Philip of Spain. The Prince was betrothed to Mary Tudor, and Menéndez became part of the military contingent that accompanied him to England for the wedding. The years of 1554 and 1555 were spent between Spain, England, and Flanders.

In 1555, Menéndez first acted on his commission in the Indies fleet. He was placed in charge of the ships going to Veracruz, and Alvaro Sánchez commanded the ships going to Panama. While the two contingents sailed out from Spain together, the return voyages were at different times. Menéndez acquitted himself well in the passage, but was arrested on his return on charges of smuggling. While convicted by the officials of the *Casa de Contratación* (House of Trade), the Council of the Indies overturned the ruling and reinstated Menéndez. Although reappointed as captain general of the next fleet, Menéndez was called into service in European waters. In 1555–1560, he was fighting corsairs and maintaining communications between Flanders, England, and Spain.

After 1560, Pedro Menéndez de Avilés concentrated his efforts on the *carrera de Indias.* Up until this time, ships sailing to the New World had routinely sailed in convoy on a more or less organized basis, especially in time of war. The decade of the 1550s was especially critical due to the ongoing warfare with the French. During

M

that decade, the Spanish perfected the large galleon. This ship often displaced 500 tons or more and was used to accompany fleets of merchants vessels through corsair-infested waters. It carried several ranks of cannon for broadside combat and was a significant fighting vessel. During the early 1560s, Menéndez drew on the experience of earlier captains general, especially his fellow Northerner, the great Admiral Alvaro de Bazán, and developed the fleet system. The fleet system had become routine by 1564 and would remain so for most of the rest of the Spanish colonial era.

Under the fleet system, merchant vessels were organized into convoys accompanied by from two to eight galleons. Ships sailing for Mexico and the Caribbean would leave Sanlúcar de Barrameda on the Atlantic coast of Andalucia in May. Entering the Caribbean through the Mona Passage, ships bound for Honduras and the Greater Antilles would leave the convoy, with the remainder of the fleet sailing on to Veracruz. Ships destined for the Isthmus of Panama and the Peruvian trade would leave Sanlúcar in August and enter the Caribbean through the Windward Islands. That fleet would then go to Nombre de Dios in Panama and off-load its goods. The goods destined for Peru would be carried across the isthmus, then reloaded on the Pacific fleet for the voyage to Callao. The isthmus fleet would winter in Cartagena, which, although it had little commercial importance, was the naval heart of the southern Caribbean. The isthmus fleet would then sail in January toward Havana and the Mexican fleet would sail in February. Both contingents would rendezvous in Havana for the final passage back to Spain.

Menéndez effectively shifted the center of the Spanish Caribbean from Santo Domingo, where it had been since the times of Columbus, to Havana, which now had to have the infrastructure to support the fleet operations for the whole of the New World. The system developed by Menéndez placed a premium on security. It was an expensive undertaking, since the crown had to pay the costs of the armed escort, offset partially by a tax placed on fleet goods. The fleet system was also rather slow, since the whole fleet would sail no faster than the slowest ship. Likewise the long winter delays in the Indies ports prohibited a fast turn-around. Yet with it, Menéndez became the unrivaled master of the *carrera de Indias*.

In 1563, Menéndez was again arrested by port officials in Seville and had to suffer imprisonment from August till January. During this same time, his son, Juan Menéndez, was lost at sea and presumed dead while commanding one of the ships of the Mexican fleet on the homeward leg. While imprisoned, Pedro Menéndez became interested in the security implications of newly reported French colonization in Florida. From as far north as Santa Helena, in modern-day Georgia, to the southern area of the peninsula, there were reports of French activity. The presence of the French posed a major threat to the fleet system, since the combined fleets returned to Spain laden with New World silver in the Gulf Stream, barely a few miles off the Florida coast. In March of 1565, Menéndez concluded a contract with the Spanish crown to undertake a settlement in Florida with the dual purpose of driving out the French and permanently establishing Spanish communities to discourage further incursions from other powers. For his efforts, Menéndez was awarded the title of *adelantado* and captain general of Florida.

At the same time Menéndez was preparing his expedition, the French were making ready a small fleet, under Jean Ribault, to send reinforcements to their Florida settlement. The French fleet departed in late May 1565. Menéndez, after months of delays and frustrations, was able to set sail from Cádiz on 27 June, with part of his fleet departing from Asturias and Santander in the north. The Cádiz fleet stopped for water and other supplies in the Canaries, and began the Atlantic crossing on 8 July. Only two weeks out the little convoy of eight ships was struck by a major storm, perhaps a hurricane. One ship was lost, three others blown off course, with one of those eventually falling into French hands. Menéndez made repairs in Puerto Rico and departed on 17 August with four ships.

On 4 September, the Menéndez fleet caught sight of the French off the Florida coast. The two fleets engaged, with the Spanish forcing the French to run. Menéndez then put ashore and established his permanent base at St. Augustine on 8 September. While the Spanish were still unloading and settling in at St. Augustine, most of the French forces put to sea in an attempt to attack the Spanish. The Spanish caught sight of the approaching French and were able to put to sea to meet them. A fight ensued, but a storm dispersed the French, driving them as far to the south as Cape Canaveral. Menéndez then marched his men overland to the French fort, La Caroline, which the Spanish had an easy time taking. Over the next few months, Menéndez was busy mopping up French stragglers. Menéndez dealt summarily with the French prisoners thus captured. At least two groups were executed on the banks of the inlet south of St. Augustine, thus giving the river its name, Matanzas (Slaughter).

Once in control of Florida, Menéndez sailed in a small boat to Cuba. There he encountered the northern half of his fleet. After many tribulations, he was able to send two relief ships north to St. Augustine. They returned with news of mutinies. Menéndez sent more supplies and men to put down the mutineers. He then began the exploration of the southwestern coast of Florida. He felt the peninsula was cut in half by a river, from the St. Johns on the east to a point on the Gulf. He wished to establish another fort on the western outlet. With word of yet more mutinies, Menéndez returned to St. Augustine in March 1566. He successfully put down the mutinies and hunted the remaining French who had evaded capture.

In August 1566, Menéndez shifted the capital of Florida from St. Augustine to Santa Elena, located in modern Georgia. In September, he promulgated 17 ordinances for the civil and military governance of Spanish Florida. Menéndez kept up a hectic pace in leading expeditions, managing the affairs of the colony while still serving as a crown official, and maintaining a presence in Cuba and Santo Domingo. In late 1566 and 1567, he was concerned with improving fortifications in the northern Caribbean and Gulf of Mexico. The provisioning of Florida and the supply of the new forts was a continual problem. Finally, in May 1567, Menéndez returned to Spain.

On his return to court, Philip II greeted the *adelantado* warmly. Menéndez had earlier been initiated into the highly prestigious military-religious order of Santiago. Philip now had him made an officer (*comendador*) administering one of the order's agricultural estates. The monarch also appointed him governor of Cuba and captain general of the new armada, which was intended to defend the Caribbean. All of these honors carried with them incomes, which were desperately needed by Menéndez to continue supporting the Florida adventure. Menéndez negotiated with the Jesuits to establish missions in Florida, and he oversaw the baptism of five Florida Indians in the cathedral of Seville.

Pedro Menéndez de Avilés was active in Spain, securing additional concessions and guaranteeing what he had gained, as well as putting together reinforcements for the Florida outposts. He was finally able to return as captain general of a small relief armada of nine ships in 1571. On his arrival in Florida, he discovered only the principal fortifications, San Mateo, St. Augustine, and Santa Elena, were still occupied. After settling matters in Florida, he went to Havana where, with three galleons, he sailed to Spain with the 1572 return fleet—never again to see Florida.

After arriving in Spain in 1572, Menéndez continued to enjoy royal favor. Philip was planning an attack on England, and Menéndez emerged as the leader of that armada. Nevertheless, the *adelantado* died in Santander before the armada was organized. His death was one of the causes for the postponement of the attack. He was buried in his home town of Avilés.

John F. Schwaller

References
Alfonso Camin, *El adelantado de la Florida* (1944); Eugene Lyon, *The Enterprise of Florida: Pedro Menéndez de Avilés and the Spanish Conquest of 1565–1568* (1974).

See also CALUSA; FLORIDA; FORT CAROLINE (FLORIDA); COUNCIL OF INDIES; LAUDONNIÈRE, RENÉ GOULAINE DE; RIBAULT, JEAN; FORT MATANZAS (FLORIDA); ST. AUGUSTINE; TEQUESTA

Metacom (Metacomet)
See PHILIP

Fort Miami (Michigan)
René-Robert Cavelier de La Salle obtained royal permission to reconnoiter the interior of North America in 1678. While carrying out this task on 1 November 1679, he and his men arrived at the mouth of the St. Joseph River seeking a convenient portage to the Illinois River. Fort Miami was built on a bluff above the river and measured 30 by 40 feet. It was used for several weeks before the expedition pushed on to the Illinois Indians. La Salle visited the fort in March 1680 and again in late January 1681, after which it was abandoned.

Russell M. Magnaghi

Miantonomo (?–1643)
Co-sachem with his uncle, Canonicus, of the strong Narragansett tribe of New England,

Miantonomo learned the pain of resisting Puritan designs. Initially, Miantonomo worked with the growing English contingent in New England. After the deaths of Captain John Stone (1634) and John Oldham (1636), for example, Miantonomo sought to locate and punish the perpetrators. Then in 1637, Miantonomo added 300–500 Narragansett warriors to the Mohegan-Puritan force marching on the Pequot village, Mystic Fort, even though he had serious doubts concerning the outcome of the attack. After the Pequot War, Miantonomo joined the Mohegans and English in signing the Hartford Treaty (Tripartite Treaty) in September 1638, which stipulated the Mohegan and Narragansett tribes would remain at peace. If disagreements challenged that peace, the English would adjudicate.

Unlike Uncas, however, Miantonomo refused to resign any more of his authority to the English. Miantonomo especially alienated the Puritans when he gave refuge to arch-heretics such as Roger Williams and Samuel Gorton. In the fall of 1640, the Massachusetts government summoned Miantonomo to answer charges of fomenting a pan-Indian conspiracy against the English. Miantonomo skillfully deflected the accusations, countering that the allegations sounded like the work of Uncas. Although Connecticut and Plymouth leaders remained skeptical of Miantonomo's loyalty, after two days of questioning, Massachusetts leaders released him with a stern warning. Rumors of a Narragansett plot continued to circulate, and though Puritan officials could not find sufficient evidence to declare war, they actively challenged Miantonomo. In 1643, Massachusetts leaders again commanded Miantonomo to appear, this time to answer charges of a conspiracy on Uncas's life. Then in June 1643, John Winthrop accepted the formal subservience of Saconomoco and Pumham (sub-sachems under Miantonomo) to English rule, thus undercutting Miantonomo's control of the Narragansett (Rhode Island) region.

Later that summer, strained relations between Uncas and Sequasson (sachem from the Connecticut River region and ally of Miantonomo) erupted into hostilities. Connecticut Governor John Haynes decided not to intervene, and Uncas seized the opportunity to inflict seven or eight deaths and wound 13. Hearing of Uncas's attack, Miantonomo asked the Massachusetts government for license to go to Sequasson's aid. Believing that Winthrop had given him the necessary assurances, Miantonomo moved

against Uncas's 300–400 men with 900–1,000 Narragansetts. Uncas turned the tables, however, and captured Miantonomo in a rout. Uncas presented Miantonomo before the Hartford government, asking for instructions. The Connecticut leaders, however, deferred to the commissioners of the newly formed United Colonies (a military alliance of Massachusetts Bay, Plymouth, Connecticut, and New Haven) who were scheduled to meet in September at Boston. After a conversation between the commissioners and community elders, the commissioners decided to return Miantonomo to Uncas and allow a "civil" execution. On the road between Hartford and Windsor, Uncas's brother slammed a tomahawk into the back of Miantonomo's head, thus ending the life of a powerful leader who challenged the New World's order.

Richard C. Goode

References

"Relation of the Indian Plot," *Collections of the Massachusetts Historical Society*, 3rd ser., 3 (1833):161–164; John A. Sainsbury, "Miantonomo's Death and New England Politics, 1630–1645," *Rhode Island History* 30 (1971):110–123; John Winthrop, *A Declaration of Former Passages and Proceedings Betwixt the English and the Narragansett* (1645); ———, *Winthrop's Journal: "History of New England," 1630–1649*, 2 vols., ed. by James Kendall Hosmer (1908).

See also NARRAGANSETT; NEW ENGLAND CONFEDERATION; PEQUOT WAR; UNCAS

Fort Michilimackinac (Michigan)

The Straits of Mackinac were an important strategic location dominating the Great Lakes. After the establishment of Detroit in 1701, unlicensed traders returned to the region because of the excellent furs traded by the Indians. After serious consideration, the French government in 1715 dispatched Constant Le Marchand de Lignery to establish a new post on the south side of the straits.

During the summer the French soldiers constructed a square palisaded fort with blockhouses and armed with six iron cannons. Within the walls resided the military garrison and some of the traders, while outside arose a small settlement of métis, Indians, and Frenchmen. The soldiers were paid with powder and bullets and traded these items for profitable furs. During the summer, hundreds of Indians came to trade and French traders traveled as far as New Mexico.

The fort served its military function well. It served as a staging area for the French attacks on the Fox of Wisconsin. It was from Fort Michilimackinac that Charles Langlade, Jr., led large war parties of Ottawa and French into Ohio to attack the English and their Indian allies in the 1750s.

With the defeat of the French in the French and Indian War, the French surrendered Fort Michilimackinac on 1 October 1761 to Captain Henry Balfour. Thirty men of the 60th Regiment (the Royal Americans) were stationed at the fort, which was duly strengthened. Due to the negative attitude of the British, the Indians grew angry and longed for the French. During Pontiac's War the fort fell to the Indians in the middle of a lacrosse game in June 1763. A number of soldiers and a trader were killed, and after some tense days, the British prisoners were returned to Montreal. The British changed their attitude and policy toward the Indians and reentered the fort in September 1764, and thereafter maintained excellent relations with the Indians.

For the soldiers and officers, life at the fort was monotonous, especially during the long winters. During the 1760s, Major Robert Rogers served as commandant and dreamed of a great interior colony. Arrested for treason and acquitted, he died in London a ruined man. Major Arent De Peyster was so bored that he kept a number of pets as a diversion. However, the resident traders like John Askin, with their black and Indian slaves and abundant provisions, found life quite pleasant.

During the American Revolution, the fort was used as a staging area for attacks on Spanish St. Louis (May 1780) and Indian raids as far south as Kentucky. However, there were also rumors the Americans planned to attack the fort, which it could not sustain. As a result, the British obtained land on Mackinac Island by treaty from the Indians in 1780 and occupied Fort Mackinac, which was located on a formidable bluff overlooking the straits, in July 1782.

The sandy site of Fort Michilimackinac remained abandoned and windswept for 70 years. Today the fort has been reconstructed and is operated as a state park.

Russell M. Magnaghi

References

David Armour and Keith R. Widder, *At the Crossroads: Michilimackinac during the American Revolution* (1978); Walter Havighurst, *Three Flags at the Straits: The Forts of Mackinac* (1966); Louise P. Kellogg, *The French Regime in Wisconsin and the Northwest* (1925); ———, *The British Regime in Wisconsin and the Northwest* (1935); N.V. Russell, *The British Regime in Michigan and the Old Northwest, 1760–1796* (1939).

See also FORT BUADE (MICHIGAN); FOX; OTTAWA; PONTIAC'S WAR; ROGERS, ROBERT

Middle Plantation, Treaty of
See VIRGINIA-INDIAN TREATY (1677/1680)

Militia

The militia in the English colonies evolved from the ancient Anglo-Saxon fyrd, which was based on the obligation of every member of society to participate in the common defense. After the Norman Conquest in 1066, the military responsibilities of the militia, as the latinized fyrd was called, gradually dwindled as medieval monarchs relied more and more on mercenaries and a hereditary warrior class to fight their wars. By 1600, the English militia was essentially moribund. Only a fraction of the middle and upper classes were enrolled; training was infrequent and ineffective; and weapons were scarce and often obsolete. The peculiar nature of the English colonial experience in North America led to a revival of the militia in the New World. Because the early English colonies were undercapitalized commercial enterprises rather than government projects, the colonists could not rely on royal military forces or expensive mercenaries for protection. As no one else would defend them, they had to defend themselves. The initial landing parties in Chesapeake Bay and New England usually included veterans of the wars in Ireland or the Netherlands, such as John Smith and Miles Standish. Their responsibility was to train the rest of the colonists in the military arts and provide military leadership in times of crisis. As the years passed and the early colonies became established, these ad hoc military arrangements were formalized by law and custom into English-style militias. (It is correct to speak of the colonial militias in the plural form because each colony had a distinct paramilitary institution, but for the sake of simplicity the singular term, militia, is used hereafter.)

The early colonial militia was a curious mix of Old World traditions and New World innovations. Certain features of the English militia which seemed appropriate for the wilderness, or which were too deeply ingrained in the English psyche to abandon, existed side by side with other features developed after considerable trial and error in conflict with the Indians. On training days and other formal occasions, for example, colonial militiamen beat drums and blew bugles, practiced the manual of arms, and paraded about their village greens in the best European tradition. But when danger threatened, these same militiamen took up muskets and hatchets, assembled into small bands, rendezvoused with Indian allies, and set out after their enemies through the endless forest.

The foundation of the militia was the town or county infantry company. A typical company was composed of most men in the community. A company was not a combat unit and rarely went into battle as such. It served primarily as a reservoir from which reasonably well-trained and well-equipped militiamen could be called up for active duty on an expedition or other assignment. Rangers, dragoons, minute companies, and other specialized units soon appeared as the colonists experimented with various ways of dealing with the unusual problems posed by the Indians. Arms and armaments evolved as well. Early colonial militiamen clanked around in helmets, armor, and carried swords, pikes, and clumsy matchlock muskets. By the middle of the seventeenth century, however, these burdensome medieval accouterments gave way to padded coats, hatchets, and lightweight flintlock muskets as the colonists discovered the importance of mobility in irregular warfare.

The colonial militia usually is described as an institution of local defense. This is misleading. It was obvious from the earliest period of settlement the militia was ineffective as a static defense force against an enemy who could choose the time and place of an attack. Consequently, astute colonial leaders quickly learned to concede the first blows to the Indians and rely on the militia primarily as an offensive or, more accurately, counteroffensive weapon. During the half-dozen major Indian wars of the seventeenth century, it was not unusual for powerful colonial expeditions of up to a thousand men to attack and lay waste native towns and fields. The destruction of the Pamunkey stronghold in Virginia in 1644 and the Great Swamp Fight in Rhode Island in 1675 were spectacular examples of the devasta-

tion wrought by militia forces on the march. Such bold strokes inflicted heavy casualties on the Indians and compelled them to scatter into the forest, concentrating on their own survival. Again and again, the militia seized the initiative and relieved the pressure on beleaguered colonial farms and villages along the frontier. Reliance on the offensive was one of the key differences between the English and American militias; since Anglo-Saxon times the militia in England had served as a shield, but in America it functioned as a sword as well.

At first, the colonial militia was highly inclusive. Males from about 16 to 60, which sometimes included slaves and indentured servants, were required to participate in training and to own or have ready access to arms and military equipment. In practice, however, actual militia duty usually fell on men 20 to 30 years of age. As the population increased and the threat posed by the Indians decreased over the course of the seventeenth century, the militia became more select. Slaves and servants were purged entirely; poorer freemen usually were dropped from active ranks and assigned to a vaguely defined reserve. Ministers, gunsmiths, and others were exempted from militia duty altogether. By the beginning of the eighteenth century, membership in the militia generally was limited to the ranks of the middling and more prosperous elements in colonial society. Everywhere the militia became a hollow shell as interest in maintaining a creditable military posture waned. Training days became memorable for speechmaking and riotous behavior, but not for training.

As the militia decayed, colonial defense was taken up by other institutions. In the late seventeenth and early eighteenth centuries, the colonies hired long-service volunteers to man isolated garrisons, serve on expeditions, and perform other onerous tasks in place of regular militiamen who were reluctant to leave their farms and mercantile establishments for the hardships and hazards of public service on a now distant frontier. Ironically, many of these semi-professional soldiers were the very same poor young men who were routinely excluded from the militia because of their supposed unreliability and their inability to equip themselves properly. Another new aspect of colonial defense was the appearance of amateur military companies, such as the Ancient and Honorable Artillery Company of Massachusetts, which usually were composed of social elites. Such organizations tended to be well trained and equipped, but seldom saw active service. Finally, regular forces of the British army were stationed in America as the titanic imperial struggle with France dominated colonial military affairs after 1689. Although the militia deteriorated in the second half of the colonial period for lack of anything particularly urgent to do, the militia tradition did not. The militia revived with remarkable rapidity during the imperial crisis of 1763–1775 and played a key role in the War of Independence.

William L. Shea

References

Douglas E. Leach, "The Military System of Plymouth Colony," *New England Quarterly,* XXIV (1951):342–364; ———, *Arms for Empire: A Military History of the British Colonies in North America, 1607–1763* (1973); Harold L. Peterson, *Arms and Armor in Colonial America, 1526–1783* (1956); William L. Shea, *The Virginia Militia in the Seventeenth Century* (1983); John Shy, "A New Look at Colonial Militia," *William and Mary Quarterly,* 3rd ser., XX (1963):175–185.

See also ANCIENT AND HONORABLE ARTILLERY COMPANY OF MASSACHUSETTS; GREAT SWAMP FIGHT; MILITIA: THE ARCHEOLOGICAL RECORD; PAMUNKEY; WAR AND SOCIETY IN COLONIAL AMERICA

Militia: The Archeological Record

While many colonial military sites have been investigated by historical archeologists, including numerous forts such as Michilimackinac, Stanwick, Necessity, and Moultrie, the Valley Forge and Morristown encampments, and the Brandywine and Monmouth battlefields, the militia as a separate institution has received limited attention. This is due in part because the specific historical associations of military objects in the archeological record is often difficult to establish. Extensive excavations at the Addison Plantation Site (18PR175), Oxon Hill, Prince George's County, Maryland, were conducted and resulted in the recovery of a rare assemblage of military artifacts associated with the county militia. The analysis of this assemblage in the context of the history of the Potomac region, and the Addison family's association with the Prince George's County militia, offers special insight into the duties of provincial militia officers and the evolution of the militia on the Potomac Frontier.

Prior to ca. 1715, the Potomac Valley, from the fall line near present day Washington, D.C., to the interior of western Maryland, was part of the colonial frontier. John Addison (?–1706) arrived in Maryland in 1674 and established himself as a leading merchant/planter on the Potomac frontier by 1689. When Prince George's County was formed in 1696, he became colonel of the new county's militia. His son, Thomas Addison (1669–1727), subsequently became the colonel of the county militia in 1714, and his son, John Addison (1713–1764), was a captain in the militia.

The Addison plantation military artifacts were recovered in and around an earthfast, or post-in-the-ground, house originally built in the late seventeenth century. The house seems to have been altered by the Addisons to serve as a militia armory. An angled 25-foot-long passage had been appended to the house's cellar, altering its plan to correspond to that of the earliest magazine at Fort Stanwick. The structure was destroyed by fire ca. 1730. The artifacts recovered included two "dog-locks"; flintlocks with an external latch or "dog" used to keep the cock in the "half-cocked" or safety position, allowing the weapon to be carried while fully loaded. This was the preferred British lock type from ca. 1625 through ca. 1675 and it remained part of the British military's armament through ca. 1715. Various items of iron firearms hardware and brass stock furniture were also recovered, including 12 triggers, one dog catch, a small cock, 18 fluted ramrod pipes, five pistol butt plates, five trigger guard fragments, nine screw plate fragments, and a fragment of a musket butt plate. These items, which did not include any complete weapons, are interpreted as having been parts in storage. The artifacts represent transitional weapon types which were replaced by the British military with the adoption of "true" flintlocks, such as the Long Land Pattern Musket, or "Brown Bess," introduced ca. 1718.

While the militia's importance in establishing and maintaining the structure of colonial society has been recognized, there has been little discussion of the nature of an officer's duties and obligations beyond the muster field. The maintenance of the militia was one of the obligations of a colonel. He supplied arms to his troops at government expense. Colonel Addison's storage of arms supplies at his plantation ensured that his troops would be adequately provisioned when needed. The operation and management of such a store would have entailed ongoing coordination of personnel, equipment, and supplies and consultation with the provincial government, necessitating a major commitment of time and effort on the Addisons' part. In addition, the establishment and maintenance of an armory on the plantation must have affected the physical organization and patterns of activity which comprised daily life on the plantation. The social respect and honor associated with militia rank were clearly earned.

While records of provincial Maryland and Prince George's County provide scant reference to militia arms storage policy, and even less detail as to the types of arms in storage, the recovered arms assemblage, which ranges in date from c. 1690 to 1730, seems to represent materials on hand for the repair and maintenance of guns held by members of the militia at their homes and outlying plantations. One of the dog locks recovered was in new, unused condition when the structure burned. The Prince George's County militia seems to have relied on the older, simpler weapon types that had proven reliable throughout the seventeenth century, rather than the more modern half-cockable flintlock used by the regular British army. The militia's apparent failure to keep pace with advancing firearms technology suggests its role was evolving from that of defense of the British Empire's borders to that of local security as Prince George's County became more settled and the frontier retreated to the west. By ca. 1730, the militia was no longer an effective, up-to-date military force required for the primary defense of Prince George's County. This period may represent the ebb-point of the militia's military role in the colony.

Neither the importance of the colonial militia, nor the details of its operation, are well documented or understood. This seems to be due, in part, to incomplete and vague records for those periods when colonial frontiers were being most aggressively pursued. As evidenced by the materials recovered from Addison plantation, the archeological record has the potential to provide important insights into the details of militia operations, which will lead to a more complete understanding of the militia as an institution and its role in our early history.

Jeffrey B. Snyder and John P. McCarthy

References

M.L. Brown, *Firearms in Colonial America: The Impact on History and Technology, 1492–1792* (1980); John P. McCarthy, Jeffrey B. Snyder, and Billy R. Roulette, Jr., "Arms from Addison Plantation and the Maryland Militia on the Potomac Frontier," *Historical Archaeology* 25 (1991):66–75; Allan R. Millett and Peter Maslowski, *For the Common Defense: A Military History of the United States of America* (1984); Harold L. Peterson, *Arms and Armor in Colonial America, 1526–1783* (1956); William L. Shea, "The First American Militia," *Military Affairs* 46 (1982): 15–18.

See also MILITIA

Mingo

The Mingos were Iroquois from New York who migrated to western Pennsylvania and Ohio during the early 1700s. By the 1740s, these Ohio Iroquois had settled along the Ohio River and its tributaries, establishing villages with Indians from western tribes such as the Shawnees, Delawares, Miamis, and Wyandots. As their numbers grew, the Ohio Indians became increasingly more important to Pennsylvania officials, who were determined to enlist them as trading partners and allies against New France.

The Ohio Iroquois (or Mingos) emerged as the spokesmen for the loose alliance of Ohio tribes. In 1747, Mingos journeyed to Philadelphia to open relations between the Ohio tribes and Pennsylvania government. Despite claims by the Iroquois Confederacy that the Ohio tribes were under their control, the Mingos convinced the Pennsylvanians they were establishing their own council fire on the Ohio River, independent of the New York Iroquois League Council.

The Mingos quickly established their leadership role. Their familial ties to the famed Iroquois Confederacy carried great weight both in the government chambers at Philadelphia and around council fires in the Ohio country, while their political independence from the Iroquois League Council guaranteed they were no threat to the sovereignty of Ohio tribes. As a result, both the English and Ohio Indians felt the Mingos were the perfect go-between. Following the diplomatic model originally established by the New York Iroquois, the Ohio Iroquois became diplomatic middlemen, facilitating improved economic and political relations between the Ohio tribes and the Pennsylvania government.

In July 1748, Mingo chiefs met with officials at Lancaster to discuss relations between the Ohio tribes and Pennsylvania. Later that summer, the Pennsylvania government dispatched Indian agent Conrad Weiser to the Ohio country for further talks. He met with the Mingos and other Ohio Indians at Logstown, the principal Indian village on the Ohio River (located about 18 miles below present-day Pittsburgh). The Logstown Conference elevated the Mingos' position as the official spokesmen for the Ohio Indians, and cemented the alliance between the Ohio tribes and the Pennsylvania government.

For the next several years, the Mingos and the Ohio tribes held fast to their English alliance. But by the mid-1750s, many of the Ohio Indians switched over to the French to stop English westward expansion. Some Mingos even joined Pontiac's War against the British in 1763.

The Mingos played an extremely important role on the Ohio frontier from the 1740s through the American Revolution. Along with influencing the movement of Indians and whites onto the lands south of Lake Erie, they facilitated diplomacy and trade between Indians and whites. The Mingos or Ohio Iroquois proved to be as adept at diplomacy in the Ohio country as their New York brethren further to the east.

Richard Aquila

References
Richard Aquila, *The Iroquois Restoration: Iroquois Diplomacy on the Colonial Frontier, 1701–1754* (1983); Randolph C. Downes, *Council Fires on the Upper Ohio; A Narrative of Indian Affairs in the Upper Ohio Valley until 1795* (1940); Francis Jennings, *The Ambiguous Iroquois Empire: The Covenant Chain Confederation of Indian Tribes with English Colonies from its Beginnings to the Lancaster Treaty of 1744* (1984); Daniel K. Richter and James Merrell, eds., *Beyond the Covenant Chain: The Iroquois and Their Neighbors in Indian North America, 1600–1800* (1987); Paul A.W. Wallace, *Indians in Pennsylvania* (1961).

See also DINWIDDIE, ROBERT; HALF-KING; IROQUOIS; WEISER, CONRAD

Minuit, Peter (1580–1638)

Peter Minuit first arrived in New Netherland in 1625. He had been sent to the colony to assist Willem Verhulst in surveying the rivers for possible new Dutch settlements. However, Verhulst soon proved himself incapable of either governing the settlers or establishing peaceful relations with the natives. Minuit seized authority and immediately dealt with the problem of widespread native disturbances. As director general, he consolidated colonists on Manhattan Island after its purchase—either by Verhulst or himself—probably between 4 May and 26 June 1626.

Under Minuit's command, Fort New Amsterdam was erected and Manhattan's defense perimeter strengthened by the purchase of Staten Island. He saw to the hydrographic mapping of the Hudson River and inaugurated years that saw, if not profits for the West India Company, a successful beginning to the aggrandizement of the fur trade. William Bradford of New Plymouth expressed envy of New Netherland's advantageous trading position at the time, but could do nothing to interfere in the trade and generally responded with good will to Dutch overtures of friendship. When Minuit was recalled to Holland in 1632, he played an important role in encouraging Kiliaen van Rensselaer to look optimistically at his investment in a patroonship around Fort Orange (later Albany) called Rensselaerswijck.

In Amsterdam, Minuit agreed with Samuel Bloemaerts in 1634 to lead a Swedish expedition to the Delaware, an area already claimed by the Dutch. In 1638, at a cost of 24,000 guilders, the Swedes sent a small fleet with about 50 colonists to a tributary of the river. There they built Fort Christina (now at Wilmington), some 15 miles from the nearest Dutch fort. In the same year, after receiving (unanswered) rebukes from the Dutch, Minuit set sail for Florida, but was lost at sea off St. Christopher in the Antilles. Meanwhile, the colony prospered until 1655, when soldiers under Director General Petrus (Peter) Stuyvesant brought it under Dutch authority.

Donna Merwick

References
Charles Gehring, "Peter Minuit's Purchase of Manhattan Island—New Evidence," *De Halve Maen* 55 (1980):6–20; Amandus Johnson, *The Swedish Settlements on the Delaware: Their History and Relations to the Indians, Dutch and English,* 2 vols. (1911); C.A. Waslager, *The English on the Delaware, 1610–1682* (1967).

See also FORT AMSTERDAM (NEW YORK); FORT CHRISTINA (DELAWARE); NEW NETHERLAND; NEW SWEDEN; FORT ORANGE (NEW YORK); STUYVESANT, PETRUS

Missiagua

See OJIBWA

Fort Mississippi (Louisiana)

See FORT DE LA BOULAYE (LOUISIANA)

Mississippi River

The Mississippi River played several roles during the colonial period: boundary, goal, and means of transportation. Before the coming of Europeans, the Mississippi served North American natives as a great highway of trade and communication. Established in the minds of Europeans as the major artery leading to the Gulf of Mexico by Hernando de Soto's expedition of 1539–1543, its connection with the Great Lakes country was established in 1674 by Jacques Marquette and Louis Jolliet; its complete southward course was traced by René-Robert Cavelier de La Salle's expedition of 1682. In La Salle's plans, it became the spine of a Canada-Louisiana connection and was subsequently so used by the French Louisiana colony from 1700–1763, which built outposts along it: Arkansas post to establish La Salle's stake in the region in 1686; Fort Mississippi to guard its mouth in 1700; Fort Rosalie in 1716 to control the Natchez Trace connection; Fort St. Pierre to control the Yazoo basin and New Orleans to establish an entrepôt on the lower river in 1718; and a pair of small forts at English Bend below New Orleans in 1746 to guard the city from possible attack by the British.

The British sought it as the goal of their westward expansion: they attempted to connect their "Upper Path" of Indian trade to it in 1698; tried to land settlers at its mouth in 1699; and maintained connections with Indian groups controlling portions of it during most of the French tenure. Nor did the Spaniards forget it. When in 1763 they were given Louisiana west of the river and the "Isle of Orleans" between Lakes Maurepas and Pontchartrain and the Mississippi by the French, they emphatically retained control of the river also as a border defense. In spite of various British smuggling schemes designed to bypass Spanish control of the river's mouth by bringing goods out to the Gulf through the lakes, the Spaniards exploited their control of the Mississippi in 1780 to first take the British outposts on the east side of the river at Manchac, Pointe Coupee, and Natchez, and then the whole of British West Florida.

Patricia Galloway

References

Jean Delanglez, *El Rio del Espiritu Santo: an essay on the cartography of the Gulf Coast and the adjacent territory during the sixteenth and seventeenth centuries,* ed. Thomas J. McMahon (1945); Frederick Austin Ogg, *The Opening of the Mississippi: A Struggle for Supremacy in the American Interior* (1904), rpt. 1969; Timothy Severin, *Explorers of the Mississippi* (1968).

See also ENGLISH BEND; LOUISIANA; NEW ORLEANS; FORT ROSALIE (MISSISSIPPI)

Mohawk

The Mohawk tribe (nation), of the Iroquoian cultural linguistic group, had its homeland in the Mohawk and northern Hudson River valleys, extending north through the Adirondacks to the St. Lawrence River. Their Iroquois neighbors to the west were the Oneidas, and their immediate eastern neighbors were the Mohicans (Mahicans), whom they decimated in the early seventeenth century. Because of their location as the easternmost tribe of the Iroquois Confederacy, the Mohawks were referred to as the "keepers of the eastern door" of the metaphorical longhouse. (The longhouse was the traditional house style of the Iroquoians: an oblong building made of a bent sapling frame covered with elm bark.) The Mohawks called themselves "people of the land of flint," or *kanien'keha'ga,* although their Algonquin neighbors in New England (Narragansetts, Massachusetts, and others) referred to them as *Mohowawogs,* which meant "man-eaters," a derogatory appellation. The Dutch and English adapted this name to the present commonly used "Mohawk." The French referred to the Mohawks by their rendition of the Huron name for these people, *Agniers.*

The first smallpox epidemics probably attacked the Mohawks in the 1630s, and the population loss was great. However, it is difficult to know what the pre-epidemic population was; it may have been as high as 4,000 people.

By the latter half of the seventeenth century, the population was around 2,000. Not as numerous as the Senecas, but more numerous than the Oneidas, Onondagas, and Cayugas, the Mohawk people exerted a great deal of authority over the Iroquois Confederacy in the seventeenth century and into the eighteenth. Their influence, despite holding only nine of the 50 Iroquois League sachem (chief) positions, stemmed partly from the prominent role of the mythical historic figure, Hiawatha, who was Mohawk, in the founding of the Iroquois League and from their geographic situation closest to the new Dutch presence from the 1610s onward. This proximity to the Dutch traders meant preferential access to European trade goods, such as firearms and metal tools, and to wampum, a southern New England Indian and European invention which was part commodity, part currency, part communication device, and came to play an important symbolic role in religious and political life among the Iroquois.

The Mohawks' close proximity to the sources of wampum and to the trade with Dutch merchants gave them the opportunity to assert themselves as leaders among the Iroquois, acting as speakers for the other tribes in dealings with the Dutch, and later the English. This led to tensions within the confederacy, especially with the Senecas and Onondagas, who preferred to establish and strengthen their own ties with the French at the expense of Mohawk-Dutch influence. In the 1640s and 1650s, the Mohawks won a political tug-of-war within the league by asserting their agenda of an all-out war against tribes more closely allied with the French than the Senecas and Onondagas. From 1649 to 1653, the Iroquois (led by the Mohawks) virtually destroyed the Huron, Petun, Neutral, Erie, and other smaller nations, also serving notice to the French that the same fate might befall them. (Many of the aforementioned peoples were assimilated into Iroquois communities.)

The Mohawks, in particular among the Iroquois, had had antagonistic relations with the French in the Saint Lawrence Valley from their first contacts in the 1610s. Mohawk depredations against the French continued until 1667, when France sent a crack regiment to put a brutal end to the Mohawk threat to their colonial settlements on the St. Lawrence. Following the peace, French Jesuit missionaries actually enjoyed a sizable popular following in Mohawk villages. More than half of the remaining Mohawks in the 1670s and 1680s moved to establish new villages near the Jesuit and French outpost settlements along the St. Lawrence. With the wars of 1687–1701, the Mohawks surviving in the Mohawk Valley again led Iroquois resistance against the French and the French reciprocated. However, most of the eighteenth century was spent in a tense neutrality between the French to the north and the New York British to the east of the Mohawk Valley. The Kahnawake Mohawks, a group which had moved to a Jesuit-sponsored village near Montreal, often sided with the French in military affairs, and the Mohawks in the Mohawk Valley were not eager to assist British military forces in the Seven Years' War, which ended in 1763.

However, the end of French rule in North America in 1763 did not bode well for either group of Mohawks, and a sizable minority moved from both the St. Lawrence and Mohawk Valley communities to the Ohio country to escape the growing British presence in the east. Both nominally British-allied and French-allied Mohawks lost the ability to play the two European powers off against each other with the British takeover of Quebec. The American War of Independence took a great toll on the Iroquois in general. Largely because of their close personal relationships with loyalist Sir William Johnson's family, the Mohawk Valley Mohawks led the other Iroquois nations in siding with the British in the Revolutionary War. They were subsequently rewarded with large land grants in the new colony of Upper Canada (Ontario). (Their loyalism defeated their chances of returning to their homeland.) The Mohawks living in the St. Lawrence Valley were relatively unaffected by the outcome of this war. By the end of the eighteenth century, there were five separate Mohawk communities, all of them in British territory and hundreds of miles away from their traditional village territory of the Mohawk Valley.

Gretchen L. Green

References
William N. Fenton and Elisabeth Tooker, "Mohawk," in *Handbook of North American Indians, the Northeast,* Vol. 15 (1978); Charles T. Gehring and William A. Starna, eds., *A Journey into Mohawk and Oneida Country, 1634–1635: The Journal of Harmen Meyndertsz van den Bogaert* (1988); Thomas

Grassman, *The Mohawk Indians and Their Valley* (1969); Daniel K. Richter, *The Ordeal of the Longhouse: The Peoples of the Iroquois League in the Era of European Colonization* (1992).

See also COVENANT CHAIN; IROQUOIS; IROQUOIS WARS; MOHAWK-MAHICAN WAR

Mohawk-Mahican War (1624–1628)

This is an early example of the "beaver wars," in which Indian tribes fought for control of trapping territories or for access to European trade goods, and it also illustrates the maneuvering for advantage of rival traders. The Mohawks and Mahicans seem to have been enemies long before the arrival of Europeans, but the fur trade gave an economic dimension to their conflict. The Mahicans occupied an area in the present state of New York, which extended along the Hudson River southward from Lake Champlain, and spoke an Algonkian dialect. The Mohawks, speaking an Iroquoian tongue, lived immediately to the west and were the easternmost members of the Iroquois Confederacy.

The Dutch established a trading post, Fort Nassau, in the heart of the Mahican country in 1614. This gave the Mahicans a favored position in the trade for European goods, and they generally succeeded in preventing their Mohawk enemies from visiting the post. In 1624, the new Dutch West India Company reestablished the post nearby, calling it Fort Orange (present-day Albany). The Dutch hoped to entice the Algonkian-speaking tribes of the north, friends of the Mahicans, to abandon the French of the St. Lawrence and trade instead with them. This posed a threat to the Mohawks from enemies better supplied with steel tools and weapons, and perhaps guns, and they struck to win access to Fort Orange. The Mohawks negotiated a treaty with their former enemies, the French of Canada (1624), and attacked the Mahicans.

Few details of the war have survived, but it is clear that after initial difficulties, the Mohawks won decisively. The Mahicans were said (in 1610) to number 1,600 warriors; the Mohawks perhaps half as many. At first the Dutch assisted their Mahican allies. In 1626, seven Dutchmen from Fort Orange accompanied a Mahican raid into Mohawk country. Although the Mohawks seem to have been without guns,

they routed the Mahicans in an ambush and killed four of the Dutch. One was roasted and eaten on the spot; the three others were burned at the stake. At this point, the Dutch drew back and left the tribes to fight it out. By 1628, the Mahicans had been so thoroughly defeated that they abandoned their lands west of the Hudson forever. Many sought temporary refuge as far away as the Connecticut River to the east.

Victory gave the Mohawks control of the approaches to Fort Orange and they determined who could trade there. Few in number and weak militarily, the Dutch had to accept this outcome. On the St. Lawrence, the French had the consolation that northern Algonkians were now barred from Fort Orange by Mohawk hostility. So despite the much cheaper prices of trade goods at Fort Orange, their Indian customers could not abandon them.

Bert M. Mutersbaugh

References

T.J. Brasser, "The Mahican," in Bruce G. Trigger, ed., *The Northeast*, Vol. 15, *Handbook of North American Indians* (1978): 198–212; George T. Hunt, *The Wars of the Iroquois: A Study in Intertribal Relations* (1940); Allen W. Trelease, *Indian Affairs in Colonial New York: The Seventeenth Century* (1960); Bruce G. Trigger, "The Mohawk-Mahican War (1624–28): The Establishment of a Pattern," *Canadian Historical Review* 52 (1971):276–286.

See also MAHICAN; MOHAWK; FORT NASSAU (NEW YORK); FORT ORANGE (NEW YORK)

Mohegan

The Mohegans lived along the Thames River in Connecticut. Though their early history is disputed by scholars, at the time of European contact the Mohegans were a subordinate branch of the Pequot tribe. Uncas, son-in-law to the Pequot grand sachem, Sassacus, challenged Sassacus for control of the Pequots. After this failed attempt at supremacy, Uncas left the tribe with followers.

Uncas, eager to defeat his enemies, the Pequots, soon joined with the English and the Narragansetts to defeat Sassacus and the Pequots during the Pequot War of 1637–1638. Connecticut's quick and decisive victory over the Pequots was due in large part to Mohegan efforts. The Pequots' loss resulted in the

Mohegans' gain as many of the captives from the war were split between the Narragansetts and the Mohegans. This agreement was a component of the Hartford or Tripartite Treaty of 1638 between Connecticut, the Mohegans, and the Narragansetts. The Mohegans and Narragansetts agreed to utilize the English as an umpire for their differences. They would not resort to arms without first obtaining approval of the English.

Though the two were allies in the war, Uncas soon looked to defeat the Narragansetts to gain control of the distribution of wampum. A rivalry between Miantonomo, the Narragansett chief, and Uncas threatened to throw the English colonies into warfare numerous times. Uncas utilized the English authorities in the 1643 war with the Narragansetts when he turned over Miantonomo to them after his capture in Mohegan territory. Miantonomo thought he had received adequate clearance by English authorities to attack the Mohegans, but they turned against him. He was later returned to Uncas with a request by the English to kill him.

Uncas's power base was greatly strengthened in the years following the Pequot War because of his relationship with the English. The English came to rely on the Mohegans, especially Uncas, to alert them to any Indian threats to their security. Uncas took advantage of this dependence by making his own enemies sound threatening to English security. With his increased power base, Uncas also served as an intermediary between subordinate bands in the area and the Connecticut authorities. Uncas's ability to extract tribute was largely based on his relationship with the English and his claim to be the successor of the Pequots. They eventually occupied most of their Nipmuck and Niantic neighbors' land as Connecticut authorities allowed him to extend his power among Indians to the north and east.

In 1675, the Mohegans sided with the English against the New England Indian alliance in the King Philip's War and substantially helped in the defeat of the Narragansetts. But not even the Mohegans' close relationship with the English civil authorities lasted. Though the Mohegans had played key roles in English victories during the Pequot War and King Philip's War, the Mohegans' usefulness to the English as warriors and trade partners diminished after 1675. English land hunger led the Mohegans to cede or sell much of their territory to Connecticut and they were confined to a reservation on the Thames River at New London. Mohegan numbers continued to dwindle as they were surrounded by English settlers and many of them escaped the area by joining the Brotherton community of Christianized Indians in New York in 1788.

Leslie Miller

References

Laurence M. Hauptman and James D. Wherry, *The Pequots in Southern New England: The Fall and Rise of an American Indian Nation* (1990); Francis Jennings, *The Invasion of America: Indians, Colonialism, and the Cant of Conquest* (1975); Neal Salisbury, *Manitou and Providence: Indians, Europeans, and the Making of New England, 1500–1643* (1982); Alden T. Vaughan, *New England Frontier: Puritans and Indians, 1620–1675* (1965).

See also CONNECTICUT; KING PHILIP'S WAR; MIANTONOMO; NARRAGANSETT; PEQUOT WAR; FORT SHANTOK (CONNECTICUT); UNCAS

Monckton, Robert (1726–1782)

Robert Monckton began his military career at the age of 15, when he was commissioned in the 3rd Foot Guards; in this capacity he served in the War of the Austrian Succession, seeing action at Dettingen and Fontenoy. He subsequently progressed rapidly through the ranks, achieving successive commissions as captain, major, and finally as lieutenant colonel of the 47th Foot. On his father's death in 1752, Monckton succeeded to the family-controlled seat in Parliament, representing Pontefract. Soon, however, he was posted to Nova Scotia.

Monckton was appointed commander of Fort Lawrence, the key British post in Acadia, situated on the isthmus of Chignecto. He saw little action during his first year, exchanging notes, deserters, and runaway horses with his French counterpart at Beauséjour, Jean-Baptiste Mutigny de Vassan. In June 1753, he was appointed to membership in the colony's council in Halifax. On 18 December of that year, he led a 200-man force to put down an insurrection by German settlers at the British outpost of Lunenberg, in the process evincing a far more humane and forgiving perspective than his more austere superior, Lieutenant Governor Charles Lawrence.

In June 1755, Monckton led the successful campaign against the Chignecto forts of Beauséjour and Gaspereau. He had spent the winter in Boston preparing for the attack, where he quarreled with John Winslow, his principal subordinate commander; relations between the two remained poor throughout the campaign. Nonetheless, Monckton succeeded in capturing both of the French forts, securing control of Nova Scotia for the British. His victory was based on surprise and intelligent deployment of superior resources. Following the French surrender, he repaired Beauséjour, improved the local roads, and reluctantly participated in the deception and deportation of more than 1,000 Acadians from Chignecto.

Monckton had led the sole British victory that year, and as a reward he was made lieutenant governor of Nova Scotia in December 1755; during the succeeding three years he served as acting governor twice. In the fall of 1758, he was promoted to full colonel and given command of an expedition to the St. John River country. His forces destroyed houses, cattle, and crops for 70 miles or so up the river. In early 1759, Jeffrey Amherst called him to New York, intending to appoint him to the command of the southern region; but James Wolfe first chose him as second-in-command for the planned Quebec expedition.

Monckton played a pivotal role in the capture of Quebec, leading the four regiments that took control of the south shore of the river at Pointe Lévy, across from the city. As a result, Wolfe was able to place his artillery in a most advantageous position. However, the siege stalled; Monckton himself led an unsuccessful attempt to land on the Beauport shore on 31 July. As the difficulties increased and tension mounted, he, James Murray, and George Townshend convinced Wolfe to launch an attack from above the city. Monckton himself commanded the landing at Anse au Foulon on 13 September, and later that day was in command of the British right on the Plains of Abraham, where he was wounded in the chest. Despite his wound and exclusion from the subsequent negotiations, Monckton was then placed in command of the city after the surrender, ruling firmly but sympathetically and acting to protect the civilian population from the British regulars.

Several months later, on 29 April 1760, Monckton was named commander of British forces in the southern provinces. In February 1761, he was promoted to major general, and on 20 March, he was named governor and commander in chief of the New York colony. During the winter of 1761–1762, Monckton commanded the army that captured Martinique in an impressive victory against a strong fortress. He was sent back to New York, and then to England in June 1763. During the subsequent imperial crisis, he was regarded as a friend of America by the Americans themselves, though this stance does not seem to have harmed his political or military career. In 1764, he was named governor of Berwick-upon-Tweed, and in 1770, commissioned a lieutenant general. He did fail to get the position of commander in chief in India, which he had sought with East India Company support in an effort to recoup losses from investments in the company. He also declined the offer to command the British army in America. He did, however, accept a land grant on St. Vincent in the West Indies, and again served briefly as a member of Parliament in 1774. In 1778, he was appointed governor of Portsmouth, and represented the town in Parliament until his death in 1782.

Ronald P. Dufour

References

Guy Frégault, *Canada: The War of the Conquest,* trans. by Margaret M. Cameron (1969); Douglas Edward Leach, *Arms for Empire: A Military History of the British Colonies in North America, 1607–1763* (1973); Stanley M. Pargellis, "Robert Monckton," *Dictionary of American Biography,* Vol. 13 (1934); I.K. Steele, "Robert Monckton," *Dictionary of Canadian Biography,* Vol. IV (1974).

See also FORT BEAUSÉJOUR (NOVA SCOTIA, CANADA); FORT GASPEREAU (NOVA SCOTIA, CANADA); FORT LAWRENCE (NOVA SCOTIA, CANADA); MURRAY, JAMES; QUEBEC, BATTLE OF; WINSLOW, JOHN; WOLFE, JAMES

Monongahela River

The Monongahela River runs in a northerly course from Fairmont, West Virginia, for 128 miles to Pittsburgh, where it joins the Allegheny to form the Ohio. Its main tributaries are the Cheat and the Youghiogheny. In the eighteenth century, the Ohio and the Allegheny were generally thought of as one river, with the point being simply the mouth of the Monongahela, rather than a confluence.

Long an avenue for the fur trade, the Monongahela became, in the mid-eighteenth century, a focus of the Anglo-French contest in the Ohio Valley. George Washington, surveying the Ohio forks in 1753, commented that the Monongahela was "extremely well designed for Water Carriage, as it [was] of a deep still Nature." Despite this appraisal, the Monongahela often ran low, and despite the fact that its banks were generally steep as it neared its northern terminus, it was also prone to flooding. Nevertheless, the forks was so pivotal it became the site of four successive forts, built in a seven-year span. The first was an uncompleted American effort, "Fort Prince George," built in 1754. It was replaced later the same year by Fort Duquesne, built by the French after they had evicted the small American force from that site. Although at times thinly garrisoned, Fort Duquesne marked the center of French power in the valley and was saved by General Edward Braddock's defeat in 1755; but it was destroyed, rather than allowed to be captured, as the French retreated before Forbes's army in late 1758. Its British successor, "Mercer's Fort," built in 1759, was the only fort of the period to face only the Monongahela, though Fort Pitt, constructed by the English in 1761—by far the largest of the forts at the point—took its river traffic through it. Fort Duquesne was badly flooded on several occasions, and so was Fort Pitt, even though it was built on slightly higher ground. The flooding problem encouraged British army engineers to recommend alternative sites in the vicinity. The last significant action to center on Fort Pitt was Pontiac's War (1763). Thereafter, with the removal of the French and Indian threat in western Pennsylvania and with the subsequent increase of tension in Boston, New York, and elsewhere on the seaboard, the British lost interest in the forks as a strategic site. In 1772, they abandoned and partly dismantled Fort Pitt, which quickly degenerated into a ruin.

The Monongahela has other military associations, as well. On its eastern bank, at present-day Brownsville, Pennsylvania, the Ohio Company constructed a depot in 1754, but it was taken by the French in the course of their move against Washington during the Fort Necessity campaign. In 1759, it was rebuilt and strengthened, as Fort Burd. Most of all, however, the Monongahela is associated with Braddock's expedition. His army forded it twice, below and later above Turtle Creek, as it neared Fort Duquesne on 9 July 1755. Later that day, in the wake of its disastrous defeat, it reversed the process, fleeing to the west bank to escape the pursuing Indians, and later, in total disarray, traversing the river yet again to move eastward in an attempt to rejoin the division commanded by Colonel Thomas Dunbar.

Paul E. Kopperman

References
William A. Hunter, *Forts on the Pennsylvania Frontier, 1753–1758* (1960); Alfred P. James and Charles M. Stotz, *Drums in the Forest* (1958).

See also BRADDOCK, EDWARD; FORT BURD (PENNSYLVANIA) FORT DUQUESNE (PENNSYLVANIA); FORT PITT (PENNSYLVANIA); PONTIAC'S WAR

Montcalm-Gozon de Saint-Veran, Louis-Joseph, Marquis de (1712–1759)

In 1756, in the beginning of the year, Louis-Joseph, marquis de Montcalm-Gozon de Saint-Veran, known to us simply as the fabled marquis de Montcalm, was chosen to lead the forces of France in North America against the British. In a letter dated 25 January at Versailles, the minister of war, the Comte d'Argenson, wrote: "The King [Louis XV] has chosen you to command his troops in North America, and will honor you on your departure with the rank of major-general."

With that simple note, the long struggle of France and England over control of Canada and the present United States east of the Mississippi entered its final, dynamic phase, and one of the most legendary figures in North America entered our history. In 1756, the marquis de Montcalm was 44 years old, having been born in the south of France in February 1712, in a region that had given royal France some of its boldest men-at-arms ever since Raymond, count of Toulouse, rode off to fight the Moslems in the First Crusade. Already, Montcalm was a battle-scarred and battle-wise veteran of the almost continual wars France fought through much of the eighteenth century, bleeding the nation and fatally bankrupting the treasury of a rich and fortunate kingdom. At the age of 17, he saw service in the War of the Polish Succession; as a captain in the Regiment of Hainault, he first smelled gunpowder at the siege of Philipsbourg in 1734, where an Austrian imperial garrison was overwhelmed by the army of France's "Great Captain," Marechal de Saxe. During the subsequent War of the Austrian Succession, the young marquis, now commanding the Auxerrois Regiment, saw more action, and almost met an early and violent death. Having been in the fury of battle at Assietta and at Piacenza in 1746, he was sabered five times, twice on his head, and taken prisoner. At Piacenza, the French were defeated by their old enemies, the Austrians, with whom they had been battling for supremacy in Italy for more than two centuries. Promoted to the rank of brigadier general after being returned to France, he again was wounded in action before the War of the Austrian Succession came to a close in 1748.

On 3 April 1756, Montcalm set sail from Brest, the historic port of France's Atlantic fleet, on board the good ship *Licorne*. A few days later, three other French officers, whose names would remain inextricably linked with that of the marquis throughout the war in America, would follow: Louis-Antoine de Bougainville, a colonel and Montcalm's trusted aide; François-Gaston de Lévis, second-in-command with the rank of brigadier; and Colonel François-Charles de Bourlamaque, who went as third-in-command.

The war in America had reached a critical turn for the French by the time Montcalm and his band of brothers sailed to the west across the blue Atlantic. In 1755, the Baron Jean-Armand de Dieskau, Montcalm's predecessor as the French commander in chief, had been defeated on the shores of Lake George by Mohawk Indians and colonial troops under the command of Sir William Johnson, at that time the most influential and respected Englishman on the northern frontier. This victory by Johnson considerably balanced the defeat in July 1755 by a British force under General Edward Braddock; Johnson's Battle of Lake George took place in September 1755. Thus, it could be said that strategically the British had taken the military initiative by the time Montcalm sailed for America.

When the marquis arrived in New France (French Canada), it was with an incurable enthusiasm to carry the war to the enemy, a gambit necessary to bolster the sagging morale of the French and their Canadian subjects, as well as retain the loyalty of their Indian allies, eternally aware of any shift in the balance of power between France and England in the northern forests. Writing to his beloved wife, Angélique, at home when he was lying off anchor before Quebec City on 11 May, he proclaimed, "I see that I shall have plenty of work! Our campaign will soon begin." Montcalm's zest for battle was spurred on by Iroquois intelligence reports that the British were preparing to follow up their victory at Lake George by inaugurating the 1756 campaigning season with a thrust up the same Lake Champlain waterway, as well as by an offensive directed at the French defenses in the Great Lakes region. This key intelligence data provided the impetus for the dynamic response of Montcalm in the months ahead.

The potential British assaults posed a grave threat. There were three main "gateways" into the "interior lines" of New France: the Great Lakes region, almost a French lake because of their control of the Mississippi Valley; the Lake Champlain waterway, which connected the St. Lawrence River to Lake Champlain; and Lake George, by means of the little-known Richelieu River; and the mouth of the St. Lawrence itself, commanded by the French bastion of Louisbourg on Cape Breton Island. Any of these three water highways could be used either as an avenue for the British to attack the French, or as a highway by which the French could strike (hopefully first) from their interior strategic position at the surrounding British foe.

In 1756, Montcalm decided to use the Great Lakes to attack the British first, "beating them to the punch" in the best tradition of American prize fighting. Hearing that the British would move against the French at Fort Carillon, which protected the Lake Champlain riverine approaches, Montcalm's Great Lakes movement was an excellent—and frustrating for the British—strategic card to play. Gathering his attacking forces at the French Great Lakes strongholds of Fort Frontenac and Fort Niagara, Montcalm set about the destruction of the main British post on Lake Ontario, Fort Ontario, at the strategic spot known as Oswego.

On 10 August, in a brilliantly conceived tactical move carried out under the protection of night, Montcalm moved his soldiers into position to take on the British garrison. With the critical element of surprise in his favor, Montcalm played his trump card: artillery. Wooden Fort Ontario had been designed to withstand a quick raid by colonial troops like Robert Rogers' dashing New England rangers or a wild foray by woodland Indians, never a concerted attack by disciplined regular troops supported by cannon. (Ironically, just a few feet of earth piled against the wooden walls of the stockade would have sufficed, for such "earthworks" would have been impervious to all but the heaviest eighteenth-century ordnance.) Even though the fort itself was supplied with cannon, Montcalm's decided the battle. After firing hotly at the French, the garrison, Sir William Pepperrell, Jr.'s, regiment, gave up the fight. Colonel James Mercer, in overall command of Oswego, ordered the men from the fortress to retire to the main British defenses, Old Oswego. Yet the fall of Fort Ontario presaged the fall of the entire British position, for its demise opened a gap in the British defenses that Montcalm took advantage of with lethal alacrity. With the death of Colonel Mercer, who had caused the fatal gap by abandoning Fort Ontario, all fight left the British, and they chose to surrender. Almost immediately after the British capitulation, the French and Montcalm were confronted by the ugly specter of their Indian allies running amok. Before Montcalm could enforce order on the warriors, who had broken into the fort's rum store, between 50 and 100 prisoners had fallen beneath the tomahawks of the Indians. Only Montcalm's personal efforts avoided greater atrocities by offering the Indians presents for saving their captives' lives. He wrote, "it will cost the king eight or ten thousand livres in presents"—a sum Louis XV would have been spared had Montcalm kept an adequate watch over his prisoners of war. It would not be the last time that Montcalm, otherwise a flawless commander, lost control of the actions of his Indian allies.

After the removal of the surviving captives, some thousand and more, without further molestation by the Indians, the French set about the systematic destruction of Oswego as a threat. On 20 August, Bougainville wrote "the stockade of the fort has been set on fire and the stone house of Oswego filled with wood and combustible material" to be blown sky high. Even "all the barges and bateaux that could not be taken away" were put to the torch.

With the removal of the British threat to French Canada by way of the Great Lakes, the war effectively came to an end for 1756. When it returned in 1757, the astute marquis again outmaneuvered his British counterpart, Lord Loudoun, the British commander in chief. Loudoun possessed the strategic vision for defeating New France but he lacked the ability necessary to carry it out. Loudoun saw correctly that the key to New France was the mighty citadel of Louisbourg on Cape Breton Island. Louisbourg was the proverbial cork in the bottle: whoever had Louisbourg could, by "popping this cork," gain access to the St. Lawrence, and a broad water highway directly to Quebec City and Montreal. This was Loudoun's campaign plan for 1757 and it virtually denuded the entire northern frontier of fighting men to achieve his aims. This offered Montcalm an opportunity he simply could not pass up.

While Loudoun was formulating his grandiose plan to take Louisbourg, which hinged on the difficult prospect of effecting a timely rendezvous with a British fleet under Vice Admiral Francis Holburne, Montcalm decided to strike where enemy forces were the weakest—the Lake Champlain waterway. Here, rather than pursuing the French after his victory in September 1755, Sir William Johnson had built Fort William Henry as a counterweight to Fort Carillon, whose construction Montcalm had hastened to serve as a base for just such a strategic offensive as he now contemplated. Once again, his attack force would comprise the veteran regiments which had sailed over from Old France: La Reine, La Sarre, Royal Roussillon, Languedoc, and Guyenne. They would be ably supported by the Independent Companies of Marines, New France's virtual standing army, as well as by the Canadian militia and the thoroughly unpredictable Indians.

Early in July 1757, Montcalm wrote home to Angélique, "I am going on the ninth to sing the war song at the Lake of Two Mountains, and on the next day at Sault St. Louis—a long, tiresome ceremony. On the twelfth I am off" against Fort William Henry. Throughout the Great Lakes and the woodland redoubt of New France, news of Montcalm's feat at Lake Ontario had spread among Native Americans. One Indian said to the marquis, "we wanted to see this famous man who tramples the English under his feet." To the 1,000 Indians assembled—Iroquois, Hurons, Abenaki, Nipissings, and members of several other nations—Montcalm had proclaimed in council at Carillon, "my children, I am delighted to see you all reunited for the good work. So long as your union lasts the English will never be able to resist you." Two days after this conference on the evening of 29 July 1757, the advance guard of Montcalm's army moved silently down Lake George toward their military objective, Fort William

Henry. Before dawn on 3 August, Montcalm and his soldiers were ready to begin the siege of the fort.

Commanding at Fort William Henry was a brave Scot by the name of Lieutenant Colonel George Monro; in overall command of the British defenses was General Daniel Webb in Fort Edward not far away. It was in this divided leadership that the marquis would find his way to victory. At the time of the French incursion, Monro had some 2,200 fighting men at William Henry, while Webb had 2,400 under his overall disposition: about 1,600 in garrison at Fort Edward and the remainder dispersed all the way from Lake George to Albany. Confronting him was Montcalm with about 7,600 men, including approximately 1,600 Indians, equal in themselves to the entire garrison at Fort Edward. It was a situation that Webb, never the most aggressive commandant, found totally daunting. As Montcalm tightened his noose around Fort William Henry, Monro plaintively called for help. On the night of 4 August, rangers (probably from Rogers' command) slipped into Fort Edward bearing this terse note for Webb, "I believe you will think it proper to send a reinforcement as soon as possible."

But help was not in the offing for Monro and his hard-pressed defenders. Thanks to Loudoun's reduction of manpower for his quixotic and rash attempt on Louisbourg, Webb, his lack of personal gallantry notwithstanding, could not muster reinforcements to support Monro. Should the British meet with a catastrophic reversal like General Braddock had suffered two years earlier—a possibility with Webb in charge—the entire New York frontier would be laid defenseless. Even if he had had the personal initiative, the cards were dealt against Webb from the start. With deplorably few troops at his command, it was impossible to relieve William Henry—the total strategic position along the frontier had doomed the stockade from the moment Montcalm landed. Despite Monro's valiant defense, Fort William Henry was doomed to fall.

The siege of the fort went off with the measured pace of a Greek tragedy. Early in the morning of 6 August, Montcalm, repeating his winning tactics at Fort Ontario, commenced firing with his artillery on Monro. Throughout the next few days, Montcalm's batteries of cannon pounded the fort, its beleaguered troops, and the women and children who would share their fate. Meanwhile, as the French guns

steadily pounded William Henry's walls to make a breach for a final infantry assault, the dreaded smallpox struck down men, women, and children alike. Finally, this double assault proved too much to bear even for the resolute Munro. With no aid coming from a despondent Webb, who could hear the thunder of Montcalm's guns from Fort Edward (on one day he railed in a letter to Loudoun, "I have not yet received the least reinforcement"—men would finally come, but not enough), Monro had no choice but to surrender. As Bougainville recorded in his journal for 9 August, "at seven in the morning the fort raised a white flag and asked to capitulate." According to Bougainville, who helped draft the articles of surrender, the British and colonial troops "should depart with the honors of war with the baggage of the officers and of the soldiers, that they should be conducted" safely by the French to Fort Edward.

Yet, in spite of Montcalm and Bougainville's careful planning, the surrender of Fort William Henry ended in horror. The Indians, as before at Fort Ontario, got into the column of prisoners and fell upon them in a savage attack. The terrified prisoners begged the Canadians and French, who were supposed to protect them, for help; their guards, through callousness or fear, did not lift a hand. At the first noise of the mayhem, Montcalm, Lévis, and other French officers rushed to the scene. Montcalm personally saved a British officer, crying "kill me, but spare the English who are under my protection." Finally, the massacre of Fort William Henry was stopped by Montcalm, but not before at least 50 were slain by the warriors.

Although the capture of Fort William Henry, and the entrenched camp next to it, culminated in the tragic slaughter commemorated later in James Fennimore Cooper's *The Last of the Mohicans,* Montcalm's capture of William Henry was a decisive victory for the marquis and the French. Coupled with Loudoun barring British initiative elsewhere with his abortive descent on Louisbourg, Montcalm's strike broke the threat of any further British action against New France in 1757. Yet it was a defensive victory above all, since Montcalm lacked the resources to make capital out of his triumph and carry the war to the enemy, even as far as Fort Edward. On 17 August, as Bougainville recorded, "this same day the demolition was completed" on the doleful William Henry, and the French returned to Fort Carillon; some Indians traveled all the way to Montreal.

In the spring 1758, after a tense winter along the frontier, the entire character of the war became defensive for the French. In London, the energetic prime minister, William Pitt, initiated offensive action against French Canada on several fronts: a drive against Louisbourg to capture the fortress as a gateway up the St. Lawrence to Quebec City and Montreal; up Lake Champlain against Fort Carillon to open the Lake Champlain route to Canada; against Fort Frontenac to wrest control of France's bastion on the Great Lakes; and to capture Fort Duquesne, the key to the Ohio River country.

Indeed, from the British standpoint, 1758 would be a year of great victories. Fort Frontenac fell to Lieutenant Colonel John Bradstreet on 29 August; Duquesne was destroyed by its garrison before it was taken by the ailing General John Forbes in winter-tinged November. Even earlier, in July, General Jeffrey Amherst had finally taken the "impregnable" Louisbourg, aided by the bold James Wolfe, thus opening for the first time in the war Quebec City and Montreal to direct assault by the St. Lawrence. Only at Montcalm's post at Carillon could the French claim a triumph in this ill-starred year.

The force Montcalm faced at Carillon was one of the largest yet seen in North America: 6,300 British redcoats with 5,000 colonial troops, some of whom, like the "Jersey Blues" were militarily the equals of His Majesty's best troops. The same could not be said of the commander the marquis faced, General James Abercromby. Abercromby was the result of the worst abuses of a system of command in which, just like the French, the top posts were the rewards of political influence, not the rewards of military aptitude. Of Abercromby, Wolfe could only say he was "a heavy man." William Parkman, a Massachusetts soldier who was the great-uncle of Francis Parkman, the great historian of the French and Indian Wars, dismissed Abercromby as "an aged gentleman, infirm in body and mind."

On 8 July 1758, British troops paid the price for the unsuitability of their chief, whom the Americans contemptuously dismissed as "Nabbycromby." Montcalm had fortified his position with all the art that ingenuity and desperation could create. In front of the fort stood a wooden breastwork fronted by an abatis, an obstacle of felled and sharpened trees. Behind all these defenses loomed the guns of the fort. Without the support of British artillery, which Abercromby incredibly held back, the infantry were ordered "to march up briskly, rush upon the enemy's fire, and not to give theirs, until they were within the enemy's breastwork." All day, in bloody fighting hardly equaled until the Civil War, the British and American colonial troops tried to smash through the stout barrier and the withering gunfire of Montcalm's troops. Of the British and American effort, Bougainville exclaimed, "the different attacks, almost all afternoon and almost everywhere, were made with the greatest of vigor." But human bravery could not rival Montcalm's ability or Abercromby's ineptitude. By the time Abercromby called off the slaughter, approximately 1,944 British and Americans were casualties; only 377 French, Canadians, and Indians had been killed or wounded. Rightly did Montcalm and his jubilant men celebrate their seemingly miraculous victory. Well could a French soldier boast of the day, "I sing of the French, of their valor and glory!" But Fort Carillon would be the last hurrah for Montcalm and his troops.

Montcalm's saving of Fort Carillon, immortal now in a painting by noted American military artist H.A. Ogden, in the fort's museum, could not compensate for the lethal body blows the French and French-Canadians had taken in 1758. With Louisbourg, Fort Duquesne, Fort Frontenac, and even old Fort Niagara in British hands, New France was fighting for its life. By the opening of 1759, French control was largely limited to a belt of territory along the St. Lawrence, with Quebec City and Montreal in real danger of enemy attack. Accordingly, Montcalm pulled back the majority of French soldiers to hold the heartland of New France, while Carillon's garrison was reduced to a rearguard under the chevalier de Bourlamaque, who had been grievously wounded the July before. Against Bourlamaque would advance Amherst, conqueror of Louisbourg. But the real thrust of British offensive strategy now was an attack directly up the St. Lawrence to the city of Quebec, led by General James Wolfe. (Amherst would take Carillon in July.)

To face Wolfe's threat, Montcalm, with the equivocal cooperation of Governor Pierre de Riguad de Vaudreuil, constructed some of the greatest defenses seen before Robert E. Lee's protection of Petersburg in the Civil War. Below Quebec, Montcalm entrenched his army with its left flank on the St. Charles River and run-

M

ning due east until the army's right was the Montmorency River. By early June 1759, Montcalm's preparations were complete. Meanwhile, on 6 June, the British under Wolfe sailed from Louisbourg cheering, "British colors on every French fort, port, and garrison in America." It would not be long before Montcalm met Wolfe in battle for the first—and the last—time.

On 26 June, due to a stunning French tactical blunder, the British fleet under Vice Admiral Charles Saunders was able to carry Wolfe and his 9,000-man army to the Isle d'Orléans, astride the St. Lawrence and within sight of Quebec City. By not fortifying an important "high ground," the mountain of Cape Tourmente, Vaudreuil and Montcalm had enabled the British, unvexed by opposing artillery fire from Tourmente, to gain a successful toehold near Quebec that would weigh heavily in the scales against Montcalm, giving Wolfe an indispensable camp from which to besiege the city. Soon, Wolfe put cannon ashore at Pointe Lévy, directly opposite the town, and he unleashed on Quebec a bombardment fiercer than any yet seen in North America.

As time went on, it became clear to Montcalm that Wolfe was attempting to draw him out from his virtually impregnable defenses and take his 16,000 men into open battle against the redcoats. This Montcalm resolutely refused to do. Even Wolfe's "scorched earth" campaign against the French-Canadian *habitants,* or settlers, did not budge Montcalm. Relying on the strength of his tactical position, on the high northern bank of the St. Lawrence, Montcalm was determined to let Wolfe exhaust himself until cold weather forced him to withdraw. Although unusually placid for the intrepid Frenchman, the marquis seemed determined to let Canadian geography do the winning for him.

Finally, on 31 July, Wolfe made the sort of precipitate move that Montcalm had hoped for. At 5:30 P.M., along the narrow beach below the falls of the Montmorency, Wolfe landed his troops at the point where the French defenses were perhaps strongest. Advanced elements of Wolfe's invasion force—grenadiers, the storm troopers of their day—sprinted ahead of the main body to capture a redoubt on the steep slope leading up to the French defenses, but to no avail. Furious French fire caused them to abandon the position and to withdraw. Wolfe, sensing his attack unravel, ordered a general retreat. Indians charged down the slopes to scalp the dead and wounded. On this day, the British vanguard of grenadiers and Royal Americans lost 443 killed, wounded, and missing, according to Captain John Knox of the British 43rd Regiment. Vaudreuil wrote to Bourlamaque, "I have no more anxiety about Quebec. M. Wolfe, I can assure you, will make no progress." Yet the governor general did not know that Wolfe possessed a tenacity little seen in American war until Ulysses S. Grant.

Ironically, it was Montcalm who helped Wolfe find his winning strategy. Before the debacle at Montmorency Falls, part of the British fleet had worked itself up under the guns of Quebec to station itself upstream and above the city. Yet Montcalm, fixated by the drama along his defensive lines, did not understand if the Royal Navy could sail up above Quebec, it could transport troops there as well. Confident the steep heights above the town presented an impossible tactical roadblock to Wolfe, Montcalm made no attempt to fortify this exposed territory.

In the early days of September, Wolfe, despairing of ever taking the city on a hill, discovered a cove, or *anse*—known now as Wolfe's Cove—from on board one of the vessels upriver with a path that led directly to the ground above Quebec, the Plains of Abraham, named for a Scotsman named Abraham Martin who had once kept his herd there. On the night of 12 September, in a feat of genius seldom rivaled in the annals of armed conflict, Wolfe achieved the tactical miracle of putting his army, one man at a time, up the path and atop the Plains of Abraham, brushing aside puny resistance from a small party of soldiers.

On the morning of 13 September, Montcalm awoke to find Wolfe's army, captured in a rare painting by American artist Frederic Remington, arrayed before him on the Plains of Abraham. Here, in the moment of supreme crisis, the marquis's great sense of judgment fled him. Instead of waiting for reinforcements to come up from the defensive lines, troops held back by the stubborn Vaudreuil, or for others led by Bougainville to come up from a distance away, Montcalm decided impetuously on an attack. Rather than waiting for more soldiers who might have doubled his army, he engaged Wolfe on about equal terms—each fielding about 4,500 men. In such a situation, the disciplined volleys of the British infantry won the day, with Wolfe dying at the moment of his victory. His last words were, "Now, God be praised, I will die in peace." Montcalm paid the ultimate price for his battlefield haste. Mortally wounded, he died the following morning, with his honored remains still resting where they were interred in the convent of the Ursuline Sisters. By the time that Bougainville received word of the British appearance on the Plains of Abraham, it was too late to come to Montcalm's aid. As Bougainville sadly recalled, "when I came within range of the battle, our army was beaten and in retreat."

There was no appealing the verdict of the Battle of the Plains of Abraham, although Lévis would later defeat Wolfe's successor James Murray outside Quebec at Sainte-Foy in April 1760, his success one of history's footnotes. Through his uncharacteristic impetuosity on the morning of the battle of 13 September and his surprising failure to fortify the Plains earlier, Montcalm had given Wolfe the window of opportunity he needed to win a decisive victory. Montcalm's strategic and tactical wisdom had failed him in the most important battle of the war for, although the conflict would not end officially until Vaudreuil surrendered Montreal to Amherst on 7 September, 1760, nothing could reverse the outcome of Montcalm's defeat that day on the Plains of Abraham.

John F. Murphy, Jr.

References

Louis Antoine de Bougainville, *Adventures in the Wilderness: The American Journals of Louis Antoine de Bougainville, 1756–1760*, ed. and trans. by Edward P. Hamilton (1964); Lawrence Henry Gipson, *The Great War for the Empire: The Years of Defeat* (1946); ———, *The Great War for the Empire: The Years of Victory* (1959).

Edward P. Hamilton, *The French and Indian Wars: The Story of Battles and Forts in the Wilderness* (1962); ———, *Fort Ticonderoga: Key to a Continent* (1964); Christopher Hibbert, *Wolfe at Quebec* (1959); Journals of the Fort Ticonderoga Museum, Ticonderoga, New York; Douglas Edward Leach, *Arms for Empire: A Military History of the British Colonies in North America, 1607–1763* (1973); Sir B.H. Liddell Hart, *Strategy: The Indirect Approach* (1968).

Francis Parkman, *A Half-Century of Conflict* (1962); ———, *Montcalm and Wolfe* (1962); Robin Reilly, *Wolfe: The Rest to Fortune* (1973); Joseph Lister Rutledge, *A Century of Conflict* (1956); C.P. Stacey, *Quebec, 1759: The Siege and the Battle* (1959); Sun Tzu, *The Art of War* [many editions]; Dale Van Every, *Forth to the Wilderness: The First American Frontier, 1754–1774* (1961).

See also Bougainville, Louis-Antoine de; Fort Edward (New York); Lévis, François-Gaston de, Duc de; Fort Ontario (New York); Oswego, Battle of; Fort Oswego (New York); Pepperrell, William, Jr.; Quebec, Battle of; Rigaud de Vaudreuil de Cavagnial, Pierre de; Seven Years' War; Ticonderoga, Battle of; Fort William Henry (New York); Wolfe, James

M

Montiano, Manuel de (1685–1762)

Don Manuel de Montiano y Sopelana was born in Bilbao, Spain, in January 1685. In 1737, after 24 years of service to the Spanish crown, he was appointed governor and captain general of Florida. He was also to act as judge of the judicial review of his predecessor, Governor Francisco del Moral Sánchez. He served in Florida for more than 12 years, the second-longest tenure of any colonial governor.

Montiano was 52 years old and held the rank both of colonel and captain of the grenadiers at the time of his assignment to Florida. An experienced military man, he was chosen in part to defend Spain's long-standing territorial claims to 32° 30' north against English incursions. In his first years of office, Montiano led the colony through a series of battles with the British. In 1740, during the War of Jenkins' Ear, he successfully defended the Castillo de San Marcos, the fort at St. Augustine, against a 38-day siege led by James Oglethorpe of Georgia. Two years later, in July 1742, Montiano led a force of 1,900 men in a reprisal against the English. He attempted to drive Oglethorpe from St. Simons Island in Georgia but suffered a major defeat at the Battle of Bloody Marsh and was forced to retreat. In 1743, when the British once more marched into Florida, Montiano refused to be provoked into open battle and again out-waited Oglethorpe from inside the castillo.

Montiano undertook extensive rehabilitation of the castillo and its outerworks immediately upon reaching Florida. By 1740, he had replaced wooden support timbers with masonry vaults, repaired the existing fortification line, and built a new stockade. He also transformed a chapel on Anastasia Island into an effective lookout to guard the ocean entrance to the city.

After the wars, he built additional protective earthenworks to the north.

Aggravating the poor relations between the English and the Spanish during this period was Montiano's decision to formalize the previous informal practice of accepting runaway slaves from the English colonies. In 1738, Montiano decreed that all fugitive slaves from South Carolina were to be granted freedom in return for conversion to Catholicism. He also petitioned the governor of Cuba to free eight Carolinian slaves who had been taken to Havana. He settled the freed blacks in Gracia Real de Santa Teresa de Mose, also known as Fort Mose, about two miles north of St. Augustine. When Governor James Glen of South Carolina pressed for the return of runaways in 1739, Montiano declined, citing a royal edict of 1733 that required he grant them religious sanctuary. During the War of Jenkins' Ear, the British captured Fort Mose. Montiano gave the blacks refuge in St. Augustine and assigned them to participate in the recapture of the fort. After the British retreat, when Montiano commended his troops, he specifically cited both the bravery of the blacks and their industry in establishing the new community at Mose. In 1742, Montiano planned to send English-speaking blacks into Georgia and the Carolinas to incite the slaves to flee and settle in Florida.

When Montiano arrived in Florida, Indian allegiance to Spain was in rapid decline. In 1739, only nine Indian villages professed loyalty to Spain, and during the wars of 1740–1742, additional Indians deserted to the British. Although he often distrusted the natives, Montiano tried to reverse this trend and establish mutually beneficial relations. He was often thwarted by his superiors abroad. In 1738, he advocated that the language policy of the Franciscans be changed to compel the friars to learn the Indian dialects. This idea was rejected by the king along with other religious reforms. After the war, Montiano proposed liberal trade with the Indians as the only way to regain their friendship. Eager to win over the Yuchi and Lower Creek, he recommended a large, well-stocked post be established in Apalachee. Although the king accepted the idea, no supplies were ever provided and Montiano was forced to set up the post with items from his meager storehouse in St. Augustine. Provisions quickly ran out and were never replenished. Shortly thereafter, Montiano tried unsuccessfully to convince the English and French to agree to prohibit the supply of arms to the tribes of Florida, Louisiana, and the southeastern English colonies. At the same time, he tried once more to regain the friendship of the Lower Creek and Yuchi. In 1748, he invited the Yuchi to St. Augustine to negotiate an alliance. With only limited funds available to supply gifts, he used personal diplomacy during the negotiations. He arranged and participated personally in an impressive funeral for an Indian boy and appointed a Yuchi chief a captain in the Spanish army. These steps toward friendship were later undermined when Montiano was unable to secure supplies to help the Indians during droughts of 1748 and 1749. During this same period, Montiano was enraged when a band of 28 Lower Creek to whom he had presented gifts later attacked a party of Spaniards and Christian Yamasee Indians in June 1748. He dispatched soldiers who killed 27 renegades.

Montiano was an innovative and compassionate administrator. He tried various ways, large and small, to better the harsh lot of the Floridians. However, due to a lack of support from his superiors, most of his efforts came to naught. To revitalize the religious life of the colony, he suggested Jesuits replace the Franciscans, who were split between Spanish and Creole factions. In an attempt to eliminate the problems associated with reliance on imported food, Montiano proposed a colonization scheme to settle 50 families from the Canary Islands as farmers close to St. Augustine. Neither idea was supported by the crown.

In 1744, Montiano devised an elaborate devaluation scheme to collect the huge back debt owed to the colony by Mexico. He asked that 132,523 special pesos, with a value of one-quarter of the Mexican peso, be minted for use only in Florida. He argued that these new coins would confuse English traders, foil illicit trade, and prevent the flight of hard money from the colony. He proposed to use the money to aid the needy, construct new buildings and defense projects, and pay debts to Cuban merchants. The king ordered the viceroy of New Spain to mint these devalued coins, but no evidence exists that the viceroy ever compiled.

In 1744, Montiano also proposed establishing a naval stores industry in Florida. He envisioned the sale of tar, pitch, and spars to the Havana Company. Two years later he advocated free trade with the English in America. He argued that English supplies were cheaper than those provided by the Spanish and defective goods, such as moldy bread or wormy flour, could be rejected before purchase. Montiano was unable to garner support for either proposal from his superiors abroad.

Montiano left Florida in November 1748 to take the position of governor of Panama and president of the *audiencia* of Panama, a panel of judges with executive powers. He retired in 1758, returning to Madrid, where he died in 1762.

Kathryn L. Utter

References

Verne Chatelain, *The Defenses of Spanish Florida 1565 to 1763* (1941); Georgia Historical Society, *Collections,* Vol. VII, Part I (1909) and Part III (1913); Jane Landers, "Gracia Real de Santa Teresa de Mose: A Free Black Town in Spanish Florida," *American Historical Review,* 95 (1990):9–30; John Jay TePaske, *The Governorship of Spanish Florida, 1700–1763* (1964)

See also ANGLO-SPANISH WAR (1739–1744); BLACK AND INDIAN MILITIAS; BLOODY MARSH, BATTLE OF; FLORIDA, BRITISH INVASION OF; OGLETHORPE, JAMES EDWARD; MORAL SANCHEZ, FRANCISCO DEL; ST. AUGUSTINE

Montreal

Montreal, the commercial and military supply center of New France, is situated on an island of the same name at the confluence of the St. Lawrence and Ottawa Rivers. It was originally the site of the Laurentian Iroquoian fortified villages of Hochelaga and Tutonoguy surrounded by productive cornfields that were visited by Jacques Cartier in 1535 and 1541. In the early decades of the seventeenth century, when Samuel de Champlain proposed a permanent settlement on the island, it was uninhabited except for summer encampments of nomadic native hunters. In 1642, Paul de Chomeday de Maisonneuve, working in the interests of the pietistic Société Notre-Dame de Montreal dedicated to "the conversion of the savages," began construction of a utopian colony known as Ville-Marie. Within a year, the 70 original colonists had erected a fort for defense against Iroquois raids, individual dwellings, a small hospital, and a chapel. In 1657, the Sulpician secular clergy became the seigneurs of the island and town and provided spiritual services, including the organization of

sedentary missions for Mohawk, Algonquin, and Nipissing peoples who were eventually assembled on their seigneury at Oka in 1721–1726. The location in fertile agricultural land and on the main waterways, which served as transport and communication arteries, determined the development of the millenarian colony into a mercantile and military Montreal. It became the headquarters of the hinterland fur trade and base of the merchants engaged in it. From Montreal explorers and traders penetrated into the Mississippi Valley, the Sioux country, and organized the Compagnie du Nord for the trade on Hudson's Bay.

Settlers living in proximity were periodically threatened by Iroquois raiding parties in the intertribal contest for domination of the fur trade. In August 1689, 1,500 warriors attacked Lachine, burning 54 farms, killing 24 settlers, and taking scores prisoner. Peace was established in 1701 between the French, their allied tribes, and the Iroquois Five Nations. Montreal had about 1,000 inhabitants by this time. The period of peace between Britain and France (1713–1744) saw expansion of military and trading posts in the Great Lakes basin, the Illinois country, and onto the western prairies, as well as an advantageous, albeit illicit, trade between Montreal, Albany, and New York.

In the Seven Years' War, when the tide turned against the French regulars, Canadian militia, and allied native warriors in the Great Lakes region and at Quebec (1759), Montreal became the focal point of Anglo-American military action. The city had only approximately 8,000 inhabitants; its commerce was stifled; and it was not fortified. Therefore, it seemed prudent to ask for terms of surrender. On 8 September 1760, the articles of capitulation guaranteed the people of the French colony the maintenance of their property rights, their civil institutions, and religious privileges. With the capitulation of Montreal, the French regime in Canada came to an end and the colony was officially ceded to the British crown by the definitive Treaty of Paris in 1763. Montreal would continue to develop as the main commercial center under British rule and soon became the metropolis.

Cornelius J. Jaenen

References

[Dollier de Casson], *Histoire de Montreal, 1640–1672* (1868); Louise Dechêne, *Habitants et marchands de Montreal au XVIIe siècle* (1974); Olivier Massicotte, *Montreal sous le regime français: 1640–1760* (1919).

See also MONTREAL, ATTACK ON

Montreal, Attack on (1760)

After the fall of Quebec in September 1759, and the failure of François-Gaston de Lévis to retake it in May 1760, there was not much doubt as to how the British would proceed to attack Montreal, France's last holding in Canada. There were three major routes the British could take to reduce the city. One was to come upriver to Montreal from Quebec. The second was to take the water route north via Lake Champlain and the Richelieu River. The third approach was from the west, sailing from Oswego across Lake Ontario, then down the St. Lawrence River to Montreal. The British took all three routes so as to press in on all the scattered French forces.

Marking the start of the summer 1760 military campaign was Lévis' inability to retake Quebec. He thereupon fell back to Montreal with his force of some 6,000 men, roughly half of whom were militia, who readily deserted. Brigadier François-Charles de Bourlamaque was in command at Sorel on the south bank of the St. Lawrence, about 50 kilometers north of Montreal. Bourlamaque, with 3,000 men, and Major Jean-Daniel Dumas on the north bank, were shadowing Brigadier James Murray's force of 2,500 which had left Quebec on 14 July. Brigadier William Haviland's 3,000 pushed up Lake Champlain, outflanking Colonel Louis-Antoine de Bougainville's contingent of 1,700 stationed on the strategic Isle-aux-Noix. After a 16-day siege, Bougainville, outnumbered and outgunned, slipped away quietly during the night of 27 August, and joined up with the other French forces from the east and south who had fallen back on Montreal. During his advance upriver, Murray had been promising protection of life and property to the militiamen who would lay down their arms. As a result, both Bourlamaque and Bougainville witnessed large-scale desertions from their forces and were unable to mass enough soldiers to attack either of the relatively small forces of the two British commanders. The British were now in full control of the southern and eastern approaches to Montreal.

The main British force of about 10,000, under the command of General Jeffrey Am-

herst, was making its way cautiously from the west. Amherst had set out by water from Oswego and crossed Lake Ontario. Sailing down the St. Lawrence, he came upon Fort Lévis, a small rocky island in the river, not far from La Présentation mission (Ogdensburg, New York). Here there was a small unit of 350 regular Canadian troops of the marine regiment. Amherst, not wishing to leave any enemy fortifications in his rear, laid siege to the timbered fort. After two weeks, French Captain Pierre Pouchot de Maupas surrendered. Amherst then had to negotiate the series of rapids on the great river. In spite of losing 55 boats of various types and 84 soldiers drowned, Amherst landed his first troops on the island of Montreal 6 September. Haviland's and Murray's forces had been waiting two weeks for their commander to join them for the assault on Montreal.

However, with the desertions of the Canadians, the French numbered only some 3,000 at Montreal, against 15,000 British and Americans and perhaps 2,000 Indians. The French had only ten or 12 artillery pieces. Montreal's fortifications were flimsy; erected primarily to defend against Indian attacks, they never could have withstood a British bombardment. Seeing that further resistance was futile, the governor general of Canada, Pierre de Riguad de Vaudreuil, held council with the highest-ranking civil and military authorities. All agreed Montreal should be surrendered to the British in order to spare any further loss of life and property, the latter an important consideration with the coming of winter.

Colonel Bougainville, who spoke English, was delegated on 7 September to discuss terms with Amherst. Although provisions for the civilians were lenient, Amherst was harsh with the military personnel, adamantly insisting they lay down their arms and not serve for the remainder of the war. The officers protested vigorously because the ban would put them on half-pay. Amherst remained deaf to their pleas, blaming the French officers for the massacre by the Indians of their British prisoners after the battle at Fort William Henry in 1757. The French now had no choice but to accept the humiliating terms, and the formal surrender of Montreal was signed 8 September 1760.

Mary Kimbrough

References

Vincent J. Esposito, ed., *The West Point Atlas of American Wars, 1689–1900* (1959);

Edward P. Hamilton, *The French and Indian Wars: The Story of Battles and Forts in the Wilderness* (1962); René Kerallain, *La Jeunesse de Bougainville et la querre de Sept Ans* (1896); Mary Kimbrough, *Louis-Antoine de Bougainville, 1729–1811: A Study in French Naval History and Politics* (1990); Francis Parkman, *Montcalm and Wolfe* (1969).

See also AMHERST, JEFFREY; BOUGAINVILLE, LOUIS-ANTOINE DE; BOURLAMAQUE, FRANÇOIS-CHARLES DE; ISLE-AUX-NOIX; LÉVIS, FRANÇOIS-GASTON DE; MONTREAL; MURRAY, JAMES; POUCHOT DE MAUPAS, PIERRE; RIGAUD DE VAUDREUIL DE CAVAGNIAL, PIERRE DE; FORT WILLIAM HENRY (NEW YORK)

Montreal, Treaty of
See IROQUOIS TREATIES OF 1700 AND 1701

Fort Moore (South Carolina)
Fort Moore was constructed by the province of South Carolina in 1715 in order to protect the storehouses of Indian traders at Savannah Town near the head of navigation on the Savannah River. The name honored former Governor James Moore, who had led two punitive expeditions against the Spanish in Florida and their Indian allies in 1702 and 1704. The town and river were named for a wandering tribe known by several names including Suwanee, Shawnee, and Savannah. The fort represented a reaction of the Carolina government to the Yamasee Indian uprising in 1715 and was meant to be a buffer against hostile Creek Indians west of the Savannah River. In 1733, Carolinians welcomed James Oglethorpe's Georgians as extra protection to its western frontier.

Fort Moore, atop a high bluff, measured 150 feet square, with walls only four feet high. Its barracks were built for 100 men, but the garrison actually numbered between 14 and 30. The South Carolina general assembly authorized a town of 300 half-acre lots to be laid out adjacent to the fort in 1721, but the ambitious plans were never realized. Instead, 20 or 30 structures, mostly storehouses, clustered haphazardly near the fort with small farms round about.

In 1730, the settlement around Fort Moore was designated New Windsor Township, one of 11 such townships on the Carolina perimeter of settlement. Essentially a traders' town, New Windsor was the point of departure for caravans trading to the Cherokee in the mountains, the Creek in the interior, and the Chickasaw in the Mississippi Valley. By the economic ties fashioned by the Carolina traders, Britain established a claim to the entire region east of the Mississippi.

The New Windsor traders began moving across the river into Georgia in 1736 when Parliament gave control of the western trade to Georgia. Although New Windsor was nearly depopulated, Fort Moore was maintained during the two colonial wars with France. During the Cherokee War of 1759–1761, it served as a refuge for refugees from the Carolina upcountry. In 1766, Fort Moore was abandoned and its garrison transferred to Fort Charlotte, some 30 miles upriver.

Edward J. Cashin

See also CREEK; SOUTH CAROLINA; YAMASEE WAR

Moral Sánchez, Francisco del
Francisco del Moral Sánchez was governor of Spanish Florida from 1733–1737. He deterred British advancement from Georgia into Spanish territory, but was removed from office under accusations of misuse of funds, abuse of authority, neglect of duty, and illicit trade.

An infantryman who advanced through the ranks during 30 years of service in Cuba, Francisco del Moral Sánchez, in a departure from normal appointive procedures, was selected for the Florida governorship by the governor of Cuba, rather than by the king. Once in Florida, Moral ordered the building of Forts San Francisco de Pupo and Picolata, where the trail to the missions crossed the St. Johns River, west of St. Augustine. Faced with insufficient men, funds, and supplies, Moral resorted to diplomacy to keep the British of Georgia out of Spanish Florida. Officials in Spain bitterly denounced Moral's accord with Georgia's James Oglethorpe that included mutual restraint of the Native Americans with the colonies' respective control, demilitarization of the St. Johns River, and the submission of border disputes to European arbitration. Moral, however, readied for war while negotiating peace.

While diplomatically and militarily holding the British at bay at the border, Moral allowed English traders to operate freely in St.

M

Augustine and he sold English goods for profit. He mixed in disputes between Iberian and Creole Franciscan friars and arrested local dignitaries with whom he quarreled. In March 1737, Manuel de Justís, appointed as interim governor, arrived with orders to remove Moral from office and impound his belongings. Moral claimed sanctuary in the Franciscan friary to avoid arrest. Auxiliary Bishop Francisco de San Buenaventura intervened to persuade Moral to surrender. Moral was imprisoned in Havana and then Spain until 1740. The Council of the Indies ultimately exonerated Moral in 1748. Although he departed Florida in disgrace, Moral's accomplishments in defense had maintained Spanish presence in the Southeast and limited British presence to north of the St. Johns River.

Susan R. Parker

References

Michael V. Gannon, *The Cross in the Sand: The Early Catholic Church in Florida, 1513–1870* (1965); John Jay TePaske, *The Governorship of Spanish Florida, 1700–1763* (1964).

See also COUNCIL OF INDIES; FLORIDA

Mortar of the Okchai (?–1774)

The Mortar was the principal warrior of the Upper Creek town of Okchai. The Mortar's proper Indian war name, given as a busk title around the time he reached puberty, was Yahatastanage, loosely translated as Wolf Warrior. By the early 1750s, the Mortar had become the spokesman for the younger warriors of Okchai and surrounding towns. He and his followers established a small settlement on the fringes of Creek territory in the 1750s, but were forced to abandon it during the Cherokee War and return to Okchai. By 1766, he was known as Otis (Otassu) Mico, a headman, thereby occupying the highest civil position in Creek town government. He was a member of the Bear Clan.

Throughout his lively career, he espoused several notable aims: lowering trade prices, curbing abusive trade practices, and forming a coalition of Indian tribes to stand firm against European expansion into Indian territory. The Mortar's willingness to be courted by France during the 1740s and 1750s, and his staunch refusal to compromise his goals, enraged the British and he was regarded as the leader of the French party among the Creeks. Most of the "conspiracies" associated with the Mortar were exaggerated by the British. His goals were not so much anti-British as they were pro-Creek.

He frequently met with the French at Fort Toulouse. There he sought to win trade concessions and to use the French to impede British expansion. He also worked tirelessly to end intertribal warfare among the Choctaw, Cherokee, and Creek. He supported the elimination of British forts in Cherokee territory, and due to his leadership, the British were not given clearance to build a fort among the Upper Creek. The British especially resented the Mortar's French proclivities after the Seven Years' War erupted. In 1759, in an attempt to garner support for Britain during the conflict, Edmond Atkin, the superintendent of Indian affairs, toured the Creek towns. Due to the Mortar's activities, Atkin refused to visit Okchai and attempted to cut off British trade to the village. At a meeting of all Upper Creek headmen at Tuckabatchee in September 1759, Atkin refused to allow the Mortar to receive the peace pipe that was circulating among the assemblage—a highly undiplomatic step that insulted all the Creek present. The stupid action nearly cost the superintendent his life, for one of the Mortar's warriors lunged at Atkin with a hatchet. The attack stunned the superintendent, but did not inflict serious injury. The other chiefs present quickly restrained the warrior and the dissidents withdrew. Following the incident, the Creek managed to maintain a precarious peace with the British for the remainder of the Seven Years' War. The incident created considerable animosity among the Upper Creek. When war broke out between the Cherokee and the British in 1760, the Mortar was involved in some of the fighting and urged Creek participation. His was a minority sentiment, however, and the Creeks remained neutral.

British forces ultimately triumphed over the French, and in 1763, France relinquished control of all its lands east of the Mississippi River. Many Creeks feared they would be made to suffer for their French contacts during the war. But all sides favored peace, including the British, who were weary of the expense and turmoil of the previous decades. British politicians realized it was essential to placate the Mortar and other disaffected headmen to secure prosperity for the new colonies they hoped to build along the Gulf coast. General Thomas Gage, the commander in chief of all British forces in America, suggested to John Stuart, who replaced Edmund Atkin as British superintendent of Indian affairs, that it might be prudent to have the Mortar assassinated.

Fortunately, Stuart followed another course. At Pensacola, the Mortar was appointed as one of five Great Medal chiefs of the Upper Creek in 1765. Medal chiefs, selected from among the most prominent headmen, were supposed to represent the British viewpoint to their people and work for peace. Britain hoped, by large presents of rum and other trade goods, to buy these men. The Mortar was never unduly impressed with his Great Medal. He resigned it twice when he felt he had been slighted by the British or when they had failed to live up to an agreement. He is the only southern Indian chief ever known to resign a Great Medal. The Mortar continued to lobby for better trade terms, constantly denounced the illegal occupation of Indian land by white settlers, and sought to build a multi-tribal alliance to stand firm against the powerful British Empire in America. His protestations against high trade prices ultimately paid off, and in 1767, the price schedule for Creek goods was renegotiated. He also continued to work against land cessions. He consistently advocated peace among all tribes, but failed to accomplish this goal due to the encouragement the intertribal wars received from the British.

In December 1774, during the Creek-Choctaw war, the Mortar and a band of 85 Creek set out for New Orleans. They hoped to purchase ammunition from the Spanish to offset a trade embargo enacted by Georgia in the aftermath of Creek attacks against Georgia settlers. A group of Choctaw attacked the party. Mortally wounded in the chest, stomach, and thigh, the Mortar died on the trade path shortly after the battle.

The Mortar's achievements were few, though significant. Under his guidance, the Upper Creek ceded less land to whites than did any other southern Indian tribe, except the landlocked Chickasaw. He won, if only for a time, what his people considered fair trade prices. His proposed coalition of southern and western tribes to oppose white expansion never got off the ground, but was the forerunner of the pan-Indian movements of the early nineteenth century.

Kathryn E. Holland Braund

References

John R. Alden, *John Stuart and the Southern Colonial Frontier* (1944); David H. Corkran, *The Cherokee Frontier: Conflict and Survival, 1740–1762* (1962); ____. *The Creek Frontier, 1540–1783* (1967).

See also ATKIN, EDMOND; CREEK; CREEK-CHOCTAW WARS; STUART, JOHN; FORT TOULOUSE (ALABAMA)

Moulton, Jeremiah (1688–c. 1760)

In 1692, four-year-old Jeremiah Moulton was captured in the January attack on York, Maine. Somehow he managed to escape, or was released, but it is unlikely he ever forgot the experience, or the attack in which his parents were killed. Thirty years later he began Dummer's War as a sergeant, quickly rose to lieutenant, and finally captain. Moulton led many patrols and raids along the Maine frontier, and commanded one of the companies sent to attack Norridgewock in August 1724. Moulton led the actual assault on the village. After the war, Moulton continued public service as representative to the General Court between 1726–1728. Moulton, promoted to colonel, commanded one of the Maine regiments sent to Louisbourg in 1745. At the conclusion of King George's War, Moulton served for many years as sheriff of York County.

Steven C. Eames

References

Charles Edward Banks, *History of York, Maine*, 2 vols. (1931–1935).

See also DUMMER'S WAR; NORRIDGEWOCK, BATTLE OF; SCOUT

Murray, James (1725–1794)

Born the fifth son of Alexander, fourth lord Elibank, and Elizabeth Stirling, James Murray was commissioned second lieutenant in Wynyard's Marines in 1740, seeing service during the War of the Austrian Succession in the West Indies, Flanders, and Brittany. In the Indies, he was fortunate to survive the Cartagena expedition, where disease ravaged the British forces more severely than did the Spanish. In 1748, Murray took part in operations at L'Orient on the coast of Brittany as a grenadier captain in the 15th Regiment.

M

With war's end, Murray's promotion prospects, like those of officers generally, slowed. Promoted major in 1749, Murray purchased the lieutenant colonelcy of the 15th in 1751, and held that rank on the unsuccessful expedition against Rochefort (1757) during the Seven Years' War. After serving as a defense witness at the court-martial of the expedition's commander, Sir John Mordaunt, Murray arrived in North America in late 1757. In 1758, he served as a brigade commander against Louisbourg, where he was described by James Wolfe as acting "with infinite spirit." In 1759, he served as a brigadier under Wolfe at Quebec, commanding the left wing of the army at the battle of the Plains of Abraham, 13 September. Murray was made lieutenant colonel and commandant of a battalion in the 60th Regiment on 24 October. The death of Wolfe meant that command devolved on Brigadier George Townshend. Townshend was too well connected to spend the winter in Canada, while his immediate junior, Robert Monckton, was recovering from wounds. The first winter of occupation, therefore, fell to Murray. As part of his somewhat limited strategy against Quebec, Wolfe had ordered an indiscriminate bombardment of the city. One of the cardinal rules of eighteenth-century warfare, however, was to never destroy quarters which might be needed for one's own troops. Over the cold and desolate winter of 1759–1760, Murray and his 4,000 men would learn the truth of this rule, and the consequences of its being abrogated. In early spring 1760, the French commander, François-Gaston de Lévis, counterattacked in the hope of retaking the capital before the arrival of the English fleet. Murray, hoping élan would compensate for material weaknesses, fell upon his enemy at Sainte-Foy on 28 April 1760. Suffering greater losses than had Wolfe the previous September, Murray gained a black mark on his otherwise competent, if unexceptional, record. In England and the colonies Murray was blamed for sacrificing so many men in what Colonel Henry Bouquet described as "that rash attempt." Lévis's victory proved hollow, however, with HMS *Lowestoft* arriving on 9 May, and additional ships on the 16th.

That summer, Murray took part in operations against Montreal on 7 September 1760, which fell to a three-pronged attack by Major General Jeffrey Amherst from Lake Champlain, Lieutenant Colonel William Haviland from Lake Ontario, and Murray from Quebec. On 27 October 1760, British-occupied Canada was divided into three military districts: Brigadier Thomas Gage commanded at Montreal; Colonel Ralph Burton at Trois Rivières; Murray at Quebec. Murray was promoted major general on 10 July 1762. After Canada was formally ceded to Britain with the Treaty of Paris, 10 February 1763, Murray became the province's first governor on 21 November 1763. As governor, Murray had the unenviable task of implementing an often inarticulate and confusing colonial policy formulated in London. He was instrumental in raising Canadian volunteers for the war against Pontiac in 1763, and generally demonstrated great sympathy for the war-ravaged Canadians. Murray showed little patience, however, for the ever-complaining English merchants and traders of Montreal. The army was not without its own sources of conflict and tension, particularly after Murray first became governor. Brigadier Frederick Haldimand questioned the authority of Colonel Burton, now that his military district had ceased to exist, and challenged Murray's authority over the army in Canada on the grounds that, though a major general, Murray's was a civilian post. Undeniably, elements of personality and the eternal competition among officers for promotion played a role in these disputes; but what they really represented were the pangs of the army learning an entirely new role: administering a colonial empire.

Leaving Canada in 1766, Murray was made colonel of the 13th Foot in 1767. In 1772, he was promoted lieutenant general and assumed command of Minorca in 1774, which he was forced to surrender after a length siege on 5 February 1782. Honorably acquitted by the subsequent courtmartial, Murray received the commendation of George III for his defense of the island. He became a full general in 1783. In 1789, he was made colonel of the 21st Foot. James Murray died on 18 June 1794, while serving as governor of Hull, Canada.

While James Murray's career may give him claim to moderate fame, other members of his family were worthy of still more note, particularly his nephews Adam Ferguson, a mainstay of the Scottish Enlightenment, and Patrick Ferguson, rifle designer and army officer killed in the American War of Independence.

Adam Norman Lynde

References

Ferdinand J. Dreer Autograph Collection, Historical Society of Pennsylvania; Thomas Gage Papers, American Series, William R. Clements Library, University of Michigan; G.S. Kimball, ed., *Correspondence of William Pitt* (1906); Douglas Edward Leach, *Arms for Empire: A Military History of the British Colonies in North America, 1607–1763* (1973); Stanley Pargellis, ed., *Military Affairs in America, 1748–1765* (1969).

See also LÉVIS, FRANÇOIS-GASTON DE; MONCKTON, ROBERT; MONTREAL, ATTACK ON; QUEBEC, FRENCH ATTEMPT TO RECAPTURE; QUEBEC, BATTLE OF

Musgrove, Mary (c. 1700–1765)

Mary Musgrove was one of the most colorful and influential figures in colonial Georgia. During her lifetime, she played many significant roles—Indian trader, interpreter, liaison between the Creek Indians and the English, and finally, the largest landowner in Georgia. Her most important contribution, however, was as a "forest diplomat."

In the colonial Southeast, early relations between the Indians and the whites were defined primarily in terms of trade and military alliances. The most successful links between the two cultures were typically traders of mixed Indian-white heritage. These *métis,* or mixed-bloods, were the forest diplomats of the south. Equally familiar with both cultures, they were able to use their influence effectively in either world. There was only one woman who earned the title "forest diplomat" in the eighteenth century—Mary Musgrove.

Mary Musgrove was born about 1700 in the Creek nation. Her mother was a full-blooded Indian and a member of the ruling clan in Coweta, one of the principal towns of the Lower Creek. Her father was a white trader from Carolina named Edward Griffin. Mary's Creek name was Coosaponakeesa, but as a young girl she was baptized and christened Mary by her father's family. She spent her childhood among her father's people in Pon Pon, Carolina. She was also taught to read and write, thereby becoming one of an exceptionally small group of literate, Christianized Indians in that period.

In 1717, Mary married Johnny Musgrove, son of a prominent Carolina trader and an Indian woman. This marriage was arranged by Mary's uncle, the powerful "Emperor" Brims of Coweta, as part of peace negotiations ending the Yamasee War. Mary and Johnny Musgrove

initially settled in the Creek nation, but in 1725, they returned to Pon Pon where they built a highly successful deerskin trade with the Creek. The couple had three sons and Mary worked alongside her husband in their trade center.

The year before the first settlers arrived in Georgia, the Musgroves requested permission from the Carolina government to open a new trade store on the Savannah River. When James Oglethorpe and the initial group of colonists arrived in 1733, the Musgroves were on hand to welcome them. Mary and her husband served as Oglethorpe's interpreters in his dealings with the local Yamacraw Indians, and their chief, Tomochichi.

Mary Musgrove began her long career as a forest diplomat during these early years spent as Oglethorpe's liaison to the Indians. She convinced the Yamacraws to accept the whites peacefully, and then encouraged them to cede a portion of their land to the trustees of Georgia. Mary was also able to help Oglethorpe secure Creek friendship. The Creek were the largest and closest Indian nation, but more importantly, they held sole title to the land south of the Savannah River.

Creek allegiance was crucial to the survival of the colony—not only to strengthen Georgia's territorial claims, but to erect a barrier between the English and their European rivals along the southern frontier. By the 1730s, Creek leaders had begun to understand their nation's role in the international struggle for control of the Southeast. The old "Emperor" Brims had proved to his people that a firm policy of Creek neutrality kept the European rivals in check. Mary Musgrove's relationship to Brims, and her influence in the nation because of her blood ties to the ruling clan, played a vital role in securing Creek loyalty.

When Oglethorpe invited the Lower Creek headmen to Savannah in mid-1733 to discuss a land cession and alliance, Johnny Musgrove served as the official interpreter. Mary was also present and she took the lead in encouraging her Indian relations to accept the English offer. Her sphere of influence as a trader's wife had now widened beyond her immediate kin to include the headmen of the other Lower Creek towns. By the end of 1733, Mary Musgrove was no longer simply the wife of a prominent Indian trader, she had become Oglethorpe's liaison to the Creek.

Johnny Musgrove accompanied Oglethorpe on a visit to London in 1734, and Mary remained in Georgia where she continued to act as interpreter for visiting Indians. She also provided meat for the colonists, regularly diverting some of her hunters to bring in venison. When colonists needed supplies, Mary used her personal credit with Charles Town merchants on their behalf. These years of service earned Mary a circle of loyal and influential friends in Georgia.

After her husband's death in 1735, Mary continued to run her trade store and act as Oglethorpe's interpreter. Three years later she married a former indentured servant, Jacob Matthews. In that same year, she received a grant from Tomochichi, chief of the Yamacraws, for a strip of vacated tribal land adjacent to Savannah. This gift would later place her in the middle of colonial Georgia's most notorious controversy.

At Oglethorpe's request, the Matthews built a second trade store, Mount Venture, on the south side of the Altamaha River about 150 miles from Savannah. This store was designed to attract the Lower Creek and provide an advance guard if the Spanish attacked the colony. In 1739, the couple established a third trade post, the "Forks," at the juncture of the Oconee, Altamaha, and Okmulgee Rivers. Both of these trade stores were destroyed during Anglo-Spanish hostilities between 1741 and 1742.

Jacob Matthews died in 1742 and Mary continued to act as interpreter at Frederica and provide warriors when requested. The two commanders who succeeded Oglethorpe, after his final departure in 1743, came to depend on Mary's skills as an interpreter and use her as their agent to the Creeks. In 1744, she married for the third time. Her new husband was an English minister, Thomas Bosomworth.

Once Bosomworth entered her life, Mary's energies gradually shifted from forest diplomacy to matters which affected her more directly. She began to use her influence among the Creek to press her claims to the land Tomochichi had given her. Neither the Savannah magistrates nor the trustees, however, were willing to confirm Mary's claim. Legalizing an Indian grant to a private citizen would have embroiled the authorities in an unwelcome dispute over the crown's claim to territorial sovereignty in the colonies.

Mary's battle with the authorities over her land claims culminated in the summer of 1749 when the Bosomworths led a group of approximately 100 Creek into Savannah. The unexpected arrival of so many Indians badly frightened the townspeople; but in the end, the Bosomworths were unable to force the magistrates' hand, and Thomas and Mary retreated back into the Creek nation.

In the following years, the Bosomworths continued to press for confirmation of Tomochichi's grant. Mary used her influence among the Lower Creek in an effort to validate it. She approached her relatives in the nation and was able to get grants from the Lower Creek giving her title to Saint Catherines, Sapelo, and Ossabaw Islands in addition to the Yamacraw tract.

The Bosomworths also enlisted the support of James Glen, governor of South Carolina. In 1752, Creek warriors had ambushed several Cherokee on the path to Charles Town. Since Carolina guaranteed the safety of all Indian allies traveling within the colony's borders, Glen and his council wanted the guilty Creeks punished. No one in Charles Town was willing to act as agent to the Creeks in this delicate affair. The Bosomworths were in Charles Town and Mary offered her services to Glen. Thomas Bosomworth was eventually named agent and Mary was appointed the official interpreter for the mission.

Mary's influence among her relatives in the Upper and Lower Creek was undiminished. After several impassioned speeches by Mary, and countless private meetings, the Bosomworths were able to avert war between the Creek and Cherokee. A treaty between these two nations was signed in Carolina the following year. It is unlikely that any other colonial agent of the period could have accomplished what Mary did on this mission. She never received payment for her services.

The Bosomworths went to England in 1754 to petition the Board of Trade for confirmation of Mary's land grant, but once again they were rebuffed. In order to raise enough money to pay their expenses home, Mary and Thomas sold a one-half interest in the three sea islands to an unwitting English investor named Isaac Levy. With the profits from this dubious transaction, the two returned to Georgia and settled on Saint Catherines Island. Bosomworth stocked the island with cattle and adopted the lifestyle of a wealthy plantation owner.

Mary Musgrove's influence in the Creek nation, and in Georgia and Carolina, did not decline over the years. When the Indian threat to Georgia became a reality during the Seven Years' War, Governor Henry Ellis moved to secure Mary's loyalty. In 1760, he finally convinced the

English to acknowledge the Bosomworth land claims. Mary agreed to accept title to St. Catherines and a lump sum settlement in exchange for relinquishing any claim to the Yamacraw tract, Sapelo, and Ossabaw.

Mary Musgrove probably died in 1765. She left no surviving children; her husband, Thomas, remarried soon after. At the time of her death, Mary was the largest landowner in Georgia. Her years of service as Oglethorpe's liaison to the Creek had been crucial to the peaceful settlement of Georgia, and until her death she remained a loyal friend to the English.

Doris B. Fisher

References

Allen D. Candler, ed., *Colonial Records of Georgia*, 26 vols. (1904–1916); Colonial Office Papers, ser. 5, Public Record Office of Great Britain; David H. Corkran, *The Creek Frontier, 1640–1783* (1967); John Pitts Corry, *Indian Affairs in Georgia, 1732–1756* (1936); E. Merton Coulter, ed., *The Journal of William Stephens, 1741–1743* (1958); ———, *The Journal of Peter Gordon, 1732–1735* (1963); Verner W. Crane, *The Southern Frontier, 1670–1732* (1929).

John T. Juricek, ed., *Early American Indian Documents: Treaties and Laws, 1607–1789. Volume XI, Georgia Treaties, 1733–1763* (1989); William L. McDowell, ed., *Journals of the Commissioners of the Indian Trade, 1710–1718* (1955); South Carolina Commons House Journals MSS; South Carolina Council Journals MSS; South Carolina Miscellaneous Records MSS; Sylvia Van Kirk, *Many Tender Ties: Women in Fur-Trade Society 1670–1870* (1983).

See also BRIMS, EMPEROR; CREEK; GEORGIA; GLEN, JAMES; OGLETHORPE, JAMES EDWARD

Mutiny, Navy

Technically, the term "mutiny" means the seizure of a ship by members of its crew. However, in some instances, the seizure was perpetrated by an officer and, on some occasions, refusal to obey an order by the captain has been construed as mutiny without seizure of the vessel.

Before the reforms of Samuel Pepys in the late seventeenth century, mutiny was frequent in ships of the Royal Navy. Disgruntlement over low and infrequent pay, bad food, conditions on board, orders to sail in unsafe vessels, or disaffection from the regime ashore caused several mutinies in that century. In January 1627, a number of ship crews refused to sail from Plymouth, England, ostensibly because of the poor condition of the ships. In 1650, some crewmen on the *Hart* mutinied in favor of the king; in 1653, the *Portland* suffered a short-lived mutiny. In each case, the disturbance was suppressed and the perpetrators lightly punished.

Following the Pepys reforms, mutinies were few. In 1696, some officers and men of the *Speedwell* attempted to seize the ship and turn to piracy in the West Indies, but were thwarted. During Lord Anson's passage round Cape Horn in 1741–1742, the small warship *Wager* became separated from the main body. The crew, weakened by scurvy, were unable to prevent the ship from running onto rocks on the coast of Chile on 15 May 1742. Discipline collapsed and all but nine of the crew threw off their obedience to the captain and sailed off in the ship's boats. Then, in 1748, the first lieutenant and lieutenant of marines of the *Chesterfield* seized the ship while the captain was ashore at Cape Coast Castle in Africa. Loyal crewmen were able to take the ship back, and the two officer mutineers and four others were executed.

The *Bounty* mutiny resulted from a breakdown of discipline rather than over conditions of the service; but the mass mutinies at Spithead and the Nore in 1797 were directly connected to the fact that the pay of sailors had not been increased since the Pepys reform. It is possible that many failed mutinies were not reported because the captain of a mutinous ship was subject to court-martial as well. Some vessels deemed lost at sea may have succumbed not to the elements, but to mutineers.

John F. Battick

See also NAVY, GREAT BRITAIN

Mutiny, Regular Army

Despite the importance of the Mutiny Act to its administration, mutinies in the English army were not the common occurrence that they were for contemporary French or Spanish forces. In part, this was because the English army was very small and was highly dispersed when quartered. Thus soldiers were unable to gather for the purpose of discussing grievances. Additionally, it was not uncommon for officers to attempt to mitigate the material sufferings of their men—the most common cause of mutiny in this

M

era—out of their own pockets. In addition, soldiers often supplemented bad pay or sparse provisions with private income from either a specific trade or common labor. For some regulars, soldiering became but a part-time trade.

Though these factors mitigated against the great mutinies that plagued the Spanish forces, the English army did have its troubles. Excessive discipline, wretched quarters, or simple regimental mismanagement could turn otherwise obedient soldiers against their officers. The minor presence of the army before 1755 meant that North America saw few such incidents. In 1763, however, the garrisons at Albany, Montreal, Quebec, Halifax, and Louisbourg mutinied. The cause was the reimposition of peacetime deductions from the soldiers' pay to cover food, fuel, and clothing expenses. The mutineers argued that American service made such reductions a hardship. Ultimately, the soldiers went back to their duties when the army cut the rate of reduction in half, a partial acceptance of the hardship of American service. It is ironic that the first "tax revolt" after the Seven Years' War was waged by the British army.

Adam Norman Lynde

References

Christopher Duffy, *The Military Experience in the Age of Reason* (1988); William Alfred Foote, "The American Independent Companies of the British Army, 1664–1764," Ph.D. Dissertation, University of California, Los Angeles (1966); Thomas Gage Papers, American Series, William L. Clements Library, University of Michigan, Ann Arbor; J.A. Houlding, *Fit For Service, The Training of the British Army, 1715–1795* (1981); Rex Whitworth, *Field Marshal Lord Ligonier, A Story of the British Army, 1702–1770* (1958).

N

Nairne, Thomas (c. 1672–1715)

Thomas Nairne, soldier, politician diplomat, and cartographer, was probably born in northeastern Scotland, moving to South Carolina by 1695. Seven years later he was involved with a raid against Florida to capture Indian slaves. He penetrated as far as the Everglades and returned to Charles Town with 35 Indians who were sold as slaves. That same year Nairne was employed by the South Carolina assembly to regulate traders among the Yamasee, and he became an active supporter of sending missionaries to the Indians. By 1706, he represented Colleton County in the assembly and led that body against Governor Nathaniel Johnson in a successful attempt to abolish acts requiring religious conformity of legislative members.

Nairne's Indian trade bill of 1707 created the post of Indian agent, and he became South Carolina's first appointee to that post. He subsequently authored that colony's Indian policy. In 1708, amid rumors of a French plan to attack Carolina overland with an Indian army from Mobile, Nairne developed an elaborate scheme to protect his province. Nairne and Thomas Welch, a Carolina trader among the Chickasaws, proposed to isolate the French at Mobile by traveling more than 400 miles through Indian country and winning over French Indian allies in the Southeast. Nairne kept a journal of his trip and outlined a "bold plan for the British to use the fur, deerskin and slave trade" to gain allegiance of the Indian tribes and then direct this British Indian alliance against the French and Spanish colonies in North America.

Nairne's plans to take control of the whole mid-continent of North America resulted in this portion of his journal being described as "one of the most remarkable documents in the history of Anglo-American imperialism." His journal also contains a wealth of ethnographical information on the customs, ceremonies, and social organization of the Chickasaws and Creeks (specifically the Talapoosas and the Ocheses). In fact, Nairne gives one of the earliest and fullest accounts in English available on these tribes.

However, Nairne's attempt to regulate traders brought him into conflict with the governor of South Carolina, and he was charged with high treason and jailed. The government denied him a seat in the assembly and discharged him as Indian agent. Nairne was never tried, and when released he traveled to England where he won the favor of the Lord Proprietors, who secured his appointment as judge advocate of South Carolina.

By 1711, he was elected to the assembly again and the following year was reappointed as Indian agent. In spite of attempts to end trader abuses, he was not successful. When the Yamasee War (1715–1717) erupted, Nairne was attempting to redress some Yamasee Indian grievances. He was awakened 15 April 1715 by war cries, captured, and tortured for three days by fire (sticking splinters into his body and igniting them) before he finally died.

William L. Anderson

References

Verner W. Crane, *The Southern Frontier, 1670–1732* (1929); J. Norman Heard, *Handbook of the American Frontier: Four Centuries of Indian-White Relationships* (1987); Alexander Moore, ed., *Nairne's Muskhogean Journals: The 1708 Expedition* to the Mississippi River (1988); John Philip Reid, *A Better Kind of Hatchet: Law, Trade, and Diplomacy in the Cherokee Nation during the Early Years of European Contact* (1976).

See also ADAIR, JAMES; ATKIN, EDMOND; CRAVEN, CHARLES; YAMASEE WAR

Nansemond

The Nansemond, whom Captain John Smith termed "a proud warlike nation" that had an estimated 200 warriors, lived along Virginia's Nansemond River, not far from the mouth of the James. They were Algonkian-speakers and during the first half of the seventeenth century were part of the Powhatan chiefdom. In September 1608, the Nansemond attacked a party of colonists who entered their river on an exploratory visit, but they were subdued when the intruding explorers discharged a retaliatory hail of musket shot. The English seized the Nansemond king's weapons, a chain of pearls, and 400 baskets of corn before sailing away. In the late fall they returned for more corn, which they again obtained through the use of force.

The Nansemond, who were active participants in the 22 March 1622 Indian uprising, captured a colonist and his wife that lived on the upper James River. They also were implicated in the 18 April 1644 uprising that claimed the lives of numerous settlers on the lower James. The Nansemond stubbornly resisted the colonists' intrusion into their homeland and seemingly retarded the spread of settlement in lower Hampton Roads. They were attacked by the combined militias of Isle of Wight and Norfolk Counties in March 1646, which culminated in their becoming English tributaries later in the year. During the early 1660s, the Nansemond sought military assistance from the colonial government, for they had problems with the Weyanocks, whose king they were accused of killing, and they had difficulty with the Pamunkey, who allegedly abducted two of their men. The Nansemond also feuded with the Tuscarora. It may have been such native infighting that led Virginia officials to reaffirm the southerly boundary line between the colonists and the territory that was left to the occupation of the Indians. In 1669, the Nansemond had 45 warriors and were living in Nansemond County.

The king of the Nansemond signed the 29 May 1677 Treaty of Middle Plantation, whereby his people became tributaries to the crown. During the 1690s, the Nansemond petitioned Virginia officials for protection against certain stronger, outlying tribes that had invaded their territory. By the early eighteenth century the Nansemond were seated near the Nottoway River's mouth; eventually they joined forces with the Nottoway Indians. In 1705 the Nansemond were credited with 30 bowmen.

Martha W. McCartney

References

Robert Beverley, *History of the Present State of Virginia* (1705), Louis B. Wright, ed. (1947); William W. Hening, ed., *The Statutes at Large: Being a Collection of All the Laws of Virginia*, 13 vols. (1809–1823); H.R. McIlwaine, ed., *Executive Journals of the Council of Colonial Virginia*, 5 vols. (1925–1945); ———, *Minutes of Council and General Court of Colonial Virginia* (1934); Helen C. Rountree, *Pocahontas's People: The Powhatan Indians of Virginia Through Four Centuries* (1980); John Smith, *Travels and Works of Captain John Smith, President of Virginia and Admiral of New England, 1580–1631*, Edward Arber, ed., 2 vols. (1910).

See also PAMUNKEY; POWHATAN; VIRGINIA-INDIAN TREATY (1646); VIRGINIA-INDIAN TREATY (1677/1680); VIRGINIA-INDIAN WAR (1622–1632); VIRGINIA-INDIAN WAR (1644–1646);

Nanticoke
See MARYLAND

Narragansett

Narragansett referred to both the Narragansett tribe and the extended sachemdom, including the Coweset, Shawomet, Pawtuxet, Manissean, Niantics, and parts of the Nipmucks and Montauks. Narragansett territory comprised much of present-day Rhode Island, but the tribe's influence was felt throughout the Long Island and Block Island Sound regions by the Pequot, Mohegans, and Wampanoags. Spared the epidemics of the late 1610s, the Narragansetts were the strongest of the southern New England Indian tribes, able to muster an army, according to Daniel Gookin, of 5,000 men. As the strongest, the Narragansett was the most aggressive tribe in southeastern New England and was not adverse to pitched battle—though it was more likely to effect covert raids than direct assaults.

Over the course of 70 years, relations with the English degenerated from anxious to inflamed. In 1622, Narragansett sachem Canonicus sent a snakeskin filled with arrows to Plymouth. The Pilgrims, interpreting this action as a threat, returned the snakeskin filled with shot and powder, symbolizing their readiness for war. With the invasion of the Puritans in the 1630s, the Pequots tried to ally themselves with the Narragansetts to repulse the Puritan onslaught, but the Puritans feared a powerful Pequot-Narragansett alliance and encouraged Roger Williams to bring the Narragansetts into league with them. Williams's mission was successfully completed in October 1636 when the Narragansetts made a covenant with the Puritans. In 1637, the Puritan-Narragansett alliance was put to the test with the advent of the Pequot War. In the war the Narragansetts backed the Puritans, but the Puritan strategy of total warfare (e.g., Fort Mystic) repulsed the Narragansetts.

Drafted by the Puritans, the Treaty of Hartford (1638) stipulated that the Narragansetts and Mohegans, long traditional enemies, would renounce hostilities against each other except with permission from the Puritans. The Narragansett-Mohegan cold war turned hot, however, when the Mohegan sachem, Uncas, accused Miantonomo, the Narragansett sachem, of an assassination plot against him. Tensions were further heightened in 1643 when Uncas threatened Sequasson, an allied sachem of the Narragansetts. Miantonomo sought Puritan permission for an attack against Uncas, but the Puritan response was noncommittal. So, in August 1643, Miantonomo attacked Uncas. In the battle the Mohegans routed the Narragansetts, and Miantonomo was captured. Uncas sent Miantonomo to the newly formed United Colonies of New England (New England Confederation), which decided to return Miantonomo to Uncas for execution.

After this rebuff, the Narragansetts tried to free themselves from the confederation's domination by submitting themselves directly to King Charles I. Although not without logic, the effort was without avail since the confederation ignored the implications and the limitations of Charles's power.

In 1645, tensions again flared between the Narragansetts and Mohegans when Miantonomo's brother, Pessacus, attacked the Mohegans to avenge his brother's death. The confederation supported the Mohegans and forced Pessacus to capitulate. The treaty signed on 28 August 1645 required the Narragansetts to remain at peace with any tribe allied with the United Colonies, pay a fine of 2,000 fathoms of wampum, and offer several hostages as collateral. Though Pessacus signed, he did not feel bound by a treaty endorsed under duress.

Over the next generation the Narragansetts continued to preoccupy the confederation. Ninigret, sachem of the Niantics, became the spokesman for the Narragansetts and exhibited a willingness to challenge the power of the confederation. Thus Narragansett-Puritan relations suffered due to a series of reports concerning Narragansett sedition, followed by Puritan demands for penance. The confederation disparaged the Narragansetts as little more than provocateurs.

Open hostilities between the Narragansetts and Puritans erupted when the Narragansetts joined King Philip's War against the Puritans. The Narragansetts did not originally favor an alliance with their old enemy, the Wampanoags, but sachem Canonchet, son of Miantonomo, refused to submit to the demands of the confederation to turn over Wampanoag refugees in Narragansett territory. This led to the confederation's declaration of war against the Narragansetts on 2 November 1675. On 19 December 1675, confederation forces attacked the Narragansett fort at the Great Swamp near South Kingston, Rhode Island. By some estimates, more than 600 Narragansett warriors, women, and children were killed when Captain Benjamin Church burned the fort and its 500 cabins. The war also cost the Narragansetts their chief sachem, Canonchet, as well as their remaining political identity and autonomy. Surviving Narragansetts fled their homeland and joined other tribes.

Richard C. Goode

References

Francis Jennings, *The Invasion of America: Indians, Colonialism, and the Cant of Conquest* (1975); Howard S. Russell, *Indian New England Before the Mayflower* (1980); John Sainsbury, "Miantonomo's Death and New England Politics, 1630–1645," *Rhode Island History* 30 (1971):110–123; William

S. Simmons, "Narragansett" in Bruce Trigger, ed., *Handbook of North American Indians, Vol. 15: Northeast* (1978); John Winthrop, *Winthrop's Journal*, ed., James Kendall Hosmer (1908).

See also CHURCH, BENJAMIN; GREAT SWAMP FIGHT; KING PHILIP'S WAR; MIANTONOMO; MOHEGAN; NEW ENGLAND CONFEDERATION; PEQUOT; PEQUOT WAR; PLYMOUTH; RHODE ISLAND; UNCAS; WAMPANOAG

Narváez, Pánfilo de (c. 1485–1528)

Pánfilo de Narváez was the first conqueror to explore the interior of the Southeast and Southwest. In 1526, the Spanish monarch rewarded the lackluster Narváez with a patent to conquer Florida. Six years before, he had been sent to Mexico to imprison disobedient Hernán Cortés, but allied with Cortés instead. Narváez sailed from Spain to Florida, but on the way lost two vessels. Some of his recruits deserted him. Finally, toward the middle of April 1528, after casting anchor in Tampa Bay, he landed about 400 men and 80 horses to carry on the royal mandate. He ordered his ships to go north to an unspecified port where they were to meet. Two months later he had covered the land distance to the Indian town of Apalachee, now Tallahassee. In order to explore the territory by sea and having lost contact with his ships, he set about in August to construct five crude vessels near Aute, just south of Apalachee. During November a storm wrecked all his boats near Galveston, Texas. All but 80 of his people (including Narváez) disappeared. The survivors continued by land toward Mexico but hunger, thirst, diseases, exhaustion, and attacks by the natives decimated them. In June 1536, or eight years after they had sailed for Florida, only four survivors were able to reach Mexico City. Among them were Alvar Núñez Cabeza de Vaca, who wrote a chronicle of Narváez's adventure, and Estebanico, a resourceful black slave.

Jose Agnacio Avallaneda

References

Gonzalo Fernández de Oviedo, *Historia general y natural de las Indias, islas y Tierra-Firme del Mar Oceano*, 5 vols. (1955); Robert S. Weddle, *Spanish Sea, the Gulf of Mexico in North American Discovery, 1500–1685* (1985).

Fort Nassau (New Jersey)

Located near what is today Gloucester, New Jersey, Fort Nassau was constructed in 1623 by the Dutch and was intermittently occupied by them over the years. The fort was situated to control the river and the territory around the fort. In this way the Dutch hoped to secure their trading rights in a region desired by both the Swedish and the English. Fort Nassau was a wooden palisade with four or five cannon. The initial group of settlers consisted of four married couples and eight seamen. After New Amsterdam was established these settlers abandoned Fort Nassau in favor of Manhattan because of the hostility of the Indians.

The Dutch returned to the site in the summer of 1633, constructed a house, and repaired the fort. Arent Corsen was named commissioner, and he purchased some land from local Indians so that he could build a blockhouse outside of the fort's walls for trade with the Indians. However, other Indians remained hostile, and the Dutch had to abandon the site sometime during the winter of 1633–1634.

During the summer of 1635, 15 Englishmen under orders from the provisional governor of Virginia occupied Fort Nassau. The Dutch heard of this rather quickly and sent a military force to evict the intruders. This was done rather easily, and the Englishmen were returned to Virginia. After this incident the Dutch seemed to have occupied the fort in 1636, and by 1640 the site was definitely occupied, since contemporary sources mention that the fort had a garrison of 20 soldiers. In 1648 the defenses of the fort were improved only to be abandoned three years later. The Swedes by this time controlled the water routes to the fort so the Dutch decided to build a new fort. Fort Casimir was constructed by them seven miles from the Swedish Fort Christina. Fort Nassau's cannon and settlers were sent to the new fort. After Fort Nassau was evacuated the Dutch destroyed it.

Anthony P. Inguanzo

References

Charles M. Andrews, *The Colonial Period of American History*, 4 vols. (1934–1938); Oliver Perry Chitwood, *A History of Colonial America* (1961); James F. Jameson, ed., *Narratives of New Netherland, 1609–1664* (1909); Albert Cook Myers, ed., *Narratives of Early Pennsylvania, West New Jersey and Delaware, 1630–1707* (1912);

Louis B. Wright, *The Atlantic Frontier: Colonial American Civilization, 1607–1763* (1947).

See also FORT CASIMIR (DELAWARE)

Fort Nassau (New York)

Fort Nassau was constructed in 1614 by Hendrich Christiansen, who was in the employ of the New Netherland Company, on a little island in the North or Hudson River known as Castle Island. The fort served as a base of operations for Dutch fur traders. The traders would obtain trade goods here and deposit the furs that they received for shipment to New Amsterdam. Fort Nassau demonstrated to Holland's competitors that the Dutch were serious about exploiting the Hudson River valley.

Fort Nassau was basically a redoubt with four bastions. It was surrounded by a deep and wide moat. The 12 men assigned to the fort had two cannon and 11 stone swivel guns at their command. Since it was on the New Netherland frontier this fort was costly to operate. In 1617, it was abandoned because of hostile Indians and the constant flooding of the Hudson River, which on several occasions covered the site of the fort with four or five feet of water. The Dutch built a much cruder redoubt near the site where Fort Orange would be built.

Anthony P. Inguanzo

References

Charles M. Andrews, *The Colonial Period of American History*, 4 vols. (1934–1938); Oliver Perry Chitwood, *A History of Colonial America* (1961); James F. Jameson, ed., *Narratives of New Netherland, 1609–1664* (1909); Michael Kammen, *Colonial New York: A History* (1978); Arthur M. Schlesinger, Jr., ed., *The Almanac of American History* (1983).

Natchez

The Natchez Indians, who called themselves Théloël, lived near the bluffs on the Mississippi River at present-day Natchez, Mississippi; Natchez was the name of one of their villages, but Europeans adopted it for the nation as a whole. The Natchez were one of the most advanced cultures of North America; linguistically related to the nearby Avoyelles and Tensas Indians, their society was composed of two ranked classes, with the higher classes further subdivided into three different levels. Unlike other southeastern woodland societies, the Natchez ruler, known as the "great sun," had arbitrary power of life and death over his subjects. They may have been related to the Quigualtam, who attacked Hernando de Soto's army near present-day Vicksburg, Mississippi, but in 1682, when René-Robert Cavelier de La Salle encountered them, they were concentrated in nine village areas near St. Catherine Creek.

Like other southeastern Indians, they seem to have suffered significant depopulation in the time between Soto's entrada and 1682 when La Salle passed through their country; sustained contact with Europeans only accelerated their decline. The Natchez responded to this demographic collapse by adopting the Tunican-speaking Tioux and Grigra into their nation. The Natchez received La Salle peacefully in 1682, but sustained contact came after 1699, when they were visited by two missionary priests coming down from Canada to meet with Pierre Le Moyne d'Iberville, sent to establish the colony of Louisiana. Because of their strategic location relative to other Indian groups and their location on the first significant bluff north of the mouth of the Mississippi (the site was considered for the capital of Louisiana), the Natchez attracted the attention not only of missionaries, but also traders and military strategists, both French and English.

The French first established a warehouse at Natchez in 1714, partly to improve trade, but also to counter growing English involvement with the Natchez. In 1708, Thomas Welch, a Chickasaw trader, convened a meeting at the Yazoos during which he claimed to have concluded alliances with the Natchez and other area tribes; in 1714, promoter Price Hughes made a tour of the Southeast that resulted in the Natchez joining the English-inspired slave raiding that had characterized English expansion in the region. Louisiana Governor Antoine Lamothe Cadillac insulted the Natchez in the fall of 1715 by refusing to smoke the calumet with them, which they interpreted as an act of war; they killed four French traders and plundered their canoes of a great body of goods. Lieutenant Governor Jean-Baptiste Le Moyne de Bienville moved against the Natchez with a force of only 35 men in spring 1716. He ended the so-called "First Natchez War" by taking Natchez chiefs hostage, successfully demanding the execution of several chiefs and Natchez assistance in building

Fort Rosalie de Natchez. Natchez became the most flourishing district in Louisiana, boasting several large and many small concessions, many of which lay very near Natchez villages.

The "Second Natchez War" broke out in fall 1722, when a disagreement over Indian debts to a French soldier led to several Indian deaths; when the commandant refused to discipline the soldier involved, a spiral of attacks on French property (including slaves and cattle) led in spring 1723 to another punitive expedition by Bienville, which once again led to the execution of a number of leading men. Relations deteriorated further after 1725, when political turmoil in Louisiana led to Bienville's recall and, in 1728, the appointment of Sieur De Chepart as commandant of Fort Rosalie. Generally hated by Frenchmen and Indians alike, he was a business partner of Governor Etienne Périer. He provoked the Natchez uprising by his insistence that the Natchez abandon their principal village so that he could establish a plantation there. The Natchez determined to drive out the French, and on 29 November 1729, they killed at least 238 French men, women, and children, and took many Frenchmen and their Negroes captives. The French war of extermination resulted in the deaths of many Natchez and the sale of many into slavery in the West Indies, but a remnant survived by taking refuge, first with the Chickasaw (which was a pretext for the Franco-Chickasaw War of 1736–1740), then with the Creek and Cherokee. They eventually established their own village in the Creek nation, and were removed to Oklahoma. The Natchez language died out in the early twentieth century.

Michael James Foret

References

Andrew C. Albrecht, "Indian-French Relations at Natchez," *American Anthropologist* 48 (1946):321–354; Verner L. Crane, *The Southern Frontier, 1670–1732* (1928), rpt. 1981; Jean Delanglez, S.J., "The Natchez Massacre and Governor Périer," *Louisiana Historical Quarterly* 17 (1934): 631–641; John R. Swanton, *The Indians of the Southeastern United States*, Smithsonian Institution, Bureau of American Ethnology Bulletin 137 (1946).

Daniel H. Usner, Jr., *Indians, Settlers, and Slaves in a Frontier Exchange Economy: The Lower Mississippi Valley Before 1783* (1992); Patricia D. Woods, "The French and the Nat-

chez Indians in Louisiana, 1700–1731," *Louisiana History* 19 (1978):401–412.

See also LE MOYNE DE BIENVILLE, JEAN-BAPTISTE; LE MOYNE D'IBERVILLE, PIERRE; NATCHEZ WAR; FORT ROSALIE (MISSISSIPPI)

Natchez War (1729–1733)

The Franco-Natchez War began on 29 November 1729, when Natchez chiefs and warriors entered Fort Rosalie de Natchez and surrounding plantations on pretext of looking for ammunition for a hunt, and killed at least 238 French men, women, and children. Although Louisiana Governor Etienne Périer tried to portray the Natchez uprising as part of a "general conspiracy" of southeastern Indians against the French, its origin lay in a larger pattern of Franco-Natchez conflict and the greed of Périer and the commandant of Fort Rosalie, one Sieur De Chepart, who was hated by both Frenchmen and Indians, but who enjoyed the governor's protection.

In August 1729, De Chepart ordered the Natchez to quit their grand village, which contained the most sacred places and objects of the Natchez, so that he could establish a plantation there in partnership with the governor. When the Natchez great sun (paramount chief) and other chiefs could not convince him to place his plantation elsewhere, they stalled for time by asking him if they could stay three more months to bring in their corn crop, which they would share with the French in gratitude for their consideration. The Natchez leadership, several of whom were related to chiefs killed according to French demands in earlier conflicts, decided to kill all Frenchmen in their country at the time they were supposed to deliver their tribute to De Chepart. Natchez ceremonial preparations for war did not go unnoticed by French settlers, who informed the commandant of their suspicions, only to be put in jail for their insolence. The Natchez even enlisted plantation Negroes in their scheme, promising them freedom for their support.

The attack went off as planned, and though the Natchez killed at least 145 men, 36 women, and 56 children, and captured almost 300 Negro slaves and 50 French women and children, they only suffered 12 killed. The Yazoos did join the Natchez in their uprising by taking Fort St. Pierre near their villages. The uprising caused a general panic in the colony, which did not respond militarily until a Choc-taw force led by Jean-Paul Le Sueur attacked the Natchez on 27 January 1730. Although the at-tackers killed more than 100 Natchez and re-covered most of the French women and children and some of the slaves, Negro cooperation with the besieged Natchez allowed them to escape into two forts on St. Catherine Creek. Joined by 200 French troops with cannons from New Orleans, the Franco-Choctaw army bombarded the Natchez forts for more than two weeks. The Natchez agreed to give up their remaining cap-tives, and the French agreed not to attack them afterwards, but planned to do so anyway; on 28 February, with their last captives handed over and the French army planning an attack, the Natchez slipped out from the Franco-Choctaw encirclement, and eventually made their way across the Mississippi River to the former lands of the Ouachita Indians, near present-day Sic-ily Island, Catahoula Parish, Louisiana.

The Natchez proved that they could still trouble the colony over the next year by making several attacks on Mississippi convoys and against Fort Rosalie; in one attack, six Natchez gained entrance to the fort and killed five French-men before being all killed but one, who was cap-tured and burned. In September 1730, the governor's brother, Périer de Salvert, arrived from France with 350 troops from the Company of the Indies and the Ministry of the Marine; French policy was to crush the Natchez com-pletely by killing them or taking them captive for sale as slaves in the islands. The French army assembled on the Red River on 4 January 1731, although they did not find the Natchez fortifica-tions until 20 January. Périer's army attacked the Natchez with cannons and mortars for four days before the Natchez sent up a flag of truce and began to negotiate terms with the French. The Natchez returned some Negroes to the French, and several chiefs went to negotiate with the French; the chiefs were told they and their people would be allowed to surrender the next day, but through a ruse they were taken captive and held for the good behavior of the remaining Natchez. On 25 January, 45 men and 450 women and children did surrender but an unknown number, which Périer put at 20, but others estimated to be as many as 150 or more, escaped. Périer de-stroyed the fortifications and returned to New Orleans with the captives. To add to everyone's troubles, an unidentified illness broke out in spring which lasted through the rest of the year and killed many Indians and Creoles.

During summer 1731, a group of Natchez established a village at the Chickasaws, but at least 150 or more remained scattered in four bands, one at the Yazoo east of the Mississippi River and three west of the river. During spring, several Natchez chiefs approached the great chief of the Tunicas about making peace for them with the French and settling with them; Governor Périer directed the Tunicas to treat with the Natchez, but only if they were dis-armed. An initial group of 30 Natchez agreed to give up their arms to the Tunicas, but when the Flour Chief arrived at the Tunicas with 150 warriors and their families, he demurred giving up their weapons on the grounds that retaining them reassured the warriors' wives. The Tunicas accepted this explanation, and in typical Indian fashion set out a feast for the visitors. Just be-fore daybreak the next morning, however, the Natchez grabbed their own and the Tunicas' weapons, and joined by some Chickasaws and Koroas hiding nearby, attacked their hosts. The Natchez lost more than 30 killed and three taken prisoner, but they killed 20 Tunicas, in-cluding the grand chief, and wounded 20 more.

At about the same time a group of almost 40 Natchez that had surrendered at the Natchez post were disarmed, but allowed their knives; when French soldiers tried to gain better control of their prisoners in the aftermath of the attack on the Tunicas, the Natchez seized a stack of guns and began an attack that resulted in the deaths of every one of the Natchez men, women, and children. After fleeing from the Tunicas, the Flour Chief assembled those of his people he could and with a force of perhaps 200 attacked the French fort at Natchitoches on the Red River in October 1731. The Natchez managed to drive the Natchitoches from their village, which they occupied and fortified. Before a relief expedition from New Orleans could reach Natchitoches, a force that included Frenchmen, a small detach-ment from the nearby Spanish post of Los Adaes, and Natchitoches, Attakapas, and Caddo Indi-ans defeated the Natchez after a siege of several weeks, during which the Flour Chief and many other chiefs were killed. Once again, however, a group of at least 50 survived the attack and made their way back to their camps along the Oua-chita; guerilla warfare continued from there as the Natchez attacked the Chacchiumas and the French settlement of Pointe Coupee through the first half of 1732.

Périer was recalled in September 1732 and replaced by Bienville, who was reappointed to this third term because of his acknowledged ability in handling Indian affairs. The last bands of Natchez holdouts were driven away or captured in separate attacks near the Natchez post and along the Yazoo during summer 1733, after which all the Natchez gathered together at the Chickasaws. The war was an epic disaster for the Natchez, who were one of the largest, most advanced, and prosperous societies of the Southeast in 1729, but constituted only a refugee village in 1733. The war was calamitous for Louisiana as well; as a result of war the Company of the Indies retroceded Louisiana to Louis XV in 1732.

Michael James Foret

References

Jean Delanglez, S.J., "The Natchez Massacre and Governor Périer," *Louisiana Historical Quarterly* 17 (1934):631–641; John A. Green, "Governor Périer's Expedition Against the Natchez Indians," *Louisiana Historical Quarterly* 19 (1936):547–577; *Mississippi Provincial Archives: French Dominion*, Dunbar Rowland, ed., and A.G. Sanders, trans., Vols. 1–3 (1927–1932), and Patricia Galloway, ed. and trans. Vols. 4–5 (1984).

Charles D. Van Tuyl, *The Natchez: Annotated Translations from Antoine Simon le Page du Pratz's Histoire de la Louisiane and a Short English-Natchez Dictionary* (1983); Patricia D. Woods, "The French and the Natchez Indians in Louisiana, 1700–1731," *Louisiana History* 19 (1978):401–412.

See also CHICKASAW; CHOCTAW; LE MOYNE DE BIENVILLE, JEAN-BAPTISTE; NATCHEZ; FORT ROSALIE (MISSISSIPPI); FORT ST. PETER (MISSISSIPPI); TUNICA

Navigation and Shiphandling

Sailors in the seventeenth and eighteenth centuries inherited and improved the navigational and shiphandling techniques of previous epochs. While astrolabe, compass, chip log, and polar star navigation were employed before 1600, more thorough knowledge of winds and currents, the Mercator projection, the sextant, and the chronometer appeared in the seventeenth and eighteenth centuries.

Voyaging experience over several generations contributed to mariners' knowledge of wind systems. This body of information became fuller with the early nineteenth-century publications of Alexander Becher and Matthew F. Maury. By 1900, captains could consult volumes and charts from national hydrographic offices with hundreds of passages laid out for all parts of the world, including average times (e.g., Melbourne-Hampton Roads, 80–100 days), and course variations for the season of the year.

In the seventeenth and eighteenth centuries, seasoned mariners utilized the sailing directions recorded by earlier explorers. For a voyage from Europe to the Western Hemisphere, the Portuguese and Spaniards perceived that Northeast trade winds would blow them to the Caribbean, between 0 and 36 degrees; the southern route. From 37 to 60 degrees in the North Atlantic, the wind spirals in clockwise fashion from the west. Easterlies are more prevalent above 60 degrees, which the Vikings took advantage of in sailing to Greenland and Vinland, as did Cabot, Cartier, and others; the northern route.

As Prince Henry and his captains found, Southeast trades from 0 to 20 degrees south made it difficult to sail from the Canaries to the Cape of Good Hope. Later masters rode the Northeast trades to South America, then hoped for a reach through the Southeast trades to the westerlies further south that could carry them to the cape and beyond into the Indian Ocean. Monsoons played around the equator in the Indian Ocean with varying effect and Southeast trades forced captains like Vasco da Gama to seek coastal wind shifts along the east African coast before heading for Calicut. Later, Dutch East Indiamen rode the strong westerlies down in the "roaring forties" nearly to Australia before shaping a northerly course for Java.

In the Pacific, the Spanish learned to fly before the westerlies from 40 to 60 degrees that blew their galleons from Manila to the Pacific Northwest coast before heading for Acapulco on coastal northerlies. After Schouten and Le Maire sighted Cape Horn in 1616, masters would catch the Northeast and Southeast trades of the Atlantic, then fight the strong westerlies from 50 degrees around the cape to 50 degrees in the Pacific before favorable Southeast trades could lift them to meet the Northeast trades from 0 to 20 degrees that could carry them to the Orient. In the eighteenth century, the voyages of Dampier, Cook, and others to untraveled parts of the Pacific added to knowledge of wind and current systems.

Current direction and force were also logged and published over the years. In the

Atlantic, the Canary current coincides with the Northeast trades as the Gulf Stream flows northeast to join the westerlies. In the Pacific, the equatorial current generally flows with the Southeast and Northeast trades, the Subarctic current with the westerlies, and the California current with the northerlies. The Indian Ocean and South Atlantic feature more variable currents.

Navigators used piloting, dead reckoning, and celestial navigation before the days of electronic instruments. In piloting, the mariner figures out where he is by checking landmarks and aids to navigation such as lighthouses. Dead or deduced reckoning is where a course is laid out on a chart and the navigator figures time and speed along that distance. By 1300, masters used the compass and Portolani (charts) described coastal landmarks and course headings. In the early 1500s the chip log came into service: a triangular piece of wood attached to a line knotted at equal intervals. Speed was estimated by the number of knots passing through a sailor's fingers as measured by a 30-second sandglass. Captains also cast experienced eyes on wind and wave patterns, scents, birds, flotsam, and jetsam. Before the age of timepieces, half-hour sandglasses kept time at sea. Celestial navigation consisted of using astrolabe or cross staff to keep the North or Pole Star the same distance above the horizon night after night. This is called sailing your westing or easting down, knowing latitudinal position. In 1735, James Harrison invented the first chronometer and in 1772, Cook took a fourth version to the Pacific. Chronometers allowed captains to calculate their longitude according to Greenwich mean time. John Hadley invented the sextant for navigational sights in 1731, and this instrument came into general use at sea by the 1750s.

Chart work was facilitated by Mercator's projection in 1569 and world map of 1587. By 1640, his charts were used for ocean navigation. With mathematical computation, he placed all lines of latitude and longitude to intersect at right angles, allowing the compass course or thumb line to be drawn straight on the chart, making it easier to plot a course, but exaggerating the size of the Arctic and Antarctic on the projection.

Ship handling methods differed little from the days of the caravel to those of the frigate. On raising anchor and desiring to bear away on the port tack, the foresails are sheeted aback, so the wind will push the bow off to starboard, while main and mizzen are sheeted to catch the wind on a reach. To come about, a ship on the starboard tack would head into the wind with yards sheeted hard on the starboard tack. As the bow passes through the eye of the wind, the foremast yards are left aback so the wind can push the bow off to starboard, while the main and mizzen are hauled around smartly for the port tack. Then on the new course, the foresails are trimmed to match the others. Wearing ship (like a jibe in a small boat) consists of putting the stern into the eye of the wind by slacking off the sails to catch the wind accordingly, running off before the wind and then trimming sails to the new wind direction as the ship heads on the new course. These maneuvers could often taken ten to 15 minutes and a mile or more of distance.

The points of sail are beat, reach, and run, with the wind coming from the bow, side, or stern, respectively. Square riggers could sail within 65 degrees of the wind direction, a modern sloop, 35 degrees.

With the aforementioned knowledge of winds, currents, navigation, and ship handling, merchant captains and naval officers sailed the seven seas seeking profit and victory.

James H. Hitchman

References
Edward V. Lewis and Robert O'Brien, *Ships* (1965); J.H. Parry, *The Establishment of the European Hegemony: 1415–1715* (1962); Alan Villiers, *The Way of a Ship* (1953).

See also SHIP DESIGN; SHIP OF THE LINE

Navy, France

In the eighteenth century, France needed an oceanic navy in order to retain and profit from its overseas colonies, the most important of which lay in the Americas. After 1697, France held one of the great sugar sources in the world, Saint-Domingue (Haiti), as well as smaller Caribbean islands such as Martinique and Guadeloupe. To the north, Canada—the St. Lawrence Valley, Acadia, and Newfoundland—with the fur trade and the fishery, was French. None of these colonies had much population, and segments of the populations (many Acadians, most slaves) had only dubious loyalties to France. So none could defend itself, yet defense was required in the face of the large, growing, and aggressive colonial population of British North

America, often backed by the imperial ambitions of Britain. Furthermore, the point in having these colonies was to enrich the kingdom by their production and trade, which France could not do without protecting that trade on the high seas. For these reasons France needed a navy capable of projecting power in the Caribbean and the North Atlantic, and capable of escorting shipping through the choke points of the Atlantic (such as the Windward Passage in the Caribbean, the Gulf of St. Lawrence, and, of course, the English Channel).

The French navy of the eighteenth century was inadequate to the task. Under Louis XIV's minister, Jean-Baptiste Colbert (1619–1683), France had built the largest navy Europe had ever seen. But when this fleet did not permit Louis XIV to invade England he lost interest in it and permitted it to wither. After 1692, the French abandoned the conception of a battle fleet superior to all rivals and instead pursued a guerilla strategy, the *guerre de course,* in which privateers harried the enemy's shipping while the navy protected one's own. The size of the navy shrank from 105 ships of the line in 1690 to 66 in 1715 and a mere 30 in 1720. Thereafter, until 1763, its size fluctuated between 30 and 77, but usually hovered around 45. This gave France a navy about one-third or one-fourth the size of its enemy, the British navy, and allowed Britain to float as many ships in American waters as the French could overall. The cardinal reason for this proportion was finance.

After the 1690s the French navy was starved for funds. The strategy of *guerre de course* attempted to make a virtue of a necessity. The finances of the French monarchy were overstrained, as frequent bankruptcies attest, and the army always enjoyed first claim on the treasury, as France had enemies to the north and east. A dedicated campaign to build up the navy would have been costly (as Louis XIV discovered in the 1670s and 1680s), and would merely have provoked Britain to expand its navy. Britain did not have to maintain an expensive army and could therefore always outspend France on the navy. Under these circumstances, naval inferiority was an immutable condition for France, and strategy and tactics had to take this into account.

Inferiority in American waters derived from more than finance, however. The French navy did not maintain year-round bases in the Americas, but instead sent annual expeditions from its ports in France, usually Rochefort but

sometimes Brest. The difficulty was that France held no colonies between Saint-Domingue and Canada. Saint-Domingue and the whole Caribbean was an expensive place to maintain a squadron, as the islands generally had to import food from afar, and tropical diseases killed off crews very quickly. Yellow fever, which is communicated by a mosquito that breeds especially well in water casks, was a disease of ports and ships in the eighteenth century, and was usually lethal to those without childhood immunity to it. Manning ships with natives of the Caribbean would have solved this problem, but the French islands had insufficient population. Canada was a healthy place by eighteenth-century standards, but the St. Lawrence can be blocked by ice for up to five months of the year. In addition, the colony was chronically short of food: feeding a squadron would have required additional annual supplies from France. Beyond this, by the 1720s the jewel in the crown of French colonial possessions in the Americas was clearly Saint-Domingue with its sugar; and Canada was about as far from the Caribbean as was France—roughly 40 days by sail. Louisbourg, which the French developed after 1713, was several days closer to the Caribbean, had a good harbor, and might have been a suitable place for a squadron. But it too could not feed itself, and drift ice, often shrouded in fog, obstructed its waters for many months of the year.

The British, with their mainland colonies in North America, easily maintained bases at costs no greater than those in Britain. Consequently, in time of war, they had ships in American waters year-round, while the French normally sent out their fleets in April and brought them home before they ran out of supplies. The British colonies, from Georgia to Massachusetts, produced enough food, timber, and other essentials that the Royal Navy did not need to rely on supplies from Britain as the French navy—and colonies—invariably had to rely on supplies from France.

The British colonies also produced quantities of able-bodied seamen to supplement the crews raised in Britain. The French colonies did not, and while manpower was a problem for all European navies in this age, it hamstrung the French more severely than the British. In both manpower and material the French had to rely on what France (and Europe) could supply, while Britain could employ the resources of the colonies its navy defended. Hence the French navy, weaker than Britain's for reasons of finance, was weaker still in American waters.

French strategy and tactics were based on the idea that ships, by reason of their scarcity, were too precious to lose. Whereas the British sought combat, and would accept a naval war of attrition, French squadrons avoided engagement when possible, and when it was not, usually fought hoping to flee. This allowed France to keep a fleet in existence throughout the century, but it did not, and could not, prevent several major British victories, and the gradual expansion of the British Empire in the Americas at French expense. The French enjoyed no significant naval victories in the wars of the Spanish Succession (1701–1713), Austrian Succession (1740–1748, known in the Caribbean as the War of Jenkins' Ear), or the Seven Years' War (1754–1763, also known as the French and Indian War). Alliance with the Spanish navy and the rebellion of most of Britain's American colonies allowed the French some naval success in the American Revolution (1776–1783).

Naval writers, under the influence of Alfred Thayer Mahan's ideas, have often chided the French for their strategy in the eighteenth century, that of the *guerre de course*. But no strategy could have countered the trend of the times. The weaknesses of the French navy were fundamental matters of economics and geography, not questions of attitude, strategy, or courage. A defensive, guerrilla approach to naval matters, with considerable reliance upon privateers, suited French resources even if it could not secure France's imperial ambitions.

John R. McNeill

References

M. Acerra, J. Merino Navarro, and J. Meyer, *Les marines de guerre européennes (XVII–XVIIIe siècles)* (1985); Paul Bamford, *Forests and French Sea Power, 1660–1789* (1956); Raoul Castex, *Les idées militaires de la marine de XVIIIe siècle* (1911); Maurice Filion, *Maurepas: Ministre de Louis XV* (1967); G. Lacour-Gayet, *La marine militaire de la France sous la règne de Louis XV* (1902); James Pritchard, *Louis XV's Navy, 1748–1762* (1987).

See also CHARLES TOWN, ATTACK ON; LOUISBOURG; PENSACOLA; SHIP DESIGN; SHIP OF THE LINE

Navy, Great Britain

Until the sixteenth century the Royal Navy was little more than a collection of fortified merchant vessels. Not until the reign of Henry VII (1485–1509), and more especially that of Henry VIII (1509–1547) were specialist warships constructed, among them the *Henry Grâce à Dieu* and the *Mary Rose*. However, until the mid-seventeenth century the navy was only intermittently active. A lack of finance both inhibited the building of warships and prevented the fleet for being mobilized except in an emergency like the Spanish Armada in 1588. The Tudor monarchy otherwise had to rely on the entrepreneurial efforts of individuals like Sir Francis Drake and Richard Grenville. This weakness continued under the early Stuart kings. The only attempted use of naval power at this time was the expedition in 1628 to help the French protestants at La Rochelle. Unfortunately, the fleet under the duke of Buckingham had neither the organization nor the knowledge of the French coast to do anything effective.

During the English civil wars (1642–1648) the navy played a subsidiary role. As a consequence, the Dutch took control of much of England's overseas trade, especially with its emerging colonies in the West Indies and North America. In response, the victorious parliamentary side, strongly influenced by the merchants of London, passed the Navigation Act of 1651 to regain control of the carrying trade. The result was the Anglo-Dutch War of 1652–1654. The greater resources available from Parliament enabled the navy to defeat the premier maritime power of Europe. Most of the fighting took place in the English Channel and North Sea, but it was during this era that the fleet paid its first visit since Drake to the Caribbean when it helped in the capture of Jamaica from Spain.

The restoration of the Stuart monarchy in 1660 saw the navy again financially constrained, resulting in a subsequent loss of effectiveness as the Second (1664–1667) and Third (1672–1674) Dutch Wars revealed. The first of these conflicts was the product of renewed trade rivalry. Although the navy had some success, it failed to prevent the Dutch from entering the Thames River in June 1667, resulting in the loss of much shipping and the destruction of the Sheerness naval yard.

However, important developments were taking place. James, duke of York, the future King James II, was a keen naval administrator and with the assistance of the indefatigable

Samuel Pepys, he secured additional dockyard facilities and improvements to the victualling that promised to give the fleet greater operational capacity. Ironically it was James II's opponents who benefitted from these reforms, following his flight in 1688 and subsequent dethronement. The triumph of William III was especially crucial since it meant that Parliament was now able to give the navy the long-term funding it had never previously enjoyed. This set the scene for the expansion of British naval power during the next 150 years. From some 40 ships in 1600, the navy had by 1697, 170 vessels in service manned by 45,000 seamen. The fleet was now able to operate not only in the Channel, but the Mediterranean, and even further afield, where the growth of the English colonies in the West Indies and North American brought additional responsibilities.

The new possibilities of naval power initiated a debate on how it should be used. One school, led by the Whigs, believed that Britain's true destiny lay in Europe and that the fleet should be subservient to that end. Principally, this meant maintaining the balance of power to prevent France from gaining control of Germany and the Low Countries. The other, Tory, school believed that the nation's real interests lay outside Europe. Trade was the source of Britain's wealth, and the navy should be primarily deployed in support of commerce and the capture of France and Spain's overseas possessions, especially in the Caribbean and North America.

For most of King William's War and that of Queen Anne, the continentalists were in the ascendant, and most of the fleet was accordingly concentrated in the Channel. After a poor start at Beachy Head in 1690, the English and their Dutch allies succeeded in wrecking French naval power at the battle of La Hogue in 1692. Thereafter, the navy played a supporting role to the land campaigns of William III and later the duke of Marlborough, though commerce protection remained an important responsibility. However, in 1710, a Tory ministry came to power determined to pursue a maritime strategy. Unfortunately, the force dispatched with Admiral Hovendon Walker to capture Quebec in June 1711 lost several transports on the rocks of the St. Lawrence and the maritime war ended in disappointment.

With the coming of peace, most of the fleet was laid up, leaving a force mainly of frigates around Britain and in the Baltic, Mediterranean, and Caribbean for commerce protection. The only vessels in North American waters were those assigned to the Newfoundland fishery. However, the outbreak of the War of Jenkins' Ear in 1739 saw a renewal of maritime warfare, since the easiest way of attacking Spain was through its vulnerable American empire. Following an early success at Porto Bello in 1739, a strong squadron was dispatched to take Cartegena in 1741, but with disastrous results. Despite Tory arguments, conducting amphibious operations across the Atlantic was fraught with difficulty. Thereafter, the entry of France into the war in 1744 meant the navy was once more primarily deployed in European waters in support of continental operations.

This situation only changed during the Seven Years' War. For once, a war between Britain and France began as a struggle for the mastery of North America rather than a contest to preserve the balance of power in Europe. Accordingly, large squadrons of warships were sent to North America almost every year, and the navy played a key role in the capture of Louisbourg in 1758, and Quebec in 1759. Substantial squadrons were also maintained in the West Indies, where the fleet assisted in the capture of Guadeloupe in 1758, Martinique in 1761, and Havana in 1762. By then the Royal Navy had almost 300 ships worldwide, manned by 84,000 seamen, an unparalleled force. It was the breaking of this naval preponderance that prompted France, and indirectly Spain, to support America during its struggle for independence.

Richard Middleton

References

Jeremy Black and Philip Woodfine, eds., *The British Navy and the Use of Naval Power in the Eighteenth Century* (1988); P. Crowhurst, *The Defence of British Trade, 1689–1815* (1977); J. Ehrman, *The Navy in the War of William III: Its State and Direction, 1689–1697* (1953); Paul Kennedy, *The Rise and Fall of British Naval Mastery* (1976); Richard Middleton, *The Bells of Victory: The Pitt-Newcastle Ministry and the Conduct of the Seven Years' War, 1757–1762* (1985); H.W. Richmond, *The Navy in the War of 1739–1748*, 3 vols. (1920).

See also ANGLO-DUTCH WAR, FIRST; ANGLO-DUTCH WAR, SECOND; ANGLO-DUTCH WAR, THIRD; CANADA, BRITISH EXPEDITION

AGAINST (1711); CARTAGENA, ATTACK ON;
DRY DOCKS; IMPRESSMENT, NAVY;
LOUISBOURG; MARINE FORCES; NAVIGATION
AND SHIPHANDLING; PORTO BELLO, EXPEDI-
TION AGAINST; SEA LAWS; SEAMEN AND SOCI-
ETY; SHIP DESIGN; SHIP OF THE LINE

Navy, Spain (1492–1699)

The development of the American territorial
defense system, as much on sea as on land, was
dependent largely on what the king of Spain was
to spend on it. Until 1521, the management of
the coastal defense was generally in the hands of
private individuals; but from this date on, the
carrera de Indias navy (initially allied to the
fleet), began to patrol to protect the merchant
ships that crossed the Atlantic to and from America. Its origin was a direct response to warlike
clashes in Europe and the first serious French
pirate attacks of the early sixteenth century.

Between the years 1526 and 1543, Spanish ships crossed the Atlantic in convoys (naval
and fleet), although only in certain years were
they accompanied by the navy all the way. After 1543, a change was brought about, only one
fleet a year departed (made up, normally, of two
naval ships), which on its arrival in the Caribbean was divided into two convoys: one headed
for the "Tierra Firme" and the other toward
New Spain. In 1551, owing to the interests of
the Spanish crown, the navy decided to try for
a better defense of *la Carrera* that was more
prevalent, cheaper, and methodical. This encompassed investing a large amount of money
in coast guard patrols. Another innovation
arose in 1561, when ships were to sail together
with the fleet in two annual convoys (April and
August). However, this was not always carried
out. The fleets from America had to leave by
March so as to arrive in Havana by April, they
then weighed anchor and set sail through the
Bahamas Channel before the month of August
and the hurricane season. Florida was of great
strategic importance to the Spanish crown because its control guaranteed the return route of
the fleets as well as controlling the entrance to
the Gulf of Mexico; however, its defense was
not taken into account until well into the seventeenth century. Toward the middle of the sixteenth century, the crown was more careful in
assuring the arrival and return of the fleets than
actively defending the coasts, so, among other
things, it neglected the growing French settlement on the coast of Florida and the rest of

North America. However, thanks to a counteroffensive, the Spanish managed to throw the
French out of Florida, thereby making the defense of the entire peninsula their major military
objective in the Caribbean. They also began to
aim at the development of a small specialized
naval force to link up the garrisons of the south
coast of North America with the most important defense bastions of the Caribbean.

Until then, the marine defense was organized with naval galleons forming patrols
around all the Caribbean ports. The restriction
of movement of these large and old ships was
a disadvantage against the speed of pirate ships.
That was the reason for the arrival of the galleys in 1578: ships more agile in shallow water
than galleons, which could not maneuver close
to the coast. However, all this was ineffective
due to the lack of adequate supplies needed for
the basic running of these ships.

Toward the end of the sixteenth century,
the idea was conceived of dividing the fleet into
two groups, making it easier to supervise the
naval defense of the Indies: the *Armada de Barlovento,* whose center of action and defense was
developed around the West Indies and the Caribbean coast, and the South Sea navy, whose
aim was the defense of the Pacific coast. The
primary objective of the *Armada de Barlovento*
was protection of the naval route through
which the Spanish convoys passed. Its activities
were hampered by lack of funds, but after the
middle of the seventeenth century and, above
all, after the decade of the eighties, the *Armada
de Barlovento* made detailed explorations along
the southern coast of the present United States.
This was precipitated by the capture of French
pirates who informed the Spanish authorities of
new French settlements in Espíritu Santo Bay
(near San Antonio, Texas). This produced a
state of alert and the immediate dispatch of
various expeditions along the Gulf coast. The
first expedition (1685), made up of one frigate
and one canoe, took its course from the mouth
of the Mississippi River and, owing to adverse
weather conditions and the inadequacy of the
boats, had a negative result. However, this expedition managed to explore and discover Pensacola Bay, Mobile, and the mouth of the Empa-
lizada River.

The following year these voyages were
continued, but now they used vessels of lesser
draught, as well as adding land expeditions
from San Luis de Apalachee. The help given
them by the natives was very effective in the

identification of these coasts (river mouths, coves, depths, etc.), and the Spanish found remains of some French settlements. Owing to the delay of this expedition, they sent another, and although they did not find the French settlement, they made a detailed survey of Santa Maria de Galvez (Pensacola), where they located good conditions for building a settlement: fertile land, abundant wood, good port locations, and pacific Indians. However, no fort was erected in this area until 1695.

Until this time the work of the *Armada de Barlovento* in the Gulf coast had consisted of exploration and survey work, after 1695 it also contributed in a more direct way to Spanish settlement by recruiting and transporting people. This was of no hindrance to them as they made most of their return trips with heavy cargos of wood that was then used in shipbuilding. The fortifying of Pensacola Bay at the end of the century through the construction of the San Carlos de Austria fort and the survey of the rivers El Almirante, Jordan, and Jovenazo secured the Spanish presence on the north Florida Gulf coast.

Almost all of the fleets' action took place in the Atlantic and Gulf of Mexico, although in the seventeenth century the Spanish tried with little success to build some defensive points along the Pacific coast, especially on the Gulf of California. A fortress was built at the mouth of the San Bruno River, but it lasted only briefly.

Pedro M. Martin-Escudero

References

Antonio Acosta and Juan Marchena, eds., *La influencia de España en el Caribe, la Florida y la Luisiana, 1500–1800* (1983); Cesáro Fernández Duro, *Armada española desde la unión de los reinos de Castilla y de Aragon* (1972); Clarence Haring, *Comercio y navegación entre España y las Indias en la época de los Habsburgo* (1979); Paul E. Hoffman, *The Defense of the Indies, 1535–1574, A Study in the Modernization of the Spanish State* (1969); Bibiano Torres Ramirez, *La Armada de Barlovento* (1981).

See also CALIFORNIA; FLORIDA; HAVANA; MENÉNDEZ DE AVILÉS, PEDRO; PENSACOLA; ST. AUGUSTINE; SHIP DESIGN

Navy, Spain (1700–1763)

In the eighteenth century, the Spanish navy in American waters had a limited function, but one of the utmost importance. Spain relied on fortifications and tropical fevers to defend its American colonies, but needed an oceanic navy to safeguard its treasure fleets from Vera Cruz to Havana and from Havana to Spain. The Spanish state depended fundamentally on Mexican silver, so the first duty of the navy was to see that the *flota* arrived safely in Seville (or Cádiz after 1717).

By the late seventeenth century, the Spanish navy had declined to inconsiderable proportions, part of a general decline in Spain under the late Hapsburgs. It could barely protect the silver fleets from pirates and certainly could not convoy safely in time of war. In 1702 the English sank most of this paltry navy at Vigo. When the Bourbon dynasty ascended the throne (1713), Spain began to rebuild its navy, almost from scratch. Initially, its purpose was to assist in Mediterranean projects, reducing rebellious Barcelona and promoting dynastic ambitions in Italy, but by the 1730s it became a regular presence in American waters. Vigorous reforming naval ministers, who usually held several other additional portfolios in the Spanish government, spent generous allotments to good effect. The navy expanded from 11 ships of the line in 1724 to 38 in 1735 and 46 by 1740. In the War of the Austrian Succession (1739–1748) the British destroyed most of the fleet, but the Spanish rebuilt it again, from 18 ships of the line in 1751 to 46 in 1756. This major program of naval construction demonstrates the commitment within the Spanish state to the navy. By 1713, Spain had lost most of its European territories, and the importance of the army shrank. Spanish power rested on its American empire, so the navy enjoyed a high priority with a budget from one-half to three-quarters as large as the army's.

The Spanish navy suffered from shortages of quality mast timber and of sailors. Neither problem was solved satisfactorily, despite recourse to the Baltic for fir and to prisons for men. Spain even paid high wages to attract foreigners into its fleets, a unique policy among European navies. Manpower and mast timber problems, rather than financial ones, limited the size of the Spanish navy to 1763.

Cuba played a central role in maintaining the Spanish naval presence in American waters. After 1737, Havana served as the home port for a squadron, the *Armada de Barlovento*, which varied in size but generally numbered around three to five ships of the line. Cuban forests provided tropical hardwoods that made excellent hulls and planking. After it opened in 1723, the royal shipyard at Havana built about two-fifths of the ships of the Spanish navy. It built more than any Spanish port, and its ships were larger, cheaper, and more durable than those built in Spain.

The Spanish navy fought defensively when it fought at all in American waters. In the only major engagement it accepted, the squadrons of Admiral Andres Reggio and Admiral Charles Knowles dueled inconclusively off of Havana while a treasure fleet slipped away (1748). This defensive posture, logical in the face of naval inferiority to Britain, worked well. The navy did manage to convoy the silver fleets past numerous eager predators, thereby keeping Spain solvent. It also protected countless merchant ships attached to the silver fleets, thereby permitting Spain to nurture a four-fold expansion in colonial trade between 1700 and 1763 and (inadvertently) a corresponding merchant elite in the Indies. It did not, and could not, prevent the British navy from assuming command of the seas and mounting some successful (and many unsuccessful) attacks on Spanish colonies. Ironically, it would be the successful merchants in the colonies, rather than the British navy, that eventually cost Spain its American empire.

John R. McNeill

References

Cesáro Fernández Duro, *Armada española desde la unión de los reinos de Castilla y de Aragon*, 15 vols. (1973 [1895–1909]); John Harbron, *Trafalgar and the Spanish Navy* (1988); José P. Merino Navarro, *La armada española en el siglo XVIII* (1981); Rolf Mühlmann, *Die reorganisation der Spanischen Kriegsmarine im 18 jahrhundert* (1975); P. Pérez-Maillana, *Politica naval española en el Atlántico, 1700–1715* (1982); J.L. Sariego del Castillo, *De Sevilla a Vera Cruz: Historia de la marina española enla América Septentrional y Pacifico* (1975); Gerónimo de Uztáriz, *Theorica y práctica de comericio y marina* (1742), rpt. 1968.

See also Navy, Great Britain; Pensacola; St. Augustine; Ship Design

Fort Necessity (Pennsylvania)

Fort Necessity was the site of one of the opening battles in the struggle for control of the Ohio Valley between the English and the French. It was located at a place called Great Meadows, 11 miles east of present-day Uniontown, Pennsylvania, and just west of Farmington. The fort was begun on 30 May 1754 by 22-year-old Lieutenant Colonel George Washington. It was formally surrendered to the French on 4 July 1754.

On 15 March 1754, George Washington was commissioned by Governor Robert Dinwiddie of Virginia as lieutenant colonel and ordered to raise troops and proceed to the forks of the Ohio (Fort Duquesne). On the evening of 27 May, while encamped at Great Meadows, Washington received word from Seneca chief Half-King that a small party of French had been sighted five miles to the west. He immediately set out with a detachment of about 40 men, met and defeated the party. The French leader, Ensign Joseph Coulon de Villiers, sieur de Jumonville, and nine of his men were killed. Washington lost one man.

Washington fell back to Great Meadows and fearing retaliation from the French sent a message to Wills Creek for reinforcements and began strengthening the fort. By 12 June the fort was finished and some reinforcements had arrived. Despite dissension within his force, Washington decided to proceed on to Redstone (Brownsville, Fayette County, Pennsylvania). Leaving a detachment of men to guard the fort he pressed on, clearing the road as he went. On 29 June he learned that a large force of French and Indians were advancing from Fort Duquesne. Due to the shortage of supplies and the great fatigue of the men, the decision was to return to Great Meadows, now called Fort Necessity. Early on 3 July word arrived that the French were in full march with about 600 men. Washington's force of about 300 men hastily prepared their defense by making a small entrenchment around the fort. The French under the command of Captain Louis Coulon de Villiers, brother of the slain Joseph, arrived about 11:00 A.M. The French moved across the open field in a file, fired a volley, and then scattered to the edge of the woods, about 60 yards away, hidden by trees and stumps. The English went into their trenches, and a steady rain fell. Firing continued until 8:00 P.M., when the French called a parley, asking for surrender. Washington had no choice but to capitulate. The rain had filled the trenches and soaked their munitions, the men were fatigued and short of supplies. The French and their Amerindian allies had also killed and driven away all the horses and cattle. Early the next morning the English marched out of their encampment, reaching Wills Creek five days later. The French demolished the works at Fort Necessity.

Several excavations were undertaken, and in 1932, Fort Necessity was restored. Then reconstructed in 1953, it became a National Battlefield site under the auspices of the National Park Service.

Evelyn C. Darrow

References

J.C. Harrington, "Metamorphosis of Fort Necessity," *Western Pennsylvania Magazine* 37 (1954):181–188; William Blake Hindman, "The Great Meadows Campaign and the Climaxing Battle at Fort Necessity," *West Virginia History* 16 (1955):65–89; William A. Hunter, *Forts on the Pennsylvania Frontier, 1753–1758* (1960); Donald Dean Jackson, *The Diaries of George Washington*, 6 vols. (1976–1979).

Charles Morse Stotz, *Outposts of the War for Empire: The French and English in Western Pennsylvania; Their Armies, Their Forts, Their People, 1749–1764* (1985); Frederick Tilberg, *Fort Necessity: National Battlefield Site, Pennsylvania* (1954).

See also COULON DE VILLIERS, JOSEPH, JUMONVILLE; COULON DE VILLIERS, LOUIS; DINWIDDIE, ROBERT; HALF-KING; WASHINGTON, GEORGE; WILLS CREEK

Fort New Casco (Maine)

Fort New Casco was erected in 1700 after the destruction of Fort Loyal. Designed by Colonel Wolfgang Romer, it was situated near the mouth of the Presumpscot River. Fortifications consisted of a 70-foot-square palisade with two bastions and two raised sentry boxes. After the outbreak of Queen Anne's War, it was the site of a council in June 1703 between Governor Joseph Dudley and Abenaki Indians who agreed to remain peaceful. However, Canadian Governor Pierre de Riguad de Vandreuil was able to assemble 500 Abenakis under Michel Leneuf de La Vallière et de Beaubassin and sent them against the British in Maine. On 10 August 1703, six war parties from this force simultaneously struck major English settlements. Chief Moxux led the attack on Fort New Casco, which was commanded by Major John March. After three Abenaki chiefs appeared under a white flag, Major March and five or six others were tricked out of the fort and ambushed. However, Major March made it safely back to the fort, which was placed under siege. The siege ended on the third day when an armed vessel from Massachusetts appeared in the harbor. The fort was redesigned and enlarged to 250 feet long and 190 feet wide by engineer John Redknap in 1705. It was never again attacked and was subsequently dismantled in 1716 to save costs.

David L. Whitesell

See also CASCO BAY; FORT LOYAL (MAINE); MAINE; MARCH, JOHN

New England Confederation

The New England Confederation, the first formal attempt to organize an intercolonial union in the northern colonies, was, as its charter proclaimed, a "confederation for amity, offence, and defence." Its founding members, Massachusetts, Plymouth, Connecticut, and New Haven, had sound practical and ideological motives for the endeavor. The brief but violent Pequot War, in 1636–1637, coupled with their isolation from England, especially during the English civil war, made them vulnerable to attack from their Indian, French, and Dutch neighbors. Intercolonial boundary and trade disputes plagued all the settlements, and no one wanted to appeal to England to adjudicate these disputes for fear that this would invite unwanted outside interference. Connecticut, New Haven, and Plymouth saw the confederation as a means of protecting themselves from possible encroachments on their territory from Massachusetts, the only confederation member boasting a royal charter. All of the colonies hoped to use the confederation to expand their territorial and trading opportunities. Finally, they intended to use the confederation to preserve and promulgate the Puritan religion. Because membership would guarantee any colony's borders from outside attack, Maine, New Hampshire, and Rhode Island were all excluded from the confederation. Massachusetts hoped to annex Maine and New Hampshire; everyone had designs on Rhode Island. Moreover, Rhode Island's religious heterodoxy had made that colony a pariah to the more "orthodox" confederation members.

The confederation charter, signed in Boston on 7 September 1643, created a league of friendship for offense, defense, advice, and aid. Acting as independent, sovereign states, its members did not pledge allegiance either to king or Parliament. The confederation operated on a federal model: each colony had two commissioners, each with an equal vote. No war could be undertaken by any member without confederation approval. Expenses and military personnel would be contributed proportionate to the population of each colony. Consequently, Massachusetts dominated the confederation. Ultimately, the commissioners could only advise the individual colonies; sovereignty rested in the individual General Courts.

The New England Confederation was strongest during the first decade of its existence. Untroubled by English interference, it kept the peace, straightened out relations with the French and the Dutch, negotiated a boundary treaty with New Netherlands governor, Petrus (Peter) Stuyvesant, in 1650, settled internal disputes, and put an end to a trade war between Connecticut and Massachusetts. The commissioners also approved the bay colony's claims in New Hampshire, Maine, and Martha's Vineyard, and allowed the expansion of Connecticut and New Haven on Long Island.

With the restoration of Charles II, the confederation steadily deteriorated, as it was forced to confront a more aggressive imperial policy. In 1672, when New Haven was subsumed by Connecticut, a new confederation charter was devised by the three remaining members. Meeting triennially instead of annually, the confederation focused on missionary activity and the adjudication of intercolonial disputes. It revived briefly during King Philip's War in 1676, but while the United Colonies managed to act in concert during the war, intercolonial squabbling increased as hostilities dragged on and the war actually undermined the confederation's effectiveness. Nearly moribund during the dominion period, it was active briefly from 1689 to 1691, organizing an expedition against the Abenakis and renewing a treaty with the Mohawks. Massachusetts's royal charter of 1691 dealt the final blow to the confederacy. Royal control made independent colonial diplomatic and military activity both unnecessary and impossible. And the religious underpinnings of the confederation were undermined by the official policy of religious toleration now emanating from London.

Sheila L. Skemp

References
Charles M. Andrews, *The Fathers of New England: A Chronicle of the Puritan Commonwealths* (1919); Francis Jennings, *The Invasion of America: Indians, Colonialism, and the Cant of Conquest* (1975); Douglas Edward Leach, *Flintlock and Tomahawk: New England in King Philip's War* (1958); Herbert L. Osgood, *The American Colonies in the Seventeenth Century, Vol. 1: The Chartered Colonies* (1904); Harry M. Ward, *The United Colonies of New England, 1643–1690* (1961); George F. Willison, ed., *The Pilgrim Reader* (1953).

See also DOMINION OF NEW ENGLAND; HARTFORD, TREATY OF; INTERCOLONIAL RELATIONS; KING PHILIP'S WAR; PURITANS

New Hampshire

The province of New Hampshire figured in the colonial wars primarily as a buffer between the French-led Indians of Canada and the more populated parts of New England, and as a major contributor to the New England expedition against Louisbourg in 1745. The province also produced Robert Rogers, whose New Hampshire "rangers" gained fame as a woodland scouting force during the Seven Years' War.

The native inhabitants of what eventually became New Hampshire can be sorted into four principal groups. By far the largest were the Pennacooks, the name given both to the Algonkian hunting/farming/fishing tribe that was centered in the Merrimack Valley near Concord, and to a larger association consisting of the central tribe and a number of semi-autonomous bands stretching northward and southward. Other groups, also of the Algonkian culture, were the roaming Sokokis north of the White Mountains, whose hunting ground extended well to the eastward into Maine; some western bands of Abenaki, known collectively as the Pigwackets, clustered in and near the upper Saco Valley in the southeastern part of the White Mountains; and the Pocumtucks of western Massachusetts, whose hunting ground extended northward into the southern Connecticut River valley of New Hampshire.

English settlement along the Piscataqua River began as early as 1623. Early efforts to establish fishing and trading colonies under the auspices of various groups of merchant venturers operating with grants from the Council for

New England were supplanted in the 1630s by migrants to the region from Puritan Massachusetts. From the early 1640s until 1680, the four original New Hampshire towns were a part of Massachusetts. The crown set up a separate royal province in 1680 to create a jurisdiction for the trial of a land dispute, but it was not until 1740 that the boundaries of the province were firmly settled and New Hampshire was given its own royal governor.

Because the immediate region of earliest English settlement was relatively clear of native inhabitants, there was no important occasion for conflict between the two cultures for much of the seventeenth century. The Pennacooks, in fact, were eager for trade with the English and for awhile welcomed the settlers as protection against the hostile Mohawks. Their sachem, Passaconaway, consistently counseled accommodation with the whites.

The tribes of northern New England, including the Pennacooks and Abenakis, took no part in the Pequot War and remained neutral during King Philip's War. In 1675, Passaconaway's son and successor, Wonalancet, even led his people out of the Merrimack Valley to the region north of the mountains in order to stay out of trouble, only to have the villages they left behind destroyed by New Englanders. After the war had ended in 1676, an episode of betrayal by Major Richard Waldron during a "field day," or sham battle in Dover, resulted in the capture and execution of some refugee Nipmucks from southern New England whom the Pennacooks had befriended. Opportunity for revenge came with the outbreak of King William's War. In the summer of 1689, raids on Dover (Waldron was among the 23 settlers killed) and Oyster River (later Durham) by Pennacook-led eastern Indians, now allied with the French, set the pattern for frontier warfare that would dominate the action in New England during both King William's and Queen Anne's Wars.

During Queen Anne's War, strings of manned garrison houses, ranging parties to intercept marauding Indian bands, and eventual organized expeditions against Quebec and Nova Scotia all helped protect the previously wide-open frontier towns. Even so, raids on coastal Maine and New Hampshire settlements, including Exeter, Dover, Kingston, and Hampton, resulted in hundreds of casualties, dozens of captivities, and massive loss of property. Such raids, threats of raids, and the more or less constant presence of small hostile bands in the surrounding forests impeded farm production and the expansion of settlement, and French privateers off the New England coast hindered the colony's fishing and the export trade.

On the other hand, the larger Anglo-French conflict in the early years of the eighteenth century prompted the British government to encourage the development of naval stores in the Piscataqua region. The export of white pine masts and other forest products thus became central to both the economy and politics of New Hampshire in the middle decades of the century.

In the interlude between the Treaty of Utrecht and King George's War, broken only by Massachusetts Lieutenant Governor William Dummer's war against the eastern Indians in the 1720s, settlement extended well up the Merrimack and Connecticut Valleys and along the tributaries of each. Renewed hostilities in the 1740s again inhibited the further expansion of settlement, but this time the province escaped significant incursion, thanks in part to a string of frontier fortifications, most of which were never put to the test. The main exception was the fort at Township No. 4 (Charlestown) on the Connecticut River, whose small garrison repulsed a 300-man raiding force in the spring of 1746. Nothing during King George's War, however, matched for drama or long-term consequence the successful New England expedition in 1745 against Louisbourg, to which New Hampshire contributed 450 men.

Militiamen from New Hampshire again participated alongside troops from neighboring provinces and British redcoats in the various northern campaigns and battles of the last French and Indian War, and were especially conspicuous in the Battle of Lake George in 1755. In 1759, the climactic year of the war, nearly a thousand New Hampshiremen were serving somewhere outside the province. New Hampshire's most distinctive contribution, however, was the body of "rangers" raised and trained for wilderness fighting in 1756 by Robert Rogers. Except for one disastrous defeat during an attempt on Fort Ticonderoga in 1758, the rangers made important contributions everywhere in the northern theater and gained a wide reputation for effectiveness.

The end of intercolonial warfare after 1760 brought on a massive pioneering movement from southern New Hampshire, Massachusetts, and Connecticut to settle most of the remaining empty lands of the province over the next 15 years.

Charles E. Clark

References

Charles E. Clark, *The Eastern Frontier: The Settlement of Northern New England, 1610–1763* (1970), rpt. 2983; Jere R. Daniell, *Colonial New Hampshire: A History* (1981); Douglas Edward Leach, *Arms for Empire: A Military History of the Colonies in North America, 1607–1763* (1973); Francis Parkman, *A Half-Century of Conflict* (1962); David Van Deventer, *The Emergence of Provincial New Hampshire, 1623–1741* (1976).

See also ABENAKI; DOVER, ATTACK ON; KING WILLIAM'S WAR; LAKE GEORGE, BATTLE OF; FORT AT NUMBER FOUR (NEW HAMPSHIRE); OYSTER RIVER; QUEEN ANNE'S WAR; ROGERS, ROBERT; FORT WILLIAM AND MARY (NEW HAMPSHIRE)

New Jersey

New Jersey, part of the Dutch colony of New Netherland, began with a trading post at the future site of Gloucester in 1623 and spread to other posts along the Delaware River and in eastern New Jersey. In 1626, the Dutch built Fort Nassau across from the present site of Philadelphia to trade with the Delaware River Indian tribes, but the fort was abandoned in 1628 in favor of a trading ship stationed in the river. Dutch settlers around these posts enjoyed relatively good relations with the Native Americans, suffering only two violent wars. Colonial competition with other European powers was the major source of trouble, though mostly bloodless, until the English took possession in 1664.

The Dutch governors had strict orders from the Dutch West India Company to avoid conflict with the natives, and most governors established fair trade policies. Because the colony did not establish a strong militia system for defense, the Dutch relied on their governors' privately hired soldiers. Wars therefore were to be avoided. Governor Willem Kieft was the exception, sparking a war with the tribes around New Amsterdam in 1643 by exploiting the Indians and having 80 Hackensack tribe members killed. Peace was restored in 1645, by which time eastern New Jersey had been abandoned and Pavonia (now Jersey City) had been devastated. Despite efforts by Kieft's replacement, Petrus (Peter) Stuyvesant, to improve relations with the natives, fighting resumed in 1655, Pavonia again being abandoned. Through stricter trade regulations, a

policy of collecting isolated farmers into fortified villages, and controlling Indian movements around Dutch towns, Stuyvesant reestablished peace in 1657. After this event, the Dutch and Indians remained at peace.

New Jersey's prominent role in the colonial competition of the seventeenth century came from competing claims by the Dutch, Swedish, and English. Swedish settlers began encroaching on Dutch claims in New Jersey in 1638, and by 1643, New Sweden claimed the western shore of the Delaware River and the lower eastern shore of the river to Cape May. Kieft's War in 1639–1645 threatened to spread to the Swedish settlements, but the Swedes avoided open conflict with the natives. New Sweden continued to expand its control, causing clashes on the western shore with Dutch settlers in 1645. By 1649, Sweden claimed the New Jersey shore from the cape to the present site of Trenton. About 90 soldiers defended New Sweden.

Governor Stuyvesant challenged Sweden's claims in 1651, marching across New Jersey with 120 soldiers, briefly occupying Fort Nassau, and then moving to the western bank of the Delaware to build Fort Casimir. After the Swedes took Fort Casimir by force in 1654, Stuyvesant sailed upriver in 1655 with more than 300 soldiers and sailors. Under company orders to eliminate New Sweden by force if necessary, Stuyvesant besieged Fort Casimir and captured the other Swedish fort, Fort Christina, without inflicting or receiving any casualties. New Sweden's Governor Johan Classon Rising surrendered the colony, and New Sweden ceased to exist.

The English also claimed this territory. In 1635, 15 Virginians occupied the empty Fort Nassau, but a Dutch naval force returned the English to Virginia. Throughout the 1640s and 1650s, Virginia and Maryland settlers continued to encroach on Dutch-held New Jersey, compelling Stuyvesant to send 60 soldiers in 1659 to southern New Jersey to prevent permanent English settlements. Finally in 1664, Stuyvesant surrendered New Netherland to an English naval force commanded by James, duke of York, and New Netherland officially passed to English control. James immediately separated New Jersey from New York. After 1664, New Jersey ceased to be an object of foreign colonial competition.

During the imperial colonial wars of 1689–1763, New Jersey's importance was as a support for its strategically critical neighbor, New York.

France did not threaten the English coastal colonies and the wars along the western and northern frontiers of New Jersey's neighbors rarely touched New Jersey. New Jersey contributed militia soldiers and money to New York's defense during all the wars, and especially after 1702, when New Jersey's governors were under standing orders to supply all possible support to New York's frontier. In addition, New Jersey sent large contingents to join the proposed invasions of Canada in every war during the eighteenth century. Throughout these colonial wars, relations with the local New Jersey tribes remained peaceful except for the occasional flare-up. War and colonial competition had receded from New Jersey's boundaries.

Mark V. Kwasny

References
Douglas Edward Leach, *Arms for Empire: A Military History of the British Colonies in North America, 1607–1763* (1973); John E. Pomfret with Floyd Shumway, *Founding the American Colonies, 1583–1660* (1970); Ellis Lawrence Raesly, *Portrait of New Netherland* (1945); Allen W. Trelease, *Indian Affairs in Colonial New York: The Seventeenth Century* (1960); Christopher Ward, *The Dutch and Swedes on the Delaware, 1609–1664* (1930).

See also FORT CASIMIR (DELAWARE); FORT CHRISTINA (DELAWARE); FORT ELFSBORG (NEW JERSEY); KIEFT'S WAR; FORT NASSAU (NEW JERSEY); FORT NORMANOCK (NEW JERSEY); NEW SWEDEN; STUYVESANT, PETRUS; SWEDE; FORT WALPACK (NEW JERSEY)

Fort New Korsholm (Pennsylvania)
Fort New Korsholm was constructed in 1647 under orders from the governor of New Sweden, Johan Bjornsson Prinz. It was constructed on an island near the mouth of the Schuykill River because of the increasing competition of the Dutch and Swedish for the fur trade of the region. (In 1633, Dutch from Fort Nassau constructed a blockhouse here, and the English constructed one in 1642. Both of these structures were abandoned due to Indian and Swedish hostility.) Nothing is known about the size of the garrison or the nature of the fort's armament, but several contemporary descriptions of the fort describe it as dominating the region, indicating that it was well armed and manned.

In response to the building of Fort New Korsholm, Petrus (Peter) Stuyvesant ordered the construction of a fort opposite it. Located on the site of present-day Philadelphia, Fort Beversrede was constructed in April 1648 and was destroyed one month later by the Swedes at Fort New Korsholm. The Dutch rebuilt the fort and the New Korsholm garrison destroyed it once again in November 1648. The Dutch held on to the site until Fort Casimir was built in 1651. Two years later the Swedes abandoned New Korsholm when it was no longer needed by them.

Anthony P. Inguanzo

See also FORT CASIMIR (DELAWARE); FORT NASSAU (NEW JERSEY); NEW SWEDEN; STUYVESANT, PETRUS; SWEDE

New Mexico
New Mexico was, until the occupation of Alta California, the most remote and northern of Spain's settlements in the New World. The wanderings of Alvar Núñez Cabeza de Vaca and his companions, survivors of the ill-fated Pánfilo de Narváez expedition of 1527, brought them near enough to the valley of the Rio Grande to hear tales of large Indian communities, stories which were quickly transmuted into fables of golden cities. A fleeting glimpse by a Franciscan monk seemed to confirm the existence of the legendary Seven Cities of Cíbola, and Viceroy Antonio de Mendoza assembled an *entrada* of conquistadors, led by Francisco Vásquez de Coronado in 1540.

The rapacious army of Spanish noblemen, adventurers, vagabonds, slaves, and Mexican Indians was sorely disappointed to find not golden cities, but the mesa dwellings of the sedentary tribes collectively known as the Pueblo Indians (so called because they lived in fixed communities, or pueblos). In the river valley lived the Pueblos, divided between the tribes of the Piro, Kere, southern and northern Tiwa, Tano, Towa, and Tewa. To the west lay the communities of the Zuni, and even further west lived the Hopi. The Pueblo settlements were small, most not exceeding 400 persons; the largest held about 2,000 inhabitants. The Indians built compact dwellings, two or three stories in height, and raised crops using irrigation. There was no level of political organization higher than the individual village. The siting of a number of Pueblo settlements atop tall mesas attests to the endemic state of warfare between the tribes, and between the Pueblos and the nomadic Utes, Navajos, and Apaches around them.

By the time a disappointed party of Spanish had left New Mexico more than a year later, having tramped over the plains of Kansas in a fruitless quest for gold, European-native relations were permanently soured. The Spaniards took Hawikuh pueblo in Zuni territory by storm and used it as their headquarters. Coronado quartered his army on the southern Tewas during the harsh winter of 1540–1541, and the ravenous mob stripped the Indians of food and blankets. After some Indian women were molested, the natives resisted. The Spanish assaulted several pueblos and executed at the stake those not slain in battle. This so terrified the Tiwas that virtually all of them abandoned their pueblos. The conquistadors began the long journey back to New Spain, leaving behind two Franciscan friars, who were quickly killed by the Indians.

The Spaniards did not return in force for 50 years, until Juan de Oñate led 400 soldiers, colonists, friars, and Mexican Indians to establish an outpost in the far north. Unlike the conquests of Mexico and Peru, the Spanish had less venal and more altruistic motivations in their colonization of New Mexico. Large numbers of natives living outside of what the Spaniards considered to be "civilized polity" prompted the viceroy to extend to the Pueblo Indians the dubious benefits of Spanish government and the Christian religion. Since New Mexico lacked gold, silver, or any other lucrative and quick source of wealth, the colony had to be subsidized from New Spain, and although it was a net drain on the economy of the viceroyalty, it was maintained largely for religious reasons.

The relationship between Spaniards and Indians was a complex one, but on the whole and at best a relationship between exploiter and exploited. Franciscan missionaries made the eradication of native religious practices, which they believed were idolatrous, their goal. They used native labor to build churches and sustain the friars in the Indians' own villages, and they freely used the whip to enforce their authority and that of the church. The civil authorities, on the other hand, constantly quarrelled with the Franciscans about jurisdiction over the Indians, and especially over allocations of native labor and tribute. At times these disputes escalated into open warfare, during which some governors encouraged Indians to defy the friars and permitted them to dance their *katchina* dances.

In 1680, drought, famine, and resentment finally forced the Indians to rebel. The revolt was the result of a pan-Indian alliance, in which traditionally hostile tribes overcame their enmities to join against the common enemy. The revolt was successful, if bloody; some 396 Spaniards, including 21 missionaries, were killed. Although the Pueblos gained only a dozen years of freedom after expelling the Spaniards, they had shaken the Europeans profoundly. The Spanish regained military control over the Pueblo, Hopi, and Zuni communities, and the nominal political allegiance of the Indians, but they never regained complete power in New Mexico. The missions were never reestablished in many Indian pueblos, and where they were, the friars tended to look the other way when Indians practiced their native religion.

New Mexico grew in strategic importance in the eighteenth century. As the French moved into Illinois and Louisiana, their influence became more pronounced among the Plains and Texas Indians. The adoption of the horse by many Native American groups had already revolutionized the way of life of many tribes. Now the musket began to change traditional patterns as well. While the Spanish prohibited selling or giving firearms to any Indians, the French had no hesitation in arming tribes like the Pawnee. Giving advanced weapons technology to one indigenous group but not others represented a shift in strategic equilibrium. The newly-armed Pawnee, for example, put pressure on the Comanches, who in turn moved into Apache territories; the Apaches in their turn stepped up their raids on Pueblo and Spanish communities. Facing "the French threat," the outer borderlands served as defensive settlements guarding New Spain and the vital silver mines at Zacatecas, Guanajuato, and Parral. Texas became the eastern, and New Mexico the northern, zone of frontier defense.

Santa Fe was the capital and Taos the northern outpost of this defensive perimeter. From here, Spanish governors of the eighteenth century were directed to probe for evidence of French civilian or military intruders, maintain the complex policy of war and peace among borderlands Indians, and support Spanish imperial policy, foreign and domestic. In 1706, Juan de Ulibarri took an expedition out onto the plains in search of reports of the presence of white men; in 1714, Juan Paéz Hurtado campaigned against the Apache and picked up more intelligence on foreign intruders. In 1719, Frenchman Charles Claude du Tisné traveled to Osage country south of the Missouri River; when word finally reached Santa Fe, the Frenchman was back in Illinois, but Governor Antonio Valverde sent out the ill-fated Pedro de Villasur party in search of the foreigners. The expedition was wiped out on the Platte River by Pawnee armed with muskets. Plans were made to reinforce New Mexico with arms and men, but peace in Europe, an unresponsive Spanish imperial bureaucracy, and fiscal problems blunted imperial borderlands defenses.

New Mexico in the eighteenth century was little more than a sleepy garrison province. Taos, Picuris, and Pecos became entrepôts for Spanish and Indian traders. Apaches, Utes, Navajos, and Comanches all came into town to exchange captives for goods, collect subsidies when the crown could afford to pay them, swear fleeting allegiance to Spain, or conduct peace negotiations. Some tribes deliberately took captives from Spanish settlements or among Pueblo or allied Indians, knowing that the Spanish would always ransom Christians or allies. Spanish-Pueblo relations improved, in part because Indian communities were much weakened by war and disease, in part because the Spanish interfered less in Indian affairs after the reconquest in 1692. The main reason for better relations was mutual need; increased depredations by Utes, Apaches, and Comanches forced natives and Europeans to cooperate in matters of defense. The Spanish relaxed their rules about guns in the hands of Indians and gave the Pueblos arms; the Pueblos in turn served loyally and bravely in military campaigns. In the 1780s, an able officer, Governor Juan Bautista de Anza, was able to engineer a series of peace treaties with the Comanche, Ute, Navajo, and Jicarilla Apaches that granted a measure of peace to the province. These so-called allied nations then helped the Spanish make war on the remaining Apache groups in New Mexico. The Spanish scrupulously maintained their alliance with the Comanche until independence in 1821.

New Mexico's conquest was a result of the early conquistador spirit, but its settlement was an act of religious faith. The Pueblo Indians, weakened by disease, famine, and war, tenaciously fought back in open revolt, and later in surreptitious and subversive rebellion. They managed to preserve a great deal of their cultural and religious heritage, and ultimately became a key element in Spanish imperial defense in the borderlands. New Mexico acted to the end of the colonial period as the northernmost outpost of Spain's empire in North America.

Peter Stern

References

John Francis Bannon, *The Spanish Borderlands Frontier, 1513–1821* (1974); Marc Simmons, "History of Pueblo-Spanish Relations to 1821," in *The Handbook of North American Indians*, ed. by Alfonso Ortiz, Vol. 9 (1979):178–193; Edward Spicer, *Cycles of Conquest: The Impact of Spain, Mexico, and the United States on the Indians of the Southwest, 1533–1960* (1962); Alfred B. Thomas, *After Coronado: Spanish Exploration Northeast of Mexico, 1696–1727* (1935).

See also CORONADO, FRANCISCO VÁZQUEZ DE; OÑATE, JUAN DE; PRESIDIO; PUEBLO REVOLT OF 1680; SPANISH MISSION SYSTEM–SOUTHWEST; TEXAS; VILLASUR, PEDRO DE

New Netherland

New Netherland was an overseas outpost within the Dutch mercantile empire of the seventeenth century. Like their Portuguese counterparts, the Dutch intended to create an empire with trading factories established for "*handel and wandel*," that is, barter. Their original ambition in New Netherland was to realize quick profits either from trade with the Amerindians or from the acquisition of commodities valued in Europe, such as furs, minerals, and precious metals. Based on the navigation of Henry Hudson in the *Half Moon* (1609), the Dutch were able to place traders in New Netherland who had no interest in locating permanent settlements when they landed. In 1621, the merchant-directors of the West India Company gained a monopoly on the right to trade and explore. They administered New Netherland until its seizure by the English in 1664.

Initially, then, New Netherland was not expected to be the same kind of "full-settlement colonization" that, for example, the English were undertaking in the New World. As a result, it was largely a trading center. In 1626, on Manhattan Island, the Dutch established Fort New Amsterdam and a small community of traders. Some 120 miles upriver along the Hudson River, they traded out of Fort Orange and, after 1652, the surrounding fur-trading settlement of Beverwijck (later Albany). In 1654, a trading post still farther inland was established at present-day Schenectady. In addition to these market settlements, the Dutch maintained a trading presence at Fort Good Hope on the Connecticut River and at Fort Casimir (New Castle, Delaware) as well as along Long Island and at Wiltwijck (Kingston).

The fact that New Netherland was not envisaged as "full-settlement colonization" had significant consequences. It meant that relations between the Dutch and the native populations were relatively harmonious. The lands of tribes like the Mohawk and Esopus were invaded—although land was always appropriated by purchase—but only to take ownership of geographical space required for trading places. The violence that European expansion caused elsewhere in northeastern North America was diminished here.

The emphasis on trade also meant that population grew slowly. In 1639, the company opened the trade to individual merchants, and an entrepreneur like Kiliaen van Rensselaer seized the opportunity to colonize, especially sending men and women to his patroonship of Rensselaerswijck near Fort Orange. He was one of many men—Petrus (Peter) Stuyvesant was another—who warned the company that New Englanders would overwhelm New Netherland if greater attention were not give to colonization. However it was only after the mid-1650s that a notably large migration, including many farm families, arrived. By 1664, the population was close to 10,000. Initial plans for New Netherland and traditional Dutch preferences regarding settlement practices were now working toward the achievement of an urban-based society much like the homeland. The resident company secretary, Nicassius de Sille, boasted that within the jurisdiction of New Netherland there were two cities (one with 14 public buildings and 342 houses), 13 villages, two forts, and three colonies.

The administration of New Netherland was in the power of the West India Company. Its purposes were carried out by a resident director general and a range of bureaucrats primarily concerned with the commercial success of the venture. Willing to see the factories abandoned if profits were not forthcoming, the company made many mistakes. However, New Netherland functioned in republican ways. The most readily available token of this was the establishment of New Amsterdam (later New York City) as a city in the mid-1650s. Slowly, the municipality had won the rights claimed by any one of the great cities of the Low Countries. Modeling itself on Amsterdam, it set about actualizing the practices that the highly decentralized and, of course, non-monarchical and (effectively) non-feudal republic of the Netherlands allowed it: a market and fairways, independence in matters of war and peace, control of justice, and other affairs within its walls.

In 1664, and without the declaration of a state of war, the English forced Petrus Stuyvesant to surrender New Netherland, and such developments became part of a very different culture. New Netherland remained under English control until 1673 when, for a short period, it reverted to the Dutch. In 1674 it became a permanent English possession, the gift of Charles II to his brother James, duke of York.

Donna Merwick

References

Van Cleaf Bachman, *Peltries or Plantation: The Economic Policies of the Dutch West India Company in New Netherland, 1623–1639* (1969); John Romeyn Brodhead, *History of the State of New York*, 2 vols. (1853–1871); Simon Hart, *The Prehistory of the New Netherland Company: Amsterdam Notarial Records of the First Dutch Voyages to the Hudson* (1959); Donna Merwick, *Possessing Albany: 1630–1710: The Dutch and English Experiences* (1990); Oliver Rink, *Holland on the Hudson: An Economic and Social History of Dutch New York* (1986).

See also FORT AMSTERDAM (NEW YORK); ANGLO-DUTCH WAR, FIRST; ANGLO-DUTCH WAR, SECOND; ANGLO-DUTCH WAR, THIRD; FORT CASIMIR (DELAWARE); ESOPUS WAR; FORT GOOD HOPE (CONNECTICUT); HARTFORD, TREATY OF; KIEFT, WILLEM; KIEFT'S WAR; LONG ISLAND; MINUIT, PETER; MOHAWK-MAHICAN WAR; NEW NETHERLAND, SURRENDER OF; NEW SWEDEN; FORT ORANGE (NEW YORK); PEACH WAR; STUYVESANT, PETRUS; WALL STREET PALISADE (NEW YORK)

New Netherland, Surrender of (1664)

The Dutch West India Company's colony of New Netherland—wedged between New England in the north and the English tobacco colonies of Maryland and Virginia in the south—had been an annoyance to England ever since its earliest settlement in the 1620s. The Dutch were not only competing with the English for dominance of world trade in Europe and the Far East, but had also gained a foothold in the New World. New Netherland had become an impediment to English hegemony along the coast of North America; a haven for smugglers and a threat to English plans for dominance of New World trade.

England never recognized the Dutch claim to New Netherland. The closest the two countries ever came to an agreement was the Hartford Treaty of 1650, which was never ratified. England based its claim on the charters of James I, which granted the region to New England and Virginia trading companies. The Dutch countered English rights to the land by referring to Spanish rights of discovery in the sixteenth century that were transferred to the Dutch by the Treaty of Westminster in 1648. The English were so distracted during their civil war in the 1640s that their overseas colonies were neglected or remained royalist, allowing the Dutch to solidify their position in the New World. New Netherland came closest to invasion by the English colonies during the First Anglo-Dutch War.

In April 1653, a delegation from New England visited New Amsterdam to complain of purported Dutch depredations in Connecticut. Dissatisfied with Director General Petrus (Peter) Stuyvesant's denial of the charges, the New Englanders returned to Boston to urge the conquest of New Netherland. All the New England colonies agreed to contribute to the venture except for Massachusetts Bay. Without Massachusetts's financial and military support, the enterprise was called off. The following year, Cromwell supplied Robert Sedgwick with four warships to take New Netherland; however, the plan was aborted when news of peace with the Dutch Republic reached the English naval force in mid-Atlantic.

After the restoration of Charles II to the throne of England, New Netherland once again became a target for English attempts to diminish Dutch commercial interests. In 1663, Charles granted all the land from the Penobscot River in Maine to Delaware Bay (excluding the New England colonies) to his brother James, duke of York and Albany. In addition to this huge gift of land, which included New Netherland, Charles gave his brother £4,000 to defray expenses incurred while taking possession of his new holdings. James commissioned Richard Nicolls in 1664 to lead a force of four ships carrying 250 soldiers to reduce New Amsterdam and bring the entire Dutch colony under English control.

If it is not already a maxim of war, it should be: That a well-executed attack during time of peace will probably succeed. Nicolls was able to surprise Stuyvesant, the director general of New Netherland, who was unprepared for such hostile actions in peacetime. Although rumors had reached Stuyvesant of the possibility of such an attempt, English diplomats had assured the Dutch government that Nicolls's objective was to correct matters in New England. The defenses on Manhattan were in poor shape. They had suffered the ravages of time since being repaired and strengthened during the first war with England a decade before. Added to the poor condition of the city's defenses was a "fifth column," the English settlers on the western end of Long Island. Although living within the jurisdiction of New Netherland, they were prepared to exploit the situation with the hope of acquiring more self-government and the right to plunder New Amsterdam if the city was stormed.

On 26 August, Nicolls arrived off Sandy Point aboard the 32-gun warship *Guinea*. When three more English ships appeared two days later, Stuyvesant wrote to his commanders at Fort Orange and the Esopus region (present-day Kingston) for assistance. He also ordered Fort Orange not to ship any furs downriver until the intentions of the English were clear. By Sunday, 31 August, Stuyvesant had received a reply to his request that the English explain their presence in Dutch waters. Nicolls wrote that he had come to claim what belonged to his sovereign, and demanded the surrender of New Amsterdam. He indicated that the property, life, and liberty of everyone who submitted to His Majesty would be respected, but those who oppose His Majesty "must expect all the miseryes of a Warr, which they bring upon themselves."

At about this same time, reports were coming in that the English had landed troops at New Utrecht (near the southwestern point of Long Island). The local farmers were ordered to assist in moving supplies and ordnance to the ferry in preparation for an assault on Manhattan. If they complied, they were promised that not even a chicken would be disturbed. The city was full of rumors generated by the exchange of letters. Stuyvesant refused to allow the burgomasters of New Amsterdam to see the letter from Nicolls, stating, in so many words, that it was none of their business. Rather than show the burgomasters a letter from Governor Winthrop of Connecticut, which urged Stuyvesant to comply with Nicolls's terms to avoid bloodshed, Stuyvesant tore it up.

When Stuyvesant polled his troops in the fort, they responded unanimously that they were prepared to fight; the officer in charge of the fort's ordnance was ordered to prepare to fire. Although Stuyvesant assumed a determined posture of resistance, the situation on Long Island was deteriorating. As news spread of the situation, New Englanders began to swell the ranks of the English force at the ferry. The possibility of plundering the riches of Manhattan also attracted hundreds of French privateers and Indians who enlisted in support of the English invasion. On 4 September, the English ships began to maneuver toward the fort; a sign that Nicolls was about to spill blood. Stuyvesant wrote to Nicolls that he had little choice but to discuss surrender terms. His decision was reinforced by a letter signed by 93 inhabitants, imploring him to accept Nicolls's terms. A day later Stuyvesant agreed to the surrender terms at his farm outside the city. On 8 September, New Amsterdam became New York.

After the fall of New Amsterdam, Nicolls acted quickly to gain control of the rest of New Netherland. He sent Sir George Cartwright north to accept the surrender of Fort Orange, which was accomplished without incident; and sent Sir Robert Carr south to take control of the Delaware. Carr's assignment provoked the first violence in the campaign against the Dutch. Although the population along the Delaware was willing to accept the terms of surrender, the commander of Fort New Amstel (present-day New Castle, Delaware) refused to yield. As a result, Carr deemed it fit to storm the fort and plunder the settlements in the Delaware Valley, including the Mennonite settlement on Delaware Bay. The terms of surrender were confirmed at the conclusion of the Second Anglo-Dutch War by the Treaty of Breda on 21 July 1667.

Charles T. Gehring

References
Notarial records of the Municipal Archives of Amsterdam; Robert C. Ritchie, *The Duke's Province: A Study of New York Politics and Society, 1664–1685* (1977); I.N. Phelps Stokes, *The Iconography of Manhattan Island, 1498–1909*, 6 vols. (1915–1928).

See also FORT AMSTERDAM (NEW YORK); ANGLO-DUTCH WAR, SECOND; LONG ISLAND; NEW YORK, DUTCH CAPTURE OF; FORT ORANGE (NEW YORK); STUYVESANT, PETRUS

New Orleans

New Orleans was founded in 1718, probably on the site of a former Indian settlement, to replace Mobile as the capital and main transshipment depot for the Louisiana colony as John Law's Company of the West began development of the Mississippi Valley interior. Not only could the new settlement control the Mississippi, but its situation on a major portage to Lake Pontchartrain and thence through Mississippi Sound to Mobile Bay enabled it to command both river drainages by water.

From the beginning, the city was laid out in the neoclassic insulae still to be seen in the "Vieux Carré," with a central parade ground where Jackson Square now stands, but no attempt was made to provide any fortification until 1730, when ditches were dug around the town boundaries to protect from Indian attack after an uprising by the Natchez. During the entire colonial period the urban development of the city was restricted to the north shore of the river, while it was supplied from farms on the south shore, from the German Coast upstream, and from a municipal fishery set up on Lake Pontchartrain.

Defended by downstream forts and fire ships at the mouth of the Mississippi in time of war, the city of New Orleans never became a strategic target for capture during the colonial period proper, in spite of the occasional alarms raised by colonial governors. The well-known "Battle of New Orleans" was a defense against British attack in the War of 1812.

Patricia Galloway

References
Marcel Giraud, *Histoire de la Louisiane Française*, 4 vols. (1953–1974); Samuel Wilson, Jr., *The Vieux Carré* (1968).

See also LOUISIANA; MISSISSIPPI RIVER; NATCHEZ WAR

New Sweden

In 1624, the Swedish king, Gustavius Adolphus, because of the activities of the Dutch, thought of establishing a colony in the New World. He

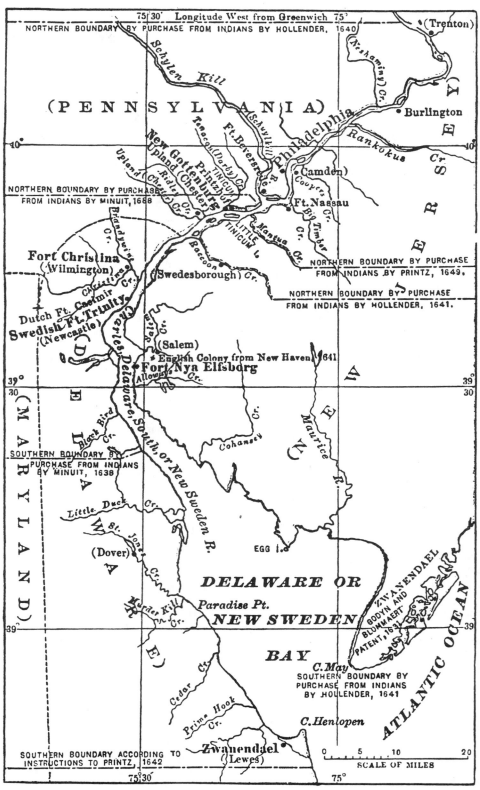

New Sweden, 1638–1655.

could never act on his inclinations because of two wars—one in Poland and then the Thirty Years' War—that occupied his attention. After the death of Gustavius Adolphus, Count Oxenstein, regent for the young Queen Christina, revived the idea of establishing a colony in the New World. With his encouragement, the New Sweden Company of traders was formed. Dutch merchants were involved rather heavily in the company, having provided half of the company's funding.

New Sweden was established 31 December 1637, when two ships and 50 colonists under the command of Peter Minuit arrived in Delaware Bay. Minuit entered into negotiations with the local Indians. The negotiations resulted in New Sweden consisting of all of the land on the eastern side of Delaware Bay, that is the Jersey shore, from Cape May in the south to a spot opposite Chester, Pennsylvania, in the north and on the western shore from Cape Henlopen to where Philadelphia is located today.

New Sweden was conceived of as a commercial venture. At first the colony consisted of trade posts so that the Swedes could obtain beaver pelts and other animal skins from the Indians. The Indians also traded agricultural products to the Swedes. From the beginning the Indian trade was profitable, with the Swedes sending home 1,200 skins in 1648.

The Swedish colonists could use whatever foodstuffs the Indians brought to the colony. Company officials wanted to turn a profit, and following the lead of the Virginians they decided to plant tobacco instead of grains. However, it never proved profitable, and tobacco growing seems to have been abandoned by 1648, since there are no reports of tobacco shipments to Sweden after that date. The colonists turned to the raising of grain and Indian corn instead.

The colonists had to turn to the cultivation of these crops because of the lack of support that they received from the company and the government. This lack of support was all the more serious because the colonists' own farms did not produce enough food, due in part to the lack of farm implements and draft animals, with the result that they had to purchase provisions from the Dutch of New Netherland and the English of Virginia. The Swedish colonists turned some of their grain into beer since a brewery was present.

Throughout the life of New Sweden the colony was plagued by a lack of settlers. Few Swedes wanted to leave their homeland for the North American colony. In 1644, there were only 90 Swedes present in the colony. Three years later the number rose to 183. Despite this impressive growth, the colony needed increased immigration to prosper. New lands could not be brought under cultivation or posts established. In various letters to their superiors in Sweden the governors of New Sweden stated that the colony needed settlers, particularly families, single women, and skilled craftsmen. One governor suggested that undesirables—debtors, army deserters, the indolent—be sent over. Some such people were sent, but the colony always needed more people.

In 1650 and 1651, severe crop failures occurred in Sweden with the result that more Swedes now expressed an interest in the North American colony. However, in 1653, the population numbered only 200 souls, and in 1655, Governor Johan Classon Rising was once again calling for the forced immigration of undesirables in order to increase the colony's population.

The Swedes constructed several forts for defense and trade. The more important of these were Fort Christina (1638–1655), Fort Elfsborg (1643–1653), and Fort New Korsholm (1647–1653). These outposts of Swedish authority in North America were usually undermanned, not maintained properly, and undersupplied with gunpowder and ammunition. This proved fatal in 1655 when the Dutch attacked New Sweden. The attack was precipitated in part by Swedish success in the fur trade, which was cutting into Dutch profits. Thus, in 1655, the Amsterdam authorities decided to do away with the Swedish colony. Petrus (Peter) Stuyvesant, the Dutch governor at New Amsterdam, was ordered to attack New Sweden, and he was given additional troops and ships for the task. Eventually, Stuyvesant led approximately 600 men and seven ships in a short, successful, and expensive campaign against New Sweden.

Anthony P. Inguanzo

References
    Israel Acrelius, *A History of New Sweden or the Settlements on the River Delaware* (1874), rpt. 1972; Charles M. Andrews, *The Colonial Period of American History*, 4 vols. (1934–1938); Amandus Johnson, *Swedish Settlements on the Delaware, 1638–1664* (1911); John A. Munroe, *Colonial Delaware: A History* (1978); Albert Cook Myers, ed.,

Narratives of Early Pennsylvania, West New Jersey and Delaware, 1630–1707 (1912).

See also FORT CHRISTINA (DELAWARE); FORT ELFSBORG (NEW JERSEY); FINN; MINUIT, PETER; FORT NEW KORSHOLM (PENNSYLVANIA); NEW JERSEY; STUYVESANT, PETRUS; SWEDE

New York

The first Europeans to inhabit New York were the Dutch, following the 1609 voyage of Henry Hudson up the river that bears his name. The Dutch West India Company founded New Netherland to generate profits in minerals, furs, timber, and other commodities. Seeking to prevent competition, it discouraged settlement beyond what was necessary to reap commercial profit; unfortunately, such a shortsighted policy prevented strong defense and invited encroachment by neighboring foreign colonies.

The weakness of the Dutch was in stark contrast to the English, particularly in New England. Industrious Puritan families prospered and multiplied, spreading their settlements westward along the coast of Long Island Sound and onto land claimed by Holland. Friction between Connecticut and New Netherland prompted Dutch governor Petrus (Peter) Stuyvesant to negotiate for a firm boundary; the English, however, recognizing the vulnerability of the Dutch, rejected a draft agreement (Hartford Treaty) in 1650. Adding to the enmity was King Charles II's 1662 charter to Connecticut, which extended that province's border through New Netherland to the Pacific Ocean.

The English mood in the second half of the seventeenth century was expansionist. With the Stuart restoration in 1660 came renewed interest in extending sovereignty to other continents and keeping pace with imperial competitors. English colonies already dotted the globe from Asia to North America, but their development had been more in spite of English policies than the result of them. The upheavals of the civil wars and interregnum behind them, the English could now devote their energies to enlarging the empire.

The empires of France, the Netherlands, and Spain offered compelling examples of the benefits of overseas possessions. Colonies provided raw materials and markets, helping the mother country maintain a favorable balance of trade. They supported military and naval forces necessary to protect shipping and conquer new lands. These advantages made Englishmen as eager as other Europeans to reap the rewards of empire. London merchants joined with noblemen, courtiers, statesmen, and the most prominent nationalist, James, duke of York, the king's brother, to press for an aggressive colonial policy.

Success in North America depended on English conquest of New Netherland. The Dutch occupied land surrounding strategic waterways and possessed an excellent deepwater port. They enjoyed a near monopoly over the beaver trade and controlled the carrying trade within much of the English empire, despite navigation acts designed to deny it to them. New Netherland separated the New England and Chesapeake colonies and profited from their trade. Determined to prevent further intrusions into their mercantile system, the English resolved to remove the Dutch from their midst in the New World.

Anticipating success, Charles granted his brother in March 1664 a patent for land encompassing New Netherland, as well as Pemaquid (in modern Maine), Nantucket, Martha's Vineyard, and Long Island. Shortly thereafter, he dispatched a small invasion force under Colonel Richard Nicolls who, by the end of August, had forced the feisty Stuyvesant to surrender. With the articles of capitulation signed, New York became an English proprietary. The Dutch reconquered the colony in 1673 during the Third Anglo-Dutch War, but relinquished it permanently the following year when the two countries concluded the Treaty of Westminster.

The origins of a much greater imperial rivalry began just as relations with the Dutch were easing. For many years, despite commercial competition, relations between the English and the French in the New World had been peaceful. Early New York governors were only dimly aware of French expansion south and west out of Canada and, surprisingly, did not seem to care. They were more concerned with promoting political stability and earning a profit for the proprietor. The myopia of the English allowed the French uncontested access to the territory and trade of the interior.

Some change occurred under Governor Edmund Andros (1674–1681), who sought to win the friendship and cooperation of the Indian nations in and around the province. His goal was a pact of nonaggression designed to bring order to New York and its colonial neighbors, recent victims of King Philip's War in New England and Bacon's Rebellion in Virginia. The culmination of his efforts came in 1677 with the signing of a treaty known as the "Covenant Chain." Though Andros intended it to be strictly a defensive alliance, the pact established a strategic relationship between the English and the powerful Iroquois confederation that endured for much of the colonial period.

Andros's successor, Thomas Dongan (1683–1688), saw most clearly the consequences of unfettered French settlement in America. Fearing that the king of England "will not have 100 miles from the sea anywhere" if the French continued their expansion, he developed an aggressive diplomacy to compete for sovereignty over the American continent. He sent trading expeditions to the Indians of the Great Lakes, a region claimed by Canada, and encouraged them to sell their furs at Albany instead of Montreal. He rejected French claims of sovereignty that were based on the work of explorers and Jesuit missionaries. Writing frequently to the Lords of Trade in London, he developed detailed proposals for building forts and improving military preparedness.

Most significantly, Dongan sided with the Iroquois in their ongoing feud with the French. He alerted the Indians to a French invasion of Iroquoia in 1684 and came to their aid after another encroachment in 1687. The latter attack induced King James II (formerly the duke of York) to declare his sovereignty over the Iroquois and to guarantee their security.

Dongan's rivalry with his Canadian counterparts portended things to come. In 1688, James was overthrown in the Glorious Revolution, bringing to power the francophobic William of Orange. As a result of the new political equilibrium in Europe, England and France fought a series of imperial wars that spread to the colonies and influenced their political, social, and economic development.

New York was in no shape to participate in the first of these wars, King William's (1689–1697). When news of James's demise reached the province, aggrieved colonists rose in rebellion against the trappings of the Stuart monarchy. They had many complaints, including high taxes, favoritism, commercial regulations, and inadequate defense. They resented the incorporation of New York into the Dominion of New England in 1688, citing among other things the inconvenience of having to conduct official business in Boston. Most serious, however, was discontent over authoritarian rule—except for the short-lived Dongan assembly, James had ruled autocratically as duke and king. Exacerbating each of these grievances was the enmity between the numerous ethnic and religious groups that comprised the polyglot colony.

Jacob Leisler, a Long Islander of German descent, emerged as the leader of the uprising. If he won the support of groups that had opposed the old regime, he failed to attract the colonial elites. The resultant power struggle hampered efforts to defend New York against French attack. Even after Leisler's hanging for treason in 1691 and the establishment of a permanent assembly, the lingering animosities between Leislerians and anti-Leislerians bedeviled politics for years to come. Subsequent governors continued to have difficulty molding a coherent war strategy.

Although the Iroquois provided temporary assistance by attacking Montreal in 1689, Canadian Governor Louis de Buade de Frontenac recovered quickly. In February 1690, he dispatched a force of 150 Frenchmen and 200 allied Indians who laid waste to Schenectady. Three years later, the French attacked south of the Mohawk River, destroying Iroquois villages and stores. In 1696, Frontenac led a raid into Onondaga, intimidating the Iroquois to the point that they never again posed a serious threat to the French. When the combatants signed the Treaty of Ryswick, which ended the fighting in 1697, fewer than 1,500 people remained in Albany County out of an original population of several thousand.

Four years later, England and France resumed fighting in the War of the Spanish Succession (1702–1713). Known in the colonies as Queen Anne's War, it left New York virtually unscathed. A principal reason was that Albany merchants, wishing to avoid high taxes, Indian raids, and financial loss, arranged a policy of neutrality with their Montreal trading partners. They had little trouble convincing colonial elites to support neutrality because of the unpopularity of Lord Governor Edward Cornbury, who had alienated virtually every faction in the colony with his incompetence and buffoonery. Not wishing to enhance Cornbury's power, the assembly denied him revenue for fighting the war.

Another reason for the relative peace was the stance of the Iroquois. Resentful of their shoddy treatment by the English during King William's War, Iroquois leaders established a more balanced diplomacy with the European powers. In 1701, they signed a treaty of friendship with Montreal that secured a promise against a French attack. Concurrently, they offered the British sovereignty over hunting grounds northwest of Lake Ontario. By playing off one European power against the other, the Iroquois reaped benefits for themselves as they contributed to the peace in New York.

The nearest New Yorkers came to participating actively in the war was in 1709, when the crown directed Governor John Lovelace (1708–1709) to command an English invasion force against Canada. The failure of the British government to provide adequate support, as well as Lovelace's untimely death, forced the English to abort the mission. Another expedition two years later met the same fate when British naval forces were defeated on the St. Lawrence River.

The Treaty of Utrecht (1713) ended the war and improved the English position in America. It awarded Newfoundland, Nova Scotia, and the Hudson Bay region to the English and confirmed British sovereignty over the Iroquois. It ushered in a period of peace that lasted for about three decades in America.

In the years following the treaty, New York governors sought to counter the growing French influence on the western frontier. They courted Indian allies and built forts along the Ohio River, the focal point of Anglo-French competition. In 1727, Governor William Burnet (1720–1728) approved the construction of Fort Oswego on the southern shore of Lake Ontario, which was effective in diverting the Indian fur trade from Montreal to Albany. He also banned the Albany-Montreal trade connection, but his opponents in the assembly—which grew steadily in power and prestige during this period—forced him to rescind the order.

The start of King George's War (1744–1748), known in Europe as the War of the Austrian Succession (1741–1748), found most New Yorkers determined to stay out of the fight. Governor George Clinton (1743–1753), an admiral in the Royal Navy, had other ideas, however. He provided guns and provisions for the successful assault of Louisbourg, a vital French outpost guarding the seaways to Canada. He criticized Albany commissaries for their lackluster support of the war effort and pressured them to cease trading with Montreal. These unpopular measures, coupled with his irritating hauteur, provoked heated opposition in the assembly and made further defense appropriations problematic.

In desperation, Clinton appointed William Johnson as colonial Indian agent and colonel of the Albany County militia. Besides sharing Clinton's imperial outlook, Johnson had more expertise and sensitivity in Indian affairs than any other Englishman. He had earned the respect of the Iroquois as an honest agent and friend; indeed, his mistress, Molly, was the sister of the famed Mohawk chief, Joseph Brant.

Clinton directed Johnson to enlist and supply Iroquois braves for an attack against Canada. Johnson's reputation and eloquent appeals induced the Iroquois to go on the warpath in 1746. Unfortunately, support from the British navy never materialized, and the expedition was called off. Henceforth the Mohawks patrolled the frontier while the remainder of the Iroquois nations provided only token support. In the end, New York escaped the brunt of King George's War, just as it had done in Queen Anne's.

The treaty of Aix-la-Chapelle, ending the war in 1748, changed little between the English and French in America. Canadian governors ordered the construction of forts throughout the west, especially along the upper Ohio River. They wooed the Iroquois, who were at odds with the British over land disputes and were repelled by Clinton's arrogance. In 1751, when William Johnson resigned his post as Indian agent because of the assembly's refusal to reimburse his expenses, the Iroquois were even more ready to leave the British fold. A Pennsylvania Indian agent noted ominously that at least three of the six Iroquois nations had "turned Frenchmen."

Fearful that the alienation of the Iroquois would coincide with the next round of warfare with France, the Board of Trade proposed that Indian and colonial representatives meet at Albany to overcome their differences. The Albany Conference convened in June 1754; besides the Iroquois sachems, 23 delegates from seven colonies were present. Largely because of the efforts of William Johnson—and 30 wagonloads of gifts—the two sides reached a tentative conciliation; nonetheless, they failed to conclude a new defensive alliance.

To strengthen England's strategic position, colonial delegates recommended the construction of a freshwater navy, appointment of a colonial Indian agent, erection of forts among the Iroquois, and creation of new colonies beyond the Appalachians. In addition, Benjamin Franklin proposed a plan for colonial union that would have improved military defense through the establishment of an intercolonial congress, headed by a crown-appointed president general. The Board of Trade and colonial assemblies rejected this recommendation, each fearing that such a congress would dilute its influence. The plan for colonial union would have to wait for another two decades, when provincial parochialism would crumble under the weight of Anglo-American tensions.

At the same time that the Iroquois were leaning away from England, the French were becoming more aggressive on the frontier. The migration of English settlers across the Appalachians forced the question of which nation—France or England—had sovereignty over the region. In 1749, the governor of New France directed the removal of the British "trespassers" in the Ohio Valley. Captain Pierre-Joseph Céloron de Blainville executed the order with gusto; in 1752, he destroyed an English trading post at Pickawillany and harassed the settlers who got in his way. In the following two years the French built Fort Duquesne (Pittsburgh, Pennsylvania) and defeated a Virginia militia force under the command of Colonel George Washington.

Unless the British acted decisively, they were in danger of losing the entire trans-Appalachian region. Major General Edward Braddock, commander of British forces in North America, met with the governors of five colonies in April 1755 to devise a strategy for dealing with the French. They decided to conduct simultaneous attacks on the most important French forts: Crown Point by William Johnson, Niagara by Governor William Shirley of Massachusetts, and Duquesne by Braddock. Additionally, Colonel Robert Monckton was to proceed from Boston to seize Acadia.

Braddock's catastrophic defeat on the banks of the Monongahela on 9 July 1755 compromised Shirley's expedition. Captured papers revealed Shirley's plan to the French, prompting them to reinforce their garrisons at Forts Frontenac and Niagara. As a result, Shirley, who succeeded Braddock as commander in chief, ordered Johnson to divert a portion of his forces for the attack on Niagara. Johnson refused, arguing that he needed the forces for his own assault at Crown Point. Threatened by the reinforced French garrisons and the stormy waters of Lake Ontario, Shirley abandoned the mission in October.

Meanwhile, Johnson had moved his force of 3,500 colonials and 400 Indians to the southern tip of Lake George, where he ordered the construction of Fort George as a precaution against a preemptive French attack. On a bend in the nearby Hudson River he also established Fort Edward.

The French commander in Canada, Baron Jean-Armand Dieskau, deployed 3,200 soldiers and braves from Crown Point. His primary objective was Fort Edward, but on hearing that Johnson's force was divided between there and Fort George, he decided to attack the latter. Although the initial skirmish, on 8 September, went well for the French, subsequent engagements that day resulted in headlong retreat. Dieskau was captured as the remainder of his disorganized force withdrew to Crown Point. That autumn the French erected a fort at Ticonderoga, a key chokepoint on Lake Champlain.

The events in America led to a British declaration of war in May 1756. Known as the Seven Years' War in Europe and the French and Indian War in the colonies, it was the decisive conflict in the long and bitter feud between the two imperial powers. Unlike the previous two wars, New Yorkers this time found themselves near the center of the fighting. Lake George and its environs became the crucible of war as English and French forces battled along the same waterways that had carried their peacetime trade.

Despite the propinquity of the war, New York was once again unprepared. The militia was poorly supplied and its training suspect. As always, available funds were scarce, along with the willingness of the assembly to appropriate them. The greatest obstacle, however, was the chronic bickering among the most important people and groups within the colony. Johnson and Shirley still fumed at each other over the events of 1755; Dutch traders flouted prohibitions against trading with the enemy; New York governors worked at cross-purposes with their counterparts in Pennsylvania and New Jersey. The political rivalry generated from these conflicts resulted in frequent changes in military command that undermined operations against the French.

Partly as a result of these problems, the English suffered a series of defeats in the early years of the war. The first came at Fort Oswego in August 1756. French commander Louis-Joseph de Montcalm, wishing to secure his line of communication to the Ohio Valley and convince the Iroquois to abandon the English, easily overpowered the weak Oswego garrison.

The French victory demoralized the English and temporarily neutralized the Iroquois.

English procrastination the following year led to more French success. The new English commander, the earl of Loudoun, wasted the summer of 1757 in an unsuccessful attempt to recapture Louisbourg. In the meantime, Montcalm traversed Lakes Champlain and George with a combined French-Indian force and siege equipment for use against Fort William Henry. The defenders surrendered on August 9; despite Montcalm's orders to the contrary, Indians butchered many of the English survivors as they retreated to Fort Edward. In November, the French and their Indian allies raided villages along the Mohawk River, inciting panic and a large-scale exodus of settlers.

In July 1758 the English suffered their most humiliating setback at Ticonderoga (Fort Carillon). Loudoun's successor, General James Abercromby, assaulted Montcalm's 3,500 defenders with a force of 15,000. He ignored the strength of Montcalm's excellent breastworks and entrenchments; the result was a stinging defeat.

Despite the Ticonderoga fiasco, the momentum of the war had begun to shift to the English. The brilliant war leader, William Pitt, had recently come to power and was developing an effective strategy for fighting the French in America. He committed himself to a staunch defense of the colonies and promised to reimburse their contributions to the war. As a result, for the remainder of the war the New York assembly was uncharacteristically responsive to requests for men and money.

Things were changing on the battlefield as well. Seven weeks after Abercromby's defeat, Colonel John Bradstreet led a lightning strike on Fort Frontenac that succeeded in denying the French a key link in the chain of western forts. The victory roused the flagging morale of the English and induced the wary Iroquois to side with them.

By 1759 the English were in command of the war. General John Prideaux, supported by 1,000 Iroquois under William Johnson, captured Fort Niagara on July 25. The victory allowed the English to sever French communications and supply from Montreal to the interior. General Jeffery Amherst seized Ticonderoga the following day; one week later his forces occupied Crown Point, which the French had abandoned. In September, General James Wolfe led a daring and successful attack on Quebec that

forced the further contraction of French forces in Canada. The French scuttled their fleet on Lake Champlain in October and prepared for the defense of Montreal.

The end came in the summer of 1760. Amherst assembled 10,000 men near Oswego for the short voyage down the St. Lawrence. On reaching the outskirts of Montreal he was reinforced by General William Haviland, who had moved north over Lake Champlain. On September 8 the great Montreal fortress fell to the English, ending the fighting in the New World. With the signing of the Treaty of Paris in 1763, the French ceded all their territory on the North American mainland to the English; for the first time in many years, New Yorkers were free from the worry of attack from the north.

Ironically, the onset of peace in the colonies revealed deep rifts within the empire that caused a constitutional crisis and eventuated in the American Revolution. New York, as well as its sister colonies, had matured politically as provincial leaders managed the manifold problems of defense, finance, and internal administration. During the first half of the eighteenth century, the assembly won control over internal finance and kept a watchful eye on royal governors. It now guarded its power jealously and resisted the efforts of royal officials to reassert imperial authority and raise colonial revenue. The latter issue was particularly divisive, as it called into question the scope of Parliament's sovereignty over colonial governments.

The imperial wars had generated other disputes as well. New York City merchants, many of whom had carried on an illicit trade with the enemy during the war, resented the tightening of the navigation acts. Residents had bitter memories of the quartering of British soldiers in private homes, and provincial soldiers resented their second-class treatment by the regulars. Land speculators and prospective settlers were indignant over British-Indian agreements limiting westward expansion into former French territories.

Imperial and colonial officials groped for solutions to these grievances, but to no avail. As a result, in little more than a decade Britain was at war again, this time against former subjects who no longer recognized the bonds of empire.

Lance A. Betros

References

Patricia Bonomi, *A Factious People: Politics and Society in Colonial New York*

(1971); David M. Ellis, et al., *A History of New York State* (1967); Alexander C. Flick, ed., *History of the State of New York*, 10 vols. (1933); Michael Kammen, *Colonial New York: A History* (1975).

Lawrence H. Leder, *Robert Livingston, 1654–1728, and the Politics of Colonial New York* (1961); E.B. O'Callaghan, ed., *Documents Relative to the Colonial History of the State of New York*, 15 vols. (1856–1887); Robert C. Ritchie, *The Duke's Province: A Study of New York Politics and Society, 1664–1691* (1977).

See also ABERCROMBY, JAMES; ALBANY CONFERENCE; AMHERST, JEFFREY, FIRST BARON AMHERST; ANDROS, EDMUND; BRADSTREET, JOHN; COVENANT CHAIN; CROWN POINT; DOMINION OF NEW ENGLAND; FORT EDWARD (NEW YORK); FORT FRONTENAC (ONTARIO, CANADA); HARTFORD TREATY; HUDSON RIVER; IROQUOIS; IROQUOIS TREATIES OF 1700 AND 1701; JOHNSON, WILLIAM; LA BELLE FAMILLE, BATTLE OF; LAKE CHAMPLAIN; LAKE GEORGE; LAKE ONTARIO; LEISLER, JACOB; LEISLER'S REBELLION; LONG ISLAND; NEW NETHERLAND; NEW NETHERLAND, SURRENDER OF; NEW YORK, DUTCH CAPTURE OF; NIAGARA, SIEGE OF; FORT OSWEGO (NEW YORK); FORT ST. FRÉDÉRIC (NEW YORK); SCHENECTADY, BATTLE OF; SEVEN YEARS' WAR; STUYVESANT, PETRUS; TICONDEROGA, BATTLE OF; FORT WILLIAM HENRY (NEW YORK)

New York, Dutch Capture of (1673)

In 1664, New Netherland had become New York. The English had completed their drive for hegemony along the Atlantic coast from Maine to Virginia. Although the map had changed, little else had been altered in the former West India Company possession when a Dutch fleet sailed into New York harbor nine years later.

When the Third Anglo-Dutch War erupted in 1672, it would seem the restoration of New Netherland would have been a prime concern for the Dutch. However, this time the Netherlands was hard pressed at home. An alliance between Great Britain and France brought a large French army to the eastern frontier of the Netherlands and a combined Anglo-French fleet off its coast in the west. The situation was desperate. Despite such adversity, characterized in Dutch history as "the catastrophic year" (*het*

rampjaar), Dutch naval commanders were able to mount an offensive in the Atlantic theater of operations. While the French armies of Louis XIV stalled when the land before Amsterdam was flooded by opening the dikes and Admiral Michiel Adriaansz de Ruyter fought the allied fleet to a draw in the English Channel, Cornelis Evertsen de Jonge of Zeeland set out on an expedition that would inadvertently restore Dutch control over its former possession in North America.

Evertsen's primary target was Saint Helena in the South Atlantic. The British-held island was used as a resupply station for its shipping lanes to the Far East; in Dutch hands it would cause serious security problems for the English East Indian Company. However, a scrape with an English squadron in the Cape Verde Islands forced Evertsen to abort his attempt on Saint Helena and focus instead on secondary targets in the Americas.

Evertsen crossed the Atlantic to Cape Orange on the wild coast of South America, where he reconnoitered Dutch possessions in Surinam. After an unsuccessful attack on the island of Barbados, he joined forces with a small squadron of warships out of Amsterdam commanded by Jacob Benckes. The combined fleet headed for Virginia. On the way Evertsen and Benckes exercised their new squadron, which was probably the largest operating in these waters at this time, by attacking in succession Montserrat, Guadeloupe, Nevis, St. Christopher, and St. Eustatius. Operating on instructions to inflict as much damage as possible to English and French shipping, the Dutch squadron sailed into Chesapeake Bay where it surprised the Virginia tobacco fleet preparing to sail for England; eleven English ships were lost, either taken as prizes or run aground and burned. With prize crews aboard the captured tobacco ships and several ships captured in the Caribbean, Evertsen's fleet had now grown to 19 ships when it entered New York Harbor on 9 August 1673.

Unlike the attack on the city in 1664, which took place during peace time, New York in 1673 had been on a war footing for more than a year. In May rumors began to filter in that a Dutch fleet had targeted the city. Captain John Manning, commander of the garrison at Fort James (formerly Fort Amsterdam), had alerted Governor Francis Lovelace of the danger. After some debate soldiers were called down from Albany to reinforce the city's defenses. However, when no hostile sails appeared that summer the troops were sent back north, and the garrison returned to its understrengthed complement of 50 to 60 soldiers.

When Evertsen and Benckes appeared off Sandy Hook, his 19 ships carrying 600 marines faced a fort with only six operational guns mounted on rotten carriages. Added to the sad shape of defenses on Manhattan, Governor Lovelace had left town for a visit with Governor John (Fitz-John) Winthrop of Connecticut only a few days before. Captain Manning, left in charge, was in a dilemma. Reports on the strength of the Dutch naval force quickly revealed the hopelessness of the situation. Manning's only recourse was to stall until Lovelace could be informed and the alarm sent out for reinforcements. Evertsen, however, was intent on moving fast. Dutch farmers from New Utrecht on Long Island had greeted the fleet as soon as it appeared in New York waters, informing the Dutch commanders of the state of the city's defenses and the absence of the governor. Manning's initial attempt to request a truce until the following day was reduced to one half-hour. When the English failed to act, Evertsen maneuvered his ships to deliver a broadside on the fort.

While Evertsen's ships exchanged fire with the fort, Anthony Colve landed his 600 marines just to the north where they were enthusiastically welcomed by the Dutch population. Captain Manning's options were quickly reduced as his cannon collapsed on their platforms after firing; in addition to this there were reports that 400 Dutch townsmen had armed themselves. They were encouraging Colve to storm the fort and warned the English defenders to keep their heads down. Manning was forced to run up the white flag of truce. As Colve marched his marines toward the fort they were joined by the armed burghers. Just short of the fort Colve paused to demand the immediate surrender of the garrison. After some confusion, Manning agreed to terms that allowed his soldiers to march out of the fort with full honors and to retain their goods and baggage. As soon as the garrison laid down their arms they were ordered back into the fort where they were incarcerated to await transport to England.

Evertsen and Benckes immediately prepared the fleet for departure. The next target was the French fishing industry on Newfoundland. Sixty soldiers were left to garrison the fort on Manhattan, renamed Fort Willem Hendick. Anthony Colve was also left behind as governor of the restored colony of New Netherland. New York was renamed New Orange; Kingston, Swanenburgh, after Evertsen's ship; Albany, Willemstad; and Fort Albany (formerly Fort Orange), Fort Nassau. The entire territory of the former New Netherland had been restored to Dutch control, with the exception of the Mennonite settlement on Delaware Bay (Lewes, Delaware). On Christmas Eve, a detachment of horsemen from Maryland burned the community to the ground rather than let it fall into Dutch hands again.

The restoration of New Netherland was short-lived. When peace was concluded with England on 19 February 1674, among the articles of the Treaty of Westminster was a provision to return the territory as the province of New York. On 10 November, Anthony Colve surrendered the colony for the final time to the new English governor, Edmund Andros.

Charles T. Gehring

References
Peter R. Christoph and Florence A. Christoph, eds., *The Andros Papers, 1674–1676* (1989); C. de Waard, ed., *De Zeeuwsche Expeditie naar de West onder Cornelis Evertsen den Jonge 1672–1674* (1928); Robert C. Ritchie, *The Duke's Province: A Study of New York Politics and Society, 1664–1685* (1977); Donald G. Shomette and Robert D. Haslach, *Raid on America: The Dutch Naval Campaign of 1672–1674* (1988); I.N. Phelps Stokes, *The Iconography of Manhattan Island, 1498–1909*, 6 vols. (1915–1928).

See also Anglo-Dutch War, Third

Fort Niagara (New York)

Situated at the juncture of the Niagara River with Lake Ontario, Fort Niagara commanded the most direct route from New France to the upper Great Lakes and the colony of Louisiana. The primary purpose of this fortification was to guard the portage around Niagara Falls, but it also provided a French presence at the western edge of the country of the Iroquois Six Nations.

The Niagara portage had been of interest to the French since the late seventeenth century. Two early posts, Fort Conti (1679) and Fort Denonville (1687–1688) proved too isolated and exposed to Iroquois hostility to be maintained. The French were not able to gain a permanent foothold until 1726 when a machicolated stone house surrounded by a wooden

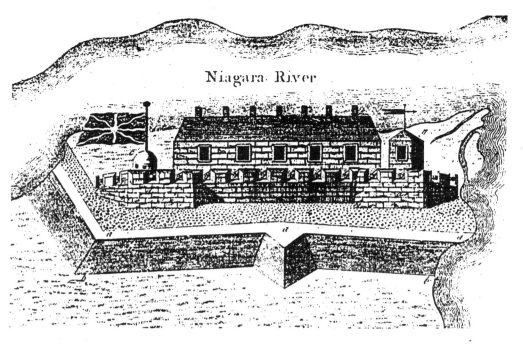

Niagara River

N

View of Fort Niagara.

stockade was established at the mouth of the Niagara River. Dubbed Fort Niagara, it gave the French control of the portage, guarded communications between the St. Lawrence Valley and the west, and effectively blocked the British from penetrating into the Great Lakes farther than Oswego, where they constructed a fort in 1727. Although Fort Niagara was strengthened during King George's War, it remained essentially a frontier post with a garrison of about 30 men.

The years immediately preceding the French and Indian War saw Fort Niagara become the primary forward base in French attempts to secure the Ohio Valley. It served as a point of departure for Pierre-Joseph Céloron de Blainville's 1749 expedition, as well as the 1753 and 1754 efforts to establish a chain of forts from Lake Erie to the forks of the Ohio. The Niagara portage was further secured in 1751 by construction of a dependent post, Fort Little Niagara, at the head of the portage above Niagara Falls.

The French and Indian War found Fort Niagara in poor condition. The stockade was worthless, and the entire design was vulnerable to artillery. British General William Shirley's unsuccessful attempt to launch an attack against Niagara in 1755 caused the French to reinforce the

post. During the winter of 1755–1756, the fortifications were reconstructed and greatly enlarged. Captain Pierre Pouchot de Maupas designed an earthen hornwork in the manner of Vauban. (A hornworks was located outside the fort and consisted of two demi-bastions at each end of a curtain, which was connected to the main structure by two parallel wings.) By mid-1756, the defenses encompassed about 12 acres, and Fort Niagara was arguably the strongest and most sophisticated fortification west of Quebec. Work on additional buildings continued until late 1757, by which time 20 buildings stood within the walls.

Fort Niagara served the French in an offensive capacity from 1756 until 1759. War parties were assembled and supplied at the post to strike the frontiers of Pennsylvania and Virginia, and they returned to Niagara with prisoners and scalps. French interests among the Seneca and the tribes of the Great Lakes were well-represented by Captain Pouchot, who commanded the post until his relief and the withdrawal of regular army troops from his garrison in the autumn of 1757. Fort Niagara was thereafter only weakly held. In the fall of 1758, its 41-man garrison nearly abandoned the place following Lieutenant Colonel John Bradstreet's descent on Fort Frontenac. The post remained in French hands only because of Bradstreet's inability to attack it.

Fort Niagara was reinforced during the spring of 1759 in anticipation of a new British assault. Captain Pouchot was sent with a small reinforcement to defend the place. On 6 July, a British force of 2,500 European and colonial troops and 1,000 warriors of the Six Nations landed near the post. The British were obliged to conduct a regular siege but, on 25 July, they forced Pouchot and his 600-man garrison to capitulate. The British thus severed New France from Louisiana and the West.

Fort Niagara was strongly garrisoned by the British for the winter of 1759–1760. In the autumn of 1760, Major Robert Rogers departed from Niagara to accept the surrender of Detroit. Fort Niagara remained headquarters for British posts in the west. It played an important role in Pontiac's War and in the American Revolution. Fort Niagara remained in British hands until 1796 when it was ceded to the United States. It continued as a United States army fortification through the nineteenth and well into the twentieth century.

Brian Leigh Dunnigan

References

Brian Leigh Dunnigan, *History and Development of the Old Fort Niagara* (1985); ———, *Siege—1759: The Campaign Against Niagara* (1986); Lawrence Henry Gipson, *The Great War for the Empire: The Victorious Years, 1758–1760* (1965); Frank H. Severance, *An Old Frontier of France*, 2 vols. (1917); Charles Morse Stotz, *Outposts of the War for Empire: The French and English in Western Pennsylvania; Their Armies, Their Forts, Their People, 1749–1764* (1985).

See also BRADSTREET, JOHN; FORT CONTI (NEW YORK); FORT LITTLE NIAGARA (NEW YORK); NIAGARA, SIEGE OF; POUCHOT DE MAUPAS, PIERRE; SHIRLEY, WILLIAM

Niagara, Siege of (1759)

The surrender of Fort Niagara (Youngstown, New York) marked the culmination of one of the few regular sieges conducted during the colonial wars of North America. The post was important because it controlled the portage around Niagara Falls and guarded French communications between the St. Lawrence Valley, the upper Great Lakes, and the colony of Louisiana.

The capture of Niagara was one of the objectives of the British campaign of 1759. Brigadier John Prideaux, 55th Regiment of Foot, was selected to lead the expedition. He was to reestablish a fort at Oswego, capture Niagara, and ultimately advance to the head of the St. Lawrence River to threaten Montreal and support General Jeffery Amherst's thrust down Lake Champlain. Prideaux moved up the Mohawk River from Schenectady in May 1759 with the 44th, 46th, and 4/60th Regiments of Foot, and the New York Regiment. Oswego was successfully reoccupied and, on 1 July, Prideaux set out along the south shore of Lake Ontario with 2,500 regulars and provincials, a small train of artillery, and nearly 1,000 Iroquois led by Sir William Johnson. The army landed four miles east of Fort Niagara on the afternoon of 6 July.

The French had anticipated an attack. Niagara was reinforced in April, and its defense entrusted to Captain Pierre Pouchot de Maupas of the Regiment de Béarn. Pouchot had previously commanded Niagara and had built new works there in 1755–1757. Following his return in 1759, Pouchot repaired the fortifications and organized his 600 defenders. French intelligence was faulty, however. Despite two heavily-armed vessels on Lake Ontario, their inability to locate the approaching British army allowed the besiegers to slip along the Lake Ontario shoreline and arrive safely.

The British, for their part, achieved surprise, but they too had been misled by their intelligence, largely provided by the Iroquois through Sir William Johnson. Prideaux had expected Fort Niagara to be a stockade. He found instead a post strongly fortified in the manner of Vauban and armed with more than 40 cannon. The British were thus forced to conduct a siege, similar in nearly every respect to those employed to reduce fortified places in Europe. Prideaux's train of artillery was barely sufficient for this task. Nor were his engineers the best in the army. The senior engineer, Captain Lieutenant John Williams, was wounded early in the siege. His successor, Ensign George Demier, lacked experience. Although Demier was assisted by other officers who understood the rudiments of siege warfare, the performance of the British engineers at Niagara was, at best, mediocre.

Prideaux, nonetheless, advanced his siege in the best European manner. His light troops and Iroquois immediately moved to cut off the fort. The posts at each end of the portage were abandoned and destroyed by the French, and their garrisons retired to Fort Niagara. The British were unable to open their trenches until the night of 9–10 July, however. The first few days of siege work were marked by frustrating errors, due largely to the inexperience of the engineers. Although the British began to bombard the fort with mortars early in the siege, it was not until 17 July that an effective battery opened fire. The French, however, despite the expenditure of much ammunition, were unable to seriously delay the sapping or muster any effective sorties against the besiegers.

The unmasking of three siege batteries on 17 July gave a boost to British morale, and Fort Niagara's defenders were soon suffering from the effects of their fire. British fortunes again declined on 20 July, however, when a provincial lieutenant colonel was wounded in the trenches, and, a short time later, Colonel John Johnston of the New York Regiment was killed. Most devastating was the death, late that evening, of Brigadier Prideaux himself when he carelessly walked in front of one of his own mortars as it was discharged. The British thus lost their two senior officers within a matter of hours. A stormy council of war selected a new leader. Sir William Johnson was chosen over the senior regular officer, Lieutenant Colonel Eyre Massey, probably because Sir William would be able to ensure the continued support of the Iroquois. Johnson prosecuted the siege with vigor, and a new battery, situated only 100 yards from the fort, was unmasked on 23 July.

The French garrison was nearly exhausted by this time, and the new battery simply hastened the inevitable collapse of morale. Pouchot continued the struggle largely because he expected aid. His call had gone to the French army in the upper Ohio Valley. On 23 July, Pouchot learned that a relief force of about 1,500 men was approaching from Lake Erie and would attempt to raise the siege. Sir William Johnson likewise heard of this threat and sent a force to block it. On the morning of 24 July, the relief force, under the dual command of François-Marie Le Marchand de Lignery and Charles-Philippe Aubry, attempted to fight its way into Fort Niagara. A mile south of Fort Niagara, at a place called La Belle Famille, they encountered 454 British under Lieutenant Colonel Massey. After a fierce 20-minute battle, the French were routed.

Pouchet at first refused to believe news of the disaster. Then, convinced, he asked for terms. On the morning of 25 July the British took possession of the gates of Fort Niagara. A storm delayed embarkation of the French garrison, which was unable to leave for captivity in New York until 26 July. Most of Johnson's army returned to Oswego to prepare for an advance to the St. Lawrence, but the unexpected delay caused by the siege of Niagara, combined with confusion and timidity in the British command, prevented the final goal of the 1759 Lake Ontario campaign from being achieved.

Brian Leigh Dunnigan

References

Brian Leigh Dunnigan, *Siege—1759: The Campaign Against Niagara* (1986); ———, "Vauban in the Wilderness: The Siege of Fort Niagara, 1759," *Niagara Frontier* XXI (1974):37–52; *George Douglas Emerson, The Niagara Campaign of 1759* (1909); Lawrence Henry Gipson, *The Great War for the Empire: The Victorious Years, 1758–1760* (1965); Frank H. Severance, *An Old Frontier of France*, 2 vols. (1917).

See also La Belle Famille, Battle of; Fort Niagara (New York); Fort Oswego (New York); Pouchot de Maupas, Pierre

Nicholas

See Orontony

Fort Nicholson (New York)

See Fort Edward (New York)

Nicholson, Francis (1655–1728)

No single British colonial administrator had more varied appointments than Francis Nicholson. Governor of Virginia, Maryland, South Carolina, and Nova Scotia, lieutenant governor of New York and Virginia, and military commander of colonial troops during Queen Anne's War, Nicholson's extensive career in colonial administration began in 1686 and lasted until 1725.

Nicholson was born on 12 November 1655 at Downholme Park in Yorkshire of unknown parents. The duke of Bolton took an interest in young Nicholson, who entered the army in 1679 and spent his early career in Tangier. His first stint in the colonies began in 1686 with an appointment as a captain of New England troops. Two years later, he was commissioned lieutenant governor of the Dominion of New England and stationed in New York under Governor Sir Edmund Andros. When news of the revolution in England spread to North America, Nicholson's handling of the local situation led to his return to England in 1689, which was more flight than just retreat.

Nicholson's most successful stint in colonial administration began in 1690 with his appointment to the lieutenant governor's post in Virginia. The royal governor, Lord Howard of Effingham, was an absentee official, and Nicholson enjoyed virtual authority. His accomplishments included the establishment of postal services, a survey of frontier conditions in the colony, the support of schools, strengthening of the clergy, and especially the establishment of the College of William and Mary. Nicholson's financial support of commissioner James Blair enhanced the conditions under which Blair was able to start the college. Nicholson's first administration was also marked by foresighted economic policies and defense measures. He pushed the crown to provide ample supplies so that the colonies would not establish their own manufacturing society and thus compete with the English. More importantly, he urged union among the separate colonies for an effective strategy against the French in Canada. It was this later policy that he fervently preached to the royal government. Here, Nicholson's thought preceded the dilemma which severely strained colonial-crown relations after 1700.

When Governor Lord Howard died in 1692, it was ironically Andros, not Nicholson, to whom the crown turned. Instead, Nicholson's lot lay in Maryland, where he was appointed governor in early 1694. As in Virginia earlier, Nicholson was a proponent of education and a strong supporter of the Anglican church. His defense mentality led him to look to the legislature for support of the New York colony, but he failed. His often virulent temper kept him in constant quarrels with colonial leaders, and although Nicholson was less than popular, he was named governor of Virginia to succeed Andros in 1698. Good fortune did not shine on Nicholson in his second tenure in Virginia, and his chief nemesis was, surprisingly, Blair. His temper again harmed his relations with the colonial aristocracy—he was charged with attempting to dominate the House of Burgesses. Yet, the governor was successful in moving the capital to Williamsburg and placed the colony on a sounder financial footing. Just as in Mary-land, he stressed colonial cooperation. He recommended to the crown that a standing army be established—at the expense of the colonists themselves. Finally, Nicholson was replaced in 1705.

After 1706, most of Nicholson's contributions to the British colonies involved military campaigns against Canada, and his career was tied to the fortunes of Samuel Vetch, another advocate of a policy of aggression against the French in Canada. Vetch pressured the crown for a British-supported attack on the French and Indians on the northern frontier. Vetch's plan was a two-prong attack, one on Quebec following the route of the St. Lawrence River, and the other on Montreal by way of Lake Champlain. Vetch would join the assault on Quebec with 4,000 British regulars and six warships, while Nicholson volunteered to lead the land forces from the south. His force consisted of 1,500 colonial troops joined by about 600 Indians. In June 1709, Colonel Nicholson moved his band to Wood Creek at the southern tip of Lake Champlain. Here he awaited word of the arrival of the British troops in Boston—troops that would not arrive. Evidence points to the force at Wood Creek as a disaster, caused by intercolonial jealousies, lack of trained troops, Indian problems, and especially disease. Discontent and desertion set in, and by October, when word finally arrived that the British were not coming, Nicholson disbanded his troops and the campaign was abandoned.

The next year, Nicholson led a representation to London before the queen to once again seek British support for a Canadian invasion. In turn, the former administrative official was made commander in chief of a force of 1,900 that achieved a conquest of Acadia without bloodshed. Vetch was appointed governor of the renamed Nova Scotia, and Nicholson was made a lieutenant general, despite his very limited military experience. When the crown agreed to still another Canadian invasion in 1711, Nicholson once again commanded a force that advanced to Wood Creek. However, a British fleet under Admiral Hovenden Walker lost more than 800 men and eight ships in the treacherous waters of the St. Lawrence, and yet another assault ended in disaster.

Once again, the British crown turned to Nicholson as governor of Nova Scotia in 1713, although his now well-known temper, a grating arrogance, and his delegation of authority to a deputy helped seal his eventual fate. Nicholson did engage briefly in an administrative role to supervise fiscal, commercial, and religious affairs in the northern colonies, but in early 1715, he was ironically replaced by Vetch, whom Nicholson had replaced in 1713.

Nicholson's final colonial appointment was in 1720 as governor of South Carolina. His stay was fairly uneventful—he again supported schools and churches. He also was able to appease the potentially hostile Cherokee. He did draw the ire of the merchant class and was recalled for the last time in the spring of 1725, in a state of ill-health and failing spirits. He died in London on 5 March 1728.

Although there is some doubt cast about his being knighted, at least one historian notes Nicholson's "remarkable instinct for political survival," a trait that enabled him to serve five colonies in administrative posts for more than thirty years.

Boyd Childress

References
John Andrew Doyle, "Nicholson, Sir Francis," in *Dictionary of National Biography*, 21 vols. (1921–1927), 14:457–458; Leonard W. Labaree, "Nicholson, Francis," in *Dictionary of American Biography*, 28 vols. (1929–1958), 7:499–502; John. W. Raimo, *Biographical Directory of American Colonial and Revolutionary Governors, 1607–1789* (1980).

Charles William Sommerville, "Early Career of Governor Francis Nicholson," *Maryland Historical Magazine* 4 (1909):101–114, 201–220; Stephen S. Webb, "The Strange Career of Francis Nicholson," *William and Mary Quarterly*, 3rd ser., 23 (1966):513–548.

See also ACADIA, BRITISH CONQUEST OF; ANDROS, EDMUND; CANADA, BRITISH EXPEDITION AGAINST (1709); CANADA, BRITISH EXPEDITION AGAINST (1711); DOMINION OF NEW ENGLAND; LEISLER'S REBELLION; MARYLAND; NEW YORK; VETCH, SAMUEL; VIRGINIA

Nipmuck
The Nipmucks were a small Algonquin tribe located in central Massachusetts in "Nipmuck country," the area between Boston and the Connecticut River valley. The Nipmuck tribe was a collection of bands that traded furs with various tribes and colonists. Their villages were without strong political ties to one another, so they were vulnerable to neighboring tribes' demands for tribute, such as the Pequots, Narragansetts, Mohegans, Wampanoags, and Mohawks. The English Christian missionary, John Eliot, afforded them some needed protection. By 1674, Eliot had created seven "praying towns." These efforts, however, did not prevent most of the tribe's participation in King Philip's War in 1675. They joined the loose-knit uprising of Indian tribes and were responsible for the destruction of several frontier communities. The tribe was devastated by the colonists' and their Indian allies' retaliation, and most surviving tribal members fled to Canada or were absorbed by tribes along the Hudson River.

Leslie Miller

References
Laurence M. Hauptman and James D. Wherry, *The Pequots in Southern New England: The Fall and Rise of an American Indian Nation* (1990); Alden T. Vaughan, *New England Frontier: Puritans and Indians, 1620–1675* (1965).

See also PRAYING INDIANS

Fort Nohoroco (North Carolina)
This was one of four forts built by chief Hancock of the Lower Town (North Carolina) Tuscarora in the Tuscarora War, 1711–1713. One of these, Fort Hancock on lower Catechna (now Contentney) Creek, was razed after a treaty with John Barnwell's South Carolina forces in the spring of 1712. Hancock withdrew north to Fort Nohoroco, on the east side of Catechna Creek in what is now Pitt County. Fighting soon resumed, and in 1713, South Carolina, again responding to North Carolina's plea, sent an expedition of friendly Indians and white officers under Colonel James Moore. After striking small tribes along the coast, Moore on 20 March led his men to Fort Nohoroco, the major Tuscarora stronghold.

Fort Hancock had been built along advanced European lines under the direction of an escaped South Carolina slave named Harry, and he may have had a hand in erecting Fort Nohoroco as well. Catechna Creek looped west, north, and east around the fort, with steep banks inside the loop. This gave defenders a distinct advantage over attackers from either of these directions. To the south, a marsh offered access only along a narrow ridge. The fort's earthen walls, with tiers of portholes for firing and blocks to close off the lower tier if required, were topped by tall log palisades angled against taller blockhouses. The fort also had interior walls, bunkers to protect noncombatants, and a moat and trenches athwart its only approach.

In what appears from Moore's brief description to have been one of the most desperate close-quarter battles ever waged on the North American continent, Moore's men on 20 March overran the trenches and moat and raised a blockhouse and battery near the fort's walls. This structure was higher than the walls and enabled attackers to fire down into the fort. Moore had a tunnel dug to a portion of the outer wall to try to blow it apart, but the effort failed owing to defective powder. A subsequent charge carried part of the outer works and made possible setting fire to a blockhouse and other parts of the fort. But it required three days of fighting within the compound for the South Carolinians to gain control. The defenders, according to Baron Christoph von Graffenried, showed themselves "unspeakably brave . . . wounded savages . . . on the ground still continued to fight. There were 200 who were burned up in a redoubt and . . . in all about 900, including women and children were dead and captured." Moore sustained 151 casualties, 47 of them killed. His victory broke the back of Tuscarora resistance.

T.C. Parramore

References
    John W. Barnwell, "The Second Tuscarora Expedition," *South Carolina Historical and Genealogical Magazine* X (1908):32–45; T.C. Parramore, "With Tuscarora Jack on the Back Path to Bath." *North Carolina Historical Review* LXIV (1987):115–138; Vincent H. Todd, ed., *Christoph von Graffenried's Account of the Founding of New Bern* (1920).

See also BARNWELL, JOHN; TUSCARORA WAR

Fort Normanock (New Jersey)
Fort Normanock was part of seven defenses built along the Delaware River at the beginning of the French and Indian War. Situated near the present town of Newton in Sussex County on an elevation overlooking the Delaware River, it was constructed from December 1755 to January 1756. The fort was intended to protect the local settlers from hostile Indian attacks. A skirmish occurred in the region on 17 November 1763, when Captain Benjamin Westbrook and a party of 11 soldiers were ambushed by unidentified Indians after they crossed the Delaware River into Pennsylvania to retrieve abandoned cattle and supplies. The captain and five men were subsequently killed in the fight.

David L. Whitesell

Norridgewock
See ABENAKI

Norridgewock, Battle of (1724)
Norridgewock was one of the best known and perhaps the most feared of Indian villages by those living in northern New England. Early Jesuits located a mission at the confluence of the Kennebec and Sandy Rivers, calling it Old Point. It was a crossroads of Indian trails leading to the Penobscot village to the east, the coast to the south, New England to the west, and Quebec to the north. Norridgewock hunting territories extended to Moosehead Lake and Mount Katahdin regions where Penobscot also hunted. New England felt that the Norridgewock Indians should be under English authority and established a trading post about 35 miles south of the Norridgewock village. The Jesuit missionaries created a strong Catholic foundation; a Father Baird had visited Norridgewock as early as 1610, Father Gabriel Druillettes, S.J. was assigned to the village in 1640 and was followed by the brothers Jacques and Vincent Bigot. Sebastien Rale arrived in 1694 already having had several years' experience living with Abenaki. He remained, living with them until his death in 1724. The French claimed that the Kennebec River was the boundary between Acadia and New England. The Bigots probably influenced the Indians to move from the west side to the east side of the Kennebec by building a church on that side of the river within the boundaries of the French claim (Acadia).

Rale remained at Norridgewock for 30 years, an unusually long time. The Indians sought guidance from Rale in their relations with the English just as they had his predecessors. The English felt that Rale could have controlled or restrained his Indians and so blamed him for Indian raids on New England frontier settlements: they put a price on his head. The Indians observed activities in the frontier settlements and quickly reported back to Rale anything that seemed unusual or that could be interpreted as an expansion of English power. Raids soon followed. The Indians felt it necessary to retaliate for any further threatened expansion of settlement on their lands. By 1720, relations worsened between the English and the Indians. Each side distrusted and feared the other.

In 1722, Colonel Thomas Westbrook was ordered to destroy Norridgewock. He led an attack on the village in the winter, but the village was deserted. The chief success was in finding Rale's correspondence to Canadian Governor Philippe de Rigaud de Vaudreuil, which they took with them. Westbrook attacked again in August 1724. An Indian account claims that a clairvoyant old woman told Rale that the village would be attacked the following day, so he should leave. Rale did not take her seriously. Norridgewock was attacked; Rale was killed. Although English, French, and Indian accounts of the attack differ considerably, the English objective was achieved. The surviving Indians scattered: some to the Penobscot, others joined St. Francis in Quebec, and a few joined other bands. Rale's greatest contribution may have been his French-Abenaki dictionary, which was taken to Boston and presented to the library at Harvard.

Both sides welcomed Dummer's Treaty, after which Abenaki raids on frontier settlements almost ceased. After the treaty, eastern Indians participated in colonial conflict by joining large armies or by attacking coastal shipping.

Nicholas N. Smith

References
O.P. Thomas Charland, "Sebastien Rale," *Dictionary of Canadian Biography*, 12 vols. (1966–1990), 2:542–545; Gordon M. Day, "The Identity of the St. Francis Indians," National Museum of Man, Mercury Series, Canadian Ethnology Service Paper no. 71; Fannie Eckstorm, "The Attack on Norridgewock," *New England Quarterly* 7 (1934):541–478; Kenneth M. Morrison, *The Embattled Northeast: The Elusive Ideal of Alliance in Abenaki-Euroamerica Relations* (1984); Samuel Penhallow, *The History of the Wars of New England, with the Eastern Indians* (1726), rpt. 1969.

See also ABENAKI; DUMMER'S TREATY; DUMMER'S WAR; HARMON, JOHNSON;

MOULTON, JEREMIAH; RALE, SEBASTIEN; WESTBROOK, THOMAS

Fort Norris (Pennsylvania)

Completed in early February 1756, Fort Norris was one in the line of forts built by Pennsylvania along the Blue Mountains. Located 15 miles east of Fort Allen, Fort Norris was named for Isaac Norris, the speaker of the Pennsylvania assembly. It was commanded by Captain Jacob Orndt and occupied by a company of 50 men. The fort was a square palisade, measuring about 75 feet on a side. Like Fort Allen, it was occupied until 1761 but saw very little military activity.

Eric Hinderaker

References
Thomas L. Montgomery, ed., *Report of the Commission to Locate the Frontier Forts of Pennsylvania*, 2nd ed., 2 vols. (1916).

See also FORT ALLEN (PENNSYLVANIA); FORT DUPUI (PENNSYLVANIA); FORT HENRY (PENNSYLVANIA); FORT LEBANON (PENNSYLVANIA)

Norteños

Norteños (Nations of the North) was a term used by the Spanish to denote the Indian tribes of the interior of Texas, west of the coast and Caddo country, and excluding the Apaches. The Norteños included various Wichita tribes that entered Texas in the seventeenth and eighteenth centuries, including the Wacos, Wichitas proper, Kichai, and Tawakonis, as well as Comanches, Tonkawas, and other small groups. As the Comanches became better known to the Spanish in the latter part of the eighteenth century, it became common for the Spanish to refer to them separately from the Norteños.

The first encounter between the Norteños and the Spanish took place on the San Sabá River, Menard County, Texas. Although the Spanish were aware that the Lipan Apaches were being pushed southward by their enemies, in particular the Comanches, they nonetheless agreed to form a mission for them near the present town of Menard. In March 1758, within months of the mission's founding, a combined force of Comanches, Tonkawas, Wichitas, Tawakonis, and others attacked the establishment, killed two Franciscans and six soldiers, and made off with livestock. In October

1759, a punitive expedition sent from San Antonio found the Norteños well fortified in a village on the Red River, at present-day Spanish Fort, Montague County. The Spanish suffered their worst defeat in Texas at the hand of the Indians, who were armed with French muskets.

During the 1760s and 1770s, a variety of Indian tribes generally referred to as Norteños continued to commit depredations against Texas settlements, particularly San Antonio. A policy of limited pursuit and gift-giving eventually led to a series of peace treaties with the Comanches, Tonkawa, and Wichitas in the 1770s and 1780s. Until the beginning of the Mexican war of independence minor depredations by Norteños occurred, but the peace generally held.

Jesús F. de la Teja

References

Elizabeth A.H. John, *Storms Brewed in Other Men's Worlds: The Confrontation of Indians, Spanish, and French in the Southwest, 1540–1795* (1975); W.W. Newcomb, Jr., *The Indians of Texas: From Prehistoric to Modern Times* (1961).

North Carolina

Present-day North Carolina was first explored by Giovanni da Verrazano, a Florentine explorer in the service of France, who landed at several points along the coast in 1524. Two years later, Lucas Vázquez de Ayllón failed in an attempt to establish a colony near the present South Carolina-North Carolina border. Hernando de Soto in 1540 explored part of present southwest North Carolina, as did Juan Pardo in 1566–1567. In 1561, Angel de Villafañe explored the region around present Cape Hatteras, while five years later Pedro de Coronas explored the Currituck region. None of these ventures led to permanent Spanish settlement.

Eventually the Spanish determined to concentrate their efforts elsewhere, and the English filled the gap. After the failure of the Roanoke Island colonies in the 1580s, English settlement attempts shifted slightly northwards, into present Virginia. Virginians sporadically explored the Albemarle Sound region in the first half of the seventeenth century, most notably John Perry in 1622. Seven years later, King Charles I granted his attorney general, Sir Robert Heath, land between latitudes 31 degrees north and 36 degrees north and named it Carolina. Heath never settled the grant, however. Permanent Virginia settlers began creeping down into the Albemarle Sound region in the 1650s. In 1663, King Charles II, recently restored to the monarchy, rewarded eight of his supporters by making them proprietors of Carolina. The grant was extended in 1665, giving the proprietors control of a region that theoretically included present-day North Carolina, South Carolina, and Georgia.

The separation of North and South Carolina was gradual. Carolina was first divided into three counties: Albemarle, Clarendon, and Craven. The latter was first settled in 1670 and evolved into South Carolina, while a middle-1660s attempt to settle Clarendon County, near the Cape Fear River, failed. Albemarle County had its own governor until 1689, when it was replaced as a unit of government by "Carolina North and East of Cape Feare." In 1691, the proprietors united all of Carolina under a single governor in Charles Town (now Charleston), with a deputy governor in the Albemarle region. This system endured until 1710, when the proprietors decided to appoint separate governors for North and South Carolina. This marks the functional division of the two colonies.

During the proprietary period Carolina and then North Carolina were poorly governed. The proprietors had little first-hand knowledge of the colony and appointed governors and deputy governors who were undistinguished, even corrupt. Conflict between these appointees and the elected assembly was constant. The situation did improve somewhat after the division of the colony. Although coastal Indians were unable to take advantage of this weakness in the 1675–1677 Chowanoc War, the later Tuscarora War (1711–1713) clearly exposed the weakness of the proprietary system. Successful prosecution of the war was possible only with substantial aid from South Carolina and from friendly Indians. North Carolina was also infested with pirates, most of whom were rooted out by 1718, largely by South Carolina and Virginia forces.

The defeat of the Tuscarora and the 1715 Yamasee War opened up large portions of the North Carolina interior to settlement. However, growth continued to be slow until 1729, when seven of the eight proprietors sold their land back to the crown and North Carolina was chartered as a royal colony. Lord Granville held on to his property until the end of the colonial period. Under royal rule the quality of government improved as the crown generally appointed a higher quality of governor than had previously been the case. The pace of settlement quickened, aided immeasurably by the generally harmonious relations between the settlers and the backcountry Indians, most notably the Catawba. At the beginning of the royal period, North Carolina had an estimated population of 35,000. By 1765, the colony had an estimated 200,000 people. With the arrival of the Great Wagon Road in the 1750s, settlement increasingly encroached on the edges of Cherokee control, eventually leading to the Cherokee War.

The part of Carolina that eventually became South Carolina was particularly plagued by attacks by the Spanish in the late seventeenth century. The North Carolina coast was plundered on several occasions by the French and Spanish during Queen Anne's War. The colony was more heavily involved in King George's War. North Carolina gave four companies of troops to the ill-fated Cartegena expedition in 1740. North Carolina's coast was also subjected to constant raiding by French and Spanish privateers. The ports of Brunswick and Beaufort were plundered in 1747, while three Spanish privateers occupied Brunswick in September 1748, before being driven away by armed townspeople.

North Carolina sent troops to the Virginia frontier early in the French and Indian War and suffered from sporadic backcountry raids from Indian tribes allied with the French. By the early part of 1760, the Cherokee, initially allied with the English, had turned to the French side. The Cherokee won a notable victory in the spring of that year when they defeated an expedition under the command of Archibald Montgomery. A later expedition, however, under the command of James Grant, routed the tribe and destroyed numerous villages. The November 1763 treaty conference at Augusta, Georgia, brought a short-lived period of stability to the North Carolina backcountry.

Jim Sumner

References

A. Roger Ekirch, *"Poor Carolina": Politics and Society in Colonial North Carolina, 1729–1776* (1981); Lawrence Lee, *Indian Wars in North Carolina, 1663–1763* (1963); Hugh T. Lefler and William S. Powell, *Colonial North Carolina: A History* (1973); Theda Perdue, *Native Carolinians: The Indians of North Carolina* (1985); William L. Saunders, ed., *The Colonial Records of North Carolina*, 10 vols. (1886–1890).

See also AYLLÓN, LUCAS VÁZQUEZ DE; CATAWBA; CHEROKEE WAR; KING GEORGE'S WAR; PARDO, JUAN; ROANOKE ISLAND; SOTO, HERNANDO DE; SOUTH CAROLINA; TUSCARORA WAR; YAMASEE WAR

Northfield Fortifications (Massachusetts)

Originally settled in 1670, Northfield was the northernmost English settlement in the Connecticut Valley prior to 1724. In 1673, a ten-foot-high stockade was built for protection of the settlers and their houses. This was the first in a series of fortifications constructed in 1685, 1686, 1688, and 1722. On 6 September 1675, Northfield was abandoned, and the town was destroyed. It was resettled in 1676, and in June 1689, suffered an Indian attack in which half the families were lost. In 1690, the town was again abandoned and not reoccupied until 1713. Attacks by Grey Lock against the northern settlements kept the town on almost constant alert during Dummer's War. In 1724, several garrison houses were constructed and all the town's fortifications were refurbished. In 1753, all the fortifications for Northfield were dismantled. However, after the beginning of the French and Indian War, four new forts were constructed.

David L. Whitesell

See also DUMMER'S WAR; GARRISON HOUSES

Nottoway

The Nottoway, Iroquoian-speakers whose territory lay along the Nottoway River in the upper Chowan drainage, resided within the Virginia-North Carolina coastal plain. They, like their neighbors, the Tuscarora and Meherrin, were agriculturalists who relied heavily on hunting and gathering. Nottoway villages, where the highest-ranking leader was the teerheer (teethha), reportedly enjoyed a nearly autonomous existence and joined forces with their neighbors only when in pursuit of a common goal.

The Nottoway's remoteness from the more thickly-settled part of the Virginia colony spared them from European intrusion until the mid-seventeenth century. However, they were seated only 32 miles from Fort Henry, a trading post and military garrison that was built at the falls of the Appomattox River in 1646. In 1650, when Abraham Wood and a party of European explorers penetrated deeply into the territory beyond the Appomattox River's head, they were accompanied by Oyeocker, brother of a Nottoway king. The Nottoway's wariness of their English visitors and suspicion of their firearms suggest that they had had little previous contact with Europeans. The great men of a Meherrin village that Wood's party visited referred to Opechancanough, the Algonquian-speaking Powhatan chiefdom's paramount leader from c. 1619–1620 to 1646, as "their great Emperor," an indication that his influence extended into the territory the Iroquoian-speaking Meherrin shared with the Nottoway. After Abraham Wood's journey of exploration, the Virginia colonists began trading regularly with the Nottoway.

In 1669, the Nottoway reportedly had 90 warriors and two towns, both of which were located in that portion of Charles City County that later became Prince George County. In 1674, they asked the Virginia government for protection against English settlers who had seated themselves within the tribe's officially allocated preserve. Three years later, the Nottoway became signatories to the Treaty of Middle Plantation, at which time they became tributaries to the crown. By the early 1680s, when colonists commenced building homesteads within the Nottoway's territory, they withdrew southeast to the Nottoway River. During the 1690s, the Nottoway began raising hogs for sale to their English neighbors, and they turned increasingly to the colonial government for protection against the Tuscaroras, who had invaded their hunting habitat near the Appomattox River.

The onset of the eighteenth century found the Nottoway complaining bitterly about the Seneca and Tuscarora as well as certain unidentified tributary tribes. In 1705, the Nottoway, who had 100 bowmen, lived on the south side of the Nottoway River in what was then Surry County. They signed a treaty with the Virginia government in 1713, and eventually joined up with remnants of the Nansemond and Weyanoke. William Byrd II, who visited the Nottoway town in 1729, said that they had an English-style fort. As the eighteenth century wore on and Nottoway's population dwindled, they began disposing of the Nottoway River acreage they had been allocated as a preserve or reservation.

Martha W. McCartney

References

Robert Beverley, *History of the Present State of Virginia* (1705), Louis B. Wright, ed. (1947); Lewis R. Binford, "An Ethnohistory of the Nottoway, Meherrin and Weyanoke Indians of Southeastern Virginia," *Ethnohistory* 14 (1967):103–218; Douglas Boyce, "Iroquoian Tribes of the Virginia-North Carolina Coastal Plain," in *Handbook of North American Indians*, Vol. 15, Bruce G. Trigger, ed. (1978).

William W. Hening, ed., *The Statutes at Large: Being a Collection of All the Laws of Virginia*, 13 vols. (1809–1823); Martha W. McCartney, "Cockacoeske, Queen of Pamunkey: Diplomat and Suzeraine," in *Powhatan's Mantle: Indians in the Colonial Southeast*, Peter H. Wood, et al., eds. (1989); H.R. McIlwaine, ed., *Executive Journals of the Council of Colonial Virginia*, 5 vols. (1925–1945); Alexander S. Salley, *Narratives of Early Carolina, 1650–1708* (1911).

See also FORT HENRY (VIRGINIA); NANSEMOND; OPECHANCANOUH; PAMUNKEY; POWHATAN; TUSCARORA; VIRGINIA-INDIAN TREATY 1677/1680

Presidio Nuestra Señora de Loreto (Texas)

See FORT LA BAHÍA (TEXAS)

Presidio Nuestra Señora de los Dolores de los Tejas (Texas)

Presidio Nuestra Señora de los Dolores de los Tejas (1716–1729) was the first of the garrisons established in Texas during the 1716 Domingo Ramón expedition that effected the permanent occupation of the province. Originally located on the east bank of the Neches River, it was subsequently moved four miles east of the Angelina River, Nacogdoches County.

Domingo Ramón, charged with establishing a Spanish presence in east Texas as a bulwark against further French penetration toward New Spain, located the presidio at a site central to the various missions being founded for the Caddo villages in the area. The complement of 25 soldiers was inadequate to the task of managing the region; many had failed to bring families, either because of young age or danger, and were insufficient in number to both assist the missionaries and to carry out maintenance chores at the new presidio. When a small French force overran the easternmost Spanish mission in Texas, San Miguel de los Adaes, in 1719, the Spanish population of east Texas, including the garrison, retreated to San Antonio.

In 1721, the marqués de San Miguel de Aguayo, leader of a Spanish expedition to secure east Texas, reestablished Presidio de los Tejas at a new site in present Nacogdoches County. At this location the garrison spent the next several years farming, ranching, and helping missionaries at neighboring missions. During his inspection tour of the presidio in 1727, Pedro de Rivera concluded that the garrison served no strategic purpose and recommended its decommission. A viceregal order to the effect was carried out in June 1730, leaving the nearby missions with no support for their efforts and leading to their eventual transfer to San Antonio in 1731.

Jesús F. de la Teja

References
Carlos E. Castadea, *Our Catholic Heritage in Texas,* 7 vols. (1936–1958).

See also Aguayo Expedition; Presidio Nuestra Señora del Pilar de los Adaes (Louisiana); Texas

Presidio Nuestra Señora del Pilar de los Adaes (Louisiana)

Presidio Nuestra Señora del Pilar de los Adaes, situated near modern Robeline, Louisiana, was founded by the marqués de San Miguel de Aguayo in 1721. This garrison was located about 17 miles southwest of Natchitoches, a trading post founded on the Red River in late 1713 by Louis Juchereau de Saint Denis. To defend Spain's dominion against French incursions and to exercise influence among native tribes of the region, Aguayo set up this presidio and staffed it with 100 men. In future years Los Adaes would serve as the Spanish capital of Texas, but its importance waned steadily as France and Spain mended their differences and moved toward a Bourbon alliance. Also, the missions in extreme east Texas and western Louisiana proved remarkably unsuccessful. When the region was inspected by *visitadors general,* inspector generals, in the late 1720s and again in the last 1760s, the three missions contained not a single resident neophyte. The latter inspector, the marqués de Rubí, found abominable conditions at the presidio. A garrison of 61 men had two functional muskets, and none of the soldiers possessed a uniform. On the recommendation of Rubí, made more feasible by the previous transfer of Louisiana from France to Spain (1762), east Texas was abandoned in 1772, with the capital and civilian population removed to San Antonio.

Donald E. Chipman

References
Donald E. Chipman, *Spanish Texas, 1519–1821* (1994).

See also Aguayo Expedition; Presidio Nuestra Señora del Dolores de los Tejas (Texas); St. Denis, Louis Juchereau de; Texas

Fort at Number Four (New Hampshire)

The northern-most military post on the Connecticut River was the fort at the settlement known as Number Four. The General Court of Massachusetts granted lands for four settlements along the Connecticut that in 1738 were determined to be within the borders of New Hampshire. Despite the controversy, Massachusetts settlers moved to the grants in the early 1740s. In November 1743, the settlers in the most exposed of the grants, Number Four, voted to build a fort. Paying for the structure was difficult. Massachusetts refused to pay because it would improve New Hampshire territory. New Hampshire refused to pay because the fort did nothing to protect its other towns situated near the coast, and in fact protected the Massachusetts towns to the south (a similar controversy broke out over Fort Dummer to the south in present-day Brattleboro, Vermont). So the settlers of Number Four paid for the fort by assessing the proprietors £300 each. In the end, Massachusetts would provide the soldiers and other military support for the fort.

Apparently, Colonel John Stoddard of Northampton supervised the building of the fort at Number Four. Although no specific reference can be found, he was the principle engineer in charge of forts on the Connecticut River, and the fort bears many of his touches. The structure covered about three-quarters of an acre, with large, connecting buildings of horizontal hewn logs built almost in a square shape. A palisade of upright logs extended around most of the fort. The palisade did not have the logs touching each other, but were planted several inches apart. Thus it only kept the enemy at a distance, while the defenders fired from the buildings within. In addition, the buildings were constructed so as to enable the defenders to fight an enemy that might penetrate the courtyard. The principle officers and leaders of the community were assigned dwellings (or rooms, as all the buildings were connected), and there was a great hall built over the main gate.

French and Indian raiding parties began incursions against Number Four in April 1746. Over the course of three weeks, mills were burned and several individuals killed or captured. Massachusetts sent soldiers to garrison the fort throughout June 1746, but the overall commander was local inhabitant and proprietor Phineas Stevens, who had been commissioned in provincial service the previous year. The first group of soldiers to arrive insisted on visiting the site where an inhabitant had been recently killed, despite the warnings of Stevens. As Stevens predicted, the soldiers were ambushed and several killed or wounded.

Massachusetts decided to withdraw its soldiers for the winter, and without this added protection, the inhabitants reluctantly withdrew as well, temporarily abandoning Number Four during the winter of 1746–1747. In March, Phineas Stevens persuaded the government to allow him to return with a company of soldiers. A short time after their return, the fort endured its greatest attack. On April 7, the uneasiness of dogs alerted the garrison to the presence of the enemy. The attacking force of French-led Indians set fire to the outbuildings. The fire spread to the grass and threatened the fort itself. The garrison split into two teams, one-half to douse the walls with water, the other to maintain a steady fire on the attackers. Eventually, 11 trenches were dug from under the buildings radiating out, deep enough for a man to stand upright and remain protected from fire. From these trenches the outside of the fort buildings were kept wet with water throughout the night.

The French and Indians constructed a crude fire cart filled with brush and pushed it toward the fort, then called for a parley. Stevens met the French officer sent to negotiate, who demanded that food be gathered for their use and then called for the immediate surrender of the fort. Stevens replied that the fort had been entrusted to him by his government and he had no intention of turning it over. The Frenchman threatened all sorts of consequences, and Stevens agreed to put it to a vote. The defenders voted unanimously to defend the structure. The French and Indians resumed their terror tactics of firing and yelling, and then called for another truce. This time the French officer re-quested that Stevens sell them some food and they would then leave. Stevens refused the unusual business transaction, and after firing a few more shots in frustration, the French force moved off to find provisions elsewhere.

News of this defense of the fort at Number Four caused quite a sensation throughout the New England colonies. Commodore Charles Knowles was so impressed that he personally sent Phineas Stevens a fancy sword in honor of his heroic stand. After King George's War, the inhabitants of Number Four would return the compliment and name the settlement "Charlestown."

During the uneasy peace that followed King George's War, the fort's readiness was maintained, as it remained the most exposed post on the Connecticut River. Charlestown endured several raids at the beginning of the last French war, particularly in 1754 and 1757. However, in 1757, Massachusetts assigned large forces to the fort, and for the remainder of the conflict, several hundred soldiers usually occupied the structure. In 1759, Robert Rogers and what remained of his force staggered into the fort after their raid on St. Francis, and in the following two years Charlestown became a major station on the Crown Point military road.

With the end of the French wars and the capture of Canada by the English government, Charlestown no longer needed the protection of a fort, and the structure was dismantled to allow for the expansion of the town. A reconstruction of the fort now sits a few miles north of the original site.

Steven C. Eames

References
Henry H. Saunderson, *History of Charlestown, New Hampshire* (1876).

See also STEVENS, PHINEAS

Nutimus (c. 1680–c. 1763)

Born in what is now New Jersey, probably on the upper Delaware River, Nutimus is said to have been a boy in 1686. His name means "striker of fish with a spear." Early in the eighteenth century, Nutimus moved to the Pennsylvania side of the Delaware River, south of the mouth of the Lehigh River, a region known as the forks of the Delaware. The region, between the Kittatinny Mountains and Tohicoon Creek, which had long supported Delawares, including

Nutimus's maternal grandparents, became a refuge not only for Delaware Indians of all dialects, but also for bands of Shawnees. Nutimus's political authority rested on both his lineage and his personal command; he was a sachem, that is, the leading civil political leader of his village. A highly regarded healer, he became the leading spokesman for the Delawares who inhabited the forks in the early eighteenth century.

In 1734, the government of Pennsylvania sought the sale of vast tracts in the forks. As an asking price, Pennsylvania offered £2 per 1,000 acres. That it would shortly sell these lands for £155 per 1,000 acres is a fact of which Nutimus could not then have been aware, but he knew the value of the land to his people, and he rejected Pennsylvania's offer. Three years later, however, under pressure not only from Pennsylvania but also from the Six Nations Iroquois Confederacy, Nutimus signed the notorious "Walking Purchase" agreement.

Nutimus protested the manner in which Pennsylvania extended the boundaries of this cession, but he was forced to yield to British and Iroquoian strength. In 1742, Nutimus moved with his people to the Susquehanna Valley, establishing a town at present Nescopeck, Pennsylvania, under Six Nations "protection." He was joined by some Shawnees and Mahicans.

There he and his people found little peace. Nutimus's name appears on a cession of the remaining Delaware lands between the Susquehanna and the Delaware in 1749. In 1753, Nutimus found renewed threats to his lands when Connecticut's Susquehanna Company, on the basis of Connecticut's colonial charter and a very dubious purchase from Six Nations "delegates," began surveying the valley for settlement. The event was inauspicious for the British, not only as a manifestation of intercolonial rivalry, but also as it, along with the Walking Purchase and other Delaware dispossessions, fed arguments for war against the British in 1755. In the wake of General Edward Braddock's defeat that year, most of the region's Indians allied with France.

Nutimus was not among them. He withdrew northward from the Susquehanna Valley into neutral Iroquois territory. He is found treating with William Johnson in 1756, seeking British recognition for the Delawares as an independent people. His last official notation is in 1757, when he signed a document at Easton. Nutimus was still alive during Pontiac's War. In 1763, although at peace with the colonies, his village on Big Island was attacked and destroyed by an expedition from Cumberland County, Pennsylvania, under Colonel John Armstrong.

Nutimus, like many Native Americans, easily embraced selected aspects of European and Euro-American culture. He was known as a good blacksmith. He and his family once possessed five African American slaves. While abandoned by many of his erstwhile followers in the wake of repeated removals and disappointments, Nutimus himself believed war with the Anglo-Americans to be fruitless. But he did seek to get the most for his people, under the circumstances. And he could lodge cutting criticisms. Pennsylvania authorities found him "troublesome." When in 1737 James Logan demanded how Nutimus, who was born in New Jersey, could claim lands in Pennsylvania, Nutimus responded with an unassailable quip, "the Indians did not consider the River as any boundary for those of the same Nation lived on both sides of it—As Nutimus thought this a trifling Question he in banter asked how he [Logan] came to have a Right here as he was not born in this Country."

Gregory E. Dowd

References

Francis Jennings, *The Ambiguous Iroquois Empire: The Covenant Chain and the Confederation of Indian Tribes with the English Colonies from its beginnings to the Lancaster Treaty of 1744* (1984); C. Hale Sipe, *Indian Chiefs of Pennsylvania* (1927); Anthony F.C. Wallace, *King of the Delawares: Teedyuscung* (1949); Paul A.W. Wallace, *The Indians in Pennsylvania* (1961); C.A. Weslager, *The Delaware Indians: A History* (1972).

See also DELAWARE; PONTIAC'S WAR; WALKING PURCHASE

Oconostota (also known as Great Warrior, c. 1712–1783)

Oconostota was a leading Cherokee warrior and spokesman in the mid-eighteenth century who became a major advocate of peace with the whites in the 1760s. He first appeared in historical literature in 1736, when he supported a French delegation that visited the Overhill Cherokee towns. Two years later, Oconostota blamed the English for his disfigurement caused by smallpox. For the next two decades he continued to court the French.

In August 1754, Oconostota and other Cherokee chiefs, unhappy with South Carolina trade, attempted unsuccessfully to break that colony's monopoly by opening commercial ties with Virginia. In 1755, he led 500 warriors to a decisive victory over the Creeks at the Battle of Taliwa, forcing the losers to leave northern Georgia to the Cherokees.

Although Oconostota was not a great orator, he had enough stature within the tribe to head delegations. In 1759, he led a large group of Cherokee chiefs to Charles Town in an attempt to prevent the outbreak of war between the Cherokees and the whites. South Carolina Governor William Henry Lyttleton ignored the peaceful intentions of these leaders, took them hostage, and marched the group to Fort Prince George. There he demanded that the tribe surrender the Indians who murdered 24 whites in exchange for the release of the chiefs. Eventually, Attakullakulla, a great eighteenth-century peace chief, secured the release of a few, leaving 24. Oconostota was one of the chiefs released, and he soon led an attack on Fort Prince George, which resulted in the immediate execution of the remaining hostages. This attack on the fort brought a punitive expedition under

Archibald Montgomery, who destroyed many of the lower towns in 1760. Oconostota and his warriors repulsed Montgomery at Etchoe, about six miles south of Franklin, North Carolina, on 1 June. Believing that he had sufficiently chastised the Cherokees, Montgomery returned to Charles Town.

Oconostota then began a siege of Fort Loudoun in Tennessee, which surrendered in early August. Although the Cherokees promised that the garrison could march away unmolested, they later attacked the retreating soldiers, killing a number exactly equal to the number of hostages killed at Fort Prince George.

Great Warrior traveled to New Orleans in 1761, where he received a French commission but failed to bring back needed supplies for war. In the spring of 1761, Colonel James Grant led approximately 2,400 men into Cherokee country. Grant's scouts detected a Cherokee ambush near the location where Montgomery had been attacked. Grant avoided the ambush and was successful against the Cherokees. He became the first white man to invade the middle settlements, where he destroyed at least 15 towns and more than 1,500 acres of corn.

Although the Cherokee War was disastrous for the tribe, it raised the status of Oconostota, who by 1764 was the effective head of the Cherokees. In 1768, Great Warrior led a delegation of Cherokees to the Iroquois, and later that year he and other leaders agreed to a new boundary line with Virginia. The ink was barely dry on the treaty before whites began crossing over the boundary and Virginia began requesting more land. Oconostota replied, "We shall give no part of our land away unless we are paid for it and indeed we want to keep the Virginians at as great a distance as possible as they are generally bad men and love to steal horses and hunt deer . . . But what are a few goods in comparison to good land. The land will last forever."

In the early 1770s, Oconostota declined a proposal from northern Indians to cooperate in an attack on the whites. In late 1773, Great Warrior visited Charles Town, where, because of his status among the Cherokees, he was inducted into St. Andrews Society, a fraternal organization of Scots founded in 1729. The following year Oconostota prevented young warriors from joining the Shawnees in another proposed attack on whites. In the spring of 1775, Oconostota, preferring land cessions to war, was one of the signatories on a deed to North Carolina lawyer Richard Henderson that turned over 20 million acres comprising middle Tennessee and most of Kentucky.

In July of 1776, young Cherokee warriors led a series of attacks on the Watauga, Holston, and Carter Valley settlements in present-day eastern Tennessee. A series of raids were also launched on the Carolina and Georgia frontiers. The Americans retaliated in the fall. William Christian devastated the Oconostota's overhill towns, and the Cherokees agreed to sign a peace treaty the following spring. At that treaty, Long Island of the Holston, the Cherokees ceded additional land to Virginia. When a Cherokee was accidentally killed at the meeting, and it appeared that negotiations might end, Oconostota insisted that the conference continue.

Although the Cherokees were technically at peace for the next three years, young warriors under the leadership of Dragging Canoe broke away from the tribe and resettled at Chickamauga. These Cherokees continued to attack the Virginia and Carolina frontier. Whites blamed all Cherokees for these incursions, and Oconostota was obliged to ask for peace again in May 1779. Encouraged by British successes in the south, the Cherokees rejoined the Revolutionary War briefly during the following year, but punitive expeditions by Colonel John Sevier and Arthur Campbell soon ended Cherokee activity.

In July 1782, Oconostota resigned his authority, designating his son, Tuckesee, as his successor, but the Cherokees found Tuckesee unacceptable. In the spring of 1783, Oconostota died. Oconostota's grave was discovered in 1972, and he was reinterred in 1987 near the Sequoyah Museum in Vonore, Tennessee.

William L. Anderson

References

John P. Brown, *Old Frontiers: The Story of the Cherokee Indians from Earliest Times to the Date of Their Removal, 1838* (1938); David H. Corkran, *The Cherokee Frontier: Conflict and Survival, 1740–1762* (1962); James C. Kelly, "Oconostota," *Journal of Cherokee Studies* III (1979):221–238; Grace Steele Woodward, *The Cherokees* (1963).

See also ATTAKULLAKULLA; CHEROKEE WAR; FORT LOUDOUN (TENNESSEE); LYTTLETON, WILLIAM HENRY; FORT PRINCE GEORGE–KEOWEE (SOUTH CAROLINA)

Oglethorpe, James Edward (1689–1785)

James Oglethorpe was the driving force behind the colonization of Georgia between 1733–1743. He was a member of the board of trustees set up to administer the colony in England. He was also the board's representative in North America and upheld its purpose to provide aid to the poor and to secure the southern English frontier from the Spanish and the French. Oglethorpe returned to England on colonial business twice, in 1734 and in 1736. His main purpose in doing so was to renew his support with the trustees and to gain financial aid from Parliament in order to increase Georgia's defensive posture. Generally unsuccessful in gaining financial support, Oglethorpe spent £91,705.13.5 of his own money to keep the colony supplied and defended. On his final return to England in 1743, Parliament reimbursed him the money he had spent to support Georgia.

The trustees hoped to create a yeoman-farmer-based colony where people defended their settlements and at the same time were able to produce wine, olive oil, and silk for export. The colonists were selected initially from the impoverished masses of Great Britain and later from the servant class, and sent to Georgia with all of their expenses paid. Slavery was banned from the colony in 1735, as the trustees felt its practice would negate their attempt at helping the poor. It was also thought that the presence of slaves would inhibit the defense of the colony, as the Spanish offered the slaves of the English freedom in Florida.

These plans failed primarily because of the poor quality of land and the smallness and inflexibility of the land grants awarded to the settlers once in Georgia. In addition, the prohibition of strong alcohol prevented the traditional use of rum as a trade commodity. Without enough land to create a cash crop or the ability to trade with other colonies or the Native Americans, the early settlers began to leave Georgia and seek their fortune in other colonies.

When he volunteered to sail with the first group of charity colonists, Oglethorpe had already spent 11 years in Parliament and 13 in the army. He was actively involved in prison reform and was a founding member of the board that set up Georgia. Oglethorpe was wealthy, politically experienced, and had a trained military mind. By the time the ship reached Yamacraw Bluff and the colonists disembarked, Oglethorpe had developed a paternalistic attitude toward the settlers and made the colony his personal responsibility as long as he was in it. Physically tough, energetic, and a fighter, Oglethorpe apparently had a charismatic quality that attracted Native Americans to him and inspired confidence among his soldiers. The southeastern frontier brought out Oglethorpe's unusual combination of qualities in a way the trustees never could have predicted.

Oglethorpe was concerned with the defense of the colony against Spanish and Native American attack and planned a series of fortified settlements around the perimeter of Savannah. This first settlement was located 17 miles up the Savannah River on Yamacraw Bluff. Building began in February 1733, and by the end of the summer, Savannah was defended by a palisade, guardhouse, two blockhouses with cannon, and a battery of cannon along the river.

Around Savannah were built eight fortified settlements: Fort Argyle, located 30 to 40 miles to the west on the Ogeechee River; Thunderbolt, located five miles to the southeast on the Wilmington River; Tybee Island, located at the mouth of the Savannah River; Skidaway Island, located to the south of Tybee Island; Hampstead, Highgate, and Acton, all located near one another inland and to the south; and Abercorn, located 15 miles northwest of Savannah. By 1737, many of these fortified settlements were rotting and their original settlers were gone, victims of the harsh living conditions and infertile land.

More enduring fortifications were established in 1736; Augusta, at the fall line of the Savannah River, became an important trading center; Frederica, on St. Simons Island, became headquarters for Oglethorpe and his regiment; Darien, along the coast near the mouth of the Altamaha River, was colonized by Highland Scots; and Ebenezer, 22 miles above Savannah, was settled in 1734 by Salzburgers, German refugees. Fort St. Andrews and Fort Frederica, built in 1736, and Fort St. Simons, built in 1738, guarded the southern coastline.

Oglethorpe realized the defense of Georgia rested with the Native Americans and lost no time entering into diplomatic relations with them. He established a friendly relationship with the Yamacraw Indians, a band of Creek who lived on the site of the first settlement, Savannah. They facilitated his meeting with representatives from eight Lower Creek tribes in May 1733. The resulting treaty gave the Georgia colonists the right to live on land the Creek did not use themselves, which eventually included much of the territory between the Savannah and St. Johns Rivers. In return, the trustees promised restitution if Georgia traders mistreated the tribe or destroyed their property. This alliance proved an enduring one for the British in Georgia.

In addition to maintaining diplomatic relations with the Lower Creek, Oglethorpe entered into alliances with the Upper Creek, Choctaw, and Cherokee. By 1739, he had created a network of Native American allegiance to Great Britain that discouraged Spanish and French incursion along the frontier. During the subsequent war with Spain, Oglethorpe employed Native American warriors as scouts, hit-and-run raiders, spies, and messengers.

Although an attempt to settle the boundary dispute between Spain and Great Britain regarding the southern frontier in North America had been made with the Treaty of Frederica in 1736, Oglethorpe was convinced that the Spanish would invade Georgia if it was unprotected. He was cautioned by the British government not to provoke the Spanish and agreed to abandon Fort St. George, near the south of the St. Johns River. On his second trip to England, 1736–1738, he appealed to Parliament for military support and got it. In June 1737, Oglethorpe was commissioned general and commander in chief of the forces in South Carolina and Georgia and given a regiment, the 42nd Regiment of Foot.

Oglethorpe and his regiment were in Georgia by the fall of 1738. The soldiers were stationed among the sea island forts, Fort St. Simons, Fort St. Andrews, and Fort Frederica. They did not settle in easily, and General Oglethorpe personally put down a mutiny at Fort St. Andrews. The trustees refused to pay any more expenses for the rangers, scouts, or forts used for

Georgia's defense once the regiment arrived. General Oglethorpe disbanded many units, but retained a number of ranger units and scout-boat crews. He paid for them with his own money.

With the declaration of war against Spain in October 1739 (War of Jenkins' Ear), the British government encouraged General Oglethorpe to harass Florida. He made several expeditions to Florida in order to familiarize himself with the territory around the Spanish stronghold at St. Augustine.

In mid-November 1739, a band of Spanish-allied Yamasee killed two trustee servants garrisoned on Amelia Island. Oglethorpe took a combined raiding party of about 200 soldiers, militia, and warriors and traveled by boat as far as the St. Johns River. Although little damage was inflicted, they familiarized themselves with the terrain. Oglethorpe garrisoned Fort St. George before returning to Frederica.

In early January 1740, General Oglethorpe and 180 soldiers and warriors, including Creek, Chickasaw, and Uchee, went south again. They traveled by sea and brought cannon. They first captured Fort Picolata, which was burned, then Fort San Francisco de Pupo. This second fort controlled the navigation on the St. Johns River, and Oglethorpe left a garrison there before returning to Fort Frederica.

Oglethorpe was anxious to capture the Spanish fort, Castillo de San Marcos, protecting the town of St. Augustine. Recently reinforced with more than 200 men and provisions from Cuba, St. Augustine was further protected by Spanish half-galleys, which were able to sail in the shallow bay. The governor of Florida, Manuel de Montiano, had deliberately avoided open battle with the British, and Oglethorpe and his men thought the Spanish weak.

Oglethorpe assembled a large army, including a regiment and volunteers from South Carolina, as well as his own regiment, various troops of rangers, and companies of foot from Georgia. Joining them were about 200 warriors, more than half of whom were Cherokee with the rest Creek, Uchee, Chickasaw, and Yamacraw. In addition, he had eight British men-of-war to blockade St. Augustine harbor. This army of approximately 1,000 regular and provincial troops and 200 warriors set off for St. Augustine in May 1740.

They captured Fort San Diego, a small outlying post 17 miles to the north of St. Augustine, and Fort Mose, located two miles from St. Augustine, in May. The siege of St. Augustine

was begun in June. This was raised after 38 days, and failed for a variety of reasons. One problem lay in the shallowness of the bay; the British men-of-war could not enter it and challenge the Spanish half-galleys. Thus, Oglethorpe's plan to position cannon on Anastasia Island, in the bay, and bombard the fort, was not carried out. Not only did the Spanish receive food, but they recaptured Fort Mose in late June, breaking the spirit of many of the troops and disgusting Oglethorpe's Indian allies. When the British naval captains fled at the onset of the hurricane season, the troops grew sick and began to desert. Oglethorpe ordered a retreat on 4 July 1740 and nearly lost control of the regiment on 21 July when he proposed returning to St. Augustine. They were back at Fort Frederica by the end of July. There were approximately 122 dead, 16 prisoners, and 14 deserters left in Florida.

For the next two years, Oglethorpe spent his own money to maintain the colony in a defensive position, for England was now engaged in the War of the Austrian Succession and its attention was focused on Europe. Nor did he get any help from South Carolina, whose assembly claimed Oglethorpe was incompetent and responsible for the failure at St. Augustine. Oglethorpe concentrated most of his defensive units on St. Simons Island, and formed his own provincial navy, with soldiers from his regiment serving as marines. He also increased his ranger units, hoping to achieve more mobility with more horsemen, but was limited by the number of horses available.

Spain, however, kept an eye on Georgia, and an attack was planned by the governor of Cuba, Juan Francisco de Güemes. The invasion force was to include 56 vessels and approximately 7,000 men. Led by Governor Montiano of Florida, the expedition was to attack and destroy the British regiment at St. Simons Island and then move up the coast, destroying settlements. Montiano was then to withdraw to Cuba and Florida and avoid British retaliation.

The attack was launched 20 June 1742 from St. Augustine. Hampered by strong winds, a number of smaller ships sought shelter in the inland passage. They encountered Fort Prince William at the tip of Cumberland Island and later anchored at the entrance to St. Andrews Sound, out of range of that fort's cannon. General Oglethorpe reached Fort St. Andrews by scout boat several days later, with reinforcements from St. Simons Island. He ordered the fort abandoned, and the soldiers withdrew to Fort Prince William. On seeing the Spanish ships sailing back to St. Augustine, Oglethorpe returned to St. Simons Island.

The main Spanish force, led by Governor Montiano of Florida, numbered between 3,000 to 5,000 men and 36 vessels. They appeared off St. Simons Island on 28 June 1742 and began their attack on 5 July. Oglethorpe had gathered together approximately 500 men, including civilians and warriors, and they awaited the Spanish at Forts St. Simons and Delegal, with a small flotilla of vessels. Although the tip of the island where these two forts stood was the most heavily fortified area in Georgia, the Spanish fleet sailed past with only five men killed. They anchored in the north end of St. Simons Sound near the mouth of the Frederica River.

That evening, while the Spanish landed one and one-half miles to the northwest, Oglethorpe ordered the forts evacuated. Three of the larger ships in the British flotilla were able to sail away, and the rest were deliberately burned. The British marched six miles to the north on an overland trail and reached Fort Frederica without being detected.

As news spread of the Spanish invasion of St. Simons Island, Georgia settlers fled to inland forts at Abercorn and Argyle. The South Carolina assembly ordered Charles Town fortified and called out the militia.

The Spanish took over Fort St. Simons as headquarters, and on 7 July sent out a reconnoitering party. This party got within one and one-half miles of Fort Frederica before being detected. The ensuing battle was won by General Oglethorpe and his hastily gathered group of provincials and warriors. Fearing a counterattack, Oglethorpe set up an ambush approximately five miles to the southeast of Frederica along the trail. The resultant fight, called the Battle of Bloody Marsh, was won by battalion soldiers. The Spanish retreated to Fort St. Simons, and the British returned to Fort Frederica the next day.

Reinforcements arrived from Fort Prince William, and Oglethorpe now had approximately 700 to 800 men at Fort Frederica. Both the Spanish and the British used Native Americans on St. Simons Island; the Yamasee were allied with the Spanish, and the Yamacraw, Creek, and Chickasaw with the British. All served in battle and as scouts.

On 9 July, the Spanish decided to reconnoiter the Frederica River in an attempt to determine if they could land their troops closer to British headquarters. Their galley retreated when it came within range of the fort's guns. On 12 July, Oglethorpe and a group of 500 attempted to conduct a night raid on the Spanish camp. This failed as the camp was alerted to their presence. Governor Montiano grew uneasy about the possibility of a British fleet coming to the aid of Georgia, and decided to abandon St. Simons Island.

Montiano had Fort St. Simons destroyed and his soldiers ferried to Jekyll Island. From Jekyll Island they were ferried to Cumberland Island, where they burned abandoned Fort St. Andrews. The Spanish fleet divided on 17 July, with the larger ships going by open sea and the smaller sailing the inside passage to St. Augustine.

Montiano made an attempt to capture Fort Prince William at the southern end of Cumberland Island on 18 July and then headed for St. Augustine. Oglethorpe was right behind him with a scout-boat flotilla. They went as far south as the St. Johns River and returned to Frederica by 22 July.

Reinforced by a relief fleet from Charles Town, Oglethorpe returned to St. Augustine and attempted to destroy the half-galleys in the harbor and land a force on Anastasia Island in late August. These efforts failed, and the fleet returned to Frederica on 4 September 1742.

The Spanish-allied Yamasee began to increase their attacks against the Georgia settlements and British-allied tribes during late 1742 and early 1743, getting as far north as the Altamaha River. General Oglethorpe led a major punitive raid against Florida in March 1743, encouraging the Lower Creek warriors to participate. These warriors ambushed Spanish soldiers outside Fort San Marcos, but did not remain with Oglethorpe's forces. After an attempted landing on Anastasia Island, Oglethorpe gave up his plans and returned to Frederica, arriving on 31 March 1743.

Oglethorpe achieved some success on this last trip south. He convinced the Creek that the Spanish were in a defensive and weak position, even though they had not been defeated. The Creek conducted raids into Florida for several years. Governor Montiano was convinced that the British were serious about invading Florida and remained on the defensive.

General Oglethorpe left Georgia permanently on 23 July 1743 and returned to England. He was married in 1744, made a major general in 1745, and led a regiment against the Stuart invasion. In 1749, he was made a Fellow of the Royal Society, and he continued to attend trustee meetings until 1749. He was a member of Parliament until 1768, and died in 1785.

The colony imagined by the trustees in England was based on humanitarian and defensive ideals that James Oglethorpe tried to put into practice in Georgia between 1733 and 1743. Although a yeoman class did not develop and slavery became legal in 1750, Georgia was able to hold on to its southern frontier. This was due in large part to the fact that Oglethorpe succeeded in creating a positive diplomatic relationship with the Native American population that enabled him to develop and maintain a convincing defensive posture against the French and Spanish in the Southeast.

Leslie Hall

References

Kenneth Coleman, *Colonial Georgia: A History* (1989); Amos Aschbach Ettinger, *James Edward Oglethorpe: Imperial Idealist* (1968); Larry E. Ivers, *British Drums Along the Southern Frontier: The Military Colonization of Georgia, 1733–1749* (1974); Phinizy Spalding, *Oglethorpe in America* (1977); Phinizy Spalding and Harvey H. Jackson, eds., *Oglethorpe in Perspective: Georgia's Founder After Two Hundred Years* (1989).

See also BLOODY MARSH, BATTLE OF; FLORIDA, INVASION OF; FORT FREDERICA (GEORGIA); GEORGIA; MONTIANO, MANUEL DE; MORAL SÁNCHEZ, FRANCISCO DEL; FORT PICOLATA (FLORIDA); FORT ST. ANDREWS (GEORGIA); FORT ST. SIMONS (GEORGIA); FORT SAN FRANCISCO DE PUPO (FLORIDA); CASTILLO DE SAN MARCOS (FLORIDA)

Ogoula Tchetoka, Battle of (1736)

French and Indian forces under command of Pierre d'Artaguette attacked the Chickasaw village of Ogoula Tchetoka on 25 March 1736. Artaguette, commanding forces from the Illinois country supported by Indian allies, was supposed to rendezvous with Jean-Baptiste Le Moyne de Bienville at the end of March, but Bienville was delayed for lack of supplies; Artaguette arrived at the Prudhomme Bluffs (Memphis) on 4 March and learned of Bienville's projected two-month delay. At the urging of his Indian allies, especially the

Iroquois, Artaguette attacked the fortified Chickasaw village of Ogoula Tchetoka to acquire provisions and obtain a secure position from which to wait for Bienville, but the Chickasaws had been alerted to French plans by Shawnee hunters, and thus were prepared for an attack. Artaguette was defeated, and died along with almost half of his 137 French troops, including Commander François-Marie Bisot de Vincennes and Jesuit chaplain Antoine Senat. English traders found Artaguette's correspondence on the field of battle, which laid the groundwork for Bienville's defeat two months later in the Battle of Ackia.

Michael James Foret

References

James R. Atkinson, "The Ackia and Ogoula Tchetoka Chickasaw Village Locations in 1736 during the French-Chickasaw War," *Mississippi Archaeology* 20 (1985):53–72; Michael James Foret, "On the Marchlands of Empire: Trade, Diplomacy, and War on the Southeastern Frontier, 1733–1763," Ph.D. Dissertation, College of William and Mary (1990):131–169; Joseph Peyser, "1740 French Map Pinpoints Battle Site in Mississippi," *Mapline* 39 (1985):1–4; ———, "The Chickasaw Wars of 1736 and 1740: French Military Drawings and Plans Document the Struggle for the Lower Mississippi," *Journal of Mississippi History* 44 (1982): 1–25.

See also ACKIA, BATTLE OF; CHICKASAW WARS; LE MOYNE DE BIENVILLE, JEAN-BAPTISTE

Ohio Company

The Ohio Company was the primary group that sought to implement Virginia's claims to the trans-Appalachian west in the period immediately preceding the French and Indian War.

The company was created in 1748 under the leadership of several politically influential Virginia leaders, drawn largely from the northern portion of the colony. Among these were Thomas Lee, Thomas Cresap, and Lawrence Washington. They planned to use the company to obtain a substantial grant of land lying along the Ohio River, to plant settlers in that area, to engage in Indian trade, and to speculatively resell much of their holdings. The company's charter, confirmed in 1749 by the British government, involved a grant of 200,000 acres with the provision that the company must undertake stated activities of trade and settlement. Key sections of the charter allowed the company to negotiate with Indian leaders and to erect fortifications on its holdings.

Between 1750 and 1752, the company employed Christopher Gist to explore the Ohio Valley in search of the best land on which to place its first settlement. In 1752 and 1753, Gist and other representatives negotiated with Indian leaders of the valley, and produced the Treaty of Logstown. This gave sanction both to trade and to construct a "strong house" at the forks of the Ohio. The company then retained William Trent, who was directed to raise men and erect a blockhouse, which became known as Fort Prince George. Begun in January 1754, it was not completed when its capture by the French in March initiated the French and Indian War.

The close ties of the Ohio Company and the Virginia government make it difficult at times to distinguish the actions of each. Company agents and investors, including Gist and George Washington, played an active role in the subsequent campaigns of 1754 and 1755, in part in hope of confirming the company's claims. But military reversals and the failure to plant settlements eventually caused the company's claims to lapse into a shadowy existence that was extinguished in 1792.

George Geib

References

Kenneth P. Bailey, *The Ohio Company of Virginia and the Westward Movement, 1748–1792* (1939).

See also DINWIDDIE, ROBERT; FORKS OF THE OHIO; GIST, CHRISTOPHER; LOGSTOWN, TREATY OF; TRENT, WILLIAM; WASHINGTON, GEORGE

Ohio Country

The Ohio country became a battleground between the colonial empires of France and Great Britain in the 1750s. Each country desired control of this region to use for future settlement. It also contained valuable resources, such as furs. Rivalry between the French and British in the area led to increased tensions between the two colonial powers and eventually culminated in the French and Indian War.

The Ohio country was located between the Ohio and Wabash Rivers and reached into the Great Lakes area. This included portions of the present-day states of Indiana, Ohio, Michigan, and Pennsylvania. The region was abundant with game, which could be used by inhabitants for food and fur pelts, and its many rivers fostered easy transportation. The junction of the Monongahela and Allegheny Rivers, in particular, was a strategic location. Control of these rivers could determine control of the entire Ohio Valley.

Several Indian groups lived in or near the Ohio country in the colonial era. During the seventeenth century, the Iroquois defeated and drove out the Indians that inhabited the area. Among these were the Shawnee, Miami, and Erie tribes. The Iroquois retained dominance in the region for about 100 years, but it remained only sparsely populated and was used primarily as an open hunting ground until more permanent settlements began in the early eighteenth century.

Beginning in the 1720s and continuing through the 1740s, large numbers of Indians began to return to the Ohio country. Among these were the Delaware, Shawnee, and Iroquois (or Mingos). There were several motivations for the migrations. Abundant game was a major attraction, but also, many Indians to the east were being displaced by large numbers of European immigrants moving into the British colonies. Finally, Indians migrated to the Ohio from the west to be closer to centers of trade.

The British and French each sought to ally themselves with the Indians of the valley. The latter were caught in the middle of the formers' imperial rivalry. Any conflict between Great Britain and France would involve the Indians, who had grown dependent on European goods. The Indians also inhabited land that the colonial powers wanted for themselves. Their sole advantage was to play the French and British against one another and hope that neither could exert domination over the region.

In the 1740s the British colonies moved forcefully into the Ohio Valley to obtain more control over the prosperous fur trade. This was shown initially, in 1747, with the formation of the Ohio Company of Virginia. The company's charter called for the construction of a fort and a settlement of 100 families. This was also a deliberate move to counter the French presence in the area and to reassert British authority. The Ohio Company eventually failed, but Virginia's interest in the region motivated another colony, Pennsylvania, to increase its own expansion into the Ohio country.

In 1748, the town of Pickawillany was established. It was originally settled by a group of Indians from the Miami tribe, but traders from Pennsylvania were welcomed immediately. The trading post soon developed into a center of British influence.

The French saw Virginia's and Pennsylvania's advances as a threat to their own security. Many believed British control of the Ohio would produce a wedge between French Canada and Louisiana. In 1749, Captain Pierre-Joseph Céloron de Blainville led a military expedition throughout the Ohio Valley. He claimed the lands for France and warned all British traders to leave the area. In 1752, the French struck at the town of Pickawillany and destroyed it. Finally, in the early 1750s, they began to construct several forts in the Ohio Valley to improve their military power.

By the early and middle 1750s, competition between the British and French over the Ohio country was at its height. Each nation held conflicting claims to the territory. The British claims were based on earlier discovery and exploration. The crown also held charter grants that, in theory, extended from the Atlantic to Pacific Oceans. However, permanent settlements in the English colonies were all east of the Appalachian Mountains. Only small groups of Englishmen (primarily traders) lived west of the mountain range.

The French claims to the area relied on the many trading posts, missions, and forts constructed in the Ohio Valley. Fort Le Boeuf was one such fort built by the French. In 1753, a very young George Washington was commissioned by Governor Robert Dinwiddie of Virginia to order the French to leave. The French refused. In 1754, they constructed a fort at the forks of the Ohio River, which the British considered an act of aggression, as its position blocked the westward expansion of both Virginia and Pennsylvania. Colonel Washington was called on to act against the French presence, but was defeated soundly at Fort Necessity.

British and French rivalry over the Ohio country culminated in the French and Indian War. Eventually, the French were defeated and removed. The Indians also became big losers, as the balance of power was then held by the British and the Indians could no longer play the British and French against one another. A trickle of settlers from the British colonies into the Ohio Valley followed the war, but European settlement was not heavy for many years to come.

Michael W. Nagle

References
Lawrence Henry Gipson, *The British Empire Before the American Revolution*, 15 vols. (1939–1970), 4; Francis Jennings, *Empire of Fortune: Crowns, Colonies, and Tribes in the Seven Years War in America* (1988); Douglas Edward Leach, *The Northern Colonial Frontier, 1607–1763* (1966); Gary B. Nash, *Red, White, and Black: The Peoples of Early North America* (1982); Richard White, *The Middle Ground: Indians, Empires, and Republics in the Great Lakes Region, 1650–1815* (1991).

See also DELAWARE; FORKS OF THE OHIO; MINGO; MONONGAHELA RIVER; SHAWNEE

Ohio Expedition of 1754

On 31 March 1754, George Washington wrote in his journal, "I received from his Honour [Lieutenant Governor Robert Dinwiddie of Virginia] a Lieutenant Colonel's Commission of the Virginia Regiment whereof Joshua Fry, Esquire, was Colonel, dated the 15th, with orders to take the troops, which were at that time quartered at Alexandria under my command, and to march with them towards the Ohio, there to aid Captain Trent in building Forts, and in defending the possessions of his Majesty against the attempts and hostilities of the French." Thus began the expedition of 1754 that was to end with the disastrous battle and surrender at Fort Necessity on 4 July, causing repercussions that changed the course of history.

The French had explored and occupied the territory of the Mississippi basin and the Ohio Valley long before the English had given it much thought. The increasing competition for the fur trade and the English encroachment and hunger for land caused the French to act by building forts from Lake Erie to the Ohio, and down the river to French New Orleans. In the autumn of 1753, concerned over the audacity of the French, land-speculating Governor Dinwiddie sent George Washington to carry a letter to the French at Fort Le Boeuf demanding that they evacuate the region immediately. The French replied, "That it was their absolute Design to take Possession of the Ohio . . ." Lieutenant Governor Dinwiddie asked the Virginia House of Burgesses for an appropriation to equip a military force to expel the French. The Burgesses declined, so Dinwiddie took matters into his own hands by asking the Ohio Company to begin building a fort, out of its own funds, at the juncture of the Allegheny and Monongahela Rivers. He also raised a force of men and put Colonel Joshua Fry in command with Washington as second-in-command.

Washington marched out of Alexandria, Virginia, on 2 April with two companies of infantry, commanded by Captain Peter Hogg and Lieutenant Jacob Van Braam. Captain Adam Stephen with a company of men joined the march about 15 days later. On 22 April, Washington reached Wills Creek and there met Ensign Edward Ward, who, under the orders of Captain William Trent, had been building a fort at the forks of the Ohio. Ensign Ward informed Washington of his surrender of the fort on the 17th to a superior body of French under the command of Captain Claude-Pierre Pécaudy de Contrecoeur. A council of war was held, and it was agreed that it would now be impossible to march on the forks of the Ohio without reinforcements, but that they should advance to Redstone Creek on the Monongahela to revamp the already existing storehouse of the Ohio Company, and clear the road for the expected heavy artillery. While they waited for reinforcements and further orders, Washington sent dispatches to notify Governor Dinwiddie and Tanaghrisson, the Half-King, of his intention to advance to Redstone. As Washington's forces marched out of Wills Creek on 30 April, reports came in that the French had rebuilt the fort at the forks of the Ohio, naming it Fort Duquesne, and that they were expecting reinforcements.

As Washington continued his march to the Redstone he received word that Colonel Joshua Fry was at Winchester, Virginia, with about 150 men and would join him in a few days, also that Colonel James Innes would soon join him with 350 men. It was also expected that Maryland would raise 200 men and Pennsylvania would raise funds to pay the soldiers. On 17 May, Washington received word from Lieutenant Governor Dinwiddie to go ahead with his plan of action.

On 24 May, Washington and his men reached the Great Meadows, cleared bushes out of the meadow, and built an entrenchment. Also on this day, two Indian runners came with a message from Tanaghrisson informing Washing-

ton that a small party of French had marched from Fort Duquesne to meet the Virginians, and that Tanaghrisson with other chiefs from the Ohio would join him shortly. Early in the morning of 27 May, Christopher Gist visited Washington's camp at the Great Meadows and reported that the French under the command of a M. La Force had visited his plantation the day before and while on his way to Washington's camp had seen their tracks only five miles away. Washington also received word from Tanaghrisson that he had seen the tracks of the Frenchmen and had traced them to their camp.

Washington, fearing the French were going to attack his camp, left a strong force to guard the camp and ammunition and set out with a band of soldiers and reached Tanaghrisson's camp a little before sunrise on 28 May. Washington and Tanaghrisson held a council and agreed to join forces in an attack on the French camp. Advancing on the camp, the forces were on the French before they could prepare their defense. Firing commenced and lasted about 15 minutes. The French were completely defeated, ten were killed, including Joseph Coulon de Villiers de Jumonville, one wounded, and 21 taken prisoner. Washington's forces lost one killed and two or three wounded, the Indians sustaining no loss. On 30 May, Washington sent a guard to march the prisoners to Winchester, and fearing that the French defeat would bring a large-scale attack, he began to erect a fort with a small palisade.

By 6 June, the fort was finished, and Washington received word from Christopher Gist that Colonel Fry had died in a fall from his horse and Washington was to take full command of the forces. During the next three weeks Washington's forces were increased by the expected reinforcements and were on the move toward Christopher Gist's plantation to hold a council with the Indians. The council was a failure due to disagreements between them over the method of conducting the campaign. In the meantime, Washington had sent out a party of men under Captain Charles Lewis to clear a road from Gist's plantation to the mouth of the Redstone.

Meanwhile, a force of about 500 French and about 4000 of their Indian allies left Fort Duquesne under the command of Louis Coulon de Villiers, a half-brother of Jumonville, advancing to attack Washington. Washington received the news by an Indian runner and recalled the road crew and sent a message to

Captain James Mackay to join him at Gist's plantation. A council was held and it was decided to fall back to the Great Meadows due to the great fatigue and hunger of the men. Arriving back at Great Meadows on 1 July they resolved to make a stand, strengthening and preparing the fort, now called Fort Necessity.

At 9 A.M. on 3 July, word was received that the French forces were only four miles off. The French arrived a little before noon and firing began, continuing until about eight in the evening, when the French requested a parley. Washington suspected this was a ruse to spy on the conditions of his camp and men, and therefore refused. The French then repeated their request with an additional proviso that an officer be sent to them and they would guarantee his safety. Washington acquiesced by sending Captain Jacob Van Braam, the only person in his troop that understood French. Van Braam returned with proposed articles of capitulation, which asked for the surrender of the fort and the English could retire with the honors of war. Due to the poor conditions of his men and the overpowering numbers of the French, Washington decided to surrender. On the morning of 4 July, Washington and his men marched out of Fort Necessity and retreated to Wills Creek, then Washington went on to Williamsburg to notify Governor Dinwiddie of the capitulation.

Evelyn C. Darrow

References

Kenneth P. Bailey, *The Ohio Company of Virginia and the Westward Movement, 1748–1792* (1939); Hugh Cleland, *George Washington in the Ohio Valley* (1955); John P. Cowan, "George Washington at Fort Necessity," *Western Pennsylvania Historical Magazine* 37 (1954) 153–177; John C. Fitzpatrick, ed., *The Diaries of George Washington, 1748–1799, Vol. 1, 1748–1770* (1925); James Thomas Flexner, *George Washington: The Forge of Experience, 1732–1775* (1965); Douglas Southall Freeman, *George Washington, Vol. 1, Young Washington* (1948).

William Blake Hindman, "The Great Meadows Campaign and the Climaxing Battle at Fort Necessity," *West Virginia History* 16 (1955):65–89; William A. Hunter, *Forts on the Pennsylvania Frontier, 1753–1758* (1960); Bunford Samuel, ed., "The Ohio Expedition of 1754 by Adam Stephen," *Pennsylvania Magazine of History and Biography* 18 (1894–1895):53–60; C. Hale Sipe, *The Indian Wars of Pennsylvania* (1929); Charles Morse Stotz, *Outposts of the War for Empire: The French and English in Western Pennsylvania; Their Armies, Their Forts, Their People, 1749–1764* (1985); Frederick Tilberg, *Fort Necessity: National Battlefield Site, Pennsylvania* (1954).

See also COULON DE VILLIERS, LOUIS; COULON DE VILLIERS DE JUMONVILLE, JOSEPH; DINWIDDIE, ROBERT; GIST, CHRISTOPHER; HALF-KING; FORT LE BOEUF (PENNSYLVANIA); FORT NECESSITY (PENNSYLVANIA); OHIO COMPANY; PÉCAUDY DE CONTRECOEUR, CLAUDE-PIERRE; WASHINGTON, GEORGE

Ohio Expedition of 1755

During the early 1750s, two empires jockeyed for position in America. By 1752, the French were seeking to establish a strong position in the Ohio Valley. Along the Great Lakes and the Ohio itself, they built a string of forts, key among them Fort Duquesne, erected in 1754 on the forks of the Ohio. The Americans themselves had designs on the region, and certainly were unwilling to be excluded from it, but their main counterthrust, Washington's "Fort Necessity" expedition of 1754, ended in humiliating defeat. The government in London then determined to commit British regulars to the effort. During the autumn of 1754 final plans were laid for the proposed enterprise. The 44th and 48th Foot were to be sent to Virginia, then on to strike Fort Duquesne. Meanwhile, the two provincial regiments, the 50th and 51st (they had been reduced in 1748 but were now raised again) were to move on Niagara. The two British regiments would join them after taking Fort Duquesne, and this combined force would sweep the French from south of the Great Lakes. Commanding this effort was to be Major General Edward Braddock, a favorite of the duke of Cumberland. Despite the ambitious nature of the enterprise, the government committed scant resources to it. The 44th and 48th were among the weakest regiments, both considerably undermanned. They were to some extent filled out, more in quantity than quality, by drafts from other regiments, and it was anticipated that once they reached Virginia, American recruits would bring them to 700 men apiece. On this small and motley force, commanded by a general whose combat experience was limited, perhaps nonexistent, the government placed its primary reliance.

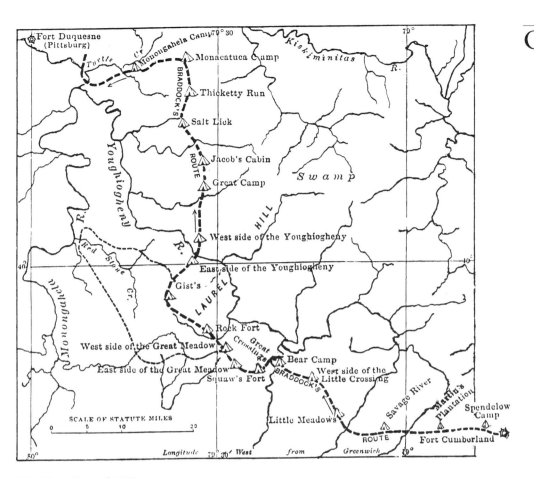

Ohio Expedition of 1755.

Once in America, Braddock refined the master strategy. Shirley was given command of the Niagara expedition, and in addition to the 50th and 51st he was allotted the New York independents, along with whatever provincials and Indian allies he could recruit. Sir William Johnson, newly designated superintendent of the northern Indians, was ordered to move on the French fort at Crown Point. His army was to consist of provincials, supported by Indians. Finally, an army of New Englanders was to sail to Nova Scotia, there to join British regulars in garrison in an attack on Fort Beauséjour at Chignecto. Command of this expedition fell to Colonel Robert Monckton.

Linchpin to the campaign was, of course, Braddock's expedition. The 44th and 48th sailed from Ireland on 8 January 1755, and after a generally smooth crossing arrived at Alexandria in mid-March, there to encamp for one month prior to departing, on 12 April, for Fort Cumberland. The bulk of the army arrived at the fort on or about 10 May, encamping at nearby Wills Creek. A shortage of supplies and wagons delayed further moves, but with the help of a supply effort masterminded by Benjamin Franklin, Braddock was able to order his men forward on 10 June.

Despite some problems with dysentery, the army that departed Wills Creek was in generally good condition, and in a return of the troops dated 8 June, Braddock accounted 1,330 men of the two regiments, and 2,041 overall fit for duty, as opposed to only 124 regulars (192 overall) sick, not counting those who had been left behind at Alexandria. Furthermore, whereas Braddock had earlier bemoaned the quality of his army, especially the provincial component, he seemed pleased with both the size and strength of his forces at this point, commenting,

"With these I flatter myself to be able to drive the French from the Ohio." However, he was also troubled by the delays that he had faced at Wills Creek, for he feared that the slow progress of his army might permit the French to reinforce Fort Duquesne. Even after the march began the army moved slowly and on 16 June, at the Little Meadows, Braddock, perhaps acting on the recommendation of George Washington, one of his aides-de-camp, decided to divide his army, pressing on with about 1,400 men while the remaining forces and most of the baggage were separated, to advance as best they could, under the command of Colonel Thomas Dunbar of the 48th. Braddock's army now advanced more rapidly, though stymied by the terrain and the forest. The men may have suffered fatigue, since they were pressed to a more rapid march, with fewer halting days. It also appears that they ran short of provisions in the final days of the march. However, there is no evidence that either of these considerations harmed the troops. On 8 July the men made camp about ten miles from Fort Duquesne. Braddock planned to decamp early the next morning, cross the Monongahela twice so as to avoid a dangerous defile, and then march nearly to the fort. He would invest it on the 10th.

As Braddock had feared, in early July the French were indeed able to get reinforcements to Fort Duquesne. The garrison then included about 600 French regulars and Canadians, and about 800 Indian warriors, most of them from Great Lakes tribes that had traditionally been pro-French, were encamped around the fort. It appears that initially there was a general reluctance to face Braddock's army, especially since rumor placed its size at 4,000 men. However, on the morning of July 9, Captain Daniel-Hyacinthe-Marie Liénard de Beaujeu, who had been assigned to assume command of the fort if it were held, rallied behind him a force that included, by the most precise French reckoning, 36 officers, 72 regulars, 146 Canadian militiamen, and 637 Indians. With this force he hoped to intercept the British as they crossed the Monongahela and force them to turn back.

By the time Beaujeu got his men organized, however, the British were already completing the second crossing of the river, and as one of them subsequently noted, the troops, safely forded, "hugg'd themselves with joy at our Good Luck in having surmounted our greatest Difficultys, & too hastily Concluded the Enemy never wou'd dare to Oppose us." Despite this optimism, about a mile further on, Braddock's army collided with Beaujeu's, and although Beaujeu was killed in an early British volley, his forces quickly gained the upper hand, as the Indians raced down the British flanks and began firing from cover, while the French blocked the way forward. Particularly damaging to the British was investment by the enemy of a small hill to the right of their line of march, and much of the fire was directed from this vantage point. Almost from the onset of action, Braddock's troops seemed disorganized. The components of the vanguard collided, and they fell back into a detachment from the main body, which Braddock had sent forward. The end result of this telescoping, combined with incessant enemy fire, was widespread confusion and panic. In the frenzy that followed, the troops fired blindly, and consequently many men were shot by their own comrades. It was only after three hours that the British were able to retreat. In a rout the troops fled, some not stopping until they found the security of Dunbar's force some 50 miles to the rear. Official returns placed British casualties at 914 men. In addition, 63 of 86 officers were killed or wounded. Sir Peter Halkett, colonel of the 44th, was among those left dead on the battlefield, and Braddock himself was mortally wounded.

With the defeat of Braddock, the master plan for rolling back the French began to unravel. Shirley, who when Braddock died became commander in chief, was a cautious general—not the last that the British were to have in the highest command during the period 1755–1783. After putting together a 5,000-man army at Oswego by late September, he decided not to proceed against Niagara. He was likely unnerved by the rout of Braddock's army, though the sickliness of his force and the lateness of the season may also have influenced his thinking.

The first year of war was not devoid of British successes. In June, Monckton's force captured, almost without bloodshed, Forts Beauséjour and St. John, the last French strongholds in the vicinity of the Bay of Fundy. The enterprise was lackluster but strategically important, for it quashed the French threat to Nova Scotia. More dramatic was the victory scored by the army under Sir William Johnson. It never reached Crown Point, and so failed to achieve the aim set out by Braddock, but on 8 September at Lake George, it crushed a French force, then proceeded to construct Fort William

Henry, which temporarily secured British control of the southern end of the lake. But Braddock's defeat was clearly the most decisive event of 1755.

The Battle of the Monongahela dramatically altered the equation of conflict. After its stunning defeat, Braddock's army quickly retreated east, to winter (although it was still July) in Philadelphia. For all practical purposes, this left the British army in North America inoperative, and although a few more regiments arrived in 1756 and many more in 1757, these were generally years of French success, and it was not until 1758 that the British regained the initiative. Braddock's defeat not only weakened the British, but it enhanced the French position in several ways. First, it secured their hold over the Ohio Valley. Second, it allowed them time to bring in reinforcements from Europe. Finally, it strengthened their position among the Indians, as they gained several allies, notably the Delawares, while tribes that had supported Britain became more neutral. As a Delaware chieftain said of his tribe, "the Greater Part remained neuter till they saw How Things wou'd go Between Braddock and the French in their Engagement." This shift set off an important chain of events. During the winter of 1755–1756, Delawares and other pro-French Indians attacked settlers on the Pennsylvanian frontier. Since the British forces were in Philadelphia, and since Pennsylvania, owing to Quaker influence, lacked a militia, there was no organized frontier defense. In the face of protests from the settlers, however, the Quaker assemblymen whose pacifism prevented them from supporting the establishment of a militia resigned their seats, and the assembly provided the necessary authorization.

The impact of Braddock's defeat was, therefore, highly complex. It was certainly the most decisive action of the first three years of warfare.

Paul E. Kopperman

References

Paul E. Kopperman, *Braddock at the Monongahela* (1977); Lee McCardell, *Ill-Starred General Braddock of the Coldstream Guards* (1958); Ronald D. Martin, "Confrontation at the Monongahela: Climax of the French Drive into the Upper Ohio Region," *Pennsylvania History* 37:133–150; Winthrop Sargent, *The History of an Expedition Against Fort Du Quesne in 1755* [Pennsylvania Historical Society, *Memoirs*, 5] (1855).

See also BRADDOCK, EDWARD; FORT DUQUESNE (PENNSYLVANIA); GAGE, THOMAS; FORT NECESSITY (PENNSYLVANIA); PACIFICISM; WASHINGTON, GEORGE

Ojibwa

The Ojibwa (or Chippewa in the American usage) played an extremely important role in colonial North America. Ojibwa oral tradition holds that their tribe early separated into three tribes (Ojibwa, Ottawa, and Potawatomi) centered around the northern tip of Michigan's lower peninsula. They formed a loose confederation called "The Three Fires." The Crees of western Canada are also closely related. The Ojibwa consider the area of Ontario around Sault Ste. Marie as their heartland. In summer, large congregations of related kin fished the rapids, gathered wild rice, and cultivated some maize. They participated in the Grand Medicine Society ceremonies and the Shaking Tent performances. In the Feast of the Dead, alliances were renewed. In short, these village activities fostered a tribal unity otherwise not apparent in any obvious tribal political structure. Experts, in fact, debate the question of just how much unity existed, and many scholars argue that the Ojibwa show at best a very loose relationship between quite distinct groups. As far as military expertise goes, the unity question is academic. Relatively large-group interaction led to an enormous increase in territories as a result of spectacular military successes against the Iroquois in the Northeast, the Fox Indians south of Lake Superior, and several plains tribes west and northwest of Lake Superior. Like most Indian groups they were decimated regularly by disease, and yet the Ojibwa population seemingly increased during the nearly two centuries of constant advance. Moreover, intermarriage with the French produced, in time, a large métis population. Their identification with the French and the fur trade guaranteed them a supply of guns. Healthy, numerous, relatively well-armed, and trained in the unforgiving woods north of Lake Superior, the Ojibwa made great soldiers. On the other hand, the Northern Ojibwa, or Saulteaux, who continued to live on the rivers running north into the Hudson and James Bays have avoided completely the warlike label. In addition, the Ojibwa, or Saulteaux, of Lake Winnipeg rather peacefully came to occupy the shores of the inflowing rivers of Lake Winnipeg, lands formerly occupied by the Crees.

The first but relatively unpublicized territorial aggrandizement occurred in the east at the expense of the Five Nations Iroquois. In 1662, the Ojibwa and some allies had annihilated a large Iroquoian war party in Lake Superior. In the 1690s, and after well-executed and fiercely-fought campaigns, the Iroquois were forced out of the lands north of Lakes Erie and Ontario that they themselves had just wrested from the Hurons. By the end of the Iroquois war, the Ojibwa occupied all the area around Georgian Bay and Lake Huron. Eastern Michigan was Ojibwa and western Michigan was Ottawa. While the Iroquois had, not doubt, several reasons for accepting neutrality in 1701, military defeats at the hands of the Missisauga Ojibwa played a major role. George Copway's *Traditional History* is the fullest Ojibwa attempt to sketch the outline of the epic struggle that gave the Southeastern Ojibwa, or Missisauga, possession of the land north of Lake Ontario. Unfortunately, traditional English, French, and American fascination with the Five Nations Iroquois have guaranteed that few readers understand why the winners of the so-called "Beaver Wars" of the pro-English Iroquois were the French and their Indian allies.

By the 1660s, the Ojibwas were also moving southwest of their Sault Ste. Marie bastion. During a lull in the Ojibwa-Dakota confrontation, the Southwestern Ojibwa, or Chippewa, moved in 1680 to La Pointe (Wisconsin) in southwestern Lake Superior. A decade earlier the Dakota had chased the Ottawa Indians and their Jesuit missionary from the area. Separate attacks by the pro-British Fox and Dakota Indians failed to dislodge the Ojibwa from that island. A decade later, the Ojibwa counterattacked by moving south toward the headwaters of the St. Croix and Chippewa Rivers to attack Fox, or Mesquakie, villages. While this movement was part of an official French desire to gain direct access to Dakota hunting territory, the Ojibwa seemed also to be moved by such motives as traditional dislike and the desire to control the wild rice areas. The Ojibwa participated in the French-sponsored Fox War that destroyed the power of the Fox Indians. As late as 1783, some Ojibwa were still pummeling the remaining Fox Indians, this time by forcing them farther south on the Mississippi to the Des Moines River.

After the destruction of the Fox Indians in 1729–1730 by a French-Indian force, the stage was set for a fight between the old allies of the Fox, the Dakota (or Sioux to use an Ojibwa designation), and the Ojibwa. William H. Warren's *History of the Ojibway People* (written in 1852–1853) chronicles the Ojibwa version of this centuries-old struggle. Dakota tradition, on the other hand, minimizes the war and emphasizes Dakota desire to enter fully into the plains culture to the west. The incredibly ferocious anger the Dakota women showed toward Ojibwas in the tales collected in the 1840s by Mary Eastman would indicate that Ojibwa "push" rather than plains "pull" caused the Dakota to leave their ancient homeland. The *Jesuit Relations* for 1640 indicates that some Dakota lived just 18 days west of Sault Ste. Marie. Nevertheless, after the Ojibwa moved west to La Pointe on Chequamegon Bay in 1680, repeated attacks by the Dakota and their Fox ally failed to dislodge the Ojibwas. While some scholars would dismiss such attacks as exceptions to a general Ojibwa-Dakota alliance that was broken only with the French expansion west in the 1730s, the Dakota-Ojibwa relations after the founding of La Pointe seemed to follow that Indian pattern where the two tribal groups were traditional enemies but there were also many periods of uneasy truce and even of alliance.

The Ojibwa-Dakota feud noticeably heated up after the Dakotas forced the closing of Fort Beauharnois on the upper reaches of the Mississippi River near the Chippewa River and destroyed a French party in 1736 on Massacre Island near Fort St. Charles on the Lake of the Woods. This general area around Fort St. Charles controlled both the southern reaches of the Hudson Bay river basin system and the headwaters of the Mississippi River, as well as forming an eastern gate to the plains. Jonathan Carver in 1766 had described this area as one of the "roads of war" of the Dakotas. In the 1740s, the Ojibwas, moving west from Fond du Lac at the extreme western end of Lake Superior, permanently gained control of the upper reaches of the Mississippi, and were moving toward the Red River and the plains. Repeated attacks by the Ojibwa from Fond du Lac also forced the Dakota out of the Mille Lacs area, a region of great religious importance for the tribe. By 1770, the Ojibwa securely occupied all of the northern area of Minnesota. While the Ojibwa suffered many military setbacks, they continued a gradual advance west and southwest at the expense of the Dakota. The last battle between them was in 1858. In the movement west, the Ojibwa also pushed the Hidatsa from the Red River area and continued to raid their later villages on the Missouri River. The Mandan and Arikara Indians of that region were also attacked. The Cheyenne were expelled from eastern North Dakota.

Another route west for Ojibwa penetration was from the Grand Portage-Thunder Bay area, up the river system to Lake of the Woods. Some Ojibwa then moved west to the plains. Ojibwa were by the end of the eighteenth century ranging far out into the plains, both north and south of the international boundary, even though at first their lack of horses left them at the mercy of the equestrian Dakota. As they moved into the Canadian and American plains regions in Saskatchewan and northern north Dakota, these Plains-Ojibwa (or Bungi), began to adapt quickly the typical plains Indian culture. Plains-Ojibwa maintained generally favorable relations with two traditional enemies of the Dakota, the Plains-Cree (who are enthnically related) and the Assiniboin, a break-away Sioux tribe. Other Ojibwa moved northwest to the Lake Winnipeg region. These Ojibwa (along with the Cree and Assiniboine) in the period before the American Revolution returned to the Lake Superior route much of the fur trade that had been going to the English merchants at the various entrepôts on Hudson Bay.

In the eighteenth century French-English confrontations in the Northeast, the various Ojibwa tribes often played various roles, mostly unimportant. In 1757, however, 160 Ojibwa from as far west as La Pointe were fighting with the French at Ticonderoga against the English. Ojibwa fought in 1759 when Quebec fell to General James Wolfe's forces. The Ojibwa predominantly participated in Pontiac's 1763 "rebellion" against the English. Indeed, the most dramatic event of that uprising was the Ojibwa capture of Michilimackinac by a ruse. Not surprisingly, Ojibwa helped destroy the Peoria Indians after one of them killed Pontiac.

Leroy V. Eid

References

George Copway, *The Traditional History and Characteristic Sketches of the Ojibway Nation* (1850); James H. Howard, *The Plains-Ojibwa or Bungi: Hunters and Warriors of the Northern Prairies* (1977); Harold Hickerson, *The Chippewa & Their Neighbors: A Study in Ethnohistory* (1989); William W. Warren, *History of the Ojibway People* (1885).

See also FORT BEAUHARNOIS (MINNESOTA); FOX; FORT LA POINTE (WISCONSIN); FORT MICHILIMACKINAC (MICHIGAN); OJIBWA-DAKOTA CONFLICT; OTTAWA; PONTIAC'S WAR; FORT ST. CHARLES (MINNESOTA)

O

Ojibwa-Dakota Conflict

For at least a couple of centuries, these two large North American Indian groups (and their allies) fought over control of northern Wisconsin-Minnesota-North Dakota. While some scholars believe that the Ojibwa and Dakota were generally at peace before French traders stirred them up in the 1730s, Ojibwa, or Chippewa, tradition alleges that a general hostility with the Dakotas started much earlier at Sault Ste. Marie. By 1680, the relatively well-armed Ojibwa had moved to La Pointe (Wisconsin) in Chequamegon Bay in southwestern Lake Superior. Attacks by Dakota and their Fox allies failed to dislodge the Ojibwa from this strategic island stronghold.

After the 1729–1730 destruction of the Fox Indians by the French and allied Indians from a number of tribes, the Ojibwa moved west against the Dakota in two tracks. The Minnesota arm of the westward-moving Ojibwas gradually edged the Dakota (or Sioux) and their Cheyenne ally on to the plains. A second arm moved northwest along the river route from the Grand Portage on northwest Lake Superior to the Winnipeg area via the Lake of the Woods. After the Dakotas destroyed a French party in 1736 near Fort St. Charles on the Lake of the Woods, the Ojibwas mounted fierce counteroffensives south and west from the Lake of the Woods area and west and southwest from the Duluth region. By the 1740s, they had gained a precarious control of the ancient Dakota heartland (Mille Lacs area) in the eastern portion of Minnesota. A generation later, there was not a Dakota village east of the Mississippi River. By then, the Ojibwas had also gained control of all the northern branches of the Mississippi River and thus were able to move due west to the plains. The second arm of the Ojibwa westward movement also headed north from Grand Portage to Winnipeg. By the end of the eighteenth century, some of these Ojibwa were allied in Canada with the Plains Cree and Assiniboin (a detached group of Siouian people) in raiding the Dakota and their allies along the international border. In time, large numbers of Plains Ojibwa, or Bungi, roamed the plains even in Saskatchewan and Alberta as they continue to clash with the northern branch of the Dakotas.

Leroy V. Eid

References

Gary C. Anderson, "Early Dakota Migration and Intertribal War: A Revision," *Western Historical Quarterly* 11 (1980): 17–36; Harold Hickerson, *The Chippewa & Their Neighbors: A Study in Ethnohistory* (1989); Helen H. Tanner, *Atlas of Great Lakes Indian History* (1987); William W. Warren, *History of the Ojibway People* (1885).

See also FOX; OJIBWA; FORT ST. CHARLES (MINNESOTA)

Old Fort Niagara (New York)
See FORT CONTI (NEW YORK)

Old Shawnee Town
Located at the mouth of the Scioto River, a tributary of the Ohio, this was the first major Shawnee village west of Pennsylvania near the Ohio River. It was founded in 1731 by Shawnee Indians from the Cumberland region. Later, many Shawnee from Pennsylvania traveled there. Its location on the Ohio River and the Great Warrior Path made it an ideal area for trade. It was a favorite rendezvous location for the Shawnee and a trading area for the British and French. In 1749 the village contained approximately 80 to 100 dwellings. However, in 1753, it was destroyed by a flood, and the Indians moved to higher ground.

Michael W. Nagle

References

Lawrence Henry Gipson, *The British Empire Before the American Revolution, Vol. IV: Zones of International Friction* (1939).

See also SHAWNEE

Oñate, Juan de (1552–1625)
Juan de Oñate was the first governor and colonizer of New Mexico. In 1598, he led a group of about 500 persons and 80 wagons loaded with provisions, plus 7,000 head of livestock he had purchased with his own funds, north of the vicinity of Santa Barbara, the northernmost frontier outpost in Mexico. By May, the caravan had forded the Rio Grande at El Paso and was crawling onward in the river valley toward the first Indian village, or pueblo. Two months later, after having traversed the heart of New Mexico, where he estimated 60,000 natives lived, he arrived at Okhe Pueblo, located in the Española Valley. Oñate chose this site as the first capital of the colony and christened it San Juan. He had lengthened the Spanish Royal Highway by more than 600 miles.

From San Juan, Oñate went to visit and conquer all the known pueblos. He also led two important expeditions, one in 1601 to the legendary Quivira, located about 600 miles from the Rio Grande in south-central Kansas, and another in 1604–1605 to the Gulf of California. On August 1607, Oñate renounced his office as a result of the great expense he incurred in sustaining the colony. He returned to Mexico where he was accused of mismanagement and abuse of power and condemned to exile from New Mexico. For the rest of his life he fought to clear his name of any fault and finally succeeded before his death. He had married Doña Isabel de Tolosa, granddaughter of Hernán Cortés, the Aztec conqueror, and great-granddaughter of Montezuma, the Aztec ruler.

Jose Ignacio Avallaneda

References

George P. Hammond, *Don Juan de Oñate and the Founding of New Mexico* (1927); Marc Simon, *The Last Conquistador: Juan de Oñate and the Settling of the Far Southwest* (1991).

See also CALIFORNIA; NEW MEXICO

Oneida
The Oneidas were a member of New York's famed Iroquois Confederacy. The five nations comprising the league were (from west to east) the Senecas, Cayugas, Onondagas, Oneidas, and Mohawks. The Senecas were designated the confederacy's "Keepers of the Western Door." The Mohawks were the "Keepers of the Eastern Door." The Onondagas, living at the geographic center, became the "Keepers of the Fire," responsible for hosting league council meetings and maintaining confederacy wampum records. The Oneidas and Cayugas were known as the "Younger Brothers" of the League.

The Oneidas lived in east central New York, around Oneida Creek, which flows into

Oneida Lake. Their homeland included the region around Wood Creek and the upper Mohawk Valley. Their hunting territory extended northward to the St. Lawrence and south to the Susquehanna. Like other Iroquois tribes, Oneida hunters also ranged far into the Great Lakes country in search of furs.

For most of the seventeenth and eighteenth centuries, the Oneidas had one principal village. In 1677, the stockaded town had about 100 longhouses. By the mid-1700s, the village was no longer palisaded, and cabins, housing one or two families, had replaced the traditional multi-family dwellings.

The Oneidas were one of the smaller Iroquois tribes. Their warrior population probably never exceeded 250 men, while their total population was generally estimated to be no more than 1,500 people. In the 1700s, the Oneidas welcomed several immigrant tribes onto their lands, including the Tuscarora from the Carolinas and various Algonquin bands from New England.

Like other members of the Iroquois Confederacy, the Oneidas followed league policy only when it was to their advantage. The Oneidas were as determined to maintain their independence from fellow confederates as they were from other Indian and white neighbors. As a result, the Oneidas often played the Onondagas and Mohawks against each other, cooperating with the other Iroquois only when it was beneficial.

Oneida warriors accompanied Iroquois war parties westward in the 1640s and 1650s to wrest control of the fur trade away from the French and Great Lakes tribes like the Hurons, Petuns, Neutrals, and Eries. In 1653, the Oneidas followed the lead of the Onondagas, Senecas, and Cayugas and made peace with the French, despite objections by the Mohawks. They even allowed Jesuits to establish a mission in their village in 1668.

When French and western Indians threatened to take control of the fur trade of the upper Great Lakes country in the 1670s, the Oneidas joined the Iroquois Confederacy's war in the west. Like other Iroquois, the Oneidas suffered great losses as the fighting escalated into King William's War. In 1696, a French army even swooped down on Iroquoia, destroying the Oneidas' village and cornfields. By 1701, the Oneidas and their fellow confederates had had enough. They agreed to a peace settlement with the French and western tribes.

For the next half-century, the Oneidas usually followed the Iroquois Confederacy's official policies regarding the English, French, and neighboring Indian tribes. Like other Iroquois, the Oneidas generally remained neutral in the colonial wars between England and France (although individual warriors did fight alongside the English in each war); they maintained peace with the tribes of the Great Lakes country; and they followed a policy of war against tribes of the south. These strategies allowed the Oneidas and the rest of the Iroquois to achieve economic, political, and military advantages from both their Indian and white neighbors.

The Oneidas' geographic location enabled them to develop especially strong ties to the English. Their proximity to Albany gave them access to Dutch (and later English) trade goods. And by the mid-1700s, the Oneidas had close diplomatic ties to English governments in New York and Pennsylvania. In 1767, Samuel Kirkland, a Presbyterian "New Light" minister, established a mission among the Oneidas. His brand of individualistic fundamentalism appealed to the Oneida warrior faction, intent on challenging the more traditional Iroquois sachems.

By the late 1760s and early 1770s, Oneida loyalties were divided between Kirkland, the colonial preacher, and William Johnson, the British superintendent of Indian affairs and long-time ally of the confederacy. During the American Revolution, this contest became a multi-faceted struggle between Calvinism and Anglicanism; revolutionary forces and loyalist forces; and warriors and sachems. Many pro-American Oneida warriors eventually wound up fighting alongside the rebels, while other factions within the confederacy joined the British. The American Revolution became a civil war for the Oneidas and for the Iroquois Confederacy.

Richard Aquila

References
Richard Aquila, *The Iroquois Restoration: Iroquois Diplomacy on the Colonial Frontier, 1701–1754* (1983); Jack Campisi and Laurence M. Hauptman, eds., *The Oneida Indian Experience: Two Perspectives* (1988); Barbara Graymont, *The Iroquois in the American Revolution* (1972); Francis Jennings, *The Ambiguous Iroquois Empire: The Covenant Chain Confederation of Indian Tribes with English Colonies from its beginnings to the Lancaster Treaty of 1744*

(1984); Allen W. Trelease, *Indian Affairs in Colonial New York: The Seventeenth Century* (1960).

See also IROQUOIS; IROQUOIS WARS; JESUITS; JOHNSON, WILLIAM

Onondaga

The Onondagas, a member of the Five Nations Iroquois Confederacy, lived in the region between Cazenovia Creek and Onondaga Creek (near present-day Syracuse, New York). Their main hunting territory included all of Onondaga County, north to Lake Ontario, and south to Chenango Forks.

By the 1600s, the Onondagas had two villages—a principal one that served as the "capital" of the confederacy, and a smaller one about two miles away. An observer in 1677 noted that the large village contained approximately 140 houses (each probably occupied by one or two families), while the smaller one had about 24 houses. At that time, their warrior population numbered about 350. By 1763, their ranks had dwindled to 150 warriors due to disease, warfare, and migration.

The Onondagas lived in the heart of Iroquois country. To their west resided the Cayugas and Senecas; to their east the Oneidas and Mohawks. Their central location allowed the Onondagas to play an important geographic and political role in confederacy matters. The Onondagas were designated the "Keepers of the Fire." As such, they were responsible for convening league council meetings and maintaining wampum records.

For most of the seventeenth and early eighteenth centuries, Onondaga policies were determined by the need for security and a role in the fur trade. Whenever Onondaga interests matched those of their fellow league members, the tribe contributed to the united action of the Iroquois Confederacy. On other occasions the Onondagas acted independently to guarantee individual tribal goals.

The Onondagas understood the differing interests of the various Iroquois tribes, and they were determined not to become pawns of either the confederacy or individual members. Not wanting to be controlled by the Mohawks with their Albany connection or the Senecas with their access to the western fur trade, the Onondagas frequently played the two tribes against each other.

The Onondagas also sought independence from both the French and English. The Onondagas' easy access to Canada via Lake Ontario or Lake Champlain coupled with their proximity to Albany enabled them to deal with both sides.

The Onondagas' diplomatic balancing act proved successful throughout most of the seventeenth and early eighteenth centuries. In the early 1600s, when all five Iroquois nations were struggling for a share of the western fur trade, the Onondagas found it convenient to join the league warfare against the French and their Indian allies of the Ohio country. But, as soon as the Onondagas realized most of their goals, they quickly abandoned the war effort, despite protests from the Mohawks.

In 1653, Onondaga leaders, accompanied by representatives from the Cayugas and Onondagas, journeyed to Canada for peace talks with New France. After that date, the Onondagas were divided into pro-French and anti-French factions, whose influence ebbed and flowed depending upon internal and external circumstances. By the mid-1650s, French missionaries were living among the Onondagas. During times of crisis, they retreated to Canada, and then returned when peace resumed. In the 1750s, numerous Onondagas moved northward to settle at La Présentation (or Oswegatchie), the mission established in 1749 on the site of present-day Ogdensburg, New York, by the Sulpician missionary, Abbe François Picquet. The mission's great success led William Johnson to remark in 1754 that one-half of the Onondagas now lived at Oswegatchie.

The Onondagas' ties to the French did not interfere with their friendly relations with the English. Like the rest of the Iroquois Confederacy, the Onondagas tried to maintain neutrality between the English and French after 1701. This diplomatic stance allowed the Onondagas and fellow confederates to officially sit out most of the eighteenth-century colonial wars, although individual warriors from each tribe did sometimes accompany English and French armies. The policy of neutrality allowed the Indians to play the two European powers off against each other, providing political, military, and economic benefits for the Iroquois.

The Onondagas' relations with neighboring Indian tribes usually followed those of the confederacy as a whole. In order to win hunting and trading privileges in the upper Great Lakes country, the Onondagas joined in the confederacy's "Beaver Wars" against the Hurons, Neutrals, Eries, and other western tribes in the mid-seventeenth century. After 1701, the Onondagas, along with the rest of the confederacy, switched to a policy of peace with the western tribes as the best means to guarantee economic and political interests. During the seventeenth and eighteenth centuries, the Onondagas also took part in the Iroquois' southern wars against the Susquehannocks and other tribes, which were waged for economic, political, and social reasons.

The Onondaga played an extremely important role on the colonial American frontier. As a member of the Iroquois Confederacy, they greatly influenced economic, political, social, and military developments in colonial America. The Onondagas' location and tribal importance placed them at the center of intrigue for Indian-white diplomacy throughout the 1600s and 1700s.

Richard Aquila

References

Richard Aquila, *The Iroquois Restoration: Iroquois Diplomacy on the Colonial Frontier, 1701–1754* (1983); Michael K. Foster, Jack Campisi, and Marianne Mithun, eds., *Extending the Rafters: Interdisciplinary Approaches to Iroquoian Studies* (1984); Barbara Graymont, *The Iroquois in the American Revolution* (1972); Francis Jennings, *The Ambiguous Iroquois Empire: The Covenant Chain Confederation of Indian Tribes with English Colonies from its beginnings to the Lancaster Treaty of 1744* (1984); Daniel K. Richter and James H. Merrell, eds., *Beyond the Covenant Chain: The Iroquois and Their Neighbors in Indian North America, 1600–1800* (1987).

See also DECANISORA; IROQUOIS; IROQUOIS WARS; FORT LA PRÉSENTATION (NEW YORK)

Fort Ontario (New York; also known as East Fort, Fort of the Six Nations)

Fort Ontario was part of the Oswego fort system originally ordered built by Governor William Burnet in 1728. The first fort, Fort Oswego on the shore of Lake Ontario, was for protection against increasing Indian attacks. The site was strategically located at the end of the Mohawk Valley-Wood Creek-Lake Oneida-Oswego River route leading from the Hudson

Valley at Albany. During the French and Indian War, General William Shirley ordered two more forts built to strengthen his Lake Ontario base, and to stop French encroachment. The new stockaded blockhouse on the east bank of the Oswego River, overlooking its junction with Lake Ontario, was named Fort Ontario. The other two forts, Oswego and George, were located on the west bank of the Oswego.

In August 1756, the French, led by General Louis-Joseph de Montcalm, laid siege to the Oswego forts. By 10 August, Fort Ontario had to be abandoned, and the British troops retreated to Fort Oswego. The French took control of Fort Ontario, training their guns on the two other forts. On 14 August those forts surrendered as well, leaving Lake Ontario entirely in French control.

In 1759, the British built on the original Fort Ontario site a new pentagonal fort with a corner bastion, regarrisoned it and later used it as a base for Tory raids into New York and for the capture of Forts Niagara and Montreal. The British abandoned the fort in 1777, but reoccupied it in 1782, remaining until 1796, when the concessions stated in the Jay Treaty forced them out.

The site was not active again until the United States occupied it in 1813, 1838–1844, and again in 1863. The fort was later converted to a training post in 1903–1905, a general hospital in World War I, and a training camp in World War II.

Elizabeth Gossman

References

Mark Boatner, *Landmarks of the American Revolution* (1973); T. Wood Clarke, *The Bloody Mohawk* (1940); James Thomas Flexner, *Mohawk Baronet: Sir William Johnson of New York* (1959); Robert West Howard, *Thundergate: The Forts of Niagara* (1968); Michael Kammen, *Colonial New York: A History* (1975); Howard Peckham, *The Colonial Wars, 1689–1762* (1964).

See also LAKE ONTARIO; OSWEGO, BATTLE OF; FORT OSWEGO (NEW YORK); SHIRLEY, WILLIAM

Opechancanough (c. 1575–1646)

Opechancanough, the "King of the Pamunkeys," as Captain John Smith referred to him, was a powerful leader of native tribes in the Chesapeake region during the early period of the Virginia settlement. The werowance, or chieftain, of the Pamunkey Indians at the time of the establishment of Jamestown, he was the subject of his half-brother, Powhatan, leader of a confederation of tribes. Nevertheless, Captain John Smith and other leaders of Virginia believed that Powhatan placed special confidence in Opechancanough, entrusting him to treat with the English. In 1617, when Powhatan moved to the Potomac, he left the government in the James River sector to Opechancanough. The only surviving English description of this remarkable Native American leader portrayed him as a large, handsome man of noble bearing.

Soon after the death of Powhatan in 1619, Opechancanough succeeded as the paramount leader of the Indian confederacy, a position he was to hold for a quarter-century. He swiftly pursued a quite different course from that of his predecessor. Certain that the Virginia colony was not about to disappear, and confronted by the settlers' steady encroachment on the traditional hunting lands of his people, Opechancanough ordered a surprise attack on the English settlements in march 1622. It was a desperate move undertaken in the hope of completely eradicating the colony; his gamble nearly succeeded. Many of the nearly 80 English settlements along the James River were taken by surprise. Only a week before Opechancanough had assured the governor of Virginia that "the Skye should sooner fall than Peace be broken." Moreover, the London company that operated the Virginia colony had recently boasted of a "perpetuall league" of peace with Opechancanough. In this atmosphere of trust and apparent accord, few settlers any longer carried arms. The "Virginia Massacre," therefore, was a devastating blow, resulting in the death of approximately one-quarter of the settlers, including six councilors. At least three outlying settlements were abandoned in the wake of the assault.

The colonists immediately struck back, sending armed units into the countryside to kill the natives and destroy their crops. A search was mounted for Opechancanough and a reward was offered for his capture, but he eluded his hunters. His people paid dearly for their attack, however, and within a year, faced with starvation and a heavy casualty toll, Opechancanough was forced to ask the Virginia authorities for peace.

Despite this setback, Opechancanough remained in command of the Indian confederation for another generation, until 1644 when, an old and feeble man, he ordered still another surprise attack against the inhabitants of the English colony. This attack, like the first, stemmed from the unrelenting pressure placed on the Indians by the land-hungry settlers. In addition, Opechancanough may have been influenced to act on learning of the English civil war; the governor of Virginia, William Berkeley, subsequently stated that Opechancanough had acted in 1644 because he presumed that the settlers would be unable to receive assistance from a distracted parent state. The immediate catalyst of the attack, however, likely was the killing of the "Chief Captain" of the Pamunkeys, slain by the English in retaliation for his murder of a settler. Opechancanough's blow—the "Virginia Massacre of 1644"—resulted in a heavier casualty toll than his previous attack, although a far smaller percentage of the colonists perished. Approximately 500 of Virginia's 8,000 residents died in the assault.

Ultimately, however, the principal losers were the Indians, including Opechancanough. In the aftermath of his attack, "that bloody Monster," as the Virginians called him, was tracked down and taken captive. He was murdered by a Virginia soldier while a prisoner in Jamestown.

John E. Ferling

References
Wesley F. Craven, *The Southern Colonies in the Seventeenth Century, 1607–1689* (1949); ———, *White, Red, and Black: The Seventeenth-Century Virginian* (1971); Ben C. McCary, *Indians in Seventeenth-Century Virginia* (1957); Richard Morton, *Colonial Virginia*, 2 vols (1960); William L. Shea, *The Virginia Militia in the Seventeenth Century* (1983).

See also PAMUNKEY; POWHATAN; VIRGINIA-INDIAN WAR (1622–1632); VIRGINIA-INDIAN WAR (1644–1646)

Fort Oplandt (Delaware)
See FORT SWANENDAEL (DELAWARE)

Fort Orange (New York)
Fort Orange was founded in 1624 by Dutch and Walloon families who were colonizing the upper reaches of the Hudson River valley on behalf of the Dutch West India Company and

Kiliaen van Rensselaer. The fort and colony were located near the site where Henry Hudson had anchored the *Half Moon* in 1609.

Fort Orange was situated so as to take advantage of the beaver and other skins trade and to provide protection for the Dutch and Walloon families who had settled on the edge of New Netherland. The fort was costly to maintain due to the presence of hostile Indians and the flooding of the Hudson River, which necessitated the constant rebuilding of sections of the fort. It consumed a sizable portion of the profits of the trade that it was supposed to encourage.

Fort Orange was constructed of logs and had four bastions. The four or five cannons that were mounted on the walls of the fort were manned by a garrison of 15 to 16 men. Just before Peter Minuit's arrival on the scene in 1626, the commander of Fort Orange, Daniel van Krieckebeeck, was killed along with three of his soldiers while assisting the Mahican Indians in a battle against the Mohawks.

The colony that surrounded the fort prospered with the aide of the company. In 1625, six more families with hogs, sheep, horses, cattle, seed, hay, and agricultural implements arrived. Within a very short time approximately 35 houses were located on the site for the benefit of the colonists. These colonists were followed by others, so that by 1630, there were 200 people present in the colony.

While the colonists were primarily engaged in agriculture and trade with the Indians, a not so insignificant brick industry developed. The colonists engaged in this activity provided bricks for local construction and at one point sold 3,000 bricks to a builder in New Amsterdam. In 1664, Fort Orange surrendered to the English and became known as Albany.

Anthony P. Inguanzo

References
Charles M. Andrews, *The Colonial Period of American History: The Settlements III* (1937); Oliver Perry Chitwood, *A History of Colonial America* (1961); J.F. Jameson, ed., *Narratives of New Netherland, 1609–1664* (1909); Michael Kammen, *Colonial New York: A History* (1975); Arthur M. Schlesinger, ed., *The Almanac of American History* (1983).

See also ALBANY; MINUIT, PETER; MOHAWK-MAHICAN WAR; NEW NETHERLAND

Fort Orleans (Missouri)

Built by the French in 1723 in the Missouri River, Fort Orleans was established to secure good relations and trade with the Missouri Indians and as a base from which to seek cooper deposits rumored to be in the area. Lacking labor and necessary materials, the fort was crudely constructed and may never have been finished. The interior buildings were made of stakes and mud with roofs of turf or straw. Jean-Baptiste Le Moyne de Bienville described it as a "little Palisaded fort." Etienne de Vénieard de Bourgmont oversaw construction and used the fort as a base from which to conduct relations with tribes of the Missouri River valley. Bourgmont's efforts were generally successful, if short-lived, in promoting French interests. He left the fort in late 1724 to escort a delegation of the region's Indians to France, and the fort was finally abandoned in early 1729.

Alan Gallay

References
Marcel Giraud, *A History of French Louisiana, Vol. V: The Company of the Indies, 1723–1731*, trans. by Brian Pearce (1987).

Orontony (?–1750)

Orontony (baptismal name Nicholas) was a Wyandot chief in the Ohio Valley. He first emerged on the historical scene in the late 1730s and rose to prominence as a leader of a 1747 intertribal uprising against the French. He was instrumental in a major eighteenth-century realignment of both native village and imperial politics in the region.

The Indians known to the English as Wyandot were a remnant of the descendants of Petuns and Hurons who had fled to the upper Great Lakes after being defeated by the Iroquois in Ontario in the mid-seventeenth century. By 1671, they had settled in Michilimackinac, were embroiled in the English-French dispute over control of the fur trade, and had developed close ties to the Jesuits. When Antoine Laumet de Lamothe Cadillac established Detroit in 1701, they moved south, over Jesuit objections, to the new trading center and built a village near Fort Pontchartrain de Detroit. With this move the Huron-Petuns began hunting south of Lake Erie in the Ohio River valley. In 1728, they moved their village to Bois Blanc Island on the south side of the Detroit

River. The Jesuits transferred their mission to this new location also.

By 1738, amid growing tension with their Ottawa neighbors, the Huron-Petun chiefs asked the French for assistance to resettle near Montreal. Two years earlier, the Hurons had made a treaty with the Catawbas, an enemy of the Ottawas, and were now afraid that if the Catawbas attacked the Ottawas, they would be accused of conspiracy in the attack. At this time Orontony emerged as a pivotal figure in village politics. He was chosen by the older leaders to represent the tribe in negotiations with the French. In arguing for assistance, Orontony stressed that he was proud that the Hurons had never shed French blood. During these negotiations, a minor, non-Christian Huron chief led his followers away from Detroit and settled them on the south side of Lake Erie, near Sandusky. By 1742, the Huron-Petuns were hopelessly divided. Orontony became disillusioned with the inadequacy of the French response, broke with the older chiefs who still favored a move to Ontario, and led his followers to Sandusky to join the earlier Wyandots. Orontony emerged as their leader.

Within months, he began to establish cordial relations with the English and to break with the French. In 1745, he allowed English traders from Pennsylvania to build a large blockhouse in the marshes of the main Wyandot village. In 1747, when five French traders came to Sandusky without Orontony's consent, he condemned them to death and had one of the scalps sent to Pennsylvania. These actions both challenged the established Huron elders who remained loyal to the French and catapulted the Wyandots into the midst of the growing imperial conflict.

By August, Orontony had gathered a wide range of Indian allies, including the Ottawas and the Miamis, into a rebellion against the French. This uprising failed when a Detroit Huron woman warned the Jesuits. Orontony was able to secure pardons from the French for himself and his Wyandot followers in the rebellion, but refused to return to the French fold.

During the following winter, Orontony welcomed two parties of Pennsylvanians into his village, where a large band of Ottawas were living with the Wyandots. In February 1748, the governor of Canada sent a messenger to Sandusky to notify Orontony that no English traders were to be allowed among his people. Orontony's response in April was to destroy the villages and blockhouse at Sandusky Bay and lead 119 warriors and their families southeast into the Ohio country, closer to the British traders. Approximately 90 of his followers settled at the forks of the Muskingum River, while Orontony and the remainder continued on to Kuskuskies on the Beaver River where he died in 1750.

Kathryn L. Utter

References

Lawrence Henry Gipson, *The British Empire Before the American Revolution: Zones of International Friction; North America, South of the Great Lakes Region, 1748–1754* (1939); Alfred T. Goodman, ed., *Journal of Captain William Trent from Logstown to Pickawillany* (1871); Charles A. Hanna, *The Wilderness Trail: Or the Ventures and Adventures of the Pennsylvania Traders in the Allegheny Path*, Vol. Two (1911); Reuben G. Thwaites, ed., *Collections of the State Historical Society of Wisconsin*, Vol. XVII (1908); Richard White, *The Middle Ground: Indians, Empires, and Republics in the Great Lakes Region, 1650–1815* (1991).

See also CATAWBA; HURON; JESUITS; FORT SANDUSKY (OHIO); FORT PONCHARTRAIN DE DETROIT (MICHIGAN); UPRISING OF 1747

Osage

Once the Osage made contact with Jacques Marquette and Louis Jolliet in 1673, the French quickly discovered their importance to the region of the lower Missouri River. The tribe numbered at least 6,200 members at contact, and perhaps as many as 12,000, but it suffered a population loss after contact. Carl Haley Chapman delineated their lands as eventually encompassing the area "between the Missouri River on the north, the Mississippi on the east, the Arkansas on the south and the branches of the Kansas River on the west." Early in the eighteenth century the tribe split into two politically distinct tribes, the Little Osage and the Big Osage. The Little Osage then began a long and close relationship with the Missouri Indians, first on the Missouri River, and then farther west near present-day Kansas City. To the south, the Big Osage maintained a village on the Osage River during the French colonial period.

A desire for trade goods induced the Osage to procure furs for the French, but Osage-French relations were often strained by Osage violence directed against Frenchmen and neighboring Indians. The violence included horse stealing, raids, robberies, and mourning-war ceremonies (raids motivated by the death of an Osage, satisfied only with the death of the first non-Osage encountered). Although the French needed the Osage as allies because of the tribe's strategic location, the Indians lived far enough from French posts that the Europeans had little chance of controlling them. The French thought of the Osage as allies, however, even if associations were strained at times. An aggressive people, the Osage fought both the friends and enemies of France, as well as their own enemies. Allied with the French during the French and Indian War, English victory meant that the Osage would have to adjust to vastly changed circumstances in their relations with neighboring peoples.

Raymond E. Hauser

References

Carl Haley Chapman, *The Origin of the Osage Indian Tribe; an Ethnographical, Historical, and Archaeological Study* (1971); Gilbert C. Din and A.P. Nasatir, *The Imperial Osages* (1983); John R. Swanton, "Osage," in *Handbook of American Indians North of Mexico*, Frederick Webb Hodge, ed. (1968) II:156–158; ———, *The Indian Tribes of North America* (1952); Robert P. Wiegers, "A Proposal for Indian Slave Trading in the Mississippi Valley and Its Impact on the Osage," *Plains Anthropologist* XXXIII (1988):187–202.

Oswego, Battle of (1756)

From its first establishment by the New Yorkers in 1727, Oswego, or Chouaguen as the French called it, had been a threat to French control of the Lake Ontario fur trade and to New France's ties with the Iroquois Six Nations. Albany area merchants and traders capitalized on the trading post's position at the entry of the Oswego River into Lake Ontario to divert Indian furs from the French at Frontenac or Niagara. This trade, and a special relationship with the Iroquois, was particularly beneficial to William Johnson. With the outbreak of hostilities between France and England in 1755, Oswego took on significant military importance as well.

To the governor of New France, Pierre de Rigaud de Vaudreuil, the Anglo-American control of Chouaguen could disrupt lines of communication with the Great Lakes Indian allies and with the French forces and posts further into the interior. To the governor of Massachusetts, William Shirley, Oswego was the vital base from which his proposed 1755 attack on the French at Niagara would be launched. Vaudreuil's plans to attack Oswego in 1755 had to be postponed in order to meet the threat posed by William Johnson's forces in the Lake Champlain area. Meanwhile William Shirley's army, in the spring and summer of 1755, found simply getting to Oswego difficult enough, let alone launching a major offensive. Throughout May, June, and July, Oswego was reinforced, fortifications were strengthened, and boats were constructed, but Shirley and the major portion of his army only arrived on Lake Ontario in mid-August. By late September, in the face of inclement weather and rumors concerning substantial French reinforcements at Niagara, Shirley decided not to strike at Niagara but proposed to make an attack on Fort Frontenac his first priority in a spring campaign. He left Oswego under the command of Lieutenant Colonel James Mercer and withdrew for the winter to face heavy criticism of his military performance, or nonperformance.

The fortifications of Fort Ontario, immediately east of the Oswego River, and Forts George and Oswego, just to the west of the river, were still extremely weak, and the winter took its toll on the garrison's provisions and morale. Rations had to be cut in half, and the forts were constantly on alert for possible attack. Shirley recognized the vulnerability of Oswego and ordered John Bradstreet on 17 March 1756, to take command of all aspects of the transportation of men and provisions from Albany to Oswego. Despite enemy harassment, Bradstreet did lead substantial *bateaux* convoys through in mid-May and early July, but the garrison remained in an extremely precarious position.

Meanwhile, rumors circulated concerning Shirley's replacement as commander of the British forces, and a leadership vacuum emerged as Lord Loudoun's assumption of the command took time to implement. Admittedly, one of Loudoun's subordinates, General James Abercromby, did take over from Shirley in late June of 1756, but a hesitant uncertainty prevailed. No such uncertainty existed on the French side, as Vaudreuil dispatched raiding parties to threaten Oswego's supply lines and then ordered the newly arrived Louis-Joseph de Montcalm to lead a force massing at Fort Frontenac, on the north side of Lake Ontario, in a major expedition against Oswego. Montcalm first appeared at Fort Carillon (Ticonderoga) to mislead the Anglo-Americans as to where the major French thrust would come, but by 29 July he had joined the 3,000-man force assembled at Frontenac for a strike across Lake Ontario. On the English side, Bradstreet's warnings, among others, about the French designs on Oswego did help in a 16 July 1756, council of war decision to send a regiment to reinforce and relieve Oswego. Almost a month later when the outpost fell, however, the regiment had moved only approximately 70 miles from Albany and was still more than 100 miles from Oswego.

By 10 August 1756, Montcalm had moved his force and 80 cannon across Lake Ontario and was a mile and one-half from the Anglo-American positions before they became aware of his presence. As the French began siege preparations, Fort Ontario was evacuated by the British on 13 August. New batteries were constructed and soon opened fire on the main Anglo-American positions, killing Mercer on 14 August. On the same day, his successor, John Littehales, surrendered to Montcalm. The French took 1,700 prisoners, largely comprising Shirley's and William Pepperrell's regiments, six armed vessels, approximately 100 pieces of artillery, munitions, and supplies, in addition to a substantial war chest. By 21 August 1756, the work of demolition was completed, and the French withdrew, having achieved a significant victory at very little cost. Casualty figures differ, at times substantially, with one claim that the French suffered 30 killed and wounded while the Anglo-Americans lost 150. The situation is further complicated by recent evidence that Montcalm heightened Indian expectations of plunder and was unable to control a resultant "massacre" of some of the captives and nonmilitary personnel.

French control of Lake Ontario was now complete, and the threat to Forts Niagara and Frontenac had been removed. Indian alliances in favor of the French had been shored up. Captured ships, provisions, and other munitions would resurface to be used by the French in later campaigns against the Anglo-American forces. Shirley would be blamed for the disaster, but Loudoun's own command was off to a very disappointing start. The tide of war was definitely running in favor of the French, the

French Canadians, and their Indian allies at this time. Oswego would eventually be revenged, but it would take almost two more years before a British victory on the Great Lakes would undermine the French hold on the region.

William G. Godfrey

References
W.J. Eccles, "Louis-Joseph De Montcalm," in F.G. Halpenny, ed., *Dictionary of Canadian Biography*, 12 vols. (1974) III:458–469; ———, "Pierre de Rigaud de Vaudreuil de Cavagnial," in F.G. Halpenny, ed., *Dictionary of Canadian Biography*, 12 vols. (1979) IV:662–674; W.G. Godfrey, *Pursuit of Profit and Preferment in Colonial North America: John Bradstreet's Quest* (1982); Francis Jennings, *Empire of Fortune: Crowns, Colonies, and Tribes in the Seven Years War in America* (1988); G.F.G. Stanley, *New France: The Last Phase, 1744–1760* (1968).

See also Bradstreet, John; Campbell, John, Lord Loudon; Lake Ontario; Montcalm-Gozon de Saint-Veran, Louis-Joseph; Fort Ontario (New York); Fort Oswego (New York); Pepperell, William Jr.; Shirley, William; Rigaud de Vaudreuil de Cavagnial, Pierre de

Fort Oswego (New York; also known as Chouaguen)

The lone permanent British outpost beyond the Atlantic watershed, Oswego posed both an economic and military threat to the survival of New France. Since 1727, British traders based there had sapped the economic vitality of Canada by providing a convenient alternative market for Amerindians who had traditionally dealt with the French, weakening the economic links binding the Franco-Amerindian alliance system. Moreover, a military presence on the shore of Lake Ontario gave the British the ability to threaten to invade Canada by way of the St. Lawrence and cut the lines of communication between Canada and its western hinterland.

At the time of its construction in 1727, the trading post at Oswego consisted of a stone blockhouse about 17.5 by 8 meters, with walls 1 meter thick. In 1741, this building was surrounded at a distance of 5 meters by a crenellated stone and clay wall 1.3 meters thick and 3.2 meters high, with small projecting towers on the northeast and southeast corners. This wall was armed with three guns firing though loopholes toward the river. Between 1728 and 1744, Oswego was garrisoned by 24 provincials. During the War of the Austrian Succession (1740–1748), this garrison was increased to 43. In December 1754, the garrison was raised to 50.

In 1755, following the outbreak of the Seven Years' War, Oswego became a base for British military operations on Lake Ontario, and expanded from a small commercial outpost into a major military installation. In the center was Fort George, the old trading post, now so dilapidated that it could not be relied on to protect its garrison from the weather, let alone withstand artillery. It was protected on the landward side by an entrenchment and ditch, which was mounted with 28 cannon.

Two new forts were built to hold the high ground that dominated Fort George. To the east was Fort Ontario, a star-shaped stockade, about 88 meters across at its widest point, surrounded by a ditch 6 meters across and 2.5 meters deep. Although constructed of sound timber, it was badly designed and "defenceless against cannon." On the heights to the west was Fort Oswego, a flimsy palisade about 40 meters square, shielded by an entrenchment on the east and south side that was used as a cattle pen. To the south of Fort George lay the "town" of Oswego, a double row of buildings extending southward along the west bank of the Oswego River, and consisting of the traders' and carpenters' houses, and the hospital, bake house, smithy, and shipyard. Although the town itself was not fortified, its approaches were covered by the "Advanced Guard"—a guardhouse protected by an entrenchment.

In August 1756, the garrison consisted of 1,124 provincials, 18 artillerymen, 100 seamen, and two engineers. As well, 138 workers and carpenters, 84 women, and 74 servants were present.

Despite the strengthened fortifications and garrison, Oswego was considered by its officers to be so weak that it "depended wholly for its defence upon a naval force upon the lake, sufficient to prevent the French from bringing artillery against the forts, which could only be done by water carriage." At the time of the siege, however, the British naval forces were still under construction and not yet strong enough to deter the French. Once the French army landed, Oswego fell after a four-day siege on 14 August 1756.

D. Peter MacLeod

References
J.G. Cooper, "Oswego in the French-English Struggle in North America, 1720–1760," Ph.D. Dissertation, Syracuse University (1961); Guy Frégault, *Canada: The War of the Conquest*, trans. by Margaret M. Cameron (1969); D. Peter MacLeod, "The French Campaign of 1756 in the Lake Ontario Theater and the Siege and Capture of Chouaguen," M.A. Thesis, University of Saskatchewan (1985); T.E. Norton, *The Fur Trade in Colonial New York, 1686–1776* (1974); Stanley Pargellis, ed., *Military Affairs in North America, 1748–1675: Selected Documents from the Cumberland Papers in Windsor Castle* (1936); George F.G. Stanley, *New France: The Last Phase, 1744–1760* (1968).

See also FORT BULL (NEW YORK); FORT CANAJOHARIE (NEW YORK); FORT ONTARIO (NEW YORK); OSWEGO, BATTLE OF

Ottawa

The Ottawa Indians, whose name means traders, are of Algonquin stock. In the early seventeenth century, they numbered 5,000 people and were located on Manitoulin Island and the Bruce Peninsula on northern Lake Huron. They had a diversified economy based on fishing, hunting, trading, farming, and gathering wild foods.

They were first visited by Samuel de Champlain in 1615, and with the defeat of the Hurons in the 1640s, the two tribes were forced to migrate westward. After settling in the vicinity of modern Ashland, Wisconsin, for a number of years, they relocated at the Straits of Mackinac where Jacques Marquette, S.J., established a mission for the two tribes. The Ottawa established a number of villages in the vicinity of St. Ignace, Michigan. While some of the Ottawa were Christians and lived near the Jesuit missions, others were not. These traditional Ottawa remained mildly hostile to the French and antagonistic toward the Hurons, who they felt had become too much like the French.

The Ottawa were excellent traders and acted as middlemen between the Hurons and French and western tribes. At times they sought to establish trade with the Iroquois, their former enemies, but were blocked by the French. In 1702, the Huron migrated to Detroit, and although some Ottawa followed them, the majority remained and dominated the Straits of Mackinac. In the 1740s, the French aided the Ottawa in their move to the Traverse Bay area, where conditions were better for farming. Pontiac, who led a rebellion of Great Lakes Indians against the British in 1763, was of Ottawa origin.

By the early nineteenth century the Ottawa were concentrated in Michigan's lower peninsula as far south as Grand Rapids. In 1836, they signed the first of several treaties with the United States government whereby they surrendered their lands for reservations status. During Indian removal, some of the Ottawa were relocated in Oklahoma. Today numbering some 8,000 people, the Ottawa are concentrated in Ontario, Michigan, Wisconsin, and Oklahoma.

Russell M. Magnaghi

References
Joseph H. Cash and Gerald W. Wolf, *The Ottawa People* (1976); Howard H. Peckham, *Pontiac and the Indian Uprising* (1947); David Armour, "Who Remembers La Fourche?" *Chronicle of the Michigan Historical Society* 16 (1980):12–16.

See also DETROIT; HURON; JESUITS; MICHILIMACKINAC; PONTIAC; PONTIAC'S WAR

Oyster River (New Hampshire; also known as Durham)
On 18 July 1694, a force of 300 French-led Penobscots and Norridegwocks assaulted the exposed frontier town of Oyster River. The French and Indians divided initially into two large parties, planning to attack the community from the north and south. The larger parties further divided into small groups of eight to ten in order to hit as many houses simultaneously as possible. However, one inhabitant, out early, was shot and killed by the raiders, and his death afforded a brief warning to some residents, as not all the attackers were in position.

For most in the town, surprise was complete and they died in their homes. The towns had 12 garrisons, and they received particular attention from the raiders. Some withstood attack, others were less prepared. One garrison had the gate flung wide open and only shut it at the last moment. The Adams garrison offered no resistance, and all 14 inside were killed. In the end, 20 buildings were destroyed, 100 inhabitants killed, and 30 captured. As the raiding party left, a group led by the chief, Moxus, broke off to continue the raid, killing a few people around Portsmouth and attacking Groton, Massachusetts.

Oyster River would rebuild, but remained a frontier town, and thus drew the continued attention of the enemy. The town was attacked again on 27 April 1706. In September 1707, ten members of a wood-cutting party were killed, and during Dummer's War there was a brief skirmish on 10 June 1724. None of these were as devastating as the 1694 attack. In addition, as with all frontier towns throughout the French war period, Oyster River suffered numerous small attacks in which isolated individuals were killed by small enemy scouting parties.

Steven C. Eames

References
Jeremy Balknap, *The History of New Hampshire* (1831), rpt. 1970.

See also ABENAKI; DUMMER'S WAR; NEW HAMPSHIRE

P

Pacifism

In the seventeenth and eighteenth centuries, pacifism was practiced only by persons of religious conviction, and its history in North America is found among Protestant sectarians, especially those in Pennsylvania. Pacifists were almost entirely the Quakers, Mennonites, Amish, Schwenkfelders, Church of the Brethren, and Moravians.

Although Pennsylvania and some other American colonies variously offered pacifists relief from military obligations, flight from such obligations in Europe was not the most common motive for sectarian immigration. Religious discrimination and economic hardships more effectively moved them to migrate.

Pacifism was not simply a matter of not fighting; pacifist ethics varied among the denominations, with the Quakers supporting the most restrictive version. Depending on one's affiliation, one might be forbidden or permitted various degrees of complicity with war. The Quakers would do little more than pay taxes to the government to support war. Mennonites and Amish would pay taxes, but would also supply substitutes and pay fines in lieu of each man's personal service in the militia. Moravians would not serve in the public militia or regular army, but would pay substitutes and even organize their own defense (fortifications, armed watch drill with weapons). Some of these scruples emerged ad hoc in America when the particular denomination in question was expected to meet some military threat to a settlement or colony.

The Quakers were extraordinary among the colonial pacifists, for whereas almost all others did not want public office and were forbidden to do more than vote, Quakers ran much of the government of Pennsylvania and became responsible for public policy in peacetime and in war. Other pacifists might rest content with exceptions for fighting or more easily reach accommodation with governments when comparatively little was expected of them; not so the Quakers.

Eighteenth-century governments did not trouble most pacifists as much as later regimes did, when the obligations of democratic citizenship made universal military service more common. Armies were small, professional, and removed from most property-owning citizens' experience. Militia service obligations existed almost everywhere, but impinged far less on a colonist's life than regular army service, and in some localities, militia service was avoidable.

The fortunes of war before 1754 favored colonial pacifists. Earlier, warfare had focused on the borders of New England and New York or the South, where there were few pacifists. Later, where pacifists were common—New Jersey and Pennsylvania through Delaware and Maryland—potential belligerents were remote or already eliminated. Many pacifists also lived in the sheltered eastern counties of these colonies. In the case of Pennsylvania, William Penn's equitable treatment of the indigenous Indians' long delayed conflict with them. The Seven Years' War ended the reprieve.

Before 1755, the Moravians had settled in the South, in communities in Georgia and later North Carolina. Their pacifism combined with Georgia's exposure to attack rendered their community there untenable by 1740, even while their industriousness made them desirable settlers. They removed to Pennsylvania. In North Carolina in the 1750s and beyond, they accommodated themselves to the government's military demands, and they remained and grew. Some Mennonites and Amish lived in Virginia but had little trouble with the colony because they willingly paid fines for non-service. The area east of the Hudson River had no conspicuous pacifist communities other than the Quakers.

The Seven Years' War and Pontiac's War ended the historical respite for pacifists, especially because Pennsylvania became a major theater of war. Almost all the sectarians suffered some casualties, but few took up arms against the Indians or French. Until the Revolutionary War then, few pacifists other than Quakers were troubled by war; America was a refuge.

Jack D. Marietta

See also QUAKER PACIFISM; WAR AND SOCIETY IN COLONIAL AMERICA

Pamunkey

The Pamunkey, an Algonkian-speaking group who inhabited the banks of Virginia's Pamunkey River, were one of the chiefdoms that the paramount leader Powhatan inherited from his parents during the late sixteenth century. In 1608, when Captain John Smith explored the upper reaches of the York River and its tributary, the Pamunkey, he observed that the village of Youghtanund, which had 60 warriors, was located on the Pamunkey's southern bank, whereas Mattapament, which had 30 bowmen, was situated on the opposing shore. Downstream, within the central basin of the York, were other native villages that were subservient to Powhatan. Smith believed that the Indians of the York River basin had an estimated 1,000 fighting men.

Initial interaction between the Pamunkey and the colonists was erratic but relatively cordial, especially after the 1614 marriage of Pocahontas (Powhatan's daughter and a Pamunkey) to an Englishman. But after Opechancanough assumed leadership of the Powhatan chiefdom in c. 1619–1620, relations between the two peoples became increasingly strained. It was during this period that the colony expanded rapidly and Virginia planters moved more deeply into native-occupied territory, clearing land and establishing homesteads. The Pamunkey were the prime actors in the 22 March 1622 Indian uprising, a bloody attempt to drive the European settlers from their soil. At Wolstenholm Town, a plantation on the James River, the Pamunkey captured approximately 20 English women whom they held prisoner for more than a year. Retal-

iatory marches against the Indians eventually reduced their strength and destroyed much of their food supply. In August 1628, Virginia's colonial government made a formal treaty with the Pamunkey, but unilaterally revoked it early in 1629. In October 1632, the colonists executed a new treaty with the Pamunkey and the Chickahominy, but trade and other association with them was prohibited by law.

On 18 April 1644, a second major Indian uprising occurred. Again, the Powhatan chiefdom's paramount leader, Opechancanough, was implicated. Especially hard hit were the settlers who lived at the head of the York River, within the Pamunkey's traditional homeland. In October 1646, after the aging Opechancanough's capture and death, Necotowance (who surviving records suggest was a Pamunkey) signed a treaty with the colonial government whereby the natives under his command became tributaries to the crown. Simultaneously, he ceded to the colonial government all of the James-York peninsula that lay east of the fall line, plus southerly territory that extended to the Blackwater River. By the time the 1646 treaty was signed, Fort Royal, a trading post and fortified military outpost, had been erected deep within Pamunkey territory. In 1649, Necotowance's successor, Totopotomoy, "commander and leeder over the Pymunckee," and two other tribal leaders requested assignment of specific tracts of land for the use of their people. Thus, between 1646 and 1649, the ancient Powhatan chiefdom appears to have disintegrated. In 1652, the Pamunkey were allocated land in the upper reaches of the Pamunkey River, King William County acreage that forms the nucleus of the reservation they still occupy. In 1669, the Pamunkey reportedly had 165 warriors.

Despite the fact that the Pamunkey signed a peace agreement with the English in March 1677, they were attacked by Nathaniel Bacon's rebels shortly thereafter. In May 1677, when the Treaty of Middle Plantation was endorsed by several native groups that inhabited Virginia's coastal plain, Cockacoeske, queen of the Pamunkey and successor to her husband, Totopotomoy, attempted in vain to restore her people to a position of primacy. During the late seventeenth century, Pamunkey leaders, exercising their rights as tributaries, approached Virginia officials in attempts to obtain justice within the framework of the colony's legal system.

During the early eighteenth century the Pamunkey interacted with the Meherrin and

Nottoway as well as the Chickahominy, Mattaponny, Rappahannock, and other Powhatan groups with which they traditionally had been associated. Although the Pamunkey's population gradually dwindled, in 1705 they were credited with 135 warriors and were said to be the strongest of the tribes that once comprised the Powhatan chiefdom. In 1735, Governor William Gooch reported that ten Pamunkey families then lived in the colony.

Martha W. McCartney

References

Charles M. Andrews, *Narratives of the Insurrections, 1675–1690* (1915); Robert Beverley, *History of the Present State of Virginia* (1705), L.B. Wright, ed. (1947); William W. Hening, ed., *The Statutes at Large: Being a Collection of All the Laws of Virginia*, 13 vols. (1809–1823); H.R. McIlwaine, ed., *Minutes of Council and General Court of Colonial Virginia* (1934); Helen C. Rountree, *Pocahontas's People: the Powhatan Indians of Virginia Through Four Centuries* (1990); John Smith, *Travels and Works of Captain John Smith, President of Virginia and Admiral of New England, 1580–1631*, 2 vols., Edward Arber, ed. (1910).

See also BACON'S REBELLION; CHICKAHOMINY; COCKACOESKE; NOTTOWAY; OPECHANCANOUGH; POWHATAN; FORT ROYAL (VIRGINIA); SMITH, JOHN; VIRGINIA-INDIAN TREATY (1646); VIRGINIA-INDIAN TREATY (1677/1680); VIRGINIA-INDIAN WAR (1622–1632); VIRGINIA-INDIAN WAR (1644–1646)

Parade Fort (Connecticut)

Parade Fort was built in New London under orders of the General Court in 1691 and fortified with guns from Fort Saybrook. Parade Fort was destroyed on 6 September 1781 during Benedict Arnold's brutal rampage on New London and Groton at the tail end of the Revolutionary War. The fort was never rebuilt.

Leslie Miller

References

Robert B. Roberts, *Encyclopedia of Historic Forts: The Military, Pioneer, and Trading Posts of the United States* (1988).

Pardo, Juan (?–?)

Juan Pardo led two expeditions to the interior of the United States in 1556 and 1557 from the coastal Spanish settlement of Santa Elena, located on Parris Island, South Carolina. Pardo had arrived in this newly established town as captain of a 250-man force sent by the Spanish king to reinforce a string of settlements intended to shield from French influence the southeastern territory bordered by the Atlantic and the Gulf of Mexico. Pardo's expeditions were intended to explore the country, to evangelize the Indians he encountered, and to find a road to the silver mines of Zacatecas, Mexico.

The first expedition departed from Santa Elena on 1 December 1556 and returned on 7 March of the next year. Accompanied by 125 soldiers, Pardo headed north as far as the Indian town of Joara, or Xuala, located near present-day Marion County, North Carolina. Conqueror Hernando de Soto had visited it in 1540. Pardo erected a fort there that he garrisoned with 30 men before returning to Santa Elena. From September 1567 to March 1568 he led his second expedition. He traversed the same area but made additional explorations as far as Satapo, an Indian village near the junction of the Little Tennessee River and Citico Creek in Tennessee. Even though, of course, he never reached Zacatecas in Mexico, he left behind five temporary forts manned by armed men, most of whom were never to return to Santa Elena.

Jose Ignacio Avallandeda

References

Charles Hudson, *The Juan Pardo Expeditions: Exploration of the Carolinas and Tennessee, 1566–1568* (1990); Eugene Lyon, *The Enterprise of Florida: Pedro Menéndez de Avilés and the Spanish Conquest of 1565–1568* (1976).

See also FORT SAN JUAN (NORTH CAROLINA); SANTA ELENA; SOTO, HERNANDO DE

Paris, Treaty of (1763)

The Treaty of Paris ended the French and Indian War in America and that part of the Seven Years' War in Europe and elsewhere fought between Britain on the one side and France and Spain on the other.

By 1763, the British had thoroughly defeated the French and Spanish, not only in America but also in Europe, India, and Africa. The peace party in England, however, led by the young George III, had been growing in strength since 1760, fearful not only of the growing national debt, but of the tremendous political popularity of the brilliant but vain and domineering prime minister, William Pitt.

In 1761, Pitt resigned when his own coalition government failed to follow his advice to declare war on Spain, which had secretly allied with France. Fortunately for Britain, though, Pitt's military plans continued to be implemented, and the Lord Bute ministry found it necessary in January 1762 to declare war on Spain. Subsequently, British expeditions took Martinique, plus Grenada, St. Lucia, and St. Vincent from France; the British had previously occupied Guadeloupe and Dominica. From Spain, British forces seized Havana in Cuba, Manila, and the Philippines. When the Spanish invaded Portugal, England's ally, British troops forced them to retreat. French Foreign Minister César de Choiseul, who had previously said, "Since we do not know how to make war, we must make peace," was at last truly ready to bring hostilities to an end. George III and Lord Bute were ready to oblige, hoping thereby to prevent the ever-popular Pitt from engineering a return to power.

Treaty negotiations immediately became public and controversial. Pitt insisted that France should surrender not only Canada but also the West Indian islands Britain had conquered. This would have not only humiliated France but left it less than a maritime and colonial power, something César de Choiseul resisted mightily. Lord Bute was less demanding than the uncompromising Pitt. In late 1762, representatives of England, France, and Spain reached tentative agreement on peace terms. France would surrender to Britain Canada and all of New France east of the Mississippi, except for New Orleans and its environs. Thereby, France explicitly renounced its claim to Acadia, Cape Breton Island, and all other islands, in the Gulf and River of St. Lawrence.

In the West Indies, Britain returned Havana to Spain, but Spain had to cede Florida and all possessions east of the Mississippi to the British. France got certain restricted fishing rights in the Gulf of St. Lawrence and off Newfoundland, plus the use of two small islands as fishing stations. In the West Indies, Britain kept Grenada and the Grenadines, but returned to France Martinique, Guadeloupe, plus Desirade, and Marie-Galante. Of the so-called neutral islands, Britain got Dominica, Tobago, and St. Vincent, while St. Lucia went to Spain.

Regarding Europe, Britain and France promised to stop assisting their respective allies. France gave up territory it had captured in Hanover, evacuated certain fortresses belonging to Prussia, promised to demolish its maritime fortress of Dunkirk, and restore Minorca to Britain. For its part, Britain returned Belleisle, off the coast of Brittany. In Africa, France ceded Senegal to Britain, which in turn restored the small Island of Goree. In India, France surrendered all the territory it had gained since the peace of Aix-la Chapelle (1748), regained certain trading stations, but renounced its claim to keeping troops in Bengal.

Although not a part of the Treaty of Paris, several other territorial arrangements sprang from it. France, to compensate Spain for the loss of Florida, signed a secret agreement turning over to its Bourbon ally New Orleans and all French lands west of the Mississippi River. France thus renounced all claims to its once mighty North American empire. Frederick the Great of Prussia, England's great ally in Europe, might well have resented the Treaty of Paris, which ended Britain's subsidy to the Prussia ruler, seemingly facing defeat at the combined hands of Austria and Russia in 1761. However, the death of Empress Elizabeth of Russia in early 1762 led to the ascension of Czar Peter III, an unabashed admirer of King Frederick. The young czar thus changed sides, bringing Sweden along with him, thus allowing Frederick to concentrate his forces against Austria and the German empire. The Treaty of Paris, ratified in February 1763, thus prepared the way for the Peace of Hubertusburg, concluded about the same time, which secured for Prussia its claim to Silesia and status as a great European power.

Ronald W. Howard

References

Lawrence Henry Gipson, *The British Empire Before the American Revolution*, 15 vols., *The Great War for the Empire: The Culmination, 1760–1763*, Vol. 8 (1958–1970); William L. Grant, "Canada Versus Guadeloupe, an Episode of the Seven Years' War," *American Historical Review* 17 (1912):735–743; Francis Parkman, *Montcalm and Wolfe: A Series of Historical Narratives*, 2 vols. (1884).

Jack M. Sosin, *Whitehall and the Wilderness: The Middle West in British Colonial Policy, 1760–1775* (1961); Ian Kenneth Steele, "The European Contest for North America," in *Encyclopedia of the North*

American Colonies, ed. by Jacob Ernest Cooke, 3 vols. (1993), II:271–288; H.W.V. Temperley, "The Peace of Paris," in *The Cambridge History of the British Empire: The Old Empire*, ed. by J. Holland Rose, A.P. Newton, and E.A. Benian (1929), I:485–506.

See also PITT, WILLIAM; SEVEN YEARS' WAR

Passage Fort (South Carolina)

This palisaded structure was built at Bloody Point on Daufuskie Island in December 1717 when one of the two scout boats at Beaufort Fort was ordered to patrol further south on the inside passage. Enclosed on three sides by the present Intracoastal Waterway, the fort was periodically manned by scouts until the scout boat service was terminated in 1764. In early 1728, a Yamasee war party surprised the fort and killed or captured the entire garrison.

Gregory D. Massey

References

Larry E. Ivers, *Colonial Forts of South Carolina 1670–1775* (1970); Robert R. Roberts, *Encyclopedia of Historic Forts: The Military, Pioneer, and Trading Posts of the United States* (1988).

Paxton Boys

Alternately portrayed by eighteenth-century observers as lawless banditti and protectors of hinterland settlers, the Paxton Boys remain perhaps the most famous ruffians in Pennsylvania history. The group, with perhaps up to 250 members, entered the historical record, and the popular imagination, when they murdered 20 Indians in Lancaster county during two raids in December 1763. Soon after, they marched toward Philadelphia, with the intent of killing another 140 Indians then under the protection of the proprietary government, before they halted under threat of violence from hastily organized colonists. The scope of their murderous assault was matched by its misplaced aggression: the Indians they killed were no enemies to the colonists of Pennsylvania, a fact the Paxton Boys either did not care about or ignored. Yet their actions led to a spirited debate about Indian affairs in Pennsylvania, and revealed deep divisions within the colonial population of the province. Benjamin Franklin in particular attacked the group in print; so did others, including an anonymous playwright who wrote a farce about the incident but warned that it would be followed by a tragedy if the Paxton Boys rode again into the capital. Yet while the opponents of the Paxton Boys seemed to win the day, the march made a deep impression on the politics of Pennsylvania, and hastened the decline of Quaker power in the province.

Whatever one's view of the Paxton Boys, their hostility toward the Indians and their march on Philadelphia reflected a split within the colony over Indian affairs. During the French and Indian War, settlers in western Pennsylvania often felt the brunt of Indian attacks; some accounts suggest that hundreds of colonists lost their lives or property. These settlers, many of them Scotch-Irish migrants to Pennsylvania, sought redress from the colonial government for their losses and protection from future incursions. But the proprietary government, long in the hands of the pacifist, eastern Pennsylvania Quakers, refused to provide the western settlers with what they desired, or so the settlers believed. Thus the Paxton Boys took it on themselves to rid the province of the dreaded specter of warring Indians.

The group's hatred of Indians appeared in their testimony. "We humbly conceive that it is contrary to the maxims of good policy," a petition they left in Philadelphia declared, "and extremely dangerous to the frontiers, to suffer any Indians, or what tribe soever, to live within the inhabited parts of this province while we are engaged in an Indian war, as experience has taught us that they are all perfidious, and their claim to freedom and independency puts it in their power to act as spies, to entertain and give intelligence to our enemies, and to furnish them with provisions and warlike stores." To stop the threat they wanted scalp bounties reinstituted, believing this would encourage other colonists to join them in their protection of outlying settlements.

In the end, colonial leaders suppressed the Paxton Boys. Franklin attacked the group's presumption that all Indians constituted a threat to the province; if a man with "a freckled Face and red Hair" murdered a woman or child, he wrote, such an act did not provide justification for revenge to kill "all the freckled red-haired Men, Women and Children, I could afterwards any where meet with." But while the logic of Franklin's point was perhaps patently clear in Philadelphia, the Paxton Boys were not prosecuted for their actions. Since the legal system of Pennsylvania dictated that crimes be tried in the vicinity they were committed, local justice officials and grand juries in western Pennsylvania made little attempt to punish the perpetrators of the murders. Ever wary of hostile Indians on the outer margins of colonial settlements, those responsible for maintaining justice in the backcountry abdicated their responsibility, with disastrous consequences for Indians in Pennsylvania, who suffered from repeated attacks from the mid-1760s until the Revolution. Some of the Paxton Boys, retaining their animosity toward the provincial government of Pennsylvania, even hired themselves out to the Susquehanna Company, a group of Connecticut settlers seeking to establish themselves in northeastern Pennsylvania and in the midst of an ongoing conflict with the proprietary government. Yet it was Indians, ultimately, who suffered most from these self-appointed protectors of backcountry settlers. Emboldened by their apparent judicial immunity, the Paxton Boys, in spite of their blatant disregard for the law, rode off unscathed into the tragic history of Indian-white relations in colonial America.

Peter C. Mancall

References

John Dunbar, ed., *The Paxton Papers* (1975); James Hutson, *Pennsylvania Politics, 1746–1770: The Movement for Royal Government and Its Consequences* (1972); James Kirby Martin, "Return of the Paxton Boys," *Pennsylvania History* 38 (1971):117–133; *Pennsylvania Colonial Records*, Vol. 9; *Pennsylvania Archives*, 1st ser., Vol. 4; Alden T. Vaughan, "Frontier Banditti and the Indians: The Paxton Boys' Legacy, 1763–1775," *Pennsylvania History* 51 (1984):1–29.

See also FRANKLIN, BENJAMIN; PENNSYLVANIA; QUAKER PACIFISM; SCALP BOUNTIES

Peach War (1655–1657)

The second of the Dutch-Indian wars, the Peach War takes its name from the murder of an Indian woman who was caught stealing peaches in a Dutch settler's orchard. This, however, was not the only motivation for Indian action as the events of 15 September 1655 make clear. On this day, while Director General Petrus (Peter) Stuyvesant led his soldiers against Swedish settlements in the Delaware Valley, several hundred Munsee-speaking Delaware men, including many from the Hackensack band, overran New Amsterdam in the hours just before dawn. Although the citizens feared that the Indians intended to massacre them, only Isaack Allerton, a Plymouth merchant living in New Amsterdam, was actually harassed during this "invasion." After breaking into his house, several Indians made a thorough search for their enemies, the "Northern Indians." This, the Indian leaders explained to the New Netherland council during a midday meeting, was their only reason for coming to the island. The sachems assured the council that they would soon relocate with their warriors to Nut (Governor's) Island. In the evening, however, the Indians remained on the island, apparently waiting for some of their comrades to avenge the murder of the Delaware woman who had been killed by Hendrick van Dyck, the owner of the peach orchard. Several Indians finally found him in his yard that evening and shot him with an arrow, although they did not succeed in killing him. The Delawares had seemingly accomplished both their aims and were preparing to leave the island, when Cornelis van Tienhoven and the armed militia raced to the beach in unruly fashion and opened fire on the Indians they found waiting there. In reaction, the Delawares returned the citizens' fire and withdrew across the Hudson River to Staten Island and Pavonia, on the New Jersey mainland, where they sought revenge by attacking the Dutch settlements there. After a three-day assault on these places, 28 farms, together with crops and livestock, were destroyed, and 50 colonists killed with another 100 captured.

On his return to New Amsterdam, Stuyvesant tackled the problem of the hostages. Relying on the services of Captain Adriaen Post, a Dutchman who apparently knew the Delaware language and had himself been held captive, Stuyvesant conducted a series of negotiations with the Hackensack chief, Pennekeck, and eventually obtained the release of about 70 hostages by exchanging a variety of trade goods, but especially gunpowder and lead, for their liberation.

Although the Hackensacks had been quick to cooperate with the Dutch, other bands continued to hold several European captives and Director Stuyvesant and the members of his council debated about what actions should be taken to remedy the situation. While warfare with the Indians was considered just and necessary, the military unpreparedness of the colony suggested caution. Furthermore, Stuyvesant and his councilors feared for the safety of the captives, but believed that continued ransom payments for their release would only encourage the

Indians to make similar demands in the future. With the directors of the Dutch West India Company in agreement, the director general and his council decided to continue to barter for the release of Dutch prisoners, while at the same time plan to attack at least one of the offending bands in the future in order to teach all a lesson.

The surviving records do not make clear whether or when the remaining hostages were returned, but five children remained in captivity two years later. Presumably, these were never returned to the Dutch, but adopted into the Delaware bands as was the custom of the eastern woodland Indians of this period. It may be that the Delawares were putting this practice into play when they took European hostages in the first place, but other evidence suggests that they held them as a surety because they fully understood that as long as they held the captives, the Dutch would not attack them.

This strategy worked, as Stuyvesant's administration never gave the Indians the punitive treatment or punishment the Dutch council thought was necessary. As time wore on, New Netherland's administration had other concerns to worry about and was never able to devote the time, resources, or energy necessary to conduct a war against the Indians. Nor was it needed, for although a formal peace treaty was never arranged that called an end to the Peach War, peace remained in the region until the end of the Dutch rule, with the exception of an uprising by the Esopus further up the Hudson River.

Paul Otto

References

Michael, Kammen, *Colonial New York: A History* (1975); Edmund B. O'Callaghan and Berthold Fernow, eds., *Documents Relative to the Colonial History of the State of New York*, Vols. I, XII, XIII (1856–1887); Allen W. Trelease, *Indian Affairs in Colonial New York: The Seventeenth Century* (1960).

See also DELAWARE; ESOPUS; STUYVESANT, PETRUS

Pécaudy de Contrecoeur, Claude-Pierre, (1705–1775)

Claude-Pierre Pécaudy, sieur de Contrecoeur, captain in the French colonial regular army, chevalier of Saint-Louis, and later member of the British governor's legislative council, constructed Fort Duquesne where the Allegheny and Mononga-hela Rivers join to form the Ohio (modern Pittsburgh, Pennsylvania), and from there commanded French forces in the Ohio region in 1754 and 1755 at the beginning of the Seven Years' War.

Born at Contrecoeur, Quebec, 28 December 1705, Claude-Pierre was the son of François-Antoine Pécaudy, sieur de Contrecoeur (c. 1676–1743), also an officer in the French colonial regular army. The younger Contrecoeur entered the army as a cadet in 1722 at the age of 16, married Marie-Madeleine Boucher (by whom he had nine children) on 10 January 1729, was commissioned second ensign later the same year, promoted full ensign in 1734, and by 1742 served as a lieutenant at Fort Saint Frédéric (now Crown Point, New York), where his father was commander. In 1748, he was promoted to captain, and the following year designated second-in-command to Pierre-Joseph Céloron de Blainville on the mission down the Ohio River valley.

Céloron's expedition awakened concern about English penetration into the Ohio region and led to a major effort to secure French domination of the area. Given command of Fort Niagara (near modern Youngstown, New York) by 1752, Contrecoeur was responsible for provisioning the forts in the area, controlling and maintaining the Niagara portage, and conserving good relations with nearby Indian tribes. The new governor, Ange de Menneville, marquis de Duquesne, in 1753 sent a force of some 2,300 men under Captain Paul Marin de La Malgue, to begin the permanent occupation of the Ohio Valley. Marin constructed Fort Presque Isle (present-day Erie, Pennsylvania) and Fort Le Boeuf (Waterford, Pennsylvania) opening up the portage from Lake Erie to the Allegheny tributary French Creek. Marin's death in October and the demand of his elderly replacement, Jacques Legardeur de Saint-Pierre, to retire led Duquesne to appoint Contrecoeur as commander in the Ohio region on 27 January 1754.

Contrecoeur had orders to descend the Ohio with virtually all his men, leaving only skeleton garrisons in the forts already built, to the Indian village the English called Logstown (now Ambridge, Pennsylvania) and there construct a major fortification to be named after the governor. If the forks in the Ohio, supposedly some 20 miles upstream, were actually a better position to block the route of English traders, Duquesne gave him the option of building there instead. Arriving near the forks on 16 April 1754 with more than 600 soldiers, Contrecoeur discovered Ensign Edward Ward and

41 men of the Virginia militia in the process of erecting a wooden stockade and the next day summoned them to surrender the position and leave French territory. As soon as Ward and his men withdrew at noon on 18 April, Contrecoeur's workers demolished the stockade and begun laying out Fort Duquesne, which he commanded until 1756. Over the next two months, Contrecoeur's men, working under the direction of the engineer Captain François Le Mercier, constructed a 150-foot-square earth and wood fortification capable of holding a permanent garrison of 300. The sides facing the rivers were simple wooden palisades, while the landward exposures were defended by a ditch and 12-foot-high earthen wall supported by eight small cannon.

Contrecoeur's command of Fort Duquesne coincided with the series of events that initiated the Seven Years' War and the greatest French successes in the Ohio region. After having a small scouting party led by Ensign Joseph Coulon de Villiers, sieur de Jumonville, ambushed by George Washington in late May 1754, Contrecoeur organized the large party of men at his disposal into a striking force the command of which he gave to Captain Louis Coulon de Villiers, brother of the slain Jumonville. Coulon trapped Washington at Fort Necessity on 3 July 1754, forcing him to capitulate and withdraw across the Alleghenies. Contrecoeur continued to strengthen his fort's defenses and repeatedly sought reinforcements and the material to solidify French gains, but found himself woefully short of manpower in the summer of 1755 when the British army under Major General Edward Braddock marched to avenge Fort Necessity with some 3,000 men and a small artillery train. Fortunately for Contrecoeur, Braddock's army bogged down crossing the Alleghenies and the British commander opted to advance with less than 1,500 men and his guns in hope of reaching Fort Duquesne before French reinforcements. Still, on the morning of 9 July 1755, Contrecoeur's designated replacement, Captain Daniel-Hyacinthe-Marie Liénard de Beaujeu, moved out from Fort Duquesne with less than 200 Canadian soldiers and around 600 Indians, leaving Contrecoeur with 100 men to destroy the place if Beaujeu failed to stop the English. Despite the disparity in numbers and despite Beaujeu's death early on, the French and Indians triumphed over the British at the battle of the Monongahela (Braddock's Defeat).

Contrecoeur spent the rest of July 1755 gathering up and storing the spoils of battle while requesting replacement on the grounds of poor health. Both Governor Duquesne and his successor, Pierre de Rigaud de Vaudreuil, warmly acknowledged Contrecoeur's contributions to French successes in 1754 and 1755 and, when he asked for the coveted Cross of Saint-Louis for himself and promotion for his two sons on 28 November 1755, both petitions were granted in record time on 1 April 1756. Contrecoeur never served actively again and in 1759 received formal retirement and the accompanying half-pay pension.

Accepting the English conquest with grace, Contrecoeur remained on his estate when peace returned; by 1769, the British governor, Guy Carleton, could refer to him as one of the most influential Canadians in the province. Following the death of his first wife, Contrecoeur married Marguerite-Barbe Hingue de Puygibault on 9 September 1768. In 1775, he was selected to serve on the legislative council but was able to participate in only one session before dying in Montreal on 13 December 1775 at the age of 69.

Ronald Martin

References
Francis-J. Audet, *Contrecoeur: Famile, Seigneurie, Paroisse, Village* (1940); Fernand Grenier, "Claude-Pierre Pécaudy de Contrecoeur." *Dictionary of Canadian Biography* 4:617–168; ———, ed., *Papiers Contrecoeur et autres documents concernant le conflit anglo-français sur l'Ohio de 1745 à 1756* (1952); William A. Hunter, *Forts on the Pennsylvania Frontier, 1753–1758* (1960); Ronald Martin, "Confrontation at the Monongahela: Climax of the French Drive Into the Upper Ohio Region," *Pennsylvania History* 37 (1970):133–150.

See also BRADDOCK, EDWARD; COULON DE VILLIERS DE JUMONVILLE, JOSEPH; COULON DE VILLIERS, LOUIS; FORT DUQUESNE (PENNSYLVANIA); FORKS OF THE OHIO; FORT NECESSITY (PENNSYLVANIA); FORT NIAGARA (NEW YORK); OHIO EXPEDITION OF 1755

Fort Pelham (Massachusetts)

Part of a defensive chain of forts erected between the Connecticut River and the New York boundary to protect the frontier, Fort Pelham was constructed in 1745 at the town of Rowe in present-day Franklin County. The fort consisted of a palisaded structure that enclosed roughly one and a half acres. Watch boxes 12 feet square and seven feet high were situated at each corner. The entire fort was surrounded by a ditch and was usually garrisoned with 20 men.

David L. Whitesell

See also FORT MASSACHUSETTS (MASSACHU-SETTS); FORT SHIRLEY (MASSACHUSETTS)

Pemaquid, Attack on (1689)

Pemaquid, a settlement older than Boston, was the site of an early fort built at a narrow neck of a peninsula on the Maine coast. The Indians especially resented the fort because they were afraid to continue to use an ancient Indian portage that cut off the long canoe trip around the peninsula. In 1688 Edmund Andros, who had attacked coastal Indians, raided Jean-Vincent d'Abbadie de Saint-Castin's Penobscot home. On 2 August 1689, a group of about 100 Maliseet and Penobscot Indians retaliated by attacking Pemaquid. The attack occurred early in the afternoon when the men had left the protection of their fort and homes to harvest hay. There were two groups of Indians, one attacked the men in the fields; the others plundered the unprotected houses before burning them. The fort held out for two days before surrendering. The fort and remaining homes were then set on fire. Those who did not escape were killed or captured.

Nicholas N. Smith

See also ANDROS, EDMUND; DOVER, ATTACK ON; MAINE; FORT WILLIAM HENRY (MAINE)

Pennsylvania

Of all the British colonies in eastern North America, Pennsylvania had perhaps the most peculiar military history. William Penn, the colony's founder, and the Quakers who found a refuge in his province and soon dominated its politics, made pacifism a central part of their political agenda. Yet while the colonial government often espoused nonviolence, at times enraging provincial officials elsewhere who wanted to draw on Pennsylvania's rapidly expanding population for men to serve in the campaigns of the crown, there were numerous skirmishes within the boundaries of Penn's province. Further, while Pennsylvanians had been largely successful at avoiding immersion into the ongoing wars between Great Brit-ain and France until the mid-eighteenth century, western Pennsylvania became one of the most important military theaters in the Seven Years' War. The colony thus witnessed the end of an age of pacifism and the emergence of an age of bel-licosity. If Penn himself might have regretted the transition, a young George Washington, who participated in events leading to the French and Indian War in western Pennsylvania, did not give voice to similar misgivings.

The shift in the province's military history ultimately was due to two related developments: the impact of colonial population growth on Indian-white relations, and continued British-French competition for North America. In most colonies, particularly Massachusetts and Virginia, hostilities between English colonists and Indians broke out within a generation of colonial settlement. No so in Pennsylvania. While there were, to be sure, conflicts between the peoples who sought to control Pennsylvania, the provincial government was more successful than most in achieving relative harmony with the Indians who lived in the region. This is not to suggest that colonists always acted honorably in their efforts to get land from Indians. Even Penn's sons became involved in the notorious "Walking Purchase" of 1737, whereby a group of Indians were defrauded of a substantial tract of land. Yet, by and large, the proprietary government of Pennsylvania made concerted efforts to purchase land from Indians, and those attempts created the goodwill necessary to sustain peace over the course of the eighteenth century, at least until the mid-1750s.

The ability of the government to control Indian-colonist relations in the province for more than 70 years is itself remarkable. While Quakers controlled the government, Pennsylvania became a haven for a wide variety of Europeans, most of them lured by the promotional efforts of Penn and his associates. And migrants did, in fact, literally pour into the province, landing at Philadelphia and then moving west in the search for land. Chief among the migrants were German-speaking peoples, themselves refugees from a war-besieged palatinate where they had been persecuted for their religious beliefs, and Scotch-Irish Presbyterians who came to Pennsylvania from northern Ireland seeking economic and religious freedom as well. For these migrants, and the thousands of others who came from throughout Europe to join them, Pennsylvania was apparently "the best poor man's country" that they had heard about.

The philosophers believed in the promise of Pennsylvania, celebrating it in their writings; so did Benjamin Franklin, who moved there from Boston early in his life. For people of European descent, life in Pennsylvania promised freedom from the trials they had experienced in Europe, including military hostility.

Yet, significantly, Indians too found Pennsylvania a refuge in the eighteenth century. While the Indians who had inhabited eastern Pennsylvania at the time of first contact with colonists—Delawares, Shawnees, and Susquehannocks in particular—had suffered a massive demographic catastrophe from the spread of Old World diseases (such as smallpox, measles, and influenza), those who survived found relative peace in central Pennsylvania, especially in the Susquehanna Valley. There, seemingly beyond the reach of land-seeking colonists, they created new villages, often multi-tribal, and a stable political and economic world. They were assisted in this task, or at least not substantially hindered, by the Iroquois, the confederacy of six tribes in New York, who claimed suzerainty over much of central Pennsylvania, including the Susquehanna Valley. Yet since the Iroquois too, like the Indians of eastern Pennsylvania, had suffered great population loss, again mostly due to epidemics for which they had no immunities, they wanted other Indians to migrate to the region. Only by keeping it peopled with Indians, the Iroquois believed, could the territory remain under their control; uninhabited territory would have been too tempting to the colonists, the Iroquois reasoned. They were correct. Colonial legal policies relating to the seizure of *vacuum domicilium*, so-called empty land, would have provided sufficient justification for colonial settlement in central Pennsylvania even without the effort to seek Indian permission.

Peaceful as relations were between Pennsylvanians and Indians in the province, however, the possibility for conflict always existed. The potential for violence grew when colonists, experiencing massive population increase, sought new lands along the margins of the settled portions of the colony. To protect outlying settlers from attacks by Indians, the colony erected a series of forts—some no more than palisaded houses, others with garrisons in attendance—throughout the hinterland. In times of conflict, especially during the Seven Years' War, these forts proved vital for the protection of the colonial population. Yet the fact that many were created when the province was not at war with Indians indi-

cates the constant fear some colonists had. Life in Penn's province might be peaceful most of the time, they reckoned, but better not to take chances.

Still, while outright violence might have been extremely localized before the mid-1750s, tensions between colonists and Indians were ubiquitous. Colonists were, to Indians, uninvited intruders on their lands. Delawares and Shawnees might not have understood how European pathogens devastated their bodies, but they certainly realized that their lives were immeasurably better before the coming of Europeans. In this sense they were correct. Even the most benevolent colonist could have been the vector for a deadly disease, especially since the smallpox bacillus could survive long ocean voyages, both on infected people and in scabs that had fallen into the crates carrying their goods. While colonists, even in Pennsylvania, might not have acknowledge the legitimacy of the Indians' hostility toward the spread of the empire in eastern North America, they knew that their presence created anxiety for Indians and that, over time, accumulated grievances, no matter how petty they might have seemed, could lead to an attack.

But it was not only Indians whom the colonists of Pennsylvania feared. From the late seventeenth century to the Revolution, the proprietary government was in a desperate struggle to protect the province from the incursions of other colonists. Legal battles over boundaries brought tension with colonists in New York to the north and Maryland to the south. While these border disputes did not erupt into any significant wars, a long-simmering dispute with Connecticut over the northern tier of Pennsylvania, claimed by Connecticut through the "sea-to-sea" clause of its 1662 charter, did lead to armed encounters, although more severe conflicts took place after the colonial period.

The assembly, under Quaker control, did its utmost to preserve peace in the colony. Members supported the creation of the Friendly Association for Regaining and Preserving Peace with the Indians by Pacific Measures. The association paid a great role in facilitating trade with Indians, and its efforts were so successful that it encountered greater resistance from colonists (who resented the benevolent treatment given to potential foes) than from the Indians residing in the colony.

Still, while the government tried to limit hostilities, those in the Quaker-dominated assembly could not control all of the peoples in the extensive province. For example, the assembly voiced its opposition to wars being carried out by the crown against its traditional enemies, but it could not prevent Pennsylvanians from volunteering to serve on privateering ventures to the West Indies or in troop brigades moving north to displace the French from eastern Canada. Even Franklin at times opposed the politics of the provincial government, as did colonists throughout North America who resented what they took to be the Pennsylvania government's lack of loyalty to the greater cause of enriching the empire. The tensions emerged forcibly in the early 1740s. When hostile French and Spanish privateers entered the Delaware River in 1745 and seemed on the verge of embroiling Pennsylvania in the conflict initiated by the War of Jenkins' Ear, the assembly refused to provide funds for the defense of the province. The legislators' action prompted Franklin, who possessed a patent for raising a defense force, to organize some volunteers to meet the challenge. The anticipated attack never came, and Pennsylvania, only minimally prepared for war in any event, continued to escape armed conflict.

But the reprieve was temporary. Within a decade, in spite of the best efforts of the Quaker politicians to prevent it, war broke out in the colony. However much William Penn and his followers wanted to remove themselves from the hostilities plaguing the larger world, the strategic location of Pennsylvania made that wish futile. When tensions between the British and the French exploded in the mid-1750s, each imperial power sought control of Penn's colony. And during the Seven Years' War, Pennsylvanians, Indians, and colonists alike found themselves in the midst of a war beyond the scope of any they had witnessed in their lives.

In the mid-1750s, the English, ever wary of the growing French presence to the west, sought to vanquish their traditional foes and the Indians allied with them. Beginning in 1753, French troops had moved into western Pennsylvania in an effort to claim the Ohio country and thus solidify their nation's hold on the territory between its valued North American possessions, Canada and Louisiana. The English, once they discovered the incursion, sought to expel the French. To do so, they mounted a campaign, under General Edward Braddock, to seize Fort Duquesne in 1755. The assembly, mired in a dispute over taxation with Robert Hunter Mor-

ris, the new governor of the province, proved unable to provide the support the general wanted; in early June 1756, several Quakers, claiming that their constituents believed "the present Situation of Publick Affairs call upon us for Services in a military Way, which, from a Conviction of Judgment, after mature Deliberation, we cannot comply with," resigned from the government. The campaign went ahead nonetheless. The attack never materialized as the English had planned; a combined force of 800 French soldiers and Indians caught the British in a poor position and routed Braddock's force of almost 1,500 troops. Within three hours almost one-third of the English were dead, and about as many wounded, and Braddock himself lay mortally wounded; he died four days later. After Braddock's defeat, many in the province, particularly in the west, believed that Pennsylvania was under threat of being taken by the French, but the colony survived the late 1750s. The threat of war, especially carried out by French-allied Delawares, seemed to fade, and by the end of the war western Pennsylvania no longer seemed in danger.

But the peace proved brief indeed. Beginning in 1763, after the French had been largely vanquished, various Indian groups in the western borderlands of British America attacked colonial settlements. While the conflict, termed Pontiac's Conspiracy by Francis Parkman, began beyond the reach of Pennsylvania, Indians soon attacked provincial outposts in the western portion of the colony. The Indians, including many Delawares and Shawnees, could not take Fort Pitt, but in June 1763, they had far better luck when they attacked Fort Venango, Fort Le Boeuf, Fort de la Presque Isle, and Fort Ligonier; colonists, terrified they would be slaughtered, migrated eastward to more established settlements, seeking assistance. In one widely publicized attack, Captain Bull, son of the Delaware leader Teedyuscung, led a foray into Northampton County that resulted in the deaths of 23 colonists.

Panic spread through the backcountry, and some colonists known as the Paxton Boys, and perhaps numbering 250, vented their hostility in a decidedly violent way: they murdered 20 peaceful Indians at Conestoga, the last distinct remnants of the Susquehannocks, and then proceeded to march onto Philadelphia to kill another 140 Indians then being held in protective custody. While the Indians, who allegedly participated in attacks on colonists, were the first target of these backwoods vigilantes, the Paxton Boys marched to the capital to confront those they held responsible for their troubles: the assembly. When the vigilantes reached the city they were rebuffed, mostly through Benjamin Franklin's ability to raise sufficient colonists to ward them off. Yet the march signaled a substantial shift in Indian-colonist relations throughout much of southern and western Pennsylvania. No longer would judicial officials in the hinterland make any substantial efforts to punish colonists who attacked Indians. While the proprietary government remained committed to interracial harmony in the province, and promised Indians that perpetrators of crimes against them would be punished to the full extent of the law, the Philadelphia-based government demonstrated that it had little control over affairs in the backcountry. Further, the events led to a crisis in government in the province, and brought about the effective end of Quaker dominance in the assembly, a process begun with the withdrawal of some Quakers from the assembly during the Seven Years' War.

War, when it came, changed forever the political structure of Pennsylvania. Yet it did more as well. For three generations, Pennsylvanians had managed, most of the time, to find peaceful solutions to the problems of population growth and Indian-colonist animosity. While it would be easy to attribute the long peacetime as due solely to the pacifist principles of the Quakers, such an attribution would be misleading. What enabled Pennsylvanians to maintain peace was a willingness on the part of the different peoples of the province to live and work together to resolve common problems. To be sure, Quaker ideology played a role, but so did the desire of many Indians to establish peaceful relations with those who displaced them. While those who engaged in warfare in the colony often did so with great passion and ferocity, the success Pennsylvania experienced during the colonial period was ultimately due to the ability of its inhabitants to avoid military encounters.

Peter C. Mancall

References

Robert Davidson, *War Comes to Quaker Pennsylvania, 1682–1756* (1957); James H. Hutson, *Pennsylvania Politics, 1746–1770: The Movement for Royal Government and Its Consequences* (1972); Francis Jennings, *The Ambiguous Iroquois Empire: The Covenant Chain Confederation of Indian Tribes with English Colonies from its beginnings to the Lancaster Treaty of 1744* (1984); Donald H. Kent, *The French Invasion of Western Pennsylvania, 1753* (1954), rpt. 1981; Ralph L. Ketcham, "Conscience, War, and Politics in Pennsylvania, 1755–1757," *William and Mary Quarterly*, 3rd ser., 20 (1963):416–439.

Peter C. Mancall, *Valley of Opportunity: Economic Culture Along the Susquehanna, 1700–1800* (1991); Gary B. Nash, *Quakers and Politics: Pennsylvania, 1681–1726* (1968); *Pennsylvania Colonial Records*, 16 vols. (1838–1853); *Pennsylvania Archives*, 138 vols. (1852–1935); Sally Schwartz, "*A Mixed Multitude*": *The Struggle for Toleration in Colonial Pennsylvania* (1987); Frederick B. Tolles, *Meeting House and Counting House: The Quaker Merchants of Colonial Philadelphia, 1682–1763* (1948); Alden T. Vaughan, "Frontier Banditti and the Indians: The Paxton Boys' Legacy, 1763–1775," *Pennsylvania History* 51 (1984):1–29.

See also FORT ALLEN (PENNSYLVANIA); FORT AUGUSTA (PENNSYLVANIA); BRADDOCK, EDWARD; DELAWARE; FORT DUQUESNE (PENNSYLVANIA); FORBES CAMPAIGN OF 1758; FRANKLIN, BENJAMIN; LANCASTER, TREATY OF; FORT LE BOEUF (PENNSYLVANIA); FORT LIGONIER (PENNSYLVANIA); LOGSTOWN, TREATY OF; OHIO EXPEDITION OF 1755; PACIFISM; PAXTON BOYS; FORT PITT (PENNSYLVANIA); PONTIAC'S WAR; QUAKER PACIFISM; SHAWNEE; SUSQUEHANNOCK; TEEDYUSCUNG; VENANGO (PENNSYLVANIA); WALKING PURCHASE

Pensacola (Florida)

When the Spanish government established a garrison at Pensacola Bay in November 1698, it began a struggle between itself, France, and Great Britain for control of the Gulf of Mexico that continued for the remainder of the colonial period. Spanish interest in the bay dated from the late 1550s, when an abortive attempt was made to establish a colony there. After its failure, Spain's interest waned until the 1680s, when French actions in the Gulf prompted a second effort.

Spanish reexploration of Pensacola Bay commenced in 1686. Reports were forwarded to Madrid that the bay could be a strategic link between St. Augustine, Apalachee, and New Spain. These reports stimulated further explorations in the early 1690s, most importantly an expedition led by Andrés de Pez and Carlos de Sigüenza y Góngora in April 1692. Three weeks of exploration convinced both men that Spain should fortify the bay, and on their return to New Spain, they forwarded this recommendation to the king and the Junta de Guerra.

As usual, Spanish funds were short and the bureaucracy was slow. In spite of royal orders that this recommendation be acted upon, it would take rumors of French action to effect Spanish occupation. After the signing of the Treaty of Ryswick in 1697, it was reported that Louis XIV planned an expedition of at least four ships to plant a colony on the Gulf. Since the harbor afforded by Pensacola Bay was assumed by the Spaniards to be the best on the northern gulf, they assumed that Pensacola was the French destination.

King Charles II issued an order on 19 April 1698 to the viceroy of New Spain to occupy Pensacola and await reinforcements from Spain. As it happened, the rumors of a French expedition were well founded. In October 1698, Pierre Le Moyne d'Iberville, accompanied by his brother, Jean-Baptiste Le Moyne de Bienville, left France with soldiers and colonists to plant a colony on the Gulf.

Two Spanish expeditions, one from Cuba commanded by Juan Jordan de Reina and the other from New Spain commanded by Andrés de Arriola, arrived at Pensacola in November 1698, two months before the arrival of the French. The Spaniards immediately began construction of a fort (or presidio), which they called San Carlos de Austria, to guard against the suspected French threat. This threat materialized on 26 January 1699.

The French may have been surprised by the presence of a Spanish garrison at Pensacola, but if they were, they did not show it. They immediately asked for permission to enter the bay so that they could purchase supplies. Arriola told them that the channel entering the bay was too narrow for their ships, at which point the French tried to sound the channel themselves to ascertain the truth of this claim. When ordered to desist by Arriola, they did so and withdrew on 30 January.

The French were gone but not forgotten. Arriola called together his officers to discuss defensive preparations. They decided that Arriola should go to New Spain to ask for reinforcements from the viceroy. During his absence, reports from local Indians reached the garrison at Pensacola that English from the Carolinas intended to take the town. When Arriola returned with meager reinforcements, an investigation of the rumors determined that what the Indians had seen were Iberville's French soldiers and colonists establishing themselves at Biloxi. To make matters worse, Arriola did not have enough men to dislodge them. The competition for control of the upper Gulf of Mexico had begun.

The French presence in the Gulf was in response to English movement into the interior from the Carolinas and the fear that this encroachment would lead to English domination of the Mississippi Valley and monopolization of the skin and fur trade in that region. Control of the Gulf and the mouth of the Mississippi River would make the Mississippi Valley far less attractive to the English. The founding of Pensacola had spurred a competition between the French, Spanish, and English that lasted for 100 years.

Jeanne T. Heidler

References

Verne E. Chatelain, *The Defenses of Spanish Florida, 1565 to 1763* (1941); Verner W. Crane, *The Southern Frontier, 1670–1732* (1929); William Edward Dunn, *Spanish and French Rivalry in the Gulf Region of the United States, 1678–1702; The Beginnings of Texas and Pensacola* (1917); Lawrence Carroll Ford, *The Triangular Struggle for Spanish Pensacola, 1689–1739* (1939).

See also FLORIDA; FRANCE-SPAIN RELATIONS; PENSACOLA AND THE WAR OF THE QUADRUPLE ALLIANCE; PEZ, ANDRÉS DE

Pensacola, English Attacks on (1707)

Queen Anne's War (the War of the Spanish Succession) changed the relationship between Spanish Florida and French Louisiana. In 1700, the accession to the Spanish throne of Philip V, the Bourbon grandson of Louis XIV, assured that those two countries would be allies in the upcoming war. Rather than competition, cooperation in the Gulf of Mexico governed Spanish and French behavior.

Once Queen Anne's War officially commenced in 1702, the French immediately suggested that the Spaniards should turn over Pensacola to them. In return, they suggested that the Spaniards could reap the benefits of a joint French-Spanish expedition against Charles Town, South Carolina, by annexing the Carolinas. The Spanish Junta de Guerra, obviously not in the thrall of its French allies, and with the approval of the new king, declined the offer. The French, undaunted, then occupied Mobile Bay, just west of Pensacola. Though the Spanish in Pensacola, commanded by Francisco Martínez, protested this encroachment, they would later appreciate the French presence.

During the next few years the French in Mobile and the Spaniards in Pensacola cooperated to an unusual degree. Though Spanish Florida bore the brunt of English aggression, the French realized that the primary goal of English attacks was to remove the Spanish buffer to French Louisiana. In 1702, Carolinians under James Moore made an unsuccessful attempt to take St. Augustine, followed in early 1704 with an attack on Apalachee. The destruction of the missions around Apalachee cut off the only land communication link between Pensacola and St. Augustine. Furthermore, the English under Moore intended the elimination of Apalachee as merely a prelude to the taking of Pensacola.

Cut off from the closest Spanish settlement in Florida, the garrison at Pensacola was forced into the arms of its French neighbors. Pensacola had never been a particularly strong settlement. In spite of encouragement from the government, few settlers had been induced to locate there. The garrison, made up primarily of convicts and derelicts, was always short of food and other supplies, which made these rather unlikely soldiers increasingly restless. This restlessness apparently boiled over in 1705 when a mysterious fire destroyed virtually the entire settlement and much of the presidio. The garrison was forced to turn to the French in Mobile for help to rebuild.

There was also the ever-present threat from the English, who were doubling their efforts to recruit Indian, especially Creek, allies in the interior so as to put Pensacola out of its misery. To forestall any further attempts on Gulf outposts, the Spanish and French governments decided to attack Charles Town in the summer of 1706. Poor planning and coordination produced a disastrous campaign that only served to make the English angry.

Planning retaliation, the Carolinians began organizing another strike at Spanish Florida in the summer of 1707. They intended to use primarily Talapoosa Creek allies led by a few Englishmen. Through their own alliances, the French heard about the intended attack several days before it began and immediately sent word to Pensacola.

The governor of Pensacola, Joseph de Guzman, ignored the warnings, and as a result when the attack came, the town was caught completely by surprise. The garrison was forced to retreat into the presidio and watch the entire town go up in smoke. The attackers then turned their attention to the fort, which was briefly penetrated before the defenders were able to repulse the Creek. In the engagement 11 Spaniards were killed and 15 taken captive.

The success of this raid only whetted the appetite of the Carolinians, who immediately planned another attack in November 1707. Once again the Spaniards were warned by the French, and this time they took the warnings more seriously. The 13 Carolinians and their 350 Creek allies intended to take the fort this time. When the Spanish garrison withdrew into the presidio, the attackers settled in for a protracted siege. As the siege dragged into December the Creek and Carolinians fell to bickering among themselves, and when rumors circulated that the French were coming from Mobile to lift the siege, the Carolina-Talapoosa alliance fell apart. By the time the French arrived on 8 December, the attackers had disappeared.

Raids continued against Pensacola for the remainder of the war, with another serious one occurring in 1711. However, weathering the storm of 1707 practically assured the retention of Pensacola in Spanish hands and the safety of French Louisiana.

Jeanne T. Heidler

References
Verner W. Crane, *The Southern Frontier, 1670–1732* (1929); William Edward Dunn, *Spanish and French Rivalry in the Gulf Region of the United States, 1678–1702; The Beginnings of Texas and Pensacola* (1917); Lawrence Carroll Ford, *The Triangular Struggle for Spanish Pensacola, 1689–1739* (1939); J. Leitch Wright, *Anglo-Spanish Rivalry in North America* (1971).

See also CHARLES TOWN, ATTACK ON; FLORIDA; GREAT BRITAIN-SPAIN RELATIONS; QUEEN ANNE'S WAR

Pensacola and the War of the Quadruple Alliance (1718–1722)
Following the War of the Spanish Succession, Spain tried to tighten its grip on Florida. The English in Carolina had been weakened by the

Yamasee War, allowing the Spaniards to feel secure enough to reoccupy Apalachee and renew alliances with the Lower Creeks. The reoccupation of Apalachee reestablished a land link with St. Augustine, facilitating communications between Pensacola and that city. However, two events occurred in 1718 that would shake Spanish security in Pensacola; the French, already established on the Gulf near Mobile, established a second settlement at New Orleans and sent a small garrison to St. Joseph Bay between Pensacola and Apalachee. Though they did not remain at St. Joseph Bay more than a few months, their intentions alarmed the Spaniards at Pensacola.

French interest in Pensacola Bay became obvious the following year on the outbreak of the War of the Quadruple Alliance in Europe, a war that placed France and Spain on opposite sides. In America, Pensacola would become the focus of the struggle between France and Spain for control of the northern Gulf of Mexico and the Mississippi Valley.

France declared war on Spain on 10 January 1719. Word was immediately sent to the French governor of Louisiana, Jean-Baptiste Le Moyne de Bienville. Before the Spanish governor at Pensacola, Juan Matamoros de Ysla, knew there was a war between the two countries he was faced with a French expedition off Pensacola.

Commanded by Bienville's brother, Joseph Le Moyne de Sérigny, the expedition consisted of three ships with more than 300 officers and men aboard. Another group, consisting of 60 French soldiers and 400 Indians, traveled overland. On arriving at Pensacola, Sérigny demanded the surrender of a battery overlooking the entrance to the bay on Punta de Sigüenza. The battery surrendered without firing a shot, allowing the ships to enter the channel. The guns of the presidio could not reach the channel, so the French were able to enter Pensacola Bay unmolested. Once inside they commenced firing on the presidio, which only briefly returned fire and then surrendered the next morning.

Matamoros, who later was criticized for not putting up a stiffer defense, did not have enough food to sustain his men for a long siege; and to make matters worse, approximately half of his men were former convicts, always on the verge of mutiny. Matamoros did secure rather generous terms from the French in that they promised to transport the entire garrison to Havana. En route, the French ships were captured by Spanish vessels intended for an assault on Charles Town, South Carolina. When the Spaniards heard about the fall of Pensacola, the governor of Cuba, Gregorio Guazo Calderón, decided to divert the expedition to retake Pensacola. The French would now learn that it was much easier to take Pensacola than to hold it.

The French intended to make Pensacola, rather than the new settlement at New Orleans, the capital of their Gulf holdings. However, they found that the defenses of the bay were horribly neglected and that many of the Spanish artillery pieces were virtually useless. The French commander at Pensacola had been able to do little to improve the dilapidated Spanish defenses. Approximately one-third of his small garrison consisted of convicts, many of whom had already deserted. Those who remained were on the verge of mutiny. Repairs of the fortifications were not completed before the arrival of the Spanish counterattack.

The Spanish fleet arrived off Pensacola on 6 August 1719, and because it had brought along the two captured French ships, it was able to move close to the battery on Punta de Sigüenza. When word reached the garrison about the surrender of Punta de Sigüenza, 50 men deserted to the Spanish side and informed the Spanish officers of the weakness of the French position. On 8 August the Spaniards demanded the surrender of the fort and took it without firing a shot.

While Matamoros reassumed control of the defenses at Pensacola and tried to strengthen them, the other Spanish officers at Pensacola decided that to forestall any future assaults on Pensacola, they should eliminate the French settlements on the Gulf. Their attempt to take control of French positions on Mobile Bay ended in failure on 18 and 19 August.

The French, in the meantime, had already made plans to retake Pensacola and were preparing an expedition for September. This expedition departed Mobile on 13 September and arrived at Pensacola Bay on 17 September. It encountered no opposition to entering the bay, but once inside, a fierce three-hour naval battle was fought until the Spanish ships asked for terms. The battery on Punta de Sigüenza then surrendered, and the faint-hearted Matamoros in the presidio soon followed.

The French under Bienville, once more in possession of Pensacola, knew that they could not hold the bay if faced with serious attempts to retake it. Bienville therefore decided to damage the Spanish fortifications to such an extent that they would not be worth retaking. He ordered the officers remaining in Pensacola not to defend the position if it were attacked.

Over the next six months many plans were made in Spain and in New Spain to retake Pensacola, but none of them came to fruition. By early 1720, the king of Spain, Philip V, had indicated that he was ready to discuss peace and hostilities were suspended, but possession of Pensacola proved to be a serious stumbling block in negotiations. Finally, in November 1720, the French agreed to return Pensacola, paving the way for a defensive alliance between the two countries.

Despite the French promise that Pensacola would be returned, they remained reluctant to relinquish the strategic bay. Not until 25 November 1722 was Pensacola finally surrendered to Spanish authorities, under whom it remained until 1763.

Jeanne T. Heidler

References
Verner W. Crane, *The Southern Frontier, 1670–1732* (1929); Lawrence Carroll Ford, *The Triangular Struggle for Spanish Pensacola, 1689–1739* (1939); John Jay TePaske, *The Governorship of Spanish Florida, 1700–1763* (1964); J. Leitch Wright, *Anglo-Spanish Rivalry in North America* (1971).

See also FLORIDA; LE MOYNE DE BIENVILLE, JEAN-BAPTISTE

Fort Pentagoet (Maine)
The site of Fort Pentagoet was originally a trading post established by the Plymouth Company in 1629. It was then occupied by the French in 1635, who erected a fort with a 60-foot-square parade ground and four 16-foot-square bastions of stone and earth. This fortified stronghold was at the site of the present town of Castine at the head of Penobscot Bay. It was intended to support the French claim to all of Maine north of the Kennebec River. Between 1654 to 1670, it was utilized by the British under the name Fort Penobscot. However, the Treaty of Breda returned the fort to the French. Shortly after reverting to French control it became the trading post of Baron de St. Castin. The fort was captured and plundered in 1674 by a Dutch privateer. Further attacks by privateers occurred in 1686 and again in 1687. After the outbreak of Indian trouble in the fall of 1688, the settlement was raided by

the English under the direction of Governor Edmund Andros. During Queen Anne's War it was raided in 1704 by a force under the command of Colonel Benjamin Church. The English finally destroyed the fort in 1722 during Dummer's War and subsequently occupied the Penobscot peninsula.

David L. Whitesell

See also CHURCH, BENJAMIN; DUMMER'S WAR

Pepperrell, William, Jr. (1696–1759)
William Pepperrell, Jr., the eighth child of a Piscataqua fisherman and landholder, was the famous hero of the siege of Fort Louisbourg in 1745. His parents, William and Margery Bray Pepperrell, settled at Kittery Point after their marriage in 1680. Only a few years before William had left Revelstoke, on the English Devon coast, for better fortunes in New England. The Brays were already landholders and shipbuilders in Piscataqua.

William, Jr. grew up in Kittery Point, and at an early age entered his father's growing business. His older brother, Andrew, was expected to inherit the business, but died unexpectedly when William was only 17 years of age. Already their company had six ships sailing to distant ports and a shop, docks, and warehouses. Most trade was concentrated in Antigua and Barbados, but vessels often sailed to Newfoundland, the Carolinas, and other ports in the West Indies where good cargoes of cotton, indigo, and cocoa could be found. Not much of the Pepperrell business was conducted directly with England, but in the years after 1713, trading became generally confined to New England and landowners up the Piscataqua River. Profits and prestige increased greatly and there developed alliances of merchants that included many of the great shopkeepers of York County, Maine, and neighboring Portsmouth, New Hampshire.

More important was the Pepperrell trade with Boston that was drawing the firm to ally with important merchants in the capital. With these connections it reached out to the French Caribbean Islands for molasses, which they marketed in Boston, and then increased their imports of Newfoundland fish for the Caribbean trade. Business conditions were often depressed in the 1720s so that William, Jr. tried various markets, including those in Spain and Portugal.

With a wider and diversified market, William, Jr. accepted election in 1724 to the house of representatives in Boston and agreed in 1727 to be elected to the council, where he would sit for 31 years. Together with his legislative service in Boston, he agreed to be justice of the inferior court of common pleas for York County in 1725, and its chief justice in 1731. His political service grew to include a commission as justice of the peace in 1728 and colonel of the local militia regiment. Even before William, Jr. went to Boston for political service, he met the daughter of Grove Hirst, a wealthy merchant like himself, and he and Mary were married in 1723. As the granddaughter of the powerful Samuel Sewall, Mary gave William, Jr. a major social position in Boston. Their daughter, Elizabeth, married Nathaniel Sparhawk in 1741, and he became a merchant associate of Pepperrell.

The mercantile empire of William Pepperrell, after his father's death in 1734, embraced the services of a large number of York County merchant seamen, many of them relatives. The Frost family, in particular, served the company, but the Dearings, the Whittemores, and Sparhawk looked after the family business. His son, Andrew, as he gained experience, acted as head of the firm's local office, possibly with the advice of Nathaniel Sparhawk.

When war with Spain and France broke out in the 1740s, Pepperrell's trade was threatened by hostile seizures, and he joined Governor William Shirley and a group of merchants of Massachusetts to organize the siege of Louisbourg in 1745. His popularity in New Hampshire and Maine made him the inevitable choice as commander of the expedition. With much publicity and great exertion, the New England colonies gave the most backing to the expedition, and within seven weeks, Commanding General Pepperrell was able to lead the militia into the French fort. Britain, at Shirley's request, supplied naval support, heavy guns, and transport, but the battle, in the eyes of New Englanders, was a regional victory. Pepperrell soon was knighted by King George II in recognition of the victory and named a colonel of a British regiment.

The siege was the high point of Sir William's career. He had thoughts of further military services in the campaigns of 1746 and 1747, but was disappointed when they were cancelled before being undertaken. He thought then of a governorship of New Hampshire, possibly of Maine (to be separated from Mas-sachusetts). In 1749, he went to England and was well received by George II. But little more was added to the recognition he had already received. He was promoted to be a lieutenant general of British forces.

On his return home in 1750, he suffered some bitter disappointments. The cancellation of his son's pending marriage to Hannah Waldo, which was to be a grand social event, was followed by Andrew's unexpected death from pneumonia in March 1751. At this crisis, his nephew, Charles Chauncey, then joined in the management of the family business as his uncle's chief assistant. But these events were almost too much for the baronet, who took little interest in the mobilizations of the French and Indian War. Differences with Governor William Shirley soured his attitude toward the mobilization in 1755. Only in the crisis over the French attack on Fort William Henry in 1757 did he come out of semi-retirement to lead briefly the colonial troops. His health was precarious during these years, but he remained a member of the council until his death, and with Chauncey's support he had the satisfaction to see the profits of his mercantile business expand. His grandson, William Pepperrell Sparhawk, succeeded to the baronage in 1774.

John A. Schutz

References
Byron Fairchild, *Messrs. William Pepperrell* (1954); John A. Schutz, *William Shirley: King's Governor of Massachusetts* (1961).

See also LOUISBOURG, EXPEDITION (1745); SHIRLEY, WILLIAM

Pequot

The Pequots, an Algonquian-speaking tribe, had grown to great strength in southern New England through conquest and later through a monopoly over the local trade market. With their territory encompassing the area between Niantic Bay and the Pawcatuck River, the Pequots controlled both European and Indian access to furs and the raw materials for wampum (the legal tender for the English). With increased demand by the English for wampum came pressures associated with becoming a part of the European economic system, including internal strife among tribal leaders. When a subchief, Uncas, lost a struggle with grand sachem Sassacus, he took his followers with him and formed the Mohegan tribe. The English declared war on the Pequots in 1637 and were joined by Pequot rivals, the Mohegans and the Narragansetts. As hostilities intensified, the English and their allies killed Pequot men, women, and children in their attempt to obliterate the tribe. The war ended with the forced signing of the Treaty of Hartford in 1638, in which surviving Pequot sachems swore to never use their tribal name again or live in the same territory. The Pequots were then divided among the Mohegan and Narragansett tribes and others were sold into slavery as far away as the West Indies. The Pequots under the Mohegans and Narragansetts did manage to disentangle themselves from their control by the 1650s. Connecticut authorities divided them into four Indian towns under two governors, forming the Paucatuck (eastern) and the Mashantucket (western) tribes. They were given land, but had to continually appeal to Connecticut authorities as English settlers encroached on their space. This struggle was only made more difficult because Pequot males contributed their talents and lives to colonial Connecticut war efforts.

Leslie Miller

References

Laurence M. Hauptman and James D. Wherry, *The Pequots in Southern New England: The Fall and Rise of an American Indian Nation* (1990).

See also CONNECTICUT; MOHEGAN; NARRAGANSETT; PEQUOT WAR; UNCAS

Pequot War (1636–1637)

One of the first successful English military campaigns against a Native American tribe, the Pequot War established the Puritans as a major force and ended the dominance of the powerful Pequot tribe in New England. Although the results of the war are clear enough, the background and actual events of the conflict are sometimes difficult to decipher since New Englanders published at least five separate reports on the conflict, each with its own perspective. In addition, other authors published their reflections in journals and general histories of Puritan New England.

Fertile in natural resources, the region now known as Connecticut captured the interest of the Narragansett, Niantic, Mohegan, Pequot, Dutch, and English. The Pequots, who settled in the region well before contact with Europeans, controlled much of the region, extending their influence from present-day New Haven to Rhode Island, from Hartford onto eastern Long Island. In June 1633, the Dutch, realizing the strength of the Pequots, signed a treaty with the Pequot sachem, Wopigwooit, for a tract of land along the eastern edge of the Connecticut River (near present-day Hartford). The Dutch envisioned a free-trade zone where all Indians could come and trade with them. In reality, however, the Dutch post, "House of Good Hope," generated portentous competition among the Indians, which the Pequots did not appreciate. In October 1633, Plymouth decided to join the wampum economy along the Connecticut River, but when it purchased land north of the Dutch on the Connecticut River it dealt with sachems subordinate to the Pequot rather than the Pequot leadership itself. The Pequot, therefore, saw the English action as a de facto repudiation of their authority. Also at this time a few Dutch traders disrupted Indian-European relations by kidnapping Wopigwooit. When the Pequots sent wampum to redeem their sachem, the Dutch merely returned the corpse. (Some believe that the Dutch orchestrated the affair to destablize the Pequot nation, thereby allowing the Dutch to better monopolize the Indian trade.) The Pequot tribe thus felt serious provocation toward the Europeans, and sought opportunities to assert their authority.

In January 1633–1634, the Pequot made their point. New England learned that either the Pequot or a vassal tribe killed Virginia merchant Captain John Stone and his crew while they were trading on the Connecticut River. After Massachusetts leaders threatened revenge, the Pequots sent a messenger, in October, to calm the tense situation. Puritan representatives received the messenger's gifts, but told him that the Pequot must send their leaders along with the murderers of Stone if they wanted an audience with New England's highest officials. The Pequot response was muted. They told the Massachusetts leaders that the Dutch had already killed the sachem who ruled at the time of Stone's death, and that all but two of the Stone conspirators had since died of smallpox. The Pequot also justified the attack on Stone by explaining that he had kidnapped two Pequots to use as guides up the Connecticut River, and that in the heat of a Pequot rescue attempt some powder had inexplicably ignited, thus destroying Stone's ship. John Winthrop recorded that the Pequot leaders related this story "with such confidence and gravity" that the Massachusetts leaders were "inclined to believe it."

It is surprising that Massachusetts leaders used the Stone incident—given Stone's history in New England—as a means of gaining the moral high ground against the Pequot. A few months earlier, Stone had been found in bed with "one Bancroft's wife." When told by the governor that he must stay offshore on his ship while in New England, Stone verbally attacked Massachusetts Judge Roger Ludlow with "brave and threatening speeches." At that point Stone was arrested and charged with adultery, but the grand jury found Stone an "ignoramus," fined him £100, and promised to execute him if he ever returned to the bay.

Massachusetts leaders understood that the Pequot needed the English about as much as the English needed the Pequot. The Pequot were at war with the Narragansett and both the Pequot and the English feared that the Narragansett would construct an alliance with the Dutch. Realizing the gravity and possibilities of the situation, the New England Puritans decided to play the role of peacemaker in the region. They negotiated a settlement between the Pequot and the Narragansett and reaped financial rewards from both. Not everyone was pleased with the peace, however. John Eliot, later known as "the Apostle to the Indians," publicly criticized the "lenient peace" that the magistrates had made with the Pequot.

During 1635 and early 1636, Massachusetts took advantage of the calm to send settlers to Connecticut. They hired, for example, Lieutenant Lion Gardener to build Fort Saybrook at the mouth of the Connecticut River. But relations quickly degenerated, and on 4 May 1636, Massachusetts Bay Governor Henry Vane sent instructions to Connecticut Governor John Winthrop, Jr., to tell the Pequots to send Stone's killers to Massachusetts for justice, and to remit the other half of "the present." Then the trip-wire was found.

In July 1636, John Gallop spied John Oldham's trading pinnace sailing erratically off the coast of Block Island. He also noted a number of Indians on deck. Assuming that the Indians had seized Oldham's ship, Gallop attacked the pinnace, killing ten to 11 Indians in the skirmish. A Massachusetts investigation determined that all of the Narragansett sachems—except Canonicus and Miantonomo—were "contrivers of Oldham's death" because Oldham was a leading advocate of peace with the

Pequot. On 8 August 1636, the Massachusetts government sent Lieutenant Edward Gibbons, John Higginson, and Cutshamekin (Massachusetts sagamore) to the Narragansett. When the three returned on the 13th, they announced that Canonicus had cleared himself and his neighbors of Oldham's murder, and had offered to assist in the revenge. On 24 August 1636, the Endicott expedition set sail to extract that revenge.

Endicott's adventures only served to make a difficult situation worse. Although the Puritans had temporarily settled matters with the Narragansett, the Pequots were outraged. And once Roger Williams successfully blocked a potential alliance between the Narragansetts and Pequots in the winter of 1637, the Pequots responded with a guerrilla campaign against the English in Connecticut. The attacks by the Pequot in Connecticut were especially threatening, given the size of the English population. Lieutenant Gardener "commanded" a force of 24 men, women, and children at Fort Saybrook, and only 250 lived in the other English settlements. So the Puritans were sensitive to any attacks. On 22 February 1637, for example, Lieutenant Gardener and ten soldiers left Fort Saybrook for provisions, but before they ventured far, some 70 to 100 Pequots attacked. Four men were killed, two wounded. In this simple clash, the Pequots had effectively decimated Gardener's Saybrook force. Then to show that they understood the English's precarious position a force of 200 to 300 Pequot warriors taunted Fort Saybrook on 9 March 1637, scoffing "Come out and fight if you dare"—underscoring the fact that the fort was under siege. Gardener requested assistance from Governor Henry Vane, and Vane responded by sending Captain John Underhill and 20 men. Then on 23 April 1637 approximately 100 Pequot warriors (Underhill recalled 200) attacked the English village of Wethersfield, up the Connecticut River from Fort Saybrook. Nine settlers were killed in the strike, and two young girls were taken captive.

By the end of April, Pequot attacks had killed approximately 30 English settlers, and the Connecticut General Court, meeting at Hartford, responded with a declaration of war. The court gave Captain John Mason command of a force of 80 to 100 Connecticut volunteers and told him to attack the Pequot strongholds. Uncas, sachem of the Mohegan, offered his assistance to Mason, and though Mason was wary, he agreed. On 15 May 1637, the Mohegans assured Mason of their intentions when they killed five to seven Pequots in a small skirmish. When Mason's force reached Saybrook, Underhill added his 20 men to the assault force, although an equivalent number of Connecticut men remained at Saybrook to protect the fort.

Lieutenant Gardener and Captain Underhill expressed their uncertainty in Mason's ability to command since Mason had limited military experience. They were especially alarmed when they learned that Mason's strategy included a frontal assault on the sachem's Pequot River fort, Weinshauks. Sachem Sassacus would clearly hold the numerical and tactical advantage if Mason sailed up the Pequot River. Mason then suggested that the force sail east from Saybrook, past the Pequot River and Weinshauks, landing in Narragansett territory—well east of the Pequots' strength. Then his force would double back, marching westward overland, attacking the Pequots from the east. While most thought this strategy superior to the former, some voiced concern that it might be sinful to disobey the original commands. Mason then asked one of the chaplains of the expedition, Reverend Samuel Stone, to pray and seek God's sanction for the new strategy.

Once the blessing was given, Mason enacted the plan. The only problem was that the Narragansett sachem, Miantonomo, was unaware of Mason's intentions and had not given approval for a landing on Narragansett lands. Once presented with the plan, Miantonomo allowed passage of the force through Narragansett territory, but told Mason that the expedition was doomed since the Pequot were too strong for the English. Later, however, Miantonomo decided to send warriors to join Mason's attack. Reports vary concerning the numbers of Indians in the force. Miantonomo apparently sent between 300 to 500, while Uncas added 50 to 100. Captain Mason noted that the entire Indian contribution was 500. Captain Underhill figured the combined Indian force at 300. Philip Vincent recorded the Indian contingent at 500 to 600. Whatever numbers used, it is clear that the 70 to 80 English were a distinct minority.

As the combined Narragansett-Mohegan-Anglo force reached Pequot territory, Mason decided to attack the fort on the Mystic River rather than Sassacus's village. Whatever the reasons behind the decision—distance to Sassacus's village or fear of Sassacus's strength—on the morning of 26 May 1637, the attacking force surrounded the palisades of the Pequot village. The English were in front, with the Narragansett and Mohegans forming a second circle behind. Once the Pequots sounded the alarm, the Puritans fired a volley through the palisades. Then, as the Puritan sources retell the events, Captain Mason led the charge toward the northeast entrance of the village, while Captain Underhill led the advance from the south. Once inside the palisades the English found that "the fort was too hot for us." So Mason entered a longhouse, seized a firebrand, and began setting fire to the houses. Once engulfed, Mason ordered his men outside the palisade and commanded that any Pequot fleeing the inferno should be "entertained with the point of a sword."

Mason recalled that the Pequot had once scoffed at the English and their religion, but "God was above them who laughed" and God "made them a fiery oven: filling the place with dead bodies." In the span of one hour the village was destroyed, and 300 to 700 Pequot men, women, elderly, and children had perished. The Puritans captured seven to 18 trying to escape, while only seven to eight Pequot successfully evaded their attackers, since the Narragansett surrounded the village so closely. The Puritans suffered two killed and 24 to 26 wounded. The Narragansett and Mohegans suffered 40 casualties.

After this battle, Mason's forces were short on provisions and deep in hostile territory with Pequot reinforcements nearby. As Mason's force tried to retreat, 300 Pequot warriors harassed the attackers. Both Mason and Underhill claimed responsibility for leading the heroic rearguard action that allowed the force to escape. Underhill boasted that with 39 men he held off the Pequots, killing 100 more in the process. Although Captain Patrick arrived with the ships at Pequot harbor, Mason was unable to evacuate the entire force, so he led the march of 20 English and most of the Indians westward to Fort Saybrook.

The devastation inflicted on Mystic Fort thrust the Pequot tribe into utter chaos. Many of the Pequots rejected Sassacus's leadership and migrated toward other tribes, such as the Manhatance (Manhatan or Manhatoes) on Long Island. Sassacus desperately tried to hold his people together and sought help from neighboring tribes. Instead of allies, however, he found more enemies. Eventually Sassacus appealed to the Mohawk, but they executed him and sent his scalp back to Massachusetts.

About two weeks after Mason returned, a Massachusetts force of 120, under the command of Israel Stoughton, arrived at Saybrook. With this infusion of troops, Mason launched an attack on the Pequot refugees, who moved slowly due to the number of children and a lack of provisions. On 13 July 1637, the English surrounded some remnants of the Pequot tribe at a swamp near present-day New Haven. For the better part of the afternoon the two sides exchanged fire, but with little consequence. Toward evening, Thomas Stanton—who knew the Pequot language—went into the swamp and negotiated the evacuation of 180 to 200 old men, women, and children (some reports put the number at 99). Although the Puritans tried to annihilate the remaining 70 to 80 Pequot men the next morning, most managed to escape. Seven Pequots were killed—although Hubbard puts the number at more than 20. Those who surrendered the night before became slaves.

Having lost 700 to 1,500 members at the hands of the Puritans and untold numbers to neighboring tribes, the remaining Pequot sachems came forward asking for peace for the 180 to 200 who remained. Under terms of the Treaty of Hartford (1638), Uncas took 80 Pequots, Miantonomo took 80, Ninigret (Niantic sachem) secured 20, and a handful were sold into slavery in the Caribbean. The treaty also stipulated that the Pequot were no longer entitled to their native lands, or their tribal name. In addition, the Hartford Treaty (or Tripartite Treaty) sealed the peace between the Mohegans, Narragansett, and Puritans.

Although pockets of Pequots rejected the treaty, the Pequot tribe ceased to exist as a strong, autonomous, recognized tribe until the twentieth century.

Richard C. Goode

References

Lion Gardener, *Lieft Lion Gardener his relation of the Pequot Warres* in *Massachusetts Historical Society Collections*, 3rd ser., 3 (1833):131–160; William Hubbard, *A Narrative of the Troubles with the Indians in New England* (1677); John Mason, *Brief History of the Pequot War* in *Collections of the Massachusetts Historical Society*, 2nd ser., 7 (1826):120–153; Increase Mather, *A Relation of the Troubles Which Have Happened in New England by Reason of the Indians There* (1766).

John Underhill, *News from America,* in *Massachusetts Historical Society Collections*, 3rd ser., 6 (1837):1–28; Philip Vincent, *A True Relation of the Late Battle Fought* in *New England in Collections of the Massachusetts Historical Society*, 3rd ser., 6 (1837):29–43; John Winthrop, *Winthrop's Journal: "History of New England," 1630–1649*, 2 vols., James Kendall Hosmer, ed. (1908).

See also CONNECTICUT; FORT CORCHAUG (NEW YORK); ENDICOTT EXPEDITION; FORT GOOD HOPE (CONNECTICUT); MIANTONOMO; MOHEGAN; NARRANGANSETT; PEQUOT; FORT SAYBROOK (CONNECTICUT); FORT SHANTOK (CONNECTICUT); UNCAS; UNDERHILL, JOHN; WILLIAMS, ROGER

Pez, Andrés de (1653–1723)

Andrés de Pez was a Spanish seaman credited with convincing the Spanish royal court of the need to occupy Pensacola Bay to prevent foreign penetration of the upper Gulf of Mexico coast. Pez was born in Cádiz, Spain, to a naval family and entered the service in the Andalucia fleet in 1673 as an ordinary seaman. In 1681, he transferred to the Windward fleet, which was charged with protecting Spanish interests in the Gulf of Mexico and Caribbean Sea. While stationed in the New World he saw action against pirates and participated in various of the seaborne expeditions that searched for René-Robert Cavelier de La Salle's Gulf Coast colony in 1687 to 1688.

His personal bravery and understanding of naval conditions in the Gulf of Mexico and Caribbean provided Pez the means for steady promotion. By 1687, he had reached the rank of captain and soon thereafter became commander of Presidio San Juan de Ulúa in Veracruz Harbor. Having escorted some of the La Salle survivors to Spain, he was promoted to the rank of admiral and knighted in the Order of Santiago. On his return to New Spain in 1692, he became commander of the Windward fleet and led an exploratory expedition to Pensacola and Mobile Bays and the Mississippi delta.

Pez continued in the Spanish navy until 1717, when he became governor of the Council of the Indies, the royal council in charge of colonial affairs. Despite the ascent of the Bourbon Philip V to the Spanish throne, Pez advocated an antipathetic policy toward the French in the Gulf of Mexico. Three years later, the king appointed him secretary of state for war and marine, in addition to his post on the Council of the Indies. He died at Madrid on 9 March 1723.

Jesús F. de la Teja

References

Robert S. Weddle, *The French Thorn: Rival Explorers in the Spanish Sea, 1682–1762* (1991).

See also COUNCIL OF THE INDIES; PENSACOLA

Philip (?–1676)

Also known as Metacom (Metacomet), Philip was the Wampanoag sachem from 1664 to 1676. The son of Massasoit, Philip succeeded his brother Alexander (Wamsutta), who died while in the custody of Plymouth leaders. When Philip became the grand sachem he quickly renewed the Wampanoag-Pilgrim peace accord. Yet Philip was a proud and wise man who realized that the English avarice for land, as well as the creation of "praying Indians," meant the decline of Indian culture. Thus he saw two choices. Either the Indians would totally submit to the English, or they would have to rise up in unified armed insurrection. Initially Philip did not challenge Plymouth, for he was still threatened by the Narragansetts, but in 1667, relations with the English began to deteriorate.

In that year, Plymouth suspected that Philip was in league with the Dutch to attack the English. Philip denied any knowledge of the alliance and asserted that Ninigret, the Niantic sachem, was the source of the rumors. When Philip's claim was proven spurious, Philip was forced to pay a fine of £40. In 1671, yet another war scare rocked Plymouth when a rumor circulated that the Wampanoags and Narragansetts were arming themselves at Mount Hope, the Wampanoag capital. Philip was hauled before the Plymouth leaders at Taunton in April 1671 and forced to cower to the English. Then in the summer of 1671, Philip sought to diminish pressure from Plymouth by playing Massachusetts against Plymouth. Unfortunately for Philip his plan miscarried. Again Philip was forced to do penance, pay a fine of £156, and sign a treaty that gave Plymouth the sole right to dispose of Wampanoag lands. A Rubicon had been passed. Philip balked at the idea that the English could dispose of his lands at their discretion. Philip began to construct a military Indian alliance.

The first attack of King Philip's War occurred on 20 June 1675, at Swansea, Massachusetts. After a series of summer raids by Philip's forces, the United Colonies of New England declared war on 9 September 1675. With this escalation, Philip sought support from the Mohawks and their Iroquois Confederation, but Philip's request was denied. Though Philip's troops pressed ever closer to Boston, they could not maintain a war of attrition, and by the summer of 1676 the end was near for Philip. On 12 August 1676, Philip was surrounded and killed by Indian allies of the English. His body was quartered and his head returned to English settlements in celebration.

Richard C. Goode

References

Francis Jennings, *The Invasion of America: Indians, Colonialism, and the Cant of Conquest* (1975); Douglas Edward Leach, *Flintlock and Tomahawk: New England in King Philip's War* (1958); Richard Slotkin and James Folsom, eds. *So Dreadful a Judgment: Puritan Responses to King Philip's War, 1676–1677* (1978); Bruce G. Trigger, *Handbook of North American Indians, Vol. 15: Northeast* (1978); Wilcomb E. Washburn, *Handbook of North American Indians, Vol. 4: History of Indian-White Relations* (1988).

See also KING PHILIP'S WAR; NEW ENGLAND CONFEDERATION; PLYMOUTH; PRAYING INDIANS; WAMPANOAG

Philip II (1527–1598)

King of Spain, son of Holy Roman Emperor Charles V, Philip II ascended the throne upon his father's abdication in 1556. His realms included the Spanish Netherlands, the Kingdom of the Two Sicilies, the Kingdoms of Spain (León, Castille, and Aragón), the Spanish Indies, and other minor holdings. After 1580 he was also king of Portugal, and its overseas holdings.

Philip was a thorough monarch who kept himself informed about all of his possessions, relying heavily on the Spanish conciliar form of government. Each of the major realms was administered by a royal council, such as the Council of the Indies, the Council of Castile, the Council of Aragón, the Council of Portugal, and the Council of State, with jurisdiction over both Italian and northern European holdings. He also relied heavily on royal secretaries who managed the flow of information through the councils and to the monarch. He regularly shifted his allegiances within this inner circle to maintain a balance of influence.

Under the rule of Philip, the Spanish world empire reached its maximum size, encompassing all of the Americas and the Philippines. When he became king of Portugal in 1580, to his realms were added outposts in China, the Spice Islands, Goa, Mozambique, Angola, and Brazil. Although united under one monarch, the two kingdoms nevertheless remained strictly separate political entities, with no direct contact between them.

During the reign of Philip II, Spain conducted an ongoing war against the Auracanian Indians of Chile. Melchor López de Legaspi conquered the Philippines. Pedro Menéndez de Avilés ended French claims to Florida and established the Spanish permanently in St. Augustine. The Indians of the northern deserts of Mexico were pacified.

The Spanish American colonies also felt the pressure from other European powers during the epoch. Leading all others were the English, principally through the efforts of John Hawkins and later Sir Francis Drake. The French attempted to settle Florida and Brazil.

John F. Schwaller

References

Geoffrey Parker, *Philip II* (1978).

See also COUNCIL OF INDIES; FLORIDA; MENÉNDEZ DE AVILÉS, PEDRO

Phips, Sir William (1651–1694)

Sir William Phips, treasure hunter, military leader, and governor of Massachusetts, was born in humble circumstances on the Kennebec River in Maine, one of the numerous children of James and Mary Phips. Apprenticed to a ship's carpenter, he came to Boston, built and captained several vessels, and married Mary Spencer Hull, the widow of a prominent merchant. But from childhood, Phips was convinced, in the words of his biographer, Cotton Mather, that "he was Born to greater Matters." Inspired by tales of sunken treasure ships, he followed a voyage of exploration to the Bahamas with a second to England. There he induced King Charles II to loan him a 20-gun ship that he sailed back to Boston in 1683 and then to the Caribbean, facing down rivals and mutineers as he went. The voyage found no treasure, but Phips persuaded a consortium headed by England's duke of Albermarle to stake him to a further expedition that in 1686, using divers and a primitive diving bell, discovered large quantities of silver in a sunken galleon off the coast of Hispaniola. Phips returned to England with nearly 30 tons of coin and bullion valued at more than £200,000 of which his personal share amounted to £11,000. Greeted with open arms and palms by his backers, he was knighted by King James II.

Phips spent the next five years of his life oscillating between old and New England. He returned to Boston in June 1688 with an appointment as provost marshal general in the newly created royal government of the Dominion of New England, only to be so coldly received by its governor, Sir Edmund Andros, that he retreated back to England and aligned himself with Increase Mather and other colonists there seeking Andros's recall. The Glorious Revolution of 1688, by which William of Orange toppled James II from the English throne, opened the way for political changes in America, and Phips was again in Massachusetts for three months following the colonists' overthrow of Andros and the dominion in April 1689. Back in London, he continued to work with Increase Mather to secure a restoration of Massachusetts's charter privileges. Not until the spring of 1690, once more in Boston, did he find a role befitting his ambitions. War with the French in Canada and their Indian allies had inflicted heavy damage on New England's frontier towns and fisheries, and plans were afoot for a counterattack directed against the French settlements in Acadia (modern Nova Scotia). Phips—visibly aggressive, eager for office, honored in England and yet a native son—appeared the ideal candidate for a command. His newly forged alliance with the powerful father-and-son team of Cotton and Increase Mather was now sealed by instant initiation into the Massachusetts elite: on 22 March, compressing into a few hours what it took mere mortals half a lifetime to achieve, Phips was named a freeman of Massachusetts, major general, and commander in chief of the forthcoming expedition on one day, and received baptism and full membership in Mather's Boston North Church on the next. A few weeks later he was chosen to the colony's council of magistrates.

Phips's seaborne expedition against Acadia in April and May of 1690 was a swift yet not wholly creditable success. At the head of a powerful force of some 700 sailors and militiamen, he had no difficulty persuading Governor Louis-Alexandre des Friches de Meneval to surrender his weakly-held post of Port Royal (modern Annapolis Royal) on 12 May on promise of the protection of private property and safe-conduct for the garrison back to French soil. The victors promptly violated these terms and plundered the town with ruthless zeal. Phips in particular was accused of looting Meneval's extensive personal possessions, a charge that led to an embarrassing confrontation with his fellow councilors on his return to Boston. Nor did he make any effort to garrison, and thereby retain, Port Royal.

Nonetheless, Phips was the hero of the hour and the natural choice to command the larger expedition now launched by the New England colonies against the much more formidable target of Quebec. Here his fabled luck ran out. The assembled fleet did not reach Quebec until early October, far too late in the season to conduct any lengthy siege; the forces landed north of the town were poorly disciplined and led; and Phips himself, instead of supporting these forces in their assault as had been planned, sailed off to waste the expedition's scanty ammunition in a showy but futile bombardment of Quebec's eastward flank. Within a week, the expedition was compelled to beat a precipitous and costly retreat.

Unabashed, Phips headed for London to petition King William for aid in a new attack on Canada. There, too, he worked with Increase Mather in negotiating for a new charter for Massachusetts: among his contributions were proposals for exploiting the timber and mineral resources of eastern New England that played a part in extending the bounds prescribed in the charter to include Maine and Acadia. Mather was permitted to nominate the officials appointed by the crown to head the new government. Phips was his choice for chief executive, and in December 1691, the former ship's carpenter, now in his fortieth year, received the king's commission as governor.

Phips and Mather reached Boston in May 1692 to face opposition on both flanks, from the many colonists who lamented the loss of the old charter's privileges and from others, mainly merchants and Episcopalians, who felt that the new government was insufficiently subordinate to the crown. In several respects, Phips's first months of office were constructive. Finding the colony enmeshed in the Salem Village witchcraft trials, he stepped in after some indecision to prevent further executions and eventually put an end to the trials. Simultaneously he worked with the colony's legislature to calm public fears about the passing of the old Puritan order by reenacting many of its laws and procedures, such as state

support for the Congregational church. To the eastward, he sought to shore up the colony's defenses by rebuilding the former English strongpoint at Pemaquid, now named Fort William Henry and equipped with 18 cannon. Several expeditions under Benjamin Church and James Converse were sent out to patrol the frontiers, leading to the signing of a peace agreement with the eastern Indians in the summer of 1693.

Overall, however, Phips's three-year governorship revealed the obverse side of the very force of character and determination to succeed that had lifted him from obscurity. Intolerant of opposition, especially when it stood in the way of his personal advantage, he engaged in hand-to-hand brawls on the Boston waterfront with Collector of Customs Jahleel Brenton and Captain Richard Short of the Royal Navy frigate *Nonsuch* when they seemed to challenge his authority. Confronted with opposition in the colony's General Court, he first sought to purge his opponents by invalidating their election and then personally invaded the lower court to drive them out. His brusque attempts to assert his authority over the militia of neighboring colonies drew angry complaints from their commanders. Other evidence later gathered by his critics charged him with using his position as governor to turn a quick profit in ventures ranging from privateering, the sale of prize vessels, and the production of naval stores, to trading with the Indians, an attempted monopoly of the fur trade, and speculation in eastern lands.

By 1693, complaints of the governor's behavior were pouring into Whitehall. Phips made matters no easier for himself by his reluctance to aid an expedition organized in England and led by Sir Francis Wheeler that arrived in Boston in July but was then forced to abandon its design of a new attack on Canada. Finally, in the fall of 1694, he was recalled to England to answer charges of misconduct. There, even as he responded with a flurry of new schemes designed to prove his worth, he died of a fever and was buried in London's Church of St. Mary Woolnoth.

Phips was a man of great personal force and vitality, much admired and as fiercely resented. Cotton Mather's eulogistic biography, *Pietas in Patriam* (1697), presents the best possible case for the defense. Yet even as Mather lauded Phips as a hero who best served his country by serving himself, he inevitably pointed up how sharply Sir William's style of leadership contrasted with the gentility of a John Winthrop or a Simon Bradstreet. Spectacularly self-made but ever seeking to make more of and for himself, Phips had the kind of personality perpetually driven to validate itself through confrontation: his life was a string of episodes in which, under cover of upholding some recently assumed authority, and regardless of ideology, he picked face-to-face quarrels that he pursued with ferocious energy. Passionate, resourceful, and plain-spoken—Mather delicately characterized him as "cutting rather like a *Hatchet* than a *Razor*"—Phips emerges as a formidable enemy and charismatic personality but a greedy and short-sighted politician and an incompetent military strategist.

Richard R. Johnson

References

A Journal of the Proceedings in the Late Expedition to Port Royal (1690); Viola F. Barnes, "The Rise of Sir William Phips," and "Phippius Maximus," *New England Quarterly* I (1928):271–294, 532–553; Richard R. Johnson, *Adjustment to Empire: The New England Colonies, 1675–1715* (1981); Alice Lounsberry, *Sir William Phips, Treasure Fisherman and Governor of the Massachusetts Bay Colony* (1941); Cotton Mather, *Pietas in Patriam: The Life of His Excellency Sir William Phips, Knt.* (1697).

See also ACADIA, NEW ENGLAND ATTACK ON (1690); ANDROS, EDMUND; CANADA, NEW ENGLAND EXPEDITION AGAINST (1690); DOMINION OF NEW ENGLAND; KING WILLIAM'S WAR

Fort Picolata (Florida)

Fort Picolata was a small wooden fort located on the east bank of the St. Johns River, seven leagues west of St. Augustine, Florida, on the old Indian trail to Spain's western province of Apalachee. It was constructed in the fall of 1734 on the orders of Governor Francisco del Moral Sánchez, who anticipated English and Indian attacks. Governor Moral spent 2,036 pesos on the construction of Picolata and its twin on the west side of the St. Johns, Fort San Francisco de Pupo. Picolata contained a blockhouse, barracks, and storehouses, and was fortified with several small cannon. Nine soldiers manned the fort. In 1735, Picolata was attacked by a band of Talapuses and Uchize Indians. They killed one Spanish soldier and badly damaged the fort. On 1 January 1740, General James Oglethorpe of Georgia, com-

manding a larger force of Creek, Chickasaw, and Uchize Indians and Highland rangers, captured Forts Picolata and Pupo after killing 12 Spanish soldiers. Although Pupo was retaken by the Spaniards in May of 1740, Picolata was destroyed. In the final days of the first Spanish regime in Florida (1565–1763), Picolata was rebuilt with a stone watchtower surrounded by a wooden stockade and earthworks. The rebuilt fort at Picolata remained in use during the British interregnum (1763–1784), the second Spanish period (1784–1821), and the American territorial period (1821–1845).

Jane Landers

References

Verne E. Chatelain, *The Defenses of Spanish Florida, 1565 to 1763* (1941); John Jay TePaske, *The Governorship of Spanish Florida, 1700–1763* (1964).

See also ANGLO-SPANISH WAR (1739–1744); MORAL SÁNCHEZ, FRANCISCO DEL; OGLETHORPE, JAMES EDWARD

Pigwacket

See ABENAKI

Pilgrim

Unwilling to tolerate the Church of England, the Pilgrims separated from the whole of English society by moving from Scrooby to the Dutch city of Leyden in 1607, and then to southern New England in 1620.

Arriving in December 1620, the Pilgrims established Plymouth Colony on the western shore of Cape Cod Bay. Threatened by the ignorance of requisite agricultural methods and tensions created by previous Indian-European interaction, the Pilgrims bettered their chance for persistence in the New world through an alliance with the Wampanoags on 22 March 1621. According to the Pilgrims' interpretation, the treaty made the Wampanoags vassals of the English monarch, guaranteed defensive aid for Plymouth, and validated Plymouth's right to exist, since the Pilgrims' charter was technically invalid north of the Virginia grant. The Wampanoags, in turn, received Plymouth's pledge of military assistance.

While Plymouth's situation with the Wampanoags was amicable, the Pilgrims' relations with other tribes in the region became increasingly militarized. For example, in 1622, Canonicus, leading sachem of the Narragansetts, sent a snakeskin filled with arrows to Plymouth to condemn the Pilgrims' interference with the Wampanoags. Governor William Bradford returned the skin filled with shot and powder. In the spring of 1623, Plymouth leaders achieved a preemptive strike against the Massachusetts tribe who, according to the Wampanoag sachem, Massasoit, had allied themselves with tribes from Cape Cod, Martha's Vineyard, and Agawam to attack Wessagusset—a non-English settlement on Massachusetts Bay. Miles Standish and eight associates assassinated the Massachusetts sachem, Wituwamet, and several of his "co-conspirators." Having flexed their military muscle, the Pilgrims spent the next few years extorting tribute from the local tribes, trading much of that tribute to the Abenaki for pelts.

With the arrival of the Puritans beginning in 1630, Plymouth's dominion over New England began to wane. Nevertheless, the Pilgrims continued exclusive relations with the Wampanoags. This was necessary since the "heretics" of Rhode Island were also making claims to Wampanoag lands. The Pilgrims forced the successors of Massasoit [Alexander and Philip] to grant Plymouth the power to allocate Wampanoag lands at their discretion. This restriction contributed significantly to the beginning of King Philip's War.

Richard C. Goode

References

William Bradford, *History of Plymouth Plantation* (1952); George D. Langdon, Jr., *Pilgrim Colony: A History of New Plymouth, 1620–1691* (1966); G. Mourt, *Journal of the Pilgrims at Plymouth* (1622); Neal Salisbury, *Manitou and Providence: Indians, Europeans, and the Making of New England, 1500–1643* (1982); Alden T. Vaughan, *New England Frontier: Puritans and Indians, 1620–1675* (1965).

See also KING PHILIP'S WAR; NARRAGANSETT; PHILIP; PLYMOUTH; PURITANS; STANDISH, MILES; WAMPANOAG; WESSAGUSSET RAID

Piscataway

See MARYLAND

Fort Pitt (Pennsylvania)

An enormous, basically earthen-work, pentagonal fort, with an extending perimeter to seal off the point of the peninsula at the confluence of the Allegheny and Monongahela Rivers, Fort Pitt was maintained by the British from September 1759 to October 1772. It succeeded Fort Duquesne and the small Fort Mercer on the same peninsula. Rivaling Fort Ticonderoga as the most formidable British post of the period, Fort Pitt ironically was never significantly challenged or fully garrisoned. France's potential to return to the upper Ohio Valley was eclipsed in August 1759, the month before construction began. A masonry wall was part of the eastern perimeter of the pentagon and shielded part of the works from torrents of flood waters in January 1762 and March 1763, but those conflagrations made it obvious that the location was impractical. The initial construction expenditure was all that justified maintenance of the site.

Fort Pitt was only attacked once, in the two months prior to the Battle of Bushy Run (5–6 August 1763) when Indians allied with Pontiac's movement (Ottawas, Wyandots, and Delawares) surrounded it. An attack from the Allegheny riverbank lasted from 28 July to 1 August, and resulted in 20 Indian casualties and the wounding of eight redcoats, one of whom later died. The Indians set fire to the roofs of a barracks and the commander's home, pillaged the gardens, and stole cattle, but they abandoned the area when Henry Bouquet's force moved toward Bushy Run; the departing siege force probably was the group that ambushed Bouquet at Bushy Run.

Fort Pitt was the logistical and command center for forts in the upper Ohio Valley. It was the base for Bouquet's Ohio expedition of October–December 1764. With its adjacent community, Pittsburgh, it was a trading post, and the site for negotiations with various tribes. After 1765, boats were built and loaded with cargo there for the Anglo-American stations in Illinois. The last credible rumor of an Indian attack arose in 1767. In 1768, the king's government abandoned its civil administration of Indian trade, and neither the army nor the colonies wanted to assume the chore. The abandonment of Fort Pitt in 1772 roughly coincided with the closing of other British frontier military posts. The structure remained sufficiently intact to be reopened as Fort Dunmore in 1774.

Louis M. Waddell

References

Clarence E. Carter, ed., *The Correspondence of General Thomas Gage . . . 1763–*

1775, 2 vols. (1933); John Wilson Huston, "Fort Pitt, 1758–1772," Ph.D. Dissertation, University of Pittsburgh (1957); Donald H. Kent, John L. Tottenham, Louis M. Wadell, et al., *The Papers of Henry Bouquet*, Vols. 3–5 (1976–1984).

See also BOUQUET, HENRY; BUSHY RUN, BATTLE OF; FORT DUQUESNE (PENNSYLVANIA); PONTIAC'S WAR

Pitt, William, First Earl of Chatham (1708–1778)

William Pitt was born in Westminster on 15 November 1708, the younger son of Robert Pitt of Boconnoc in Cornwall. He was educated at Eton and Trinity College, Oxford. He suffered severely from gout and on medical advice left the university without taking a degree and spent some time in France and Italy. On his return to England he was still suffering from the hereditary disease, and as it was necessary for him to have some form of employment he obtained a cornetcy in the King's Own Regiment of Horse on 9 February 1731. Four years later he ran for Parliament and in February 1735 succeeded his elder brother, Thomas, and became the member for Old Sarum. He then joined William Pulteney's party of "patriots" in opposition to Robert Walpole.

He spoke for the first time in the House of Commons on 29 April 1736, when he supported a motion for a congratulatory address to George II on the marriage of the Prince of Wales. Its intentional satire was so offensive that he was shortly afterwards dismissed from his cornetcy in the army. Pitt became an aggressive parliamentarian, speaking out against the convention with Spain, and it is generally accepted that this speech, made on 8 March 1739, first showed his power as an orator. He was reelected at the general election in May 1741, and continued to serve as the member for Old Sarum.

Pitt spoke out against Walpole, and among the principles that he fought against was the practice of paying Hanoverian troops with English money, and the system of foreign subsidies—a stand that made him very popular in the country.

In 1745, Pitt actively supported the cause for the raising of new regiments during the Jacobite rebellion, and although Prime Minister Henry Pelham wanted to have Pitt as the secretary of war, the king opposed his appointment. Following the resignation of Pelham and then his return to power, Pitt was appointed joint vice-treasurer of Ireland, and following this he gave his support to the employment of the Hanoverians in Flanders. On 6 May 1746, he was promoted to the important post of paymaster general of the forces, and on 24 May was made a member of the Privy Council. At this time he refused to accept the customary financial gains that normally accompanied his post and in so doing secured himself a great deal of public confidence.

In January 1751, Pitt defended the new treaties with Spain and Bavaria and strongly opposed the plan for the reduction of the British navy. His support for major changes increased his standing in Parliament, but after the death of Pelham in March 1754, the promotion that he had hoped to receive was denied him. On 14 November 1754, he obtained permission to bring in a bill for the relief of Chelsea outpensioners that passed through both Houses without opposition. Pitt was dismissed from his office on 20 November 1755, and throughout that year hostilities continued between the English and the French in North America. With the deterioration of the situation Pitt, as an M.P., supported the government in making the army and navy more effective. The disastrous events such as the loss of Minorca, the capture of Calcutta by Surajah Dowlah, and the atrocities committed at the Black Hole of Calcutta, together with the defeat of General Edward Braddock at Fort Duquesne, caused the government to fall. The king, finding that the control of the government was in the hands of an administration that had failed, agreed that Pitt should take control, and in December 1756, he became secretary of state for the southern department and leader of the House of Commons. Unfortunately, Pitt was distrusted by the king and only weakly supported in the House of Commons and found it difficult to carry on the government. He took vigorous measures to increase the strength of the army, dismissed the Hessian troops, and brought in a bill for the establishment of a national militia. Pitt had been absent from office due to a severe attack of gout and returned as leader of the House on 17 February 1757. King George II refused an appeal for clemency by Pitt in the case of Admiral George Byng and, urged on by the duke of Cumberland, the king dismissed Pitt from office on 6 April 1757. Following 11 weeks of turmoil, the king agreed to Pitt's return, and with the help of Lord Mansfield, an alliance was reached between Pitt and his former adversary, the duke of Newcastle. Pitt became secretary of state with "supreme direction of the War and of foreign affairs."

With Pitt in control again, the business of government progressed, and having been re-elected as a member for Bath in a by-election in July 1757, he spent the next four years bringing the country to a period of new power in the world. Pitt himself planned expeditions and raised loans for war expenses. There followed a succession of victories, with the decisive battle of Minden on 1 August 1759. Robert Clive's victory at Plassey in India ensured that the English were in control of Bengal. In North America, Louisbourg and Fort Duquesne had been taken from the French, and then General James Wolfe achieved his victory at Quebec on 13 September 1759, thus effectively ending the French domination in Canada. In the same year, the French navy was almost entirely destroyed.

Pitt's conduct of the war led to the reestablishment of the English as a major nation in the eighteenth century, and at the close of the reign of George II, Pitt was at the zenith of his glory.

On the accession of George III, Pitt was persuaded to form an alliance with one of the king's favorites, and although there were moves to reach a peace with France, Pitt remained firm in his belief that only the "complete humiliation of France" would suffice. As a result of continued disagreement Pitt resigned from his office. He refused an offer to become governor of Canada and also that of chancellor of the Duchy of Lancaster; however, he did accept a substantial pension and the title of Baroness Chatham for his wife. As the reasons for his resignation had been misrepresented, Pitt wrote to the town clerk of the City of London putting his side of the story, and as a result, on Lord Mayor's day, he made a triumphant progress to the Guildhall during which time the king and queen "were scarcely noticed."

He continued in Parliament as the member of Bath and on 9 December 1762, he made a speech lasting three hours and 26 minutes denouncing the proposed treaty with France and Spain. He also refused to present the address prepared by the Bath corporation congratulating the king on the peace treaty.

At the beginning of 1765, his health deteriorated, and he spent several months in retirement in his home at Hayes. On 14 January 1766, Pitt returned to the House of Commons, and in a controversial speech, denied the right of the mother country to tax the colonies, and insisted that taxation was "no part of the governing or legislative power." Following his speech he was accused of causing sedition in America, which he naturally denied.

Pitt refused to form a coalition with the marquis of Rockingham. This decision was considered to be out of character, but was made at a time when his health had again deteriorated and he had become increasingly eccentric. His illness prevented him from attending the House of Commons except on infrequent occasions, and on 30 July 1766, he was persuaded to take the sinecure office of lord privy seal. He was then raised to the peerage and became Viscount Pitt of Burton Pynsent of Somerset and earl of Chatham.

There followed a period when, between bouts of illness, he appeared and made spirited speeches, and on 26 May 1774, he implored the ministers to adopt a more gentle mode of governing America. At the beginning of the following year, on 20 January 1775, he proposed an address to the king requesting that the British troops be "recalled from Boston." In his speech he fully justified the "resistance of the colonists." Regrettably, although he was supported by a number of prominent politicians, the motion was defeated by 68 votes to 13. Following a meeting with Benjamin Franklin on 1 February 1775, Chatham introduced a bill for "settling the trouble in America," and again the bill was defeated, but Chatham had the text of the bill printed and circulated to the general public. On 30 May 1777, although in great pain, he attended the House and unsuccessfully moved an address to the crown requesting the stopping of hostilities in America saying "You may ravage, you cannot conquer. It is impossible. You cannot conquer the Americans."

During the following summer Chatham fell from his horse while out riding at Hayes. However, he recovered and attended the House and made two further speeches in November 1777. On 5 December, he again appealed for the withdrawal of troops from America and spoke against the employment of Indians against the American people. The motion was again defeated. Chatham continued to advocate a change of policy toward the Americans, and in March 1778, Lord North unsuccessfully attempted to induce him to join the government.

His health continued to worsen and on 7 April 1778, against the advice of his physician,

Chatham insisted on being present at a debate in order to voice his disagreement with the American policy. He made a short speech, and when rising to speak a second time he fell backwards in a fit. He was taken from the House to a house in Downing Street and later moved to his home at Hayes where he lingered for a few weeks. He died on 11 May 1778, in his seventieth year.

Alan Harfield

References

Francis Thackeray, *History of the Earl of Chatham* (1827).

See also SEVEN YEARS' WAR

Fort Pleasant (West Virginia)

Fort Pleasant was located on the south branch of the Potomac River at the present town of Old Fields, five miles north of Moorefield in Hardy County, West Virginia. The palisaded fortification was built in 1756 under orders from George Washington, and it appears on a Washington map of operations for 1756. The fort contained several portholed blockhouses and a number of cabins housing a garrison of 60 men. In its early years it was called Fort Van Metre after its builder, and after the town of Moorefield was established nearby, the fort was also known as the Town Fort. The bloody Battle of the Trough, in which Indian attackers decimated the garrison, took place a short distance below the fort. George Washington visited the area in 1784 when the fort was still standing.

Thomas Costa

References

Louis K. Koontz, *The Virginia Frontier, 1754–1763* (1925)

Plymouth

Plymouth Colony (1620–1691) began as a small English settlement with the arrival of the Pilgrims on the *Mayflower* in Plymouth Bay, 16 December 1620.

On 17 February 1621, the Pilgrims gathered to appoint Miles Standish (1584–1656) as their supreme military commander. Advances to strengthen the settlement's defense system typified the first few months of Standish's leadership. A palisade surrounded the east side of the hill to the harbor and southward from the hill to the town brook. To secure the wall of the pale, flankers embraced the top of the hill and a fort formed where the walls came together. John Pory (1572–1635), a visitor in 1622, said that this defensive perimeter on the west and north sides of the town extended 2,700 feet in length and was stronger than any he had seen in Virginia.

Two events prompted the completion of the fort and palisade that Pory observed in 1622—the news in a letter that the Virginia colony at Jamestown had been massacred by the Indians and a gesture of war by the Narragansett Indians, a powerful tribe to the west of Plymouth. Standish divided his forces, finished the palisade for town protection, mounted existing artillery on the blockhouse, and instructed his men in the proper use of firearms.

The Plymouth colonists built a platform on Fort Hill overlooking the bay and surrounding country and installed their cannon there. They had a minion, a cannon weighing more than 1,200 pounds, having a bore three and one-quarter inches in diameter and possessing a range of 340 yards. Also a saker (or sacre), a larger cannon weighing 1,500 pounds, having a three-and-one-half-inch bore and firing 360 yards, was placed on the platform. Rounding out the armament were two bases, much smaller guns weighing only 202 pounds each and having bores of one and one-quarter inches.

Until 1627, all of the colonists resided within the village of Plymouth surrounded by the palisade. Two rows of houses along a street leading from the hilltop fort to the harbor formed the main thoroughfare. The bottom story of the fort served as the meetinghouse, where Sundays were spent in prayer and hymn singing. Muskets were carried by the men to the service for common defense against Indian attack.

Between 1630 and 1640, only two new towns were established as increasing friction with the Narragansett Indians alarmed the colonists. Gradually, these kinds of concerns ended with Plymouth improving its militia. In 1680, Governor Josiah Winslow (1629–1680) reported to England that Plymouth Colony counted 1,200 "enlisted men" from 16 to 60. This number would have included almost all of the adult males of the colony at that time.

While Plymouth was asked by Massachusetts Bay Colony to supply a militia against the Pequots in 1637 (a request that Plymouth refused, fearing its own survival if Massachusetts failed in the war), it was not until 1675 and King

Philip's War that the settlement risked its existence against the powerful Wampanoag tribe.

Ever since the spring of 1621 when chief Massasoit (1580?–1661) and his warriors first appeared at Plymouth Plantation and signed a treaty with John Carver (1576–1621), promising peace in exchange for protection, friendship prevailed. The first indication of trouble came in 1662 when Wamsutta reversed the land policy. The Plymouth General Court sent an armed force led by then-Major Josias Winslow to bring in Wamsutta after he delayed coming to Plymouth for questioning. Some question remains whether or not Winslow actually ambushed Wamsutta and took him prisoner, but the fact is that the chief died shortly thereafter of cholera. Rumors circulated quickly that Wamsutta's successor, his brother Philip (1638–1676), was angry and plotting trouble. Plymouth authorities summoned Philip to appear at Plymouth in August. Philip came and professed his love for the colony and pledged himself to continue his father's covenant with Plymouth. Philip refused to give up his firearms and he began to initiate unification talks with neighboring tribes.

The direct events leading to King Philip's War came with the murder of an Indian called John Sassamon (?–1674/5). Sassamon, heading toward Plymouth to report Philip's war plans, was murdered by three Indians, two of whom were from Philip's tribe in January 1674–1675. After their conviction and execution, Philip attacked.

King Philip's War caused considerable physical devastation, suffering, and loss of life in Plymouth. Approximately 5 to 8 percent of its adult men were lost in the war. Through now-Governor Winslow, Plymouth supplied leadership to the war effort.

Plymouth Colony contributed 150 infantrymen divided into two companies to Winslow's army, which was supposed to number 1,000. On 10 December 1675, the Plymouth companies joined with troops from Massachusetts at Rehoboth. While the main army operated in the western portion of the colony, Captain Benjamin Church (1639–1718), commanding a detachment of English soldiers and friendly Indian warriors, protected the southern and eastern sides of Plymouth. Early in August 1676, this roving band encountered Philip and a small group of his warriors at the Sakonnet River. Philip was killed, quartered, and left to rot on the ground.

After King Philip's War, the military significance of Plymouth declined in proportion to the Indian threat. Many of the adult male Indians captured were sold into slavery outside of the colony. By 1686, Plymouth was added to the Dominion of New England, and in 1691, when Massachusetts received a new charter, it became part of that colony, losing its separate identity.

John S. Erwin

References

John S. Erwin, "Captain Myles Standish's Military Role at Plymouth," *Historical Journal of Massachusetts*, xiii (1985):1–13; George D. Langdon, *Pilgrim Colony: A History of New Plymouth, 1620–1691* (1966); Douglas Edward Leach, "The Military System of Plymouth Colony," *New England Quarterly*, xxiv (1951):342–364; Herbert L. Osgood, *The American Colonies in the Seventeenth Century*, 3 vols. (1957); Jack S. Radabaugh, "The Militia of Colonial Massachusetts," *Military Affairs*, xviii (1954):1–18; Darrett Bruce Rutman, "A Militant New World 1607–1640," Ph.D. Dissertation, University of Virginia (1959).

See also CHURCH, BENJAMIN; KING PHILIP'S WAR; NARRAGANSETT; NEW ENGLAND CONFEDERATION; PILGRIM; PURITANS; STANDISH, MILES; WAMPANOAG; WAR AND SOCIETY IN COLONIAL AMERICA

Fort Pontchartrain de Detroit (Michigan)

Antoine Laumet de Lamothe Cadillac, former commandant at Fort Buade, saw the advantages of settling the Detroit area as a means of blocking Iroquois and British traders and developing a trade monopoly for himself. On 24 July 1701, with royal permission, he founded Fort Pontchartrain de Detroit, named after the French minister of the marine, Count Pontchartrain, and for the fact that it was at the narrowest point of the Detroit River.

The palisaded fort was a civilian settlement covering 37 acres. Cadillac convinced the Huron, Chippewa, Mississagua, Miami, and Ottawa to settle around the post and engage in the fur trade. Unfortunately, this mix of Indians caused various problems and hostilities that eventually led to the disastrous Fox War in 1712. Detroit flourished even after Cadillac's departure and eventually had a population of approximately 500 *habitants.*

On 29 November 1760, Major Robert Rogers took possession of the fort for the British from the French commandant, François-Marie Picoté de Belestre. Peace did not last long for the British. In May 1763, the Ottawa leader, Pontiac, led the Great Lakes Indians in a rebellion against the British. Anticipating trouble, Major Henry Gladwin took action to keep the Indians out, and for the next five months the garrison was under siege. Shocked and surprised by this turn of events, the British subsequently developed excellent trade relations with the Indians, and there was no future trouble.

In 1778, during the American Revolution, Detroit's defenses were strengthened with the construction of Fort Lernoult. The original French fort and settlement were completely destroyed by a disastrous fire in June 1805.

Russell M. Magnaghi

References

C.M. Burton, ed., "Cadillac Papers," *Michigan Pioneer and Historical Collections* 33 (1903):36–75 and 34 (1904):11–302; Jean Delanglez, "Cadillac at Detroit," *Mid-America* 30 (1948):152–176 and (1948):233–256; ———, "The Genesis and Building of Detroit," *Mid-America* 30 (1948):75–104; H.J. Nelson, "Walled Cities of the United States," *Annals of the Association of American Geographers* 51 (1961):1–22; M.M. Stimson, "Cadillac and the Founding of Detroit," *Michigan History* 35 (1951):129–136.

See also FORT BUADE (MICHIGAN); DETROIT; FOX FORT (ILLINOIS); PONTIAC; PONTIAC'S WAR; ROGERS, ROBERT

Pontiac (c. 1720–1769)

Biographical information concerning Pontiac's life is not plentiful, nor is much of it reliable. Historians generally accept 1720 as an approximate time of his birth. Pontiac was born into the Ottawa nation although he may not have been a full-blooded Ottawa. One of his parents may have been either a Chippewa or a Miami. Not only are the facts concerning his ancestry unclear, so also are those that surround the place of his birth and his early years. He probably was born in an Ottawa village located somewhere on the Maumee River in what is now Ohio and reared in that vicinity.

Nothing is known of the particular details of his formative years. Pontiac lived in the Great Lakes region all his life, and his upbringing, character, and values clearly reflected the culture of the nations who inhabited that area. By the time he was a grown man, he apparently was a classic example of the young warrior-aristocrat. Pontiac was a tattooed, painted war chief who drank the blood and ate the hearts of brave enemies and generally comported himself in a fashion that clearly identified his station in life in his Ottawa nation.

Until 1746, little is known of the precise details of his life, but, in that year, he joined the Indian forces allied with the French and soldiered in the war against Great Britain. At the end of King George's War, he continued to live in the Detroit area where his French benefactors encouraged his friendship and where he steadily rose in influence among his people. Pontiac again joined the struggle against France's enemies in North America during the French and Indian War and may have participated in the defeat of British General Edward Braddock in 1754. He also played an active role in other phases of that frontier war, and acquitted himself with distinction even though he remained an obscure figure to his enemies. Pontiac was virtually unknown in the English-speaking world when the war that bears his name began. The fact that the war for empire in North America had not gone well for France was obvious to all, and the Indian allies of the French were restive and fearful of the effects of British occupation of their homeland. Then, once the terms of the Treaty of Paris were announced to France's Indian allies in the Great Lakes country and their fears were realized, the dismay among the defeated and despondent tribes palpably mounted.

In 1763, as the crisis that bears his name was about to explode on the frontier, Pontiac was approximately 40 years old, in good health, physically vigorous, an experienced soldier, and renowned among his brethren as a powerful orator. His skills as a speaker were prominent among the assets that helped him rise to a position of significant influence among the Great Lakes nations. Another of the assets that helped him rise to a leadership role was that he was the titular leader of a semi-religious secret society known as the *Metai.* His influence among the Ottawa was especially enhanced by his activities in the *Metai.* Not long before the devastating news of the scope of the French defeat reached him and his contemporaries, Pontiac spent a good deal of time in seclusion pondering the Indians' fate at the hands of the hostile white invaders, and he earned a reputation as a man who had a clear vision of what the future held in store for the hard-pressed tribes. He furthermore was profoundly affected by the words he heard uttered by a messianic Delaware Indian known only as the Prophet in 1762, and when the news of France's humiliation in North America reached him, Pontiac was ready to act.

Pontiac was not a man to reveal his thoughts prematurely to his actions. Observers noted that the great chief was a cautious man who used different aides to handle his incoming and outgoing messages. As a result, even his closest associates were usually unaware of his innermost thoughts. Now, in 1763, after long deliberation, Pontiac was prepared to state his views openly and forcefully. He called a council of representatives of all the nations of the lakes area in April of 1763. The well-attended meeting was held on the River Ecorse, about eight miles from Detroit, and it lasted nearly a month. Here, using his indisputable talents as an orator, Pontiac found it a relatively simple task to persuade his auditors that the time was at hand to strike a heavy blow against their traditional white enemies.

As the assault on English garrisons in the Great Lakes country got underway, Pontiac chose to shoulder the imposing task of reducing Fort Detroit, which was the principal British base west of Pittsburgh. He at first plotted to take the fort by a ruse. He arranged to have a dance to cement Indian-British friendship held within the fort, and when the day for the dance arrived, he and many of his followers entered Detroit carrying concealed weapons. They intended to use the commotion caused by the celebration as a means to launch a surprise attack on an unwary garrison. The commandant of Detroit, Major Henry Gladwin, apparently received some sort of warning and was prepared. Gladwin and all his men appeared under arms. Finally, after assessing Gladwin's obvious security preparations, Pontiac chose not to spring the attack. The garrison was too well prepared to defend itself. He withdrew his forces.

With his plan of a quick and easy attack on Detroit frustrated, Pontiac turned to the only means open to him to take the post. He began a siege. Siege warfare was not one of the Indian nations' tactical strengths, but it must be noted that Pontiac subsequently directed one of the

longest sieges of a fortified position ever undertaken by North American Indians. While his assault on Detroit eventually proved fruitless, the Indian nations enjoyed breathtaking victories elsewhere. Forts Sandusky, Miami, St. Joseph, Ouiatenon, Michilimackinac, Presqu'ile, Le Boeuf, and Venango fell in rapid succession before the surprise onslaught of the outraged and inspired nations. Even though most of the forts taken by the Indians were small and thinly garrisoned, the Indians' spirits were manifestly buoyed by their triumphs, and yet they also fully understood that until Detroit was taken, their campaign was inconclusive. Ultimately, Pontiac's efforts to take Fort Detroit proved inadequate, the offensive lost its momentum, the British regrouped and eventually counterattacked, and Pontiac's vision of a final victory over his white enemies was unattainable. He made peace in October 1763.

After the war with the whites faltered and an uneasy peace returned to the frontier, Pontiac lived in a village on the Maumee River. Even though he lived in a world that was now dominated more than ever before by the white aggressors he loathed, Pontiac lived quietly and in relative obscurity. During a visit to Cahokia in 1769, he was attacked by a Peoria Indian who mortally wounded him. The reason for the assault on Pontiac is unknown. The Peorias, however, fled to the nearby British fort for protection, thereby fostering the suspicion that Pontiac had been the victim of an assassination plot. Pontiac's remains were carried across the Mississippi River to St. Louis, where he was buried at a site that has long since been lost to history.

Larry G. Bowman

References

John R. Cuneo, *Robert Rogers of the Rangers* (1959); Frederick W. Hodge, *Handbook of American Indians North of Mexico*, 2 vols. (1907, 1910); Francis Parkman, *History of the Conspiracy of Pontiac* (1902); Howard H. Peckham, *Pontiac and the Indian Uprising* (1947); Milo M. Quaife, ed., *The Siege of Detroit, Including the Journal of Pontiac's Conspiracy and John Rutherfurd's Narrative* (1958); Dale Van Every, *Forth to the Wilderness: The First American Frontier, 1754–1774* (1961).

See also DETROIT; FORT LE BOEUF (PENNSYLVANIA); FORT MICHILIMACKINAC (MICHIGAN); OTTAWA; PONTIAC'S WAR; FORT DE LA

PRESQUE ISLE (PENNSYLVANIA); THE PROPHET; FORT ST. JOSEPH–ST. JOSEPH RIVER (MICHIGAN); FORT SANDUSKY (OHIO); VENANGO (PENNSYLVANIA)

Pontiac's War (1763)

Pontiac's War was one of the more desperate wars on the American frontier prior to the American Revolution. At the conclusion of the French and Indian War, the Indian nations who had traditionally allied themselves with the French faced a disturbing reality. The long alliance with the French was at an end, and the unreconciled tribes understood that they would have to establish a rapport with another imperial power that had been their hereditary enemy. No one expected the 1760s to be an easy or placid time on the frontier.

France's policies toward the Indian nations of New France had been benign and generally profitable for both parties. While it may be argued that French policy was calculated to serve national ends, the net result was that the Indian fared better at the hands of the French than did those confronted by the white advance out of British colonial America. Once the scope of the French defeat in America became apparent and the French prepared to evacuate New France, the Indians genuinely lamented the exit of their European ally. Not only were the Indians of the Great Lakes region dismayed by the departure of their old comrades, they were also understandably apprehensive about the arrival of a new order dominated by their erstwhile foes. New ties concerning trade, diplomacy, and social conventions would have to be constructed and no one, red or white, fully understood the complexity of the situation as the political realities of the frontier dramatically altered in the early 1760s.

The Great Lakes Indians' fears were not unrealistic ones. They had, for example, witnessed a disturbing event in 1760; Robert Rogers, one of their more notable adversaries in the recent war, led a military detachment to Detroit where he raised the British flag over an installation that had always been French. From that point forward, rumor after rumor swept through the Indian nations that kept them in a state of turmoil and uncertainty over what the future held for them.

Discontent among the pro-French Indian nations was endemic. As early as 1761, the Senecas of New York circulated a war belt among the tribes of the Detroit vicinity seeking allies for a continuation of the struggle against Great Britain. Little support for the Senecas materialized among the nations in the mid-Great Lakes region, although the tribes were clearly unhappy with their circumstances. At this point, Pontiac, a rising chieftain among the Ottawa nation, probably did not favor open cooperation with the Senecas, but he was, as were many of his peers, alarmed by the unwelcome changes that disordered his world.

Once the war with the French was ended, it became the responsibility of Sir Jeffrey Amherst, the British commander in chief in North America, to devise a strategy to deal with the Indians in the territories newly acquired from France. Amherst was not favorably disposed to the Indians, and he apparently did not comprehend the need for a policy that would allay their fears and win their gratitude. Two men in particular, George Croghan and William Johnson, attempted to persuade Amherst to pursue a constructive policy toward the Indians. Croghan and Johnson were widely experienced in frontier diplomacy, and they wisely advised Amherst to authorize substantial quantities of gifts to the Indians as a means to emulate French policy and thereby win the loyalty of the dissident tribes. Amherst bridled at the suggestion to reward his former enemies and declared that he did not "... see why the Crown should be put to that expense. Services must be rewarded; it has ever been a maxim with me. But as to purchasing the good behavior either of the Indian or any others, [that] is what I do not understand. When men of whatsoever race behave ill they must be punished not bribed." And so, even before peace was officially established in 1763, Amherst embarked on a policy that virtually guaranteed unrest among the recalcitrant Indians. His obstinate and shortsighted policy made war with the Indians nearly inevitable.

By the spring of 1763, it was obvious that the tribes of the Great Lakes country from western New York to the Illinois River were fundamentally dissatisfied with the British, their Indian policy, and their condescending attitudes. At this juncture, two men came to the forefront and had a profound effect on the Indians' thinking. One, a Delaware who was commonly referred to as the "Prophet," was a mystic who had a vision that caused a sensation among his brethren; the other, Pontiac, was an imposing chieftain among the Ottawa nation. Both men were impressive figures who, working independently of one another, proved to be catalysts that spurred the tribes to rise against the British. The Prophet had been deeply troubled by the white man's advance into his homeland. He was certain that if he could communicate directly with the "Master of Life" he could discover an answer to the Indians' perplexing dilemma posed by the grasping white man. Eventually, the Prophet had a religious experience with the Master of Life in which the deity directed the Prophet to preach to the Indians and to cause them to unite. The master declared that the Indians were to return to their ancient ways, shun the white man's technology, live virtuous lives, and he, the master, would improve their fortunes in a renaissance of Indian culture. Once his experience with the Master of Life was ended, the Prophet, a dynamic figure who apparently wept constantly while he spoke, traveled about from village to village delivering the master's message to his children. He had a stunning impact on the Indians of the Great Lakes area and certainly seemed the prophet all had sought. His message made sense, and he spoke with what nearly everyone accepted as the sanction of the master himself. The Prophet's words electrified the Indian nations at a time they were yearning to hear a nationalistic anthem; the Prophet answered the deep-seated emotion.

Pontiac was similarly concerned about the future, and he too was moved by the Prophet's words. He too had brooded over the ominous actions of the new imperial power that occupied his homeland, and after a long period of meditation, the great Ottawa decided the time for action had arrived. He called for a council of all the tribes of the western Great Lakes nations. Pontiac's summons were widely heeded, and in April 1763, representatives of nearly all the nations assembled on the River Ecorse, about eight miles below Detroit. The council lasted for nearly a month, and Pontiac, using his gifts as an orator, plus his interpretation of the Prophet's powerful message, persuaded the delegates that the time for decisive action was at hand. Pontiac did modify the Prophet's message somewhat. He remained faithful to the Prophet's lessons in all areas save one. The Prophet taught that all white men were the cause of the Indians' downfall, and that all white men must be spurned. For obvious political reasons, Pontiac argued that the Master of Life's warnings about the white man did not include the French colonials who remained in North America. These French descendants were not to be feared or harmed. Only the British, their colonial lackeys, and the few Indian nations who supported them were the enemies Pontiac wanted annihilated. Pontiac apparently had little difficulty in convincing his fellow delegates that

his differentiation between the French and the British did not pervert the master's directives.

After a good deal of debate, the members of this fateful council decided on war with the British. Now their task was to return to their villages, deliver the message that war was necessary, and to build support for such an enterprise. Each nation had agreed to undertake certain military operations; now each nation had to develop the wherewithal to fulfill its goals in the upcoming struggle.

Great Britain's military presence in the newly acquired western lands was anchored by the installations at Forts Pitt and Detroit. In addition to these posts, there were about a dozen smaller, lightly-garrisoned forts in the immediate vicinity that would also be the objects of the Indians' attentions, but possession of Pitt and Detroit were vital to the outcome of the war for either side.

Pontiac personally took on the responsibility of reducing Fort Pontchartrain de Detroit. His plan was a simple one. Pontiac arranged for a ceremonial dance to be held within the walls of Detroit, and he plotted to use it as a means to get an armed body of his followers inside who, on a prearranged signal, would launch a surprise attack on the fort's personnel. On 7 May 1763, Pontiac and several hundred of his followers entered Detroit carrying concealed weapons that they hoped to use that day once the dance had begun. Detroit's commandant, Major Henry Gladwin, was prepared for all eventualities. Perhaps he had been warned of Pontiac's intentions, or he was fortuitously suspicious; Gladwin's men were armed and ready. After surveying the situation, Pontiac decided not to spring the assault and eventually withdrew his forces from the fort. Pontiac was soundly berated by several of his lieutenants for calling off the attack, and because of the furor his aborted attack had caused among his younger followers, he allowed some minor forays against local settlers who had unwisely chosen to remain outside the fort's protection. Then, on 10 May, Pontiac asked for a parley with Gladwin. Gladwin refused because he sensed treachery. One of his subordinate officers, Captain Donald Campbell, volunteered to meet the Indians. Gladwin did not think Campbell's idea a good one, but he did not deny Campbell permission to leave the fort and sally forth to meet with Pontiac's deputies. Once he arrived at the meeting site, Campbell was seized and made a hostage. Pontiac then demanded that Gladwin surrender Detroit. Gladwin promptly rejected the ultimatum. So, at that point, Pontiac began a siege of Detroit that proved to be both the longest assault on a fortified position ever staged by North American Indians—and a failure.

While the attack on Detroit was getting off to an inauspicious beginning, the Indians enjoyed enormous successes elsewhere. Less than a week after the siege of Detroit commenced, Fort Sandusky (on the south shore of Lake Erie) was taken by a group of Ottawas and Hurons who surprised its garrison and its commander, Christopher Pauli. The small detachment of 20 men was quickly overwhelmed, and the complete, easy victory at Sandusky fed the enthusiasm of the Indians as they rapidly moved against other British outposts.

More victories for Pontiac's loosely confederated forces emerged. On 28 May 1763, a force, commanded by Lieutenant Abraham Cuyler, en route from Niagara with supplies for Detroit, put in at Point Pelee on the western end of Lake Erie. Cuyler's command consisted of ten *bateaux* and 96 men. Not long after making camp, the command was all but overwhelmed by an Indian force that rushed them from the nearby forest. Cuyler, a handful of his men, and two *bateaux* escaped. The remainder of the men and boats were taken by the Indians. The English fort among the Miamis, near modern-day Fort Wayne, Indiana, fell next. Its commander, Robert Holmes, was decoyed out of the fort by his Miami mistress, who evidently bore him no love, and killed. Holmes's tiny force of 11 men tried to resist the Indians but finally capitulated when they were threatened with total destruction. On 1 June 1763, Fort Ouiatenon (Lafayette, Indiana) was taken by a mixed force of Weas, Kickapoos, and Mascoutens who managed to seize its commander, Lieutenant Edward Jenkins, and then, with Jenkins under restraint, coaxed the 20-man garrison into surrendering. Farther to the north, Fort Michilimackinac soon became another victim. The fort's commander, George Etherington and his 35 men, like most other frontier posts, had no knowledge of the outbreak of hostilities and were caught completely by surprise and nearly annihilated. Michilimackinac's commander and his men turned out to watch a lacrosse game between local Chippewas and visiting Sauks. Once the game reached a fever pitch, the ball was purposefully thrown into the compound and the players rushed past the sentries after it. Once inside, the men were armed by women who had smuggled weapons into the fort con-

cealed beneath their clothing. A few of the English survived when local French settlers gave them shelter, but most were slaughtered in the first few minutes of the assault. Then, during the remainder of June, in rapid succession, Forts Venango (Franklin, Pennsylvania), Le Boeuf (Waterford, Pennsylvania), St. Joseph (Niles, Michigan), and Presqu'ile (Erie, Pennsylvania) were destroyed by mixed forces of Senecas, Ottawas, Hurons, and Chippewas. By the last part of June, with the exception of Fort Pontchartrain de Detroit, the entire British military establishment west of Fort Pitt had been overrun by the Indians' offensive. Small military installations had been seized, settlements laid waste, and dozens of successful ambushes had been staged; the Indians appeared to be on an unstoppable spree of military triumphs.

In spite of all the Indians' successes, nearly everyone understood that the Great Lakes Indians could not claim final victory until Detroit capitulated. Gladwin remained poised and steadfast in his defense of Detroit and occasionally harried his besiegers with small counterattacks of his own. One of Gladwin's several sorties out of Detroit resulted in the death of a nephew of Wasson, chief of the Saginaw Chippewas. Wasson was outraged by his nephew's death and demanded that Pontiac deliver Captain Campbell over to his revenge. Pontiac acceded, and Wasson killed and scalped Campbell. After killing the hapless Campbell, Wasson threw the corpse into the river, and it floated past Detroit. The defenders of Detroit were infuriated by Campbell's murder and their resolve to hold the fort at all costs was reinforced. Pontiac knew that his assault on Detroit was becoming a stalemate and he also understood that some of his allies' resolve was faltering. He needed a victory to end the war and none was in sight. The war superficially appeared to be going well for Pontiac's forces when in fact it was not. If the struggle was not soon ended, reinforcements for the British would soon arrive, and the prospect of victory then became less likely.

Reinforcements were, in fact, on the way to the beleaguered frontier. A relief force of 460 men under the command of Henry Bouquet had departed from Fort Niagara to relive and then reinforce the defenders of Fort Pitt. Fort Pitt had been under nearly constant pressure since the outbreak of hostilities, but its commander, a determined professional soldier named Simeon Ecuyer, had refused to be intimidated. The Dela-

P

wares had demanded that he surrender the fort; Ecuyer refused, and sent smallpox-infected garments to the Indians and apparently unleashed an epidemic among them that caused their withdrawal from the immediate vicinity of Pitt.

The relief column led by Bouquet was attacked about 30 miles from Fort Pitt by a force composed of Delawares, Shawnees, Mingos, and Hurons. On 5 and 6 August 1763, near an area called Bushy Run, Bouquet fought a series of heavy skirmishes with the Indians who sought to check his advance. The Indians were finally driven off, and the Battle of Bushy Run, as it was called, was a turning point in the war. Bouquet marched on to effect the relief of Fort Pitt, and the Indians' hopes for a final victory faded. The tide of events now favored the British.

While the attempt to deny relief to Fort Pitt was faltering, the siege of Fort Detroit remained inconclusive. Pontiac could not devise a strategy that promised success. His leadership was openly called into question, and his enemies remained defiant. In September 1763, the schooner *Huron*, after beating off a canoe-borne attack by Ottawas while it was anchored below Detroit, arrived at Detroit carrying supplies for the beleaguered garrison. It was apparent that the Indians had control of the surrounding countryside, but it was equally apparent that they could do nothing to interdict the movement of armed vessels to and from the area. Winter was coming, dissent was rife among the nations, final victory eluded Pontiac, and the British forces, even though they had been badly battered, were rallying for counterattacks. At this point, Pontiac began witnessing the distressing sight of individual bands of his former allies negotiating peace with Gladwin. Finally, in October 1763, Pontiac, recognizing that he would not prevail against his enemies, made peace and ended the ill-fated war that had begun in such a promising fashion.

Larry G. Bowman

References
Frederick W. Hodge, *Handbook of American Indians North of Mexico*, 2 vols. (1907, 1910); Franklin B. Hough, ed., *Diary of the Siege of Detroit in the War with Pontiac* (1860); M. Agnes Narvarre, ed., *Journal of Pontiac's Conspiracy, 1763* (1921); Francis Parkman, *History of the Conspiracy of Pontiac* (1902); Howard H. Peckham, *Pontiac and the Indian Uprising* (1947); Milo M. Quaife, ed., *The Siege of Detroit, Including the Journal of Pontiac's Conspiracy*

and John Rutherfurd's Narrative (1958); Robert Rogers, *Concise Account of North America . . .* (1765); Dale Van Every, *Forth to the Wilderness: The First American Frontier, 1754–1774* (1961).

See also AMHERST, JEFFREY; BOUQUET, HENRY; BUSHY RUN, BATTLE OF; DELAWARE; DETROIT; ECUYER, SIMEON; HURON; FORT LE BOEUF (PENNSYLVANIA); FORT MICHILIMACKINAC (MICHIGAN); OTTAWA; FORT PITT (PENNSYLVANIA); PONTIAC; FORT DE LA PRESQUE ISLE (PENNSYLVANIA); THE PROPHET; FORT SANDUSKY (OHIO); VENANGO (PENNSYLVANIA)

Porto Bello, Attack on (1739)
In 1739, in the face of growing resentment of Spanish interference with British commerce in the Caribbean, British Prime Minister Sir Robert Walpole reluctantly acceded to hostilities against Spain. During the War of Jenkins' Ear, the first phase of what became known in America as King George's War and in Europe as the War of the Austrian Succession, the British moved against Spanish possessions in the West Indies.

Porto Bello, a fortified harbor on the north side of the Isthmus of Panama, was the initial target of an attack by newly promoted Vice Admiral Edward Vernon. The port was a well-known base for the Spanish *guarda costas* that so aggravated British merchants by enforcing Spanish mercantilist regulations and harassing commerce. Vernon, who had been one of the most vociferous advocates for war, sailed from England before the official declaration of hostilities and arrived at Jamaica in October 1739.

On 21 November, Vernon, with six ships-of-the-line, sailed into Porto Bello harbor, making directly for the town. Unexpectedly becalmed opposite the Iron Castle, one of three fortifications protecting the harbor, Vernon ordered a bombardment followed by an assault. Landing under the walls of the fort, British sailors and marines gained entry through the embrasures and captured the poorly manned and equipped garrison. The other fortifications and the town itself fell the following day. Vernon destroyed the forts before sailing away, having captured a number of Spanish vessels, including three of the hated *guarda costas*. Additional loot included several brass cannon and 10,000 Spanish dollars.

News of Vernon's success at Porto Bello created a sensation in England. Medals featuring the admiral's likeness and the motto, "He took Porto Bello with six ships" became extremely popular. Encouraged by the victory, the government ordered Vernon to mount a more ambitious expedition against the Spanish and sent out additional vessels and a large force of soldiers to reinforce him. Vernon opposed such large-scale campaigns, favoring more limited naval operations, but early in 1741, his force augmented with several thousand North American colonial troops, the admiral commenced the ill-fated attack on Cartagena.

Thomas Costa

References

Douglas Edward Leach, *Arms for Empire: A Military History of the British Colonies in North America, 1607–1763* (1973).

See also ANGLO-SPANISH WAR (1739–1744); CARTAGENA, EXPEDITION AGAINST; VERNON, EDWARD

Port Royal, Acadia (Annapolis Royal, Nova Scotia)

Established as a French habitation on the Bay of Fundy in 1605–1606 by Jean Bencourt, sieur de Pontrincourt, Port Royal remained a French stronghold for a century and a half. It was first raided in 1613 by Captain Samuel Argall (1572–1639), who was acting under orders from Governor Thomas Dale of Virginia to destroy all French settlements as far north as 45 degrees latitude.

In 1635, the Port Royal region became the seigneury of Charles de Menou d'Aulnay de Charnisay (1605–1650), who erected a fort there in 1636, making it the principal settlement in Acadia. Charnisay's claim became the cause of a territorial feud with Charles Saint-Etienne de La Tour, who launched an attack on Port Royal in 1643.

In 1654, the New England colonies raised an expedition against French garrisons at Penobscot and Port Royal. Robert Sedgwick (1590–1656), leader of the expedition and commander of all Massachusetts militia, forced the surrender of both garrisons without resistance.

In 1690, Sir William Phips (1651–1695) of Massachusetts, led a naval expedition to Acadia and in a bloodless encounter siezed Port Royal, which he plundered and departed, intent on attacking Quebec.

On 10 April 1706, Daniel d'Auger de Subercase (1655–1712) was appointed governor of Acadia. It became Subercase's policy to establish Port Royal as a base and haven for French privateers preying on New England's shipping. Port Royal attracted numerous West Indies buccaneers who were encouraged to raid English commerce. Governor Thomas Dudley (1576–1652) of Massachusetts organized an expedition to eradicate the "nest of spoilers." Colonel John March led a force of 1,300 Massachusetts men from Boston on 13 May 1707, in 24 vessels defended by the *Province Galley* and the royal frigate *Deptford*. Squabbles among March's undisciplined rabble prevented effective action. Port Royal's garrison of 156 men under Governor Subercase resisted successfully. With the expedition a shameful failure, March withdrew his force to Casco Bay where he was met by reinforcements from Dudley. March then set off for a second attempt at Port Royal, which also ended in failure. The entire expedition was viewed as a fiasco. When the first returning contingent arrived in Boston, they were presented with a wooden sword and greeted in the streets with the contents of chamber pots being poured on their heads.

The year 1709 marked the false start of another expedition against Acadia. A congress of provincial governors convening at Rehoboth, Rhode Island, on 14 October 1709, laid plans to mount a joint attack on Port Royal. Queen Anne was urged to grant approval for resuming the expedition, based on unanimous accord for the united colonial action.

Colonel Francis Nicholson was appointed commander in chief of the expedition. A British naval squadron consisting of 36 vessels under Captain George Martin, including four men-o-war and a star bomb ketch arrived to assist. Nicholson's military force consisted of a regiment of Royal Marines and 3,500 provincial volunteers. The New Englanders had been recruited with promises of cash bounties and firearms presented as gifts on behalf of the queen. The expedition finally sailed from Boston on 18 September 1710.

Nicholson's siege of Port Royal began on 24 September. Confronted by vastly superior numbers (outnumbering the French five to one), and a disciplined siege operation, Governor Subercase was forced to surrender Port Royal's citadel on 1 October 1710. The fortress was promptly renamed Annapolis Royal in honor of Queen Anne. Colonel Samuel Vetch (1668–1732) was appointed adjutant general of the English garrison, and subsequently governor. In

P

acquiring Port Royal, the English established a claim to all Acadia and freed the New England coast from French privateers. Vetch was relieved of any fear of French counterattack by the terms of the Treaty of Utrecht, signed 11 April 1713, which confirmed England's possession of the area. Vetch's successor, Lawrence Armstrong, was replaced in 1739 by Paul Mascarene (1684–1760), who continued to serve as acting governor of Nova Scotia from 1740 to 1749.

Annapolis Royal was not attacked again until 1744. After François Du Pont Duvivier's successful surprise attack on Canso, French forces struck at Annapolis Royal in September/October 1744. Local Acadians failed to respond to Duvivier's call to arms. Mascarene, receiving unexpected assistance from a band of Micmacs led by the Abbe Antoine Simon Millars, was able to grimly hold out until reinforcements arrived from New England to raise the siege. The governor of New France, Jacques-Pierre de Taffanel de La Jonquière, ordered the duc d'Anville to attempt another attack on Annapolis. Hampered by contrary winds, Anville's fleet was blown off course and prevented from threatening Annapolis.

In the spring of 1745, a combined force of French and Micmac Indians again attacked Annapolis Royal. Mascarene's defenders were reinforced by a company of Gorham's Rangers, who were ever eager to collect Governor William Shirley's bounty on enemy Indian scalps. The French were under orders to not molest the Acadians, and Mascarene did not attempt to involve them in his defense, either. Both combatants allowed them to go about the vital business of harvesting their crops. Discouraged at making no progress, Duvivier departed by ship, leaving behind a token siege force under Captain Michel de Gannes. Unable to accomplish any effective results, Gannes shortly withdrew to Louisbourg, ending the last attack on Annapolis Royal.

John D. Hamilton

References
John Bartlet Brebner, *New England's Outpost: Acadia Before the Conquest of Canada* (1927); John G. Reid, *Acadia, Maine, and New Scotland: Marginal Colonies in the Seventeenth Century* (1981).

See also ACADIA; ACADIA, BRITISH CONQUEST OF (1710); ACADIA, NEW ENGLAND ATTACK ON (1690); ACADIA, NEW ENGLAND ATTACK ON (1707); CASCO BAY; MARCH, JOHN; NICHOLSON, FRANCIS; VETCH, SAMUEL

Port Royal (South Carolina)

Port Royal Sound, South Carolina, is the deepest natural harbor on the south Atlantic coast and the dominant geographical feature of the Carolina Sea Islands. Consequently, it was the objective of many sixteenth-century maritime explorers and subsequently the center of much colonial military activity. (The name also attaches to one of the largest of the Sea Islands and a present-day small town of late nineteenth-century origins.)

Port Royal Sound may have been first discovered by Spanish Captain Pedro de Salazar on his voyage from Hispaniola in 1514 or 1516. The Spaniards referred to the region as "Santa Elena," from the 1525 voyage of Captain Pedro de Quexos. In its Anglicized version, St. Helena, it is one of the oldest continuously used European placenames in North America. The area around Port Royal Sound is also one of the possible sites of the first Spanish municipality in the continental United States, the lost colony of San Miguel de Gualdape in 1526. A French expedition was in the vicinity in 1546 and a Spanish expedition, commanded by Captain Angel de Villefañe, was among the Sea Islands in 1560. In 1562 the French expedition led by Captain Jean Ribault of Dieppe arrived. The French named the harbor Port Royal and left there the first Protestant (Huguenot) colony in North America. The Charlesfort colony at Port Royal was abandoned in 1563 and destroyed in 1564 by a Spanish expedition from Cuba commanded by Captain Hernando Manrique de Rojas.

Following the conquest of Florida, the death of Jean Ribault and the establishment of St. Augustine by Pedro Menéndez de Avilés in 1565, the Spaniards established the Ciudad de Santa Elena on Port Royal Sound in 1566. It was the official capital of the Florida colony from 1566 to 1573. In 1576, the Escamacu Indian rebellion began near Santa Elena and forced the evacuation of all the Spanish missions and settlements north of St. Augustine. The town and fort at Santa Elena were rebuilt (1577–1580), but were permanently abandoned by the Spaniards in 1587 following the destruction of St. Augustine by Sir Francis Drake.

Spain maintained consistent claims to the Port Royal region throughout the sixteenth century and intermittent activity from Florida was noted by English explorers Captain William Hilton in 1663 and Colonel Robert Sandford in 1666. Colonel Sandford left the first English settler of South Carolina, Dr. Henry Woodward, at Port Royal. Woodward was imprisoned by the Spaniards at St. Augustine, freed by the English pirate Robert Searles, and marooned on the West Indian island of Nevis. There he was picked up by the English fleet from Barbados that settled Charles Town in 1670.

With the permanent settlement of South Carolina, the Port Royal area became the southern frontier of English America until the founding of Georgia in 1733. In 1686, Henry Erskine, Lord Cardross, founded the Scotch settlement of Stuart Town on Port Royal Island, and the Yamasee tribe of Georgia moved to the headwaters of Port Royal Sound to be near its trading partners. Yamasee raids on Florida, instigated by Scottish traders, prompted a Spanish retaliation and the destruction of Stuart Town in August 1686.

By 1698, Carolina land grants marked the beginning of permanent English settlement of the Port Royal area. The region became the center of important military activity during Queen Anne's War (1702–1713). Governor James Moore assembled his expedition against St. Augustine on the south end of Port Royal Island in 1702 and left at that location a permanent lookout post to prevent Spanish retaliation in 1703. In 1706, a log blockhouse was constructed at the site and occupied by a garrison of 106 men. This location became the center of trade between the English and the Indians, and in 1711, the town of Beaufort was chartered, the second-oldest town in South Carolina.

English encroachment on lands south of Port Royal Sound, set aside for the Yamasee tribe by an act of 1707, and constant abuse of the Indians by the Charles Town traders, erupted in the Yamasee War (1715–1717). The Yamasee War, one of the largest and most dangerous Indian wars in colonial history, began on good Friday, 15 April 1715, at the Yamasee village of Pocotaligo on the headwaters of Port Royal Sound. It involved the entire Creek Indian confederation reaching into present-day Alabama and Mississippi. The Port Royal frontier was destroyed and abandoned and the region's leader, Indian Commissioner Thomas Nairne, was tortured to death during the initial outbreak. Governor Charles Craven defeated the Yamasee at the Salkehatchie Fight in June 1715, and Colonel John "Tuscarora Jack" Barnwell burned the main Yamasee towns at Pocotaligo and Coosawhatchie. The Yamasee abandoned the Port Royal area and sought refuge among their old enemies in Florida. In January 1716, the Carolinians secured an alliance with the Cherokees, and in November 1716, they signed a truce with the Creeks. The Yamasee, however, aided by the Spaniards, continued to raid among the Sea Islands, making the resettlement of the Port Royal area difficult.

Colonel Barnwell organized the "Carolina Scouts," waterborne patrols based on Port Royal Island, to protect the Sea Islands. In 1721, he built Fort King George on the Altamaha River (Darien, Georgia), the first English settlement in Georgia. In 1724, Barnwell died and the mantle of frontier leadership passed to Colonel John Palmer. In 1728, in response to the massacre of the crew of one of the Carolina Scout boats at Bloody Point, Daufuskie Island, Palmer led a raid on St. Augustine that destroyed the Yamasee towns in Florida and finally ended the Yamasee War.

In 1733, the Carolinians built Fort Prince Frederick on Port Royal Island, but real security was provided by the settlement of Savannah. The establishment of a plantation economy based on rice was disrupted by runaway slaves seeking freedom at St. Augustine and by the Stono Rebellion of 1739. These local disturbances contributed to the outbreak of the War of Jenkins' Ear (1739–1742). Georgia Governor James Oglethorpe's failure at the siege of St. Augustine led to the death of Colonel John Palmer at the Battle of Fort Mosa and, in 1742, the islands around Port Royal Sound were evacuated on the approach of a Spanish invasion fleet from Cuba. The original Spanish objective in 1742 was to conquer Port Royal Sound, seize Port Royal Island, and call for a general slave insurrection in the Carolina lowcountry. The Spaniards, however, were defeated by Oglethorpe at the Battle of Bloody Marsh. Spanish privateers commanded by Don Francisco Lorando and Don Julien de Vega occasionally used Port Royal and St. Helena Sounds to harass commerce from the port of Charles Town from 1740 through 1744. The *Beaufort Galley*, an oar and sail coastal gunboat, was built in 1742 to protect the Sea Islands around Port Royal Sound from Spanish privateers.

The War of Jenkins' Ear was followed by King George's War against France, and in

1748, Port Royal Sound was designated a royal naval station. A careening wharf was built near the town of Beaufort and the H.M.S. *Adventure* and the H.M.S. *Rye* were stationed there during 1748 and 1749. The last recorded Indian raid in the Port Royal area occurred during this war when a party of 20 Creeks, encouraged by the French, slipped passed Georgia patrols to harass plantations on Port Royal Island in 1752.

King George's War was followed by the French and Indian War (1754–1763) during which the Port Royal area was protected by the construction of Fort Lyttleton. Fort Lyttelton was a large installation mounted with 21 cannons. Its completion was delayed until near the end of the war. From the Treaty of Paris in 1763 to the end of the colonial era, the Port Royal area remained at peace. The frontier had moved on, and military matters became less important than economic and political matters.

Lawrence S. Rowland

References

Jeannette Thurber Conner, ed., *The Colonial Records of Spanish Florida*, 2 vols. (1925); Verner Crane, *The Southern Frontier, 1670–1732* (1929); Paul E. Hoffman, *A New Andalucia and a Way to the Orient: The American Southeast During the Sixteenth Century* (1990); George C. Rogers, Jr., *Charleston in the Age of the Pinckneys* (1969); Lawrence S. Rowland, "Eighteenth Century Beaufort: A Study of South Carolina's Southern Parishes to 1800," Ph.D. Dissertation, University of South Carolina (1978).

A.S. Salley, *Warrants for Land in South Carolina, 1670–1710* (1973); Robert M. Weir, *Colonial South Carolina: A History* (1983): Peter H. Wood, *Black Majority: Negroes in Colonial South Carolina from 1670 Through the Stono Rebellion* (1974).

See also ANGLO-SPANISH WAR (1739–1744); BEAUFORT FORT (SOUTH CAROLINA); CHARLESFORT (SOUTH CAROLINA); FORT FREDERICK (SOUTH CAROLINA); FORT LYTTLETON (SOUTH CAROLINA); FORT PRINCE FREDERICK (SOUTH CAROLINA); RIBAULT, JEAN; SANTA ELENA; YAMASEE WAR

Port Royal Fort (South Carolina)

See BEAUFORT FORT (SOUTH CAROLINA)

Portsmouth, Treaty of (1713)

For Europeans the Treaty of Utrecht brought peace to both Europe and America and ended the War of the Spanish Succession. In North America, England gained from France Nova Scotia, Newfoundland, and Hudson Bay; France retained Quebec (New France). When the Indians discovered that they had no part in that treaty, they pressured Massachusetts for a treaty to end the war known in America as Queen Anne's War. The Penobscot, Kennebec, and Maliseet Indians signed the treaty recognizing their allegiance to Great Britain on 28 July 1713. The Indians retained rights to their land, and for hunting, fishing, and fowling, as well as all their "lawful liberties and privileges."

The French missionaries found it difficult to accept defeat and considered the Indian lands to be in New France. Indians claimed that the English were not keeping treaty obligations. Indians split: some recognized treaty obligation; others retained French loyalty. The peace was short-lived.

Nicholas N. Smith

See also ABENAKI; UTRECHT, TREATY OF

Pouchot de Maupas, Pierre (1712–1769)

Pierre Pouchot de Maupas was born in Grenoble, France, in 1712. In 1733, he entered the army as a volunteer engineer and on 1 May 1734 was commissioned lieutenant *en second* in the Béarn Regiment. An infantry officer, Pouchot had a talent for engineering that was utilized by his superiors in Europe and America. His earliest campaigns were in Italy during the War of the Polish Succession (1733–1738). He subsequently served on Corsica (1738–1739) and in Germany, Flanders, and perhaps Italy during the War of the Austrian Succession (1740–1748). Much of his duty involved siegework and fortification. He rose steadily in rank: lieutenant (1739), assistant major (1743), and captain (1745). In 1749, Pouchot obtained a company in the 2nd battalion.

The 2nd battalion of Béarn was sent to New France in 1755. Pouchot arrived at Quebec on 23 June and proceeded to Fort Frontenac. Because all of the army's engineers had been lost aboard the *Alcide*, which had been captured by the British off Newfoundland, Pouchot was the most experienced field engineer in the colony. He was immediately put to work retrenching the camp at Frontenac. In September, Governor Pierre de Rigaud de Vaudreuil ordered him to Niagara to convert the stockaded post into an earthen fortification.

Pouchot's work at Niagara was interrupted in July 1756, when he went with his battalion to besiege Oswego. There another accident placed him in a position of responsibility. Engineer Captain Jean-Claude-Henri de Lombard de Combles was killed by an allied Indian. His assistant, Lieutenant Jean-Nicolas Desandrouins, had no experience in siegecraft, so Pouchot was ordered to direct operations, a task he performed efficiently. In September he was assigned to command Fort Niagara.

Pouchot's appointment set a precedent and created jealousy among officers of the *troupes de la marine* who had traditionally held command of the wilderness posts. The assignment provided an opportunity for Pouchot to display a talent for Indian diplomacy. His efforts, aided by French successes at Oswego in 1756, and Fort William Henry in 1757, kept the western Iroquois and other nations in the French interest. Pouchot continued to fortify Niagara which, when completed in September 1757, was the strongest fortification west of Quebec.

Despite Pouchot's popularity with the Indians, completion of the fortifications removed Governor Vaudreuil's chief reason for giving command of Niagara to a *troupes de terre* officer. Pouchot was relieved in October by Captain Jean-Baptiste Mutigny de Vassan, of the marine. He spent the winter in Montreal, devoting much of his time to completing a detailed map of the French and English frontiers.

The 1758 campaign found Pouchot leading a *piquet* of Béarn on the expedition of François-Gaston de Lévis down the Mohawk River. When this operation was cancelled, Pouchot rushed his men to Fort Carillon, rejoining Montcalm's army on the eve of the battle of July 8. Pouchot then worked on field defenses at Ticonderoga before returning to Montreal in November.

The loss of Fort Frontenac in August 1758 threatened the Lake Ontario frontier. Montcalm wanted Pouchot to return immediately to Niagara, but he was not sent until March 1759. When the English appeared before his post, on 6 July, Pouchot and his 600-man garrison resisted for 19 days before capitulating on 25 July. He was taken to New York, but exchanged and returned to Montreal in December.

The final campaign found Pouchot in similar circumstances. He was ordered to Fort Lévis in the upper St. Lawrence River where he took command in March 1760 and prepared to block Amherst's thrust against Montreal. His garrison of fewer than 400 soldiers and sailors was besieged by Amherst's 10,000 men from 17 July until the 25th, when Pouchot surrendered his shattered fort. He again went to New York and from there to France, arriving at Le Havre on 8 March 1761.

A paroled prisoner of war, Pouchot returned to Grenoble. There he learned that he was being sought concerning the financial malfeasances in New France. He went to Paris in February 1762 and quickly established his innocence. Pouchot did not participate further in the trials of the *affaire du Canada*. Another blow to his career came later that year when the Béarn Regiment was disbanded. Pouchot thus became an officer without a regiment. It was probably at this time that he began to prepare mémoires of his service in North America. Although it was intended to vindicate his conduct, and contains particularly harsh criticism of the financial administrators of New France, the work is essentially a narrative of the war with much information on geography and the Indians. The text was incomplete when, in 1768 or early 1769, Pouchot took the opportunity for further military service as an engineer on Corsica. There, on 8 May 1769, the day before the decisive French victory at Ponte Novu, he was killed by partisans while reconnoitering a strategic road.

Pouchot's incomplete writings were left to his heirs, who saw to their publication in 1781 as *Mémoires sur la dernière guerre de l'Amérique septentrionale*. It was the only history of the war in America from the French perspective published during the eighteenth century. One writer characterized Pouchot as "the French Mante."

Pierre Pouchot was perhaps the most influential company officer of the *troupes de terre* to serve in America during the Seven Years' War, and also one of the most capable. He was universally acknowledged to be a good engineer and the best qualified officer in the colony to defend a fortified place. This reputation earned him command at two hopeless sieges, both of which he conducted with honor. Pouchot was also a rare example of a European officer who possessed an aptitude for working with France's Indian allies. He did everything possible to keep the Iroquois in the French interest, but in the end, could not compete with Sir William Johnson and English resources.

Pouchot was respected by colonial and army officers alike. Inevitably, he was drawn into the conflict between Governor Vaudreuil and Louis-Joseph de Montcalm. Indeed, Montcalm, who had expressed a good deal of warmth toward Pouchot, distanced himself in the spring of 1759 after the captain expressed optimism for Vaudreuil's plans for defending the Ohio. Pouchot proved overly optimistic about the campaign and the fidelity of the Iroquois. He was deceived when they promised to warn him of any threat to Niagara, but then allowed an English army to pass through their country. Pouchot's shortsightedness in the 1759 campaign was the only aspect of his American service that drew criticism from his fellow officers.

Pierre Pouchot's greatest legacy is his *Mémoires*. While the work presents a comprehensive account of the war, it is most valuable for the events in which he participated. Pouchot was an astute observer of events, places, and customs. His descriptions of the Indians are precise and objective by the standards of his time. He was a talented mapmaker and left at least three plans of Fort Niagara, one of the siege of Fort Lévis, and a detailed map of the territory over which French and English forces clashed from 1754 to 1760.

Brian Leigh Dunnigan

References
H.R. Casgrain, ed., *Collection des manuscrits du Maréchal de Lévis*, 12 vols. (1889–1895); Edward P. Hamilton, trans. and ed., *Adventure in the Wilderness: The American Journals of Louis Antoine de Bougainville, 1756–1760* (1964), rpt. 1990; Gabriel du Maurès de Malartic and Paul Gaffarel, eds., *Journal des campagnes au Canada de 1755 à 1760 par le comte de Maurès de Malartic* (1890); Peter N. Moogk, "Pouchot, Pierre," *Dictionary of Canadian Biography*, 12 vols. (1966–1991) III:534–537.

Edmund B. O'Callaghan, ed., *Documents Relative to the Colonial History of the State of New York*, 15 vols. (1856–1877), Vol. 10; Pierre Pouchot, *Mémoires sur la dernière guerre de l'Amérique septentrionale*, 3 vols. (1781); ———, *Memoirs on the Late War in North American Between the French and English*, 1755–1760, trans. and ed. by Franklin B. Hough, 2 vols. (1866); ———, *Memoirs on the Late War in North America*, trans. by Michael Cardy, ed. by Brian Leigh Dunnigan (1994).

See also FORT FRONTENAC (ONTARIO, CANADA); LA BELLE FAMILLE, BATTLE OF; FORT LÉVIS (NEW YORK); FORT NIAGARA (NEW YORK); RIGAUD DE VAUDREUIL DE CAVAGNIAL, PIERRE DE

Powhatan (c. 1550–1618)

Powhatan (throne name; personal name: Wahunsonacock) was paramount chief (*mamanatowick*) of the Algonquian-speaking Indians of the Virginia coastal plain. At an unknown date he inherited six tribes near the falls of the James, Pamunkey, and Mattaponi Rivers. Then, through warfare or intimidation, he added tribes to the east and north until by 1608, he ruled over some 30 groups altogether.

It is probable that Powhatan only heard about the Spanish in their abortive mission (1570–1571) or their subsequent visits (1570s, 1580s). He must also have heard about the English colonists from Roanoke Island who wintered in 1585 with the Chesapeakes, his enemies. His subordinate chiefs dealt with the Jamestown colonists in 1607, and Powhatan met an Englishman (John Smith) only in December 1607. By then he had received considerable intelligence about the newcomers.

Powhatan's policy was initially to make allies of the English. However, by the fall of 1608 he probably gave it up, after the English insisted on exploring all over his dominions and also visiting the enemy Monacans against his wishes. After the English attacked him in his capital town in January 1609, he withdrew all assistance to the colony and allowed his subjects to snipe freely at Englishmen. The terrible "starving time" of 1609–1610 was the result at Jamestown.

In 1610, a tougher commander, Lord de la Warre, arrived in Virginia, reorganized the colony, and began expanding English landholdings in spite of Indian resistance. Diplomatic relations between the Powhatans and English ceased altogether in this first Anglo-Powhatan War (1610–1613), but since no massed Indian attacks occurred, very few of the English perceived that a war was in fact going on. Powhatan appears to have been aging rapidly and losing his taste for organized hostilities. When his daughter Pocahontas was captured and held for ransom in 1613, his spirit seems to have broken. In the ensuing peaceful years, he told Englishmen that he was tired of war and wanted to live quietly. The English took advantage of his semi-retirement and continued expanding their plantations. Indians objecting to it found another leader: Powhatan was overshadowed in his last years by his second younger brother and eventual successor, Opechancanough.

Helen C. Rountree

References

Helen C. Rountree, *Pocahontas's People: The Powhatan Indians of Virginia Through Four Centuries* (1990); ———, *The Powhatan Indians of Virginia: Their Traditional Culture* (1989); John Smith, *The Complete Works of John Smith, 1580–1631*, Philip L. Barbour, ed. (1986).

See also CHICKAHOMINY; OPECHANCA-NOUGH; POWHATANS; SMITH, JOHN

Powhatans

Powhatan Indians, the Algonquian-speaking native people of eastern Virginia who by 1608 were organized into a paramount chiefdom (not a confederacy) by the man Powhatan. Anthropologists differ on whether the term "Powhatans" should apply to all the groups under the influence of Powhatan or only to more loyal tribes nearer his home territory on the James and York Rivers.

The Indians of southeastern Virginia met the Spanish first at a Jesuit mission of 1570–1571 that they wiped out, and an avenging party in 1572. By that time they were already organized under fairly powerful chiefs. In subsequent decades, as Spanish reconnaissance continued, English visits began, and regular attacks from inland Indians occurred, the man Powhatan expanded his holdings until by 1607 he dominated the James, York, and Rappahannock River basins and heavily influenced the Virginia Delmarva Peninsula and the south bank of the Potomac River. His relations with the Maryland Algonquian-speakers (Nottoways, Meherrins) were warily friendly. His declared enemies were the Virginia Piedmont Siouan-speakers (Monacans, Mannahoacs), possibly the Iroquoian-speaking Susquehannocks, and definitely the unidentified but probably Iroquoian-speaking Massawomecks and Pocoughtaonacks from far up the Potomac River.

The very early, best-documented, years of the Jamestown colony show Indians alternately feeding and raiding colonists whom they wanted to make into allies but who exasperated them by insisting on exploring while remaining unable to support themselves. By 1610, when the colony was reorganized and became better supplied from England, the distrust and violence reached the point that warfare may be said to have started (1610–1614). A truce ensued, springing from the marriage of Pocahontas, but the English soon afterward discovered tobacco as a cash crop. From then on, Virginia became an expansion-oriented agricultural colony, which made conflict with native landholders inevitable.

Powhatan's Potomac River fringe had been persuaded into neutrality by 1610; now the Delmarva Peninsula groups were wooed into being English allies by 1621. The remainder of Powhatan's organization, especially the James River tribes who had lost their best farmland, made a mass attack that started a new war with Virginia (1622–1632). Powhatan being dead, the leader was his second brother, Opechancanough, who acted under the aegis of the new paramount chief, Opitchapam/Otiotan. Once that war wound down into a stalemate, the English began expanding again, with floods of new immigrants pouring into the territory of the diminished Powhatans. The lower York River basin was occupied and claims were starting in the Rappahannock and Potomac Valleys when the Powhatans rose in one last effort, a new war with Virginia (1644–1646). That war ended decisively in the death of the now-paramount chief, Opechancanough, and the making of a treaty with his more compliant successor, Necotowance.

In spite of official treaty protection of Indian lands, the English moved in north of the York River and took over the rest of the Virginia coastal plain by the 1670s. The much diminished Powhatans posed no real threat to them anymore, but nevertheless the internal troubles erupting in Bacon's Rebellion caused all Indians to be blamed and the Pamunkey tribe in particular suffered two gratuitous attacks. To reassure them and others in the wake of the rebellion, the Treaty of 1677 was made, a treaty which is still in force.

The still-diminishing Powhatans were harassed along with the frontier English by various "foreign" Indians, especially the Senecas, in the years that followed. Their relations with the Tuscarora, on the other hand, were friendly enough that the English felt threatened. Powhatan men served regularly as scouts for the militia. The English took over all negotiations with other Indians, however, and the Powhatans lacked even a symbolic role in making the Treaty of Albany in 1722. Thereafter their military role was minimal: there is no record of their serving in the later intercolonial wars, though they did serve with the American forces in the Revolution.

Helen C. Rountree

References

Helen C. Rountree, *Pocahontas's People: The Powhatan Indians of Virginia Through Four Centuries* (1990); ———, *The Powhatan Indians of Virginia: Their Traditional Culture* (1989).

See also APPOMATTOCK; CHICKAHOMINY; NANSEMOND; NOTTOWAY; OPECHANCA-NOUGH; PAMUNKEY; RAPPHANNOCK; VIRGINIA-INDIAN TREATY (1646); VIRGINIA-INDIAN TREATY (1677/1680); VIRGINIA-INDIAN WAR (1622–1632); VIRGINIA-INDIAN WAR (1644–1646)

Praying Indians

Although the missionary impulse was a primary objective of their migration to southern New England, Puritans did not act on this until Thomas Mayhew, Jr., began to proselytize the Indians of Martha's Vineyard in 1642. John Eliot, the "Apostle to the Indians," followed suit in 1646 when he began a 30-year missionary campaign to the Indians of Massachusetts. Eliot borrowed the French method of segregating converted Indians into enclaves called "Reserves." The English named Puritan Indian villages "praying towns." By 1674, the Puritans had created 14 praying towns with a total population estimated as high as 4,800. The oldest and strongest communities in Massachusetts were Natick, Punkapoag, Hassanemesit, Okommakamesit, Wamessit, Nashobah, and Magunkaquogt.

The Puritan mission to the Indians combined conversion, acculturation, and military objectives. Puritans forced on their converts such "Christian criteria" as permanent physical structures, European agricultural methods, English civil polity, personal hygiene procedures, and dress codes. These standards allowed Puritans to distinguish between hostile and friendly Indians by location and sight. Christianized Indians were not only easier to identify, their towns, lying on the outskirts of Puritan possessions, served as a barrier against hostile tribes. Praying Indians also served their fellow

Puritans by informing them of impending attack. In April 1675, for example, Waban, the principle ruler of Natick, warned Massachusetts Bay of Philip's forthcoming assault. Throughout King Philip's War, Praying Indians from the older Massachusetts praying towns remained loyal to the Puritans and performed as scouts and soldiers. After King Philip's War in 1676, the Puritans disbanded most praying towns, transformed a few into reservations, and essentially suspended Indian missions. Solomon Stoddard would revive New England Indian missions in the 1730s.

Richard C. Goode

References

James Axtell, *The Invasion Within: The Contest of Cultures in Colonial North America* (1985); Henry Bowdin, *John Eliot's Indian Dialogues: A Study in Cultural Interaction* (1980); Daniel Gookin, *An Historical Account of the Doings and Sufferings of the Christian Indians of New England* (1836); Neal Salisbury, "Red Puritans: The 'Praying Indians' of Massachusetts Bay and John Eliot," *William and Mary Quarterly* 31 (1974):27–54; Alden T. Vaughan, *New England Frontier: Puritans and Indians, 1620–1675* (1965).

See also KING PHILIP'S WAR; PURITANS

Presidio

The presidio was a fort established to provide frontier defense against hostile Indians on the Spanish borderlands. The word presidio derives from the Roman *praesidium*, connotating a garrisoned place. The term presidio, however, did not come into common usage in the Spanish language until the 1570s, when it was applied to Spain's garrisoned forts in Morocco. There it took in the added meaning of a Christian outpost in a heathen land, as well as a place of confinement for criminals sentenced for serious offenses.

After the swift and total conquest of the Aztec empire in 1519, Spanish explorers headed north and south from central Mexico to explore the new land. The discovery of silver at Zacatecas, several hundred miles north of Mexico City, caused a rush of miners and explorers into an area occupied by fierce nomadic bands generically known as "Chichimecas." Presidios were strategically sited along the roads into the silver lands. They resembled miniature medieval castles, designed to withstand siege and bombardment, in the classic Spanish manner. As such, they were useless for the guerrilla-style hit-and-run tactics of the Chichimeca war parties. Eventually, the presidios evolved into bases for the mobile cavalry that was needed to counter the nomadic Indians of the borderlands. Some 30 presidios were established during the Chichimec War, and 15 additional forts between 1580 and 1600. These were lightly-manned garrisons, usually consisting of no more than 14 men apiece. Inadequately financed, ill-equipped, and poorly-officered, these forts contributed little to the eventual pacification of the Chichimecs. But the establishment of the presidio as a nucleus for Spanish civil, military, and religious settlement continued in the next phase of European advance north into the borderlands.

The colonization of New Mexico, Sinaloa, and the western Sierra Madre was marked by numerous Indian revolts. In response, the viceregal government in Mexico City established new presidios in the early eighteenth century to protect roads, missions, mines, and civilian towns. The new presidios were more heavily manned, having garrisons of 15 to 30 troopers. Still, their uncoordinated and poorly-supported efforts made little progress in protecting the frontier. In 1693, and again in 1729, Spanish officials inspected the presidios and made recommendations to reform frontier defense. These recommendations, codified in the *reglamento* (ordinance) of 1729, resituated presidios closer to frontier areas, replaced some forts with civilian settlements, created *compañías volantes* ("flying companies," or light cavalry units), and shifted the emphasis of the presidial company from garrison and convoy duties to offensive operations.

By 1730, there were 23 presidios, with a strength of 1,006 officers and men trying to police a vast frontier stretching from Sonora in the west to eastern Texas. The 1729 *reglamento* established the site of each, regulated the annual pay for officers and common soldiers, and set out the armaments, duties, and responsibilities of the company. Subsequent inspections and political and military changes in American and Europe brought about further reforms later in the eighteenth century. A new *reglamento* was promulgated in 1772, and an *instrucción* in 1786. Each dealt with the establishment and shifting of forts, political and military strategy in relation to borderlands Indians tribes, and the logistics of maintaining the garrisons.

The presidio itself took the form of a simple walled enclosure adorned with a few guard towers, often built of adobe brick instead of stone. Within its walls, surrounding a central plaza, were quarters for the officers and men, a chapel, and storehouses for food and equipment. Until the *reglamento* of 1772, there was no standardization for presidios, and most were in a constant state of disrepair due to lack of funds. Most of the presidial soldiers were recruited from frontier towns, and a high percentage were mestizos and mulattoes, soldiers of mixed European, Indian, and African heritage. Armed with a sword, long lance, and short musket, the soldiers carried a leather shield to stop Indian arrows, and also wore protective armor in the form of leather jerkins, called *cueras*; for which the presidio soldiers were known as *soldados de cuera*. Life in the frontier garrisons was harsh and unrelenting. Besides the danger from Indian attack, soldiers were usually behind in their pay, short of supplies, and inadequately equipped to fight against a swift and elusive enemy. Not surprisingly, desertion rates were high, and there were instances of revolt against commanding officers. The proximity of French territory, or of nomadic Indian bands who valued fighting skills were temptations to which many soldiers succumbed.

At the end of the eighteenth century, the Spanish defenses consisted of 22 presidios, manned by almost 3,000 men, including the *presidiales*, five light cavalry companies, and a company of Spanish regulars sent to fight in the Americas. After 1800, an enfeebled Spanish government could not properly finance the presidio system, and it gradually deteriorated. Independence from Spain completely destroyed the garrisons, as Spanish officers left the country and a weakened central government in Mexico City was unable to pay its soldiers. But during the colonial period, the presidio played a key role as a nucleus of frontier settlement throughout the Spanish borderlands.

Peter Stern

References
    Max Moorhead, *The Presidio: Bastion of the Spanish Borderlands* (1975).

See also ARMY, SPANISH

Fort de la Presque Isle (Pennsylvania)
French penetration of the Ohio Valley, which would trigger the climactic struggle for colonial

supremacy in North America, began with the establishment of a fort at Presque Isle on the south shore of Lake Erie. For most of the French and Indian War, this post would guard the beginning of the portage from Lake Erie to the upper Allegheny River and provide the main point of supply and communication between the posts on the Great Lakes, particularly Niagara, and French forces operating in the Ohio Valley.

The military expedition that was to establish a chain of posts from Lake Erie to the forks of the Ohio was dispatched early in 1753 by Ange de Menneville, the marquis de Duquesne, and governor of New France. The forts were intended as tangible symbols of French authority, particularly over "La Belle Rivière" or the Ohio River. With no direct water route to the area, it was necessary to secure one of several portage routes. The original plan had been to utilize a portage from Lake Erie to Chautauqua Lake and thence to the Allegheny. This was the route used by Pierre-Joseph Céloron de Blainville during his 1749 expedition. The location of the new post was changed before the end of the month to a site farther west, a well-sheltered bay known as Presque Isle for the long, curving peninsula that protected it from Lake Erie. From this point, a road would carry traffic 15 miles to the Rivière aux Boeufs or French Creek.

Construction of the new fort began on 15 May 1753 under the direction of Captain François Le Mercier, an artillery officer. It was situated on a substantial bluff overlooking the bay. Fort de la Presque Isle, as the new post was called, was erected in the form of a square with four bastions. Rather than being constructed as a stockade, however, the walls were built of horizontal logs. The few contemporary accounts of the post indicate that the fortifications were only roughly finished. The walls enclosed log quarters and storehouses and a stone powder magazine.

From the time of its construction until 1759, Fort de la Presque Isle served its role of, in the words of Louis-Antoine de Bougainville, "an essential storehouse, the first between Niagara and the Belle-Rivière." The portage proved to be difficult to use and maintain, but it nonetheless carried the men and supplies for the French war effort in the Ohio. Fort de la Presque Isle was initially spared destruction in July 1759, when Captain François-Marie Le Marchand de Lignery rushed to raise the siege of Fort Niagara, burning the posts at Venango and Le Boeuf as he hastened to Lake Erie. When Captain Pierre Robinau de Portneuf learned of the defeat of

Lignery's army near Niagara on 24 July, however, he burned his weak wooden fort and, in August, withdrew with his garrison to Detroit.

The site of Presque Isle was soon visited by the British, the first being Captain Charles Lee, who crossed the portage that fall with dispatches from Niagara to British forces at Pittsburgh. Colonel Henry Bouquet arrived at Presque Isle from Pittsburgh with his army in the summer of 1760. Bouquet forwarded troops to relieve the garrison of Niagara and constructed a new Fort Presque Isle. This post was maintained by the British to secure communications between Niagara and Pittsburgh until its capture and destruction by Indians during Pontiac's War on 21 June 1763. Although Fort Presque Isle was to have been reestablished later that year, this was not done.

Brian Leigh Dunnigan

References

Lawrence Henry Gipson, *The Great War for the Empire: The Victorious Years, 1758–1760* (1965); Walter O'Meara, *Guns at the Forks* (1965); Max Schoenfeld, *Fort de la Presqu'ile* (1989); Charles Morse Stotz, *Drums in the Forest* (1958); ———, *Outposts of the War for Empire: The French and English in Western Pennsylvania; Their Armies, Their Forts, Their People, 1749–1764* (1985).

See also BOUGAINVILLE, LOUIS-ANTOINE DE; BOUQUET, HENRY; FORT NIAGARA (NEW YORK); OHIO COUNTRY; PONTIAC'S WAR

Fort Prince Frederick (South Carolina)

Fort Prince Frederick was built on the west bank of the Beaufort River, an estuary of Port Royal Sound, between the years 1731 and 1734. It was built to guard the southern approaches to the South Carolina colony along the inland passage (the modern Atlantic Intra-Coastal Waterway) between Charles Town and St. Augustine, Florida. Fort Prince Frederick replaced the earlier log blockhouse called Beaufort Fort (1706–1721) located two miles to the north. The fort was 125 feet by 75 feet with walls of local "tabby" masonry construction. Inside the walls were barracks and a powder magazine. Fort Prince Frederick was garrisoned by the Independent Company of Foot (1731–1736), a detachment of the 42nd Regiment of Georgia (1738–1744) and intermittently by regular and provincial troops thereafter. It was also one of the supply bases for the waterborne patrols known as the "Carolina Scouts" that roamed the inland passage from Carolina to Florida between 1721 and 1742. Fort Prince Frederick was the base for the "Beaufort Galley," one of the two oar-and-sail-propelled coastal gunboats built by the South Carolina province in 1742 to guard against Spanish privateers. In 1748, Fort Prince Frederick was superseded as the area's principal military installation by the establishment of the Royal Navy's Port Royal station and careening wharf, and the arrival of the H.M.S. *Adventure* and the H.M.S. *Rye*. By 1758, Fort Prince Frederick had fallen into disrepair and was replaced by the larger Fort Lyttleton (1758–1779) on Spanish Point, one mile to the north. The foundations of Fort Prince Frederick are well maintained and can be clearly seen on the grounds of the U.S. Naval Hospital, Beaufort, South Carolina.

Lawrence S. Rowland

References

Larry D. Ivers, *Colonial Forts of South Carolina 1670–1775* (1970); ———, "Scouting the Inland Passage, 1685–1737," *South Carolina Historical Magazine* 73 (1972):117–129; Lawrence S. Rowland, "Eighteenth Century Beaufort: A Study of South Carolina's Southern Parishes to 1800," Ph.D. Dissertation, University of South Carolina (1978).

See also BEAUFORT FORT (SOUTH CAROLINA); FORT FREDERICK (SOUTH CAROLINA); FORT LYTTLETON (SOUTH CAROLINA); PORT ROYAL (SOUTH CAROLINA)

Fort Prince George–Keowee (South Carolina)

In 1753, South Carolina Governor James Glen built Fort Prince George, which was located just across the Keowee River from the Cherokee town of Keowee (near present-day Clemson, South Carolina). The Cherokees had requested a fort for many years to protect their women and children while they were fighting elsewhere for the British. As the French expanded southward out of the Ohio Valley and northeast from New Orleans, the English began to appreciate the need for the Cherokees as a buffer against the French.

Military and Indian labor constructed this first fort on Cherokee land out of earth and wood. It measured 200 feet square with a ditch running around the exterior five feet deep and five feet wide. Construction began in October and was completed in December 1753. When Raymond Demeré took command of the post in 1756, he began such an extensive renovation that many authorities have mistakenly credited that as the year the fort was built.

Fort Prince George played a pivotal role in the Cherokee War of 1760–1761. When the Cherokees retaliated for tribesmen murdered by whites, South Carolina Governor William Henry Lyttleton took more than 20 chiefs who came to Charles Town in a peace delegation as hostages. Lyttleton refused to release the chiefs until 24 Cherokees who had murdered whites on the frontier were turned in. In February 1760 in an attempt to free the hostages, Oconostota (Great Warrior) led an attack on the fort, killing its commander, Richard Coytmore. The soldiers responded by massacring the hostages, thus beginning the Cherokee War of 1760–1761. During the war, troops under Colonel Archibald Montgomery and Colonel James Grant destroyed the lower and middle towns. Shortly after the war, no longer threatened by the French, who had lost all of their colonial possessions, the English evacuated the fort (1768).

William L. Anderson

References

David H. Corkran, *The Cherokee Frontier: Conflict and Survival, 1740–1762* (1962); J. Norman Heard, *Handbook of the American Frontier: Four Centuries of Indian-White Relationships* (1987); Chapman J. Milling, *Red Carolinians* (1940); Grace Steele Woodward, *The Cherokees* (1963).

See also CHEROKEE WAR; GLEN, JAMES; FORT LOUDOUN (TENNESSEE); LYTTLETON, WILLIAM HENRY; OCONOSTOTA

Fort Prince George–Palachacola (South Carolina)

Built in 1723 on the west bank of the Savannah River, about fifty miles from the river's mouth, Fort Prince George guarded the main trail to Charles Town from the south and southwest. The former site of a Palachacola village, the Indian trade was occasionally conducted there, though, Fort Moore, upriver, remained the premier trading post on the Savannah. The fort was occupied by rangers at least until 1742.

Alan Gallay

References

Larry E. Ivers, *Colonial Forts of South Carolina 1670–1775* (1970).

See also FORT MOORE (SOUTH CAROLINA);
RANGERS; SALTCATCHERS FORT (SOUTH
CAROLINA)

Fort Prince William (Georgia)

Fort Prince William was one of a series of garrisons built along the southern frontier by Georgia's military commander, James Edward Oglethorpe, to protect English territorial claims. It was erected in April 1740 at the southern tip of Cumberland Island to provide a backup for Amelia Fort across Cumberland Sound. The new garrison consisted of a plank-sided house and a small stockade armed with eight cannons. During the Spanish invasion of Georgia in 1742, Oglethorpe evacuated the original Cumberland garrison at Fort St. Andrews, and concentrated his forces at Fort Prince William.

When the Spanish retreated after their defeat on Saint Simons Island in July 1742, Fort St. Andrew was destroyed. Fort Prince William, with a garrison of less than 100 men, was the final English target for the Spanish forces. On 18 July, determined rangers successfully defended the fort against a Spanish attack. The following year, the fort was one of the staging areas for Oglethorpe's counterattack on the Spanish in Florida. In 1748, Fort Prince William was rebuilt by the Georgians and a new battery was installed.

Doris B. Fisher

References

Allen D. Candler, ed., *Colonial Records of Georgia*, 26 vols. (1904–1916); Colonial Office Papers, ser. 5, Public Record Office of Great Britain; Larry E. Ivers, *British Drums on the Southern Frontier: The Military Colonization of Georgia, 1733–1749* (1974).

See also BLOODY MARSH, BATTLE OF;
RANGER; FORT ST. ANDREWS (GEORGIA);
FORT ST. SIMONS (GEORGIA)

Privateering

Throughout the colonial period Great Britain, Spain, France, and other European powers attempted to augment the power of their navies on the high seas by mobilizing the business community to fit out their own vessels as warships. These private men-of-war, also known as privateers, cruised in every intercolonial war during the 1600s and 1700s, in European as well as American shipping lanes. Because they added to their nation's seapower without draining the national treasury, privateers were encouraged by European and colonial officials. Merchants in Europe and America eagerly dispatched their vessels, and thousands of mariners served on board, in hopes of making windfall profits while simultaneously demonstrating laudable patriotism. Colonial privateering expanded in each imperial conflict as Britain's New World possessions developed from outposts of empire into sizable cities, towns, and agricultural communities. By the mid-eighteenth century, privateering played the leading role in America's contribution to Britain's war effort. Disrupting an adversary's maritime commerce continued to dominate American naval thinking well after independence, and privateers plied the seas in large numbers during the Revolutionary War and the War of 1812. To understand the nature and impact of imperial warfare on colonial America, an examination of privateering is essential.

Privateering was and still is often confused with the infamous activity of piracy. Since in both cases heavily armed and manned vessels attempted to earn large profits by attacking and capturing richly-laden merchantmen, such confusion is perhaps understandable. Actually, there was a great difference between these two forms of maritime enterprise. Privateering was legal and was the object of increasing government regulation as it expanded in scope and importance from the sixteenth to the eighteenth centuries. Piracy, on the other hand, was a capital crime and declined at the end of the 1600s until it was finally stamped out of its strongholds in the Caribbean and Indian Ocean shortly thereafter. There was also a substantial difference in the types of people who participated in each endeavor. Governments encouraged privateering, and some of the most important and respected merchants in Europe and America responded by investing heavily in private men-of-war. The queen of England was not infrequently an investor in privateering ventures in the late sixteenth century. As a criminal activity, piracy attracted a clientele largely restricted to disgruntled sailors and other marginal men.

Privateering played an important role in the founding of England's New World empire during Queen Elizabeth I's reign. The slaving and privateering exploits of Sir John Hawkins and Sir Francis Drake in the Caribbean prompted increased interest in American colonization among England's governing circles. Sir Walter Raleigh's attempts to establish a settlement at Roanoke Island were financed in part by privateering expeditions against the Spanish, and all three of the 1580s voyages included forays into the Caribbean as part of their itinerary. Roanoke was selected as the site because it was originally thought to be an ideal privateering base: close to Spanish shipping lanes but difficult to find because of the Outer Banks. The link between privateering and colonization continued after the end of Queen Elizabeth's war with the Spanish (1585–1603). When the Virginia Company dispatched three ships carrying settlers to establish what became the first permanent English colony at Jamestown, Captain Christopher Newport, a veteran privateering officer, commanded the expeditionary force.

Privateers operated in a world dominated by the political economy of mercantilism. The purpose of warfare in that world was to expand or protect a nation's trade. Privateering made it possible to achieve this goal during the prosecution of the war itself. The desire for acquisition did not have to be postponed until the peace conferences at the conclusion of the hostilities. European governments viewed privateers as a way to augment national wealth and cripple the enemy's ability to wage war simultaneously. Thus the ends became the means. The lure of profits at the expense of an adversary's commerce appealed to the merchant communities in Europe as well as in the New World. Thus the inability of Great Britain, Spain, and the other colonial powers to afford the staggering expenditures necessary for large, powerful navies that could control the sea-lanes gave rise to privateering, and private property exerted an important influence in the maritime strategy of the imperial powers.

Large seaports dominated American privateering because only major cities possessed the extensive resources necessary for cruising operations. Privateering voyages required entrepreneurial ability, shipping, and manpower. The organization of cruises called for experienced merchants who were unafraid of taking risks and who commanded sufficient capital to acquire a strong vessel, substantial ordnance, and enough victuals for a long voyage. They need skilled captains with established reputations to attract large crews. Once a privateer captured an enemy merchantman, the owners' business skills were crucial because income did not materialize until the prize was condemned in a vice-admiralty court and the vessel and cargo were sold at a profit. Business correspondents, warehouse facilities, and market information were all necessary for success. Clearly, this was a business for experienced merchants, not amateurs.

In addition to business skills, shipping and manpower were also more available in the larger ports. Although some vessels were constructed specifically for privateering, most private men-of-war were converted merchantmen. Thus communities with large merchant fleets were better able to dispatch privateers than their smaller neighbors. Because privateers captured and did not sink their prey, large crews for boarding parties were essential. The principal ports more easily supplied the enormous number of men needed for privateering crews. Although full complements were often difficult to secure because of competition from the merchant marine and the Royal Navy, bigger cities offered the amplest supply of men.

Privateering was a popular wartime enterprise in America, and Newport, New York, Boston, Philadelphia, and Charles Town, as well as the island ports in the British West Indies, responded strongly to government encouragement of private men-of-war. Merchants in Newport began that city's strong tradition of privateering during Queen Anne's War (1702–1713), when they dispatched a privateer within 11 days of the arrival of the declaration of war. Newport became a privateering center, and William Wanton, owner of the first private warship, established his family as one of that colony's leading political and economic forces. Rhode Island's interest in privateering continued throughout the 1700s. When the War of Jenkins' Ear erupted in 1739, Newport responded with enthusiasm at the chance to dispatch private men-of-war. During the privateering boom accompanying the French and Indian War (1754–1763), Rhode Island authorities successfully petitioned London to obtain the colony's own vice-admiralty court to facilitate speedy prize adjudication. Rhode Islanders continued to fit out privateers in the American Revolution, though this enterprise suffered during the Royal Navy's three-year occupation of Newport.

Manhattan merchants also established a strong tradition of privateering. Their privateers captured numerous French and Spanish vessels worth thousand of pounds sterling during Queen Anne's War, and New York became the leading privateering port in America during the wars of 1739–1748 and the French and Indian War. The British occupation of New York hindered privateering operations during the Revolution, but Manhattan again became a leading privateering center during the War of 1812.

The valuable cargoes embarking from West Indian ports made the Caribbean the center of New World privateering operations from the sixteenth century until the end of the Napoleonic Wars. Jamaica, Barbados, Antigua, and other island colonies fitted out scores of private men-of-war during the imperial conflicts. Caribbean predators wreaked havoc with the enemy's sugar commerce during the wars of King William and Queen Anne (1689–1697 and 1702–1713), and according to the *Boston Evening-Post*, were eager to seize rich Spanish prizes in 1739: "'Tis said, that upon the first Advice of a War, all Business will be laid aside in Jamaica, but that of Privateering, the Men waiting with Impatience to have their Hands untied."[27 August 1739]. Given the extensive privateering activity in the Caribbean during the French and Indian War, the American Revolution, and the French revolutionary and Napoleonic era (including the War of 1812), it appears that the privateers' hands were seldom tied.

Although Newport, New York, and the British West Indian ports played the leading roles in American privateering, other communities had strong supporting parts. Boston and the Essex County, Massachusetts, ports launched numerous privateering voyages throughout the period. Despite the importance of a sizable Quaker mercantile community that largely avoided privateering, Philadelphia also dispatched many private men-of-war throughout the colonial and revolutionary conflicts. Charles Town also fitted out private warships, though its participation in privateering was limited by the lack of locally-owned shipping and a shortage of mariners.

British colonial privateers sailed Atlantic waters from Newfoundland to the Spanish Main but concentrated on Caribbean sea-lanes where the pickings were richest. The staples of the Indies—sugar, molasses, coffee, indigo—fetched better prices than the fish and fur shipped from New France. Spanish treasure ships, though elusive, were also alluring. American privateers seriously disrupted Spanish and French commerce throughout the intercolonial wars. American warships captured thousands of enemy vessels, and successful investors, captains, and crews received substantial income. Privateering could

be very profitable. Successful privateers earned profits of nearly 150 percent during the 1700s.

Privateering was synonymous with imperial warfare during the mercantilist world of the seventeenth and eighteenth centuries. As long as nations needed to mobilize private capital to augment sea power, and naval fleets could not control wartime shipping lanes, privateering dominated American maritime conflict and exerted a major influence on colonial commerce. Merchants and mariners correctly believed that they could make their fortunes from the decks of a private man-of-war.

Carl E. Swanson

References

Kenneth R. Andrews, *Trade, Plunder and Settlement: Maritime Enterprise and the Genesis of the British Empire, 1480–1630* (1984); James G. Lydon, *Pirates, Privateers, and Profits* (1970); Richard Pares, *War and Trade in the West Indies, 1739–1763* (1936); David J. Starkey, *British Privateering Enterprise in the Eighteenth Century* (1990); Carl E. Swanson, *Predators and Prizes: American Privateering and Imperial Warfare, 1739–1749* (1991).

See also DRAKE, FRANCIS

Proclamation Line of 1763

The Proclamation Line of 1763 is a fixture found in most historical atlas maps and texts purporting to describe the territorial divisioning of eastern North America on the eve or opening of the American Revolution. It was, however, an historical ephemera that faded from the scene almost as soon as it had been mentioned in the hastily issued Royal Proclamation of 7 October 1763. In that omnibus document the bounds and governments of four new colonies, Quebec, East Florida, West Florida, and Grenada, were promulgated, officer and soldier veterans of the war against France were rewarded with grants of land proportional to their rank, and imperial policies on Indian trade and land were formalized. The Proclamation Line grew out of the latter. So that the "Nations or Tribes of Indians with whom We are connected and who live under Our Protection should not be molested or disturbed in the Possession of . . . their Hunting Grounds," King George III reserved the "Lands beyond the Heads or Sources of any of the Rivers which fall into the Atalantick Ocean from the West and

North-West, or upon any Lands whatever. . . . not having been ceded to, or purchased by Us." Traditionally, the Proclamation Line has been drawn along the Appalachian water-divide from upstate New York to northern Florida. The vast interior lying west of the line is thus presented as an Indian reserve from which white settlement was excluded. Clearly this traditional model is an oversimplification since it neglects the proclamation's provision detailed in the underlined phrases quoted above. The king's advisers and colonial leaders knew that vast areas lying well to the east of the Appalachian divide were unquestionably Indian land that had not yet "been ceded to, or purchased" by the crown. The intention of the proclamation was to make a clear and unequivocal statement regarding Britain's Indian land acquisition policy. It was that Indian lands could only be acquired by the imperial government in the name of the king "at some publick Meeting or Assembly of the said Indians to be held for that Purpose by the Governor or Commander in Chief of Our Colonies . . ." Such "publick Meeting" between the southern colonial governors and the "kings, headmen, and warriors of the Chickasaws, upper and lower Creeks, Chactahs, Cherokees, and Catawbas" had been ordered to convene in Augusta, Georgia, in the months prior to the drafting of the proclamation. The "Congress of the Four Southern Governors, and the Superintendent of That District, With The Five Nations of Indians at August, 1763" served as the model for a long series of formal Indian "Congresses" which led to the creation of the Indian Boundary Line that clearly and legally separated the Indians' land from that open to white settlement in the Revolutionary era. The Indian Boundary Line eventually stretched from the Mississippi near the Yazoo River's mouth, east across the Gulf coastal plain, around the coastal zone of the Florida peninsula, north across Georgia and the Carolinas, west across the Virginias and Kentucky to the Ohio River at the juncture of Kentucky. From the mouth of the Kentucky, the Indian Boundary Line followed the Ohio River upstream and crossed the state of Pennsylvania from its southwest to northeast corner and crossed central New York state to the Mohawk River near present-day Rome and continued north to end at the St. Lawrence River. Needless to say, the Indian boundary, and not the Proclamation Line of 1763, came to represent a factor of the greatest possible moment to the Indians, pioneers, and British administrators concerned with the orderly and peaceful settlement of America's first west. In conclusion, it is emphasized that the Indian Boundary Line was conceived of and adopted as the key element in Britain's Indian land policy long before the expediency of Pontiac's frontier war led to the hasty issuance of the Proclamation of 7 October 1763. The Indian Boundary Line's evolution was primarily guided by the two royal superintendents for Indian affairs, Sir William Johnson in the northern district, and John Stuart in the southern.

Louis De Vorsey, Jr.

References
Louis DeVorsey, Jr., *The Indian Boundary in the Southern Colonies, 1763–1775* (1966); *Journal of the Congress of the Four Southern Governors, and the Superintendent of That District, with the Five Nations of Indians, at August, 1763* (1764); 7 October 1763, [Establishing New Governments in America] By the King. A Proclamation.

See also AUGUSTA, CONGRESS OF; JOHNSON, WILLIAM; PONTIAC'S WAR; STUART, JOHN

The Prophet (?–?)

The Prophet was a Delaware Indian who rose to a position of significant influence among the disgruntled Indians of the Great Lakes country in the days immediately preceding Pontiac's uprising in the early 1760s. Little is known about the Prophet's early years or his fate after he drifted back into the obscurity from which he momentarily arose. What is known, however, is that the Prophet delivered a powerful and compelling message to his brethren and called on them to spurn the white man's way and technology.

Not long before the events of Pontiac's War, the Prophet had an experience that profoundly altered his life and the lives of hundreds of those who chose to heed his message. The Prophet contacted the "Master of Life." After a long period of brooding about both the Indians' impending fate at the hands of the white invader and how to reach the Master of Life to seek deliverance, the Prophet had a dream in which he was instructed to embark upon a long journey. This he did, and after several days, he came to a spot in the wilderness where three trails converged. Not knowing which one to take, he chose the widest of the three, which eventually led him to a pit of fire that seemed to advance in his direction. He retraced his steps and took a second trail and found another pit of fire. The Prophet again backtracked, and upon following the third trail, he came to the base of a luminous white mountain where he encountered a beautiful woman. She instructed him to bathe and to ascend the mountain. On reaching its peak, he saw three villages. The Prophet chose to enter the most attractive of the villages, where he was greeted by a man dressed in white who led him into the presence of the Master of Life.

The Master of Life greeted him kindly and spoke. He said to the Prophet: "I am the Master of Life, and since I know what thou desirest to know, and to whom thou desirest to speak, listen well to what I am going to say to thee and all Indians." The master directed that all Indians were to cease using alcohol to the point of madness, to take one wife and remain with her for life, to cease running after other men's wives, and to end the making of war on all other Indians. In addition, the master also instructed the Prophet to teach the Indians to halt the practice of praying to Manitou, since he was the prince of evil, and for all Indians to foreswear the white man's trade goods. The master's message was simple. His Indian children were not on the path to heaven, and, until they rid themselves of the evil influence of the white man, their road to paradise was hopelessly blocked. The master also assured the Prophet that, if the Indians would revive the old ways of living, a better time for all Indians would be created.

After his visit with the Master of Life, the Prophet descended the mountain and returned to his people to broadcast the master's words. It was a dynamic revelation that the Prophet brought to the dissident Indians, who were in a state of profound distress. The messianic words of this mysterious and charismatic man electrified them. The Prophet wept constantly while he delivered his orations, and the Indians, who were always respectful of great speakers, were awed and inspired by his statements. The Prophet may have had a smattering of Christianity somewhere in his background. He often used imagery related to Christian traditions, but his message was unmistakable and true to the revelation he had received from the Master of Life. The Prophet taught that all white men were the enemies of the Indians' hopes for return to the older and better ways of life. Chief Pontiac of the Ottawa nation was among the many of the Prophet's auditors who were affected by the words the holy man brought from the Master of Life. At a time when the entire Indian frontier was in a state of ferment, the Prophet came on the scene and added significantly to the xenophobia rising among the nations harassed by the penetration of English/American civilization into their homelands. Pontiac eventually modified the Prophet's message by declaring that the French still in the Great Lakes area were exempt from the Master of Life's blandishments. Pontiac probably made this compromise for the sake of both diplomatic and military considerations. When the war finally came in 1763, the French descendants were exempted from the destruction the Prophet encouraged on all white men. Nevertheless, the Prophet had a profound impact on the turbulent frontier at a time when most of the Indian nations instinctively understood that they were at a vital crossroads in their struggle to survive the depredations of the white man.

Larry G. Bowman

References

Francis Parkman, *History of the Conspiracy of Pontiac* (1902); Howard H. Peckham, *Pontiac and the Indian Uprising* (1947); Milo M. Quaife, *The Siege of Detroit, Including the Journal of Pontiac's Conspiracy and John Rutherfurd's Narrative* (1958); Robert M. Utley and Wilcomb E. Washburn, *Indian Wars* (1985); Dale Van Every, *Forth to the Wilderness; the First American Frontier, 1754–1774* (1961).

See also DELAWARE; PONTIAC'S WAR

Province Fort (Maine)

Part of the effort by Massachusetts in 1743 to establish adequate defenses for several settlements on the frontier, Province Fort was designed for the protection of the inhabitants of New Marblehead, now South Windham. The fort was completed in the summer of 1744. It consisted of a palisaded fort 50 feet square with hemlock walls one foot thick and two watchtowers. The fort withstood five Indian attacks between 1747 and 1756. It was also known as Salmon Falls Fort.

David L. Whitesell

Provincial Troops

Colonial military campaigns were carried out by provincial troops, volunteers who were recruited for a single campaign. Because the militia rarely functioned outside a colony, provincial armies did the real fighting. The men who filled the ranks of provincial armies were drawn from surplus manpower that was temporarily available for military service and were commanded by officers whom the legislature or governor commissioned every year. While soldiers might reenlist and officers be recommissioned, provincial armies were recreated each year. This fact shaped the organization, composition, discipline, and effectiveness of provincial armies during the French and Indian War and helped create a mythology about American soldiers that played a part in the colonies' decision to declare independence from Great Britain.

Provincial armies were organized roughly like a British regular unit. The company was the basic unit—40 to 100 men, led by three commissioned officers and seven noncommissioned officers. Ten companies formed a battalion, and a regiment was composed of from one to four battalions. The regiment was led by three field officers. A single-battalion regiment might range from 400 to 1,000 men and officers.

The men who enlisted in a provincial army varied widely, but generally reflected the social and economic composition of the colony in which they were recruited. In Massachusetts, soldiers tended to be native-born, younger than the age at which men usually married, and either agricultural laborers or farmers who were living in or near their birthplace when they enlisted to fight. By contrast, the Virginia Regiment raised in 1756 was composed chiefly of poor, unemployed men, most of whom were recruited in Maryland and Pennsylvania.

Colonial governments used inducements and a draft in order to fill their regiments. They offered high wages and a bounty on enlistment. A Connecticut volunteer, for example, earned more than twice the amount paid to a British regular, and Virginians were paid £10 on enlistment, a sum equal to about half the annual cash income of a small tobacco planter. Still, colonial governments had to enact draft laws. In Massachusetts, the law required all able-bodied men to report to their local militia unit, where a predetermined number of men were selected for duty in the provincial army. All men between the ages of 21 and 50 "who have no visible way of getting an honest Livelihood" were subject to the draft in Virginia.

American soldiers were governed by the Rules of War and the British Mutiny Act, just as the redcoats were. But American officers shared neither the legal assumptions nor the class biases of British officers. Therefore, military law in an American provincial regiment tended to be pragmatic and paternalistic, to the disgust of British officers.

There were occasions when British regulars and provincial troops were expected to cooperate. Although some British and American officers tried to make these joint operations work smoothly, friction between the armies was commonplace. According to British officers, American soldiers refused to perform hard labor without extra pay, to stay in the field beyond their enlistment term, or to take orders unquestioningly. For their part, Americans regarded British offices as snobbish aristocrats and the redcoats as impious ruffians. The British thought the Americans cowardly and the Americans viewed the British as incompetent.

However, for all their real and exaggerated imperfections, provincial soldiers did fight well, especially in 1758. Together with General Edward Braddock's defeat in 1755, this led Americans to believe they could defeat British regulars. With their wartime experience fresh in mind, Americans dared to contemplate armed resistance, firm in the conviction that the British army represented arbitrary royal authority.

Alan Rogers

References

Fred Anderson, *A People's Army: Massachusetts Soldiers and Society in the Seven Years' War* (1984); Douglas Edward Leach, *Roots of Conflict: British Armed Forces and Colonial Americans, 1677–1763* (1986); Alan Rogers, *Empire and Liberty: American Resistance to British Authority, 1755–1763* (1974); James Titus, *The Old Dominion at War: Society, Politics, and Warfare in Late Colonial Virginia* (1991).

See also ARMY, GREAT BRITAIN; BRADDOCK, EDWARD; MILITIA

Pueblo
See NEW MEXICO

Pueblo Revolt of 1680
The revolt of the Pueblo Indians of New Mexico was the most serious Native American uprising the Spaniards faced during the colonial

period in New Spain. Following the disappointing end of the Coronado expedition of 1540, the Spanish withdrew from the valley of the Rio Grande, leaving behind embittered and wary Indian nations who were fully aware of the rapacious and destructive nature of the European intruders. The conquistadors had taken advantage of their Pueblo hosts, demanding food and supplies, abusing Indian women, and taking and executing captives in their fruitless search for the Seven Cities of Gold.

The Spaniards returned in 1598, when Juan de Oñate led a group of colonizers into the valley to settle New Mexico. The Rio Grande Valley was the northernmost outpost of Spanish colonization, with thousands of leagues of hostile territory between New Mexico and Mexico City. Populated by nine nations collectively known as the Pueblo Indians (so-called because they lived in settled villages, as opposed to the nomadic hunting tribes of the borderlands), the valley was viewed as a fertile ground for missionary activity by the Franciscans missionaries. But the Pueblo tribes proved stubbornly resistant to evangelization. The Spaniards who lived there were small farmers and cattle ranchers. Although New Mexico, with its lack of precious metals, was more of an agrarian colony than a mining enterprise, the Spanish still attempted to impose on the native peoples many of the odious institutions upon which their colonial enterprise in Central Mexico had been built. The *encomienda* and *repartimiento*, to extract tribute in the form of food and labor, were applied to the Pueblo Indians, albeit in a half-hearted manner. Still, the governor and the friars had to be supplied with corn and wheat, as well as wood, water, and personal servants. Worse still, the Spanish, in their crusading zeal, were determined to stamp out native religious practices and beliefs as forms of heresy, and to impose Christianity on a people whose culture and religion were deeply bound up with the natural world around them.

At the end of the seventeenth century there were about 2,350 Europeans in New Mexico, including Spaniards, *mestizos*, and mulattoes, most living in or near Santa Fe. There were also some 33 Spanish missionaries living in Indian villages. The Pueblo Indians numbered between 25,000 and 30,000 inhabitants in the eastern pueblos, divided among the nations of the Piro, Kere, southern and northern Tiwa, Tano, Towa, and Tewa.

It could not escape the notice of many Indians that there was a great deal of discord among the Spaniards. The governor and the friars were usually at odds with each other concerning jurisdiction over the natives, particularly over the collection of tribute and labor from the Indians. Each side accused the other of economically exploiting the natives. Bernardo López, who was governor from 1659 to 1662, required the inhabitants of several pueblos to bring him quotas of hides, salt, and piñon nuts so that he could resell them. The Franciscans in turn wanted Indians to work in the mission fields to support them. Successive governors charged the friars with abusing their charges; the padres, like the Jesuits in Sonora, often enforced their authority with whippings in the villages. To undermine the missionaries with whom they were feuding, some governors encouraged the Indians to continue their native religious practices, which included dancing, costumed and masked, as *katchina* spirits, strewing sacred cornmeal, and offering prayer sticks.

The late 1660s brought drought and crop failure in the valley. The drought on the plains drove bands of Utes, Navajos, and Apaches to raid the Pueblo villages, increasing the pressures on a beleaguered people. The hard times also increased cooperation between the civil and military authorities, and Indian religious ceremonies were suppressed. Forty-seven native leaders from the Pueblos were accused of witchcraft and idolatry, and were punished. The Pueblo villages, which had been hereditary enemies when the Europeans arrived, overcame their mutual hostility and began to plot revolt. Popé and Catiti, two shamans of San Juan and Santo Domingo pueblos, and El Ollita, a war chief from San Ildefonso, met secretly to unite the villages in a conspiracy to expel the Spaniards from the valley. At first the Indians plotted to present the Spanish authorities with an ultimatum. Their conspiracy was soon joined by a number of mixed-blood inhabitants, who understood the mentality of the Spaniards. Plans for an ultimatum turned to talk of expelling the Spanish completely.

Eventually, leaders from most of the valley pueblos agreed to participate in the uprising. A careful plan to isolate Santa Fe from the northern and southern settlements was worked out. Timing was crucial: the Indians planned to strike just before the irregular supply caravan from Mexico arrived, so that the Europeans would be low on horses, weapons, and ammunition. Despite precautions, word of the conspiracy reached Governor Antonio de Otermín in Santa Fe. Two messengers from Tesuque, who were to carry word to the other Pueblos when the moment to strike had arrived, were captured and interrogated. On 10 August 1680, the revolt broke out when the padre at Tesuque was murdered by armed men whose faces were painted for war. His soldier escort managed to escape and carry word to Santa Fe.

Pent-up hatred for the Europeans exploded. Although the Indians' original intentions had been to offer Spaniards a chance to escape, vengeance gained the upper hand. Many of the Franciscans refused to leave their missions, intent on saving the souls of their villagers. Twenty-one of the 33 missionaries were killed, along with 375 Spanish settlers. The survivors fled to Santa Fe, which the Pueblos knew was too strong for them to take by storm. Instead, they concentrated on cutting off the water supply of the town in order to force the Spanish to withdraw. On 21 August, Governor Otermín ordered the evacuation of Santa Fe, and the Spaniards pulled back to El Paso del Norte. The Indians could have attacked the weakened colonists, but let them pass, reinforcing the idea that their original intent had been not to destroy, but to expel the Europeans.

Indian unity, which had been forged by the necessity of rebellion, disintegrated quickly after the Spanish left. Tewa, northern Towa, Kere, and Tano villages had fought effectively together, but pan-Indian unity was short-lived. Some among the Pueblos wished to extirpate every vestige of the hated Europeans, but many other Indians appreciated the animals and plants the Spanish had transplanted to New Mexico, and resisted giving up horses, cattle, fruit, and olive trees. When after some punitive expeditions the Spanish returned from El Paso in 1692 to reoccupy Santa Fe, there was no united resistance from the Indians, and the Spanish reconquered each Pueblo settlement in turn. But they never forgot the shock of the revolt in 1680, and thereafter the Spanish trod very lightly in New Mexico. They reestablished formal political and military control over the Indian tribes, who never again rose in revolt, but the missionaries never reentered many villages. In those where they reoccupied their mission churches, they tended to look the other way when Indian dances were held. A wary tolerance held sway in New Mexico thereafter, reinforced by the increasing aggression of Apaches, against whom Indians and Europeans had to join forces. The great Pueblo Revolt was the largest and most successful pan-Indian revolt against the Spanish in Mexico, and the last.

Peter Stern

References

Joe Sando, "The Pueblo Revolt," in the *Handbook of North American Indians*, ed. by Alfonso Ortiz, Vol. 9 (1979):194–197; Edward Spicer, *Cycles of Conquest: The Impact of Spain, Mexico, and the United States on the Indians of the Southwest, 1533–1960* (1962); *Revolt of the Pueblo Indians of New Mexico and Otermín's Attempted Reconquest, 1680–1682*, annotated by Charles W. Hackett, trans. by Charmion Shelby, 2 vols. (1942).

See also NEW MEXICO, OÑATE, JUAN DE; SPANISH MISSION SYSTEM–SOUTHWEST

Puritans

Originally an epithet, Puritans were exceptionally scrupulous religionists who denounced the continuance of Catholic rites and regalia within the Church of England's worship services. In addition to challenging Anglican practices, Puritans also differed with one another. The spectrum ran from those who wanted to make only minor changes in religious convention, to radicals seeking to alter both church and state. The type that migrated to Massachusetts Bay in 1630 under the direction of John Winthrop, and throughout the great migration of the 1630s, were non-separating Congregationalists. This group rejected Anglicanism's episcopal form of church government, but did not favor an overt break from the English church or crown.

Backgrounds to the Puritan's colonization ideology are two-fold. In the mid-sixteenth century, the English undertook the colonization of Ireland, not only to protect it from Spanish invasion but also for profit. The English colonization approach included aggressive military rule, justified by the discounting of indigenous peoples. Hence the English depicted the Irish as barbaric pagans who required civilization under the tutelage of the English. This sanction for the hostile treatment of an indigenous people would be used by the Puritans in seventeenth-century New England.

The Puritans' sense of mission also colored their colonization approach. The English believed that their country was elect of God. Yet the Puritans feared that Catholic retentions of the English church, promoted by Archbishop William Laud, along with the "secularization" of daily life, threatened England's chosen status. So a portion of the Puritans migrated to New England with the idea that they were the righteous remnant sent by God to create a Bible commonwealth, which would serve as the "city on the hill" that the motherland could and should imitate. The Indians, however, were problematic in this scenario. The Puritans did not believe that they should ignore the Indians, but neither were they certain how the Indians were an essential element in the "errand." One solution was to depict the Indians as satanic forces placed by God in the "New Canaan" to test the Puritans. As the Puritans arrived in New England they put their colonization and mission theories into practice and created a militarized context.

The Indians also had their preconceptions of the Puritans due to their experiences with Europeans. Still, the Puritans were the aggressors. Their quest for land led to constant pressure on the Indian tribes of southern New England, especially the Massachusetts, Narragansetts, Wampanoags, Pequots, and Nipmucks. The Puritans primarily purchased land, but they also used the theory of *vacuum domicilium* that allowed them to commandeer fallow Indian lands. Conversion into "Praying Indians" also allowed the Puritans to dominate the local tribes.

The constant strain the Puritans put on Indian land and culture contributed to at least three major phases of Indian-Puritan hostility. The first battle was with the Pequots. As the Puritans pressed for Indian lands southwest of Massachusetts Bay, they came into conflict with the Pequot tribe. In 1637, the pressures exploded into outright war when the Puritans, with the help of the Narragansetts and Mohegans, virtually exterminated the Pequot tribe as an autonomous political entity.

The second conflict was with the Narragansetts. In 1643, Uncas, sachem of the Mohegans, claimed that the Narragansett sachem, Miantonomo, tried to have him killed. Although both Miantonomo and Uncas were allies of the Puritans, the newly-formed United Colonies of New England—which consisted of Massachusetts, Connecticut, Plymouth, and New Haven and designed to address military affairs with the Indians—handed Miantonomo over to Uncas for execution. In 1645, Miantonomo's brother, Pessacus, sought revenge on the Mohegans, but was effectively thwarted when the commissioners reinforced the Mohegans against the threats of the Narragansetts. Ninigret, sachem of the Niantics and spokesman for the Narragansetts, challenged Puritan authority over the next two decades. Thus the Puritans' view of the Narragansetts declined from ally in 1637, to potential enemy in the 1660s.

The most devastating of all the Indian-Puritan hostilities came with the advent of King Philip's War in 1675. Metacom, known to the Puritans as Philip, led an uprising of southern New England Indian tribes—including the Wampanoags, Narragansetts, Pocumtucks, Pocassets, and Nipmucks—against the Puritans. Praying Indians, Pequots, and Mohegans assisted the Puritans in the conflict. Though the Puritans prevailed, they suffered dearly. Half of the Puritan towns were severely damaged—12 completely destroyed. One out of every 16 military-aged males was killed.

Within the space of two generations, the Puritans managed to subdue the major Indian tribes in southern New England either by alliance or military conquest. Yet the years after King Philip's War also witnesses the beginning of the end for the Puritans. The English crown revoked the charters of the Puritan colonies and installed a royal governor. The ethos that made Puritanism a unique phenomenon also began to subside.

Richard C. Goode

References

James Axtell, *The European and the Indian: Essays in the Ethnohistory of Colonial North America* (1981); ———, *After Columbus: Essays in the Ethnohistory of Colonial North America* (1988); Nicholas Canny, "The Ideology of English Colonization: From Ireland to America," *William and Mary Quarterly* 30 (1973):575–598; Francis Jennings, *The Invasion of America: Indians, Colonialism and the Cant of Conquest* (1975); Cotton Mather, *Magnalia Christi Americana, or The Ecclesiastical History of New England* (1702); Wilcomb E. Washburn, ed., *Handbook of North American Indians*, Vol. 4, *History of Indian-White Relations* (1988).

See also Connecticut; King Philip's War; Massachusetts; Mohegan; Miantonomo; Narragansett; New England Confederation; Pequot War; Philip; Pilgrims; Praying Indians; Plymouth; War and Society in Colonial America; Winthrop, John

Q

Quaker Pacifism

Quakers were the most numerous and the most rigid pacifists in colonial America. For that reason, and because they held public offices, they generated the most controversy and left by far the largest pacifist record. Except for those in Pennsylvania and Rhode Island, Quakers suffered for their pacifism as few others did.

Quakers encountered difficulties because they would not serve in the colonial militias, and more importantly, would not pay for a substitute nor pay any fines for refusing to serve. In peacetime as well as war, they might have property distrained or suffer other penalties for their refusal. Additionally, they could not assist armies in the field nor take compensation for items commandeered by commissaries and the like. Some Quakers from time to time objected even to paying taxes that supported war, although the Society of Friends never required that refusal.

On the other hand, unlike other sectarians, Quakers did not balk at government service and conspicuously held office in Rhode Island, New Jersey, and Pennsylvania. In Pennsylvania, they institutionalized pacifism; Pennsylvania never had compulsory military service before the American Revolution.

Quakers in Pennsylvania and Rhode Island were least troubled by government demands. In New York and New Jersey, they legally escaped impositions for decades, and at other times unenthusiastic magistrates overlooked them. Elsewhere, they balked at laws that required pacifists to labor on fortifications, provide substitutes, or pay fines; and were prosecuted.

In Pennsylvania, Quakers who dominated the legislature had to reconcile their obligations to the state with their pacifism. They determined to levy taxes on the crown's behalf that the crown, and not Quakers, spent for war; they felt religiously disengaged as long as they did not spend the money, but instead "rendered it unto Caesar." With King George's war, however, they overstepped that bound and spent for war as well as levy. In the Seven Years' War, confronted by a protest from more scrupulous Quakers and by the outrage of settlers in western Pennsylvania and the British government, Quakers resigned from the legislature and left others to become the majority there. With that change, pacifist lineaments of Pennsylvania began to fade until the American Revolution when the Quakers were completely eclipsed.

Jack D. Marietta

See also PACIFISM; PENNSYLVANIA

Quapaw

The Quapaw (Arkansas) met their first Europeans in 1673, when Jacques Marquette and Louis Jolliet appeared among them at their villages on the lower Mississippi River near its juncture with the Arkansas River in the present state of Arkansas. The Quapaw desire for trade goods ensured a cooperative reception for the French, but the long-range implications for the Indians were disastrous. Early in the contact period, the Quapaw enjoyed a population estimated at between 6,000 and 15,000, but by 1763, their numbers had been reduced to fewer than 700. European diseases explain much of the decline.

The Quapaw maintained four great villages in 1673, three on the Mississippi River and one on the Arkansas River. "Given their number and the strategic location of their settlements," David W. Baird noted, "the Quapaws were reckoned as one of the tribes whose allegiance was critical to any European power aspiring to dominate the Mississippi River valley." Although the smallpox epidemic of 1698 devastated the Quapaw to the point where they were able to field just 300 warriors, the French cultivated the willing tribespeople into unusually dependable allies. The Quapaw promoted French interests when they fought such traditional enemies as the English-allied Chickasaw, although the small-scale Quapaw raids had little impact on the outcome of the English-French struggle. The French also enlisted the Quapaw in what Baird described as "the largest military force ever assembled in the Mississippi Valley," an army of 3,600 that expected to destroy the Chickasaw in 1739–1739. As was so often the case with Indian participants in European military operations, the Quapaw abandoned the venture after many weeks of campaigning because it failed to engage the enemy. By 1763, the Quapaw were reduced to just three small villages that they located on the Arkansas River for security reasons.

Raymond E. Hauser

References

W. David Baird, *The Quapaw Indians: A History of the Downstream People* (1980); John R. Swanton, *The Indian Tribes of North America* (1952); Cyrus Thomas, "Quapaw," in *Handbook of American Indians North of Mexico*, Frederick Webb Hodge, ed. (1968), II:333–336.

See also ARKANSAS POST (ARKANSAS); CHICKASAW WARS

Quartering

After the revolutionary settlement of 1689, the British Parliament passed an annual Mutiny Act that prohibited the quartering of soldiers on private citizens against their will. Whenever troops moved into areas where barracks were not available, the act stipulated that the commanding officer was to apply to the local magistrate, who would designate public buildings in which the troops were to be sheltered. The owners or innkeepers were compensated according to a per diem rate set by Parliament.

The situation in North America was so different that the law was of little use. There were fewer public houses, the daily allowance was too low, and major sections of the act were not extended to the colonies. Still, Americans held to the view that an Englishman's home was his castle and that forced quartering in private homes was a violation of the British constitution. However, British officers in America contended that legal restraints did not apply in wartime. For many Americans, this raised fears that the civil government would be overwhelmed by military power.

The issues surrounding the quartering of soldiers in America came to a head during the Great War for Empire. Major General Edward Braddock, the first commander in chief of the British forces in North America, told the Pennsylvania assembly in 1755 that assigning quarters was his right, and he threatened to "take due care to burthen those colonies the most, that show the least loyalty to his Majesty." Braddock's death and the headlong retreat of his army in July forced the assembly to confront the issue sooner than expected. The legislature passed a bill very much like the Mutiny Act, but the Privy Council disallowed the law. Attorney General William Murray argued that the Pennsylvania law would "Cramp the Public Service and obstruct the defense of the Province."

Therefore, when the new commander in chief, Lord Loudoun, arrived in the American colonies, the stage was set for another confrontation between the British army and colonial legislators. The city officials of Albany, New York, clashed with the army during the summer of 1756. The New York assembly had appropriated money to build barracks, but the troops arrived in Albany before construction began. Because there were not enough public houses to accommodate Loudoun's soldiers, the general insisted that they be quartered in private homes. The mayor refused, claiming the order was illegal. But, faced with British bayonets and political pressure from Lieutenant Governor James DeLancey, the mayor's resistance collapsed. British soldiers were quartered in every house in the town.

The army's use of force, the city council argued, "assumed a Power over us Very inconsistent with the Liberties of a free and Loyal People. We conceive," the council concluded, "that his Majesties Paternal Cares to Release us from the threat of France have in a great measure been Made use of to oppress us." Disgruntled colonists in Charles Town, Philadelphia, and Boston agreed.

A Quartering Act for the colonies finally was passed by Parliament in 1765. Soldiers were to be housed in barracks, public houses, or vacant buildings rented by the governor and council. No mention was made of quartering in private homes. In this way, Parliament hoped to quiet American complaints.

The New York assembly initially refused to comply with the Quartering Act; it said only American legislatures could enact such a law. In 1774, the First Continental Congress listed the Quartering Act as one of those arbitrary laws "which demonstrate a system formed to enslave America." In short, as a result of the struggle over quartering during the Great War for Empire, many Americans found cause for making a revolution.

Alan Rogers

References

Fred Anderson, *A People's Army: Massachusetts Soldiers and Society in the Seven Years' War* (1984): Douglas Edward Leach, *Roots of Conflict: British Armed Forces and Colonial Americans, 1677–1763* (1986); Alan Rogers, *Empire and Liberty: American Resistance to British Authority, 1755–1763* (1974).

Quartermaster General

The office of quartermaster general (QMG) did not appear in the organization of the British army until 1689. It initially combined the functions of the two earlier offices, scoutmaster general and provost marshal general. However, the office and duties of the provost marshal were later placed under the adjutant general, another very important staff officer, in charge of personnel and all matters relating to disciple.

As the primary staff officer under the commander in chief, the quartermaster general had responsibility over intelligence, troops movements and encampments, field equipment, and transportation generally. By the mid-eighteenth century, the quartermaster general usually commanded a division in the field as well as acting as chief supply officer. In fact, he often served as chief of staff for the commanding general, in charge of working out all the details of every operation in conjunction with the commissary general of discipline, and the master general of ordnance in charge of guns and ammunition.

Combining both administrative and command functions, the quartermaster general might divide his many and detailed administrative duties among capable deputies (DQMG) and assistant deputies (ADQMG) at the various military bases. Every regiment had a quartermaster on its command staff to coordinate supply with headquarters, and the quartermaster general's office employed hundreds of civilians as artisans, warehouse workers, wagoners, and boatmen.

The office of quartermaster general was first established in America during the French and Indian War. A member of General Edward Braddock's staff, Lieutenant Colonel John St. Clair, held the king's commission as deputy quartermaster general in America. Wounded in the ambush that took Braddock's life in 1755, St. Clair never fully recovered. He at first shared quartermaster duties, and in 1758 was replaced by Lieutenant Colonel James Robertson and Lieutenant Colonel John Bradstreet, both of whom were DQMGs in New York. During the French and Indian War, St. Clair, Robertson, and Bradstreet dispensed thousands of pound sterling among numerous vendors for crucial supplies and transportation services.

In fact, the success or failure of British arms in the wilds of America depended especially on the effectiveness of the quartermaster general's department. "In this Country," wrote John Campbell, the earl of Loudoun and commander in chief in America in 1756, "the Qr Mr General has a great deal of bussiness, more than in any Service I ever was in, which arises from the Variety of Services going on at the same time in so many different Places." The quartermaster general's office in America continued to be maintained following the Treaty of Paris of 1763 because of the enlarged responsibilities of the British army. However, many of the quartering duties formerly exercised by the quartermaster general were assumed by the barrack master general, appointed by the commanding general under the Quartering Act of 1765.

Ronald W. Howard

References

William G. Godfrey, *Pursuit of Profit and Preferment in Colonial North America: John Bradstreet's Quest* (1982); Milton M. Klein and Ronald W. Howard, eds., *The Twilight of British Rule in Revolutionary America: The New York Letter Book of General James Robertson, 1780–1783* (1983); John Knox, *An Historical Journal of the Campaigns in North America for the Years 1757, 1758, 1759 and 1760*, Arthur G. Dougherty, ed., 3 vols. (1914–1916); Stanley M. Pargellis, ed., *Military Affairs in North America, 1748–1765* (1936); Colonel H.C.B. Rogers, *The British Army of the Eighteenth Century* (1977).

See also BRADDOCK, EDWARD; BRADSTREET, JOHN; CAMPBELL, JOHN; ROBERTSON, JAMES

Quebec

Quebec, capital of New France and its main port, strategically located at a narrowing of the St. Lawrence River above the Isle d'Orléans, is noted for its promontory Cap-aux-Diamants, which has been effectively fortified since early colonials times. Originally the site of the Laurentian Iroquois village of Stadaconna when Jacques Cartier visited it in 1535–1536 and 1541–1554, it takes its name from the native appellation for the narrows, which soon found its way onto French maps. Cartier abandoned his small advance settlement of Charlesbourg-Royal (Cap Rouge) in the spring of 1542, as Jean-François de La Rocque, sieur de Roberval, arrived with the authority of lieutenant general and the main group of 200 settlers. The severe winter of 1542–1543, the outbreak of scurvy among the settlers, the hostility of the Laurentian Iroquois, and internal squabbling culminated in the abandonment of the settlement in the summer of 1543. When Cartier's nephews visited the site in 1580 to engage in the fur trade, Stadaconna and other Iroquoian villages had disappeared.

In 1608, the royal geographer, Samuel De Champlain, founded a *habitation* at Quebec (population 28) in the interest of the fur monopoly held by the associates of sieur de Monts in what was now Algonkian hunting territory. Quebec grew very slowly during the period of initial settlement under the aegis of the Company of New France, or the One Hundred Associates (1627–1663). The post was turned over in July 1629 to the Kirke brothers, and Thomas Kirke was left in charge as governor until it was retroceded to France in 1632 by the Treaty of Saint Germain-en-Laye. It became the headquarters of the Canadian Jesuit missions in 1633, and four years later the first *réduction*, or Indian reserve, was organized in nearby Sillery. In 1635, the Jesuits founded a college, the oldest post-secondary institution in North America, and in 1639, Sisters Hospitallers arrived to open a hospital and Ursulines to provide education for French and Indian girls. The first bishop arrived 20 years later, in 1659, and quickly took over supervision of welfare, hospitalization, and educational work, and founded a seminary for training secular priests.

In 1663, King Louis XIV assumed personal control over the colony, and Quebec's role was greatly enhanced as the seat of royal administration. A governor arrived as the king's representative to take charge of military and Indian affairs and organize a sovereign council having both legislative and judicial duties. Within a couple of years, a royal intendant arrived to assume control of colonial finances and the judiciary. Ministry of Marine troops were also sent out to deal with the Iroquois threat. In 1674, Quebec became the seat of a vast diocese embracing the entire northern continent. By this time, the town had several thousand inhabitants, divided socially and physically between the upper and lower towns. The lower town, at the foot of the promontory along the river, was the home of the merchants and artisans, while the upper town, surrounded by a stone wall dominated by a viceregal Château St. Louis, the episcopal palace, seminary, cathedral, and Jesuit and Ursuline establishments, was the seat of political and social power. On the intermediary slope stood the intendant's palace and a brewery.

Town regulations in 1676, representing some of the earliest urban legislation on the continent, required buildings be built of stone with fire walls, access to chimneys that were to be cleaned regularly, maintenance of proper latrines and drains, collection and disposal of garbage, restrictions on the keeping of animals within the town, and provision for a weekly farmers' market.

Although the colony was intermittently at war with the Five Nations Iroquois from 1609 to 1701, Quebec was never attacked directly by the Iroquois. English adventurer Sir William Phips attacked Quebec with a force of 32 ships and 2,000 colonial troops in 1690, the War of the League of Augsburg (known as King William's War in North America). Governor Louis de Buade de Frontenac would not be frightened into surrender, announcing he would not respond "save from the mouths of my cannon" along the wall of the upper town. In 1711, during the War of the Spanish Succession (Queen Anne's War), another expedition was launched to capture Quebec under Sir Hovenden Walker, who led an armada of ships and some 8,000 troops into the St. Lawrence estuary. But stormy weather and unreliable pilots wrecked the naval expedition with the loss of about a thousand lives near the entrance of the river. There was a period of peace from 1713 to 1744, during which time the town of Quebec expanded beyond the walls as it became an important service center, administrative center, and port. Following the War of the Austrian Succession (1740–1748), barracks were built to house some of the French regular troops sent out by the Ministry of War.

In 1759, a British expedition with heavy naval support laid siege to the city of about 10,000 inhabitants. The naval bombardment over the next two months succeeded in demolishing the major buildings of the town and the inhabitants who had not fled to the surrounding countryside were on the verge of starvation. On 13 September, General James Wolfe managed to land a force on the Plains of Abraham behind the town and engage Louis-Joseph de Montcalm, the marquis de Montcalm's troops in a premature encounter that proved disastrous for the French. Both Wolfe and Montcalm were killed. The French army retreated behind the walls of the capital. François-Gaston de Lévis assumed command and negotiated a conditional surrender permitting his army to retreat to Montreal for the winter, while the British navy sailed home. In the spring of 1760, Lévis marched on Quebec and succeeded in drawing out the British to engage in a battle at Saint-Foy, an encounter that proved as disastrous for the British as the previous year's battle had been for the French. They retreated behind the walls of Quebec. Contrary to popular belief, neither of the two battles at Quebec in 1759–1760 were decisive. It was the arrival of the British fleet in 1760 that confirmed the British hold on Quebec and so on the entire colony.

Quebec remained the administrative center during the period of British military rule (1759–1764) and became the capital of the crown colony of Quebec after the Treaty of Paris in 1763. Its commerce expanded quickly, particularly exports of wheat and timber to Britain. In 1775–1776, Quebec was again attacked by a large force after refusing to join in the American Revolution. In November 1775, General Richard Montgomery boasted that he would eat Christmas dinner in Quebec or in hell. He was killed trying to scale the walls of the old capital. The following May, a British fleet came to the rescue. The demoralized attackers retreated hastily. Quebec could still boast that it had never been taken by assault.

Cornelius J. Jaenen

References

Guy Frégault, *Canada: The War of the Conquest,* trans. Margaret M. Cameron (1969); Hilda Neatby, *Quebec: The Revolutionary Age, 1760–1791* (1966); Ian K. Steele, *Guerillas and Grenadiers: The Struggles for Canada, 1689–1760* (1969); Brian Young and John A. Dickinson, *A Short History of Quebec* (1988).

See also CANADA, BRITISH EXPEDITION AGAINST (1711); CANADA, NEW ENGLAND EXPEDITION AGAINST (1690); FRONTENAC, LOUIS DE BUADE DE; JESUITS; KIRKE BROTHERS; MONTCALM-GOZON DE SAINT-VERAN, LOUIS-JOSEPH; PHIPS, WILLIAM; QUEBEC, BATTLE OF; QUEBEC, FRENCH ATTEMPT TO RECAPTURE; ST. LAWRENCE RIVER; WOLFE, JAMES

Quebec, Battle of (1759)

The Battle of Quebec is usually regarded as the most important military engagement in the French and Indian War. It was surely the most dramatic. Following a siege of 80 days, the British under Major General James Wolfe caught the French off-guard and were able to scale the steep cliffs upriver of the fortress city. Lieutenant General Louis-Joseph, the marquis de Montcalm, ordered his troops out of their entrenchments to challenge the British, and the first set-piece battle ever fought in North America took place on the morning of 13 September 1759, on the Plains of Abraham, located just to the west of the city's front gates.

The battle itself lasted less than half an hour and involved fewer than 10,000 soldiers, but the fighting was especially fierce, much of it hand-to-hand. Among the many casualties were the two rival commanders themselves, Generals Wolfe and Montcalm, both of whom were mortally wounded. Montcalm's army was not destroyed. Most of his soldiers managed to escape and regrouped in Montreal, and the war would drag on yet another year. Yet the French had lost Quebec, plus the confidence of many Canadians, and much of their Indian support. Indeed, the British victory on the Plains of Abraham that fateful September morning contributed mightily to the fall of Montreal in 1760 and the surrender of French North America in 1763.

The capture of Quebec City was just one of several British triumphs in 1759, affirming William Pitt's grand strategy for defeating France and its allies, not only in North America but also in the West Indies, India, and Europe. Taking charge of the failing British military effort in 1756, Pitt spared no expense and made it clear from the outset that Britain would capture and keep French colonies throughout the world. The prime minister was especially interested in North America, where this latest war with France had first begun in 1754 and where the marquis de Montcalm, military commander in New France since 1756, had taken the war to the British and defeated them time and time again.

Two successive British commanders in chief, first Major General John Campbell, earl of Loudoun, and then Major General James Abercromby, proved no match for the clever Montcalm. While Loudoun imposed at least some semblance of order on the American military enterprise, Montcalm's successes at Oswego (1756) and Fort William Henry (1757) made the British commander appear sluggish and even ineffectual, especially in the eyes of the imperious prime minister. Pitt instructed Loudoun to make haste and attack Fort Louisbourg, the French citadel on Cape Breton Island in the Gulf of St. Lawrence. Bad weather and a late start forced the Scottish earl to abort the Louisbourg campaign, and Pitt angrily recalled him in late 1757. Command thus devolved upon the truly inept General Abercromby, who, in July 1758, repeatedly ordered suicidal frontal assaults against Montcalm at Fort Carillon (Ticonderoga), located on the southern shore of Lake Champlain. His poorly led army of 15,000 was mangled and routed by 4,000 troops well entrenched and well led by Montcalm.

Although Abercromby failed at Fort Carillon, Major General Jeffrey Amherst succeeded in 1758 in conquering the French brigadiers assigned Amherst for the Louisbourg expedition, particularly distinguishing himself. In Amherst and Wolfe, Prime Minister Pitt believed he had at last found competent military leaders for America. British successes at Louisbourg, Fort Frontenac, and Fort Duquesne convinced Pitt that New France could be conquered in 1759. Pitt knew that the military demands of the European theater reduced the number of troops and amount of supplies France could send to Canada, and of those that were sent, the Royal Navy was increasingly successful in intercepting them. So New France was vulnerable, and Pitt planned a three-fold attack aimed at its very heart.

Amherst replaced the discredited Abercromby as commander in chief and assembled about 14,000 soldiers near Albany. His primary objectives were Fort Carillon (Ticonderoga) and Crown Point on Lake Champlain, though collateral expeditions were also sent against Fort Niagara and to reestablish Fort Oswego. Once that was done, British forces from those two operations might combine and sail across Lake Ontario and down the St. Lawrence to attack Montreal. Ideally, Amherst's forces should also smash through Fort Carillon and Crown Point and join forces with yet another British expedition attacking Quebec, the capital of New France.

The Quebec campaign was entrusted to James Wolfe, whose family background was respectable middle class and thoroughly military. Wolfe's only brother died in battle in 1744, and his father, who rose to the exalted rank of lieutenant general, died in March 1759, while James was en route to North America. Tall, gangling, awkward acting and awkward looking, hatchet-faced, with a receding chin, Wolfe was a zealous officer whose regiment was one of the best trained in the service. Although tough and demanding, Wolfe was respected and admired by his soldiers; he was fearless in battle and bore the wounds to prove it. He was also eccentric, rather moody, always sickly, and preoccupied with death, especially his own. Thomas Gray's "Elegy in a Village Church Yard" was his favorite poem, which he was fond of quoting. After the capture of Fort Louisbourg, Wolfe had returned to England, taken the baths for his health, and become engaged to be married. He was not anxious to return to America, preferring the European theater. However, command of the Quebec expedition, with the rank in America of major general, was too good an opportunity for the 32-year-old soldier to pass up.

The young commander certainly faced a daunting chore. Known as the Gibraltar of America, Quebec was fixed high atop a stony, triangular-shaped promontory jutting into the northern shore of the St. Lawrence and bounded on the northeast by the St. Charles River. Quebec was located 300 miles from the mouth of the St. Lawrence and 158 miles downstream from Montreal. Given the wreckage that attended Admiral Hovenden Walker's unsuccessful attempt to attack Quebec in 1711, the French claimed that heavy English warships and troop transports could not negotiate the treacherous shoals of the unfamiliar St. Lawrence. But even if a few British vessels did make it to Quebec, the fortress city was generally thought unassailable, protected by its steep cliffs, more than 100 cannon, positioned in both the upper town bastion

Q

Plan of the
CITY OF QUEBEC
1759.

Scale of Yards

0   50   100   200   300   400

Reference.

1. Notre Dame de la Victoire
2. Cathedral
3. Jesuit's College
4. Convent of the Ursuline Nuns
5.   "   "   Recollect Friars
6. Commandant's House
7. Bishop's Palace

River   St.   Charles

River

PLACE OF ARMS
TO DEFEND THE HEAD
OF THE BOOM

BATTERY
TO DEFEND
THE BOOM

St. Roch's BRIDGE OF BOATS

BOOM OF LOGS

Ford at Low Water

St. Roch's
Chapel

The King's
Storehouse

Intendant's
Palace

Jetty of Masonry

BATTERY
BATTERY
BATTERY
BATTERY

Hotel Dieu

Seminaire

PALACE
GATE

DAUPHIN'S
REDOUBT

ST. JOHN'S
GATE

KING'S
REDOUBT

ST. URSULA'S
BASTION

ST. LOUIS GATE

POWDER
MAGAZINE

POWDER
MAGAZINE

POWDER MAGAZINE

POWDER MAGAZINE

ST. LOUIS
BASTION

CARE
DIAMOND
BASTION

LA GLACIÈRE
BASTION

Citadel

FORT
ST. LOUIS

PLACE
D'ARMES

THE
KING'S
YARD

BATTERY
BATTERY
BATTERY
BATTERY

DAUPHIN'S BATTERY

ROYAL BATTERY

QUEEN'S C. BATTERY

C. DIAMOND BATTERY

River   St.   Lawrence

and the lower town commercial district, along with an army of 15,000 composed mainly of Canadian militiamen, but also including five battalions of well-trained French regulars, and about 1,000 Indians. Moreover, the accomplished and experience Montcalm was organizing Quebec's defenses.

Coming from the British Isles and various American colonies, the different components of the Quebec expedition gathered in the spring of 1759 at Cape Breton Island. General Wolfe found himself in charge of 8,500 seasoned British regulars, plus four companies of American rangers, the only provincials with him. His brigadiers—Colonels Robert Monckton, James Murray, and Charles Townshend—were all like Wolfe himself, young but proven in battle. Unlike Wolfe, they were all sons of noble families. His friend, Colonel Guy Carleton, served as quartermaster general. Supporting Wolfe's army was the largest collection of naval vessels hitherto assembled in North America, involving well over one-fourth of the entire British navy. There were 49 warships, including 21 ships of the line, plus 119 transports and supply vessels, manned by more than 13,000 sailors and marines, all under the overall command of Vice Admiral Sir Charles Saunders, an unassuming and thoroughly competent officer.

Much to the surprise and chagrin of the French, this formidable fleet had little difficulty navigating the long and broad tidal estuary that is the lower St. Lawrence. Rear Admiral Philip Durell led the way. Durell lured local pilots to his vessels by flying the French flag and then made them guide the flotilla through the trickiest part of the river, known as the Traverse, running upstream from Cape Tourmente to the lower end of the long Isle d'Orléans. By the last of June, British transports were debarking troops on the Isle d'Orleans, whose western end juts into the Quebec basin, beyond which the St. Lawrence channel narrows considerably. One evening shortly thereafter, Pierre de Rigaud de Vaudreuil, the marquis de Vaudreuil, governor general of New France, launched eight so-called fire ships, each laden with combustibles, against the multitude of British vessels anchored in the Quebec basis, near the Isle d'Orleans. Unfortunately for the French, the fire ships were lit prematurely, and British sailors bravely grappled the exploding crafts ashore without any damage being done to the Royal Navy.

General Montcalm had anticipated that the fire ships would fail. The French commander did not like Vaudreuil, partly because the vainglorious governor interfered in military affairs and partly because the civil government was notoriously corrupt. Blaming Vaudreuil and his cronies for having never properly fortified Quebec, Montcalm had decided that the walled city might well turn into a trap during a prolonged siege, despite its formidable natural defenses. Accordingly, only the regular garrison of 1,200 or so soldiers, under chevalier Jean-Baptiste-Nicholas-Roch de Ramezay, remained in Quebec itself. Montcalm deployed the bulk of his French regulars and the Canadian militia across the St. Charles River from Quebec all along the low bluffs of the Beauport Shore, a six-mile stretch running down the northern bank of the St. Lawrence from the St. Charles to the Montmorency River. Terribly outnumbered, French warships near Quebec beat a hasty retreat to Montreal, but 700 French sailors remained to maintain the artillery pieces on the surrounding heights.

The Beauport Shore was a very strong defensive position, with shoal waters keeping British warships a good half-mile from either the mouth of the St. Charles or the shoreline, and with a high waterfall making it impossible for any vessel to enter the Montmorency. But in order to concentrate troops on the Beauport Shore, Montcalm, somewhat against his better judgment, agreed with Governor Vaudreuil that the French should not try to defend the southern bank of the St. Lawrence, which the British shortly occupied. At Pointe Lévy, just across the river from Quebec, Brigadier Monckton, following Wolfe's instructions, installed siege guns that began to reign death and destruction upon the capital city, especially devastating the lower town commercial district. Even the less accessible upper town fortress, standing some 250 feet above the river, began to sustain severe damage from Wolfe's heavy artillery.

The bombardment blew some buildings apart and set fire to many others. Frightened civilians fled the besieged city, and French morale undoubtedly suffered as the destruction of Quebec continued, day after day. Yet neither the soldiers on the Beauport Shore nor their upriver supply lines to Montreal were much threatened by British shelling. Indeed, Montcalm had decided to pursue a purely defensive strategy, designed to wear the invaders down and keep them at bay until the onset of winter drove the Royal Navy from the icy St. Lawrence, thereby forcing Wolfe to give up the siege. It all seemed

Battle of Quebec, 1759.

to make good sense, even to Governor Vaudreuil, who seldom missed an opportunity to criticize Montcalm behind his back. True, the French had many more soldiers than the British, but almost two-thirds of them were untrained Canadians, including old men and boys, good enough perhaps if entrenched properly, or for fighting in the woods, but hardly fit to take on British regulars in open field combat, something Montcalm wanted to avoid at all costs.

There was one tragic flaw in Montcalm's strategy. Like everyone else, the marquis accepted the conventional wisdom that the combined effect of French artillery and dangerous cross-currents would keep British warships from sailing through the Quebec basin and into the narrow upriver channel beyond the fortress city. Should British warships somehow get upstream, French supply lines would be threatened, and Montcalm would either have to come out and fight or else weaken his Beauport entrenchments to protect his supplies. However, Montcalm expected the impetuous Wolfe to assault the Beauport encampment.

Interestingly enough, Wolfe initially worked up several battle plans, one of which called for slipping a small force on land above Quebec while attacking all along the Beauport Shore. But that would require dangerously dispersing his troops and ran the risk of being defeated in detail. Instead, Wolfe opted on 8 July to send Brigadier Townshend with a detachment to the heights on the west side of the Montmorency falls, thereby flanking the French left, under Major General François-Gaston de Lévis, Montcalm's second-in-command. This was also a hazardous maneuver, virtually inviting the French to attack Wolfe's forces, divided now into three camps located on Isle d'Orléans, Pointe Lévy, and the east side of the Montmorency, respectively. Montcalm was tempted, but sobering second thoughts on the capacity of the Canadian militia convinced him to stay behind his barricades. Townshend's artillery could now harass the French left, but it did little real damage.

As the blasting of Quebec continued, the siege settled into a stalemate that both the British and the French found most irritating. Almost every day, a few more Canadian militiamen deserted and returned to their farms and homes. On the other hand, Canadian *coureurs de bois* and their Indian friends remained fairly active, stalking the edges of the British camps, killing and scalping sentries and scouting parties whenever the opportunity presented. Having warned the Canadian settlers not to assist the French army, Wolfe began to unleash his American rangers, whose services he had previously disdained but shortly came to appreciate. Homes and barns were burned, farm animals slaughtered, and more than a few civilians were killed.

Meanwhile, Admiral Saunders and the British navy once again proved conventional wisdom wrong. On 18 July, in the middle of the night, Captain John Rouse maneuvered two warships, two armed sloops, and two transports with troops and provisions past Quebec's big guns, thanks in part to the surging tide and to the protection provided by the powerful British batteries at Pointe Lévy. On 20 July, Colonel Carleton and 600 troops from Captain Rouse's transports raided upriver at Pointe-aux-Trembles, though they found few of the supplies rumored stored there. Montcalm was mortified and worried, for he had not planned on fighting upriver. However, the British did not have enough troops to mount significant attacks both above and below Quebec. The French already had a boat bridge over the St. Charles, and if necessary could move troops from the Beauport Shore most expeditiously. The key for Montcalm was not to let the British take them by surprise. So the Marquis immediately dispatched 800 troops to guard the north shore between Quebec and Cape Rouge, a distance of just over 12 miles.

The stalemate looked like it just might be breaking up. Governor Vaudreuil convinced Montcalm to give his fire ships one more try. Late on the night of 27 July, the French launched several schooners and shallops and 72 rafts all chained together and filled with combustibles of all kinds, including grenades, overloaded cannon, muskets and pistols, plus tons of miscellaneous metal objects. This time the fire ships were not lit until within musket range of the British fleet, anchored between Pointe Lévy and Isle d'Orléans. Only the courageous efforts of British sailors, once again grappling the blazing and exploding vessels away from their intended targets, kept the huge fire raft from damaging their fleet.

Two days later, Wolfe, desperate to bring Montcalm into open battle, planned a frontal assault against what he thought was a lightly-manned advanced French redoubt well below the Beauport bluff entrenchments and not too far from the Montmorency River. If that redoubt were taken, Wolfe reasoned, the French would be obliged to come out of their lines to regain it. Then, Brigadier Monckton's troops held in reserve on the beach, and Brigadiers Townshend and Murray's troops from east of the Montmorency, would combine and storm the bluffs. On 31 July, the British began a massive artillery barrage against the Beauport Shore, especially the French left under chevalier de Lévis. But the Canadian militia, well entrenched, did not break and run as Wolfe had hoped, and the British grenadiers and American rangers who led the assault encountered stiff resistance from the advanced redoubt, which proved to be fully manned. Moreover, once the redoubt had fallen to the British, the grenadiers, disregarding their orders to sit tight and wait, moved on against the French on the bluffs, where they were caught in a withering cross fire that drove them back to the beach and their boats.

The British were beaten badly, with 450 killed or wounded, mostly grenadiers. The French reported only 70 casualties. While Montcalm and his soldiers rejoiced, Wolfe denounced his grenadiers, tried to blame the navy for not doing enough, and chastised his brigadiers for not bringing up their troops quickly enough. Then, he took to his bed for several weeks, physically ill and sick at heart. His brigadiers, especially Townshend, resented Wolfe's blaming them, and Admiral Saunders protested Wolfe's critical comments about the Royal Navy. Wolfe apologized to Saunders, but not to his aristocratic brigadiers, especially not to Townshend, who took to drawing unflattering caricatures of his commander. Wolfe did assume full responsibility for the defeat, and also seemed absolutely convinced that his career was ruined beyond redemption. Wolfe's self-pity was doubtlessly exaggerated by personal illness, including scurvy and probably tuberculosis of the kidneys, a particularly debilitating and painful combination.

Wolfe had good reason to be depressed. He was no closer now than a month before to defeating Montcalm and capturing Quebec. About a third of his soldiers were sick, suffering from assorted "fevers" and the enervating effects of scurvy, the latter due to the lack of fresh fruit and vegetables. British morale hit rock bottom when rumors spread that Wolfe, whose constant travels back and forth among the three major encampments had previously kept confidence high, had himself died. By the end of August, Wolfe had recovered enough to move his Montmorency headquarters, but he was far from well. Stymied by Montcalm, the sickly young general increasingly took out his anger and frustration on the Canadians within his grasp. The shelling of Quebec, which served no tactical or strategic purpose, was renewed in early August with special fury, and British regulars began to join American rangers in attacking Canadian settlements. They burned several thousand homesteads, took hundreds of prisoners, and butchered a number of civilians. British ships enlarged their operations upstream, riding the tide from Quebec to Cape Rouge and back daily, with troops debarked occasionally to harass Montcalm's supply lines and probe French defenses along the north shore.

British depredations in the countryside and the disruptions of supplies dampened French euphoria over the Beauport attack. Increasing numbers of Canadian militiamen abandoned French lines and returned to protect their homes, even though Montcalm warned he would send his Indian allies to punish deserters and their families. Moreover, news that Niagara in the west and Ticonderoga and Crown Point in the east had fallen to the British led the French to believe that General Amherst would be moving next against Montreal, to which Montcalm dispatched chevalier Lévis with 800 troops, though by doing so he greatly weakened his own defenses at Quebec. Montcalm also transferred a few hundred more troops upriver and put all 3,000 or so there under the command of his young friend, the chevalier de Bougainville, already celebrated for his mathematical genius. Above all else, Montcalm implored Bougainville to keep close watch on Admiral Charles Holmes, whose 22 vessels were patrolling for French ships. Holmes's squadron also carried Brigadier Murray and 1,200 troops who raided Canadian villages on both sides of the St. Lawrence above Quebec.

As August ended, Montcalm knew that the British warships would have to leave the St. Lawrence shortly and that Wolfe would probably make another major attack before his naval support left. But where would he attack? Wolfe described the dilemma that both he and Montcalm faced in a letter to his mother:

> My antagonist has wisely shut himself up in inaccessible entrenchments, so that I can't get at him without spilling a torrent of blood, and that perhaps to little purpose. The Marquis de Montcalm is at the head of a great number of bad soldiers, and I am at the head of a small number of good

ones, that wish for nothing so much as to fight him; but the wary old fellow avoids an action, doubtful of the behavior of his army.

In fact, having consulted with his brigadiers, Wolfe was planning a final attack. To Townshend, Monckton, and Murray, Wolfe proposed variations of another frontal assault against Montcalm's lines. The brigadiers all rejected moving against the Beauport Shore; instead, they insisted upon landing upriver and attacking Quebec on land from the west. "The General [Montcalm] might fight us on our own terms," they pointed out. "We shall be betwixt him and his provisions, and betwixt him and their Army opposing General Amherst."

Wolfe readily agreed with his brigadiers and began planning the operation. Of course, the odds were against British success. Montcalm knew something was coming when the British began breaking up the Montmorency encampment and moving troops and guns first to Isle d'Orléans and then to Pointe Lévy. But were the British giving it all up and simply leaving, preparing to strike upriver, or trying to cloak yet another attack against the Beauport Shore? Until he knew for sure, the marquis was not about to weaken the Beauport Shore defenses further. He did learn that approximately 4,000 British troops were marching from Pointe Lévy upstream, probably headed for the transports Admiral Saunders had recently run past Quebec's guns. Either this was an elaborate ruse or the British were going to land upriver. Montcalm again warned Bougainville to follow Admiral Holmes carefully and moved the crack Guyenne regiment of French regulars onto the Plains of Abraham, just in case. Nevertheless, the French commander felt that Wolfe would likely hit Beauport Shore once again, probably the center this time, which is exactly what Wolfe had proposed and what his brigadiers had turned down.

Wolfe disagreed with his brigadiers on where exactly their troops should land on the north shore. The brigadiers recommended Pointe-aux-Trembles, about 30 miles upriver from Quebec. Wolfe thought that was too far, and after reconnoitering from the opposite shore, he selected Anse au Foulon (Foulon cove), less than two miles from the city, where a twisting path led up the steep hillside. After rain storms delayed operations for several days, on 12 September at 1:00 a.m., almost 4,000 British troops, massed on the south shore just opposite Cap Rouge, were quietly ferried to Holmes's ships.

Although detachments had been left on Isle d'Orleans and along the south shore at Pointe Lévy and other places, Wolfe was committing his fittest soldiers to the upriver invasion. They were composed of light infantry, four regular regiments, a detachment of Highlanders, and the Louisbourg grenadiers. At 9:00 P.M. on 12 September, the troops boarded flatboats, and along with the rest of Holmes's squadron, rode the onrushing tide upstream some 20 miles to Pointe-aux-Trembles, suggesting an attack would be made there. About 2:00 A.M. on the 13th, driven by the rapidly ebbing tide and a strong southward wind, the ships and flatboats began moving swiftly down the river. At 4:00 A.M., well before any hint of dawn, the advanced 30 flatboats, carrying 1,800 troops, with Wolfe, Monckton, and Murray among them, came to shore—a few at Anse au Foulon, but most others further downstream at Sillery and even at Cap-aux-Diamants, right next to Quebec. Brigadier Townshend was in charge of the reserves on the ships and on the south shore who were to land as soon it was clear that Monckton's battalion had secured the shore and heights.

Admiral Holmes, whose job it was to supervise the landing, warned Wolfe that "The distance of the landing place, the impetuosity of the tide; the darkness of the night; and the great chance of exactly hitting the very spot intended without discovery or alarm; made the whole extremely difficult." However, the fates were smiling on the British, for everything that might easily have gone wrong for them went right, and vice-versa for the French.

To begin with, Bougainville, who with a thousand troops had been following Holmes and his ships back and forth from Cap-aux-Diamants to Pointe-aux-Trembles for weeks, was completely worn out. So on the night of 12–13 September, the young general decided to keep his force at Cap Rouge rather than follow Holmes downstream again; rumors later spread that Bougainville had spent the night with the wife of a friend.

Moreover, Bougainville failed to alert the many sentry camps along the north shore that a previously scheduled supply expedition from Montreal had suddenly been canceled. Consequently, French guards who spotted the British flatboats in the dark were likely to mistake them for the supply convoy. At least one sentry verbally challenged them from shore, but a quick-thinking Highlander officer replied in fluent French, "Provision-boats. Don't make a noise; the English will hear us." The sentry asked nothing else, and the British continued downriver.

British success at Quebec also depended upon the crafty Montcalm not anticipating what Wolfe was doing, and he did not, until it was too late. Surprise was complete, thanks largely to the effective deception worked by Admiral Saunders, whose ships busily placed buoys opposite Beauport on 11 September, as if to mark where transports should land. Then, on the evening of the 12th, Saunders blasted away at the Beauport Shore, making it appear that an assault was forthcoming. The admiral also kept his marines with their red coats moving about the decks, thereby giving the appearance his ships were filled with British regulars. Saunders's warships kept lowering whaleboats, seemingly filled with soldiers, threatening first one and then another part of the Beauport Shore with imminent assault.

With all this going on before his very eyes, Montcalm thought that British activity upriver had just been a feint to cover the approaching assault against Beauport. Perhaps for that reason, the Guyenne regiment of French regulars, although scheduled once again to reinforce the heights and western approaches to Quebec, remained at Beauport on 12 September. Even the warning shots indicating something was definitely wrong at Quebec did not worry Montcalm much. Probably just part of the upriver diversion, he thought. Only when the dawn brought enough light for him to observe Saunders's ships calmly at rest did Montcalm suspect that the British had made a substantial landing upriver.

Meanwhile, in the absence of the Guyenne regiment, the heights above the Anse au Foulon were lightly defended. That particular sentry post was commanded by Captain Louis Du Pont Duchambon de Vergor, friend of the notoriously corrupt intendant of New France, François Bigot. Not much of a soldier and given to hard drinking, Vergor was in command of less than 70 men, most of whom were as inattentive as their lackadaisical leader. Captain William Delaune and 24 volunteers were the first British soldiers to make their way from Foulon cove up the narrow path to the heights, followed by Colonel William Howe and his light infantry. Delaune's soldiers were not challenged until they were near the very top. By pre-arrangement, a French-speaking Highlander stalled the sentry just long enough for his compatriots to surround the camp and take it by storm, wounding Vergor himself.

Still weak and shaky from his illness, Wolfe followed Howe's troopers up the path, surveyed the terrain, and directed his soldiers to move east along the cliffs and then north across the plateau lands known as the Plains of Abraham, named after a former river pilot and farmer. For almost five hours, the British kept unloading at Anse au Foulon and directing troops up the path to the plateau. By 9:00 A.M., Wolfe's army was in battle formation stretched across the cornfields, grasslands, and clumps of trees for almost half a mile, lined up two abreast and backed by two artillery pieces, looking directly at the west walls of Quebec just over a half-mile away. Anchoring the south (or right) front line were the Louisbourg Grenadiers, next stood Bragg's 28th battalion, with the center manned by Kennedy's 43rd and Lascelles's 47th. Holding the north (or left) front line were the Highlanders, better known for wielding their claymores than for firing their muskets. Murray commanded the left, Monckton the right, with Townshend in charge of the left flank and reserves. Altogether, Townshend reckoned Wolfe had 4,441 soldiers confronting the western walls of Quebec.

While crossing the boat bridge spanning the St. Charles, Montcalm could see the British troops gathering on the Plains of Abraham. He sent back a message for his regulars and militia units at Beauport to hasten and join him in Quebec City. The British were clearly preparing for a siege, already digging their trenches. "There they stand," Montcalm said, "where they have no right to be." Wolfe was daring the French to come out and fight, and Montcalm, at long last outmaneuvered, was foolishly going to oblige him. The marquis reasoned rightly that the west walls of Quebec were weak and not equipped to resist a siege, but he did not have to move out and attack the invaders as quickly as he did. He could have waited, allowing the Canadians and Indians to harass the British flanks from the surrounding woods, and then attack only after he had assembled significantly more troops and cannon than Wolfe had. In fact, the British were very vulnerable on the Plains of Abraham, especially if Bougainville should arrive on the scene and attack from the west.

Yet Montcalm, tired and angry, having gone for weeks with little sleep, felt he could not wait. He knew that if the British entrenched they would be much harder to dislodge. As for Bougainville and his troops, if the young commander were not pinned down upriver, surely he would have appeared already. The Beauport troops were slow in arriving, thanks in large part to the indecisive and obstructive nature of Governor Vaudreuil, who was reluctant to weaken further the Beauport line; moreover, the garrison commander at Quebec refused to turn cannon over to Montcalm for use outside the city because he feared a British assault on the lower town.

In the light of all this, Montcalm should have waited. Yet Wolfe was where he should not be! In his favor, Montcalm had most of his French regulars, about 2,000, plus another 2,500 or so enthusiastic Canadians and Indians. If he waited too long, the unreliable Canadians and Indians might become less willing to fight, and the British would certainly dig in. He also had six cannon ready, four more than Wolfe. No, Montcalm would not wait for more cannon and more men; he wanted to defeat Wolfe before the pompous Vaudreuil could arrive and take the credit.

The marquis deployed his troops on the ridge just beyond the west gates of Quebec. French regulars of the Béarn and Guyenne regiments formed twin columns in the center, with the Languedoc and La Sarre regiments lined up on the right and flanked by provincial troops from Quebec and Montreal. On the left were the Royal Roussillon, flanked by colonial troops from Montreal and from Three Rivers. Montcalm's flank commanders, Brigadier Senezergues on the right and Lieutenant Colonel Fontbonne on the left, were untested and did not have the confidence of their chief, who deeply regretted not having the dependable General Lévis in this crisis. Montcalm's force of 4,500 was a little larger than Wolfe's, but the British had twice as many regulars as the French, and regular troops understood how to move and fire from formation. By mixing Canadians with his regular line regiments, Montcalm hoped to keep the colonials under fighting discipline.

As both armies stood hardly 300 yards apart, the battle began with the ritualistic but deadly artillery exchange. The British, significantly outgunned, suffered the worst of it as several volleys of grapeshot ripped through their lines before Wolfe ordered them to the ground. Both Montcalm and Wolfe moved about the field freely, encouraging their soldiers and seemingly oblivious to the shot flying about them. Good commanders were expected to do this to inspire confidence in their men. Dressed in his brightest uniform, scarlet and gold, Wolfe probably expected he would be killed that day. In fact, he was shot twice, first in the hand and then in the belly, but he kept moving about the field and directing his soldiers.

True to their training, the British regulars held their fire and stood their ground as Montcalm ordered his troops to advance. The intermixing of Canadians and regulars began causing confusion in the French lines, with the Canadians running ahead of the regulars and falling down to reload, thereby getting in the way of the slower but methodical French regulars. As smoke engulfed the Plains of Abraham, the white coats were less than 40 yards away when Wolfe finally gave the order to fire. The French reeled and stumbled, feeling the full fury of the double-shot from the British muskets, even as the two English cannon cut bloody swaths through Montcalm's ranks. Ordering the British to charge, Wolfe himself led the Louisbourg Grenadiers into the stunned and confused French lines until a third shot, probably from a Canadian sniper, tore deep into his chest. As blood filled his lungs, Wolfe was told that the French were running away. He ordered that a British regiment be sent to block the French retreat across the St. Charles. Thinking Montcalm's army was destroyed and his mission accomplished, Wolfe's last words reportedly were, "Now God be praised, I will die in peace."

Had Wolfe's final order been carried out, the Seven Years' War might well have ended that day. The French were in full rout, with the Highlanders in hot pursuit, lopping off heads and arms with their broadswords. But confusion also reigned among the British regulars. General Monckton, second-in-command, had been seriously wounded too, and General Townshend, next in line to command and in charge of the reserves on the left flank, did not learn of Monckton's incapacity for more than an hour. Meanwhile, Brigadier Murray, who thought that Townshend was dead, took command and concentrated on securing the field rather than blocking the retreating French. Furthermore, Canadian troops in the wooded areas north of the plateau provided excellent cover fire for the French retreat across the St. Charles and into their Beauport Shore fortifications. The French kept their battalion colors, but they had been badly defeated and knew it. Montcalm was dying, shot in the thigh and groin. He suffered throughout the day and night, expiring the next morning in Quebec City.

General Townshend, who had assumed command about an hour after the French charge, found it difficult to restore order among the British troops. Nor did he pursue the French troops across the St. Charles River, or even assault Quebec City. Instead, he continued the British entrenchments. General Bougainville and his 3,000 soldiers reached Quebec about noon, saw the British in command of the Plains of Abraham, and retreated without making so much as a fight. Townshend was not about to go after them. On the evening of 13 September, after advising the garrison commander to surrender Quebec, Governor Vaudreuil and Intendant Bigot led the French regulars and Canadians out of the Beauport entrenchments, traveled north and then west around the English lines, and on the evening of the next day arrived at the French post, Jacques-Cartier, where General Lévis took command.

Altogether, the French suffered more than twice the casualties of the British, with 200 dead and at least 1,200 wounded. On 18 September, Quebec formally surrendered, along with its garrison of 2,200 soldiers and sailors. The French fleet, bearing Wolfe's corpse back to England, departed, as did several thousand soldiers, leaving Brigadier Murray in charge at Quebec with a garrison of almost 5,000. "Measured by the numbers engaged the battle of Quebec was but a heavy skirmish," wrote the historian Francis Parkman; "measured by results, it was one of the great battles of the world."

Ronald W. Howard

References

Donald Barr Chidley, *The French and Indian War: An Informal History* (1969); Gordon Donaldson, *Battle for a Continent: Quebec 1759* (1973); W.J. Eccles, "The Battle of Quebec: A Reappraisal," *French Colonial Historical Society, Proceedings* 3 (1978):70–81; Lawrence Henry Gipson, *The British Empire Before the American Revolution*, 15 vols. (1958–1970).

Edward P. Hamilton, ed. and trans., *Adventure in the Wilderness; The American Journals of Louis Antoine De Bougainville, 1756–1760* (1964); ———, *The French and Indian Wars: The Story of Battles and Forts in the Wilderness* (1962); Basil H. Liddell Hart, "The Battle That Won an Empire," *American Heritage* 11 (1959):24–31, 105–108; Francis Jennings, *Empire of Fortune: Crowns, Colonies, and Tribes in the Seven Years War in America* (1988).

John Knox, *An Historical Journal of the Campaigns in North America for the Years 1757, 1758, 1759 and 1760*, Arthur G. Dougherty, ed., 3 vols (1914–1916); James G. Lydon, *Struggle for Empire: A Bibliography of the French and Indian War* (1986); Stanley M. Pargellis, ed., *Military Affairs in North America, 1748–1765* (1936); Francis Parkman, *Montcalm and Wolfe: A Series of Historical Narratives*, 2 vols. (1884); Howard H. Peckham, *The Colonial Wars, 1689–1762* (1964).

James L. Stokesbury, "Quebec Falls!," *American History Illustrated* 10 (1975):4–11, 42–48; Ian Kenneth Steele, "The European Contest for North America," in *Encyclopedia of the North American Colonies*, ed. by Jacob Ernest Cooke, 3 vols. (1993), II:271–288.

See also BOUGAINVILLE, LOUIS-ANTOINE DE; COUEURS DE BOIS; LÉVIS, FRANÇOIS-GASTON DE; MONCKTON, ROBERT; MONTCALM-GAZON DE SAINT-VERAIN, LOUIS-JOSEPH; MURRAY, JAMES; PITT, WILLIAM; RANGERS; RIGAUD DE VAUDREUIL DE CAVAGNIAL, PIERRE DE; ST. LAWRENCE RIVER; SEVEN YEARS' WAR; WOLFE, JAMES

Quebec, Capture of (1629)
See KIRKE BROTHERS

Quebec, French Attempt to Recapture (1760; also known as Battle of Sainte-Foy, Second Battle of Quebec)

The French attempt to recapture Quebec took place on 28 April 1760, on the Plains of Abraham and adjacent lands to the north and west of the plateau. Assuming command of French forces after General Louis-Joseph de Montcalm's death, Major General François-Gaston de Lévis led some 7,000 troops from Montreal to challenge the British who had captured Quebec six months before. Brigadier James Murray, the military governor of Quebec, assembled 3,600 troops outside the west gates of the fortress city and attacked the French in what was the last major field engagement of the French and Indian War. Lévis and his troops won the battle handily but were unable to take Quebec by siege. After three weeks, they had to retreat following the timely arrival of British warships escorting reinforcements and supplies for Murray's beleaguered garrison.

Contrary to popular thinking at the time and since, the first battle of Quebec did not end the Seven Years' War. Montcalm had been killed and the capital city surrendered, but 7,000 or so soldiers, 2,000 of them French regulars, escaped after the British chased them from the field on 13 September 1759. The French army in Canada, whose destruction had been the primary military objective of General James Wolfe, remained largely intact. Canadian militiamen were definitely tired of fighting and had little confidence in their civil and military leaders, but thousands of the *habitants* remained with the French regulars; their farms and homesteads devastated by warfare, they simply had no place else to go. Add to them the several thousand troops still under Generals Louis-Antoine de Bougainville, François-Charles de Bourlamaque, and Lévis, plus the Indians, several hundred of whom could be counted on to fight. So despite recent reversals, General Lévis believed that Quebec could still be reclaimed and the British defeated, particularly if France were to send warships and a few thousand reinforcements next spring.

Lévis saw the Canadian winter as his ablest ally. It was even more severe than usual. The British garrison—as well as most civilians in Quebec—suffered grievously from the cold and snow and the growing scarcity of food and fuel. The city itself was in ruins. Hardly a building had escaped the ferocious bombardment or fires, and many elegant structures were reduced to rubble. The influx of *habitants* from the countryside compounded the basic problems of keeping warm and fed. Soldiers sent out in search of wood returned with frostbitten fingers and toes; sentries froze at their posts. Fresh food was a rarity; farms for miles around had been pillaged and grain destroyed. Leathery salt pork was generally available, but its nutritional value was limited. Scurvy ravaged the garrison, with scarcely anyone untouched by the debilitating malady. By early spring, of the 7,000 soldiers left with Murray, less than one-half were fit for duty; more than a thousand had died, mostly from complications brought on by the pernicious scurvy. What solace there was came from liquor, which inspired a wide range of lawless behavior, disruptive of both military discipline and public order.

Despite the many hardships, Governor Murray began to establish a series of outposts to the south and west, knowing full well that the French would be back in force sooner or later. In February, the sickly British troops even beat back a small French detachment sent to occupy Pointe Lévy, located just opposite Quebec on the south shore. In fact, Lévis had hoped to attack in force the British at Quebec, but the St. Lawrence was frozen solid, and the French lacked the portable food supplies necessary to sustain their soldiers as they made the 160-mile trek from Montreal to Quebec through the cold and snow. So the campaign against Quebec had to wait until the spring thaw, which would begin a few weeks earlier in Montreal than in Quebec. Given the distress of the British garrison, General Lévis felt certain he could retake Quebec, and if the French could get reinforcement and warships up the St. Lawrence before the British in the spring, Canada would be saved.

Lévis began assembling troops and ships for the Quebec expedition in early April. He would take 7,000 soldiers, half of them French regulars, two frigates, ten transports, a supply ship, and a schooner carrying artillery. On 15 April, the St. Lawrence was open enough for the little fleet to begin following the ice downstream. On 26 April, the river became so clogged with ice that General Lévis decided to debark near Pointe-aux-Trembles and march the rest of the way through the mud and melting snow. A violent spring storm struck just as the French were unloading, overturning boats and drowning several men. One survivor climbed onto an ice floe and was rescued the next day by an alert British sentry at Quebec. From the grateful Frenchman the British learned that General Lévis was much nearer than they had suspected. By the evening of 27 April, the French reached Sainte Foy, just a few miles west of Quebec.

Like Montcalm before him, Governor Murray doubted that Quebec's walls could withstand much of a siege. Therefore, on the morning of 28 April, Murray began deploying his troops outside the western gates on the ridge known as Buttes á Neveu, much as Montcalm's had done six months before. Murray's troops were outnumbered 3,600 to 7,000 under Lévis, but the British were in a stronger position on the high ground and had the support of 22 cannon, many more than Lévis had in place. As Lévis's troops moved onto the plateau and began to dig trenches, Murray abandoned the Buttes á Neveu and charged the French. Moving forward through the spring slush and mud, British soldiers stumbled, dropping their muskets on the wet ground, and their cannon mired down. Lévis wisely had his soldiers fall back, drawing pursuing redcoats into the knee-deep snow of Sillery woods. After an hour of ferocious fighting, the British left began to give way, and Murray's troops had no choice but to abandon their artillery pieces and begin an orderly retreat back inside the gates of Quebec.

The Second Battle of Quebec had lasted two hours. Both sides suffered about equally, but Murray had lost fully one-third of this troops. Fortunately for the British, General Lévis did not feel strong enough to storm Quebec immediately, thereby giving them enough time to fortify the west walls with dozens of cannon, many of them hauled from the lower town; more than 150 would be in place within two weeks. Meanwhile, the French dug in, having neither the big guns nor powder necessary to do real damage to Quebec's fortification. Everything depended on who got resupplied and reinforced first, the British or the French. All eyes were on the St. Lawrence, where on 6 May, the first of several British warships appeared. A French supply fleet of 20 to 30 ships had sailed from Bordeaux on 14 April, but most of the ships either turned back or were captured. Meanwhile, a British squadron had left England in March and broke the siege of Quebec in mid-May. Losing control of the St. Lawrence and almost out of ammunition, General Lévis had no choice but to retreat on 16 May. As in the First Battle of Quebec (13 September 1759), the Royal Navy had once again been the margin of British victory in New France.

Ronald W. Howard

References

Donald Barr Chidley, *The French and Indian War: An Informal History* (1969); Gordon Donaldson, *Battle for a Continent: Quebec 1759* (1973); W.J. Eccles, "The Battle of Quebec: A Reappraisal," *French Colonial Historical Society, Proceedings* 3 (1978):70–81; Lawrence Henry Gipson, *The Great War for Empire: The Triumphant Years* (1958).

Edward P. Hamilton, ed. and trans., *Adventure in the Wilderness; The American Journals of Louis Antoine De Bougainville, 1756–1760* (1964); ———, *The French and Indian Wars: The Story of Battles and Forts in the Wilderness* (1962); John Knox, *An Historical Journal of the Campaigns in North America for the Years 1757, 1758, 1759 and 1760*, Arthur G. Dougherty, ed., 3 vols. (1914–1916).

James G. Lydon, *Struggle for Empire: A Bibliography of the French and Indian War* (1986); Stanley M. Pargellis, ed., *Military Affairs in North America, 1748–1765* (1936); Francis Parkman, *Montcalm and Wolfe: A Series of Historical Narratives*, 2 vols. (1884); Howard H. Peckham, *The Colonial Wars, 1689–1762* (1964); James L. Stokesbury, "Quebec Falls!," *American History Illustrated* 10 (1975):4–11, 42–48.

See also MURRAY, JAMES; LÉVIS, FRANÇOIS-GASTON DE; QUEBEC, BATTLE OF (1759)

Queen Anne's War (1702–1713)

Queen Anne's War refers to the New World theater of the War of the Spanish Succession. With the Spanish inheritance at issue, the war in North America was thus both local and international. From Flanders and the Rhine to North American fronts in New England, along the Carolina frontier, and in the Caribbean, an Anglo-centered European coalition fought to prevent the union of the French and Spanish crowns.

During the brief interval of peace following the inconclusive Nine Years' War of 1689–1697 (King William's War in the colonies), Versailles made an apparent effort to hem in the English and link the French and Spanish colonies. Between 1699 and 1702, new military settlements were established along the Gulf coast at Biloxi and Mobile, a truce was negotiated with the Iroquois Confederacy, and a military post was established at Detroit to secure French control of the Great Lakes. In America, as in Europe, the French seemed to be on the diplomatic and military offensive.

In fact, the French situation was precarious. Canada's economic lifeline of Atlantic fish and western fur was threatened. English traders were active in the colony's trading hinterlands at Hudson Bay, along the Great Lakes, and in the Mississippi Valley. To the east, expansion from Maine pressured Acadia, and New Englanders were penetrating the coastal fisheries. With but 15,000 inhabitants facing a population 20 times its number to the south, Canada was vulnerable both in its heartland along the St. Lawrence and on its strategic flanks.

Despite little inclination by either side to initiate hostilities in 1702, Canada was forced to mask its weakness with a show of force. After some hesitation, Governor Philippe de Rigaud de Vaudreuil launched a series of spoiling raids in 1703. With the New York front neutralized by the Iroquois truce, the full weight of the assault fell on New England.

When Massachusetts Governor Joseph Dudley failed to secure an "Iroquois-type" neutrality in a meeting with the Abenakis and Micmacs at Canso, Maine's coastal settlements were devastated by an estimated 500 French and allied raiders. During "six terrible days" following 10 August, more than 130 settlers fell victim as settlements at Wells, Cape Porpoise, Winter Harbor, Scarborough, Spurwink, Purpooduck, and Falmouth were overwhelmed or besieged. Subsequent Franco-Amerindian raids ravaged the New England frontier from the Maine coast to New Hampshire.

New England, however, was far better organized for war than in 1689. Preceding the conflict, Massachusetts militia had reinforced the Maine outposts, Connecticut units were sent to western Massachusetts, and even previously reluctant Rhode Island voted arms and prepared a ship. Relying on the experience of King Philip's War, "flying columns" equipped with snowshoes and utilizing friendly (or coerced) Indian allies, probed enemy territory to gather information and disrupt raiders.

A few spectacular French victories obscured the general success of New England's countermeasures. The surprise assault at Deerfield in February 1704, in which 40 inhabitants were killed and another 111 taken captive, marked a breakdown in local security after months of false alarms. However, Deerfield was the exception. More common was the subsequent relief of Lancaster, Haverhill, and later Deerfield by the rapid deployment of neighboring militia. Although New England's defensive "roof" continued to spring leaks, an outer ring of designated frontier garrison towns, protected by permanent garrisons of 40 to 50 volunteer militia, created a mutually supporting defense system.

Once the first wave of guerilla raids subsided, New England was anxious to take the initiative. As early as 1704, the "old Indian fighter" Benjamin Church, conducted a sweep by 400 men to ambush isolated raiding parties and attack enemy settlements along the Maine coast. In retaliation for Deerfield, the French

outpost of Grand Pré was burned and the dikes broken to flood the fields; but when Church failed to attack the larger settlement at Port Royal, he was roundly criticized. New England was ready for a more aggressive strategy.

Rather than dissipate its strength against the screen of Indian villages protecting Canada, New England planned to attack the core of French strength on the St. Lawrence and in Acadia. Quebec and Port Royal each served as supply bases and rallying points for guerilla raids against the New England frontier, and for privateers who ravaged the colonies' maritime commerce.

Two regiments of volunteer militia were raised in 1707, and 1,000 men with artillery prepared to move against Port Royal. In two separate attempts, in May and again in August, the New Englanders were repulsed after a desultory show of force. Clearly, aid from all the northern colonies, as well as imperial assistance, would be required. By 1709, that combination seemed to be in place.

Prominent among the advocates of a more aggressive policy was recently arrived Scottish merchant Samuel Vetch. Previously involved in an unsuccessful scheme to establish a colony at Darien, Vetch quickly ingratiated himself into colonial society through trade and marriage. As both merchant and colonizer, Vetch had developed a continental perspective. Nor was he alone. At frontier outposts under the threat of constant attack, and in seaport communities devastated by French privateers, the logic of an assault against Canada was obvious. As New Yorker Robert Livingston advised, "strike at the head and all the rest must follow."

Vetch had considerable (and illegal) trade interest in Canada and had been sent by Governor Dudley to negotiate prisoner exchanges in Quebec. Armed with firsthand knowledge of the St. Lawrence and of Canadian defenses, in 1708, he offered his information and a plan of attack to the Board of Trade; Canada, defended by only a "handfull . . . vastly dispersed," would quickly fall to a coordinated colonial-imperial attack if the crown would allocate a force of but two regiments and six ships. With the war in Europe stalemated, the plan was approved.

The planned invasion was a replay of a failed attempt by Sir William Phips in 1690 and was a prelude to the final assault on Canada 50 years later. A colonial force from New England would join the regulars and warships for an assault on Quebec. Meanwhile, a strong diversionary attack of colonial militia and Iroquois would operate from Albany under Colonel Francis Nicholson to pin down the French at Montreal. Canada's defenses would thus be divided and its two major strongpoints would fall in turn. But if the plan was to succeed, New York must participate.

Iroquois neutrality in 1701 had meant the neutrality of New York as well. The Five Nations were simply exhausted after a generation of war against Canada and its allies; in New York, Anglo-Dutch conflict, political scandals of Governor Edward Cornbury's administration, and continuing dissension from the Leisler era led to a "prudent defense." Neither New York nor the Five Nations would sacrifice neutrality to fight an inconclusive guerilla war, but a chance to destroy Canada was another matter.

In a masterful publicity move promoted by expansionists Philip Schuyler and Robert Livingston, four Iroquois chiefs were sent to ask the queen for aid against the French. Although the Seneca refused to take part, several hundred league warriors joined in the abortive expeditions of 1709 and 1711. Then, when each of those invasion plans went awry, New York and the Five Nations simply reverted to neutrality and to their "cold war" with Canada.

In effect, the 1709 expedition was over before it began. While colonial governments gathered men and material through the summer, the expected aid from London failed to appear. Finally, in September, word came that the force intended for Canada had been diverted to Portugal; there would be no imperial assistance. It was even more frustrating to learn that this decision was made in May, yet it was August before messages were prepared for the colonies. Hopes for a renewed effort in 1710 were similarly frustrated when six ships, but only one regiment, arrived from England. Making the best of a poor situation, a combined colonial-imperial force of 3,500 men under Nicholson captured Port Royal in Acadia and its garrison of 300.

Nonetheless, the queen remained committed to action against Canada; so too was the newly elected Tory government, which wished victories of its own to offset those won under the Whigs by John Churchill, duke of Marlborough. A fleet of 15 warships and 46 transports under the joint command of Admiral Sir Hovenden Walker and Brigadier John Hill was sent in the summer of 1711 to replicate the 1709 plan. This project, too, was "ill-fated" from the start.

The 6,000 regulars, 5,000 seamen, and 1,500 colonials gathered at Boston overwhelmed the town's 9,000 inhabitants, leading to acute shortages and spiralling costs. There was persistent conflict between the British military and colonials over prices, supply, and desertions. Even worse, few experienced pilots could be found who knew Canadian waters. Walker would have to use impressed Boston navigators and captured Frenchmen to take his ships through the narrow and poorly chartered waters of the St. Lawrence.

Despite its apparent strength, the expedition arrived off the St. Lawrence on 20 August with a sense of foreboding. Driven by a fresh wind and heavy seas, navigation was complicated by dense fog and unpredictable currents. Three days later, as he retired for the night, Walker assumed the fleet was off the south shore. He was, in fact, crossing a great southward loop in the river and bearing down on its northern bank. About midnight on the 23rd, eight transports and a sloop drove onto the breakers with a loss of more than 800 men.

Vetch, in command of the colonial troops and familiar with the St. Lawrence, wanted to continue; but with several hundred miles of uncharted river still ahead, a council of war agreed with Walker to abort the mission. The fleet with its troops returned to England. In New York, where 2,000 colonials and Iroquois assembled at Wood Creek to move against Montreal, Colonel Nicholson threw his wig to the ground in disgust and dispersed his force.

Along the southern frontier, as in New England, a buffer of Indian allies screened Bourbon possessions. But the growing influence of Carolina traders among the Yamasee, Creek, Chickasaw, Cherokee, Yazoo, and Alabama tribes threatened this Indian barrier. In response, French posts at Biloxi (1699) and Mobile (1702) established an uneasy alliance with Spanish Pensacola (1699) to block English expansion along the Gulf coast and lower Mississippi River. In Spanish Florida, mission settlements and military posts formed a wilderness barrier for the colony's major strongpoint at St. Augustine, where some 300 poorly-equipped troops guarded the Atlantic approaches to the Bahamas Channel.

War in 1702 gave official sanction to an already planned expedition by Carolina's Governor James Moore against St. Augustine. In

Q

September, 1,000 English and Yamasees sacked the town and lay siege to Castillo de San Marcos. When their four cannon had no impact on the stone fort, Moore decided to starve out the garrison and the "one thousand mouths" of its civilian refugees. Governor Joseph de Zuñiga y Cerda, in anticipation of a siege, gathered the population, their valuables, and four months' provisions.

For eight weeks, each side waited for aid, until a convoy from Havana closed the harbor and decided the issue. Besieged in turn, Moore burned his ships and the town and retreated overland. Although casualties were light, the attack cost £26,000, the ships, and Moore's reputation.

To recoup his losses, Moore organized a raid by 1,500 Yamasees in 1703 that devastated Spain's Apalachee mission frontier. At the stockaded village of Ayubale, Franciscan friar Angel de Miranda and the defenders were tortured and killed when they surrendered after a vigorous defense. More than 300 Indian slaves were taken and perhaps 1,000 others were resettled along the Savannah River. With no native population to serve, the Spanish abandoned their last post in west Florida at Fort San Luis near Tallahassee. Over the next few years the Timucua mission villages east of Apalachee, the Tocabagga to the south, and the Guale mission frontier along the Georgia coast were destroyed in turn. Forced on the defensive in the wilderness, Bourbon offensive operations against South Carolina must come by sea.

Unpredictable weather, difficult logistics, and problems in coordinating land and maritime units plagued seaborne operations throughout the Americas. A Franco-Spanish assault on Charles Town in 1706 had one of its six ships, the *Brilliante*, carrying 200 men and the commanding officer, driven off by a Dutch raider. After an initial success by the remaining force, 160 men were caught by surprise while roasting captured chickens on the beaches and were routed. When the *Brilliante* finally arrived, its force was defeated in turn, and the ship was captured. In all, 320 prisoners were taken, and subsequent plans to attack Charles Town were shelved.

By 1707, South Carolina had formed an effective system of outer defenses. Small coastal vessels patrolled to St. Augustine, while a barrier of protective Indian villages, warning beacons, and permanently garrisoned "watch stations" guarded the interior and captured runaway slaves. Once defenses were secured, the English, as in New England, adopted an offensive strategy aimed at the major centers of Bourbon power. Pensacola was attacked twice in 1707, and Indian trader Thomas Nairne was urging an assault on Mobile. Like Vetch and Livingston, Nairne was a continentalist who advocated English control from the Great Lakes to the Gulf.

But internal dissension proved stronger than Bourbon defenses. A controversy between Nairne, as newly appointed Indian agent, and South Carolina Governor Nathaniel Johnson over the enforcement of trade regulations led to Nairne's imprisonment and distracted attention from military expeditions. When Carolina was finally ready to act, the colony was diverted by Indian war. Trade abuses, slave raids, and encroaching settlement led to conflict with the North Carolina Tuscaroras in 1711 and with the Yamasee in 1715, in which Nairne was an early victim. By 1713, Europe was at peace, but in North America the struggle for control of the wilderness interior was just beginning.

At sea, as on land, the outnumbered and outgunned Bourbon powers relied on a strategy of hit-and-run raids against isolated targets. Privateers acting alone or in combination with French naval forces attacked commerce and ravaged coastal settlements. Brutally effective in the short term, their impact was selective. Chesapeake tobacco fleets were devastated until convoys were established by 1706, while the Newfoundland fishing fleet dropped from 171 ships to 16 and its trade fell by one-quarter. Philadelphia and New York, which had no compensating expenditures for military expeditions as did Boston, also suffered. Eventually, however, the security of a permanent squadron stimulated colonial trade. As French naval power disintegrated, the British could launch amphibious operations from Canada to the Indies almost at will

English preparations in the Caribbean actually predated hostilities, as Admiral John Benbow brought a squadron of ten ships to Jamaica in November 1701. This was countered by a fleet of 35 sail under the count de Chateau-Renault at Martinique early in 1702. Equally ravaged by disease, neither side took action until much of the French force left to convoy the Spanish treasure fleet. Benbow then encountered the remaining French force under Admiral Jean du Casse in a running fight in August.

An apparent English victory was lost when several English captains refused to follow the "cabin boy" admiral, who later died from wounds suffered in the battle. In a subsequent court-martial, two captains were executed and a third was dismissed from the service. A similar instance of apparent military snobbery occurred in 1708 when two captains were dismissed after refusing to follow orders of Commodore Charles Weger.

Fleet action, however, was unusual, and J.H. Parry's assessment that the "age of buccaneers had ended for the age of navies" was only partially true. With the Spanish content to remain on the defensive, most fighting was confined to a series of bitter raids along the Anglo-French Atlantic periphery extending from the Bahamas through the Leeward Islands.

In July 1702, Leewards Governor Christopher Codrington, the younger, drove the French off jointly-owned St. Christopher. When the French meekly surrendered, Governor Jean-Baptiste de Gennes was accused of cowardice. Stripped of his titles and offices, de Gennes was cleared only after his death in an English prison. Although Codrington wanted the French inhabitants exiled to more distant St. Dominique, they were only sent to nearby Martinique. There they formed a surplus population used to supply French privateers.

Codrington then proposed a major attack on Martinique before its defenses could consolidate, but Commodore Hovenden Walker tarried two months with his squadron at Barbados, and the opportunity lapsed. Finally, in March 1703, a combined colonial-imperial force of 3,500 attacked Guadeloupe. Despite the advice of his officers and of Jesuit missionary and self-educated military engineer Father Jean-Baptiste Labat, who designed much of the island's defenses, Governor Charles Auger retreated into the interior. Frustrated by this "Fabian strategy," Codrington plundered the island and two months later withdrew.

In retaliation, a French expedition under the Comte de Chavagnac savaged St. Kitts for a week in February 1706, and a month later Pierre Le Moyne d'Iberville attacked Nevis. Now it was the English who evacuated their fortifications and fell back to their mountain "deodard," or retreat, where they collected their families and valuables. Angered when the slaves put up a stouter defense than their English owners, Iberville imposed severe terms. More than 3,000 slaves were taken as booty, and he demanded another 1,400 or their cash equivalent. Some English captives, taken as security, remained prisoners six years after the war ended when the ransom went unpaid. Subsequent French raids then devastated Montserrat, Barbuda, and Antigua.

Slaves and mill works were prime targets as both sides sought plunder and the destruction of their rival's sugar industry. Nonetheless, the islands generally prospered during the war. Slave imports into the Leewards reached 1,000 annually, the highest to date, and sugar production doubled. The same was true for Martinique and Guadaloupe. Prosperity, however, was unevenly distributed. Throughout the sugar islands of both sides, large planters benefited at the expense of the smaller owners, who were less able to withstand the constant raids.

On several occasions domestic society simply broke down. Wartime tensions, plus the growing demands of imperial military and economic influence, led to open conflict. Antigua's abrasive Governor Daniel Parke, who challenged land claims and trade rights of the local elite, was brutally killed along with 11 soldiers by a mob of leading citizens in 1706. On French Martinique, the governor was ousted by a mob after trying to enforce trade restrictions. In the Bahamas, Franco-Spanish raids in 1703–1704 virtually eliminated organized government and turned the islands into a buccaneer haven under the pirates Barrow and Harnigold.

After a decade of often bitter but generally inconclusive fighting, the war ended with the Treaty of Utrecht in 1713. The French and Spanish crowns remained separate; Spain granted the *asiento* to Britain for 25 years and lost Gibraltar and Minorca. In the colonies, France surrendered Acadia, Hudson Bay, Newfoundland, its half of St. Kitts, and recognized the Iroquois as "subjects" of Britain. Boundaries and clauses, however, were vaguely drawn and poorly understood. In the Americas, a stalemated war and an ambiguous peace provided the ingredients for a new round of fighting a generation later.

David R. Farrell

References
Richmond Bond, *Queen Anne's American Kings* (1952); Donald Chard, "The Impact of French Privateering on New England, 1689–1713," *American Neptune* 35 (1975): 153–165; Verner W. Crane, *The Southern*

Q

Frontier, 1620–1732 (1928); Nellis M. Crouse, *French Struggle for the West Indies 1665–1713* (1966); Samuel Drake, *Border Wars of New England* (1897).

Gerald Graham, ed., *Walker Expedition to Quebec in 1711* (1953); Francis Jennings, *The Ambiguous Iroquois Empire: The Covenant Chain Confederation of Indian Tribes with English Colonies from its beginnings to the Lancaster Treaty of 1744* (1984); Douglas Edward Leach, *The Northern Colonial Frontier 1607–1763* (1966); Lawrence H. Leder, *Robert Livingston, 1654–1728, and the Politics of Colonial New York* (1961).

W.R. Meyer, "English Privateering in the War of the Spanish Succession," *Mariners Mirror* 69 (1983):435–446; William Thomas Morgan, "The Five Nations and Queen Anne," *Mississippi Valley Historical Review* 23 (1926):169–189; J.H. Owen, *War at Sea Under Queen Anne* (1938); George Waller, *Samuel Vetch: Colonial Enterpriser* (1960).

See also ACADIA, BRITISH CONQUEST OF (1710); ACADIA, NEW ENGLAND ATTACK ON (1707); AYUBALE; CANADA, BRITISH EXPEDITION AGAINST (1709); CANADA, BRITISH EXPEDITION AGAINST (1711); CHARLES TOWN, ATTACK ON; CHURCH, BENJAMIN; DEERFIELD; HAVERHILL; LE MOYNE D'IBERVILLE, PIERRE; NAIRNE, THOMAS; PENSACOLA (FLORIDA); RIGAUD DE VAUDREUIL DE CAVAGNIAL, PIERRE DE; ST. AUGUSTINE, SIEGE OF; UTRECHT, TREATY OF; VETCH, SAMUEL

R

Raiding Party

Traditional warfare waged by Native Americans east of the Rocky Mountains often involved the raiding party, defined by Harold E. Driver as "a single small military engagement of short duration." These expeditions varied in size from as few as a half-dozen warriors, perhaps smaller on occasion, to as many as 20 or even 50 combatants. A continuous state of war existed between enemies engaging in raiding warfare, and peace could only exist as a temporary armistice. War leaders often were self-selected after supernatural endorsement, and expeditions consisted of volunteers who were motivated by revenge, adventure, prestige, and economic advantage. Tactics involved stealth, surprise, and ambush carried out by a group of individuals fighting independently against enemy men, women, and children. Weapons included the bow and arrow, lance, knife, and war club, as well as the gun. In a successful raid, the numerically superior invaders obtained prisoners or trophies, such as arms, legs, or scalps, without losing any members of the expedition. Raids began and ended with certain ceremonies, including torturing captives to death, although adoption was possible. Raids increased dramatically in size and became more deadly and more frequent during the colonial period. Differences in martial goals and objectives meant that European military leaders were often frustrated when they attempted to employ Native Americans in their large military operations of extended duration.

Raymond E. Hauser

References

James Axtell, "Who Invented Scalping?," *American Heritage* XXVIII (1977):96–99;

Harold E. Driver, *Indians of North America* (1961); Alice C. Fletcher, "War and War Discipline," in *Handbook of American Indians North of Mexico*, Frederick Webb Hodge, ed., (1986), II:914–915; Raymond E. Hauser, "Warfare and the Illinois Indian Tribe During the Seventeenth Century," *The Old Northwest* X (1984–1985):367–387; Keith F. Otterbein, "Why the Iroquois Won: An Analysis of Iroquois Tactics," *Ethnohistory* XI (1964):56–63.

See also INDIAN WARFARE; SCALPING; SCOUT

Rale, Sebastien (also spelled Rasle, 1652?–1724)

Sebastien Rale was born in Pontarlier, France, in late 1651 or early 1652. As a boy he was trained in Jesuit schools, entered a Jesuit seminary, and in 1677 took his vows. Rale taught school for a few years, then in 1689, he was ordained as a priest and in July sailed for New France. Initially assigned to the mission at St. Francis de Sales, Rale learned the Abenaki language and began his famous dictionary. In 1692, he was sent to the Illinois country, but returned to Quebec in 1695 to receive his next assignment to the mission at Norridgewock on the Kennebec River.

Rale would spend the rest of his life at Norridgewock, building a church, administering to the Indians, seeking converts. As the Norridgewocks had long fought for the French against the English, Rale found himself thrust into the middle of that conflict. Pressure from the English forced Rale and the Norridgewock tribe to move to Canada in 1705. They returned to the village toward the end of Queen Anne's War in 1711.

Tension between the New England colonies and the Indians continued despite the peace treaty. Sebastien Rale in particular found himself the focus of controversy. He was upset that the English tried to woo his Indians away from Catholicism, and the English in turn believed the Jesuit was the main cause of their failure to separate the Norridgewocks from the French. In January 1722, Colonel Thomas Westbrook led a raiding party to Norridgewock. Rale and those remaining in the village fled into the woods, but Westbrook captured his personal papers, including his dictionary. Personal letters also seized confirmed English suspicions, as they appeared to show Rale encouraging the various tribes to unite against the English.

Growing tension and bloody incidents eventually escalated into Dummer's War during the summer of 1722. Two years later, in August 1724, a force of provincial soldiers led by Johnson Harmon, Jeremiah Moulton, John Brown, and Joseph Bean marched toward Norridgewock. On the 23rd they attacked the village. The surprise was complete, and an estimated 80 Indian men, women, and children were killed, and among the dead was the Jesuit priest, Sebastien Rale.

Steven C. Eames

References

Mary R. Calvert, *Black Robe on the Kennebec* (1991); Francis Parkman, *A Half-Century of Conflict*, in *France and England in North America*, Vol. II (1983).

See also ABENAKI; DUMMER'S WAR; HARMON, JOHNSON; NORRIDGEWOCK, BATTLE OF; WESTBROOK, THOMAS

Fort Raleigh (North Carolina)

Fort Raleigh is the twentieth-century name for the fort built shortly after the arrival of the Ralph Lane colony on Roanoke Island in the summer of 1585. The fort was designed to protect the short-lived colony from attack by either Indians or the Spanish. It was built on the north end of the island and was apparently completed by 25 August, when Richard Grenville left for the return trip to England.

There are no contemporary drawings or detailed descriptions of the fort. Much of what we know about Fort Raleigh comes from archaeological research, especially that undertaken by the National Park Service since the end of World War II. This research suggests that the fort was square, augmented with bastions on the sides of the square, which formed a star shape, and was less than 100 feet to a side. Although at least one structure was inside the enclosure, it is not clear how many of the colony's buildings were built inside the fort. Some observers argue that the excavated fort is too small to have been Lane's primary fort and that the location of that fort is still to be determined.

When John White returned to Roanoke Island in 1587, he found the fort "rased downe," although the nearby houses were still standing. Recent archaeology suggests that the fort may have been reasonably intact on White's arrival. Portions of the fort were still visible for centuries.

Jim Sumner

References

David N. Durant, *Raleigh's Lost Colony* (1981); Jean Carl Harrington, *Archaeology and the Enigma of Fort Raleigh* (1984); Charles W. Porter III, *Fort Raleigh National Historic Site, North Carolina* (1956); David Beers Quinn, ed., *The Roanoke Voyages, 1589–1590*, 2 vols. (1955); ———, *Set Fair for Roanoke: Voyages and Colonies, 1584–1606* (1985).

See also ROANOKE ISLAND

Rangers

During the late Middle Ages, the word "range" came into common English usage as a verb to describe a particular task that was assigned to military or law enforcement forces. To range was to patrol a designated area. Men assigned to forces whose principal mission was to range were called "rangers." The term was probably first used about the beginning of the fourteenth century for those men who were hired as a constabulary to range the king's forests in England. Since the beginning of the English settlements in North America, the word "range" was used to describe the movement of soldiers when they patrolled an area to prevent its use by hostile Indians.

The English colonies in America had great difficulty in defending against the Indians' hit-and-run tactics. Initially, the colonial governments tried stationing small, immobile garrisons in forts situated on the major avenues of approach into the settled areas. However, the In-

Rangers and (center) Company Officer

Rogers' Rangers, 1756–1760. Reproduced from Plate No. 97, Military Collector & Historian, *Vol. VII, No. 1, Spring 1955, by permission of the Company of Military Historians.*

dians quietly bypassed the forts and raided and ambushed the surprised settlers. A system of rangers soon evolved to deal with the problem.

The use of small, private units of rangers by plantation owners may have been common in Virginia and Maryland by the 1630s. In 1634 and 1635, Edward Backler was hired as a "rainger" for Kent Island, a Virginia settlement in the upper Chesapeake Bay, in present-day Maryland. His probable duty was to give warning of the approach of Indians and Marylanders, both of whom were raiding that settlement.

By 1648, the colony of Maryland was employing rangers to patrol the most exposed portions of its frontier. During the period 1675 to 1692, Maryland militia commanders often used small units of rangers to protect the remote plantations, but these units were raised and disbanded in response to each crisis. In 1693, Maryland organized small "parties" of full-time, regular rangers that included a few Indian trackers and guides. They ranged the frontier between modern Washington and Baltimore until 1701.

In 1676, during a major Indian war, Virginia established a screen of forts along its frontier. Part of each garrison served as rangers. That system was used again from 1679 to 1682, but maintaining the forts was too expensive. From 1683 to 1686, regular "troops" of rangers mustered biweekly or monthly and patrolled the frontier. With the lessening of Indian incursions small "parties" of rangers were maintained to serve as regular provincial units, patrolling Virginia's frontier from 1691 to 1698, and again from 1711 to 1716.

The northern colonies also used the ranger system of defense against Indians. Although official documents of that period seldom designate ranging soldiers as "rangers," it appears that they were commonly nicknamed as such. By 1670, the colony of Plymouth had a small party of rangers under the supervision of Captain Thomas Willet. During King Philip's War (1675–1676), small parties of soldiers ranged along the outskirts of the New England settlements on the lookout for the approach of Indian war parties. Independent ranging companies, made up of both white and allied Indian men from Plymouth and Massachusetts, were recruited to take the offensive and raid and ambush in the Indians' lands. Some of these companies became extremely efficient in conducting forest warfare.

One of the best known of the New England ranger leaders was Benjamin Church. He commanded ranging companies for Plymouth during 1675–1676, 1689, and 1690. During 1696, and again in 1704, he commanded Massachusetts ranging forces composed of from four to 12 companies of whites and friendly Indians. His rangers were extremely successful. He became a legend in the northern colonies, and he probably influenced many of the successful ranger commanders who followed him.

By the year 1700, rangers were conducting all of the types of operations that are now considered as ranger specialties: reconnaissance, raids, and ambushes. During their operations they used the best available means of transportation. If the circumstances permitted, they rode horseback. However, horses were used for transportation only; when in action they normally dismounted and fought on foot as infantry. They also used boats whenever possible. Amphibious reconnaissance and raids by rangers were common in New England by the late seventeenth century. Ranging units in the northern colonies commonly operated during winter on snowshoes and ice skates. Rangers considered themselves elite soldiers, and civilians recognized them as such.

The rangers' area of operations was the unending forest that overlaid the mountains, valleys, hills, coastal lowlands, and swamps of eastern North America. The ideal ranger recruit was the hunter or farmer who resided on the frontier, a man who could shoot well and who felt comfortable in the forest. However, men with those qualifications were very independent; excellent leadership was required to secure their best performance. Thus, the efficiency of the ranger units usually varied with the skill of the commanders and the quality of the recruits.

Normally, rangers were not uniformed or equipped by their government. Instead, they were given higher wages than other soldiers, and were required to outfit themselves. They normally furnished their own clothing, weapons, equipment, and food. Their governments sometimes issued those items and took the costs out of their wages. Ranger clothing was usually the working man's clothing of the period. Modifications, such as adding leggins and shortening coats, were necessary for forest operations. The most common headgear were brimmed hats, Scotch bonnets, and fur caps. Their primary weapon was a flintlock musket with the barrel cut short for easier handling. Hatchets and knives were carried as weapons and essential tools in the forest. Cumbersome military trappings such as swords and pikes were seldom used.

Following the Yamasee War of 1715–1717, the Carolinas were the most exposed of the southern colonies, and small companies of rangers began patrolling their frontiers. South Carolina continued to use regular units of rangers for more than 20 years. In early 1733, it loaned the Company of Southern Rangers to the new colonists of Georgia. The company remained there under the command of James

McPherson until 1738. McPherson was one of America's most experienced ranger leaders, commanding ranger companies for a total of 14 years.

The colony of Georgia, under the leadership of James Edward Oglethorpe, relied heavily on rangers to protect its frontiers. Rangers were also used for offensive operations. During the War of Jenkins' Ear and King George's War (1739–1748), Georgia rangers, on the British payroll, took part in several battles and skirmishes with Spaniards and their Indian allies in the coastal forests and marshes.

South Carolina, New York, and Massachusetts also used rangers on their frontiers during King George's War. In Nova Scotia, ranger companies recruited in New England and commanded by John, and later Joseph, Gorham were engaged in hit-and-run warfare with the French and their Indian allies throughout the war and beyond. The Gorham family had a long history of ranger leadership beginning about 1704 and extending to 1764.

The French and Indian War, 1754–1763, saw the greatest use of rangers in North America. Almost every English colony maintained companies of rangers to patrol the frontiers against hostile Indians. For the first time, the British army operated in strength in the American forests, and it was forced to place great reliance on rangers for reconnaissance, raiding, and ambushing. Ranger companies suffered with General Edward Braddock on the Pennsylvania frontier at the beginning of the war, and ranger companies were in Canada at the successful conclusion of the war. Rangers accompanied the British army and navy to the Caribbean during 1761 and 1762 for the invasions of French Martinique and Spanish Cuba. The army attempted to avoid the need for American rangers by converting entire British regular infantry battalions into ranger units, calling them "light infantry" and equipping and training them in ranger style. However, the effort was only partially successful, and the more efficient American ranger companies remained on the British payroll. By conducting raids and ambushes at all hours and even in the worst of weather, the ranger companies frustrated and terrorized the French.

The best known and perhaps the most successful ranger leader during the French and Indian War was Robert Rogers, whose companies served near the Canadian border. During the period 1756–1760 Rogers' Rangers raided and ambushed French forces and their Indian allies in all seasons. During the legendary 1759 St. Francis raid, his rangers quietly moved about 150 miles through trackless forests, surprised and destroyed an Indian town, and withdrew over another route under constant pursuit by French and Indians. He conducted history's first ranger training school during which young British regular officers were taught the fundamentals of ranger operations. He wrote a detailed set of "Rules for the Ranging Service" that are applicable for ranger operations today.

Rangers maintained a special status during the colonial period and beyond. They were given the most exhausting, dangerous missions. They had to operate over the most difficult terrain during all types of weather. In return they were given higher wages, escaped the spit and polish of the regular infantry, and enjoyed the prestige of serving with the elite. Many exploits of early American rangers became legend long before the end of the colonial period. Men who had served under such leaders as Benjamin Church, James McPherson, and Robert Rogers enjoyed the admiration of their communities throughout the remainder of their lives.

Larry E. Ivers

References

John R. Cuneo, *Robert Rogers of the Rangers* (1959); Samuel Drake, *The Border Wars of New England* (1910); Larry E. Ivers, *British Drums on the Southern Frontier: The Military Colonization of Georgia, 1733–1749* (1974); Harvey H. Jackson and Phinizy Spalding, eds., *Forty Years of Diversity: Essays on Colonial Georgia* (1984); Francis Parkman, *A Half-Century of Conflict*, 2 vols. (1922).

See also CHURCH, BENJAMIN; COUREURS DE BOIS; LIGHT INFANTRY; ROGERS, ROBERT; SCOUT

Rappahannock

When English colonists arrived in Virginia in 1607, four groups of Native Americans were living along the Rappahannock River below the fall line: the Cuttatawomen, the Moraughtacund, the Toppohanock, and the Nautaughtacund. The Rappahannock, as the groups generally became known, were Algonquian-speakers and were part of the Powhatan chiefdom. Captain John Smith estimated that they had 335 warriors. Although the colonists' initial encounter with the Rappahannock was cordial, they appear to have participated in the 1622 Indian uprising and may have been implicated in the 1644 attack.

During the early 1650s, when colonists began seating land along both sides of the Rappahannock River, a group of Rappahannock Indians withdrew to the vicinity of Fleets or Cat Point Creek, on the north side of the river. A second community of Rappahannock, called the Totosha or Tanks (Little) Rappahannock, were then living on Totusky Creek. In 1653, the Virginia government allocated to the Rappahannock a tract of land between Totusky and Rappahannock Creeks, and local officials agreed to build their king an English-style house. But within two years, relations between the Rappahannock and their English neighbors had deteriorated to the point that the militias of Lancaster, Northumberland, and Westmoreland Counties made a retaliatory raid against the Rappahannock Indian towns. Although a treaty was signed with the Rappahannock in September 1656, a steady flow of settlers into the Rappahannock River basin made further inroads into the natives' territory. In 1662, the legal boundaries of the Rappahannock's land between Totosky and Rappahannock Creeks were clearly defined. Even so, by 1669, the Rappahannock abandoned the land they had been assigned and withdrew to the headwaters of the Mattaponi River. The group, which continued to bear the name "Rappahannock," then had only 30 warriors, whereas the Totosky (Totusky) had 40.

In 1677, the Rappahannock signed a treaty whereby they became tributaries to the crown and subservient to the queen of Pamunkey. But by 1678, the Rappahannock had asserted their independence. In 1683, when the Seneca commenced preying on Virginia's tributary tribes, the Rappahannock were living on the ridge between the Mattaponi and Rappahannock Rivers. At that juncture, colonial officials encouraged the Rappahannock to unite with the Nanzattico for their mutual protection. During spring 1684, the Rappahannock relocated to the land bordering Portobago Bay, where they took up residence on part of a preserve that had been allocated to the Nanzattico. In 1705, Robert Beverley reported that the Rappahannock, who were then residing in Essex County, were "reduc'd to a few Families, and live scatter'd upon the English Seats."

Martha W. McCartney

References

Robert Beverley, *History of the Present State of Virginia* (1705), Louis B. Wright, ed. (1947); William W. Hening, ed., *The Statutes at Large: Being a Collection of All the Laws of Virginia*, 13 vols. (1809–1823); H.R. McIlwaine, ed., *Minutes of Council and General Court of Colonial Virginia* (1924); Nell M. Nugent, ed. *Cavaliers and Pioneers: Abstracts of Virginia land Patents and Grants*, 3 vols. (1969–1979); John Smith, *Travels and Works of Captain John Smith, President of Virginia and Admiral of New England, 1580–1631*, Edward Arber, ed. (1910).

See also PAMUNKEY; POWHATAN; SENECA; SMITH, JOHN; VIRGINIA-INDIAN TREATY OF 1677/1680; VIRGINIA-INDIAN WAR (1622–1632); VIRGINIA-INDIAN WAR (1644–1646)

Rasle, Sebastien
See RALE, SEBASTIEN

Fort Reading (North Carolina)
Fort Reading was established during the early part of the Tuscarora War as a safeguard for inhabitants near the Pamlico River. It was located on the plantation of Lionel Reading, not far from the present city of Washington, North Carolina, and had a ten-man garrison

Jim Sumner

Recruitment, Army
The idea underlying all forms of recruitment in the age of absolutism was the concept that the armed forces were composed of the dregs of society who had no place else to go. Recruiting practices as well as the attitude toward the soldiery were determined by that assumption, even though modern research has corrected that prejudice to a large degree. In the British army, recruitment took three different forms: impressment, service in lieu of other punishment, and enlistment of volunteers.

Impressment
In 1704, the British Parliament passed the first Impressment Act for the army. It instructed justices of the peace to enlist for a period of usually five years "such able-bodied men, as have not any lawful employment or calling, or visible means for their maintenance [sic] livelihood." Unlike naval pressing, army impressment stood under the con-

trol of the local civil authorities. The act was renewed every year between 1704 and 1711. It was in effect between 1746 and 1758, and again from 1756 to 1758. Since potential recruits had the benefit of a hearing before the local justices, impressment produced very few recruits and was greatly resented, since these hearings carried a great potential for abuse. It was reintroduced in 1778 and 1779. In 1708, some 5,825 men were impressed, but that number fell to about 2,200 for the years 1778–1779, of which about half actually joined the colors. The act was allowed to lapse in 1780 because of the expense involved, public opposition, and lack of success.

Service in Lieu of Other Punishment

Since the end of the thirteenth century, particular offenders could be granted pardons in return for military service by the king of England, and the Mutiny Acts of 1701 and 1703 confirmed this practice. Throughout the eighteenth century, acts for the relief of debtors stipulated that they could join the military as a means of escaping prison. In 1744, an act of Parliament gave magistrates the power to offer enlistment instead of corporal punishment to vagrants, while other acts allowed parishes to hand over to the army such men as had left their families dependent on the parish. Under an act of 1777, convicted smugglers could be taken into the army or navy in lieu of other punishment. The military establishment always resented having criminals pushed on them, and during peacetime these acts were rarely used. When invoked in times of war, the numbers recruited in this fashion were still relatively small. Between 1763 and 1774, only four men were given that opportunity in Essex, and 14 between 1775 and 1781. In all of England and Wales between 1776 and the end of 1781, some 764 men were pardoned to military service, an insignificant number among the total of 73,310 men raised between September of 1775 and September 1780.

Enlistment of Volunteers

Kidnapping and other forms of illegal recruitment were rare in the British army, and the vast majority of soldiers were volunteers who served for life. Recruiting parties induced volunteers to sign up by offering an enlistment bounty of usually one and one-half guineas and the promise of eligibility as Chelsea pensioners after 20 years of service. But even here the boundaries were fluctuating, since many a volunteer may have joined the ranks to escape punishment for crimes committed or entered the service out of economic necessity to escape hunger and deprivation.

Robert A. Selig

References

Stephen R. Conway, "The Recruitment of Criminals Into the British Army, 1775–81," *Bulletin of the Institute of Historical Research* 58 (May 1985):46–58; Arthur N. Gilbert, "Army Impressment During the War of the Spanish Succession," *The Historian* 38 (1976):689–708; ———, "Charles Jenkinson and the Last Army Press, 1779," *Military Affairs* 42 (1978):7–11.

See also IMPRESSMENT, ARMY

Redoubt

Redoubts are defensive fortifications placed beyond the perimeter of defense on a high point in the terrain to guard the main defensive lines, to warn of an approaching enemy, to impede his advance, or to hinder the offensive preparations of the enemy. They can also be raised within the defensive system at a particularly advantageous point in the terrain. A redoubt usually consists of raised earthen walls, a ditch, and defensive obstacles such as an abatis or a parapet around it. When placed outside the defensive network, they usually lack a glacis, since that would facilitate an attack on them. Located about a musket shot away from the main defensive works, they can take various forms, i.e., square- or star-shaped, and are manned by detached guards of infantry and sometimes artillery. The marquis de Feuquières called for the length of the sides to be between 60 and 120 feet, and the ditch surrounding the redoubt about ten feet wide and ten feet deep. The parapet was to have two or three banquets and be at least ten feet thick.

An attacking party sometimes would also raise temporary redoubts to protect its workmen employed in digging trenches or otherwise occupied in the preparation of a siege from fire and/or sallies by the defenders.

Robert A. Selig

References

Antoine de Pas, Marquis de Feuquières, *Memoirs Historical and Military: Containing a Distinct View of All the Considerable States of Europe*, 2 vols. (1730), rpt. 1968, 2.

See also ABATIS

Red Shoe (also known as Soulouche Oumastabé, Soulier Rouge; c. 1705–1747)

Soulouche Oumastabé, Soulier Rouge, Red Shoe—these names did not reflect a personal name but were instead a title given to Choctaw war leaders, probably referring to the ceremony of making a warrior during which young men wore red-dyed moccasins. The Choctaw leader who became most indelibly identified with this name was apparently at least partly a product of the new alignments of power within the tribe brought about by the presence of Europeans in the old Southwest in the late seventeenth and eighteenth centuries.

Born in the early eighteenth century into an unimportant family of the western division of the Choctaw tribe, Red Shoe was still an ordinary warrior, but had apparently become known for his war exploits when he became speaker for the French-created "Great Chief" of the nation in the late 1720s. To attain this role, which called for him to make speeches voicing the chief's sentiments, he must have had a good deal of skill as a speaker. In a society where leadership depended on persuasion and generosity rather than coercion, he therefore was already equipped with an important talent. In his role as speaker he acted, on the chief's encouragement, in setting up trading opportunities with the English traders among the Chickasaws when French presents to the chiefs dwindled at the end of the decade; the chief, Mingo Tchito, then theatrically renounced his French alliance after an insult from the Mobile commandant, and the French were forced to woo him back with a trading house.

When the Natchez revolt broke out in 1729, Choctaws were called on to help the French in punishing the Natchez. Red Shoe was the organizer of the initial Choctaw contingent that managed to obtain custody of the French women, children, and slaves taken prisoner in the uprising, and he was able to profit from the trade goods the French were forced to offer for their return. In this way he began to build a faction by having the wherewithal to demonstrate generosity.

The Natchez, however, had been allowed to escape to the Chickasaws, and the Chickasaws would not give them up, so the French were interested in inducing Choctaws to attack the Chickasaws and thereby force a settlement. Conservative Choctaws, including Mingo Tchito, were unwilling to break peace with the Chickasaws. Red Shoe undertook to do it with a small band of young warriors, attacking a Chickasaw hunting party in 1732 and thereby earning a medal from the French in return for Chickasaw scalps and prisoners. With the medal he also achieved a place on the roster of chiefs receiving regular gifts from the French, but the alliances implied by this state of affairs were not permanent, nor did they represent Red Shoe's aims.

Red Shoe shared the western division's common ethnic origins and existing alliances with the Chickasaws. In spite of occasional actions against the Chickasaws, he was instrumental in using Chickasaw friendships in an attempt to establish his faction and sometimes the Choctaws as a whole as a neutral group, able to sustain alliances with both French and English colonies and to enjoy thereby the results of their competition for Indian trade, as the Alabama tribe to the east had done. Thus his actions favored now the French, now the English. He participated on the French side in both Chickasaw wars, in 1736 and 1740, yet in 1734 he persuaded the eastern chief, Alibamon Mingo, to join with him in inviting English traders to visit the Choctaws, and in 1738, he visited Carolina. His efforts to maintain his Chickasaw connections backfired when in 1740, as the French army approached Chickasaw country—abortively, as it turned out—from the Mississippi River, Red Shoe had sent a company of Choctaws to the Chickasaws to establish peace and reassure the Chickasaws that Choctaw support for Jean-Baptiste Le Moyne de Bienville's campaign would not be significant. Killed as spies, these Choctaws had to be avenged under traditional Choctaw custom, and Red Shoe was thus forced into several years of war on the Chickasaws as the French, ironically, made peace with them.

This war was, however, instrumental in restoring to Red Shoe the gifts from the French due to his medal by the early 1740s, when the French turned once more against the Chickasaws to force them to a more advantageous peace. When a new French governor, Pierre de Rigaud de Vaudreuil, took over in 1743, and restructured the redistributive system of Indian presents, however, Red Shoe was excluded from a scheme that seemed to bid fair to unite the Choctaws, Chickasaws, and Creeks in a French-sponsored peace. But war between England and France in 1744 and a subsequent British blockade reduced the flow of French trade goods to a trickle and forced the formerly loyal Choctaw chiefs to make their own Chickasaw-English peace. Vaudreuil was forced to call upon Red Shoe to break that peace with attacks on the Chickasaws. This Red Shoe did, but only to induce the Chickasaws to make a peace with him; other Choctaw chiefs opposed to this move attacked a Chickasaw peace delegation. In response, Red Shoe ordered the unthinkable: the killing of three Frenchmen.

The series of events thus initiated grew into the Choctaw civil war, and it lasted from 1746 to 1750. The French demanded Choctaw deaths, beginning with Red Shoe, for their men, but the pro-French Choctaws instead attacked Englishmen, dreading the chain of death that intratribal revenge would start. Meanwhile, Red Shoe hastened negotiations with the English government in South Carolina that had begun with trader James Adair's overtures in 1745, sending his brother to treat with Governor James Glen for an assured government-sponsored trade in return for the expulsion of the French. By the time the first English packtrain arrived in the spring of 1747, many Choctaws, unable to get French trade goods because of the blockade, were ready to join Red Shoe. But this wily negotiator was killed by an assassin as he escorted the packtrain into the nation, and the English alliance fell apart. It would not be seriously renewed as the Choctaws were precipitated into a full-scale civil war that did not end until hundreds had died and several important villages had been destroyed in the name of the French alliance.

In many ways, Red Shoe clearly fits the mold of the intercultural "broker," a person who is not entirely successful in his own culture and who seizes such advantages as can be gained by doing business with another. He is mentioned several times in the French documents as being of a "low caste," or a family of little influence in the Choctaw tribe, and this meant that he had to take advantage of the very few routes to power that were available in Choctaw society through individual achievement alone. Certainly he was a very capable person, a strong warrior, persuasive speaker, and skilled manager of people. But there was a certain aggressiveness in his character, obvious to Frenchmen and Choctaw alike, that was not in harmony with the role that represented the greatest recognition available to southeastern Indian males: that of "peace" or civil chief.

His aggressiveness was used by peace chiefs like Mingo Tchito and Red Shoe's contemporary, Alibamon Mingo, but when he tried to construct his own power base, beyond the temporary leadership role of the war chief, he found himself in an innovating role without the ramified network of kin and neighbor alliances that supported the civil chief. Only several generations later, when European contact began to become sustained and face-to-face, could such "new men" as Red Shoe exploit a real need for their services, as traditional Choctaw relationships were no longer sufficient to bear the stress of contact.

Patricia Galloway

References

Patricia Galloway, "Choctaw Factionalism and Civil War, 1746–1750," *Journal of Mississippi History* 4 (1982):289–328; Richard White, "Red Shoe: Warrior and Diplomat," in David G. Sweet and Gary B. Nash, eds., *Struggle and Survival in Colonial America* (1981):49–68.

See also ADAIR, JAMES; CHICKASAW WARS; CHOCTAW; CHOCTAW CIVIL WAR; NATCHEZ WAR; RIGAUD DE VAUDREUIL DE CAVAGNIAL, PIERRE DE

Fort Redstone (Pennsylvania)

See FORT BURD (PENNSYLVANIA)

Fort Repentigny (Michigan)

In 1750, Governor Jacques-Pierre de Taffanel de La Jonquière of New France became alarmed by reports that traders and Indians were avoiding Fort Michilimackinac and trading furs to the English. As a result he granted Louis Legardeur de Repentigny and his partner, Captain Louis de Bonne de Missègle, 18 square miles along the St. Mary's River that controlled access between Lakes Huron and Superior.

Repentigny constructed a small palisaded fort enclosing three buildings in the summer of 1751. Jean Baptiste Caddote was hired as the tenant farmer, livestock was introduced, and a few acres were farmed. In return for this development, Repentigny and Bonne were given a trading monopoly.

With the start of the French and Indian War in 1754, Repentigny and Bonne left to fight, while Cadotte remained to work the farm with his Chippewa wife. At the end of the war, Lieutenant John Jamet led a detachment of troops from Fort Michilimackinac to take possession of the fort for the British. On 10 December 1762, a mysterious fire engulfed the entire fort except Cadotte's house. In the nineteenth century, Repentigny's descendants unsuccessfully sought to reclaim the grant.

Russell M. Magnaghi

See also FORT MICHILIMACKINAC (MICHIGAN)

Requisition System

During the colonial war in America, there were several requisition systems by which the military was supplied. Because of its primary role of protecting the British nation, the Royal Navy by 1700 had a well-defined administrative and logistical service, under the Lords Commissioners of the Admiralty. The British army, on the other hand, regarded primarily as a domestic peacekeeping force, had little structure beyond the regimental level.

During the wars of the eighteenth century, British regiments were drawn together under a commander in chief and command staff. The two senior staff positions were the quartermaster general and the adjutant general. By the French and Indian War (1754–1763), the quartermaster general had become what today would be called the chief of staff, coordinating troop movements and supply through the commissary general in charge of food and forage, the ordnance master general in charge of arms and ammunition, and the board of engineers who supervised various types of construction.

The War Department and the Admiralty, speaking for the Cabinet, which handled wartime strategy, determined how many ships and sailors and regular regiments would be committed to a particular operation. The Admiralty relied on its own well-developed procurement and transportation establishment for the needs of the navy, but the logistical demands of the French and Indian War went well beyond the capacity of the lightly-staffed War Department, forcing the Treasury Department to undertake the primary responsibility for supplying British troops abroad, both regular and provincial regiments. The Treasury Department did so by awarding contracts to British merchants for all sorts of provisions, especially food and money, the latter drawn upon to pay for services and supplies purchased locally. British contractors, in turn, had American partners who dealt directly with the commanding general's chief supply officer (usually the deputy quartermaster

general), whose assistants directed supplies to the quartermasters of various regiments.

Until 1756, provincial troops assigned to fight along side and support British regulars in America were supplied by commissaries contracted and paid by special committees appointed by the colonial government involved. During the French and Indian War, this complex and inefficient system broke down and caused considerable hardship. At the urging of Major General John Campbell, the colonial governments, led by Massachusetts Bay, finally agreed in late 1756 to allow provincials to be provisioned by regular army commissaries. The colonial assemblies resisted General Campbell's generous offer until they were reassured that regular provisioning would not bring provincials under the control of the British army or endanger the reimbursements promised by the Pitt Ministry for colonial expenses.

Despite the centralizing of the requisition system, British troops, both regular and provincial, still suffered grievously at times because of the distances and difficulties involved in transporting food, clothing, and equipment through the American wilderness.

Ronald W. Howard

References

Edward Pierce Hamilton, *The French and Indian Wars: The Story of Battles and Forts in the Wilderness* (1962); Douglas Edward Leach, *Roots of Conflict: British Armed Forces and Colonial Americans, 1677–1763* (1986); Stanley M. Pargellis, ed., *Military Affairs in North America, 1748–1765* (1936); Francis Parkman, *Montcalm and Wolfe: A Series of Historical Narratives*, 2 vols. (1884); Howard H. Peckham, *The Colonial Wars, 1689–1762* (1964); Colonel H.C.B. Rogers, *The British Army of the Eighteenth Century* (1977).

See also QUARTERMASTER GENERAL; ROBERTSON, JAMES; SUPPLY

Rhode Island

Colonial Rhode Island was, from its inception, plagued by dissent from within and unremitting aggression from its neighbors. Its four original towns—Providence and Warwick on the mainland, and Newport and Portsmouth on the island of Aquidneck—were all founded as refuges from religious persecution. Providence was founded in 1636 by Roger Williams, whose extreme separatism resulted in his banishment from Massachusetts. Anne Hutchinson's "Antinomians," who represented the mystical strain of Puritan thought, founded Portsmouth in 1638. A year later, a group of dissenters led by merchant William Coddington left Portsmouth to found the seaport town of Newport. And in 1643, after successive quarrels with leaders in Massachusetts, Portsmouth, Newport, and Providence, a group of settlers who followed the lead of "Familist" Samuel Gorton established Warwick.

If the Rhode Island settlements were troubled by internal dissension, they were in danger of being utterly destroyed by external aggression. Thanks to Roger Williams, their relationship with the Narragansett Indians was relatively untroubled. But Connecticut, Portsmouth, and Massachusetts, motivated in part by their antipathy toward religious heterodoxy, in part by simple greed for more land, made the colony the target of constant encroachments. In 1643, the New England Confederation was established. Rhode Island asked to be included in the organization, but its pleas were pointedly ignored. Even though Roger Williams had used his good offices to keep the Narragansetts neutral during the Pequot War, Rhode Island remained an outlaw colony in the eyes of its New England neighbors.

Rhode Island's only recourse was to appeal to London, which it managed to do with surprising success. Roger Williams secured a parliamentary patent in 1644. By 1657, thanks in large part to the need to unite against external aggression, the colony's inhabitants had resolved their political differences and could claim to be a relatively cohesive unit. In 1663, John Clarke traveled to England and obtained a royal charter. But the charter, while it gave Rhode Island legal standing and the ability to withstand repeated incursions from hostile colonies, did not halt rival claims to Rhode Island territory.

With the onset of King Philip's War in 1675, the colony's security was threatened once more. Governor William Coddington refused to be drawn directly into the affair, but he allowed the New England Confederation to take military action against the Narragansetts in Rhode Island, even providing vessels to transport troops into the colony. The confederation used Aquidneck as a base from which to launch its attacks on the mainland, and Rhode Island inhabitants—including Roger Williams—joined the fight. By the end of the war, many settlements had suffered severe losses, but their losses were nothing compared to the wholesale destruction experienced by the Narragansetts. Rhode Island did not participated officially in the war, but it certainly profited, in the long run, from the opening up of new lands that accompanied the Narragansett's decimation.

Rhode Island briefly lost its political identity in 1687, when it became subsumed in Edmund Andros's Dominion of New England. But by 1694, it won crown recognition of its charter, its political existence guaranteed, the colony was ready to lay the foundations of its economic success. Helped by the firm guidance of Governor Samuel Cranston and led by an increasingly aggressive merchant community in Newport, Rhode Island entered an era of international war with surprising optimism. It successfully fended off efforts by neighboring governors to assume command of local militia units by supporting England's war efforts voluntarily. During King George's War (1744–1748), the government fitted out the sloop *Tartar* at public expense and participated in the intercolonial expeditions against Louisbourg and Cape Breton Island. During the French and Indian War (1754–1763), the colony joined the efforts to subdue Ticonderoga and Louisbourg. By 1757, 10 percent of Rhode Island's male population was actively involved in the war effort. But despite its significant military contributions, Rhode Island's detractors never tired of complaining that the "pacifist colony," now dominated by Quakers, was not doing its fair share.

Involvement in England's imperial wars profoundly affected the economic development of Rhode Island in general and Newport in particular. While the wars were expensive, the colony's leaders soon learned to finance them with paper money, hoping to be reimbursed by London at war's end. Many individual entrepreneurs profited from their ability to obtain government contracts. The shipping industry expanded. Merchants used privateers, flags of truce, and trade through neutral ports to carry on an often lucrative, if always risky, commerce with the enemy during time of war. Nevertheless, by the French and Indian War such opportunities had become increasingly hazardous. Stiffer competition, especially from the British West Indies, and a stricter and more aggressive British navy, which looked askance at much of the colony's trade with the French, led to huge losses and even bankruptcy for many of Newport's leading merchants. As the home government grew more willing to listen to exaggerated complaints by Rhode Island's detractors that the colony harbored military deserters and was the center of illegal trade activity, it also became more determined to tighten its restrictions and to avoid compensating the colony for its expenses at war's end. A hostile government in England, an unusually severe postwar depression, and the growth of a confident and well-placed community of merchants in Providence all helped lead to the ultimate loss of Newport's hegemony in the years following the Treaty of Paris. While the French and Indian War did not cause the rise of Providence, it certainly hastened the process that would ultimately transfer the colony's leadership from Aquidneck to the mainland.

Sheila L. Skemp

References

Sydney V. James, *Colonial Rhode Island: A History* (1975); Francis Jennings, *The Invasion of America: Indians, Colonialism, and the Cant of Conquest* (1975); Herbert L. Osgood, *The American Colonies in the Seventeenth Century: The Chartered Colonies* (1904); Irving B. Richman, *Rhode Island: Its Making and Meaning, 1636–1683* (1902).

See also DOMINION OF NEW ENGLAND; GREAT SWAMP FIGHT; KING PHILIP'S WAR; NARRAGANSETT; NEW ENGLAND CONFEDERATION; PEQUOT WAR; WILLIAMS, ROGER

Ribaut, Jean
See RIBAULT, JEAN

Ribault, Jean (1520–1565)
A French sailor and soldier born in Dieppe, France, Jean Ribault was a fervent Protestant who led two expeditions to colonize Florida (the southeast region of the present United States) with French Huguenot colonists. These fruitless attempts, which cost him his life, should be understood in the context of the French religious wars of the second half of the sixteenth century. After the failure of the 1562 expedition, led together with René de Laudonnière, and the departure of a second led by the latter in 1564, he was given the command of a new fleet much bigger than those before (1,000 men and 7 ships) whose objective was to rein-

force the new colony of Fort Caroline founded by Laudonnière some months before. The expedition left Dieppe on 22 May 1565, after various delays that would prove fatal, as the Spanish had time to send a fleet to Florida under the command of Pedro Menéndez de Avilés. When Ribault arrived with reinforcements at Fort Caroline, on the St. Johns River, the Spanish (1,000 men and 4 ships), blocked the French ships, forcing them to flee. Ribault tried in vain to counterattack with his largest ships and 600 men at the recently founded Spanish fort, St. Augustine. Menéndez knew that his biggest enemy was Ribault and decided to pursue him; after destroying Fort Caroline (20 September 1565), and throwing out the French prisoners with Laudonnière at the head, he put to the sword nearly 200 Huguenots who had sailed into a cove later named Matanzas, 18 miles from St. Augustine (29 September). A little while after, Ribault, who had sailed up the coast in command of a decimated and hungry crew unawaredly stopped at the same place where days before the above-mentioned slaughter took place. Menéndez, on discovering Ribault's whereabouts, thanks to his Indian friends, confronted the French captain, and held a long and unsuccessful negotiation that ended on 12 October with the killing of the majority of the French, including Ribault.

Felipe del Pozo-Redondo

References

Eugene Lyon, *The Enterprise of Florida: Pedro Menéndez de Avilés and the Spanish Conquest of 1565–1568* (1976); Jean Parker Waterbury, ed., *The Oldest City: St. Augustine, Saga of Survivals* (1983); Antoine Tibesar, ed., "A Spy's Report on the Expedition of Jean Ribault to Florida, 1565," *The Americas* 11 (1955):589–592.

See also CHARLESFORT (SOUTH CAROLINA); FLORIDA; LAUDONNIÈRE, RENÉ GOULAINE DE; MENÉNDEZ DE AVILÉS, PEDRO; PORT ROYAL (SOUTH CAROLINA); SANTA ELENA

Fort Richmond (Maine)
First erected in 1719, Fort Richmond was later enlarged in 1723 and further updated in 1740. It was situated on the west side of the Kennebec River about 25 miles from the coast at the present town of Richmond. It was designed to safeguard the settlements of the lower Kennebec

River and Merrymeeting Bay. Although not directly attacked, a skirmish occurred in the area during Dummer's War. At the end of that war a trading house was established at the fort to conduct business with the Indians. The fort was basically dismantled by 1755.

David L. Whitesell

See also DUMMER'S WAR

Rigaud de Vaudreuil de Cavagnial, Pierre de, Marquis de Vaudreuil (1698–1778)

A Canadian-born French nobleman, Vaudreuil was the last governor general of New France and the director of the defense of Canada against the British during most of the Seven Years' War. The son of Philippe de Rigaud de Vaudreuil, who governed that colony between 1703 and 1725, he was commissioned ensign in the colonial garrison in 1708 at the age of ten, and propelled by family influence to the rank of captain in 1715.

The young captain formed part of a delegation that circumnavigated Lake Ontario and conducted negotiations with the Senecas and Onondagas in 1721 to secure permission to construct Fort Niagara. In 1727, he served in an expedition against the Fox that took him to Michilimackinac and Green Bay. Vaudreuil began his second career as a colonial administrator in 1733, with a successful, if uneventful, term as governor of Trois Rivières that ended in 1742. Possessed of a solid background in administration, military affairs and Amerindian relations, he was appointed governor of Louisiana.

He arrived in New Orleans in 1743, and within a year was forced to cope with the challenges posed by the outbreak of the War of the Austrian Succession. The forts of the colony were in bad condition, artillery and munitions in short supply, the garrison weak, and Louisiana itself surrounded by increasingly pro-British Amerindian nations. Vaudreuil did what he could to set the defenses in order, against a much-apprehended British invasion that never arrived. In spite of his best efforts, the difficulties of navigation on the Mississippi continued to pose a greater obstacle to a potential enemy than the small French garrison.

During the war, the Choctaw, the largest nation in lower Louisiana, were drawn by an increasingly influential pro-British faction toward alliance with the British, and began to attack French traders and settlements. Vaudreuil possessed neither the military power to compel, nor the trade goods to purchase, the allegiance of the Choctaw. He resorted to vigorous diplomacy and supporting pro-French elements of that tribe in attacks on British traders and an ugly civil war between Choctaw factions. This fratricidal strife lasted until 1750, and ended with the survivors firmly in the French alliance.

As governor of Louisiana, Vaudreuil was responsible for French interests throughout the Mississippi basin, and deeply concerned by the penetration of British traders into upper Louisiana and the possibility that they might establish a permanent presence in the Ohio Valley. He proposed several times that a French fort be built there, where it would be "the key to the colony and a barrier to the ambitions of the English," but lacked both the necessary resources and support from France. Vaudreuil was, however, able to reinforce the Illinois garrison and send officers to each major tribe in the Illinois area to strengthen their ties with the French. When the French finally took decisive action in the Ohio Valley in the 1750s, the situation there had deteriorated to the point that the establishment of a strong French presence provoked open warfare with the British.

Vaudreuil left Louisiana in 1753 and returned to France. After two years in Paris, he was appointed governor general of New France, and landed at Quebec on 23 June 1755.

Once again he found himself responsible for the uncertain destiny of a colony at war. As governor general, Vaudreuil was commander in chief of the French armed forces in North America and responsible for the defense of Canada. The first clash between the French and British had taken place in the Ohio Valley in 1754. The French had won that encounter, but a year later the colony was threatened by four British offensives. With the garrison of this isolated colony heavily outnumbered by British troops on land, and threatened with blockade by sea that might at any moment interrupt the flow of supplies without which New France could not survive, the outlook for the French was hardly encouraging.

So serious was the plight of Canada and so great the stress of governing the colony under wartime conditions that the new governor general became extremely discouraged, and in 1756, seriously considered asking for recall or declaring himself an invalid, abandoning his career, and returning to his estates in France. Instead, Vaudreuil persevered and pursued an

R

aggressive strategy that made the best possible use of the limited human and material resources available to him and of the geography of northeastern North America.

British armies could reach Canada only by traversing the wide belt of mountains and forests that separated French and British North America. The rival colonies were linked by river systems that gave the French interior lines of communications along a network of waterways and channeled British attacks along three linear axes of advance. Canadian militiamen were available to man the fleets of canoes and *bateaux* that carried troops and supplies along these waterways from the central colony to the frontiers. Thousands of Amerindians were willing to serve alongside the French as scouts and raiders. Regulars from the colonial garrison and metropolitan battalions provided soldiers trained in conventional warfare.

Displaying the same ruthlessness against Anglo-American colonies as he had against the pro-British Choctaws, Vaudreuil used his Amerindian allies (together with some Canadians) to take the war to the enemy, compel them to divert resources to defend themselves, deny them the luxury of an inviolate base area from which to prepare offensives against Canada, and perhaps bring the war to a conclusion, with French North America intact—"Nothing," he wrote in 1756, "would more effectively sicken the peoples of these colonies [of the war], and make them desire to return of peace."

As the irregulars flayed the Anglo-American border settlements, Vaudreuil used his conventional forces to defend the central colony. In this theater, he remained on the defensive, even when acting aggressively. With Canada under constant threat of invasion by numerically superior British forces, Vaudreuil sought to conserve his limited resources by avoiding direct confrontations with the British main body, and taking advantage of interior lines of communication to achieve local superiority for a series of limited offensives that drove the British back over the St. Lawrence watershed and destroyed their advance bases on the frontier before they could be used as staging points for invasions of Canada.

Vaudreuil, however, lacked an equally sound strategy for dealing with opponents on a second front, against the officers of the metropolitan troops that had been sent to Canada to reinforce the colonial garrison. This was a serious problem, since circumstances forced him to depend upon these officers to implement his strategy.

As commander in chief, the strategic direction of the war was in Vaudreuil's hands. Tactical control of the French forces, on the other hand, was entrusted to senior metropolitan officers. This was necessitated by the fact that the colonial garrison was organized in independent companies, led by subalterns, while the metropolitan battalions, led by lieutenant colonels, were accompanied by a number of general officers, all of whom outranked the colonials. Unfortunately for Vaudreuil, while the metropolitan officers were experienced in handling large bodies of troops in conventional warfare, their individual abilities were counterbalanced by defeatism and lack of familiarity with North American conditions.

The persistent recalcitrance of Louis-Joseph Montcalm, marquis de Montcalm, the commander of the metropolitan regulars, was a continual source of concern for Vaudreuil. Not only did he consistently challenge Vaudreuil's authority, he disagreed with Vaudreuil's basic strategy and would have preferred to suspend operations on the frontier and concentrate French forces in the central colony in hope of saving a fragment, instead of forcing the British to fight past a series of obstacles to reach Canada.

Constantly at odds with Montcalm, Vaudreuil was more fortunate in his subordinates in the colonial service. François Bigot, the intendant, responsible for the civil and military administration of the colony, mixed public and private affairs in a way that was conventional for civil servants in the eighteenth century, but would be considered rather creative today. But he was an efficient bureaucrat, who presided over a well-organized administrative machine that in spite of every difficulty managed to keep the French forces adequately provided with munitions and provisions. Bigot's confederate, Joseph Cadet, continued to transport supplies to Canada after the French navy had ceased to escort convoys. Vaudreuil could also rely on an experienced cadre of veteran Canadian officers, in particular François-Charles de Bourlamaque. In each of his victories, Montcalm was assisted by one or both of these officers, whose presence compensated for some of his failings as a commander.

Vaudreuil characterized his conduct of the war as cautious and conservative, informing the minister of marine in 1755 that "War in this country is different from the war in Europe. We are obliged to act with great circumspection so as not to leave anything to chance; we have few men, and however small the numbers we may lose, we feel its effects." His offensives against the British were noted for the collection of detailed and accurate intelligence, careful planning and preparation, swift execution, and successful results.

On his arrival in 1755, Vaudreuil found his resources badly strained by the need to defend two frontiers, on Lake Ontario and Lake Champlain. He intended to carry out a plan by his predecessor to destroy Oswego, but the need to redeploy his forces on Lake Champlain to block an invasion compelled him to remain on the defensive. In 1756, however, the destruction of Oswego eliminated the threat of a British offensive on Lake Ontario, and allowed Vaudreuil to concentrate all of his forces on Lake Champlain to destroy Fort William Henry in 1757, and halt a British offensive at Fort Carillon in 1758. So successful was Vaudreuil's direction of the war that during the early years of the conflict, at times it seemed as if British, rather than French, North America was threatened with defeat and conquest.

The survival of New France depended less on inflicting defeats upon the British than in holding out until hostilities ended in Europe. New France lacked the recuperative powers of the British colonies. For with their large populations and economic strength, together with much more generous assistance and reinforcements from Britain, the British in North America could suffer severe defeats, year after year, and still bounce back, rebuild their forts, and send new armies of regulars and provincials back again and again to hammer at the gates of Canada until finally they succeeded. Canada, on the other hand, remained vulnerable to a single defeat. Vaudreuil's forces were stretched too thin to prevent the capture of Fort Duquesne and Fort Frontenac in 1758. But it was only in 1759 and 1760 that the British were once again able to make simultaneous attacks on the St. Lawrence, Lake Champlain, and Lake Ontario approaches to Canada.

It was at Quebec that the French met with decisive defeat. Even if the British offensive up Lake Champlain had succeeded, only the conquest of Quebec could give them control of Canada. Vaudreuil's greatest error as governor general was to fail to apply the strategy of defense in depth that he employed in the interior

and adequately fortify the lower St. Lawrence. Batteries at key points along the river could delay an enemy fleet, a factor of critical importance, since besiegers had only a limited time in the river before they would be compelled to withdraw by the onset of winter. Failure to do so allowed James Wolfe and Charles Saunders to ascend unopposed to Quebec. This mistake was shared with others, but as governor general, Vaudreuil held the ultimate responsibility.

Vaudreuil confided the tactical direction of the defense of Quebec to Montcalm and François-Gaston de Lévis. His second major error of the war was to allow Lévis to leave to organize the defense of Montreal after the fall of Fort Niagara. However necessary the defense of that town might be, Lévis's departure left the direction for the defense in the hands of Montcalm, in whom Vaudreuil had entirely lost confidence. In each of his previous victories, Montcalm had been supported by Lévis and Bourlamaque. Now he was on his own, without a reliable senior subordinate, and the results proved unfortunate. When Wolfe took up a precarious position on the Plains of Abraham, Montcalm disregarded Vaudreuil's instructions to await the concentration of the entire French army before taking action, and lost the battle in a single disastrous charge. After the Battle of the Plains of Abraham, Vaudreuil attempted to rally the French forces to continue to resist, but the surviving officers preferred to retreat. With Montcalm dead, command of the metropolitan battalions based to Lévis, and Vaudreuil's difficulties with French officers ended. In 1760, Vaudreuil and Lévis planned to attempt to recover Quebec. Lévis won the Battle of Sainte-Foy and besieged Quebec, but success depended on the arrival of assistance from France that never came. Instead, the Royal Navy lifted the siege, and Lévis withdrew toward Montreal.

With French possessions reduced to the town of Montreal, surrounded by an overwhelming British force under Jeffrey Amherst, Vaudreuil was forced to surrender. Amherst adamantly refused to grant the French the honors of war on account of atrocities committed against British civilians by Amerindians allied to the French. Unhappy with the terms offered by the British, Vaudreuil's senior metropolitan officers wanted to make a token gesture of resistance, in order to secure more honorable terms and protect their reputations and careers.

Vaudreuil had received strict orders to make the preservation of the honor of the French army his first priority if he were compelled to negotiate a capitulation. To accept Amherst's terms meant courting the wrath of the king, but to resist would expose the town of Montreal to siege and storm and Canadian civilians and the last French troops to pointless death. Rather than quibble over points of honor, Vaudreuil made certain that the rights of Canadians to their religion, property, and laws were safeguarded by the articles of capitulation. On 8 September, he surrendered Canada to the British.

Rather than acclamation as a hero who had defended New France under the most difficult conditions, Vaudreuil found himself under arrest in 1762 and made a scapegoat for the loss of Canada. Acquitted within a year and granted a pension to compensate him for his arrest and trial, Vaudreuil lived out the remainder of his life at his Paris residence. It is ironic, and more than a little unjust, that Montcalm, rather than Vaudreuil, is now best remembered as the leader of the defense of Canada during the Seven Years' War.

D. Peter MacLeod

References

Bill Barron, ed., *The Vaudreuil Papers: A Calendar and Index of the Personal and Private Records of Pierre de Rigaud de Vaudreuil, Royal Governor of the French Province of Louisiana, 1743–1753* (1975); Luca Codignola, "Montcalm, Vaudreuil e la Guerra per bande (1755–1758)," in Luca Codignola, ed., *Canadiana: aspetti della storia e della letteratura canadese a cura de Luca Cogignola* (1978):41–55; Jean Delmas, ed., *Conflits de societés au Canada français pendant la guerre de sept ans et leur influence sur les operations* (1978).

W.J. Eccles, "Pierre de Rigaud de Vaudreuil de Cavagnial, Marquis de Vaudreuil," in F.G. Halpenny, ed., *Dictionary of Canadian Biography, Vol. IV, 1771 to 1800* (1979):662–674; ———, "Louis-Joseph de Montcalm, Marquis de Montcalm," in F.G. Halpenny, ed., *Dictionary of Canadian Biography, Vol. III, 1741 to 1770* (1974):458–469; Guy Frégault, *Canada: The War of the Conquest*, trans. by Margaret M. Cameron (1969); ———, *Le Grand Marquis: Pierre de Rigaud de Vaudreuil et la Louisiane* (1952).

Francis Jennings, *Empire of Fortune: Crowns, Colonies, and Tribes in the Seven Years War in America* (1988); D. Peter MacLeod, "The Canadians Against the French: The Struggle for Control of the Expedition to Oswego in 1756," *Ontario History*, Vol. LXXX (1988): 144–157; George F.G. Stanley, *New France: The Last Phase, 1744–1760* (1968); Richard White, *The Roots of Dependency: Subsistence, Environment, and Social Change Among the Choctaws, Pawnees, and Navajos* (1983).

See also BOURLAMAQUE, FRANÇOIS-CHARLES DE; CHOCTAW; CHOCTAW CIVIL WAR; FORT DUQUESNE (PENNSYLVANIA); FORT FRONTENAC (ONTARIO, CANADA); LÉVIS, FRANÇOIS-GASTON DE; LOUISIANA; MONTCALM-GOZON DE SAINT-VERAN, LOUIS-JOSEPH; SEVEN YEARS' WAR; FORT WILLIAM HENRY (NEW YORK)

Right of Conquest

While most Europeans of the sixteenth through eighteenth centuries endorsed the concept of the "right of conquest," their colonial practices toward Indians differed markedly. Indeed, the concept of ownership of land through military conquest or successful invasion had been a part of European diplomatic and political thinking since the Roman world. However, the American colonies experienced vastly different applications of this theory in policies that various colonial authorities established.

In the thirteen British colonies the theory of right of conquest was generally accepted, as evidenced in colonial attitudes of superiority, but was not always immediately employed regarding Indian lands. In addition, demographics and geographic location played important roles in determining how and when Indian lands were seized. Generally, while European populations remained small and were militarily weaker than surrounding tribes, the practical application of the right of conquest was set aside. As colonial populations increased, so did aggressive and domineering behavior toward Indians and their lands. Generally, as European populations grew, Indian populations decreased due to disease and warfare. Such decline among Indians strengthened colonial populations. Finally, when nearby Indians ceased to threaten colonial security, colonial officials employed the theories of the right of conquest and seized Indian lands with little or no resistance.

Yet, seizures of Indian lands also varied according to geographic location. In New England, Puritans settled in an already depopulated area, and because of their strict religious beliefs, took a harsh stance regarding Indians and Indian culture. New England colonists depersonalized Indians in order to rationalize seizures of Indians lands—in effect a variation on the right by conquest theme wherein civilization conquered the uncivilized.

In contrast to New England, southern colonial land acquisitions were products of flexible attitudes toward Indian character; the "noble" versus "savage" Indian. These conflicting images divided over the "right" of Englishmen to claim Indian lands as their own; when colonial desire for land was greatest, the image of savagery prevailed. Ultimately, these shifting viewpoints resulted in land purchases, or, like the New Englanders, denial of Indian humanity and subsequent seizure of land.

Situated midway between New England and the far southern colonies was Maryland. While geographically and culturally a southern colony, Maryland set its own course of land acquisitions. In the beginning of settlement, Lord Baltimore (Cecil Calvert) established guidelines for his colonists to follow regarding Indian relations. While designed to maintain peace between colonists and Indians, Baltimore's rules also softened the harsh philosophy and practice of right of conquest. Indeed, while this theory supported Baltimore's exclusive control of all land in Maryland, he realized the impracticality of seizing Indian lands outright. Instead, lands in Maryland were purchased from Indians during the early years (c. 1630s–1640s), and later were acquired through the treaty-making process, once Marylanders gained superiority over the local tribes. Ultimately, colonial will was imposed on severely reduced tribes through the legislative process.

In addition to the prescribed purchase of Indian lands, Baltimore prohibited private individuals from taking Indian lands, whether through purchase, gift, or force. This injunction further reinforced Baltimore's control over all land in the colony, and was not much different than similar laws in other colonies. Yet, colonists did manage to acquire Indian lands outside of proprietary control. Allowing cattle to trample Indian crops and seizing Indian lands when the tribesmen retaliated was a common means of land acquisition in Maryland and throughout the colonies. Likewise, surrounding Indian villages with colonial settlement, then seizing the land when the natives left for seasonal migrations, was another means of rapid land acquisition. Yet, the justification for these and other methods of land seizures relied on that basic premise—that colonial lands belonged to the British through right of conquest.

Overall, while the theory of right of conquest was the underlying justification for all colonial land acquisitions, colonies used varied means to acquire those lands. Indeed, most colonial lands were acquired through purchase, treaty making, and trickery. Only on occasion was outright military force or aggression the primary means of colonial land acquisition, thus masking, but not significantly altering, the theory of right of conquest.

Debra R. Boender

References

James Axtell, *The European and the Indian: Essays in the Ethnohistory of Colonial North America* (1981); Debra Ruth Boender, "Our Fires Have Nearly Gone Out: A History of Indian-White Relations on the Colonial Maryland Frontier, 1633–1776," Ph.D. Dissertation, University of New Mexico (1988); Richard Beale Davis, *Intellectual Life in the Colonial South, 1585–1763,* 3 vols. (1978), I.

Francis Jennings, *The Invasion of America: Indians, Colonialism, and the Cant of Conquest* (1975); Francis Paul Prucha, *The Great Father: The United States Government and the American Indian* (1984); W. Stitt Robinson, *The Southern Colonial Frontier, 1607–1763* (1979); Neal Salisbury, *Manitou and Providence: Indians, Europeans, and the Making of New England* (1982).

Roanoke Island (North Carolina)

Roanoke Island, located between the North Carolina mainland and the barrier islands known as the Outer Banks, was the site of the first English attempts to colonize the New World. It was first explored by a two-ship expedition in the summer of 1584, shortly after Walter Raleigh, the expedition's sponsor, had acquired a patent from Queen Elizabeth granting him the right to establish a colony. The next summer, Raleigh put together a seven-ship expedition, under the overall command of Richard Grenville. After losing valuable supplies on the trip from England, Grenville returned to England, leaving a 108-man military colony on the island, under the command of Ralph Lane. The colony suffered from food shortages, spent an excessive amount of time looking for metal, and alienated previously friendly Indians. Thus, when Sir Francis Drake unexpectedly arrived in the spring of 1586 with a large fleet, fresh from a series of raids against Spanish properties in Florida, Lane elected to abandon the colony and return to England.

Ironically, Grenville arrived with supplies only a few weeks after Lane's departure. In order to maintain an English presence in the area, he left 15 men on Roanoke Island and also returned to England. These men were quickly attacked by hostile Indians and killed.

Raleigh then decided to switch his focus north to the Chesapeake region, an area that promised more security from the Spanish and better agricultural conditions. This colony was planned to be more self-sufficient than the earlier attempt, and would be under the command of artist and Lane colony veteran John White. It was scheduled to make a brief stop at Roanoke Island in the summer of 1587 in order to consult with the men left by Grenville. However, for reasons never fully explained, Simon Fernandes, captain of the fleet, refused to transport the colony to the Chesapeake.

The White colony was thus stranded on Roanoke Island. It consisted of about 117 settlers, including 17 women and nine children. Two babies were born in short order, including White's celebrated granddaughter Virginia Dare, on 18 August. When hostilities with the Indians resumed, White made a difficult trip back to England for more supplies. His return to Roanoke Island was delayed repeatedly by England's war with Spain. When he finally arrived in August 1590, he found the colony abandoned. Bad weather intervened, and White was compelled to leave. Later attempts at finding the so-called "Lost Colony" were haphazard and unsuccessful. Many historians are convinced that the majority of the colony eventually made its way to the Chesapeake region, where they lived until slaughtered by Powhatan in 1607, shortly before the arrival of the Jamestown colony.

Despite their failure, the Roanoke voyages produced important books, drawings, and maps, adding considerably to the English knowledge of North America.

Jim Sumner

References
David Durant, *Raleigh's Lost Colony* (1981); Michael Foss, *Undreamed Shores:*

England's Wasted Empire in America (1974); Paul Hulton, *America 1585: The Complete Drawings of John White* (1984); David Beers Quinn, ed., *The Roanoke Voyages, 1584–1590*, 2 vols. (1955); ———, *Set Fair for Roanoke: Voyages and Colonies, 1584–1606* (1985).

See also FORT RALEIGH (NORTH CAROLINA)

Robertson, James (c. 1717–1788)
Born in Scotland to middle-class parents, James Robertson enlisted in the British military as a volunteer and rose through the ranks to reach the position of lieutenant general, one of the few commoners to achieve that exalted rank. Robertson came to America with Sir John Campbell, earl of Loudoun, commander in chief of British forces from 1756 to late 1757. A valued member of Loudoun's staff, Robertson remained in America and served under succeeding commanders James Abercromby, Jeffrey Amherst, and Thomas Gage. Following the French and Indian War, Robertson was appointed barrack master general of the British army in America and became a colonel-commandant of the 60th Regiment in 1776. During the American Revolution, Robertson rose from brigadier general to major general and to lieutenant general. In 1780, he was appointed civil governor of occupied New York, but the authority he exercised in that province continued to rest on his military position. Robertson returned to England in April 1783 and died in London in 1788.

Not much is known about Robertson's early life, or even when he entered the British army. He either entered or shortly moved to the marines, a decidedly new and secondary military branch, where he was apparently promoted from sergeant to second lieutenant in 1739. Serving in the West Indies during the War of Jenkins' Ear, Robertson won promotion to first lieutenant on 9 April 1742, having been among the few in his regiment to survive the disastrous British expedition against Cartagena. Robertson is known to have served in the Scottish Highlands during the Jacobite uprisings of 1745–1756, where he apparently made the acquaintance of Campbell. He was appointed captain in September 1745, transferred to a regiment headed by Loudoun, and served with his regiment on constabulary duty in Ireland.

Robertson's association with Loudoun brought him to America in 1755 as a major in the 62nd Regiment, known as the Royal Americans. Although a junior officer, Robertson served on Loudoun's staff as supply officer. In 1756, Robertson supervised the transfer of Loudoun's troops and supplies to America, where he would make his career as a hard-working staff officer serving a succession of commanding generals from 1756 until the end of the America Revolution. As a supply officer, Robertson understood early on the most crucial factors in the French and Indian War were obtaining supplies and moving both troops and provisions through the American wilderness. In fact, Robertson became Loudoun's chief aide, obtaining the rank of lieutenant colonel in America. He also served as acting deputy quartermaster general in the place of the sickly incumbent, Sir John St. Clair. Under commanding General James Abercromby, Robertson became deputy quartermaster general and continued to hold that position after General Jeffrey Amherst succeeded Abercromby as commanding general in late 1758.

Robertson also became General Amherst's chief aide, having considerable responsibility, especially with regard to procurement and transportation. He helped Amherst plan the 1759 campaign against Ticonderoga and Crown Point, and as Amherst's chief of staff, Robertson was primarily in charge of getting troops and materials from New York City to Albany, thereby involving himself in a multitude of procurement arrangements. Among other important duties, Robertson served as Amherst's inspector general, evaluating all public accounts before Amherst endorsed them for payment. A skilled troubleshooter, Robertson mediated the dispute between the artillery and engineers over gun platforms during the Ticonderoga expedition, persuaded New York troops to return guns loaned them by the royal armory, convinced the Pennsylvania assembly to raise troops during Pontiac's War, and supervised the military transfer of Florida from Spanish to British rule. Indeed, Robertson was becoming what historian John Shy called "the apparently indispensable staff officer to be found in almost any headquarters, the man who seems to be running the organization by sheer energy and factual knowledge of every problem."

Unlike most other British officers, Robertson won his rank not by influence but by merit.

However, his former commanders, Loudoun and Amherst, were influential and became Robertson's chief patrons. In 1760, Amherst secured for Robertson a lieutenant colonelcy in the 15th Regiment, and General Gage, who succeeded Amherst as commanding general in America, found Robertson every bit as invaluable as Sir Jeffrey had. Gage urged that Robertson be appointed barrack master general, a position created by the Quartering Act passed by Parliament in 1765. In fact, many of the suggestions embodied in the Quartering Act had been made by Robertson himself, whose long service in America made him a respected expert advisor on such matters. As barrack master general, Robertson oversaw a large department charged with the care of the permanent barracks in America. This entailed buying furniture and bedding, cooking stoves and utensils, and fuel and candles. During the years from 1768 to 1774, Robertson, as barrack master general, dispensed at least £100,000 for supplies and services.

As a most important member of the British general staff, Robertson moved in the highest economic and social circles in America. By the time of the American Revolution, he had become fairly wealthy through his various business connections. He owned several thousand acres of land in New York and had loaned out several thousand pounds sterling. At long last, in 1776, he became a colonel-commandant of a regular regiment, which disqualified him from continuing as barrack master general. Robertson remained, however, on the command staff of both Generals Gage and Howe as the War for Independence began. He served as commandant of Boston in 1775, commanded a brigade during the Battle of Long Island, and became commandant of occupied New York City in 1776.

The American Revolution definitely expedited Robertson's rise in rank from brigadier general to major general to lieutenant general. However, the rupture between Britain and its American colonies threatened everything, including Robertson's respected position in the British military establishment and his colonial investments. He urged compromise, once the military struggle began, and became a primary exponent, along with lawyer William Smith, of the resurrection of civil government in New York under British auspices. Smith and Robertson sold their idea to the North ministry, and in 1780, Robertson was named civil governor of New York. But the opposition of commander in chief Henry Clinton prevented Robertson from acting as civil governor, Clinton instead preferring that Robertson administer the occupied portions of the province as lieutenant general on his staff. The death of his only daughter in childbirth, plus the failure of the British in America, plunged the aging general into the depths of depression. He left America in early 1783, and died in London in 1788.

Ronald W. Howard

References

William G. Godfrey, *Pursuit of Profit and Preferment in Colonial North America: John Bradstreet's Quest* (1982); Virginia D. Harrington, *The New York Merchant on the Eve of the Revolution* (1935); Milton M. Klein and Ronald W. Howard, eds., *The Twilight of British Rule in Revolutionary America: The New York Letter Book of General James Robertson, 1780–1783* (1982).

Douglas Edward Leach, *Roots of Conflict: British Armed Forces and Colonial Americans, 1677–1763* (1986); Stanley M. Pargellis, ed., *Military Affairs in North America, 1748–1765* (1936); Ian Kenneth Steele, "The European Contest for North America," in *Encyclopedia of the North American Colonies*, ed., Jacob Ernest Cooke, 3 vols. (1993), II:271–288.

See also CAMPBELL, JOHN; CARTAGENA, EXPEDITION AGAINST; INSPECTOR GENERAL; QUARTERMASTER GENERAL

Rogers, Robert (1731–1795)

By its very nature, modern warfare offers little in the way of romance; however, the exploits of hard-hitting assault and reconnaissance units (commandos, chindits, American special forces, Soviet *spetsnaz*) are replete with elements of derring-do. These groups are generally light infantry specializing in long-distance penetration of enemy-held territory; self-contained and deliberately independent of extensive logistics trains. They pride themselves on speed, surprise, initiative, and resourcefulness. Their prime utility is to disrupt enemy supply and support areas, gather intelligence, serve as flanking forces, or operate as rear guards for a retiring friendly force.

An early prototype for these groups was that band of troops known collectively as Rogers' Rangers, of the French and Indian War (1754–1763). Comprised of selected levies from the American provinces, and leavened with an interspersing of attached British regulars and Indians, the rangers were officially activated in 1755 and served intact until the war's end.

No single individual so characterized the ranger type as did the unit commander himself, Major Robert Rogers. It can be said that he cut a mold from which other charismatic leaders (e.g., O.C. Wingate in Burma) were later cast. He was born in 1731 to Scotch-Irish settlers living in Massachusetts's lower Merrimack Valley, and grew up along the frontier to the west of the middle valley, in New Hampshire.

Having established itself as a separate political entity only late in the seventeenth century, New Hampshire was a wild and dangerous place during Rogers's formative years. Only seven years before his birth, New Hampshiremen and others had destroyed Norridgewock town on neighboring Maine's Penobscot River; many Abenaki inhabitants of that town had subsequently dispersed to the Canadian mission of St. Francis. In 1725, colonial survivors of the vicious fight with Pigwacket Indians at Lovewell's Pond in Maine had come straggling back to the Merrimack with accounts of their frightful adventure. Tales from such events must have been part of local lore when Rogers, at age 14, first enlisted in the militia, called out to fight other bands of Abenakis and their cohorts.

The frontier environment was fluid, agrarian, one in which squatters' rights, self-reliance, and self-defense were tenets of daily existence. Six feet tall in stature and by all accounts a physically rugged individual, Rogers was in his element. He presumably developed his legendary tracking skills during his youth and early manhood. By his twenties, he was homesteading near present-day Dunbarton Center, a settlement crossroads between Portsmouth and the fort at Number Four, below Charles Town on the Connecticut River. He also became enmired in transactions and charges related to counterfeiting, but he was acquitted. It was the kind of shortcoming that would eventually attach more and more to his later reputation. When the call arose soon after this episode for recruits to join a 1755 British expedition against Crown Point, he may have fairly leapt at the opportunity to leave his troubles behind him.

Because the New England contingent in which he was a company commander had been delayed in its march to the New York theater of operations, Rogers was not involved in William (later Sir William) Johnson's desperate repulse of the French under Jean-Armand Dieskau at the Battle of Lake George (8 September 1755). However, seeking to rationalize inaction in pursuit of the retiring French force, Johnson chose him to scout for the presence of the enemy and their Indian allies; checked but hardly destroyed, the French had withdrawn northwards, to Ticonderoga and Crown Point, both of which they heavily fortified. Rogers's career as a ranger began with this phase of the campaign.

He soon became famous for his ability to enter the wilderness, pinpoint enemy outposts, bring back seized material or prisoners/scalps, and return with generally few casualties. While his exploits would carry him as far as the Michilimackinac and Ohio countries, most of his wartime ranging took part in present-day Essex, Warren, and Washington Counties, New York. This is a vast area of some 3,500 square miles: rocky, forested, cut through by numerous lakes and streams, and traversed then by few roads or tracks. In the struggle for mastery of the continent, whichever side could force its way through this strategic terrain would then be astride either the vital northward routes, the Richelieu and the St. Lawrence, or southward down the Hudson. Because both sides were stalemated in this area through most of the war, Rogers's tactics and mobility made him immediately conspicuous.

From 1755 to 1759, Rogers and his men, gradually expanded from one company to more than seven, were a formidable foe. Clad in the green of woodsmen, adorned with characteristic headgear "cropped to leave only a skull covering and a flap in front," well-armed with regulation muskets and both tomahawk and knife, they must have been fearsome to encounter in the forest. Whether traveling in groups of three or four, or 50, or more than 100, they could slip up the environs of Lake George by whaleboat, canoe, skates, snowshoes, or on foot. In distinct contrast to most colonial levies, Rogers and many of his men continued in the field, year after year, through all weather and seasons. He seems to have been one of the few noteworthy provincial figures, besides George Washington and John Bradstreet, to have chosen an active military career for the entire war.

He codified his methods, which were mostly successful. He could suffer grievous losses, such as at "The Battle of the Snowshoes," or experience significant attrition and deprivation, such as after "The Battle of the St. Francis," yet he was always soon back again in the thick of things. It is perhaps because he reached such heights of public esteem that his end seems to be so ignominious.

It was expensive keeping a force like the rangers fitted and supplied. Rogers unwisely took on the financial burden to do so; in this, he may have been encouraged by his superiors. As had his predecessors—William Johnson, William Shirley, Lord Loudoun, and James Abercromby—General Jeffrey Amherst as North American commander in chief made the rangers his eyes and ears in the Lake George arena. It was Amherst who sent the rangers on their mission to St. Francis, who utilized them again in the various operations that reduced French fortifications along the Richelieu, and who authorized Rogers to accept Detroit's surrender once all French activities east of there had been suppressed. From the nature of these missions, as well as the tenor of his correspondence with the ranger leader, it is clear that Amherst held Rogers in high regard. However, when the accounts for pay and equipment came due, Amherst either would not or could not reimburse him adequately. Rogers also failed to get sufficient compensation from the various colonial assemblies, including New Hampshire's, which he had served. The financial difficulties that would hound him into penury began at this time.

He emerged from the war a full-fledged hero. He also had become a married man; his new wife of 1761 was the former Elizabeth Browne, daughter of Portsmouth, New Hampshire's, Episcopalian rector. He seemed only to require a suitable venue for continuing his life on an heroic scale.

Neither an overland traverse from Ohio to Fort Pitt, nor brief service against the Cherokee in Carolina, nor gallantry in rescuing his small detachment from Pontiac's besieging forces at Detroit in 1763 propelled Rogers into any position that was secure or lasting. He tried his hand at wilderness trading partnership, then land speculation; both ended in failure, and the latter venture brought him to the disapproving attention of an influential rival speculator, Sir William Johnson.

The late war, with all its distresses and vagaries, had at least guaranteed Rogers disciplined activity as well as patrons such as Amherst. In the reorganization of British North American operations that followed the war, Amherst's place was taken by General Thomas Gage. Gage had certainly been less than enthralled by the daring ranger's military exploits; moreover, the general allied himself with Johnson, now the appointed overseer to His Majesty's loyal Indian subjects. Neither Gage nor Johnson were dangerously corrupt, yet in the spirit of the times both were committed to preserving the status quo of their personal interests, which paralleled the crown's. They would not tolerate any threat to their authority.

Rogers, meanwhile, had slipped away from his creditors and reached England during 1765. He spent that same year utilizing his yet-considerable prowess to track down another sort of prey: royal favor. One can imagine Rogers in Hanoverian London, living off his recent reputation among the clamorous throng of courtiers, schemers, and other lobbyists. During this busy year, he also managed to write his memoirs of the French war, which were generally well received. He sold at least part of his proposal, to search for a Northwest Passage to the Orient through the Great Lakes, to Charles Townshend, who had replaced Pitt at the War Ministry. When Rogers returned to America in early 1766, it was as the new commandant for the post at the straits between Lakes Huron and Michigan, Michilimackinac.

His leadership style and organizational skills won him a small coterie of followers among the military people and civilian traders at the post. Though in combat he had been a mortal adversary to the Indians, peacetime showed him to have astute methods for dealing with them on a daily basis; he was even able to settle disputes between some of the regional tribes. Had he continued in his position, it is likely he would have written new discoveries onto the contemporary maps (although the Northwest Passage would have eluded him), and fixed a place for himself in the annals of exploration. However, he soon ran afoul of several underlings with ties to Gage or Johnson; trumped-up charges of treason, misappropriation of funds, etc., led to his being relieved of duties, imprisoned, then brought to Montreal for a trial that began 20 October 1768. The charges were that Rogers had,

> contrary to his Duty and Allegiance to his King and Country, formed designs of a Traiterous and Dangerous nature of Deserting to the French . . . [and had] undertaken expensive Schemes and projects, and lavished away money amongst the Savages, contrary to his Instructions . . .

That he was acquitted was a small victory indeed, because he was neither completely exonerated nor reinstated to his position. At a time when his fellow Americans were getting a rude introduction to independence in the form of such events as the Boston Massacre and Tea Party, Rogers returned again to England; from 1769–1775, he remained there, suffering the degradation of debtors' prison and practically having to beg His Majesty's officials for a pension at half-pay from the war. His life plans seem to have become no more than a means toward an end unknown even to himself; he drifted back to America in 1775, a vague embodied reminder of some previous generation's heroism and causes.

He wandered, that seminal year of 1775, between the two fires of the rudimentary patriot forces and the loyalists or British, between Philadelphia, Albany, Boston, and New York. He seemed half-asleep to the notion there was revolution in the air, seeking as he did a further source of income or possible land grants. Both sides were suspicious of his motives, remembering who he had been and uncertain how to make use of him in his current lowered status. Even General Washington, often willing to turn a blind side to the shortcomings of useful subordinates, had Rogers watched, interrogated, and finally imprisoned as a suspected enemy agent. As the Continental Congress was in the process of turning him over to New Hampshire authorities for disposition, he escaped to the British. In August 1776, as his forces were about to descend on Long Island, General Richard Howe (younger brother to the Viscount Howe, whom Rogers had accompanied against Ticonderoga some 18 years previously) elevated Rogers to a new command: He was to raise a battalion to be called the Queen's Rangers.

This would prove to be his last chance at regaining any semblance of glory under arms. While the Queen's Rangers would later establish some laurels for themselves under John Graves Simcoe, during Rogers's brief tenure they seem to have been utilized as little more than Tory bushwhackers. Higher authorities dismissed him in 1777; in 1778, Elizabeth Rogers made public her intention to divorce him. The rest of his life can be accounted in stray bits, but rather seems like a deteriorating spiral through dissolution to oblivion. Rogers died in London in 1795, age 63.

It is probably useless, albeit interesting, to speculate on how Rogers might have otherwise ended. Those characteristics which made him such a force in the woods, on the march, above the din of musketry: supreme self-confidence, almost boundless endurance, driving ambition, and cold-blooded ruthlessness . . . none of these had been sufficiently leavened by civility or prudence; he was unable to make appropriate transition from the field to the politic sphere of balanced accounts and patronage for life. Certain elements in him were never tempered, and if this provided for him a tragic end, it has also preserved forever the wild excitement that yet attaches to his name.

Roy Marokus

References

John R. Cuneo, *Robert Rogers of the Rangers* (1959); Robert Rogers, *Journals of Major Robert Rogers*, ed. by Howard H. Peckham (1961).

See also FORT PONTCHARTRAIN DE DETROIT (MICHIGAN); PONTIAC'S WAR; RANGERS; ST. FRANCIS, BATTLE OF; SAINTE-THÉRÈSE, BATTLE OF; SCOUT; SNOWSHOES, BATTLE ON

Fort Rosalie (Mississippi)

In 1716, Jean-Baptiste Le Moyne de Bienville constructed a fort among the Natchez, a populous Indian chiefdom occupying fertile lands along the lower Mississippi River. Fort Rosalie, named in honor of the colonial minister's wife, was originally a rectangular palisade (measuring about 100 by 160 feet) built on a high hill and enclosing bark-roofed officers' quarters, guardhouse, barracks, and a magazine. During the 1720s, the fort was garrisoned by 30 men and had two small iron cannons and a brass swivel gun.

Beginning in 1719, the Company of the Indies encouraged French settlement at two concessions in the Natchez area where tobacco cultivation had proved successful. The presence of a large French farming population intermingled with Indian villages and fields led to a series of violent clashes in 1722 and 1723. Continued demands for Natchez lands by the French commandant at Fort Rosalie, Captain De Chépart, precipitated an attack on the French fort and settlement on the morning of 28 November 1729. The Natchez killed about 235 French colonists, captured another 250 French women and children and black slaves, and burned the fort and other structures. The scale of this disaster

discredited Governor Etienne Périer's Indian policy and brought Bienville to power as royal governor.

During the French siege of the Natchez that followed in February 1730, the fort was rebuilt, eventually including earthworks and a palisade. In mid-1731, baron de Crenay and his garrison were briefly besieged by a Natchez force, until 30 attackers were captured and placed in irons during a parley inside the fort. An uprising by the captives was quelled only when Crenay fired his artillery on the guardhouse.

After the Natchez War, Fort Rosalie continued as a military post until 1763, although the rainy climate kept the garrison of 50 men constantly occupied repairing the eroding earthworks.

Gregory A. Waselkov

References

Philip P. Boucher, *Les Nouvelles Frances: France in America, 1500–1815, An Imperial Perspective* (1989); Dumont dit Montigny, *Mémoires historiques sur la Louisiane* (1753); Antoine Simon Le Page Du Pratz, *The History of Louisiana* (1744); Dunbar Rowland and Albert G. Sanders, eds., *Mississippi Provincial Archives, French Dominion*, 3 vols. (1927–1932); Patricia D. Woods, *French-Indian Relations on the Southern Frontier, 1699–1762* (1980).

See also LE MOYNE DE BIENVILLE, JEAN-BAPTISTE ; NATCHEZ WAR; FORT ST. PETER (MISSISSIPPI)

Fort Royal (Virginia)

In 1645, in the aftermath of Indian attack the previous year, the Virginia assembly ordered the construction of three forts to defend against further Indian encroachment. Fort Royal was situated on the Pamunkey River in King William County, Fort Charles at the falls of the James River, and Fort James on a high ridge overlooking the Chickahominy River. The following year, the burgesses added a fourth fort to list: Fort Henry, erected at the falls of the Appomattox River, on the site of the present city of Petersburg. There was also an unnamed fort constructed south of the James River, in Nansemond County.

About 100 men were assigned to each of the first three palisaded blockhouses, with 40 garrisoning Fort Henry. The garrisons of these forts consisted of men serving a specific term at a set salary, many of whom must have been poor free laborers, for indentured servants could not leave their valuable labor, and planters would not. The troops were probably young landless men who jumped at the chance for a salary and adventure.

Their duty was twofold. Garrisons of the four forts on the north side of the James River were to prevent Indian raiding parties from moving down the peninsula toward the more settled area. In addition, whenever the opportunity presented itself, they were to join forces and move against chief Opechancanough, leader of the 1644 attack. The garrison of the Nansemond fort, joined by militia of the counties south of the James River, conducted an expedition against Indians in the Roanoke River area to the southwest.

Soon after construction of the first three forts, a message came via a captive of the Pamunkey Indians that Opechancanough wished an end to hostilities. Setting a trap for the chief, Governor William Berkeley declared a truce and arranged a meeting at Fort Royal. On the appointed day, as the Indians approached, the garrison rushed out of the fort and killed a number of Indians, but Opechancanough escaped.

Following the failure to kill Opechancanough, the assembly authorized an expedition to hunt him down, and a force of 60 militia set off from Fort Royal. Governor Berkeley himself joined the hunt, and the party captured Opechancanough and carried him to Jamestown. After an irate colonist shot the chief in the back, the English designated a successor with whom they signed a treaty in 1646.

The cost of these forts strained the colony's limited funds, and the assembly thus enacted a statute granting large tracts of land to individuals in return for promises to maintain and man the forts. Under this system the forts were soon abandoned and the land continued in private hands.

Thomas Costa

References
William L. Shea, *The Virginia Militia in the Seventeenth Century* (1983).

See also BERKELEY, WILLIAM; FORT HENRY (VIRGINIA); OPECHANCANOUGH; PAMUNKEY; VIRGINIA-INDIAN TREATY (1646); VIRGINIA-INDIAN WAR (1644–1646)

Royal Regiment of Artillery

Britain's Royal Regiment of Artillery was (and still is) not a single regiment as such, but rather a corps consisting of that entire arm. Prior to the start of the eighteenth century most European armies did not maintain standing units of artillery. In England, a train of artillery was raised for each new war around a small cadre of master gunners. In 1714, the train that had been raised for the War of the Spanish Succession was disbanded. The following year, another train was hastily raised for the Jacobite Rebellion; but the crisis passed before an effective artillery force could be formed. That experience underscored the need for standing artillery units.

In 1716, John Churchill, the duke of Marlborough, was the master general of ordnance. On his recommendation, King George I authorized the formation of two standing artillery companies at Woolwich. In 1722, two more companies were added, and the whole organization was designated the Royal Regiment of Artillery. By the end of the War of the Austrian Succession in 1748, the RA had grown to 12 companies. In 1757, just after the start of the Seven Years' War, the RA had 24 companies organized into two battalions. At the end of the war in 1763, RA strength stood at 34 companies in three battalions. Ten of those companies were in the New World, with seven in Canada, one in America, and two in Havana.

At the higher levels, British artillery had a complicated and cumbersome command and control structure. Up until 1855, both the artillery and the engineers came under the Board of Ordnance, rather than under the War Office like the rest of the British army. Artillery commanders at home and abroad reported directly to the master general of ordnance in London. This arrangement often made for awkward coordination during military operations.

Unlike some of the more fashionable regiments in the British army, the Royal Artillery was a thoroughly middle-class establishment. It was one of the few regiments never to use the system of purchasing commissions. In the early years, the RA used an apprentice system to train its future officers. From 1741 to 1939, artillery and engineer officers were trained at the Royal Military College at Sandhurst. The RMA was known as "The Shop" for the technical nature of its curriculum.

The first RA company to serve in the New World arrived in Jamaica in December 1740. Several months later it moved to Cuba, and returned to England in 1742. In 1746, that same company was sent to garrison Louisbourg after the fort had been beaten into submission by colonial militia artillerymen. After Louisbourg was returned to the French in 1748, the RA company moved to Halifax, Nova Scotia. In 1749, the first RA company raised in North America was formed at St. Johns, Newfoundland. The first two RA companies in America proper arrived in New York and Albany in 1757.

The second siege of Louisbourg in 1758 was the Royal Artillery's major fight during the French wars. Three hundred twenty-four gunners and officers in seven RA companies manned a siege train of 88 guns, 52 mortars, and six howitzers. They poured some 18,000 rounds of shot and shell into the French fort, which mounted 229 pieces of ordnance. The RA also had three companies servicing a 29-piece siege train at Quebec in 1759. During General James Wolfe's attack on the Plains of Abraham, 50 RA gunners under Lieutenant John Yorke hauled two light 6-pounders up the cliffs to support the British. Yorke is thought to be the officer in the artillery blue uniform supporting the dying General Wolfe in Benjamin West's painting, *The Death of Wolfe.*

David T. Zabecki

References

James Alex Browne, *England's Artillerymen* (1865); Captain Francis Duncan, *History of the Royal Regiment of Artillery,* Vol. I (1872); Lieutenant Colonel M.E.S. Laws, *Battery Records of the Royal Artillery: 1716–1859* (1952).

See also ARTILLERY; LOUISBOURG, SIEGE OF (1758); QUEBEC, BATTLE OF (1759); WOLFE, JAMES

Russian America

In the last decade of the sixteenth century and continuing through the seventeenth, the Russian empire expanded through the forested lands of Siberia toward the Pacific Ocean. Russian tsars, often couching that expansion in the rhetoric of the Enlightenment and its search for scientific knowledge, used Cossacks as "frontier guards" and *promshlenniki* (private traders) to secure the region east of the Urals. Trade in sable furs, most of them taken as tribute from the peoples of Siberia and traded in Europe, sustained that expansion. Virtually stripping the furs from each successive zone over the next

half-century, the Russian fur trade reached the Okhotsk Sea by 1650. By the 1710s, it had also expanded to the Kamchatka peninsula.

Far distant from European markets, Russian fur traders in eastern Siberia came to depend on the traffic in their goods to China, possible through only one portal far to the interior in Kyakhta. (China, even under the Manchus, was able to maintain control of foreign trade as well as exports by allowing it only at selected sites that included Kyakhta in the north and Canton (Guangzhou) in the south. This system held, for the most part, until the Opium War of 1838 and the subsequent "Unequal Treaties" negotiated between the 1840s and 1860s that allowed for the opening of the China trade.) Because the Manchu rulers of China were enamored with furs in general and sea otter pelts in particular, at least some Russians in Kamchatka made tremendous profits in the trade. Having exhausted the local supply of sea otters within a short period, Russian *promshlenniki* extended out into the Pacific into the Aleutian Islands. In the early 1740s, when the government-sponsored expedition led by Vitus Bering and Alexei Chirkov sighted the American mainland and returned with hundreds of sea otter pelts, an explosion in Russian trading activity in the far northwest corner of America ensued. Between 1743 and 1800, no fewer than 101 trading expeditions left from Russian territory in search of Aleutian and Alaskan sea otter furs.

Promshlenniki contacts with Aleuts were highly varied. A few were quite harmonious and without acrimony, but a majority appear to have been quite contentious. Violence often attended contact. Russians entered Aleut villages, forcibly taking furs and supplies, and even holding women, children, and the elderly hostage while they forced hunters to procure furs for them. Aleut resistance to such treatment was at first scattered, but by the early 1760s, they began to act in concert and successfully attacked several Russian ships. While effective in the short run, those measures triggered a harsh response. In the mid-1760s, Ivan Soloviev systematically attacked Aleut villages, killing residents and destroying tools, houses, and foodstuffs. In the harsh environment of the Alaska peninsula, the loss of the means to survive was nearly as telling as the immediate death toll. Wedged between Russian advances from the west and hostile Eskimos to the east, Aleuts after the 1760s found it difficult to avoid impressment by Russians and had to employ measures other than direct military assaults to resist Russians, who, as with other native peoples in North America, introduced devastating diseases. Estimates of aboriginal Aleut population place their number at 15,000 to 25,000. By 1834, ill treatment by the Russian traders and introduced diseases had reduced their number to fewer than 2,500, and by 1848, after a smallpox epidemic, to approximately 900.

Throughout the eighteenth century, Russian activity in the Aleutians and Alaska was largely sponsored by private companies, and competition among them was intense. As the traders ventured farther eastward toward the Alaskan coast, however, the voyages became increasingly expensive to mount and risky, given the nature of the North Pacific, the ill-equipped vessels, and inexperienced crews. Gradually, over the half-century of trade, several powerful merchant houses emerged out of the competition. The most prominent, the Golikov-Shelikhov Company, was reorganized as the Russian-American Company in 1799, and from that date monopolized the Alaska trade under a charter from new Tsar Paul I. The earlier Golikov-Shelikhov Company sought assistance from his mother, Tsarina Catherine II, but she preferred to encourage competition among the traders as well as avoid any possible direct confrontation with other European powers that had begun moving into the region in the 1780s. Still, the Golikov-Shelikhov Company, under Gregory Shelikhov, pushed forward, and in 1784, established the first permanent Russian base in Alaska on Kodiak Island. The outpost there consisted of Shelikhov, his wife, and 192 men. Shelikhov hoped to set up a series of permanent posts intended to provide depots for his company's fur trade. On Kodiak, the Eskimos at first left them alone. Not long after the Russians had established themselves, though, the Eskimos gathered to begin an assault on the Russian position. Shelikhov beat them to it and used small cannonfire to batter a surrender out of the Eskimos.

Believing that the settlement would survive, Shelikhov returned to Russia to recruit finances, employees, and official sanction for his enterprise. There he hired Aleksandr Baranov to oversee operations of his company in Alaska. Baranov arrived at Kodiak in 1791 and embarked on a path that was to make him the virtual government of Russia's Alaskan empire. Baranov's strategies for managing his

Russian employees were unorthodox at best. While he forbade his employees from drinking on the job, he promoted the production and consumption of a brew of crab apples, rye meal, and cranberries. Baranov himself lead in the drinking. He also gave sanction for his men to develop relationships with native women, so long as they kept them above board; once established the relationships had to be maintained, though children were to remain with the mother should the employee return to the Russian mainland. (A great many Russians stayed on, contributing to a significant Creole population.) Moreover, Baranov tolerated no prostitution. Baranov claimed that he was a father figure to the Aleuts, upon whom he depended heavily for their skills in hunting, but his paternalism had a hollow ring to it, given the state of subjugation in which the Russians attempted to hold the Aleuts.

By the mid-1790s, though, furs around Kodiak began to thin out substantially, and Baranov embarked on a plan to establish a second settlement at Yakutat Bay. In 1796, he sent a group of settlers and traders—serfs, convicts, and "shanghaied" men from Kamchatka—to Yakutat. The glacial bay was unsuitable for any agriculture necessary to support a self-sufficient outpost and the settlers were none too enthusiastic about the venture. Still, the greatest problem for the Russians was that the Yakutat settlement impinged on the territory guarded by the powerful Tlingits. In part because of the strategic location of their territory and a long history as traders between native nations to the north, east, and south, Tlingits had a strong sense of nationalism and took great care to protect their monopoly. Interior tribes, for example, could only pass through Tlingit territory with an escort, and even then only nobles could do so.

In addition to their accustomed position as middlemen in precontact trade systems, Tlingits also played British and independent American traders against the Russians. The Americans in particular exhibited few qualms about trading firearms for furs with the Tlingit; a factor that made the Russian occupation of Yakutat even more tenuous. In 1805, the Yakutat Tlingit destroyed the Russian settlement and drove the Russians from the bay.

Simultaneous to the foray into Yakutat Bay, Baranov had designs on another outpost farther to the south, and in 1796, ventured down to about six miles north of present-day

Sitka. There he found evidence that other Europeans had begun to trade with the Tlingit (British and Americans in particular since the late 1780s). Anxious to stave off their advance, he paid a small sum of money to the Tlingits for the rights to establish a post. Shelikhov's death the next year in Russia delayed Baranov's plans for expansion until 1799. In that year, the newly reorganized company known as the Russian-American Company sponsored Baranov's venture to the south. The company operated under an official charter from the tsar and was modeled after the British East India Company—a monopoly on business but a privately funded company with limited powers of government in the territory. This allowed Russia to claim the territory as its own, but if necessary it could disavow any action because the company was not a full representative of the state. The tsar awarded the company the authority to settle anywhere north of 55 degrees as well as anywhere to the south so long as the company did not run into conflict with other European powers. The company also was responsible for making the peoples of the region loyal subjects of the tsar and for assisting Russian Orthodox priests in mission efforts. Neither of the latter were particularly successful.

In 1799, then, Baranov left Kodiak with nearly a thousand Aleuts and a hundred Russians with their Aleut and Eskimo wives to set up a post at the site near present-day Sitka. Many died during the voyage as their canoes capsized in the surf, but a large enough contingent arrived to complete the task. Baranov returned to Kodiak with most of the Aleuts and some of the Russians. For the next few years the post functioned in the heart of Tlingit territory, but in June 1802, no longer willing to suffer the presence of Russian traders in their midst, the Tlingit attacked and destroyed the post, killing or capturing most of the Russian and Aleut occupants. A British vessel anchored in the bay transported escapees back to Kodiak, but the captain demanded nearly a million rubles of Baranov as ransom, although they eventually settled on 200,000 rubles. Russians accused the captain of fomenting the attack, but Tlingit desires to hold their trade monopolies figured just as large as one British captain's plans to thwart Russian advances into the region.

In 1804, Baranov returned to Sitka with a very large contingent of Aleuts and Russians, backed by a Russian warship then touring Russian outposts. Baranov ordered the Tlingit settlement bombarded. On the ruins he built a new post and kept it well staffed. Known as Sitka, it became the largest settlement in Russian America and eventually became the capital of the Russian presence in the region. Russian relations with the Tlingit remained uneasy, with sporadic armed conflict between the two as late as 1855.

Under Baranov, though, the Russian-American Company by 1812 extended its reach all the way down to Fort Ross (short for Russian), some 50 miles outside present-day San Francisco. The Russian claim to northern California was at best tentative, and the area served as a diplomatic buffer to more essential claims in what was to become Alaska.

For native peoples the Russian presence had a varied effect. For the Aleuts and Eskimos, the rapacious behavior of the *promshlenniki* led to their virtual subjugation. The Tlingit, on the other hand, resisted Russian occupation of their territory fiercely and throughout the period of Russian occupation (until the sale of the territory to the United States in 1867), posed a constant threat to the viability of Russian outposts. Even Sitka was a distant outpost in a Tlingit-dominated territory.

As the trade in furs waned in the 1830s, Alaska natives and Russians suffered. Tlingits managed to maintain their position as middlemen in trade relationships, but people like the Haida, just to the south of Tlingit-held territory, moved to providing arts and crafts for other native nations and to producing potatoes for Russian consumption. The annual fairs at Sitka, which ran from 1841 to 1865, became the prime market.

By 1839, the Russians had also reconciled themselves to trading with their rival, the Hudson's Bay Company, for basic staples such as grains and livestock. From the 1840s to the sale of the territory to the United States in 1867, Russian-America's fur production dropped, it became an increasing liability to the Russian empire and to the Russian-American Company. Not until the advent of salmon canning, lumbering, and mining after the 1880s did Alaska reemerge as part of an empire rich in desirable resources.

The Russian presence in Alaska, however, did prompt international action. Russians had attempted to keep their activities in the Aleutians secret, but could not. By 1788, James Cook took note of the Russian trade in sea otter pelts to

China and his crew's casual trade in those furs helped initiate British and American interests in the region. The Spanish, too, worried about Russian expansion into California, and by the 1760s and 1770s had moved to establish posts as far north as San Francisco; they also sent ships to the Queen Charlotte Islands north of Vancouver Island. In 1792, Spain and Britain became embroiled in a controversy over the claim to territory at Nootka Sound on the northwest side of Vancouver Island. The diplomatic settlement provided for a short-lived joint occupation of the territory, but even that fell apart by the middle of the decade. Spain withdrew to California, leaving what became Oregon, Washington, and British Columbia to the British and Americans, the Russians agreeing to keep to the area above 55 degrees north latitude.

Russian America was thus an important component of Russian eastward expansion, of the final struggles over colonial American territories among Euro-American powers, and illustrative of the varieties of Euro-American and Native American contact experiences.

Chris Friday

References

Robert Howe Bancroft, *History of Alaska, 1730–1885* (1886); Robert Fortuine, *Chills and Fever: Health and Disease in the Early History of Alaska* (1989); James R. Gibson, *Feeding the Russian Fur Trade: Provisionment of the Okhotsk Seaboard and the Kamchatka Peninsula, 1639–1856* (1969); Claus-M. Naske and Herman E. Slotnik, *Alaska: A History of the 49th State*, 2nd ed. (1987); Wayne Suttles, ed., *Handbook of North American Indians*, Vol. 7, *Northwest Coast* (1990).

Ryswick, Treaty of (1697)

This agreement formally ended King William's War, known in Europe as the War of the League of Augsburg. Negotiations were conducted in the summer of 1697 at Ryswick, the Netherlands, between representatives of France and the members of the league. These negotiations produced a series of individual agreements that were signed on 20 September 1697. These accords primarily dealt with conditions in Europe, and the specific provisions were largely dictated by the goals of Louis XIV. His aim was to dominate both Europe and America by placing an ally on the throne of Spain to succeed the ailing Charles II. To accomplish this goal he was willing to prohibit further support of James II, and recognize William III as the legitimate ruler of England.

The situation between France and England in America was largely ignored by the treaty. Essentially, conditions were returned to those that had existed at the outbreak of hostilities in 1689. This approach involved the restitution of all territory conquered during the war. This restored the English fort on Hudson Bay, allowed the French to hold Placentia harbor in English-dominated Newfoundland, and gave Acadia back to the French. However, the treaty did not set an official boundary between Acadia and New England. This problem was addressed by a joint Anglo-French committee in the few years of peace before the outbreak of Queen Anne's War or the War of the Spanish Succession in 1702.

David L. Whitesell

See also KING WILLIAM'S WAR

S

Sailor
See SEAMEN AND SOCIETY

Fort St. Andrews (Georgia)
One of several forts guarding Georgia's southern flank from Spanish invasion, Fort St. Andrews was constructed on the order of James Edward Oglethorpe in 1736. Situated on the northwest side of Cumberland Island, its purpose was to protect the settlements of Darien and Frederica, to the north. A starwork configuration, the fort measured 65 feet by 130 feet, excluding its bastions. A battery for cannon was constructed below the fort.

Provincial rangers patrolled the inland passage as far south as the St. Johns River in scout boats. Soldiers carried messages between Fort St. Andrews and Fort Prince William at the southern tip of Cumberland Island, and they patrolled the beaches.

Newly arrived British regimental soldiers unsuccessfully attempted to mutiny in 1738. This was brought about by the primitive living conditions and lack of extra pay traditionally given for a sea voyage. General Oglethorpe led the officers in regaining control.

Approximately 15 ships, separated from the Spanish invasion fleet at the southern tip of Cumberland Island, sheltered off the fort in St. Andrews Sound in June 1742. General Oglethorpe ordered the fort abandoned, and the troops retreated south to Fort Prince William. Later in July, the Spanish forces camped at the abandoned fort on their return trip to Florida and burned it down.

Rangers were stationed at the ruins of Fort St. Andrews for several years, but it was never rebuilt.
Leslie Hall

References

Kenneth Coleman, *Colonial Georgia: A History* (1989); Larry E. Ivers, *British Drums Along the Southern Frontier: The Military Colonization of Georgia, 1733–1749* (1974); Phinizy Spalding, *Oglethorpe in America* (1977).

See also BLOODY MARSH, BATTLE OF; OGLETHORPE, JAMES EDWARD; FORT PRINCE WILLIAM (GEORGIA)

St. Augustine (Florida)
San Agustín de la Florida was established in September 1565 by Pedro Menéndez de Avilés, the Spanish conquistador from Asturias. It is the oldest continuously occupied European city in what is today the mainland United States. St. Augustine was created to forestall French settlement in the Southeast and guard the route of the treasure fleets returning to Spain. Immediately after founding this town, Menéndez captured the French Fort Caroline, located near the mouth of the St. Johns River, and killed its leader, Jean Ribault, and many of his Protestant followers, securing Spain's claim to the area.

The terms of Menéndez's contract with Philip II charged him to establish two or three fortified towns in the territory of La Florida, which the Spaniards conceived to stretch from the Florida Keys north to Newfoundland and west to Mexico. Although Menéndez established a second town the following year at Santa Elena (present-day Parris Island, South Carolina), this settlement eventually succumbed to Indian attacks, and St. Augustine remained the political, military, and religious hub of Spanish Florida.

St. Augustine was laid out on the Spanish grid system with rectilinear streets and a central plaza, around which were built the most significant government buildings and the Catholic church. St. Augustine's primary function was defensive, and it was an important garrison outpost for Spain. When the English challenged Spain's claim to sole sovereignty in the Southeast by establishing a colony in Carolina in 1670, the Spaniards had to fortify their position and began the construction of an imposing stone fortress at the northern end of St. Augustine, the Castillo de San Marcos. That structure was never captured, and enabled the Spaniards to endure the attacks of Carolinians James Moore in 1702, and John Palmer in 1728, and the major land and naval assault against the city coordinated from Georgia by General James Oglethorpe in 1740. The castillo also sheltered the colony's residents from Indian attacks in the 1740s and 1750s, and in 1812, the city withstood yet another siege, this time during the so-called Patriot Rebellion led by land-hungry Georgians. An extensive, long-term program of archaeology, directed by Dr. Kathleen A. Deagan of the Florida Museum of Natural History, has uncovered much of the city's material past. Extensive historical documentation is also available for St. Augustine, and the multidisciplinary studies of this city make it one of the best understood Spanish cities in the New World.

An older image of St. Augustine as an impoverished colonial backwater of the Spanish empire is being revised by the new interdisciplinary scholarship focused on the city. Inventories and wills from the sixteenth century reveal an unexpected level of wealth in many city households, and by the seventeenth century, some citizens had developed flourishing cattle ranches in the countryside. By the eighteenth century, St. Augustine had developed into a rather cosmopolitan place with a polyglot population. Its population was composed of a mix of Europeans, American Indians, and Africans, and race mixture was common in St. Augustine, as it was in other Latin American cities. A colonial port city, St. Augustine was linked by economics and politics to the Caribbean islands of Cuba and Hispaniola, as well as to Mexico, and to Spain itself. St. Augustine also developed important connections with the Indian nations of the hinterlands through its system of missions, treaties, and trade. Although St. Augustine was technically bound by Spain's strict mercantile policies, archaeological and historical evidence prove that the Spanish city also carried on a fairly regular trade with first English, and later, American, ports such as Charles Town, Savannah, Baltimore, and Philadelphia. Ships from these ports and other Caribbean locations stopped often in St. Augustine, and during periods of economic disruption or embargoes across the border, St. Augustine's economy benefitted from a brisk transshipment trade.

St. Augustine became a British city in 1763 when, by the terms of the Treaty of Paris, Spain ceded Florida to its arch enemy. The entire Spanish colony, including Spaniards, Indians, and Africans, evacuated Florida. Most of the exiles went to Cuba, although a small number resettled in Campeche, Mexico. The British interregnum lasted only 20 years, and by a second treaty, Spain recovered Florida in 1784. Many of the British settlers who had established homesteads and plantations in Florida remained to add a new element to the population mix in St. Augustine. Over the next decades, Spain complained of the territorial ambitions of the United States, but could do little to forestall the loss of Florida. In 1819, Spain signed the Adams-Onis Treaty ceding Florida to the United States, and St. Augustine became an American city, although it retains much of its Latin American appearance.

Jane Landers

References

Kathleen A. Deagan, *Spanish St. Augustine: The Archaeology of a Colonial Creole Community* (1983); Eugene Lyon, *The Enterprise of Florida: Pedro Menéndez de Avilés and the Spanish Conquest of 1565–1568* (1974); John Jay TePaske, *The Governorship of Spanish Florida 1700–1763* (1964).

See also FLORIDA, BRITISH INVASION OF; MENÉNDEZ DE AVILÉS, PEDRO; OGLETHORPE, JAMES EDWARD; ST. AUGUSTINE, BATTLE OF; ST. AUGUSTINE, SIEGE OF; SAN MARCOS, CASTILLO DE

St. Augustine, Battle of (1728)

In the spring of 1728, Colonel John Palmer, of the South Carolina Commons House of Assembly, led a force of 100 Carolinians and another 200 Indian allies in a raid on St. Augustine. Their main targets were the Yamasee Indian villages on the outskirts of that Spanish city. In 1715, the Yamasees in Carolina had waged a major war that almost eradicated white settlements. Although reinforcements succeeded in crushing the uprising, the Yamasee continued their fight through the 1720s. Some of the Yamasee, and the fugitive slaves who had joined their cause, escaped to Spanish Florida where they received sanctuary based on their religious conversion, and from Florida they continued to raid Carolina homesteads. Palmer's retaliatory raid concentrated on one of the main Yamasee villages, Nombre de Dios. On 9 March 1728, Palmer's raiders killed 30 Yamasee and wounded many more. They also captured 15 others, including the wife and children of the chief, Francisco Iospogue. Palmer's Indian captives were later sold into slavery. Although Governor Antonio de Benavides offered his Indians allies refuge within the walls of the Castillo de San Marcos, to their disgust he refused to engage the enemy, despite its smaller size. Before returning to Charles Town on 13 March, Colonel Palmer burned the village of Nombre de Dios and sacked and destroyed its church, further discrediting the Spaniards in the Indian view.

Jane Landers

References

Verne E. Chatelain, *The Defenses of Spanish Florida, 1565 to 1763* (1941); Verner W. Crane, *The Southern Frontier, 1670–1732* (1928); John Jay TePaske, *The Governorship of Spanish Florida, 1700–1763* (1964).

See also Castillo de San Marcos; Florida; Port Royal (South Carolina); Yamasee War

St. Augustine, Siege of (1702)

An unsuccessful siege of the capital of Spanish Florida by English forces from Carolina from 8 November to 29 December 1702 (New Style), was one of the first large engagements of the century-long, international struggle for dominance of the North American continent between Great Britain and Spain.

Settlers from Barbados had established Charles Town in 1670 in Spanish-claimed territory. The English presence in Carolina threatened the Spanish missions established along the Georgia coast; raids between the rivals ensued. During the 1690s, the tensions between Spain and England subsided as the expansionist policies of France's Louis XIV imperiled both Spanish and English interests. But with the death in 1702 of the childless Charles II of Spain, En-

gland joined Holland and Austria in the War of the Spanish Succession to prevent Bourbon control of the Spanish throne. The Carolina assembly moved quickly to authorize an attack against Florida. Carolina's governor, James Moore, set out in September 1702, with a force numbering between 800 and 1,200 (sources disagree) settlers and Native American allies.

Florida's governor, Joseph de Zúñiga y Cerda, learned on October 27 of the enemy's approach from a courier sent from Apalachee (Tallahassee vicinity). The infantry of the St. Augustine garrison was badly equipped, inexperienced, and understaffed; the artillery deficient. Spanish mission villages on Amelia Island and at the mouth of the St. Johns River sustained the first English assault on the night of 3–4 November 1702. On 6 November, Zúñiga ordered the residents of St. Augustine and Spanish Indian allies into Castillo de San Marcos. Approximately 1,500 persons entered the fortress. At 8 P.M., Moore arrived by sea and took the town unopposed. On 10 November, Colonel Robert Daniel's force arrived overland from the west after advancing up the St. Johns River. Meanwhile, Spanish troops had succeeded in driving cattle through the English lines to refuge in the Castillo's moat to supply badly needed food.

The English forces headquartered themselves in the town's Franciscan friary, situated "a cannon shot" to the south of the castillo, and also occupied the mission village of Nombre de Dios, a half-mile north of the fortress. To deprive the English forces of sheltered positions for harassing the castillo, Zúñiga and his council of war ordered the burning of all buildings located within musket range (750 feet) of the fortress. The 9- and 12-pounder guns brought by the Carolinians proved ineffective against the castillo's thick, porous walls built of local shellstone (coquina), and Moore had to dispatch Daniel to Jamaica for more men and bigger guns. On 24 November, the English stepped up fire on the fort with round and bar shot. Spanish gunners responded with 80 shots of 16-pound and 18-pound cannonballs during a 24-hour period, directing some of their fire at the English ships in the harbor. On 25 November, the English set fire to buildings in the southern part of the town. By 19 December, the English had advanced within a pistol shot of the fort.

Four Spanish men-of-war from Havana arrived at St. Augustine on 27 December, but refused to give battle to the cornered English ships. On 29 December the English began their retreat.

Abandoning a plan to escape by sea, the invaders burned four of their vessels and deserted four others. Moore and 500 men marched northward along the beach while the rest of the English force withdrew by land. The Carolinians set fire to the town's remaining buildings as they departed; fewer than 20 structures survived the siege. Zúñiga wanted to pursue the English, but his council of war voted against such an expedition. Moore was later accused of retaining the plunder from St. Augustine for himself by sending it to Jamaica. In 1703–1704, a discredited Moore attacked Spanish outposts in western Florida and further disrupted Spanish relations with Native Americans in the region.

St. Augustine's resistance to the English invasion force maintained Spanish presence in the Southeast and perpetuated the international contest. But the English had destroyed the mission system; Spanish influence in the region was severely reduced.

Susan R. Parker

References

Luis Rafael Arana and Albert Manucy, *The Building of Castillo de San Marcos* (1977); Charles W. Arnade, *The Siege of St. Augustine in 1702* (1959); Converse D. Clowse, *Economic Beginnings in Colonial South Carolina, 1670–1730* (1971).

See also APALACHEE; AYUBALE; QUEEN ANNE'S WAR; ST. AUGUSTINE; CASTILLO DE SAN MARCOS (FLORIDA); SOUTH CAROLINA

Fort St. Charles (Minnesota)

Fort St. Charles was founded by Pierre Gaultier de Varennes et de La Vérendrye in 1732 as the second in a chain of fur-trading posts built by the French in the eighteenth century as part of their west and northwest push from Lake Superior into the Manitoba and Saskatchewan regions. Located in the northwest angle of modern-day Minnesota on the west shore of the Lake of the Woods, the fort operated for a couple of decades as a kind of western capital, increasingly limiting the number of furs going to the established British posts on Hudson Bay. Although a hundred miles north of the headwaters of the Mississippi River, the fort figured prominently in the relentless Ojibwa displacement of the Dakota Indians in northern Minnesota and North Dakota.

Leroy V. Eid

References

"Under Northern Skies," in Theodore Blegen, *The Land Lies Open* (1949):61–73; Grace Lee Nute, *Rainy River Country* (1950).

See also OJIBWA-DAKOTA CONFLICT

Saint Denis, Louis Juchereau de (1676–1744)

Louis Juchereau de Saint Denis was a French-Canadian trader and explorer who occupied western Louisiana for the French and led Spanish forces to occupy east Texas. The son of Nicholas Juchereau, seigneur de Beauport, and Marie Thérèse Giffard, Louis Juchereau was born near Quebec and inherited his brother's seigneury de Saint Denis on the latter's death in 1694.

Having served in Canada, where he rose to the rank of captain, Saint Denis sailed for France in 1698 to take part in Pierre Le Moyne d'Iberville's Louisiana expedition. In 1700, he accompanied Jean Baptiste Le Moyne de Bienville on an expedition up the Red River that established contact with the Caddo Indians known as the Natchitoches. Soon thereafter he became commandant of Fort de la Boulaye (Fort du Mississippi), from which post he established permanent trade relations with Indian groups as far west as present-day east Texas. After Fort de la Boulaye was abandoned in 1707, he remained in the region as an Indian agent and later resigned his commission to become a trader in the New Orleans area.

In 1713, the governor of Louisiana, Antoine de la Mothe, sieur de Cadillac, chose Saint Denis to lead an expedition to open an overland trade route to northern New Spain. During the expedition's winter layover at the Natchitoches village, he established a trading post that would become Louisiana's westernmost French settlement. In July 1714, Saint Denis arrived at the Spanish outpost of San Juan Bautista on the Rio Grande. He was subsequently taken to Mexico City, where his story convinced viceregal officials of the need to occupy east Texas. Hired to guide the Spanish expedition of soldiers and missionaries, Saint Denis abandoned the Spanish once they had reached east Texas and returned to Louisiana.

In April 1717, he returned to San Juan Bautista with merchandise, but was arrested and held in Mexico City until his escape in November. Returning to Louisiana to settle, in 1721, he was joined by his wife, Manuela Sánchez, a granddaughter of San Juan Bautista's commandant. Saint Denis established a profitable trading business with local Indian groups as well as the Spanish, served as commandant of Fort Saint Jean Baptiste at Natchitoches, received the Order of Saint Louis in 1721, amassed considerable property, and often served as an intermediary between the French and Spanish until his death in 1744.

Jesús F. de la Teja

References

Robert S. Weddle, *The French Thorn: Rival Explorers in the Spanish Sea, 1682–1762* (1991).

See also CADDO; FORT DE LA BOULAYE (LOUISIANA); TEXAS

Sainte Foy, Battle of

See QUEBEC, FRENCH ATTEMPT TO RECAPTURE

St. Francis, Battle of (1759)

Within the annals of American military history, there are more than a few striking examples of what can be considered "epic" small-unit actions. Some of these have involved aggressive defense of strategic strongpoints (the Texans at the Alamo, the 20th Maine at Little Round Top, etc.); others have taken the form of tactical maneuvering (Arnold's expedition up the Kennebec against Quebec, the 1st Marine Division at the Chosin Reservoir, etc.). While casualties in such operations have often been significant, and defeat or retreat of the units a frequent occurrence, negative results have more often than not contributed to the "epic" lore that trails after the event.

Robert Rogers's march to and attack on the Abenaki Indian mission at St. Francis, as well as the subsequent travails that he and his rangers suffered on their return to the British frontier in the fall of 1759, fit into the above category.

In North America, the strategic situation had improved remarkably for the British. By the summer of 1759, they had captured Louisbourg fortress, opening the way for a water-borne assault on Quebec. In response, the French had retreated northward down the Champlain Valley, leaving Ticonderoga to its fate. The French were also experiencing a squeeze on the resupply of their Great Lakes and Mississippi Valley posts after their loss of Forts Frontenac (27 August 1758) and Duquesne (25 November 1758) to John Bradstreet and John Forbes, respectively. The right and left wings of the Canadian defensive lines were in ruins, with General James Wolfe on the St.

Lawrence set to push hard at the center.

Before the British commander in chief on American soil, Jeffery Amherst, could set his plans for a complementary thrust against Montreal, he had to ascertain Wolfe's situation. Scouts were sent across the marshy woodland country northeastward from Champlain, but these were effectively blocked by Abenakis operating from their base at St. Francis, close to the mouth of the river of the same name, between Montreal and Trois Rivières. Thereupon, Amherst directed Major Rogers to "[remember] the barbarities that have been committed by the enemy's Indian scoundrels. Take your revenge . . ." Of course, Rogers was to spare women and children.

Albeit with a specific goal in mind, Rogers's detail could be described in later terminology as a "reconnaissance in force." One of Rogers's lieutenants, John Stark, had been to St. Francis as a captive some five years earlier; however, he was not present on the current venture. The force consisted of rangers, several British regulars, and some Stockbridge Indians; there is no record that any of these had personal familiarity with the ground they were to cover. It was generally understood that the French were positioned in some depth between the Isle-aux-Noix, at Champlain's outflow into the Richelieu, and the lower St. Francis, with ranging parties of unknown size or composition between. There was significant risk, therefore, that as Rogers plunged into unknown ground, he could be attacked on either flank or from the rear. He would have to proceed with speed and arrive at his destination with the element of surprise intact.

Crown Point, on Lake Champlain below Ticonderoga, had also fallen to the British by default; Rogers and approximately 200 rangers, regulars, and Stockbridge Indians, debarked in whaleboats from the former location during the evening of 13 September 1759. By 24 September, the party was already two days overland from where they had beached their boats (Missisquoi Bay, at present-day Vermont's far northwestern corner). This was not accomplished without considerable cost: the expense of one-fifth their number through accident and disease, as well as their wooden flotilla, which the French discovered and destroyed. Rogers was thus cut off entirely from his logistical support; any other commander, adrift in uncharted enemy territory, with limited supplies and the countryside alerted to his presence, might have lost his head and retreated in disorder. Considering what eventually befell the group, in retreat they would likely have been caught and slaughtered piecemeal, without having reached their objective. Rather than panic, Rogers coolly appraised the situation. Bolstered by a council of war, he elected to strike for St. Francis, then move across country to sanctuary at the fort at Number Four, on the middle Connecticut River.

Rogers dispatched a plea to General Amherst asking that provisions be forwarded to the Connecticut. Then he and his men slogged onward through wet low-lying country. Bivouacs were hasty affairs, uncomfortable and only briefly occupied. The St. Francis River was laboriously crossed by a human chain formed through swift and chilling water. Finally, having eluded contact with their foe for more than 20 days, 150 miles from their start, the party came within sight of the Abenaki mission on the evening of 5 October.

The St. Francis Indians had not made suitable dispositions to guard against the encroaching Anglo-American threat; in fact, faulty intelligence had lulled them into fatal complacency. They expected Rogers's attack to be directed elsewhere. Theirs was, after all, a substantial settlement nearly a century old. Their orderly huts and chapel attested to this. (That they were also a scourge of the New England colonists was given ample testimony by the numerous scalps visibly displayed about the town.) Only desperate men would risk taking on such a place.

Indeed, it was a desperate band of some 142 men who were now poised to implode upon that attitude.

Nerves tautened, stripped of any save the most utilitarian encumbrances, and with the emotional edge of unsuspected fury squarely on their side, the rangers dressed their thin line and moved forward against the village in the predawn hours of 6 October. At a given signal, the attack commenced; doors were stove in and firebrands thrown at will. It was close-in work, with muskets and pistols fired at short range. Knives and tomahawks were brandished with fearsome effect, but it could scarcely have been called hand-to-hand combat because the rangers' opponents offered little real resistance. Some burned alive in the flames, while others who momentarily escaped were cut down by marksmen on the riverbank. It was over rather quickly. The warrior strength of the Abenakis had been almost annihilated.

Booty from the village amounted to some captive white women, corn, and perhaps some sacramental things from the mission. More important, Rogers gleaned from the survivors the information that French and Indian war parties were not far off. The attack on St. Francis was of necessity a hit-and-run affair: Filling their packs with available corn, with their few captives and casualties in tow, they began their own arduous flight from enemy territory.

If they had been filthy and exhausted on 6 October, their condition could only have deteriorated as they ascended the St. Francis River approximately as far as where the city of Sherbrooke now stands, in Quebec's eastern townships (L'Estrie). Their food gave out in the vicinity of Lake Memphremagog, and as they moved southeastwardly, they were forced to break into smaller parties; it was hoped that in this fashion, opportunities to find game might increase. Unfortunately, this did not occur. The north country autumn, replete with miserably cold, damp weather and shortened daylight hours, offered up little more than the merest bits of sustenance. Also, their trail was fresh if they were not; some of them fell prey to the most hideous retribution as the French and Indians tracked them down.

Rogers's group, by traveling down the Passumpsic River, reached the junction of the Wells and Connecticut Rivers on or around 20 October, after two weeks of privations. It was there that they had expected to be replenished with stores Amherst had authorized sent from Number Four under a Lieutenant Stevens. Neither Stevens nor his goods were to be found; whatever his reasons (and he was later court-martialed for his actions), he had left the rendezvous site prematurely.

Again, Rogers in adversity proved his mettle. Summoning what can only have been a superior reservoir of strength, he and a couple of the survivors pushed down the Connecticut on an improvised raft. On 31 October, they reached Number Four at last. Assistance was immediately sent back upstream for those left at Wells River, now increased by other stragglers.

Of the force that left St. Francis in ruins, Rogers eventually lost one-third. Besides the approbations of the British and New England, what had he accomplished?

Certainly, he created a diversion by drawing French attention away from the line of the St. Lawrence. However, much more distracting must have been the chaotic, fluid situation that resulted from the capitulation of Quebec to Wolfe's successors on 18 September. And he could not have caused much disruption in

French troop movements, because the season's campaign had ended with the summer.

Nevertheless, Rogers and his men had shown that a highly-trained, superbly-led band of resolute troops could survive extreme conditions and achieve its mission. Its goal had been no more ambitious than to destroy the Abenakis on their home ground and return. New Englanders had been driving this tribe further afield for several decades; whether justified in their marauding or not, the Abenakis would never again exert a unified deadly threat on the frontier.

Roy Marokus

See also FORT AT NUMBER FOUR (NEW HAMPSHIRE); RANGERS; ROGERS, ROBERT; SAINTE-THÉRÈSE, BATTLE OF

Fort St. Frédéric (New York)

The no-man's land between Albany and Montreal lay largely unoccupied during King William's War and Queen Anne's War. In 1730, Charles de Beauharnois de la Boische, governor of New France, recommended the construction of a fort at the head of Lake Champlain. Louis XV gave his assent and work commenced on Fort St. Frédéric (named for the minister of the marine) in 1731. Largely complete by 1742, the fort included a four-story stone citadel from which cannon could control passage of the lake. Despite incentives offered by the French government, little civilian settlement took place.

To the south, New England and New York colonists regarded Fort St. Frédéric with alarm; it appeared to them to be a dagger pointed toward Albany. During King George's War, Massachusetts Governor William Shirley drew up plans—which were not carried out—for an assault on the fort. In 1745, French and Indian war parties left Fort St. Frédéric on their way to attack Saratoga. Meanwhile, the annual cost of maintaining the fort had risen to 76,000 livres.

At the start of the French and Indian War, William Johnson mustered colonial militia and Indian warriors in order to capture the French fort. Forewarned of Johnson's intentions, Baron Jean-Armand Dieskau left Fort St. Frédéric with both French regular troops and Indian allies; they fought Johnson's men at the Battle of Lake George, in which Dieskau was captured and the French were put to flight. Johnson did not pursue the retreating enemy, and Fort St. Frédéric was not attacked in 1755. Late in the same year, Pierre de Rigaud de Vaudreuil recommended

that another, larger fort be built at Carillon, 15 miles to the south of Fort St. Frédéric. The construction of Fort Carillon (in 1756 and 1757) reduced the importance of Fort St. Frédéric, which became a backup to the larger fort at Carillon.

Both Fort Carillon and Fort St. Frédéric were saved from capture in 1758 by Louis-Joseph de Montcalm's victory over General James Abercromby (8 July 1758), and the French presence in the Lake Champlain Valley was preserved. But in 1759, General Jeffery Amherst moved methodically north, and General François-Charles de Bourlamaque abandoned both Fort Carillon and Fort St. Frédéric; the retreating French blew up the powder magazines of both forts. Amherst proceeded to build a much larger fortress slightly inland from Fort St. Frédéric—this became Fort Crown Point. From 1731 to 1756, Fort St. Frédéric loomed large in the thinking of both the British and French commanders; although there was never a battle on its location, the fort stood as a swinging door between New France to the north and New York to the south.

Samuel Willard Crompton

References

Russell P. Bellico, *Sails and Steam in the Mountains: A Maritime and Military History of Lake George and Lake Champlain* (1992).

See also AMHERST, JEFFERY; BOURLAMAQUE, FRANÇOIS-CHARLES DE; CROWN POINT; DIESKAU, JEAN-ARMAUD; JOHNSON, WILLIAM; LAKE CHAMPLAIN; LAKE GEORGE, BATTLE OF; SARATOGA, BATTLE OF; FORT TICONDEROGA (NEW YORK)

Fort St. George's (Maine)

The land along the St. George's River in Maine (now Thomaston) was settled around 1719. In order to protect the settlers, two blockhouses were built, surrounded by a palisade, with a covered way to the water. As the settlement, particularly the provincial fort, introduced an English presence on Penobscot Bay, the French and their Indian allies attempted to destroy it several times. During Dummer's War the fort was attacked on 12 June 1722, and again two months later, at which time the French-led Indians besieged the blockhouses for 12 days. On 25 December 1723, a 30-day siege began, eventually lifted by the arrival of provincial forces led by Colonel Thomas Westbrook. In 1725, John Gyles took command of the fort and conducted major negotiations to end the conflict.

After Dummer's War, Fort St. George's, while remaining a military post, became an important truck house or trading post. However, to reinforce its military purpose, another blockhouse was added to the structure. King George's War brought more assaults. The buildings of the settlement were burned in an attack on 19 July 1744, but the inhabitants remained safe behind the walls of the fort. In September 1747, another siege was conducted. This time the enemy attempted to tunnel under the walls, but failed when the tunnel walls caved in.

During the last French war, Fort St. George's withstood two major attacks, one in 1755, and another, undertaken by a force of 400 French-led Indians, in August 1758. In the latter case, intelligence of the impending attack enabled reinforcements to arrive just before the assault. With the French wars over, the military post would be discontinued in 1762. General Henry Knox would later build his mansion near the site of the fort.

Steven C. Eames

References

Henry E. Dunnack, *Maine Forts* (1924); Steven C. Eames, "Rustic Warriors: Warfare and the Provincial Soldier on the Northern Frontier, 1689–1748," Ph.D. Dissertation, University of New Hampshire (1989).

See also DUMMER'S TREATY; DUMMER'S WAR; GYLES, JOHN; MAINE; WESTBROOK, THOMAS

St. Inigoes Fort (Maryland)

When St. Mary's Fort fell into disuse, the need for a new fortification developed, not to defend against Indians, but against incoming vessels. A new fort, St. Inigoes Fort, was erected on the peninsula at the mouth of St. Inigoes Creek, two-and-one-half miles south of St. Mary's City. St. Inigoes Fort served to remove the trading business—Indian, intercolonial, and international—from the colony's seat. In addition, the fort was a place for colonists to congregate in the event of an Indian alarm, and it sometimes housed the colonial assemblies and the provincial court. Even the local gunsmith and surgeon settled there to practice their respective trades. Taxes were collected at St. Inigoes Fort, and so was booty captured in engagements with colo-

nial enemies (of which there were very few). After its construction, St. Inigoes Fort served as the central fortification for the colony and as an official extension of St. Mary's City.

Debra R. Boender

See also ST. MARY'S FORT (MARYLAND)

Fort St. Joseph–St. Clair River (Michigan)

Fearing the intrusion of English traders into the Great Lakes country, Governor Jacques-René de Brisay de Denonville ordered a fort built at the site of modern Port Huron, Michigan. Daniel Greysolon Dulhut with the aid of 50 *coureurs de bois* constructed Fort St. Joseph in the autumn of 1686 on a hill above the St. Clair River at its narrowest point at the mouth of Lake Huron. The palisaded fort was one arpent square (.85 acre), without bastions. Baron Louis-Armand de Lahontan commanded the fort during 1687. The garrison traded with the Indians, and the Hurons and French used it as a base against the Iroquois. The fort was abandoned in 1688.

Russell M. Magnaghi

See also DENONVILLE, JACQUES-RENÉ DE BRISAY DE

Fort St. Joseph–St. Joseph River (Michigan)

Fort St. Joseph (known also as the St. Joseph River post, the Miami post, and St. Joseph of the Miamis) was built in late 1691 by Ensign Augustin Legardeur de Courtemanche by order of New France's governor general, Louis de Buade de Frontenac. It was strategically located on the east bank of the St. Joseph River about 20 miles south of its mouth on Lake Michigan. The French garrison and its resident Indian allies (at first the Miamis, then the Potawatomis) controlled the southern end of Lake Michigan and the nearby St. Joseph River–Kankakee River portage, a vital link in the water route to the Illinois and Mississippi rivers. Frontenac's purpose in establishing this fort was to prevent the Iroquois and the English "from sticking their noses in" the region and from "penetrating as far as Michilimackinac and ruining completely all our trade with the Ottawas."

Fort St. Joseph's trading post and warehouse annually produced as many as 400 bales of furs. These buildings, the commander's and troops' quarters, and later its stone jail, were all protected by a wooden palisade. In 1693, the fort withstood an attack by 300 Iroquois, who suffered heavy casualties and withdrew from the region. The garrison in the 1720s numbered 18 *troupes de la marine*, including eight officers. Hundreds of Miami and Potawatomi warriors provided the bulk of the fighting forces for the garrison. The fort served as a major staging area for campaigns in distant locations, such as the 1730 campaign against the Fox in Illinois and the one against the Chickasaws in Louisiana in 1739 and 1740.

In 1761, Fort St. Joseph was ceded to the English. The fort was captured by the Potawatomis in November 1763 during Pontiac's War and was never garrisoned again. During the American Revolution, a Spanish-led raiding party from St. Louis destroyed the fort in 1781.

Joseph L. Peyser

References

Dunning Idle, "The Post of the St. Joseph River During the French Regime 1679–1761," Ph.D. Dissertation, University of Illinois (1946); Gérard Malchelosse, "Le poste de la Rivière Saint Joseph (Michigan) (1691–1781)," in *Les Cahiers des Dix* (1958):139–186, translated as "The St. Joseph River Post (Michigan)," in *French Canadian and Acadian Genealogical Review*, VII (1979):173–209.

George Paré, "The St. Joseph Baptismal Register," *Mississippi Valley Historical Review*, XIII (1926):201–239; Joseph L. Peyser, "New Cartographic Evidence on Two Disputed French-Regime Fort Locations," *Indiana Military History Journal*, V (1980):6–17; ———, *Letters from New France: Selected Translations and Readings on the "Pays d'en haut," 1686–1783* (1992).

See also FOX FORT (ILLINOIS) AND SIEGE; FRONTENAC, LOUIS DE BUADE DE; OTTAWA; PONTIAC'S WAR

St. Lawrence River

The St. Lawrence is the principal route of a water system 1,900 miles long, from the Gulf of St. Lawrence to the St. Louis River in Minnesota, which empties into the head of Lake Superior. The St. Lawrence acquires its name at the foot of Lake Ontario, and from that point downstream to Montreal is the most difficult section to navigate; rapids alternate with broad, shallow lakes, often no more than ten feet deep. In colonial times, Montreal was considered the head of ocean-going transport, and the section of the river from that city to Quebec represented the heart of New France. This relatively easy stretch, 170 miles long, averages only two and one-third miles in breadth. The third section of the river, the 240-mile-long estuary from the foot of the Isle d'Orléans to Anticosti Island, varies in width from eight to 70 miles. At its widest point, the river empties into the Gulf of St. Lawrence.

The St. Lawrence was both the lifeline of New France and its downfall, being the colony's sole route to Europe. Whoever controlled the river controlled Canada. Because of the great width of the estuary, there were few settlements along its banks. Enemy ships could pass through its waters with impunity from shore-based artillery. It was at Quebec, from whose heights guns can command passage on the narrowing river, that a settlement was made by Samuel de Champlain in 1608. Although the river teemed with fish, Quebec, because of its distance upriver, could not compete with Grand Banks fishing, which was much closer to the home markets.

The shape of the land concessions, or seigniories, was determined by the river. Since the river was the sole means of transportation for the *habitants* living between Quebec and Montreal, all had to have access to it; therefore, the seigniories tended to have a narrow river frontage whose boundaries often extended inland for several miles. Most of the residents of New France lived along this section of the river, which could be defended against hostile ships.

Founded in 1640 by the Compagnie du Saint Sacrement on an island in the river, Montreal controlled the fur trade. There, the high-quality furs from the northern interior and the Great Lakes region could be loaded directly onto ships sailing for France. Montreal was not far downstream from the confluence of the Ottawa and St. Lawrence Rivers at Lachine. The Ottawa River was long the preferred trade route, with portages into Lake Huron so as to avoid the hostile Iroquois to the south of Lake Ontario in present-day New York. From Montreal to the foot of Lake Ontario, the several series of rapids had to be navigated either by Indian birchbark canoe, or later by the French-designed *bateau*, a shallow draft vessel.

The St. Lawrence is a tidal river, with a rise of 17 feet at Quebec, but negligible at Trois Rivières. The Jesuits established a school of navigation at Quebec that produced river pilots, and the Ministry of Marine charted the river's hazards and installed navigation markers from Quebec to the Gulf of St. Lawrence. These measures alleviated some of the perils posed by the river, such as shoals, dangerous currents, and fogs.

Because of its northern latitude, the St. Lawrence had a limited shipping season; the river was usually frozen over from November until late March or April. This posed a danger to the colony, dependent as it was on France for most of its manufactured goods and for wine. During wartime, British ships often lay in wait for the French supply convoys. The British hastened the fall of New France in May 1760 by arriving first to resupply their garrison in Quebec besieged by the French forces. The French were then forced to retreat to Montreal, whose defenses were totally inadequate to resist shipborne artillery. A second British force converged on Montreal via the Lake Ontario-upper St. Lawrence route. A third British army came down the Lake Champlain-Richelieu River route into the St. Lawrence, joined the other two at Montreal, and France's North American colony fell because the French had not the means to control the river.

Mary Kimbrough

References
W.J. Eccles, *France in America* (1973); Theo L. Hills, *The St. Lawrence Seaway* (1959).

See also LAKE ONTARIO; MONTREAL; QUEBEC; QUEBEC, BATTLE OF

Fort St. Leon (Louisiana)
See ENGLISH BEND (LOUISIANA)

Fort St. Louis (Texas)
Fort St. Louis was founded by René-Robert Cavelier, sieur de La Salle, in 1685. The precise location of the fort has been the subject of considerable controversy, but there is now convincing archaeological evidence that it was situated precisely at the site identified by Herbert Eugene Bolton in 1915. It was established on the right bank of Garcitas Creek, a tributary of Matagorda Bay. La Salle's colony was soon threatened by disease, desertions, and internal factionalism. The survivors, except for five children, were killed in late 1688 or early 1689 by Karankawa Indians. The wooden buildings were burned by the Spanish in 1690.

Donald E. Chipman

References
Kathleen Gilmore, "La Salle's Fort St. Louis in Texas," *Bulletin of the Texas Archaeological Society,* 55 (1984):61–72; Robert S. Weddle, *The French Thorn: Rival Explorers in the Spanish Sea, 1682–1762* (1991).

See also KARANKAWA; FORT LA BAHÍA (TEXAS)

Fort St. Louis at Pimiteoui (Illinois)
Of the three seventeenth-century forts that the French built in the Illinois country, this was the last and the one concerning which there is the most documentation. Following René-Robert La Salle's murder in 1687 in what is now eastern Texas, his associates, Henri de Tonti and François La Forest, were given the Fort St. Louis concession at Starved Rock. They operated this fort as a fur-trading outpost for several years, but in 1691 decided that the outpost should be moved about "twenty-five leagues" down the Illinois River. It is not clear precisely why this decision was made, but several interrelated factors seem to have borne on it: the area around Starved Rock was being depleted of game and firewood; hostile Fox and Iroquois were a source of anxiety; the Kaskaskia Indian tribe wished to migrate downriver. All French actions in the Illinois country during the seventeenth century were related in some way to Indian movements.

The site that Tonti and La Forest selected for the new Fort St. Louis was one with which Tonti was familiar, for it was not far from the site of the earlier Fort Crevecoeur. The fort was built during the winter of 1691–1692 on the northwestern shore of Lake Peoria (or Pimiteoui) just above where the lake emptied into the Illinois River. Contemporary descriptions leave little doubt about the physical aspects of this fort. It was a wooden palisaded quadrilateral with a bastion in each of the four corners. Inside the palisade were a number of log buildings that were used for housing and for storing peltries and European trade goods. Outside of the fort stood a mission chapel that served both Frenchmen and Indians.

The purpose of the fort at Pimiteoui was largely economic, i.e., it was principally a fur-trading outpost, and no French troops were stationed there. In addition to the fur trade, however, the fort provided a center for the missionary work of French Jesuit priests. Closely associated with the fort were villages of Kaskaskia and Peoria Indians. The mission of the Immaculate Conception, which Father Jacques Marquette had begun with the Kaskaskia tribe further up the Illinois River in 1674, was formalized at Pimiteoui during the 1690s. Parish registers, which are still extant, were begun by Father Jacques Gravier, and in 1695 he recorded the first baptism at Pimiteoui—Pierre Accault, infant son of Michel Accault and Marie Rouensa, daughter of a Kaskaskia Indian chief.

During the mid-1690s, Fort St. Louis at Pimiteoui was a flourishing center of French colonialism in the Illinois country. By the end of the decade, however, this outpost was in decline. A glut of beaver pelts provoked a series of confusing and contradictory royal edicts; Tonti and La Forest moved on to other ventures; the Fox Indians commenced hostilities against the French and their Indian allies; the Kaskaskia Indian tribe moved further south. With the founding of mission and trading centers at Cahokia (1699) and Kaskaskia (1703), the focus of French colonialism in the Illinois country moved from the Illinois River valley to the middle Mississippi Valley. A new era had begun in the French colonial history of mid-North America.

Carl J. Ekberg

References

Clarence W. Alvord, *The Illinois Country: 1673–1818* (1920); Pierre-François Xavier de Charlevoix, *Histoire et description generale de la Nouvelle France avec le Journal Historique d'un Voyage fait par ordre du Roi dans l'Amerique Septentrionale*, 6 vols. (1744); Louise Kellogg, ed., *Early Narratives of the Northwest, 1634–1699* (1917); Theodore C. Pease and Raymond C. Werner, eds., *The French Foundations, Illinois State Historical Collections*, Vol. XXIII (1934); Reuben G. Thwaites, ed., *The Jesuit Relations and Allied Documents*, Vols. LXIV and LXVII (1900).

See also FORT CREVECOEUR (ILLINOIS); FOX FORT (ILLINOIS); ILLINOIS; ST. LOUIS AT STARVED ROCK (ILLINOIS)

Fort St. Louis at Starved Rock (Illinois)

René-Robert Cavelier de La Salle (1643–1687) was the first person to plan the construction of a European fort in the Illinois country; this proposed fort was to serve as a base for his envisioned fur-trading empire. In 1680, his first attempt, Fort Crevecoeur, was a signal failure. After his epic journey from Lake Michigan to the mouth of the Mississippi River and back in 1682, La Salle and his principal lieutenant, Henri de Tonti, selected a new location for their proposed fort. This was atop Le Rocher (The Rock), as the French called it in colonial times. Located on the south bank of the Illinois River near present-day Utica, Illinois, this site had several distinct advantages. The high sandstone bluff was a naturally defensible location; it controlled the strategic Illinois River at a point where the river descended through a series of rapids; the important Kaskaskia Indian village was situated just across the river.

During the winter of 1682–1683, La Salle and Tonti began work on a fort that La Salle described as being located on an "inaccessible rock" with a circumference of "600 feet." The fort was an irregular palisaded structure made of white oak posts that were 22 feet high where the bluff sloped away from the river and 15 feet high on the river side. There were no bastions, and there was no ordnance of any kind. "Fort St. Louis" appears clearly marked and located on Jean-Baptiste Franquelin's map of French North American drawn in 1688.

An interesting description was made of Fort St. Louis and its setting by Henri Joutel, a survivor of La Salle's last and fateful expedition. After La Salle's murder in what is now east Texas in 1687, Joutel made his way northward up the Mississippi and Illinois River valleys, finally arriving at Fort St. Louis with the news of La Salle's death. Remaining at the fort for some period of time to recuperate from his exertions, Joutel later wrote this description of his place of sanctuary:

> It is only fortified with Stakes and Palisades, and some houses advancing to the edge of the Rock. It has a very spacious Esplanade, or Place of Arms. The Place is naturally strong, and might be made so by Art, with little expense. Several of the natives live in it, in their Huts.

With La Salle's death, control of Fort St. Louis devolved upon his associates, Tonti and La Forest, to whom King Louis XIV eventually granted possession of the fort and the local fur trade concession. The high point of Fort St. Louis at Starved Rock was the period of the late 1680s, and in the early 1690s, Tonti and La

Forest decided for a variety of reasons to relocate the fort at Pimiteoui, lower down on the Illinois River. The name "Starved Rock" for "Le Rocher" stemmed from a later episode in intertribal Indian warfare and relates in no way to La Salle or Fort St. Louis.

Carl J. Ekberg

References
    Clarence W. Alvord, *The Illinois Country: 1673–1818* (1920); Henri Joutel, *Joutel's Journal of La Salle's Last Voyage, 1684–1687*, ed. by Henry R. Stiles (1906); Pierre Margry, ed., *Decouvertes et establissements des francais dans l'ouest et dans le sud de l'Amerique Septentrionale, 1614–1698*, Vols. 1 and 2 (1876, 1879); Francis Parkman, *La Salle and the Discovery of the Great West* (1908).

See also Fort St. Louis at Pimiteoui (Illinois)

Fort Ste. Marie (Louisiana)
See English Bend (Louisiana)

St. Mary's Fort (Maryland)
When, in 1634, St. Mary's was chosen as the site for permanent settlement in Maryland, a fort was erected in a cove there, situated in such fashion so as to protect the fledgling colony against Indians. This fort, dubbed St. Mary's Fort, probably looked very much like the palisaded Indian towns found throughout the region, which consisted of trees trimmed into huge stakes driven into the ground to form a wall. St. Mary's Fort was incorporated into a palisaded area 120 yards square. Colonists mounted one piece of ordnance and six murtherers (small and somewhat primitive cannons) on the walls of the fort, which, along with the squared shape of the walls of the fort, were probably the only major features to distinguish the English fort from the Indian palisades.
    St. Mary's Fort was deemed necessary to the protection of the colony, yet not all colonists chose to live within its walls. Indeed, space inside the fort was limited. It did, however, serve as the site of the first colonial assemblies and was where the first colonial laws were passed and posted. Yet the fort was never actively called upon to defend the colony.
    Over the next several years, St. Mary's Fort at St. Mary's City served as the primary defensive post of the colony (if only in theory), and

as the only port of call for traders entering and leaving the colony. Yet the fort did not survive long, as it was quickly discovered that the Indians in southern Maryland posed little threat to the already growing numbers of colonists. No longer needed for defense, upkeep of the fort lapsed, and within about ten years it was no longer in use.

Debra R. Boender

References
    Debra R. Boender, "Our Fires Have Nearly Gone Out: A History of Indian-White Relations on the Colonial Maryland Frontier, 1663–1776," Ph.D. Dissertation, University of New Mexico (1988); Raphael Semmes, *Captains and Mariners of Early Maryland* (1937).

See also Maryland; St. Inigoes Fort (Maryland)

Presidio San Miguel de los Adaes (Texas)
See Presidio Nuestra Señora del Pilar de los Adaes (Louisiana)

Fort St. Peter (Mississippi)
A French-built palisaded fort on the Yazoo River about 12 miles from Vicksburg, Fort St. Peter (which was known by numerous names) was mainly a trading outpost built around 1719. The fort was overshadowed by the more important military establishment of Fort Rosalie at Natchez. The Yazoo and Koroa Indians destroyed the fort and killed the inhabitants in 1729 during the Natchez War.

Alan Gallay

See also Natchez War; Fort Rosalie (Mississippi)

Fort St. Simons (Georgia)
Fort St. Simons was constructed at the order of James Edward Oglethorpe in 1738 on the southern tip of St. Simons Island. It was built within 400 yards of Fort Delegal, and the two guarded the entrance to St. Simons Sound against Spanish invasion. By 1742, this area was the most heavily fortified in Georgia, with the two forts and their adjacent ground containing 15 cannon and infantry trenches. Oglethorpe's regiment, the 42nd Foot, rotated be-

tween Fort St. Simons and Fort Frederica, six miles to the north on St. Simons Island.

On 28 June 1742, the main Spanish invasion fleet of 36 ships and boats appeared off the southern tip of St. Simons Island. On 5 July, they sailed past the battery of cannons and anchored in St. Simons Sound. That night, as they landed their troops one and one-half miles to the northwest, General Oglethorpe ordered the forts evacuated. The seaworthy British ships sailed away, and those too damaged were burned. The troops marched overland to Fort Frederica.

On 6 July, the Spanish occupied Fort St. Simons and made it their headquarters. By 15 July the Spanish had left St. Simons Island, having burned the fortifications. These were not rebuilt.

Leslie Hall

References
    Kenneth Coleman, *Colonial Georgia: A History* (1989); Larry E. Ivers, *British Drums Along the Southern Frontier: The Military Colonization of Georgia, 1733–1749* (1974); Phinizy Spalding, *Oglethorpe in America* (1977).

See also BLOODY MARSH, BATTLE OF; FORT FREDERICA (GEORGIA); MONTIANO, MANUEL DE; OGLETHORPE, JAMES EDWARD; FORT ST. ANDREWS (GEORGIA)

Sainte-Thérèse, Battle of (1760)
Early in May 1760, Major General Jeffery Amherst, first baron Amherst (1717–1797), learned that Major General François de Lévis, chevalier de Lévis (1719–1787), had marched on Quebec with all available troops, including sizeable contingents from the Richelieu River forts at Chambly, Saint-Jean, and Isle-aux-Noix. On 27 May, Amherst ordered Major Robert Rogers (1731–1795) to lead 275 Rangers and 28 British regulars from the light infantry regiments past Colonel Louis-Antoine de Bougainville's (1729–1811) garrison on Isle-aux-Noix to attack the forts at Saint-Jean and Chambly and destroy as many supplies and *bateaux* as possible. Amherst hoped that this would weaken local French strength and even persuade Lévis to divert troops from his operations against Brigadier General James Murray (1721/22–1794) at Quebec.

Rogers and 250 men left Crown Point in four vessels and a number of *bateaux* at the be-

ginning of June 1760. On 3 June, Rogers landed 50 rangers under Lieutenant Robert Holmes at Missisquoi Bay with orders to attack the French post at "Wigwam Martinique" on the Yamaska River west of the Richelieu. Four rangers were also dispatched overland to Quebec with a letter for Murray. Rogers and the remaining 200 rangers crossed to the northwest shore of Lake Champlain the next day and landed near the Chazy River. Despite a diversion by several vessels commanded by Captain Alexander Grant (1734–1813) of the 77th Highlanders Battalion, Bougainville's patrols discovered the rangers' whereabouts and he sent out a party of about 350 French, Canadians, and Indians under a Canadian officer, Pierre Pépin *dit* La Force (b. 1725). At 11:30 in the morning on 6 June, La Force attacked the rangers' left and attempted to drive them toward the lakeshore. Rogers, however, sent 70 men through a bog by the lake, and when this party fell on the French rear, he led the main body of rangers forward. The French retreated for a mile and took refuge in a cedar swamp. La Force was wounded and his men carried off up to 40 casualties, while Rogers's losses amounted to 14 dead and ten wounded.

The Anglo-Americans regrouped on nearby Isle La Motte and were reinforced by a company of Stockbridge Indians. On 9 June, 220 rangers landed at the mouth of the Chazy River and marched north parallel to the west bank of the Richelieu to Fort Saint-Jean. After a reconnaissance of the fort at about midnight on 15 June, and being fired on by the sentries, Rogers decided that the post was too well guarded for a successful assault. Accordingly, he led a night march further downriver to Sainte-Thérèse, a village and stockaded post with two storehouses at the upper end of the Chambly rapids, five miles south of Fort Chambly. Supplies for the forts on the upper Richelieu were unloaded at Chambly, moved by road past the rapids, and then reloaded on *bateaux* at Sainte-Thérèse.

At daybreak on 16 June, Rogers and a few of his men rushed the gates while a haycart was passing through them and captured the 24 soldiers inside without a shot being fired. Simultaneously, rangers seized 78 soldiers and civilians in the outlying houses. Only a few young men escaped to warn Fort Chambly. Rogers had the village, fort, *bateaux,* canoes, wagons, supplies, and livestock burned or destroyed and set the women and children free on the road to

Montreal. After interrogating the prisoners, Rogers decided that there was little point in trying to surprise Fort Chambly, so the force crossed the Richelieu and returned to Lake Champlain by a route to the east of the river. As they marched along the shores of Missisquoi Bay on 20 June, the rangers were attacked by the advance guard of a force of 800 men dispatched by Bougainville to intercept them. The French were driven off, and Rogers reached the rendezvous later that day. After Holmes arrived on 21 June, the last of the rangers embarked on the waiting vessels.

Rogers failed to destroy Chambly or Saint-Jean, and Harris's 50 men lost their way while trying to attack Wigwam Martinique, but Amherst considered the audacious raid a success. The rangers and light infantry destroyed some of Bougainville's valuable supplies and transport, and the prisoners provided Amherst with valuable information about the state of Lévis's army, the exact strength of the garrisons on the Richelieu, and the lack of French troops at Montreal. In addition, the local *habitants* were shaken by this unexpected attack, and Lévis himself was obliged to leave his headquarters outside Quebec in order to inspect the Richelieu River forts and revive Canadian morale.

Martin L. Nicolai

References
Henri-Raymond Casgrain, ed., *Collection des manuscrits du maréchal de Lévis* (1888–1894); Edward P. Hamilton, ed., *Adventure in the Wilderness: The American Journals of Louis Antoine de Bougainville, 1756–1760* (1964); H.M. Jackson, *Rogers' Rangers: A History* (1953); Robert Rogers, *Journals of Major Robert Rogers* (1765); John C. Webster, ed., *The Journal of Jeffery Amherst, Recording the Military Career of General Amherst in America from 1758 to 1763* (1931).

See also AMHERST, JEFFERY; BOUGAINVILLE, LOUIS-ANTOINE DE; FORT CHAMBLY (QUEBEC, CANADA); ISLE-AUX-NOIX; LAKE CHAMPLAIN; MURRAY, JAMES; RANGERS; ROGERS, ROBERT

Salmon Falls, Battle of (1690)

In the winter of 1689–1690, the governor of New France, Louis de Buade de Frontenac, launched three raiding parties against the English colonies. The first struck Schenectady, New York, and the second attacked the small frontier community of Salmon Falls. Situated on the west bank of the Salmon Falls River, which divides New Hampshire from Maine, the struggling community was exposed and ill-prepared. The attacking force was rather small, numbering 52, fairly divided between French and Indians, but with leaders like Joseph-François Hertel de La Fresnière and the Norridgewock chief Hopehood, they were very efficient. Dividing into three parties, the raiders attacked at dawn, taking three garrisons by surprise, burning houses and mills. Thirty inhabitants were killed and 54 captured. Pursuit forces caught Hertel's band near a river in Berwick, Maine. Hertel turned on the far bank and a fire fight continued until dark with losses on both sides. The French and Indians slipped away in the dark and, with dead and wounded to take care of, the pursuit was called off. Hertel's force would later join up with Frontenac's third raiding party when they attacked and destroyed Fort Loyal in Casco Bay (Portland, Maine).

Steven C. Eames

References
Cotton Mather, *Decennium Luctuosum* (1699), rpt. in Charles H. Lincoln, ed., *Narratives of the Indian Wars, 1675–1699*, 1913.

See also FALMOUTH, BATTLE OF; FORT LOYAL (MAINE); FRONTENAC, LOUIS DE BUADE DE; SCHENECTADY, BATTLE OF

Saltcatchers Fort (South Carolina)

Located on the west side of Salkehatchie (Saltcatchers) River, less than a mile east of present-day Yamasee in Beaufort County, this stockade fort was built between 1728 and 1731 by Captain James McPherson and his company of southern rangers. The rangers' mission was to patrol the region between Combahee River and Savannah River, defending the Beaufort settlers against Yamasee raids. In 1734, the fort was demolished, and the garrison was relocated to Fort Prince George–Palachacola.

Gregory D. Massey

References
Larry E. Ivers, *Colonial Forts of South Carolina 1670–1775* (1970).

See also FORT PRINCE GEORGE–PALACHACOLA (SOUTH CAROLINA); RANGERS; YAMASEE WAR

Presidio San Agustín de Ahumada (Texas)
Presidio San Agustín de Ahumada (1756–1772), a garrison located near the mouth of the Trinity River, Chambers County, Texas, was established to defend the upper Texas coast from seaborne encroachment and protect Mission Nuestra Señora de la Luz. The presidio was commonly referred to as Orcoquisac, a reference to the Akokisa Indians of the area.

Spanish exploration of the lower Trinity first took place in 1745–1746, following rumors of French traders in the area. It was not until 1754, however, that a group of Frenchmen was caught trading with area tribes by an agent of the Spanish governor, Jacinto de Barrios y Jáuregui, who was similarly engaged. Akokisa assertions of a French promise to send 50 families and a priest convinced Spanish authorities to take preemptive action. Governor Barrios occupied the site with a temporary garrison of soldiers from other Texas presidios in 1755, while he organized a permanent garrison and mission, both of which were in place by the end of the following year.

The swampy location of the place combined with increasing resistance to subordination by the Akokisa to make the post unsuccessful. Plans to establish a civilian settlement were never carried out. French abandonment of direct trading in the area and the transfer of Louisiana to Spanish control contributed to neglect. As part of his 1766–1767 inspection tour of the frontier garrisons, the marqués de Rubí recommended abandonment of the site. The garrison, which was composed of 31 men, including the captain, was reduced to three in 1771 after two transfers to San Antonio. The three left with the missionaries a few weeks later. When the final order for abandonment was issued in 1772, Orcoquisac was already deserted.

Jesús F. de la Teja

References
Herbert E. Bolton, *Texas in the Middle Eighteenth Century: Studies in Spanish Colonial History and Administration* (1970); Donald E. Chipman, *Spanish Texas, 1519–1821* (1994).

San Antonio (Texas)
San Antonio (1718–) is the oldest continuously occupied urban center in Texas. Founded near the headwaters of the San Antonio River, Bexar County, as San Fernando de Béxar, the town's charter dates to 1731, when 15 families from the Canary Islands (Isleños) were settled on a site adjacent to Presidio San Antonio de Béxar. San Antonio remained the only Texas community with civilian local government throughout the colonial period. Following the closing of Presidio Los Adaes as part of a Spanish reorganization of the northern frontier after acquisition of Louisiana from France in 1763, San Antonio became the provincial capital.

Royal authorities considered civilian settlement of the San Antonio area important to the defense and development of the region, and Isleño immigrants were seen as a convenient source of settlers. The expense and lack of suitability of European families for life on the Indian frontier ended further crown-sponsored immigration efforts, leaving the city to develop through increases in the neighboring garrison and natural growth. The 55 Isleño men, women, and children who were given *hidalgo* (minor nobility) status, adapted to their new home by learning frontier skills from the approximately 250 military settlers already living in and around the presidio. Intermarriage between the groups, the strengthening of the garrison toward the end of the century, and the transfer of some east Texas settlers in 1773 produced a population of approximately 2,000 by the end of the eighteenth century.

The largest Texas settlement until the late 1830s, San Antonio was also the most exposed to hostilities, particularly from Lipan Apaches and Comanches. The severity of depredations, especially in the 1730s and 1760s, led to occasional petitions to abandon the site and severely hampered economic development. San Antonio was also the place, however, where important treaties were signed with the Apaches in the 1740s and the Comanches and Norteño Indians in the 1770s and 1780s. During the Mexican war of independence, San Antonio was the site of a garrison uprising in 1811 and a battle between a rebel-filibuster force and a royalist army in 1813.

During times of peace, the civilian population moved into the countryside to establish a number of cattle ranches along the San Antonio River basin, relying on agricultural fields adjacent to the city for the corn, bean, and sugar cane crops that were the mainstays of the population. Isolation and freight costs resulted in a policy of subsistence agriculture, the town's farmers producing enough for the civilian and military population of the area. Animal husbandry, however, served as an important export activity, with hides, dried beef, and, in the 1770s and 1780s, beeves being sent to the interior parts of New Spain, and sometimes to Louisiana.

Jesús F. de la Teja

References

Gerald E. Poyo and Gilberto M. Hinojosa, *Tejano Origins in Eighteenth-Century San Antonio* (1991).

See also NORTEÑOS; PRESIDIO DE SAN ANTONIO DE BÉXAR (TEXAS); TEXAS

Presidio San Antonio de Béxar (Texas)

Presidio San Antonio de Béxar (1718–1836) housed a garrison established near the headwaters of the San Antonio River, Bexar County, Texas, to protect local missionary activity and communication lines between Spanish east Texas and the Rio Grande. Never an entirely walled structure, Presidio de Béxar consisted of barracks, captain's and other soldiers' homes, and storehouses surrounding a plaza (now covered by San Antonio city hall) adjacent to the civilian settlement. The presidio survived the Mexican independence movement and continued to serve as the principal military establishment in Texas until it surrendered to Texas independence forces on 4 June 1836.

Governor Martín de Alarcó founded Presidio de Béxar on 5 May 1718, as a *villa* (town), but the outpost had trouble attracting civilian settlers. The number of soldier/settlers fluctuated during the first years at about 30 officers and men. As a result of an expedition to protect Texas from French encroachment in 1719, the new governor, the marqués de Aguayo, reinforced Spain's Texas outposts and placed them on more solid footing. The garrison at Béxar was increased to 54 officers and men, who, along with the families of many, made up the nucleus of San Antonio's population.

Fluctuations in garrison size took place during the mid-eighteenth century in response to Indian hostilities and French withdrawal from Louisiana. In 1756, Béxar's garrison was reduced by 22 men, who were made part of the garrison of a new presidio assigned to the Apache mission at the San Sabá River. Reorganizations of Texas outposts following the outbreak of hostilities with the Comanches and Norteños in the late 1750s, and the 1763 Treaty of Paris, led to the temporary reinforcement of Béxar in the 1760s and expansion of the garrison to 80 men in 1773. By 1781, the command had grown to 100, the unit's approximate strength well into the nineteenth century.

Jesús F. de la Teja

References

Gerald E. Poyo and Gilberto M. Hinojosa, *Tejano Origins in Eighteenth-Century San Antonio* (1991).

See also AGUAYO EXPEDITION; NORTEÑOS; SAN ANTONIO; TEXAS

Fort Sandusky (Ohio)

Two forts, one French on the north shore of Lake Sandusky, a second British on the lake's south shore, bore the name Sandusky. Wyandots (Hurons) were most numerous of the region's people, but Delawares, Shawnees, Six Nations Iroquois, Caughnawagas, and others also hunted, traded, and planted in the area throughout the mid-eighteenth century. The French erected their post in November or December 1750, as part of their effort to restrict British trading activities. Twenty troops garrisoned the small palisaded enclosure, south of present-day Port Clinton, Ohio. They withdrew in November 1753, on orders from their superiors.

Ten years later, Britain's Fort Sandusky, which stood near what is now Bay Bridge, Ohio, had a less happy end. Erected to secure communications with Detroit, the British did not bother to gain permission for use of the site from the Indians. Under orders from Fort Pitt's commander, Colonel Henry Bouquet, and at the desire of General Jeffery Amherst, Lieutenant Elias Meyer established the fort in August 1761, and left its garrison of 15 under the command of Ensign H.C. Pauli, who finished the construction in November. British visitors to the post that year included Sir William Johnson and George Croghan. While local Indians frequented the blockhouse to trade and to request gifts, Pauli noted rumors of plots against it in 1762. On 16 May 1763, seven Wyandot and Ottawa visitors surprised and captured Pauli within its walls. Before plundering the storehouses and magazine, and before burning the blockhouse to the ground, other warriors slew the remaining 27 British soldiers and civilians in one of the first episodes of "Pontiac's War." Pauli, carried to the villages investing Detroit, managed to escape into that garrison on 3 July.

Gregory E. Dowd

References

Howard Peckham, *Pontiac and the Indian Uprising* (1947); Erminie Wheeler-Voegelin, *Indians of Northwest Ohio: An Ethnohistorical Report on the Wyandott Potawatomi, Ottawa, and Chippewa of Northwest Ohio* (1974); ———, "An Ethnohistorical Report," in Ermine Wheeler Voegelin and Helen Hornbeck Tanner, eds., *Indians of Northern Ohio and Southeastern Michigan* (1974).

See also BOUQUET, HENRY; DETROIT; OTTAWA; PONTIAC'S WAR

Sandusky Bay (Ohio)

Sandusky Bay was located on the southwestern portion of Lake Erie in the present-day state of Ohio. In the 1740s, chief Angouirot of the Hurons settled in this area. The French originally explored this region, and by 1749, English traders were also frequenting the area. Both the French and British established trading posts here. In 1763, a fort was constructed, but it was destroyed by a fire during Pontiac's War.

Michael W. Nagle

See also PONTIAC'S WAR; FORT SANDUSKY (OHIO)

Fort San Francisco de Pupo (Florida)

San Francisco de Pupo was a small wooden fort located on the west bank of the St. Johns River, seven leagues west of St. Augustine, Florida, on the old Indian trail to Spain's western province of Apalachee. It was constructed in the fall of 1734 on the orders of Governor Francisco del Moral Sánchez, who anticipated English and Indian attacks. Governor Moral spent 2,036 pesos on the construction of Pupo and its twin on the east bank of the St. Johns, Fort Picolata. Pupo was described as 20 yards square and surrounded by a shallow entrenchment. It contained a blockhouse, barracks, and storehouses, and was fortified with several small cannons. Nine soldiers manned the fort. In the summer of 1738, Lower Creeks allied to the English attacked Fort Pupo, did some damage to the structures, and killed two soldiers. On 1 January 1740, General James Oglethorpe of Georgia commanded a larger force of Creek, Chickasaw, and Uchize Indians and Highland rangers that captured Pupo and Picolata after killing 12 Spanish soldiers. Pupo was retaken by the Spaniards in May 1740.

Jane Landers

References

Verne E. Chatelain, *The Defenses of Spanish Florida 1565 to 1763* (1941); John Jay TePaske, *The Governorship of Spanish Florida 1700–1763* (1964).

See also FLORIDA, INVASION OF; MORAL SÁNCHEZ, FRANCISCO DE; OGLETHORPE, JAMES EDWARD; FORT PICOLATA (FLORIDA)

Presidio San Francisco Xavier (Texas)

Presidio San Francisco Xavier (1751–1756) held a garrison organized to protect the three Franciscan missions established for central Texas Indian tribes on the San Gabriel River, Milam County. At the request of a number of small tribes seeking Spanish protection from the Lipan Apaches, missionaries from San Antonio set up operations on the banks of the San Gabriel, then known as the San Xavier, in the spring of 1746. In 1748, the viceroy ordered a temporary guard of 30 men, to be taken from the presidios of Los Adaes and La Bahía, assigned to the new establishment. The formal order for a garrison did not come until 1751; it called for 50 soldiers as well as civilian settlers, all with families, who were to be granted land and water rights in the vicinity of the mission.

Felipe de Rábago, appointed commander of the presidio, immediately ran into trouble with the missionaries. His personal conduct and that of other members of the garrison, combined with lack of cooperation and resistance to the missionaries' requests for assistance, produced a decree of excommunication against the whole garrison. Soon after, in mid-1752, Rábago was implicated in the murder of the husband of a woman with whom he had had sexual relations, and in the murder of one of the missionaries. These crimes, the drying up of the San Marcos River, and the outbreak of an epidemic among remaining mission Indians threw the whole central Texas enterprise into turmoil.

By 1755, the missions had been abandoned by the neophytes, and the presidio was in a state of disrepair. The new commander, Pedro de Rábago y Terán, took it upon himself to transfer the whole establishment to the San Marcos River. There the garrison remained until late

1756 when royal authorities ordered it to become part of the new presidio for the Apache mission on the San Sabá River.

Jesús F. de la Teja

References

Herbert E. Bolton, *Texas in the Middle Eighteenth Century: Studies in Spanish Colonial History and Administration* (1970); Donald E. Chipman, *Spanish Texas, 1519–1821* (1994).

See also Presidio Nuestra Señora de los Delores de los Tejas (Texas); Presidio Nuestra Señora del Pilar de Los Adaes (Louisiana)

Fort San Juan (North Carolina)

Fort San Juan was built by Spanish captain Juan Pardo in December 1566, close to the Indian village of Xualla, at the foothills of the Appalachian Mountains, near the present-day town of Marion. Pardo left shortly afterward, leaving a garrison of 30 men under the command of Sergeant Hernando Moyano (also spelled Boyano). Moyano used the fort as a base for several bloody attacks against the Cherokee Indians. The fort was subsequently overrun by Indians in 1568.

Jim Sumner

See also Pardo, Juan

Castillo de San Marcos (Florida)

The Spanish-built Castillo de San Marcos, the stone fort at St. Augustine and the oldest masonry fort in the continental United States, was constructed in the last quarter of the seventeenth century. Florida was a low-lying peninsula of forbidding wilderness. An interior of impenetrable swamps and forests was bounded by a 1,200-mile coastline cut by broad estuaries and dangerous harbors exposed to tropical storms and violent winds. The climate was marked by excessive heat and humidity. Except for a few isolated spots of high ground in the interior where native populations were hostile, the soil was sandy and swampy and not suitable to agriculture.

Although Florida itself had little appeal, it was vital to the protection of the great commercial route that linked the rich Latin American colonies to the mother country, and St. Augustine became the keystone in Spain's defense of Florida. Ships that carried the riches that had made Spain the most powerful nation in sixteenth-century Europe followed a great circle route guided by wind and current, called the Bahama Channel, that passed close by the tip of Florida. Spain, thus, had to defend Florida to prevent pirates and other enemies from using its many harbors as bases from which to attack the treasure fleets.

Pedro Menéndez de Avilés established St. Augustine in 1565 as the northern most outpost of Spain's vast New World empire. Strategically located on a sheltered harbor in northeast Florida, the colony could serve as a base for the protection of Spanish colonial commerce in the Bahama Channel and as a staging point for military operations to both the north and south. The harbor was bounded on the east by 14-mile-long Anastasia Island, which provided protection from coastal storms. The entrance was a narrow, shallow channel between the island and the mainland requiring expert navigation and favorable tides and winds to pass through. The town sat approximately one mile north of the confluence of the San Sebastian and Matanzas Rivers on a short peninsula of land on the west side of the harbor. In colonial times, a small stream, with wide marshes along both banks, flowed for a mile west of St. Augustine, emptying into the San Sebastian River. To the north a narrow tongue of land widened into hard-to-penetrate pine barrens, cypress swamps, palmetto scrub, and oak groves.

During its first 100 years, St. Augustine was defended by a succession of nine wooden forts, which could be built quickly and cheaply, but were short-lived, falling prey to heat and humidity, shoddy construction, and fire. By the mid-1660s, the ninth and last fort was so rotten as to be useless, leaving St. Augustine nearly without defenses. For years, the governors in Florida had pleaded for the construction of a stone fort as a bulwark against pirate attacks and English encroachments from the north, but to no avail. As Spain's wealth and power diminished, neither the viceroy in New Spain nor the monarch in Europe was willing to commit the needed resources. Then, in May 1668, the English pirate, Robert Searles, staged a daring midnight raid, sacking and nearly destroying St. Augustine and gaining damaging knowledge of the city's weaknesses. Almost one-fourth of the Spanish population was killed, including 60 soldiers, out of a total of 130 in all of Florida. This attack shocked the Spaniards, and when two years later the English established Charles Town within striking distance of Florida, Queen Mariana ordered the construction of the castillo.

In 1671, the queen ordered Don Manuel de Cendoya to Florida as governor with specific instruction to construct the fort. She also commanded the viceroy of New Spain to provide Cendoya with an initial 12,000 pesos ($18,960) for this purpose, and to pay to Florida an additional 10,000 pesos a year until the fort was completed.

Local workers in Florida had no experience in masonry construction, so Cendoya recruited skilled labor in Cuba, including Ignacio Daza, a military engineer schooled in Italian-Spanish principles of fortifications; a master of construction; two master masons; seven masons; eight stonecutters; and 12 carpenters. In Florida, he drafted Indians from the Guale, Timucua, and Apalachee tribes as the primary unskilled labor, some of whom later became carpenters. Spanish peons, convicts, and English prisoners from Carolina rounded out the workforce. Some prisoners proved to be skilled workers, were promoted to positions of responsibility, and became permanent residents. Wages ranged from one reale (12 $1/2$ cents) a day for the Indian laborers to three pesos a day for military engineer Daza. The workforce fluctuated, but at its height, totalled approximately 150 men, 100 of whom were Indian laborers.

Cendoya chose to build the castillo on the site of the last wooden fort, immediately to the north of the city. History had proven that this location, on the west side of the Matanzas River and west of the northern tip of Anastasia Island, took maximum advantage of the harbor's natural defenses. Occupying a narrow strip of high ground, this site enabled the guns of the fort to command both the harbor entrance to the east and the only land access to the north.

The fort was built of coquina, a hard durable stone created from shells of the mollusk Donax and found along the upper east coast of Florida. In August 1671, Cendoya opened a quarry nine miles from the location of the castillo. Rock was taken by wagon across land to a marshy creek and from there ferried by raft to the building site. At the same time, Cendoya built two kilns next to the old fort, in which oyster shells were heated white hot to make quality lime. By the spring of 1672, 7,000 pounds of lime and great piles of stone had been stockpiled.

Daza designed a straightforward fort slightly larger than the old wooden fort. The central plaza was a hollow square surrounded by solid masonry walls 30 feet high and 12 feet thick, with diamond-shaped bastions at each corner. Two sides of each bastion were of a greater length, creating an angle from which the cannons could defend every adjacent part of the fort walls with a deadly crossfire. The walls were packed with rubble and sand to support the weight of the 50 cannons of various types and weights with which the fort was equipped. Each bastion also contained rooms on the ground floor for storing guns and ammunition. A ravelin, a triangular outerwork, shielded the only entrance. A moat, with two drawbridges, surrounded the fort, including the ravelin. Two gates on the seawall let tidal water in and out. Beyond the moat, a man-made embankment shielded the lower forts walls and offered protection entering and leaving. Courtyard structures underwent significant changes during the fort's 300-year history. Surviving plans from 1675, however, show a 24-by-90-foot rectangular, one-story building along the west wall, originally partitioned for a guardroom, armory, and provision magazine, and soon after repartitioned to include quarters for a lieutenant. No other quarters were planned, as soldiers lived in St. Augustine except when on guard duty, usually a 24-hour shift.

Actual construction began with the groundbreaking on Sunday, 2 October 1672. The first stone was laid on 9 November, but after an initial burst of progress, problems and slowdowns plagued the project. Illness felled Indian laborers, peons, and townspeople. Cendoya left in 1673 and was not replaced for two years. Supply ships were lost, and laborers had to be taken off construction and sent to Indian villages for food. The viceroy in New Spain repeatedly refused to release funds. When Governor Hita Salazar arrived in 1675, he had to work without an engineer and with an incompetent master of construction and received no subsidy during his entire four-year term. Yet, by the time he left in 1680, he had raised all four walls, built two bastions, and mounted cannons on the palisade. The castillo could be used as a defense. When Juan Cabrera arrived in 1680 to replace Salazar as governor, he recruited an experienced foreman who, along with an engineer from Cuba, conducted an inspection of the fort that revealed errors in construction. Both the bastions and parapets had to be rebuilt. Still, by 1686, in spite of repeated raids by the English, pirates, and Indians, the main part of the castillo was essentially complete. In

S

1688, escaped slaves from Charles Town arrived in St. Augustine and were hired as free labor to work on the fort at a wage of four reales a day. Seven years later, Governor Laureano de Torres put the finishing touches on the outerworks to protect against siege guns and scaling ladders. In 1695, after 25 years of construction and at a cost of approximately $150,000, the castillo was completed. One year later, the soldiers in the fort anonymously warned the governor they would surrender if the English attacked because they were starving.

Even before completion, the fort proved its worth as a defense against attack, as a refuge for the townspeople, and as a base of offensive operations. In 1686, when pirates threatened St. Augustine, the colonists sought protection in the fort, and the attackers retreated without attempting a siege. In the same year, Cabrera sent troops north to attack a Scottish colony at Port Royal, South Carolina.

Then, in 1702, during the War of the Spanish Succession (Queen Anne's War), the castillo successfully came through its baptism of fire. Charles Town had flourished while the castillo was being built, and by 1702, Governor James Moore of South Carolina felt strong enough to attack St. Augustine. Yet, even with a force of 800 soldiers and Indians that vastly outnumbered the Spanish fighting men, the English were unable to capture the fort. Taking their cattle and food, and with good wells inside the walls, 1,400 townspeople and 410 soldiers waited out a 50-day siege within the fort. When Spanish men-of-war arrived to block the harbor, Moore retreated, burning the city to the ground. The castillo was unscathed, and often throughout the following years, the townspeople slept within its walls.

The Spanish learned from this experience. During the next few years, in an effort to protect the town, they constructed strong earthenworks, palisades, and redoubts out from the castillo to the north and west. The first of these, the Cubo Line, was built in 1704 and extended west from the fort to the San Sebastian River. St. Augustine became essentially a walled city. In 1728, Colonel John Palmer led South Carolina troops to the gates of St. Augustine, but was discouraged from attacking by the defenses of the castillo.

By 1737, when Manuel de Montiano was appointed governor, the courtyard structure was in ruins, and the wooden palisades were rotten. At the time of Montiano's appointment,

Antonio de Arredondo was also sent to Florida to participate in diplomatic negotiations with the English, who were becoming increasingly aggressive, and to assist in the preparation of military defenses. The two men recommended extensive rehabilitation and modernization of the castillo and brought in an experienced engineer, Pedro Ruiz de Olano, from Cuba. By the end of 1739, eight masonry vaults, covered with four feet of fill, replaced timber-supported rooms along the east side. A six-inch bed of mortar was spread over the entire renovated roof of the fort, enabling the cannoneers to maneuver heavy guns at will. The Cubo Line was repaired, and a new stockade was built outside to strengthen the covered way. Military reinforcements brought the size of the garrison to approximately 750 soldiers.

In early 1750, Governor James Oglethorpe of Georgia invaded Florida in a major campaign of the War of Jenkins' Ear. After attacking Fort Mose to the north of St. Augustine, Oglethorpe approached the city on 13 June, and the 2,000 residents fled to the protection of the castillo and its defensive lines around the city. The South Carolinians were unable to enter the harbor and were forced to batter the fort and the city from Anastasia Island. The attack lasted for 38 days, but the British guns were ineffective against the massive walls. In the middle of the siege, Spanish soldiers were able to leave the castillo undetected and retake Fort Mose, inflicting major losses on the Scottish troops left there. Oglethorpe eventually retreated, at the onset of the hurricane season, after a desperate assault attempt from the north was driven back, and six Spanish half-galleons arrived from Havana with needed supplies for the fort.

The Spanish quickly repaired the slight damage done to the castillo during the siege. In 1743, Montiano built additional earthenworks to the north. During the next few years, decorative touches were added, and in 1752, the royal coat of arms was placed above the gate. In 1756, the castillo was officially declared finished in honor of King Ferdinand VI. Seven years later, Spain relinquished Florida and the castillo in order to regain Cuba, which had been captured by the British.

St. Augustine became a regimental headquarters for the English, who repaired the palisades, gate, and earthenworks of the castillo and added second stories to some interior rooms. During the Revolution, the British incarcerated prisoners from South Carolina in the castillo, including Lieutenant Governor Christopher Gadsden. Because of its alliance with France, Spain regained Florida and the fort in 1783 at the end of the war. Less than 40 years later, as a result of the Treaty of 1819, Florida was ceded to the United States, and the castillo was renamed Fort Marion. In 1837, during the Second Seminole War, Osceola and 82 of his followers were imprisoned in one of the southwest rooms. Twenty of the Indians crawled through a narrow opening in the wall to freedom. The Confederacy held the fort for 14 months during the Civil War. From 1875 through 1878, it served as a prison for southern Plains Indians. In 1900, the fort was deactivated as a military post and in 1924 was declared a national monument. In 1942, the original name, Castillo de San Marcos, was restored.

Kathryn L. Utter

References
Luis Rafael Arana, "Conservation and Reutilization of the Castillo de San Marcos and Fort Matanzas," *Florida Historical Quarterly* (1986):72–91; Verne Chatelain, *The Defenses of Spanish Florida 1565 to 1763* (1941); J.C. Harrington, Albert Manucy, and John M. Goggin, "Archaeological Excavations in the Courtyard of Castillo de San Marcos, St. Augustine, Florida," *Florida Historical Quarterly* (1955):101–139; Albert C. Manucy, *The Building of Castillo de San Marcos* (1945); ———, ed., *The History of Castillo de San Marcos and Fort Matanzas from Contemporary Narratives and Letters* (1955).

See also FLORIDA, BRITISH INVASION OF; MONTIANO, MANUEL DE; ST. AUGUSTINE; ST. AUGUSTINE, BATTLE OF; ST. AUGUSTINE, SIEGE OF

Fort San Mateo (Florida)
Fort San Mateo was founded by Pedro Menéndez de Avilés on 23 September 1656, after having captured a French garrison on the same site (Fort Caroline). The first Spanish commander was Gonzalo de Villaroel. A few days after its capture by the Spanish, the fort was burned when the French, under Jean Ribault, counterattacked. The fort was rebuilt and served as an important auxiliary to the fortress at St. Augustine. There was an attempted mutiny in both forts in 1566, due to the failure of supply ships to arrive. The next year, San Mateo was at-

tacked and burned by a French expedition under Dominique de Gourgues, aided by local Indians. The fort served as a refuge for the population of St. Augustine during Sir Francis Drake's raid in 1586. The purpose of the settlement changed with time, until it served more as a mission than a defensive site. The fort was located north of St. Augustine, on the south bank of the St. Johns River, some ten miles east of modern-day Jacksonville.

John F. Schwaller

See also FORT CAROLINE (FLORIDA); DRAKE, FRANCIS; MENÉNDEZ DE AVILÉS, PEDRO; RIBAULT, JEAN

Santa Elena (South Carolina)
Located on modern-day Parris Island, South Carolina, Santa Elena (1566–1587) marked the northernmost point of effective Spanish control in the province of La Florida.

The area was first visited in 1521 by Spanish explorers on slaving expeditions sent out from Santo Domingo. In 1526, one such explorer, Lucas Vázquez de Ayllón, guided by Francisco de Chicora, a Guale Indian captured on a previous expedition, returned with 500 settlers, including the first black slaves to be brought to the North American mainland. Ayllón's expedition ended in failure, and a later colonizing attempt led by Angel de Villafañe in 1561 was similarly unsuccessful. In 1562, French Protestants led by Jean Ribault and René de Laudonnière established a fort, Charlesfort, in the area. Starvation, desertion, and disease took a similar toll, and an expedition to the area sent from Havana in 1564, led by Hernando Manrique de Rojas found only an abandoned blockhouse and one 17-year-old survivor.

In response to French and English Protestant challenges to Spain's dominance, in 1565, Pedro Menéndez de Avilés erected a Spanish fort, San Felipe, and founded a settlement, Santa Elena, across the bay from the burned French fort. From here, in 1566, Captain Juan Pardo left in an attempt to discover a water passage to the Pacific and to discover rich mines he believed lay between La Florida and New Spain. Although the search for precious metals proved futile, Pardo's expedition reached as far inland as present-day Tennessee.

In 1576, the settlement was destroyed by a rebellion of a confederation of Guale and Orista tribes, and the Spanish survivors and missionaries were evacuated to St. Augustine. Reprisals by Menéndez de Avilés's nephew, Pedro Menéndez Marquéz, succeeded in quelling the Indian resistance, and the town was reestablished in 1580. At one time, Santa Elena vied with St. Augustine for dominance of the province. The colony was spared an attack by English corsair Francis Drake in 1586, but by 1587, Santa Elena was considered to be a liability and was abandoned for good.

Sherry Johnson

References

Paul S. Hoffman, *The Spanish Crown and the Defense of the Caribbean, 1535–1585: Precedent, Patrimonialism, and Royal Parsimony* (1980); Eugene Lyon, *The Enterprise of Florida: Pedro Menéndez de Avilés and the Spanish Conquest of 1565–1568* (1976); J. Leitch Wright, Jr., *The Only Land They Knew: The Tragic Story of the American Indians in the Old South* (1981).

See also AYLLÓN, LUCAS VÁZQUEZ DE; CHARLESFORT (SOUTH CAROLINA); GUALE; MENÉNDEZ DE AVILÉS, PEDRO; PARDO, JUAN; PORT ROYAL (SOUTH CAROLINA); RIBAULT, JEAN

Fort Saraghtoga (New York)

Fort Saraghtoga was built in 1709 by Colonel Francis Nicholson. Located at the present-day town of Easton, it was to protect the military road leading to Fort Edward (Fort Nicholson) throughout Queen Anne's War. The fort housed 450 men, was 150 feet by 140 feet, and was armed with six 12-pounder and six 18-pounder cannon. Fort Saraghtoga was destroyed in 1713.

Elizabeth Gossman

See also FORT EDWARD (NEW YORK); NICHOLSON, FRANCIS

Saratoga, Battle of (1745)

During the summer of 1745, most of the colonial soldiers and militia had departed New York on the expedition against Louisbourg. With most of the soldiers away, the French and their Indian allies began to increase their raids in central New York, resulting in a great deal of lost property and colonial lives.

William Johnson, an Indian trader in the Mohawk Valley, retaliated by inciting the Iroquois against the French. Johnson himself led many of the raids during the summer and fall of 1745.

The raids accomplished little other than to anger the French, who stepped up their attacks in the fall of 1745. They penetrated as far as Saratoga, and eventually to Albany.

The Saratoga attack consisted of 400 French soldiers and 220 Indians, primarily Caughnawaga and Abenakis from St. Francis, Montreal, and St. Frédéric. They moved with ease through the Mohawk Valley, meeting little to no resistance. They reached Saratoga, about 30 miles north of Albany, in November. The Mohawk Indians, who were aligned with the British, did not attempt to stop this force as it moved through their territory, for the Caughnawaga were Iroquois who had separated themselves from the league many years earlier.

With no serious opposition, the combined force of French and Indians attacked Saratoga in the early morning hours. They destroyed every structure within the town except for one sawmill located far from the site of the battle. The destruction of Saratoga was helped in part by the occupants of the town. The citizens became so terrified that they set fire to their own fort and fled down the Hudson River toward the safety of Albany. In all, the French and Indians killed or captured more than 100 individuals.

John M. Keefe

References

Donald Chidsey, *French and Indian War* (1969); Allan W. Eckert, *Wilderness Empire* (1969); Gene Gurney, *Pictorial History of the United States Army in War and Peace, from Colonial Times to Vietnam* (1966); Edward P. Hamilton, *The French and Indian Wars: The Story of Battles and Forts in the Wilderness* (1962); Maurice Matloff, *American Military History* (1985).

See also CAUGHNAWAGA; JOHNSON, WILLIAM; KING GEORGE'S WAR

Fort Saratoga (New York; also known as Fort Clinton, Fort Hardy, Fort Vroomen)

Located on Fish Creek, south of Schuylerville, the Fort Saratoga site was first occupied by Fort Vroomen, which was built by Bartolomeus Vroomen in 1689. This fort had an occasional garrison and was destroyed by the French in 1695. In 1709, it was rebuilt as Fort Saratoga, and later rebuilt again in 1721 under Captain Philip Livingston. The structure was square, palisaded, and had a blockhouse armed with cannon at each angle. The post was manned by militiamen at this time.

Although there was a third rebuild in 1739, it was burned down in 1744 by a group of about 400 French and 200 Indians. After burning the fort at Saratoga, this group continued on, plundering the Hudson Valley down to Albany. More rebuilds followed: one in 1745 as Fort Clinton (after Governor Charles Clinton), and another in 1757 by engineer Colonel James Montressor, this one known as Fort Hardy (after Governor Charles Hardy). The Fort Hardy site covered 15 acres, had two 120-foot barracks, and three storehouses. It was abandoned sometime after the end of the French and Indian War.

Elizabeth Gossman

References
Mark Boatner, *Landmarks of the American Revolution* (1973); Michael Kammen, *Colonial New York: A History* (1975).

Fort Sault Ste. Marie (Michigan)
See FORT REPENTIGNY (MICHIGAN)

Savannah
See SHAWNEE

Fort Saybrook (Connecticut)
In 1632, the earl of Warwick granted title to land at the mouth of the Connecticut River to several English gentlemen, including Lords Sale and Brooke, for which it was named. John Winthrop, son of the Massachusetts governor, was appointed Saybrook's governor for the first year. He dispatched 20 men to occupy the point, establish a settlement, and build a fort on the left bank of the river. Lion Gardener, a skilled engineer, came from England to plan and head construction efforts. With their strategic location, the English were able to keep the Dutch from reaching their own fort, Fort Good Hope, which was located just a few miles up the river at Hartford. In fact, this point controlled the only waterway in the Hartford region. The Dutch remained at Fort Good Hope, although they were increasingly isolated by growing numbers of English.

George Fenwick, an English gentleman and an agent of the land title holders, governed the colony for several years. In 1637, the small garrison at the fort found itself under attack by the Pequots during the Pequot War, and so the fort was reinforced with additional men. By agreement of the General Court, Fenwick sold the fort to colonial authorities at Hartford in December 1644. Fire destroyed the fort during the winter of 1647. The replacement structure was built nearer the riverbank and made of stone and earth. The fort soon fell into disuse as New London and New Haven replaced Saybrook as important shore points. Periodic repair of the facility was required to keep it functional. With the Revolutionary War at hand in the 1770s, repair efforts were again undertaken, but the fort was never ready for action. Saybrook Point was a strategic location during the War of 1812, so the fort was partially restored and renamed Fort Fenwick after its early leader. After the War of 1812, Fort Saybrook fell into a state of permanent disuse, and all remnants of its existence disappeared by 1871.

Leslie Miller

References
"Coast Forts in Colonial Connecticut," *The Coast Artillery Journal* 69 (1928):237–244; Bruce Grant, *American Forts Yesterday and Today* (1965); Robert B. Roberts, *Encyclopedia of Historical Forts: The Military, Pioneer, and Trading Posts of the United States* (1988).

See also CONNECTICUT; FORT GOOD HOPE (CONNECTICUT); PEQUOT WAR; WINDSOR BLOCKHOUSE (CONNECTICUT); WINTHROP, JOHN (FITZ-JOHN)

Scalp Bounties
While the act of scalping itself existed in North America before Europeans ventured there in the early modern period, colonists turned this ritualistic practice into a business through the advent of scalp bounties. These bounties were payments, often quite generous, which were bestowed on colonists who brought scalps back from conflicts with Indians and turned them over to colonial authorities. Initially intended to encourage colonists to kill putatively hostile Indians, the bounties became, within the commercial economy of eastern North America, a way for some colonists to enhance

revenues even when there was no great danger from Indians.

Scalp bounties existed in many, if not all, of the English colonies in North America, and other Europeans, too, adopted the custom. As early as the 1630s, the English paid Mohegan Indians for the scalps of Pequots, and the Dutch offered remuneration in wampum for the heads of Raritan Indians in New Amsterdam. In times of war the bounties became further incentive for soldiers to carry out the wishes of those in command. While the practice of taking scalps was perhaps new to English warriors in the seventeenth century, it did not represent an enormous departure from the military tactics of the Elizabethan period. After all, English military leaders in Ireland had already been busy cutting off the heads of the hostile native Irish in order to terrorize the population; this tactic had been seemingly perfected by Sir Humphrey Gilbert in the late sixteenth century when he decapitated battle victims and laid out their heads on both sides of a path leading to his tent "so that," Thomas Churchyard recorded, "none could come into his tente for any cause but commonly he must passe through a lane of heddes, which he used *ad terrorem*" to intimidate the survivors.

Yet cutting off the heads of battle victims and paying colonists, many of them civilians, for Indian scalps did represent an historic shift. Most significant, the use of scalp bounties encouraged those who would, in all likelihood, have shied away from such acts to assault the bodies of dying or deceased Indians. Indeed, since scalp bounties rewarded colonists for the skins they had taken off Indians, there emerged a backwoods cottage industry involved in the production of scalps. At times, would-be scalp hunters scalped Indians who were already dead, or divided the scalps they had into several pieces to claim they had scalped more Indians than they actually had. With the desire for profit so firmly established among the English, an act intended to subdue Indians became, over time, a way for hinterland settlers to increase their revenue without suffering undue risks from Indians. Rather than solving the initial problem of vanquishing hostile Indians, colonial officials eventually had to cope with the fraud associated with the trade in scalps.

While scalp bounties thus integrated human flesh into the market, they remained a different type of commodity as well. The story of Hannah Duston, described in a brief but fast-paced narrative by one of New England's most famous clerics, Cotton Mather, demonstrates the importance of these rewards in colonial society. Taken captive in Haverhill, Massachusetts, in 1697, near the end of King William's War, Duston witnessed the destruction of her home and the murder of her newborn child, and was forced to walk miles through the woods only days after giving birth. She awoke one night when the group holding her, several of them women, slept, and finding justification for her actions in the Book of Judges, she and two of her fellow captives fell upon the Indians, killing and scalping ten of them. "[C]utting off the scalps of the ten wretches," Mather wrote, "they came off and received fifty pounds from the General Assembly of the province as a recompense of their action, besides which they received many presents of congratulation from their more private friends. But none gave them a greater taste of bounty than Colonel [Francis] Nicholson, the governor of Maryland, who, hearing of their action, sent them a very generous token of his favor." While Duston became celebrated for her bravery, the fact that her story included prominent mention of the reward she received was perhaps more notable, for it taught a lesson to a public eager to read captivity accounts: scalping Indians was profitable, regardless of the gender (or age) of the victims.

Over time, scalp bounties became more sophisticated, no doubt a response to the growing sophistication of the trade in scalps. When Massachusetts, which had passed its first law intended to reward those who brought in scalps in 1694, revised its statute in 1704, the act prescribed different reward for the scalps of Indians, depending on their gender and age; it further prevented payments for scalps of Indians under ten years old, and later acts there and elsewhere raised the minimum age to 12 or higher. In Pennsylvania, however, where Indian attacks against colonists troubled provincial officials in the late colonial period, Lieutenant Governor John Penn authorized payments for scalps of Indians as young as ten in 1764, although the colony paid more for the scalps of men than those of women: the scalps of male Indians ten or older brought 134 pieces of eight; the scalps of females ten or older brought 50 pieces of eight. Such bounties pleased the Paxton Boys, a band of backcountry Pennsylvania vigilantes, who believed that "reward for Indian scalps" would "encourage the seeking them in their own country as the most likely means of destroying or reducing [the Indians] to reason"; they hoped the bounties sufficient "to the dangers attending enterprises of this nature."

While the modifications in laws, and their greater specificity, were no doubt intended to limit the violence of colonists against Indian women and children, the presence of these laws throughout the eighteenth century indicated the continued perception among colonists that Indians were a threat to their existence. Wedding the pursuit of scalps to the market economy, however, gave colonists in hinterland areas further reason to attack Indians. If successful, they would not only gain fame and status but, as they knew from colonial statutes and widely read captivity narratives, fortune as well.

Peter C. Mancall

References

James Axtell, "Scalping: The Ethnohistory of a Moral Question," in James Axtell, ed., *The European and the Indian: Essays in the Ethnohistory of Colonial North America* (1981):207–241; Alden T. Vaughan and Edward W. Clark, eds., *Puritans Among the Indians: Accounts of Captivity and Redemption, 1676–1724* (1981).

See also DUSTON, HANNAH; HAVERHILL (MASSACHUSETTS); INDIAN WARFARE; INDIAN WARFARE, EUROPEAN ACCOUNTS OF; LOVEWELL, JOHN; PAXTON BOYS; SCOUT

Scalping

According to the *Oxford English Dictionary*, scalping is the cutting "off the scalp (of a person): chiefly said of the North American Indians." Yet such a definition does little to capture the symbolic meaning of scalping in early America. By the late seventeenth century, if not earlier, few acts of violence were as famous, or infamous, as scalping. The practice, laden with cultural significance for Indians, came over the course of the colonial period to symbolize relations between the peoples competing for power in eastern North America. The act, chilling as it was, soon became a customary part of colonial warfare as well, particularly in encounters with Indians.

Archaeological evidence indicates that scalping had existed long before European colonization of North America began. Significantly, not all of those who were scalped died immediately; skulls have been found that indicate partial scalp regrowth after scalping, a remarkable phenomenon given the injury to the head while the victim's scalp was removed.

Scalping fascinated European explorers who traveled through North America. The Stadaconans showed Jacques Cartier evidence of scalping near Quebec in 1535; traveling in Apalachee country, Hernando De Soto witnessed the act in west Florida in 1540. By the mid-sixteenth century, Jacques Le Moyne de Morgues provided a description of scalping as it was practiced by Timucua Indians in the Southeast. "In these skirmishes those who fall are immediately dragged out of the camp by those entrusted with this responsibility," he wrote in 1564, "and they cut the skin of the head down to the skull (*capitis cutim ad cranium*) with pieces of reed sharper than any steel blade, from the brow in a circle to the back of the head; and they pull it off while, gathering the hair, which is still attached to it and more than a cubit long, into a knot at the crown; and what there is over the brow and back of the head they cut off in a circle to a length of two fingers, like the fringe around a skullcap; on the spot (if there is enough time) they dig a hole in the ground and kindle a fire with moss." Once dried, the warriors made the scalp "hard like parchment" and then "triumphantly" returned to their communities.

Le Moyne's description of scalping, as well as the vivid testimony of other observers, emphasized the ritualistic aspects of the act. To scalp an enemy in conflict was, for many Indians, a symbolic act of the greatest importance. And the rituals involved with scalping did not end at the battle site. Significantly, elaborate ceremonies often ensued when Indians returned home with scalps. Dried scalps became important items in their own right, often decorated and displayed in ritually determined ways; women greeted warriors returning with scalps and thus joined in the celebration of the warrior's victory. As James Axtell has aptly pointed out, in a world where "the honors of war were so eagerly sought and so highly valued," scalps convinced those who were not present at the battle of the fortitude of the victors. Since to many Indians scalps represented, in Axtell's words, "the transference of power and identity into the victor's hand," it is not surprising that elaborate ceremonies took place to commemorate the act.

Colonists too recognized the special significance of the act and some, especially those held captive by Indians, believed it a punishment inflicted largely on the English. "Now having killed two of my children," a captured Elizabeth Hanson wrote in an account of her ordeal, "they scalped them (a practice common with these people, which is whenever they kill any English people they cut the skin off from the crown of their heads and carry it with them for a testimony and evidence that they have killed so many, receiving sometimes a reward of a sum of money for every scalp. . . ."

Yet while Indians developed rituals associated with scalping, the act of cutting off the forehead and bringing it back home did not long remain solely in the hands of Indians. Over the course of the colonial period many colonists also became enraptured by the power of scalping, and they turned to it with a flourish, often receiving reward for the scalps they brought back. Like Indians, colonists often displayed scalps, at times riding triumphantly through the streets of settlements, including Boston and New York, with scalps recently taken in combat. Thomas Penn, governor of Pennsylvania in the late 1750s, even considered sending a scalp taken at Kittanning to the British Museum, presumably for display to a much larger English audience. Significantly, by the end of the colonial period, English colonists participated in scalping Indians for the reward, monetary and cultural, that they felt such acts would bring. Whatever horror scalping had originally suggested to colonists about the savagery of Indians had apparently lessened dramatically. While an act of Indian invention, colonists found scalping an acceptable method of displaying the bellicosity that lay at the heart of the colonization effort.

Peter C. Mancall

References
James Axtell, "Scalping: The Ethnohistory of a Moral Question," in James Axtell, *The European and the Indian: Essays in the Ethnohistory of Colonial North America* (1981):207–241; James Axtell and William C. Sturtevant, "The Unkindest Cut, or, Who Invented Scalping," *William and Mary Quarterly*, 3rd ser., 37 (1980):451–472; Alden T. Vaughan and Edward W. Clark, eds., *Puritans Among the Indians: Accounts of Captivity and Redemption, 1676–1724* (1981).

See also INDIAN WARFARE; INDIAN WARFARE, EUROPEAN ACCULTURATION OF; RAIDING PARTY; SCALP BOUNTIES

Schenckingh's Fort (South Carolina)

In May 1715, during the Yamasee War, this fort was built on the cattle ranch owned by Benjamin Schenckingh, located on the south bank of the Santee River, 20 miles northwest of present-day Moncks Corner in Berkeley County. A month later, a war party of Catawba Indians and their allies attacked the fort and its force of 30 men. Using the pretense of conducting negotiations, the Indians gained entry, whereupon they killed or captured most of the defenders, and burned the fort.

Gregory D. Massey

References
Larry E. Ivers, *Colonial Forts of South Carolina 1670–1775* (1970).

See also CATAWBA; YAMASEE WAR

Schenectady, Battle of (1690)

In 1690, the French forces in Canada decided to launch a series of assaults on the northern frontier of America. A three-pronged strike was decided on: the first contingent led by Jacques Le Moyne de Sainte-Hélène and Nicolas d'Ailleboust de Manthet was to move into position at Montreal; a second force at Trois Rivières on the St. Lawrence was under the command of Joseph-François Hertel de La Fresnière; and would attack Salmon Falls, New Hampshire; the third force, made up mostly of about 50 French and 60 Abenakis led by Captain Pierre Robinau de Portneuf, was to head for Quebec by way of the Chaudiere River. Once in the area the third force was to begin assaults on the coastal settlements of Maine. The object of this offensive was two-fold; to demoralize the English colonists and to prevent any further advance on New France by ridding the area of English settlements. As a byproduct of the raid it was hoped that the surrounding Indian tribes would be impressed by the French strength and the British weakness.

Unfortunately for the French, the attack did not work according to plan. The physical separation of the three forces, coupled with the harsh conditions, prohibited intercommunication and close coordination between the three groups. Sainte-Hélène's Montreal group struck first. By February of 1690, only 200 men out of the 160 French and 199 converted Iroquois that began the journey made it to the upper Hudson Valley. The French had chosen to attack at Albany because it was embroiled in a public political struggle stemming from the new provincial government led by Jacob Leisler. It was believed that Albany lacked any kind of support from the lower colony. Yet, Albany retained a small English garrison along with a number of Connecticut militiamen; its outward appearance seemed solid.

Because of the possible strength of the Albany garrison, the Iroquois persuaded Sainte-Hélène to launch an attack on Schenectady instead. Twenty miles from Albany, on the southern bank of the Mohawk River, the village of Schenectady stood encircled by a palisade of vertical stakes. The only line of communication between Schenectady and Albany was a small, rarely used cart path. Not only was the village physically isolated, but Schenectady was decidedly hostile toward Albany. Political rivals, the two towns eyed each other with suspicion. It was this physical isolation and political division that made a coordinated system of defense along New York's frontier an impossibility.

Rumors of an impending assault on Schenectady had reached Albany by that winter of 1690, and a small contingent of troops was sent to protect the town. Along with the troops, the Albany convention (city and county officials) cautioned the people of Schenectady to realize the seriousness of their situation. However, this warning went unheeded. The winter of 1690 was fierce, and Schenectady did not believe that any sort of attack would be forthcoming. Furthermore, the people of Schenectady saw the Albany forces as not only unnecessary but as an insult as well; the troops were unceremoniously sent back to Albany. As a further show of independence from the Albany convention, the people discharged the guards from Schenectady's gates and replaced them with snowmen, claiming that the snowmen were the only sentinels Schenectady needed. The townspeople were soon to discover their mistake.

A blizzard began at Schenectady on 8 February 1690, continuing throughout the day and into the night. Believing in their ultimate safety, most of the townspeople were asleep by 11:00 P.M. and were unaware of the French and Indian force that was moving down from Montreal toward them. In the early morning hours of 9 February, the French force passed through the unguarded gates of the village. Once inside the stockade, they divided into groups of six or seven and moved into position completely surrounding the village. Sud-denly a war cry arose, and the attack began. The raiding party proceeded to break down doors and take people by surprise as they lay in their beds. Men, women, and children all fell victim to the attack, as any resistance meant death for the entire household. Only one household, that of the Sanders family, was left untouched, as the family had previously shown kindness to several French captives. In the end, 60 people were killed, 27 were taken captive, and the rest of the village was left to escape down the road to Albany, many of whom froze or starved along the way. After the killing had ceased the French force remained in the village plundering houses and slaughtering livestock. When the raiding party finally left at noon of the next day they took with them 40 of the best horses they could find and killed the rest.

Although the English losses were heavy, the French left unhurt 20 Mohawks who lived in the village. This was to show the Mohawk that the French harbored no ill-will toward the Indians and that they hoped for a future Mohawk alliance. However, this was not to be, as the Mohawks joined a militia force in pursuit of the retreating French party. The militia force proved too slow, and the raiding party made it back to Montreal where they proclaimed complete success.

With the raid on Schenectady the French hoped to pull the sentiments of the Five Nations away from British influence and to extend their own alliance system; by doing this they hoped also to raise the sagging morale in New France. In reality, the raid only succeeded in alarming the British settlements and alerting them to future assaults. As a result, the British began to take the offensive with a series of their own attacks on French settlements such as La Prairie.

Elizabeth Gossman

References

James Thomas Flexner, *Mohawk Baronet* (1959); Robert West Howard, *Thundergate: The Forts of Niagara* (1968); Michael Kammen, *Colonial New York: A History* (1975); Howard Peckham, *The Colonial Wars, 1689–1762* (1964); William Smith, Jr., and Michael Kammen, eds., *The History of the Province of New York* (1972).

See also ALBANY; FALMOUTH, BATTLE OF; KING WILLIAM'S WAR; LA PRAIRIE, BATTLE OF (1690); LA PRAIRIE, BATTLE OF (1691); LEISLER'S REBELLION; SALMON FALLS, BATTLE OF

Fort Schuyler (New York)

Fort Schuyler was built at the same time as the much larger Fort Stanwix on the Mohawk River. It was located about 16 miles below Fort Stanwix, on the site of present-day Utica. The fort did not have a permanent garrison, since it was built only to provide shelter for supply parties that traveled up the river.

Elizabeth Gossman

Fort Schuyler (New York; on Hudson–Lake Champlain route)

See FORT ANNE (NEW YORK)

Schuyler, Peter (Pieter) (1657–1724)

Peter Schuyler was born 17 September 1657. One of ten children, he rose to be a merchant, deacon of the Dutch church in Albany, judge, justice of the peace, and lieutenant in the cavalry of the Albany militia, all by 1686. New York Governor Thomas Dongan gave Albany a city charter on 22 July 1686, and appointed Schuyler as Albany's first mayor, a position he held until 1694. He joined the Governor's Council in 1692, and sat on it until 1720 when he was dismissed because of political maneuvering behind his back. During his tenure on the council, he served as acting governor three times due to his seniority on the council: for two months in 1701; for three days in 1709; and finally, between July 1719 and September 1720. Politically, Schuyler proved to be a survivor, staying on good terms with succeeding governors until his death in February 1724, and even being offered a knighthood by Queen Anne during his visit to England in 1711. He declined the honor.

Schuyler served the colony of New York during the colonial wars in two capacities: militia officer and chairman of the board of commissioners for Indian affairs. In the militia, he started as a lieutenant, but rose to the rank of colonel, the highest rank then given by the English government to a colonist of New York. As mayor and ranking militia officer of Albany, Schuyler was responsible for the defense of the city from 1686 until 1694, after which he concentrated on his duties as Indian commissioner.

He gained his position as Indian commissioner due to his appointment as mayor of Albany. At that time, the city officials were the commissioners to the Five Nations of the Iroquois Confederacy. Albany was the gateway to the western Indian trade, and therefore became the site for all negotiations with the Five Nations. New York Governor Edmund Andros set up the board of commissioners in Albany in 1675, and when Albany was incorporated, the city officials continued to serve as commissioners. Only between 1696 and 1698 was there a board of commissioners separate from the Albany city officials, but after 1698, the board reverted to Albany's leaders.

After Schuyler's tenure as mayor, he remained chairman of the board due to his special relationship with the Iroquois, who affectionately gave him the name "Quidor," meaning "the Indians' friend." He earned this name by knowing their culture and learning their language, by leading them in combat, by dealing fairly with them, and by supplying them with food from his own farm. Schuyler served as chairman of the board until his death, except for one short interruption. In 1710, he left for England, and while he was gone, the board was reorganized and he was left off of it. The council, however, petitioned Governor Robert Hunter to reinstate him, which Hunter did. In 1698, during an earlier reorganization of the Board, political feuds in New York almost led to Schuyler's removal, but the Iroquois urged his retention, and he remained chairman of the board.

Schuyler's position as commissioner gave him great power over the Iroquois and the other colonies. New York's governors only allowed negotiations with the Iroquois Confederacy in Albany and through the auspices of the board, and therefore Schuyler was, in effect, the agent to the Five Nations for all the colonies until 1723, when Albany's monopoly ended. Iroquois delegates then went to Boston to negotiate directly with the New England colonies, though Schuyler accompanied the Iroquois party, thus retaining his special relationship with the Five Nations.

As militia officer and chairman of the board of commissioners, Schuyler played a pivotal role in the colonial wars that began in the 1680s. In 1687, even before a state of war existed between the English and French, Governor Dongan ordered Mayor Schuyler to prepare Albany's defenses and militia, enlist about 40 Indians as scouts, and assure the Iroquois of English protection. Meanwhile, Schuyler met with leaders of the Five Nations, gave them presents, and reassured the Indians that reinforcements would arrive. The next year, 1688, he strove to counter a growing French influence among the tribes caused by the presence of Jesuit priests.

Finally, war erupted in 1689, and Schuyler continued to prepare for war, improving the wooden palisades around the city. When threatened by attack, Schuyler forbade anyone capable of carrying arms to leave the city without permission, and he instituted fines for those who refused to take their turn on watch. Internal political turmoil also ensued in 1689 after the removal of King James II in England, and Governor Edmund Andros was put in jail in New York. Schuyler, some Mohawk warriors, and a detachment of Connecticut militia prepared to defend Albany from the self-appointed governor, Jacob Leisler. Only when Leisler proposed an attack on Canada did Schuyler cooperate, going to Massachusetts and Connecticut to ask for help. The plan collapsed in 1690. That same year, the French and their Indian allies attacked Schenectady, 20 miles northwest of Albany, and panic struck Albany. The raiders, however, returned to Canada, and Schuyler's brother, Captain John Schuyler, raided La Prairie, across the St. Lawrence River from Montreal. Meanwhile, Schuyler successfully countered French attempts to entice the Five Nations from their allegiance to the English crown.

In June 1691, Major Peter Schuyler raided into Canada with 260 men, about half English and Dutch militia and half Iroquois warriors. He entered Canada in late July and decided to strike La Prairie. Leaving 50 men behind to guard his canoes, he struck out across country and arrived 1 August near the French fort, which was defended by close to 800 French regulars, Canadian militia, and Indian allies. Schuyler's force surprised and scattered the Indians and Canadians outside the fort, but about 400 French regulars counterattacked and forced Schuyler's men into a ditch, where they repulsed two French attacks. Schuyler then led his own counterattack, marching behind the French. A wild melee ensued on the plains outside the fort, where, as Schuyler put it, they "fought them fairly." Beaten, the French retreated into the fort. Schuyler decided his men had done all they could, and they headed back for the canoes, blundering into a French and Indian ambush. Schuyler dramatically informed his men "there was not other choice, fight or dye," whereupon he led them in a charge, and the opposing forces fought at close quarters for about an hour. A final furious charge by the raiding party broke

through the French center, and Schuyler's force turned about and fought the enemy in the other direction. Finally the Franco-Indian force recoiled, and Schuyler admitted with understatement, "to say the truth we were all glad to see them retreat." Schuyler's party reached their canoes, waited five hours for stragglers to arrive, and then rowed off. On 9 August, they arrived in Albany with all of their wounded. Schuyler admitted to 43 dead and 25 wounded and claimed to have killed 200 of the enemy.

This 1691 raid had several good effects. It impressed the French, and the Canadian governor, Louis de Baude de Frontenac, described the action as the "most hot and stubborn ever known in Canada." More importantly, the action impressed the Iroquois, who admitted the English could fight, and admired Schuyler as a man of action. When Schuyler received reinforcement in late 1691, the Iroquois were more impressed. These events helped solidify Schuyler's hold on the allegiance of the Five Nations.

Governor Benjamin Fletcher arrived in 1692 and put Major Richard Ingoldsby in command at Albany, relegating Schuyler to second-in-command. Then, on 8 February 1693, about 350 French regulars and Canadian militia and 200 Indian allies struck three Mohawk villages near Schenectady. Warning arrived in Albany the day of the attack, and Major Ingoldsby called out the local militia. Schuyler went to calm the Mohawks, who were enraged that no English soldiers were in pursuit. Within four days of the initial attack, Schuyler had command of 200 militia at Schenectady, where he awaited orders from Ingoldsby to pursue. The Indian warriors who joined Schuyler threatened to leave if the militia did not march and finally Schuyler began the pursuit without orders, though the necessary orders arrived a few hours later.

The French began to retreat, and Schuyler pursued, leading 250 militia soldiers and about the same number of Iroquois warriors through the cold and snow. The Anglo-Indian force caught up with the French force, and both sides spent 17 February fighting and fortifying their camps, which were within sight of each other. On the 18th, the French retreated again, but Schuyler's militia refused to pursue farther without provisions. A small detachment followed but could not engage the enemy. Provisions arrived the next day, and Schuyler resumed the pursuit, but when they caught the French, Schuyler's Indian allies refused to attack due to a French threat to kill their Mohawk captives. The French safely crossed a river, and Schuyler had to break off the pursuit and return to Albany. Altogether, Schuyler reported eight dead and 14 wounded. Schuyler also had recovered almost 50 prisoners, and subsequently the French released almost all their prisoners in their haste to return to Canada.

This expedition helped ease Iroquois fears that the English would not protect them. They were especially pleased with Governor Fletcher's response. News of the 8 February attack arrived in New York City on the 12th, and by the 17th, Fletcher had arrived in Albany with about 300 soldiers. He immediately sent men and supplies to support Schuyler, but Schuyler, unaware that Fletcher's force was nearby, had already ended the pursuit. Schuyler's reputation with the Five Nations also improved, and Fletcher too was impressed, recommending him for a captaincy in the regular army. The request was never approved.

When not raiding, Schuyler used his reputation and position as Indian commissioner to keep the Five Nations allied to the English. From the beginning of the war, Schuyler recommended more presents to console the Indians for their losses in the constant raiding, and urged reinforcements for the defense of the frontier and the Indian allies. In a council in 1692, Schuyler urged the Five Nations to attack Canada, but the Iroquois leaders responded that they expected to see more English activity. This response probably induced Schuyler to react so quickly to the February 1693 raid.

After 1693, Schuyler held regular councils with the Iroquois, showering them with gifts and supplying them with food, often bought with his own money because he could never get enough from the New York government. Due almost solely to his efforts, influence, and reputation with the Five Nations, the Iroquois Confederacy stayed loyal to the English until the end of the war in 1697. In the process, he ruined his own finances.

While leading raids and negotiating with the Five Nations, Schuyler kept the New York governors and council informed of Indian and enemy activities along the New York-Canadian border, dispatching Indian and English scouts at his own expense, and reporting information gained at the Indian councils. Thus, the governors had a reliable source of intelligence on the current situation along the northern frontier.

The Treaty of Ryswick ended hostilities in 1697, and news of the treaty arrived in New York in 1698. Governor Fletcher sent Schuyler and Dominie Dellius to Canada to negotiate with Governor Frontenac concerning the implementation of the treaty and to arrange a prisoner exchange of French, English, and Indian captives. Taking the released French prisoners, Schuyler and Dellius arrived in Canada in May 1698. They met Frontenac, who released some of the English prisoners, but refused to return the Iroquois because he was in direct negotiations with them and did not recognize English sovereignty over them. Schuyler and Dellius returned home, collecting more English prisoners and gathering information on Canadian militia forces and defenses, which Schuyler reported to the governor. Schuyler and Dellius brought with them 25 freed English captives. By the next year, a new Canadian governor had finally returned the Iroquois prisoners.

The competition between Canada and New York for control of the Five Nations occupied Schuyler's full attention between 1698 and the opening of the next war in 1702. Richard Coote, the earl of Bellomont, New York's next governor, was displeased with the negotiations held with the Five Nations in 1698, and with Schuyler, who was under suspicion of abusing his position for personal profit. Despite these problems, Bellomont did not interfere with Schuyler's position on the Indian board, recognizing that Schuyler was indispensable. The Iroquois reinforced this point by generally criticizing English actions in the previous war, but praising their friend "Quidor," the only person who had come to their aid and had fought by their side.

Despite Schuyler's presence at the meetings in 1698–1699, the English began to lose their grip on the Five Nations. By 1700, after having suffered continued attack by Canada's Indian allies, the Iroquois were ready to sue Canada for peace. After a series of intense meetings between the French, New York's commissioners, Iroquois delegates, and French Indian allies, a preliminary treaty of peace between the French, their Indian allies, and the Five Nations was signed in September 1700. Schuyler managed to prevent an alliance between the Five Nations and Canada, and instead retained their friendship. In 1701, the Five Nations met in council with Lord Edward Cornbury, the new governor of New York, and told him they were glad to see that "Quidor" had good relations with the new governor.

Iroquois neutrality in Queen Anne's War, which raged in North America between 1702–1713, worked to New York's advantage because neither French-Canadian nor English forces dared violate Iroquois territory. Schuyler believed this neutrality was the best policy, even though it meant Canada could concentrate its forces against New England. He considered another war of raids a useless expenditure of effort and lives. Until the colonies could unite and attack Canada itself, Schuyler believed border clashes should be avoided. Meanwhile, he tried unsuccessfully to negotiate with Canada on Massachusetts's behalf for a similar treaty of peace with France's native allies, and he sent warnings to the New England governors whenever he received word from his Indian scouts of impending attack by French allies. As late as 1708, he was still trying for a treaty for Massachusetts.

Throughout these years of neutrality, Schuyler again spent his own money lavishly to hire spies and scouts, and to supply the Iroquois with food and other supplies.

In 1709, Colonel Samuel Vetch proposed a plan for a united colonial attack on Montreal and Quebec. Schuyler believed the time was opportune for such an attack, and he convinced the reluctant Five Nations to join the proposed expedition. The plan called for a colonial and Indian force to attack Montreal from New York, while a British fleet joined a colonial army to attack Quebec. Schuyler, now a colonel, was appointed second-in-command under Colonel Francis Nicholson of the army destined to attack Montreal. Schuyler also had command of one of the two New York regiments of militia, and the Indian allies were attached to his regiment. Schuyler was sent ahead toward Lake Champlain in June 1709 with the forces already assembled, and there he awaited the opening of the campaign. The British, however, diverted the promised fleet to Portugal, thus ending the proposed campaign, and by October the army near Lake Champlain had been sent home. The Five Nations were disappointed and alarmed because their neutrality was imperiled. They negotiated with the Canadian government and reestablished their neutrality, and in return got a Canadian guarantee not to attack Albany.

Schuyler had supported Vetch's plan because he believed that as long as the French held Canada, a lasting peace was impossible. Therefore, Schuyler decided to accompany colonel Nicholson and five Mohawk chiefs to England to impress the Mohawks with England's might and to plead at the court of Queen Anne for a renewed effort to eliminate the French. One Mohawk died at sea, but Schuyler, Nicholson, and the other four arrived in England in 1711. While the Mohawks created a sensation in the court, Schuyler had a personal meeting with the queen, and received presents and a portrait. He declined the Queen's offer of a knighthood.

Impressed with the importance of supporting the Indian allies and the colonial efforts against Canada, the home government decided to send another fleet and an army for a new campaign against Canada in 1711. The plan called for attacks against Quebec by sea and against Montreal by land from New York. Schuyler again persuaded the Five Nations to participate by countering the presence of French officers such as Charles Le Moyne de Longeuil, and by convincing the Iroquois to let him destroy a fort built by the French on Indian territory. After this event, the French momentarily relinquished their efforts to sway the Five Nations.

The Iroquois nations, however, decided to play both ends against the middle. They sent Schuyler 800 warriors, while they sent warnings to Canada of the intended expedition. The Iroquois by this time were more interested in extending their power to the west, but New York's Governor Robert Hunter refused to support such a move. Thus, relations between New York and the Iroquois remained cool.

Colonel Nicholson again commanded the Montreal wing, with Schuyler again commanding a regiment of militia and Indians. By mid-September, Nicholson and Schuyler were near Lake Champlain with more than 2,300 men. Then the fleet met disaster in the St. Lawrence River, where eight transports went aground and 800 men perished. The fleet sailed for home, and by early October, the army near Lake Champlain had disbanded.

Hostilities soon ended in 1712, and peace between Canada and the English colonies reigned until 1744. Schuyler's talents, however, remained in demand because Albany remained the reserved place for all negotiations with the Five Nations, and other English governors wanted to talk with the Iroquois. In particular, the southern governors feared the French might influence the Iroquois to attack the southern colonies or intervene in local wars between the southern colonists and local tribes. In 1712, the Iroquois offered to mediate between North Carolina and the Tuscarora, but received no response. When the Tuscarora had been badly weakened, they asked for asylum within the territory of the Five Nations, and permission was

S

granted after negotiations between Governor Hunter and his commissioners and the Five Nations. The Tuscaroras became the sixth nation in the confederation.

In 1715, Schuyler, Hunter, the Iroquois, and the southern governors were still holding conferences concerning the continued fighting between North Carolina and neighboring tribes, and Iroquois interests in these regions. As late as 1720, Schuyler met with the Iroquois nations, extracting a promise from the Iroquois not to attack any Indian tribes allied to the British in the south. In 1722, at age 65, he still attended a conference between the Iroquois and the governors of Virginia and Pennsylvania.

The French continued to exert their influence over the Iroquois throughout this period. In 1720, they built a fort at Niagara, and the Iroquois asked Schuyler, who at that time was in New York City presiding as acting governor, to go personally and tear this fort down as he had done in 1711. Schuyler did not feel he could leave New York City, and the fort remained, increasing French influence with the Six Nations. Schuyler did hold a conference later in 1720 to renew the friendship between the British and the Six Nations, but the Senecas did not arrive until after Schuyler had left. British dominance over the entire confederation continued to weaken. In 1721, he and the new governor, William Burnet, held another conference with the Iroquois. The governor decided to create a new English settlement only 60 miles from Niagara to offset the French. Partly due to Schuyler's reputation, his son, Peter Schuyler, Jr., was selected to lead this expedition.

Peter Schuyler died in 1724, having spent his adult life helping defend the northern frontier and working with the Iroquois Confederacy. The French in Canada feared and respected him, recognizing his courage and influence over the Iroquois, and his efforts to lessen the savagery of the frontier war. The Iroquois showed their admiration through the name "Quidor." They recognized that he treated them with respect, and though he did not adopt their customs, he dealt honestly with them and opened his own home and granaries to them when they were in need. Perhaps most importantly, he campaigned alongside them, which gained their trust and admiration.

The clearest proof of his lasting reputation among the Iroquois nations occurred decades after his death. When William Johnson, the renowned Indian commissioner of the mid-1700s, first won the hearts of the Iroquois, he was given the title "Quidor." As late as the beginning of the American Revolution in the 1770s, when the Continental Congress proposed a conference with the Six Nations, they demanded the presence of one of his descendants. Peter Schuyler accomplished much good for Albany and the English during almost 40 years as a militia officer and chairman of the board of commissioners for Indian affairs.

Mark V. Kwansy

References

Berthold Fernow, *Albany and Its Place in the History of the United States: A Memorial Sketch* (1880); Codman Hislop, *Albany: Dutch, English, and American* (1936); Francis Jennings, *The Ambiguous Iroquois Empire: The Covenant Chain Confederation of Indian Tribes with English Colonies from its beginnings to the Lancaster Treaty of 1744* (1984); Douglas Edward Leach, *The Northern Colonial Frontier, 1607–1736* (1966); Lawrence H. Leder, "Robert Livingston (1654–1728), Secretary for Indian Affairs, and His Papers," *Pennsylvania History* 23 (1956):5–14.

John J. McEneny, *Albany, Capital City on the Hudson: An Illustrated History* (1981); Joel Munsell, *The Annals of Albany* (1853); Edmund B. O'Callaghan, John R. Brodhead, and Berthold Fernow, eds., *Documents Relative to the Colonial History of the State of New York*, 15 vols. (1856–1887), Vol. III: "Major Peter Schuyler's Journal of His Expedition to Canada."

Francis Parkman, *Count Frontenac and New France Under Louis XIV* (1983); Howard H. Peckman, *The Colonial Wars, 1689–1762* (1964); Colonel Nicholas Reyard and Lieutenant Colonel Charles Ludwick, "A Narrative of an Attempt Made by the French of Canada Upon the Mahaques Country, Being Indians Under the Protection of Their Majesties Government of New-York" (1693); Mary Lou Rustig, *Robert Hunter, 1666–1734: New York's Augustan Statesman* (1983).

George W. Schuyler, *Colonial New York: Phillip Schuyler and His Family*, 2 vols. (1855); Allen W. Trelease, *Indian Affairs in Colonial New York: The Seventeenth Century* (1960); G.M. Waller, "New York's Role in Queen Anne's War, 1702–1713," *New York History* 33 (1952):40–53.

Scout

A "scout" referred to any armed force moving
beyond the frontier line, from defensive patrols
marching among frontier communities to extended raids striking deep into enemy territory.
Scouts were the cardinal element of warfare on
the northern frontier, the essence of *la petite
guerre*. Although the term "ranger" is usually
associated with such activity, especially with the
fame of Rogers' Rangers, the British military
apparently did not promote the use of that title
until the French and Indian War. There are one
or two rare references to provincial soldiers
"ranging" the woods before the 1750s, but in
all official references, especially in New England, including government documents, letters, and journals, the term "scout" is used as
a designation.

To "scout" means to observe the motions
and obtain intelligence concerning an enemy, but
la petite guerre of the New World added a combat emphasis as well. Scouts can be identified as
defensive or offensive by their primary goal and
scope of operation. Defensive scouts operated
"on the backs of the towns," or close to the frontier communities, and their mission involved four
major objectives: first, they had to look for signs
of enemy raiding parties, usually revealed by
their tracks or campsites, and warn the towns;
second, they protected the inhabitants while they
performed their labors; third, they pursued the
enemy after they had struck; and finally, they
ambushed known trails and fords used by enemy
raiding parties and Indian fishing sites. Of
course, the possibility always existed that the
patrol itself could be ambushed.

While defensive patrols may seem complicated, with their simultaneous objectives of
warning, protection, pursuit, and ambush, offensive raids can be viewed in rather simple terms—
they were either intelligence-gathering probes or
search-and-destroy missions. Despite the reports
of friendly Indians and other outside sources,
small companies of soldiers sent on deep probes
into enemy territory became the most common
method of gathering intelligence, especially for
the New England colonies. Numbering around
ten to 15 men to reduce the chance of detection,
these probes attempted to locate Indian villages
and determine occupancy, and chart major trails,
all to pave the way for larger raids.

These larger raids were nothing less than
search-and-destroy missions. New France targeted Iroquois villages in New York and frontier communities in New England to discourage
their expansion east and north. It was this sort
of large, offensive raid, involving French-led
Indian forces that caused the destruction of such
towns as York, Maine, and Deerfield, Massachusetts. The raiding parties against New England in the early wars were led by officers from
the *troupes de la marine* companies stationed in
New France, and the participants were drawn
principally from the eastern tribes, St. Francis
and other Christian Indians, Canadian militia
from Montreal and Trois Rivières, and a handful of eastern-based *coureurs de bois*.

To many historians, nothing illustrates the
chasm between the ineffectiveness of the English
provincials and the superiority of the French
more than the inability of the English to emulate their enemy and assault French communities. But as far as can be determined, the provincial governments never considered raids
against French villages as an efficacious form of
offensive strategy. The English considered the
French and the Indian tribes as separate enemies
and devised separate strategies to defeat them.
The final solution to the French problem was
the reduction of Canada itself, and thus it is
unreasonable to assume the English provincials
incapable of emulating their Canadian counterparts when they never attempted, or even contemplated, such an action. The eastern Indians,
however, offered a tempting target for provincial raiding parties.

The purpose of these raids was threefold:
to disrupt the economy of the Indians, to intimidate Indian raiding parties with the presence of
provincial soldiers on their invasion routes, and
to destroy warriors through ambush and battle.
Of course, strategies are generally easier to devise than to execute, and so it was in the case
of the provincial raids. Of the three major goals,
the disruption of the Indian economy proved
the easiest to achieve. The eastern Indians depended upon hunting and fishing to provide for
their subsistence, and specific locations within
the tribe's territory became associated with

waterfowl or shellfish. The provincial governments knew the locations of these areas and regularly ordered their commanders to scout and ambush them. The destruction of food stores during attacks on villages was also an assault on the Native American economic system. Indeed, critics of English scouting efforts seem to gauge success by one criteria—body count. Raids were only successful if they resulted in a large number of enemy killed, but attrition, not scalps, proved to be the real purpose of the raids and patrols.

Provincial raiding parties also sought to discourage French and Indian forces by their presence in the woods. At the very least, the English hoped the evidence of large parties scouting the woods would create second thoughts among enemy raiders. Determining if these efforts accomplished their purpose can be difficult. When intimidation succeeded, there were no attacks, but there is no difference between successful intimidation and simple inactivity on the part of the enemy. In both cases nothing happens. Despite this percipient problem, there is evidence to indicate provincial presence in the woods achieved results.

The final purpose of the raiding parties, the killing of Indians through ambush, proved to be the most difficult, as well as the most hazardous. Indian fishing and hunting grounds, fords, and warrior paths, as well as the villages themselves, were all targets for ambuscade or attacks, but the provincial forces rarely found their foe where they expected. Although provincial soldiers experienced some success in this regard, to "search out and destroy the enemy" was indeed easier said than done. In addition, like defensive patrols, the very real possibility existed that the English raiding parties themselves could be ambushed.

Offensive scouts varied greatly in size, from a handful of men to large companies numbering several hundred. But all operated on the march, or at least were supposed to operate, in a similar manner. As the main party followed a trail or a river, smaller scouts would be constantly detached to the flanks and the front to investigate signs of enemy activity and to prevent ambush. Emphasis was placed on keeping open formations, since any bunching could be disastrous if the enemy opened fire from ambush.

For the English colonies, Benjamin Church became the first successful leader of offensive raids. Using a combined force of about equal numbers of Indians and whites, mostly recruited from Plymouth, Church participated in four major raids during King William's War and Queen Anne's War, striking not only Indian villages, but French fishing communities in Nova Scotia. Others would follow his example, including James Converse, Johnson Harmon, Winthrop Hilton, Jeremiah Moulton, John Lovewell, and John Goffe. The most famous commander of English raiding parties, Robert Rogers, would draw on the experience of Church and these other well-known scout leaders.

The success or failure of raids into enemy territory depended on many components beyond the quality of the commander and the soldiers. The weather obviously played a role. A heavy downpour forced soldiers to halt their march in order to protect their food, powder, and weapons, and prolonged rain not only created swollen rivers, but often produced illness among the men. The knowledge of the guides or "pilots" who led the scouts into the mountains and forests also contributed. The New England governments used local inhabitants—hunters, Indians, and former captives—to pilot their raiding parties, but faulty memory or changes in terrain could abort missions.

In addition to the weather and the quality of the pilots, difficulties in the procurement of provisions could create serious problems for long-range scouts. Food and replacement clothing had to be gathered and prepared and then transported by the soldiers, usually in knapsacks ("snapsacks"). Smaller scouts could also hunt as they marched. While hunting and fishing did supplement the food supplies of smaller parties, success was haphazard at best. Game animals could prove scarce during certain times of the year and under some weather conditions, and larger groups of men moving through the woods had a tendency to drive the game before them. Under most circumstances, therefore, raiding parties had to husband their supplies for the duration of the scout. But even with strict frugality and careful conservation, unforeseen shortages could force the termination of a scout and endanger the health of the soldiers. On many occasions, raiding parties and scouts returned to the settlements in a ragged, starving, and sick condition. Shortages of food were a hazard all soldiers experienced when they marched into the woods—the English were not exceptional in this respect. A major French raid against the western Iroquois in 1684 found their provisions short due to mismanagement in transportation, and as a result, many of the soldiers fell dangerously ill. In 1747, a force of apparently starving French and Indians laid siege to the fort at Number Four in New Hampshire. Frustrated in their attempts to extort food from the defenders, the French force moved off to find provisions elsewhere.

The number and effectiveness of scouts did not remain static during the French wars. The use of defensive patrols protecting the immediate communities remained customary throughout the period for both French and English, but the number and character of offensive scouts changed considerably. The New England colonies entered King William's War unprepared for the French wars. The territorial limits and close proximity of enemy villages in King Philip's War proved a poor precedent for the demands of this wider conflict. As a result, the aggressive use of raiding parties, with a few exceptions, found limited success during King William's War. Military forces were drastically reduced in winter to save money, and provincial officers had to master the procedures and logistics of long-distance marches. The French, on the other hand, enjoyed considerable success with their large raiding parties launched at New England towns.

But by Queen Anne's War, the English colonies greatly increased their use of scouts, both defensive and offensive. These "constant marches" kept the Indians away from their territories, forcing them to remove to Canada and thus increase the travel distance to the English frontier. In addition, the increased presence of provincial soldiers in the woods probably forced a change in French and Indian tactics from the larger forces used in King William's War to smaller parties that were less easy to detect and posed fewer logistical problems. The French found their Indians more reluctant to venture to the English frontier in larger parties because those that did often sustained casualties from the numerous patrols operating throughout the region. After Queen Anne's War, larger French and Indian raiding parties usually focused their attention on the growing number of provincial forts.

Two other changes greatly enhanced the English scouting effort. The first innovation was the introduction of winter raids. Winthrop Hilton led the first such English raid in February 1704, after which winter raids, when the Indians were most vulnerable, became routine, and increased patrols and scouts all year long kept the enemy off-balance.

The second element, commencing simultaneously with the winter marches, was the encouragement of scalp hunters. Bounties for Indian scalps had been offered in previous wars, but the governments of Massachusetts and New Hampshire now offered a larger reward for those who served without government pay. The parsimonious provincial assemblies seized on the concept of soldiers who would be paid only if successful. The concept of scalp hunting would prove popular and increased the number of soldiers in the woods, but Governor Joseph Dudley had reservations. Essentially, these men were speculators recognizing little government control.

Eventually, the government exerted some control on scalp hunters by regularizing their position. Companies of "snowshoe men" were raised in frontier communities commanded by officers with provincial commissions. (The commission in snowshoe companies was a provincial rank, and was considered separate from the local militia rank, even though the men belonged to both. The former was military in nature, the latter political.) Unlike scouts taken from provincial forces posted on the frontier, snowshoe companies received wages only when they were actually on a raid, but were paid for scalps as volunteers. Thus the government subordinated the scalp hunters through the commissions and wages. Many of the more famous and successful scout commanders operated under this system, including Johnson Harmon, who commanded the snowshoe men from York, Maine, and John Lovewell.

The English continued to improve their scouting performance during the remainder of the French and Indian Wars. During Dummer's War, the aggressive use of large provincial forces marching against the Indian villages of Norridgewock and Pigwacket eventually broke the power of these eastern tribes, and the officers who led these raids became heroes to the frontier communities struggling for their existence. And of course, the service of Robert Rogers in the last French war is another prime example.

Steven C. Eames

References

Steven C. Eames, "Rustic Warriors: Warfare and the Provincial Soldier on the Northern Frontier, 1689–1748," Ph.D. Dissertation, University of New Hampshire (1989); Patrick M. Malone, *The Skulking Way of War: Technology and Tactics Among the New England Indians* (1991).

See also CHURCH, BENJAMIN; CONVERSE, JAMES; COUREURS DE BOIS; GOFFE, JOHN; HARMON, JOHNSON; HILTON, WINTHROP; LOVEWELL, JOHN; MOULTON, JEREMIAH; RAIDING PARTY; RANGERS; ROGERS, ROBERT; SCALP BOUNTIES

Sea Laws (1588–1763)

The sea laws of the period 1588 to 1763 evolved from earlier codes, cases, treaties, and ordinances. In this century and a half of expanded commerce and numerous wars, emerging nations with maritime and colonial interests adjusted their oceanic practices according to the requirements of the moment, sometimes as neutrals, other times as belligerents, adhering to and modifying the sea laws. The general categories of sea laws treated here may be stipulated as commercial, including rules of trade, contraband, blockade, and seizure; and territorial, meaning the extent of neighboring sea claimed by a nation-state.

Authorities differ about the existence of an accepted body of marine law in the seventeenth and eighteenth centuries. Carl J. Kulsrud, *Maritime Neutrality to 1780* (1986), believed that nations generally adhered to a corpus of codes and cases, while Richard Pares, *Colonial Blockade and Neutral Rights, 1739–1763* (1938), contended that reasons of state induced neutrals and belligerents to act in somewhat uniform ways. The belligerent nation usually espoused the seizure of enemy goods and ships, leaving the ships and goods of genuine neutrals alone. The neutral power often argued that since its ships were neutral, that the goods they carried should be treated the same way regardless of their ownership, origin, and destination, and that neutral goods on enemy ships should be exempted also, as long as they were not items of war. Each power prohibited trade with its colonies, e.g., the English Navigation Acts of the mid-seventeenth century aimed at the Dutch, and the Spanish laws of empire that the British violated. However, exceptions existed, e.g., the Dutch trade to the French West Indies, which the British tolerated in the 1740s and opposed in the 1750s.

Codes of commerce and seizure may be traced to the Phoenicians in 2000 B.C., Graeco-Roman practice and the Rhodian Sea Laws of the Third Century, B.C. In the Middle Ages, several codes existed: among them the *Consolato del Mare* (1070, 1494, Barcelona); Oléron (France, c. 1226); Visby (Baltic, 1320); Black Book of the Admiralty (English, mid-1300s). Of these, the most influential was the *Consolato del Mare*, which defined some 300 points, such as the conduct of merchants, captains, and sailors, judicial procedures, damages, breach of contract, and prize shares. In regard to relations between belligerents and neutral shipping, the *Consolato* held to a principle that has endured to the present: the belligerent may seize enemy goods off a neutral ship or capture an enemy ship, but not a neutral ship with enemy goods or neutral goods on an enemy ship. The rule held that both neutrals and belligerents had rights in time of war: the right to capture enemy property and the right of neutral trade.

Because nations and national navies hardly existed until the late sixteenth century, belligerents often used private navies and privateers. In the Middle Ages, admiralty, prize and consulate courts arose to decide ship seizure cases. These courts ranged from the Mediterranean to the Baltic, but those that cast the longest shadow were the English, as the island nation rose in sea power.

These courts did not follow legal theory, rather, they interpreted the maritime precedents in light of the desires of their sovereigns. Crown decrees, such as the French Ordinances of 1584 and 1681, often indicated a more severe approach such as "enemy ships, enemy goods." Treaties usually revealed some concessions and cooperation, e.g., the principle of free ships, free goods, in the Franco-Spanish agreement of 1659, and the Anglo-Dutch accord of 1674.

As British sea power vanquished the Spanish, Dutch, and French, and commercial/dynastic wars spread to the colonies, so Admiralty courts devised the Rule of the War of 1756. The British did not interfere with neutral (Dutch) trade between belligerent (French) ports, but did object to Dutch trade with French colonial ports in the West Indies that were closed to foreigners in time of peace. This led to the doctrine of continuous voyage, i.e., that if goods were ultimately to land in a belligerent (French) port, they could be seized even if they were transshipped at a neutral (Dutch) port such as St. Eustatius. British alternation on this rule could be seen during the Napoleonic Wars, where the doctrine was not enforced in the *Polly* case of 1800 and was in the *Essex* case of 1805. During the U.S. Civil War, the British acquiesced to the application of the doctrine in the *Bermuda, Peterhoff,* and *Springbok* cases, perceiving the precedent would help them later on, as it did in World War I.

While it is clear that rights of seizure existed prior to 1600, and these rights were extended after 1700, scholars disagree over the existence of doctrine regarding blockade and contraband. Blockades occurred from ancient times onward, but became more frequent in the seventeenth century due to the improved sea-keeping quality of warships. Opinions regarding the conduct of tight or loose blockade appeared in a Spanish-Austrian agreement of 1725. Lists of contraband and free goods were agreed upon in this treaties: Anglo-Spanish, 1604; Anglo-Dutch, 1625; among others.

Neutrals responded to British practices with various agreements. The leagues and convoys of armed neutrality in 1613, 1691, 1756, and 1780 failed to have much effect. The Paris Treaty of 1856 refined the principals of neutral rights over contraband, blockade, and seizure more in favor of neutrals, most of which were ignored in the world wars of the twentieth century.

The doctrines of territorial sea may be traced to the Romans, who held the sea common to all mankind in the Justinian Code of 529 A.D. In the Middle Ages, Venice and Genoa attempted to control their territorial waters. Barolus of Venice argued for a 100-mile limit in the mid-fourteenth century. After the Treaty of Tordesillas in 1495 divided the known world between the Spaniards and Portuguese, the English, Dutch, and French corsairs challenged this claim as the Swedes expanded in the Baltic, so new declarations about the territorial sea appeared.

In 1608, Hugo Grotius wrote his famous treatise, arguing for *mare liberum*, or an open sea, partly on behalf of the Dutch East Indian Company against Portuguese protectionism. As Anglo-Dutch competition increased, Selden proposed in 1635 a *mare clausum*, or closed sea, referring not to the broad oceans, but to a nation's right to local control of fisheries, similar to Alberico Gentili's plea for a common sea and national coastal control in 1605.

Generally, the Spanish argued for the line of sight doctrine, i.e., the state controlled the adjacent waters as far as the eye could see from shore. The Danes held for a league distance rule of four nautical miles. The Dutch proposed the cannon shot rule as early as 1610; you claimed as far as a cannon shot could reach, about a mile at that time. Cornelius van Bynkershoek, the Hollander, wrote the most noteworthy justification for this principle in 1702. Later in that century, the British established a three-mile

limit, and by 1782, Ferdinando Galiani equated the three-mile and cannon shot rules. From the eighteenth to the twentieth centuries, due to British and American sea power, the three-mile limit became widely, although not completely, accepted. After 1945, various nations began to plead for 12-, 20-, and 200-mile limits to protect fisheries and minerals, so that by the mid-1970s, most nations agreed to 200-mile limits, which caused many exceptions for innocent passage and difficulties of enforcement.

In the evolution of sea laws from ancient times to modern that attempted to reconcile the claims of neutrals and belligerents, the contenders of the seventeenth and eighteenth centuries contributed the Rule of 1756, the free ships, free goods principle, and concepts of contraband, blockade, and territorial sea, all modified and applied in the nineteenth and twentieth centuries.

James H. Hitchman

References

Philip C. Jessup and Francis Deák, *Neutrality. Its History, Economics and Law*, Vol. I: *The Origins* (1935); Sayre A. Swarztrauber, *The Three-Mile Limit of Territorial Seas* (1972).

See also PRIVATEERING

Seamen and Society

Most British seamen came from the lowest classes of society and were recruited from all parts of the country. Their reasons for becoming seamen were various. The desire for adventure was always strong in an island population, but going to sea also offered an escape for lovers, husbands, debtors, and anyone fleeing from the law. However, most seamen served out of economic necessity, since it was generally a hazardous life with poor conditions and modest remuneration. Another disadvantage was separation from one's family, especially for those in the trans-Atlantic, African, and East Indian trades. The majority of seamen were probably young and single, but many had dependents who were often left to the charity of neighbors or the harsh regime of the poorhouse. The men themselves, confined for long periods in cramped conditions, naturally gave vent to their instincts once on shore. This helped foster the image that sailors were a fickle, boisterous, and immoral group who had wives in every port and were constantly drunk. Certainly it was no coincidence that English seaports had the highest number of brothels and bars of any towns.

During peacetime most sailors found employment in the merchant marine. This offered numerous and varied opportunities from the shipping of Newcastle coal to the arduous African and East Indian trades. Service with the Royal Navy, in contrast, was not popular because of the harsh discipline and low pay. Thus, in 1750, the merchant marine had 609,000 tons of shipping, employing around 36,500 men. The navy, in contrast, had only 10,000 personnel, though the position changed dramatically during the Seven Years' War, when the fleet required between 60,000 and 80,000 sailors.

Although society accorded seamen a grudging respect for a difficult and dangerous job, in times of national emergency they could be impressed without legal redress, reflecting the low esteem in which they were held. Life was cheap and mariners' lives were among the cheapest. Admittedly, the merchants brought parliamentary pressure on the Admiralty to restrain the use of the press in the interests of their trade; and many commentators pleaded for better treatment of seamen to induce more of them to volunteer, so doing away with the need for impressment. The sailors themselves made every attempt to avoid capture, often with the connivance of their merchant employers. However, the almost complete absence of mutinies on board ship suggests that seamen in general were a conservative group. They rarely challenged those in command or voiced political discontent. Fisticuffs with the local press-gangs was the limit of their protest.

Richard Middleton

References

Peter Kemp, *The British Sailor: A Social History of the Lower Deck* (1970); C.C. Lloyd, *The British Seaman* (1968); G.J. Marcus, *Heart of Oak; A Survey of British Sea Power in the Georgian Era* (1975); N.A.M. Rodger, *The Wooden World: An Anatomy of the Georgian Navy* (1986).

See also DISCIPLINE, NAVY; IMPRESSMENT, NAVY; NAVY, GREAT BRITAIN

Seneca

The Senecas were the westernmost of the five Iroquois nations that comprised the Iroquois Confederacy. They lived primarily in what is now western New York state between the Genesee River and Canandaigua Lake. By the 1700s, they also had some settlements near Niagara.

The Senecas' hunting territory extended from Lake Ontario in the north to the headwaters of the Finger Lakes in the south. Seneca hunters traveled eastward to the highlands between Seneca Lake and Cayuga Lake, and roamed far to the west into the upper Great Lakes country.

The Seneca population—approximately half of the entire Iroquois population—lived in two main villages and several smaller ones. In 1656, the principal villages contained 100 or more houses, while the smaller ones had 20 to 30 houses each. Throughout most of the 1600s and 1700s, the Senecas could field about 1,000 warriors, making them the largest and perhaps strongest of the Iroquois tribes.

Geography determined the Senecas' role in the Iroquois Confederacy. The Five Nations referred to themselves as the "People of the Longhouse" and likened their homelands to a longhouse sheltering all Iroquois people. The Senecas were designated the "Keepers of the Western Door," while the easternmost Mohawks were called "Keepers of the Eastern Door." The Onondagas, in the geographic center, were the "Keepers of the Fire," responsible for convening league councils and keeping wampum records. Sachems, or representative chiefs, from the Senecas, Cayugas, Onondagas, Oneidas, and Mohawks met annually at the league council house at Onondaga, the capital of the confederacy.

The Senecas' location gave them access to the valuable furs of the upper Great Lakes country, and brought them into direct contact with the French and various tribes of the region. It also gave the Senecas leverage in both directions. Western tribes could not trade with the Dutch or English at Albany without passing through Seneca territory, and eastern Iroquois or English and French traders could not journey to the western lands without Seneca permission. Their strategic location allowed the Senecas to play a significant role in political, economic, and diplomatic matters on the northern colonial Indian frontier.

Like other tribes of the Iroquois Confederacy, the Senecas conducted diplomacy at both the tribal and league level. They followed league policy only when it was compatible to Seneca interests. On all other occasions, the Senecas operated independently of the confederacy.

During the 1640s and early 1650s, the Senecas and fellow members of the confederacy launched major wars against the Hurons, Neutrals, Petuns, and Eries. At stake was control of the valuable western fur trade. Having achieved their western aims by the early 1650s, and in need of protection against Susquehannock raiders from the south, the Senecas joined with other members of the confederacy seeking peace with New France. Despite the objections of the Mohawks, who feared improved French relations would attract Iroquois traders to Canada instead of Albany, peace was ratified. In 1656, a French Jesuit even visited the Senecas, but no permanent mission was established until 1668.

By the late 1670s, relations between the Senecas and French began to cool. The Susquehannocks' defeat in 1675 made the French alliance less imperative, and the Senecas were growing increasingly concerned about French and western Indian encroachments in the upper Great Lakes country. In 1680, the Senecas attacked the Illinois and French traders in the region. This sparked 20 years of warfare between the Senecas and the French and western tribes, which became intertwined with King William's War. By the end of the century, the Senecas and their fellow confederates were reeling from French and Indian attacks, so the league agreed to peace in 1701.

For the next half-century, the Senecas adhered to the Iroquois Confederacy's official policy of neutrality between the French and English. This diplomatic balancing act kept the Iroquois out of the eighteenth-century colonial wars and enabled them to wring political and economic advantages from both sides. The Senecas also followed the league's policy of rapprochement toward the powerful tribes of the Great Lakes country, and warfare against tribes of the south.

Of all the Five Nations, the Senecas (particularly the Chenussios of the westernmost Seneca village) developed the closest ties to the French and western tribes. During the early 1700s, the French agent, Louis-Thomas Chabert de Joncaire, lived among them, cultivating good relations with New France. After 1735, Philippe-Thomas Chabert de Joncaire continued the work begun by his father. Pro-French Senecas supported the building of the French fort at Niagara in the 1720s. And despite the confederacy's neutral stance, numerous pro-French Senecas joined French war parties during the various colonial wars, including the French

and Indian War. The Chenussios also played a major role in the Indian war against the British in 1763, commonly known as Pontiac's War. Those Senecas sacked British posts at Venango, Le Boeuf, and Presque Isle, and won a devastating victory over the English at Devil's Hole (on the Niagara portage). When the Indian war drew to a close, the Senecas were forced to cede lands around Niagara to the British.

Throughout their history, the Senecas were among the most powerful and politically active Iroquois. Like the rest of the confederacy, they played a major role in the history of colonial America. Their geographic location, military strength, and diplomatic connections to Indians and whites made them a significant force throughout the Great Lakes region.

Richard Aquila

References
    Richard Aquila, *The Iroquois Restoration: Iroquois Diplomacy on the Colonial Frontier, 1701–1754* (1983); Barbara Graymont, *The Iroquois in the American Revolution* (1972); Francis Jennings, *The Ambiguous Iroquois Empire: The Covenant Chain Confederation of Indian Tribes with English Colonies from its beginnings to the Lancaster Treaty of 1744* (1984): Daniel K. Richter and James H. Merrell, eds., *Beyond the Covenant Chain: The Iroquois and Their Neighbors in Indian North America, 1600–1800* (1987); Anthony F.C. Wallace, *The Death and Rebirth of the Seneca* (1969).

See also CHABERT DE JONCAIRE, LOUIS-THOMAS; CHABERT DE JONCAIRE, PHILIPPE-THOMAS; IROQUOIS; IROQUOIS TREATIES OF 1700 AND 1701; IROQUOIS WARS; FORT KANADESAGA (NEW YORK); FORT NIAGARA (NEW YORK); PONTIAC'S WAR; SENECA, FRENCH ATTACK ON THE

Seneca, French Attack on the (1687)

Following Joseph-Antoine Le Febvre de La Barre's humiliating peace with the Iroquois in 1684, in which he abandoned France's allies in the west, particularly the Illinois, the new governor, Jacques-René de Brisay, the marquis de Denonville, was instructed by the king of France to secure a permanent peace in Canada by humbling the Iroquois and reestablishing alliances with the Illinois and others whom La Barre had abandoned. Denonville attacked the Seneca in 1687, both to humble them and to prevent the

Lieutenant Governor of New York, Thomas Dongan, from stealing France's Great Lakes trade by routing it through Albany.

In 1682, while the western Iroquois were fighting the Illinois, Decanisora, an Onondaga diplomat, persuaded Governor General Louis de Buade de Frontenac that the Iroquois had no inclination to interfere with the French, thus keeping them out of the conflict. Decanisora was back in Quebec the next year to convince Governor La Barre that the Iroquois wanted to keep the peace with New France despite their war with the Illinois. Senecas undermined his efforts by attacking the French fort of Saint-Louis-des-Illinois. La Barre responded with a brief and ineffective campaign, which was followed by his recall to France.

When Dongan organized expeditions to Michilimackinac, Denonville recognized that their success would tempt the western Indians to the British side. With the king's support, but only half the army that he had been promised, Denonville moved against the Senecas in June 1687. The French force included 1,600 continental soldiers, nearly 1,000 Huron-Petun, Ottawa, and Potawatomi allies, and 400 Canadians. An ineffectual Seneca attack on the French invaders did little damage, and the Senecas withdrew, leaving their largest village, Gannagaro, in ashes. Denonville destroyed the Senecas' other great villages, burning hundreds of thousands of bushels of corn, slaughtering the pigs, and pilfering their graves. Although he met few people, the French governor declared the land conquered, claimed it for France, and built a fort at Niagara, briefly stationing 100 men there.

French colonials suffered the retaliation of the Senecas and other Iroquois long after the French troops returned to France. In 1689, Iroquois besieged Fort Frontenac, and attacked Montreal and Lachine. Iroquois raiding parties made travel, trade, and even farming very dangerous for French colonials in the early 1690s. Still, the French attack did reduce the Senecas' food supply, and they suffered difficult times for a long while. The Five Nations became dependents of New York, unable to use the French as a counter to the British. One troublesome consequence of the war was that Denonville, following the king's orders, shipped 36 Iroquois prisoners to France to row in the royal galleys. Only 13 eventually returned, following a peace settlement. Another consequence was that the French realized that forcing the Iroquois to submit would require a much larger military commitment from France.

Sean O'Neill

See also DECANISORA; DENONVILLE, JACQUES-RENÉ DE BRISAY, MARQUIS DE; DONGAN, THOMAS; FORT FRONTENAC (ONTARIO, CANADA); IROQUOIS TREATIES OF 1700 AND 1701; LACHINE, BATTLE OF (1689); FORT NIAGARA (NEW YORK); SENECA

Seven Years' War (1754–1763)

The Seven Years' War in America (also termed the French and Indian War or Fourth Intercolonial War) ensued from rival claims to the Ohio Valley and Acadia by Britain and France. The War of the Austrian Succession had left these disputes unresolved when hostilities ceased in 1748. Tensions steadily mounted, and violence occasionally flared as the French tried to halt British expansion at the Appalachian crest and the isthmus of Chignecto.

From 1748 to 1754, the French reoccupied the fortress of Louisbourg on Cape Breton Island and strengthened or rebuilt Fort Gaspereau (Nova Scotia), Fort St. Frédéric (New York), Fort Niagara (New York), and Fort Toulouse (Alabama). They also placed new garrisons at Fort Beauséjour (Nova Scotia) and Fort La Présentation, or La Galette, (New York). Challenged for control of the fur trade by Pennsylvanians who diverted a large volume of pelts to the Miami town of Pickawillany (Ohio), 200 *coureurs de bois* and Ottawas drove out the British interlopers when they overran and burned that palisaded village on 21 June 1752. A year later, French troops began constructing in western Pennsylvania Fort Presque Isle, Fort Le Boeuf, and Fort Venango along the portage route from Lake Erie to the juncture where the Allegheny and Monongahela Rivers form the Ohio, where another fort was to be built in early 1754.

Virginia's government claimed the forks of the Ohio as its own, and funded an expedition under Lieutenant Colonel George Washington to fortify the site before the French could. An advance party of 41 men under Ensign Edward Ward started digging earthworks there in early 1754, but surrendered on 17 April when more than 500 French arrived and trained artillery on them. Claude-Pierre Pécaudy de Contrecoeur, the French commander, allowed Ward's detachment to leave in peace and then began erecting Fort Duquesne (Pennsylvania).

The war's first bloodletting occurred during the chilly dawn of 28 May, when 40 Virginians commanded by Washington attacked a patrol of 34 French 50 miles southeast of Fort Duquesne. At a cost of one dead and one wounded, Washington's men killed or captured all but one of the soldiers. Washington consolidated his 300 provincials and 100 regulars nearby at Fort Necessity, Pennsylvania, which was attacked by 500 French and 400 Indians on 3 July. The French peppered the Anglo-American troops with a galling fire that killed or wounded a quarter of them as they lay in muddy trenches during a day of pouring rain. The French accepted Washington's capitulation the next day, allowed him to march his troops home under arms, and burned Fort Necessity to the ground.

Britain's government resolved to expel the French from western Pennsylvania, northern New York, and the Isthmus of Chignecto in 1755. Whitehall sent 1,300 troops under General Edward Braddock to Virginia and ordered its American garrisons, then barely half full, brought to full strength with colonial volunteers. *Rage militaire* swept Anglo-America, which furnished more than 2,000 recruits for the regular army and 6,500 soldiers in provincial units for the upcoming campaign.

After months of back-breaking labor hewing a road across the Appalachian wilderness, 2,500 redcoats and provincials under Commander in Chief Braddock converged on Fort Duquesne. Two hundred fifty French launched a last-minute raid to harass the British, in which they were joined by about 600 Indians. Early on 9 July, the French vanguard collided unexpectedly into Braddock's advancing grenadiers, who fired first and killed the French commander, Captain Daniel-Hyacinthe-Marie Liénard de Beaujeu. After the Indians and Canadians took cover and shot back, the main British force hurried forward and crashed headlong into the advance guard as it was withdrawing. Confusion reigned among the ambushed troops, who endured heavy fire from an unseen enemy for three hours as their officers tried to reform their ranks for a counterattack. The regulars finally broke and left Washington's Virginians to cover their retreat. British casualties numbered more than 800, compared to 39 for the French. After Braddock died of wounds on 11 July, his successor marched the decimated regulars to Philadelphia, where cynics sneered that the king's soldiers had taken up winter quarters in August.

Rank as commander in chief devolved upon Massachusetts Governor William Shirley, who had been ordered to attack Fort Niagara, but never advanced beyond Oswego for lack of supplies. Shirley's subordinate, Colonel William Johnson of New York, received orders to take Fort Carillon (New York), which the French had just begun constructing, and then to besiege Fort St. Frédéric. Johnson's 3,000 provincials and 300 Iroquois came under attack at their base on Lake George from a force of 1,600 French and Indians led by Baron Jean-Armand de Dieskau on 8 September 1755. Dieskau mauled a reconnaissance party of 500 Yankees and Iroquois, whose chaotic retreat spread panic through Johnson's army, and might have overrun the Anglo-American camp had not Colonel Phineas Lyman of Connecticut assumed command from the wounded Johnson and animated the troops to repel repeated French assaults. Abandoning their equipment and the wounded Dieskau, the French retreated in confusion after losing about 230 casualties, compared to 262 for Johnson's troops. Johnson concluded the campaign by building Fort William Henry nearby, but left Fort Carillon and Fort St. Frédéric unmolested.

Only in Nova Scotia did British arms enjoy unqualified success during 1755. Commanding 2,000 New Englanders and 300 regulars, Colonel Robert Monckton dislodged the French from the Chignecto peninsula and captured about 1,000 prisoners by taking Fort Beauséjour on 16 June, and Fort Gaspereau the next day. Monckton's troops then deported about 6,000 of Nova Scotia's 16,000 French civilians, or Acadians, who refused to swear allegiance to Britain. Although never again the scene of major fighting, Nova Scotia remained beset by raiding parties of Indians and Canadian partisans, who forced Britain to protect the colony with large bodies of regulars, provincials, and rangers that were sorely needed in the war's more active theaters.

The backcountry from Maine to Virginia also endured an incessant succession of Indian incursions. By mid-1756, Indians had killed at least 376 civilians and captured another 276, but lost fewer than 100 of their own number. Long accustomed to self-defense from earlier conflicts, settlers in New England and New York held firm, but the untested frontiersmen of Pennsylvania and Virginia often succumbed to panic and abandoned their homes.

The first effort to deter Indian attacks came in early 1756, when Major Andrew Lewis led

236 Virginia militia to burn Shawnee villages on the Ohio River. Lewis's food supplies ran out in mid-winter, and his half-starved expedition disintegrated from mass desertion. In reality, few of France's Indian allies lay within reach of British offensive operations. Anglo-Americans succeeded only twice in retaliating against their tormentors: at Kittanning in 1756 and St. Francis in 1759 (see below).

After two years of hostilities in North America, George II declared war with France on 17 May 1756. George's declaration came too late for his navy to interdict a French squadron bound for Canada with two fresh regiments and a new commanding general, Louis-Joseph de Montcalm. Britain's Cabinet also ordered reinforcements to America, and replaced Shirley as commander with John Campbell, fourth earl of Loudoun, who landed at New York on 23 July.

Lord Loudoun discovered that his understrength forces had neither the training nor the logistical base to take the offensive, and he devoted his energies to solving the army's administrative problems. The campaign of 1756 brought only two victories for Loudoun's army, and both were minor. On 3 July, a supply column of 400 American *bateaux* men under Captain John Bradstreet were ambushed by a superior force of French and Indians near Fort Oswego, but after three hours under attack, they fixed bayonets and routed their attackers with cold steel. On 30 August, Colonel John Armstrong's Pennsylvania militia burned the Delaware village of Kittanning, killed about 50 Indians, and rescued 11 white prisoners.

Unlike Loudoun, Montcalm assumed command of battle-ready regulars and hardened Canadian militia who were aggressively harassing British outposts and had disrupted Oswego's supply line by capturing Fort Bull and its 105 defenders on 27 March 1756. Montcalm followed up this minor victory by besieging the exposed garrison at Oswego harbor, which surrendered on 9 August. In one fell swoop, the British lost four armed ships, 70 cannon, and 1,606 soldiers and sailors, including two regiments of regulars.

Montcalm struck even deeper into New York the next year when he besieged Fort William Henry on Lake George with 6,200 French and 1,800 Indians. Lieutenant Colonel George Monro's 2,100 defenders resisted for seven days, until French batteries were within a hundred yards of their ramparts and the final assault was imminent, before surrendering on 9 August

1757. Monro accepted a parole for his troops in which his regulars and provincials agreed not to bear arms for 18 months. Montcalm's Indians fell upon the unarmed troops as they evacuated the post on 10 August, however, and could not be restrained from killing about 30 wounded men left behind in the hospital and seizing 529 soldiers to sell as forced laborers to Canadian civilians. Montcalm paid for the release of every prisoner he could locate and repatriated them, but some Indians dragged soldiers infected with smallpox back to their villages and unwittingly spread several epidemics among tribes in the Ohio Valley and Great Plains.

Despite having lost almost 4,000 troops killed or captured since his arrival, Lord Loudoun had greatly strengthened Britain's military forces by mid-1757. He had established a reliable system of supplying his garrisons, more than replaced his casualties with colonial volunteers for the Royal American Regiment and other regular units, and created a corps of hard-fighting rangers under Major Robert Rogers to gather intelligence and harass the French with partisan warfare. By 30 June 1757, Loudoun had assembled 11,000 soldiers at Halifax, Nova Scotia, for an assault against Louisbourg. Unfavorable weather kept the British fleet in harbor for a month, and when the seas cleared, word came that a powerful French squadron had arrived at Cape Breton Island. After his naval advisors recommended against undertaking the amphibious operation, Loudoun cancelled the project on 4 August. His troops returned to New York too late in the season to undertake another expedition, and Loudoun sent his men into winter quarters without having struck a single blow at the French.

As Britain's military fortunes reached their nadir in 1757, George II summoned William Pitt to be prime minister on 29 June. Pitt's fighting spirit and grim determination galvanized both Britons and Anglo-Americans. Pitt was reluctant to send substantial numbers of troops to North America because of Britain's manpower needs in Europe and the Caribbean, so he encouraged the colonies to provide provincial troops by promising that Parliament would reimburse their mobilization expenses. Most American legislatures enthusiastically contributed men once they were free of the war's financial burdens; in both 1758 and 1759, the colonies raised 21,000 provincials, and as a result, fewer than 4,000 reinforcements had to be sent from Britain before Canada fell.

Pitt also lost confidence in Lord Loudoun after the aborted expedition against Louisbourg and dismissed him in December 1757. Loudoun was a cautious strategist and never popular among Anglo-Americans, but he nevertheless had transformed the ineffectual forces inherited from Shirley into an army capable of waging war in the wilderness far from its base of supply. Much of the credit for ultimate victory lay with his painstaking administrative work.

General James Abercromby assumed rank as commander in chief in March 1758; by summer he was ready to hurl 42,000 troops against Montcalm, who could muster less than 7,000 regulars, perhaps 12,000 militia, and possibly 2,000 Indians. For the first time since 1755, the British had the manpower and logistical means to fight on three fronts. Pitt ordered Abercromby to capture Fort Carillon and Fort St. Frédéric on Lake Champlain. General Jeffery Amherst received command of the amphibious force assigned to besiege Louisbourg, whose fall would deny the French navy its primary base for blocking a seaborne invasion of Canada by the St. Lawrence River. The task of crossing the mountains and taking Fort Duquesne fell to Brigadier General John Forbes.

To drive the French from Lake Champlain, Abercromby launched an armada of 800 *bateaux* and 90 whaleboats carrying 15,000 troops. Their first objective, Fort Carillon, was held by about 3,500 men under Montcalm. On 7 July, Abercromby's provincials and rangers swept through Montcalm's outermost defenses and inflicted about 350 casualties on the French. Montcalm had ensconced his remaining infantry behind a moat-and-log barrier covered by the fort's guns. Assured by his engineers that the French lines were weak, and fearful that enemy reinforcements were nearby, Abercromby did not take time to breach Montcalm's defenses with artillery before ordering his regulars into a frontal assault on 8 July. Exposed to withering fire before a ten-foot barrier, the regulars suffered more than 1,600 casualties in the series of courageous, but futile, charges. Abercromby retreated to Fort William Henry that night.

With his regulars decimated and in no shape for further combat, Abercromby approved a plan by Lieutenant Colonel John Bradstreet to attack Fort Frontenac, on Lake Ontario's northern shore, which served as Canada's main depot for the trade goods needed to retain the loyalty of western Indians. Bradstreet plunged into the wilderness on 14 August with 3,700 provincials

and 150 regulars. His force covered 430 miles, including 84 miles of portages, in just 11 days and reached its objective on the 25th. He subdued the post two days later and captured 110 troops, 76 pieces of artillery, and nine warships. Frontenac's loss temporarily cut Canada's supply lines with the Ohio Valley and cost the French trading goods valued at £70,000 intended for their Indian allies.

Britain's second major campaign of 1758, Amherst's expedition against Louisbourg, embarked from Halifax with 14,200 regulars. Owing to the Royal Navy's success in intercepting French warships and supply convoys, the French could not attack Amherst at sea and were unprepared for a lengthy siege. On 8 June, Brigadier General James Wolfe's brigade tried to land at Gabarus Bay in the face of heavy artillery fire, and were on the point of withdrawing when a light-infantry officer spied a distant, rocky cove unoccupied by the French. As his men crashed ashore amid pounding surf, in which many drowned, Major George Scott and ten soldiers scrambled up the crags to meet 70 oncoming French. Though French bullets tore three holes in his coat and hit half his men, Scott held off the enemy until the beachhead was secured. Wolfe then stormed the shore batteries and drove the French within Louisbourg's walls.

For six weeks, the British slowly extended their siege lines closer to Louisbourg and bombarded the fortress ferociously. When Governor Augustin Boschenry de Drucour surrendered on 26 July, France lost 3,000 soldiers, 2,600 sailors and marines, and five ships of the line mounting 340 guns. Louisbourg's fall, furthermore, gave the British navy mastery over the Gulf of St. Lawrence, and sharply reduced the flow of much-needed military supplies to Canada.

The final offensive of 1758, an assault on Fort Duquesne by General Forbes across Pennsylvania, fell far behind schedule due to the enormous difficulties of hacking a road through the mountains and protecting convoys over 200 miles of an enemy-infested supply line. On 11 September, the French killed or captured 270 Highlanders and provincials under Major James Grant sent to reconnoiter Fort Duquesne. On 12 October, the forward supply base at Fort Ligonier, 40 miles from Fort Duquesne, held off an attack by 570 French and Indians, but suffered the loss of all its cattle and packhorses. Heavy rains washed out Forbes's military road and brought British operations to a standstill just as winter was beginning.

By mid-November, when Forbes had become resigned that he could advance no further than Fort Ligonier, a former British soldier captured in a French uniform revealed that Fort Duquesne's garrison was too weak to withstand a siege. Although so dangerously ill that he would die within four months, the general led 2,500 picked men in a winter's march of nine days across the final chain of ridges to Fort Duquesne. The French garrison retreated after blowing up the post on 24 November. One day later, Forbes entered the smoldering ruins amid the gruesome sight of Indian victory poles spiked with the skulls of Highlanders killed at Grant's defeat. The year 1758 ended with a new post, Fort Pitt, under construction at the forks of the Ohio.

The tide had begun to turn against the French in 1758, and Pitt promoted the generals responsible for the year's greatest victory, the fall of Louisbourg. The prime minister named Jeffery Amherst as commander in chief, and directed him to sweep the French from northern New York, capture Montreal, and, if possible, press on to Quebec. Amherst's most energetic subordinate at Louisbourg, James Wolfe, received command of the expedition ordered to invade Canada through the St. Lawrence Valley and besiege Quebec.

Amherst ordered Brigadier General John Prideaux to reoccupy Oswego and then take Fort Niagara with a force of 2,200 regulars and 3,500 provincials. By 7 July, Prideaux had Fort Niagara under fire, but 2,000 French and Indians were rushing to break the siege. Sir William Johnson of New York, who assumed command after Prideaux died in the front lines, routed the relief column on 24 July. Fort Niagara's 600 troops surrendered the next day. Fearful that Johnson would cross Lake Ontario and attack Fort Toronto in Canada, the French burned and abandoned that post.

Because both his provincials and supplies arrived very late, Amherst could not leave his base on Lake George until 21 July. Brushing aside enemy skirmishers, he marched to Fort Carillon only to see it blown up in his face on the 26th. Amherst occupied the ruins, afterward known as Fort Ticonderoga, and pushed on to Fort St. Frédéric, which he found destroyed on 4 August. Halting to build Fort Crown Point from the rubble of St. Frédéric, Amherst allowed his offensive to bog down until winter's approach made an advance on Canada impractical. Amherst nevertheless sent 200 rangers

under Major Robert Rogers against the Abenaki Indian village of St. Francis, which Rogers burned on 6 October.

James Wolfe also began his expedition to Quebec late, and he labored under the added disadvantage of having just 9,000 troops instead of 12,000 as planned, when he landed east of that city on 27 June. Montcalm adopted a strategy of watchful waiting that forced the British to sacrifice lives probing his strong points while civilian guerrillas slowly whittled away his numbers. Exasperated by the Canadian militia's harassing tactics, Wolfe retaliated by sending his light infantry and rangers on an orgy of devastation that destroyed hundreds of small farms, but only stiffened Canadian resistance. By autumn, Wolfe's army had suffered 700 casualties, was continually beset by vengeful partisans, and would be forced to withdraw unless it could lock Montcalm's army in mortal combat before winter froze the St. Lawrence River.

Wolfe's staff discovered that west of Montcalm's shore batteries lay an unguarded path leading up the high cliff to Quebec. If British troops could slip past the French artillery and scale the heights undetected, they could force Quebec's garrison into open battle on the Plains of Abraham. On the evening of 12 September, Wolfe's infantry rowed up the St. Lawrence and safely passed Montcalm's artillery after several officers who spoke French bluffed their way past enemy sentries. By next morning, 4,500 British troops had clambered up to the Plains of Abraham and were challenging Quebec's garrison to sally forth. Without waiting for nearby reinforcements, Montcalm marched out to fight. Both sides were approximately equal in numbers, but the British lines held fast and drove the French back within the city. Both commanders fell mortally wounded, but Wolfe died the victor. Quebec formally capitulated on 18 September.

General James Murray assumed command from Wolfe and watched his isolated garrison wither pitifully as malnutrition, disease, and the severe Canadian winter took their toll on his men. One thousand redcoats died at Quebec that winter, and by spring so many were hospitalized that only 4,000 troops were fit for duty. Canada's governor, Pierre de Rigaud de Vaudreuil, meanwhile, consolidated his forces at Montreal, and in spring 1760, he ordered François-Gaston de Lévis to retake Quebec with 7,000 troops, including eight regular regiments. On 28 April at Sillery, Lévis routed Murray's soldiers, who suffered 1,000 casualties, and brought Quebec under siege. Enemy fire and disease continued to ravage the surrounded garrison, which shrank to 2,500 men fit for duty, but Murray kept Lévis at bay until 16 May, when the siege was broken by a British naval convoy.

Quebec's relief enabled Amherst to coordinate a three-pronged offensive to crush French resistance in 1760. On 14 July, 2,500 regulars under Murray began marching up the St. Lawrence toward Montreal. Amherst left Oswego on 10 August with 10,000 troops and captured 300 French troops at Fort Lévis on 25 August. Brigadier General William Haviland marched north from Crown Point with 2,500 men and took Chambly on 1 September. The three armies converged at Montreal, where Canada's remaining military forces were concentrated, and compelled Governor Vaudreuil to surrender on 8 September. Canada's remaining garrisons capitulated peacefully.

As Canada collapsed, full-scale hostilities were erupting in South Carolina. The Cherokees had invited the British to build Fort Prince George (South Carolina) and Fort Loudoun (Tennessee) in their territory, and even sent warriors to scout for Forbes in 1758, but they became alienated by abusive treatment received from Fort Prince George's garrison, and because the British failed to arrest the murderers of several warriors killed in Virginia while returning from the Forbes campaign. French agents encouraged a war faction to avenge these injuries, and in April 1759, there began a series of raids on South Carolina in which 23 settlers perished by early July.

Governor William Henry Lyttleton marched South Carolina militia into the Cherokee country and intimidated the Indians into giving a hostage for each colonist killed until their murderers were surrendered for trial. In February 1760, the Cherokees killed Fort Prince George's commander after inviting him to a parley, and then besieged the garrison, which retaliated by massacring the hostages. Cherokee raiding parties once again spread terror through the South Carolina frontier and besieged Fort Loudoun.

Amherst responded by sending 1,200 Highlanders under Lieutenant Colonel Archibald Montgomery to relieve Fort Loudoun and restore peace. Montgomery's regulars and a provincial force advanced as far as the Little Tennessee River, where they stood off a large attack near the Indian town of Etchoe, but suffered 100 casualties. Montgomery then abandoned hope of reaching Fort Loudoun and withdrew. The regulars at Fort Loudoun surrendered on 7 August after being assured of safe conduct eastward, but were attacked on the 10th, when the Cherokees killed a number equal to the hostages massacred at Fort Prince George in February and held the remaining 113 for ransom.

Lieutenant Colonel James Grant undertook a second expedition with 2,500 Highlanders and provincials in June 1761. The failure of French agents to provide ammunition crippled Cherokee resistance, however, and after Grant's men fought their way through an ambush near Etchoe on 10 June, the Indians could do nothing to prevent their enemies from burning 15 towns. Grant's rampage through the Smoky Mountains led the Cherokees to sue for peace, which was negotiated the following December.

As the Cherokee uprising subsided, French diplomats were concluding an alliance with Spain that would draw thousands of Anglo-Americans to fight in the Caribbean. On 15 August 1761, the two Bourbon kingdoms signed a secret pact obligating Spain to enter the war against Britain by 1 May 1762, unless peace had already been ratified. Britain declared war with Spain on 4 January 1762, however, and ordered Amherst to dispatch 6,000 regulars and 2,000 provincials to join 6,600 troops under the duke of Albemarle in an assault on Cuba.

Albemarle's forces gained a foothold east of Havana on 7 June after the Royal Navy had silenced two shore batteries blocking their approach. On the next day, 8,000 enemy troops, spearheaded by Spanish cavalry, swept down from the heights above the beachhead, but were repulsed with heavy losses. The British invested Havana's chief citadel, El Morro Castle, on 10 June and then settled down to a long siege, which was twice threatened when Spanish infantry sallied out of El Morro and charged Albemarle's entrenchments.

More dangerous than Spanish bullets were the island's tropical diseases, which had killed over 1,000 British and hospitalized 40 percent of the survivors by 17 July. Only the arrival of more reinforcements from Amherst in North America ensured that British manpower would be sufficient to continue the siege. On 30 July, after their engineers had bored through El Morro's solid rock foundation and blown a breach in its wall, British infantry charged through the smoking debris and took the castle by storm. Havana's remaining bastions were silenced by 11 August, and the city surrendered on 13 August. As a military triumph, Havana's fall equalled the conquest of Louisbourg or Quebec, but it came at a terrible price: barely half of the Anglo-Americans present at the siege returned to the colonies alive.

By mid-1762, as peace discussions were imminent, France launched the war's last American campaign to seize Newfoundland's valuable fisheries as a bargaining chip at the negotiating table. Sailing from Brest, four French ships of the line convoyed 800 infantry across the Atlantic and managed to elude the British navy in the foggy waters off eastern Canada. By 24 June, the French arrived at the British colony, which was held by an understrength garrison of 240 infantry and 70 artillerymen, and they forced the main garrison at St. John's to capitulate on 27 June.

Sir Jeffery Amherst ordered his brother, Lieutenant Colonel William Amherst, to retake the island. The younger Amherst stripped Nova Scotia of 900 regulars and 500 provincials, commandeered ten transports, and landed at Newfoundland on 12 September. Because the French government assumed a British counterattack could not be launched before the next summer, by which time Newfoundland would have served its purpose as a diplomatic pawn, it had recalled its naval forces to Europe before Amherst arrived. Without armed ships to defend St. John's harbor, the French were trapped. After minor skirmishing that cost the British 52 casualties, Amherst accepted the French surrender and took 689 prisoners on 18 September 1762.

France and Spain lacked the military means of ousting Britain from its conquests and were compelled to renounce title to numerous colonies. In the secret Treaty of Fontainbleau, ratified 13 November 1762, France compensated Spain for its sacrifices by ceding the port of New Orleans and all its territorial claims west of the Mississippi. Spain thereafter agreed to cede East and West Florida in exchange for a British evacuation of Cuba. To regain their captured islands of Guadeloupe and Martinique, French diplomats bargained away Canada and all of Louisiana lying east of the Mississippi to Britain, except for the islands of St. Pierre and Miquelon off Newfoundland, but retained fishing rights off the Grand Banks. Having thus redrawn the map of North America, the Treaty of Paris formally ended hostilities on 10 February 1763.

The Seven Years' War produced the largest military mobilization and heaviest casualties of any conflict borne by a mature colonial society in North America. Outnumbered more than 20 to one by British colonists, French Canadians sent well over half of all males of military age on campaign in most years. Beginning in 1755 with the expulsion of 6,000 Acadians (nearly one of every 12 French Canadians), the civilian population suffered heavily. The British navy's interruption of seaborne trade greatly exacerbated the famine conditions that existed in 1757 and 1758, and Wolfe's ravaging of the St. Lawrence Valley in 1759 produced more damage than Canadians had ever endured during the bloody Iroquois Wars.

The war exacted fewer sacrifices from Anglo-Americans, of whom just one-fifth of eligible males had to be mobilized each year, but its cumulative impact was substantial. By 1763, at least 60,000 British colonists had served in provincial units and another 11,000 as regulars. Including privateersmen, the royal *bateaux* corps, and rangers, Britain's 13 colonies probably sent one-third to two-fifths of all free adult males into military service during the war. In retrospect, it was during the Seven Years' War that the 13 colonies ceased to be mere colonial dependencies, and came of age: for it was then that they emerged as a truly significant element of the military resources that enabled Britain to supplant Spain and France as Europe's foremost imperial power.

Thomas L. Purvis

References

Fred Anderson, *A People's Army: Massachusetts Soldiers and Society in the Seven Years' War* (1984); Guy Frégault, *Canada: The War of the Conquest* trans. by Margaret M. Cameron (1969); Lawrence Henry Gipson, *The British Empire Before the American Revolution, The Great War for the Empire*, 3 vols. (1946–1954): *The Years of Defeat, 1754–1757; The Victorious Years, 1758–1760;* and *The Culmination, 1759–1763;* Francis Jennings, *Empire of Fortune: Crowns, Colonies, and Tribes in the Seven Years War in America* (1988).

Douglas E. Leach, *Arms for Empire: A Military History of the British Colonies in North America, 1607–1763* (1973); James G. Lydon, *Struggle for Empire: A Bibliography of the French and Indian Wars, 1739–1763* (1986); Richard Middleton, *The Bells of Victory: The Pitt-Newcastle Ministry and the Conduct of the Seven Years' War, 1757–1762* (1985); Francis Parkman, *France and England in North America*, 7 vols. (1865–1892).

Fort Seybert (West Virginia)

Situated at the south fork of the southern
branch of the Potomac River, 12 miles northeast
of Franklin in Pendleton County, West Virginia,
Fort Seybert was erected sometime after May
1755. Named for prominent local landowner
Jacob Seybert, the fort consisted of several log
huts enclosing a hollow square. In April 1758,
it underwent a siege by a French and Indian
force that had taken Fort Upper Tract. Fort
Seybert's garrison surrendered after three days
on promises that their lives would be spared,
but the Indians killed 20 and carried off another
ten after burning the fort. Fort Seybert was later
rebuilt by order of the Virginia assembly.

Thomas Costa

References
    Otis K. Rice, *The Allegheny Frontier:
West Virginia Beginnings, 1730–1830* (1970).

See also FORT UPPER TRACT (WEST VIRGINIA)

Fort Shantok (Connecticut)

Fort Shantok was a fortified village built on
the west bank of the Thames River in New
London County, Connecticut, by the Mohegan
Indians. Constructed around the time of the
Pequot War (1636–1637) on the site of an
earlier Indian fortification that had not included a village within its walls, Fort Shantok

occupied a raised triangular promontory between Shantok Creek and the Thames River.
The enclosure, built of tall wooden stakes, was
approximately 600 feet long by 300 feet wide
at its base. Fort Shantok was the stronghold of
the sachem Uncas, a kinsman of the Pequot
grand sachem, whose unsuccessful efforts to
seize power within the Pequot tribe on five
occasions had resulted in his exile.

Sheltered and encouraged by the Narragansetts, Uncas lent his support to the English in
their war against the Pequots and with their aid
and support established a rival "tribe," the Mohegan, comprised of a handful of dissident Pequots and River Indians. Although initially quite
small (some have estimated Uncas had no more
than 100 followers at most), the Mohegans were
granted by the English control over some 80
Pequot men with their families at the end of
the war. Other refugees joined them. The Pequots were placed in five small villages along the
Thames River south of Fort Shantok. The main
Mohegan village within the fort served as both
a refuge against the Narragansetts, who attacked
in 1645, and as a site for wampum manufacture,
a mainstay of the Mohegan economy.

With the loss of Mohegan sovereignty after
the death of Uncas in 1684, Fort Shantok was
temporarily abandoned, but later reoccupied.
The site is now part of Fort Shantok State Park.
Excavated by Bert Salwen (1962–1970) and
Lorraine Williams (1968, 1970), artifacts from
Fort Shantok span more than a century of postcontact history and have provided important information about cultural change in Pequot-
Mohegan society in the seventeenth and early
eighteenth centuries.

Alfred A. Cave

References
    William Burton and Richard Lowenthal,
"The First of the Mohegan," *American Ethnol-
ogist* I (1974):589–599; Carroll Alton Means,
"Mohegan-Pequot Relationships," *Archaeolog-
ical Society of Connecticut Bulletin* 21 (1947):
26–33; Neal Salisbury, *Manitou and Providence:
Indians, Europeans, and the Making of New
England, 1500–1643* (1982); Lorraine E. Will-
iams, "Ft. Shantok and Ft. Corchaug: A Com-
parative Study of Seventeenth-Century Culture
Contact in the Long Island Sound Area," Ph.D.
Dissertation, New York University (1972).

See also MOHEGAN; NARRAGANSETTS;
PEQUOT WAR; UNCAS

Shawnee

The Shawnee Indians, known as the Savannahs in the south, belonged to the Algonquian linguistic group. Their closest relatives were the Kickapoo, Sauk, and Fox. In the early historic period, their numbers ranged from approximately 2,000 to 4,000 people. Originally located in the Ohio Valley, around the mid- to late seventeenth century they were driven out of the region by the Iroquois. The tribe moved southward from Ohio, hence the name Shawnee; meaning Southerner. They were actually not a single tribe, but rather a confederation of several tribes. They migrated more than most Indian groups and were well known because of their numerous branches that eventually came into contact with most of the southern and eastern colonies.

After they were driven from the Ohio Valley, the Shawnee divided into two primary branches. One group was located near the Cumberland River in Tennessee. After several years in the Cumberland region many Shawnee migrated again. During the early 1730s, they traveled to an area north of the Ohio River, because of war with the Cherokee. They settled at what became known as Old Shawnee Town, located at the mouth of the Scioto River.

The second branch of the Shawnee had traveled to South Carolina. They did not stay long, but settled near the Savannah River. Beginning in the 1680s, many of these Shawnee migrated in small groups to Pennsylvania and lived with the Delaware Indians. Finally, during the middle of the eighteenth century, the two branches of the Shawnee were reunited in the Ohio Valley. The Ohio region became a Shawnee stronghold for many years, where they consistently resisted white settlement in the area.

The Shawnee were traditionally made up of five separate divisions. Each performed specific functions and were responsible for particular duties. The Chillicothe and Thawekila were responsible for political affairs, and usually supplied the political leaders for the tribe. The Maquachakes were healers and counselors. They were concerned with health and medical problems that faced the entire tribe. Religious ritual and leadership was provided by the Piquas. Finally, the Kispokis supplied war chiefs and were responsible for training and preparing the tribe for war. Each division held a semi-autonomous status and occupied separate towns and villages.

The family unit was very important for education of children and survival. Games and rituals were taught to children at an early age. These activities were aimed at developing strength and hardiness for the young members of the tribe.

Within the tribe itself, there was a strict division of labor that was not unlike other eastern tribes. Hunting was the primary occupation for adult males. Females were responsible for farming (primarily maize), construction of housing, and preparation of food.

The Shawnee were definitely a nomadic group, but they did spend their summer months in villages, where they grew crops. Temporary villages were usually located near rivers or other sources of water. Women prepared the housing and took care of the fields as the men hunted nearby. In the winter, the villages were abandoned. They broke into small family groups, and the men often went on extended hunts in search of food.

Politically, the Shawnee were primarily associated with the French, with whom they conducted a mutually profitable trade. During the French and Indian War, they fought against the British. They often met with the French or other Indian groups to establish communication networks and plan for their common defense. French forts became meeting places where ammunition was available and raids were often organized. However, not all Shawnee supported the French. There was a minority of militants within the tribe that attempted to unite the Indians to resist all European powers. Despite these militants, the French and Shawnee became allies because most considered the British their common enemy. Following the war, the Shawnee continued to be violently opposed to white settlement in the Ohio Valley, which led them to side with the British during the Revolutionary War.

Michael W. Nagle

References

Colin G. Calloway, "We Have Always Been the Frontier: The American Revolution in Shawnee Country," *American Indian Quarterly* 16 (1992):39–52; Jerry E. Clark, *The Shawnee* (1977); Gregory E. Dowd, *A Spirited Resistance: The North American Indian Struggle for Unity, 1745–1815* (1992); Lawrence Henry Gipson, *The British Empire Before the American Revolution*, 15 vols. (1939–1970), 4–5; John R. Swanton, *The Indian Tribes of North America* (1952); Richard White, *The Middle Ground: Indians, Empires, and Republics in the Great Lakes Region, 1650–1815* (1991).

See also BUFFALO CREEK, SHAWNEE ATTACK ON; OLD SHAWNEE TOWN; PONTIAC'S WAR

Ship Design

European ship design evolved gradually through the centuries, influenced as much by war and commerce as by technology and materials. Scholars ascertained vessel types in the ancient and medieval periods from seals, coins, pottery, tapestries, and excavations. Plans, models, and paintings provided more precise evidence from the seventeenth century onward. Generally, the age of sail ran from 4,000 B.C. to the mid-nineteenth century before being eclipsed by steam and iron.

Most vessels from the Mediterranean differed from those of the North Sea until after 1600. Ancient civilizations such as Egypt produced the galley, powered by oar and sail. Norsemen developed the longship for war and the beamier *knarr* for cargo, both pointed at bow and stern, capable of rowing and better at sailing than the galley. Mediterranean ships were usually carvel-planked, edge to edge, with smooth surface. Northern vessels were clinker-built, with the lower edge of each plank overlapping the upper edge of the plank beneath. Both types used steering oars.

In the period 1200 to 1400, the one-masted ship with one square sail prevailed. The great changes in this period were the stern rudder (c. 1200), the deep-draft hull, and the bowsprit. In the Mediterranean, lateen sail usage spread after European contact with the Muslim world. The single-masted, square-sailed cog of 1400, with plump lines and castles fore and aft, looked surprisingly akin to the typical Roman cargo carrier of 50 A.D. Galleys continued as vessels of war in the southern sea until vanquished at the Battle of Lepanto in 1571.

The three-masted, full-rigged ship appeared by 1450. This development coincided with the increased demands of commerce and exploration in the fifteenth century, providing a more versatile, seaworthy craft. Rigs of these vessels gradually changed upward from three to six sails: Spritsail under the bowsprit, foresail, and topsail on the foremast, mainsail, and topsail on the mainmast, and lateen on the mizzen. The types were the *carrack* (largest, with high freeboard, bow, and stern castels), the *galleass* (combination of ship and galley), the *caravel* (smaller, 50 to 60 tons, changing from all-lateen rig to ship rig, called the *caravela redonda*), and the *galleon* (square and lateen-rigged ship, but with lower bow castle, smaller and more weatherly than the *carrack*). The square stern replaced the round stern in the 1600s.

Guns, iron, then brass muzzleloaders, fired from the upper deck in the fourteenth and fifteenth centuries as carriages improved. About 1500, guns were placed between decks, firing through ports. The demicannon, culverine, and saker, among other types of the 1540s, became the 32-, 18-, and 6-pounders of the 1700s. Some vessels, like the famous *Henry Grâce à Dieu* of 1514, carried four masts, the additional one called a bonaventure and lateen rigged, which faded by 1613. By 1523, the English shifted from clinker to carvel planking. Naval vessels differed little from merchant vessels in this period, as navies consisted mainly of called-up merchant ships. However, in 1487, *Regent* and *Sovereign*, of 100 and 800 tons, respectively, were built as strictly naval vessels. Perhaps the vindication of fifteenth- and sixteenth-century ship design may be seen in the world-ranging exploits of Columbus's *Santa Maria*, Magellan's *Trinidad*, and Drake's *Golden Hind*, all around 100 tons and 85 feet, stem to sternpost.

As with the fifteenth-century Spanish *caravels*, the ships of Henry VIII and Elizabeth were surprisingly fast sailors. Fine of entry and line, the Elizabethan vessels carried a length-to-beam ratio of about 2.3 to 1. They revealed high poops, lots of sheer, and lower forecastles with beaked bows, galleon type. About half of the British vessels attacking the Spanish Armada were under 360 tons, a ton being a measure of carrying capacity, not weight.

In the seventeenth century, ships displayed more ornamentation, characteristics of design differed from country to country, rigging altered, and the sheer of hull line began to flatten. In sails and rigging, the spritsail-topsail appeared above the bowsprit on a modified flagstaff, and the mizzen squaresail flew above the lateen. To shorten sail in severe weather, bonnets and reef points were used. Bonnets were removable lower strips of sail, and reef points were short lines for tying up sections of sail. Reef points and bonnets dated from the Middle Ages, but as topsails came into use, reef points proved to be more practicable. Fore and aft staysails, hoisted in smaller Dutch boats in the 1500s, appeared aboard ships in the 1650s, greatly adding to their weatherliness and maneuverability. Topgallant sails and studding sails could also be seen before the end of the century. Figureheads, gunport wreaths, and decorated quarter and stern galleys distinguished the ships of one nation from another.

In hull shape, the English broke away from the flat stern about mid-century and utilized the "round tuck," where planking bent gracefully in convex fashion into the rudder and post and up into a squarish stern housing. Examples of early seventeenth-century English ships are *Prince Royal* (1610) and *Sovereign of the Seas* (1637), both designed and built by Phineas Pett. *Prince Royal*, a three-decker, carried 56 guns, looked very Elizabethan, but was larger than earlier sisters. *Sovereign of the Seas* was heavier yet, boasted 100 guns, and looked sturdier and flatter in shape than its predecessors. The longest ship on English rolls in 1602 was *Merhonour* at 153 feet.

In the 1660s, naval architecture and organization set lasting precedents. Samuel Pepys began to keep a record of naval design for the Navy Board as Charles II and the duke of York continued the organization of the Royal Navy begun by Henry VIII. The chief fighting distinctions were the development of the single column battle formation from Oliver Cromwell's time, and the ship of the line of 50 guns and more to withstand the give and take of sustained broadsides. To sustain heavier throw weight, naval vessels carried their maximum beam near the waterline and displayed apple-cheeked bows, traits continued into the nineteenth century. Larger ships were steered by whipstaffs (attached at 90 degrees to the tiller from the poopdeck), or block and tackle rigged to tillers. Also, during the latter half of the seventeenth century, the English experimented with sheathing of wood, felt, and lead to deter dry rot and the teredo worm. Lead near iron fittings in water led to electrolysis, a problem not solved until Lord Anson's time in 1761 with the introduction of copper sheathing and nails below the waterline. Documentation from this period also came from the paintings of the Van de Veldes, father and son.

The Dutch, emerging from Spanish domination and competing with the English, devised the best cargo carriers in the seventeenth century. The combination of location, town councils, ship carpenters' guilds, and necessity induced the popularity of the *buss* for herring, the *hoeker* for cod, the *hekboot* for whaling, the *fluyt* for lumber, and the *retourschip* for the East India Company. If the French, Swedes, and Spaniards continued the square stern and carvel planking, and the British devised the round tuck, the Dutch continued with clinker-built topsides and perfected the distinctive *fluyt* stern

with planks curved in convex fashion into the sternpost. *Fluyts* were most often 350 to 600 tons, ship-rigged, lightly built, with flatter bottoms and shallower draft for Baltic and Dutch harbors, and accentuated tumble home (topsides curved inward) to avoid higher toll collections in the Danish Sound. Vessels in this period now indicated a length-to-beam ratio af about 5 to 1. Dutch vessels were usually smaller and cheaper to build and operate than those of other states, allowing them to dominate the European carrying trade in the 1600s.

The French navy became powerful under Minister of Marine Jean-Baptiste Colbert, from the 1660s to 1692, when defeat at La Hogue sent it into decline. France's maritime interest was always peripheral in contrast to England and Holland. Colbert's central administration organized shipbuilding centers at Brest, Toulon, and Rochefort, and a timber procurement program. French ship design and documentation became the envy of others for nearly a century. French ships were larger and wider for the number of guns they carried than those of their adversaries, e.g., *Couronne* of 72 guns was as large as *Royal Sovereign* with 100. Their stern- and stemposts were more vertical and horizontal lines finer than their rivals. French ships received more ornamentation than the English or Dutch. Louis XIV's cargo carriers evolved from the single-masted cog and double-masted *houlke* to medium-sized *barques*, small *galions* (pinnaces) and ships called *nef* or *vaisseau*.

Even though France possessed vast forests, the trees of the Pyrenees and Auvergne were not well suited for masts. Their naval bases sat apart from great rivers, so it was costly and risky to transport timber, e.g., on the leg from Le Havre to Brest, the British could intercept. The French failed to appreciate the possibilities of masts from Canada, buying oak in Italy and fir from Riga, Memel, Stettin, Danzig, and St. Petersburg, with frustrating results because the Dutch controlled most of the carrying trade and British merchant houses like Thornton, Pierson, and Tooke dominated the Baltic timber contracts.

The British also suffered from timber hunger, especially after 1650, a problem that flared until the advent of steam and iron warships in the mid-nineteenth century. While the Britons cherished their heart of oak from Sussex and Gloucester's Forest of Dean, they procured spruce spars from Norway, fir sticks from the Baltic, and pine masts from North America, where agents imprinted the king's broad arrow on vast stands of trees. The Navy Board contract system provided for timber purchases, often corrupt, rarely in sufficient quality or quantity, for vessels laid down at Chatham and Deptford. Access to adequate timber and naval stores was essential to the security of these maritime nations, and they exerted great efforts to secure this supply, employing secret agents, alliances, and attacks, from Cromwell's anti-Dutch Baltic policy of 1659 to the British assault on Copenhagen in 1807.

The Spanish augmented depleted forests and Biscayan shipbuilding with wood from their overseas empire. Although poorly situated for deepwater commerce, Seville controlled trade with the Indies. Spanish ships were famous less for their design and construction than for the materials they contained. The Spanish regarded merchantmen as *naos* and warships as *navios*. Many were constructed at colonial shipyards in Manila, Acapulco, and Havana, with durable Philippine teak and Honduran mahogany. At least one-third of the seventeenth-century Spanish merchant marine was built in the West Indies, with one-third launched in Spain and one-third purchased from other nations. Havana yards constructed ships from the 1620s onward, launching 74 of 221 *navios* Spain commissioned in the eighteenth century. The gigantic ship of the line *Santissima Trinidad* consumed 3,000 trees.

In the eighteenth century, Dutch maritime influence followed the Spanish, Portuguese, and Swedish decline. British seapower increased, challenged again by the French and then by the Americans.

The standardization of types became more pronounced in the eighteenth century as part of government and East Indian Company "establishment," or building program regulations. Naval vessels were classified into six rates. The size of a first-rate man-of-war of 100 guns increased from 1,550 tons to 2,000 between 1677 and 1745. A 74-gun ship of the line, the most popular design from the mid-eighteenth century through the Napoleonic wars, was designated as a third-rate, 200-feet-long-by-50-foot beam, with two gundecks, 600 crew, and a mainmast 36 inches at the base. It was difficult to build longer ships because of the limits of wood construction, which allowed "hogging," or the buckling of a ship in the middle.

The word *frigate* may have come from the Mediterranean by way of Dunkirk as a term for a medium-size vessel of good speed whose broadside could daunt any vessel smaller than a ship of the line. Frigates are mentioned from the 1640s onward in naval lists, but as a class, French and British frigates appeared in the 1750s. They were ship-rigged, featured one gundeck with from 28 to 44 guns, and classified as fifth-rates. USS *President* ran 173 feet on the lower deck, 44 feet in the beam, and 14 feet in depth of hold, carried 44 guns and easily made 13 to 14 knots, the fastest of all American frigates at the end of the century.

An outstanding feature of the eighteenth-century ships is the leveling out of the sheer line compared to earlier designs. *Royal George* of 1715, and *Terrible* of 1747, illustrated this trend. Other changes included massive strengthening of hulls, more powerful cannons, decline in decoration, and adoption of the gaff-rigged spanker or driver for the lateen on the mizzenmast. Figureheads became more varied and pilasters framing quarter and stern galleries were the main type of decoration. Yellow (oiled) hulls with black (tar) trim continued to be the main color combination for most vessels of the naval powers. The steering wheel began to replace the tiller on larger ships around 1715.

Merchant vessels also altered in design and average size through the years. East Indiamen increased from some 400 tons burden in 1708 to 500 tons in 1730 and 1,200 tons by 1800. In Britain, the bark proved its versatility. Captain James Cook's *Endeavor* was a bark originally used as a Whitby collier. These vessels were called barks even though they were ship-rigged, because prior to the nineteenth century, terms like *bark* and *sloop* had nothing to do with rig, but rather with size and use. *Endeavor* was 366 tons burden, with full bilges, bluff bows, and scant ornamentation.

While more varieties existed on the continent and in the British Isles, the North American colonies generally exhibited this type of vessel; the full-rigged ship, sloop, cutter, ketch, brig, snow, pink, schooner, pinnace, and shallop. The ship featured three masts, square sails on all masts, with spanker and staysails. The sloop was ship-rigged but considerably smaller in size and used as a courier by the navy. The cutter, often called a sloop, had one mast with gaff main, two staysails, and perhaps a square topsail. The ketch, used for fishing or for mortar bombardment, had two masts, with the taller in front of the shorter, looking like the hull lacked a foremast. The brig, evolved after 1700, was favored by American merchants as an efficient cargo vessel, with two masts, squaresails, and spanker. The snow was a brig with a short mast added a foot or so behind the mainmast to carry a spanker. Pinks featured a narrow, high stern gallery and varied rigs. The schooner emerged from the Dutch fore- and - afters of the 1600s and revealed gaff-rigged fore and aft sails on two masts, with staysails. This rig became most popular in America because it was maneuverable and economical; it could point higher into the wind and required less crew than square riggers. The pinnace was a lightly-built coaster, and shallops were open workboats.

The first vessel built of seagoing ability in the British North American colonies was the 50-foot, 30-ton, single-masted *Virginia*, constructed in Maine at the mouth of the Kennebec River in 1607 by homesick settlers. The Dutch at New Amsterdam built *Onrust* in 1615, about 45 feet long. In 1631, Massachusetts Bay colonists launched *Blessing of the Bay*, a 30-ton bark.

Colonial shipbuilding began as an industry in 1650, and up until the 1770s, 85 to 90 percent of all hulls were built in Massachusetts. Oak for keel and ribs, pine for spars and masts abounded, locust tree nails proved durable, while cordage, sails, and other naval stores often came from England. The four wars from 1689 to 1763 stimulated colonial shipbuilders to replace British losses. English merchants and contractors financed two out of three colonial vessels, which could be built for £2 to £4 less a ton than they could in England. On the eve of the American Revolution, from one-quarter to one-third of British registered ships were built in the North American colonies, and Boston ranked among the top ten ports in the British Empire for volume of commerce. By the mid-eighteenth century, Massachusetts launched about 120 ships a year; Rhode Island, 70; Connecticut, 50; Pennsylvania, 20; Virginia and Maryland 15 each. New England ships featured more tumble home, carrying capacity, and shallow draft than Chesapeake vessels known for their flared bows and raked masts. American builders utilized British designs, not French, and while American ships were faster, their hulls contained neither the quality of construction nor the seasoning of woods noticed in the better British ships.

While no American plans exist, several British diagrams for smaller vessels afford an idea of types probably built in the colonies. *Swift* (1721) was a 60-foot brig with a 19-foot beam, an 8-foot draft, rated at 90 tons. In later years, the typical American trading brig ranged from 100 to 250 tons, 65 to 90 feet long; the schooner somewhat smaller.

Colonials built naval vessels, as well. *Falkland*, a forty-gun ship, was launched at Portsmouth, New Hampshire, in 1694. In the four wars for empire, Americans built and manned privateers of 300 to 400 tons, boasting 14 to 18 guns (e.g., *Bethel*, of Boston, 1748) marauding for Spanish and French prizes until the Treaty of Paris in 1763.

The period from 1600 to 1760 developed the standardized rig and hull designs that continued to the end of the days of sail. Sheer flattened, weight increased, hulls strengthened but did not lengthen, lines faired and sails proliferated on loftier masts. As Spanish supremacy gave way to Anglo-Dutch rivalry in the seventeenth century, with a French challenge, so British seapower in the next century withstood threats from the French and the Americans. The need to secure oak, pine, and fir influenced foreign policy as well as construction quality. Ship design advanced from the *caravel* and *galleon* to the *fluyt*, frigate, and ship of the line, beyond which lay the clipper, the packet, and the age of steam and steel.

James H. Hitchman

References

Robert G. Albion, *Forests and Seapower: The Timber Problem of the Royal Navy, 1652–1862* (1926); Romola Anderson and R.C. Anderson, *The Sailing Ship: Six Thousand Years of History* (1963); Paul W. Bamford, *Forests and French Seapower, 1660–1789* (1936); Howard I. Chapelle, *A History of American Sailing Ships* (1935); G.S.L. Clowes, *Sailing Ships: Their History and Development*, Part I, *Historical Notes*, 5th ed. (1959).

Joseph A. Goldenburg, *Shipbuilding in Colonial America* (1976); John D. Harbron, "The Spanish Ship of the Line," *Scientific American* 251 (1984); Samuel Eliot Morison, *The European Discovery of America*, 2 vols. (1971); J.H. Parry, *The Spanish Seaborne Empire* (1966); R.W. Unger, *Dutch Shipbuilding Before 1800* (1978).

See also ARTILLERY, FRANCE; ARTILLERY, GREAT BRITAIN; DRY DOCKS; HAVANA; NAVY, FRANCE; NAVY, GREAT BRITAIN; NAVY, SPAIN; SHIP OF THE LINE

Ship of the Line

Ships of the line were warships capable of engaging the largest enemy vessels in a line of battle and were effectively the battleships of the seventeenth- and eighteenth-century Royal Navy. Since the 1650s, the tactic of forming a line had been considered the best method of engaging an enemy, as it allowed each warship to approach broadside, permitting the maximum use of firepower. A line of battle was also easier to control than a melee of individual ships.

The first large warships of the Royal Navy were those constructed by the early Tudor monarchs, notably Henry VIII (1509–1547). Thereafter they constituted the heart of the fleet. Ships of the line were normally rated by their ordnance rather than their tonnage. One-hundred-gun ships were designated first-rate, those with 90 guns second-rate, 70 and 80 guns were classified as third-rate, while those with 50 to 60 guns were fourth-rate.

Tonnages varied, even for ships of the same class and design. In the seventeenth century, 50-gun ships were usually about 500 tons, while those with 100 guns were normally around 1,200 tons. However, during the eighteenth century, tonnages steadily increased to accommodate heavier ordnance. By 1750, first-rates were approximately 2,000 tons, and even fourth-rates were frequently more than 1,000 tons.

Crew sizes similarly varied. The smaller fourth-rates normally carried around 350 men, while a first-rate might have 800. All carried marines for storming parties and to maintain discipline, since in wartime half the crew might be impressed.

The most common armament of a ship of the line was the 32-pounder, which could project solid shot of that weight for several hundred yards. However, first-rate vessels carried a tier of 42-pounders, while smaller vessels often had only lighter 18- and 24-pounders. The third- and fourth-rate ships had two gundecks, whereas the larger first- and second-rates had three. These latter ships were the most prestigious in the fleet. They were also the least seaworthy, being top heavy because of their extra deck. They were also susceptible to flooding in choppy seas if the portholes on their lowest gundeck were opened for firing. First-rate ships, in particular, only put to sea in the summer and were rarely used outside the Channel. Most admirals preferred to command from more seaworthy third-rates.

None of these ships were built to a standard design, a department in which the British lagged behind the French. Master shipwrights in both the royal and merchant yards constructed vessels according to personal whim and available materials. Until the 1750s, the commonest ships of line were the 50-, 60-, 70-, 80-, 90-, and 100-gun vessels. However, in 1747, during the First and Second Battles of Finisterre, the Royal Navy captured a number of 64- and 74-gun ships from the French. These were found to be more maneuverable and of superior design to their British equivalents, and when Lord Anson (1697–1762) became head of the Admiralty in 1751, he determined to introduce them into the fleet. Although the Navy Board, which administered the royal yards, was generally hostile, a number of 74-gun vessels were subsequently built. Anson's faith in them was fully vindicated at the Battle of Quiberon Bay in 1759, where they proved especially effective in confined and rocky waters. This persuaded Anson to order several 64-gun vessels to replace the navy's 50-gun ships, which were now clearly too small for a line of battle.

Until the Seven Years' War, few of the navy's line of battleships saw service in North America outside the Caribbean. The Admiralty allotted only a few single-gundeck frigates to patrol the northern waters. However, from 1755, several powerful squadrons were regularly sent to mainland North America in consequence of the war with France. In 1757, 12 ships of the line went with Admiral Francis Holburne to attack the strategic fortress of Louisbourg. The next year a similar operation was mounted with 16 ships of the line under Admiral Edward Boscawen while in 1759 another 14 went with Admiral Charles Saunders to help General James Wolfe capture Quebec. The dispatch of so many line-of-battle ships necessitated the building of a new naval base at Halifax so that the fleet could winter in North America. By 1762, the Royal Navy had more than 100 ships of the line in commission, exclusive of some 20 50-gun ships. Almost a quarter of them were in the Caribbean or western Atlantic.

Richard Middleton

References

Daniel A. Baugh, *British Naval Administration in the Age of Walpole* (1965); J. Charnock, *A History of Marine Architecture*, 3 vols. (1802); Brian Lavery, *The Ship of the Line*, 2 vols. (1983–1984); N.A.M. Rodger, *The Wooden World: An Anatomy of the Georgian Navy* (1986).

See also ARTILLERY, FRANCE; ARTILLERY, GREAT GRITAIN; DRY DOCKS; IMPRESSMENT, NAVY; NAVY, FRANCE; NAVY, GREAT BRITAIN; SHIP DESIGN

Fort Shirley (Massachusetts)

Built in 1744 at the present town of Heath in Franklin County after the beginning of King George's War, it was intended to protect the frontier between the Connecticut River and the New York boundary. The fortification was 60 feet square and consisted of 12-foot-high walls of pine. It was named in honor of Governor William Shirley.

David L. Whitesell

Fort Shirley (Pennsylvania)

Located on upper Aughwick Creek, near its juncture with the Juniata River, Fort Shirley was apparently built on the site of Indian trader George Croghan's home, which he had earlier fortified. Croghan began building a stockade around this home in October 1755, and when he received a captain's commission in December, along with instructions to build several posts on the western side of the Susquehanna, the site of his earlier fortification appears to have been chosen for Fort Shirley. It was well placed, since it stood near one of the main Indian paths leading toward the eastern settlements.

These far western forts were among the earliest manned in Pennsylvania, and Croghan commanded a garrison of 75 men at Fort Shirley until March 1756, when he was succeeded by Captain Hugh Mercer. During the first phase of the war, the residents on the Aughwick and Juniata were cut off from the rest of the colony, and the protection and refuge offered by Fort Shirley and its companion outposts were extremely important. In late August 1756, Colonel John Armstrong gathered his forces at Fort Shirley for the successful campaign he led against the Delaware town of Kittanning in September. Armstrong's victory apparently forestalled a planned attack against Fort Shirley by Delaware Indian leader Captain Jacobs, who had recently succeeded in capturing Fort Granville.

By the fall of 1756, Governor William Denny was forced to acknowledge that the far western outposts were too isolated to be supplied or defended effectively, and in October, he ordered Fort Shirley evacuated.

Eric Hinderaker

See also CROGHAN, GEORGE; DELAWARE; FORT GRANVILLE (PENNSYLVANIA); KITTANNING, BATTLE OF; FORT LYTTLETON (PENNSYLVANIA)

Shirley, William (1694–1771)

British colonial governor of Massachusetts and of the Bahama Islands, William Shirley was the eldest son of a Sussex County, England, country gentleman and London textile merchant. The Shirleys were distantly related to the Pelham and Onslow families and had accumulated a modest fortune at the time of William's birth in Preston, Sussex County. Educated locally and at the Merchant Taylors' School in London, he went then to Pembroke College, Cambridge, and the Inner Temple, and was called to the bar in 1720.

For some years, Shirley worked as a clerk in the London city government and practiced law. About 1719, he married Frances Barker, the daughter and heir of a London merchant, who apparently bought him an estate that he proceeded to lose during the ill-fated speculation of the South Sea enterprises (the South Sea Bubble). His personal losses, the general depression, and his own dissatisfaction with his state in life forced him to consider the American colonies for opportunities. With promises of patronage help from his countryman, Thomas Pelham-Holles, the duke of Newcastle, a secretary of state, he migrated to Boston with his wife and family of eight children.

The appointment he won with Newcastle's help was judge of the vice-admiralty court. He was able to exchange it for the post of advocate general of that court and the opportunity to practice law for supplementary income. For the coming eight years he searched for other positions, but developed in New England a large law practice, powerful friends in the Maine timber trade, and wealthy associates in Boston who wanted to replace the Massachusetts governor, Jonathan Belcher, with another person. Shirley and his wife, who went to London as his agent, connived to make him the governor's replacement in 1741.

Shirley succeeded to the governorship at a time of great bitterness over two local banking projects, silver and land—both had the purpose of easing the credit shortage. Belcher had aggravated the crisis by taking sides with the silver bankers, purging offices of opponents and calling a new election of the house of representatives. The Boston crisis occurred at a time when the Walpole ministry in England had its own crisis over a trade war with Spain. The war broke out in the Caribbean, went poorly for England, and colonial cooperation was necessary. Shirley's English friends were relying on his help in Massachusetts, and the combination of a banking crisis and the Caribbean war permitted them to replace Belcher with Shirley as governor and seize control of the ministry in England.

Shirley used the opportunity of crisis to build a political coalition in Massachusetts and to win military contracts, army commissions, and goodwill for the colony in England. He was able to cool down the overheated politics of the colony and get monetary reforms legislated that reduced the inflation of the paper currency. His supporters exploited the war with France in 1745 to organize a military expedition to Fort Louisbourg on Cape Breton Island. With the aid of the British navy, the colonial forces easily stormed the fortress and convinced themselves and England that all Quebec should be conquered. Several mobilizations occurred in 1746 and 1747, but the Treaty of Aix-la-Chapelle in 1748 returned the fortress to France, much to Shirley's sorrow.

Shirley exploited the war preparations of the 1740s to bring much wealth to Massachusetts and stimulate interest in the annexation of Canada. In 1749, he was sent to France, however, to develop a plan to divide North America between France and Britain. The conferences in Paris lasted for three years, but failed, much to Shirley's satisfaction, though he may not have desired the acquisition of all of Canada.

While he was in Paris, France erected fortifications along the western frontier of the British colonies. These forts had the purpose of discouraging American colonization and exploration. The threat was first felt by Virginia when its land speculators were harassed by French troops near Fort Duquesne (Pittsburgh) in 1753 and 1754. George Washington of Virginia was forced to capitulate at Fort Necessity in a battle with the French that forced Britain to defend the American colonies' western frontier.

Shirley's mind was divided at first on how to deal with the crisis. He urged the Massachu-setts legislature to join a conference at Albany that would organize the colonies into a military union for defense. But the so-called Albany Plan of 1754 won only the support of Massachusetts, and even that colony hesitated over the future power of England in America. Shirley then turned to a military solution. Anticipating the plans of General Edward Braddock, he helped organize a campaign that would blunt French penetration into northern New York, in western Pennsylvania, and on the Bay of Fundy. It was intended as limited war for the recovery of the British frontier.

Shirley's plan received the approval of Braddock, but it also depended upon the general's leadership and financial support. When Braddock was killed in wilderness Pennsylvania, Shirley was unable to rally enough American help as Braddock's successor to win a decisive victory in 1755. In fact, the British ministry recognized the validity of his military assumptions but was indecisive about the extent of a possible war. The period of indecision in early 1756 permitted sufficient intercolonial opposition to rise up against Shirley, and time for the French to win a major victory at Oswego in 1756.

When the British finally sent out an army in the summer of 1756, Shirley's military policies were so discredited that he was recalled to England. Charges of bungling a campaign and illegal use of funds faced him. Fortunately, the charges proved insubstantial, and by 1759, he was given the honorary military rank of lieutenant general and the governorship of the Bahamas.

His nearly eight years as the Bahamian governor were not thought of as a sinecure. Shirley applied the governing skills he learned in Massachusetts to the problems at hand. He brought the royal council up to full strength, called the assembly into session from time to time, and appointed men to government vacancies. His investigation of the admiralty court showed shortcomings in enforcing the law: he discovered much smuggling and sought help from the English government and persuaded some of his Massachusetts friends to emigrate and serve later on his executive staff. With the assembly he worked to distribute land to the poor and to encourage new crops, open new ports and roads, and improve the laws. He suggested to the home government the opening of free ports in the Caribbean and

S

urged expenditures on defense. Slight political repercussions over the Stamp Act shook the Bahamas in the mid-1760s, but Shirley's methods were moderate and conciliating in maintaining peace.

Shirley resigned in 1767 in favor of his son, Thomas, who then served successively as governor of the Bahamas, Dominica, and the Leeward Islands. Late in life, Thomas was knighted and given the rank of lieutenant general. William Shirley returned to Massachusetts in 1768 and lived on his estate in Roxbury, where he died in 1771. Three of his daughters married into Boston families—the Ervings, Temples, and Hutchinsons—who became prominent in pre-Revolutionary times.

John A. Schutz

References
John A. Schutz, *William Shirley: King's Governor of Massachusetts* (1961); George A. Wood, *William Shirley, Governor of Massachusetts, 1741–1756* (1920).

See also ALBANY CONFERENCE; BRADDOCK, EDWARD; KING GEORGE'S WAR; SEVEN YEARS' WAR

Sickness and Mortality

British regular units were constantly in North America after 1664, with independent companies being established in New York (1690), Nova Scotia (1702), and South Carolina (1720). Several regiments were stationed in the West Indies during Queen Anne's War, and afterward, the 38th Foot remained in Antigua, with independent companies in Jamaica and Bermuda. Large British forces took part in the Admiral Hovenden Walker and Admiral Edward Vernon expeditions (1711, 1741–1742), and in 1746, British regiments relieved the Americans who had taken Louisbourg.

Most of these major enterprises were attended by widespread illness, and mortality rates tended to be high. Pepperrell's 2,500-man army suffered few casualties in taking Louisbourg, but almost half of the troops died of dysentery and other illnesses during the subsequent fall and winter. Vernon's poorly managed enterprise saw the death of about 10,000 British men and officers, mainly from yellow fever (the force scarcely saw combat) and perhaps nine-tenths of his 3,600-man

provincial contingent also succumbed. But despite these disasters, and despite the regular presence of British troops in the New World, British medical literature prior to 1750 dealt little with problems associated with cold (Canada) or tropical areas, and army staff had to learn most lessons during the French and Indian War.

The main medical, as well as military, disaster of 1755 was the Battle of the Monongahela. Ironically, General Edward Braddock's army enjoyed generally good health throughout the expedition, although there were some outbreaks of camp diseases, especially dysentery, at Fort Cumberland and while the army was on the march. The two British regiments serving under Braddock were, however, shattered by the battle, and took more than a year to recover. After that debacle, the British army was largely inactive for fully two years. Provincial troops in central New York suffered heavily in a smallpox epidemic during the fall of 1756, but few regulars died, although many contracted the illness. Throughout the spring of 1757, the army was healthy, perhaps more so than at any other point of the war, but during the summer, a major outbreak of smallpox, which began in New York and spread to forces arriving at Halifax, helped to stymie Lord Loudoun's plan for an expedition against Louisbourg and Quebec. During the fall, the number of men in affected regiments that were categorized as unfit was 17 to 27 percent, among the highest during the war in North America.

The army posture was far more aggressive in 1758 to 1760, leading to great success, but at a high cost in lives and health. Abercromby's army was healthy at the time of its move against Ticonderoga, but it was decimated in battle, sustaining almost 2,000 casualties—by far the highest total of any engagement in the war—and many survivors healed slowly, reflecting the severity of their wounds. The British fared much better in their move against Louisbourg. Although there was much sickness among the forces at Halifax during the winter of 1757–1758, the army was in generally good health by the start of the expedition, and took only about 500 casualties during the course of it, while suffering relatively little from illness. The third major enterprise of 1758, the Forbes expedition against Fort Duquesne, was also attended by generally good health. Most of the 300 casualties suffered by the British came at Grant's Hill, and although there were a few outbreaks of illness among the troops, especially the provincials, they caused little mortality. The main medical element in the expedition was in fact the progressive incapacitation of Forbes himself, by the disease that killed him in March 1759.

The focus of the campaign of 1759 was the General James Wolfe expedition. Again, the army entered the campaign in generally good health, and it held up well during the expedition, though taking heavy casualties at Montmorency Falls and on the Plains of Abraham. During the subsequent winter at Quebec, however, the troops suffered severely from frostbite and even more so from scurvy, which killed perhaps 500. The army that was defeated at Sainte-Foy was in poor condition, so much so that subordinates questioned James Murray's decision to confront the enemy.

After Montreal was taken, essentially ending the war in North America, the British focused their attention on the West Indies. Previously, there had been only one major enterprise in that area, the conquest of Guadeloupe (1759). The Guadeloupe expedition was mounted almost entirely from Britain, leaving intact the army that was serving in North America. Although some casualties were taken in an earlier abortive attack on Martinique, the losses at Guadeloupe were small. However, during 1759, more than 500 men died from disease. The expeditionary medical staff was small and inexperienced, and there are indications that cost-consciousness may have handicapped it, but probably even a larger and abler staff could have done little to reduce mortality. By contrast, the Martinique expedition of 1761–1762 was conducted as well as any could be in the eighteenth century. Much of the attacking force was drawn from North America, and so was the entire expeditionary hospital, which was large, experienced, and well-supplied. The assault on Martinique took place during the winter, and there is some possibility that it was scheduled so as to coincide with the healthiest season. The forces remained relatively healthy until spring. Just as the regiments were turning sickly, many of them joined the duke of Albemarle's expedition, the greatest medical disaster of the war. Much of Albemarle's hospital was brought from Europe, and it may not have meshed well with the medical personnel who joined at Martinique. Illness became widespread in April, but Albemarle initially underestimated the danger. The assault on Havana took place during the summer, and besides casualties, yellow fever cost heavily then, as through the fall. Heavy mortality (3,000 in August–September 1762 alone) forced cancellation of a planned expedition to New Orleans. Many soldiers who survived illness were weakened, and were later discharged.

The commitment to Albemarle of many regiments that had been serving in North America, and the decimation of these regiments, slowed the response to initial attacks by Pontiac's coalition and limited the scope of the eventual response. Most of the men who fought with Henry Bouquet at Bushy Run were veterans of Havana, and in bad health. At the close of the war the British army in North America was still small, compared to what it had been in 1760. Only the breaking of some regiments, drafts, and consolidation brought the regiments up to establishment, and the established number was far lower than it had been during wartime.

During the French and Indian War, about 6,000 British soldiers died in North America, while in the West Indies, despite the narrow time frame of action, the losses were almost equal to that figure. Despite contemporary assessments, which many historians have accepted, the ratio of ten deaths from disease to every battle-related death is far off, at least as regards North America, where during the war about one-third of all deaths resulted from wounds. The West Indian ratio was very different, however, as it was in all eighteenth-century warfare. The impact of illness on warfare was most obvious in the Indies, but health factors consistently played a role in North American campaigns as well.

Paul E. Kopperman

See also MEDICAL SERVICES

Six Nations
See IROQUOIS

Fort of the Six Nations (New York)
See FORT ONTARIO (NEW YORK)

Smith, John (c. 1579–1631)
John Smith, soldier and explorer in early America, was the son of a farmer in Willoughby, Lincolnshire, England. Temperamentally ill-suited to a life as a yeoman or tradesman, he fled to the Continent in pursuit of more adventurous

callings when he was about 16 years of age. During the next seven years he served as a soldier in the religious struggles in Holland and central Europe. In the latter theater he served with considerable valor, winning promotion to the rank of captain and achieving glory within his army for his deeds, the most famous of which was his slaying of three Turkish military commanders in hand-to-hand combat. For his heroism, Prince Zsigmong of Transylvania awarded Smith an armorial insignia—the equivalent of an English coat of arms—emblazoned with the likenesses of the three Turks whom he had slain. Soon thereafter Smith's good fortune deserted him. He was captured in an engagement at Rottenton and sold into slavery in Turkey. He endured nearly a year of bondage before he escaped by murdering his master.

Smith arrived back in England in time to sign on with the London Company, a joint stock enterprise with a charter empowering it to plant a colony in North America. He was one of 105 "planters" who sailed for America in December 1606. During the voyage, Smith was arrested and sentenced to death for reasons that remain mysterious. He was saved by Captain Christopher Newport, the commander of the expedition, and by the discovery that the officers of the London Company had appointed him to be a resident councilor in America.

During the initial 15 months of the existence of the Virginia colony, Smith served principally as a commander of exploratory expeditions into the countryside surrounding Jamestown. He was also assigned the task of bartering with the Indians. In December 1607, while on a foray up the Chickahominy River, his party was ambushed; two of his men were slaughtered and Smith was captured, though not before he had killed two of his attackers. A prisoner for several weeks, Smith ultimately was released by Powhatan, the paramount chief of about a dozen Indian tribes in this region of the Chesapeake. Smith later fashioned the story that he was freed as a result of the intervention of Pocahontas, Powhatan's comely daughter. In fact, the Indian leader likely spared his captive for reasons of diplomacy and from fear of English retaliation should Captain Smith be executed. A few months after his return to Jamestown, Smith was elected president of the diminutive English colony, a post he was to hold for nearly a year, until August 1609.

Virginia had struggled since its inception 18 months before. Two in three of the original settlers had already perished; nearly one-half of all the planters sent to America during the previous two years had died, mostly from disease and lack of food. Smith succeeded in stabilizing matters by inaugurating aggressive policies. By bluster and frequent shows of force, he sought to intimidate the Indians. The policy was a success. While skirmishes and bloodshed occurred, the Indians were persuaded to provide much needed food for the desperate settlers. Smith also governed his own denizens with an iron fist. During his years in command, the condition of the colony improved dramatically. Only 18 of 200 inhabitants of Jamestown perished during his rule, more than one-half of those in a single accident.

Smith remained in Virginia for only a few weeks following the end of his presidency. Shortly after he relinquished power, he was seriously injured in an accidental gunpowder explosion. He was also surrounded by enemies, former subjects who hated him for the harsh policies he had imposed; one group of conspirators even attempted to assassinate him as he lay incapacitated, recovering from his wounds in the powder accident. In the fall of 1609, Smith returned to England, never again to return to Virginia. A measure of his effectiveness as the leader of Virginia can be discerned from developments that followed his departure from America. There were 500 colonists residing in Virginia when he sailed for home; six months later, only 60 remained alive.

During his remaining years, Smith was best known as a historian. A bachelor residing in London, Smith published several histories of Virginia, narratives laden with accounts of his experiences in the young colony, including his charming stories of his relationship with Pocahontas. His most influential work was *The Generall Historie of Virginia, New-England, and the Summer Isles* (1624). Smith returned to America only once, sent as an employee of the Plymouth Company to explore the region he named New England. A celebrity who had attained the status of a gentleman, Smith appears to have lived quietly and happily during his final years. He died in the summer of 1631 following a brief illness.

John E. Ferling

References

Philip L. Barbour, ed., *The Complete Works of Captain John Smith (1580–1631)*, 3 vols. (1986); ——, *The Three Worlds of Captain John Smith* (1964); Karen Kupperman, ed., *Captain John Smith: A Select Edition of His Writings* (1988); Bradford Smith, *Captain John Smith* (1953); Alden T. Vaughan, *American Genesis: Captain John Smith and the Founding of Virginia* (1975).

See also POWHATAN; VIRGINIA

Smuggling

Smuggling, succinctly defined as illegal clandestine trading, made its appearance in America at the very beginning of English involvement in the New World. Spanish colonial officials, for example, certainly viewed Sir John Hawkins's slaving and trading expeditions with Santo Domingo in the late sixteenth century as smuggling operations. Throughout the colonial period, smuggling was a fact of business life as Britain, Spain, France, and Holland vied for commercial supremacy in Atlantic shipping lanes. Illegal trading also served as an irritant between London and the colonies and played a prominent part in the disintegration of imperial relations after 1763.

Illicit commerce resulted from the exclusive trading arrangements that were part of the political economy of mercantilism. Orthodox economic thought maintained that wealth was fixed, and for one nation to get richer, another had to become poorer. New World colonies altered the equation and brought added wealth to Europe. As a result, colonial powers staked out possessions in the Americas to supply specie or raw materials to the mother country and to act as markets for European goods. To ensure this newfound wealth did not augment a rival's treasury, exclusive imperial trading arrangements were formulated. With few exceptions, subjects of one New World empire could not legally trade with those of another. Yet profits could frequently be made by smuggling the goods of rival colonies.

During the first half of the eighteenth century, much illegal commerce concerned the molasses trade. Vessels from Boston, Newport, New York, Philadelphia, and other northern colonial ports carried foodstuffs, lumber products, and livestock to Saint-Domingue, Martinique, Guadeloupe, and other French islands in exchange for molasses. Since French cognac interests barred molasses, the principal ingredient of rum, from markets in France, American merchants could obtain molasses more cheaply in the French islands than in the British West Indies.

French plantation owners benefited from lower prices and more certain supplies of provisions from British North America than similar commodities shipped from France or Canada. British North Americans gained expanded markets for their produce and lucrative routes for shipping, managerial, and financial services.

Spanish colonial markets were also attractive to British businessmen. In addition to the provisions trade, merchants in Britain wanted to expand their sales of manufactured goods in the Spanish empire. During the 1730s, powerful interests in England, led by the South Seas Company, advocated the expansion of illegal trade with the Spanish colonies. British imperial officials normally winked at illegal trade during peacetime; after all, smuggling expanded Britain's overseas trade. Spanish officials adopted a different view, however. The attempts by *guarda costas*, Spanish coast guard vessels, to stamp out smuggling operations by searching British vessels at sea and seizing illegal traders provoked violent confrontations, and eventually caused the Anglo-Spanish War (1739–1744).

The lax attitude of British colonial officials toward smuggling with the Spanish and French changed abruptly during hostilities. Many imperial policy makers viewed such illicit commerce as a form of treason. During the wars of 1739–1748 (France entered the War of Jenkins' Ear in 1744 as Spain's ally; this conflict is frequently called King George's War), London officials received numerous complaints of Americans trading with the enemy. During the subsequent French and Indian War (1754–1763), these complaints became a constant refrain. Smuggling became a serious problem that jeopardized British strategy for winning the war in the Caribbean. With the Royal Navy's superiority in West Indian shipping lanes, British strategists planned to blockade and starve enemy islands into submission. The clandestine arrival of American foodstuffs undermined this strategy.

American merchants devised several methods to trade with the enemy during imperial conflicts. Illicit traders embarked for neutral Caribbean islands to exchange their goods. The proximity of the West Indies facilitated this traffic. British colonial merchants also used documents (called flags of truce) issued by imperial officials to engage in illegal trade. Flags of truce enabled American vessels to sail legally to enemy ports to exchange prisoners of war. Issuing flags of truce soon degenerated into a wholesale smuggling business. Colonial governors, led by Pennsylvania's William Denny, sold countless passes to American merchants who loaded their vessels to the gunwales with North American produce for sale to the enemy islands. A single French prisoner was thought to be sufficient to legalize such commerce. Private men-of-war facilitated the flag of truce trade. After London authorized British warships to end the abuse of these passes by seizing illegal flag of truce ships, privateers pretended to seize illegal traders and escorted them home to North American ports. Many privateers also carried flags of truce in the waning years of the conflict, as French prizes became increasingly scarce because of successful British cruising operations.

The Royal Navy began seizing colonial smugglers during the closing years of the French and Indian War. This policy of interdicting illegal traders was continued after the war ended in 1763. Imperial administrators who had witnessed the navy's effectiveness in stifling trade with the enemy now viewed the Royal Navy as an effective instrument to enforce the Navigation Acts. In addition, the navy could also be useful in enforcing new measures, such as the Sugar Act of 1764, that were designed to raise a revenue in America to help defray the costs of the French and Indian War. Using the navy to end illegal trade was extremely unpopular in America, and Royal Navy seizures prompted violent protests in North American ports. Thus smuggling, which had been pervasive throughout the colonial period during peace and war, also played an important role in the coming of the American Revolution.

Carl E. Swanson

References

Thomas C. Barrow, *Trade and Empire: The British Customs Service in Colonial America, 1660–1775* (1967); Richard Pares, *War and Trade in the West Indies* (1936); Neil R. Stout, *The Royal Navy in America, 1760–1775: A Study in the Enforcement of British Colonial Policy in the Era of the American Revolution* (1973).

See also PRIVATEERING

Snowshoes, Battle on (1758)

Following General Louis-Joseph de Montcalm's reduction of Fort William Henry and the sub-

sequent massacre at that place (8 August 1757), a relative calm descended upon the Lake George theater of operations; except for occasional probes, this calm would remain largely intact until the disastrous Lord Howe/James Abercromby assault on Ticonderoga the following summer.

Lord Loudon's 1757 expedition to Louisbourg had practically died aborning. Key elements from the New York frontier, including Robert Rogers' Rangers, had been stripped from their upper Hudson posts to join the Louisbourg fiasco. It is likely that the absence of the rangers contributed to the debacle at Fort William Henry. Rogers returned to Albany and thence to Fort Edward, which had been spared by Montcalm. Loudon had been replaced by Lord Howe, who would not advance to the limits of the British frontier until winter was over; in the meanwhile, command at Fort Edward was under Lieutenant Colonel William Haviland, with whom Rogers found himself temperamentally unsuited to cooperate.

Late in that winter of 1757–1758, Haviland planned separate scouts toward Ticonderoga by two large parties. He then committed several errors as the operations developed:

1. He failed to maintain tight security over planning;
2. He sent the groups out sequentially, so that any enemy forces roused by the first would stand a good chance of colliding with the second; and
3. He reduced the second group's manpower by more than half, even after the likelihood dramatically increased that his plans had been discovered.

The first party that went out was led by Israel Putnam of Connecticut, later to be one of the heroes at Bunker Hill (1775). He lost at least one of his men either through capture or desertion, and it is speculated that this individual informed the French that Rogers would soon be under way with the second group. Rogers was to have been assigned 400 men, but left Fort Edward with only 180. Though at loggerheads with his superior, he had no choice but to obey Haviland's orders. In Rogers's own words:

> I acknowledge that I entered upon this service . . . with no small uneasiness of mind. . . . [Colonel Haviland] probably

had his reasons [for sending us out under such circumstances]; and can doubtless justify his conduct; but that is no consolation to the friends of those brave men, who were thus thrown in the way of an enemy, of three times their number.

He set out northward on 10 March 1758, with four companies of rangers, their commissioned officers, and three British regular officers (who—it was hoped—would learn the methods of woodland warfare to impart to their own light infantry unit tactics). The route crossed Lake George, frozen at that time of year. Some of the advanced parties traveled on skates, but while progress was rapid, concealment on the lake ice was poor. Therefore, the decision was made to get into the rear of Ticonderoga through the snows of the intervening rugged hills, on snowshoes. (Snowshoes were, after all, not an advanced logistical adjunct, but rather an accepted mode of travel at that latitude; indeed, the 1704 raid by the French on Deerfield, Massachusetts, had been conducted by a force that wore such implements.)

During the afternoon of 13 March, Rogers and his men were descending the frozen bed of Trout Brook, which flows northeastward as a tributary to the Lake George outflow. They found themselves in a short valley between a range of high hills to their right and left; had they proceeded a little more than a mile further, they would have gotten to the point where the valley and the brook spill outward onto the Champlain basin. There could not have been much daylight left on that late winter day when Rogers's scouts discovered a party of about 40 French and Indians unsuspectedly coming up Trout Brook in their direction. With his advanced section under Captain Charles Bulkeley now positioned as his right wing, Rogers deployed his men along the rising ground that bordered the stream. They would take the enemy in the flank, in ambuscade.

The devastation from almost 200 marksmen firing point-blank on the thin French and Indian line was sudden, horrific, and near-complete. The few survivors fled downstream with Bulkeley's group in hot pursuit. Yet how quickly did this seeming rout turn to disaster for the attackers! Those that the rangers had ambushed were only a scout for the follow-on force of some 250 under Captain Louis-Philippe Le Dessu d'Hébécourt, from Fort Carillon at Ticon-

deroga. Bulkeley and those with him were cut down; the remaining rangers, once flush with victory, now must have recoiled in horror as they found themselves pressed against the hills in their right rear. Firing was then general as the sun set to their left and the woods darkened. The mortal combat that ensued had as its background a gloomy, smoke-filled dusk, replete with variously-pitched cries and screams.

Extreme pressure was placed on Rogers's flanks, forcing them up the lower slopes of the 400-meter eminence across whose foot the Trout Brook ran. On the reverse slope of this high hill lay Lake George and the escape route to safety; amid the fury below its summit, it became apparent to the rangers who were still alive that the trap had closed: some 20 men on the right gathered about Lieutenant William Phillips, who bargained with the enemy for terms. Less than a dozen others, including Rogers, broke off and scattered. Phillips managed finally to escape, but those that surrendered with him were butchered.

While the battle still raged, Rogers had thrown off his outer jacket. In one of the jacket pockets was left his original commission as ranger commander, signed by Governor William Shirley of Massachusetts in 1755. This prize, once back at Ticonderoga, momentarily gave the overjoyed French the notion that their bushranging nemesis had been terminated. Rogers, still very much alive, had shaken his pursuers and reached the lake. Traditionally, he slid down either the precipice now called Rogers' Slide, some two miles south of the battlefield, or the slightly closer and less steep Rogers' Rock. However he got to the lake, he was eventually joined by the remnants of his force; this amounted to just over 50 men.

If he had lost some 70 percent of his command, Rogers could point to the fact the operation had been conducted under another's imprimatur and that he had expressed his caveat beforehand. Moreover, he had brought some survivors out of the wilderness. It had been a short, sharp fight which accomplished only what it put into the historical record. Rogers's reputation was in no way compromised, and the coming summer would see him chosen by Lord Howe to lead in the Ticonderoga campaign of 1758.

Roy Marokus

See also LAKE GEORGE; LIGHT INFANTRY; RANGERS; ROGERS, ROBERT; SCOUT

Sokoki

The Sokokis or Sokwakis were a western Abenaki group who inhabited the middle and upper Connecticut Valley from Northfield, Massachusetts, to Bellows Falls, Vermont. The French sometimes called them Loups, and for a long time, English writers assumed they occupied the Saco River in Maine, until anthropologist Gordon Day identified their proper location. They extended their hunting territories as far north as the St. Lawrence River and were among the first Abenaki refugees to migrate to the French mission village at St. Francis.

Like most other Abenaki tribes, the Sokokis came under the influence of French missionaries, traded at French posts, and allied themselves to the French during the colonial wars. They probably also received English goods after John Pynchon opened his trading post at Agawam (Springfield, Massachusetts) in 1636. They appear in French records in the 1640s, fighting the Mohawks and the Algonquins and Montagnais, and they were at the forefront of an abortive alliance of New England tribes that the French hoped to form against the Iroquois in 1650–1651. The Sokokis enjoyed a reputation as formidable warriors in the seventeenth century, but their location in the Connecticut Valley rendered them vulnerable to assault and proved untenable as warfare escalated.

A Sokoki village at Fort Hill on the banks of the Connecticut River near Hinsdale, New Hampshire, dispersed following an Iroquois attack in 1663, and many Sokokis took refuge among neighboring tribes. Sokokis remained in their homelands through King Philip's War. Indian forces camped in Sokoki territory in the spring of 1676, and Sokokis were almost certainly among the victims of an English attack on an Indian village at Turner's Falls that year.

In subsequent years, increasing pressure from English settlers prompted more and more Sokokis to sell their lands and migrate northward, where they amalgamated with other Abenaki communities in Vermont, New Hampshire, and Quebec, and lent their aid to the Franco-Abenaki war effort. The Abenaki village at Cowass higher up the Connecticut River probably absorbed many of the migrants, and Sokokis added a substantial element to the surviving Abenaki communities at Missisquoi on Lake Champlain and St. Francis in Quebec.

Colin G. Calloway

References

Colin G. Calloway, *The Western Abenakis of Vermont, 1600–1800: War, Migration, and the Survival of an Indian People* (1990); Gordon M. Day, "The Identity of the Sokokis," *Ethnohistory* 12 (1965):237–247; William A. Haviland and Marjory W. Power, *The Original Vermonters: Native Inhabitants Past and Present* (1981); Peter A. Thomas, "In the Maelstrom of Change: The Indian Trade and Cultural Process in the Middle Connecticut River Valley, 1635–1665," Ph.D. Dissertation, University of Massachusetts (1979).

See also ABENAKI; KING PHILIPS' WAR; ST. FRANCIS, BATTLE OF

Soto, Hernando de (1497–1542)

Probably the best-known Spanish conqueror in North America, Soto was the first to explore the Southeast extensively. A dashing cavalier and a marginal noble from the Extremadura region, he signed with the Spanish crown a contract to colonize La Florida that extended from the Atlantic coast to Mexico. Soto was a veteran in the Indies. After having been active in Panama and Nicaragua in 1532, he accompanied Francisco Pizarro in vanquishing the Inca emperor. There, in Peru, Soto collected an impressive booty that supported his ambitions for greater political and social power away from Pizarro. In 1535, he left Peru for Valladolid, where the Spanish court was being held. In that city he received from the monarch his title of *adelantado de la Florida* and governor of Cuba, and married his beloved and able Doña Isabel de Bobadilla.

Using Cuba as a base, Soto readied great loads of food and supplies, about 240 horses, more than 600 persons, including women and black slaves, and nine ships to carry them. On this island he replaced many of his original Iberian recruits. By the end of May 1539, he had landed in Tampa Bay and was marching to the town of chief Ocita, where he camped. On 15 July, Soto marched inland toward Ocale in search of precious metals. He found instead plenty of corn, a staple that was to support his explorers the rest of the way, and he heard news of rich Apalachee. He marched to that well-provided province, setting up his winter encampment in today's Tallahassee. He ordered brought up to a nearby port the two ships and the 100 men left behind at Tampa Bay. On finding the safe port of Ochuse (Pensacola), Soto sent the two ships back to Havana to bring up supplies. News of a rich land ruled by a woman guided him to the Indian town of Cofitachequi, located near present-day Augusta, Georgia. There he found quantities of river pearls, a ruling woman indeed, but no treasures. Continuing on his quest for the illusory gold, he followed a course that went across South Carolina, the corners of North Carolina and Tennessee, and headed south to Mabila in south central Alabama. In this palisaded town the Indians attacked Soto and killed 72 of his soldiers at the cost of the loss of many of their own native people. Disappointed by not having any tangible proof of success, Soto headed northwest instead of going south to meet his waiting ships. In December he reached Chicaza in northeast Tennessee, where he set up his winter encampment. The natives attacked again, killing 12 Spaniards.

In March 1541, Soto moved to the west, crossed the Mississippi, wandered around and reached Utiangue in south-central Arkansas, where he established his third and last winter camp. In the next spring Soto died by the great river that he had reached again after traveling southeast. Luis de Moscoso took the lead and tried to reach Mexico by land. A fruitless trek through eastern Texas convinced the Spaniards to return to the Mississippi River and to camp at Aminoya, located not far from where Soto had died. There, Moscoso had five vessels built to escape to Mexico. On July 1543, they started down the river toward its delta. Two months later and more than four years after they had left Cuba for Florida, 311 survivors reached Panuco in Mexico. Soto's expedition did not accomplish its goals. However, his men left invaluable information on the Southeast and its native inhabitants. By dint of his failure, he altered the Spanish perception of the American land.

Jose Ignacio Avallaneda

References
John R. Swanton, *Final Report of the United States De Soto Expedition Commission* (1985); James Lockhart, *The Men of Cajamarca; A Social and Biographical Study of the First Conquerors of Peru* (1972).

See also FLORIDA

South Carolina

Throughout much of its early history, South Carolina was one of the southernmost of the British North American colonies. Strategic considerations and military vulnerability, therefore, profoundly affected its development as competing powers struggled to control adjacent areas. For, as Francis I, king of France during the early sixteenth century, is supposed to have remarked on being told that Portugal and Spain had claimed all newly discovered lands, he had not seen the clause of Adam's will which disinherited him. Nor had the Englishmen. The ensuing scramble for space in the New World in which to project or maintain political power and cultural traditions involved Native Americans as well as Europeans; and the results reconfigured the globe. The military history of South Carolina to 1763 is therefore a small but significant part of a much larger whole.

The land that came to be known as South Carolina was the home of numerous Native American groups in the fifteenth century. Constituting perhaps 40 or 50 tribes, the total population was at least 20,000. Not a great deal is known about conflicts among the Indians before white men arrived. Presumably warfare was intermittent. Evidence from a later date and other areas suggests that small war parties periodically sallied forth in search of captives or trophies at the expense of other tribes. Prestige usually seems to have been the most important object, not the extermination of the enemy nor the acquisition of his lands. In 1540, however, Spanish explorer Hernando De Soto encountered a chiefdom, Cofitachequi, in central South Carolina that may have subjugated or allied itself with neighboring tribes. What is more certain, is that even this early, Soto's men encountered villages that had been depopulated by European diseases. Indians continued to succumb at an appalling rate to microbes to which they had not developed immunities, and by the 1760s, as one royal official observed, in a province that had once been "swarming with tribes of Indians, there remain now, except the few Catawbas, nothing of them but their names, within three hundred miles of our sea coast. . . ." Nevertheless, several more remote groups continued to be militarily significant. Chief among them were the Cherokee of the southern Appalachian Mountains and the Creek of southern Georgia and Alabama. Together they numbered nearly 50,000 in 1685. During most of the colonial period, the Cherokees tended to be friendly toward the English. The Creek, who were frequently at odds with the Cherokee, usually favored neutrality, which enabled them to play off competing European powers against each other.

The European invasion of the area began with Spain, though France was not far behind. Fanning out from bases in the Caribbean, Spanish conquistadors overran much of Latin America during the first half of the sixteenth century. As part of this process, Lucas Vázquez de Ayllón planted a short-lived colony somewhere on the coast of South Carolina or Georgia, perhaps Winyaw Bay. Disease, slave revolts, and Indian attacks soon led to Ayllón's death and the collapse of this venture.

Several abortive Spanish attempts to reconnoiter and settle the Port Royal area of South Carolina followed, but it was a French Huguenot, Jean Ribault, who made the first settlement there in 1562. Leaving a few men to hold a small fort, he returned to France. Religious turmoil at home delayed him, and his men abandoned the post. René de Laudonnière, Ribault's subordinate, then established Fort Caroline on the St. Johns River in Florida. Ribault arrived to reinforce this outpost just in time to encounter Pedro Menéndez de Avilés, an able and energetic Spanish seaman who was under orders to oust the French and establish a Spanish colony in Florida. Defeating the Frenchmen, Menéndez executed the Protestant prisoners, including Ribault, and founded the town of St. Augustine.

Spanish forts and missions soon spread throughout the area, and, for a time, the settlement at Port Royal, which was growing more rapidly than St. Augustine, served as a base for further Spanish exploration of the interior of South Carolina. But Indian attacks on Port Royal and English depredations at St. Augustine eventually forced the Spanish to pull back. Southeastern North America seemed to offer neither gold nor silver, and Spanish Florida never fulfilled its founder's expectations. It remained a sparsely populated military outpost. Although at least one mission existed in South Carolina as late as the 1680s, most Spanish authorities regarded their tenuous hold on Florida as useful primarily for keeping French and English interlopers out and thereby safeguarding the Bahama Channel, through which treasure ships from Latin America rode the Gulf Stream northward before crossing the Atlantic.

For nearly 200 years, Spain refused to recognize any but its own claims to southeastern North America, but the English were ready to challenge these pretensions from at least the 1580s on. Partly in an attempt to keep Spaniards from "flowinge all over the face of . . .

America," as one Englishman put it, Sir Walter Raleigh established the abortive venture at Roanoke Island off the coast of North Carolina; and similar strategic considerations figured in the even less successful effort by the attorney general of England, Sir Robert Heath, to settled "Carolina" with Huguenots under a grant from Charles I in 1629. Little concrete except the name Carolina seems to have resulted from these plans. In 1663, however, Charles II regranted the area to eight Lords Proprietors, some of whom had facilitated his restoration to the English throne three years earlier. In 1665, the king enlarged the boundaries of this grant and included the entire area from Albemarle Sound southward to beyond St. Augustine, from sea to sea. This huge grant, which gave the proprietors a claim on the upper Gulf coast, may have been designed to put diplomatic pressure on Spain. If so, the ploy worked, for in 1670, Spanish authorities agreed to the Treaty of Madrid, which supposedly recognized the right of Englishmen to settle as far south as the site of modern Charleston.

Despite such negotiations, settling South Carolina proved to be a dangerous enterprise. The first expedition sailed (in August 1669), headed for Port Royal, but one of the vessels overshot the mark and some of its party fell into Spanish hands on the coast of Georgia. Not surprisingly, the settlers concluded that they were in the "very chaps of the Spaniards," and when a local Indian chief, the Cacique of Kiawah, suggested that the settlement be made in his area, the leaders agreed. They moved to a site on the Ashley River, where they established themselves in a palisaded village. Spanish authorities sent an expedition to dislodge them, but the tricky entrance to the harbor and a storm thwarted these efforts. The English outpost survived. Ten years later, the Carolinians moved to a more convenient location at the confluence of the Ashley and Cooper Rivers, where they laid out and fortified Charles Town. Meanwhile, the Spanish in St. Augustine began rebuilding Fort San Marcos with stone instead of timber.

Spanish attempts to convert the Indians to Christianity involved resettling them in mission compounds and therefore, frequently, some coercion. The Carolina proprietors planned to adopt a more liberal policy. Their fundamental constitutions, which were to be "the compass . . . to steer by," called for wide religious toleration, even of indigenous belief systems, provided the

Native Americans acknowledged the existence of a god. The proprietors also sponsored a visit to London by two Indians whom they renamed "Honest" and "Just." And when it appeared that local traders were abusing Native Americans, the proprietors sought to remedy the situation by giving themselves a monopoly of the trade with the Westo Indians. Local traders wrecked these plans by waging war on the tribe in the 1680s and virtually exterminating it. Many of the Westos who survived became slaves.

Their interest in slaves soon further complicated matters for Carolinians. In the hope of attracting substantial settlers from other colonies, especially Barbados, the Carolina proprietors legalized slavery from the outset, and some early immigrants brought a few slaves with them. But the lack of staple crops made their ownership less profitable. Until the end of the century, South Carolinians therefore appear to have sought slaves chiefly as commodities, and they developed a thriving business exporting Indian slaves to the West Indies and elsewhere. But during the 1690s and early 1700s, the simultaneous development of two staples—rice and naval stores—greatly increased the demand for labor. South Carolinians began importing Africans in record numbers, and by about 1708, a majority of the population was enslaved. Throughout the remainder of the colonial period, slaves continued to outnumber whites, sometimes by more than seven to one in the low-country plantation districts. Members of "a fierce, hardy and strong" race whose enslavement, as contemporaries recognized, could be expected to instill "a secret rancor," slaves constituted a major security problem in peace as well as in war, when they might act as a potential fifth column to assist an enemy. These considerations were not lost on the Spanish in Florida, who had few slaves of their own.

Except for an attack on South Carolina that destroyed a Scottish settlement at Port Royal in 1686, the Spanish did not move against South Carolina in force during the last two decades of the seventeenth century. Indeed, Spain and England were even allied against France during King William's War (The War of the League of Augsburg in Europe, 1689–1697). But the respite on the southern frontier ended in 1699, when the French established a post at Biloxi; Mobile and New Orleans followed by 1718. Meanwhile, the king of Spain died, and Louis XIV of France sought to install his grandson on the Spanish throne. To block this potentially threatening enlargement of French power, England went to war at the head of "a Grand Alliance" of European powers. In 1702, South Carolinians, under Governor James Moore, attacked and burned St. Augustine, but failed to capture the fort; the following year, Moore—by then no longer governor—financed and led another expedition, composed largely of Indians, which laid waste the Spanish missions in northwestern Florida, paying themselves in plunder. The Spanish and French attempted to retaliate in 1706 with a joint expedition against Charles Town, which proved to be a fiasco. Despite a Carolina-backed Indian attack on Pensacola in 1707, the major contenders were unable to do much more on the southern frontier during the remainder of Queen Anne's War (The War of the Spanish Succession in Europe, 1702–1713).

Native Americans, however, mounted their most serious threat to the Carolinians. In North Carolina, which became a separate colony with the appointment of its own governor in 1710, the Tuscarora Indians attacked white settlements at New Bern. Two relief expeditions from South Carolina were necessary to defeat the Indians, who soon moved north to join the Iroquois Confederacy. In South Carolina, the Yamasee, who had been victimized by unscrupulous traders and land-hungry settlers, struck at Port Royal in 1715. Within weeks, almost all the southern Indians except the Cherokee had joined in the attack, and the defensive perimeter around Charles Town shrank to barely 30 miles in diameter. But the initial neutrality, and later assistance, of the Cherokee contributed to a white victory. Approximately 400 South Carolinians died in the war, which set back settlement of the southern parishes for nearly a generation. The Yamasees withdrew to Spanish Florida, from which they continued sporadic raids against South Carolina for more than a decade.

Queen Anne's War in general, and the Indian wars in particular, made South Carolinians painfully aware of their military problems. Adding insult to injury, pirates captured ships just outside the harbor at Charles Town and terrorized the town. Although local authorities were able to wage a successful campaign against the buccaneers, the proprietors were clearly unable to contribute much to the defense of the colony. Indeed, they sought to lease its southern portions for a buffer colony, the Margraviate of Azilia, but the deal fell through. Thus in 1719, when word arrived that a Spanish fleet was preparing to attack Charles Town, local leaders staged a bloodless revolt against the proprietary government and requested that the crown assume control of the province. Royal officials responded by appointing an interim governor and buying out the proprietors' rights. Locked in a second hundred years' war with France, British authorities considered South Carolina too strategically important to be left adrift and relatively defenseless.

South Carolinians were expanding on several fronts during the early eighteenth century. Rice production increased more than tenfold from 1700 to 1740, when a record crop of 43,000,000 pounds was exported. Rice became the third most valuable commodity exported from the North American colonies, while South Carolinians were well on their way to becoming, on a per capita basis, the richest of all mainland Americans. Their geographic aspirations were equally ambitious. Indian traders had penetrated as far as the Mississippi River in the late seventeenth century. In fact one of them, Thomas Nairne, had mapped the entire southeastern area of North America in pursuit of an imperial vision that involved the expulsion of the French and Spanish. Nairne died in the Yamasee War, but ideas closely related to his persisted. In particular, during the 1720s and 1730s, South Carolinians adopted a number of approaches designed to improve their security and strengthen their position vis-á-vis European rivals. To conciliate Native Americans, the government once again sought to monopolize the Indian trade, but protests from private traders forced a retreat. After 1731, the trade was privately conducted under regulations supervised by a public commissioner. More important, assiduous lobbying by Carolinians contributed to several decisions made in London: to send an independent company of troops to South Carolina with the first royal governor in 1721, to build a fort on the Altamaha River in what is now southern Georgia, and to instruct the governor of South Carolina to establish a number of defensive settlements on the frontiers. These settlements were to take the form of compact townships settled, with public assistance, by white immigrants who would be predominantly small farmers, and therefore good material for the local militia. Nine of the projected 11 townships eventually materialized; a tenth became the southernmost British colony when these plans fused with the philanthropic ideas of the Georgia trustees. Viewing Georgia

as a military buffer between themselves and Spanish Florida, South Carolinians gladly assisted with its settlement.

Unfortunately, the next attempt at cooperation between South Carolinians and Georgians led to more recriminations. During the 1720s and 1730s, the British and Spanish governments strengthened their respective positions in the New World, but both hoped to prolong the peace. Thus Spain only protested British activities in Georgia. In Central and South America, however, British traders sought to smuggle slaves and goods in excess of the quotas established by the Treaty of Utrecht in 1713, and Spanish officials tried to curb them. The resulting friction precipitated a war in 1739. This conflict, known as the War of Jenkins' Ear, widened into King George's War, a general European struggle that lasted until 1748. During it, French and Spanish naval forces disrupted the rice trade and thereby caused considerable economic hardship in South Carolina. More important in the long run, Spanish authorities in Florida promised freedom to slaves who escaped from South Carolina. As many as 100 tried in the Stono Rebellion of 1739. Though eventually suppressed, it proved to be the most serious slave revolt in the North American colonies. Alarmed South Carolinians quickly adopted a more comprehensive code of laws governing slave behavior and sent troops on an expedition against Florida under the command of General James Oglethorpe. After its ignominious failure, Carolinians blamed him, and he them. Thus when Spanish forces moved against Georgia by land and sea in 1742, South Carolinians offered little help. Oglethorpe's men, however, turned the Spanish back at the Battle of Bloody Marsh. Thereafter, Spain, which was well past the peak of its power by this time, did little more in the area except retain Florida.

France was the major enemy. The Great War for the Empire (The Seven Years' War in Europe) began in 1754; shortly thereafter, the governor of South Carolina proposed an attack on Fort Toulouse, the French bastion near modern-day Montgomery, Alabama. Informed that Canada was to be the main theater of action, he mounted a less ambitious demonstration against the Cherokee Indians, with whom some misunderstandings had developed. It failed, and before the Cherokee were ready to agree to peace terms, South Carolinians had to request and received help from two contingents of British regular troops. Cooperation between the provincials and the regulars turned out to difficult, and their respective commanders fought a bloodless duel after operations were completed. South Carolinians were certain, as the local assembly declared, that no one "could have exerted themselves more vigorously" during the war. What the British commander thought of their efforts revealed itself most clearly when he assured Parliament in 1775 that he would "undertake to march from one end of America to the other with 5,000 men."

It would be a mistake, of course, to overestimate the strength of the connection between these local misunderstandings and the coming of the Revolution, but one can scarcely exaggerate the significance of military matters in the history of colonial South Carolina. The inconclusive nature of so many of the struggles on the southern frontier—like "giants wrestling with their fingertips," as some historians have described the contest—gives a misleading impression of its importance; its very inconclusiveness prompted Carolinians to be ever-mindful of military considerations. Whether this made them militaristic in a conventional sense is more difficult to assess. The notion that English authorities intended to establish a military empire with "garrison governments" in the late seventeenth century cannot really be tested in South Carolina; by the time the first royal governor (an old soldier, to be sure) was appointed, that policy, if it ever existed, was being abandoned. Furthermore, as a group, colonial South Carolinians made a poor showing militarily, no matter how brave individuals may have been. By law, most adult males were required to serve in the militia, but the white population of the low country was never large enough to make it a very effective force. Moreover, as African American numbers increased, slave patrol duties usurped many of the other functions of the militia. Thus, during the Cherokee War, South Carolina was forced to recruit troops in North Carolina.

Interestingly enough, however, the vulnerability of the colony helped not only to augment the power of the local assembly but also to promote a unique political style. Under the proprietors, the lower house of the legislature began a quest for power that would make it, by the mid-eighteenth century, the dominant voice in the colonial government. To finance Governor Moore's expedition against St. Augustine, for example, the assembly issued paper money and thereby established a precedent. Taking advantage of similar military exigencies, the Commons House encroached upon the governor's right as commander in chief of the armed forces to oversee the construction of fortifications, and so forth. Fear of attack, if not military necessity, triggered the successful revolt against proprietary control; and fear of internal slave rebellion—which might be instigated by ever-present foreign enemies—contributed to a garrison-state mentality. Unity among the defenders was essential, divided command dangerous, and a momentary lapse an invitation to disaster. Serious factional discord could prove to be a fatal luxury. This consideration, coupled with a number of contributing factors, prompted South Carolinians to develop an unusually harmonious political system by the mid-eighteenth century. The impact of that system on later developments is beyond the scope of this essay; but if, as one official body observed, South Carolina was militarily a "weaker part" among the colonies, its feebleness had ironically powerful and long-lasting effects.

Robert M. Weir

References

Verner Winslow Crane, *The Southern Frontier, 1670–1732* (1929), rpt. 1981; Larry E. Ivers, *British Drums on the Southern Frontier: The Military Colonization of Georgia, 1733–1749* (1974); Marion Eugene Sirmans, *Colonial South Carolina: A Political History, 1663–1763* (1966); Robert M. Weir, *Colonial South Carolina: A History* (1983); J. Leitch Wright, *Anglo-Spanish Rivalry in North America* (1971).

See also ADAIR, JAMES; ANGLO-SPANISH WAR (1739–1744); ATKIN, EDMUND; AYLLÓN, LUCAS VÁZQUEZ DE; BARNWELL TOWNSHIP SYSTEM; CATAWBA; CHARLES TOWN, ATTACK ON; CHEROKEE; CHEROKEE WAR; CREEK; FRONTIER, SOUTHERN; GLEN, JAMES; LYTTLETON, WILLIAM HENRY; MENÉNDEZ DE AVILÉS, PEDRO; NAIRNE, THOMAS; OGLETHORPE, JAMES EDWARD; PORT ROYAL (SOUTH CAROLINA); RIBAULT, JEAN; ST. AUGUSTINE; SANTA ELENA; SOTO, HERNANDO DE; SPANISH MISSION SYSTEM–SOUTHEAST; STONO REBELLION; TUSCARORA WAR; WACCAMAW; WESTO; WOODWARD, HENRY; YAMASEE WAR

Spain

See ARMY, SPAIN; CALIFORNIA; FLORIDA; NAVY, SPAIN (1492–1699); NAVY, SPAIN (1700–1763); NEW MEXICO; ST. AUGUSTINE; SAN ANTONIO; SPANISH MISSION SYSTEM; TEXAS

Spain-France Relations
See FRANCE-SPAIN RELATIONS

Spain–Great Britain Relations
See GREAT BRITAIN–SPAIN RELATIONS

Spanish Mission System–Southeast

For 50 years after Juan Ponce de Leon made a chance landing on the southeastern shores of North America, Spain exhibited only cursory interest in Florida. The coast was inhabited by hostile Indians who successfully repulsed explorations by Spanish missionaries, and the land was virtually useless except as a navigational point on the *carrera de las Indies*.

Spain's indifference ended abruptly in 1564, when French Huguenots erected Fort Caroline at the mouth of the St. Johns River. The French intrusion threatened Spanish shipping lanes, and within a year, Spain routed the fort's inhabitants and began a serious effort to colonize Florida. San Augustin became the first presidio in the region, and soon garrisons and missions were scattered along the coast from Tampa Bay to the Carolinas.

The Spanish never had adequate funds to build forts or towns in the Southeast, so they created a mission system, reinforced by garrisons, to ensure friendly relations with the Indians. Without sufficient soldiers or settlers, the Spanish became dependent upon Indian allies to protect them, and Spanish missionaries used whatever means they could to influence the local tribes.

The missions also served a crucial role in the economic system established by the Spanish. Because there were so few settlers, the *adelantado* at San Augustin instituted an obligatory tribute system among the Indians. Skins, maize, pottery, and other goods were demanded, and by the end of the sixteenth century, labor tribute was required as well. The missions acted as distribution points in the network of trade and tribute that branched out from the presidio.

Dominican and Franciscan friars had made several ill-fated attempts to convert the coastal tribes, but little was accomplished prior to 1565. Nombre de Dios, the first Catholic vicariate in North America, was founded at St. Augustine in that year, and it served as the flagship of the Spanish mission system because of its proximity to the *presidio*. However, missions were not built among the Indians until the Jesuits arrived in 1567.

The Jesuits built their first missions at Tequesta on the tip of the peninsula, and at San Antonio among the Calusa on the Gulf coast. Then they entered Guale and Orista. None of these early missions was very successful in converting the Indians, and in 1570, the Guales and Oristas rebelled and forced the withdrawal of the remaining Jesuits. In 1570, there was not a single cleric in Spanish Florida.

The next decade witnessed widespread unrest among the Indians. Local officials tried in vain to attract religious orders to Florida. Finally, in 1578, the Franciscans sent friars to rebuild the missions. These new missions soon began to resemble fortifications, complete with firing apertures along the tops of the walls. The mission Indians were never armed by the Spanish.

From 1578 to 1583, the Franciscans built two separate chains of missions. One led from St. Augustine north along the Atlantic coast, and the other stretched westward across the peninsula. The Guale and Orista tribes were temporarily subdued and the missions in good repair. Despite the destruction of the St. Augustine presidio in 1586 by the English, the Franciscans continued their work among the Indians.

Through gifts, entreaties, and patience, the friars succeeded for a time where the *conquistadores* had failed—they converted hundreds of Guale, Timucuan, and Apalachee Indians. They preached the virtues of monogamy, wearing clothes, working hard, and living peacefully. Like their Jesuit predecessors, the Franciscans instructed the Indians in their native languages. Unfortunately, the missionaries' dreams of converting semi-nomadic hunters into sedentary farmers were short-lived.

The friars had a habit of interfering in tribal politics, and in 1597, the Franciscans at Guale intervened once too often. The mission Indians rebelled. The missions along coastal Georgia were destroyed and most of the friars murdered before soldiers stopped the uprising. Retaliatory raids against the coastal Indians finally reduced them to total submission in 1601.

When the Franciscans returned in 1602, they found the formerly warlike tribes cowed. At this point, the Spanish clergy introduced the "reduction system" to Florida and the coastal missions. Indian converts who had previously been allowed to remain in their own territory

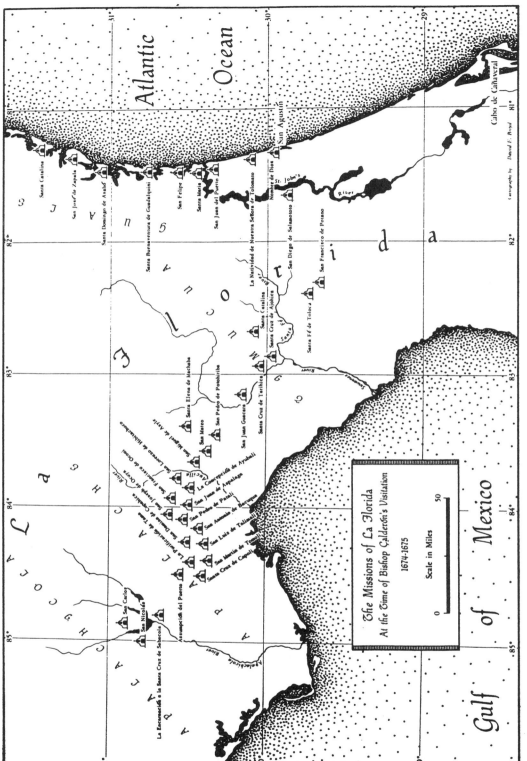

Map reproduced from Michael V. Gannon, The Cross in the Sand: The Early Catholic Church in Florida, 1513–1870 (Gainesville: University of Florida Press, 1965). Reprinted by permission of author and University of Florida Press.

were now forced to live in villages near the Spanish settlements to be trained in the ways of European civilization.

The missions once again became an integral part of Spain's plan to secure Florida. The mission villages not only kept the Indians docile, they provided a bulwark against the frequent encroachments of rival European powers. But the Spanish reduction system had deadly consequences for the southeastern Indians—the crowded living conditions in mission villages accelerated the spread of Old World diseases. Epidemics in the late sixteenth century had been devastating to many of the interior tribes in northern Florida, but it was not until the establishment of the mission villages that the coastal Indians began to die off.

By the end of the seventeenth century, disease and English slave raids had destroyed the Spanish mission system from north Florida to the Carolina coast. All that Spain retained was the peninsula, and by 1710, Carolinians had systematically laid waste to the Florida missions down to St. Augustine. Although the Yamasee and Lower Creek sought Spanish protection in the following years, and Spanish Indians continued to harass English settlers along the southern frontier, Spain's plans for hegemony in the Southeast disappeared along with its missions.

Doris B. Fisher

References

Antonio de Arrendondo, *Arredondo's Historical Proof of Spain's Title to Georgia*, ed., Herbert E. Bolton (1925); Andres Gonzalez de Barcia Carballio y Zuniga, *Barcia's Chronological Narrative of the History of Florida* (1951); Herbert E. Bolton, *The Spanish Borderlands: A Chronicle of Old Florida in the Southwest* (1921); Jeannette T. Connor, ed., *Colonial Records of Spanish Florida* (1925).

John B. Elliott, ed. *Contest for Empire, 1500–1775* (1975); Robert L. Gold, *Borderland Empires in Transition: The Triple-Nation Transfer of Florida* (1969); Charles Hudson, *The Southeastern Indians* (1976); John Tate Lanning, *The Spanish Missions of Georgia* (1935); Jerald T. Milanich and Susan Milbrath, eds., *First Encounters: Spanish Explorations in the Caribbean and the United States, 1492–1570* (1989).

See also APALACHEE; APALACHEE REVOLT; AYUBALE; CALUSA; CHACATO TROUBLES; FLORIDA; GUALE; PRESIDIO; ST. AUGUSTINE; TIMUCUAN REVOLT; TOLOMATO PRESIDIO (GEORGIA)

Spanish Mission System–Southwest

In the words of historian Herbert Eugene Bolton, the primary function of missions from the standpoint of the Roman Catholic church, was "to spread the Faith, first, last, and always." But missions also served the state. They were intended to make the Indians more tractable by Hispanicizing them and turning them into responsible, taxpaying citizens.

The mission system in New Mexico and Texas had its origins in northern Mexico during the second half of the sixteenth century. In a conflict known as the Chichimeca War (1550–1590s), missions and presidios represented Spain's institutional response to new circumstances encountered on the northern frontier of New Spain (colonial Mexico). Ideally, by employing a combination of force and persuasion, the two institutions would work in tandem to mold non-sedentary cultures into Christianized subjects of the king. The ideal, however, was often not realized. Frequent clashes between presidial commanders and missionary clergy, especially in Texas, undermined crown objectives and sowed discord among the mission neophytes.

Accompanying the advance of missions and presidios were civil settlements, which also helped secure the frontier. By 1570, the mining town of Santa Bárbara, situated near the headwaters of the Río Conchos in southern Chihuahua, served as the staging area for expeditions to New Mexico. Spanish settlement of that province was initiated in 1598 by Juan de Oñate, with continuous occupation lasting until 1680.

In 1680, Spanish influence spread from Taos in the north to Isleta in the south, from Zuñi in the west to Pecos in the east. Scattered among the missions of the province were some 16,000 partially Hispanicized Indians and 32 Franciscan friars. While there was no formal presidio, regular soldiers were stationed at Santa Fe. A massive, coordinated Indian revolt broke out in August 1680, forcing the entire Spanish community to retreat to El Paso del Norte (modern-day Ciudad Juárez). More than 400 Spaniards died in the Pueblo Revolt, and New Mexico was not reconquered until the mid-1690s. With the restoration of Spanish control, a formal presidio was established at

Santa Fe, and missionary activity resumed for the remainder of the colonial period.

The Spanish directed renewed attention to Texas during the decade of the Pueblo Revolt. In response to the discovery of René-Robert Cavelier de La Salle's Fort St. Louis (1689), two missions were founded in east Texas in the early 1690s. From the first mission in 1690 to the last in 1793, there were close to 40 mission sites in Texas. They ranged from Santa Cruz de San Sabá in the west to San Miguel de los Adaes in the east, from the San Gabriel missions in the north to Espíritu Santo de Zúñiga (La Bahía) in the south. But in reality, only the five missions at San Antonio and a single one at Goliad may be deemed successful.

Secularization of the San Antonio missions began in 1793 and accelerated in the following year. Former missions became parishes and passed under the control of non-order (secular) clergy, where they remained until the end of the colonial era in 1821.

Donald E. Chipman

References

John F. Bannon, *The Spanish Border-lands Frontier, 1513–1821* (1970); Marion A. Habig, *The Alamo Chain of Missions: A History of San Antonio's Five Old Missions* (1969); Charles W. Hackett, intro. and notes, and Charmion C. Shelby, trans., *Revolt of the Pueblo Indians and Otermin's Attempted Reconquest, 1680–1682*, 2 vols. (1942); George P. Hammond and Agapito Rey, *The Rediscovery of New Mexico, 1580–1594* (1966); Robert S. Weddle, *San Juan Bautista: Gateway to Spanish Texas* (1968).

See also NEW MEXICO; PRESIDIO NUESTRA SEÑORA DE LOS DELORES DE LOS TEJAS (TEXAS); PRESIDIO NUESTRA SEÑORA DEL PILAR DE LOS ADAES (LOUISIANA); PUEBLO REVOLT; SAN ANTONIO; TEXAS

Spotswood, Alexander (1676–1740)

Alexander Spotswood was the son of Robert and Catherine Spotswood. He was born in Tangier in 1676, where his father was an army surgeon. Spotswood had a successful military career and was eventually appointed lieutenant governor of Virginia in 1710, and served until 1722.

Spotswood's first goal was to regulate the production of tobacco. In 1713 the Tobacco Act was passed. This set a standard for tobacco quality and was very controversial. It was attacked by many in Virginia because it added extra costs and time to the process of tobacco production.

Spotswood's Indian policy was shown by his support of the Indian Act of 1714. This created the Virginia Indian Company, which worked to improve the colony's relations with Indians. By colonial standards the policy was progressive, but by today's standards, it appears ethnocentric. Spotswood hoped to educate and Christianize Indians. He also wanted to encourage them to abandon their nomadic lifestyle and adopt a more settled way of life.

Spotswood also had to directly react to Indian aggression during the Tuscarora and Yamasee Wars. In September 1711, the Tuscarora attacked a European settlement in North Carolina and killed approximately 130 settlers. The lieutenant governor convinced other Indians not involved in this attack to refrain from becoming involved. He also sent supplies to North Carolina and led a group of Virginia militiamen to protect Virginia's border with North Carolina.

Then, in May 1715, the Yamasee killed 90 settlers in South Carolina. The colony requested aid, and Spotswood replied immediately. He called a special session of the Virginia assembly and sent guns, ammunition, and then men to help the colony.

By 1715, Spotswood was at odds with several members of Virginia's House of Burgesses. Differences eventually were calmed, but not before the Tobacco Act and Indian Act were repealed. This was a tremendous blow to the lieutenant governor's prestige. Tension continued to exist between the two for the remainder of his tenure.

Spotswood also encouraged westward expansion. He wanted to extend Virginia's border and made frequent journeys to investigate the land. One goal was to establish forts in the western mountain ranges to expand trade with distant Indian tribes. In 1716, he led an expedition called the "Knights of the Golden Horseshoe," in which he and several others toured Virginia's Piedmont region.

In 1722, Spotswood was removed from office after several years of conflict with Virginia's governing council. In 1724, he returned to England where he met and married Anne Butler Brayne, with whom he had four children. The family then returned to Virginia in 1730 when Spotswood was named deputy postmaster general of the American colonies. Under his direction, the postal service was extended south of Pennsylvania to Williamsburg, Virginia, for the first time. He held this position until his death.

In 1739, war broke out between Spain and England. Spotswood proposed to recruit volunteers from the colonies to fight. He was commissioned brigadier general and began his work. In 1740 he traveled to Annapolis and became ill. He died in Annapolis on 7 June 1740.

Michael W. Nagle

References
Leonidas Dodson, "Alexander Spotswood," *Dictionary of American Biography*, Vol. XVII (1935); Walter Havinghurst, *Alexander Spotswood: Portrait of a Governor* (1967); Richard L. Morton, *Colonial Virginia*, 2 vols. (1960), 2.

See also TUSCARORA WAR; YAMASEE WAR

Springfield, Burning of (1675)

At the time of King Philip's War in 1675, Springfield was the most important settlement along the upper Connecticut River. It consisted of 40 dwellings housing a population of 500 with nearly as many barns, a saw mill, several corn mills, and a jail. Three structures had been designated as garrison houses. About a mile away, on Long Hill, lay the permanent village of the Agawam Indians. It was from here that the attack on Springfield originated on 5 October.

Until the eve of the assault, the loyalty of the Agawams remained unquestioned, despite a succession of Indian attacks in August and September on other settlements along the river, including Brookfield, Squakeg, and Deerfield. Closer at hand, on 26 September, Major John Pynchon's house and mill at Stony Brook, opposite Springfield, were burned. Only the timely arrival of a mounted messenger from Windsor on 4 October averted a massacre. This warning had been obtained from an Indian, Toto, employed at Windsor, who as a result of his nervous behavior was questioned and confessed his knowledge of a plan to attack the town. The vulnerability of Springfield had increased that morning when the provincial forces commanded by Major Pynchon left for Hadley in preparation for an attack on a suspected Indian target farther north. With the arrival of the warning, the citizens were called to the garrison houses and a messenger sent to Hadley.

On the morning of the 5th, Lieutenant Thomas Cooper and Constable Thomas Miller set forth to investigate the truth of the warning. As they approached the Indian village, they were ambushed. Miller was killed on the spot and Cooper mortally wounded but able to return on his horse to a garrison house. The Indians immediately attacked the town. Between 100 and 500 Indians participated, the larger figure indicating a sizeable reinforcement of the Agawams by Indians raised from other villages. Failing to storm the garrison houses, they set fire to all the uninhabited buildings in the center of town.

When news of the impending attack reached Major Pynchon, he promptly put Captains Samuel Appleton's and Joseph Sill's companies, aggregating 200 men, on the road back to Springfield. The first attempt to relieve the besieged, however, came from Westfield. Major Robert Treat with a small Connecticut force arrived on the west bank but, could not directly intervene, owing to Indian fire and a lack of boats. By forced marches, Major Pynchon's troops reached Springfield between 2 and 3 P.M. When they appeared, the Indians withdrew without further fighting.

Though escaping with minimal loss of life— only three dead and three or four wounded— most of the town lay in ashes. Thirty-two houses, 25 barns, and all the mills were burned. Unlike many other towns, Springfield was not abandoned. For the survivors, the following winter was filled with privation, principally overcrowding and short food. Immediately after the attack Major Pynchon was allowed to resign his commission because of his disagreement with the New England Confederation Commissioners' offense-minded policy—they wanted to pursue the Indians, while he feared leaving the towns unguarded. Appleton, who assumed command, returned to Hadley with the field forces on 12 October though leaving, against instructions, a small detachment as a garrison. Eventually the field forces were dissipated in garrisons and the offensive policy abandoned.

Richard P.W. Williams

References
George W. Ellis and John E. Morris, *King Philip's War* (1906); Douglas Edward Leach, *Flintlock and Tomahawk: New England in King Philip's War* (1958); Henry Burt, *First*

Century of the History of Springfield: Official Records from 1636–1736 (1899); Increase Mather, History of King Philip's War (1862); William Hubbard, History of the Indians Wars in New England from the First Settlement to the Termination of the War Against King Philip in 1677 (1865).

See also DEERFIELD; HATFIELD FORT (MASSACHUSETTS); KING PHILIP'S WAR; NEW ENGLAND CONFEDERATION

Squanto (?–1622)

Kidnapped by Thomas Hunt from Patuxet in 1614, Squanto was supposedly sold into slavery in Malaga, Spain, but by 1617, he had managed his way into England and the employment of John Slany. Squanto returned to New England in 1619 as a guide and mediator for Thomas Dermer's ill-fated expedition designed to reopen English trade with the southern New England Indians. When the natives attacked Dermer's group in 1620, Squanto escaped, but was later captured by the Wampanoags.

While a prisoner, Squanto established himself as an authority on Europeans. Realizing the marked decline in the Wampanoag population due to recent epidemics, Squanto convinced Massasoit, the Wampanoag sachem, that an alliance with Europeans would give the Wampanoags sufficient strength to stave off the Narragansett onslaught. The founding of the Plymouth Bay colony by the Pilgrims in 1620 offered Massasoit the opportunity to exploit Squanto's advice. Squanto acted as an intermediary for both Pilgrims and Wampanoags in the negotiations that led to an alliance.

The treaty was put to the test in the summer of 1621 when Corbitant, sachem of a small faction of Wampanoags, conspired with the Narragansetts and attacked Massasoit's village, seizing Squanto. The Pilgrims upheld their part of the treaty by defending Massasoit. In the process, the Pilgrims rescued Squanto and established their military power throughout the region.

Freed from the Wampanoags for his role in the treaty, Squanto moved to Plymouth and served as the separatists' guide, interpreter, and general adviser. Squanto's best-known contribution to the Plymouth Colony was his advice on the planting of corn. In 1622, Squanto tried to augment his status by playing the Wampanoags and Pilgrims against each other while portray-

ing himself as the only mediator. Once his motives were discovered, Squanto had to seek refuge among the Pilgrims from the wrath of Massasoit.

Richard C. Goode

References

William Bradford, Of Plymouth Plantation (1901); G. Mourt, Journal of the Pilgrims at Plymouth: Mourt's Relation (1622); Neal Salisbury, "Squanto: Last of the Patuxets," in Struggle and Survival in Colonial America, David Sweet and Gary B. Nash, eds. (1981); Frank Shuffelton, "Indian Devils and Pilgrim Fathers: Squanto, Hobomok, and the English Conception of Indian Religion," New England Quarterly 49 (1976):108–116; Alden T. Vaughan, New England Frontier: Puritans and Indians, 1620–1675 (1965).

See also PILGRIM; PLYMOUTH; WAMPANOAG

Standish, Miles [Myles] (c. 1584–1656)

Miles Standish was captain general of the Pilgrim army for nearly 40 years. Born in Lancashire, England, he served as a soldier of fortune in the Low Countries, returning to England in 1609. In 1620, he was hired by the Pilgrims to join their expedition to the New World. While he remained a "stranger," his military expertise and his devotion to the colony's survival made him an indispensable member of the Pilgrim community. He led the first landing party on Cape Cod, was elected captain general of the small but effective Pilgrim army in 1621, became an assistant in 1633, and was colony treasurer from 1644 to 1649.

Standish helped give shape to Plymouth's Indian policy. He ordered the militia system on the English model, demanding that all able-bodied men serve as potential soldiers. He began drilling his forces as soon as the Mayflower party came ashore, and by 1622 had organized them into four squadrons, each with specialized duties, to defend the tiny settlement. He also helped erect a fort, which held a gun platform for his cannon, and supervised the building of a stockade to protect the exposed and outnumbered Pilgrim community.

Known as "Captain Shrimpe" by his detractors, he was short, had red hair, a florid complexion, and a fiery temper. He was thin-skinned and quick to take umbrage at the smallest slight. He never trusted the Indians and always sought to overwhelm them with a show of power, as he remained convinced that force alone could secure the breathing room the Pilgrims needed if their venture was to survive. While he tried to work with the sachems, seeking to make them discipline their own people, his primary goal was to undermine Indian autonomy, using the sachems to effect English ends.

Standish led a number of expeditions against Indian, French, and English threats to the Pilgrim community. His most controversial venture occurred in 1622, near Wessagusset (now Weymouth), the home of a small group of adventurers sent by Englishman Thomas Weston to trade with the Indians. As "strangers," Weston's men posed both an economic and religious threat to the Pilgrims. Not long after the party's arrival, the Pilgrims learned that some Indians, led by Massachusetts sachem Wituwamat, were plotting a general uprising against all English settlements. Standish and eight of his men traveled to Wessagusett to warn Weston's men of the alleged conspiracy, but the traders were singularly unimpressed by the Pilgrims' evidence. Undaunted, Standish lured Wituwamat and three other Indians into a Wessagusett house, assassinating all four of his victims. Later, three more unsuspecting Indians were also murdered. Although the incident earned a strong protest from Pilgrim spiritual leader John Robinson, Standish had accomplished his objectives. His actions threatened to provoke Indian hostilities, driving Weston's men from Wessagusett. His show of force temporarily cowed, even if it alienated, his Indian adversaries.

Standish set the tone for Indian relations in the colony and helped protect the settlement from potential hostilities. His tendency to use military rather than diplomatic means to deal with his opponents, however, helped sow the seeds of discord between the English settlers and the Native Americans.

Sheila L. Skemp

References

William Bradford, *History of Plymouth Plantation, 1620–1647* (1912); Kate Caffrey, *The Mayflower* (1974); Francis Dillon, *The Pilgrims* (1975); Frances Jennings, *The Invasion of America: Indians, Colonialism and the Cant of Conquest* (1975); Douglas Edward Leach, "The Military System of Plymouth Colony," *New England Quarterly* 26 (1951):342–364; Harold L. Peterson, "The Military Equipment of the Plymouth and Bay Colonies, 1620–1690," *New England Quarterly* 20 (1947):197–208; Neal Salisbury, *Manitou and Providence: Indians, Europeans, and the Making of New England, 1500–1643* (1982).

See also PILGRIM; PLYMOUTH; WESSAGUSSET RAID

Fort Stanwix (New York)

Fort Stanwix was constructed at the headwaters of the Mohawk River near the present-day town of Rome, New York. At that same location, the French had earlier constructed a fort to protect their trade with the Indians. As British settlements moved inland from the Atlantic seaboard, they discovered the strategic importance of the area, and in 1757 began construction of a new fort. The location was strategically important because it was located at the portage between the Mohawk River and Wood Creek. This led to Oswego and was astride the main avenue of approach from Canada through the Iroquois country and into the Mohawk Valley. Originally, it was intended to replace Oswego as the guardian of the Mohawk.

In July 1757, Lieutenant Colonel John Bradstreet began to plan an attack against Fort Frontenac. At the same time, he was ordered by Brigadier John Stanwix to begin construction of a fort at the headwaters of the Mohawk River. Here work began in August 1757, and the fort was completed the following year.

John M. Keefe

See also BRADSTREET, JOHN

Stevens, Phineas (1706–1756)

Phineas Stevens made his military reputation during King George's War on the upper Connecticut River as a leading settler of Number Four and the commander of the fort in that isolated frontier town. Stevens was born in Sudbury, Massachusetts, on 20 February 1706. The family moved to Rutland, where they were introduced to frontier warfare during Dummer's War. On 14 August 1723, Phineas and three younger brothers were walking to their field when a party of French Indians ambushed them. Two of the brothers were killed, while Phineas and his four-year-old brother were carried into captivity. Phineas, according to family legend, carried his young brother on his back to prevent the Indians from having an excuse to kill him. Like other captives, Stevens was able to observe and learn the habits and methods of native scouting parties. His father redeemed him in 1724.

Stevens married in 1734, and then became one of the proprietors of a new settlement granted by Massachusetts on the Connecticut River called Number Four. Stevens became one of the first settlers to move there in 1743. Commissioned in the militia in 1743, Stevens would be given provincial rank in 1745 and named to command the fort in his community. He moved his family back to Rutland in 1746 when the settlement was temporarily abandoned, and moved them back again in 1748. During King George's War he commanded the fort at Number Four during several attacks. English Commodore Charles Knowles was so impressed with Stevens that he gave him a fancy sword.

In 1749, the governor of Massachusetts appointed Stevens to travel to Canada to negotiate the release of English captives. In 1752, he repeated this service, this time winning the release of John Stark, who would later gain fame in the American War for Independence. During this period he also served as leading selectman and town treasurer for the town of Charlestown, as Number Four was now called (apparently to return the favor of acknowledgement given Stevens and the community by Charles Knowles).

At the start of the last French war, Stevens was again given a provincial commission and named to command the fort. In 1755, he moved his family out of harm's way once more, this time to Deerfield, Massachusetts. That same year he served as a provincial officer in the expedition sent to Nova Scotia, participating at the surrender of Fort Beauséjour in June. The following year, Stevens caught a fever and died at Chignecto.

Steven C. Eames

References

Jeremy Belknap, *The History of New Hampshire* (1831), rpt. 1970.

See also FORT BEAUSÉJOUR (NOVA SCOTIA, CANADA); DUMMER'S WAR; FORT AT NUMBER FOUR (NEW HAMPSHIRE); KING GEORGE'S WAR

Stono Rebellion (1739)

As a staple-producing colony, South Carolina had long relied on slave labor. The rice boom of the 1730s resulted in increased importation of Africans, most of them from the southwestern coast of that continent, the areas of Portuguese Angola and the kingdom of Kongo (present-day Angola). During this decade the new arrivals totalled more than one-half of the slave population in South Carolina. This rapid influx coincided with increased instability and unrest among the slaves. To many white Carolinians, fearful of the black majority, the root of the problem was the Spanish in Florida.

For runaway slaves, the most secure haven was St. Augustine. Indeed, the Spanish practice of harboring and encouraging runaways had been a sore point for Carolinians since the early 1720s. Tensions increased in 1738, when Spanish authorities announced a royal edict that granted freedom to slaves who fled English colonies. Because many recent arrivals to South Carolina were from the kingdom of Kongo, a Christian country where Portuguese was spoken among the educated, it is possible that some slaves viewed the Spanish proclamation as a promise of religious freedom as well as freedom from bondage. Also in 1738, the Spanish established a camp for fugitives a short distance north of St. Augustine. Known as "Mose," this settlement received new inhabitants in November when about 70 slaves escaped from the Beaufort area. The Spanish governor, Manuel de Montiano, flatly refused to return the fugitives to their owners.

These troubles were part of a general dispute between England and Spain that culminated in the War of Jenkins' Ear. During the weekend of 8–9 September, news of a declaration of war reached Charles Town. Along with the outbreak of formal hostilities, the city was in the throes of a yellow fever epidemic that killed many residents. In mid-August, moreover, newspapers announced the Security Act: Beginning on 29 September, all white men were to carry firearms to church on Sunday or be subject to a fine.

Thus it was probably no coincidence that an uprising under the leadership of a slave named Jemmy began on Sunday morning, 9 September. Early that morning, about 20 slaves attacked Hutchenson's store at Stono. They killed the storekeepers and took arms and powder. From there they advanced to a Mr. Godfrey's house, which they plundered and burned, killing Godfrey and his son and daughter. They then turned south along Pons Pons, the principal road leading to St. Augustine. Reaching Wallace's Tavern shortly before dawn, they spared the owner "for he was a good Man and kind to his Slaves." One settler, Thomas Rose, was saved by his slaves, who hid him from danger. Others living in the area were not as fortunate. With a cry of "Liberty," the rebels "marched on with Colours displayed, and two Drums beating, pursuing all white people they met with, and kiling [sic] Man Woman and Child when they could come up to them." Along the road they encountered the lieutenant governor of South Carolina, William Bull, who was riding to Charles Town with four other men. The slaves pursued Bull, but he escaped and warned the countryside.

Unaware of the importance of this encounter and having marched ten miles, the rebels, who now numbered between 60 and 100, "halted in a field, and set to dancing, Singing and beating Drums, to draw more Negroes to them, thinking they were now victorious over the whole Province." While white Carolinians viewed these activities as a mindless celebration, the dancing perhaps held military significance. Dancing was part of the African military culture; it promoted the coordination and reflexes needed for hand-to-hand combat. If, as one scholar has speculated, the slaves from the kingdom of Kongo possessed military experience, then this dancing may have served a function similar to close-order drill for Euro-American armies.

In any event, the rebels' initial jubilation was short-lived. That afternoon, a force of militia and planters surprised the camp. The skirmish was brief. "The Negroes were soon routed," a contemporary account reported, "though they behaved boldly." Several survivors were taken prisoner, briefly interrogated, and then shot. Others fled to their plantations, hoping they had not been missed. Upon discovery, they were shot immediately. Still, more than 30 rebels escaped. Within a week, ten slaves had moved 30 miles southward. A party of mounted planters encountered the rebels, who "fought stoutly for some time and were all killed on the Spot." Their withdrawal from the initial skirmish to fight again another day was consistent with central African military tactics. Other rebels remained at large until the following spring; and one of the leaders was not apprehended for three years. The last fugitives were all executed upon capture. During the Stono uprising, more than 20 whites and an undetermined number of slaves lost their lives.

In response to this crisis, the Carolinians enacted a new slave code in May 1740. The code defined slaves as "chattels," or personal property, and outlined provisions for their treatment.

In the belief that better conditions would lessen the motivation for future revolts, the laws prohibited owners from working slaves on Sunday, or more than 15 hours per day. A white found guilty of killing or maiming a slave could receive a stiff fine. At the same time, the code attempted to regulate the conduct of slaves. Restrictions were placed on their freedom of movement and their right to assemble. In an effort to strengthen the patrol system, the patrols would henceforth be drawn from the militia. The law forbade slaves from learning to read and write. Finally, hoping to curb the growing black majority, the South Carolina assembly placed a prohibitive duty on future slave imports that lasted through most of the 1740s.

South Carolinians did not forget the role played by the Spanish. In 1740, they joined James Oglethorpe, governor of Georgia and the commander of military forces on the southern frontier, in an expedition to seize St. Augustine. The siege, however, proved a fiasco.

The Stono Rebellion was the largest slave uprising to occur in colonial North America. South Carolina suffered no further comparable revolts, in part because the duty reduced importations and thus new Africans among the slave population, and because the slave code restricted the personal freedom of blacks.

Gregory D. Massey

References

"An Account of the Negroe Insurrection in South Carolina," in Allen D. Candler and William J. Northen, eds., *The Colonial Records of the State Georgia*, Vol. 22, Part II (1913):232–236; M. Eugene Sirmans, "The Legal Status of the Slave in South Carolina, 1670–1740," *Journal of Southern History* XXVII (1962):462–473; John K. Thornton, "African Dimensions of the Stono Rebellion," *American Historical Review* 96 (1991):1101–1113; Robert M. Weir, *Colonial South Carolina: A History* (1983); Peter H. Wood, *Black Majority: Negroes in Colonial South Carolina from 1670 through the Stono Rebellion* (1974).

See also AFRICAN AMERICANS; ANGLO-SPANISH WAR (1739–1744); BLACK AND INDIAN MILITIAS; MENÉNDEZ, FRANCISCO

Strategy

Strategy can be defined as "the planning for, coordination of, and concerted use of the multiple means and resources available to an alliance, a nation, a political group, or a commander, for the purpose of gaining advantage over a rival." It is the art of winning campaigns and sustained operations through effective maneuver and surprise. The word is derived from the Greek term *strategos*, meaning the art of the general. It gained common acceptance toward the end of the eighteenth century, but has expanded far beyond its narrow military sense. As wars became more complex, political, military, technological, psychological, and economic factors formed an interdependent and inseparable complex determining national policies.

While early modern European writers thought the principles of strategy to be immutable, i.e., concentration of forces, surprise, proper movement of forces, and their security from attack and unity of objective, modern authors argue that, since no two military situations are the same, these principles need to be changed according to the conditions and needs of war, and that the only sound guide in war is flexibility and common sense.

The first early modern author to emphasize the larger aspects of war was Niccolò Machiavelli in his *Art of War* in 1520, in which he argued for the close relationship of the civilian and military spheres. But his ideas stood contrary to the concept of the absolutist state. The systematic study of strategy, now within strictly military confines, dates from the eighteenth century, when military writers began to analyze the examples of antiquity to define the principles of strategic planning. Nevertheless, the foundations of ancient strategy, tactics, and battle had to be relegated to a secondary role, as the internal organization and purposes of the standing armies of the age of absolutism dictated the nature of their composition, cumbersome supply structure and slowness of movement, all of which did not allow military leaders to take full advantage of their studies of strategy. The concept of the inhabitants of a state as subjects rather than as citizens and the great expense involved in raising and maintaining large bodies of soldiers led to a reluctance to risk them in battle, as well as the idea that war was an affair of the monarch. The pitched battles of earlier times, the search for the enemy and his engagement, was replaced by careful maneuvering, and battle as a means of last resort. This resulted in a preoccupation with defense and fortifications and a strategy of limited aim. Superior strategy was defined as victory without battle, maneuvering for position and a system of supply lines that allowed a combatant to outlast his opponent. The aim was no longer to destroy the enemy in battle, and risk defeat and annihilation, but rather gain terrain and the occupation of key points of fortifications. In the spirit of the times, war became scientific and mathematical, to be waged with geometric precision and won without battle.

A temporary break with these generally accepted patterns came with the wars of Frederick the Great. Surrounded and greatly outnumbered by his enemies, Frederick had to try to always keep the initiative, to destroy his enemies before they could reinforce each other, and to avoid long, drawn-out wars. Taking advantage of his central position while avoiding the dissipation of his superior and highly disciplined army, he developed the strategy of interior lines, which allowed him and his state to survive. But even he could not escape the limitations imposed on a statesman/warrior of the eighteenth century. His battles were not battles of annihilation; pursuit of a beaten enemy after battle was impossible; a levy en masse was still unthinkable.

After the end of the Seven Years' War, European military thinking returned to more traditional ways. The experiences of the American Revolutionary War were dismissed by the military elite as not applicable to Europe, and it was the French Revolution with its fundamental changes in society that introduced the concept of the citizen/soldier, and thus revolutionized the art of war as well. Political goals determined Napoleon's wars as much as military objectives. His aim was nothing short of the annihilation of the enemy. The armies of revolutionary France gave him the opportunity to succeed, and his tactics and strategy exerted a predominant influence on the military leaders of the nineteenth century.

Robert A. Selig

References

John I. Alger, *Definitions and Doctrine of the Military Art* (1985); Peter Paret, "Colonial Military Experience and European Military Reform at the End of the Eighteenth Century," *Bulletin of the Institute of Historical Research* 37 (1964):47–59; ———, ed., *Makers of Modern Strategy: From Machiavelli to the Nuclear Age* (1986).

See also TACTICS, INFANTRY

Stuart, John (1718–1779)

John Stuart was Great Britain's superintendent of Indian affairs for the southern district of North America from 1762 until his death during the Revolutionary War. The son of an Inverness merchant, this Scotsman immigrated to Charles Town, South Carolina, in 1748 to seek his fortune. He initially failed as a merchant, but he soon won fame through his service as captain of a provincial military company among the Cherokee. As early as 1756, when Carolinians were building Fort Loudoun among the Overhill towns, Captain Raymond Demeré commended Stuart's diplomatic abilities, writing to the South Carolina governor that the Scotsman was "extreamly beloved by the Indians." In 1757, Stuart gained the trust of Attakullakulla and other leading Cherokee and thus helped counter French influence among the tribe. Even after Anglo-Cherokee relations soured in 1760, producing the devastating Cherokee War, Attakullakulla helped Stuart escape following the surrender of Fort Loudoun. Perhaps Stuart appealed to many Cherokee leaders because, like themselves, he believed in the need for what he so often called "order and regularity." In Stuart's view, much Indian-white conflict could be avoided if the imperial government would centrally administer all aspects of frontier life, including trade and land transfers. This perspective shaped Stuart's entire career, and it ultimately brought him into conflict with colonial leaders who opposed such centralized control, both on the frontier and in the colonies themselves.

Stuart's British superiors never fully adopted his approach to government, but costly frontier turmoil during the Seven Years' War convinced them that trade abuses and unauthorized encroachments on Indian land had to be eliminated. Consequently, the British appointed superintendents of Indian affairs for the northern and southern districts of North America to coordinate British-Indian relations. The first superintendent for the region south of Pennsylvania and the Ohio Valley, Edmond Atkin, was appointed in 1756. Atkin shared Stuart's belief in the need for tight control of frontier life, but he lacked Stuart's diplomatic skills. On Atkin's death in 1761, those familiar with Stuart's experience among the Cherokees promoted him as the ideal candidate for Atkin's position. First General Jeffrey Amherst, and then London authorities concurred, and the Scotsman was officially appointed as the new superintendent early in 1762.

To lay a foundation for future British-Indian relations, the new superintendent convened a postwar congress including four southern governors and more than 800 Indians from all the major southern tribes at Augusta in November 1763. The Indians' complaints about trade abuses and encroachments on their land confirmed Stuart's belief in the need for centralized frontier administration. The governors also seemed to agree, recommending, along with Stuart, that the trade should be on "a general, safe, equitable footing . . . which we are afraid will never be done by respective provinces." Another positive result of the congress, in Stuart's view, was a diffusion of tension between the British and the Creek. As compensation for their recent frontier depredations, the Lower Creeks granted to Georgia a major land cession between the Savannah and Ogeechee Rivers. Upper Creek leaders did not, at first, join in making this offer, but Stuart used his considerable diplomatic skills to convince Emistisiguo, his principal Upper Creek supporter, that the Upper Creek should affirm the cession. In the following year, Emistisiguo accomplished this, but only with the understanding that Stuart would prevent settlers from crossing the new boundary line. Indeed, in the coming years, Emistisiguo, Attakullakulla, and other Indian leaders of southern tribes remembered British promises at Augusta and looked primarily to Stuart as their protector against colonists' threats to their people's economic, social, and political life.

Soon after the Augusta Congress, Stuart and others who favored more stable frontier conditions were disappointed that the British government, in its famous Proclamation of 1763, prohibited colonies from restricting their number of licensed traders. Such restriction, they believed, would be the best means to prevent cutthroat competition, declining trade prices, an increase in the use of cheap rum as a trade item, trade "in the woods" outside the Indian towns, and mounting Indian debts, all of which were weakening Indian societies and destabilizing Indian-white relations. As usual, however, Stuart made a virtue of necessity and used the British government's proposed "Plan for the Future Management of Indian Affairs" of 1764 as a guide until he received further instructions. The plan did not provide for the centralized trade regulation that Stuart advocated, since an unlimited number could enter the trade, and since provincial, rather than imperial, authorities were to license traders and, if necessary, bring legal action against them. Nevertheless, the plan did allow the superintendent to adopt uniform trade regulations for the entire district and to appoint commissaries, or assistants, among the various tribes who would help provincial officials enforce these regulations.

Stuart further hoped to regulate the trade by creating tribal hierarchies that would be responsible to him. Inspired by the example of French-Indian relations, Stuart gave "Great" and "Small" medals to pro-British Indians and enhanced their authority through frequent recognition and presents. Stuart hoped that the medal chiefs would then cooperate with his commissaries to implement a centrally coordinated regulatory system. At last, it seemed, "renegades" of all races who threatened peace and prosperity could be controlled.

Until 1766, Stuart continued his efforts to implement this system with support from General Thomas Gage. Then, although the shifting British administrations had not adopted the plan of 1764, or any other system of frontier administration, the earl of Shelburne instructed Stuart and the colonial governors to "restrain the Traders and other loose and irregular People" who by trade abuses and boundary violations had created the "too just resentment of the Indian tribes." Stuart interpreted this as a mandate to continued general trade regulation coordinated by himself as superintendent.

By 1768, the commissaries had apparently had some success in enforcing Stuart's trade regulations. In that year, however, the British government, primarily as an economy measure, ordered Stuart to withdraw his commissaries and gave exclusive authority over trade regulation to the provinces where the traders originated. This dealt a severe blow to Stuart's hopes, and it brought protests from some Indian leaders and even from some provincial governors who realized how ineffective provincial regulation had been in the past.

Nevertheless, Stuart continued after 1768 to use frontier crises to convince his British superiors to adopt his own approach to frontier government. By 1770, with Gage's support, he began to return commissaries to various Indian nations, ostensibly as emergency measures. London officials soon began to see more logic in Stuart's recommendations in the early 1770s, when rapid encroachment of settlers on Indian lands and continued trade abuses promoted tension and violence throughout the southern frontier. At last, by the time of the Georgia-Creek conflict of 1774, Stuart's British superiors were coming to agree with him that rebellious colonists who caused turmoil both in the colonies and on the frontier needed to be tightly controlled.

Thanks to his diplomatic abilities, his sincere regulatory efforts, and his gifts of goods and prestige, Stuart had won for the British the real strategic advantage of Indian loyalty by the eve of the Revolutionary War. After Lexington and Concord, his influence over the Indians was soon the source of rumors in South Carolina and Georgia that Stuart would incite Indian attacks on the colonies. Leading Carolinians vilified the superintendent as the embodiment of British threats to American liberty. After fleeing to St. Augustine and eventually establishing himself at Pensacola, the superintendent then seemed to fulfill the colonists' worst fears by organizing Indian and loyalist forces until his death in March 1779. Stuart's successors continued to cultivate British influence among the southern Indians. By the time the British evacuated the Floridas in 1783, many Indians felt they had lost both a protector and an essential source of trade goods and presents. Well into the nineteenth century, however, Scottish merchants in Spanish Pensacola, many of whom had had connections with Stuart, continued to supply southern Indians with the goods and the encouragement that they needed to continue their struggle against the new states. Therefore, ironically, Stuart's efforts among the southern Indians left a legacy, not of "order and regularity," but of violent conflict that ultimately helped lead to Indian removal.

J. Russell Snapp

References
John R. Alden, *John Stuart and the Southern Colonial Frontier* (1944); William S. Coker and Thomas D. Watson, *Indian Traders of the Southeastern Spanish Borderlands: Panton, Leslie and Company and John Forbes and Company, 1783–1847* (1985); David H. Corkran, *The Creek Frontier, 1540–1783* (1967); J. Russell Snapp, "Exploitation and Control: The Southern Frontier in Anglo-American Politics in the Era of the American Revolution," Ph.D. Dissertation, Harvard University (1988).

See also ATKIN, EDMOND; ATTAKULLAKULLA; AUGUSTA, CONGRESS OF; CHEROKEE WAR; EMISTISIGUO; FORT LOUDOUN (TENNESSEE); PROCLAMATION LINE OF 1763

S

Stuyvesant, Petrus (c. 1610–1672)

Petrus (Peter) Stuyvesant served as director general of New Netherland from 1647 to 1664. On behalf of the West India Company, he sought to exploit the commercial potential of the venture and, by 1664, his careful administration had served to create a colony of promising fur-trading and farming communities. In that year, however, an English fleet seized New Netherland, forcing Stuyvesant's surrender. He returned to Holland to defend his actions and then sailed back to New Netherland—now New York—where he lived quietly on his farm until his death.

Stuyvesant was born in Friesland, the son of a Reformed church minister. He began his career with the West India Company and learned the skills he would later need in New Netherland: the ability to command the company's marines at sea and at fortified overseas trading stations, and the capacity to oversee a small bureaucracy of accountants and clerks. In 1639, he was serving as the company's commissary of stores on the island of Curacao, but was then promoted to director general. In 1644, he led an attack on St. Martin, an island in Spanish possession, and sustained a wound that resulted in the amputation of his right leg below the knee. To recover his health he returned to Rotterdam.

In 1646, Stuyvesant was commissioned as director general of New Netherland and arrived the next year. Although he immediately set about righting the distresses of colonists and natives experienced under his predecessor, Willem Kieft, enmities lingered until the early 1650s. In 1653, the burghers of New Amsterdam (later New York City) won from him the right to conduct a court of inferior jurisdiction, and in effect to administer an independent city. Always a tough negotiator, Stuyvesant was nevertheless diplomatic in his relations with both nearby native tribes and Europeans settled on the borders of New Netherland. His insoluble problem was with the English to the north, that is, New England, as well as English-speaking settlers on Long Island. Despite the Hartford Treaty of 1650, they continued to encroach on the lands of the colony and lay claim to the entire territory. In 1664, a squadron sent by King Charles II of England forced Stuyvesant's surrender of the colony to the British.

Donna Merwick

References

Edmund B. O'Callaghan, *The History of New Netherland: or, New York Under the Dutch*, 2 vols. (1845–1848); Edmund B. O'Callaghan and Berthold Fernow, eds., *Documents Relative to the Colonial History of the State of New York*, 15 vols. (1856–1887), 1–2; Robert C. Ritchie, *The Duke's Province: A Study of New York Politics and Society* (1977); *Peter Stuyvesant, The Last Dutch Governor of New Amsterdam*, ed. by John S.C. Abbott (1873).

See also Fort Casimir (Delaware); Hartford Treaty of 1650; Kieft, Willem; New Netherland; New Netherland, Surrender of

Supplies, Impressment of

During the colonial wars of America, military officers, both provincial and regular, occasionally impressed, that is, took by force, but with reasonable compensation or promise of reasonable competition, provisions or services from the civilian population. Such impressment of goods and services was supported by both parliamentary legislation and provincial practice. However, colonial Americans generally despised the practice, especially when invoked by the British army or navy.

During wartime, soldiers and civilians competed for limited provisions, thereby driving prices higher. Considerable inflation usually accompanied every war. Because it created other problems, impressment was used only as a last resort. For example, in 1692 as Massachusetts prepared an expedition against New France, the provincial government recognized that certain provisions could not be had on the open market. Therefore, it empowered a four-man committee to enter any warehouse and take whatever was needed, paying a fair price for the products, of course. In preparation for the Louisbourg expedition in 1745, the Massachusetts government once again authorized impressment of materials not easily secured on the open market, at the price the procurement committee wanted to pay.

British naval and army officers often interpreted the high prices of much-needed provisions as nothing less than examples of unscrupulous profiteering by colonial Americans. They raised the threat of impressment repeatedly when goods or services were not forthcoming, and impressment was invoked on numerous occasions, though, again, only as a last resort. The vastly enlarged involvement of the British military in America during the French and Indian War intensified the problems of securing provisions or services in local markets.

British officers especially wanted colonial farmers to make their wagons, horses, and themselves available to move the supplies along with the soldiers during a campaign. When the Pennsylvania legislature dragged its feet in providing both provisions and transport service, Lieutenant Colonel John St. Clair, General Edward Braddock's deputy quartermaster general, "stormed like a Lyon Rampant" and threatened to "march his Army into Cumberland County to cut the Roads, press Horses, Wagons, &ca." Regarding the road building that had to be done, St. Clair made it clear he "would not suffer a Soldier to handle an Axe, but by Fire and Sword oblige the Inhabitants to do it, and take every man that refused to the Ohio." Exasperated by the difficulty of obtaining provisions generally, St. Clair further claimed he "would kill all kind of Cattle and carry away the Horses, burn the Houses, &ca., and that if the French defeated them by the Delays of the Province that he would with his Sword drawn pass through the Province and treat the Inhabitants as a Parcel of Traitors. . . ." Other British officers, especially supply officers, expressed similar sentiments throughout the French and Indian War.

Wagons, horses, and the services of farmers to drive them were impressed, as were a variety of other provisions, especially food and forage. But impressment, though actually applied much less than it was threatened, aroused deep resentment among American colonists and made procurement all the more difficult in the long run. Farmers whose goods were impressed often felt cheated by what they were paid, if they were paid. Their wagons and horses "leased" by the British sometimes were not returned, or when they were returned, were broken down or worn out. The legality of impressment was challenged repeatedly in local American courts, especially in Albany, New York, the primary staging area during the last colonial war with France. Impressment was not outright stealing, but more than a few colonial Americans felt it amounted to about the same thing.

Ronald W. Howard

References
Milton M. Klein and Ronald W. Howard, eds., *The Twilight of British Rule in Revolutionary America: The New York Letter Book of General James Robertson, 1780–1783* (1983); John Knox, *An Historical Journal of the Campaigns in North America for the Years 1757, 1758, 1759 and 1760,* Arthur G. Dougherty, ed., 3 vols. (1914–1916); Douglas Edward Leach, *Roots of Conflict: British Armed Forces and Colonial Americans, 1677–1763* (1986); Stanley M. Pargellis, ed., *Military Affairs in North America, 1748–1765* (1936).

See also OHIO EXPEDITION OF 1755; QUARTERMASTER GENERAL; REQUISITION; SUPPLY

Supply

Supplying the British army in colonial America was not much of a problem before the French and Indian War (1754–1763). In fact, there were relatively few regular regiments in British North America during King William's War (1689–1697), Queen Anne's War (1702–1713), and King George's War (1744–1748). The fighting that occurred—except for hit-and-run raids—involved provincial regiments raised for specific expeditions and supplied by commissaries hired and paid by committees of the respective colonial governments involved. But during the French and Indian War, or the "Great War for the Empire," as Lawrence Henry Gipson called it, British regulars did the bulk of the fighting, with provincials providing significant support. Supplying increasingly larger numbers of British soldiers in America became extremely expensive and problematic. For the most part, arms and ammunition, tents and blankets, and clothing had to be shipped from England, no easy undertaking because of the 3,000-mile ocean voyage involved. Supporting troops in Europe and India, as well as supplying the Royal Navy, the British government expected the American colonists to contribute as much as possible to clothing and especially to feeding and sheltering regular army regiments, as well as maintaining provincial soldiers. The colonists were seldom as forthcoming as British officers wanted them to be. Not only were the Americans generally reluctant to contribute much financially to their own defense; they were repeatedly accused of profiteering at the expense of the British Treasury. For their part, the Americans were angered by the British for impressing goods or else contracting the use of horses and wagons but not returning them in good condition or paying fully for them. Nevertheless, despite colonial profiteering and obstructiveness, the British, through the offices of both the quartermaster general and commissary general, became remarkably adept at getting what was needed to quarter, sustain, and transport troops in America.

During the French and Indian War, New York was the initial destination of all British supplies, including arms and ammunition, though munitions were redistributed through subsidiary ports like Boston, Philadelphia, and Norfolk. The Treasury awarded contracts to various British merchants for supplying food, clothing, and money to the regular army in America. Known as "Treasury Whigs" because their political loyalty depended less on convictions than on contracts, such British merchants had American partners who purchased food and forage and various other goods on the local market as well as distributed vast amounts of military supplies from England. Fortunes were made, in both England and America, through associations with these lucrative government contracts. The demand for supplies stimulated the local economy, presenting opportunities for economic gain, but also resulting in terrific inflation, which led to hardships.

Ronald W. Howard

References

Fred Anderson, *A People's Army: Massachusetts Soldiers and Society in the Seven Years' War* (1984); William G. Godfrey, *Pursuit of Profit and Preferment in Colonial North America: John Bradstreet's Quest* (1982); Virginia D. Harrington, *The New York Merchant on the Eve of the Revolution* (1935); Milton M. Klein and Ronald W. Howard, eds., *The Twilight of British Rule in Revolutionary America: The New York Letter Book of General James Robertson, 1780–1783* (1983); Stanley M. Pargellis, ed., *Military Affairs in North America, 1748–1765* (1936); Francis Parkman, *Montcalm and Wolfe: A Series of Historical Narratives*, 2 vols. (1884); Howard H. Peckham, *The Colonial Wars, 1689–1762* (1964).

See also QUARTERMASTER GENERAL; REQUISITION SYSTEM; SUPPLIES, IMPRESSMENT OF

Susquehannock

This Iroquoian-speaking people inhabited the lower Susquehanna River, in what is now Lancaster County, Pennsylvania, when John Smith in 1608 recorded the name "Susquehannock," probably a Powhatan word, of which the meaning is uncertain. The Delawares called them "Minquas." The French called them both "Andastes," a Huron term, and "Ganastogues," a related Huron or Five Nations term. The latter term came into English as Conestoga. We do not know what the Susquehannocks called themselves.

As early as 1608 they traded French goods at the head of Chesapeake Bay. In the late 1620s and early 1630s, seeking a direct Dutch outlet for their pelts, they waged war on the interposed Delawares. They won access to Dutch traders on the lower Delaware River in 1634, and soon after made a lasting peace with the Delawares. The arrival of the Swedes and the erection of Fort Christina (Wilmington, Delaware) in 1638 gave them another trading partner. Although the Swedes energetically built blockhouses along the river, they proved less able than the Dutch to meet Indian trade demands.

Susquehannock trade connections with Virginia meant tensions with the new colony of Maryland in 1634. Maryland's charter threatened the stake of the Virginia trader William Claiborne, who had begun a lucrative trade from the Chesapeake with the Susquehannocks in 1630. To forestall the end of his business, Claiborne may have turned to the Susquehannocks for assistance against Maryland. Maryland feared as much, arrested Claiborne, and went to war with the Susquehannocks.

In 1643, Maryland launched a frightening raid on the Susquehannocks. With Swedish arms and help, the Susquehannocks decisively threw back a second incursion in 1644. Desultory warfare continued until 1652, when Maryland and the Susquehannocks made peace. The Susquehannocks lost their Swedish allies with the Dutch conquest of New Sweden in 1655. In 1658, the Susquehannocks supplemented their Maryland trade by confirming a peace with the Dutch, with whom they could trade at the new Dutch post at New Amstel (now New Castle, Delaware). In 1658, with access to trade in both English Maryland and Dutch New Amstel, Susquehannocks looked forward to rivaling the Mohawks as middlemen in the trade with the west. But by the end of 1675, they had ceased to exist as an independent people.

Their "disappearance" is the subject of controversy, and several explanations have been offered. The first, disease, was a factor, but not a decisive one. Susquehannocks suffered from devastating epidemics—an unknown "purple rash," perhaps typhus or scarlet fever, in 1636–1637, and smallpox in 1661. After each of these episodes, however, Susquehannocks remained a force. They were strong enough in 1644 to repulse Maryland, and strong enough in 1663, as we shall see, to fend off the Senecas.

A second and older interpretation, which continues to claim careful advocates, holds out a military explanation. It sees the event in terms of the Iroquois quest for furs. The "Beaver Wars," beginning in 1647 with Huron-Susquehannock alliance against the Five Nations, featuring a massive, but unsuccessful, Seneca assault on the Susquehannocks and their Delaware allies in 1663, but vaguely ending with a poorly documented Iroquois conquest of the Susquehannocks by 1675—explain the Susquehannock decline. But the gaps in the record, particularly the lack of direct evidence of a successful Iroquois invasion of the Susquehanna Valley, have troubled even the interpretation's advocates.

As early as the 1850s, an alternative military explanation emerged, but it did not win converts until the mid-twentieth century. This new wisdom insists that Europeans, not the Five Nations, destroyed the Susquehannocks. It holds that the Five Nations were too weak and too neglected by their allies, particularly New York (British after 1664), to destroy the Susquehannocks in the 1660s. In 1666, it points out, the Susquehannocks shattered an Onondaga army. Peace with France in 1668 did not leave the still-undersupplied Five Nations in a better position to eliminate the Susquehannocks, who gained arms from Maryland. The "disappearance" of the Susquehannocks, this third interpretation reasonably continues, resulted most directly from the documented actions of Maryland and Virginia, not the poorly documented actions of the Iroquois. Maryland, seeking an end to its war with the Iroquois in 1674, and realizing that such an end would endanger the Susquehannocks, convinced the Susquehannocks to remove southward the next February to Piscataway Creek, on the Maryland side of the Potomac River, south of the current Washington, D.C.. The timing was disastrous, for the Susquehannocks' new homes came under militia assaults in the events surrounding Bacon's Rebellion in 1675–1676. The climactic assault was a combined Maryland and Virginia militia raid on the well-fortified Susquehannock Piscataway town in 1675. One thousand militia trapped 100 Susquehannock warriors and their families, laid siege, and slaughtered five chiefs who came out to parley. After six weeks, the Susquehannocks escaped, fanned out, and counterattacked. But the counterattacks were well met, and the Susquehannocks were dispersed. Virginians sold Susquehannock captives as slaves in Massachusetts.

This interpretation, unlike the older vision, has the advantage of an identifiable and decisive battle that finally dispersed the Susquehannas. But it leaves open two lacunae. How did the Susquehannock resisters of the Senecas in 1663, still numbering around 700 warriors *after* the smallpox epidemics, dwindle to the 100 warriors opposing Maryland and Virginia in 1675; and why did the Susquehannocks, if so formidable, agree so readily to Maryland's offer to sanctuary in 1675? Only the Five Nations were at war with the Susquehannocks in the intervening years. Nor are catastrophic diseases reported for the period. The new wisdom successfully shifts much weight to the British colonies, but it leaves room to reasonably imagine, even to suppose, a hefty Five Nations role in the Susquehannock's demise.

After the British assaults of 1675, seeking aid from whomever they could, the Susquehannocks approached New York. The new governor, Edmund Andros, mediated with the Iroquois, and the remaining Susquehannocks, sacrificing their tribal identity, merged with the Iroquois and the Delawares after a conference in Shackamaxon (now Philadelphia) in 1677.

One band of Susquehannocks, the Conestogas, reemerged in 1692 to settle near some of its old lands. Although joined by other refugees, including Shawnees, it remained a distinct people until at least 1763. By then the Conestogas had a village bearing their name near Lancaster, Pennsylvania. Here Pennsylvania's frontier vigilantes, the Paxton Boys, attacked them on 14 December 1763. Surviving unarmed Conestogas fled to Lancaster for protection, but here too, the Paxton Boys killed them.

Gregory E. Dowd

References

George T. Hunt, *The Wars of the Iroquois: A Study in Intertribal Trade Relations* (1939); Francis Jennings, "Glory, Death, and Transfiguration: The Susquehannock Indians in the Seventeenth Century," *Proceedings of the American Philosophical Society* 112 (1968):15–53; Helen Hornbeck Tanner, ed., *Atlas of Great Lakes Indian History* (1986); Elizabeth Tooker, "The Demise of the Susquehannocks: A 17th Century Mystery," *Pennsylvania Archaeologist* 54 (1984):1–10; Paul A.W. Wallace, *Indians in Pennsylvania* (1961).

See also BACON'S REBELLION; FORT CHRISTINA (DELAWARE); IROQUOIS; IROQUOIS WARS; MARYLAND; MARYLAND, INDIAN FORTS IN; NEW SWEDEN; PAXTON BOYS; SWEDE

Sutler

Sutlers sold food and other items to provincial soldiers who were eager to make their camp life bearable. It was a necessary but difficult relationship. Soldiers depended on sutlers for fresh vegetables, meat, and rum in order to supplement their sparse, monotonous rations. A soldier's good health and perhaps his life hinged on what the sutlers had to sell, and at what price. As a result, soldiers often were preoccupied with food and money. For their part, sutlers sometimes were forced to bring suit against officers whose lifestyles outran their purses, an expensive and time-consuming affair for small businessmen.

Alan Rogers

See also CONTRACTOR, ARMY; SUPPLY

Fort Swanendael or Swanendael Massacre (Delaware; also known as Fort Zwaanendael, Fort Oplandt, Fort Hoarkill, Fort Whorekill)

The short-lived colony of Swanendael, established on the western shore of Delaware Bay near the present site of Lewes, Delaware, was founded by a syndicate of private Dutch investors as a base for commercial agricultural and whaling operations. This colony lay within the boundaries of the Dutch West India Company and was allowed under a provision designed to encourage the investment of private interests if they did not directly compete with those of the company.

A group of 28 Walloon men, supplied with the equipment and materials necessary to build a small fortification, comprised the initial settlement. A few reinforcements joined the colony from New Amsterdam several months later. The

expedition landed in the spring of 1631 and proceeded to construct a fort consisting of a blockhouse made of yellow bricks imported from the Netherlands and a cookhouse surrounded by a four-sided palisade measuring 17 by 20 feet. Rather than use the supplies from home, which included granite blocks, the fort was built only partially from stone, the palisade being made entirely of wood.

This settlement soon met with disaster. Some time in their first planting season, 33 of the 34 settlers were killed by the Great Siconese, a group of Lenni Lenape who spoke Southern Unami and lived in the vicinity of the settlement. The incident began with the Dutch custom of erecting the coat of arms of the Netherlands on a wooden post. A few days later, a local sachem took down the tin coat of arms intending to construct a pipe with the metal. When the leader of the colony, Gilles Honset, discovered what had happened, he demanded reparation from the local inhabitants. Fearing that a sacred object had been carelessly handled, the Indians quickly dispensed judgement by beheading the offender. Honset was uncomfortable with the severity of the punishment, but was pleased that the Indians had responded to his demands. He was unaware, however, that his duty, according to native justice, was to satisfy the bereaved friends and relatives of the one beheaded by offering a gift of wampum to remove their sorrow.

As a consequence of Honset's diplomatic neglect, the mourning clansmen soon paid a visit to the colony to avenge the death of their relative. One day, they came quietly to the Dutch settlement in small groups, a few gaining entrance to the fort under the pretense of desiring to trade furs. Once inside, they killed Honset with an axe and stabbed the only other occupant of the fort. The rest of the colonists, working in the fields, were similarly killed. One settler who was in the woods at the time escaped to New Amsterdam to tell of the massacre. In the meantime, the Indians raided the settlement's supplies, finding the rum and brandy. They proceeded to drink all of it, and during their festivities began a fire that burned half of the storehouse.

The site lay abandoned by Europeans until 6 December 1632, when it was visited by one of the shareholders of the Swanendael project, David De Vries. His expedition originally intended to reinforce the colony, but on receiving word of its destruction just before departure from the Netherlands, he decided to come to

Delaware Bay anyway in order to continue whaling operations and to investigate firsthand the site of the Swanendael disaster. When he arrived, he proceeded to meet with the local inhabitants, and rather than seek retribution, sought reconciliation through an Indian ceremony and treaty of friendship that was sealed by the exchange of gifts.

Although De Vries was impressed with the Delaware region and went to great lengths to keep the peace with the Indians in order to re-establish a colony there, his business partners did not share his enthusiasm. Soon after his return to the fatherland, they dissolved their agreement and abandoned Swanendael.

Paul Otto

References

Charles McKew Parr, *The Voyages of David De Vries* (1969); Robert B. Roberts, *Encyclopedia of Historic Forts: The Military, Pioneer, and Trading Posts of the United States* (1988); C.A. Weslager in collaboration with A.R. Dunlap, *Dutch Explorers, Traders, and Settlers in the Delaware Valley, 1609–1664* (1961).

Swede

The first Swedes to settle in America arrived in March 1630, under the auspices of the New Sweden Company; a company initially composed of both Dutch and Swedish investors. The company's main interests included the purchase of land on the west side of the Delaware River, construction of a fort, to establish trade with the natives, production of agriculture, and the establishment of a claim on land that had previously been explored and sporadically occupied by the Dutch and English.

The first expedition of the New Sweden Company was led by Peter Minuit, the former governor of New Netherland. Two Swedish vessels carried a crew of Swedish and Dutch sailors, provisions, trade goods, and 24 soldiers up the Delaware to its tributary, Minquas Kill. Minuit, with his experience in America through the Dutch West India Company, shrewdly purchased land from the Lenni-Lenape (Delaware) Indians. A deed of sale was signed by five Delaware sachems on 29 March 1638. It transferred to the New Sweden Company an area from Minquas Kill north to the Schuylkill River (about 27 miles) south to Duck Creek (or Bombay Hook, about 40 miles) and stretched west-

ward indefinitely. For the duration of the New Sweden colony, relations between the Swedes and the Delaware would remain friendly but, according to C.A. Weslager, not always "peaceful or harmonious."

Fort Christina was built near a rock ledge two miles up the Minquas Kill (Wilmington, Delaware). When news of the Swedish intrusion reached New Amsterdam, Governor Willem Kieft promptly sent a letter of protest to Minuit. Minuit dutifully ignored it. Thus began a series of disputes over land ownership and trading rights on the Delaware between the Dutch, Swedes, and English that lasted until the English conquest in 1664.

The New Sweden Company became a totally Swedish venture in 1641 when the Dutch investors bowed out, citing economic losses. A new governor, Peter Ridder, purchased additional land from the Delaware Indians. New Sweden's holdings stretched from the falls at Trenton to Cape Henlopen on the western shore, and on the east side from Raccoon Creek to Cape May. By October 1641, there were freemen, a few skilled workmen, a blacksmith, a tailor, a millwright, a minister, soldiers, horses, cows, sheep, and goats at Fort Christina.

Rivalry over the fur trade continued to cause a war of words on the Delaware. According to Governor Kieft, the Swedes had ruined Dutch trade with the Indians by undercutting prices. But the New Sweden colony blamed an English settlement at Varken's Kill (Salem Creek, New Jersey) for the loss of trade. Together, in 1641, the Swedes and Dutch formed an unlikely alliance to peacefully remove the English traders. The English farmers were allowed to remain, albeit under scrutiny.

Between 1643 and 1653, the governor of New Sweden was Johan Printz. A physically large man (said to have been nearly seven feet tall and weighing close to 400 pounds), Printz was a powerful force on the Delaware. On his arrival, he counted the adult male population of New Sweden to be 135. Printz brought his family, more colonists, another minister, and a group of "forest destroyer Finns." Three classes of colonists came to New Sweden; criminals who were sent unwillingly, peasants who came to cultivate the land, and civil officers and soldiers.

In regard to the Indians, Printz was instructed to purchase more land from the Delaware, Christianize them, and establish fur trade with the Minquas. While the Delaware Indians were mainly agrarian and fishing people, their rivals, the Minquas, were skilled hunters and trappers. The White and Black Minquas lived along and west of the Susquehanna River, and traveled on the Delaware River tributaries to trade their furs with the Swedes, Dutch, and English. The Minquas had often attacked Delaware villages before the Europeans arrived, and they exercised a kind of overlordship over them.

Printz's instructions in regard to the Dutch and English included peaceful domination of the trade on the Delaware. To this end he constructed two new strategic forts in 1643. Fort Elfsborg was built at Varken's Kill (New Jersey) and New Fort Gothenborg on Tinicum Island (Pennsylvania). And since he was the first magistrate having legislative, judicial, and executive power, he established the seat of government on Tinicum Island near Fort New Gothenborg and his estate.

Over the next few years, a colony was established midway between Fort Christina and Fort New Gothenburg called Upland (Chester, Pennsylvania), and one named Finland near Markus Hook. There, Swedish and Finnish farmers were encouraged to raise tobacco and corn, and to breed cattle. A small fort named New Korsholm (Philadelphia) was erected for Indian trade on the south side of the Schuylkill River opposite the Dutch Fort Beversrede. Some distance inland on the Schuylkill, Printz built a blockhouse named New Vasa (West Philadelphia), and one-quarter mile yet farther, another called Mölndal was the site of the first water-powered grist mill in Pennsylvania.

When Petrus (Peter) Stuyvesant replaced Governor Kieft at New Amsterdam in 1647, the controversies between the Dutch and Swedish intensified. Land was purchased and repurchased from the Delaware Indians by both groups. Stuyvesant built Fort Casimir (New Castle, Delaware) in 1651 downriver from Fort Christina to increase trade. Families from Holland settled near it, and the English settlers continued to move into the area from the north.

Meanwhile, due to misfortunes at sea and military campaigns of the homeland, New Sweden was left without reinforcements of colonists and supplies for many years. In 1652, the people of New Sweden were "abandoned wanderers, without a sovereign," according to Printz. His many requests for help from the crown went unanswered, and Printz left New Sweden on a Dutch vessel in November 1653.

But in January of that same year, a resupply expedition had left Göttenborg for New Sweden. Aboard the ship was the new governor, Johan Rising, additional colonists numbering 350, plus the long-awaited supplies. The new expedition was attacked by pirates, ran across foul weather, and suffered dysentery before arriving at Fort Elfsborg on May 18. They found it abandoned and in ruins. Rising committed a major blunder when he boldly sailed upriver, fired upon, demanded surrender, and took possession of the Dutch Fort Casimir. Since the attack took place on Trinity Sunday, 23 May, Rising aptly renamed it Fort Trinity. Farther upriver, at Fort Christina, they found the colonists in poor standing. The 300 new immigrants were the largest number to reach New Sweden at one time in its history, and they were warmly welcomed.

There was not an immediate Dutch retaliation to Rising's actions. However, when in September 1654, a Swedish vessel, the *Gyllene Hajen* (*Golden Shark*), mistakenly sailed up the Hudson River believing it to be the Delaware, New Amsterdam's Governor Stuyvesant avenged the capture of Fort Casimir. He seized the ship and confiscated the cargo. Governor Rising was notified, but replied he would not come to Manhattan to negotiate a settlement, nor would he return Fort Trinity.

After months of preparation, by August 1655, Governor Stuyvesant had gathered an army of several hundred men, a fleet of seven armed ships, and was ready to sail for the Delaware River. Not only would Fort Casimir be retaken, but the entire Delaware River would hence belong to the Dutch.

Though the Delaware warned Governor Rising of the pending attack, there was little the Swedes could do, as they were vastly outnumbered. On 10 September 1655, Fort Trinity once again became Fort Casimir. Next to be taken by the Dutch was Fort Christina. Both forts were captured without bloodshed. On 15 September, capitulation papers were signed by Governor Rising.

Governor Stuyvesant, fearing an Indian insurrection in defense of the Swedes, offered Rising the right to remain on the Delaware. Instead, Rising preferred to return to Sweden to lodge an official protest. In total, 37 people comprised of officers, soldiers, and colonists returned to Sweden with Rising in 1655. The colonists who remained took an oath of allegiance to the Dutch, but were allowed to continue to practice the Lutheran religion and for the most part, govern themselves.

No formal colonization attempts by Sweden were undertaken in America after this; however, Swedish settlers continued to immigrate to the Delaware Valley. Thereafter, they accepted whatever authority that had been established in the location of the settlement.

Linda M. Thorstad

References

Amandus Johnson, *The Swedish Settlements on the Delaware 1638–1664*, 2 vols. (1911); Peter Lindeström, *Geographia Americae*, trans. by Amandus Johnson (1925); Sally Schwartz, "Society and Culture in the Seventeenth-Century Delaware Valley," *Delaware History* 20 (1982):99–122; Carl Sprinchorn, "The History of the Colony of New Sweden," Parts I & II, *Pennsylvania Magazine of History and Biography* 7 (1883):395–419; 8 (1884):17–44, 129–159, 241–254; C.A. Weslager, "The Swede Meets the Red Man," *Bulletin of the Archaeological Society of Delaware* 8 (1957):1–12.

See also FORT CASIMIR (DELAWARE); FORT CHRISTINA (DELAWARE); DELAWARE; FORT ELFSBORG (NEW JERSEY); FINN; KIEFT, WILLEM; MINUIT, PETER; FORT NEW KORSHOLM (PENNSYLVANIA); NEW NETHERLAND; NEW SWEDEN; STUYVESANT, PETRUS

S

T

Tactics, Infantry

Tactics is the art of maneuvering troops to one's advantage in battle to defeat the enemy, i.e., the art of fighting battles. It consists of "the planning, training, and control of the ordered arrangements (formations) used by military organizations when engagement between opposing forces is imminent or underway." The word is derived from the Greek *taktos*, meaning ordered or arranged.

During the seventeenth and eighteenth centuries, infantry tactics were determined both by the weapons carried as well as the composition of the armed forces. As pikemen finally disappeared and the flintlock with its fixed bayonet replaced the older matchlock musket and the plug bayonet around 1700, new tactical formations and battlefield organizations were introduced. While matchlock formations featured ranks at least six deep, the more efficient flintlock allowed the number of ranks to be reduced to three. At the same time, the files closed up and a greater volume of fire could be delivered on a broader front. Concurrently, battalions were divided into 18 tactical subunits called platoons, while companies remained administrative units until 1728. The essential features of this battlefield organization remained intact until the mid-nineteenth century.

Eighteenth-century armies were aggregations of battalions, drawn up in several lines for battle. Throughout the century, British tactics were heavily influenced by continental European models, primarily the Prussian example. This meant that eight of the ten companies of a battalion (regiment and battalion being almost synonymous terms) would be formed three deep in battle, with the grenadier and light infantry companies detached into separate battalions for use as shock troops; the grenadiers on the right and the light infantry on the left. Called linear tactics, the three lines of soldiers made up the line of battle. Success in battle depended on the speed and compact movement of the rigid close-order lines. The movement of a line or a portion of a line of battle around a common pivotal point was called a wheeling movement and formed the standard evolution of the seventeenth and eighteenth centuries. Thus the most important part of training consisted of close-order drill and the handling of arms. The need for strict discipline was contingent on the make-up of the armies, i.e., men supposedly inclined to desertion, as well as by the need for machine-like execution of movement by large numbers of soldiers facing each other at point-blank range. The flintlock musket still remained a highly inaccurate weapon, and the basic concept of infantry assault was based on the movement of a mass of men toward the objective and the delivery of one or more volleys at the last possible moment and the shortest possible range. Volley of fire was more important than accuracy, and victory in battle was determined by the final charge with the bayonet. The concept of aimed fire did not enter British tactics until mid-century under the impact of the colonial wars.

In the American colonies, such tactics proved disastrous, and important, if only temporary, changes in British tactics resulted from the experiences of the French and Indian Wars, where General Edward Braddock's defeat at the Monongahela River in 1755 led to the raising of the 60th Royal Americans under Colonel Henry Bouquet, and Thomas Gage's regiment of light infantry in 1758. The aim of reformers like Bouquet and Gage was a self-reliant, independent, and individual fighter who was a good marksman. This complete departure from conventional wisdom, which had resulted in the creation of the 90th regiment as a light infantry unit in 1759, and culminated in Lord Jeffrey Amherst's battle drill and organization in 1760, did not survive the peace of 1763. The light infantry companies of 1770 were such only in name, as Prussian tactics became the standard of the British army again.

Robert A. Selig

References

John I. Alger, *Definitions and Doctrine of the Military Art* (1985); John A. Houlding, *Fit for Service: the Training of the British Army, 1715–1795* (1981); H.C.B. Rogers, *The British Army of the Eighteenth Century* (1977).

See also BOUQUET, HENRY; GRENADIER; LIGHT INFANTRY; STRATEGY; WEAPONS, FIREARMS

Tanaghrisson
See HALF-KING

Teedyuscung (c. 1700–1763)

Born not far from Trenton, New Jersey, in about 1700, Teedyuscung grew up on the edge of British settlements. Around 1730, he crossed the Delaware River and settled near the northern limits of the Delaware Indian communities that embraced the "forks of the Delaware," the confluence of the Lehigh and the Delaware. Witness to both the Walking Purchase fraud of 1737 and the subsequent migration west of most Forks Delawares in 1742, Teedyuscung remained near the Delaware River, and in 1749 or 1750 he joined the Moravian Christian mission at Gnadenhütten. In 1750, he and his wife were baptized "Gideon" and "Elizabeth." By 1754, however, his new faith had waned, and he led a faction away to settle his town of Wyoming on the Susquehanna River.

Teedyuscung broke briefly with the British during the Seven Years' War. In December 1755, Teedyuscung formed a war party and raided British settlements on the upper Delaware River, north of the Kittatinny Mountains. Already highly regarded as a speaker, he now gained status as a warrior. From this basis, Teedyuscung built his reputation among the British as a "King of the Delawares," a sovereignty he may have expanded to include ten nations, although the records claiming this may have been designed to discredit him. In actuality, he had become a headman of the Susquehanna River Delawares, who now withdrew upriver to Tioga. But even on the Susquehanna, his power was limited; no warrior or village was obliged to obey him.

By the following spring, many of the Susquehanna Delawares inclined toward peace. Teedyuscung traveled to the French Fort Niagara for aid, but found the garrison impoverished. Nutimus, who had not broken with Britain, secured a peace with Britain's William Johnson at the Iroquois Onondaga Council in June 1756, and it appears that he willingly began to yield authority to the increasingly likeminded Teedyuscung. Teedyuscung, moving rapidly, sounded Pennsylvania at a council at Easton in July 1756. In November, Teedyuscung met again with Pennsylvania at Easton. Although his purpose was to make peace, Teedyuscung, apparently with the support of Pennsylvania's Quaker party and prompted by an ill-considered question from Governor William Denny, went beyond his prepared speeches to denounce the Walking Purchase of 1737 as a leading cause of Delaware disaffection. The denunciation got him into trouble with both the Six Nations and Pennsylvania's Proprietary party. No formal peace was secured at Easton, but most of the parties departed with expressions of peaceful intent.

In 1757, however, Teedyuscung again prevaricated, and sought French supplies at Niagara. He again found the garrison poor, and after convincing France of his friendship, he returned to treat with the British at the Easton Conference of 1757. Here he and his followers, who spoke neither for all of the Susquehanna Delawares nor for any of the upper Ohio Delawares, made peace with the British. In March 1758, he escorted emissaries from the Ohio region to Philadelphia, where peaceful expression produced little result. At the great, and perhaps greatly overrated, Easton Conference in the summer of 1758, Teedyuscung spent more time discussing the Walking Purchase claim than he did discussing peace, but he gained little thereby. His Susquehanna Delawares did confirm the peace with Britain, but they could still not control all their people, and, more importantly, their Ohio kinsmen were inadequately represented.

The limits of Teedyuscung's power, already apparent to Pennsylvania, became more clear in 1760, when he could not persuade even Delawares and Iroquois on the upper Susquehanna to allow a Pennsylvania peace delegation to pass through their towns on a journey to British Fort Pitt. Taking up the mission himself, Teedyuscung arrived at Pitt in time to attend the treaty, but so vacant was his authority that he was not asked to speak.

Teedyuscung spent his last years defending Wyoming town against Connecticut settlers claiming the land under both Connecticut's charter and a highly dubious Susquehanna Company purchase from Six Nations delegates. Backed by the Six Nations and Pennsylvania, Teedyuscung hoped to win this fight. He and his people several times ordered out the Yankees, including an armed force of 119 men in 1762. But on 19 April 1763, an unknown party murdered Teedyuscung, burning him to death in his cabin and setting fire to his entire village. Although the Six Nations have long been charged with the murder, it would seem to have been against their interests, since by defending Wyoming, Teedyuscung was also defending a Six Nations claim. Anthony F.C. Wallace has argued that the Susquehanna Company had better motives for his death. The circumstances point that way. Two weeks after Teedyuscung's murder, Connecticut people occupied his vacant town. Six months later, these Wyoming Yankees reeled under Indian assaults, led by Teedyuscung's son, in "Pontiac's War."

Gregory E. Dowd

References
Francis Jennings, *Empire of Fortune: Crowns, Colonies, and Tribes in the Seven Years War in America* (1978); Anthony F.C. Wallace, *King of the Delawares: Teedyuscung, 1700–1763* (1949).

See also DELAWARE; EASTON CONFERENCE; FORT NIAGARA (NEW YORK); NUTIMUS; PENNSYLVANIA; PONTIAC'S WAR; WALKING PURCHASE

Tequesta (Tekesta)
The Tequesta were an indigenous group who inhabited the southeastern coastal marshes of the Florida peninsula around Biscayne Bay at the time of contact with the Spanish. It has not been established with certainty whether the tribe was related to Muskogean-speaking people of the North American continent, or to the Taino (Arawak) of Cuba and the Antilles. The Tequesta were a semi-sedentary tribe, who lived in wattle-and-daub huts in seasonally established villages, and subsisted by hunting and gathering marine resources and native flora.

Like their Calusa neighbors, the Tequesta's first contact with Europeans came in the early sixteenth century. Spanish adventurers on slaving and trading raids visited the area, although the first official contact is credited to Juan Ponce de Leon in 1513. Relations between the Tequesta and Europeans usually were hostile, and the tribe was particularly feared by sailors for their cruel treatment of captives.

In 1567, Pedro Menéndez de Avilés established a fort and a mission outpost in Tequesta territory, and lay brother Francisco Villareal arrived to begin conversion of the native people. Less than a year later, the Tequesta rose in revolt. The survivors were taken to San Antonio de Carlos to serve among the Calusa, and the Spanish abandoned their settlement attempts in the area. As late as 1673, the bishop of Santiago de Cuba, Gabriel Díaz Vara Calderón, identified 13 Tequesta villages, but added that no successful Spanish mission or fort existed in the southern peninsula. A Jesuit mission was attempted in the area in 1743, but met the same fate as previous missionizing efforts.

Like other Florida tribes, the Tequesta suffered from the effects of European diseases, internecine warfare, and from population pressure related to emigration of northern tribes. Most likely the few Tequesta who survived into the eighteenth century were absorbed into groups identified as "Coast" Indians, and were resettled into villages near St. Augustine during the border wars with the British and their Indian allies. A conglomeration of surviving Tequesta, Calusa, Ais, and Jeaga was probably removed to Cuba in 1763, when Florida was ceded to Great Britain.

Sherry Johnson

References
John M. Goggin, "The Tekesta Indians of Southern Florida," *Florida Historical Quarterly* 18 (1940):274–284; John H. Hann, ed. and trans., *Missions to the Calusa* (1991); Eugene Lyon, *The Enterprise of Florida: Pedro Menéndez de Avilés and the Spanish Conquest of 1565–1568* (1976); John R. Swanton, *The Indians of the Southeastern United States. Smithsonian Institution Bureau of American Ethnology Bulletin* 137 (1946); David Hurst Thomas, ed., *Spanish Borderlands Sourcebooks* (1991).

See also CALUSA; FLORIDA; MENÉNDEZ DE AVILÉS, PEDRO; ST. AUGUSTINE; SPANISH MISSION SYSTEM—SOUTHEAST

Texas

Hispanic Texas, a province known to the Spanish as Tejas or the New Kingdom of the Philippines, lay north of the Medina River and east of its headwaters; it extended northward to the Red River and eastward into present-day Louisiana. The shores of the future Lone Star state were first viewed by a Spanish sea expedition in 1519, but permanent occupation of the province did not take place until 1716. Direct Spanish presence and influence lasted until 19 July 1821, when the flag of Castile and León was lowered for the last time at San Antonio.

During the 105 years of permanent occupation, the Spanish presence in Texas centered around missions, civil settlements, and presidios (military garrisons). From first to last, the province contained only eight presidios, with no more than five in operation at any one time. The eight presidios were: Nuestra Señora de los Dolores (1716–1719) in east Texas; San Antonio de Béxar (1718–1821) at San Antonio; Presidio de los Tejas (1721–1728) in east Texas; Nuestra Señora del Pilar de los Adaes (1721–1772) near present-day Robeline, Louisiana; Nuestra Señora de Loreto (1722–1821 at three sites), originally near Matagorda Bay; San Francisco Xavier (1751–1757 at two sites), originally near present-day Rockdale, Texas; San Agustín de Ahumada (1756–1771) near present-day Anahuac, Texas; San Luis de las Amarillas (1757–1770) near present-day Menard, Texas.

Spain maintained a military presence in Texas for two primary reasons. It wished to counter foreign influence—French to 1762 and American after 1803—and the actions of potentially hostile Indian groups. The latter were not important over the last 40 years of Spanish Texas, and are not considered herein.

In 1685, René-Robert Cavelier, sieur de La Salle, founded Fort St. Louis on the banks of the Garcitas Creek, a small stream flowing into Matagorda Bay. By the late 1680s, Spain had dispatched six land and five sea expeditions in search of La Salle's elusive colony. Success came in 1689 when Alonso de León discovered the remains of the failed French venture. By then, La Salle, a victim of assassination, had been dead for two years. The French threat appeared to have been almost chimerical, and the Spanish abandoned Texas in 1693.

In 1719, three years after the permanent occupation of Texas, a brief conflict in Europe, known there as the War of the Triple Alliance, spilled over into Texas. From the French outpost at Natchitoches, Phillipe Blondel and six soldiers easily captured the poorly defended Los Adaes mission, situated near present-day Robeline, Louisiana. This confrontation, known derisively in Texas history as the "Chicken War," resulted in the complete abandonment of east Texas for approximately two years. The Spanish reoccupied east Texas in the early 1720s and maintained a military presence there until 1772, when the capital and civilian population were relocated to San Antonio.

Spanish settlers reoccupied east Texas within a few years and founded the town of Nacogdoches in 1779, but a military garrison was not assigned to the town until the 1790s. Troops stationed there helped guard the frontier against filibustering expeditions into Texas. Subsequently, Spanish forces assembled in Mexico scored a decisive victory over foreign interlopers and Spanish expatriates at the Battle of the Medina River in August 1813.

The end of the Spanish period in Texas was not related to any significant military action within the confines of the present state. Texas's incorporation into the new Mexican nation, which lasted until 1836, resulted from events that transpired within the heartland of Mexico and Spain itself.

Donald E. Chipman

References

John F. Bannon, *The Spanish Borderlands Frontier, 1513–1821* (1970); Donald E. Chipman, *Spanish Texas, 1519–1821* (1992); Odie B. Faulk, *The Last Years of Spanish Texas, 1778–1821* (1964); Max L. Moorhead, *The Presidio: Bastion of the Borderlands* (1975); Robert S. Weddle, *San Juan Bautista: Gateway to Spanish Texas* (1968).

See also AGUAYO EXPEDITION; NORTEÑOS; PRESIDIO NUESTRA SEÑORA DE LOS DELORES DE LOS TEJAS (TEXAS); PRESIDIO NUESTRA SEÑORA DEL PILAR DE LOS ADAES (LOUISIANA); ST. DENIS, LOUIS JUCHEREAU DE; PRESIDIO SAN AGUSTÍN DE AHUMADA (TEXAS); SAN ANTONIO; PRESIDIO SAN FRANCISCO XAVIER (TEXAS); SPANISH MISSION SYSTEM–SOUTHWEST

Fort Ticonderoga (New York)

French Governor Pierre de Rigaud, marquis de Vaudreuil, gave orders in September 1755 to construct a fort to prevent an attack by the British and their American allies on the southern frontier of Canada. The site of the fort, to be raised under the direction of French military engineer Michel Chartier de Lotbinière, was, along with the mouth of the St. Lawrence River, New France's most vulnerable flank. In upper New York state, Lake George empties into Lake Champlain to the north. From Lake Champlain, the Richelieu River flows directly into the St. Lawrence between Montreal and Quebec—the tender heart of New France itself. Clearly, anyone—French or English—who held that vital spot where Lakes George and Champlain met virtually controlled a water highway straight into the French colony. This Vaudreuil, as governor of New France, knew all too well.

Thus it was that in the fall of 1755 that Lotbinière, who had never built a fort before, commenced the raising of one of the most important fortresses in American history. When he started his assignment on the rugged peninsula that juts out between the two lakes, he found that he was "obliged to operate in the midst of a wood without being able to see, while surveying, more than thirty yards ahead of me." Nevertheless, schooled in the great tradition of the marquis de Vauban, father of modern French military engineering, Lotbinière pursued his project with determination. Assisting him in his endeavor were the regular French regiments of La Reine (the Queen's), distinguished by the royal crowns on its flag, and of Languedoc, first raised in 1672, the year of Louis XIV's Dutch war. Helping these soldiers in their labors were civilian workers, perhaps members actually of the French Independent Company of Marines, or of the Quebec militia.

In spite of the obstacles nature put before him, Lotbinière's work progressed. By February 1756, there were already 12 cannon placed, with eight more ready to be mounted; to these French the fort was known as Carillon, from the tingling sound of the waterfall nearby. (In French, *carillon* means "bells" or "chimes.") By mid-July, some 30 artillery pieces were in their positions, the four bastions already standing, and work was progressing on the walls connecting these four corner bastions. An additional two separate bastions, or *demi-lunes*, would also be added to the fort, attached to the outer face of the walls.

It was well that Lotbinière was moving ahead with his duty, for in the summer of 1756, Louis-Joseph, marquis de Montcalm, new commander of the French forces in North America after the Baron Jean-Armand de Dieskau's defeat at Lake George in 1755, visited the fort. Montcalm wanted to get the job done more quickly, for he intended to make the rising fortification militarily useful as soon as possible. As he had taken the fight to the enemy by seizing the British Fort Oswego on Lake Ontario in 1756, the French commander, whose southern French blood made him an aggressive commander, decided in 1757 to use Carillon to attack the British at Fort William Henry, whose wooden walls had been begun by Sir William Johnson after he crushed Dieskau at the Battle of Lake George in September 1755.

The campaign of 1757 opened inauspiciously enough for the French. In March, Vaudreuil's brother, François-Pierre de Rigaud, attempted an abortive assault on the stout Fort William Henry that only served to diminish the prestige of the stone-walled French post at Carillon. It was up to Montcalm to redeem French honor. Using Fort Carillon as a jumping-off point for his offense, Montcalm mustered a force from the regular regiments of La Reine, La Sarre, Languedoc, Béarn, Guyenne, and the Royal Roussillon, soldiers from the Independent Company of Marines, and Quebeçois militia. Going along with the French were Indian auxiliary forces, who were about to perpetuate one of the greatest massacres in the blood-soaked saga of war on the frontier. On 1 August 1757, the invasion force left Carillon, no longer a guardian to protect the French but now a gate through which to carry the war to the enemy!

Six thousand Canadians and French advanced, with an estimated 1,600 Indians, "a great assembly of savages," as the Jesuit missionary Pierre Roubaud, who was there, described them. From 4 August to 8 August, Montcalm besieged Fort William Henry. Finally, Lieutenant-Colonel George Monro, commander at Fort William Henry, despaired of help from the British at Fort Edward, not far away, and surrendered. Although promised a safe-conduct by Montcalm, the Indians fell on the British in a massacre immortalized by James Fennimore Cooper in his *The Last of the Mohicans*, and killed or took prisoner some 80 of the unsuspecting British. It was only the personal intervention of Montcalm, who ran in among the Indians crying, "kill me, but spare the English who are under my protection," who brought the killing to an end, helped by a flying squad of French grenadiers and officers, including François-Charles de Bourlamaque and François-Gaston de Lévis.

It was now obvious to the English that, with the destruction of Fort William Henry, the fort of Carillon could not remain in French hands. Not only did it block any successful thrust up the Lake Champlain waterway to Canada, it also, under the inspired leadership of a Montcalm, provided an opening to launch attacks at will against the colony of New York, especially with the Hudson River only a short trip overland from Lake George. If the French reached the Hudson, the British colonies could be cut in two. Therefore, in faraway London, Prime Minister William Pitt the Elder decreed the destruction of Fort Carillon to be a primary strategic objective for the coming year of 1758. Tragically, the commander, General James Abercromby, owed his command not to military talent but to political influence. Commented James Wolfe, the conqueror of Quebec, Abercromby was "a heavy man;" "an aged gentleman, infirm in body and mind," wrote William Parkman of Massachusetts.

On 8 July 1758, this "aged gentleman" presided over one of the worst British catastrophes before Singapore in World War II. Montcalm had planned his defenses with the eye of an accomplished military engineer, like Robert E. Lee at Petersburg in the Civil War. Well in advance of the fort, Montcalm placed his men along a wooden obstacle wall, in front of which was an abatis, a man-defying defense of sharpened stakes. Although Abercromby possessed sufficient artillery to demolish these wooden defensive works, he chose to assault them at the point of the bayonet. Some seven times, his brave men charged the French, only to be thrown back with chaotic losses. Before this callous commander called off the attacks, some 1,900 out of his 15,000-man army were killed, wounded, or missing. Of Montcalm's 3,600 defenders, some 377 were listed as casualties. As Louis-Antoine de Bougainville, who served as Montcalm's chief of staff wrote, "at seven o'clock the enemy thought only of retreat, covered by the fire of the light troops [rangers], which was kept up until dark."

Yet, even with Montcalm's impressive triumph over Abercromby, ironically, Fort Carillon's moment of triumph marked the end of its military significance. While the British were frustrated at Ticonderoga—as they called Carillon—Lord Jeffrey Amherst had gained the vital gateway to the St. Lawrence, fortress Louisbourg. In 1759, Quebec itself was besieged by Wolfe, who had valiantly fought under Amherst the year before. When the British under Amherst again moved against Carillon by July 1759, the French commander, the chevalier de Bourlamaque, rather than have the now strategically irrelevant fort in the hands of the enemy, blew up Fort Carillon instead. Amherst entered the shattered hulk of the fort on 27 July 1759, a year to the day after he had accepted the capitulation of Louisbourg.

John F. Murphy, Jr.

References

Louis-Antoine de Bougainville, *Adventure in the Wilderness: The American Journals of Louis-Antoine de Bougainville, 1756–1760*, ed. and trans. by Edward P. Hamilton (1964); Lawrence H. Gipson, *The Great War for the Empire: The Victorious Years, 1758–1760* (1949); Edward P. Hamilton, *Fort Ticonderoga: Key to a Continent* (1964); Bruce Lancaster, *Ticonderoga: The Story of a Fort* (1959); Douglas E. Leach, *Arms for Empire: A Military History of the British Colonies in North America, 1607–1763* (1973); Francis Parkman, *Montcalm and Wolfe* (1962); Francis Russell, *The French and Indian Wars* (1962).

See also ABATIS; ABERCROMBY, JAMES; BOUGAINVILLE, LOUIS-ANTOINE DE, COMTE DE; BOURLAMAQUE, FRANÇOIS-CHARLES DE; CROWN POINT; OSWEGO, BATTLE OF; PITT, WILLIAM; RIGAUD DE VAUDREUIL DE CAVAGNIAL, PIERRE DE; TICONDEROGA, BATTLE OF; FORT WILLIAM HENRY (NEW YORK); WOLFE, JAMES

Ticonderoga, Battle of (1758)

On 8 July 1758, the sun shone on one of the largest battles fought in American history until the First Battle of Bull Run in the beginning months of the Civil War. Built by the French under military engineer Michel Chartier de Lotbinière in 1755, the fort, known then by its Gallic incarnation of Carillon, had virtually controlled the crucially strategic water highway of Lake George and Lake Champlain, which formed the heart of the riverine passage from the Hudson River in the colony of New York up to the St. Lawrence River in the heart of New France. As such, whoever controlled Carillon stood in an excellent position, whether he spoke English or French, of striking deep into the core of enemy territory. Just the previous summer of

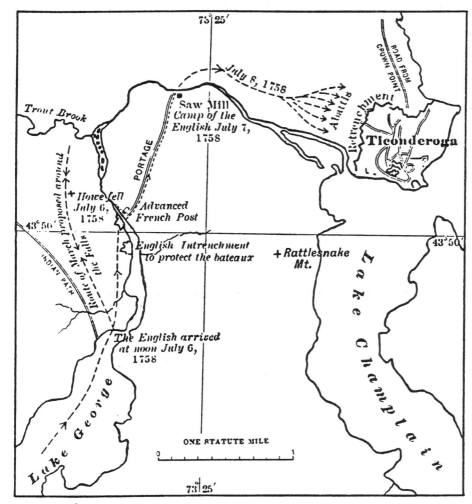

Fort Ticonderoga.

1757, Louis-Joseph, the marquis de Montcalm, commander in chief of French forces, had used Fort Carillon as his base for the utter destruction of Fort William Henry, one of the most important British strongholds on the Anglo-French border.

Now, in the summer of 1758, acting under the strategic guidance of William Pitt the Elder, Fort Carillon stood marked for destruction by what was probably the largest army Great Britain had yet put into the field against the French. Confronting the fortress was a British juggernaut composed of some 6,300 British regulars, including the renowned Black Watch, the 42nd Highlanders, supported by about 9,000 colonial soldiers, of whom the New Jersey Blues were numbered among the best. Included in the British army were specialist troops, whose cre-

ation marked the introduction of guerilla warfare—albeit reluctantly—into "official" British military thinking. With the traditionally armed and accoutered "redcoats" were the light infantry of George Augustus, Lord Howe, and Lieutenant Colonel Thomas Gage, allied to the New England rangers of Robert Rogers. The "light infantry" and Rogers' Rangers, their uniforms and equipment stripped down to the barest essentials, were intended to neutralize the fast-striking Indians and Canadian militia fighting with the French.

Unfortunately, the commander of the British army, General James Abercromby, was not the equal of his men. A political hack who owed his supreme command to political ties in London, Abercromby was held in virtually complete disrespect by the men serving under him.

The heart of the army—and its confidence—reposed in Abercromby's second-in-command, Lord Howe, whom Pitt hoped to have in operational command once the offensive against Fort Carillon actually got under way. Of Howe, Pitt had written, he was "a character of ancient times; a complete model of military virtue." Howe would need all these qualities and more, for facing the British at Carillon was Montcalm himself, the most talented French commander of the war, who had destroyed the British bastion of Fort Oswego on the Great Lakes the year before he had demolished Fort William Henry.

Under Montcalm's orders at Carillon were the cream of the French forces in New France. According to the journal of Louis-Antoine de Bougainville, Montcalm's aide, Carillon's defenders were composed of the French regulars of the Béarn, Berry, La Reine, Guyenne, La Sarre, Languedoc, and Royal Roussillon regiments, aided by Canadians and Indians. Primary among the Canadian contingent were the Independent Companies of Marines, who could trace their lineage back to the era of Cardinal Richelieu. Now, the marines were considered as the regular army of the French colony. In Bougainville's estimate, they numbered about 525 men.

On the morning of 5 July, the British invasion army swept north up Lake George toward its objective, Fort Carillon, arrayed in three majestic waterborne columns. Yet, almost as soon as the British started out, devastating tragedy struck at them. On 6 July, the advance guard under Howe was surprised by 130 French, Canadian, and Indian volunteers led by guerrilla leader Ensign Jean-Baptiste Levrault de Langis Montegron at Trout Brook, on the way to the fort. Rogers, who was some distance to Howe's front, had violated one of his own cardinal rules of operations, "no matter whether we travel in big parties or little ones," there had to be many scouts, "so the main body can't be surprised and wiped out." As a result of Rogers letting the French get between him and "the main body," Howe was killed in the ensuing skirmish.

With the death of Howe, the heart went out of the British and Americans. The psychological blow was only equalled by the fact that now Abercromby was in full charge of the offensive.

Two days later, Abercromby sent the disheartened British and allied forces against the French and Montcalm. Forming as if on parade, the soldiers marched against the log wall, topped with sand bags, that Carillon's defenders had built across the peninsula jutting into Lake Champlain. Although Abercromby had enough artillery to blow the wooden rampart into matchsticks, he let his men march on murderously unsupported by cannonfire.

Against the oncoming enemy, Montcalm opened fire with every musket of the troops behind the French defenses and as many of the cannon of Fort Carillon as could be brought to fire on the attackers. As Bougainville recorded, "half an hour after noon the English army advanced on us," driving back some forward French elements into the protection of the formidable French lines. Four British columns resolutely pushed against the French lines, while "their light troops and better marksmen, who, protected by the trees, delivered a" lethal fire on the defenders.

At the start of the engagement, Abercromby tried to outflank the French by an amphibious surprise attack, but when it was discovered, they were "received in fine style" by French soldiers "and, the cannon of the fort having smashed two of these barges, they withdrew and did not appear again during the action." It was the general's only tactical initiative of the entire day, and still the cannon remained, unlimbered and unfired, behind the British attackers.

"The different attacks, almost all afternoon and almost everywhere," Bougainville wrote "were made with the greatest of vigor." Around five o'clock the moment of crisis came. Two British columns stormed the position on the French right held by the regiments of Guyenne, Béarn, and La Reine. Here Highlanders hacked at the abatis (the felled and pointed trees) with their broadswords in a blood frenzy to get at the enemy. "Even those who were mortally wounded," Lieutenant William Grant later wrote, "cried to their companions not to lose a thought upon them, but to follow their officers and mind the honor of their country." In this, the high water mark of the battle, just like in Pickett's charge at Gettysburg, Captain John Campbell and a handful of Scotsmen succeeded in climbing the breastwork, but were bayonetted by the French. Montcalm himself led a flying squad of reserves to stem the British tide.

Toward six, the maddened attackers tried to break through at the French center, then the left. All attempts were bloodily repulsed. Bougainville wrote, "at seven o'clock the enemy thought only of retreat, covered by the fire of the light troops, which was kept up until dark." In Francis Parkman's sad eulogy, "as twilight came on, the last combatant withdrew, and none were left but the dead."

By General Abercromby's incompetence, 1,944 British and Americans were casualties. (Colonel William Johnson and some 450 Indians had arrived early in the day but took no real part in the action.) For the French, the "butcher's bill" included 377 killed and wounded. It was a small wonder that Montcalm and his men regarded the victory of 8 July as miraculous. Bougainville received a slight wound in the battle he chronicled so dramatically.

John F. Murphy, Jr.

References

Louis-Antoine de Bougainville, *Adventures in the Wilderness: The American Journals of Louis-Antoine de Bougainville, 1756–1760*, ed. and trans. by Edward P. Hamilton (1964); Edward P. Hamilton, *Fort Ticonderoga: Key to a Continent* (1964); ———, *The French and Indian Wars: The Story of Battles and Forts in the Wilderness* (1962); Journals of the Fort Ticonderoga Museum, Ticonderoga, New York; Douglas Edward Leach, *Arms for Empire: A Military History of the British Colonies in North America, 1607–1763* (1973); Francis Parkman, *Montcalm and Wolfe* (1962); François Sully, *Age of the Guerrilla: The New Warfare* (1968).

See also ABERCROMBY, JAMES; BOURLAMAQUE, FRANÇOIS-CHARLES DE; LIGHT INFANTRY; MONTCALM-GAZON DE SAINT VERAIN, LOUIS-JOSEPH; PITT, WILLIAM; ROGERS, ROBERT; FORT TICONDEROGA (NEW YORK)

Timucuan Revolt (1656)

For eight months in 1656, revolt swept western Timucua, leaving most of the settlements of Potano and Utina provinces prostrate. Among revolts of Spanish Florida, this one is unique in that the friars were not one of its targets. The revolt was directed only at the governor and his agents, the soldiers. The governor instead was to accuse certain of the friars of complicity in the revolt.

The revolt's immediate cause was Governor Diego de Rebolledo's summons of many of the natives from the interior provinces to the defense of St. Augustine from a perceived threat

of Oliver Cromwell's England. The governor's orders injudiciously ignored social distinctions that separated the native ruling class from ordinary Indians. Because of a shortage of food at St. Augustine, Rebolledo ordered all the Indians to come to St. Augustine bearing 75 pounds of maize on their backs. The chief of Santa Cruz de Tarihica, in the province of Utina, objected to sending his leading men loaded down in that fashion while there were ordinary Indians available for such chores. When Tarihica's chief informed the other Timucuan leaders of his stand, all agreed not to send any leading men to St. Augustine so burdened. When the governor repeated the order unchanged, the former head chief among those inland Timucua, the chief of San Martin de Ayaocuto, whose village was located at Itchetucknee Springs, assumed leadership of the defiance of the governor. To express that defiance, he had the soldier who brought the orders and six other soldiers killed. At that point, a friar journeyed from St. Augustine to meet with the revolt's leader at Santa Helena de Machaba in the province of Yustaga to try to persuade him to end the rebellion and come to terms with the governor to forestall greater evils that would result from continuation of the revolt. San Martin's chief refused to bow to the governor's demand, insisting that he and his people were not throwing off their allegiance to the king or to the law of God.

At least nine of the western Timucua mission settlements, representing all three provinces, participated actively in the revolt, and possibly more, as the governor put 11 chiefs to death in crushing the revolt. The chiefs of Santa Fe and San Francisco in Potano, the chiefs of Machaba, Potohiriba, and San Mateo in Yustaga, and the chiefs of Tarihica, San Francisco de Chuaquin, and San Juan de Guacara followed San Martin's chief in revolt. Although the Yustaga invited the Apalachee to join, and although there was strong sentiment in Apalachee for revolt, Apalachee did not participate at all.

Little is known about the specifics of the crushing of the revolt. The governor's initial efforts met no success. Many, if not all, the friars remained at their posts. Although they were not in any physical danger, the friars found themselves reviled by a majority of the Indians, short of food, and often forsaken and alone in their friaries as the natives devoted themselves entirely to their dances and preparations for war. To crush the revolt, the governor dispatched Sergeant Major Adrian de Canizares y

Osorio with 60 soldiers. Slowly he gathered intelligence that enabled him to defeat or capture the 11 rebel leaders who were executed. Available records provide no information on his encounters with the rebels or how those executed were captured. San Martin and San Juan de Guacara were left completely depopulated, and Santa Fe and San Francisco Potano left prostrate. While San Juan de Guacara, Santa Fe, and San Francisco were revivified, the governor's attempt to resurrect San Martin by coercing Chamile's people to move to the site of San Martin in 1657 proved unsuccessful, and neither Chamile nor San Martin and Chamile's two satellites, Cachipile and Chuaquin, were ever heard of again.

Among the rebels, the Tarihica and Yustaga settlements appear to have fared the best, surviving long after the revolt. Many Yustaga apparently sought refuge in Apalachee during the crushing of the revolt. Yustagans were employed to resurrect Guacara and to revivify the two Potano settlements as well.

The revolt proved disastrous for the governor who had caused it. Despite the governor's efforts to shift blame for the revolt to the friars, the crown was so alarmed by reports of the disruption and destruction caused by the governor's actions that it ordered his immediate removal and arrest in mid-1657. Rebolledo died in detention not long thereafter before going to trial.

John H. Hann

References
John H. Hann, "Demographic Patterns and Change in Mid-Seventeenth Century Timucua and Apalachee," *Florida Historical Quarterly* 64 (1986):371–392; ———, "Translation of the Florida Friars Response to the Rebolledo Visitation," *Florida Archaeology* (not yet published); Fred Lamar Pearson, Jr., "Timucuan Rebellion of 1656: The Rebolledo Investigation and the Civil-Religious Controversy," *Florida Historical Quarterly* 59 (1983):260–280.

See also APALACHEE; FLORIDA; ST. AUGUSTINE; SPANISH MISSION SYSTEM–SOUTHEAST

Tolomato Presidio (Georgia)

Tolomato was the site of a fort and a Franciscan mission to the Guale Indians located on the southeastern coast of Georgia. In 1597, Tolomato became the center of an indigenous uprising when Franciscan friars sought to deprive a Guale warrior of his right to succession to the chieftainship because of his polygamous practices. During the revolt. Tolomato and a half-dozen missions/military outposts were destroyed.

Sherry Johnson

References
Michael V. Gannon, *The Cross in the Sand: The Early Catholic Church in Florida, 1513–1870*, 2d. ed. (1983)

See also GUALE

Fort Tombecbé (Alabama)

In preparation for a campaign against the Chickasaws, a supply depot was established on a high bluff overlooking the Tombigbee River early in 1736. On the arrival of Governor Jean-Baptiste Le Moyne de Bienville and his French and Choctaw army in April, construction began on a permanent fort built in an angle of land formed by the confluence of the river and a small creek, with two palisaded curtain walls and three bastions protecting the land approach. Inside were numerous half-timber structures: a guardhouse, officers' quarters, prison, powder magazine, barracks, bakehouse, and storehouse. The fort was garrisoned by 40 to 50 men.

Resupply of the fort proved difficult, since all munitions and trade goods arrived in boats laboriously rowed 200 miles upstream from Mobile during the winter.

Fort Tombecbé had been strategically placed near the eastern villages of the Choctaws, astride two paths used by British traders visiting that tribe. After 1736, the garrison effectively closed that market to the British, except during the Choctaw civil war from 1746 to 1750. A faction of the Choctaws, mainly from their western villages, attempted to break the French trading monopoly, an effort that was finally defeated when Commandant Joseph Louis Boucher de Grand Pré led a detachment from Fort Tombecbé and burned five western Choctaw forts. Apart from this interruption, the commandants at Fort Tombecbé personally controlled most of the Choctaw trade by issuing permits to selected French traders, and by directly dispensing liquor and merchandise to Indians at the fort in exchange for deerskins.

The fort was extensively rebuilt in 1760. English troops took possession on 22 November 1763, and renamed it Fort York. They withdrew a year later, but reoccupied the fort from 1766 to 1768. From 1794 to 1797, a Spanish earthworks named Fort Confederation, also established to provide trade goods to the Choctaws, was located on the same spot.

Gregory A. Waselkov

References

Patricia K. Galloway, "Choctaw Factionalism and Civil War, 1746–1750," in *The Choctaw Before Removal*, ed. by Carolyn K. Reeves (1985): 120–156; James W. Parker, "Archaeological Test Investigations at 1SU7: The Fort Tombecbé Site," *Journal of Alabama Archaeology* 28(1):1–104; Dunbar Rowland, Albert G. Sanders, and Patricia K. Galloway, eds., *Mississippi Provincial Archives, French Dominion*, Vols. 4–5 (1984).

Joe Bassette Wilkins, "Outpost of Empire: The Founding of Fort Tombecbé and de Bienville's Chickasaw Expedition of 1736," *Proceedings of the Twelfth Meeting of the French Colonial Historical Society, Ste. Geneviève, May 1986*, ed. by Philip Boucher and Serge Courville (1988):133–153.

See also CHOCTAW; CHOCTAW CIVIL WAR

Fort Toulouse (Alabama)

French officials decided to build Fort Toulouse, or the Alabama post, in 1717, near the confluence of the Coosa and Tallapoosa Rivers, where they join to form the Alabama River. Here, in the midst of Alabama, Coosa, and Tallapoosa Indian villages that comprised the Upper Muscogulges (known to the British as the Upper Creek), was established the easternmost outpost of the Louisiana colony. There had been open hostilities since 1703 between the British-supplied Alabamas and the French and their Indian allies at Mobile. The expulsion of British traders from the Upper Muscogulge towns during the Yamasee War in 1715 temporarily disrupted the colonial balance of power throughout the interior Southeast, providing the French an opportunity to expand their influence.

Arriving in September 1717, Lieutenant Vitral de La Tour set to work his 25 soldiers and their Alabama hosts constructing the wooden palisaded and bastioned fort on a bluff overlooking the Coosa River. This Vauban-style fort originally measured about 150 feet on each side, but underwent numerous alterations and repairs during succeeding decades. A dry moat was added, probably in 1725, and the entire fort was enlarged in 1735. However, erosion of the river bluff gradually undermined the fort and eventually forced the French to rebuild 100 feet to the south of the old structure. The new fort (which has been archaeologically excavated) closely resembled the original 1717 plan, measuring about 150 feet on each side, lacking a moat, with palisades and bastions constructed of quartered vertical posts. Inside were five structures, including two barracks and a vaulted powder magazine. Each bastion had sentry platforms where swivel guns and 4- and 6-pounder cannons were mounted.

Due to the fort's location, isolated from other French settlements but relatively close to the British colonies of South Carolina and Georgia, desertion was a constant problem. The most serious incident occurred in 1721, when eight deserters from Mobile fled to Fort Toulouse and persuaded two-thirds of that garrison to mutiny. The officers appealed for assistance to the neighboring Alabama Indians, who soon killed or captured all of the deserters. French officials subsequently limited garrison rotation at this remote outpost and encouraged soldiers to marry and settle there after their terms of enlistment had expired. By 1755, in addition to the garrison of 40 men and officers, a civilian community of 100 men, women, and children had grown up around the post.

Fort Toulouse played a very important role in colonial southeastern diplomacy and trade. For 46 years, the presence of this outpost legitimated French claims to eastern Louisiana and discouraged British expansion westward. Because the fort's warehouses provided the Creek with an alternative to the British traders who visited their villages selling guns, liquor, and cloth, pro-French and pro-British factions arose among that powerful and numerous native people. The delicate balance that evolved prevented open warfare and allowed the Creeks to retain their political independence for many decades. Despite the best efforts of French and British officers and agents, neither side ever gained a decisive advantage in the region, and no battles took place at Fort Toulouse (although the Cherokee did receive considerable aid and assistance from the post during the siege and capture of British Fort Loudoun in 1760).

Late in 1763, Fort Toulouse was abandoned, since the British did not intend to occupy the post, and the colonists, along with several villages of Alabama Indians, relocated west of the Mississippi River. Fort Jackson was built on the same site in 1814, and a treaty ending the Creek-American War was signed there.

Gregory A. Waselkov

References

Bill Barron, *The Vaudreuil Papers* (1975); Jean-Bernard Bossu, *Travels in the Interior of North America, 1751–1762* (1962); Verner W. Crane, *The Southern Frontier, 1670–1732*, with an Introduction by Peter H. Wood (1981); Wilbur R. Jacobs, ed., *The Appalachian Indian Frontier: The Edmond Atkin Report and Plan of 1755* (1967); Daniel H. Thomas, *Fort Toulouse: The French Outpost at the Alabamas on the Coosa*, with an Introduction by Gregory A. Waselkov (1989).

See also CREEK; FORT LOUDOUN (TENNESSEE); LOUISIANA; YAMASEE WAR

Treaties
FOR PARTICULAR TREATIES, SEE UNDER INDIVIDUAL NAMES

Fort Trent (Pennsylvania)
In the early months of 1754, Governor Robert Dinwiddie of Virginia acted to try to forestall the French effort to claim control of the forks of the Ohio River. As a force of French regulars and Canadian *habitants* was engaged in constructing the string of posts from Presque Isle to Fort Le Boeuf, Dinwiddie dispatched Captain William Trent, along with a force of 70 militiamen, to build a fort at the forks of the Ohio before the French could reach the spot.

On 17 February, Trent's company reached the forks of the Ohio and immediately began to build Fort Trent. With the construction well underway, Trent took about 30 men and returned to Wills Creek, Maryland, leaving the fort-building project in the hands of 41 men under the command of Ensign Edward Ward. Meanwhile, the French forces at Forts Le Boeuf and Venango, on the upper Allegheny River, had been alerted to the Virginians' arrival; on 16 April, Captain Claude-Pierre Pécaudy de Contrecoeur arrived at the forks of the Ohio with a flotilla of about 60 *bateaux* and 300 canoes, carrying perhaps a thousand soldiers and allied Indians along with 18 cannons. Ward counted the odds and chose to surrender. According to one tradition, the Virginians were

permitted to march off with all their possessions and tools, but another version has it that, when Ward dined with Contrecoeur on the evening of 17 April, they got along so well that Ward agreed to sell the French commander all their carpentry tools. In any case, the Virginians abandoned the site to the French on 18 April and ended the short-lived history of Fort Trent, which was soon replaced by Fort Duquesne.

Eric Hinderaker

References

C. Hale Sipe, *The Indian Wars of Pennsylvania* (1929); Francis Jennings, *Empire of Fortune: Crowns, Colonies, and Tribes in the Seven Years War in America* (1988).

See also DINWIDDIE, ROBERT; FORT DUQUESNE (PENNSYLVANIA); FORKS OF THE OHIO; FORT LE BOEUF (PENNSYLVANIA); PÉCAUDY, CLAUDE-PIERRE, DE CONTRECOEUR; TRENT, WILLIAM; VENANGO

Trent, William (1715–1787)
William Trent, Indian trader and land speculator, was the son of a Pennsylvania and New Jersey officeholder. His unfortunate association with military affairs began in King George's War, when the company he had recruited and commanded was ambushed north of Albany in April 1747. Trent's force took heavy casualties before being rescued by another unit.

The next years, by using borrowed money, Trent entered into a large-scale trading partnership with the more experienced George Croghan. Trent spent the rest of his life trying to make good on this and related trading and land deals. His involvement in arms was a means to those commercial goals. In the early 1750s, he repeatedly warned Pennsylvania and Virginia officials that the French intended to establish firm control of the Ohio country. His cries fell on apathetic ears. He and other traders lost capital and trading goods to hostile French and Indians, particularly after the June 1752 attack on Pickawillany.

In fall 1753, Trent plainly told Virginia authorities that if they did not occupy such key points as the Ohio River forks, where the Allegheny joined the Monongahela, the west was lost. Trent's prospects improved in early 1754, when the Ohio Company of Virginia, bent on settlement of the upper Ohio, built a storehouse at Wills Creek, Maryland, with a view to cutting a road to the forks. Trent was to construct an intermediate fortified store at Redstone (Browns-ville, Pennsylvania) on the Monongahela.

Simultaneously, George Washington's failure to warn away the French belatedly galvanized Virginia into action. Pennsylvania, wary about Virginia's intentions, withheld cooperation. Trent was commissioned by Virginia to build a regular fort at the forks, with Washington to follow him with reinforcements, and the Virginia assembly to convene to raise more.

The effort proved too little too late. Trent, using personal funds, raised about half the hundred authorized soldier/builders, arriving at the forks in February. He began to build, hampered by lack of provisions and the notable noncooperation of a principal aide, John Frasier. Indians hired to hunt for food brought in little, as they were apprehensive of the French descending on the site from Presque Isle on Lake Erie. With food almost gone, Trent returned east to the settlements, seeking supplies, leaving the unfinished "Fort Trent" or "Fort Prince George's" (the latter after the future George III) in the care of Ensign Edward Ward.

The French and Indian allies came down from the lake in force in mid-April, compelled Ward's surrender, and began to build their own strategic bastion, Fort Duquesne, on the site. Trent was blamed for the loss by the military tyro Washington, on route to his relief, and by Virginia Governor Robert Dinwiddie, both of whom had invested in the Ohio Company. Dinwiddie ordered Trent court-martialed, but it is hard to see what else Trent or Ward could have done. Trent subsequently furnished Washington with supplies for his ill-starred efforts that culminated at Fort Necessity.

Trent successfully sued Dinwiddie for his expenses, and for the latter's public remarks against him, and got further satisfaction by serving John Forbes as Indian scout overseer during Forbes's successful 1758 march against Duquesne. Trent settled at the site, now Fort Pitt, but lost more goods in Pontiac's War. His attempts for himself and other "suffering traders" to be compensated in land or otherwise for years of losses failed.

Trent attended key Indian meetings at Logstown, Easton, and elsewhere, but lack of command of Indian languages compromised his usefulness. Trent was no military hero in motivation or accomplishment. He did sound the alarm in the right quarters against the French threat to the west, and tried to protect British colonial interests—and his own—with tardy and inadequate support.

There is no large body of Trent papers. Much of his military-related activity is scattered in Virginia and Pennsylvania state papers, and in works on fellow traders such as Croghan and Christopher Gist, and in the writings of Washington and Henry Bouquet. A 1947 biography by Sewell Swick is good on context, but more detail could be provided today on Trent himself.

Paul Woehrmann

References
    Sewell Elias Slick, *William Trent and the West* (1947).

See also BOUQUET, HENRY; CROGHAN, GEORGE; DINWIDDIE, ROBERT; FORBES CAMPAIGN OF 1758; GIST, CHRISTOPHER; MONONGAHELA RIVER; FORT NECESSITY (PENNSYLVANIA); OHIO COMPANY; OHIO COUNTRY; PONTIAC'S WAR; FORT DE LA PRESQUE ISLE (PENNSYLVANIA); FORT TRENT (PENNSYLVANIA): WASHINGTON, GEORGE

Trois Rivières, Treaty of (1645)

This treaty provided a temporary truce between New France and the Mohawks. In concluding the treaty, the French sought to decrease the almost constant attacks by the Iroquois since 1636 against their settlements in New France. By 1644, these attacks were a serious threat to both the French settlements and their Indian allies. During that year, 80 Iroquois warriors assaulted the island of Montreal for three days and succeeded in capturing a party of Algonquins near Trois Rivières. Authorities in New France were reluctant to engage in military operations against the Iroquois and instead pursued a policy of mediation.

On 12 July 1645, a conference was convened at the Trois Rivières between three Mohawk chiefs and Governor Charles Huault de Montmagny. The Mohawks presented the French with 16 proposals in the form of wampum belts. At the second meeting on 14 July, Montmagny accepted these as conditions for peace between the Mohawks and French. To confirm the treaty, two French delegates accompanied the Mohawks back to their settlements. The Mohawks were encouraged to persuade the four other Iroquois nations to negotiate peace with New France. This effort was not successful because the Senecas and Onondagas continued their attacks on New France. On 18 September, another conference was held that reaffirmed the treaty and established commercial relations between the two parties. The treaty proved to be only a temporary reprieve from warfare, as the Mohawks renewed their attacks by 1647.

David L. Whitesell

See also IROQUOIS; IROQUOIS WARS; MOHAWK; ONONDAGA; SENECA

Tunica

The Tunica Indians, descendants of Soto's Quizquiz, migrated south along the Mississippi River several times in the historic period, eventually settling at a place later known as Trudeau on the east bank near the French settlement of Pointe Coupée. They were among Louisiana's most faithful allies and were considered an integral part of the colony' defense force. They took an active part in France's war against the Natchez, 1729–1731, and suffered the deaths of many chiefs and people in April 1731, when a band of Natchez, on pretext of making peace with the French, killed many Tunicas as they slept. They were attacked again with loss of life in June 1731. Like other local nations, they stayed behind to guard the settlements when Louisiana troops and militia took part in the second campaign of the Franco-Chickasaw War (1739–1740).

At Trudeau, which lay near the strategic confluence of the Red and Mississippi Rivers, the Tunicas served as important commercial middlemen as well, involved in trading European and native trade goods to their European and Indian neighbors, as well as the important trade in horses from east Texas into Louisiana. Sometime after England gained control of the east bank of the Mississippi in 1763, the Tunicas migrated across the river to Marksville, where they absorbed several other tribes. In 1980, the federal government formally recognized the Tunica-Biloxi tribe.

Michael James Foret

References
Jeffrey P. Brain, *Tunica Treasure* (1979); ———, *Tunica Archaeology* (1988); ———, *The Tunica-Biloxi* (1989).

See also CHICKASAW WARS; LOUISIANA; NATCHEZ WAR

Tuscarora

The Tuscarora were the largest and most impor-

tant tribe in the eastern half of North Carolina. It is not certain when the tribe, members of the Iroquoian linguistic family, migrated into present North Carolina. By the end of the sixteenth century, however, they controlled much of the region between the Roanoke and Neuse Rivers. Surveyor John Lawson counted 15 Tuscarora villages and 1,200 warriors in 1701. Other observers counted as many as 2,000 Tuscarora warriors.

These villages were largely independent of each other until the pressures of white settlement and contact with Virginia traders forced them into closer confederation. By the end of the seventeenth century, the Tuscarora were heavily involved in the trading of furs and slaves. Abuses of this trade, including the loss of Tuscarora as slaves, eroded relationships between the tribe and white settlers, and led to a number of skirmishes. The Tuscarora War, which began in 1711, was a result of trade abuses and encroaching white settlement.

Not all Tuscarora took part in the war. A large group under the leadership of chief Tom Blunt occupied the region near the Roanoke River and were not directly threatened by encroaching white settlement. An equally large body of Tuscarora, under the leadership of chief Hancock, was located closer to the areas of white expansion, especially New Bern, which was settled in 1710. It was these Tuscarora who initiated the war, while those under Blunt's leadership remained neutral.

The remnants of the defeated Tuscarora ended up in New York as the sixth nation of the Iroquoian Confederacy. Their defeat opened up for settlement a large part of the North Carolina interior. Blunt's friendly Tuscarora were rewarded for their loyalty by confinement in a series of inadequate reservations. In 1752, Moravian Bishop August Gottlieb Spangenburg visited the area looking for land, and especially noted their abject poverty, stating that they were "much despised and will probably soon come to an end." Some 300 remained in North Carolina at this time. A handful served with English forces during the Cherokee War. Eventually, they sold their North Carolina land and went north to live in New York.

Jim Sumner

References
F. Roy Johnson, *The Tuscaroras*, 2 vols. (1967, 1968); John Lawson, *A New Voyage to Carolina*, ed. by Hugh T. Lefler (1962); T.C. Parramore, "The Tuscarora Ascen-

dancy," *North Carolina Historical Review* 59 (1982):307–326; Douglas L. Rights, *The American Indian in North Carolina* (1947).

See also CHEROKEE WAR; IROQUOIS; NORTH CAROLINA; TUSCARORA WAR

Tuscarora War (1711–1713)

The Tuscarora War, 1711–1713, probably arose from grievances of small North Carolina coastal tribes against colonists. The Tuscarora, occupying the colony's inner coastal plain, seem not to have been menaced or significantly injured by whites up to that time. Tuscarora of the upper towns, those along the Roanoke, Tar-Pamlico, and upper Neuse Rivers, enjoyed a thriving fur trade with Albemarle Sound and James River colonists and remained neutral in the war. The lower towns, on the lower Neuse and a northern branch called Catechna (now Contentney) Creek, comprised the militants.

Smaller tribes to the east were jostled and afflicted in a variety of ways by white encroachment. In 1695, whites had begun settling beyond Albemarle Sound, first on the lower Pamlico River, and, after 1700, west of the long-recognized Blackwater-Chowan River dividing line between white and Indian territory. In 1710 came an influx of Swiss-Palatine settlers to the lower Neuse-Trent River region and problems for the Coree, Neusiok, and other tribes of that area. By now, the Carolina government was hearing frequent complaints from these and other tribes as, no doubt, did chief Hancock, recognized as leader of the lower towns.

There were hints of Tuscarora uneasiness as early as 1703, and rumors in mid-1711 that rebels under Thomas Cary sought to draw the Tuscarora (probably chief Tom Blunt's upper towns) into the brief "Cary Rebellion" against Governor Edward Hyde. At any rate, civil conflict offered the lower towns a unique opportunity to strike. (Hancock may have perceived Bath and Albemarle County settlements as separate colonies; they were certainly antagonistic to each other.) Unusually dry weather, meaning poor corn crops and scarce game and furs, were perhaps other Tuscarora incentives to strike.

When Hancock sent 500 men against the colonists on 22 September, he held Surveyor General John Lawson and Swiss-Palatine leader Baron Christoph von Graffenried prisoners at Catechna Town, his seat on Catechna Creek.

Lawson was executed by Hancock's order for alleged misdealings with the Coree, and perhaps other tribes, but Graffenried was spared. Hancock apparently did not intend a war—though certainly risking one—but an admonition that there must be a treaty limiting white encroachment. A pact between Hancock and Graffenried before his October release amounted to a separate peace between the Indians and Swiss-Palatine settlers.

Hancock, on behalf of Coree, Wilkinson's Point, Pamlico, Bear River, "and others of the region," besides his own Tuscarora, sought in the pact to be "good friends" with whites. Graffenried's colony must remain within its grant and acquire no further land. Indians might "hunt where they wish" without hindrance, except near farms, where they might injure or drive away cattle. Wares and provisions must be sold to them at reasonable prices. Swiss-Palatine houses bearing a large letter N ("sign of Neuse") on their doors would be spared from attack. Finally, Graffenried should arrange with Hyde a four-day truce during which peace talks between militant tribes and English settlers might begin.

Hancock's 22 September raid killed more than 120 whites in both English and Swiss-Palatine settlements. The conflict quickly degenerated into full-scale war, owing to an unauthorized counterattack before Graffenried's release, from the New Bern vicinity led by English trader William Brice.

Graffenried, on returning to New Bern, was apparently unable to contact Hyde in Albemarle, all intervening settlers having fled to hastily erected forts at rivermouths. But his pact with Hancock held firm, and the Swiss-Palatine settlers, mostly refugees at New Bern, were not further molested by the Indians. (Some of the baron's people, however, allied with Brice and others in periodic clashes with the Indians.)

Meanwhile, the Hyde government, otherwise almost catatonically inactive, sent agents to Charles Town and Williamsburg for help. Virginia Governor Alexander Spotswood sent some material aid, but abandoned a plan to send 200 militia when he found that Hyde meant to tax any provisions they brought with them into North Carolina. South Carolina, however, sent a force of friendly Indians under veteran Indian-fighter John Barnwell and other whites. This force, initially more than 500, reached North Carolina in late January 1712, on the 29th attacking the Tuscarora village of

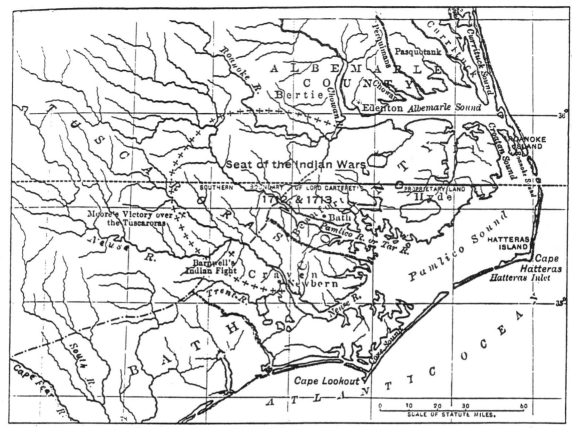

Tuscarora war.

Torhunta, in what is now Wayne County. The South Carolinians won a tense battle, though it was soon clear to some that Torhunta was a neutral town defended at the time only by women and old men. (Barnwell left South Carolina under the impression that the whole Tuscarora nation was at war with the whites.)

From Torhunta, Barnwell's force, diminished by defections, marched northeasterly to Bath Town at the mouth of Pamlico River. This route was well outside the sphere of Hancock's influence and brought further fights between the South Carolinians and neutral Tuscarora. But Tom Blunt maintained his neutrality and Barnwell's force, reduced to some 200, reached Bath Town on 9 February. Hundreds of refugees crammed the few houses there or camped nearby.

After rest and resupply, Barnwell, adding some 200 North Carolina recruits, headed southwest toward Catechna Creek on 27 February. He arrived there, 20 miles above New Bern, on March 2, and laid siege to nearby Fort Hancock. The creekside fort, built under direction of a fugitive South Carolina slave named Harry, was in state-of-the-art European style with trenches, split-log portholed walls, four circular outworks, and mazes of blocking tree limbs and canes angled "to run into peoples' legs."

Barnwell equipped his men with cylindrical bundles of sticks (fascines) for protection and directed a charge against heavy musket and arrow fire. This failing, he readied a second attack, but was deterred by threats from the fort to kill the 58 white and black hostages. Negotiations led to the release of 12 whites, the rest to be delivered within 12 days at a point six miles above New Bern. Barnwell must withdraw, a cease-fire prevailing in the interval, after which a treaty would be arranged.

Perhaps because Hancock mistrusted Barnwell's motive in retiring to New Bern (possibly to bring Graffenried into the war), no hostages were delivered on the prescribed day, and Barnwell, on 8 March, led his troops back to Catechna Creek. A party of his Yamasee were sent to Core Town, on the Neuse opposite Catechna Creek, where they killed some Coree and reportedly "cooked and ate the flesh of" one. Near Fort Hancock, Barnwell's force was joined by a body of men sent by Governor Hyde with a pair of three-pounder cannon, bringing his strength to 153 whites and 128 Yamasee.

By 7 April, Barnwell had a battery within range of the fort. The attackers, digging trenches, worked their way to the fort's moat, but efforts to tunnel from there to the walls failed. The ensuing ten-day siege was described by Barnwell as remarkable for such "variety of action, sallies, attempts to be relieved from without" and assaults on his trenches as were never seen in Indian wars. On 17 April, he called on Hancock for a cease-fire, proposing that the Tuscarora turn over Hancock and certain others to the English within ten days as hostages for the performance of other terms. The fort must be demolished, hostages released, the Indians agreeing to pay North Carolina annual tribute, restrict planting to the Neuse-Catechna Creek area, and limit hunting and fishing to land between the Neuse and Cape Fear Rivers. These conditions were accepted.

The Tuscarora soon released 32 hostages and handed over some of their leaders, though Hancock was said to have fled to Virginia. Barnwell, persuaded that the peace terms would be substantially fulfilled, began preparations at New Bern to return to South Carolina. Loath to return empty-handed, however, he invited the Tuscarora and their allies to meet him at the Core Town site to receive rewards for the safe return of captives. When a "goodly number" arrived. Barnwell's men attacked them, killed some 40 or 50 men, and seized nearly 200 women and children for sale as slaves. He then left for Charles Town with the war flaring up anew. North Carolina leaders were outraged with Barnwell both for accepting a treaty when he might have destroyed the Tuscarora war-making capacity, and for breaking it as he departed.

A second appeal to South Carolina brought another Indian-white expedition. This one, under Colonel James Moore, assaulted the Tuscarora stronghold at Fort Nohoroco on Catechna Creek in March 1713, and achieved a costly but decisive victory. Hancock, captured and turned over to the whites by chief Tom Blunt, was promptly murdered by them. Many Tuscarora fled to Virginia or the Iroquois Confederacy. Tom Blunt signed a treaty with North Carolina in April 1713, and received a reservation on the lower Roanoke River. Guerrilla fighting between whites and bands of Indian militants continued for some years. The preceding 60 years, during which the North Carolina colony remained a fringe of the eastern sounds, was followed by a 60-year rush to the Appalachians and beyond.

T.C. Parramore

References

John Barnwell, "Journal of John Barnwell," *Virginia Magazine of History and Biography* 5 (1898), Part I:391–402, VI (1898), Part 2:42–55; T.C. Parramore, "The Tuscarora Ascendancy," *North Carolina Historical Review* 59 (1982):307–326; ———, "With Tuscarora Jack on the Back Path to Bath," *North Carolina Historical Review* 64 (1987):115–138; Vincent H. Todd, ed., *Christoph von Graffenried's Account of the Founding of New Bern* (1920); Louis B. Wright and Marion Tinling, eds., *The Secret Diary of William Byrd of Westover, 1709–1712* (1941).

See also FORT BARNWELL (NORTH CAROLINA); BARNWELL, JOHN; FORT NOHOROCO (NORTH CAROLINA); NORTH CAROLINA; SPOTSWOOD, ALEXANDER; TUSCARORA

T

U

Uncas (1588?–1683)

Unable to attain authority through traditional means, Uncas quickly learned how to use the English to reach the status he desired. In the process, Uncas helped define the future of Indian-Anglo relations and the distribution of power in New England.

Uncas believed he was destined to lead his Pequot people. Both his mother's and father's family included sachems in their genealogies. And in 1626, Uncas added prestige to his leadership claims by marrying the daughter of Sassacus. Uncas was impatient, however, and repeatedly challenged his father-in-law's authority. Eventually, Sassacus became exasperated with Uncas's impertinence and forced Uncas to migrate to the Mohegans. Uncas attained revenge in May 1637, however, when he joined his Mohegan forces to the English troops in the Pequot War, and helped reduce his Pequot nation to near extinction.

Uncas immediately started taking advantage of this situation by allowing Pequot refugees to joint his Mohegan tribe. This direct violation of the Mohegan-Narragansett-Anglo alliance placed Uncas's life in jeopardy. Fearful of English reprisals, Uncas initially dodged a summons to appear before Puritan leaders and explain his actions, but eventually he accepted the Treaty of Hartford (Tripartite Treaty) in September 1638, which allowed the Puritans to divide the remaining Pequots among the various allied tribes. Perceiving how to wield power as an Indian in a Puritan-dominated New England, Uncas then told the Massachusetts leadership "this heart (laying his hand upon his breast) is not mine, but yours; they are all yours; command me any difficult thing, I will do it."

This abasement before English authority actually empowered Uncas. In 1643, for example, Uncas used his English connections to topple one of his competitors, Miantonomo. In the spring of that year, Uncas claimed that Miantonomo had hired a Pequot assassin to kill the Mohegan sachem. Miantonomo argued that this was another of Uncas's ploys to gain English sympathy and support, and that Uncas's wounds were, in fact, self-inflicted. Unlike other appearances before the Puritan leaders, this time Miantonomo was unable to remove suspicion. Miantonomo certainly did not help his case when he apparently killed the alleged Pequot assassin to silence the truth. Then, in the summer of 1643, Uncas seized an opportunity when he captured Miantonomo in a rout of Narragansetts coming to Sequasson's aid. Again, employing his humble, subservient role before the English, and capitalizing on Puritan fears of Miantonomo, Uncas gained permission to execute the Narragansett sachem.

After Miantonomo's execution, the United Colonies provided Uncas with protection so that Miantonomo's brother and new Narragansett sachem, Pessacus, could not extract revenge. Even when Uncas tested the limits of his power among the Indians of New England vis-à-vis the English (e.g., a 1661 attack on subservient tribes), a quick humbling confession would restore English favor upon him. By using the English to his advantage, Uncas undoubtedly reached a higher level of power and influence in New England than he ever would have as sachem of the Mohegan.

Richard C. Goode

References

John W. De Forest, *History of the Indians of Connecticut from the Earliest Known Period to 1850* (1851); Neal Salisbury, "Indians and Colonists in Southern New England after the Pequot War: An Uneasy Balance," in *The Pequots in Southern New England: The Fall and Rise of an American Indian Nation*, ed. by Laurence M. Hauptman and James D. Wherry (1990):81–95; John Winthrop, *Winthrop's Journal: "History of New England," 1630–1649*, 2 vols., ed. by James Kendall Hosmer (1908).

See also MIANTONOMO; MOHEGAN; NARRAGANSETT; PEQUOT; PEQUOT WAR; FORT SHANTOK (CONNECTICUT)

Underhill, John (1597–1672)

In a region known for its "steady habits," John Underhill personified the colonial New England tradition of killing Native Americans. Born in England, he gained his military knowledge in the Netherlands. Moving to New England in 1630, the Massachusetts community put his expertise to use. In August 1636, Underhill served as John Endicott's second-in-command in the inept expedition to Block Island and the Pequot territory. The next year, Massachusetts Governor Henry Vane selected Underhill to command a 20-man force ordered to strengthen Lieutenant Lion Gardener's contingent at Fort Saybrook (Underhill implied that he was given command of the fort). After the Connecticut General Court declared war on the Pequot nation on 1 May 1637, Underhill added his Massachusetts troops to John Mason's Connecticut volunteers. Assisted by a large contingent of Narragansett and Mohegan Indians, Mason and Underhill led the attack on the Pequot's Mystic Fort on 26 May. Mason reported that Underhill suffered a loss of nerve on the battlefield, and one of his subordinates, a Master Hedge, had to seize the initiative and lead Underhill's detachment. Nonetheless, Underhill's men did enter the fort from the southern entrance and helped set fire to the longhouses. "Great and doleful," boasted Underhill, "was the bloody sight to the view of young soldiers that never had been in war, to see so many souls lie gasping on the ground, so thick in some places that you could hardly pass along." Between 300 and 700 Pequot men, women, and children died in the attack.

After the Pequot War, Underhill's personal life became tumultuous. He raised more than a few Puritan eyebrows when he announced that he experienced a religious conversion while smoking his pipe. Then he joined the Antinomians, using his spiritual liberties to act in an incontinent manner with a neighbor's wife. After the community excommunicated and banished him in 1638, he offered a highly visible and emotional confession and was restored in 1639–1640. In 1641, he then tried his hand at local politics, but embarrassed himself once again. Underhill finally relocated his niche in society when he left the Puritan community in 1642 to assist Willem Kieft, governor of New Netherlands, in solving his "Indian problem." In 1644, Underhill led a massacre of 420 Indians living on Long Island and the surrounding New Amsterdam area.

Richard C. Goode

References
John Underhill, *News from America*, in *Massachusetts Historical Society*, 3rd ser., 6 (1837):1–28; John Winthrop, *Winthrop's Journal: "History of New England," 1630–1649*, 2 vols., ed. by James Kendall Hosmer (1908).

See also ENDICOTT EXPEDITION; KIEFT, WILLEM; KIEFT'S WAR; PEQUOT WAR; FORT SAYBROOK (CONNECTICUT)

United Colonies Confederation

See NEW ENGLAND CONFEDERATION

Fort Upper Tract (West Virginia)

A French and Indian War stockade commanded by James Dunlap, Fort Upper Tract was built early in 1756 by order of George Washington. Located just west of the southern branch of the Potomac River at the present town of Upper Tract in Pendleton County, West Virginia, Fort Upper Tract was captured in April 1758 by a party of French and Indians. Dunlap and 22 men were killed. After burning Fort Upper Tract, the attackers moved on to take Fort Seybert. Altogether, they killed or captured about 60 men from both forts.

Thomas Costa

References
Otis K. Rice, *The Allegheny Frontier: West Virginia Beginnings, 1730–1830* (1970).

See also FORT SEYBERT (WEST VIRGINIA)

Uprising of 1747

In 1744, the Huron chief Orontony led a group of followers from Detroit south to the Ohio country. They joined another party of Huron, led by the minor chief, Angouirot, who had settled on Sandusky Bay on Lake Erie in 1738. These migrants, who became known as Wyandots, were angry with the French and dissatisfied with their tribal leadership. The French were demanding that their Indian allies engage in constant warfare, while at the same time providing fewer and fewer trade goods at increasingly higher prices. The French also had been unwilling or unable to mediate intertribal disputes arising between the Huron and other Indians in the Detroit area, primarily the Ottawas. The established tribal elders continued the alliance with the French in spite of these unfavorable conditions. Orontony, Angouriot, and their followers rebelled, including many women who took on active roles in the opposition.

Soon after Orontony moved to Sandusky Bay, he began to establish ties with the English and allowed traders from Pennsylvania to build a large blockhouse in the marshes of the main Wyandot village. Other Indian tribes in the Great Lakes region were equally disenchanted with the French, and Orontony began to envision a peace between villages outside the old French alliance.

In June 1747, five French traders, unaware of the presence of the English among the Wyandot, arrived at Sandusky. Angered at their entrance into the village without his consent, Orontony condemned them to death and had one of the scalps sent to Pennsylvania. The governor of Canada repeatedly and unsuccessfully ordered Orontony to surrender the murderers. Instead, the Wyandot leader organized a rebellion to capture Detroit and the upper French posts, and ultimately to terminate French dominion in the region. By August, 17 tribes had joined the Wyandot in a coordinated region-wide plan to massacre the French. The Wyandot and Ottawa were to seize the fort and houses at Detroit and kill the occupants; Potawatomi to destroy the French mission and villages on Bois Blanc island; Miami to seize the French traders and the post at Fort Miami; Fox to attack Green Bay; the Sauk to seize Michilimackinac; and Mingo to destroy the French village at the junction of the Miami and St. Joseph Rivers. Other tribes were to destroy posts and kill traders in their own areas.

The uprising was damaged when a group of Indians precipitiously murdered a Frenchman near Detroit. This attack was unauthorized, and a council was called among the Wyandot and Ottawa at the fort to decide if the operation should be changed. An Indian woman overheard their discussion and alerted a Jesuit priest. The commandant at Detroit, Paul-Joseph Le Moyne, chevalier de Longueuil, notified both the French and the tribes throughout the region that the plan had been discovered. The Indians at Detroit withdrew, but various other attacks proceeded as planned. The Ottawa killed three Frenchmen at Michilimackinac; the Saulteaux attacked two French canoes on Lake St. Clair; the Miami seized eight French at the trading post on the Maumee and burned the building; the Fox murdered several traders at Green Bay; and the Wyandot attacked Bois Blanc Island. In this latter attack, five Indians were captured and imprisoned in Detroit. Various other random hostilities continued, but the momentum of the uprising dissipated.

On 22 September, reinforcements arrived at Detroit from Montreal, and some participants in the revolt, including the Potawatomis, asked the French for a pardon. Orontony, however, never reconciled with the French, and the Ohio Valley continued to seethe with hostility. In 1748, Orontony burned the village at Sandusky and moved his followers to Pennsylvania, where he died in 1750. The French Governor, Jacques-Pierre de Taffanel, marquis de La Jonquière, adopted a conciliatory policy that gradually restored the alliance along the Great Lakes, but rebellion continued in the region of the Ohio and Wabash Rivers, and opposition leadership passed to the Miamis.

Kathryn L. Utter

References

Lawrence Henry Gipson, *Zones of International Friction: North America, South of the Great Lakes Region, 1748–1754* (1939); Alfred T. Goodman, ed., *Journal of Captain William Trent from Logstown to Pickawillany* (1871); Charles A. Hanna, *The Wilderness Trail: Or the Ventures and Adventures of the Pennsylvania Traders in the Allegheny Path*, Vol. 2 (1911); Reuben G. Thwaites, ed., *Collections of the State Historical Society of Wisconsin*, Vol. 17 (1908); Richard White, *The Middle Ground: Indians, Empires, and Republics in the Great Lakes Region, 1650–1815* (1991).

See also HURON; ORONTONY; OTTAWA; FORT PONTCHARTRAIN DE DETROIT (MICHIGAN); SANDUSKY BAY; TRENT, WILLIAM

U

Utrecht, Treaty of (1713)

With the Canadian invasion of 1711 failing so miserably, the British government seized the opportunity to follow up the negotiations begun with France in 1712 at Utrecht in the Netherlands. Spain was also represented, but the French and British were the dominant world powers. The Treaty of Utrecht, signed in April 1713, brought an end to Queen Anne's War and began an uneasy truce for the next 30 years between the two nations on the northern frontier of colonial America.

The English realized major territorial gains from the Peace of Utrecht in the West Indies, but especially on the North American continent. Initially, the British gained the island of St. Kitts, which both nations had claimed for years. While the French retained Canada and the strategic Cape Breton Island and Prince Edward Island, the British now held territory on Hudson Bay, Newfoundland, and Acadia. Britain also gained Gibraltar and Minorca territorially as well as the *asiento,* which gave them exclusivity over the slave trade to South America. Clearly, the British were the major winners in the spoils of war, but the English colonists saw themselves with little advantage and were severely disappointed in the final outcome at Utrecht.

The acquisition of Newfoundland represented not only domination to the northern approach to the St. Lawrence, but it also would serve as the base for Britain's interests in the Atlantic fisheries, thus providing the mother country with a significant economic advantage. The same is true for the addition of the Hudson Bay region, where French fur traders had enjoyed the advantage economically. This also represented a victory for the Hudson's Bay Company, as it was to its disadvantage that the French operated the fur trade so successfully.

The acquisition of Acadia provided for potential British expansion, but it also cost the French their base for Indian attacks on the northern reaches of New England and privateer attacks on Atlantic shipping. Meanwhile, the French and Spanish held their considerable territory on the southern frontier.

The treaty signed at Utrecht proved less settling for the British colonials—even more as time passed. The problem focused on ambiguities over the boundaries of Acadia, a clear understanding of the area gained along Hudson Bay, and misunderstandings over Newfoundland fishing rights. While these disputes between the nations had a greater impact on the economic life of the colonies, perhaps of even greater concern was the status of the Indian tribes allied to France and Britain.

On the surface, the Treaty of Utrecht accomplished Britain's major objectives—an end to the war, territorial and economic gains, and diminished French power. Yet despite the obvious British advantage, the negative impact on its colonies would be another step on the road to eventual revolution.

Boyd Childress

References

Fred L. Israel, *Major Peace Treaties of Modern History, 1648–1967* (1967); Douglas Edward Leach, *Arms for Empire: A Military History of the British Colonies in North America, 1607–1763* (1973); ———, *The Northern Colonial Frontier, 1607–1763* (1966); Justin McCarthy, *The Reign of Queen Anne* (1902); George Macauley Trevelyan, *The Peace and the Protestant Succession* (1948).

See also CANADA, BRITISH EXPEDITION AGAINST (1711); QUEEN ANNE'S WAR

Camp Van Schaick (New York)
See FORT HALF MOON (NEW YORK)

Vaudreuil de Cavagnial, Pierre de Rigaud de
See RIGAUD DE VAUDREUIL DE CAVAGNIAL, PIERRE DE

Venango (Pennsylvania)
Third in a chain of posts constructed by the French to connect Lake Erie with the Ohio Valley, Venango was little more than a fortified supply depot. Its location at the juncture of the Rivière aux Boeufs (French Creek) with the Allegheny River made it the logical staging area for the French move to the forks of the Ohio.

Venango was the site of an Indian village and, as early as 1741, the trading post of John Fraser. The activities of merchants such as Fraser were a major reason for the French to establish posts in the region. Fraser had been warned to depart by Pierre-Joseph de Céleron de Blainville in 1749, and Philippe-Thomas Chabert de Joncaire early in 1753. Joncaire took possession of Fraser's house in August. George Washington stopped at Venango on his journey to warn the French to leave the Ohio Valley and learned much of their intentions.

The French, intent on securing the forks of the Ohio, were slow to erect fortifications at Venango. A defensible redoubt was constructed in 1755, and a larger fort was completed in 1757. It was similar to the posts at Presque Isle and Le Boeuf. Named Fort Machault in honor of the minister of marine, it was a square with four bastions. The enclosure was a rectangle of roughly 75 by 105 feet with stockaded bastions and curtains incorporating the rear walls of the barracks.

When Captain François-Marie Le Marchand de Lignery destroyed Fort Duquesne in November 1758, he withdrew to Venango. Lignery assembled his troops and Indians at Venango for a counterattack in 1759. On 12 July, however, just as Lignery was convening with the warriors, he received news of a British attack on Fort Niagara. His communications with New France were placed in jeopardy by this development. Lignery immediately led his army to Niagara, only to be defeated a mile from its walls on 24 July. Fort Machault was destroyed as the French moved toward Niagara.

When Colonel Henry Bouquet moved his British troops from Pittsburgh to Lake Erie in 1760, he constructed a blockhouse at Venango. It was maintained until late May 1763, when the local Seneca joined the uprising sweeping the Great Lakes. Fort Venango was captured and burned, and its garrison died to the last man. The post was not reestablished by the British.

Brian Leigh Dunnigan

References
Lawrence Henry Gipson, *The Great War for the Empire: The Victorious Years, 1758–1760* (1965); Walter O'Meara, *Guns at the Forks* (1965); Max Schoenfeld, *Fort de la Presqu' ile and the French Penetration into the Ohio Country, 1753–1759* (1989); Charles Morse Stotz, *Drums in the Forest* (1958); ———, *Outposts of the War for Empire: The French and English in Western Pennsylvania; Their Armies, Their Forts, Their People, 1759–1764*

(1985); George Washington, *The Journal of Major George Washington, Sent by the Hon. Robert Dinwiddie . . . to the Commandant of the French Forces on the Ohio* (1754).

See also BOUQUET, HENRY; CHABERT DE JON-CAIRE, PHILIPPE-THOMAS; FORT DUQUESNE (PENNSYLVANIA); FORKS OF THE OHIO; FORT MACHAULT (PENNSYLVANIA); FORT NIAGARA (NEW YORK); PONTIAC'S WAR; WASHINGTON, GEORGE

Vernon, Edward (1684–1757)

Son of James Vernon, secretary of state under William III, Edward Vernon was born in London in 1684. Entering the Royal Navy as a message boy aboard the *Shrewsbury* in 1700, Vernon was promoted to lieutenant in 1702. After service in the Mediterranean, he attained the rank of captain in January 1705/1706, and subsequently served in the West Indies for four years, taking part in operations against Spanish vessels in 1710.

After service in the Baltic, Vernon retired on half-pay and in 1722 was elected to parliament as member for Penrhyn. During the Parliamentary debates of the 1730s over war with Spain, Vernon became a conspicuous advocate of hostilities, insisting that Spanish Caribbean possessions were vulnerable to attack. In 1739, even before the official declaration of war, Vernon was promoted to vice admiral and sent out to the West Indies, arriving in Jamaica in October with a force of five ships of the line.

Vernon chose the fortified town of Porto Bello on the north end of the Isthmus of Panama as his first target. The town was known as a haven for *guarda costas*, vessels notorious for enforcing Spanish mercantilist regulations against British shipping. Arriving off the town on the night of 20 November 1739, Vernon commenced his attack on the following day. His warships bombarded one of the forts guarding the entrance to the harbor, which the Spaniards had allowed to fall into neglect. A landing party quickly seized the stronghold, and the other forts and the town itself were taken the following day. Vernon's total haul included a number of vessels, including three *guarda costas,* as well as a quantity of gold, and the English public greeted news of his victory with great enthusiasm.

Returning to Jamaica, Vernon advocated continued naval operations to harass the Span-iards, but the British government, fired by his success at Porto Bello, insisted on planning a land operation against Vernon's wishes. Accordingly, the ministry sent out a large expeditionary force which, augmented by American colonial troops, was to proceed against a Spanish fortification. Vernon chose Cartagena, a Spanish stronghold on the north coast of South America, and launched the attack in March 1741.

The advance went awry from the beginning. The commander of the land forces, Brigadier General Thomas Wentworth, proved wholly inept. Advancing slowly along the coast toward the town, the British and American forces were decimated by disease. When the final attack against the strongpoint commanding the town took place, the Spaniards beat it off easily, inflicting heavy casualties, and the British returned to Port Royal.

Next, Vernon embarked on an attack on Cuba, but it too failed, again chiefly owing to Wentworth's incompetence. Eventually the long-smoldering enmity between naval and army commanders burst into flame, and both men were recalled to England, charging each other with responsibility for the miserable record of British operations in the West Indies.

Following his return to England, Vernon again sat in Parliament as a member for Ipswich. Always an independent, Vernon continued to castigate the government, writing a number of anonymous pamphlets dealing with naval policy. In 1745, he was promoted to admiral of the white and appointed to command the ships of the North Sea fleet, but turned the post over to a successor after becoming angered at his seeming mistreatment by the Admiralty. Vernon subsequently appeared before an inquiry regarding some vitriolic pamphlets he had allegedly written, and the king struck his name from the list of flag officers. He remained a member of Parliament, however, and continued to criticize the government until his death in 1757.

Thomas Costa

References
Basil Williams, *The Whig Supremacy, 1714–1760* (1962).

See also CARTAGENA, EXPEDITION AGAINST; PORTO BELLO, ATTACK ON

Vetch, Samuel (1668–1732)

Historians have traditionally cast Samuel Vetch as a merchant, entrepreneur, adventurer, soldier of fortune, and expansionist, but his career can be best described as opportunist. Realizing British colonial aims and New England's fear of Franco-Indian attacks on the northern frontier, Vetch seized the opportunity to press the crown for an aggressive policy to invade Canada in order to provide a solution to both concerns.

Samuel Vetch was born on 9 December 1668, at Edinburgh, Scotland, the son of a Presbyterian minister. The family fled first to England and then to the Netherlands, where Samuel and his older brother William were educated. The two brothers entered the army under the Prince of Orange and were later commissioned as officers and engaged in battles across Europe. In 1698, Captain Vetch was assigned to an expedition to Panama. When trouble arose with the Spanish, the English colony was evacuated to New York. Thus began Vetch's career as an advocate of colonial expansion.

When Vetch settled in Albany, he had the good fortune to marry Margaret Livingston, daughter of the prominent Robert Livingston, then secretary of Indian affairs. The opportunist Vetch became heavily involved in trade with the Indians, which indirectly extended into illegal commerce with French settlers in Montreal. In 1702, he moved to Boston, where colonial Governor Joseph Dudley appointed him one of a set of commissioners seeking a truce with French authorities in Quebec. While his mission was a diplomatic failure, he established an illegal arms trade with the French and Indians of Acadia. This led Vetch into trouble with the Massachusetts General Court, where he was fined. Again grasping the opportunity, Vetch traveled to England, where, in 1708, the Privy Council vacated his conviction and ordered a new trial. Safe in London, Vetch escaped any further legal hassle over his questionable trading activities.

Nowhere is Vetch's opportunism more evident than in his efforts to promote a combined British-colonial attack on Canada. Queen Anne's War had begun in 1702 and had developed on a worldwide scale, including North America. In 1708, Vetch penned a document he presented to the Board of Trade: "Canada Survey'd" was a proposal to invade Canada with colonial troops supplementing British regulars. Vetch drew on his considerable experience with the region to resurrect Sir William Phips's 1690 attack plan. The plan drew immediate attention and then support from the government. In turn, Vetch was promised the governorship of Canada. Accompanied by former Virginia Governor Francis Nicholson, Vetch sailed for Boston in April 1709.

Vetch organized a force in Boston that would be joined by British regiments to invade Quebec following a route through the St. Lawrence. Nicholson gathered militia and colonial regulars at Albany to attack Montreal by way of Lake Champlain, and by early summer had established a camp at Wood Creek on the southern end of the lake. As summer grew into early fall, both Vetch and Nicholson realized British support was not on the way, and the campaign was abandoned. Another assault began in September of the next year and was successful in taking Port Royal and Acadia almost without opposition. In October, Vetch was named governor of Nova Scotia (as Acadia was renamed), as well as military commander of British troops in the region. Vetch's command was fairly uneventful, but in 1711, still another invasion plan materialized, and in July, Vetch joined the British forces in Boston. Nicholson would again lead an assault on Montreal, following the Lake Champlain route Vetch had proposed in 1708. When the expedition sailed from Boston in late July, Vetch was in command of the colonial troops accompanying the British regulars.

Just as the 1709 expedition had been, the Canadian invasion of 1711 was a dismal failure. Under the incompetent British General John Hill and Rear Admiral Hovenden Walker, the British ships could not navigate the treacherous St. Lawrence. On the night of 22 August, eight transport ships and more than 800 British troops were lost. Although Vetch and others insisted the mission should go forward, a decision to abandon it ended yet another abortive venture to eliminate the French threat.

Vetch returned to his post as governor in Nova Scotia as the war ended. A controversy arose when Nicholson was appointed to replace Vetch. In the fall, he left for Boston to defend his conduct, and in the spring of 1714, Vetch sailed for London, where he successfully lobbied for reappointment. In January 1715, Nicholson was recalled to England and replaced by Vetch, who remained governor until 1717. He finally returned to England in 1719, where he unsuccessfully sought relief for his seriously depleted finances. He died on 30 April 1732, a prisoner in king's bench for debt.

Samuel Vetch was a colonial merchant whose advocacy of a policy of aggression to

V

remove the French and Indian threat on the northern border of New England made him a recognized leader in the British colonies in North America. His life was marked by opportunities, which Vetch used to full advantage to rise to a colonial governorship.

Boyd Childress

References

J. Bartlet Brebner, "Vetch, Samuel," in *Dictionary of American Biography*, 28 vols. (1928–1958), 10:260–262; Douglas Edward Leach, *Arms for Empire: A Military History of the British Colonies in North America, 1607–1763* (1973); Robert Hamilton Vetch, "Vetch, Samuel," in *Dictionary of National Biography*, 21 vols. (1921–1927), 20:293–296; Samuel Vetch, "Canada Survey'd," in *Calendar of State Papers, Colonial Series, America and the West Indies, June 1708–1709*, Vol. 24, no. 60 (1922):41–51; George Macgregor Waller, *Samuel Vetch: Colonial Enterpriser* (1960).

See also ACADIA, BRITISH CONQUEST OF (1710); CANADA, BRITISH EXPEDITION AGAINST (1709); CANADA, BRITISH EXPEDITION AGAINST (1711); NICHOLSON, FRANCIS; QUEEN ANNE'S WAR

Villasur, Pedro de (?–1720)

Pedro de Villasur was commander of a disastrous Spanish colonial military expedition. The Spanish were fiercely possessive of their New World empire, which in theory encompassed all the New World. Although they could not enforce their claim on most of North America, which had been colonized in turn by the French, the Dutch, and the English, they were extremely sensitive to encroachments on their northern borderlands, which were the outer defense for the colony of New Spain and its precious silver mines around Zacatecas and Guanajuato.

The northernmost outpost of this empire was in New Mexico. From there, Spanish military commanders watched uneasily for signs of French influence among the nomadic tribes that roamed the vast expanses west of the Mississippi and Missouri Rivers. Evidence of French intrusion included trade goods and firearms. While the Spanish had always strived to keep guns out of the hands of Apaches and Comanches, the French had no compunctions against arming rival groups like the Pawnee.

In 1720, word arrived from Mexico that the English and French were at war with Spain in Europe. Governor Antonio Valverde of New Mexico learned early in the year that a French party had traveled from the Illinois country to trade among the southern Pawnee of the plains. The Frenchmen left muskets among the Indians, a development that greatly disturbed the Comanche, who quickly brought word of the expedition to Valverde in Santa Fe. In late June 1720, the governor sent an expedition under the command of his Lieutenant General, Pedro de Villasur, consisting of 42 soldiers, 60 Indian allies, three civilian settlers, a chaplain, an interpreter, and a chief Indian scout, out onto the plains in search of the alleged French intruders.

Heading northeast, the party passed through Jicarilla Apache and Carlana Apache territory, crossed the Arkansas River on rafts, and reached El Cuartelejo in southeastern Colorado, where they stopped to rest. By August, the Spaniards had reached the junction of the North and South Platte Rivers, in present-day Nebraska. Sighting a Pawnee village, Villasur sent a Pawnee captive to make contact with the Indians. But he was greeted with hostility, and fled back to the Spanish. Undeterred, Villasur's party made camp across the river from the hostile Pawnee and sent another emissary across with gifts. The man shouted back that the Indians were friendly, but that they would not let him return. He also reported there were no "Spaniards" (meaning Europeans) present in the camp. Some of the Indians visiting the Spanish camp, however, spoke of a white man, and Villasur sent a note in French across the river. The only result was the return of an old linen flag and a paper with illegible writing.

Uneasy that their emissary had been detained, Villasur's officers urged caution and retreat. At sunrise on 14 August, a party of Pawnee crossed the river and attacked the expedition, stampeding the horse herd and firing muskets at the disorganized Spanish and their Indian allies. A fierce battle raged until the survivors fled, leaving behind 32 dead Spaniards (including Villasur) and a dozen slain Indians. They had managed to inflict heavy losses on the Pawnee, who did not pursue them. Whether or not Frenchmen were actually present among the Pawnee was never clearly established.

The remains of the party limped back to Santa Fe, where their dismal report shocked Governor Valverde. Not only had hostile Indians with guns virtually wiped out a Spanish military expedition, but he had lost a third of his best soldiers. When his report reached Mexico City, plans were drawn up to reinforce New Mexico, but before funds and troops could be raised, the warring powers in Europe made peace. The Spanish never forgot the worst military disaster that had ever befallen them in the borderlands.

Peter Stern

References

John Francis Bannon, *The Spanish Borderlands Frontier, 1513–1821* (1974); Alfred B. Thomas, *After Coronado: Spanish Exploration Northeast of New Mexico, 1696–1727* (1935).

See also NEW MEXICO

Virginia

Virginia represented Great Britain's first successful attempt to colonize North America. Capitalizing on the early interest in colonial plantations that characterized Queen Elizabeth I's reign and spilled over into the early Stuart court, influential English courtiers pursued royal grants to sanction colonial settlement. A group of Londoners acquired the rights to colonize the southern portion of the continent from 34 and 45 north latitude in letters patent from King James I on 10 April 1606. Initially, this grant encompassed all of the territory from the Passamaquoddy Bay in Maine to the Cape Fear River in North Carolina, with the Atlantic and Pacific Oceans serving as eastern and western boundaries respectively. On receiving approval of their charter from the king, seven of the investors formed the Virginia Company of London on the joint-stock model and began preparations for an expedition to the New World.

After eight months of intense activity, three ships under the command of Captain Christopher Newport, the *Susan Constant, Godspeed,* and *Discovery,* with 104 prospective colonists, set sail for the Chesapeake Bay. A varied conglomeration of sailors, soldiers, company officials, gentlemen, and boys, the adventurers were poorly suited to carve a settlement out of the hostile North American wilderness. Before the expedition even reached the Chesapeake sickness, hunger, and a quarrel between company councilors Edward Maria Wingfield and John Smith that led to the latter's arrest and confine-

ment, presaged the discord and confusion that would mark the colony's early years.

The convoy arrived in the Chesapeake in April 1607. After a short series of exploratory ventures, on 13 May 1607, the councilors chose a small peninsula on the north bank of the James River as the site for their permanent habitat and named it Jamestown. Despite its precarious location—the settlement was plagued by insects, brackish water, and unfriendly Indians—Jamestown emerged as the center of colonial activity in Virginia until the late seventeenth century.

Under the stewardship of the London Company, Virginia made slow but steady progress. In 1613, John Rolfe devised a viable method of growing tobacco and gave the colony a cash crop. Quasi-military arrangements solved early defensive, labor, and leadership problems. Diplomacy and the sagacious rule of the Indian leader Powhatan over a confederacy of local tribes allowed the English and Virginia's native population to live in relative harmony. But by 1618, the colony had not yet turned a profit for the London Company, its white population had not stabilized, and the harsh conditions of colonial life had failed to attract large numbers of colonists. Responding to these difficulties, the London Company undertook its most ambitious reorganization. The "Great Charter" that resulted from the 1618 reorganization eschewed military rule in favor of a general assembly and reaffirmed a recently created "headright" system that allowed those buying passage to Virginia to receive 50 acres of land plus 50-acre grants for each additional passage purchased in return for a modest 2 shilling annual quitrent. These reforms led to the creation of the first colonial legislature in North America and went a long way toward making Virginia more attractive to British adventurers. Adoption of the headright system attracted indentured servants who bound themselves for four to seven years of service. Liberal opportunities for planters to extend the term of service and high mortality rates made indentured servitude the preferred form of labor for most of the seventeenth century. When African laborers were introduced to Virginia by the Dutch in 1619, a second pool of bound servants became available to Virginia's planters. Thus, developments in 1618 and 1619 laid the foundations of home rule, large land acquisitions, and bound servitude—characteristics that would define the very nature of colonial Virginia.

Divided leadership, changing company policies, and devotion to a single staple-crop economy characterized the latter stages of the formative period of colonial settlement and severely impeded Virginia's chances of becoming a profitable enterprise. A further obstacle presented itself with Powhatan's death in 1622, as leadership changes in the confederacy witnessed the rise of a militant faction and precipitated the Virginia-Indian War of 1622–1632, which reduced the white population of the colony by one-third, further depleted the London Company's coffers, and hardened Virginians' attitudes toward the Indian.

The creation of a staple-crop economy; the potential of Tidewater, Piedmont, Appalachian, and trans-Appalachian Virginia; and the maintenance of a settlement for nearly two decades, however, promised much for Virginia's future. Such prospects attracted the interest of the British monarchy. Capitalizing on the London Company's dismal record and recent Indian troubles, James I moved toward bringing the colony under more direct royal control. James's early death in 1625 allowed his successor, Charles I, to make Virignia a royal colony in that year.

As a royal colony, Virginia prospered moderately under the vigorous leadership of its governors, especially Sir John Harvey (1630–1635) and Sir William Berkeley (1642–1652; 1660–1676). By mid-century, the colony had become a rather stable entity. Creation of a strong militia led to the systematic destruction of the Indian population. War raged briefly between 1644 and 1646, as Opechancanough waged a last, desperate campaign. The war ended with Opechancanough's capture and murder. After 1646, Berkeley pursued a shrewd policy toward the Indians that excluded them from participation in the colony's affairs. By the late seventeenth century, historian Robert Beverley would cheerfully write that "the *Indians* [his emphasis] of Virginia are almost wasted."

As the English removed the Indian presence, the colony underwent a remarkable growth spurt. New settlements moved out in all directions from the center at Jamestown. By the 1670s, the English had placed outposts on the Eastern Shore, in the Northern Neck, on the southside frontier, and had begun a concerted westward expansion. The new settlements filled the needs of a growing population made up of fledgling planters, indentured servants, and African laborers. Tobacco production remained the primary economic endeavor of these Virginians despite Berkeley's vigorous attempts at diversificiation.

In order to facilitate the proliferation of new settlements, Virginians created new counties as early as the 1630s and provided for their organization, protection, and leadership. The jewel of this early period of growth and development was the creation of a county court system. County courts became the center of local affairs, as their judges served in a variety of administrative and judicial capacities. At the highest levels of government, the governor implemented royal policy with the assistance of a group of influential councilors and the members of the House of Burgesses sitting as the general assembly.

By the 1660s, the tremendous growth had taken its toll on the stability of the colony. Overproduction plunged the tobacco economy into destructive boom-and-bust cycles. Population increased, and rapid settlement placed stress on the colony's elite as newly arrived planters and former indentured servants jostled for limited positions in the governmental establishment. The assembly, too, had grown jealous of the autonomy gained during the period of neglect that accompanied the English civil war. Replaced during the war, but loyal to the Stuarts, Sir William Berkeley assumed control of a very different colony when he resumed his position as governor in 1660. Berkeley also found himself at odds with a new Stuart conception of empire. In 1676, the tense situation erupted into open revolt as disgruntled members of Virginia's under-elite used specious fears of renewed Indian attacks on the frontier to voice their displeasure with Berkeley's government. Following the leadership of Nathaniel Bacon, these Virginians captured Jamestown, ousted the governor, and took control of the general assembly. Berkeley quickly received aid from England and suppressed the rebellion brutally. The violent interlude drew the notice of Whitehall, and Berkeley was recalled to England and replaced by a commission of three.

In the decade following Bacon's Rebellion a new political order emerged. The rowdy under-elite that responded to Bacon's call emerged as a major voice in Virginia politics by the 1690s. Berkeley's successors and subsequent governors responded to changes in British imperial policy and gradually began to give the general assembly a greater role in colonial politics. Expansion of the assembly was mirrored by physical growth and proliferation of new local offices—measures designed to soothe the restless and now stable free white population.

Accompanying the expansion of counties and offices, Virginians began to embrace slavery (a labor alternative that had been becoming more attractive since the 1660s) as the preferred form of service.

The early eighteenth century witnessed another period of vigorous development. Increases in population, the rise of a close partnership between Virginia planters and English creditors, the institutionalization of slavery, and consolidation of gentry hegemony ushered Virginia into what historians have called its "Golden Age." During the "Golden Age," the general assembly fortified its autonomy through effective negotiations with the royal governors. The gentry flourished during this period and demonstrated its prosperity with the construction of Georgian mansions and a growing record of indebtedness. Until mid-century, the gentry suffered no serious threats to its leadership or the deferential system that supported it.

A major challenge to gentry hegemony arose during the mid-eighteenth century when Virginia, historically and officially an Anglican province, witnessed the rise of New Light congregations as the "Great Awakening" spread to the South. Slowly but steadily, for the rest of the colonial period, evangelical ministers chipped away at the deferential system through their condemnations of gentry excess. Their ideas were especially forceful in the backcountry, which would become a major concern of gentry patriarchs in the years preceding the American Revolution.

Despite the religious upheaval, the gentry remained in firm control of Virginia society and politics. Scions of well-placed families such as Thomas Jefferson, George Washington, Patrick Henry, James Madison, George Mason, James Mercer, Carter Braxton, and Edmund Pendleton emerged as leading figures in the political arena in the pre-Revolutionary era. In the decade of crisis that preceded the Revolution, these leaders served their political apprenticeships, learning the skills that would propel them to powerful positions in national affairs after 1776.

By 1776, Virginia's population topped the half-million mark. Approximately 200,000 of those residents were slaves. Agriculturally, tobacco remained the major cash crop; however, corn and wheat exports had begun to rival production in the middle colonies. Virginia merchants were begining to thrive, but on the eve of the Revolution, five-sixths of Virginia's economy depended on the export of agricultural goods. Accordingly, Virginia relied on English imports for most of its manufactured necessities. In 1784, Thomas Jefferson conservatively estimated that Virginians owed in the vicinity of £2,000,000 sterling to British creditors.

As relations began to deteriorate between England and its North American colonies after the Seven Years' War, Virginia's politicians moved slowly and conservatively, first into resistance and, reluctantly, in 1776, into revolution. Throughout the resistance, however, Virginia played a pivotal part in colonial affairs. Staunch support of Massachusetts in the wake of the Coercive Acts and unflinching leadership in the Continental Congresses thrust the Old Dominion's political leaders into the forefront of the revolutionary struggle. The Virginia constitution and declaration of rights both preceded the drafting of the Declaration of Independence and served as prototypes for other, similar endeavors in the Revolutionary and early national periods.

Militarily, Virginia played a pivotal role in the history of Britain's 13 North American colonies. The fort at Jamestown and the early military structure of Virginia's government marked the most important aspects of early seventeenth-century British military involvement in North America. The Virginia militia became a formidable fighting force after Opechancanough's raid in 1622. In the eighteenth century, aggressive expansionist endeavors by Virginians into the Ohio Valley sparked the conflicts that opened up the campaigns on the continent. Washington's defeat at Fort Necessity essentially began hostilities in North America. Virginia, as did other colonies, contributed mightily to the war effort. During the American Revolution, Virginia was active in two major phases of the war. In 1775, Virginian forces clashed with those loyal to Governor John Murray, Lord Dunmore in the vicinity of Hampton Roads. After clearing out militia units from Kemp's Landing on 15 November 1775, Dunmore's troops occupied Norfolk by 23 November. A determined resistance under the direction of William Woodford, however, cleared the British out of Norfolk by 15 December. During the southern campaign, Banastre Tarleton's nearly successful raid on Charlottesville and the pivotal siege of Yorktown in 1781 marked the major activities in Virginia. After the surrender at Yorktown, the battle phase of the Revolutionary War came to an end.

V

Virginia's emergence as one of England's most important colonies epitomizes the development of British North America. The social and political settlements fleshed out in the Old Dominion set the standard for the growth of the Chesapeake colonies and influenced similar experiments in the lower South. One of the largest and wealthiest colonies, Virginia, accordingly, assumed a role of central importance in the early years of American nationhood.

Mark F. Fernandez

References

Richard R. Beeman, *The Evolution of the Southern Backcountry: A Case Study of Lunenburg County, Virginia, 1746–1832* (1984); Robert Beverley, *The History and Present State of Virginia*, ed. by Louis B. Wright (1947); Warren M. Billings, *Jamestown and the Founding of the Nation* (1991); ———, *Virginia's Viceroy: Their Majesties' Governor General, Francis Howard, Baron Howard of Effingham* (1991); ———, "The Growth of Political Institutions in Virginia, 1634–1676," *William and Mary Quarterly*, 3rd ser. (1974):225–242; ———, comp., *The Old Dominion in the Seventeenth Century: A Documentary History of Virginia* (1975); Warren M. Billings, John Selby, and Thad Tate, *Colonial Virginia: A History* (1986); Philip Alexander Bruce, *The Institutional History of Virginia in the Seventeenth Century*, 2 vols. (1910).

Wesley Frank Craven, *The Southern Colonies in the Seventeenth Century* (1949); Rhys Isaac, *The Transformation of Virginia, 1740–1790* (1982); Thomas Jefferson, *Notes on the State of Virginia*, ed. by William Peden (1934); Susan Myra Kingsbury, ed., *The Records of the Virginia Company of London*, 4 vols. (1906–1935); Edmund S. Morgan, *American Slavery, American Freedom: The Ordeal of Colonial Virginia* (1975); Richard L. Morton, *Colonial Virginia*, 2 vols. (1960).

William L. Shea, *The Virginia Militia in the Seventeenth Century* (1982); Thad Tate and David Ammerman, eds., *The Chesapeake in the Seventeenth Century: Essays on Anglo-American Society and Politics* (1979); Wilcomb E. Washburn, *The Governor and the Rebel: A History of Bacon's Rebellion in Virginia* (1957).

See also BACON, NATHANIEL; BACON'S REBELLION; BERKELEY, WILLIAM; CHICKAHOMINY; COCKACOESKE;

NANSEMOND; NOTTOWAY; OPECHANCANOUGH; PAMUNKEY; POWHATAN; RAPPAHANNOCK; SMITH, JOHN; VIRGINIA-INDIAN TREATY (1646); VIRGINIA-INDIAN TREATY (1677/1680); VIRGINIA-INDIAN WAR (1622–1632); VIRGINIA-INDIAN WAR (1644–1646)

Virginia-Indian Treaty (1646)

The Third Anglo-Powhatan War (1644–1646) ended with a treaty between Virginia and Necotowance, the new paramount chief of the Powhatan Indians. The treaty was passed as Act I of the October 1646 Grand Assembly (Hening, *Statutes* I:323–326); no record survives of the negotiations leading up to it.

The treaty provided that Necotowance's people were now tributaries under English military protection. They were to prove their loyalty by paying a tribute in beaver skins, staying out of English territory except on business with the governor, returning captured English guns and prisoners, and returning all runaway servants to come to them in the future. To contact the governor, they were to present themselves only at certain English forts, wearing special striped coats. English territory was to be the peninsula between the James and York Rivers and also the south bank of the James River. The English governor was also later to open the north bank of the York River below the Poropotank River after notifying the Indians. Everything else in Virginia remained in Indian hands.

The treaty of 1646 is significant for two reasons. In it, the Powhatans formally acknowledged defeat at English hands for the first time. It was also the first agreement to set boundaries between English and Powhatan holdings. The treaty remained officially in force until 1677, when it was replaced with a new one. But its land provision was violated immediately and unilaterally by the English in Act VI of the same session (Hening, *Statutes* I:328–329). That act allowed English people to settle *anywhere* north of the York River whenever their governor gave his permission.

Helen C. Rountree

References

William Waller Hening, comp., *The Statutes at Large, Being a Collection of All the Laws of Virginia from the First Session of the Legislature*, 13 vols. (1809–1823), 1.

See also COCKACOESKE; NANSEMOND; POWHATANS; VIRGINIA-INDIAN WAR (1644–1646)

Virginia-Indian Treaty (1677/1680)

Once Bacon's Rebellion had subsided, the commissioners sent from England to investigate felt it necessary to reassure the tributary Indians. Accordingly, in 1677, they drew up a treaty on behalf of King Charles II, which was signed by the Pamunkeys and Weyanocks (Algonquian-speakers) and the Nottoways (Iroquoian-speakers). Because of sundry difficulties, the treaty was not ratified until 1680, when it was additionally signed by the Appomattocks and Nanzaticos (Algonquins), Saponis and Monacans (Siouans), and Meherrins (Iroquoians).

The new treaty's provisions overlapped those of its predecessor of 1646. The Indians were tributaries to be protected militarily in exchange for tribute in beaver skins. But their loyalty was less a matter of returning captured English property than of giving warning of "strange" Indians on the frontiers and joining the English in fighting such enemies. Indian civil rights were specifically to be upheld in the colony (a matter of colonial law since the 1650s), a necessity for people now surrounded by English settlers. Indian lands were to extend for a three-mile radius around Indian towns—a dictum that was not only impossible to enforce (due to English squatters and Indian voluntary sales), but also nearly impossible to survey in the first place for those Indians like the Chickahominy, who lived in dispersed, rather than nucleated, settlements.

The major significance of the 1677/1680 treaty is that it is still in force in Virginia. The two surviving reservations, the Pamunkey and Mattaponi, have autonomous governments directly answerable to the governor of Virginia, and still bring him tribute in game each fall.

Helen C. Rountree

References

"Commissioners Appointed Under the Great Seale of England for the Virginia Affairs," in "Articles of Peace between the most Mighty Prince . . . Charles II . . . And the several Indian Kings and Queens &c . . . the 29th day of May: 1677 . . . [1680]," *Virginia Magazine of History and Biography* 14 (1906):289–296; Martha W. McCartney, "Cockacoeske, Queen of Pamunkey: Diplomat and Suzeraine," in *Powhatan's Mantle: Indians in the Colonial Southeast*, Peter H. Wood, Gregory A. Waselkov, and M. Thomas Hatley, eds. (1989):173–295.

See also APPOMATTOCK; BACON'S REBELLION; MARYLAND; NANSEMOND; PAMUNKEY; VIRGINIA

Virginia-Indian War (1622–1632)

The records about this war are uneven, necessitating near-speculation in places. The best-documented years are those at the war's beginning, when English correspondence about it was copious and preserved afterward in the records of the Virginia Company of London. Before that, company records are spotty concerning Indian affairs, and after the company's dissolution in 1624, such affairs fell to the Virginia colony, many of whose records were burned in the American Civil War.

The combatants were the Algonquian-speaking Powhatan Indians and the English of Jamestown colony. The war was their second. The colony had established itself in the Powhatan chiefdom's heartland on the James River, and since 1610 had successfully expanded along that river. Its move to raising tobacco as a cash crop in the late 1610s committed it to rapid expansion into Indian territory. The Indians thus lost their best farmland along the James and, in future, the other rivers. They also lost the middle sector of their territories, making it hazardous to go from the woods, in which they still gathered nuts and hunted, to the river, in which they still collected fish, shellfish, and tuckahoe tubers. Added to these territorial problems was the colony's fresh impetus for missionizing Indians after 1619, which the Powhatan chiefs and priests recognized as a political threat, and the already-religious commoners simply found insulting. Thus the stage had been set for serious conflict for some years before 1622, though the English failed to see it and assumed that the "massacre" was a retaliation for the death of the great warrior Nemattanew (Jack of the Feather) a short time before.

The Powhatans were led by Opechancanough, originally chief Powhatan's second brother and heir, and an astute, charismatic politician in his own right. As Powhatan aged and became less aggressive toward the English, so the hostile Opechancanough rose in power, until by 1614, he was known to be in command militarily. He apparently began organizing mass resistance to the English thereafter; it was he who finally succeeded in incorporating the independent Chickahominy tribe into the Powhatan polity in 1616. Powhatan's death in 1618 brought the first brother, Opitchapam (now renamed Otiotan), to the chieftaincy, but this "lame and decrepit" man was also overshadowed. Opechancanough's demands on outlying tribes made some of them nervous enough that in 1619, the Patawomecks staged a sort of show of solidarity with the English in order to retain their neutrality. When Opechancanough ordered the Eastern Shore chief to send a poisonous plant to use on the English in 1621, that chief went over to the English side altogether.

Thus when war broke out—a year late because of that well-publicized defection—it was mainly the James and York River Powhatans who were involved; the Rappahannock River Indians may have been sympathetic, and the Potomac River people remained neutral. There were other chinks in Opechancanough's armor: several Indians (often combined by historians into one name "Chanco") who had had extensive friendly contact with the English gave warning of the mass attack to come.

The war began with the famous "massacre" on 22 March 1622, in which about one-fourth of the English in the colony were killed. Assuming that the English would take this vicious "hint" and go home, Opechancanough did not follow up that attack with others; even sniping did not resume until September. The English thus had breathing space to regroup—and send home to their very populous country for more people. The next summer, under a temporary truce, the English hostages (all female by then) were returned, after which hostilities resumed, each side raiding the other and killing people of all ages and sexes, burning houses and cutting down crops. The biggest battle of the war occurred in July 1624, at Pamunkey, with Patuxets from what is now Maryland attending as observers. There, the Powhatans were raising extra corn for their James River tribes, who were too harassed to do so. In a pitched battle, the English outflanked the Indians and set about cutting down the corn, after which the Indians gave up and melted away with terrible loss of "face."

The succeeding years show a pattern of desultory summer raids conducted by two enemies who were increasingly tired of the fight. The Powhatans could not be starved out of a country in which they were expert foragers, and the constant trickle of new English into the colony could not be stopped. A temporary peace, which no one intended to keep, was made in 1628 (no provisions from it survive),

but it was not until 1632 that a "permanent" arrangement was made (also with no provisions surviving). Interestingly, that arrangement was specifically with the Pamunkeys and Chickahominies, not with "the Indians" in general, but the truce was nonetheless real. Peace was therefore restored, but both sides knew it to be a peace that would become increasingly fragile as the English resumed their flooding into Virginia and taking of Indian lands to raise tobacco.

Helen C. Rountree

References

J. Frederick Fausz, "The Powhatan Uprising of 1622: A Historical Study of Ethnocentrism and Cultural Conflict," Ph.D. Dissertation, College of William and Mary (1977); Susan Myra Kingsbury, ed., *The Records of the Virginia Company of London*, 4 vols. (1906–1935); Henry Reade McIlwaine, comp., *Minutes of the Council and General Court of Virginia, 1622–1632, 1670–1676* (1924); William S. Powell, "The Aftermath of the Massacre," *Virginia Magazine of History and Biography* 66 (1958):44–75; Helen C. Rountree, *Pocahontas's People: The Powhatan Indians of Virginia Through Four Centuries* (1990).

See also APPOMATTOCK; CHICKAHOMINY; OPECHANCANOUGH; PAMUNKEY; POWHATAN; POWHATANS; RAPPAHANNOCK; VIRGINIA-INDIAN WAR (1644–1646); WAR AND SOCIETY IN COLONIAL AMERICA

Virginia-Indian War (1644–1646)

The records about this war are very sparse, owing to the large-scale destruction of Virginia's colonial and (southeastern) county records in the American Civil War. The general outlines of the conflict are clear enough, but details are frequently lacking.

In this war, unlike the previous Virginia-Indian War (1622–1632), there was only one cause: territorial competition. English attitudes toward the Powhatans had hardened. What missionizing the English did for the remainder of the seventeenth century was on a small, local scale and was directed at Indian young people. Indian adults were another matter in English eyes: they could either come aboard as laborers or leave. And in the decade following the truce of 1632, there was an ever-increasing flood of

Englishmen into Virginia to espouse these views. The Virginia colony's outlook toward the land and its Indian owners was now entirely economic. And since the basis of that economy, tobacco, ate up a phenomenal amount of "new" land, the English regarded Indians who did not cooperate with the English takeover as hostile—a perfectly accurate assessment.

The Powhatans had already lost their prime farmland on the James River; after 1632 they saw it taken up wholesale on the lower York River. In 1640, Englishmen began trying to settle on the best land along the Rappahannock and Potomac. Losing that land meant not only losing the most productive croplands, but also losing free access between the forest and the rivers, both major food-producing zones in the Powhatan economy. The embittered James and upper York River tribes had already seen it happen on the James; the tribes on the more northerly rivers were now faced with the beginnings of it. The Rappahannock River people joined the Indian side when war came. The Potomac River people once more remained neutral, probably because they—and the Yeocomicos who had left Maryland and joined them—felt threatened by the new colony at St. Mary's and hesitated to open hostilities with the Virginia English.

Again the leader of the Powhatans was Opechancanough. He was now very old and so frail he had to be carried about, but his mind was apparently clear. Unfortunately, he—or his followers—had not absorbed a major lesson from his earlier campaign. When his men conducted their "massacre" on 18 March 1644, and in the James River area again, he did not (or could not) incite them to follow up their victory with more raids. Thus, once more, the English got a breathing space in which to regroup. Their casualties were also less disastrous this time: the death toll was about the same (nearly 400), but it was a much smaller proportion of the current English population.

Details of the ensuing war are few. The English retaliated so strongly in the James River valley that by 1646, nearly all the Powhatan tribes had fled altogether; the southside tribes to the Blackwater River, the Chickahominies to Pamunkey Neck. Only the Appomattocks and the Powhatans later returned. The Pamunkeys and their neighbors in the upper York basin held fast, as did the Rappahannock River people. Another war of attrition seemed to be in store for both sides, even though the badly outnumbered Powhatans were at a disadvantage. But the war ended after only two years. The Powhatans were still a paramount chiefdom; Opechancanough was their commander in chief, and he apparently had no charismatic, militarily astute heir. When Governor Sir William Berkeley made a sudden raid on his fort and succeeded in capturing him (he subsequently died at Jamestown), the old chief's lackluster successor, Necotowance, and the Powhatans became permanently subjugated to the English.

Helen C. Rountree

References

Robert Beverley, *This History and Present State of Virginia* (1707) rpt. 1947; Joseph Frank, ed., "News from Virginny, 1644," *Virginia Magazine of History and Biography* 65 (1957):84–87; William Waller Hening, comp., *The Statutes at Large*, 13 vols. (1809–1823), 1; Helen C. Rountree, *Pocahontas's People: The Powhatan Indians of Virginia Through Four Centuries* (1990).

See also BERKELEY, SIR WILLIAM; CHICKAHOMINY; OPECHANCANOUGH; PAMUNKEY; POWHATAN; RAPPAHANNOCK; VIRGINIA-INDIAN WAR (1622–1632).

Fort Vroomen (New York)
See FORT SARATOGA (NEW YORK)

Waccamaw

Located on the Waccamaw and Pee Dee Rivers in the early eighteenth century, little is known about the Waccamaw. They briefly participated in the Yamasee War against South Carolina in 1715, but apparently established a peace with that colony that was then broken in 1720. The only surviving source of the latter conflict noted that a runaway black slave had inspired the Waccamaw to hostilities. Their numbers decline thereafter from around 600 to 300. Some of the survivors probably joined the Catawba, though as late as 1755, they retained their separate identity.

Alan Gallay

References
    John R. Swanton, *The Indian Tribes of North America* (1952).

See also CATAWBA; YAMASEE WAR

Walker, Hovenden

See CANADA, BRITISH EXPEDITION AGAINST (1711)

Walking Purchase (1737)

Surrounding this Pennsylvanian acquisition of Delaware Indian land is a five-pointed controversy that divided some Delaware Indians against Pennsylvania and the Six Nations, that set two eighteenth-century Pennsylvania political parties furiously against each other, and that still stands historian against historian. The land in question, known as the "forks of the Delaware," encompassed a large group of Delawares, whose main spokesman was Nutimus. In 1727,

Nutimus granted a small tract of the land to James Logan, Pennsylvania's *de facto* Indian superintendent. Logan acquired the tract privately, violating Pennsylvania's charter, which gave the sole right to purchase Indian lands to the proprietors: John, Richard, and Thomas Penn. He had an interest in seeing the land cleared of its Indian title. The Penns also had such an interest. In debt, they had already sold tracts in the encumbered region to prospective immigrants.

In the fall of 1734, John and Thomas Penn, with Logan, failed to persuade Nutimus to sell the lands. The next spring, at a meeting with the Delawares in Pennsbury, Logan brought forth a highly dubious copy of a deed, dated 1686, which alleged that the Delawares had then sold to William Penn, not only the forks, but the entire west bank of the Delaware. Here begins one point in the controversy: The copy may well have been a fake. The Indians did recall a deed in 1686, but they did not recall such an extensive cession. Neither the original deed of 1686 nor the copy produced by Logan at Pennsbury have survived, thus it is impossible to verify them. Other purported copies of these deeds have survived, but they do not correspond with other available data surrounding William Penn's purchases in the 1680s. The Delawares initially refused to confirm the deed, but they were not as strong as the forces Pennsylvania mustered against them. In 1736, Logan secured the backing of the powerful Six Nations. The Six Nations agreed to become the sole arbiters of the Indian lands in Pennsylvania.

In August 1737, the overawed Forks Delawares met with Logan in Philadelphia. They agreed to sign the Walking Purchase Deed, a newly-drawn confirmation of the disputed deed of 1686. Here begins a second point in the controversy: The new deed contained a mislabeled map. Shown to the illiterate but geographically knowledgeable Delawares, it deceived them into believing that they were ceding lands south of their villages, when the written language indicated that they were yielding lands north of Tohiccon Creek, lands that included their villages. Moreover, not all boundaries were clearly determined by the signed document. To determine the full extent of the cession the parties had to participate in a "walk."

This walk of 1737 marks a third point in the controversy: The direction of the walk on the deed is rendered unclear by blanks in the manuscript. The walk itself was performed by known colonial athletes on cleared trails. In that day and a half, they took in 64 miles, amounting to 55 crowflight miles. Far beyond anything the Delaware signers of the Walking Purchase Deed had imagined, the Walking Purchase took away virtually all their lands. The Delawares did not wait for the walk to be finished before they started protesting, and after it was done they did not move. By 1740, however, Pennsylvania had issued patents on the lands, and settlers moved in. A Delaware petition to the justice of the peace of Bucks County failed.

Nutimus had one last hope, the Iroquois. But in 1742, the Iroquois sided with Pennsylvania, which raised the fourth point in the controversy: Onondaga's speaker Canasatego now claimed that the Delawares had no right to dispose of the lands in the first place, because they had been conquered and "made women" by the Iroquois. No such conquest is known in the record. Much of the historiographic argument about it surrounds the proper interpretation of the Delawares' status as "women" of the Iroquois. But whatever the earlier relationship between the people, in 1742, Canasatego and Pennsylvania agreed that the Delawares were Iroquois subjects without authority over land. Canasatego ordered them to leave the forks and to retire to lands that the Six Nations set aside for them in the Susquehanna Valley. The Forks Delawares remained subjects from at least this point until their rebellion in the Seven Years' War.

The influence of the Walking Purchase on the Seven Years' War involves the last point in the controversy, for the Quaker party charged the Proprietary party with causing, through the Walking Purchase, the Delaware Indians' disaffection from Pennsylvania in 1755. That charge, first raised by the Delaware Teedyuscung, but invoked by Israel Pemberton, Charles Thomson, and Benjamin Franklin, brought the Walking Purchase into prominence in histories of Pennsylvania. The proprietors denied skullduggery; a poorly conducted commission headed by Sir William Johnson supported their denials in 1762; and historians have argued both sides since. It now appears that the Quaker party charge has great merit, but it must be qualified. The Walking Purchase clearly involved much fraud, but it cannot be held solely, or even mainly, responsible for Delaware hostility against the British in 1755. Not all Delawares to go to war in 1755 had once inhabited the Walking Purchase lands. Nor were the Penns and Logan the only Britons to give the Delawares cause for war.

Gregory E. Dowd

References

Francis Jennings, *The Ambiguous Iroquois Empire: The Covenant Chain and the Confederation of Indian Tribes with English Colonies from its beginnings to the Lancaster Treaty of 1744* (1984); Anthony F.C. Wallace, *King of the Delawares: Teedyuscung, 1700–1763* (1949); Paul A.W. Wallace, *Conrad Weiser: Friend of Colonist and Mohawk* (1945).

See also DELAWARE; NUTIMUS; PENNSYLVANIA; TEEDYUSCUNG

Walley, John (1644–1712)

John Walley is another example of a prominent politician given military responsibilities far above his abilities. Born in England in 1644, Walley became prominent in Plymouth Colony and instrumental in the founding of Bristol, Rhode Island. Through his early career, Walley accumulated many honors and political positions. He became a member of the Ancient and Honorable Artillery Company of Massachusetts in 1671, governor's assistant in Plymouth from 1683–1686, captain of the Bristol militia in 1684, and served as a councilor under Sir Edmund Andros.

This political prominence led to his selection as commander of the land forces for the Quebec expedition of 1690. The plan called for the land forces to disembark and attack the town while the fleet shelled the city. Walley seemed to lose his nerve once he and his soldiers were ashore. When the New Englanders pushed back the French forces sent to oppose or harass the landing, many expected Walley to order an immediate assault on the town. But time passed with no command, and the adrenaline of the provincial soldiers began to dissipate.

The Reverend John Wise searched for Walley throughout the army and finally found him in an obviously depressed state. Wise asked him what he was doing, and Walley replied, "I cannot rule them. To Whom I replyed sire you must not expect when men are let loose upon an Enemie that they should attend all the Ceremonies martial and that are in fashion in a field of Peace But Sir said I what do you intend to doe he replyed I thing they intend to lodge here all Night." Wise urged an immediate attack because the men were "Warme by to Morrow they will Stiffen and Coole." The attack never occurred, and Wise later found Walley wandering about "swallowed up with thoughts which I can deem from first to last to be only the Invincible Arrest of fear." Walley's paralysis was noticed by others as well. As one anonymous participant concluded, "but what is an army of Lyons when they must not go on Except a frighted Hart shall lead them?"

To give Walley his due, half his soldiers were sick on the transports, the powder supplies were low (an anticipated shipment of powder from England had failed to arrive), and had he ordered the attack, the provincials would have found that large French reinforcements had just entered Quebec after a forced march from Montreal. There is every indication that his indecision and anxiety attack, while not expected in a military commander, probably saved many New England lives.

Walley's experience at command did not hurt his social and political position. He would serve on the Governor's Council from 1693–1694, and 1696–1706; as commissioner of war 1693–1694; and become judge of the superior court of judicature with rank of major general of militia. But he would never take the field in a military capacity after 1690. John Walley died on 11 January 1712.

Steven C. Eames

References
Anon., "Phips Expedition to Canada," *Massachusetts Historical Society Proceedings*, Vol. 15; Steven C. Eames, "Rustic Warriors: Warfare and the Provincial Soldier on the Northern Frontier, 1689–1748," Ph.D. Dissertation, University of New Hampshire (1989); "Narrative of Mr. John Wise," *Massachusetts Historical Society Proceedings*, Vol. 15.

See also ANCIENT AND HONORABLE ARTILLERY COMPANY OF MASSACHUSETTS; CANADA, NEW ENGLAND EXPEDITION AGAINST (1690)

Wall Street Palisade (New York)

In 1653, due to trouble with the English colonies of New England and local Indians, it was decided by Petrus (Peter) Stuyvesant, governor of New Netherland, and the burgomasters of New Amsterdam to build a palisade along the northern edge of the Dutch settlement. (At this time it was also decided to build walls along both riverfronts of the settlement. Residents of the city with riverfront property were ordered to build a wall of planks along New Amsterdam's riverfront. Thus, when the Wall Street palisade and the riverfront walls were completed, New Amsterdam was completely enclosed.) Funds for the palisade were raised from the citizenry, who were also required to assist in the construction. The palisades' logs were 12 feet long and 18 inches in circumference. They were sharpened at one end. At regular intervals, logs 21 inches in diameter were placed in the palisade with rails attached to them. The costs for the logs and the rails was 20 stivers each. When completed, the palisade and bastions were mounted with brass cannons at various points. There were two gates—one on the East River road, and the other where Wall Street and Broadway meet today.

Anthony P. Inguanzo

See also NEW NETHERLAND; STUYVESANT, PETRUS

Fort Walpack (New Jersey)

Fort Walpack was one of the four forts built in 1755 by Governor Jonathan Belcher to improve defenses along the frontier. Located in Walpack Township, Sussex, the exact location of the fort is unknown. The palisaded fort was 50 feet square, and in addition to a small blockhouse, it enclosed a wooden church. It was designed to provide essential defensive measures during the French and Indian War.

David L. Whitesell

Wampanoag

Also known as the Pokanokets, the Wampanoags claimed southeastern Massachusetts, including Cape Cod, the easternmost section of Narragansett Bay, Nantucket Island, and Martha's Vineyard. Before being decimated by the epidemics of 1617–1619, the Wampanoag population may have reached a peak of 24,000, making it one of the strongest tribes in southern New England. Yet some Wampanoag villages lost upwards of 90 percent of their population to the epidemics, thereby effecting a social, economic, and political collapse. The Wampanoags, therefore, became susceptible to the Narragansetts, who, c. 1620, forced Massasoit (Osamequin), sachem of the Wampanoags, and ten of his *pineses*, or war captains, into a vassal state and the forfeiture of their lands in the Narragansett Bay area.

Acting on the advice of Squanto, Massasoit and his brother, Quadequina, capitalized on the arrival of the Pilgrims in 1621, establishing a treaty of mutual protection that would tenuously hold until 1675. Plymouth offered an end to the ritual humiliation and oppressive tribute demanded by the Narragansetts. Yet the Pilgrims practiced an aggressive military strategy that did not relate well with the Wampanoag's symbolic and ceremonial perception of war. The Pilgrims also had an avarice for exclusive rights to, and disbursement of, Wampanoag lands.

After Massasoit died in 1662, his son, Wamsutta, known to the English as Alexander, became the Wampanoag sachem. Wamsutta, however, died in 1664, when Josiah Winslow escorted Wamsutta to Plymouth to answer charges of improperly selling land to Rhode Island "heretics." Wamsutta's brother, Metacom, also known as Philip, became the next Wampanoag sachem. Philip would acquiesce to the English until June 1675, when he led a war (King Philip's War) against the English. By August 1676, Philip would be killed and much of the Wampanoag tribe annihilated, scattered, or sold into slavery.

Richard C. Goode

References

Francis Jennings, *The Invasion of America: Indians, Colonialism, and the Cant of Conquest* (1975); G. Mourt, *A Journal of the Pilgrims at Plymouth: Mourt's Relation* (1622); Neal Salisbury, *Manitou and Providence: Indians, Europeans, and the Making of New England, 1500–1643* (1982); Bruce

Trigger, ed., *Handbook of North American Indians: Vol. 15, Northeast* (1978); Alden T. Vaughan, *New England Frontier: Puritans and Indians, 1620–1675* (1965).

See also KING PHILIP'S WAR; PHILIP; PILGRIM; NARRAGANSETT; SQUANTO

War and Society in Colonial America

War was a chronic preoccupation of colonial Americans. As such, it had a significant impact on the development of colonial society from its earliest seventeenth-century origins. War, and the threat of it, dictated where the original settlements were situated, laid out, and constructed, and influenced how and where they expanded. It colored relationships between the European colonists and their Native American neighbors; in turn, this affected how settlers viewed their new environment. War strengthened the colonists' sense of community, uniting these contentious people. Furthermore, war, in all of its aspects, was one of the primary determinants in shaping the colonists, both as individuals, and collectively, as a society.

Colonial society was neither forged on the crucible of war nor was it especially martial in character. The basic colonial defense establishment—community-based militia—mirrored its parent society's general antimilitarism. Yet even limited preparedness demanded such a proportion of colonial resources that military affairs became a principle concern. Over time, the colonists' response to war, and the myths and traditions that grew up around war, became essential elements of the colonial ethos, part of what made the colonists Americans. When hostilities broke out between England and the colonies in 1775, defense of these ideas were elemental to why Americans revolted; they also would control how they fought their Revolution. Moreover, so central were these ideas in defining the national character that, in generalized form, their influence may be observed even today.

To appreciate the strength of these ideas and the impact and influence that war had on colonial society, it is first necessary to understand those often incomprehensible people, the colonial Americans. They were, wrote historian Michael Kammen in a book of the same title, a "people of paradox." He could not have been more correct. They were at once a people of conflict and consensus, of rigidity and flexibility, of simplicity and complexity. They fled the Old World for the opportunities of the New, but for education, philosophy, heroes, and even military advice they turned back to the Old. They studied the classic literature of Greece and Rome and hanged their neighbors as witches. They migrated for religious freedom and brought intolerance; they bitterly opposed tyranny and made African men and women slaves. Avowedly Christian, their God was the fierce warrior chieftain of the Old Testament Hebrews. They came seeking peace and considered war distasteful, but when they went to war—as they often did—they fought knowing that God was on their side, unrestrained by any rules save His.

To modern eyes, the colonists appear as a mass of contradictions; yet, among themselves, they juxtaposed these clearly disparate views into a relatively cohesive, harmonious society. This was due, in large measure, to their practical nature. Early on, colonists quickly learned that they could count on little assistance from Europe; early seventeenth-century Britannia barely ruled the Channel and was only a shadow of the great naval power it would soon become. Isolated in tiny New England coastal communities and along the Virginia tidewater, the colonists lay vulnerable to assault; at any moment a hostile fleet might anchor offshore, or the morning's stillness be shattered by war whoops. Necessity forced them to make do with what little they had or could create; they had to—or die. So they became increasingly self-sufficient, adapting Old World ideas, practices, and traditions to New World conditions just as they adopted ways and customs of Native Americans and displaced Africans in order to survive. Accordingly, self-sufficiency and self-preservation helped define their ideas, their world view, their self-perception and self-confidence—both as individuals and as a society—in ways that cannot be measured, except by their actions.

The men and women who began peopling British North America from the early seventeenth century came to the New World not as conquerors, but as civilian-colonists. Unlike the Spanish conquistadors, who carved out an empire by sheer force of arms, English settlers generally aimed at colonization: the creation of new communities and commercial ventures, all in harmony with the natives. True, this difference ultimately mattered little to dispossessed Native Americans, and economic exploitation (differing in degrees) played a significant role in the establishment and development of the new colonies. And that some colonists clanked ashore struggling under the weight of body armor and broadswords speaks more of conflict than harmony. But landing on unknown shores unarmed would have been the height of foolishness, and the colonists were anything but fools.

They were, for the most part, thoughtful, intelligent, eminently practical people; they were also tough. For those men and women who pitched and yawed across the ocean in small, leaky ships, death and suffering from childbirth, disease, and violence formed a part of everyday life. So, prior to boarding ship, they prepared themselves long and well for any eventuality, especially war. These colonists, after all, were products of a tumultuous, violent epoch in European history. Often ignored is the fact that English colonization of North America paralleled England's brutal pacification of Ireland and the bloody Thirty Years' War (1618–1648). The colonists' understanding of war derived from fundamental and ancient sources and was influenced greatly by the endless ferocity of Old World religious and secular strife, not the still-to-come Age of Reason.

For them, war occurred with such regularity that it was not considered an aberration but a part of life. "To every thing there is a season, and a time to every purpose under heaven," they read in Ecclesiastes (3.1.8), ". . . A time to love, and a time to hate; a time of war, and a time of peace." This Biblical perspective was apt, for among Europeans of the period, both devoid and otherwise, conventional wisdom accepted a providential explanation for floods, droughts, famines, and wars. War was perceived as having been "ordained by the Almightie himselfe," wrote Elizabethan playwright and soldier Barnabe Rich in 1604, "as a scourge upon the people, to make them feele and know their sinnes." No small wonder people who maintained that divine winds destroyed the Spanish Armada (1588) also believed that it was the hand of God that slew thousands of Native American Indians with European-transmitted diseases in the early seventeenth century, thereby opening the New World to them.

Another reason for such intense preparation was that conflict in the New World was a distinct possibility. England defeated the armada, but victory brought no respite from hostilities. Since the colonists transgressed upon lands claimed by the Spanish, amphibious raids from Spain's numerous American possessions posed a constant menace. As a deterrence, and because of philosophic and practical reasons, the colonists sought accord with the Indians. But periodic skirmishes and a major war that almost wiped out the Virginia colony (1622) reinforced their need for defensive measures. Therefore, when colonist met Indian, one hand extended an olive branch, but the other firmly grasped a sword. This was not warlike, but prudent. To the aspiring colonists, weapons of war were essential tools: they would have no more crossed the ocean without hoes or Bibles than to have left their blunderbusses, crossbows, and pikes at home.

Ironically, so thorough was their preparation in addressing defense requirements that some scholars have colored the early transoceanic migrations and colonial experience in a martial hue. To be sure, the colonists bore arms, constructed rude palisades around their shelters, and engaged veterans of the continental and Irish wars as military advisors. And when they warred against the Native American Indians, they did so with an unbridled ferocity. Yet, for all of the colonists' concerns with military affairs and the seemingly constant violence, colonial society can hardly be considered as martial in nature, or even warlike in character. In fact, just the opposite is true.

This becomes evident upon scrutinizing the colonists' defense policies and basic military establishment. The armed forces of any community—be it tribe, colony, or nation—mirror the values, social and cultural characteristics, fears, technologies, ideologies, and countless other aspects of the parent society. Captured in this reflection, of course, are images of the society's attitudes toward and conceptions of the military, and of war in general. These attitudes may be observed through the military organization a society selects (individual warrior, militia, or professional), the primary doctrine for this military (offensive or defensive), and in many additional ways, including how this military actually fights on the battlefield.

The initial settlements (at Jamestown, Plymouth, and Massachusetts Bay) were not products of cross-Atlantic military assaults on hostile New World beachheads, but colonizing efforts by civilians for whom a professional military was anathema. Thus, as civilian-colonists whose only thoughts were of self-protection, their fundamental military organization was simple, defensive in nature, and based on the long-held English tradition of a citizen-soldiery, or militia. Militia represented a classical (and biblical) tradition of free people dropping scythes and shouldering weapons to defend hearth and home against invaders; then, the battle won, of returning to resume cutting hay. For a people with neither resources nor inclination—based on both religious and secular philosophical convictions—to maintain full-time defenders, a community-based militia wholly made up of citizen-soldiers dovetailed perfectly with their basic credos.

This American tradition of citizen-soldiery continues into modern times, yet, in part, this heritage has been clouded by myth. Two stand out: every male colonist ready to do militia service, and each colonist as intrepid woodsman and Indian fighter. These myths have been reinforced so strongly through the mediums of popular culture (literature, movies, television) that fact and fiction have blurred, but the reality was quite different.

Initially, militia service was universal. Varying slightly from colony to colony, every able-bodied man from 16 to 60 was expected to keep and maintain a firearm and sufficient ammunition, and to willingly appear for regularly schedule drill. In the early days, when coastline and frontier were one, a group spirit, high morale, and some military proficiency existed. But as the frontier—and with it the constant friction between Euro-American and Native American cultures—pushed westward, the sense of urgency passed and interest in drilling waned. Along the ever-changing frontier, survival was paramount, so martial skills were vigorously maintained; in the older, seaboard communities, however, they atrophied. Weekly militia drills gave way to monthly, then biannual musters, and the number of occupational exemptions from duty increased steadily. Much like contemporary English militia assemblies, colonial muster days devolved into social events, and Bacchus, not Mars, commanded these drunken carousals. Every generation of colonials experienced renewed fervor for militia training, usually responding to a crisis, but when it passed, so did the enthusiasm.

An increasing population and the diminution of immediate threats meant that universal service was no longer a necessity; as a result, the militia bifurcated. One branch was the general militia; something of a home guard. By the mid-seventeenth century its role was more political and social than military. This branch with its clubby, political atmosphere and election of officers produced that strain of democracy long associated with colonial militia. For actual campaigning, however, colonial magistrates and legislatures found it less disruptive to a colony's economy, militarily advantageous, less distasteful (especially among colonies with high numbers of pacifistic sects such as the Quakers and Anabaptists), and cheaper to field units of volunteers. From this volunteer branch came militia companies raised for specific campaigns and contingents of provincials who later served alongside British regulars in the colonial wars.

This dual militia system, though not defined as such by the colonials, proved a practical arrangement for the type of war fought in the colonies until the Revolution. Primarily comprised of young men with neither land nor families of their own and down-and-outers always attracted to the military, volunteers received land bounties as pay; since ownership of property ensured full community membership, this proved a powerful enticement. These volunteers filled colonial needs for a regular army without the expense, waste, and fear a professional military produced. Enlisting for one campaign, which usually lasted one season, they returned home to their community's welcome. Herein, it should be noted, lay the genesis of several American conceptions regarding the military and war that remain as legacies through today.

The first was one of the great attainments of colonial American society: civilian control of the military. The Bible and history taught colonials that a professional military controlled by one man (Caesarism) or by a small group (Praetorianism) was an invitation to tyranny. Actually anticipating events in post-Cromwellian England (the Glorious Revolution of 1689), colonial magistrates, by tightly controlling the purse strings, made subordination of the military fundamental to the colonial way of war. When royal governors, beginning in the late seventeenth century, sought to usurp this prerogative, they found bitter opposition—what some scholars believe were the first stirrings of colonial independence. Another legacy of the dual militia system, however, proved less of an achievement. Dependence upon volunteers for actual campaigning and the disintegration of any real military role for the home guard militia fostered a separation between community and military. War increasingly became the "other guy's business," and economic factors,

high birth rates, and immigration furnished a ready source of "other guys." In other words, as historian John Shy summarized it, "every man's duty easily became no one's responsibility." Yet, even as universal service declined, it gained great currency in colonial and, later, American military mythology.

So, too, did that classic image of the colonist as rugged, forest-wise Indian fighter. Folklore, historian John K. Mahan noted, "has enshrined the sharpshooting frontiersman as the conqueror of North America." And, to be sure, such men did exist, since most myths have some basis in fact. Such seventeenth-century colonials as John Church, Lion Gardener, and John Underhill (precursors of the legendary Daniel Boone and fictional Natty Bumppo) adapted European firepower to Native American Indian hit-and-run guerrilla tactics with considerable success. But they were unusual, and unless such a leader emerged, militiamen continued to be routinely ambushed and slaughtered.

The typical seventeenth- and eighteenth-century colonial militiaman knew how to load and fire a musket, since most still shot for the table, but otherwise he was hapless in the forest. In the French and Indian War (1754–1763), for instance, British General Lord Loudoun arrived in America believing all colonials to be skilled woodsmen and Indian fighters. Loudoun quickly "discovered that the average provincial soldier," wrote historian Stanley Pargellis, ". . . had never been trained, either in the discipline of arms or in frontier warfare." American Indians were tough opponents, well-instructed from youth in woodcraft, hunting, and martial skills in a culture that extolled the warrior ethos. Already uneasy about entering a forbidding dark forest filled with hobgoblins and spirits, the fear engendered by these native fighters made each crossing of the treeline a frightening experience for militiamen. This fear, when combined with the colonists' poor discipline, continued lack of battlefield success, and racial and religious sense of superiority and mission, plus the violence inherent to the times, would have a dire and direct effect on how colonials actually waged war.

Frustrated by Amerindian tactics, fueled by fear, revenge, and self-preservation, and acting under the belief that God sanctioned their actions, when the colonists went to war they sought to destroy the Indian as a people, waging a small-scale version of "total war" in the forests. Urged on by their ministers, they began attacking native villages with a religious zeal,

"Cutteinge downe their Corne, burneinge their howses, and Sutch lyke," killing men, women, and children. Here they borrowed a page from the example they knew best, that of the English pacification of Ireland. There, brutality was the chosen strategy. The English relied on the tactics of deforestation and destroying the Irish food supply, burning homes and villages, and slaughtering both the Irish and their livestock indiscriminately. "We spare none of what quality or sex soever," one early seventeenth-century English commander in Ireland wrote, "and it hath bred much terror in the people." Such was the Irish influence on colonial-Indian relations, that the "doctrine that the only good Indian is a dead Indian," suggested historian Howard Mumford Jones, "first took shape in the belief that the only good Irishman is a dead Irishman." Transplanted in the New World, this doctrine of "total war" became the dominant strategy against the Native Americans—up to and including the last major confrontation at Wounded Knee (1891)—and forever influenced American military policy against non-whites.

The manner in which the colonials fought the Indians had other long-term implications. To varying degrees, colonists believed that God accompanied them on campaign and approved of their actions. They were crusaders, and God acted through them, for they were fighting for His ideals. This concept of fighting for an ideal rather than for a specific material goal (although land gains resulted from victory) would reach full maturity during the American Revolution when ideas—freedom, liberty—became primary objectives. The crusading impulse was thus cemented into American martial methods. It continued into modern times as the primary reason Americans go to war, fighting *for* Manifest Destiny, abolitionism, states' rights, and democracy, or *against* national socialism, communism, and totalitarianism.

But Americans, who have expended vast amounts of blood and treasure combatting what they perceive as an evil, or to right a wrong, have had little patience since colonial times for wars fought over specific geopolitical ends. As the English began exercising suzerainty over the colonies, and European wars spilled over into the New World, many colonial volunteers served with the British forces. But as time passed, they questioned their involvement in European balance of power wars. Why fight—and die—for some New World fort that would prove little more

than a bargaining chip when the inevitable European treaty was drawn up?

Their time and service alongside British regulars also was important in other ways, serving to further define the colonists as American. During war, some subtle and some not-so-subtle differences between English and colonial military policy and practices cropped up. These were certainly not the sole differences between the two societies, but, due to the significance of military affairs, the most apparent. For instance, volunteer militiamen who fought beside British regulars considered themselves Englishmen; those from the old country, however, treated their colonial cousins shabbily, not as fellow Englishmen, but as inferior provincial bumpkins. "The Americans," General James Wolfe charged, "are in general the dirtiest, the most contemptible, cowardly dogs that you can conceive," and he was not alone in that view. The English, for the most part, haughtily ignored established colonial practices, tried to run roughshod over the legislatures, and derided colonial military experience learned over time at great cost. Accepted as conventional wisdom, these attitudes would strongly influence British political and military behavior in the 1770s.

Likewise, Americans who fought with the English through the end of the French and Indian War (1763) also learned a great deal, and not all of it was negative. At first they may have stood in awe of the British army, naturally gawking at the precise organization, uniformed discipline, and the whole regalia of an eighteenth-century professional European army; but after spending time with this army on campaign, they would no longer be overawed. Serving side by side with the British, living in the same camps, sharing the same miserable rations, slit trenches, and conditions, colonials came to know their future enemies, and surely they compared themselves with them: not as potential opponents, but as men. Their perception of the British army as an unthinking instrument of drill-deadened men and haughty officers wedded to inflexible tactics may not have been entirely true, but it was this perception that they held and passed along upon returning home. After their war experiences, cries that "the British were coming" would not send them scurrying away, but forward into battle.

When war broke out in 1775, and Congress commissioned George Washington to form an army, what might be described as an American way of war already existed. Combining myth and reality, lessons often painfully learned, and fused by time and practicality, it was central to the American ethos and revolutionary ideology, and, as such a principal tenet, would not be disregarded no matter what the cost. Yet what made eminent sense for irregular, low-intensity conflict along the frontier, actually hindered the pragmatic Washington in his efforts to fight a high-intensity, European-style war. The absolute loathing Americans held toward a regular professional army was but one example. Washington fully concurred with this sentiment in time of peace, since history showed such an army more a threat to than a protector of civil liberty. But his countryman's "policy to be prejudiced against them in time of *War*," he wrote in 1778, left him baffled. Nonetheless, it also speaks highly of these ideals that no matter how strongly Washington and his lieutenants criticized and protested these policies, for the most part they continued serving and fighting for their freedom and that of their country.

The colonial American society's conceptions of war, however, were more than simply influences on the revolutionary way of war; they remain part of the American character through the present, a legacy and link to our earliest heritage. It is an often contradictory legacy, befitting its people, of antimilitarism and a readiness to fight and die when freedom is threatened, of equally principled people going off to war and of those refusing to serve, of fighting for secular ideas with the zealousness of holy warriors, of democracy and discipline, of myth and reality, and of complaints, disagreements, and iconoclasm, and a strict adherence to civil authority by the military. The true strength of this legacy may be seen even today.

John Morgan Dederer

References

Fred Anderson, *A People's Army: Massachusetts Soldiers and Society in the Seven Years' War* (1984); Daniel J. Boorstin, *The Americans: The Colonial Experience* (1958); Peter Brock, *Pacifism in the United States: From the Colonial Era to the First World War* (1968); Emma Lewis Coleman, ed., *New England Captives Carried to Canada between 1677 and 1760 during the French and Indian Wars*, 2 vols. (1925); H. Trevor Colbourn, ed., *Fame and the Founding Fathers: Essays by Douglas Adair* (1974); Lawrence Delbert Cress, *Citizens in Arms: The Army and the Militia in American Society to the War of 1812* (1982); Marcus Cunliffe, *Soldiers and Civilians: The Martial Spirit in America, 1775–1865* (1968).

John Morgan Dederer, *War in America to 1775: Before Yankee Doodle* (1990); John Ferling, *A Wilderness of Miseries: War and Warriors in Early America* (1980); Howard Mumford Jones, *O Strange New World—American Culture: The Formative Years* (1964); Michael Kammen, *A People of Paradox: An inquiry Concerning the Origins of American Civilization* (1972); Douglas Edward Leach, *Arms for Empire: A Military History of the British Colonies in North America, 1607–1763* (1973); ———, *Roots of Conflict: British Armed Forces and Colonial Americans, 1677–1763* (1986).

Allan R. Millett and Peter Maslowski, *For the Common Defense: A Military History of the United States* (1984); Edmund Sears Morgan, ed., *Puritan Political Ideas, 1558–1794* (1965); Stanley Pargellis, ed., *Military Affairs in North America, 1748–1765: Selected Documents from the Cumberland Papers in Windsor Castle* (1969); David Beers Quinn, *The Elizabethans and the Irish* (1966).

William L. Shea, *The Virginia Militia in the Seventeenth Century* (1983); John W. Shy, *A People Numerous and Armed: Reflections on the Military Struggle for American Independence* (1976); ———, *Toward Lexington: The Role of the British Army in the Coming of the American Revolution* (1965); Richard Slotkin, *Regeneration Through Violence: The Mythology of the American Frontier, 1600–1860* (1973).

Alden T. Vaughan, *New England Frontier: Puritans and Indians, 1620–1675*, Rev. ed. (1975); Alden T. Vaughan and Edward W. Clarks, eds., *Puritans Among the Indians: Accounts of Captivity and Redemption, 1676–1724* (1981); Stephen Saunders Webb, *The Governors-General: The English Army and the Definition of Empire, 1569–1681* (1979).

See also ANGLO-INDIAN RELATIONS; FRONTIER; JUST WAR; MILITIA; PACIFISM; PLYMOUTH; PURITANS; VIRGINIA-INDIAN WAR (1622–1632)

War of Jenkins' Ear

See ANGLO-SPANISH WAR (1739–1744)

War of the Austrian Succession

See ANGLO-SPANISH WAR (1739–1744); KING GEORGE'S WAR

War of the League of Augsburg

See KING WILLIAM'S WAR

War of the Spanish Succession

See QUEEN ANNE'S WAR

Warren, Peter (1703?–1752)

Peter Warren was born in Ireland in 1703 or 1704. His parents were Roman Catholics and his father had fought for James II, but as a youth he became Protestant and escaped the penal restrictions on Catholics in Ireland. Warren entered the Royal Navy in 1716. It was of immense help that two relatives, Matthew Aylmer and Sir John Norris, were high-ranking officers who became admirals of the fleet. By 1727 Warren was a captain. He commanded station ships at Charles Town, Boston, and New York; at each port he invested wisely, and at New York, in 1731, he married well—to Susannah DeLancey. Vast wealth came from prizes he captured during the wars of the 1740s, and his investments in America, Ireland, and England were almost all profitable. A thorough study by Julian Gwyn describes his extensive holdings and his dependence on relatives to manage them while he was absent at sea. His brother-in-law, Stephen DeLancey, nursed his interests carefully; his nephew, Sir William Johnson, who managed his Mohawk Valley estates, served him less well.

Warren's fame comes from the Anglo-Spanish War (1739–1744), and above all from the Louisbourg expedition during King George's War (1744–1748). Early in the war he was at the siege of St. Augustine in 1740, served in the Caribbean, and commanded North American station ships. In 1742, he persuaded the Admiralty to rotate the station ships to the Caribbean in the winter—a system West Indians liked but Americans did not. In early 1745, while in the Caribbean, Warren received a request from Governor William Shirley of Massachusetts to support the Louisbourg expedition. At first Warren declined for lack of authorization, but subsequently he received instructions from the duke of Newcastle to cooperate with American governors against the French, so he immediately sailed to Cape Breton, arriving there April 23. Commodore Warren's fleet, which grew from three to 12 warships (two of them captured French ships) and several provincial guardships, blockaded Louisbourg while William Pepperrell's soldiers bombarded the fortress. Victory came 17 June 1745.

Commanders of joint land-sea operations were notoriously likely to disagree. Warren, perhaps because he had an American wife, American property, and years of American service, maintained good relations with Pepperrell's New England irregulars, but nevertheless, there was some friction, and Pepperrell deserves as much credit as Warren for not letting misunderstandings hurt the expedition. In early May, Warren became impatient with the pace of the siege, for he had to worry that the weather might drive him away, and perhaps a superior French fleet might arrive. He urged Pepperrell to attack the Island Battery. The New Englanders bungled the attack, but Warren did not criticize the Americans—at the time (in 1775, with the American Revolution underway, the earl of Sandwich, the first lord of the Admiralty, told the House of Lords Warren complained that the Americans were terribly incompetent, but how accurately Sandwich reported Warren's opinions is uncertain). Warren and the navy captured many valuable French merchantmen that, not knowing Louisbourg had changed hands, sailed up to the fort to be easily taken, but Americans resented the navy's dividing £428,000 in prize money, of which Warren received one-eighth, while New England soldiers got nothing.

Honors followed Louisbourg: rear admiral of the blue, governor of Louisbourg, member of Parliament. As an MP, he helped secure reimbursement for American expenses in the Louisbourg expedition. Vice Admiral George Anson and he defeated Admiral Jacques-Pierre de Taffanel de La Jonquière off Cape Ortegal 3 May 1747 (and shared more prize money).

He died suddenly 29 July 1752; his wife and four of their six children survived him.

Joseph A. Devine, Jr.

References

Louis Effingham de Forest, ed., *Louisbourg Journals, 1745* (1932); Julian Gwyn, *The Enterprising Admiral: The Personal Fortune of Admiral Sir Peter Warren* (1974); Herbert W. Richmond, *The Navy in the War of 1739–1748*, 3 vols. (1920).

See also ANGLO-SPANISH WAR (1739–1744);
JOHNSON, WILLIAM; KING GEORGE'S WAR;
LOUISBOURG EXPEDITION (1745); PEPPER-
RELL, WILLIAM, JR.; SHIRLEY, WILLIAM

Washington, George (1732–1799)

Born into a family of modest colonial gentry in
Westmoreland County, Virginia, George Washington was the eldest son of Augustine Washington by his second wife, Mary Ball. Events
that occurred in his childhood abruptly changed
his life situation and brought him into contact
with three men who influenced him materially
and in varying degrees, Lawrence Washington,
Colonel William Fairfax, and Governor Robert
Dinwiddie of Virginia. At the death of his father
in 1743, Washington came under the protection
of his elder half-brother, Lawrence Washington.
Lawrence had inherited Augustine's estate, was
a member of the Virginia House of Burgesses,
and adjutant general of the Virginia militia.
Lawrence had also married Anne Fairfax,
daughter of Colonel William Fairfax, a cousin
and agent of Lord Thomas Fairfax.

In 1748, George Washington was invited
to accompany George William Fairfax, the son
of Colonel William Fairfax, on a surveying expedition of the lands of Lord Fairfax. Later in
1748, Washington was appointed official surveyor of Culpepper County, Virginia. The death
of his half-brother Lawrence on 26 July 1752,
left George the family heir, eventually leading to
ownership of a large plantation on the Potomac
River called Mount Vernon. He also was appointed one of the adjutant generals in Lawrence's stead by Governor Dinwiddie, a more or
less ornamental office that overlooked the militia of his district.

Governor Dinwiddie, a stockholder of the
Ohio Company, as were Augustine and Lawrence Washington and the Fairfaxes, became
increasingly alarmed at the encroachment of the
French in the Ohio Valley, who were building
a chain of forts from Lake Erie to the Ohio, and
on down to New Orleans. The Ohio Company's grant from the British crown was contingent upon building a fort at the forks of the
Ohio and establishing a settlement there. In
1753, Dinwiddie received orders from the
crown to send an emissary to the upper Ohio.
The emissary was to contact friendly Indians,
find out where the French were posted, their
strength, and to carry a letter warning the
French to leave the Ohio region. George Washington, having ties to the Ohio Company, was
chosen as emissary.

After Washington's arduous trek to the
French Fort Le Boeuf, and his return to Virginia
with an unsatisfactory answer that stated the
French were determined to continue with their
course of action, Dinwiddie tried to get the Virginia House of Burgesses to apportion funds for
a military force to expel the French. The Burgesses declined to act, so Dinwiddie persuaded
the Ohio Company to pay for and build a fort
at the forks of the Ohio. Dinwiddie also raised
troops in Virginia, naming Joshua Fry as commander, and Washington as second-in-command. They were instructed to proceed to the
forks of the Ohio to assist in the building and
fortification of the new fort and to defend against
any hostilities of the French.

By 22 April 1754, Washington was already
on the march to the Ohio, Joshua Fry was to join
him later with more enlistments. Word came that
Captain William Trent had had to surrender the
fort at the forks to a superior force of French,
who finished the fort and named it Fort Duquesne. After a council of war, it was decided to
go on to Redstone Creek for a meeting with
friendly Indians, and to await further orders. On
28 May, Washington ambushed and defeated a
small advance party of French, killing several
men, including young Ensign Joseph Coulon de
Villiers de Jumonville, and taking the rest prisoners, one of whom, a M. La Force, was commander of the French party. Fearing retaliation,
Washington hastened to build a fort at Great
Meadows, calling it Fort Necessity.

On 6 June, Washington received word that
Joshua Fry had died in a fall from his horse, and
Washington took full command of the forces.
He continued clearing a road and strengthening
the fort when he received word that a large
force of French were advancing to Great Meadows, commanded by Louis Coulon de Villiers,
a half-brother of Jumonville. On 3 July, Washington and his men were surrounded and defeated, surrendering the fort on 4 July.

What started as small skirmishes between
France and England over possession of the Ohio
Valley lands now escalated into an all-out war.
Britain sent regular troops to American, and in
order to remove any conflict over command
between regulars and provincials, the Virginia
troops were reduced to the status of independent companies. Washington was removed
from command in the fall of 1754 and faced
with being demoted to mere captaincy of a com-

pany. He angrily resigned his commission in October 1754, feeling he could not honorably serve at a lesser rank.

General Edward Braddock soon arrived in America with orders to take Fort Duquesne, and his subsequent need for a man who knew the terrain and problems led him to select Washington for the job. Braddock invited Washington to join his staff as a volunteer aide-de-camp, thus avoiding the question of rank. Recognizing the advantages of serving under the noted British general, Washington agreed to accompany Braddock. By the end of the first week of June 1755, the forces were on their way out of Wills Creek, now named Fort Cumberland. Movement was slow due to the required road building over rough terrain for the heavy artillery. Meanwhile, Washington fell ill, and Braddock ordered him to stay in camp, but not wanting to miss the attack on Fort Duquesne, he joined the forces on 8 July, two miles from the Monongahela River and 12 miles from Fort Duquesne. On 9 July, after Braddock's men crossed the Monongahela, the French suddenly appeared, the war cry was raised, the British panicked, and the rout was complete. Braddock fell mortally wounded, just after ordering a retreat, the second-in-command was killed, and the confusion so great no one knew who was in command. Washington, with a few other men, assisted Braddock from the field. He died on the retreat to Fort Cumberland.

After Braddock's defeat, the British turned their efforts toward the north, leaving the frontiers of Virginia, Maryland, and Pennsylvania unprotected from forays by the Indians. On 14 August 1775, Washington accepted command, with a rank of colonel, of a reorganized Virginia regiment, with orders to build and garrison a string of forts along the Virginia frontier. For two years, Washington did his best in defending 350 miles of frontier against Indian attacks in spite of chronic shortages of provisions, clothing, and equipment.

In 1758, Washington accompanied Brigadier General John Forbes on his expedition to Fort Duquesne. Reaching the fort on 25 December, Forbes and his men found it burned and abandoned. Now in British possession, the fort was rebuilt and named Fort Pitt. Forbes sent Washington to Williamsburg for supplies. When he finished his task, he resigned his commission and saw no further action during the war.

On 6 January 1759, George Washington married a wealthy widow, Martha Dandridge Custis, and retired from military life. He spent the intervening years between the French and Indian War and the Revolutionary War as a prosperous gentleman planter. As a young man of 21 at the beginning of his military career he made some rash and foolhardy decisions, but his experiences shaped him into a self-reliant and steady individual. His men respected his fairness as a leader, and his coolness and fortitude in the face of danger and hardship. These qualities would later sustain him as commander in chief of the Continental army during the American Revolution, and as the first president of the United States.

Evelyn C. Darrow

References

Charles Henry Ambler, *George Washington and the West* (1971); Kenneth P. Bailey, *The Ohio Company of Virginia and the Westward Movement, 1748–1792* (1939); Hugh Cleland, *George Washington in the Ohio Valley* (1955); John P. Cowan, "George Washington at Fort Necessity," *Western Pennsylvania Historical Magazine* 37 (1954):153–177.

John E. Ferling, *The First of Men: A Life of George Washington* (1988); James Thomas Flexner, *George Washington: The Forge of Experience, 1732–1775* (1965); John Clement Fitzpatrick, ed., *The Diaries of George Washington, 1748–1799*, Vol. 1 (1925); Douglas Southall Freeman, *George Washington, A Biography*, Vol. 1 *Young Washington* (1948); Edward Pierce Hamilton, *The French and Indian Wars: The Story of Battles and Forts in the Wilderness* (1962); William A. Hunter, *Forts on the Pennsylvania Frontier, 1753–1758* (1960).

Donald Dean Jackson, *The Diaries of George Washington*, Vol. 1, *1748–1765* (1976); Bunford Samuel, ed., "The Ohio Expedition of 1754 by Adam Stephen," *Pennsylvania Magazine of History and Biography* 18 (1894–1895):43–50; C. Hale Sipe, *The Indian Wars of Pennsylvania* (1929); H.M. Smith, Jr., "Fort Necessity," *Virginia Magazine of History and Biography* 41 (1933): 204–214; Charles Morse Stotz, *Outposts of the War for Empire: The French and English in Western Pennsylvania; Their Armies, Their Forts, Their People, 1749–1764* (1985); Frederick Tilberg, *Fort Necessity: National Battlefield Site, Pennsylvania* (1954).

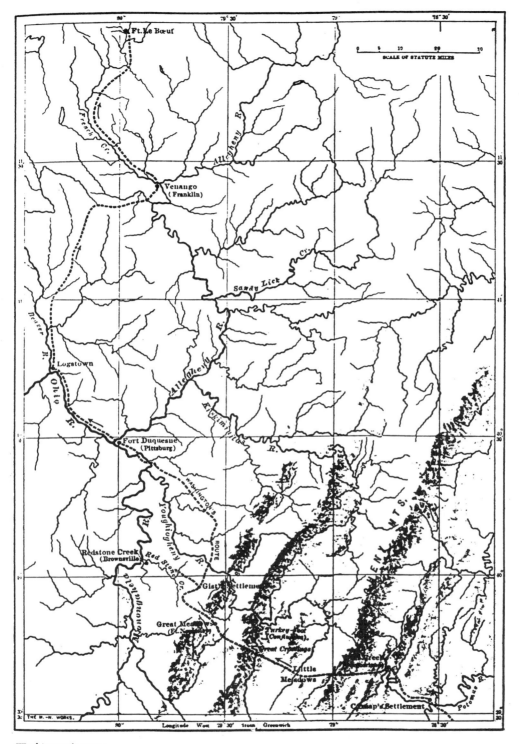

Washington's route.

See also BRADDOCK, EDWARD; COULON DE
VILLIERS, LOUIS; COULON DE VILLIERS DE
JUMONVILLE, JOSEPH; FORT CUMBERLAND
(MARYLAND); DINWIDDIE, ROBERT; FORT
DUQUESNE (PENNSYLVANIA); FORBES CAM-
PAIGN OF 1758; FORT LE BOEUF (PENNSYLVA-
NIA); FORT NECESSITY (PENNSYLVANIA); OHIO
COMPANY; OHIO EXPEDITION OF 1754; OHIO
EXPEDITION OF 1755; TRENT, WILLIAM

Weapons, Firearms

The study of firearms holds a particular fascination for many, and the period of the colonial
wars offers a bewildering variety of designs and
mechanisms. Although it marks the beginning
of mass production, there was little standardization of military weapons anywhere during
most of the seventeenth century. While calibers
and lock mechanisms would begin to be regulated in the 1680s and 1690s, European nations
would not establish standard issue weapons for
their soldiers until the first quarter of the eighteenth century. For those without direct access
to manufacturing, in particular colonists and
natives, procurement of suitable weapons became a constant headache.

Ignition Systems

There were basically six different ignition systems used during the colonial wars period, and
three of those were being phased out as the wars
began. The prevalent means of setting off the
powder charge in the barrel of a weapon in the
sixteenth and seventeenth centuries involved the
use of a lighted "match," or rope soaked in potassium nitrate. The matchlock system was extremely simple and cheap to produce, and thus
attractive to governments faced with the problem of arming growing numbers of soldiers. The
glowing match, held in the jaws of the serpentine
(the cock of the harquebus), was lowered into the
powder in the flashpan by means of a lever. The
drawbacks to the system were numerous, including real problems in wet weather. But on the methodical battlefields of Europe, with plenty of
time to light the match, it worked fairly well.

The wheel lock was an alternative ignition
system developed for use where care of the match
proved impossible, particularly on horseback.
The wheel lock produced spark by pressing a
piece of pyrite against a rapidly revolving rough
metal wheel (the power was provided by a spring
that was wound with a handle). Although less
susceptible to weather, the wheel lock was a very

complex mechanism, prone to breakdown and
difficult to repair, especially in a frontier area.

More successful were ignition systems involving the use of flint. The Dutch developed the
snaphaunce. The terms comes from schnapp-haan
or "pecking cock" (the jaws holding the flint became known as the "cock," and drawing it to the
rear known as "cocking"). The snaphaunce employed a separate pan cover and steel, which was
suspended over the cover. When released by the
trigger, the cock flew forward so the flint would
hit the steel. This would also push back the pan
cover exposing the powder to the sparks.

Although all three of these ignition systems
would be used in the New World, by the start of
the colonial war period (c. 1680), European
gunmakers were replacing them with more efficient flint systems employing a one-piece steel (or
"frizzen," to use the modern term). Spain introduced the patilla or miquelet lock, distinguished
by an L-shaped frizzen, and also featuring a large
ring on the jaw screw (located on the cock and
used to tighten the flint). Like the wheel lock, the
patilla suffered from complexity, or too many
small parts to make it practical.

The English, or "dog" lock used the L-
shaped rizzen, but added an external safety
catch, or "dog," which hooked on to the back
of the cock. Although an improvement, it remained vulnerable to damage. The ultimate
flint ignition system emerged in France around
1610–1615. This French or "true" flintlock had
all its parts covered except the frizzen spring. It
also used an internal safety or "half-cock" position, which enabled the weapon to be carried
primed and loaded with greater safety (and
making the dog catch superfluous). Proven to
be more efficient and reliable than its predecessors, the smoothbore, flintlock musket was
adopted in western countries by the last decade
of the seventeenth century, and it would remain
the principle military arm until the 1840s.

Loading procedures changed throughout
the early French war period as ignition systems
were simplified, and new techniques developed
in the numerous dynastic and colonial wars.
During the seventeenth century, the main charge
was carried in wooden tubes hung from a shoulder belt, called "bandeleroes" or bandoleers.
The top was pulled out with the teeth and the
charge poured down the barrel. Both top and
tube were attached to the bandoleer by cords
and simply hung open after use. A ball was then
removed from a leather pouch, also attached to
the shoulder belt, dropped in the muzzle with

some cloth wadding on top to prevent the ball from rolling out again, and then both were pushed down the barrel with a rammer. For speed loading, several lead balls could be placed in the mouth for easier access (the dangers of lead poisoning obviously being unknown).

Eventually, the use of paper cartridges would simplify the process and eliminate the need for wooden chargers and bullet pouches. Both ball and main charge were rolled together in a paper tube, the tube torn with the teeth, powder poured down the barrel, and ball and paper (which now served as the wadding) rammed down on the powder. Although the use of paper cartridges was not reflected in military manuals until the 1730s, it appears they already were becoming popular during King William's War.

Once the main charge had been rammed home, priming powder was poured into the pan, then the frizzen closed over it. Until the 1730s, priming was always carried in a separate container, either a bottle-shaped flask or, more commonly in the case of provincial soldiers and Indians, a powder horn. Although the printed manuals do not reflect it until much later, by 1745, it was becoming common to prime from the cartridge, a practice that increased loading speed considerably. Soldiers on the Louisbourg campaign, for example, were ordered to "allow as much powder in each cartridge as will be sufficient to prime too." When priming from cartridge, the procedure had to be reversed: the pan primed and the hammer closed, then the rest of the charge poured down the barrel.

A piece of flint, wrapped in sheet lead or a square of leather and held tightly in the jaws of the cock, ignited the weapon when it struck the face of the hammer and pushed it forward. As the flint hit the hammer, or frizzen, it scraped off tiny pieces of metal. Red hot from the friction, these "sparks" fell on the priming powder in the pan, ignited it, and the resulting flame found the main charge in the barrel through the flash hole. In order to produce these sparks, the metal in the hammer had to be hardened (rehardening was a common repair for blacksmith/gunsmiths), and the flint had to be sharp.

Soldiers also needed cleaning equipment to maintain their firearms, usually a "worm and priming-wire." Without cleaning, the powder fouling in the barrel would eventually render the weapon useless by preventing the ball from being rammed home. The "worm," which screwed on the end of the rammer, gripped a cleaning patch or two and enabled the barrel to be wiped

out. The priming-wire kept the flash hole clear, otherwise, flame from the priming powder would not ignite the main charge—a "flash in the pan." In addition to cleaning equipment, soldiers often had lock covers (a piece of leather molded to shape and tied around the lock) and a tompion, or wooden plug, for the muzzle to keep rain or snow from wetting the powder charge.

Calibers

The provenance of the word "caliber" is debated, but it seems likely to come from the Latin *qua libra* or "what is the weight?" Early weapons had been made with little thought to consistency in the diameter of the inside of the barrel, but by the mid-seventeenth century, European governments had learned the advantages of standardizing calibers to ease the ammunition supply problem. However, in doing so, various governments adopted different methods of measuring caliber.

The English and Dutch based caliber on the number of balls that could be cast from a pound of lead, thus a "16 balls" meant 16 shots to the pound. The bore size could refer to either the diameter of the ball or the measurement inside of the barrel. For ease of loading and to compensate for powder fouling, firearms generally employed a ball that was actually much smaller than the bore of the barrel, the difference being called "windage." Thus a musket with a 10-bore barrel, like the standard British infantry musket, generally loaded a 12-bore ball. Obviously, a great deal of confusion can result if references are not specific. The alternate method of determining caliber, used by the French and Spanish, was to measure the bore (or the ball) in hundredths of an inch, with a 10-bore barrel measuring out to be about .78. Both measurements are still in use today. Rifles and pistols generally use a measurement to record caliber (.38, .45, 9mm.), while shotguns use the old English method (12 gauge means a 12-bore; the term gauge was substituted for bore in the late nineteenth century).

Styles and Sizes

By the late seventeenth century, weapons manufacturers had settled on some distinct styles and sizes of firearms. Although some national variations did exist (explained below), all of the following styles were recognized and used throughout the colonial wars by all involved.

Musket

The basic infantry weapon was the musket. Originally a matchlock using a support stick to support its weight, the infantry musket had been lightened by the mid-seventeenth century to allow the elimination of the support. It still was heavy (12–16 pounds), with a long barrel, and fired the largest ball of any hand-held weapon.

Fusil

The "fusee" or "fusil" was a light musket primarily given to troops who guarded supply trains, troops who soon became known as "fusileers." Because of the ever-present danger of surprise attack, train guards could not rely on lighting their matches, therefore, the fusee always employed the flintlock system. Although almost as long as a musket, a smaller caliber and a thin stock lightened its weight, and thus it remained the primary weapon of light infantry and officers.

Carbine

Primarily used by cavalry, the carbine or "musketoon" was distinguished by a shortened barrel, as much as 20 inches shorter than a musket.

Blunderbuss

A very short, large caliber weapon used to spray slugs or shot in a wide pattern at short distances. The blunderbuss was used for boarding actions on ships, coach guards, and indoor settings—anywhere where the action was very close and accuracy was the least of worries.

Fowler

A hunting weapon employing a very long barrel to pattern the shot better. Some fowlers were seven-and-one-half-feet long. Although used mostly with shot, fowlers could shoot a round ball.

Trade Musket

Developed for trade with native populations by the Dutch, French, and British, trade muskets were distinguished by their utilitarian looks and purpose. A no-nonsense gun, simply (and cheaply) made with minimum hardware and minimum finish.

Pistol

Flint pistols tended to be bulky, and used mostly by cavalry (who carried them in saddle holsters), on ships, or in close combat. Like the blunderbuss, they were not known for accuracy at long distances.

Great Britain

The Glorious Revolution did more than bring a new government to power in England, it finally standardized calibers in the military. Expecting to use his new empire in his struggle with Louis XIV, William III had the British army adopt the Dutch calibers to ease logistical problems. British muskets were 10-bore (.78) using a 12-bore ball (.75), carbines and fusils 16-bore (.66), and pistols either 16- or 28-bore (.56). The English were using a combination of snaphaunce and matchlocks at the time of the Glorious Revolution. By the age of Queen Anne, they had switched to a mixture of English and true flintlocks. In 1718, the Long Land Service Musket made its appearance. Nicknamed the "Brown Bess," it served as the standard infantry arm (with a couple of variations) through the Napoleonic Wars. It boasted a 46-inch barrel that was held to the stock by metal pins.

France

The French adopted the true flintlock before the English and Spanish, replacing their matchlocks with the more reliable ignition in the 1670s. However, like their rivals, they did not designate a standard pattern musket until the early eighteenth century. In 1717, the French introduced a .69 caliber musket with a 46-inch barrel (carbine, fusil, and pistol caliber was set at .67). The French introduced numerous improvements throughout the century, but generally, French muskets can be distinguished by a sloping line along the butt of the stock (unlike the English musket with its straight line), and the use of metal barrel bands to attach the barrel to the stock, which allowed the stock to be thinner, reducing the weight of the weapon.

Spain

Spanish terms for their military weapons can introduce some confusion. Because they had enjoyed so much success with their old, heavy, matchlock Mosquete, they apparently wanted to retain that name for the massive, stick-supported musket. So when they lightened the weapon to allow its use without support, and added the flint patilla lock, they borrowed from the French and called it a fusile. But as the French and English used the term fusil to describe a light musket, the Spanish fusile was their standard infantry weapon, while the lighter weapon was called escopeta. The Spanish also had a carabina and pistola. All of these weapons used the patilla lock until the early eighteenth century, when they switched to the true flintlock. In 1728, they introduced their new infantry musket (fusile), and took the standardization of calibers one step further than the English and French. They made all their martial weapons the same caliber (.75 barrel firing a .69-caliber ball), even carbines and pistols, and simplified their logistical problems tremendously.

English Colonies

Weapons in the English colonies created no end of problems. In one respect this difficulty is surprising, because of all the western societies, conditions in the English colonies had encouraged the most widespread use of firearms. In Europe, weapon ownership was a privilege, a sign of independence and wealth. In France only the nobility had the right to bear arms; the English linked a property qualification with owning a weapon; and in both countries only the privileged classes had the right to hunt. Furthermore, before the refinement and increased production of firearms in the seventeenth century, only the wealthy could afford them. However, the American colonies were founded at a time when firearms were becoming more efficient and cheaper to produce, which brought their cost within reach of individuals of more modest means. The English transplants found that the environment of the New World encouraged the use of firearms, especially as the natives would not stand still for the "push of pike." Consequently, the ownership of firearms by all adult males in the community was mandated by law. More than a privilege or a convenience, the ownership of a firearm was a social and civic responsibility. The militia acts made weapon ownership a prerequisite for the status of "freeman," as every young man who turned 16 and every servant had three months to equip themselves with musket and ammunition.

However, controlled by English mercantile policies that denied them an industrial base of their own, the English colonies were constantly hampered in their war efforts by an inability to provide an adequate supply of weapons and munitions for their soldiers. For many the cost of owning a weapon was prohibitive. The militia acts attempted to compensate for such cases by ordering those unable to procure a weapon to provide corn or other "vendible goods" equal to one-fifth greater value than the average price of a firearm, this amount to be determined by the officers of the company. These goods were then sold and a suitable weapon purchased, with any excess money returned to the soldier along with the weapon. Those too poor even to provide the necessary

goods had to be armed out of the town stock of firearms. If single, they were assigned work by the town constable to pay off the debt, while married men in such circumstances were expected to provide a weapon for themselves, and return the town musket as soon as possible.

In addition to cost, the natural attrition common to all mechanical devices contributed to weapon shortages. A recent study of the British military in the eighteenth century found that the average life expectancy of muskets used in the British army was eight to ten years, at which time they were supposed to be reconditioned and repaired. But rarely were they returned to army ordnance until the muskets had become dangerous to load. After reconditioning, these old weapons often were shipped to the colonies. Therefore, the life expectancy of weapons in the colonies depended on age and source, as well as the quality of original manufacture and the responsibility of the owner. Many soldiers appeared at musters with muskets that were unusable because they had not, or could not, be repaired. Military service on the frontier could be hard on fragile stocks and lock mechanisms, not to mention losses of muskets due to enemy fire or capture.

Firearms were also ruined through carelessness, and destroyed or captured in enemy raids on frontier communities. But beyond destruction, attrition, and expense, shortages usually occurred simply because the population exceeded the available supply of weapons. Colonial assemblies continued to reissue militia acts that demanded all adult males own a weapon, but there never were enough firearms in the colonies to make this ideal a reality.

The problem of procuring suitable weapons was aggravated by the mercantile policies of the English government. Colonies, in mercantile theory, provided raw materials and in return purchased manufactured goods. Both the colonial monopoly on the production of these raw materials and the production of finished goods in the mother country was protected by law; therefore, the English government generally discouraged manufacturing in its colonies. Because of this policy, and despite some limited iron foundries such as those at Saugus, Massachusetts, the English provinces lacked a suitable means of iron and steel production, and without iron and steel, firearms could not be manufactured. Throughout the colonial period provincial soldiers were dependent on European sources, particularly England, for new firearms or metal parts for repair and replacement. Indeed, this demand from the New World would help accelerate, in true mercantile fashion, the growth of the iron and gunmaking industry in England.

In one respect, the English colonies were somewhat ahead of their European contemporaries in recognizing the superiority of the flintlock, or "firelock," system. As early as 1646, the Plymouth general court allowed only flintlocks or wheel locks for town property. In 1677, Massachusetts placed an order for 500 "new snaphaunces of firelock muskets," and at the start of King William's War requested 1,000 "fuzies" from England. By the 1690s, provincial laws insisted that soldiers provide themselves with "firelock" (i.e., flintlock) weapons.

Provincial soldiers carried a bewildering variety of firearms. Even if it had been financially feasible, and it was not, without an established gunmaking industry, standardization of weapons was impossible for the New England colonies. The calibers of provincial firearms varied as much as the weapons themselves. The militia acts of New England required members of the militia to procure a weapon of "musket or bastard musket bore." The exact meaning of "bastard musket bore" has eluded modern scholars, but apparently meant a smaller caliber, probably the Dutch carbine caliber (16-bore barrel) that the British would later adopt for their own carbines and fusils. Many hunting guns or fowling pieces also utilized the French .69 caliber.

Most New England men owned a weapon that served both for hunting and military service, and they preferred a lighter caliber that consumed less powder and lead. Military fusils with 16-bore barrels were popular, as well as 13-bore fowling pieces and 20- or 24-bore trade guns. Mixed with 10-bore military muskets and odd-size miscellaneous weapons, this hodgepodge of calibers created logistical problems even greater than the supply of the weapons themselves.

Native Americans

A key element in trade with the Indians was the trade musket. Although cheaply made, the Indians were not fools enough to purchase inferior weapons. Plain they were, but completely functional. Like European colonists, the natives preferred a dual purpose weapon that would serve for both hunting and war with an even smaller caliber to reduce the consumption of powder and lead. Gradually reduced in size throughout the colonial period, Indian trade guns eventually would employ a 24-bore ball,

enabling the Indians to get twice as many shots out of a pound of lead than the typical British soldier. This was a crucial factor, as natives had to consider both weight of shot (carried through the woods), and availability of lead. They felt that a ball a half-inch in diameter would kill game and men as easily as a ball three-quarters of an inch in diameter, and would allow them to squeeze more shots out of meager supplies. In addition to supply, natives also experienced tremendous difficulty in keeping weapons in repair. Although some tribes developed some repair ability, generally speaking, without access to European gunsmiths, an Indian's broken musket often stayed broken (the availability of gunsmiths often became an important point of discussion during peace treaties).

Steven C. Eames

References

Howard L. Blackmore, *British Military Firearms, 1650–1850* (1961); Sidney Brinckerhoff and Pierce Chamberlain, *Spanish Military Weapons in Colonial America, 1700–1721* (1972); M.L. Brown, *Firearms in Colonial America: The Impact on History and Technology, 1492–1792* (1980); Harold L. Peterson, *Arms and Armor in Colonial America, 1526–1783* (1956); Carl P. Russell, *Guns on the Early Frontiers* (1957).

See also ARMY, FRANCE; ARMY, GREAT BRITAIN; ARMY, SPAIN

Weapons, Naval

Naval Cannon

The Royal Navy obtained its cannons, small arms, gun carriages, ammunition, and all other appurtenances thereunto from the Board of Ordnance, an office dating from Tudor times. Most of the guns used by the British armed services were cast by private individuals and companies. The ordnance board's staff "proofed" (tested) the guns, stored, issued, and received them and their accessories back from the ships of the navy, as well as from the army. The Tower of London was the Board's principal office, but it also operated the Royal Arsenal at Woolwich, as well as secondary depots near the major naval dockyards at Portsmouth, Chatham, and Plymouth.

Cast in iron or bronze (the term "brass" was used by the Navy Board and the Board of

The Sea Gunner
Published
By
John Seller.

Rammerhead   Ladle
Spunge   Rammerhead
Gunners Rule
Shot
Quoins
Carriage
Trucks   Hooks

a Cascable deck
b Base Ring
c Touchole
d The Chamber
e Reinfourd Ring
f Trunions
g Cornish Ring
h Trunion Ring

Ordnance, though today the metal used would be termed bronze), naval guns by the seventeenth century were smooth-bore muzzle-loaders and, except for the smallest (swivel guns) were mounted on stout wooden carriages fitted with wooden wheels or "trucks." Until the eighteenth century, nomenclature was based on terms ranging from the "cannon-of-seven" (42-pounder), the largest carried on ship, through demi-cannon (32-pounder), 24-pounder, culverin (18-pounder), 12-pounder, demi-culverin (9-pounder), 8-pounder, 6-pounder, saker (5- $1/4$ pounder), minion (4-pounder), 3-pounder, and falconet (1-$1/2$ pounder), the lightest. A myriad of modifiers indicated variations in length, weight, and proportion. Thereafter, standard specifications were established by the Board of Ordnance according to the nominal weight of the ball the bore could take so that in a list of 1782, the guns were classed simply as 42-, 32-, 24-, 18-, 12-, 9-, 6-, 4-, and 3-pounders. There

were variations in length, the long version of a gun having a greater range of fire.

The growth of the fleet in the 1650s, a result of Oliver Cromwell's aggressive foreign policy, called for a vast increase in the number of guns to be procured by the ordnance board, and the transition began from the traditionally favored but heavier bronze to the cheaper though less reliable iron gun. By the early eighteenth century, almost all navy vessels carried iron guns. Flagships, however, were still outfitted with guns of bronze, at least where they could be seen by the admiral on board, probably because bronze guns were richly decorated with ciphers, badges, dolphins, and inscriptions. By the end of the eighteenth century, bronze cannon had disappeared from the decks of Royal Navy ships.

Ship cannon were employed primarily to smash opposing ships, shatter timber, penetrate into their hulls to slay and maim men, and to knock down rigging and hence sails, thereby reducing an opponent's ability to sail and maneuver. With two exceptions, the cannonade and the swivel gun, the naval cannon did not change in basic design or operation from the sixteenth through the late eighteenth centuries. Mounted on its four-trucked carriage, it was manhandled with block and tackle into firing position through the gunport, trained (turned from side to side) by a long crowbar (handspike), and elevated by a wedge (quoin) under its inboard end. The cannon was fired either by applying slowmatch, a glowing ember at the end of a length of saltpeter-impregnated rope, or by actuating a flintlock mounted on the gun, thus igniting powder in the touchhole. The flash passing down the narrow hole to the chamber inside the breech of the gun, the powder charge was ignited to drive the spherical projectile down the bore and toward the target. The recoil of the gun in firing brought it rapidly backward to be checked by the breaching rope. This conveniently brought the gun into the proper position for loading the next round.

The size of a gun's crew was a function of its weight; the massive 32-pounder needed a crew of as many as 15 to load, haul into firing position, and aim. A seaman designated "gun-captain" gave orders to the gun crew, primed, aimed, and fired the piece. Loading was a matter of swabbing out the bore to eliminate burning materials from the previous discharge, inserting the new powder charge, ramming it well into the chamber, then doing the same with the cannonball and wadding. The latter was a plug of old rope, straw, or waste cloth done up in a canvas bag and used to keep the ball from rolling back out the muzzle. The "powder monkey," usually a ship's boy, brought the powder charge, protected in a cylindrical leather box, up from the magazine well below the waterline to the noise, smoke, and hell of the gun position in battle. Earlier, the powder had been ladled into the muzzle from an open barrel and rammed home behind a wad, but in the eighteenth century, powder was prepared ahead of time in paper cartridges of the proper weight for each size of gun. Occasionally, a fragment of burning paper remained in the chamber and, if not extinguished by a moist sponge rammed down the bore, could ignite the next powder charge to the injury of the gun's crew. Captain Sir Charles Douglas, in 1755, devised a powder cartridge made of flannel which, by burning completely when the gun fired, removed this hazard.

The basic missile fired from these cannons was solid shot, a ball of solid iron. A few shot were stored on racks or shot garlands, circules of rope, beside the guns, but the full supply of round shot was stored in shot lockers low down inside the hull at the bow and stern. Because the shot could not be cast perfectly round, a certain "windage" or space was intentionally left inside the bore of a gun by giving it a slightly larger diameter than the shot. When a close engagement, i.e., firing at point-blank range, was contemplated, the guns might be double-shotted, that is, two solid shot were loaded one behind the other to increase the smashing effect of gunfire.

Variations on the solid shot were bar shot, chain shot, grapeshot, canister (or case shot) and langrage. Bar and chain shot, the latter a pair of cannonballs connected by a short length of chain, was intended to rip through the rigging of an enemy vessel and slow it down or limit its maneuverability. Grapeshot consisted of a number of half-pound iron balls bound into a wood and rope cartridge or a canvas bag of a diameter appropriate for the gun. It was intended to wreak minor damage on an enemy's upper works, but chiefly to kill and maim its crew at greater range than either the swivel or musket could reach effectively. Canister consisted of a light metal cylinder or can containing a great number of lead musket balls and was employed to murderous effect at very close range either as a preliminary to boarding the enemy, or to thwart boarders massing to assault one's own ship. Langrage was a similar charge made up of odds and ends of broken metal saved specifically for the purpose.

The swivel gun was a light piece firing a half-pound ball and mounted on a swivel either atop the upper rail of the forecastle and poop deck, or from the "tops" aloft at the lower mastheads. It had a crew of two and was meant as a man-killer, to weaken the weather deck gun crews of an opponent, to pick off officers, and in general to demoralize the enemy. An early, breech-loaded version was carried in sixteenth-century ships but seems to have disappeared in the seventeenth century to reappear as a muzzle-loader in the early eighteenth. In this later emanation, it was aimed by means of a long bar extending from the breech end of the piece. Lacking carriage, trucks, breechrope, etc., it could be easily and quickly aimed upward or downward over a wide arc for maximum effect.

Personal Weapons and Small Arms

Officers carried swords as personal arms from the very beginnings of navies. In the Royal Navy, a standard pattern of sword did not come into existence until the very early nineteenth century. In the seventeenth and early eighteenth centuries, the preferred pattern seems to have been the short, curved "hunting" sword with a single edge and brass hilt. In the eighteenth century, an officer might have at least two swords, a "small sword" for ceremonial occasions, and a more substantial sword for combat. The small sword usually had a blade of triangular cross-section with an ornate hilt and guard. Toward the end of the century, this developed into an elaborate weapon with an engraved blade, enamel or incised work on the hilt, guard, and pommel, and with a "sword knot," a loop of gold braid twined around the guard and handle. In battle, the officer would carry a double-edged blade, stouter in section, either straight like an infantry sword or a slightly shorter, curved blade like a military hanger. Warrant officers such as boatswains, sailing masters, etc., wore the more ordinary sword all the time.

In the first half of the eighteenth century, the scabbard was hung by two short straps from a belt about the waist. The belt was worn under the coat, and the scabbard poked through one of the pleats in the coattails. When the front of the coat was cut away about mid-century, the sword belt was worn under the coat and over the waistcoat. Toward the end of the century, the sword was slung from a broad belt worn diagonally across the body from the right shoulder, either between the coat and waistcoat, or over both.

In battle, some seamen were armed for hand-to-hand combat with boarding pikes, boarding axes, and cutlasses. The pike was a pole about six feet in length and tipped with a leaf-shaped blade some six inches long. The boarding axe was similar to a tomahawk, with a curved chopping edge on one end of the head and spike at the other. The cutlass was a single-edged, stout blade, either straight or with a slight curve and a plain, semi-basket hilt and guard. The cutlass, axe, and pike were issued only when boarding was contemplated. Normally, they were stored in an arms locker or chest.

Small arms, i.e., muskets and pistols, were issued to ships by the Board of Ordnance. The arms list of a first-rate ship in 1684 lists 150 muskets and 40 pistols. These "sea service" weapons were generally more cheaply made than those issued to army troops, on the assumption that sailors would seldom have to use them. Presumably, the marines' muskets were of a better quality, but sources do not so specify. In battle, muskets were fired from the "tops" of the masts or from the spar deck at officers and gun crews of enemy ships. The basic pattern for most of the eighteenth century was an older design of the Queen Anne period with a slightly shorter barrel than the infantry model, a flat butt plate and a rounded trigger guard. The flintlocks were more crudely made than the infantry version. Some sea service muskets issued in 1745 have the stock extended to the muzzle and therefore could not have mounted the socket bayonet. The barrels and rings were treated—"blackened"—to inhibit rust, and wooden ramrods were provided for the same reason long after metal ramrods were issued to troops ashore. In 1760, a new model of sea service musket was issued with an improved lock of the army pattern. At the same time, the stock was cut back short of the muzzle so that the bayonet could be mounted. Bayonets were identical to the infantry pattern, with a triangular cross-section blade.

A unique naval firearm, the musketoon, was issued from the late seventeenth through the eighteenth century. This was a large member of the blunderbuss family of firearms with a 28- to 30-inch barrel, and an inch-and-a-half bore flaring to two inches at the muzzle. The weapon weighed an imposing 18 pounds but was very probably rested on a gunwale or railing to fire. Its flintlock was a standard sea service device, and it could not mount a bayonet. The arms list of a first-rate ship of 1684 lists ten of these. Another firearm issued to ships was the "volley gun." This consisted of seven barrels of .45 caliber, six around a central barrel, all fired at once by a standard flintlock. The piece weighed 12 pounds and must have been very difficult to reload in battle.

At one time, a tower inventory listed 10,000 sea service pistols in reserve. Like the sea service musket, these were cheaply made to a standard pattern with blackened barrels and bands, a curved-handled stock, iron ramrod, and flintlock. The musketoon, the volley gun, and pistols were essentially boarding weapons.

John F. Battick

References

Brian Lavery, *The Arming and Fitting of English Ships of War, 1600–1815* (1987);

W.E. May and A.N. Kennard, *Naval Swords and Firearms* (1962); Peter Padfield, *Guns at Sea* (1973).

See also ARTILLERY, FRANCE; ARTILLERY, GREAT BRITAIN; NAVY, GREAT BRITAIN; SHIPS OF THE LINE

Webb, Daniel (c. 1700–1773)

In an era when an officer could receive his first commission at the age of 16 or younger, Daniel Webb entered the army at a relatively late age. This was mitigated by the fact that his ensigncy, obtained in 1721, was in the 1st Regiment of Foot Guards. The following year he was promoted captain lieutenant, and from 1725 to 1732, he served as a captain in Grove's Regiment. In 1732, Webb left the life of an infantry officer, and entered the 4th Horse, with which regiment he would serve for the next 20 years. In 1742, Major Webb was present with the regiment at Dettingen, and after Fontenoy, 1745, was promoted lieutenant colonel.

At the outbreak of the Seven Years' War, Webb was appointed to command of the 48th Foot, then in America. He had little time to relive his youth in the infantry, for when he joined his regiment in 1756, Colonel Webb did so as a major general and third-in-command to Lord Loudoun, commander in chief in North America. Arriving in New York on 7 June 1756, Webb held supreme command for just nine days before Major General James Abercromby arrived on the 16th. Together, the two generals traveled to Albany where Major-General William Shirley was unaware of his removal from command. At a war council on 20 June, it was decided that, as the French were likely to soon undertake operations against Fort Oswego, Webb was to hold the 44th Foot in readiness to march to its relief. Beyond this, Abercromby was hesitant to move until Loudoun arrived from England, which he did not do until 22 July. Arriving in Albany on the 28th, Loudoun confirmed the decisions taken on 20 June. For his part, Webb was in no hurry to move, only arriving at German Flats on 17 August. There he learned that Fort Oswego was threatened by enemy forces. In actuality, it had fallen three days before. On 18 August, Webb sent reinforcements forward to the Great Carrying Place, but did not himself arrive there until the 20th. After waiting 12 days, in which time Oswego's fall was confirmed, Webb ordered the newly constructed works at the carrying place destroyed. Hoping to delay any French advance from Oswego, he also had Wood Creek blocked with the same logs and refuse that Shirley had had it cleared of.

The following winter was a difficult one for Major General Webb. In December, he was struck with what Loudoun described as "a very slight fit of the palsy, which did not last a minute, and to another man would have been of very little consequence." Palsy had killed many of Webb's kin, and while the attack itself was physically slight, it plunged him into the depths of depression. By June, Webb was still so ill that he was forced to leave a meeting between himself, Loudoun, and Colonel James Provost, "the Colonel's voice and impetuosity overcame him so much that he could not bear it." A humorous situation, but for the fact that Loudoun had no choice but to leave an ill and depressed Webb in command of northern New York while he undertook operations against Louisbourg. Weakened physically and emotionally, and his force weakened by the demands of Loudoun's operations off Cape Breton, Webb was in no condition to face the assault against Fort William Henry coming that year. Headquartered at Fort Edward, Webb reinforced Lieutenant Colonel George Monro at William Henry with 200 regulars and 800 provincials in late July. This measure brought the strength of Monro's command to 2,200, and further weakened Webb's to 1,600. He was thus unable to reinforce William Henry further, a fact of which he warned Monro before and during the subsequent siege. The consequence was the siege, capitulation, and tragic massacre of the garrison of Fort William Henry, 9 August 1757. Loudoun was no more successful in his efforts against Louisbourg, and both he and Webb were recalled in December 1757.

Personal shortcomings aside, General Webb's failure in America demonstrated the weaknesses of the British army and the type of officer it spawned in the eighteenth century. A highly decentralized institution in which the regiment was paramount, the British army created competent, occasionally brilliant, regimental officers. Daniel Webb and James Wolfe were both creatures of this system. That Wolfe was an exceptional regimental officer cannot be denied, yet in 1755, Webb had 30 years experience as a regimental officer, while after 1757 he did not fade away, but served, in 1758, as quartermaster general to the army in Germany. Promoted major general in 1759, Webb commanded a brigade at Warburg, 31 July 1760, and was raised to lieutenant general in 1761. Capable and brave as they were, both Webb and Wolfe failed, as strategists at least, when chosen to act independently. Interestingly, both men were struck with severe physical and psychological distress when their failings became evident to themselves. Their failure was perhaps inevitable, for the army, in peacetime not gathering its forces at even regimental strength for long periods, failed to provide practical experience for future generals. The command of an army was merely the command of a regiment, writ large. For Webb, it must have been particularly frustrating being a cavalry officer in what was very much an infantry war. Colonel of the 8th Foot in 1766, Daniel Webb was in his element when he took command of the 14th Dragoons in 1772, a year before his death in 1773.

Adam Norman Lynde

References

Lawrence H. Gipson, *The British Empire Before the American Revolution*, Vol. 6, *The Great War for the Empire: The Years of Defeat, 1754–1757* (1946); Douglas Edward Leach, *Arms for Empire: A Military History of the British Colonies in North America, 1607–1763* (1973); Stanley Pargellis, ed., *Military Affairs in North America, 1748–1765* (1969).

See also ABERCROMBY, JAMES; CAMPBELL, JOHN; LAKE GEORGE; SHIRLEY, WILLIAM; FORT WILLIAM HENRY (NEW YORK)

Weiser, Conrad (1698–1760)

A native of Affstat, Würtemberg, Conrad Weiser was one of 14 children born to John Conrad Weiser and Anna Magdalina Ubellin. Two months after his mother died in 1709, his father gathered eight children and accepted an offer from Queen Anne to relocate in British North America. In the company of more than 400 other Palatine refugees, they reached New York on 23 June 1710. By then the adolescent Weiser had suffered two emotional shocks in the loss of his mother and his homeland; a third transpired in the spring of 1711 when his father remarried. In his *Autobiography*, Weiser described the marriage as "unfortunate"; he blamed his stepmother for driving him and his siblings away from home. Family unhappiness may have been one reason he took up residence among the New

York Mohawks to learn their language. That decision proved momentous, for it was as an interpreter that he rendered his greatest service to his new country.

Like many German refugees having difficulty finding land in New York, Conrad Weiser migrated to Pennsylvania. In 1729, he settled at Tulpehocken with Ann Eva, his wife of nine years, with whom he eventually would have 14 children. Like most ambitious colonials, Weiser engaged in numerous activities that he hoped would support his family. Although his basic livelihood came from farming, by 1733 he had become overseer of the poor in Tulpehocken Township. Thanks to his Mohawk education, he had mastered Iroquois sufficiently to qualify as a provincial interpreter. From 1732 onward, he was present at most conferences involving Pennsylvania and the Indians; his abilities pleased both the Iroquois tribal council at Onondaga and James Logan, Pennsylvania's provincial secretary.

The ambitious Weiser actively sought land for himself and his family; ultimately he became one of the moving spirits behind the development of Reading, Pennsylvania. From his troubled adolescence onward, religion was important to him; in the late 1730s, he associated with the community at Ephrata headed by Conrad Beissel, but he eventually broke with them. His numerous official activities introduced him to a number of religious leaders, including Archbishop Augustus Spangenberg, Count Nicholas Zinzendorf, and David Zeisberger of the Moravians, as well as his son-in-law, Henry Muhlenberg, who was a Lutheran minister. His journeys in the interest of forest diplomacy led him north to Onondaga and the Iroquois councils or to Albany, west to Logstown and meetings with the Ohio tribes, and frequently eastward to Philadelphia. Sometimes his companions were scientists such as John Bartram and Lewis Evans, British Indian department officials such as George Croghan and Daniel Claus, or curious young men such as his son Samuel or Benjamin Franklin's son, William. Apparently, he hoped the provincial interpreter's position would become a family tradition, since he placed Samuel with the Brant family among the Mohawks.

After 1745, he added defense concerns to his commitments as he labored to protect the Pennsylvania frontier against pro-French Indian attack. He became lieutenant colonel of the 1st battalion of the Pennsylvania Regiment in 1756. After two years he resigned the military commission, but continued to help acquire wagons and supplies for the western expeditions of John Forbes and Henry Bouquet. Throughout his long residence in Tulpehocken he served in various judicial capacities; he also used legal measures in seeking judgments against those who owed him debts. His final contribution both to frontier peace and Indian affairs took place in 1758 with the Treaty of Easton, when he worked for a settlement with both the Six Nations and the Delawares. Thereafter he carried on his activities as best he could until he became ill in July 1760; he died at home on 13 July 1760.

James H. O'Donnell

References
    Paul A.W. Wallace, *Conrad Weiser: Friend of Colonist and Mohawk* (1945); Joseph S. Walton, *Conrad Weiser and the Indian Policy of Colonial Pennsylvania* (1900); C.Z. Weiser, *The Life of (John) Conrad Weiser* (1876).

See also EASTON CONFERENCE OF 1758; LANCASTER, TREATY OF; MOHAWK

Wells (Maine)

The heavily fortified village of Wells, on the southwest coast of Maine, was in a practical sense the permanent eastern "frontier" of New England between 1690 and 1713. It was the settlement remotest from Boston that was able to remain intact during King William's and Queen Anne's Wars.

Settled in 1643 by the Reverend John Wheelwright and his Antinomian parishioners, Wells served occasionally as a meeting place for the provincial government of Maine before the absorption of the Maine towns by Massachusetts in 1652.

Like most of the Maine coastal settlements, Wells suffered heavily in King Philip's War. Unlike most of them, it learned its lesson sufficiently to prepare for successful defense through the years of warfare that lay ahead.

During King William's War, French and Indian forces descending from St. Castine made two attempts on Wells, one in 1691, and one in July 1692. In the second, about 30 men clustered in Joseph Storer's garrison house, where the whole remaining community had taken refuge within the palisade, combined with the crew of two Massachusetts sloops anchored in a nearby creek, to hold off a 500-man French and Abenaki raiding party.

Early in Queen Anne's War, on 10 August 1703, Wells was one of seven Maine settlements simultaneously attacked, and lost 39 persons killed or taken captive. Later in the war, another raiding party killed several Wells people and captured a young bridegroom, Elisha Plaisted, during his own wedding celebration.

Throughout this period of protracted warfare, the settlement survived to emerge in 1713 as the most vigorous and permanently well-fortified town in Maine.

Charles E. Clark

References
    Edward E. Bourne, *History of Wells and Kennebunk* (1875); Charles E. Clark, *The Eastern Frontier: The Settlement of Northern New England, 1610–1763* (1970); Francis Parkman, *A Half-Century of Conflict* (1892).

See also KING PHILIP'S WAR; KING WILLIAM'S WAR; QUEEN ANNE'S WAR

Wessagusset Raid (1623)

In April 1623, ten men from Plymouth Colony made a surprise raid on a village of the Massachusett Indians at Wessagusset, on the southern shore of Boston Bay. Plymouth had been warned by its ally Massasoit (d. 1660/1661), sachem of the Wampanoag, that the Massachusett were organizing a plot to destroy the English. The quarrel involved a trading post, unconnected with Plymouth, built at Wessagusset in the summer of 1622 by a London merchant named Thomas Weston (c. 1575–c. 1644). Weston had left the post without effective leadership, and his employees had rapidly squandered their supplies. By the winter of 1622–1623, the starving men were reduced to begging or stealing from the nearby Massachusett. To rid themselves of the nuisance and the threat of the fur traders, the Massachusett determined to surprise and kill them. But fearing retaliation from Plymouth, 25 miles away, the Massachusett were urging other tribes to join in attacking the 90-odd settlers there. Massasoit advised Plymouth to strike first and kill the leaders of the Massachusett war faction. Seeing no alternative, Plymouth leaders dispatched ten men to Wessagusset under the pretense that they had come to trade for furs.

The raiding party, commanded by Captain Miles Standish (c. 1584–1656), and including Hobbomock, Plymouth's Indian interpreter, sailed to Wessagusset on 4 April. Two days later,

Standish and four companions managed to lure four Massachusett, including two *pineses,* or war captains, Wituwamet and Pecksuot, inside the post and killed them in a fierce struggle. Three more braves were killed before warning reached the Massachusett village, where three Englishmen were killed in retaliation. The next day, after an indecisive skirmish in the woods, the English sailed away, Weston's employees abandoning their stockade. The raid did achieve its purpose in ending the Massachusett conspiracy.

Bert M. Mutersbaugh

References

Charles Francis Adams, *Three Episodes of Massachusetts History,* 2 vols. (1892), rpt. 1965; William Bradford, *Bradford's History of Plymouth Plantation, 1606–1646,* ed. by William T. Davis (1969); Edward Winslow, *Good News From New England* (1624), in *The Story of the Pilgrim Fathers,* ed. by Edward Arber, 1897.

See also PLYMOUTH; STANDISH, MILES

Fort West (Virginia)

In 1609, John Smith sent Captain Francis West with a party of men up to the falls of the James River. On an island in the river near the foot of the present Ninth Street in Richmond, Virginia, they constructed Fort West. Attacked by Indians, the men soon returned to Jamestown. A trading post was established on the site in 1637.

Thomas Costa

Westbrook, Thomas (c. 1680–1744)

Thomas Westbrook achieved fame as the commander of New England provincial forces during Dummer's War. The son of a member of the New Hampshire Governor's Council, and a native of Portsmouth, New Hampshire, Westbrook was a prominent merchant and land speculator. In January 1722, he led a raiding party to Norridgewock, seizing Sebastien Rale's Abenaki dictionary and personal letters. Promoted colonel, Westbrook commanded all the forces raised for the Maine-New Hampshire frontier line, and remained in that post for the duration of Dummer's War. After the war, he moved to Falmouth, Maine, and died in February 1744. In 1815, the town of Westbrook, Maine, was named in his honor.

Steven C. Eames

References

Steven C. Eames, "Rustic Warriors: Warfare and the Provincial Soldier on the Northern Frontier, 1689–1748," Ph.D. Dissertation, University of New Hampshire (1989); William Blake Trask, ed., *Letters of Colonel Thomas Westbrook and Others Relative to Indian Affairs in Maine, 1722–1726* (1901).

See also DUMMER'S WAR; NORRIDGEWOCK, BATTLE OF; RALE, SEBASTIEN

"Western Design" (1654–1656)

The term employed by Oliver Cromwell for the expedition aimed at seizing important points in the West Indies from which the Spanish empire in the New World could be placed at mercy. It ended in failure save for the capture of Jamaica.

Command of the naval forces was given to General-at-Sea [Admiral] William Penn; command of the embarked soldiers to General Robert Venables. Ordered to work in unison, their inability to do so contributed directly to the failure of the expedition. Some 2,500 soldiers, many the castoffs of New Model Army regiments, were embarked in a fleet of about 40 vessels that sailed from Portsmouth on 26 December 1654. Reaching Barbados on 29 January 1655, the soldiers were sent ashore to rest and become acclimated. Another 5,000 men were recruited in the English West Indies islands, and on 31 March, the fleet set sail for Santo Domingo, intending to seize the city as a base for further attacks on Spanish shipping and colonies.

Landings began on 14 April, but so far to the west of the city that four days were wasted in the approach. The defenders staged successful guerilla attacks on the ill-equipped and poorly led English troops, who were forced to retreat. Venables resumed the offensive with some support from the ships of the fleet. However, the van of the army marched into an ambush, broke in terror, and most of the remainder fled in confusion. The soldiers, demoralized and soon decimated by disease, were reembarked, and on 2 May, the expedition sailed for Jamaica, reaching that island on the 11th. A few of the troops, all volunteers, were landed, and with close support from the ships, very quickly overawed the small Spanish garrison, which abandoned its fortifications. Due to Venables's tardiness in following up this early success, the populace of Santiago de la Vega, the capital of the colony (modern Spanish Town), were allowed to flee into the mountains with virtually all of their food supplies and possessions. As a result, the expedition was soon faced with serious food shortages.

When expected store ships failed to appear in timely fashion, the commanders determined that nothing further could be accomplished with the forces at hand, and so Penn, with the greater part of the fleet, sailed on 25 June for England. Penn reached Portsmouth on 31 August; Venables arrived ten days later. Both were confined in the Tower of London, then dismissed from the service by Cromwell. Venables went into retirement; Penn later served the restored Charles II.

The fiasco of the Western Design seriously impeded Cromwell's foreign policy, brought on a declaration of war by Spain, and forced the lord protector to join France as the minor partner to Mazarin in his war with Spain. It also added heavily to the indebtedness of his regime. But the main prize was England's largest and richest colony in the West Indies, Jamaica. The fortification of Port Royal gave England a major naval base in the Caribbean from which attacks, both legitimate and otherwise, were launched on French and Spanish colonies in the Caribbean.

John F. Battick

References

John F. Battick, "Cromwell's Imperial Vision, A Re-evaluation of the Western Design," *Barbadoes Museum & Historical Society Journal* 34 (1972):76–84; ———, "Cromwell's Diplomatic Blunder: The Relationship between the Western Design of 1654–55 and the French Alliance of 1657," *Albion* 5 (1973):279–298; S.A.G. Taylor, *The Western Design*, 2nd ed. (1969); Granville Penn, *Memorials of the Professional Life and Times of Sir William Penn*, 2 vols. (1833).

Westo

In December, 1674, a party of Westo arrived at the Carolina plantation of Dr. Henry Woodward with goods to trade. The Westo must have had information as to Woodward's importance, for he held the key role in the colony's relations with its Indian neighbors as diplomat and official interpreter. The Westo already were familiar with Europeans and the advantages of establishing relations with them, as they conducted a profitable exchange with the Virginia traders. When Woodward encountered them, they were well-armed and believed to terrorize their smaller neighbors.

The Westo escorted Woodward to their town on the west side of the Savannah River above modern-day Augusta, Georgia, where they greeted him with a volley from fifty to sixty small arms. (Like many southeastern Native Americans, the Westo had palisaded their town.) Woodward later noted that "The chaife of the Indians made long speeches intimateing their own strength (and as I judged their desire of freindship with us.)" In the evening, they "oyled my eyes and joynts with beares oyl," gave him presents of deerskins and feted him with enough "food to satisfy at least half a dozen of their owne appetites." Westo intentions were clear: they wished to establish a trade relationship with Carolina in the place of Virginia. This would greatly shorten the distance they had to travel to exchange goods; moreover, the main enemy of the Westo was the Cherokee, who also traded with Virginia—a Carolina trade would be safer and more secure.

While Woodward visited with the Westo, two Savannah Indians (also known as Shawnee), arrived to establish relations with the Westo, but used the occasion to introduce themselves to Woodward. These Savannah lived in the vicinity of the Apalachicola River, near the Gulf of Mexico, where they carried on a trade with the Spanish. The Savannah approached Woodward about establishing a trade with the English—an event that eventually had disasterous consequences for the Westo.

The Westo supplied Carolina with Indian slaves who they captured from other tribes and exchanged for manufactured goods. Despite the financial benefits to Carolina, relations with the Westo quickly deteriorated and the two were at war by 1680. The colony's proprietors in England blamed Carolina for the war. They urged colonial officials to make a peace with the Westo that would "allow them to be supplied by us with necessarys by way of Trade which will make us usefull to them." For the colony's protection, the Westo were to be restricted to conducting trade at two fortified plantations and barred from entering the settled areas. The proprietors even instructed the governor to put the terms of peace into a written treaty in the Westo language.

The proprietors were unhappy with their colonial appointees who carried on gruesome wars with the Indians to obtain slaves. Yet the proprietors were not driven solely by humanitarian concerns, as they sought monopolization of the Westo trade for themselves. The proprietors, like their appointed colonial officials, were preeminently interested in making money, and saw the exploitation of Indians as the easiest way to accomplish their ends. The colony's officials saw through the hypocrisy and resented the proprietor's intrusion into their profit-making schemes. Seeing little reason to sacrifice their economic interests for the sake of the proprietors, they ignored the restrictions on trade and enslavement of innocent Indians, and elevated the Savannah to the place of the much-reduced Westo as their chief partners.

The partnership secured, in 1681, the colonial officials broke the peace with the Westo. The proprietors were dismayed to learn that the Westo were attacked while "in treaty with the government . . . put to death in Cold blood and the rest Driven from their country." The colony's leaders claimed that they had attacked the Westo to protect their new allies, the Savannah, but the proprietors had received reliable information that, in fact, the Westos had been so reduced from the earlier conflict that they were unable to carry on a war with the much more numerous and powerful Savannah, and that the war was simply an excuse to obtain slaves.

Surviving free Westo apparently affiliated with the tribes that soon became known as the Creek Confederacy, the latter including, in part, tribes that earlier had fled from the Westo. As for the Savannah, the Yamasee would soon replace them as Carolina's chief ally and partner in enslaving Indians. In time, Carolina would turn on the Yamasee, as they had on the Westo and Savannah, which would engulf the colony and the region in the so-called Yamasee War (1715–1717).

Alan Gallay

References

Records in the British Public Record Office Relating to South Carolina 1663–1684 (1928); William James Rivers, *A Sketch of the History of South Carolina to the Close of the Proprietary Government by the Revolution of 1719. With an Appendix Containing Many Valuable Records Hitherto Unpublished* (1856); Henry Woodward, "A Faithful Relation of my Westoe Voyage," in *Narra-*

tives of Early Carolina, 1650–1708, ed., Alexander S. Salley (1911): 125–134.

See also AUGUSTA; SHAWNEE; SOUTH CAROLINA; WOODWARD, HENRY

Fort Whorekill (Delaware)

See FORT SWANENDAEL (DELAWARE)

Castle William (Massachusetts)

Castle William was located on strategic Castle Island in Boston harbor. The first fortification at this site was initiated by Governor John Winthrop and members of his council in the spring in 1634. They commissioned a rudimentary structure of mud walls. After a French warship ventured into Boston harbor in 1644, the original fort was upgraded with 10-foot-thick walls of pine logs, stone, and earth enclosing a 50-foot-square compound. This was further enlarged and improved in 1665. After being destroyed by fire in 1673, a new fort consisting of four stone bastions mounting 38 guns was erected. This fort served as the site of confinement of Governor Edmund Andros in 1689. It received the name of Castle or Fort William by Sir William Phips. After his appointment as governor in 1692, a completely new fort with four bastions and 54 guns of various sizes was built. This was upgraded under the supervision of Wolfgang Romer from 1701 to 1703 to include 100 guns. It underwent further renovation in 1740 with the addition of Bastion Shirley and 20, 42-pound guns.

The fort became more important after the Seven Years' War, as Britain increased its military presence in Boston. Castle William was used by the British to safeguard the stamps during the Stamp Act crisis. During the winter of 1768–1769, it housed a British regiment due to lack of adequate shelter in Boston. After the Boston Massacre, all British troops were withdrawn to the fort to prevent further trouble. It was destroyed by the British during their evacuation of Boston in March 1776.

David L. Whitesell

See also ANDROS, EDMUND; WINTHROP, JOHN

Fort William (Massachusetts)

Located on Winter Island in Salem's harbor. Fortifications were begun in 1643, but were infrequently maintained by the town. During Queen Anne's War it was renamed Fort Ann by the settlers. However, the town refused to repair or maintain the fort. In 1735, the General Court provided £600 for the renovation of the fort to mount 15 cannon. Thoroughly renovated in 1775, it was redesignated as Fort Number Two.

David L. Whitesell

Fort William (Pennsylvania)

See FORT LEBANON (PENNSYLVANIA)

Fort William and Mary (New Hampshire)

Fort William and Mary was first proposed in 1697 as a replacement for the small fort protecting Portsmouth harbor, but the New Hampshire assembly was astonished at the £6,000 price tag, and put off the project until the start of Queen Anne's War. Construction began under the supervision of the English military engineer for the colonies, Wolfgang W. Romer. Although Romer would dispute his contentions later, Lieutenant Governor John Usher reported the fort completed in 1705, and asked the British government for the cannon to mount in its emplacements.

The building and maintenance of this fort would be a constant source of controversy throughout the history of provincial New Hampshire. In July 1708, George Vaughn, agent for New Hampshire, reported that the fort had never really been completed and was decaying because the province could not afford to pay for its upkeep. Vaughn said the fort was made of sod which "moulders and cannot endure the stormy weather and searching frosts of that countrey." In answer to a query from the Board of Trade, Romer agreed that the fort had never been completed. He said fishermen anchored off the island and stole the protective lead aprons off the cannon, and if they could do it, the French certainly could. Romer indicated the garrison usually consisted of four men, even though close to 30 cannon were mounted.

New Hampshire governors would continue to contend with the assembly to pay the upkeep of the fort for the rest of the colonial period. Captured by New Hampshire militia in December 1774, the name would eventually be changed to Fort Constitution.

Steven C. Eames

References

Jeremy Belknap, *The History of New Hampshire* (1831), rpt. 1970; Steven C. Eames, "Rustic Warriors: Warfare and the Provincial Soldier on the Northern Frontier, 1689–1748," Ph.D. Dissertation, University of New Hampshire (1989).

Fort William Henry (Maine)

Fort William Henry was the second of three English forts at the remotest New England outpost of Pemaquid, Maine. It lasted only four years, from its construction in 1692 by direction of Sir William Phips, the Massachusetts governor, to its conquest and destruction by a French and Indian force in 1696.

The structure, mounting 18 cannon and consisting of high stone walls six-foot thick, a 29-foot corner tower, a large bastion, and two smaller internal towers, is described by Cotton Mather in Book Eight of *Magnalia Christi Americana*. Phips was so proud of it he thought it could "resist all the Indians in America," though in actuality it was rather badly built.

The fort stood on the site of the wooden palisaded Fort Charles, which had fallen to a Penobscot Indian siege in 1689, early in King William's War. Even before the new fort was entirely completed, a combined French and Indian sea and land expedition arrived at Pemaquid with the intention of reducing this latest English threat to Acadia, but abandoned the effort after surveying what was apparently a powerful stronghold.

In August 1696, however, the French naval commander, Pierre Le Moyne d'Iberville, laid siege to the fort with three warships, about 100 French soldiers, and several hundred Indians. The commander of the fort, Captain Pasco Chubb, was notorious among the eastern Indians for having killed two sachems the previous February after luring them into the fort under a pretense of truce. Thus fired up, the Penobscots accompanying Iberville were eager for the kill. Warned by the French on the second day of the siege that indiscriminate massacre would follow if the fort were taken by force, Chubb surrendered the garrison on condition of safe passage to Boston. Iberville's forces razed the fort to its foundations.

A smaller stone fort, Fort Frederick, was built there in 1729 in connection with the resettlement of Pemaquid and other eastern Maine towns. Since 1902, the site has been a state memorial featuring a replica of the largest tower of Fort William Henry. Since 1974, it has been the site of extensive archaeological work.

Charles E. Clark

References
    Robert L. Bradley, *The Forts of Maine, 1607–1945: An Archaeological and Historical Survey* (1977); Justin Winsor, ed., *Narrative and Critical History of America*, Vol. 5 (1887).

See also CHUBB, PASCO; KING WILLIAM'S WAR; LE MOYNE D'IBERVILLE, PIERRE; PEMAQUID, ATTACK ON

Fort William Henry (New York)

Located at the head of Lake George, Fort William Henry was the most advanced British post in the Lake Champlain corridor between 1755 and 1757.

In 1755, a provincial army led by Sir William Johnson advancing toward Fort St. Frédéric ground to a halt at the head of Lake George. Plans to build a small stockaded fort were rejected in favor of a more elaborate post. William Eyre, a British military engineer, planned the fort and supervised its construction between September and November 1755. When Johnson and his army departed, they left behind a garrison of 208 provincials. The new post was named Fort William Henry, after two members of the British royal family, but was called Fort George(s) by the French.

Fort William Henry consisted of four bastions linked by curtain walls that formed a somewhat irregular square, about 120 meters across at its widest point. The ramparts were of earth, about 3 meters high, 4.5 meters broad, and faced with heavy logs. The parapet was 1.6 meters high, and about 4 meters across on the curtains, and 5 on the bastions. The fort stood on a high sandy bank 7 meters above the lake. The northwest side was covered by the lake; the southwest side was protected by a marsh; and the northeast and southeast sides by a ditch 2.5 meters deep and 9 wide that ran from the north to the south bastion. An elevated area to the east was occupied by an entrenched camp.

Johnson and Eyre believed Fort William Henry would "maintain his majestys possession of this important pass," the most direct route between the French and British colonies, and serve as a base for further operations against the French. The road built by Johnson was as im-

portant as the fort, since it speeded passage over the portage to the Hudson River, and facilitated further British campaigns even after Fort William Henry itself had been destroyed.

In 1756, a provincial army assembled at Fort William Henry in preparation for an advance down Lake Champlain. By August, there were 2,600 provincials at Fort William Henry and 2,700 at Fort Edward. The attack was called off after word arrived of the fall of Oswego. In 1757, an army led by Louis-Joseph, the marquis de Montcalm, besieged the fort, which was invested on 3 August. A British army passed over the site in 1758 en route to attack the French fort at Carillon. In July 1759, work began on a new post, Fort George, on the site of Fort William Henry. The British advance to the head of Lake Champlain and the establishment of Forts Ticonderoga and Crown Point made it redundant, and only the southernmost bastion was ever completed.

D. Peter MacLeod

References
    Guy Frégault, *Canada: The War of the Conquest*, trans. by Margaret M. Cameron (1969); Lawrence Henry Gipson, *The British Empire Before the American Revolution*, Vol. 7, *The Great War for the Empire: The Victorious Years, 1758–1760* (1949); Francis Jennings, *Empire of Fortune: Crowns, Colonies and Tribes in the Seven Years War in America* (1988); Stanley Pargellis, ed., *Military Affairs in North America, 1748–1765: Selected Documents from the Cumberland Papers in Windsor Castle* (1936); George F.G. Stanley, *New France: The Last Phase, 1744–1760* (1968).

See also FORT EDWARD (NEW YORK); JOHNSON, WILLIAM; LAKE CHAMPLAIN; FORT TICONDEROGA (NEW YORK); FORT WILLIAM HENRY, SIEGE OF

Fort William Henry, Siege of (1757)

The siege of Fort William Henry in August 1757, and the subsequent "massacre," the largest of its kind in colonial America, demonstrated the benefits and hazards of mixing European and Indian warfare. This successful siege also marked the pinnacle of French fortunes in the Seven Years' War.

Built in 1755, after the battle of Lake George stalled an intercolonial English campaign against Fort St. Frédéric (Crown Point), Fort William Henry was the political accomplishment of William Johnson and the engineering success of Captain William Eyre. The fort was also the first English establishment to invade the Richelieu River watershed, which the French argued marked the boundary between the empires.

Besides protecting the northern colonial frontier, the fort was to defend the new road cut from the Hudson River to Lake George, and to safeguard boatbuilding on the south end of the lake. To achieve these objectives and provide a supply base for an advancing army or a defensive point for one in retreat, Eyre chose to build at the lake's edge, on a sandy, 20-foot-high hillock to the west of the army's well-located camp. Pine logs formed the outside and inside shell and cross-bracing for the 30-foot-thick sand walls that rose ten feet high before narrowing to create protected cannon platforms and parapets. The corner-bastioned earthwork fort, designed to accommodate 500 men, was primarily built with shovels. The walls were completed in 44 days by as many as a thousand men who, in the process, dug a 30-foot-wide defensive ditch around three sides of the fort; the lake itself controlled access to the fourth. [see plate]

The first serious test of the fort came in March 1757, when a superbly equipped guerrilla force of 650 Canadian militia, 300 *troupes de la marine*, 300 Indians, and 250 French regulars attacked the garrison of 474 British regulars and colonial rangers. Failing to surprise the alert garrison under Captain Eyre, the attackers, under Pierre de Rigaud de Vaudreuil, succeeded only in burning boats, storehouses, and other outbuildings during four days of fighting. The strength of this earthen fort and its well-tended cannon had been amply demonstrated.

Fort William Henry was the central target of the Canadian offensive that same summer. Louis-Joseph de Montcalm's army of nearly 8,000 included 1,800 Indians from 33 tribes, drawn from as far away as Lake Superior and the Mississippi Valley. Scouting and raiding parties effectively screened the advance of this army, so that the commandant at Fort William Henry, Lieutenant Colonel George Monro of the 35th British Regiment, had little reliable information. On 23 June, he authorized a major scouting expedition down Lake George to capture prisoners and gather information. Colonel John Parker of the New Jersey Blues led this expedition of some 350 men from his and the New York Regiment in 22 whaleboats. Fewer than 100 of the men, and only four of the boats, returned safely after being ambushed near Sabbath Day Point by about 600 far-west Indian allies of New France.

The ruin of Parker's expedition prompted General Daniel Webb to visit Fort William Henry and plan a defensive strategy. It was now clear that the French could not be challenged on the waters of Lake George. Some 2,000 troops were decided on as appropriate to defend Fort William Henry. Since the fort could hold only 500 men, most were stationed in a new breastwork on the defensible site of the 1755 camp, to the east of the fort. Webb returned to Fort Edward, petitioned the northern colonies for reinforcements, and sent a thousand men under Lieutenant Colonel John Young north to the threatened fort, bringing its garrison to 2,372 by 2 August.

The next morning, Montcalm's attacking fleet, 250 *bateaux* and 150 Indian canoes, was visible beyond the fort's effective cannon range. Meanwhile, Brigadier François-Gaston de Lévis led nearly 3,000 Indians and Canadians overland to encircle Fort William Henry, severing communications with Fort Edward. After viewing the defenses, which included 24 cannon and 17 swivel guns, Montcalm decided against a direct assault. His invitation to surrender, which included a warning that the Indians might prove uncontrollable once they had suffered losses, was rejected by Monro later that day.

The main French force spent the first three days of the siege establishing its camp out of cannon range to the northwest, building a road and entrenchment from shore to the site of the first battery, and landing and positioning artillery. Most of the casualties during this period were in skirmishes between Indians and those in the entrenched English camp. The fort's cannon assisted the camp's defenders, but were primarily directed at disrupting the siege preparations of the French regulars and Canadian militia. Disgruntled Indians, who felt they were bearing the brunt of the fighting without being consulted on strategy, confronted Montcalm on 5 August. He responded by promising that the first battery of nine cannon and a mortar would be ready to fire the next morning, and by disclosing that he had intercepted a letter from General Webb that advised Monro to surrender because help could not come quickly enough.

Intense effort readied a second French battery for the morning of 7 August, meaning that 17 cannon, two mortars, and two howitzers were firing on a fort that was increasingly out-

A. The Dock | C. Fort William Henry | E. The Enemys 1:ˢᵗ Battery | F. Their 2ᵈ Battery of 10 Guns | G. Their Approaches
B. The Garrison Gardens | D. The Different Morass | of 9 Guns & 2 Mortars | and 3 Mortars | H. Two Intended Batterys

A PLAN of Fort William Henry and the English Camps & Retrenchments with the French different Camps and Attack there upon

PART OF LAKE GEORGE

A Scale of this Plan of 200 Yards.
100   300   500   700

I. The Place where they landed their Artillery | the main Body of ye Army | M. Mr de la Corne with | English Troops Encamped | Retrenchment was made
K. Mr Moncalms Camp with | L. Mr de Levis Camp with | 3000 Regulars & Canadians | 1500 Canadians & Indians | before they was ordered by Gl | O. the bridge over ye Morass
 | | N. The Ground where the | Wild to the Place where the | P. The English Retrenchment

gunned as more of its own artillery became disabled. Indeed, as the siege progressed, one of the greatest dangers inside Fort William Henry was from their own cannon, exploding from metal fatigue or from loading an overheated cannon with standard measures of gunpowder. After a morning of more intense firing, Montcalm pressed his psychological advantage by forwarding the discouraging letter to Monro, three days after it had been intercepted. When the fighting resumed, the fort was severely pounded, with exploding howitzer shells killing a number in the fort and an unsuccessful sortie from the camp resulting in the deaths of about 50 in that party and 21 of the Canadians and Indians.

The astonishing progress of the French was apparent the next morning; despite continual cannonfire from the fort, they had dug 250 yards down a slope, across a swamp, and were preparing a battery to place nine more cannon within only 150 yards of the fort. An inspection late on 9 August told Monro that the fabric of the fort had withstood the cannonade extremely well, but all his larger cannon had exploded, and his men were exhausted by five days without sleep.

On the morning of 9 August 1757, Monro's council of war unanimously recommended negotiating a surrender. Montcalm, impressed with the bravery of the defenders, offered them the latest version of the European honors of war. The defeated were to be allowed to march back to Fort Edward, to keep their muskets and belongings, and to be accompanied by beating drums and flying colors, as well as one of their own brass cannon. In return, the garrison became "parolees" who agreed not to fight the French or their allies for 18 months, and Monro was to arrange the return of all French, Canadians, and Indians held prisoner. Montcalm explained the agreement to a council of Indian chiefs, who reportedly approved terms that clearly deprived their warriors of promised scalps and booty.

The French took possession of the fort at noon, but that did not prevent Indians from killing several severely wounded English who had been left there. As the English parolees were assembled in their camp, Indians snatched horses, kettles, and other prizes. Monro ordered all liquor "destroyed," but the methods are not recorded. Montcalm posted guards in the camp, excluded Indians for the night, and announced that the English would march in the morning. English and French secretly cooperated in an attempt to have the English march to Fort Edward that night, but cancelled the plan when the Indians became aware of it. Colonel Joseph Frye of the Massachusetts Regiment noted: "All the Remainder of this night the Indians were in great numbers round our lines and seemed to shew more than usual malice in their looks which made us suspect they intended us mischief."

Next morning, as the English prepared for the 16-mile march to Fort Edward, Indians returned to the camp in search of plunder. Acceptable plunder was whatever the Indians thought was neither the private property of an English soldier nor the ammunition, stores of war, or provisions, which had been reserved by the French. As the British regulars began to move out with their small French escort, warriors within the camp killed and scalped 17 of the wounded soldiers of the Massachusetts Regiment. Other warriors dragged away Indians who had been with the American colonial forces, as well as black soldiers and servants. As some of these were paraded as trophies in the nearby Indian camps that flanked the road to Fort Edward, more of the 1,600 warriors raced to capture proof of their participation in a great victory. The war whoop was sounded as the warriors charged to claim packs, guns, money, and clothes from the terrified parolees, and also from families of the regulars and others who were not formally within the terms of parole. Those who resisted were summarily killed.

The "massacre" lasted only a few moments, and then became a chase for prisoners. The French commanders, Lévis and Montcalm, arrived and tried to protect the English by bargaining for them, by harboring those who had escaped, and even by confiscating them from their Indian captors. A few more English were killed by Indians who chose to take scalps rather than surrender prisoners.

Apparently Montcalm's Indian allies were disgusted, and most left for home immediately, with or without prisoners, effectively ending the campaign. Many English soldiers fled to the woods and made their own way to Fort Edward. Their reports of an extensive slaughter of everyone who could not initially be accounted for, spread terror throughout the northern colonies. On 15 August, after their demolition of Fort William Henry was complete, the French escorted about 500 of the former garrison, including most of the regular officers, to Fort Edward. Montcalm's accompanying letters to General Webb and General Loudoun blamed the victims for the incident, promised to recover and return those taken away by the Indians, and presumed that the conditions of the surrender were still in force. More than 200 prisoners were redeemed by the Canadian governor and promptly returned, and approximately 40 others made their way home over the next five years. At least 70 people had died in the "massacre," and the fate of another 105 is unknown.

The incident, most widely remembered through James Fenimore Cooper's fictional *The Last of the Mohicans*, had been provoked by the Indians' sense of betrayal at the hands of their French allies. This attack was on a defeated enemy who, by a new and alien convention of humaneness, had suddenly been freed after a bloody week-long battle. Indian resentment was confirmed by subsequent French confiscation of some prisoners and Canadian redemption of others. Indians from the far west, who also returned home carrying smallpox, would not return in comparable numbers to aid New France again. Nine months later, after most of the parolees recovered by the Canadian government had been returned, the English commander in chief declared the capitulation terms null and void. The Fort William Henry incident also led General Jeffery Amherst to deny the honors of war to the French at Louisbourg (1758) and Montreal (1760), and encouraged his anti-Indian policies, which prompted Robert Rogers's raid on St. Francis (1759), and helped provoke Pontiac's War (1763).

Ian K. Steele

References

Thomas Chapais, *Le Marquis de Montcalm (1712–1759)* (1911); Lawrence H. Gipson, *The British Empire Before the American Revolution*, 15 vols. (1936–1970), Vol. 7,

The Great War for the Empire, the Victorious Years, 1758–1760; Francis Parkman, *Montcalm and Wolfe*, 3 vols. (1905); Ian K. Steele, *Betrayals: Fort William Henry and the "Massacre"* (1990).

See also BOURLAMAQUE, FRANÇOIS-CHARLES DE; FORT EDWARD (NEW YORK); JOHNSON, WILLIAM; LAKE GEORGE, BATTLE OF; LÉVIS, FRANÇOIS-GASTON DE; MONTCALM-GOZON DE SAINT-VERAIN, LOUIS-JOSEPH; FORT ST. FRÉDÉRIC (NEW YORK); WEBB, DANIEL; FORT WILLIAM HENRY (NEW YORK)

Williams, Roger (c. 1603–1683)

Roger Williams received his B.A. at Cambridge in 1627 before emigrating to New England in 1631. There, his extreme separatist notions, coupled with his attacks on the bay colony's charter, evoked the wrath of the Massachusetts General Court. He fled to Providence, Rhode Island, in the winter of 1636, and was soon joined by other settlers who were drawn to his belief in "soul liberty."

At the heart of Williams's philosophy was his insistence that religious and secular affairs must be completely separate. Moreover, he argued that it was futile, even blasphemous, to force a particular religious belief on anyone. Only voluntary adherence to God's word merited salvation.

The consequences of Williams's beliefs were far-reaching. If government was entirely secular, then no nation could claim to be a "godly nation;" none could claim to be morally superior, nor could any government impose its values on another. Sovereignty rested on the people of any given nation, not on God. Thus, no state could rightfully interfere with the internal affairs of another, for "who can question the *lawfulnesse* of other formes of *Government, Lawes*, and *punishments* which differ, since constitutions are mens ordinances." Williams argued that removing religious ideology from governmental purview would eliminate one of the most common causes of war. He was not a pacifist. He even accepted a commission in the Rhode Island militia during King Philip's War. But he argued that only defensive war could be justified in God's eyes. Williams preferred to settle disputes by relying on arbitration and voluntary agreements between nations.

Roger Williams had practical as well as ideological reasons for his devotion to "soul liberty." Particularly after the English government moved toward a policy of toleration, Rhode Island's founder used his pleas for religious liberty as an instrument with which to bludgeon the intolerant bay colony. His most famous book, *The Bloudy Tenant of Persecution* (1644), was written with an eye to seeking favor with the home government as he sought to protect Rhode Island's settlers from the incursions of its predatory neighbors.

Williams's separatist notions led him to question the bay colony's claims to property rights in the New World. As early as 1633, he argued that Christianity did not give any person or government a superior right to the land. No one, he contended, could be lawfully deprived of his property without his consent. Williams's respect for Indian territorial claims allowed him to enjoy unusually amicable relations with New England's Native Americans. When he fled to Providence, he was careful to purchase his land from Indian sachems Canonicus and Miantonomo, and negotiated a similar purchase for Anne Hutchinson's followers on Aquidneck Island. He quickly learned to converse in the Algonkian tongue, acted as an interpreter and mediator between the English colonists and the Indians, and wrote his *Key to the Indian Languages*, an invaluable cultural and linguistic "dictionary," in 1643.

Williams's relationship to Massachusetts and its governor, John Winthrop, was curious and somewhat problematic. The bay colony cast an avaricious eye on Rhode Island territory. And Massachusetts, with the other members of the New England Confederation, resented and feared the religious liberty that festered just beyond their borders. They refused to allow Rhode Island to join the confederation, and made frequent forays into territory claimed by Williams and his followers, prompting him to travel to England in 1643 in order to seek legal recognition of the colony. Nevertheless, Williams remained on good personal terms with Winthrop, often acting as a negotiator for the bay colony in its dealings with the Narragansett Indians. He was of inestimable help during the Pequot War, splitting the Narragansetts from the Pequots, and devising a successful military strategy against the isolated Pequot nation. He also used his influence to avert war between the Narragansetts and the New England Confederation on several occasions.

Sheila L. Skemp

References

Hugh Brockunier, *The Irrepressible Democrat: Roger Williams* (1940); Jack L. Davis, "Roger Williams Among the Narragansett Indians, *New England Quarterly* 43 (1970):593–604; James E. Ernst, *The Political Thought of Roger Williams* (1929); ———, *Roger Williams, New England Firebrand* (1932); Edwin Gaustad, "Roger Williams and the Principle of Separation," *Foundations* 1 (1958):55–64; Edmund S. Morgan, *Roger Williams: The Church and the State* (1967); Alan Simpson, "How Democratic Was Roger Williams?," *William and Mary Quarterly*, 3rd ser., 13 (1958):53–67.

See also MIANTONOMO; NARRAGANSETT; NEW ENGLAND CONFEDERATION; PEQUOT; PEQUOT WAR; RHODE ISLAND; WINTHROP, JOHN

Wills Creek (Maryland)

Located at the juncture of Wills Creek and the north branch of the Potomac River on the border of Virginia and Maryland, Wills Creek was named after an Indian named Will and his family who had lived in the area for many years.

Previously part of Lord Fairfax's grant, the site was bought in 1750 by the Ohio Land Company of Virginia as headquarters for its land and fur-trading activities. Chosen by the company for its strategic location on the extreme western frontier, it was on an established Indian path from the Potomac to the Ohio River, providing easy access to the western lands and the fur trade. The company built a small storehouse on the Virginia side of the Potomac and stocked it with supplies for the traders and fur trappers. On the Maryland side of the Potomac a larger building was erected to store munitions and as a residence for the company's agents.

As hostilities escalated between Britain and France over control of the Ohio Valley, Governor Robert Dinwiddie of Virginia in 1754 received orders from England to construct a fort at the site. Governor Dinwiddie also requisitioned all of the Ohio Company's buildings, guns, stocks, and equipment for British use. The new fort was called Fort Mount Pleasant and later named Fort Cumberland in honor of the duke of Cumberland.

Here, George Washington mustered his men before and after their defeat at Fort Necessity. Fort Cumberland was later used as headquarters for General Edward Braddock in his campaign of 1755.

Evelyn C. Darrow

References

Kenneth P. Bailey, *The Ohio Company of Virginia and the Westward Movement, 1748–1792: A Chapter in the History of the Colonial Frontier* (1939); Will H. Lowdermilk, *History of Cumberland, Maryland* (1878), rpt. 1976; Robert B. Roberts, *Encyclopedia of Historic Forts: The Military, Pioneer, and Trading Posts of the United States* (1988); Charles Morse Stotz, *Outposts of the War for Empire: The French and English in Western Pennsylvania; Their Armies, Their Forts, Their People, 1749–1764* (1985).

See also BRADDOCK EDWARD; FORT CUMBERLAND (MARYLAND); DINWIDDIE, ROBERT; FORT NECESSITY (PENNSYLVANIA); OHIO COMPANY

Windsor Blockhouse (Connecticut)

Plymouth settlers heard of good economic prospects in the Connecticut River valley from River Indians and sent Edward Winslow to explore the region in 1632. A year later, a company of settlers led by William Holmes traveled to the valley in search of new opportunities. Though the Dutch at their Fort Good Hope, commanded by Jacob van Curler, ordered the group to turn back, they continued unscathed and settled just north of the Dutch at Windsor, on the left bank of the Connecticut River. The settlers immediately built a fort and established a trading post. While the River Indians were relieved to have the presence of the English settlers to counteract the powerful Pequots, the Pequots resented the English intrusion in the area. So the settlers were the targets of Pequot attacks in 1637 during the Pequot War. The whole settlement was built like a fortress, with palisades and ditches constructed for additional protection. Much to the chagrin of the Dutch, English trade with the Indians flourished in the area. The English pushed the Dutch completely out of the Connecticut River valley in 1664 and established settlements throughout the region.

Leslie Miller

References

"Coast Forts in Colonial Connecticut," *The Coast Artillery Journal* 69 (1928):237–244; Robert B. Roberts, *Encyclopedia of Historic Forts: The Military, Pioneer, and Trading Posts of the United States* (1988).

See also CONNECTICUT; FORT GOOD HOPE (CONNECTICUT); PEQUOT WAR

Winslow, John (1703–1774)

John Winslow was the second son of Isaac Winslow and Sarah Wensley, and the grandson of Governor Edward Winslow of Plymouth Colony. Though a member of one of Massachusetts's most prestigious families, he himself was barely literate. His military career began when he was commissioned captain of a provincial company in the abortive Cuban expedition of 1740. Through the influence of Governor William Shirley of Massachusetts, he transferred soon thereafter to the British army. He subsequently served as a captain in the 40th foot Regiment at Annapolis Royal, Nova Scotia, and at St. John's, Newfoundland. In 1751, he exchanged positions with a half-pay captain of Shirley's former regiment and returned home to Massachusetts, serving in the General Court from 1752–1753. In 1754, he was promoted to major general of the militia by Shirley. Because of his previous experiences and his popularity as a leader, Shirley then appointed him commander of an 800-man expeditionary force to the Kennebec River area. The mission's goals were to consolidate British positions, prevent further French encroachments, and maintain Indian alliances. Winslow constructed Fort Western (Augusta, Maine) and Fort Halifax (Winslow, Maine), and explored territory far enough to the northwest to evaluate the feasibility of a route for a possible future attack on Quebec. He also had an interest of his own in this area; the long-dormant Plymouth Colony patent, which lay claim to the region, and with which Winslow had personal connections, had been recently revived.

A year later, Shirley created a new provincial regiment to aid Governor Charles Lawrence of Nova Scotia in ridding the area of French influence; he turned to the ever-popular Winslow to head the force, appointing him commander and lieutenant colonel. Winslow played an important role in the capture of Fort Beauséjour that summer, and he was in charge of the force that captured Fort Gaspereau on 18 June. His journals, moreover, provide an important eyewitness source for the campaign. Winslow was bitter over his failure to be appointed commander of the expedition, and he fought constantly with the tactless British commander, Colonel Robert Monckton. Winslow was subsequently stationed at the Canadian town of Grand Pré, and he took part in the British removal of the French inhabitants of the peninsula. Though he carried out his orders with both care and compassion, the deportation policy offended his colonial, and personal, sensibilities. By November he had shipped more than 1,500 Acadians to Pennsylvania, Maryland, and other southern colonies.

Winslow then returned to Massachusetts. The following year, 1756, Shirley appointed him to command provincial troops against Fort St. Frédéric, near Crown Point. Again, however, Winslow ran afoul of the British high command. In particular, he objected to the earl of Loudoun's proposed integration of provincial troops with the regulars. There were two principal points of contention. The provincials had enlisted only to serve under their own officers, and the officers feared they would lose rank, since they held their posts only by colonial commission. The provincials nearly mutinied and the officers nearly revolted, but Winslow agreed to the integration after Shirley pleaded with him to cooperate with Loudoun. Winslow then found himself in command of about 7,000 provincial troops in the area around Fort Edward and Fort William Henry. He lacked sufficient time to prepare his force adequately, however, and he was then restrained by Loudoun's excessive caution. The entire expedition was depleted by illness and death and accomplished little of import, and in the end Winslow whiled away the autumn without seeing action.

Winslow returned to Massachusetts in 1757, resuming his local political career and representing Marshfield in the General Court in 1757–1758, and again from 1761–1765. In 1762, he served as a member of the St. Croix River boundary commission, and was instrumental in surveying and supervising Kennebec River development. In 1766, he moved to Hingham.

Winslow apparently never received adequate pay for his services, and he put in fruitless claims to the end of his life, both to the colonies and to England, for pay or preferment. Apparently in recognition of this injustice, after his death his name remained on the half-pay lists for his wife's benefit until 1787.

Ronald P. Dufour

References

Guy Frégault, *Canada: The War of the Conquest*, trans. by Margaret M. Cameron (1969); Barry Moody, "John Winslow," *Dictionary of Canadian Biography*, Vol. 4 (1974); Stanley M. Pargellis, "John

Winslow," *Dictionary of American Biography*, Vol. 20 (1936); John Clarence Webster, *The Forts of Chignecto: A Study of the Eighteenth Century Conflict between France and Great Britain in Acadia* (1930).

See also ACADIA; FORT BEAUSÉJOUR (NOVA SCOTIA, CANADA); CAMPBELL, JOHN; CHIGNECTO ISTHMUS; FORT EDWARD (NEW YORK); FORT GASPEREAU (NOVA SCOTIA, CANADA); FORT HALIFAX (MAINE); MONCKTON, ROBERT; FORT ST. FRÉDÉRIC (NEW YORK); SHIRLEY, WILLIAM; FORT WILLIAM HENRY (NEW YORK)

Winthrop, John (1588–1649)

John Winthrop was the first governor of Massachusetts Bay. Born in Suffolk, England, he matriculated at Trinity College, Cambridge, but did not earn a degree. He practiced law and acted as lord of Groton Manor before he made the decision to join the Puritan expedition to the New World in 1629. He was one of the men responsible for transferring the New England Company's charter to Massachusetts, thus giving the bay colony an autonomy not enjoyed by other American settlements.

Winthrop's early challenges as governor of the bay colony were more domestic than foreign. Early quarrels over the respective powers of the magistrates and the General Court, the nature of public office, taxation, and land distribution disturbed the governor's tranquility, but the threat of Indian attack or foreign invasion seemed relatively remote. Nevertheless, Winthrop was a colonel of the Middlesex trainband, a local militia unit, which met twice a year for military exercises and drills. He was also careful to articulate his view of the Puritan right to own and occupy land in the New World. All men, he argued, had the "natural right" to unused, untended land. Those men who "improved," enclosed, or settled on the land could claim ownership to it. Hunting territory, which he characterized simply as "wasteland," was available for those who would make proper use of it.

In 1636, the colony had its first taste of Indian warfare with the so-called Pequot War. While many contemporaries accused Massachusetts of instigating the war, Winthrop defended his government's actions. For him, the ultimate victory of the Puritan forces provided evidence of English superiority and of God's favor. Nevertheless, he realized that a united military policy was in the interest of all New England settlers, and in 1637, he advocated the formation of a confederation to help formulate and carry out such a policy. In 1643, the New England Confederation, composed of the colonies of Massachusetts Bay, Plymouth, Connecticut, and New Haven, was created. John Winthrop was the first president of the confederation.

In 1643, Winthrop also became involved in a dispute between two French rivals for the governorship of Acadia (New Brunswick and Nova Scotia). Winthrop chose to throw his support to Charles Saint-Étienne de La Tour in his bid for power against Charles de Menou d'Aulnay. He allowed La Tour to hire ships and men in Massachusetts to use against his rival. Winthrop had no authority to make such a unilateral decision. The matter rightfully belonged in the hands of the New England Confederation, and the following year, the commissioners condemned Winthrop's actions and offered Aulnay compensation. In 1646, Massachusetts apologized for its interference.

Winthrop was always an advocate of the interests of Massachusetts. He supported both the Pequot War and defended the colony's aggressive actions against the neighboring colony of Rhode Island, even though he remained on good terms with the colony's founder, Roger Williams. He never shrank from any opportunity to expand the territorial holdings of Massachusetts, and was generally successful in the pursuit of his endeavors.

Sheila L. Skemp

References

Charles M. Andrews, *The Fathers of New England: A Chronicle of the Puritan Commonwealth* (1919); Edmund S. Morgan, *Puritan Dilemma: The Story of John Winthrop* (1958); Harold L. Peterson, "The Military Equipment of the Plymouth and Bay Colonies, 1620–1690" *New England Quarterly* 20 (1947):197–208; Darrett B. Rutman, *Winthrop's Boston: A Portrait of a Puritan Town, 1630–1649* (1965); John Winthrop, *The History of New England from 1630–1649*, ed. by James Savage (1972).

See also MASSACHUSETTS; NEW ENGLAND CONFEDERATION; PEQUOT WAR; PURITANS; WILLIAMS, ROGER

Winthrop, John (also known as Fitz-John, 1638–1707)

John Winthrop, soldier and governor of Connecticut, and known to his contemporaries as Fitz-John, was born in Ipswich, Massachusetts, the eldest son of John and Elizabeth Reade Winthrop. He attended Harvard College, but left for England in 1657, before graduating, to join the parliamentary army. Winthrop rose to the rank of captain and served under General George Monck in Scotland and in Monck's 1660 march on London that set in motion Charles II's restoration to the throne.

Winthrop returned to New England in 1663 and settled down to the life of a country gentleman in New London, Connecticut. In 1672, he was appointed commander of the New London County militia and the following year led Connecticut troops sent to Long Island to resist a Dutch attack. He took part—but saw no battlefield action—in the war of 1675–1676 against the Indians. In 1686, he and his brother, Waitstill, accepted appointment to the governing council of the newly created royal government of the Dominion of New England, serving under Joseph Dudley and then Governor Sir Edmund Andros. While decidedly sympathetic to stronger royal influence in New England, Winthrop managed to steer clear of the unpopular policies that led, in 1689, to the dominion's overthrow. Instead, he was called upon the next year to command the 850-man expedition sent by New York and Connecticut to attack the French in Montreal as part of a two-pronged land-and-sea assault on Canada. Winthrop showed little capacity and less enthusiasm for the task, and the expedition advanced only a hundred miles north of Albany before turning back, pleading sickness and inadequate supplies. Blamed (and briefly imprisoned) by the New Yorkers for this debacle, Winthrop was exonerated by the Connecticut government.

Winthrop's later life was spent in political rather than military service. Sent as Connecticut's agent to London in 1693, he effectively protected the colony from further schemes for consolidating the northern colonies. Returning in 1698, he was immediately chosen the colony's governor, an office he held until his death in 1707. As such, he was often called upon to organize Connecticut's frontier defenses against Indian attack—and to resist demands for aid from neighboring colonies. Throughout his life, Winthrop found it difficult to match up to the expectations demanded of him by his family

name and his presumed expertise as an English-trained soldier. For a time he swam with the tide of genteel royalism enveloping New England. In his last years, however, he showed considerable diplomatic and administrative talents in reconciling his adopted colony's autonomy with the spread of England's imperial authority.

Richard R. Johnson

References

Richard S. Dunn, *Puritans and Yankees: The Winthrop Dynasty of New England, 1630–1717* (1962); Lawrence Shaw Mayo, *The Winthrop Family in America* (1948); J. Hammon Trumbull and C.J. Hoadly, *The Public Records of the Colony of Connecticut* (1852–1870), Vols. 2–5; Winthrop's letters in Massachusetts Historical Society, *Collections*, 5th ser., 8 (1882), and 6th ser., 3 (1889).

See also ANDROS, EDMUND; CANADA, NEW ENGLAND EXPEDITION AGAINST (1690); DOMINION OF NEW ENGLAND; LEISLER'S REBELLION

Wolfe, James (1727–1759)

James Wolfe was born on 2 January 1727 at the Vicarage at Westerham, Kent, the eldest son of Edward and Henrietta Wolfe. His father had been commissioned as a second lieutenant of marines in 1701–1702, and died in the rank of lieutenant general on 26 March 1759, six months before his son was killed at Quebec. James Wolfe was brought up at Westerham in a house now known as Quebec House, and about 1737, the family moved to Greenwich, where he attended school.

He was given a commission as a second lieutenant in his father's regiment, the 44th Regiment of Foot, on 3 November 1741. He soon transferred to the 12th Regiment of Foot as an ensign on 27 March 1742, and embarked for Flanders with the 12th Foot a month later. After being quartered in Ghent until February 1743, he was present with his regiment at the Battle of Dettingen on 27 June, and was serving as acting adjutant and had his horse shot from under him. Although only 16, he was commissioned as adjutant on 2 July and promoted to the rank of lieutenant on 14 July.

In the winter of 1743–1744, he was stationed at Ostend with his regiment and on 3 June 1744, transferred again when he obtained a company in the 4th Regiment of Foot (Barrel's). In October, he lost his brother, and again spent the

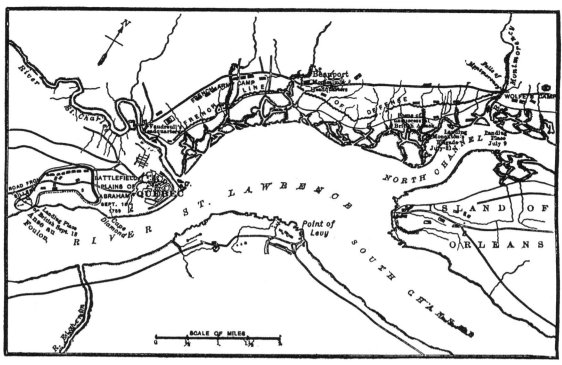

Wolfe at Quebec.

winter at Ghent. A year later, on 12 June 1745, he was appointed brigade major, and for the following three years served on the staff. In September, he accompanied the regiments that had been recalled to England to oppose the young pretender. Wolfe was present at the Battle of Falkirk and then moved on to Aberdeen. He continued to serve on the staff and was present at the Battle of Culloden, during which his regiment lost about one-third of its men.

Wolfe returned to the Netherlands and served as brigade major in Mordaunt's brigade in the campaign that followed. He was wounded at the action at Laeffelt. He returned home for the winter to recuperate and rejoined the army in the field in March and remained until the end of the year with the troops stationed at Breda.

His next move was to the 20th Regiment of Foot (Lord George Sackville's), where he obtained a majority from 5 January 1748, and actually joined the regiment at Stirling in February. With his colonel away, Wolfe had command of the regiment while it was stationed in Glasgow in March and while it was in Perth from November. Lord Bury became colonel of the regiment on 20 March 1749–1750, and

Wolfe was given the lieutenant colonelcy. He was then in command of a regiment of men, although he had not yet reached the age of 23. He wrote on 6 November 1751, "The care of a regiment of foot is very heavy, exceeding troublesome, and not at all the thing I delight in." He had been refused leave to study by the duke of Cumberland and therefore spent the winter of 1750–1751 in London and only returned to his regiment, stationed at Banff, in April 1752. In June of that year, he was granted leave of absence and spent his time in Dublin and then in Paris, where he studied French, riding, and fencing, and was recalled to his regiment owing to the sudden death of the major.

After spending the summer road-making around Loch Lomond, the regiment moved to Dover, and the next four years were spent in various quarters in the south of England.

The regiment moved about, serving at Exeter, Canterbury, and in camp in Dorsetshire. On 15 December 1755, Wolfe issued his "Instructions for the 20th Regiment," which set out a plan of action should the French land. He was often severe on officers and soldiers, but as his regiment became one of the elite foot regiments of the army, there were plenty of officers who wished to learn soldiering eager to join his regiment.

He was considered to be one of the best officers of his age and rank in the service, and although he had hopes of the colonelcy of the 20th Regiment, when it became vacant in April 1755, he was passed over. Again in May 1756, the regiment became known as "Kingsley's" and fought as such at Minden. In February 1757, Wolfe accepted the post of quartermaster general in Ireland, a post that was normally held by a colonel, but Wolfe was still judged to be too young to be given that rank. The appointment permitted him to stay with his regiment, which was then stationed in Dorset, and had been increased in strength by having a second battalion added in the spring of 1757.

In September 1757, William Pitt approved a plan for an expedition to be sent against Rochefort, the French port. The expedition was commanded by Sir John Mordaunt and included both battalions of the 20th Regiment of Foot. James Wolfe was appointed as quartermaster general for the force. The expeditionary force arrived off the French coast on 20 September and remained there for ten days, achieving little except for the occupation of Ile d'Aix. Wolfe returned home, indignant that nothing had been achieved. He wrote dismissively of the whole operation, commenting that "the public could not do better than dismiss six or eight of us from the service. No zeal, no ardour, no care and concern for the good and honour of the country." Although the expedition had failed, Wolfe had been noticed for his "zeal and ardour" and a report of his work had been given to the king. Wolfe was given a brevet colonelcy on 21 October 1757. On 7 January 1758, Wolfe was at Exeter and, on being summoned to London, made the journey of 170 miles in just 32 hours. He was offered the command of a brigade in an expeditionary force that was to be sent to Louisbourg, and although he knew that his health might be ruined, he accepted and was given his letter of service as a "Brigadier in America," which was dated 23 January. He embarked on 12 February and arrived at Halifax, Nova Scotia, on 8 May. On 28 May, the expedition left with a land force consisting of more than 11,000 regular soldiers and 500 provincials under the command of General Jeffrey Amherst. The naval force arrived off Louisbourg on 1 June, but due to bad weather was unable to land for a week. A landing was attempted, and although the force commanded by

Wolfe met with stiff French opposition at the point of landing in Freshwater Bay, and came under heavy gunfire, some of his men reached the rocks at one end of the bay. Wolfe diverted the remainder of his force, landed, climbed the cliff, and took the nearest battery with a bayonet attack. The French withdrew to Louisbourg. Following a short siege, the French garrison, numbering 5,637 soldiers and sailors, surrendered. The news of the fall of Louisbourg was greeted with delight in England.

Wolfe attempted to persuade Amherst to attack Quebec or to send help to General James Abercromby, who had been repulsed at Ticonderoga. Amherst moved to reinforce Abercromby, and Wolfe was dispatched with three battalions to destroy the French fishing settlements in the Gulf of St. Lawrence. Having completed this task, he considered that he had permission to leave, and at the end of the campaign returned to England. Although an order had been sent to him to remain in America, he had already sailed for home. On reaching England on 1 November 1758, he joined the 2nd Battalion of the 20th Regiment of Foot at Salisbury which, by this time, had been renumbered and was now the 67th Regiment of Foot. He had wanted a cavalry command and service on the Continent, but as neither were offered, he wrote to William Pitt and offered himself for further service in America. It was agreed that he should command an expeditionary force to be sent up the St. Lawrence River to attack Quebec. Amherst was to advance on Montreal while Wolfe was to carry out his attack. He was given the rank of major general in America from 12 January 1759, and was permitted to select his own staff officers. He was suffering with rheumatism and spent some time at Bath, where he became engaged to Katherine Lowther. Before leaving for America he dined with William Pitt, and on 17 February he left Spithead on the flagship of Admiral Charles Saunders and arrived at Halifax, Nova Scotia, on 30 April. There followed a period of preparation, and in June the expedition left Louisbourg. On 27 June, the troops landed on the Isle d'Orleans, which was about four miles from Quebec.

The attacking force consisted of nearly 9,000 men, making up ten battalions forming three brigades. In addition, there were three companies of grenadiers from the Louisbourg garrison, three companies of light infantry, and six companies of New England rangers. Quebec was well-defended, with more than a hundred guns and had a garrison of 2,000 regular troops, with a further 14,000 at Beauport nearby. In addition, the French had more than 1,000 Indians serving their cause.

On 30 June, Wolfe occupied Pointe Lévy with one brigade, and on 12 July, the batteries that he had established nearby opened fire on the town. Despite tempting the French by dividing his force, they failed to attack. On his arrival he informed the Canadian civilians that if they took no part in the coming contest they would be left in peace; however, they helped harass his troops, and he then retaliated by burning their settlements.

Following a reconnaissance on 18 July, it was decided that an attempt on the left bank was too difficult, and on 31 July, he launched an attack on the east end of the French camp at Beauport, but it was beaten back by the French army, and Wolfe had to withdraw his attacking force.

During the latter part of August, Wolfe was ill with fever and told his doctor that although he could not cure his complaint, he wished him to give him something so "that I may be without pain, for a few days, and able to do my duty; that is all I want."

Although he usually formed his own plan and carried it through, on this occasion he consulted his brigadiers. They rejected his three proposed plans and gave one of their own, which Wolfe initially accepted; however, the proposed landing was postponed due to bad weather. By 10 September, Wolfe had decided on a daring plan which was to land his troops at Anse au Foulon (now known as Wolfe's Cove), which was only one and a half miles from Quebec. The wooded cliffs were steep and would be guarded by only a few of the enemy. The plan was not a popular one, and the three brigadiers sent him a joint request asking for specific orders, thus revealing a degree of disagreement between Wolfe and his subordinates.

After dark on 12 September, 1,700 men embarked in boats and soon after 2 A.M., the light infantry landed and scaled the cliff and overcame the French guard. The main body of troops, with Major General Wolfe, followed. In the meantime, the ships of the fleet commenced a bombardment of the French positions at Beauport. The British force on the heights had been increased to 4,500 men with two artillery pieces and was ready for the French counterattack.

The French commander, Louis-Joseph de Montcalm, was only able to muster, due to desertion, a force about equal to that of the British. Wolfe issued what was to be his last order, in which he wrote:

The officers and men will remember what their country expects from them, and what a determined body of soldiers are capable of doing against five weak battalions, mingled with a disorderly peasantry. The soldiers must be attentive to their officers, and resolute in their execution of their duty.

Wolfe hoped to bring the French to battle and advanced to the Plains of Abraham, an open area about one mile from Quebec. The British army had six battalions as a front line, with two battalions on the left flank, and one held in reserve.

Montcalm attacked in three columns at about 10 A.M. and his troops were within forty paces of the British front before the British opened fire, and then followed with a charge. Wolfe, wearing his distinctive uniform, went to high ground on the right where he had an advance post of Louisbourg grenadiers. He had already been wounded on the wrist and in the groin, and was then hit for a third time by what has been recorded as a shot from a French sharpshooter. With the help of some grenadiers, he walked about a hundred yards to the rear, and then had to lie down. The third hit had been a chest wound, and he realized that he had been mortally wounded.

He asked how the battle was progressing and was told that the French had retreated and were being pursued. He died shortly thereafter.

Montcalm, who had also been wounded, died soon after Wolfe, and Quebec surrendered to the British on 18 September. Brigadier Robert Monckton had been wounded, and Brigadier George Townshend assumed temporary command. In his report of the British success he barely mentioned the death of General Wolfe, however; the majority of the British force mourned the loss of a general who had compassion for those under his command.

The body of James Wolfe was brought to England and buried in the crypt of St. Alfege Church, Greenwich.

Alan Harfield

References
A.G. Bradley, Wolfe (1895); W.T. Waugh, *James Wolfe, Man and Soldier*

(1928); Beckles Willson, *The Life and Letters of James Wolfe* (1909).

See also AMHERST, JEFFREY; LOUISBOURG, SIEGE OF (1758); MONCKTON, ROBERT; MONTCALM-GOZON DE SAINT-VERAN, LOUIS-JOSEPH; PITT, WILLIAM; QUEBEC, BATTLE OF

Fort Wolstenholme (Virginia)

Built in 1619 on the east side of the James River several miles east of Jamestown, Fort Wolstenholme was part of the Martin's Hundred plantation. Named for John Wolstenholme, one of the prominent shareholders in the Martin's Hundred Society, the fort was an irregular, four-sided palisade approximately 131 feet long and 86 feet wide. A watchtower stood at each angle. In 1622, the fort was partially burned when Indians under chief Opechancanough attacked the settlers along the James River, killing most of the inhabitants of Martin's Hundred. By the end of 1622, about 20 people had returned to the site, and scattered returns took place over the next decade, but the fort itself was probably not reoccupied.

Thomas Costa

References
    Ivor Noel Hume, *Martin's Hundred* (1982).

See also OPECHANCANOUGH; PAMUNKEY

Woodward, Henry (c. 1646–c. 1690)

An unusually adventurous Englishman—able to parley with anyone while being faithful to no one—Dr. Henry Woodward virtually created the lower south's Indian trade and diplomacy; he pioneered English expansion in Carolina and established the cycle of alliance and betrayal that would characterize Anglo-Indian relations in this region. Born about 1646, Woodward trained as a surgeon and entered military service. He accompanied Captain Robert Sandford when Sandford explored coastal Carolina in 1666 for the province's Lords Proprietors. Woodward volunteered to stay on at Port Royal to learn Indian languages and establish friendly relations with the local Cusabo. Acting as solitary tenant at will of the colony for the proprietors, Woodward entered Indian society and was adopted by the chief. Kidnapped by the Spanish and carried off to St. Augustine, he escaped in 1668 and traveled through the Caribbean as ship's surgeon on a privateer, getting a firsthand look at the Indian, Spanish, and English societies in the larger region.

After returning to Carolina in 1670, Woodward acted as the colony's official interpreter. In July of that year, he made a mysterious tour inland and met a king who claimed to be emperor over the region, also making informal treaties with this man and the smaller chiefs around him. In spring of 1671, the proprietors rewarded him with £100, promising him further gain as he continued to serve their interests. Woodward also serviced some private interests. Searching for precious metals, he acted as special agent for proprietor Anthony Ashley Cooper, first earl of Shaftesbury, and went on a secret mission for Sir John Yeamans in Virginia for much the same reason.

Woodward went on an official mission in 1674, when Lord Ashley ordered him to get a treaty either with the inland Westo or Kashita (in the interior of the colony), a move that would militarily strengthen the tiny English settlement against the Spanish in Florida. Meeting a party of ten Westo in the same year, Woodward decided to accompany them on an unprecedented tour inland toward the Savannah River, where he gained more knowledge of the land and inhabitants. He signed a treaty of alliance with the Westo, thus opening trade for furs, deerskins, and Indian slaves from other tribes who could be sold to labor-hungry sugar planters in the West Indies.

Woodward's Westo Treaty of 1674 triggered English settlement in Carolina. Colonists were free to expand with a lessened threat of war from the Spanish or unallied Indians, and were able to realize the colony's first profits through the Indian trade, which would be Carolina's only real source of revenue until the first quarter of the eighteenth century. The treaty raised, however, two dilemmas that would plague Anglo-Indian relations: the problem of regulating Indian trade so that allied Indians would not resent the terms of the trade (perhaps defecting to the Spanish or French), and the explosive potential for intertribal warfare that the traffic in Indian slaves created.

Woodward himself capitalized on the advantages and uncertainties of the Anglo-Indian alliance, which would degenerate into warfare within six years. The Westo treaty created a monopoly on Indian trade for the proprietors and their servants—of whom Woodward was the most beloved—thus limiting the sphere of Indian trading too narrowly for many settlers, who would have preferred an open season on furs and slaves. Woodward became an Indian trader, but was accused by other traders of destabilizing Indian relations by encouraging the Westo to raid their coastal Cusabo neighbors for more slaves to sell to the English; he seemed to be playing all sides against each other. Charles Town authorities forbade Woodward to trade, and defied the proprietors' terms of trade. Using the Westo as scapegoats (and as a source for even more captives to sell to the West Indies), traders declared war on the tribe in 1680, employing other Indians as warriors against them. In 1683, the proprietors learned that fewer than 50 Westos remained alive.

The Westo War signaled the failure of proprietary control over Indian affairs and weakened Woodward's favored position in the colony. He was fined for his shady dealings with the Westo, and censured by the proprietors. He returned to England to plead his case, and was pardoned and reinstated. His new commission encouraged him to travel over the Appalachian Mountains, which he did in the summer of 1685, tarrying along the Chattahoochee River with the Creek in what the Spanish regarded as their territory. By following his extraordinary instructions, Woodward ran afoul not only of the Spanish, but also Henry Erskine, Lord Cardross, who had established a Scottish settlement at Port Royal and claimed exclusive rights to trade southward into the Spanish area of Guale.

Woodward and Cardross squabbled over whether the English or the Scottish were more destabilizing factors in the region, until the Spanish made their own move by attacking Carolina in the fall of 1686, Despite this flurry of activity along the coastline, the region Woodward had explored a year earlier would provide a more lasting sphere of conflict among European and Indian powers. The Lower Creek would migrate from the Chattahoochee, where they had entertained Woodward, to the upper Altamaha River about 1690. They would be trading partners and military allies for the English until 1715, when they decided that the English would do to them what they had done to the Westo: use them both as allies *and* as expendable victims as it suited their convenience. Woodward himself dropped out of the picture in 1686; the next extant record of him is his will, probated in Charles Town in March 1690.

Joyce E. Chaplin

References
J.W. Barnwell, "Dr. Henry Woodward

and Some of His Descendents," *South Carolina Historical and Genealogical Magazine*, 8 (1907):29–41; Verner W. Crane, *The Southern Frontier, 1670–1732* (1929).

See also FORT AMONG THE APALACHICOLA (ALABAMA); PORT ROYAL (SOUTH CAROLINA); WESTO

Wyatt, Francis (1588–1644)

A member of a prominent Kentish family, Sir Francis Wyatt served as governor of Virginia from 1621 to 1626, and again from 1639 to 1641. Born in the year of the Spanish Armada, Wyatt was knighted in 1603. In 1618, he married Margaret, daughter of Sir Samuel Sandys, and this connection brought him to Virginia. His wife's uncle, Sir Edwin Sandys, became treasurer of the Virginia Company following the reorganization of the group in 1619. Sandys embarked upon a creative program of revitalization for the colony, and in 1621, he appointed his niece's husband governor to succeed George Yeardley. Wyatt arrived in Virginia in that year, directing the colony's affairs from his residence at Jamestown.

He had been in the post a scant six months when the Powhatan Indians under Chief Opechancanough attacked the Virginia colonists, killing between one-fourth and one-third of the English inhabitants. Wyatt presided during the ensuing retrenchment and dissolution of the Virginia Company in 1624, attempting to preserve the colonial assembly. He returned to England in 1626 after his father died, then came back to Virginia in 1639, succeeding the unpopular John Harvey as governor and arriving with the crown's official confirmation of the assembly. He served until 1641 when he was succeeded by Sir William Berkeley. Wyatt returned to England, where he died in 1644.

Thomas Costa

References
Wesley Frank Craven, *The Dissolution of the Virginia Company* (1932).

See also JAMESTOWN; OPECHANCANOUGH; VIRGINIA; VIRGINIA-INDIAN WAR (1622–1632)

Wyandot
See HURON

Y

Yamasee

See YAMASEE WAR

Yamasee War (1715–1717)

By the turn of the eighteenth century, many of the southeastern Indian tribes had become an integral part of the Carolina deerskin trade, and several moved closer to Charles Town because of the English trade. The Upper Creek established a settlement midway between the Tallapoosa, Alabama, and Ocmulgee Rivers. The Lower Creek moved to the banks of the Ocmulgee River, and the Yamasee relocated less than 100 miles from Charles Town.

All of the tribes involved in the Carolina trade complained bitterly about the white traders in their nations, but the Yamasee were the tribe whose anger and resentment was recorded most frequently. The Indian commissioners attempted to reassure the Yamasee; however, there was little they could do, or would do, to control unscrupulous dealers. Carolinians along the Indian frontier often wrote to England about the "idle and dissolute traders" among the Indians.

By 1715, Indian debt to the traders was estimated at more than £50,000, an amount that would require decades to repay. Pressure by their own creditors led many traders to kidnap free Indian women and children and sell them as slaves. These abductions and other widespread abuses played a major role in weakening the English hold on their Indian allies and ultimately led to revolt by many of the subject Carolina tribes.

On Good Friday, 15 April 1715, the Yamasee War began with a coordinated attack on all the white traders in Indian towns. Those who escaped the initial massacre warned the settlers along the southern borders of the colony. By early summer, frightened colonists from the outsettlements were pouring into Charles Town, as Creek, Yamasee, Apalachee, Savannah, and Saraw attacked the colony from the north and south.

A counterattack in June, led by Carolina Governor Charles Craven, successfully vanquished the Yamasee in the southern region of the colony, and soon Charles Town merchants were shipping captive women and children to the slave markets in the Caribbean. Most of the Yamasee women and children had fled to St. Augustine before hostilities began, and after the English victory, the remaining members of the tribe joined them.

From their base in Spanish Florida, the Yamasee and their Lower Creek allies invaded St. Paul's parish and burned 20 plantations. St. Helena and St. Bartholomew were almost totally deserted, and those who remained found that St. Paul's had suddenly become the Carolina frontier. With most of the Yamasee across the border, the war became almost entirely a Creek effort. In August, the head warrior of Coweta, Chigelley, led a force of several hundred Creek and Apalachee against Charles Town and came within a few miles of the town before being repulsed.

Carolina's only chance for survival lay in convincing the Cherokee, the largest tribe in the Southeast and traditional enemies of the Creek, to remain loyal to the English. In January 1716, Creek emissaries arrived in the Cherokee towns to ask for support in their war against the whites. The Cherokee not only refused to join the Creek, they murdered the emissaries. This overt aggression assured Cherokee allegiance to the English for the rest of the war and contributed to Creek-Cherokee enmity for more than half a century.

From early 1716 until a peace was negotiated in 1717, the Creek and their allies conducted scattered raids in Carolina, but there were no more large-scale battles. The Creek were most likely the instigators of the Yamasee War, and they bore the brunt of the actual fighting. With their northern flank exposed following the Cherokee defection, and cut off from English trade, the Creek soon gravitated to the other two European powers along the southern frontier. The Lower Creek moved back to their old grounds along the Chattahoochee and made overtures to the Spanish. The Upper Creek began to accept trade offers by the French.

During the Yamasee War, "Emperor" Brims of Coweta embarked on a deliberate policy of neutrality that was to govern Creek actions for several generations. After the war ended, the Creek maintained their contacts with both the Spanish and French. Brims and his heirs became the custodians of the southern balance of power, and they retained this role until the end of the colonial period.

In January 1717, messengers came to Charles Town from both the Upper and Lower Creek requesting peace talks. The following summer an English peace delegation was sent to Coweta with a caravan of packhorses loaded with trade goods. The Creek and Carolinians finally agreed to end hostilities in November 1717. By then, however, the French had completed Fort Toulouse on the Coosa River at the invitation of the Upper Creek, and the English were never able to dislodge their rivals from this strategic position. The Spanish were alternately welcomed and rebuffed by the Creek at Coweta until a new trade agreement with Carolina was signed, and pro-Spanish sentiment among some of the Lower Creek remained throughout the colonial period.

The Yamasee War was one of the most destructive attacks sustained by any of the English colonies, and even though South Carolina survived, the Indian alliances on which it depended for trade and protection had shifted unalterably. Southern frontier diplomacy would continue to revolve upon the pivot of Creek loyalty for many decades to come, and the presence of the French and Spanish among the Creek remained a source of alarm to the English. The English not only suffered devastating losses of life, property, and Indian trade during the Yamasee War, but in terms of empire, their influence on the southern frontier declined dramatically.

Doris B. Fisher

References
Boston News, 13 June 1715; *Calendar of State Papers, Colonial Series* 28, Public Record Office of Great Britain; *Colonial Records of North Carolina*, ed. by William L. Saunders (1886); *The Carolina Chronicle of Dr. Francis Le Jau*, ed. by Frank L. Klingberg (1956); David H. Corkran, *The Creek Frontier, 1540–1783* (1967); Verner W. Crane, *The Southern Frontier, 1670–1732* (1928).

Larry E. Ivers, *Colonial Forts of South Carolina 1670–1775* (1970); *Mississippi Provincial Archives*, ed. by Rowland Dunbar and Albert G. Sanders (1927–1932); John R. Swanton, *Early History of the Creek Indians and Their Neighbors* (1922); J. Leitch Wright, *Anglo-Spanish Rivalry in North America* (1971).

See also BRIMS OF COWETA; CHEROKEE; CRAVEN, CHARLES; CREEK; CREEK-CHEROKEE WAR; FRONTIER, SOUTHERN; NAIRNE, THOMAS; ST. AUGUSTINE, BATTLE OF; SOUTH CAROLINA

York, Attack on (1692)

York, Maine was settled very early. Over the years it received its share of Indian raids, and the people developed methods for their protection. By 1692, there were four fortified houses for people to go to during times of crisis.

The years 1689–1690 saw Indian attacks on many northern New England frontier settlements. In November 1690, a truce was signed at Sagadahoc that was to be renewed the following May. No Indians came to the proposed meeting. Several Indians in the area, who said that they had forgotten about the proposed meeting, were sent to the chiefs to arrange for another meeting at Wells, Maine, but failed to return. An uneasy period set in on the frontier. In June, after the Wells Fort had been reinforced with an additional 35 men, Indians attacked and then raided Cape Neddock, captured a vessel, and burned houses. Summer and fall passed without further action. With the coming of winter, the settlers relaxed.

Early on the morning of 6 February 1692, a surprise attack was made on York. More than 160 people were unable to reach the safety of the four fortified houses and were killed or captured.

However, when the garrisoned houses refused to surrender, the Indians released the same number of old women and children as the Indian prisoners Captain Benjamin Church had released at Pejepscot in 1690. Then they departed.

Nicholas N. Smith

References

Charles E. Banks, *History of York, Maine*, Vol. 1 (1931); Samuel Adams Drake, *The Border Wars of New England* (1897); Henry E. Dunnack, *Maine Forts* (1924); Allan Forbes, *Towns of New England and Old England, Ireland and Scotland*, Vol. 2 (1926); William Williamson, *The History of Maine*, Vol. 1 (1832).

See also CHURCH, BENJAMIN; GARRISON HOUSES; KING WILLIAM'S WAR; WELLS (MAINE)

Y

Z

Fort Zwaanendael (Delaware)
See Fort Swanendael (Delaware)

Index

653, 668, 672–673, 674–677, 684, 686,
727, 746, 759, 791, 805
Albany, Treaty of (1677), 422
Albany, Treaty of (1722), 364, 584
Albany Conference (19 June-11 July 1754), **13–15**,
48, 309, 496, 701
Albany Plan of Union, 14–15, 235
Albany Purchase of 1754, 189
Albemarle, Duke of, 691, 703
Albemarle Sound, 508, 710
Alberta, 530
Alcide, 580
Aleut, 643–645
Aleutian Islands, 643
Alexander. *See* Wamsutta
Alexandria, 523, 525
Alexandria Conference (1755), 176
Fort Algernon (Virginia), **15**, 113
Algonquin, 148, 223–224, 229, 317, 341, 360,
366, 457, 531, 539, 708, 747, 765
Alibamon Mingo, 9, 131, 132, 133, 627
Allegheny Mountains, 176, 189, 276, 295, 385, 548
Allegheny River, 147, 169, 213, 271, 289, 355,
357, 368, 386, 409, 448, 521, 523, 566,
586, 686, 746, 757
Fort Allen (Pennsylvania), **15–16**, 507
Allerton, Isaack, 546
Allouez, Claude, 297
Alrichs, Jacob, 107
Altamaha River, **16**, 62, 206, 236, 263, 272, 333,
464, 517, 519, 579, 712, 810
Alvarez de Pineda, Alfonso, 204
Ambridge, 110
Amelia, 62
Amelia Fort (Florida), 588
Amelia Island, 208, 264, 518, 649
American Bottom, 299
Amherst, Jeffery, First Baron Amherst, 3, **16–19**,
51, 72–73, 74, 80, 85, 93, 158, 190,
257, 275, 276, 286, 290, 303, 309–310,
361, 381, 382, 392–394, 407, 434, 448,
453, 458, 462, 498, 502, 573, 581, 602,
607–608, 633–634, 636–637, 639, 651–
652, 653, 659, 662, 689–692, 724, 736,
740, 800, 807
and Cherokee War, 121
spreads smallpox among Indians, 18, 73–74
Amherst, William, 692
Aminoya, 709
Ammunition, **19–21**
artillery, 46–47
Fort Amsterdam (New York), **21–22**, 26, 330, 332
Anastasia Island, 210, 264, 455, 519, 664–665,
666
Ancient and Honorable Artillery Company of Massachusetts, **22**, 47, 440, 770
Andover, 137
Andros, Sir Edmund, 4, **22–25**, 141, 168, 179,
180, 195–196, 202, 214, 249, 272, 313,
342, 370, 386, 410, 427, 494, 500, 504,

549, 556, 563, 629, 674–675, 729, 770,
795, 805
Fort Andros (Maine), 138
Androscoggin, 1
Androscoggin River, 138
Angelina River, 87, 510
Anglo-Dutch War, First (1652–1654), **25–26**, 278,
322, 387, 477, 490
Anglo-Dutch War, Second (1664–1667), **26–28**, 65,
278, 414, 477, 491
Anglo-Dutch War, Third (1672–1674), **28–29**, 278,
414, 477, 494, 499–500
Anglo-Indian Relations, **29–33**. *See also* Au-
gusta; Augusta, Congress of; Barnwell,
John; Buffalo Creek, Shawnee Attack
on; Burd, James; Cherokee War;
Cockacoeske; Covenant Chain;
Dummer's War; France-Indian Rela-
tions; Frontier; Frontier, Northern;
Frontier Southern; Half-King; Iroquois;
Johnson, Sir William; King Philip's
War; Lancaster, Treaty of; Logstown,
Treaty of; Maine; Narragansett; New
England Confederation; Norridgwock,
Battle of; Nutimus; Pequot War; Ply-
mouth; Pontiac's War; Powhatan; Pray-
ing Indians; Proclamation Line of
1763; Prophet; Right of Conquest;
South Carolina; Stuart, John;
Tuscarora War; Virginia; Virgina-In-
dian War (1622–1632); Virginia-Indian
War (1644–1646); Wampanoag; War
and Society in Colonial America;
Yamasee War
Anglo-Spanish War (1718–1721), 33, 333
Anglo-Spanish War (1739–1744), 16, **34–35**, 128,
154, 206, 280–281, 283, 334, 435,
455–456, 477, 478, 518, 551, 565,
576–577, 588, 636, 663, 666, 705,
712, 721, 758, 778
battle of Bloody Marsh, 68
expedition against Cartagena, 104–106
Georgia and, 264–266
Massachusetts in, 429
Angouirot, 663, 755
Fort Ann (Massachusetts). *See* Fort William
(Massachusetts)
Annapolis Royal. *See* Port Royal (Nova Scotia,
Canada)
Fort Anne (New York; also known as Queen's Fort,
Fort Schuyler, Mud Fort), 35, 360
Queen Anne, 577, 674, 677, 791
Anse au Foulon, 448, 608–609, 808
Anson, Lord George, 177, 416, 465, 699, 778
Anticosti Island, 99, 655
Antigua, 182, 590, 617, 702
Antonelli, Juan Bautista, 293
Anville, Duc d'. *See* La Rochefoucauld de Roye,
Jean-Baptiste Louis Frédéric de, duc
d'Anville

Apache, 44, 87, 89, 487–488, 507, 594, 661, 663, 664, 760
Apalachee, 35–37, 56, 101, 151, 152, 204, 205, 206, 234, 275, 282, 470, 552, 554, 555, 616, 649, 663, 665, 714, 743–744, 811
   Apalachee revolt, 37
   and Chacato troubles (1674–1675), 111–112
   attack Creek (1702), 81
   English attack (1704), 36–37, 56
Apalachee Revolt, 36, 37–38
Apalachicola, 38, 111
Apalachicola River, 112, 794
Fort Among the Apalachicolas (Alabama), 38
Appleton, Samuel, 718
Appomattock, 38–39, 765
Appomattox River, 38–39, 295, 509–510, 641
Aquidneck Island, 628–629, 801
Arawac, 204
Arawak, 737
Arbousset, General, 114
Arellano, Tristan de Luna y. See Luna y Arrellano, Tristan de
Argall, Sir Samuel, 223, 278, 322, 577
Argenson, Comte d'. See Voyer, Marc-Pierre de, Comte d'Argenson
Argyle, 519
Fort Argyle (Georgia), 517
Arikara, 529
Arizona, 145
Arkansas, 87, 126, 128, 709
Arkansas Indians. See Quapaw (Arkansas)
Arkansas Post (Arkansas), 39, 400
Arkansas River, 39, 130, 536, 597–598, 760
Arke, 418
Armada de Barlovento, 479–480
Armstrong, Edward, 271, 356
Armstrong, John, 103, 170, 356, 383–384, 513, 688, 700
Armstrong, Lawrence, 578
Armstrong system of artillery, 46
Army, France, 39–41, 581
   battalion strength, 41
   relations between regulars and Canadian soldiers, 40
   Troupes de la Marine, 242
Army, Great Britain (1688–1763), 41–43
   Board of General Officers, 42
   War Office, 42
Army, Spain, 44–45
Arriola, Andrés de, 553
Arrowsic, 412
Artaguette, Pierre d', 8–9, 126, 128, 375–376, 401, 520
Artaguette Diron, Jean-Baptiste Martin d', 373
Articles of War, 177
Artillery, 285–286, 451
Artillery, France, 45, 400
Artillery, Great Britain, 45–48, 273
   brass, 46
   Royal Regiment of Artillery, 642–643

Art of War, 723
Fort Ascension (Illinois). See Fort Massac (Illinois)
Ashley River, 180, 710
Ashpelon, 293
asiento, 13, 283, 334, 617, 756
Askin, John, 439
Assiniboin, 529
Fort Assumption (Tennessee), 128, 375
Atkin, Edmond, 9, 32, 48–49, 460–461, 724
Atkinson, Theodore, 14
Attakapa, 473
Attakullakulla (also known as Little Carpenter), 49–50, 118, 119, 120, 121–122, 159, 515, 724
Aubry, Charles-Philippe, 357–358, 503
Aucilla River, 35
Auger, Charles, 617
Auger de Subercase, Daniel d', 5–6, 8, 577
Aughwick Creek, 405, 700
Augusta, 50–51, 155, 264, 517
Augusta, Congress of (1763), 51–54, 107, 120, 153, 155, 192, 509, 724
Fort Augusta (Georgia), 50, 54–55, 263
Fort Augusta (Maine), 55
Fort Augusta (Pennsylvania), 55–56, 170, 271, 291
Augusta, Treaty of (1763), 51
Augustus, William, Duke of Cumberland, 432
Aute, 470
Avoyelle, 471
Ayllón, Lucas Vázquez de, 56, 204, 508, 667, 710
Aylmer, Matthew, 778
Ayubale (Florida), 56, 616
Azlor y Virto de Vera, Joseph de, second marqués de San Miguel de Aguayo, 12, 357, 511, 661

Backler, Edward, 621
Bacon, Nathaniel, 57, 58–60, 66, 139, 250, 295, 762
Bacon's Rebellion (1675–1677), 31, 57–60, 66, 101, 139, 249, 272, 322, 417, 420, 421, 424, 494, 542, 583, 729, 762, 765
Badine, 378
Bahamas Channel, 44, 479, 615, 664, 710
Bahamas Islands, 33, 435, 617, 700–701
Baillie, Robert, 62
Baird, Father, 506
Baja, 89
Balfour, Henry, 439
Balize Post (Louisiana), 60, 400
Barbados, 420, 499, 579, 590, 617, 649, 711, 793
Barbuda, 617
Fort Barnwell (North Carolina), 60
Barnwell, John, 10, 60–61, 262, 333, 505, 579, 749–751
Barnwell Township System, 61–62
Baron de la Galisonière, Roland, 338
Barrack Master General, 637
Barrett, Lemuel, 85
Fort Barrington (Georgia), 16, 62, 162

Boucher de Niverville, Jean-Baptiste, 337
Bougainville, Louis-Antoine de, Comte de, 69–71,
      319, 450–453, 454–455, 458, 586, 607–
      613, 659–660, 740, 742
Fort de la Boulaye (Louisiana), 71, 373, 379,
      399, 650
Bouquet, Henry, 65, 71–74, 80, 103, 190, 212,
      384, 462, 566, 575–576, 586, 662, 703,
      735, 747, 757, 792
    Battle of Bushy Run, 85–86
    spreads smallpox among Indians, 18
Fort Bourbon (Manitoba, Canada), 377
Bourbon, Louis-Joseph de, Prince de Condé, 382
Bourbon Family Compact, 226
Bourlamaque, François-Charles de, 74–75, 319,
      450, 453, 458, 612, 632–633, 653, 740
Bow and Arrow, 75
Braam, Jacob Van, 523–524
Brackett, Anthony, 75
Brackett's Wood, Battle of (1689), 75–76, 138
Braddock, Edward, 48, 76–78, 79, 85, 157, 158,
      169, 174, 176, 185, 226, 236, 257,
      259, 267, 268, 271, 273, 276, 281,
      307, 362, 388, 405, 430, 434, 449,
      450, 497, 513, 524–527, 548, 551,
      567, 571, 593, 598, 599, 623, 687,
      701, 702, 727, 735, 780, 802
Braddock's Defeat. See Ohio Expedition of 1755
Braddock's Road, 212
Bradford, William, 443, 566
Bradstreet, John, 73, 78–81, 111, 238–239, 335,
      453, 498, 501–502, 537–538, 599, 639,
      688, 689, 720
Bradstreet, Simon, 196, 564–565
Braintree, 346
Brandt, Randolph, 421–422
Brant, Catherine, 157
Brant, Joseph, 157, 326, 496
Brant, Molly, 327, 363, 496
Breda, Treaty of (1667), 28, 279, 411, 491, 556
Brent, Giles, 418
Brenton, Jahleel, 564
Briand, Pont, 366
Brilliante, 616
Brims of Coweta (?-c. 1730), 81–82, 463, 812
British Columbia, 90
British South Seas Company, 34
Broad Creek, 420
Broad River, 113, 155
Brookfield, 67, 164, 201, 340, 348, 718
Brown, John, 4, 620
Browne, Charlotte, 433
Bruce, Peter Henry, 325
Bruce Peninsula, 539
Brûlé, Etienne, 148
Brunswick, 412, 509
Fort Buade (Michigan), 82, 298, 570
Buffalo Creek, Shawnee Attack on (1754), 82
Buisson de Saint-Cosme, Jean François, 401
Bulkeley, Charles, 707

Fort Bull (New York), 82–83, 366, 688
Bull, Captain, 551
Bull, William, 264, 722
Bull, William, Jr., 49, 123
Bulman, Alexander, 83
Bungi. *See* Ojibwa
Fort Burd (Pennsylvania), 72–73, 83, 449
Burd, James, 83–84, 384
Fort Burke (Massachusetts), 84
Burke, John, 84
Burlington Island Fort (New Jersey), 84
Burnet, William, 84, 250, 496, 533, 678
Burton, Ralph, 462
Bushy Run, Battle of (1763), 18, 72, 85–86, 214,
      566, 703
Busse, Christian, 295
Butler, Walter, 297
Butte des Morts, 218
Buttes á Neveu, 612–613
Byerly, Andrew, 85
Byng, George, 567
Bynkershoek, Cornelius van, 683
Byrd, William (Sr.), 57
Byrd, William, 39, 129, 510
Byrd's Fort (Virginia). *See* Fort Dinwiddie
    (Virginia)

Cabeza de Vaca, Alvar Núñez, 204
Cabrera, Juan, 665–666
Cabrillo, Juan Rodriguez, 89
Cachipile, 744
Cadaraqui River, 238
Caddoes, 87, 473, 507, 510
Caddote, Jean Baptiste, 627
Cadet, Joseph, 632
Caen, Emery de, 355
Caesar, 87–88, 118
Caffetalaya, 135
Cahokia, 88, 114–115, 299, 572, 657
Cahokia-Fox Raid (1752), 88–89
Calcutta, 567
Calderón, Gregorio Guazo, 555
California, 89–91, 646
Callière, Louis-Hector de, Chevalier de, 316, 351
calumet, 254
Calusa, 91–92, 714, 737
Calvert, Cecil, Lord Baltimore, 417, 635
Calvert, Leonard, 417–418
Campbell, Donald, 574–575
Campbell, John, 742
Campbell, John, Lord Loudoun, 3, 49, 79, 92–93,
      239–240, 266, 297, 307, 392, 387–388,
      430, 434, 451–452, 498, 537, 598–599,
      602, 628, 636–637, 639, 688–689, 702,
      706, 775, 790, 800, 803
Canada, British Expedition Against (1709), 93–94,
      190, 504, 614–615, 677, 759
Canada, British Expedition Against (1711), 95–96,
      143, 428, 478, 504, 600, 602, 615, 677,
      756, 759

Canada, British Expedition Against (1746–1747), **96–97**

Canada, New England Expedition Against (1690), **97–99**, 240–242, 346, 427, 564, 600, 770–771

Canajoharie, 237

Fort Canajoharie (New York), **99**

Canandaigua Lake, 684

Canarsee, 330–331

Canasatego, 168, 364, 770

Fort Canaseraga (New York), **99**

Canavest, 422–423

Cáncer, Luis de, 204

canister, 47

Canizares y Osorio, Adrian de, 743–744

cannoniers-bombardiers, 40

Canonchet, 469

Canonicus, 193, 437, 469, 559, 565–566, 801

Canso, 272, 335, 395–396, 578, 614

Canso, Battle of (1744), 78–79, 100

Cap-aux-Diamants, 600, 608

Cape Breton Island, 6, 40, 92–93, 100, 261, 272, 274, 389–397, 429, 450–451, 544, 602, 604, 629, 688, 701, 756, 778

Cape Canaveral, 436

Cape Cod, 566, 719, 772

Cape Fear River, 508, 751, 761

Cape Hatteras, 508

Cape Henlopen, 493, 731

Cape May, 485, 493, 731

Cape Neddock, 812

Cape Ortegal, 778

Cape Porpoise, 411, 614

Cape Tourmente, 454, 604

Cape Verde Islands, 27, 499

Capricieux, 394

Cap Rouge, 600, 606–608

Captivity, European, **100–101**

Captivity, Indian. *See* Indian Warfare, Captivity

Captivity Narratives, **101–103**

Fort Carillon (New York). *See* Fort Ticonderoga (New York)

Carlana Apache, 760

Carleton, Guy, 604, 606

Carlisle, Camp Near (Pennsylvania), **103**, 356

Carlos, 91

King Carlos III, 233

Carolana, 71

Carolina Scouts, 579, 587

Carolina Troop of Rangers, 208

Fort Caroline (Florida), 44, 47, **104**, 232, 367, 431, 436, 630, 647, 667, 710, 714

Carondelet, Francisco de, 60

Carr, Sir Robert, 491

Carrera de Indias, 435–436, 479

Cartagena, 416

Cartagena, Expedition Against (1741), 34, **104–106**, 429, 461, 478, 509, 577, 636, 758

Carteret, Philip, 23

Cartier, Jacques, 101, 223, 228, 278, 457, 671

cartridges, 47

Cartwright, Sir George, 491

Carver, John, 570

Carver, Jonathan, 528

Cary, Thomas, 749

Casco, 343, 411

Casco, Treaty of (1678), 342

Casco Bay, 7, 8, 75, 106, 138, 144, 196, 202, 214, 217, 577, 660

Fort Casimir (Delaware), 26, **106–107**, 191, 470, 485, 486, 489, 491, 728, 732

Casse, Jean du, 616

Castle Island, 471

Catawba, 9, 49, 77, 107, 213, 280, 289, 313, 314, 509, 536, 591, 672, 709, 769

at Congress of Augusta (1763), 53

Catawba River, 49, 121, 276

Catechna Creek, 505, 749–750

Catechna Town, 749

Cat Island, 378

Catiti, 594

Catskill, 198–200

Catskill Mountains, 197

Caughnawaga (Kahnawaké since 1980), **107–108**, 166, 174, 229, 313, 445, 662, 668

cavalry, 273

Cavelier de La Salle, René-Robert, 12, 130, 142, 156, 224, 231, 232–233, 329, 357, 378, 397, 437, 444, 471, 561, 656, 657, 717, 738

Cayuga, **108–109**, 310–315, 316, 422, 423, 445, 530–531, 532–533, 684

Cayuga Creek, 385

Cayuga Lake, 684

Cazenovia Creek, 532

Celebre, 394

Céleron de Blainville, Pierre-Joseph, 126, 128, 145, 147, 226, 497, 501, 522, 547, 586, 757

Cendoya, Manuel de, 665

Chabert de Joncaire, Louis-Thomas, 109, 110, 163, 685

Chabert de Joncaire, Philippe-Thomas, 109, **110**, 409, 685, 757

Chabert de Joncaire de Clausonne, Daniel-Marie, **110–111**, 385

Chacato, 36, 111–112

Chacato Troubles (1674–1675), **111–112**

Chacchiuma, 473

Chamberlain, John, 403

Chambers, Thomas, 199

Chambly, 335, 365

Fort Chambly (Quebec, Canada), **112–113**, 366, 659–660, 691

Chamile, 744

Champlain, Samuel de, 1, 223, 229, 297, 354–355, 360, 457, 539, 600, 655

Chaouacha, 11, 401

charcoal; in gunpowder, 19, 47

Fort Charity (Virginia). *See* Henrico Forts (Virginia)

King Charles I, 65, 176, 179, 355, 417, 418, 469, 508, 710, 762
King Charles II (England), 26, 59, 66, 139, 168, 179, 195, 240, 378, 413, 420, 483, 489, 490, 494, 508, 553, 563, 696, 710, 726, 765, 794, 805
King Charles II (Spain), 646, 649
King Charles V, 148
King Charles VII, 161
King Charles IX, 104, 367
Fort Charles (Maine), 796
Fort Charles (Virginia), **113**, 295, 641
Charlesfort (South Carolina), **113–114**, 232, 578
Charlestown, 512
Charles Town, 9, 36, 44, 48, 51, 52, 66, 71, 121, 123, 125, 134, 150–151, 154, 155, 159, 161, 208, 234, 264, 286, 287, 301, 302, 464, 467, 508, 515, 519, 553, 555, 579, 586, 587, 589–590, 598, 649, 665–666, 710, 711, 721, 749, 778, 810, 811
    fortifications in, 325
Charles Town, Attack on (1706), **114**, 205–206, 272, 554, 616, 711
Fort Charlotte (South Carolina), 459
Charron de La Barre, Claude, 173
Charrua, 204
Charry, Jean-Antoine, Marquis Desgouttes, 393–394
Charter of Liberties and Privileges, 180
Chartier de Lotbinière, Michel, 739, 740
Fort de Chartres (Illinois), 88, **114–116**, 219, 375, 400, 401
Chateauqué, Antoine de Moyne de, 374
Chateau-Renault, Comte de, 616
Chattahoochee River, 38, 151, 152, 252, 810, 812
Chaudiere River, 672
Chaussegros De Lery, Gaspard-Joseph, 82–83
Chautauqua Lake, 586
Chavagnac, Louis-Henride, Comte de, 617
Chazy River, 659
Cheat River, 448
Chebucto Bay, 336
Checochinican, 168
Chenango Forks, 532
Chenussios, 685
Chépart, Captain De, 641
Chequamegon, 297
Chequamegon Bay, 318, 365, 528–529
Cherokee, 9, 31–32, 49, 54, 77, 81, 87–88, 107, **116–121**, 150–151, 154, 159, 213, 237, 267, 268, 276, 280, 287, 295, 306, 314, 383, 387–388, 399, 402, 407, 459, 460, 464, 472, 505, 509, 515–516, 517, 579, 587, 591, 615, 639, 694, 709, 711, 712, 724, 745, 794, 811–812
    at Congress of Augusta (1763), 51–54
    relations with Creek, 152–156
    relations with South Carolina, 162
    Trail of Tears, 121
    and Yamasee War, 152

Cherokee War (1759–1761), 9, 49–50, 107, 119–120, **121–123**, 178, 268, 287, 407, 459, 460, 509, 515, 587, 691, 713, 724, 745, 748
Chesapeake, 582
Chesapeake Bay, 59, 258, 424, 761
Chesterfield, 465
Chevert, François de, 69
Cheyenne, 529
Chicacoan, 420
Chicaza, 709
Chichimeca, 584–585
Chichimeca War, 585, 716
Chickahominy, **123–124**, 542, 543, 765–767
Chickahominy River, 123–124, 641, 704
Chickasaw, 9, 39, 50, 108, 120, **124–127**, 152, 154, 209, 231, 236, 252–253, 280, 299, 330, 335, 374–376, 379, 399, 401, 459, 467, 471, 473, 474, 518, 519, 520, 565, 591, 598, 615, 626–627, 655, 663, 744
    Battle of Ackia (1736), 8–9
    at Congress of Augusta (1763), 51–54
    kinship with Choctaw, 124
    relations with Choctaw, 124–129, 130–134
    relations with France, 8–9, 125–129
    Savannah River, band on, 50
    Trail of Tears, 127
Chickasaw Wars (1736, 1739–1740), **127–129**, 132, 146, 147, 376–377, 401–402, 472, 598, 626, 748
    African American involvement in, 11–12
    Battle of Ogoula Tchetoka, 520
Chickasawhay River, 132
Chicken, George, 81, 118
Chicora, Francisco de, 667
Chigelley, 81, 811
Chignecto, 447, 687
Chignecto Isthmus, 77, **129**, 261
Chikasahha, 125, 126, 128
Chillicothe, 694
Chimney Island, 380
Chincklacamoose, 55
Chininqué. *See* Logstown
Chippewa. *See* Ojibwa
Chippewa River, 528
Chirkov, Alexei, 643
Chisca, 36
    and Chacato troubles (1674–1675), 111–112
Fort Chiswell (Virginia), **129–130**
Chiswell, John, 129
Chitimacha, 373–374, 401
Chittenago Creek, 99
Choctaw, 32, 48, 49, 81, 120, 125, 127, **130–134**, 152, 231, 253, 268, 280, 314, 374–376, 379, 399, 401–402, 460, 517, 591, 626–627, 631, 744
    at Battle of Ackia, 9
    at Congress of Augusta (1763), 51–54
    kinship with Chickasaw, 124
    in Natchez War, 11

relations with Chickasaw, 125–129, 130–134
relations with Creek, 152–153
slave raiding against, 130–131, 155
See also Creek-Choctaw Wars
Choctaw-Chickasaw War (1752), 125–127, **134**
Choctaw Civil War (1746–1750), 9, 48, 126–127, 133, **135–136**, 254, 627, 631, 744
Choiseul, César de, 544
Choiseul, Étienne-François, Duc de, 281
Chomeday de Maisonneuve, Paul de, 457
Chota, 116, 119, 388
Chouart Des Groseilliers, Médard, 149
Chowan River, 749
Chowanoc War, 508
Fort Christanna (Virginia), **136**, 267
Christianity; Missionizing of Native Americans, 30, 37–38
Christiansen, Hendrich, 471
Fort Christina (Delaware), 106, **136–137**, 167, 203, 443, 470, 485, 493, 728, 731–732
Queen Christina, 493
Chuaquin, 744
Chubb, Pasco, **137**, 350, 413, 796
Church, Benjamin, **137–139**, 144, 202, 307, 411, 426, 428, 469, 556, 564, 570, 614, 622–623, 680, 813
  attacks Acadian settlements (1707), 8
  Battle of Brackett's Wood (1689), 75–76
  in King William's War, 344, 348–350
Church, John, 775
Churchill, John, Duke of Marlborough, 414, 615, 642
Churchyard, Thomas, 670
Cibola, 204
Claiborne, William, 728
Clapham, William, *55*, 72, 291
Clark, Thaddeus, 404
Clarke, George, 280
Clarke, John, 629
Claus, Daniel, 791
Fort Clinton (New York). *See* Fort Saratoga (New York)
Clinton, Charles, 669
Clinton, George, 326–327, 334, 337, 496
Clive, Robert, 568
Cockacoeske, Queen of the Pamunkey, 124, **139–140**, 542
Cockspur Island, 162
Coco, 329, 357
Coddington, William, 629
Codrington, Christopher, the younger, 617
Cofitachequi, 709
Colbert, Jean-Baptiste, 224, 232, 240, 476, 696
Colden, Cadwallader, 163
Coligny, Gaspard de, 113, 367
College of William and Mary, 24, 136, 504
Colorado, 760
Colorado River, 89–90
Columbus, Christopher, 111, 223, 695
Colve, Anthony, 369, 500

Comanche, 44, 487–488, 507–508, 661–662, 760
Combahee River, 150, 660
Compagnie du Nord, 377, 457
Compagnie du Saint Sacrement, 655
compañías volantes, 585
Company of Louisiana, 373
Company of New France, 312
Company of One Hundred Associates, 278, 354, 600
Company of Pejepscot Proprietors, 215, 216
Company of Surgeons, 433
Company of the Indies, 374, 400, 473–474, 641
Company of the West, 131, 374, 491
Concord, 59
Fort Condé (Alabama), 140, 389
Conejohola, 423
Conestoga, 551, 728–729
Conferences. *See* under individual names.
Congaree, 60, 62, 107
Congresses. *See* under individual names.
Connecorte, 49
Connecticut, 97–98, **140–142**, 332, 335, 344, 352–353, 365, 371, 385, 387, 396, 426, 438, 446–447, 482–483, 484, 490–491, 494, 513, 546, 550, 558–561, 614, 629, 669, 673, 675, 698, 718, 754, 804, 805
  in conquest of Acadia (1710), 5
  in Dominion of New England, 23–24, 179
  in King Philip's War, 339–340
  in King William's War, 345
  in Pequot War, 193
Connecticut River, 67, 140, 182, 201, 214, 215, 217, 270, 292, 332, 340, 347, 427, 438, 446, 483, 484, 489, 511, 548, 558, 559, 638, 652, 669, 700, 708, 718, 720–721, 802
Conococheague Creek, 387
Conoy, 168, 313, 420, 423
Conoy Island, 422–423
Consolato del Mare, 682
Fort Conti (New York; also known as Old Fort Niagara, Fort Denonville), **142–143**, 171–172, 500
Contoocook River, 186
Contractors, Army, 143
Converse, James, 138, **143–144**, 261, 348, 411, 564, 680
Cook, James, 645
Cooper, Anthony Ashley, Earl of Shaftesbury, 809
Cooper, James Fennimore, 452, 739, 800
Cooper, Thomas, 718
Cooper River, 710
Coosa, 101
Coosa Indians, 745
Coosa River, 52, 118, 151, 745, 812
Coosawhatchie, 579
Coote, Richard, Earl of Bellomont, 316, 353, 676
Copano, 329
Copley, Lionel, 422
Corbitant, 719
Corchaug, 144–145

Huck, Richard, 434
Hudson, Henry, 279, 296, 410, 488, 494, 535
Hudson Bay, 171, 226, 279, 303, 350–351, 372,
        379, 457, 496, 527, 528–529, 613, 617,
        646, 650, 756
Hudson Bay, 378
Hudson Bay Company, 279, 377, 756
Hudson River, 79, 149, 190–191, 197, 198, 200,
        215, 279, 292, **296**, 303, 311, 312, 316,
        318, 331, 359–360, 410, 426, 443, 444,
        446, 471, 497, 505, 533, 534–535, 546,
        668, 732, 740, 797, 798
Hughes, Price, 471
Hunt, Thomas, 719
Fort Hunter (New York), 246, 272, **296–297**, 326
Fort Hunter (Pennsylvania), 291, **297**
Hunter, John Dunn, 102
Hunter, Robert, 296, 674, 677–678
Huron, 31, 82, 108, 148, 173, 218, 223–224,
        229, 249, 279, **297–298**, 302, 306,
        311–312, 318, 323, 324, 341, 351,
        360, 365, 445, 451, 528, 531, 533,
        535, 536, 539–540, 570, 575–576, 662,
        663, 685, 686, 728, 755
Huron, 576
Hurtado, Juan Paéz, 487–488
Hutchins, Thomas, 73, 85
Hutchinson, Anne, 629, 801
Hutchinson, Thomas, 14
Fort Hyde (North Carolina), 298
Hyde, Edward, Lord Cornbury, 676, 749, 751

Ignacio, Juan, 66
Ile la Motte, 360
Illinois, 114–116, 125, 126, 128, 156, 218, 231,
        279, 299, 324, 337, 401, 487, 520,
        631, 656
Illinois Indians, 88, 108, 132, 163, 218, 219, **299–
        300**, 313, 318, 330, 437, 686
Illinois River, 156, 219, 299, 330, 437, 573, 654,
        656–657
Impressment, Army, 300
Impressment, Navy, 173, **300–301**, 338, 429
Impressment Act (1704), 624
Independent Companies of Marines, 40, 362, 451,
        739, 742
Independent Company of Foot, 63, 263, 333, 586
India, 544
    source for saltpeter, 19
Indiana, 521
Indian-France Relations. *See* France-Indian
        Relations
Indian–Great Britain Relations. *See* Anglo-Indian
        Relations
Indian Presents, 51, 53, 244, **301–302**, 337
Indian River, 420
Indian Slave Trade, 31, 36, 286, 374, 400, 401,
        420, 467, 558, 649, 716, 748, 794–795,
        809–810, 811
Indian Trade, 30–32, 50, 51, 54, 112, 117, 121,

125, 148, 156–157, 168, 170, 186, 240,
        243–244, 246, 250, 268, 302–304, 515,
        794–795, 809–810, 811
Indian Uprising of 1747. *See* Uprising of 1747
Indian Warfare, 75, 304–305
Indian Warfare, Captivity, 305–307
Indian Warfare, European Acculturation of, 307–308
Infantry, 308
Ingle, Richard, 418
Ingoldsby, Richard, 37, 675
Ingram, Joseph, 59
Inland Passage, 208
Innes, James, 158, 523
Inspector General, 309–310, 637
Intercolonial Relations, 308–309
Iowa, 219, 299
Iowa Indians, 218
Iroquois, 23, 55, 77, 97, 98, 107, 109–110, 112,
        136, 142–143, 148–149, 158, 162–163,
        171–172, 173, 175, 184, 229, 242, 251,
        258, 279, 289–290, 296, 297, 298, 306,
        309, **310–315**, 324, 326–328, 341–342,
        358, 359, 361, 364, 366, 377, 385–386,
        418, 420–423, 442, 444–445, 451, 457,
        495, 496, 498, 500–503, 513, 515, 527–
        528, 530–533, 535, 537, 550, 562, 570,
        581–582, 600, 613–614, 617, 655, 656,
        662, 668, 672, 674–678, 684–686, 687,
        708, 711, 729, 736–737, 747, 748, 751,
        769, 791
    Caughnawaga, 107–108
    Covenant Chain, 149–150
    Delaware, relations with, 167–170, 189
    Esopus, relations with, 197
    French, relations with, 39–40, 223–225
    Fox seek sanctuary among, 218
    in King George's War, 337
    and King Philip's War, 202
    in King William's War, 343, 345–346, 347,
        350–351, 353, 358–359
Iroquois Treaties of 1700 and 1701 (with New
        York and New France), 109, 150, 163,
        279, 314, **315–317**, 351, 495, 528, 531–
        532, 613–615, 676, 685
Iroquois Wars (1641–1701), 31–32, 108, 109,
        163, 249, 303, 312, **317–319**, 528,
        533, 692, 729
Isle-aux-Noix, 70, 74, **319**, 360, 458, 651, 659
Isle d'Orléans, 454, 600, 604, 606, 608, 655, 807
Isle La Motte, 659

Jacobite Rebellion, 567, 636, 642
Jacobs, Captain, 271, 355–356, 700
Jacques-Cartier, 611
Jamaica, 105, 182, 370, 576, 590, 616, 642, 702,
        758, 793–794
Fort James (New York; also known as Fort
        Amsterdam, Fort George at the Battery),
        22, **321**, 370, 499–500
Fort James (Virginia), 124, 295, 321–322, 641

Matthews, Jacob, 464

Fort Matuxon (Virginia). *See* Fort Manaskin (Virginia)

Maumee River, 571–572, 755

Fort Maurepas (Mississippi), 231, 373, 378–379, 399, **432**

Maurepas, Jean-Frédéric de, 280

May, Cornelis Jacobsen, 84

Mayami, 91

Mayflower, 569, 719

Mayhew, Thomas, Jr., 584

Mazarin, Jules, 224, 794

McDowell's Mill, 356

McGillivray, Alexander, 192

McGillivray, Lachlan, 52–54

McIntosh, Lachlan, 121

McKee, Thomas, 297

McNair and Company, 268

McPherson, James, 622–623, 660

Medal chiefs, 131, 461

Medical Services, 432–434

Medina River, 738

Meherrin, 509–510, 542, 583, 765

Meherrin River, 136

Mémoires sur la dernière guerre de l'Amérique septentrionale, 581

Ménard, René, 108

Mendon, 339, 340

Mendoza, Antonio de, 486

Menéndez, Francisco, 435

Menéndez, Juan, 436

Menéndez de Avilés, Pedro, 44, 47, 91, 104, 205, 232, 282, 293, 367, 431, **435–437**, 563, 578, 630, 647, 664, 667–668, 710, 737

Menéndez Marquéz, Pedro, 668

Menominee, 88, 218, 317

Menou d'Aulnay de Charnisay, Charles de, 577, 804

Fort Mercer (Pennsylvania), 449, 566

Mercer, Hugh, 700

Mercer, James, 451, 537

Merchant Adventurers of London, 354

Merrimack, 484

Merrimack River, 183, 186, 214, 269, 294, 402

Merrymeeting Bay, 412

Mesquakie. *See* Fox

Metacom (Metacomet). *See* Philip

Metacom's War. *See* King Philip's War

Metai, 571

Meyer, Elias, 55, 662

Miami, 163, 169, 173, 218, 219, 290, 302, 313, 316, 351, 386, 410, 442, 521–522, 536, 570, 571, 575, 654–655, 686, 755

Fort Miami (Indiana), 146, 330, 572

Fort Miami (Michigan), **437**, 755

Miami River, 134, 330, 755

Miantonomo, 193, **437–438**, 447, 469, 559, 560–561, 596, 753, 801

Michigamea, 299

Michigan, 438–439, 521, 527–528, 539–540, 654

Michilimackinac, 82, 149, 171, 316–317, 535,

631, 654, 686, 755

Fort Michilimackinac (Michigan), 82, **438–439**, 441, 529, 572, 575, 627, 640

Micmac, 1, 4, 6, 8, 129, 183, 224, 229–230, 276, 279, 323, 335, 337, 372, 578, 614

Middleborough, 340

Middle Cherokee, 116, 123, 155, 407

Middle Plantation, Treaty of. *See* Virginia-Indian Treaty (1677/1680)

Milborne, Jacob, 345, 346–347, 369, 371

Miles, Captain, 291

Militia, 21, 41, 223, 230, **439–441**, 451, 564, 569, 722, 774

Militia: The Archeological Record, 441–442

Millars, Antoine Simon, 578

Mille Lacs, 528–529

Miller, Thomas, 718

Minas, 428

Minden, 568

Mingo, 72, 73, 85, 214, 289–290, **442–443**, 521, 576, 755

Mingo Tchito, 626–627

Minisink, 198

Ministry of the Marine, 40, 115

Minnesota, 63, 231, 528–529, 650, 655

Minorca, 544, 567, 617, 756

Minqua. *See* Susquehannock

Minquas Kill, 731

Minuit, Peter, 21, 84, **443–444**, 493, 535, 731

Miquelon, 281, 390, 692

Miranda, Angel de, 616

Missaquash River, 63, 367

Missiagua. *See* Ojibwa

Missisquoi, 184, 708

Missisquoi Bay, 651, 659–660

Missisquois, 1

Mississippi, 124

Fort Mississippi (Louisiana). *See* Fort de la Boulaye (Louisiana)

Mississippi River, 88, 115–116, 126, 128, 130, 132, 140, 194, 204, 213, 231, 232, 246, 252, 254, 279, 299, 303, 372–373, 378, 399, **444**, 471, 473, 479, 491, 528–529, 536, 544, 597, 626, 631, 654, 657, 692, 709, 712, 748

Missouri, 299

Missouri Indians, 219, 299, 330, 535, 536

Missouri River, 114, 299, 488, 529, 535, 536, 760

Mobile, 40, 45, 51, 54, 60, 81, 118, 126, 132, 135, 140, 152, 155, 205, 206, 224, 231, 233, 399, 467, 479, 554, 613, 615, 616, 711, 745

Mobile Bay, 388–389, 491, 554, 555

Mobile Indians, 130, 388, 399, 401, 432

Mobile River, 130, 140, 231, 373, 379, 388, 399

Mobilien, 254

Modockawando, 180

Mohawk, 102, 108, 149, 164, 175, 197, 198–200, 202, 246, 249, 251, 296–297, 310–315, 316, 318, 324, 326, 337, 347, 349, 360, 362–363, 364, 365–366, 371, 410, 444–

693, 753, 754, 802
Pequot River, 560
Pequot War (1636–1637), 101, 140–141, 144–145,
    275, 284, 426, 438, 446–447, 469, 482,
    484, 558–561, 569, 596, 629, 669, 693,
    753, 801, 802, 804
    Endicott Expedition, 192–194
Percy, George, 15
Périer, Etienne, 11, 132, 374, 401, 472–473, 641
Périer de Salvert, Antoine-Alexis, 473
Perry, John, 508
Peskeompscut, 201–202
Pessacus, 469, 753
Peters, Richard, 14
Petersburg, 295
Pett, Phineas, 696
Petun, 108, 312, 318, 445, 531, 535, 685, 686
Pez, Andrés de, 552, 561–562
Phélypeaux Maurepas, Jérôme, Comte de
    Pontchartrain, 173, 231, 373–374, 377–
    379, 390, 399, 570
Philadelphia, 71, 157, 211, 235, 302, 392, 442, 493,
    527, 551, 552, 589–590, 598, 616, 736
Philip, 23, 67, 141, 201–202, 284, 313, 339–341,
    426, 562, 566, 570, 584, 596, 772
King Philip II, 431, 435, 437, 562–563, 647
King Philip III, 205, 234
King Philip V, 206, 207, 553, 556, 561
Philippe, duc d'Orleans, 114
Philipps, Richard, 78
Philipse, Frederick, 370
Phillips, William, 707
Phips, Sir William, 7–8, 19, 97–98, 197, 215, 225,
    240–241, 273, 345, 346, 348–349, 352,
    365, 371, 411, 427, 563–565, 577, 600,
    614, 759, 795, 796
Piankatank River, 59
Piankeshaw, 219
Pichon, Thomas, 63
Pickawillany, 226, 337, 386, 522, 686, 746
Fort Picolata (Florida), 459, 518, 565, 663
Picoté de Belestre, François-Marie, 266, 571
Picquet, Abbe François, 366, 532
Picuris, 488
Pigwacket, 1, 184, 402, 403–404, 483, 638, 681
Pilgrim, 4, 339, 426, 469, 565–566, 569, 719–
    720, 772
Pima, 44
Piqua, 694
Piro, 486, 594
Piscataqua River, 483, 556
Piscataway, 259, 313, 420–423, 424
Piscataway Creek, 58, 424–425, 729
Pitkin, William, 14
Fort Pitt (Pennsylvania), 18, 72, 80, 83, 85–86,
    147, 157, 170, 190, 211, 214, 275, 276,
    384, 449, 551, 566–567, 574–576, 639,
    690, 737, 747, 780
Pitt, William, First Earl of Chatham, 3, 51, 79, 92–
    93, 211, 226, 239, 271, 300, 334, 392,

416, 453, 498, 544, 567–569, 601–602,
    628, 688–689, 740–742, 807
    campaign orders for 1759, 17
    campaign orders for 1760, 18
    promotes career of Jeffery Amherst, 17
Pittsburgh, 147
Pizarro, Francisco, 708
Placentia, 377
Plains of Abraham, 448, 454–455, 462, 601, 608–
    611, 633, 690, 703, 808
Plaisted, Elisha, 792
Platte River, 488
Fort Pleasant (West Virginia), 569
Plymouth, 30, 98, 99, 137, 141, 284, 339–340,
    371, 426, 438, 443, 469, 482–483, 562,
    565–566, 569–570, 622, 680, 719–720,
    770, 772, 774, 786, 792, 802, 803, 804
    in Dominion of New England, 23–24, 179
    in King William's War, 345
Plymouth Company, 556, 704
Pocahontas, 100, 123, 306, 542, 582, 583, 704
Pocasset, 339–340, 596
Pocock, George, 416
Pocotaligo, 579
Pocoughtaonack, 583
Pocumtuck Indians, 67, 164, 483, 596
Point Pelee, 575
Pointe Coupée, 400, 473, 748
Pointe Lévy, 448, 454, 604, 606, 608, 612, 808
Pointe-aux-Trembles, 606, 608, 612
Pomeroy, Seth, 363
Ponce de Leon, Juan, 91, 204, 714, 737
Pon Pon, 463
Pons Pons, 721
Fort Pontchartrain de Detroit (Michigan), 173–
    174, 218, 298, 535, 570–571, 572, 574–
    576, 755
Pontiac, 18, 30, 51, 72, 276, 327, 529, 540, 571–
    573, 573–576, 592
Pontiac's War (1763), 32, 72, 103, 170, 190, 214,
    230, 237, 251, 276, 303–304, 315, 330,
    385, 439, 443, 449, 462, 502, 513, 529,
    540, 551, 566, 571, 573–576, 586, 591–
    592, 637, 639, 655, 662, 663, 685, 703,
    737, 747, 757, 800
    Battle of Bushy Run, 85–86
Popé, 594
Poropotank River, 764
Fort du Portage (New York). See Little Fort
    Niagara (New York)
Portland, 465
Port Nelson, 350
Portobago Bay, 624
Porto Bello, Attack on (1739), 34, 104, 478, 576–
    577, 758
Port Royal, Acadia (Annapolis Royal, Nova
    Scotia), 4–8, 94, 95, 203, 223, 225, 240,
    270, 272–273, 278–279, 296, 335, 345,
    411, 413, 415, 427–428, 563–564, 577–
    578, 614, 759

Villareal, Francisco, 737
Villaroel, Gonzalo de, 104, 667
Villasur, Pedro de, 488, **760–761**
Ville-Marie, 457
Vincent, Philip, 560
Virginia, 11, 20, 38, 49, 51, 72, 73, 92, 96, 120,
        129, 139, 147, 149, 170, 175–176,
        205, 212, 249, 268, 272, 275, 282,
        289–290, 295, 313, 315, 321, 364,
        383, 385–386, 387–388, 396, 407, 417,
        420, 423, 440, 468, 470, 493, 499,
        501, 503, 504, 508, 509–510, 515,
        520–524, 522–524, 534, 542, 548, 569,
        577, 582–584, 621–622, 623–624, 678,
        686, 691, 698, 701, 704, 717–718,
        728–729, 746, 751, **761–764**, 779–780,
        794, 802, 810
    Edmund Andros's Administration, 24
    Bacon's Rebellion, 57–60, 249
    Cartagena, in expedition against (1739), 105
    Cherokee, trade with, 117
    in Cherokee War (1759–1761), 121–122
    Dutch attack (1673), 29
    Native Americans, relations with, 30
    and Yamasee War, 150
Virginia Company of London, 322, 589, 704, 761–
        762, 765, 810
Virginia Indian Company, 136, 717
Virginia-Indian Treaty (1646), 139, **764**
Virginia-Indian Treaty (1677/1680), 39, 139, 468,
        510, 542, 583, 624, **765**
Virginia-Indian War (1622–1632), 31, 39, 65, 123,
        294, 295, 322, 468, 534, 542, 583, 762,
        765–766, 774, 809, 810
Virginia-Indian War (1644–1646), 65, 124, 295,
        468, 534, 583, 642, 762, **766–767**
Voyageur, 378
Voyer, Marc-Pierre de, Comte d'Argenson, 449
Fort Vroomen (New York). *See* Fort Saratoga (New
        York)
Vroomen, Bartolomeus, 668
Vroomen, Jacob, 99

Waban, 584
Wabash River, 218, 219, 330, 521, 755
Waccamaw, 11, **769**
Waccamaw River, 769
Waco, 507
Waddell, Hugh, 178
Wading River, 144
Wager, 465
Wainwright, Francis, 413
Walachy, 237
Waldo, Samuel, 392
Waldron, Richard, 101, 181, 484
Walker, Sir Hovenden, 95, 225, 428, 478, 504,
        600, 602, 615, 617, 702, 759
Walker, Thomas, 432
Walking Purchase (1737), 168, 251, 513, 549, 736,
        769–770

Wall Street Palisade (New York), **771**
Walley, John, 98, 346, **770–771**
Fort Walpack (New Jersey), **771**
Walpole, Sir Horace, 78, 334
Walpole, Sir Robert, 106, 263, 567, 576, 701
Walton, Shadrach, 95
Wamessit, 584
Wampanoag, 30, 67, 102, 141, 164, 249, 275,
        284, 339–341, 426, 468–469, 505, 562,
        565–566, 596, 719, **772**, 792
Wamsutta, 562, 566, 570, 772
Wando River, 114
Wanton, William, 589
Waoraneck, 197
Wappinger, 200, 331, 410
War and Society in Colonial America, 772–777
Ward, Edward, 523, 547, 686, 746–747
Ward, Nancy, 117
War Office, 42
War of Jenkins' Ear. *See* Anglo-Spanish War (1739–
        1744)
War of the Austrian Succession. *See* Anglo-Spanish
        War (1739–1744); King George's War
War of the League of Augsburg. *See* King
        William's War
War of the Spanish Succession. *See* Queen
        Anne's War
Warranawankong, 197
Warren, Peter, 97, 326, 335–336, 396–397, 429,
        778–779
Warrior's Path, 65
Warwick, 340, 628–629
Warwick's Fort (Virginia). *See* Fort Dinwiddie (Vir-
        ginia)
Warwick, Earl of, 669
Warwick, William, 175
Washington, 90
Washington, George, 145, 146, 147, 157, 158,
        169, 175–176, 185, 213, 214, 236, 267,
        289, 368, 388, 397, 449, 481, 497, 522–
        524, 526, 548, 549, 569, 639, 686, 701,
        747, 754, 757, **779–782**
Washington, Lawrence, 105, 520, 779
Wasson, 575
Wateree, 107
Waterville, 144
Wawenock, 1
Waxhaw, 60, 107
Wea, 575
Weapons, Firearms, **782–786**
    calibers, 783
    English colonies, 785–786
    France, 784
    Great Britain, 784
    ignition systems, 782–783
    Native Americans, 786
    Spain, 784–785
    styles and sizes, 783–784
    supply of, 42–43
Weapons, Naval, **786–790**

cannon, 786–788
personal weapons and small arms, 789
Webb, Daniel, 361, 452, **790–791**, 798, 800
Wecquaesgeek, 331
Weetamoo, 340
Weger, Charles, 617
Weinshauks, 560
Weiser, Conrad, 214, 289, 364, 443, **791–792**
Welch, Thomas, 467, 471
Wells (Maine), 144, 164, 202, 261, 348, 351, 411, 614, **792**, 812
Wells River, 652
Wentworth, Thomas, 105, 758
Wessagusset, 792
Wessagusset Raid (1623), 566, 720, **792–793**
Fort West (Virginia), **793**
West, Francis, 793
West, Thomas, Lord de la Warre, 167, 582
Westbrook, Benjamin, 506
Westbrook, Thomas, 83, 261, 292, 507, 620, 654, **793**
Fort Western (Maine), 285, **803**
Western Design (1654–1656), **793–794**
Westfield, 718
West Florida, 73
West Fort (Connecticut). *See* Litchfield Forts (Connecticut)
West Indies, 347
Westminster, Treaty of (1648), 490
Westminster, Treaty of (1654), 26
Westminster, Treaty of (1674), 29, 494, 500
Westo, 101, 151–152, 711, **794–795**, 809–810
Weston, Thomas, 720, 792
Westo Treaty (1674), 809
Westo War (1680–1683), 31
West Virginia, 295, 383, 385, 569, 754
Wethersfield, 559
Weyanock, 468
Wheeler, Sir Francis, 347, 427, 564
Wheelwright, John, 792
White Mountains, 184, 483
White, John, 620, 636
Whitehall, Treaty of (1686), 6, 195
Whitmore, Edward, 392–393
Fort Whorekill (Delaware). *See* Fort Swanendael (Delaware)
Wichita, 87, 299, 507
Wickford, 284, 340
Wicomico, 420
Wigwam Martinique, 659–660
Fort Willem Hendick (New York), 500
Willet, Thomas, 622
Castle William (Massachusetts), 47, 215, 430, **795**
Fort William (Massachusetts), **795–796**
Fort William (Nova Scotia, Canada), 272, 275
Fort William (Pennsylvania). *See* Fort Lebanon (Pennsylvania)
William and Mary, 24, 97, 141, 179, 195, 196, 279, 342–343, 369, 370, 426, 478, 495, 563, 646

Fort William and Mary (New Hampshire), 216–217, **796**
Fort William Henry (Maine), 137, 215, 216–217, 348–350, 377, 411, 413, 564, **796–797**
Fort William Henry (New York), 17, 69, 175, 227, 239, 266, 274, 360, 526–527, 602, 633, 687–688, 689, 706, 739–742, 797, 803
Fort William Henry, Seige of (1757), 2, 74, 93, 146, 269, 361, 381, 451–452, 458, 498, 557, 581, 688, 790, **797–801**
William of Orange. *See* William and Mary
Williams, Ephraim, 175, 362, 431
Williams, Eunice, 102
Williams, John, 102, 166, 502
Williams, Roger, 30, 438, 469, 559, 629, **801–802**, 804
Williamsburg, 59, 62, 322, 504, 749
Wills Creek (Maryland), 65, 77, 158, 481–482, 523–524, 525–526, 746, 780, **802**
Wilmington, 136
Wilmington River, 517
Wiltwyck, 187, 198–200, 489
Winchester, 388, 523
Windsor, 718
Windsor Blockhouse (Connecticut), 141, **802**
Wingfield, Edward Maria, 322, 761
Winnasoccum, 420
Winnebago, 88, 218, 317
Winnipesauke, 1
Winslow, 290
Winslow, Edward, 802, 803
Winslow, John, 63, 129, 290, 448, **803–804**
Winslow, Josiah, 284, 340, 569–570, 772
Winter Harbor, 215, 614
Winter Island, 795
Winthrop, John, 22, 438, 558, 564, 595, 669, 795, 801, 804
Winthrop, John (also known as Fitz-John), 345, 365, 371, 491, 500, 805
builds Fort Ann (New York), 35
leads New England Expedition Against Canada, 97–98
Winthrop, John, Jr., 559
Winyaw Bay, 56, 710
Wisconsin, 63, 218, 219, 224, 297, 365, 439, 528–529, 539
Wise, John, 98, 771
With, Witte de, 25–26
Wituwamet, 566, 720, 793
Woburn, 144
Wolcott, Roger, 396
Wolfe, James, 17, 43, 48, 69, 285, 286, 392–393, 448, 453–455, 462, 498, 568, 601–612, 633, 643, 689–690, 699, 703, 740, 776, 790, **805–809**
Fort Wolstenholme (Virginia), **809**
Wolstenholme, John, 809
Wonalancet, 484
Wood, Abraham, 39, 295, 509–510